THE WEST

Key Eras in the Transformation of the West

Western civilization has undergone many transformations throughout its history. Map 1 shows the Roman Empire at its greatest extent, an era when the basic intellectual, religious, political, and geographic outlines of what we call the West today were drawn. During the Carolingian Empire, seen in Map 2, Europe experienced greater political cohesion, as the Carolingian armies successfully reunified most of the western European territories of the ancient Roman Empire. A distinctive Latin Christian (or Roman Catholic) culture began to emerge in this region, distinguishing it further from Orthodox Christian culture of the Byzantine Empire in the east. Map 3 shows Europe after the Congress of

Map 1
Roman Empire at Its Greatest Extent, ca. 117 C.E.

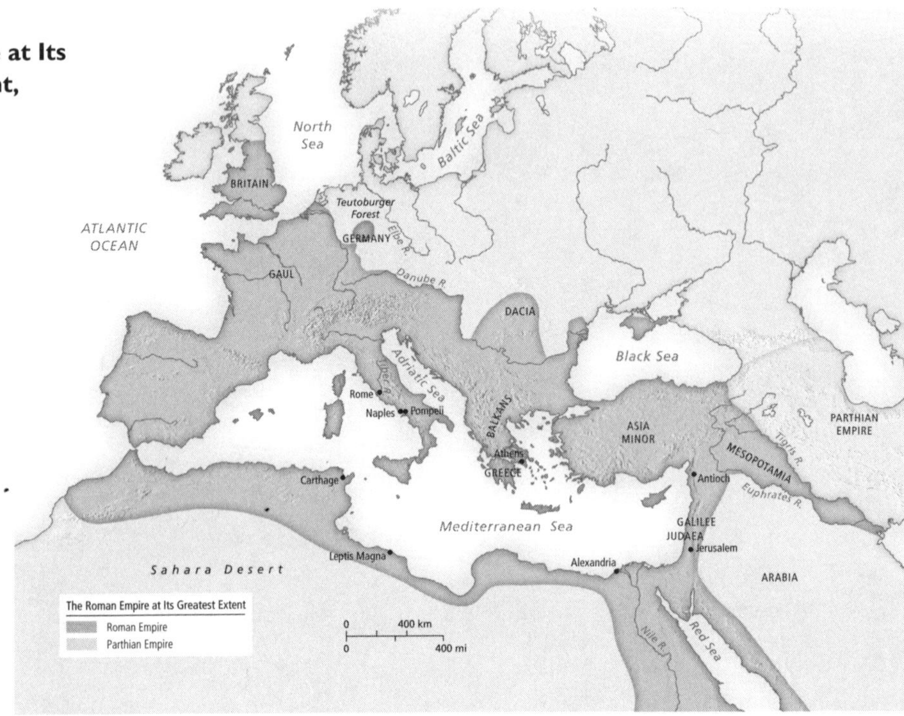

Map 2
Carolingian Empire

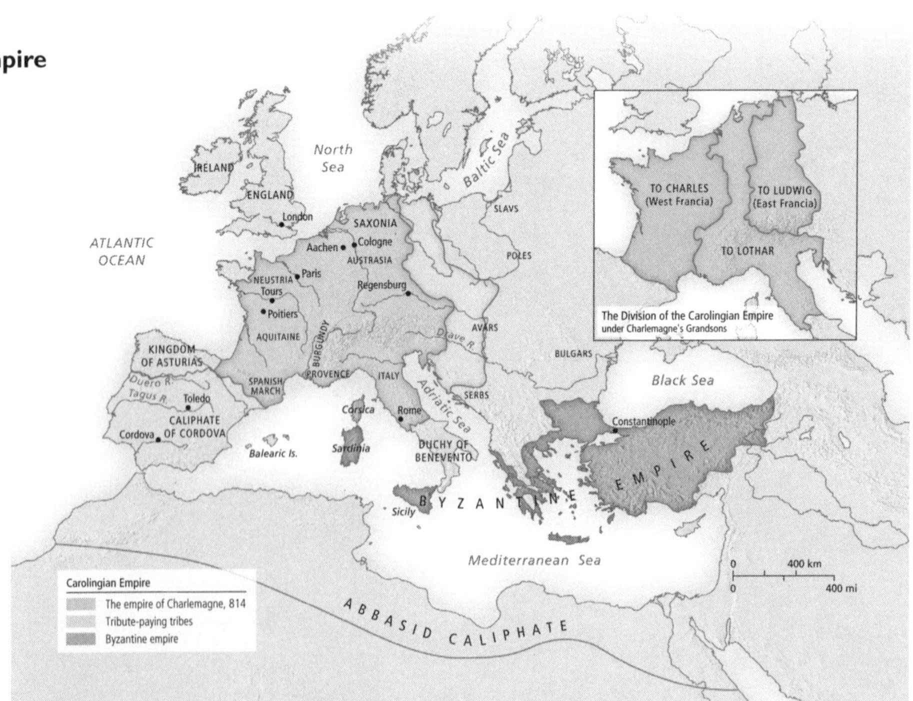

Vienna in 1815, when the major European powers re-drew the map of Europe after the defeat of Napoleon and the dismantlement of the massive empire France had acquired under his leadership. The settlement agreed upon at Vienna was intended to maintain a balance of power in the West. Map 4 shows Europe after World War I, when the map of Europe changed dramatically, with the collapse of the old authoritarian empires and the creation of independent nation-states in eastern Europe. What neither Map 3 nor Map 4 can show, however, is the expansion of "the West" beyond European borders to embrace cultures on other continents, including Australia, Africa, and North America.

■ **MAP 3**
Europe After the Congress of Vienna, 1815

■ **MAP 4**
Europe After World War I

THE WEST

ENCOUNTERS & TRANSFORMATIONS

VOLUME I: TO 1715

BRIAN LEVACK
University of Texas at Austin

EDWARD MUIR
Northwestern University

MICHAEL MAAS
Rice University

MEREDITH VELDMAN
Louisiana State University

PEARSON
Longman

New York San Francisco Boston
London Toronto Sydney Tokyo Singapore Madrid
Mexico City Munich Paris Cape Town Hong Kong Montreal

Vice President and Publisher: Priscilla McGeehon
Acquisitions Editor: Erika Gutierrez
Development Manager: Lisa Pinto
Senior Development Editor: Dawn Groundwater
Executive Marketing Manager: Sue Westmoreland
Supplements Editor: Kristi Olson
Media Editor: Patrick McCarthy
Production Manager: Donna DeBenedictis
Project Coordination and Electronic Page Makeup: Elm Street Publishing Services, Inc.
Interior Design: Pearson Education Development
Cover Designer/Manager: John Callahan
Cartography: Maps.com
Photo Researcher: Photosearch, Inc.
Manufacturing Buyer: Roy L. Pickering, Jr.
Printer and Binder: Von Hoffmann Corporation / Owensville
Cover Printer: Phoenix Color Corporation

Please visit our website at http://www.ablongman.com/levack

ISBN 0-321-18809-8 (Volume I preliminary version)
ISBN 0-321-18810-1 (Volume II preliminary version)

1 2 3 4 5 6 7 8 9 10—VHO—06 05 04 03

Brief Contents

Detailed Contents

CHAPTER 3

Building the Classical World: Hebrews, Persians, and Greeks, 1100–336 B.C.E. *3-2*

CHAPTER 4

The Hellenistic Age, 336–31 B.C.E. *4-2*

CHAPTER 5

Enclosing the West: The Early Roman Empire and Its Neighbors, 31 B.C.E.–235 C.E. *5-2*

Documents

Maps

Features

JUSTICE IN HISTORY

THE HUMAN BODY IN HISTORY

PLACES OF ENCOUNTER

Chronologies

Preface

We wrote this textbook to answer questions about the identity of the civilization in which we live. Journalists, politicians, and scholars often refer to our civilization, its political ideologies, its economic systems, and its cultures as "Western" without fully considering what that label means and why it might be appropriate. The classification of our civilization as Western has become particularly problematic in the age of globalization. The creation of international markets, the rapid dissemination of ideas on a global scale, and the transmission of popular culture from one country to another often make it difficult to distinguish what is Western from what is not. *The West: Encounters & Transformations* offers students a history of Western civilization in which these issues of Western identity are given prominence. Our goal is neither to idealize nor to indict that civilization but to describe its main characteristics in different historical periods.

The West: Encounters & Transformations gives careful consideration to two basic questions. The first is how did the definition of the West change over time? In what ways did its boundaries shift and how did the distinguishing characteristics of its cultures change? The second question is by what means did the West—and the idea of the West—develop? We argue that the West is the product of a series of cultural encounters that occurred both outside and within its geographical boundaries. We explore these encounters and the transformations they produced by detailing the political, social, religious, and cultural history of the regions that have traditionally been considered a part of the West.

Defining the West

What is the West? How did it come into being? How has it developed throughout history? Many textbooks take for granted which regions or peoples of the globe constitute the West. They treat the history of the West as a somewhat expanded version of European history. While not disputing the centrality of Europe to any definition of the West, we contend that the West is not only a geographical realm with ever-shifting boundaries but also a cultural realm, an area of cultural influence extending beyond the geographical and political boundaries of Europe. We so strongly believe in this notion that we have written the essay "What Is the West?" to encourage students to think about their understanding of Western civilization and to guide their understanding of each chapter. Many of the features of what we call Western civilization originated in regions that are not geographically part of Europe (such as northern Africa and the Middle East), while ever since the fifteenth century various social, ethnic, and political groups from non-European regions (such as North and South America, eastern

Russia, Australia, New Zealand, and South Africa) have identified themselves, in one way or another, with the West. Throughout the text, we devote considerable attention to the boundaries of the West and show how borderlines between cultures have been created, especially in eastern and southeastern Europe.

Considered as a geographical and cultural realm, "the West" is a term of recent origin, and the civilization to which it refers did not become clearly defined until the eleventh century, especially during the Crusades, when western European Christians developed a distinct cultural identity. Before that time we can only talk about the powerful forces that created the West, especially the dynamic interaction of the civilizations of western Europe, the Byzantine Empire, and the Muslim world.

Over the centuries Western civilization has acquired many salient characteristics. These include two of the world's great legal systems (civil law and common law), three of the world's monotheistic religions (Judaism, Christianity, and Islam), certain political and social philosophies, forms of political organization (such as the modern bureaucratic state and democracy), methods of scientific inquiry, systems of economic organization (such as industrial capitalism), and distinctive styles of art, architecture, and music. At times one or more of these characteristics has served as a primary source of Western identity: Christianity in the Middle Ages, science and rationalism during the Enlightenment, industrialization in the nineteenth and twentieth centuries, and a defense of individual liberty and democracy in the late twentieth century. These sources of Western identity, however, have always been challenged and contested, both when they were coming into prominence and when they appeared to be most triumphant. Western culture has never been monolithic, and even today references to the West imply a wide range of meanings.

Cultural Encounters

The definition of the West is closely related to the central theme of our book, which is the process of cultural encounters. Throughout *The West: Encounters & Transformations,* we examine the West as a product of a series of cultural encounters both outside the West and within it. We show that the West originated and developed through a continuous process of inclusion and exclusion resulting from a series of encounters among and within different groups. These encounters can be described in a general sense as external, internal, or ideological.

External encounters

External encounters took place between peoples of different civilizations. Before the emergence of the West as a clearly defined entity, external encounters occurred between such diverse peoples as Greeks and Phoenicians, Macedonians and Egyptians, and Romans and Celts. After the eleventh century, external encounters between Western and non-Western peoples occurred mainly during periods of European exploration, expansion, and imperialism. In the sixteenth and seventeenth centuries, for example, a series of external encounters took place between Europeans on the one hand and Africans, Asians, and the indigenous people of the Americas on the other. Two chapters of *The West: Encounters & Transformations* (Chapters 12 and 19) and a large section of a third (Chapter 23) explore these external encounters in depth and discuss how they affected Western and non-Western civilizations alike.

Internal encounters

Our discussion of encounters also includes similar interactions between different social groups *within* Western countries. These internal encounters often took place between dominant and subordinate groups, such as between lords and peasants, rulers and subjects, men and women, factory owners and workers, masters and slaves. Encounters between those who were educated and those who were illiterate, which recur frequently throughout Western history, also fall into this category. Encounters just as often took place between different religious and political groups, such as between Christians and Jews, Catholics and Protestants, royal absolutists and republicans.

IDEOLOGICAL ENCOUNTERS

Ideological encounters involve the interaction between comprehensive systems of thought, most notably religious doctrines, political philosophies, and scientific theories about the nature of the world. These ideological conflicts usually arose out of internal encounters, when various groups within Western societies subscribed to different theories of government or rival religious faiths. The encounters between Christianity and polytheism in the early Middle Ages, between liberalism and conservatism in the nineteenth century, and between fascism and communism in the twentieth century were ideological encounters. Some ideological encounters had an external dimension, such as when the forces of Islam and Christianity came into conflict during the Crusades and when the Cold War developed between Soviet communism and Western democracy in the second half of the twentieth century.

The West: Encounters & Transformations illuminates the variety of these encounters and clarifies their effects. By their very nature encounters are interactive, but they have taken different forms: they have been violent or peaceful, coercive or cooperative. Some have resulted in the imposition of Western ideas on areas lying outside the geographical boundaries of the West or the perpetuation of the dominant culture within Western societies. More often than not, however, encounters have resulted in a more reciprocal process of exchange in which both Western and non-Western cultures or the values of both dominant and subordinate groups have undergone significant change. Our book not only identifies these encounters but also discusses their significance by returning periodically to the issue of Western identity.

Coverage

The West: Encounters & Transformations offers both balanced coverage of political, social, and culture history and a broader coverage of the West and the world.

BALANCED COVERAGE

Our goal throughout the text has been to provide balanced coverage of political, social, and cultural history and to include significant coverage of religious and military history as well. Political history defines the basic structure of the book, and some chapters, such as those on building the classical world, the age of confessional divisions, absolutism and state building, the French Revolution, and the coming of mass politics, include sustained political narratives. Because we understand the West to be a cultural as well as a geographical realm, we give a prominent position to cultural history. Thus we include rich sections on Hellenistic philosophy and literature, the cultural environment of the Italian Renaissance, the creation of a new political culture at the time of the French Revolution, and the atmosphere of cultural despair and desire that prevailed in Europe after World War I. We also devote special attention to religious history, including the history of Islam as well as that of Christianity and Judaism. Unlike many other textbooks, our coverage of religion continues into the modern period.

The West: Encounters & Transformations also provides extensive coverage of the history of women and gender. Wherever possible the history of women is integrated into the broader social, cultural, and political history of the period. But there are also separate sections on women in our chapters on classical Greece, the Renaissance, the Reformation, the Enlightenment, the Industrial Revolution, World War I, World War II, and the postwar era.

THE WEST AND THE WORLD

Our book provides broad geographical coverage. Because the West is the product of a series of encounters, the external areas with which the West interacted are of major importance. Three chapters deal specifically with the West and the World.

- Chapter 12, "The West and the World: The Significance of Global Encounters, 1450–1650"
- Chapter 19, "The West and the World: Empire, Trade, and War, 1650–1850"
- Chapter 23, "The West and the World: Cultural Crisis and New Imperialism, 1870–1914"

These chapters present substantial material on sub-Saharan Africa, Latin America, the Middle East, India, and East Asia. Our text is also distinctive in its coverage of eastern Europe and the Muslim world, areas which have often been considered outside the boundaries of the West. These regions were arenas within which significant cultural encounters took place. Finally we include material on the United States and Australia, both of which have become part of the West. We recognize that most American college and university students have the opportunity to study American history as a separate subject, but treatment of the United States as a Western nation provides a different perspective from that usually given in courses on American history. For example, this book treats the American Revolution as one of four Atlantic Revolutions, its national unification in the nineteenth century as part of a broader western European development, its pattern of industrialization as related to that of Britain, and its central role in the Cold War as part of an ideological encounter that was global in scope.

Organization

The chronological and thematic organization of our book conforms in its broad outline to the way in which Western civilization courses are generally taught. We have limited the number of chapters to twenty-nine, an effort to make the book more compatible with the traditional American semester calendar and to solve the frequent complaint that there is not enough time to cover all the material in the course. We have also made some significant changes in organization:

- Chapter 2 covers the period from ca. 1600 to 550 B.C.E. and is the first in a Western civilization textbook to examine the International Bronze Age, a period important in its own right because it saw the creation of expansionist, multiethnic empires, linked by trade and diplomacy, and sharing the same military technology.
- In Chapter 4 the Roman Republic, in keeping with contemporary scholarship, has been incorporated into a discussion of the Hellenistic world, dethroned slightly to emphasize how it was one of many competing Mediterranean civilizations.
- Chapter 12 covers the first period of European expansion, from 1450 to 1650. It examines the new European encounters with the civilizations of sub-Saharan Africa, the Americas, and East Asia. By paying careful attention to the characteristics of

these civilizations before the arrival of the Europeans, we show how this encounter affected indigenous peoples as well as Europeans.

- Chapter 16 is devoted entirely to the scientific revolution of the seventeenth century in order to emphasize the central importance of this development in the creation of Western identity.
- Chapter 19, which covers the second period of European expansion, from 1650 to 1850, studies the growth of European empires, the beginning of global warfare, and encounters between Europeans and the peoples of Asia and Africa.
- Chapter 27, "The Holocaust, the Bomb, and the Legacy of Mass Killing," explores the moral fissure in the history of the West created by World War II. This unique chapter looks in detail at the age of mass destruction inaugurated, in very different ways, by the Holocaust and by the aerial bombings of civilian centers that culminated in the use of the atomic bomb in August 1945.

Features and Pedagogical Aids

In writing this textbook we have endeavored to keep both the student reader and the classroom instructor in mind at all times. The text includes the following features and pedagogy, all of which are intended to support the themes of the book.

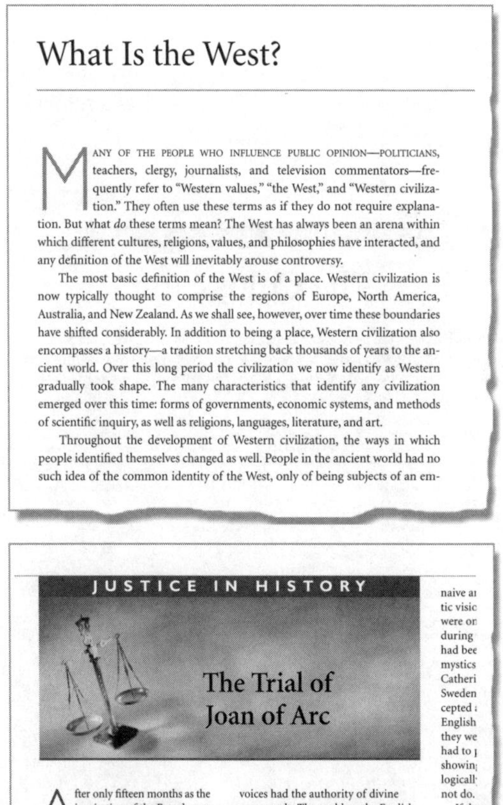

What Is the West?

MANY OF THE PEOPLE WHO INFLUENCE PUBLIC OPINION—POLITICIANS, teachers, clergy, journalists, and television commentators—frequently refer to "Western values," "the West," and "Western civilization." They often use these terms as if they do not require explanation. But what *do* these terms mean? The West has always been an arena within which different cultures, religions, values, and philosophies have interacted, and any definition of the West will inevitably arouse controversy.

The most basic definition of the West is of a place. Western civilization is now typically thought to comprise the regions of Europe, North America, Australia, and New Zealand. As we shall see, however, over time these boundaries have shifted considerably. In addition to being a place, Western civilization also encompasses a history—a tradition stretching back thousands of years to the ancient world. Over this long period the civilization we now identify as Western gradually took shape. The many characteristics that identify any civilization emerged over this time: forms of governments, economic systems, and methods of scientific inquiry, as well as religions, languages, literature, and art.

Throughout the development of Western civilization, the ways in which people identified themselves changed as well. People in the ancient world had no such idea of the common identity of the West, only of being subjects of an em-

WHAT IS THE WEST?

The West: Encounters & Transformations begins with an essay to engage students in the task of defining the West and to introduce them to the notion of cultural encounters. "What Is the West?" guides students through the text by providing a framework for understanding how the West was shaped. Structured around the five questions of What? When? Where? How? and Why?, this framework encourages students to think about their understanding of Western civilization. The essay serves as a blueprint for using this textbook.

JUSTICE IN HISTORY

Found in every chapter, the goal of this feature is to present a historically significant trial or episode in which different notions of justice (or injustice) were debated and resolved. The *Justice in History* features illustrate cultural encounters within communities as they try to determine the fate of individuals from all walks of life. Many famous trials dealt with conflicts over basic religious, philosophical, or political values, such as those of Socrates, Jesus, Joan of Arc, Charles I, Galileo, and Adolf Eichmann. Other *Justice in History* features show how judicial institutions, such as the ordeal, the inquisition, and revolutionary tribunals, handled adversarial situations in different societies. These essays, therefore, illustrate the way in which the basic values of the West have evolved through attempts to resolve disputes, contention, and conflict.

Each *Justice in History* feature includes two pedagogical aids. "Questions of Justice" help students explore the historical significance of the episode just examined. These questions can also be used in classroom discussion or as student essay topics. "Taking It Further" provides the student with a few references that can be consulted in connection with a research project.

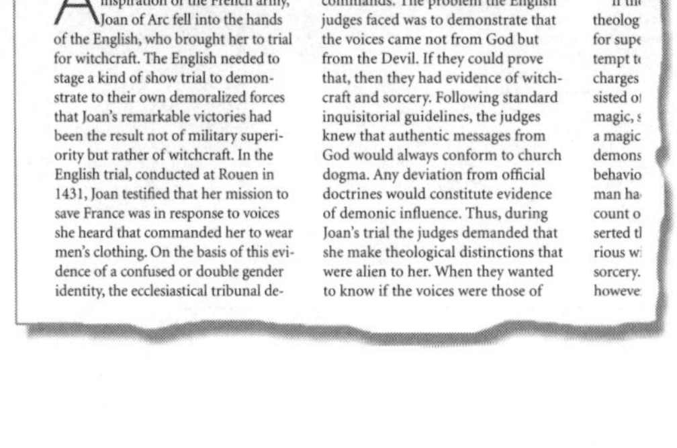

JUSTICE IN HISTORY

The Trial of Joan of Arc

After only fifteen months as the inspiration of the French army, Joan of Arc fell into the hands of the English, who brought her to trial for witchcraft. The English needed to stage a kind of show trial to demonstrate to their own demoralized forces that Joan's remarkable victories had been the result not of military superiority but rather of witchcraft. In the English trial, conducted at Rouen in 1431, Joan testified that her mission to save France was in response to voices she heard that commanded her to wear men's clothing. On the basis of this evidence of a confused or double gender identity, the ecclesiastical tribunal de-

voices had the authority of divine commands. The problem the English judges faced was to demonstrate that the voices came not from God but from the Devil. If they could prove that, then they had evidence of witchcraft and sorcery. Following standard inquisitorial guidelines, the judges knew that authentic messages from God would always conform to church dogma. Any deviation from official doctrines would constitute evidence of demonic influence. Thus, during Joan's trial the judges demanded that she make theological distinctions that were alien to her. When they wanted to know if the voices were those of

THE HUMAN BODY IN HISTORY

Shell Shock: From Woman's Malady to Soldier's Affliction

Broken in mind as well as body, the casualties of World War I forced medical practitioners to think anew about the connections among emotional anguish, physical disabilities, and gender roles. Doctors discovered to their horror and surprise that in the trenches of total war, men's bodies began to act like women's. Pouring into hospital units came thousands of men with the symptoms of a malady that before the war was considered a woman's disease—hysteria.

The word *hysteria* comes from the Greek word *hystera*, for "womb" or "uterus," and for much of Western history doctors believed that women were doomed to suffer from hysteria because of their physical makeup—because they were afflicted with wombs. Physicians long considered the uterus to be an inherently weak and unstable organ, prone even to detach itself from its proper place and wander about the body causing havoc. By the end of the nineteenth century, however, the diagnosis had changed. Doctors continued to regard hysteria as primaril
were more inclined to view it
emotional disorder. The sym
included bouts of shrieking,
pression or breakdown, and
clear physical cause—rangin
somnia to the inability to wal

With war came thousands
of hysteria—men who could
healthy limbs who could not
were nibbling at their bodies.
symptoms as signs of coward
ness to avoid doing their dut
accounting for 40 percent of
zones alone, doctors realized
demic of male hysteria.

The war illustrated that h
uterus or the weak female ne
environment of immobility
length of time a soldier had
horror of his combat experi
ducing breakdowns. Instead
his level of immobility. Men
found themselves in positio
ment. Deprived of the abilit
mine their future, to act, ma

Yet the reincarnation of w
woman's malady as a soldier's

THE HUMAN BODY IN HISTORY

Found in most chapters, these features show that the human body, which many people tend to understand solely as a product of biology, also has a history. These essays reveal that the ways in which various religious and political groups have represented the body in art and literature, clothed it, treated it medically, and abused it tell a great deal about the history of Western culture. These features include essays on the classical nude male body, the signs of disease in the Black Death, bathing the body in the East and the West, and the contraceptive pill. Concluding each essay is a single question for discussion which directs students back to the broader issues with which the chapter deals.

PLACES OF ENCOUNTER

Found in four chapters of the book, these features show that cultural exchanges between groups of people often occurred in specific places. The four features discuss the Roman Colosseum, Protestant and Catholic churches at the time of the Reformation, the French salon during the Enlightenment, and the twentieth-century soccer stadium. Accompanied by innovative visuals and graphics, these features reinforce the theme of encounters and also show that culture, which students often think of in abstract terms, has a material dimension. The essay concludes with a question for discussion.

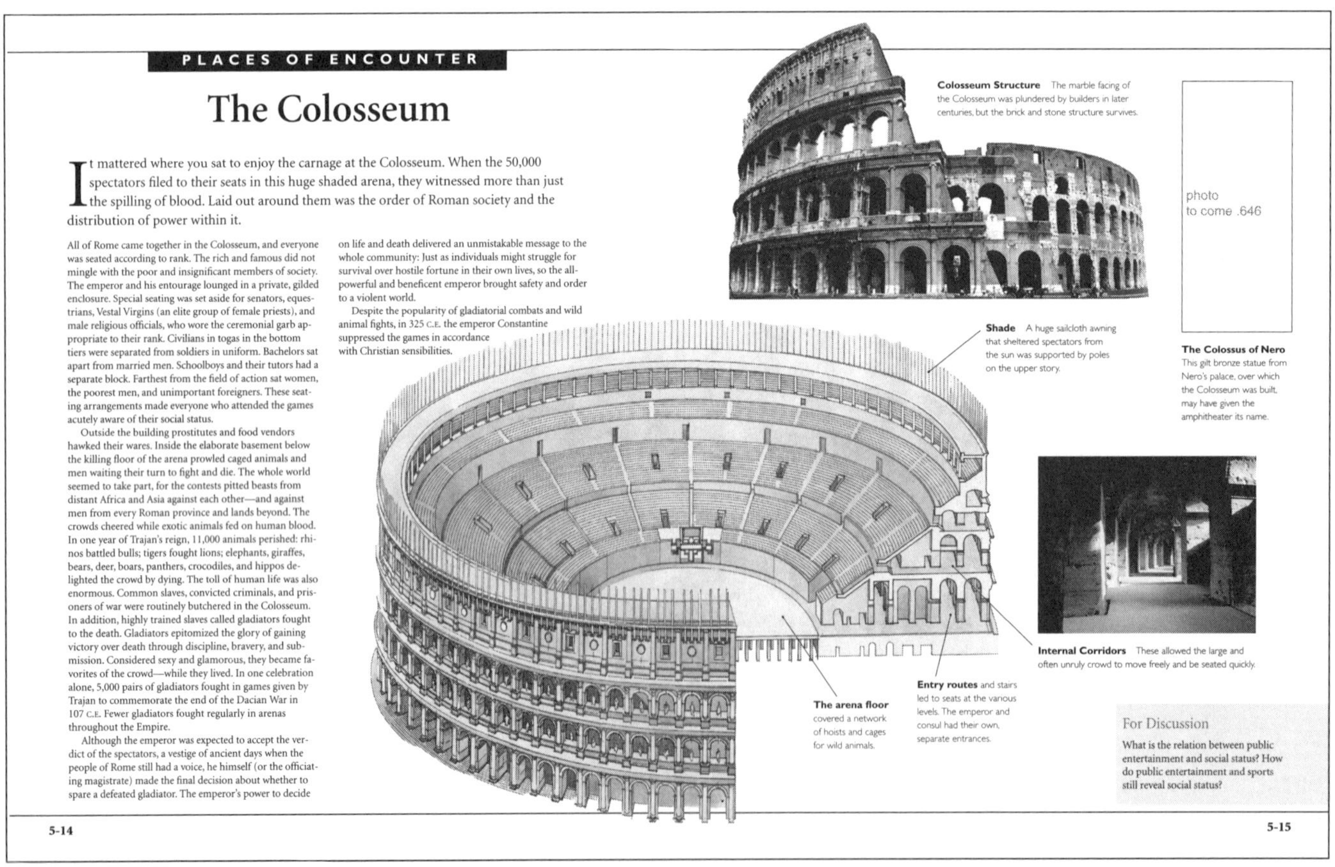

PLACES OF ENCOUNTER

The Colosseum

It mattered where you sat to enjoy the carnage at the Colosseum. When the 50,000 spectators filed to their seats in this huge shaded arena, they witnessed more than just the spilling of blood. Laid out around them was the order of Roman society and the distribution of power within it.

All of Rome came together in the Colosseum, and everyone was seated according to rank. The rich and famous did not mingle with the poor and insignificant members of society. The emperor and his entourage lounged in a private, gilded enclosure. Special seating was set aside for senators, equestrians, Vestal Virgins (an elite group of female priests), and male religious officials, who wore the ceremonial garb appropriate to their rank. Civilians in togas in the bottom tiers were separated from soldiers in uniform. Bachelors sat apart from married men. Schoolboys and their tutors had a separate block. Farthest from the field of action sat women, the poorest men, and unimportant foreigners. These seating arrangements made everyone who attended the games acutely aware of their social status.

Outside the building prostitutes and food vendors hawked their wares. Inside the elaborate basement below the killing floor of the arena prowled caged animals and men waiting their turn to fight and die. The whole world seemed to take part, for the contests pitted beasts from distant Africa and Asia against each other—and against men from every Roman province and lands beyond. The crowds cheered while exotic animals fed on human blood. In one year of Trajan's reign, 11,000 animals perished: rhinos battled bulls; tigers fought lions; elephants, giraffes, bears, deer, boars, panthers, crocodiles, and hippos delighted the crowd by dying. The toll of human life was also enormous. Common slaves, convicted criminals, and prisoners of war were routinely butchered in the Colosseum. In addition, highly trained slaves called gladiators fought to the death. Gladiators epitomized the glory of gaining victory over death through discipline, bravery, and submission. Considered sexy and glamorous, they became favorites of the crowd—while they lived. In one celebration alone, 5,000 pairs of gladiators fought in games given by Trajan to commemorate the end of the Dacian War in 107 C.E. Fewer gladiators fought regularly in arenas throughout the Empire.

Although the emperor was expected to accept the verdict of the spectators, a vestige of ancient days when the people of Rome still had a voice, he himself (or the officiating magistrate) made the final decision about whether to spare a defeated gladiator. The emperor's power to decide on life and death delivered an unmistakable message to the whole community: Just as individuals might struggle for survival over hostile fortune in their own lives, so the all-powerful and beneficent emperor brought safety and order to a violent world.

Despite the popularity of gladiatorial combats and wild animal fights, in 325 C.E. the emperor Constantine suppressed the games in accordance with Christian sensibilities.

Colosseum Structure The marble facing of the Colosseum was plundered by builders in later centuries, but the brick and stone structure survives.

photo
to come .646

The Colossus of Nero This gilt bronze statue from Nero's palace, over which the Colosseum was built, may have given the amphitheater its name.

Shade A huge sailcloth awning that sheltered spectators from the sun was supported by poles on the upper story.

Internal Corridors These allowed the large and often unruly crowd to move freely and be seated quickly.

The arena floor covered a network of hoists and cages for wild animals.

Entry routes and stairs led to seats at the various levels. The emperor and consul had their own, separate entrances.

For Discussion

What is the relation between public entertainment and social status? How do public entertainment and sports still reveal social status?

5-14 5-15

PRIMARY SOURCE DOCUMENTS

In each chapter we have presented a number of excerpts from primary source documents in order to reinforce or expand upon the points made in the text and to introduce students to the basic materials of historical research.

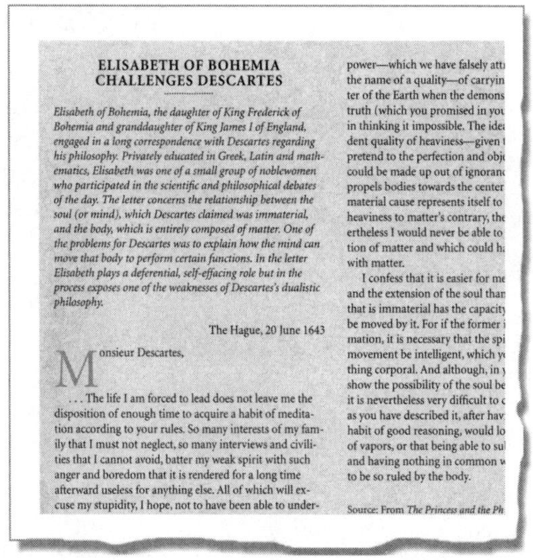

ELISABETH OF BOHEMIA CHALLENGES DESCARTES

Elisabeth of Bohemia, the daughter of King Frederick of Bohemia and granddaughter of King James I of England, engaged in a long correspondence with Descartes regarding his philosophy. Privately educated in Greek, Latin and mathematics, Elisabeth was one of a small group of noblewomen who participated in the scientific and philosophical debates of the day. The letter concerns the relationship between the soul (or mind), which Descartes claimed was immaterial, and the body, which is entirely composed of matter. One of the problems for Descartes was to explain how the mind can move that body to perform certain functions. In the letter Elisabeth plays a deferential, self-effacing role but in the process exposes one of the weaknesses of Descartes's dualistic philosophy.

The Hague, 20 June 1643

Monsieur Descartes,

. . . The life I am forced to lead does not leave me the disposition of enough time to acquire a habit of meditation according to your rules. So many interests of my family that I must not neglect, so many interviews and civilities that I cannot avoid, batter my weak spirit with such anger and boredom that it is rendered for a long time afterward useless for anything else. All of which will excuse my stupidity, I hope, not to have been able to under-

power—which we have falsely att
the name of a quality—of carryin
ter of the Earth when the demons
truth (which you promised in you
in thinking it impossible. The ide
dent quality of heaviness—given
pretend to the perfection and obj
could be made up out of ignoran
propels bodies towards the center
material cause represents itself to
heaviness to matter's contrary, th
ertheless I would never be able to
tion of matter and which could h
with matter.

I confess that it is easier for me
and the extension of the soul tha
that is immaterial has the capacit
be moved by it. For if the former
mation, it is necessary that the sp
movement be intelligent, which y
thing corporal. And although, in
show the possibility of the soul b
it is nevertheless very difficult to
as you have described it, after hav
habit of good reasoning, would lo
of vapors, or that being able to su
and having nothing in common w
to be so ruled by the body.

Source: From *The Princess and the Ph*

MAPS AND ILLUSTRATIONS

Artwork is a key component of our book. We recognize that many students often lack a strong familiarity with geography and so we have taken great care to develop maps that help sharpen their geographic skills. Complementing the book's standard map program, we include maps focusing on areas outside the borders of Western civilization. These maps include a small thumbnail globe that highlights the geographic area under discussion in the context of the larger world. Fine art and photos also tell the story of Western civilization and we have included over 350 images to help students visualize the past: the way people lived, the events that shaped their lives, and how they viewed the world around them.

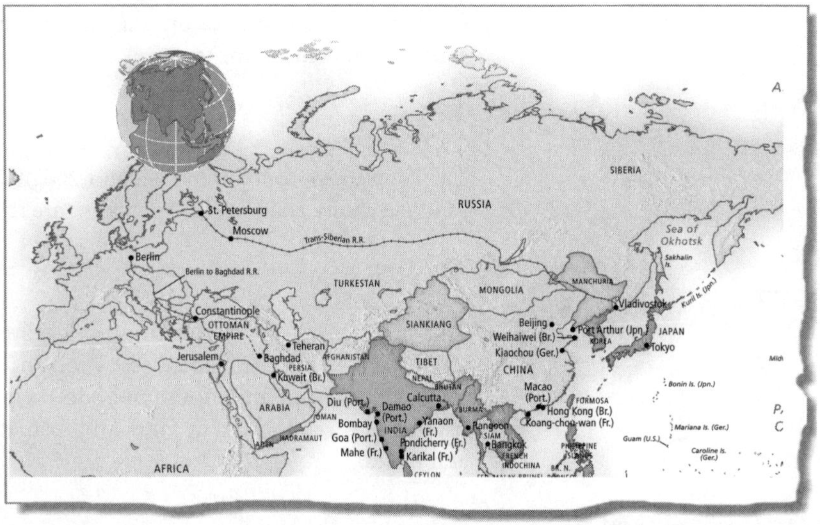

CHRONOLOGIES AND SUGGESTED READINGS

Each chapter includes chronological tables and suggested readings. Chronologies outline significant events and serve as convenient references for students. Each chapter concludes with an annotated list of suggested readings. These are not scholarly bibliographies aimed at the professor, but suggestions for students who wish to explore a topic in greater depth or to write a research paper. A comprehensive list of suggested readings is available on our book-specific website, www.ablongman.com/levack.

GLOSSARY

We have sought to create a work that is accessible to students with little prior knowledge of the basic facts of Western history or geography. Throughout the book we have explained difficult concepts at length. For example, we present in-depth explanations of the concepts of Zoroastrianism, Neoplatonism, Renaissance humanism, the various Protestant denominations of the sixteenth century, capitalism, seventeenth-century absolutism, nineteenth-century liberalism and nationalism, fascism, and modernism. Key concepts are identified in the chapters with a degree symbol (°) and defined as well in the end-of-text Glossary.

A NOTE ABOUT DATES AND TRANSLITERATIONS

In keeping with current academic practice, *The West: Encounters & Transformations* uses B.C.E. (before the common era) and C.E. (common era) to designate dates. We also follow the most current and widely accepted English transliterations of Arabic. Qur'an, for example, is used for Koran; Muslim is used for Moslem. Chinese words appearing in the text for the first time are written in *pinyin*, followed by the older Wade-Giles system in parentheses.

Supplements

FOR QUALIFIED COLLEGE ADOPTERS

Instructor's Resource Manual

0-673-97563-0

Each chapter contains a chapter outline, significant themes, learning objectives, lesson enrichment ideas, discussion suggestions, and questions for discussing the primary source documents in the text.

Test Bank

0-673-97564-9

This supplement contains more than 1,200 multiple-choice, true/false, and essay questions. Multiple-choice and true/false questions are referenced by topic and text page number.

TestGen-EQ Computerized Testing System

0-673-97565-3

This flexible, easy-to-master computerized test bank on a dual-platform CD includes all of the items in the printed test bank and allows instructors to select specific questions, edit existing questions, and add their own items to create exams. Tests can be printed in several different fonts and formats and can include figures, such as graphs and tables.

Companion Website

www.ablongman.com/levack

Instructors can take advantage of the Companion Website that supports this text. The instructor section includes teaching links, downloadable maps, tables, and graphs from the text for use in PowerPoint™, and a link to Supplements Central.

Supplements Central™

http://suppscentral.ablongman.com

A helpful website where instructors can download supplements including: Instructor's Manuals, Test Banks, TestGens, Power Point™ presentations, as well as CourseCompass®, WebCT, and Blackboard materials. Instructors will need to request a password from their sales representative to gain access.

PowerPoint™ Presentations

These presentations contain an average of 15 PowerPoint™ slides for each chapter and may include key points and terms for a lecture on the chapter, as well as full-color slides of important maps, graphs, and charts. The presentations are available for download from www.ablongman.com/levack.

Text-Specific Transparency Set

0-673-97568-1

A set of full-color transparency map acetates drawn from the text.

History Video Program

A list of over 100 videos from which qualified adopters can choose. Restrictions apply.

History Digital Media Archive CD-ROM

0-321-14976-9

This CD-ROM contains electronic images and interactive and static maps, along with media elements such as video. It is fully customizable and ready for classroom presentation. All images and maps are available in PowerPoint™ as well.

Course Compass

http://cms.abacon.com/coursecompass
http://www.ablongman.com/technologysolutions

Focus on teaching the course, not the technology! Course Compass combines the strength of Longman content with state-of-the-art technology that simplifies online course management for you.This easy-to-use and customizable programs enables you to tailor the content and functionality to meet your individual needs. You can create an online presence—for ANY course you teach—in under an hour. This course contains several dozen primary sources, Western civilization maps from Longman textbooks, and the map exercises from both *Mapping Western Civilization* and *Western Civilization Map Workbook,* all of which you can customize for your own class and text.

BlackBoard

http://cms.abacon.com/blackboard
http://www.ablongman.com/technologysolutions

Longman's rich Western civilization content is available in BlackBoard's course management system. The BlackBoard format enables you to quickly and easily customize any course to meet your specific needs. This course contains several dozen primary sources, Western civilization maps from Longman textbooks, and the map *Workbook,* all of which you can customize for your own class and text.

WebCT

http://cms.abacon.com/webct
http://www.ablongman.com/technologysolutions

WebCT offers a host of online course management tools. You can customize your own WebCT course with Longman content in a number of ways. Available content includes several dozen primary sources, Western civilization maps from Longman textbooks, and the map exercises from both *Mapping Western Civilization* and *Western Civilization Map Workbook,* all of which you can customize for your own class and text. Contact your sales representative for more information.

Discovering Western Civilization Through Maps and Views

0-673-97499-5

Created by Gerald Danzer, University of Illinois at Chicago, and David Buissert, this unique set of 140 full-color acetates contains an introduction to teaching history through maps and a detailed commentary on each transparency. The collection includes cartographic and pictorial maps, views and photos, urban plans, building diagrams, and works of art. Available to qualified college adopters.

FOR STUDENTS

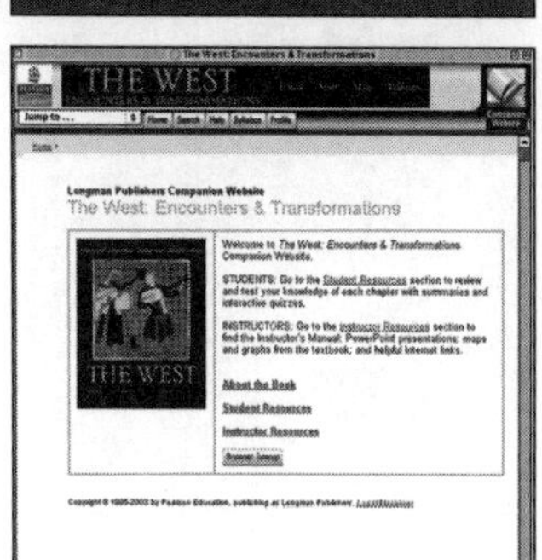

Study Guide

Volume I 0-673-98252-1
Volume II 0-673-98253-X

Containing activities and study aids for every chapter in the text, each chapter of the *Study Guide* includes a thorough summary; learning objectives; identification, completion, multiple-choice and thought questions; and critical-thinking questions based on primary source documents from the text.

Companion Website

www.ablongman.com/levack

Providing a wealth of resources for students using *The West: Encounters & Transformations,* this Companion Website contains chapter summaries, interactive practice test questions, and Web links for every chapter in the text.

Research Navigator and Research Navigator Guide

0-205-40838-9

Research Navigator is a comprehensive website comprising three exclusive databases of credible and reliable source material for research and for student assignments: EBSCO's ContentSelect Academic Journal Database, the New York Times Search by Subject Archive, and "Best of the Web" Link Library. The site also includes an extensive help section. The Research Navigator Guide provides your students with access to the Research Navigator website and includes reference material and hints about conducting online research. **Free to qualified college adopters when packaged with the text.**

Multimedia Edition CD-ROM for *The West: Encounters & Transformations*

0-321-18788-1

This unique CD-ROM takes students beyond the printed page, offering them a complete multimedia learning experience. It contains the full annotatable textbook on CD-ROM, with contextually placed media—audio, video, interactive maps, photos, and figures—that link students to additional content directly related to key concepts in the text. The CD also contains the *Study Guide,* Map Workbooks, a primary source reader, and more than a dozen supplementary books, most often assigned in Western civilization courses, including Plato, *The Republic,* and Machiavelli, *The Prince.* **Free to qualified college adopters when packaged with the text.**

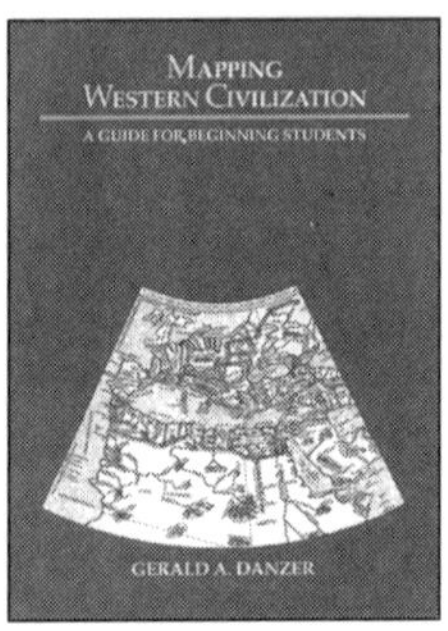

Mapping Western Civilization: Student Activities

0-673-53774-9

Created by Gerald Danzer, University of Illinois at Chicago, this FREE map workbook for students is designed as an accompaniment to *Discovering Western Civilization Through Maps and Views.* It features exercises designed to teach students to interpret and analyze cartographic materials such as historical documents. **Free to qualified college adopters when packaged with the text.**

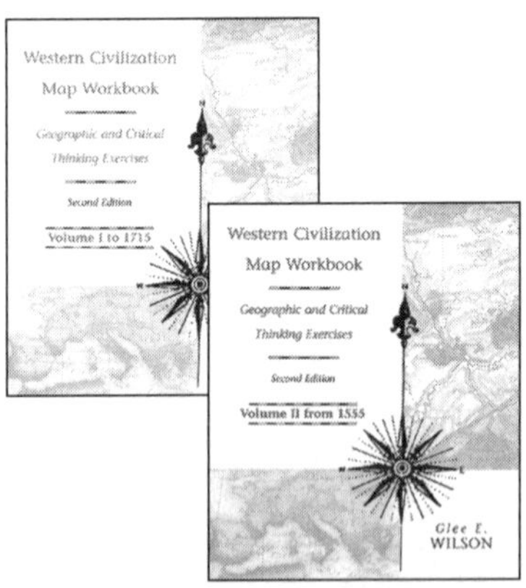

Western Civilization Map Workbook

Volume I 0-321-01878-8

Volume II 0-321-01877-X

The map exercises in these volumes by Glee Wilson test and reinforce basic geography literacy while building critical-thinking skills. **Free to qualified college adopters when packaged with the text.**

Full-Color Longman Western Civilization Timeline

0-321-13004-9

Noting key events and trends in political and diplomatic, social and economic, and cultural and technological history, this fold-out illustrated timeline provides a thorough and accessible chronological reference guide for Western civilization. **Free to qualified college adopters when packaged with the text.**

Longman Atlas of Western Civilization

0-321-21626-1

This 52-page atlas features carefully selected historical maps that provide comprehensive coverage for the major historical periods. Each map has been designed to be colorful, easy-to-read, and informative, without sacrificing detailed accuracy. This atlas makes history—and geography—more comprehensible.

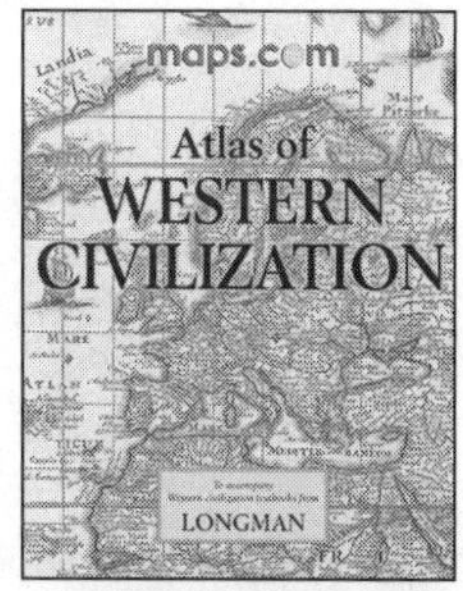

A Short Guide to Writing About History, Fourth Edition

0-321-09300-3

Written by Richard Marius, late of Harvard University, and Melvin E. Page, Eastern Tennessee State University, this engaging and practical text helps students get beyond merely compiling dates and facts; it teaches them how to incorporate their own ideas into their papers and to tell a story about history that interests them and their peers. Covering both brief essays and the documented resource paper, the text explores the writing and researching processes, identifies different modes of historical writing, including argument, and concludes with guidelines for improving style.

Everything You Need to Know About Your History Course

0-321-06628-6

This helpful supplement by Sandra Mathews-Lamb, Nebraska Wesleyan University, shows students how to become better history students by giving them direction on how to take good notes; how to write a paper or an exam; how to read maps, graphs, and charts; how to read primary and secondary sources; and more.

Longman World History—Primary Sources and Case Studies

Longmanworldhistory.com

The core of this website is its large database of thought-provoking primary sources, case studies, maps, and images—all carefully chosen and edited by scholars and teachers of world history. The content and organization of the site encourage students to analyze the themes, issues, and complexities of world history in a meaningful, exciting, and informative way. Offered at a significant discount to *The West: Encounters & Transformations* users, professors can visit the site for a free three-day trial.

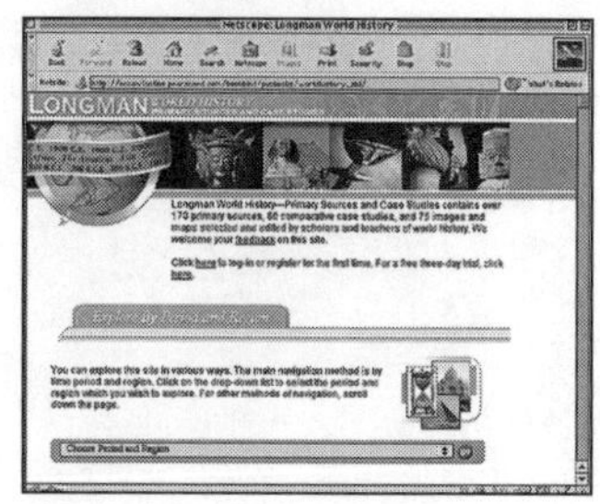

PENGUIN-LONGMAN PARTNERSHIP

The partnership between Penguin Books and Longman Publishers offers your students a discount on the titles below when instructors bundle them with any Longman survey. Visit www.ablongman.com/penguin for more information.

PEARSON Longman

PENGUIN PUTNAM INC.

Available titles

Peter Abelard, *The Letters of Abelard and Heloise*
Dante Alighieri, *Divine Comedy: Inferno*
Dante Alighieri, *The Portable Dante*
Anonymous, *The Song of Roland*
Anonymous, *The Epic of Gilgamesh*
Anonymous, *The Koran*
Anonymous, *Vinland Sagas*
Aristophanes, *The Knights, Peace, The Birds, Assemblywomen, Wealth*
Louis Auchincloss, *Woodrow Wilson* (Penguin Lives Series)
Jane Austen, *Emma*
Jane Austen, *Pride and Prejudice*
Jane Austen, *Persuasion*
Jane Austen, *Sense and Sensibility*
Edward Bellamy, *Looking Backward*
Richard Bowring, *Dairy of Lady Murasaki*
Charlotte Brontë, *Jane Eyre*
Charlotte Brontë, *Villette*
Emily Brontë, *Wuthering Heights*
Benvenuto Cellini, *The Autobiography of Benvenuto Cellini*
Geoffrey Chaucer, *The Canterbury Tales*
Marcus Tullius Cicero, *Cicero: Selected Political Speeches*
Miguel de Cervantes, *The Adventures of Don Quixote*
Bartolome de las Casas, *A Short Account of the Destruction of the West Indies*
René Descartes, *Discourse on Method and The Meditations*

Charles Dickens, *Hard Times*
Charles Dickens, *Great Expectations*
John Dos Passos, *Three Soldiers*
Einhard, *Two Lives of Charlemagne*
Olaudah Equiano, *The Interesting Narrative and Other Writings*
Jeffrey Gantz (tr.), *Early Irish Myths and Sagas*
Peter Gay, *Mozart* (Penguin Lives Series)
William Golding, *Lord of the Flies*
Kenneth Grahame, *The Wind in the Willows*
Grimm & Grimm, *Grimms' Fairy Tales*
Thomas Hardy, *Jude the Obscure*
Herodotus, *The Histories*
Thomas Hobbes, *Leviathan*
Homer, *The Iliad*
Homer, *Odyssey: Revised Prose Translation*
Homer, *Odyssey Deluxe*
Lemisch, *B. Franklin*
Primo Levi, *If Not Now, When?*
Machiavelli, *The Prince*
Karl Marx, *The Communist Manifesto*
John Stuart Mill, *On Liberty*
Jean-Baptiste Molière, *Tartuffe and Other Plays*
Charles-Louis Montesquieu, *Persian Letters*
Sir Thomas More, *Utopia and Other Essential Writings*
Sherwin Nuland, *Leonardo DaVinci*
George Orwell, *1984*
George Orwell, *Animal Farm*
Plato, *Great Dialogues of Plato*
Plato, *The Republic*
Plato, *The Last Days of Socrates*
Marco Polo, *The Travels*
Procopius, *The Secret History*
Jean-Jacques Rousseau, *The Social Contract*
Sallust, *The Jugurthine Wars, The Conspiracy of Cataline*
William Shakespeare, *Hamlet*
William Shakespeare, *Macbeth*
William Shakespeare, *The Merchant of Venice* (Pelican Series)
William Shakespeare, *The Merchant of Venice* (Signet Classics)
William Shakespeare, *Othello*
William Shakespeare, *The Taming of the Shrew*
William Shakespeare, *Twelfth Night*
William Shakespeare, *King Lear*
William Shakespeare, *Four Great Comedies: The Taming of the Shrew, A Midsummer's Night Dream, Twelfth Night, The Tempest*
William Shakespeare, *Four Great Tragedies: Hamlet, Macbeth, King Lear, Othello*
William Shakespeare, *Four Histories: Richard II, Henry IV: Part I, Henry IV: Part II, Henry V*
William Shakespeare, *The Tempest*
Mary Shelley, *Frankenstein*
Aleksandr Solzhenitsyn, *One Day in the Life of Ivan Denisovich*
Sophocles, *The Three Theban Plays*
St. Augustine, *The Confessions of St. Augustine*
Robert Louis Stevenson, *The Strange Case of Dr. Jekyll and Mr. Hyde*
Suetonius, *The Twelve Caesars*
Jonathan Swift, *Gulliver's Travels*
Tacitus, *The Histories*
Voltaire, *Candide, Zadig and Selected Stories*
Goethe, *Faust, Part 1*
Goethe, *Faust, Part 2*
Edith Wharton, *Ethan Frome*
M. Willet, *The Signet World Atlas*
Gary Wills, *Saint Augustine* (Penguin Lives Series)
Virginia Woolf, *Jacob's Room*

Acknowledgments

In writing this book we have benefited from the guidance of many members of the superb editorial staff at Longman. Our first acquisitions editor, Bruce Borland, encouraged us to write a book emphasizing the theme of cultural encounters, while Jay O'Callaghan and Erika Gutierrez helped us refine that theme as the book progressed. Dawn Groundwater, our senior development editor, gave us valuable line-by-line criticisms of all our chapters and helped us keep our audience in mind as we revised them. Lisa Pinto, the director of development, read our chapters at different stages of composition and made sure that our arguments were logical and consistent. Priscilla McGeehon, publisher for the social sciences, facilitated the progress of the project at a number of crucial junctures. Susan Gallier superintended the copyediting and proofreading with skill and efficiency, while Jullie Chung helped us locate the most appropriate illustrations. Sue Westmoreland, the executive marketing manager for history, offered many creative ideas for promoting the book.

The authors wish to thank the following friends and colleagues for their assistance: Joseph Alehermes, Kenneth Alder, Karl Appuhn, Sharon Arnoult, Nicholas Baker, Paul-Alain Beaulieu, Paula Baskovits, Timothy Breen, Peter Brown, Peter Carroll, Patricia Crone, Tracey Cullen, Arthur Eckstein, Susanna Elm, Benjamin Frommer, Dena Goodman, Matthias Henze, Stanley Hilton, Kenneth Holum, Mark Jurdjevic, Werner Kelber, Cathleen Keller, Anne Kilmer, Jacob Lassner, Robert Lerner, Nancy Levack, Richard Lim, David Lindenfeld, Sarah Maza, Laura McGough, Roderick McIntosh, Susan K. McIntosh, Glenn Markoe, William Monter, Randy Nichols, Scott Noegel, Monique O'Connell, Carl Petry, Michael Rogers, Karl Roider, Sarah Ross, Michele Salzman, Paula Sanders, Regina Schwartz, Ethan Shagan, Julia M. H. Smith, and James Sidbury.

We would also like to thank the many historians who gave generously of their time to review our manuscript at various stages of development. Their comments and suggestions have helped to improve the book. Thank you:

Henry Abramson, *Florida Atlantic University*
Patricia Ali, *Morris College*
Joseph Appiah, *J. Sergeant Reynolds Community College*
Sharon L. Arnoult, *Midwestern State University*
Arthur H. Auten, *University of Hartford*
Clifford Backman, *Boston University*
Suzanne Balch-Lindsay, *Eastern New Mexico University*
Wayne C. Bartee, *Southwest Miami State University*
Brandon Beck, *Shenandoah University*
James R. Belpedio, *Becker College*
Richard Berthold, *University of New Mexico*
Cynthia S. Bisson, *Belmont University*
Richard Bodek, *College of Charleston*
Melissa Bokovoy, *University of New Mexico*
William H. Brennan, *University of the Pacific*
Morgan R. Broadhead, *Jefferson Community College*
Theodore Bromund, *Yale University*
April A. Brooks, *South Dakota State University*
Nathan M. Brooks, *New Mexico State University*
Michael Burger, *Mississippi University for Women*
Susan Carrafiello, *Wright State University*
Kathleen S. Carter, *High Point University*
William L. Combs, *Western Illinois University*
Joseph Coohill, *Pennsylvania State University—New Kensington*
Richard A. Cosgrove, *University of Arizona*
Leonard Curtis, *Mississippi College*
Miriam Davis, *Delta State University*
Alexander DeGrand, *North Carolina State University*
Marion Deshmukh, *George Mason University*
Janusz Duzinkiewicz, *Purdue University North Central*
Mary Beth Emmerichs, *University of Wisconsin, Sheboygan*
Steven Fanning, *University of Illinois at Chicago*
Bryan Ganaway, *University of Illinois at Urbana-Champaign*
Frank Garosi, *California State University—Sacramento*
Christina Gold, *Loyola Marymount University*
Ignacio Götz, *Hofstra University*
Louis Haas, *Duquesne University*
Linda Jones Hall, *Saint Mary's College of Maryland*
Paul Halsall, *University of North Florida*
Donald J. Harreld, *Brigham Young University*
Carmen V. Harris, *University of South Carolina at Spartanburg*
Mark C. Herman, *Edison Community College*
Curry A. Herring, *University of Southern Alabama*
Patrick Holt, *Fordham University*
W. Robert Houston, *University of South Alabama*
Lester Hutton, *Westfield State College*
Jeffrey Hyson, *Saint Joseph's University*

Paul Jankowski, *Brandeis University*
Padraic Kennedy, *McNeese State University*
Joanne Klein, *Boise State University*
Theodore Kluz, *Troy State University*
Skip Knox, *Boise State University*
Cynthia Kosso, *Northern Arizona University*
Ann Kuzdale, *Chicago State University*
Lawrence Langer, *University of Connecticut*
Oscar E. Lansen, *University of North Carolina at Charlotte*
Michael V. Leggiere, *Louisiana State University at Shreveport*
Rhett Leverett, *Marymount University*
Alison Williams Lewin, *Saint Joseph's University*
Wendy Liu, *Miami University, Middletown*
Elizabeth Makowski, *Southwest Texas State University*
Daniel Meissner, *Marquette University*
Isabel Moreira, *University of Utah*
Kenneth Moure, *University of California, Santa Barbara*
Melva E. Newsom, *Clark State Community College*
John A. Nichols, *Slippery Rock University*
Susannah R. Ottaway, *Carleton College*
James H. Overfield, *University of Vermont*
Brian L. Peterson, *Florida International University*
Hugh Phillips, *Western Kentucky University*
Jeff Plaks, *University of Central Oklahoma*
Thomas L. Powers, *University of South Carolina, Sumter*
Carole Putko, *San Diego State University*
Barbara Ranieri, *University of Alabama at Birmingham*
Elsa M. E. Rapp, *Montgomery County Community College*
Marlette Rebhorn, *Austin Community College*
Roger Reese, *Texas A&M University*
Travis Ricketts, *Bryan College*
Thomas Robisheaux, *Duke University*
Bill Robison, *Southeastern Louisiana University*
Mark Ruff, *Concordia University*
Frank Russell, *Transylvania University*
Marylou Ruud, *The University of West Florida*
Michael Saler, *University of California—Davis*
Timothy D. Saxon, *Charleston Southern University*
Daniel A. Scalberg, *Multnomah Bible College*
Ronald Schechter, *College of William and Mary*
Philip Skaggs, *Grand Valley State University*
Helmut Walser Smith, *Vanderbilt University*
Eileen Solwedel, *Edmonds Community College*
Sister Maria Consuelo Sparks, *Immaculata University*
Ilicia J. Sprey, *Saint Joseph's College*
Charles R. Sullivan, *University of Dallas*
Frederick Suppe, *Ball State University*
Frank W. Thackery, *Indiana University Southeast*
Frances B. Titchener, *Utah State University*
Katherine Tosa, *Muskegon Community College*
Lawrence A. Tritle, *Loyola Marymount University*
Clifford F. Wargelin, *Georgetown College*
Theodore R. Weeks, *Southern Illinois University*
Elizabeth A. Williams, *Oklahoma State University*
Mary E. Zamon, *Marymount University*

BRIAN LEVACK
EDWARD MUIR
MICHAEL MAAS
MEREDITH VELDMAN

Meet the Authors

Brian Levack grew up in a family of teachers in the New York metropolitan area. From his father, a professor of French history, he acquired a love for studying the past, and he knew from an early age that he too would become a historian. He received his B.A. from Fordham University in 1965 and his Ph.D. from Yale in 1970. In graduate school he became fascinated by the history of the law and the interaction between law and politics, interests that he has maintained throughout his career. In 1969 he joined the History Department of the University of Texas at Austin, where he is now the John Green Regents Professor in History. The winner of several teaching awards, Levack teaches a wide variety of courses on British and European history, legal history, and the history of witchcraft. For eight years he served as the chair of his department, a rewarding but challenging assignment that made it difficult for him to devote as much time as he wished to his teaching and scholarship. His books include *The Civil Lawyers in England, 1603–1641: A Political Study* (1973), *The Formation of the British State: England, Scotland and the Union, 1603–1707* (1987), and *The Witch-Hunt in Early Modern Europe* (1987 and 1995), which has been translated into eight languages.

His study of the development of beliefs about witchcraft in Europe over the course of many centuries gave him the idea of writing a textbook on Western civilization that would illustrate a broader set of encounters between different cultures, societies, and ideologies. While writing the book, Levack and his two sons built a house on property that he and his wife, Nancy, own in the Texas hill country. He found that the two projects presented similar challenges: It was easy to draw up the design, but far more difficult to execute it. When not teaching, writing, or doing carpentry work, Levack runs along the jogging trails of Austin, and he has recently discovered the pleasures of scuba diving.

Edward Muir grew up in the foothills of the Wasatch Mountains in Utah, close to the Emigration Trail along which wagon trains of Mormon pioneers and California-bound settlers made their way westward. As a child he loved to explore the broken-down wagons and abandoned household goods left at the side of the trail and from that acquired a fascination with the past. Besides the material remains of the past, he grew up with stories of his Mormon pioneer ancestors and an appreciation for how the past continued to influence the present. During the turbulent 1960s, he became interested in Renaissance Italy as a period and a place that had been formative for Western civilization. His biggest challenge is finding the time to explore yet another new corner of Italy and its restaurants.

Muir received his Ph.D. from Rutgers University, where he specialized in the Italian Renaissance and did archival research in Venice and Florence, Italy. He is now the Clarence L. Ver Steeg Professor in the Arts and Sciences at Northwestern University and former chair of the History Department. At Northwestern he has won several teaching awards. His books include *Civic Ritual in Renaissance Venice* (Princeton, 1981); *Mad Blood Stirring: Vendetta in Renaissance Italy* (Johns Hopkins, 1993 and 1998); and *Ritual in Early Modern Europe* (Cambridge, 1997).

Some years ago Muir began to experiment with the use of historical trials in teaching and discovered that students loved them. From that experience he decided to write this textbook, which employs trials as a central feature. He lives beside Lake Michigan in Evanston, Illinois. His twin passions are skiing in the Rocky Mountains and rooting for the Chicago Cubs, who manage every summer to demonstrate that winning isn't everything.

Michael Maas was born in the Ohio River Valley, in a community that had been a frontier outpost during the late eighteenth century. He grew up reading the stories of the early settlers and their struggles with the native peoples, and seeing in the urban fabric how the city had subsequently developed into a prosperous coal and steel town with immigrants from all over the world. As a boy he developed a lifetime interest in the archaeology and history of the ancient Mediterranean world and began to study Latin. At Cornell University he combined his interests in cultural history and the Classical world by majoring in Classics and Anthropology. A semester in Rome clinched his commitment to these fields—and to Italian cooking. Mass went on to get his Ph.D. in the Graduate Program in Ancient History and Mediterranean Archaeology at University of California at Berkeley.

He has traveled widely in the Mediterranean and the Middle East and participated in several archaeological excavations, including an underwater dig in Greece. Since 1985 he has taught ancient history at Rice University in Houston, Texas, where he founded and directs the interdisciplinary B.A. Program in Ancient Mediterranean Civilizations. He has won several teaching awards.

Maas's special area of research is Late Antiquity, the period of transition from the Classical to the Medieval worlds, which saw the collapse of the Roman Empire in western Europe and the development of the Byzantine state in the east. During his last sabbatical, he was a member of the Institute for Advanced Study in Princeton, New Jersey, where he worked on his current book, *The Conqueror's Gift: Ethnography, Identity, and Imperial Power at the End of Antiquity* (forthcoming). His other books include *John Lydus and the Roman Past: Antiquarianism and Politics in the Age of Justinian* (1992); *Readings in Late Antiquity: A Sourcebook* (2000); and *Exegesis and Empire in the Early Byzantine Mediterranean* (2003).

Maas has always been interested in interdisciplinary teaching and the encounters among different cultures. He sees *The West: Encounters & Transformations* as an opportunity to explain how the modern civilization that we call "the West" had its origins in the diverse interactions among many peoples of antiquity.

Meredith Veldman grew up in the western suburbs of Chicago in a close-knit, closed-in Dutch Calvinist community. In this immigrant society, history mattered: the "Reformed tradition" structured not only religious beliefs but also social identity and political practice. This influence certainly played some role in shaping Veldman's early fascination with history. But probably just as important were the countless World War II reenactment games she played with her five older brothers. Whatever the cause, Veldman majored in history at Calvin College in Grand Rapids, Michigan, and then earned a Ph.D. in modern European history, with a concentration in nineteenth- and twentieth-century Britain, from Northwestern University in 1988.

As Associate Professor of History at Louisiana State University, Veldman teaches courses in nineteenth- and twentieth-century British history and twentieth-century Europe, as well as the second half of "Western Civ." In her many semesters in the Western Civ. classroom, Veldman tried a number of different textbooks but found herself increasingly dissatisfied. She wanted a text that would convey to beginning students at least some of the complexities and ambiguities of historical interpretation, introduce them to the exciting work being done now in cultural history, and, most important, tell a good story. The search for this textbook led her to accept the offer made by Levack, Maas, and Muir to join them in writing *The West: Encounters & Transformations.*

The author of *Fantasy, the Bomb, and the Greening of Britain: Romantic Protest, 1945–1980* (1994), Veldman is also the wife of a Methodist minister and the mother of two young sons. They reside in Baton Rouge, Louisiana, where Veldman finds coping with the steamy climate a constant challenge. She and her family recently returned from Manchester, England, where they lived for three years and astonished the natives by their enthusiastic appreciation of English weather.

THE WEST

What Is the West?

MANY OF THE PEOPLE WHO INFLUENCE PUBLIC OPINION—POLITICIANS, teachers, clergy, journalists, and television commentators—frequently refer to "Western values," "the West," and "Western civilization." They often use these terms as if they do not require explanation. But what *do* these terms mean? The West has always been an arena within which different cultures, religions, values, and philosophies have interacted, and any definition of the West will inevitably arouse controversy.

The most basic definition of the West is of a place. Western civilization is now typically thought to comprise the regions of Europe, North America, Australia, and New Zealand. As we shall see, however, over time these boundaries have shifted considerably. In addition to being a place, Western civilization also encompasses a history—a tradition stretching back thousands of years to the ancient world. Over this long period the civilization we now identify as Western gradually took shape. The many characteristics that identify any civilization emerged over this time: forms of governments, economic systems, and methods of scientific inquiry, as well as religions, languages, literature, and art.

Throughout the development of Western civilization, the ways in which people identified themselves changed as well. People in the ancient world had no such idea of the common identity of the West, only of being subjects of an empire. But with the rise of Christianity and Islam between the third and seventh centuries C.E., the notion of a distinct civilization in these "Western" lands subtly changed. People came to identify themselves less as subjects of a particular empire and more as members of a community of faith—whether that community comprised followers of Christianity, Judaism, or Islam (see Chapter 7). These communities of faith drew lines of inclusion and exclusion that still exist today. From about 1,000 to 5,000 years ago, Christian monarchs obliterated polytheism (the worship of many gods), strove to expel Muslims from Christian kingdoms, and marginalized Jews (see Chapter 9). Europeans developed definitions of civilization that is not include Islamic communities. The Islamic countries themselves erected their own barriers, isolating themselves from the West. During the Renaissance in the fifteenth century an identity based on a continuous historical experience dating back to the ancient world was added to these religious definitions of the identity of the West.

The Temple of Hera I at Paestum, Italy: Greek colonists in Italy built this temple in the sixth century B.C.E. Greek culture was one of the foundations of the civilization of the West. Greek ideas and artistic styles spread throughout the ancient world both from Greek colonists, such as those at Paestum, and from other peoples who imitated the Greeks.

The definition of the West has also changed as a result of European colonialism, which began about 500 years ago. When European powers assembled large overseas empires, they introduced Western languages, religions, technology, and culture to many distant places in the world, making Western identity a transportable concept (see Chapters 12, 19, and 23). In some of these colonized areas—such as North America, Argentina, Australia, and New Zealand—the European newcomers so outnumbered the indigenous people that these regions became as much a part of the West as Britain, France, and Spain. In other European colonies, especially in European trading outposts on the Asian continent, Western culture failed to exercise a widespread influence.

As a result of colonialism Western culture sometimes merged with other cultures. Brazil, a South American country inhabited by large numbers of indigenous peoples, the descendants of African slaves, and European settlers, epitomizes the complexity of what defines the West. In Brazil, almost everyone speaks a Western language (Portuguese), practices a Western religion (Christianity), and enjoys the benefits of Western political and economic institutions (democracy and capitalism). Yet in Brazil all of these features of Western civilization have become part of a distinctive hybrid civilization, in which indigenous, African, and European elements have been blended. During Carnival, for example, Brazilians dressed in indigenous costumes dance in African rhythms to the accompaniment of music played on European instruments.

A Satellite View of Europe
What is the West? Western civilization has undergone numerous definitions throughout history.

For many people today, the most important definition of the West involves abhorrence to a certain set of values, the "Western" values. Values are the moral and philosophical principles that are held in esteem by a particular culture. The values typically identified as Western include universal human rights, toleration of religious diversity, equality before the law, democracy, and freedom of inquiry and expression. These values have a long history. Yet these values have not always been embraced by Western societies. For example, the rulers of ancient Rome extended the privileges of citizenship, the right to own property, and the ability to participate in trade to a select few inhabitants of their empire (see Chapter 5)—thus only the privileged enjoyed the benefits of equality before the law. The majority of medieval Europeans, who were Christian, expressed an intense intolerance for religious diversity expressed in the Crusades against Muslims and heretics and pogroms of Jews (see Chapter 9). As late as the nineteenth century, white men living in the United States enslaved blacks and into the twentieth excluded women from voting and equal access to jobs. And in Nazi Germany and the Soviet Union, totalitarian regimes terrorized their own population and millions of others beyond their borders (see Chapter 25). The history of the West is riddled with examples of leaders who stifled free inquiry and who censored their followers. What are we to make of this contradiction in values? This text highlights and examines these contradictions, demonstrating how hard values were to formulate in the first place and how difficult they have been to preserve.

The Shifting Borders of the West

The geographical setting of the West has also shifted over time. This textbook begins about 12,000 years ago in Mesopotamia and the Middle East. At that time crops were harvested, animals were domesticated, and vast trading networks were being established. Cities, kingdoms, and empires gave birth to the first civilizations. By about 500 B.C.E., the civilizations that are the culture ancestors of the modern West had spread from the Middle East to include the Mediterranean basin—areas influences by Egyptian, Hebrew, Greek, and Roman thought, art, law, and religion. By the first century C.E. the Roman Empire drew the map of what historians consider the heartland of the West: most of the western and southern Europe, the coastlands of the Mediterranean Sea, and the Middle East.

The West is now usually thought to include western Europe and North America. However, the borders of the West have in recent decades come to be less about geography than identity. When Japan, an Asian country, accepted some Western values such as human rights and democracy after World War II, did it become part of the West? Or consider the Republic of South Africa, which until 1994 was ruled by the white minority, people descended from European immigrants. The oppressive regime violated human rights, rejected full legal equality for all citizens, and jailed or murdered those who questioned the government. Only when that government was replaces through democratic elections and a black man became president did South Africa grant full rights to non-Europeans. To what degree was South Africa part of the West before and after these developments?

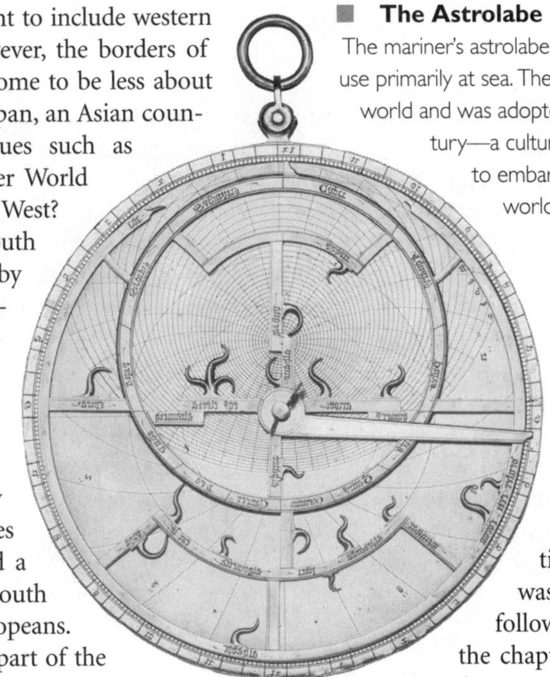

The Astrolabe

The mariner's astrolabe was a navigational device intended for use primarily at sea. The astrolabe originated in the Islamic world and was adopted by Europeans in the twelfth century—a cultural encounter that enabled Europeans to embark on long ocean voyages around the world.

Russia long saw itself as a Christian country with a tradition of culture, economic, and political ties with the rest of Europe. The Russians have intermittently identified with their western neighbors, but their neighbors were not always sure about the Russians. After the Mongol invasions of the thirteenth and fourteenth centuries much of Russia was isolated from the rest of the West (see Chapter 10) and during the Cold War from 1949 to 1989 (see Chapter 27–29) Russian communism and the Western democracies were polarized. When was Russia "Western" and when not?

Thus, when we talk about where the West is, we are almost always talking bout the Mediterranean basin and western Europe (and later, North America). But we will also show that countries that border "the West," and even countries far from it, might be considered Western in many aspects as well.

Asking the Right Questions

So how can we make sense of the West as a place and an identity, the shifting borders of the West, and Western civilization in general? In short, what has Western civilization been over the course of its long history—and what is it today?

Answering these questions is the friendly challenge this book poses. You may be alarmed to learn that there are no simple answers to any of these questions. On the other hand, you may be relieved to discover that there is a method for finding answers that have meaning for the different periods of history covered in this book. The method is straightforward. Always ask the *what,* the *when,* the *where,* the *who,* the *how,* and the *why* questions of the text. If you do so, you will surmount the challenge the book poses. To aid you, every chapter addresses the question of "What is the West," or "How was the West made" at its beginning following the story or event that opens the chapter. We revisit the question in the Conclusion at the end of every chapter. For example, in Chapter 11 we look at how the Italian Renaissance helped refashion the very concept of Western civilization. In the Conclusion, we see that the Renaissance interest in the history of the ancient world transformed the idea of the West from one defined primarily by religious identification with Christianity to one created by a common historical experience.

The "What" Question

What is Western civilization? The answer to this question will vary according to time and place. In fact, for much of the early history covered in this book, Western civilization as we know it today did not exist as a single cultural entity. Rather, a number of distinctive civilizations were taking shape in the Middle East, northern Africa, and Europe, each of which contributed to what later became Western civilization (see Chapter 1–3). But throughout time the idea of Western civilization slowly began to form. Thus our understanding of Western civilization will change from chapter to chapter. For example, in Chapters 12, 19, and 23, we examine how the place of the West changed through the colonial expansion of the European nations. In Chapter 16 we learn how the West came to prize the values of scientific inquiry for solving human and philosophical problems, an approach that did not exist before the seventeenth century but became central to Western civilization.

The "When" Question

When did the defining characteristics of Western civilization first emerge, and for how long did they prevail? To explore these questions you will want to refer to the dates that frame each chapter, as well as the numerous short chronologies offered in each chapter. These resources will help you keep track of what happened when. Dates have no meaning by themselves, but the connections *between* them can be very revealing.

For example, dates show that the agricultural revolution that permitted the birth of the first civilizations (see Chapter 1) unfolded over a long span of about 10,000 years—which is more time than was taken by all the other events and developments covered in this book. Wars of religion (see Chapter 14) plagued Europe for nearly 200 years before Enlightenment thinkers articulated the ideals of religious toleration (see Chapter 17). The American Civil War—the war to preserve the union as President Abraham Lincoln termed it—took place at exactly the same time as other wars were being fought to achieve national unity in Germany and Italy (see Chapter 21).

By learning when things happened, you can identify the major causes and consequences of events, and thus you can see the transformations of Western civilization. For instance, the ability to produce a surplus of food through agriculture and the domestication of animals was a prerequisite for the emergence of civilizations. The violent collapse of religious unity after the Protestant Reformation in the sixteenth century led some Europeans to propose the separation of church and state two centuries later. And during the nineteenth century many Western states—in response to the enormous diversity among their own peoples—became preoccupied with maintaining or establishing national unity.

THE "WHERE" QUESTION

Where has Western civilization been located? Geography, of course, does not change very rapidly, but the idea of where the West is does. The location of the West is not so much a matter of changing borders but of how people identify themselves. The key to understanding the shifting borders of the West is to study the peoples within the countries

Map I Topographical Map of the West

The geographical borders of the West have not changed substantially throughout history, but the concept of where the West is has changed.

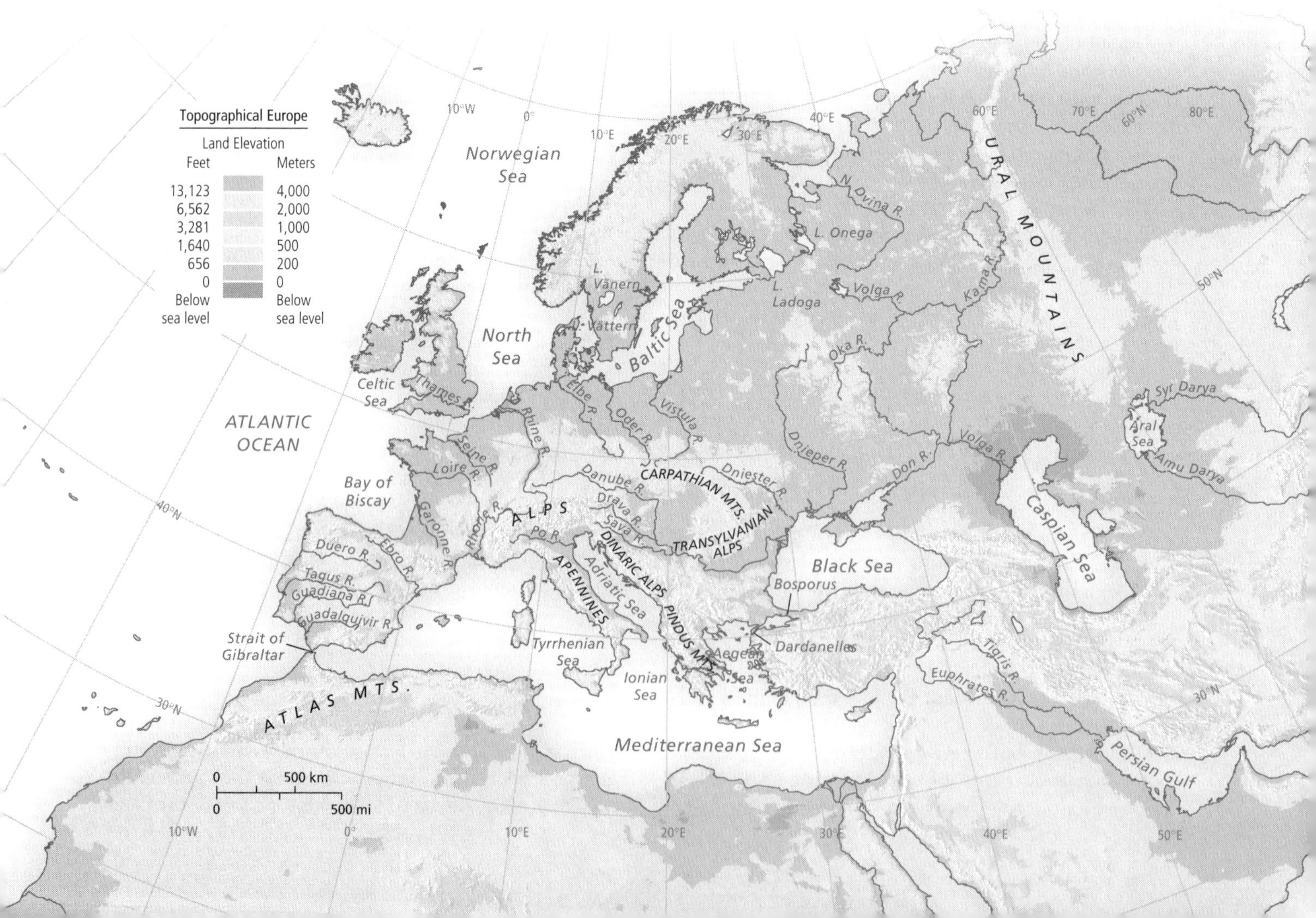

Cortés Meets Montezuma
As the Spanish fought, traded, and intermarried with the native peoples of the Americas during the fifteenth and sixteenth centuries, each culture changed.

around the West. These groups include Muslims and the peoples of eastern Europe (such as the Soviet Union during the Cold War). In addition, the chapters help you trace the relationships between the West (as it was constituted in different periods) and other, more distant civilizations with which it interacted. Those civilizations include not only those of East Asia and South Asia but also the indigenous peoples of sub-Saharan Africa, the Americas, and the Pacific islands (see Chapters 12, 19, and 23).

THE "WHO" QUESTION

Who were the people responsible for making Western civilization? Sometimes they were anonymous, such as the unknown geniuses who invented the mathematical systems of ancient Mesopotamia. At other times the makers of the West were famous—emperors such as Julius Caesar, creative thinkers such as Galileo Galilei, or generals such as Napoleon. But history is not only made by great and famous people. Humble people, such as the many millions who migrated from Europe to North America or the unfortunate millions who suffered and died in the trenches of World War I, can also influence the course of events.

Perhaps most often in this book you will encounter people who were less the shapers of their own destinies than the subjects of forces that conditioned the kinds of choices they could make, often with unanticipated results. When during the eleventh century farmers throughout Europe began to employ a new kind of plow to till their fields, they were merely trying to do their work more efficiently. They certainly did not recognize that the increase in food they produced would stimulate the enormous population growth that made possible the medieval civilization of thriving cities and magnificent cathedrals. In answering the who question, you will always want to evaluate how much individuals and groups of people were in control of events and how much events controlled them.

THE "HOW" QUESTION

How did Western civilization develop? This is a question about processes—about how things change or stay the same over time. This book will help you identify these processes in several ways. First, we have woven the theme of encounters throughout the story. What do we mean by encounters? Here is an example from Chapter 12: When the Spanish *conquistadores* arrived in the Americas some 500 years ago, they came into contact with the cultures of the Caribs, the Aztecs, the Incas, and other peoples who had lived in the Americas for thousands of years. As the Spanish fought, traded with, and intermarried with the natives, each culture changed. The Spanish, for their part, borrowed from the Americas new plants for cultivation and responded to what they considered serious threats to their worldview. Many native Americans, in turn, adopted European religious practices and learned to speak European languages. At the same time, they were decimated by European diseases to which they had never been exposed.

They also witnessed the destruction of their own civilizations and governments at the hands of the colonial powers. Through many centuries of interaction and mutual influence, both sides became something other than what they had been.

The European encounter with the Americas is an obvious example of what was, in fact, a continuous process of encounters with other cultures. These encounters often occurred between peoples from different civilizations, such as the struggles between Greeks and Persians in the ancient world (see Chapter 3) or between Europeans and Chinese in the nineteenth century (see Chapter 23). Other encounters took place among people living in the same civilization. These include interactions between lords and peasants, men and women, Christians and Jews, Catholics and Protestants, factory owners and workers, and capitalists and communists. Western civilization developed and changed through a series of external and internal encounters.

Second, features in the chapters can also help you formulate answers to the question of how Western civilization developed. For example, each chapter contains an essay titled "Justice in History". These essays discuss a trial or some other episode involving questions of justice. Some "Justice in History" essays illustrate how Western civilization was forged in struggles over conflicting values, such as the discussion of the trial of Galileo in Chapter 16, which examines the conflict between religious and scientific concepts of truth. Others show how efforts to resolve internal cultural, political, and religious tensions helped shape Western ideas about justice, such as the essay on Spanish *auto da fé* in Chapter 14, which illustrates how authorities attempted to enforce religious conformity. At the end of each "Justice in History" feature, you will find several questions tying that essay to the theme of the chapter. These questions will also ask you to explore the value-based conflicts or disputes embodied in the incident described in the essay.

Some chapters include two other features as well. Essays titled "The Human Body in History" demonstrate that even the body, which we typically understand as a product of genetics and biology, has a history. These essays show that the ways in which Western people understand their bodies, how they cure them, how they cover and uncover them, and how they adorn them tell us a great deal about the history of Western culture. We explore, for example, how the bodies of World War I soldiers afflicted with shell shock were treated differently from women experiencing similar symptoms of hysteria (see Chapter 24). Shell-shocked soldiers gave people a sense of the horrors of war and stimulated powerful movements in Europe to outlaw war as an instrument of government policy.

The "Places of Encounter" features show how encounters between different groups of people were not abstract historical processes but events that occurred in actual places, such as in the nineteenth-century soccer stadium (see Chapter 23). In the nineteenth century soccer was a sport reserved for gentlemen, but in the great industrial cities it became the favorite sport of the industrial workers. In the soccer stadiums they began to experience their common identity as a class.

THE "WHY" QUESTION

Why should you study Western civilization? Because everything around you depends on it—the education you receive, the books you read, the language you speak and those you study, the legal system that protects you, and the political one that guarantees you certain rights. The buildings you inhabit, the music and art you enjoy, and the science and technology that provides you with health, comfort, and prosperity are all artifacts of Western civilization. To appreciate all that, to contribute to it more fully yourself, and when necessary to question and critique it, requires that you understand the West was sometimes very different from the present—it was like a foreign country—and how it was sometimes very much like the present, the foundation upon which your world was made.

CHAPTER

1

The Beginnings of Civilization, 10,000–2000 B.C.E.

Chapter Outline

- Culture, Agriculture, and Civilization
- The Birth of Civilization in Southwest Asia
- The Emergence of Egyptian Civilization
- The Transformation of Europe

IN 1991 HIKERS TOILING THEIR WAY ACROSS A GLACIER IN THE ALPS BETWEEN Austria and Italy made a startling discovery: a man's body stuck in the ice. They alerted the police, who soon turned the corpse over to archaeologists. The scientists determined that the middle-aged man had frozen to death about 5,300 years ago. Otzi the Ice Man (his name comes from the Ötztal Valley where he perished) quickly became an international celebrity as the world's oldest freeze-dried human.

The scientists who examined Otzi believe that he was a shepherd herding flocks of sheep and goats to mountain pastures when he died. A few grains of wheat on his clothing suggested that he lived in a farming community. Copper dust in his hair hinted that Otzi may also have been a metalworker, perhaps looking for ores during his journey. An arrowhead lodged in his back indicated a violent cause of death, but the exact circumstances remain mysterious.

Otzi's gear was state-of-the-art for his era. His possessions showed deep knowledge of the natural world. During thousands of years of careful observation and interaction with the environment, Otzi's ancestors had learned what materials were best suited to specific tasks. Otzi benefited from their experience—but made use of new technology as well. He wore leather boots insulated with dense grasses chosen for protection against the cold. The pouch around his waist contained stone tools and fire-lighting equipment. Over his carefully stitched leather leggings, loincloth, and knee-length tunic, he wore a raincoat of woven grasses selected for their water resistance. The wood selected for his bow offered special strength and flexibility. In his light wooden backpack Otzi carried containers to hold burning embers, as well as dried meat and nutritious seeds to eat on the trail. The arrows in his quiver featured a natural adhesive that tightly bound bone and wooden points to the shafts. The most noteworthy find among

Wall Plaque: This Sumerian wall plaque shows King Ur-Nanshe of the city of Lagash. He carries a basket of bricks that will be used to build a temple. Cuneiform writing identifies the king and his project. In the lower right corner he drinks a beer to celebrate the completion of the temple.

Otzi the Ice Man
This artist's recreation shows Otzi in his waterproof poncho carrying his state-of-the-art tools.

Otzi's possessions was his axe. Its handle was made of wood but its head was copper—a remarkable innovation at a time when most tools were made of stone. Otzi was ready for almost anything—except the person who shot him in the back.

Otzi lived near the end of what archaeologists call the Neolithic Age, or "New Stone Age," when people made refinements in tool-making techniques over those of previous ages. For example, Neolithic artisans carved remarkably delicate arrowheads and blades that could be used for a variety of tasks, from hunting to sewing. The Neolithic Age was a long period of revolutionary change lasting from about 10,000 to 3000 B.C.E. that altered human existence on Earth forever. Even the most advanced technological developments of the twentieth century did not reshape human life as profoundly as did the technological and social shifts of the Neolithic era.

This chapter traces humanity's first steps toward the civilizations that developed in Southwest Asia, Egypt, and Europe—regions that made fundamental contributions to the development of Western civilization. First we will consider the most fundamental encounter of all—the relationship between humans and the natural world. Many thousands of years of human interaction with nature led to food production through agriculture and the domestication of animals. This revolutionary achievement let humans develop new, settled forms of communities: villages, cities, and eventually kingdoms and empires. Civilizations with quite different religious and political systems grew from the foundations of agriculture and the domestication of animals. The growth of civilization also depended on constant interaction among communities who lived far apart. Once people were settled in a region, they began trading for commodities that were not available in their homelands. As trade routes extended over long distances and interactions among diverse peoples proliferated, ideas and technology spread.

In this chapter we will address several major questions about humanity's first civilizations: (1) What is the link between the food-producing revolution of the Neolithic era and the emergence of civilizations? (2) What transformed the earliest settled communities in Southwest Asia into the first cities, kingdoms, and empires in history? (3) How did civilization take shape along the Nile River in Egypt? (4) How and why did food production and the use of metals transform the lives of the men and women who first populated Europe?

Culture, Agriculture, and Civilization

Anthropologists use the term *culture* to describe the knowledge and adaptive behavior created by a group of people that helps them to mediate between themselves and the natural world through time. Indeed, culture° encompasses all the different ways that humans collectively adjust to their environment and organize and transmit their experiences and knowledge to future generations.

In the animal world, any successful adaptation takes a very long time. The paleontological record is full of vanished species—such as the woolly mammoth and the giant tree sloth—that failed to adapt quickly enough to changing environments and new predators. Humanity has survived by assessing constant changes in the natural world and making the necessary adjustments to these new circumstances. Our evolution as a species over the last several million years has depended on this adaptability. We are not as strong as rhinoceroses or as fast as cheetahs, but through culture we have an advantage over all the other creatures with whom we share the planet—the ability to adapt to new environments extremely quickly.

More specifically, humans possess three crucial adaptive mechanisms. The primary adaptive behavior of humans is language. Language allows us to exchange information and share experiences from one generation to the next, a skill that animals lack. We do not simply respond biologically. We can imagine powerful forces at work in our lives that we cannot see, and we can discuss our ideas. This ability to think abstractly and to share our thoughts through spoken language lets us employ our innate curiosity productively. We accumulate knowledge and use it to modify the world in which we live.

Our ability to speak and to put ideas into action drives us to create new technologies, the second adaptive mechanism that gives humans a competitive advantage over other species. Humans are careful observers of nature, acquiring knowledge from our experience that helps us respond creatively to the challenges that we encounter. As a result, we constantly refine our tools so that they become more efficient. With these tools we build shelters that allow us to live in a wide range of environments, from the icy Arctic to tropical rain forests. We create calendars that help us track time, and we write textbooks that interpret the past and give it meaning. We devise technologies—everything from Otzi's humble gear to space stations orbiting Earth—that alter natural processes, exploit natural resources, and help us understand our world.

Perhaps the most important adaptive mechanism of all is our capacity to experience and to express emotions such as love, pity, guilt, and shame. This ability shapes our collective behavior. We organize ourselves into families and other groups in which these feelings play an integral role. Thanks to our emotions we have the capacity to create long-lasting social relationships, such as families and friendships that have profound meaning for us. These bonds are the foundation of all human communities. Patterns of social relationships are transmitted through the generations, forming the backbones of our cultures and our civilizations. Emotional bonds enable communities to survive even while responding to challenges and change.

Culture is the medium through which these transmissions and adaptations take place over time. We can understand a people's culture as a web of interconnected meanings that enable them to understand themselves and their place in the world and transmit their experience and knowledge to future generations. Each culture is distinctive; thus we use labels—"Greek culture" or "American culture." Yet all cultures constantly borrow from their neighbors and change over time.

We often use *culture* and *civilization* interchangeably, yet in the history of human development, civilization has a specific definition. Archaeologists define civilization° as a society differentiated by levels of wealth and occupation in which people lived in cities. With cities, human populations achieved the critical mass necessary to develop specialized occupations, as well as a level of economic production high enough to sustain complex religious and cultural practices. In earlier village communities, social classes—groups considered to have different degrees of importance and status—developed when the people to whom food and other vital resources were distributed became dependent upon the elites who distributed them. With the appearance of stark differences in wealth, the lines between social classes became more rigid. Rulers emerged who dictated the distribution of economic resources. As villages evolved into cities, their social organization grew more complicated. The labor of most people supported a small group of political administrators and religious leaders, as these city elites used taxation and control of trade to gain access to the economic resources of the countryside. Thus, as we will see shortly, in early civilizations three kinds of power—economic, political, and religious—converged. A city's rulers controlled the mechanisms of not only government and warfare but also the distribution of food and wealth. They augmented their authority by building temples to the gods and participating in religious rituals that linked divinity with kingship.

The Emergence of Hunter-Gatherer Societies

Between 200,000 and 100,000 years ago—after several million years of biological evolution—physically and intellectually modern humans, known as Homo sapiens sapiens° ("most intelligent people"), first appeared in Africa and began to spread to other continents. Scientists refer to this stage of human history as the Paleolithic Age, or Old Stone Age, because people made tools by cracking rocks and using their sharp edges to cut and chop. These people were our direct ancestors, but they were not alone on the planet. Other less advanced species of humans had been evolving for about four million years, and they too had migrated from Africa to many regions across the globe. *Homo sapiens sapiens* coexisted with these less advanced peoples, such as Neanderthals, for thousands of years during the Paleolithic Age.

Homo sapiens sapiens' use of tools shows the difference between their mental capacities and those of other less advanced groups. The tools of the non–*Homo sapiens sapiens* groups remained virtually unchanged over the hundreds of thousands of years of their evolution. By contrast, those of *Homo sapiens sapiens* demonstrated quick adaptation to new environments and practical needs. They learned quickly through experience and observation and shared their knowledge through language. Their ability to develop new tools enabled *Homo sapiens sapiens* to live almost everywhere on the planet. For example, hunters learned to make razor-sharp blades with which to skin hides, which in turn could be used to make warm clothes suitable for cold climates. *Homo sapiens sapiens,* thus, successfully adapted to a broad range of environments, including tropical jungles, dry savannas, and mountain woodlands.

These humans developed other skills as well. They mastered the art of making fire, which they used to cook food and keep warm. They scavenged for wild food and became shrewd observers of the natural environment. They followed migrating herds of animals, hunting with increasing efficiency as their weapons improved. Archaeologists have unearthed skillfully crafted arrowheads, spear tips, and other blades, as well as fishhooks and harpoons carved from bone. These tools show that Paleolithic peoples learned to exploit the natural resources of a wide variety of ecological zones. They also created beautiful works of art by carving bone and painting on cave walls. Sadly, their music, poems, languages, and beliefs have all vanished from the human record.

By 45,000 years ago, these humans had reached most of Earth's habitable regions, except for Australia, the islands of the South Pacific, and North and South America. They continued to live as nomadic hunter-gatherers, foraging for wild foods, fishing, and tracking herds of game. But about 15,000 years ago, when the last Ice Age ended, the Earth's climate became warmer, causing changes in vegetation. The hunter-gatherer life slowly began to change as well. Humans began to interact with the natural environment in new ways. The warmer climate allowed cereal grasses to spread quickly over large areas; hunter-gatherers learned to collect these wild grains and grind them up for food. Sometimes, groups of hunter-gatherers settled in semipermanent camps, returning to them regularly to take advantage of the wild foods that flourished during different seasons. They established some camps near rivers and wetlands, where wild grains grew and provided a reliable source of food to supplement their hunting and fishing. When people learned that the seeds of wild grasses could be transplanted and grown in new areas, the domestication of plants was under way.

CHRONOLOGY

Prehistory to Civilization

4.5 MILLION YEARS AGO	Humans originate in Africa
1 MILLION YEARS AGO	Humans learn to control fire
200,000 YEARS AGO	Origins of anatomically modern humans
150,000 YEARS AGO	Modern humans (*Homo sapiens sapiens*) appear
45,000 YEARS AGO	Modern humans spread through Europe, Africa, and Asia
13,000 YEARS AGO	Ice Age ends
10,000 YEARS AGO	Food production begins
3000 B.C.E.	Sumerian civilization develops in Mesopotamia
2500 B.C.E.	Egyptian civilization begins

THE FOOD-PRODUCING REVOLUTION

Until about 8000 B.C.E., human beings acquired their food in the same ways they had since our species began evolving. They hunted, fished, and gathered foods that grew in the wild. But over the course of the next 8,000 years, a revolutionary change took place. Farming crops and herding domesticated animals gradually replaced hunting and gathering as the source of virtually all human nourishment. The long transition to food production° brought about the most profound change in human society since the appearance of *Homo sapiens sapiens:* Food production made civilization possible (see Map 1.1).

There was no single reason for the shift to food production, but archaeologists agree that population growth, ecological changes brought about by the warming environment, and the dwindling of game due to overkill by hunters all increased the demand for food. Driven by need, humans began to recognize that cultivation of the earth and domestication of animals could provide a dependable food supply. By trial and error they learned to plant crops in accordance with the seasons and natural growing cycles. They also discovered that if they fertilized, weeded, harvested, and stored their crops at the right times and under favorable climatic circumstances, they would get bigger yields. In hunter-gatherer societies men hunt and fish while women generally collect wild foods. Thus it was probably women who first observed how plants spread in nature and first discovered that they could achieve the same effect by sowing seeds.

At the same time that people discovered the benefits of planting seeds, they also began domesticating pigs, sheep, goats, and cattle, which eventually replaced wild game as the main source of meat. Domestication° involves more than just taming wild animals. It requires entering into a complex process of control and intervention that lasts through several of the animals' generations. Domestication occurs when humans manipulate the breeding of animals in order to serve their own purposes—for example, making wool (lacking on wild sheep), laying extra eggs (not done by undomesticated chickens), and producing extra milk (wild cows produce only enough milk for their offspring).

Hunters had practiced some techniques of domestication when they began to spare the females and young males of a wild herd in order to maintain a steady food supply. Perhaps some young animals were captured alive and taken back to the camp, where they were partially tamed as pets. As flocks of animals were penned, the effects of breeding eventually were noticed and systematically developed. The first signs of goat domestication occurred about 8900 B.C.E. in the Zagros Mountains in Southwest Asia. Pigs, which adapt very well to human settlements because they eat

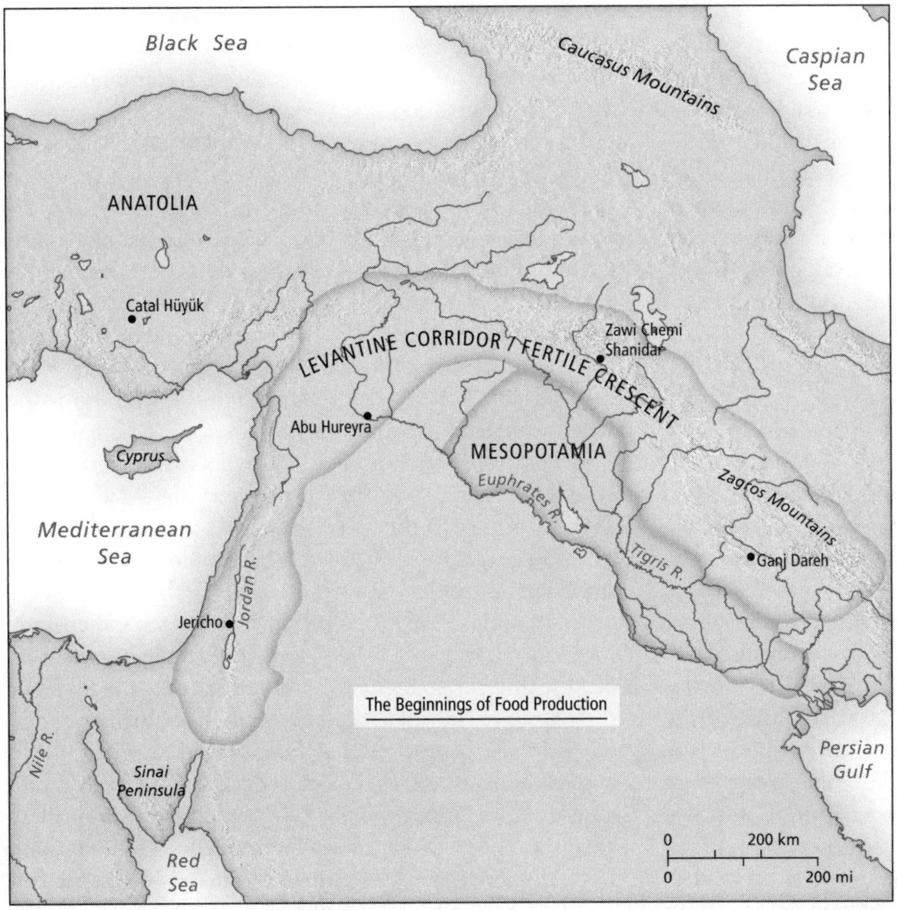

Map 1.1 The Beginnings of Food Production
This map shows early farming sites discovered by archaeologists where the first known production of food occurred in ancient Southwest Asia (the Middle East).

garbage, were first domesticated around 7000 B.C.E. By around 6500 B.C.E domesticated cattle, goats, and sheep had become widespread.

Farming and herding required hard work, but the payoff was enormous. Even simple agricultural methods could produce about fifty times more food than hunting and gathering. Thanks to the increased food supply, more newborns survived past infancy. Populations expanded, and so did human settlements. When the food-producing revolution began, humans numbered only about eight million people. Today, about 6.5 billion people live on the planet. Food production made this growth in world population possible.

In Southwest Asia, food production fostered the development of two new kinds of human communities that now exist around the globe: agricultural societies° and pastoralist societies°. In agricultural societies, people live in fixed communities. They plant crops and perhaps maintain herds of domesticated animals, often grazing them in meadows some distance away. In pastoralist societies, people lead a nomadic way of life, constantly moving their flocks from place to place in search of pasture where the animals can graze. Pastoralism developed in ancient Southwest Asia as a response to the arid conditions of most of the region. It spread widely around the globe from its Southwest Asian origins, but few traces of it exist in the archaeological record.

With the mastery of food production, human societies developed the mechanisms not only to feed themselves, but also to produce a surplus, which could then be traded for other resources. Such economic activity allowed for economic specialization and fostered the growth of social, political, and religious hierarchies. As villages developed and then grew into cities, the first human civilization emerged.

The Birth of Civilization in Southwest Asia

By 6000 B.C.E., settled communities that depended on farming and herding had become the norm throughout Southwest Asia. With better and more plentiful food, such communities expanded steadily. Prosperity further stimulated commerce, and merchants from different regions began traveling regularly to one another's villages to trade. Mesopotamia, the dry floodplain bounded by the

Tigris and Euphrates Rivers, became the meeting place of ideas and peoples from across an enormous geographical area. The cultures of these trading communities remained quite distinct—they had different ways of building houses, decorating pottery, and selecting locations for their settlements. Historians assume that their beliefs and languages differed as well. Over time, however, these Mesopotamian village communities began to resemble one another and a more uniform culture developed. The development of this more uniform culture set the stage for the emergence of civilization in Southwest Asia.

The First Food-Producing Communities

In Southwest Asia, where sufficient annual rainfall enabled crops to grow without irrigation, people began cultivating food in three separate areas. Archaeologists have named the first area the Levantine Corridor° (also known as the Fertile Crescent°)—a twenty-five-mile-wide strip of land that runs from Jericho in the Jordan River valley of modern Israel to the Euphrates River valley in Iraq. The second region was the hilly land north of Mesopotamia at the base of the Zagros Mountains in the western part of modern Iran. The third was Anatolia, or what is now the central region of Turkey. Although humans mastered agriculture and domestication of animals independently in these three areas, contact among traders may have accelerated the spread of crops and knowledge about food production. Examination of human settlement in each of these three regions illuminates the diverse processes by which human beings learned to control their natural environment and to organize their societies.

The small settlement of Abu Hureyra in Syria on the Euphrates River, which was inhabited from about 9500 to 5000 B.C.E., illustrates how agriculture developed over a long period at a single site. The first settlers here fed themselves primarily by hunting gazelles and gathering wild cereals. But sometime between 8000 and 7700 B.C.E., they began to plant and harvest a small number of grains. By 7000 B.C.E. Abu Hureyra had grown into a farming settlement, covering nearly thirty acres that sustained a population of about 400. A few generations later, the inhabitants of Abu Hureyra began herding sheep and goats to supplement their meat supply. These domesticated animals became the community's primary source of meat when the gazelle herds were depleted about 6500 B.C.E.

Families in Abu Hureyra lived in small dwellings built of mud brick containing several rooms. The inhabitants discovered that crop rotation—planting different crops in a field each year—would result in much higher yield. Archeological evidence shows that many women in the community developed arthritis in their knees, probably from crouching for hours on end as they ground grains. Thus we assume that while men hunted and harvested crops, women performed the labor of grinding the grains. This division of labor along gender lines indicates a growing complexity of social relations within communities.

At the other end of the Levantine Corridor, the farming village of Jericho began to develop rapidly after 8500 B.C.E. Located at an old hunting-gathering site along a stream in the Jordan River valley near modern Jerusalem, Jericho expanded to encompass nearly ten acres after its inhabitants started cultivating crops, including wheat, barley, lentils, and peas. In addition, they learned a valuable lesson: If they let a field lie fallow for a season, the soil would be richer and more productive the following year.

Archaeological evidence shows how Jericho's growing wealth enabled the community to develop. The inhabitants developed more complex political, religious, and economic structures. Fairly sophisticated engineering projects, such as the digging of a nine-foot-deep ditch around the village as a flood control device and the erection of a massive stone wall to protect against attackers, indicate the emergence of some form of political organization. Other findings hint at religious beliefs. Jericho's people buried their dead within the settlement, sometimes under the floors of their houses. They placed plastered skulls of their deceased on the walls, a practice that may suggest worship of the family's ancestors. Archaeological evidence also reveals that long-distance commerce played a part in the lives of these villagers. They exchanged agricultural goods for turquoise from the Sinai Peninsula, shells from the Mediterranean and Red Seas, and most important of all, obsidian from Anatolia. This volcanic stone was the most important commodity in the Neolithic Age because it could be used for making sharp-edged tools such as arrowheads, spear points, and sickles for harvesting crops.

The second region of village settlement, the lands at the foot of the Zagros Mountains north of Mesopotamia, reveals a different sort of development pattern from that exhibited in either Jericho or Abu Hureyra. Archaeologists have unearthed a hunter-gatherer camp at Sawi Chemi Shanidar, dating to about 9000 B.C.E. In this settlement, the domestication of animals long predated the development of agriculture. The settlers herded animals, but they did not cultivate crops for more than a thousand years. At the site of Ganj Dareh, a similar pattern occurred. First occupied as a seasonal camp in 8500 B.C.E., Ganj Dareh became a permanent mud-brick village with a few two-story houses by 7000 B.C.E. Its villagers herded cattle and goats. Evidently they slaughtered most male livestock but kept the females for breeding.

The third region of early settled communities, Anatolia, followed patterns more like those of the Levantine Corridor. Around 8500 B.C.E. a few simple settlements appeared. The villagers raised pigs and traded obsidian for materials from far away, such as the highly prized blue lapis lazuli stones from northeastern Afghanistan. A thousand years later, about 7400 B.C.E., Anatolians began cultivating a variety of crops, including wheat and lentils. They started herding sheep at roughly the same time as the Abu Hureyra villagers, and domesticated dogs for hunting, herding, and protection. Many new villages sprang up in this region during the next millennium. The farmers lived in rectangular houses. More than mere huts, these houses featured plastered walls, hearths, courtyards, and ovens for baking breads.

Some time after 6000 B.C.E. Anatolian communities grew more complex, with the emergence of religious beliefs and social hierarchies. For example, the Anatolian town of Çatal Hüyük consisted of thirty-two acres of tightly packed houses that the townspeople rebuilt more than a dozen times as their population expanded. Çatal Hüyük controlled the obsidian trade from Anatolia to the Levantine Corridor. The wealth from this trade fostered the emergence of social differences. For example, we know that the townspeople buried some of their dead with jewelry and other riches, a practice that indicates distinctions between wealthy and poor members of the society. In addition, the community was wealthy enough to sustain what appears to be some type of communal religious practice. The walls of several buildings display paintings of bulls and women giving birth to bulls, while the homes contain altars decorated with horns and figurines of rams and bulls.

The long-distance obsidian trade sped up the development of communities in the Levantine Corridor, the Zagros Mountains, and Anatolia. Enterprising merchants began carrying the valuable stone from the rich deposits of Anatolia to the Levantine Corridor, the Zagros Mountains, and the Sinai Peninsula. In village markets, they traded obsidian for turquoise, for decorative shells from the Mediterranean and Red Seas, and for timber from the hills of Lebanon. These trade networks of the Neolithic Age laid the foundation for commercial and cultural encounters that would shape the development of civilizations for the next 5,000 years.

CHRONOLOGY

	Mesopotamia and Anatolia
9500–5000 B.C.E.	Settled community at Abu Hureyra develops on the Euphrates River
8500–7000 B.C.E.	Humans domesticate animals at Ganj Dareh
8500–6000 B.C.E.	Humans domesticate animals, engage in agriculture, and create settled communities in Anatolia
6000 B.C.E.	Çatal Hüyük in Anatolia prospers from trade and agriculture
5300–3000 B.C.E.	Villages develop into cities in Mesopotamia; Sumerian culture emerges
4600–2500 B.C.E.	Uruk in Mesopotamia becomes powerful, with temples, kings, and economic regulation
3200 B.C.E.	First known written documents in cuneiform appear
2350 B.C.E.	Akkadian king Sargon conquers Sumer and other lands
2100 B.C.E.	Akkad falls; Ur becomes powerful in Mesopotamia
2000 B.C.E.	Amorites begin to enter Mesopotamia
1900 B.C.E.	Assyria grows powerful through trade and conquest
1800 B.C.E.	Babylonian civilization emerges; Hammurabi prepares his Law Code

SUMER: A CONSTELLATION OF CITIES IN SOUTHERN MESOPOTAMIA

About 5300 B.C.E. the villages in Sumer, an ancient name for southern Mesopotamia, began a dynamic civilization that would flourish for 3,000 years. At the height of this civilization, Sumerians (who called themselves "the black-headed people" because of their characteristic dark hair) lived in thriving cities governed by leaders who controlled agricultural production, regulated long-distance trade, and presided over the worship of the gods.

The Origins of Sumerian Cities

Sumerian civilization was linked to water. Over centuries, the Sumerians learned to control the unpredictable waters of the Tigris and Euphrates Rivers. In the process, they developed the structures of civilization. Initially, Sumerian villagers dug their own small channels to divert floodwaters from the two great rivers to irrigate their dry lands. Then they discovered that by combining the labor force of several villages, they could build and maintain irrigation channels on a large scale. These channels directed the rushing floodwaters of the rivers every spring in time for planting. The lands irrigated by river water provided rich yields of crops that fed Sumer's growing population. Villages blossomed into cities that became the foundation of Sumerian civilization.

By 2500 B.C.E., about twelve major cities in Sumer had emerged that controlled the Mesopotamian floodplain in an organized fashion. They used the floodwaters of the Tigris and Euphrates Rivers in order to irrigate agricultural lands, create new fields, and increase the food supply. Some cities achieved impressive dimensions. Uruk, for example, covered about two square miles by 2500 B.C.E. and had a population estimated at between 10,000 and 50,000 people, including the peasants living in the countryside. Many villagers living in the countryside surrounding the main cities labored to provide food for the urban populations as well as for themselves.

Sumerian Economic and Political Life

Sumerian cities served as the economic centers of southern Mesopotamia. Craft specialists such as potters, toolmakers, weavers, and artists gathered in these urban settings to purchase food, swap information, and sell their goods. By providing markets for outlying towns, the cities spun a web of economic interdependence. Long-distance trade, made easier by the introduction of wheeled carts drawn by oxen, enabled merchants to bring timber, ores, and luxury items unavailable in Mesopotamia from Anatolia, the Levantine Corridor, Afghanistan, and Iran. With the introduction of the potter's wheel, Sumerian artisans could mass-produce containers for trade and storage of grain and other commodities. Fishermen thrived as well. They fished on the rivers of Mesopotamia and in the Persian Gulf and traded their catch in the markets of villages and cities.

Within the cities, centralized authorities directed the necessary labor for irrigation and water control. The rulers of Uruk, for example, organized large-scale irrigation projects with canals leading to the rivers. They also maintained warehouses for storing surplus grains, and they distributed food to workers who labored on building projects for the king. Ultimate power to direct labor lay in the hands of the king. The people dedicated all the resources of the kingdom to supporting him and maintaining the city's ziggurat, the temple where everyone gathered to worship the city's main gods. Monumental temples and palaces demonstrated the king's power over the economic and human resources of the city—as well as the vast inequality of wealth between governing elites and the peasant workers. Archaeological excavations reveal that Uruk's elite—its priests, aristocrats, important civil administrators, and wealthy merchants—lived in luxurious houses near the temples, while everyone else crowded into small mud-brick houses with few comforts. Similar divisions characterized Sumer's other cities as well.

The economic resources of their cities enabled kings to supply armies and lead them into battle. Sumerian kings frequently waged war against one another in an effort to increase their territory and power. Long walls punctuated by tall gates and towers protected the inhabitants of Sumerian cities from the attacks of rival cities and the persistent raids of nomadic pastoralists who hovered on the outskirts of settled lands.

Rivalry among the kings prevented Sumerian cities from uniting politically, but the kings maintained diplomatic relations with one another as well as with rulers throughout Southwest Asia and Egypt, primarily to protect their trading networks. Safe trade links helped tie each Sumerian city to the common culture of Sumerian lands.

Through trade and warfare and from the many diplomats, soldiers, travelers, and slaves who passed through Mesopotamia's cities, the Sumerians knew much about the natural resources, economic organization, and customs that characterized the foreign peoples around them. The world known to them extended from India in the east to the Caucasus Mountains in the north; to Egypt and Ethiopia in the south; and to the Mediterranean Sea in the west. Sumerians strongly believed that the gods favored them over all other peoples, and they developed intense prejudices against their neighbors, accusing them of cowardice, stupidity, and treachery.

Sumerian Religious Life

Religion—powerfully influenced by Mesopotamia's volatile climate—played a central role in daily life. Sumerians knew firsthand the famine and destruction that could come from sudden floods, storms, and winds. They envisioned each of these natural forces as a god who, like a human king or queen, had to be pleased and appeased. Sumerians believed that in order to survive they must continually demonstrate their subservience to the gods, and their practice of constantly feeding these deities with sacrifices was one way of doing so.

Some scholars maintain that an important reason for the growth of Sumerian cities was the desire to "nourish" the gods, primarily through sacrifices of meat. The need to fulfill such expensive religious obligations may have led Sumerians to develop the complex economic and political arrangements that are the hallmarks of Sumerian civilization. It is clear that the bulk of each city's resources went to maintaining the temples, priests, and herds of sacrificial animals. Every day priests carried several sumptuous meals to the statues of the gods. The deities would consume the "immaterial essence" of the food, and then the priests and temple attendants would eat the leftovers. Ordinary people offered smaller gifts of nourishment to the gods at family shrines. By performing the right rituals and giving the appropriate offerings, Sumerians hoped that the gods would answer their humble prayers. For instance, one queen made a private offering to a goddess on behalf of her son, pleading, "May the statue, to which let my mistress the goddess turn her ear, speak my prayers."[1] There were, however, no guarantees of divine assistance.

Each Sumerian city was protected by one god or goddess. The deity's temples served as the center of the city and the focus of religious life. In Uruk, for example, two enormous temples dominated the community: the Ziggurat of Anu (the supreme sky god) and the Temple of Heaven Precinct. This latter complex of buildings contained a colonnaded courtyard and a large limestone temple dedicated to Inanna (also known as Ishtar), the goddess of love and war and the city's special guardian. All Sumerian cities had similar tem-

THE CLASH BETWEEN CIVILIZATION AND NATURE: THE TAMING OF ENKIDU

The Sumerians saw their civilization as tightly linked to nature, as this passage from the tale of Gilgamesh suggests. This excerpt tells how Enkidu, Gilgamesh's companion, first became civilized. Originally living like a wild animal, Enkidu prevents hunters from trapping game. But city officials send him a prostitute who tames him by having sex with him for a week. The prostitute represents natural forces controlled by the city. As a result of this epic sexual encounter, Enkidu loses his ability to talk to the animals. Then, by consuming cooked food and beer and wearing cloth garments for the first time, he becomes a civilized man. The episode teaches that civilization imposes control on natural forces, transforming them in the process—a metaphor for the Sumerians' civilization.

In the wilderness the goddess Aruru created valiant
Enkidu . . .
He knew neither people nor settled living . . .
He ate grasses like gazelles,
And jostled at the watering hole with the animals . . .
Then Shamhat [the prostitute] saw him—a primitive,
A savage fellow from the depths of the wilderness! . . .
Shamhat unclutched her bosom, exposed her sex,
And Enkidu took in her voluptuousness.
She was not restrained, but took his energy . . .
For six days and seven nights Enkidu stayed aroused,
And had intercourse with the prostitute,
Until he was sated with her charms.
But when he turned his attention to the animals,
The gazelles saw Enkidu and darted off,
The wild animals distanced themselves from his body . . .
Enkidu knew nothing about eating bread for food,
[nor] of drinking beer he had not been taught to.
The prostitute spoke to Enkidu, saying:
"Eat the food, Enkidu, it is the way one lives.
Drink the beer, as it is the custom of our land."
Enkidu ate the food until he was sated,
He drank the beer—seven jugs!—and became expansive
and sang with joy!
He was elated and his face glowed.
He splashed his shaggy body with water,
And rubbed himself with oil and turned into a human.
He put on some clothing and became like a warrior.
He took up weapons and chased lions so shepherds could
rest at night.
With Enkidu as their guard, the herders could lie down.

Source: Excerpts from Kovacs, Maureen Gallery, translator, *The Epic of Gilgamesh,* with an Introduction and Notes.

ples that towered over the city, reminding all the inhabitants of the omnipresent gods who controlled their destiny.

Sumerians believed that everything in the universe, from the mightiest god to the most insignificant pebble, contained a divine presence. They assumed, however, that the mightiest gods took human form. The all-powerful king Anu, the father of the gods, ruled the sky. Enlil was master of the wind and guided humans in the proper use of force. Enki ruled the Earth and rivers and guided human creativity and inventions. Inanna was the goddess of love, sex, fertility, and warfare. Ninhursaga, another female divinity, was considered a source of royal power. Sumerians also worshiped hundreds of lesser gods at home and in shrines throughout their cities and in the countryside.

Sumerians told exciting stories about their gods and heroes. One of the most popular figures in Sumerian ballads was the legendary king Gilgamesh of Uruk. Part god and part man, Gilgamesh—accompanied by his stalwart companion, Enkidu—embarked on many adventures that delighted Mesopotamian audiences for thousands of years. Originally told in the Sumerian language, the tales of Gilgamesh and Enkidu excited the imaginations of other Mesopotamian peoples as well, who later recorded them in their own languages.

The vastly entertaining story of Gilgamesh reveals Sumerian concerns about the proper behavior of a king and the limits of human ambition. The tale describes how the gods created Enkidu to be Gilgamesh's companion and balance the king's rash disposition. Together the two men battled monsters and set out on long journeys in search of adventure. When Enkidu died, Gilgamesh tried to find the secret of immortality, but learned that humans cannot live forever. As a result of his travels, Gilgamesh becomes a wiser king and his subjects benefit from his new wisdom.

Sumerian Cultural Achievements

Sumerian culture exerted an enormous impact on the peoples of ancient Southwest Asia, and remnants of it continue to influence today's world. Some archaeologists believe that the Sumerians invented the wheel. They also devised the potter's wheel, the wagon, and the chariot, which proved essential for daily transportation and warfare.

Perhaps the Sumerians' most important cultural innovation was their development of writing. The Sumerians

■ **Cuneiform Texts**

The first of these clay tablets, left, written in cuneiform, or "wedge-shaped" letters, is early in the development of the script. Dating from about 3000 B.C.E., it lists what are probably temple offerings under the categories day one, day two, and day three. The second text, below, was produced in Babylonia about 1750 B.C.E. It contains problems in geometry. Unlike the first tablet, which is written in the Sumerian language, the geometry tablet is in the Semitic language spoken by the Babylonians.

devised a unique script used to record their language. Historians call the symbols that were pressed onto clay tablets with sharp objects cuneiform°, or wedge-shaped, writing. The earliest known documents written in this language come from Uruk about 3200 B.C.E. In the following excerpt, a Sumerian storyteller marvels at the invention and usefulness of writing:

> *This speech was too difficult; its contents were too long;*
> *The Messenger's mouth was too slow; he could not repeat it.*
> *Since the Messenger's mouth was too slow, and he could not repeat it,*
> *The Lord of Kulab patted some clay and set down the words as on a tablet.*
> *Before that day, there was no putting of words on clay;*
> *But now, when the Sun rose, it verily was so:*
> *The Lord of Kulab had verily put words on clay!*[2]

Researchers believe that the roots of cuneiform writing date back 10,000 years, when people began to cultivate crops and domesticate animals in Southwest Asia. To keep track of quantities of produce and numbers of livestock, villagers began using small clay tokens of different shapes to represent and record these quantities. Each marker had a separate meaning. For example, cones and spheres indicated certain quantities of grain, and an oval meant a container of oil. New shapes could be added to represent new commodities. The tokens took the uncertainty out of transactions, reducing conflict because parties to a transaction no longer had to rely simply on memory or spoken agreements.

About 3400 B.C.E. people began to store these tokens in small clay envelopes and to impress their markings on the outsides of the envelopes to convey what was inside. After several centuries, people stopped using the envelopes entirely and simply impressed the shapes on a flat piece of clay or tablet to record transactions. Eventually, traders started impressing information about quantities or objects directly onto clay with a pointed stick, thus eliminating the need for tokens entirely. As commodities and trading became more complex, the number of symbols multiplied. By 3000 B.C.E. the number of symbols had been streamlined from about a thousand to approximately 500, but learning even 500 signs required intensive study. The scribes, the people who mastered these signs, became valued members of the community. Sumerian cuneiform writing spread, and other peoples of Mesopotamia and Southwest Asia began adapting it to record information in their own languages.

The Sumerians also made impressive innovations in mathematics. The first numerals (symbols for numbers) emerged around the same time as writing. Derived from the impressions of tokens, numerals proved to be valuable in the royal bureaucracy and in trade. Over time, the Sumerians became highly skilled in mathematics. Archaeologists have found many Sumerian tablets used as school texts that contain problems in advanced algebra and plane and solid geometry. They also show multiplication tables, square and cube roots, and exponents, as well as other practical information such as how to calculate compound interest on loans. Sumerian numeracy has left a lasting imprint on Western culture. It was the Sumerians who developed a counting system based on sixty in multiples of ten—a system still in use in the way we tell time—and it was the Sumerians who divided the circle into 360 degrees.

In addition to mathematics, the Sumerians excelled in many other fields. They were skilled architects, as their ziggurats and city walls reveal. Their irrigation systems show their mastery of hydraulic engineering. They also developed detailed knowledge about the movement of the stars, planets, and the moon—especially as these movements pertained to agricultural cycles. But despite their invention of writing, they recorded none of their architectural, technological, and astrological knowledge. Instead, they passed it orally from generation to generation. The Babylonians, members of a civilization that arose later in Mesopotamia, inherited this knowledge, expanded it, and ultimately shared it with the Greeks, the Persians, the Phoenicians, and other peoples of later ages. In this way scientific traditions that began in ancient Sumer contributed to the scientific thought of Western civilization.

FROM AKKAD TO THE AMORITE INVASIONS

Around 2340 B.C.E., the political independence of Sumer's cities ended. Conquered by a warrior who took the name Sargon ("true king"), Sumer's cities found themselves swallowed up by Mesopotamia's first great empire. Sargon came from Akkad, a region in Mesopotamia north of Sumer. Sargon's people, the Akkadians, had lived in Mesopotamia for more than a thousand years.

The Akkadians began to migrate into Mesopotamia from their original homes somewhere in the Levantine Corridor during the late fourth millennium B.C.E. Their settlements grew in size, and although they intermingled with the native Sumerian population they preserved their own language and customs. During the third millennium B.C.E., a number of Akkadian cities grew strong. The inhabitants of these cities spoke Akkadian, a Semitic language that became the common language of trade throughout ancient Mesopotamia and Southwest Asia until about 500 B.C.E. The Akkadians' most significant contribution to Western civilization, however, came with their creation of a new kind of political entity: the multiethnic empire.

By bringing cities with very different languages, culture, and traditions under his rule, Sargon (r. ca. 2340–ca. 2305 B.C.E.) created a dynamic empire that endured for more than a century (see Map 1.2). The realm that Sargon had established reached its greatest extent about 2220 B.C.E. The empire's diverse subjects, including peoples in Mesopotamia, Syria, Anatolia, and western Iran, struggled to win back their independence, but Akkadian kings crushed their revolts.

Controlling such a large empire posed new challenges for Akkadian rulers. To surmount them, Sargon and his successors imitated and expanded upon the governing methods they observed in individual Sumerian cities. For example, to secure the loyalty of their many subjects, Akkadian kings presented themselves as symbols of unity in the form of semidivine figures. After a king's death, his subjects worshiped him as a god. Some monarchs claimed to be gods while they were alive.

Raising the revenues to meet the costs of running their enormous empire presented another problem for Akkadian kings. The king paid for all the public buildings, irrigation projects, and temples throughout his realm, as well as for the immense army required to defend, control, and expand the empire. Monarchs generated revenues in several ways. A key source of revenue was the leasing out of the vast farmlands that belonged to the king. Kings also required conquered peoples to pay regular tribute in the form of trade goods, produce, and gold and silver. In addition, Akkadian kings depended on the revenue generated by commerce. They placed heavy taxes on raw materials imported from foreign lands. In fact, most Akkadian kings made long-distance trade the central objective of their foreign policy. They signed treaties with foreign kings and sent military expeditions as far as Anatolia and Iran to obtain timber, metals, luxury goods, and construction materials. Akkadian troops protected these international trade routes and managed the maritime trade in the Persian Gulf, where merchants brought goods by ship from India and southern Arabia.

The cities of Mesopotamia prospered under Akkadian rule. A wealthy upper class developed that owned a great deal of private property obtained from trade and agriculture. Even so, Akkadian rulers could not hold their empire together for reasons that historians do not completely understand. One cause was marauding tribes from the Zagros Mountains, who repeatedly infiltrated the kingdom and caused tremendous damage. Suddenly Akkadian kings lost control of their lands and a period of anarchy began about 2103 B.C.E. "Who was king? Who was not king?" lamented a

■ Map 1.2 Sargon's Empire, 2220 B.C.E.
Sargon of Akkad created a large empire that included many distinct ethnic groups. For the first time in history, rulers had to struggle with the resistance of subject peoples.

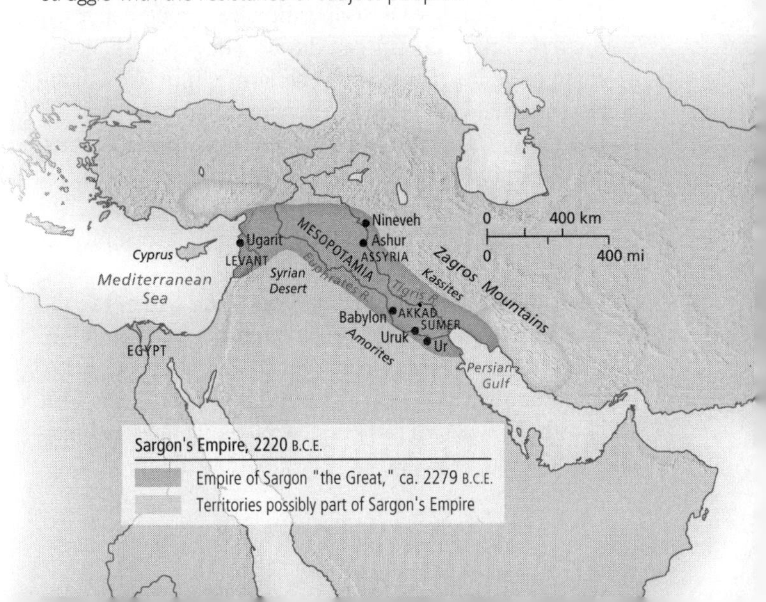

writer during this time of troubles. The kingdom finally collapsed about 2100 B.C.E.

With the fall of Akkad, the cities of Sumer regained their independence, but they were quickly reunited under Ur-Nammu, king of the Sumerian city of Ur. Ur-Nammu established a powerful dynasty that lasted for more than a century. The kings of Ur strengthened the central government by turning formerly independent cities and their territories into provinces and appointing administrators to govern them. To prevent these provincial governors from becoming too powerful and possibly developing royal ambitions, the kings routinely rotated them to new administrative posts.

Ur's kings also centralized economic production in their empire. The royal administration controlled most long-distance trade and developed a vigorous industry in woolen garments and leather goods. Ur's rulers supported many thousands of artisans and laborers who were paid in beer and various agricultural products. The materials the artisans produced were traded throughout Southwest Asia. Wealth also flowed to the kings of Ur from farming and herding. The kings owned huge herds of livestock that grazed on royal estates, but ordinary individuals were not permitted to possess agricultural lands. Most of Ur's citizens worked either as tenant farmers on estates owned by the king and the political leaders, or as slaves. Each year government officials collected tens of thousands of cattle and hundreds of thousands of sheep and redistributed them to temples throughout the kingdom for use in sacrifices.

The most important innovation in Ur occurred in the realm of the law. Ur-Nammu compiled the first known collection of laws in the history of Western civilization. His laws reveal his determination to provide social justice for his subjects. He established courts in which a panel of judges made decisions about family controversies and business disputes such as debt, inheritance, contracts, and the sale of property and slaves. The custom of writing down laws so that citizens and later generations could refer to them became a strong tradition in Western civilization.

The kings of Ur used political innovations, economic centralization, and legal codification to strengthen their hold over Sumer's cities; they did not, however, challenge or change the key facets of Sumerian culture. Ur's monarchs continued the long Mesopotamian tradition of building elaborate temple complexes featuring ziggurats, palaces, and tombs to demonstrate their piety. Like earlier Mesopotamian rulers, Ur's kings considered themselves gods. They placed their tombs in the temple complex of the moon god Nanna, Ur's special protector.

Despite their sophisticated governmental structures, the kings of Ur could not stave off political fragmentation. About 2000 B.C.E., seminomadic peoples known as Amorites began invading Mesopotamia from the steppes to the west and north. They seized fortified towns, taking food and supplies and causing widespread destruction. By 2004 B.C.E. they had destabilized the economy of Mesopotamia as well as of other regions of Southwest Asia. Peasants fled from the fields, and with no food or revenues, inflation and famine overcame the empire. Ur collapsed, and Mesopotamia shattered once again into a scattering of squabbling cities. Taking advantage of the political turmoil, tribes of Amorites settled in Mesopotamian lands, because food was more abundant there than on the steppe. They abandoned their nomadic way of life in favor of agriculture.

THE LEGEND OF KING SARGON

The Akkadian king Sargon inspired many legends. The following story tells how his mother, a priestess, bore him in secret and put him in a basket in the river, from which a water bearer rescued him. The document explains how Sargon eventually became king of the Mesopotamians through the favor of the goddess Ishtar. The tale of a baby found in the bulrushes who achieves greatness was a Sumerian story already old in Sargon's day. A similar tale about the prophet Moses would be recorded in the Hebrew Bible more than a thousand years later. The recurrence of such literary motifs over a period of more than 3,000 years indicates the pervasive influence of Sumerian culture on subsequent civilizations of Southwest Asia.

Sargon, the mighty king, king of Agade, am I.
My mother was a high priestess, my father I knew not . . .
My mother, the high priestess, conceived me, in secret she bore me.
She set me in a basket of rushes, with bitumen she sealed my lid.
She cast me into the river which rose not over me.
The river bore me up and carried me to Akki, the drawer of water. . . .
Akki, the drawer of water, took me as his son and reared me.
Akki, the drawer of water, appointed me as his gardener.
While I was a gardener, Ishtar granted me her love.
And for four and [. . .] years I exercised kingship.
The black-headed people I ruled, I governed. . . .

Source: From *Chronicles Concerning Early Babylonian Kings*, by L. W. King. London: British Museum, 1907.

NEW MESOPOTAMIAN KINGDOMS: ASSYRIA AND BABYLONIA

Within a few generations, the Amorites absorbed the culture of the Mesopotamian urban communities they had conquered. Two new kingdoms, Babylonia and Assyria, emerged in the lands once controlled by Sumer and Akkad

Ziggurat of Ur
Built of mud bricks, the Ziggurat of Ur was the focal point of religious life. This vast temple was built by King Ur-Nammu of the Third Dynasty (2113–2096 B.C.E.) and restored by the British archeologist Sir Leonard Woolley in the 1930s. Similar structures have been found in all the major cities of ancient Sumer and were typically surrounded by public buildings and palaces of the elite.

Aerial View of the Ziggurat Ur
This photograph reveals how the great temple dominated the flat cityscape that surrounded it.

and coexisted for more than two centuries. The phenomenon of invaders absorbing the culture of sophisticated communities they conquered and then creating something new would often be repeated as Western civilization evolved.

Assyria: A Kingdom of Commerce

Ashur, the major city in Assyria, had its start on the upper Tigris River some time before 2000 B.C.E. Ashur's inhabitants, called Assyrians, spoke a Semitic language related to Akkadian. International commerce formed the basis of the Assyrian economy, and Ashur held a privileged place as a hub of trading routes.

Assyria's power began to expand around 2000 B.C.E., perhaps due in part to the discovery of bronze making. Bronze is an easily worked but very hard metal, made by combining molten copper with small quantities of tin. It quickly became very highly valued both for military and ornamental uses. Because the sources of copper and tin were in southern Arabia, Anatolia, and Afghanistan, trade in metals became increasingly important throughout Southwest

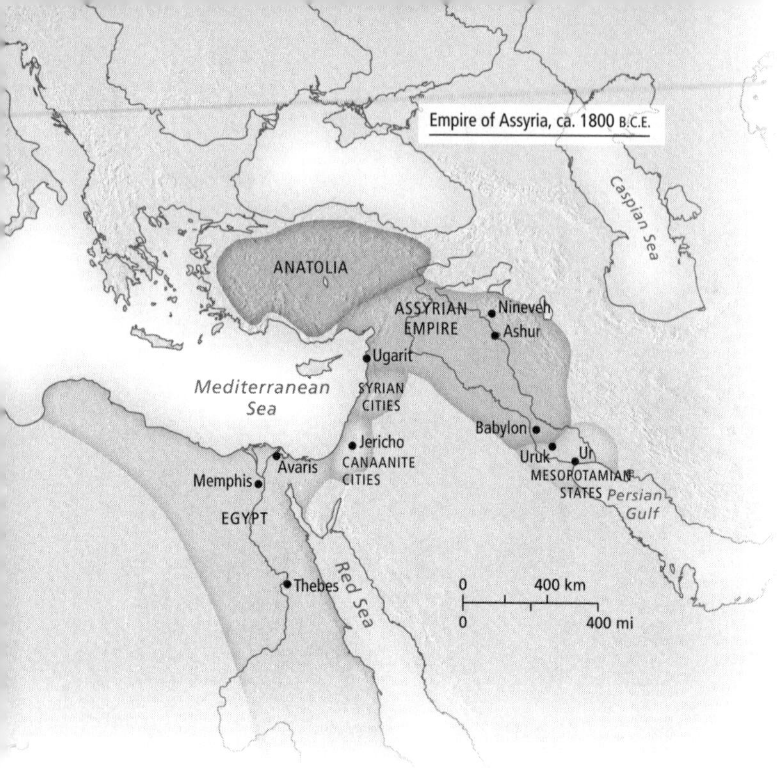

■ **Map 1.3 Empire of Assyria, ca. 1800 B.C.E.**
The Assyrians combined warfare and commerce to create their empire in Mesopotamia and Anatolia.

Asia. The Assyrians controlled much of the metals trade among these various regions.

By 1900 B.C.E. the Assyrians had established an extensive trading network that reached as far as Anatolia and Syria (see Map 1.3). They also controlled and operated about a dozen trading colonies throughout these regions. Assyrian merchants sent donkey caravans to these colonies loaded with tin (obtained in Afghanistan) and textiles (acquired in southern Mesopotamia) to exchange for copper, gold, and silver. In order to encourage long-distance commerce, Assyrian kings did not tax silver, gold, copper, tin, barley, and wool. The whole process of trading was recorded by Assyrian scribes who kept commercial records dealing with accounting, credit, prices, and transportation costs.

An assembly of leading merchants called "the City" amassed great power in Assyria. The City controlled diplomatic relations with foreign kingdoms, established economic policy, and determined taxes on commerce. It also passed binding legal decisions that affected the entire region. By contrast, the authority of Assyrian kings was limited to performing religious duties, maintaining the system of justice, and building irrigation works, walls, and other public projects.

By 1762 B.C.E., however, independent Assyria had ceased to exist. It, and all of Mesopotamia, fell under the rule of King Hammurabi of Babylon, one of humanity's first great empire builders.

Babylon: A Kingdom of Law and Order

The kingdom of Babylonia, a mixture of Sumerian and Amorite cultures, emerged about 1800 B.C.E. as the dominant power in southern Mesopotamia. To secure their rule and enrich their coffers, Babylonian kings embarked on the conquest of neighboring lands. Their capital city, Babylon, grew wealthy. Under the leadership of King Hammurabi (r. 1792–1750 B.C.E.), Babylonia gained control of all of Mesopotamia, including the Assyrian realm. Impressed by his own victories, Hammurabi called himself "King of the Four Quarters of the World."

Hammurabi also called himself the "King of Justice," a title he deserves, because his historical legacy is a rigorous system of justice codified in law. The Law Code of Hammurabi, the most complete surviving legal text of ancient Mesopotamia, demonstrates the careful thought this monarch devoted to matters of justice.

The 282 civil, commercial, and criminal laws contained in the Code unveil the social assumptions and specific concerns of Babylonia's rulers. For example, the irrigation system on which Babylonian agriculture depended is a frequent focus of the Code. Many laws related specifically to damages and personal responsibility with regard to irrigation. Similarly, the Code buttressed Babylon's social hierarchy by drawing legal distinctions between classes of people. The crimes of aristocratic elites were treated far more leniently than were the offenses of nonaristocrats, while slaves were given no rights at all.

At the same time, however, Hammurabi's Code introduced one of the fundamentals of Western jurisprudence: the idea that the punishment must suit the crime. For example, one law reads: "If a man has opened his channel for irrigation and has been negligent and allowed the water to wash away a neighbor's field, he shall pay grain equivalent to the crops of his neighbors."[3] Through its introduction of such abstract principles as "an eye for an eye," Hammurabi's Code helped shape legal thought in Southwest Asia for a millennium. It later influenced the laws of the Hebrews, and through the Hebrew Bible continues to mold ideas about justice to this day.

The great temples of Mesopotamian cities influenced the lives of Babylonians by providing the opportunity to worship the gods upon whom success depended. In addition, the priests at the temples controlled large tracts of land in the name of the gods they served. The farmers who labored on these lands gave their produce to the priests, and the temples enjoyed great prosperity. Other groups in Babylonian society also grew wealthy.

Babylonian society contained a private sector of merchants, craftspeople, farmers, and sailors. These free people, who were not tied to the temples or the king, grew prosperous. For example, merchants traveling by land and sea brought textiles and metals as well as luxury items such as gold and silver jewelry and gems from Anatolia, Egypt, Iran,

Afghanistan, and lands along the Persian Gulf and Red Sea. This private sector enjoyed a degree of personal freedom unique in ancient Mesopotamia.

The most important person in Babylonian society, however, was the king. Babylonian monarchs had the responsibility of building and repairing city walls, temples to the gods, irrigation systems to improve agriculture, and warehouses for storing grain. Hammurabi and his successors imposed increasingly heavy taxes on their subjects. These financial demands provoked great resentment, and when Hammurabi died, many Babylonian provinces successfully revolted. As a result, Babylonian rulers were weakened by loss of revenues. They tried to maintain their control by increasing the number of bureaucrats. This only made the government top-heavy, and by 1500 B.C.E. it collapsed.

CHRONOLOGY

	Egyptian Civilization
CA. 5000 B.C.E.	First agricultural communities on Nile
CA. 3500 B.C.E.	Hierakonpolis and other kingdoms established
CA. 3100 B.C.E.	Narmer unifies Upper and Lower Egypt
CA. 3000–2200 B.C.E.	Old Kingdom
2200–2040 B.C.E.	First Intermediate Period
CA. 2040–1785 B.C.E.	Middle Kingdom
1785–1560 B.C.E.	Second Intermediate Period; Hyksos rule in delta

The Emergence of Egyptian Civilization

As the civilizations of Mesopotamia rose and fell, another emerged far to the south, in Egypt—a long and narrow strip of land in the northeast corner of the African continent. Egypt's lifeline is the Nile, the world's longest river, which flows north into the Mediterranean Sea from its origin in east Africa 4,000 miles away. The northernmost part of Egypt, where the Nile enters the Mediterranean, is a broad and fertile delta. In ancient times, Egypt controlled an 850-mile strip of land along the Nile. Until the completion of the Aswan Dam in 1970 C.E., the river flooded annually from mid-July to mid-October, leaving behind rich deposits of silt ideal for planting crops. In its ancient days, the Nile abounded with fish, water birds, and game on the shore. The rich banks of the Nile provided an ideal setting for agriculture and settled communities.

Historians organize the long span of ancient Egyptian history into four main periods: Predynastic (10,000–3000 B.C.E.), the Old Kingdom (3000–2200 B.C.E.), the Middle Kingdom (2040–1785 B.C.E.), and the New Kingdom (1600–1100 B.C.E., discussed in Chapter 2). Times of political disruption between the kingdoms are called intermediate periods. Despite these periods of disruption, the Egyptians maintained a remarkably stable civilization throughout millennia.

Women's Work and Leisure This sculpture from the Old Kingdom, made about 2400 B.C.E., shows a woman grinding grain by hand and then sieving it to remove the chaff. Small particles of stone from the grinding block entered the wheat and ground down everyone's teeth, as skeletal remains show.

THE BEGINNINGS OF SETTLED LIFE

Human beings had lived as hunter-gatherers in Egypt for tens of thousands of years before they began to settle in agricultural communities. Like the other civilizations we have discussed, the Egyptians were originally hunter-gatherers who slowly turned to growing crops and domesticating animals. Small villages, in which people could coordinate their labor most easily, appeared along the banks of the Nile between 5000 and 4000 B.C.E.

By 3500 B.C.E., Egyptians could survive comfortably through agriculture and herding. With hunting and foraging for food no longer a major focus of everyday life, the transition to settled life was complete, and Egyptian society began to develop in many new ways. Small

JUSTICE IN HISTORY

Gods and Kings in Mesopotamian Justice

Mesopotamian kings placed a high priority on ruling their subjects justly. Shamash, the sun god and protector of justice, named two of his children Truth and Fairness. In the preface to his law code, Hammurabi explained the relationship between his rule and divine justice:

> *At that time, Anu and Enlil [two of the greatest gods], for the well-being of the people, called me by name, Hammurabi, the pious, god-fearing prince, and appointed me to make justice appear in the land [and] to destroy the evil and wicked, so that the strong might not oppress the weak, [and] to rise like Shamash over the black-headed people [the people of Mesopotamia].*[4]

Courts in Mesopotamian cities handled cases involving property, inheritance, boundaries, sale, and theft. A special panel of royal judges and officials handled cases involving the death penalty, such as treason, murder, sorcery, theft of temple goods, or adultery. Mesopotamians kept records of trials and legal decisions on clay tablets so that others might learn from them and avoid additional lawsuits.

A lawsuit began when an individual brought a dispute before a court for trial and judgment. The court consisted of three to six judges chosen from among the town's leading men, who typically included merchants, scribes, and officials in the town assembly. The judges could speak with authority about the community's principles of justice.

Individuals involved in the dispute spoke on their own behalf and presented testimony through witnesses, written documents, or statements made by leading officials. Witnesses took strict oaths to tell the truth in a temple before the statue of a god. Once the parties presented all the evidence, the judges made their decision and pronounced the verdict and punishment.

Sometimes the judges asked the defendants to clear themselves by letting the god in whose name the oath was taken make the judgment. The accused person would then undergo an ordeal or test in which he or she had to jump into a river and swim a certain distance underwater. Individuals who survived were considered innocent. Drowning constituted proof of guilt and a just punishment rendered by the gods.

The following account of one such ordeal comes from the city of Mari, about 1770 B.C.E. In this case a queen was accused of casting spells on her husband. The maid whom she forced to undergo the ordeal on her behalf drowned, and we do not know whether the queen received further punishment:

> *Concerning Amat-Sakkanim . . . whom the river god overwhelmed . . . : "We made her undertake her plunge, saying to her, 'Swear that your mistress did not perform any act of sorcery against Yarkab-Addad her lord; that she did not reveal any palace secret nor did another person open the missive of her mistress; that your mistress did not commit a transgression against her lord.' In connection with these oaths they had her take her plunge; the river god overwhelmed her, and she did not come up alive."*[5]

This account illustrates the Mesopotamian belief that sometimes only the gods could make decisions about right and wrong. Kings willingly allowed the gods to administer justice in their kingdoms. In this way, divine justice and royal justice became part of the same system.

By contrast, the following trial excerpts come from a homicide case in which humans, not gods, made the final judgment. About 1850 B.C.E., three men murdered a temple official named Lu-Inanna. For unknown reasons they told the victim's wife, Nin-dada, what they had done. King Ur-Ninurta of the city of Isin sent the case to be tried in the city of Nippur, the site of an important court. When the case came to trial, nine accusers asked that the three murderers be executed. They also requested that Nin-dada should be put to death because she had not reported the murder to the authorities. The accusers said:

> *They who have killed a man are not worthy of life. Those three males and that woman should be killed in front of the chair of Lu-Inanna, the son of Lugal-apindu, the religious official.*

In her defense, two of Nin-dada's supporters pointed out that she had not been involved in the murder and therefore should be released:

■ **The Law Code of Hammurabi**
This stone copy of Hammurabi's code stands taller than seven feet. Written in Babylonian cuneiform script, it shows Hammurabi receiving the law directly from the sun god, Shamash, seated on a throne. The god wears a crown of horns, a scepter, and a ring, and has flames coming from his shoulders. Hammurabi stands because his status is lower than Shamash's. He raises his hand in a gesture of respect and speaks directly to the god.

> *Granted that the husband of Nin-dada, the daughter of Lu-Ninurta, has been killed, but what had the woman done that she should be killed?*

The court agreed with this latter argument on the grounds that Nin-dada was justified in keeping silent because her husband had not provided for her properly. Then the members of the Assembly of Nippur faced the three murderers and said:

> *A woman whose husband did not support her . . . why should she not remain silent about him? Is it she who killed her husband? The punishment of those who actually killed him should suffice.*

In accordance with the decision of the court, the defendants were executed.

This approach to justice—using witnesses, evaluating evidence, and rendering a verdict in a court protected by the king—demonstrates the Mesopotamians' desire for fairness. This court decision became an important precedent that later judges frequently cited. ■

Questions of Justice

1. How would a city benefit by letting a panel of royal officials make judgments about life-and-death issues? How would the king benefit?
2. These trials demonstrate that the enforcement of justice in Mesopotamia depended on the interaction of religious, social, and political beliefs. How does this interaction help us understand Mesopotamian civilization?

Taking It Further

Greengus, Samuel. "Legal and Social Institutions of Ancient Near Mesopotamia," in *Civilizations of the Ancient Middle East,* ed. Jack M. Sasson, vol. 1, 469–484. 1995. Describes basic principles of law and administration of justice, with a bibliography of ancient legal texts.

Kuhrt, Amelie. *The Ancient Middle East: ca. 3000–330 B.C.,* vol. 1. 1995. An authoritative survey combining archaeological and textual evidence.

towns grew quickly in number along the Nile, and market centers connected by roads emerged as hubs where artisans and merchants exchanged their wares. After the potter's wheel was introduced from Mesopotamia, the production of pottery became more sophisticated. Some towns specialized in producing certain kinds of pots for trade, such as the elegant clay vessels found in the tombs of the wealthy along the Nile. As the quality of tools improved, artisans made ever more intricate copper, gold, and silver vessels.

These technological advances had drastic ecological consequences, however. As potters cut down more and more trees to burn in their kilns and as flocks of sheep and goats devoured the grasses and plants on the forests' edge, the ecological balance of grassland and desert collapsed. Farmers were pushed to cultivate land closer to the banks of the Nile River.

With this ecological shift, the social balance of Egyptian communities changed as well. The men who controlled the fertile river banks grew wealthy from the increase in grain production. As wealth grew in the fourth millennium B.C.E., social divisions widened between rich and poor Egyptians. Rich people built large houses and tombs and filled them with expensive items such as jewelry and fine pottery. Archaeologists have discovered clusters of such graves, a clue that generations of prosperous families were buried together and that the community viewed lineage as vital. At the same time, the wealthy members of the community began to experiment with mummification to preserve their bodies after death. Thus, not even death erased the distinctions between rich and poor.

To meet these wealthy landowners' demand for luxuries, professional merchants traded busily up and down the Nile. Assembling donkey caravans (camels would not come into use for another 3,000 years), they traveled to the Red Sea, Sinai, Mesopotamia, Palestine, Syria, and Nubia for gold, silver, ivory, copper beads, and other prized goods. These voyages established the foundations of long-lasting international trade routes.

Between 3500 and 3000 B.C.E., during the Predynastic period, energetic trade along the Nile River resulted in a shared culture and unified way of life. Towns along the Nile grew into small kingdoms. Despite shared social structures, religious beliefs, and ideas, rulers of these small kingdoms constantly warred with one another, attempting to grab more land and extend their power. The big gobbled up the small, and by 3000 B.C.E., all the towns had been absorbed into just two kingdoms: Upper Egypt in the south and Lower Egypt in the north. These two then united, forming what historians term the Old Kingdom. There is no written record or other evidence to show how the process of political unification unfolded, but Egyptian legends give some clues. According to tradition, King Narmer of Hierakonpolis (the "City of the Falcon") in Upper Egypt united the two kingdoms around 3100 B.C.E. Narmer established control from Aswan, a city in the southernmost part of Egypt, all the way north to the Mediterranean Sea.

UNITED EGYPT: THE OLD KINGDOM, CA. 3000–2200 B.C.E.

With the unification of Egypt under one king, a new era dawned for this civilization. Soon after Narmer brought all of Egypt under his command, cultural and political power moved north from Hierakonpolis to the newly built capital city of Memphis. There the Egyptian kings established themselves as the focal points of religious, social, and political life. Under the kings' careful supervision, the Old Kingdom stabilized and took on many of the characteristics of early civilizations we have seen in Mesopotamia, such as semidivine kingship, literate bureaucracies, a centralized

Narmer the Unifier of Egypt
This piece of slate, twenty-nine inches long, is carved on both sides. Carved pieces of stone, called palettes, were originally crafted in the Predynastic period as holders for cosmetics, but they evolved into objects with important religious and symbolic functions. This sample shows King Narmer of Hierankopolis, who lived about 3100 B.C.E. With his right hand he holds a mace and is about to smash the skull of an enemy. He stands on two dead enemies, as a servant behind him carries his sandals. A falcon god, Horus (Hierankopolis means "City of the Falcon"), sits in a papyrus plant holding an enemy's severed head. Narmer wears the White Crown of Upper Egypt and a bull's tail, symbolizing his virility. On the other side, he wears the Red Crown of Lower Egypt, which he has conquered.

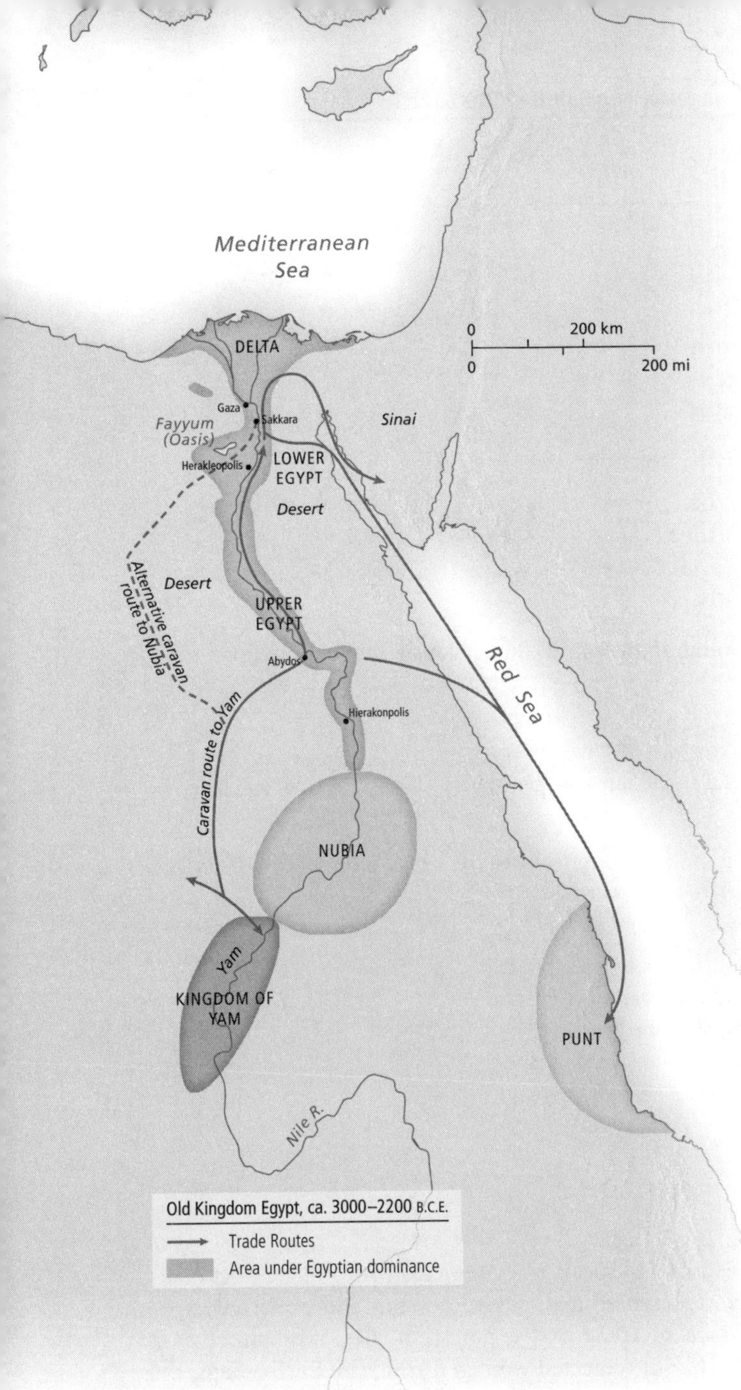

Map 1.4 Old Kingdom Egypt, ca. 3000–2200 B.C.E.
During the Old Kingdom, Egyptians traded with the kingdom of Yam, Nubia, and the land of Punt. Egyptian rulers built pyramids in lower (northern) Egypt.

economy, and strong support of long-distance trade (see Map 1.4).

Egyptian monarchs considered themselves to be gods as well as kings, believing that Ra, the sun god and creator of the universe, had chosen them to rule as his representatives. A text called *King as Priest of the Sun* explains the king's role: "Ra has placed the king on the earth of the living for ever and eternity to judge humanity and to pacify the gods, to realize Right and annihilate Wrong; he gives divine offerings to the gods, funerary offerings to the transfigured dead, the name of the king is in the sky like that of Ra. . . ."[6]

In their role as religious leaders, kings claimed to control even the Nile and its life-giving floods. To the Egyptians, the presence of the kings meant that cosmic order reigned, and that the kingdom was protected against forces of disorder and destruction. The rulers steadily amassed more power, and by 2600 B.C.E. they owned the largest and richest agricultural lands.

The power of the kings was highly centralized. Authority began with the king and passed to his court officials and then to provincial governors who delegated power to the mayors of cities and villages. Administrators collected Egypt's surplus produce—coinage would not be invented for another 2,500 years—and then the kings' officials redistributed it wherever it was needed: to feed the armies that protected Egyptian territories and long-distance trade and the peasants who labored on public works such as temples, roads, and irrigation projects.

A complex bureaucracy organized the enormous resources controlled by the pharaohs. The job of keeping records of the kings' possessions and supervising food production fell to the scribes, who were trained in hieroglyph writing. This form of writing involved a set of several thousand signs called hieroglyphs, literally "god's words." Hieroglyphs represent both sounds (as in our alphabet) and objects (as in a pictorial system). The hieroglyph system was very complex; all the more so because it diverged from the spoken Egyptian language. Consequently, learning hieroglyphs for literary or administrative purposes meant acquiring a second language and took years of schooling to master. It was worth the effort, however, for knowledge of hieroglyphs gave scribes and administrators great power. For 3,000 years, the royal bureaucrats kept the machinery of Egyptian government running despite the rise and fall of dynasties.

Scribes kept their records on papyrus, a durable and lightweight paper made from the pulp of the stalk of the papyrus plant, which grows in abundance along the banks of the Nile. Egyptians began to manufacture papyrus paper about 3000 B.C.E., and it quickly became an essential tool for the kings' bureaucracy. The government kept a monopoly on papyrus, and merchants exported it to Southwest Asia, where scribes used papyrus as well as clay tablets to record information.

Like bureaucrats, priests in the king's service grew powerful. Priests came from elite families, often the king's, and their positions passed from father to son. They owned vast estates, including the temples to the god they served, and they became enormously wealthy. In addition, they often played a major role in political life. Kings sought their

Photo to come .083

The elder of the house of Meni, he says: the crocodile in the water against him, the snake on the land against him

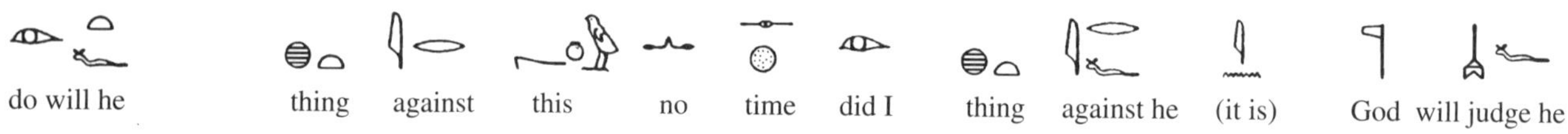

who does anything to this (tomb)! Never have I done anything to him. It is God who will judge.

Hieroglyph Writing

One consequence of long-distance trade with Mesopotamia was the importation of the idea of writing, which became firmly established in Egypt about 3100 B.C.E. Egyptian script combines pictures and signs for sounds. Egyptians wrote on paper made from papyrus reeds, plentiful on the banks of the Nile. They also wrote on wood and pottery, and they carved on walls. *Hieroglyph,* the word used for Egyptian writing signs, means "sacred carving" in Greek. Writing came into use for keeping business records. As a tool for organization it helped unify Egypt. (Source: From Regine Schulz and Matthias Seidel, *Egypt, the World of Pharaohs,* Koenemann, 1998, p. 347).

advice to ensure that in their leadership they were implementing the will of the gods.

Religious Beliefs in the Old Kingdom

Egypt's religion was polytheistic°. Ra, the sun god, was at the center of the belief system. Embodying the power of Heaven over Earth, Ra had created the universe and everything in it. He journeyed across the sky every day in a boat, rested at night, and returned in the morning to resume his eternal journey. By endlessly repeating the cycle of rising and setting, the sun symbolized the harmonious order of the universe that Ra established. The sun's reappearance at dawn every day gave Egyptians the hope of life after death.

Evil, however, constantly threatened the order of the universe in the form of Apopis, a serpent god whose coils could trap Ra's boat like a reef in the Nile. Ra's cosmic journey could continue only if proper worship and justice existed among humans. To make this possible, Ra created Egypt's kings, who shared in his divine nature and who ruled as his representatives on Earth.

Egyptians worshiped many gods in addition to Ra. Ptah, the patron of craftsmen, embodied the impulse to create and to speak. Min, depicted with a huge, erect phallus, represented male sexual potency and protected expeditions of trade and exploration. Bes, symbolized as a dwarf lion, protected women during childbirth. Hapy, the god of the annual Nile floods that enabled agriculture, was depicted as a man with pendulous breasts carrying armloads of crops.

Egyptians also worshiped Osiris, the son of the sky and the Earth, as god of the dead. According to Egyptian belief, Osiris was murdered by his brother Seth, god of chaos, after Osiris married their sister Isis, goddess of fertility. Seth cut Osiris into pieces and scattered them over the Earth, but Isis gathered the pieces and restored Osiris to life. The death and resurrection of Osiris symbolized the natural cycles of regeneration and rebirth that the Egyptians witnessed each spring as their fields bore new crops. After his regeneration, Osiris became king of the underworld, where he judged the dead. Egyptians associated this powerful deity with mummification, by which they tried to preserve bodies after death. Representations of Osiris appeared in pyramids, where the mummies of pharaohs rested for eternity.

THE HUMAN BODY IN HISTORY

The Mummy

The burial practices of the ancient Egyptians provide a window into their society. They reveal Egyptian attitudes about life, death, and the afterlife. Egyptians believed that a person could have an afterlife only if the person's body remained in recognizable form after death.

The Egyptians also thought that every human possessed three spirits active after death: the Ka, Ba, and Akh. The Ka was a person's life force, created at birth but set free at death to live in his or her tomb after death, where the spirit inhabited the deceased's statue and cared for the body. The Ba could take many shapes and travel outside the tomb, and it accompanied the corpse to final judgment. The Ba comprised all the qualities that made a person unique; without a body to return to, the Ba and the deceased's personality would vanish forever. The Akh represented a person's immortality and lived among the stars. These three spirits could survive only if the body did not decay, and so preserving the corpse became a central issue in burial practice.

Egyptians began experimenting with embalming or mummification between 3000 and 2600 B.C.E. and continued to develop the art for the next 3,000 years. The rise of Christianity in Egypt in the second and third centuries C.E. ended the practice of preserving corpses. Ancient records and modern scientific investigation have uncovered the secrets of mummification. Embalming took place within seventy days after death. By means of a metal hook, highly trained experts extracted the brains through the nostrils and discarded them. Sometimes they filled the skull with linen cloth and resin. Through an incision below the ribs the embalmers removed all the organs except for the heart. (That organ represented a person's life and would be examined by the gods on Judgment Day.) The embalmers wrapped the liver, lungs, stomach, and intestines individually and placed them in separate containers within a chest carved from alabaster. Next the embalmers thoroughly dried the corpse by packing it with natrun, a natural compound of sodium carbonate and bicarbonate. After drying for forty days, the skin shriveled and the embalmers padded the body with aromatic packing materials to re-create as lifelike an appearance as possible. The priests then added hairpieces and artificial eyes. They applied a layer of resin over the face and body followed by a coat of paint—red for men and yellow for women.

Customarily, embalmers placed magical amulets on the corpse to protect the deceased in the next world. They also decorated the body with expensive jewelry and insignia of rank. Then they tightly wrapped the corpse in long strips of linen. Before placing the corpse in a shroud, they fitted the face with a painted linen mask. The masks of royalty were made of gold.

Finally the corpse was placed in its coffin, which was painted with a stylized portrait of the deceased. The dead person's family and friends carried the coffin to the tomb. After the proper prayers, the priest conducting the burial ceremony touched the eyes, ears, nose, and mouth painted on the coffin to enable the dead person to see, hear, smell, and breathe for eternity. Then the priest and family sealed the tomb. When prepared in such a fashion, a body could last forever. ■

Mummy of Ramesses II
Both a science and an art, mummification preserved the body of King Ramesses II (r. 1279–1213 B.C.E.) for more than 3,000 years. This near-perfect example of a mummy is the product of an Egyptian tradition of preserving the body after death that began at the beginning of Egyptian history.

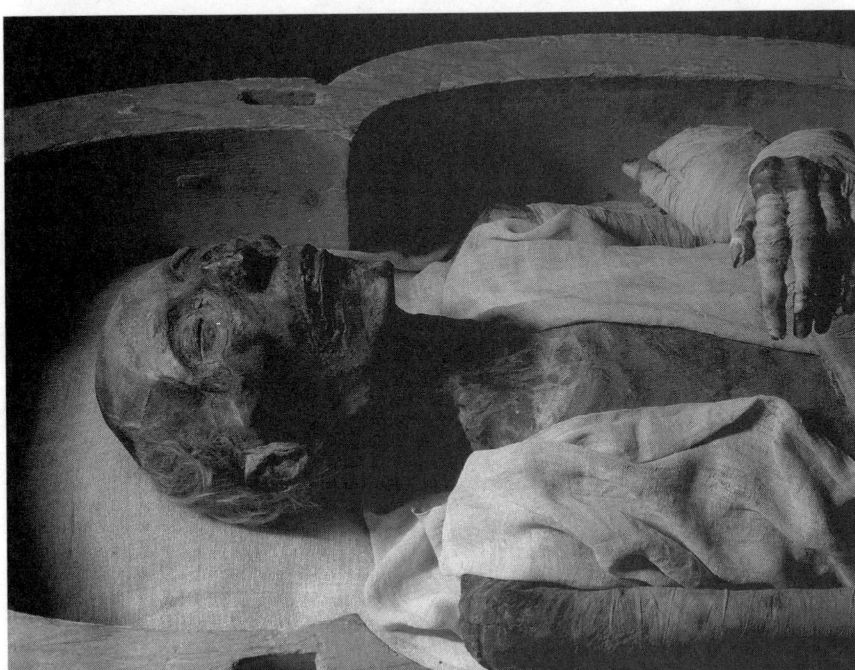

For Discussion

What does the practice of mummification reveal about Egyptian attitudes toward death and the boundaries between life and death?

Shabtis

Shabtis were small carved figures placed in tombs to serve the deceased in the afterlife. This elaborate group of shabtis in a Theban tomb, around 1900 B.C.E., shows officials assessing a herd of cattle for taxation purposes and scribes seated in a small pavilion taking careful notes. The deceased sits with them, watching a farmer being beaten by an official.

The Pyramids

With their emphasis on the afterlife, Egyptians took great pains to provide proper housing for the dead. Many tombs were built as monuments to the dead person's wealth and social status. These structures provided not only a resting place for the corpse but a symbolic entryway to the next life. Members of the elite were buried in expensive tombs filled with ivory furniture and other luxurious goods, but kings had the grandest tombs of all.

Burial customs in the Old Kingdom grew ever more elaborate. For the first several centuries of the Old Kingdom, kings built their tombs in the city of Abydos, in the homeland of the first kings. The tombs consisted of an underground room with a special compartment for the royal corpse. The king's treasures filled nearby underground rooms. Above the ground sat a small palace featuring courtyards and halls suitable for a royal afterlife. The earliest of these tombs, dating to about 2800 B.C.E., contains the bones of animals and people sacrificed to accompany the ruler into the next world. These included servants, entertainers, women, dogs, and pet lions. The practice of killing attendants ended a few centuries later.

About 2680 B.C.E., architects began building a new kind of royal tomb. The defining feature was a great four-sided monument of stone in the shape of a pyramid. Elaborate temples in which priests worshiped statues of the king surrounded the monument. The structure also included compartments where the king could dwell in the afterlife in the same luxury he enjoyed during his life on Earth. King Djoser, the founder of the Old Kingdom, built the first pyramid complex at Saqqara near Memphis. Known today as the Step Pyramid, this structure rests above Djoser's burial place and rises high into the air in six steps, which represent a ladder to heaven.

For the next 2,000 years, kings continued building pyramids for themselves and smaller ones for their queens, with each tomb becoming more architecturally sophisticated. The walls grew taller and steeper and contained hidden burial chambers and treasure rooms. The Great Pyramid at Giza, built around 2600 B.C.E. by king Khufu (or Cheops), stood as the largest humanmade structure in the ancient

The Pyramids

The cemetery of King Djoser, built at Saqqara about 2690 B.C.E., is the oldest monumental structure in the world built entirely of cut stone. The pyramid has steps and is surrounded by courts and chapels.

world. It consists of more than two million stones that weigh an average of two and a half tons each. Covering thirteen acres, it reaches more than 481 feet into the sky.

Building the pyramid complexes was an unending and enormously costly task. In addition to the architects, painters, sculptors, carpenters, and other specialists employed on the site throughout the year, stone masons supervised the quarrying and transportation of the colossal building blocks. Peasants, who were organized into work gangs and paid and fed by the king, provided the heavy labor when the Nile flooded their fields every year. As many as 70,000 workers out of a total population estimated at one and a half million sweated on the pyramids every day. Entire cities sprang up around pyramid building sites to house the workmen, artisans, and farmers. The construction of enormous pyramids stopped after 2400 B.C.E., probably because of the expense, but smaller burial structures continued to be built for many centuries.

THE MIDDLE KINGDOM, CA. 2040–1785 B.C.E.

Around 2200 B.C.E. the Old Kingdom collapsed, dragged down by economic decline, the deterioration of royal authority, and a cycle of terrible droughts that triggered a breakdown of law and order. As the kingdom endured years of famine, rulers lost their power to control Egypt, and provincial governors seized political and religious power in their provinces.

For 200 years, anarchy and civil war raged in Egypt during what historians call the First Intermediate Period. Finally, the governors of Thebes, a city in Upper Egypt, set out to reunify the kingdom. In 2040 B.C.E., Mentuhotep II consolidated his rule and established a vigorous new monarchy, initiating the Middle Kingdom (see Map 1.5).

Rulers in the Middle Kingdom defined a new role for themselves. They still viewed themselves as gods, but their rule became less despotic. The highly centralized bureaucracy that regulated most aspects of everyday life was open to men of any social standing, as long as they could read and write hieroglyphs. Wealth spread more widely, and private tombs were no longer the monopoly of the royal elite. Although they continued building large temple complexes to house themselves in the afterlife, these structures were not as grandiose as the Old Kingdom pyramids. Even more important, many Middle Kingdom kings directed more of Egypt's resources toward their subjects' welfare.

The kings also launched many public-works projects for the benefit of their subjects. For example, Amenemhet I (r. 1991–1962 B.C.E.) and his successors transformed the marshy Fayyum Oasis, fifty miles southwest of Memphis, into a well-irrigated agricultural community that yielded abundant crops even in dry years. In the planned city of Kahun, near the Fayyum Oasis, the houses were laid out on a grid pattern, with larger homes for the officials. Each of

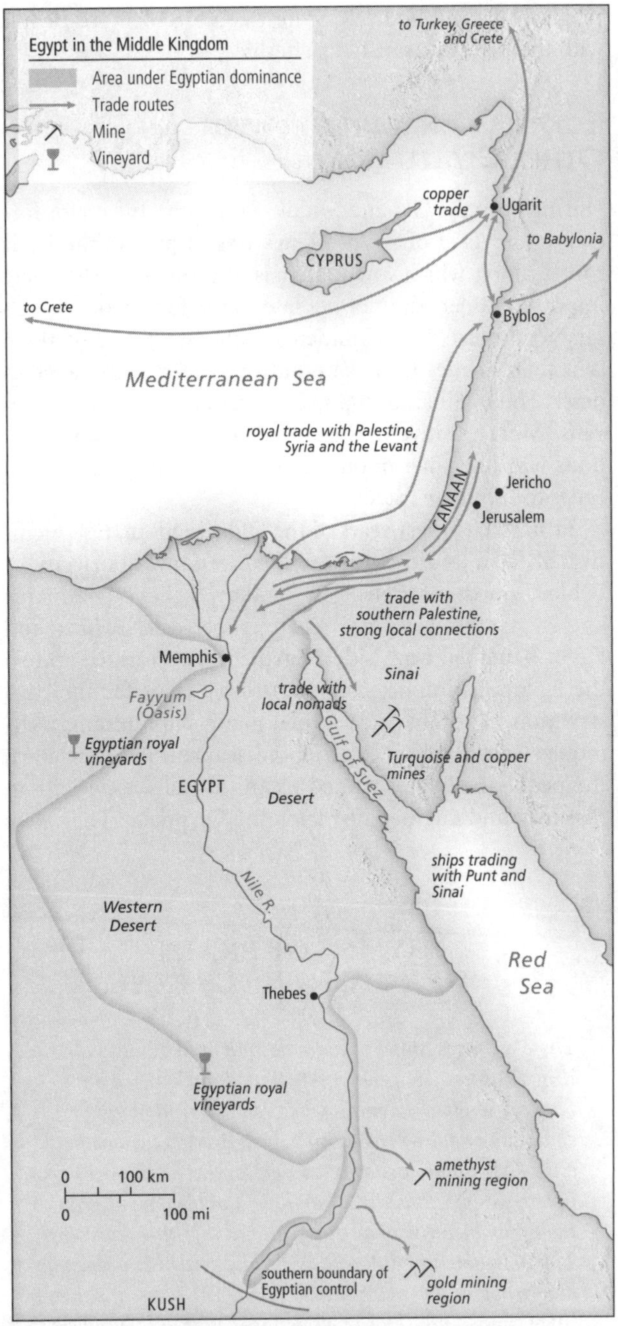

Map 1.5 Egypt in the Middle Kingdom
During the Middle Kingdom, Egyptian merchants traded extensively with Southwest Asia and the cities of the eastern Mediterranean. Turquoise and copper mines in the Sinai were heavily exploited.

these had its own granary, from which workers in the community received regular allotments of grain.

Even the religious life of the Middle Kingdom was characterized by greater concern for the lives and needs of ordinary people. Because it stressed moral conduct more than the performance of rituals open only to the wealthy, the religion of the Middle Kingdom comforted more people with the hope of a satisfying afterlife.

EGYPTIAN ENCOUNTERS WITH OTHER CIVILIZATIONS

During both the Old and Middle Kingdoms, the major foreign policy goal of Egypt's kings was to protect the trade routes along which raw materials and luxury goods were imported. Rulers did not hesitate to use force when necessary to protect their commercial interests. Some of them sent their armies to make punitive attacks in the western desert and in Sinai to stop raiders from robbing trade caravans. More positively, kings tried to maintain good relations with the chief trading cities of Syria and Palestine in order to stimulate trade.

From the earliest years of the Old Kingdom, Egypt cultivated friendly ties with the Mediterranean port city of Byblos, north of Beirut in modern Lebanon, an area known as the Levant. Exchanges between Byblos and Egypt benefited both sides. Egypt had no forests, and so the Egyptians imported timber from Byblos for the construction of tombs and learned many shipbuilding techniques from Byblos's experienced seamen. For their part, the people of Byblos gained technical skills, especially in masonry and engineering, from the Egyptians. They were also influenced by Egypt's religious beliefs. The Egyptian god of writing, Thoth, became Taut in Byblos, while Byblos's god of craftsmen, Kothar, was believed to have his home in the Egyptian city of Memphis.

During the Old and Middle Kingdoms, Egyptian interactions with Nubia, the territory to the south, also proved economically important. Egyptian merchants systematically exploited its natural resources of gold, timber, and animal skins. They also enslaved many Nubians and transported them for labor in Egypt. Agents of Egyptian rulers, called Keepers of the Gateway of the South, tried to protect the merchants by keeping the peace with the warlike Nubian tribes. When diplomacy failed, Egyptian armies would invade for short periods of time to create peaceful conditions. Slowly, Egyptian monarchs made their presence more permanent. About 1900 B.C.E., king Amenemhet built ten forts at strategic locations where trade routes from the interior of Africa reached the Nile River. Egyptian merchants placed the gold, ivory, and other natural resources that reached these forts into boats, which they sailed northward along the Nile to Egypt. Egyptians came to depend on the vast resources of Nubia.

Commercial connections between Egypt and other African lands were less important. Egyptian merchants traded with the land of Punt (modern Somalia) for spices and rare woods, and they opened turquoise mines in the

HYMNS OF PRAISE TO A VICTORIOUS KING

These passages come from a collection of hymns of praise to King Sesostris III of the Middle Kingdom. Written on a papyrus scroll, the hymns were probably read aloud in an elaborate ritual when Sesostris, who lived in the northern city of Memphis, visited a town in southern (Upper) Egypt. References to "Two Lands" and his "double crown" refer to the symbolic unity of all of Egypt that this king represents. The Bowmen are raiders from Nubia, evidently a considerable problem during Sesostris's reign. The praise includes more general allusions to other enemies as well. Needless to say, the king triumphs over all of them and wins the universal devotion of his subjects.

I.

Hail to you, Son of Re [the sun god], our Horus,
Divine of Form!
Land's protector who widens its borders,
Who smites foreign countries with his crown;
Who holds the Two Lands in his arms' embrace;
Who subdues foreign lands by a motion of his hands;
Who slays Bowmen without a blow of the club;
Who shoots the arrow without drawing the string;
Whose terror strikes the Bowmen in their land,
Fear of whom smites the Nine Bows.
Whose slaughter brought death to thousands of Bowmen,
Who had come to invade his borders. . . .
His majesty's tongue restrains Nubia.
His utterances make Asiatics flee. . . .

II.

How the gods rejoice:
You have strengthened their offerings!
How the people rejoice:
You have made safe their frontiers!
How your forbears rejoice:
You have enriched their portions!
How Egypt rejoices in your strength:
You have protected its customs!
How the people rejoice in your guidance:
Your might has won increase for them! . . .

Source: From Miriam Lichtheim, *Ancient Egyptian Literature: The Old and Middle Kingdoms,* Volume 1.

Sinai. During the Old Kingdom, some merchants traded for skins, ivory, incense, and slaves among the peoples living in the Kingdom of Yam, located at the tributaries of the Nile River in the interior of eastern Africa. Because the peoples of the interior of Africa attacked Egyptian merchants and took their goods, this trading activity proved too dangerous, and the Egyptians abandoned trade with Africa south of Nubia during the Middle Kingdom.

With the desert on both sides of the Nile Valley protecting Egypt from invasion by foreign enemies, the Egyptians developed a distinctive culture characterized not only by economic prosperity but also by a powerful sense of self-confidence and optimism. Attracted by Egypt's stability and prosperity during both the Old and Middle Kingdom eras, peoples from different lands sought to settle in the Nile Valley. They came from Syria, Nubia, and the deserts that border the Nile River. They took Egyptian names and assimilated into Egyptian culture. The government settled these immigrants, as well as war captives, throughout the kingdom where they could mix quickly with the local inhabitants. This willingness to accept newcomers into their kingdom lent Egyptian civilization even more vibrancy. During the last years of the Middle Kingdom, many merchants and large numbers of settlers moved into Egypt from Syria and Palestine. Around 1750 B.C.E., one such group from Syria, called the Hyksos, took control of Egypt and changed the direction of Egyptian history. As we shall see in Chapter 2, the Second Intermediate Period was marked by both foreign invasion and internal division.

CHRONOLOGY

	Neolithic Europe
CA. 45,000 B.C.E.	*Homo sapiens sapiens* begin to spread throughout Europe
CA. 7000–2500 B.C.E.	Agriculture spreads through Europe
CA. 5000 B.C.E.	Linear Pottery culture emerges in northern Europe; cultures grow diverse
CA. 4500 B.C.E.	Copper is first mined in Europe
CA. 3500–2000 B.C.E.	Battle Axe cultures and megalith–building cultures flourish
CA. 3300 B.C.E.	Otzi the Ice Man dies

The Transformation of Europe

Europe, which has become the core territory of Western civilization, occupies the westernmost part of the Eurasian land mass stretching from western Russia to the Atlantic Ocean. Because the climate was colder and forests had to be cleared, food production was more difficult in Europe than in the floodplains of Mesopotamia and the Levantine Corridor. Consequently people made the transition from hunting and gathering to food production very gradually. The food-producing revolution that had begun in Southwest Asia around 8000 B.C.E. spread to Europe a thousand years later when farmers, probably from Anatolia, ventured to northern Greece and the Balkans. It took another 4,000 years for the inhabitants of Europe to clear forests and establish farms and grazing lands. By 2500 B.C.E., most of Europe's hunting and gathering cultures had given way to farming societies. This transition to food production laid the economic foundations of subsequent European cultures (see Map 1.6).

Food production in Europe spread slowly but steadily in two interrelated ways: through the migration of groups who knew how to farm and breed livestock and by the adoption of agriculture and animal domestication by hunter-gatherers. Archaeologists have discovered thousands of small outposts of food producers in Europe who were greatly outnumbered by the hunter-gatherers around them. In these frontier settlements, farmers and hunter-gatherers traded food, hides, and tools. Perhaps necessity eventually compelled hunter-gatherers to abandon their old ways of life. Clearing the lands for farming meant the forests disappeared in many areas, and so hunter-gatherers who depended on forest animals and plants had to adapt

Map 1.6 Neolithic Cultures in Europe
During the Neolithic period, most of the peoples of Europe changed their way of life from hunting and gathering to food production. In the process, many new cultures developed.

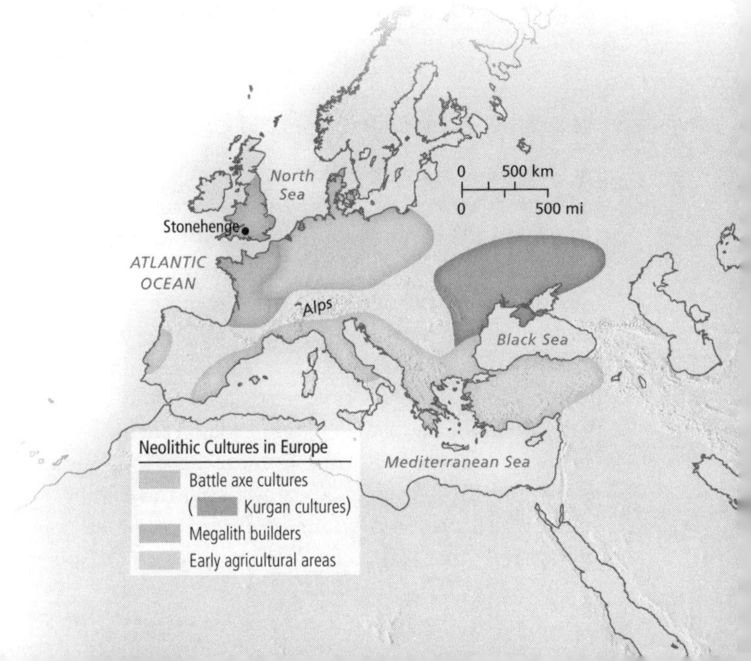

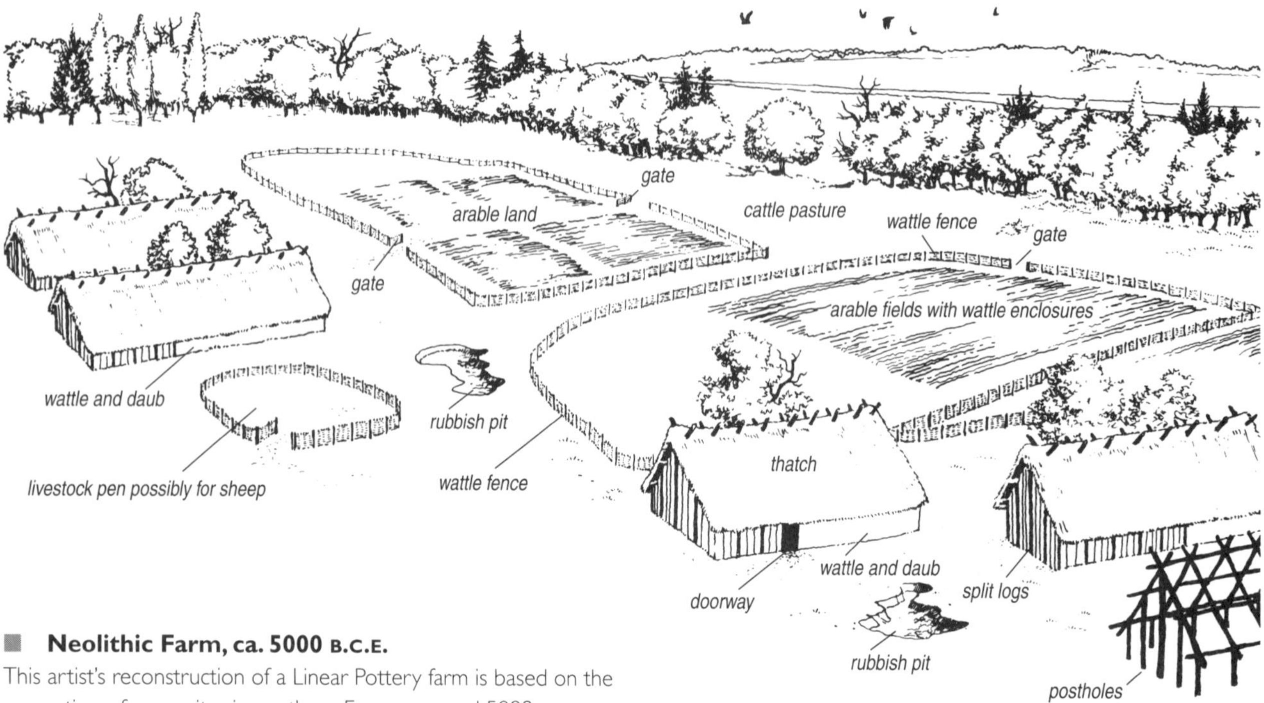

Neolithic Farm, ca. 5000 B.C.E.
This artist's reconstruction of a Linear Pottery farm is based on the excavation of many sites in northern Europe around 5000 B.C.E.

to farming and animal domestication for their survival. Hunting continued to supplement food production in Europe during the Neolithic Age, but it would never again stand as the primary way to obtain food.

As farmers and herders spread across Europe, people adapted to different climates and terrain. A variety of cultures evolved from these differences. We will never know the names these people called themselves, the languages they spoke, or their religious beliefs because no writings or oral traditions have survived from their time. So, archaeologists have named the different cultures of Neolithic Europe after some distinguishing feature of their pottery, tools, methods of constructing houses, or burial customs.

THE LINEAR POTTERY CULTURE

By 5000 B.C.E. one of the most important of these cultures, the Linear Pottery culture, had spread across Europe from Holland to Russia. Archaeologists call it the Linear Pottery culture because its people decorated their pottery with parallel lines. Their customs varied slightly in different regions, but they shared many similarities as well. For example, the Linear Pottery farmers lived in small villages of about sixty people. They built clusters of permanent family farmsteads made of timber and thatch, and rebuilt them over many generations. These farm families cultivated barley and other grains and kept sheep, goats, dogs, and, most important, cattle, which provided wealth and prestige. From gifts of jewelry and other luxury goods left in graves, archaeologists theorize that women were held in high esteem, perhaps because the people in these communities traced ancestry through them.

After about 4500 B.C.E., villages consisting of several hundred people began to appear in northern Europe, and the trend toward cultural diversity accelerated. In different regions, people used different kinds of pottery and probably spoke distinct languages.

As Linear Pottery settlements slowly spread, competition for farmlands and grazing lands stiffened. Archaeologists believe that men who controlled the livestock—the source of wealth and prestige—developed political authority. These early European elites tried to increase their influence by seizing the lands and herds of others. Conflicts broke out among groups, and people fortified their villages with defensive works. These struggles marked the beginnings of warfare in Europe.

At the same time that the power of elites in Linear Pottery communities was growing, they began building communal stone tombs called *megaliths* ("large stones") in the regions from Scandinavia to Spain and on islands in the western Mediterranean. Archaeologists disagree about the meaning of the megaliths. Some believe that these tombs were the burying places of the elites who controlled the livestock and lands in Linear Pottery communities. They argue that the tombs symbolized the power of these influential, wealthy families—and perhaps new religious beliefs involving these family groups in the afterlife. Other archaeologists, however, reject the religious interpretation of the megaliths. Instead, they argue that farming communities built the structures to announce their claim to frontier lands, for which they competed with hunting-gathering communities. The megalith builders may also have wished to display their power and wealth to families with whom they were competing for prestige.

The best-known example of a megalithic structure is Stonehenge, a monument in England. People began to build Stonehenge about 3000 B.C.E. as a ring of pits. Later generations reconstructed it several times, adding large stones. Stonehenge took its final form about 1600 B.C.E., when builders positioned immense stones, each weighing several tons, in standing positions. Stonehenge possibly measured the movement of stars, the sun, and the planets, and perhaps served as a place for religious ceremonies of some kind.

Around the same time Europeans began experimenting with metallurgy, the art of using fire to shape metals such as copper into items such as tools or jewelry. The idea of shaping metals probably originated when potters noticed that bits of metal ore that accidentally mixed with pottery clay melted in the hot kilns and then hardened again after cooling. Knowledge of metallurgy spread slowly across Europe from the Balkans, where people started to mine copper about 4500 B.C.E. Metallurgy would eventually prove as revolutionary as food production, but its beginnings were very modest. At first, people worked with copper only part of the year. Otzi the Ice Man, for example, may have been both a shepherd and a coppersmith. Gradually, as copper tools and ornaments became more widely used, metalworkers became specialists. As villages became larger, wealthier inhabitants demonstrated their social status by wearing precious copper jewelry. Trade in metals flourished, changing Europe's economy by creating long-distance trading networks. In turn, these networks provided the basis for cultural encounters—for the meeting and blending of different cultural assumptions and ideas.

THE BATTLE AXE CULTURES

Between 3500 B.C.E. and 2000 B.C.E. the Battle Axe cultures flourished in Europe. Fanning across Europe, they gradually replaced the Linear Pottery cultures. Battle Axe peoples cultivated many different types of crops, lived in rectangular single-family thatched dwellings, and used stone and copper battle axes. They may also have been the first peoples to domesticate the horse.

One of the better-researched Battle Axe cultures is that of the Kurgan peoples, who made their homes on the edges of the Russian steppes beginning about 3000 B.C.E. Their name comes from a burial custom in which each male corpse was buried under a mound of earth (*kurgan* in Russian) with a copper or stone axe. Kurgans were a warrior culture in which weapons not only were used for fighting but had an important symbolic meaning as well, although the symbolism is not clearly understood by archaeologists. Because Kurgans had to cross long distances to trade for the copper they needed for their weapons, their culture spread far to the west and south. They traveled by means of wheeled carts and domesticated horses that they obtained from seminomadic pastoralists whom they encountered on the steppe. One of the most important things the Kurgan peoples may have carried with them was a language that was the ancestor of the tongues spoken by half the world's population today.

Historians of languages believe that the majority of the languages spoken today in Europe, the Americas, and other lands colonized by Europeans, as well as several languages spoken in Southwest Asia such as Persian and Armenian, descend from an ancient family of languages that Europeans spoke about 5,000 years ago. Historians call this family of languages Indo-European. All Indo-European languages share similarities in vocabulary and grammar inherited from their ancient parent language.

Stonehenge
This megalithic monument consists of two circles of standing stones with large blocks capping the circles. It was built without the aid of wheeled vehicles or metal tools, and the stones were dragged from many miles away.

Many historians believe that Indo-European languages began to develop among the ancestors of the Kurgan peoples, who first lived in southern Russia more than 5,000 years ago. When the Kurgan peoples began to migrate from southern Russia about 3500 B.C.E. they spoke the Indo-European parent language, which then spread throughout Europe in the course of their migrations. The spread and development of Indo-European languages represents a foundation of Western civilization: the languages we speak.

TECHNOLOGY AND SOCIAL CHANGE

As the peoples of Europe developed their diverse cultures, their societies became socially stratified. Historians link the emergence of social hierarchies to technological and economic change. One important tool that helped alter human relationships in early Europe was the plow. European farmers had used wooden plows to cultivate their fields as early as 3600 B.C.E., but the use of plows did not become widespread until about 2600 B.C.E. Once plow technology took hold, however, agricultural life in Europe underwent substantial changes over the course of a mere 200 years. European soils are heavy and difficult to cultivate; hence, the use of plows meant that fewer people were needed to cultivate land. With more people available to clear forest lands, new settlements sprang up and farming communities spread into new regions.

The expansion of land under cultivation led to the development of new ways of organizing society. Because farmers could move out from old family-controlled lands and start new homes, opportunities for individual initiative and the accumulation of wealth increased. Some farmers could afford trade goods of high prestige, and they passed their lands and possessions to their descendants, who used their inherited resources to acquire even more wealth. By exchanging these expensive and prestigious objects, men cultivated friendships and loyalty, established political and military ties, and formalized mutual obligations. Growing divisions resulted between rich and poor, the powerful and the subordinate.

Such changes were evident in western Europe between about 2600 and 2400 B.C.E. For the first time, individual graves played a prominent role in burial customs, which may indicate the emergence of new forms of authority based on the preeminence of individual men in the community, particularly those who controlled land and inheritances. The tombs contain weapons and luxury goods such as jewelry and drinking cups, suggesting not only that these individuals were wealthy and powerful men who could afford expensive symbols of their prestige and power, but also that they were warriors as well as or instead of farmers. As influential warriors gained power, wealth, and influence in their communities, they emerged as political leaders, and they passed their wealth, political power, and social status down to their sons. These families came to dominate their societies. Today we call these elite groups nobles or aristocrats. The presence of male-dominated groups, designated by birth, that controlled the greatest wealth and enjoyed the greatest privileges in society remained unchallenged in Europe until the eighteenth century.

CONCLUSION
Civilization and the West

Civilization is a recent phenomenon in human history. Humans with intellectual capacities equal to our own have existed on the planet for about 200,000 years, but the elements that produced civilization in ancient Southwest Asia and Egypt began to appear only about 10,000 years ago. Western history claims the cultures that developed in these regions as remote ancestors.

This chapter has described the change in human patterns of life from nomadic hunting and gathering to living in settled communities in which food was produced through agriculture and domestication of animals. This transformation took more than 8,000 years. The changes in food production led to the development of village settlements. Powerful elites emerged, and an individual's social status and gender defined what kind of work he or she performed.

Soon human communities took on new characteristics. In Southwest Asia and Egypt, civilizations arose by about 3000 B.C.E. that were based on cities that devoted their resources to irrigation, warfare, and worship. The invention of writing enabled communities to record their laws and traditions. It also reinforced the long-distance trade linking communities together throughout Southwest Asia and beyond. Long-distance trade among these cities led to the encounters of different peoples. They exchanged new food production technologies, advances in crafts, new approaches to government and administration, and stories and religious ideas.

These changes unfolded over many centuries and did not happen everywhere at the same time. In Europe new patterns of wealth, prestige, and inheritance had begun reshaping some communities by the end of the Neolithic Age, but Europeans did not yet live in cities. Without the critical mass of people and possessions that accompanied city life, Europeans could not yet develop the specialized religious, economic, and political classes that characterize a "civilization." The West did not yet exist, but from the civilizations of Southwest Asia, Western civilization would inherit such crucial components as systems of writing and numeracy, the idea of a law code based on abstract principles, and perhaps gender-based divisions of labor and power.

By 3000 B.C.E., the rulers of Egypt and Mesopotamia had spun a web of interrelated economies and shared political interests. For the next millennium, civilizations waxed and waned. Cities such as Ur and Ashur grew powerful under the watchful eyes of ambitious kings who constantly fought with one another. But these kings did not yet possess the skills needed to rule vast empires for an extended period of time. As we will see in the next chapter, they would soon learn.

Suggestions for Further Reading

For a comprehensive list of suggested readings, please go to www.ablongman.com/levack/chapter1

Andrews, Anthony P. *First Cities.* 1995. An excellent introduction to the development of urbanism in Southwest Asia, Egypt, India, China, and the Americas.

Bogucki, Peter. *Forest Farmers and Stockherders: Early Agriculture and Its Consequences.* 1988. A clear synthesis of archaeological evidence from northern Europe.

Cunliffe, Barry, ed. *The Oxford Illustrated Prehistory of Europe.* 1994. An important synthesis of recent research by leading archaeologists.

Fagan, Brian. *People of the Earth: An Introduction to World Prehistory.* 1998. A comprehensive textbook that introduces basic issues with a wealth of illustrations and explanatory materials.

Harris, David R., ed. *The Origins and Spread of Agriculture and Pastoralism in Eurasia.* 1996. A collection of detailed essays by noted experts that draw on the latest research.

Kemp, Barry J. "Unification and Urbanization of Ancient Egypt," in *Civilizations of the Ancient Middle East,* ed. Jack M. Sasson, vol. 2, 679–690. 1995. Describes the emergence of towns and political unification of the early phases of Egyptian history.

Kuhrt, Amelie. *The Ancient Middle East: ca. 3000–330 B.C.,* vol. 1. 1995. An authoritative and up-to-date survey that combines archaeological and textual evidence in a lucid narrative with rich documentation.

Murnane, William J. "The History of Ancient Egypt: An Overview," in *Civilizations of the Ancient Middle East,* ed. Jack M. Sasson, vol. 2, 691–718. 1995. A good place to start for a "big picture" of ancient Egyptian history.

Quirke, Stephen. *Ancient Egyptian Religion.* 1992. A brilliant synthesis and explanation of basic Egyptian beliefs and practices.

Redford, Donald B. *Egypt, Canaan, and Israel in Ancient Times.* 1993. A distinguished Egyptologist discusses 3,000 years of uninterrupted contact between Egypt and southwestern Asia.

Schmandt-Besserat, Denise. *How Writing Came About.* 1996. A highly readable and groundbreaking argument that cuneiform writing developed from a method of counting with tokens.

Shaw, I., ed. *The Oxford History of Ancient Egypt.* 2001. Provides excellent discussions of all aspects of Egyptian life.

Spindler, Konrad. *The Man in the Ice: The Discovery of a 5,000-Year-Old Body Reveals the Secrets of the Stone Age.* 1994. A leader of the international team of experts interprets the corpse of a Neolithic hunter found in the Austrian Alps.

Trigger, Bruce G. *Early Civilizations: Ancient Egypt in Context.* 1995. A leading cultural anthropologist examines Old and Middle Kingdom Egypt through comparison with the early civilizations of China, Peru, Mexico, Mesopotamia, and Africa.

Notes

1. J. N. Postgate, *Early Mesopotamia: Society and Economy at the Dawn of History* (1992), p. 132.
2. H. Vanstiphout, "Memory and Literacy in Ancient Western Asia," in David R. Harris, ed., *The Origins and Spread of Agriculture and Pastoralism in Eurasia* (1996) p. 2185.
3. *Code of Hammurabi* (trans. J. N. Postgate), 55–56. Cited in Postgate, *Early Mesopotamia,* p. 160.
4. Samuel Greengus, "Legal and Social Institutions of Ancient Near Mesopotamia," in *Civilizations of the Ancient Middle East,* ed. Jack M. Sasson, vol. 1 (1995), p. 471.
5. Ibid., p. 474.
6. Translated in Stephen Quirke, *Ancient Egyptian Religion* (1992), p. 38.

CHAPTER

2

The International Bronze Age and Its Aftermath: Trade, Empire, and Diplomacy, 1600–550 B.C.E.

Chapter Outline

IN 1984, SCUBA-DIVING ARCHAEOLOGISTS BEGAN TO EXCAVATE THE WRECK OF A RICH merchant ship that sank about 1300 B.C.E. at Uluburun, off the southern coast of Turkey. Its cargo of raw materials and exotic luxury objects reveals a prosperous world of international trade and cultural exchange. A partial inventory includes ebony logs, ostrich eggshells, elephant tusks, and a trumpet carved from a hippopotamus tooth from Egypt. From the Middle East came exquisitely worked gold jewelry as well as nearly a ton of scented resin, perhaps intended for use as incense in religious worship. The ship's stone anchors had been made in Syria. Finely painted storage jars from the island of Cyprus held pomegranates and probably olive oil. The archaeologists also recovered swords, daggers, and arrowheads; scrap gold and silver that might be sold in any port; and hinged wooden writing boards with a thick wax surface on which business accounts could be recorded.

The most valuable portion of the cargo that the divers lifted from the ocean floor, however, consisted of 354 flat copper bars, each weighing about fifty pounds, and several bars of tin. When melted and mixed together, these metals produce bronze°. This alloy, which is much tougher than copper or tin, lends itself to the making of dishes, jewelry, tools, and especially weapons. The use of bronze ushered in a new era in the ancient world.

About 3200 B.C.E. people living in northern Syria and Iraq began making bronze. The technology spread slowly throughout the Middle East and into Egypt and Europe. Because deposits of tin and copper are not always present in the same areas, merchants traded over long distances to obtain the ores with which to forge the prized alloy. As they traded, they spread knowledge about

House of the Admiral: This lively wall painting, which may depict a religious celebration, comes from the so-called "House of the Admiral" on the island of Thera, midway between Crete and Greece. The painting is about twenty-two feet long and a foot and a half high. Created about 1500 B.C.E., before a volcanic explosion destroyed the settlement on Thera, this painting shows scenes of busy maritime activity outside a harbor town.

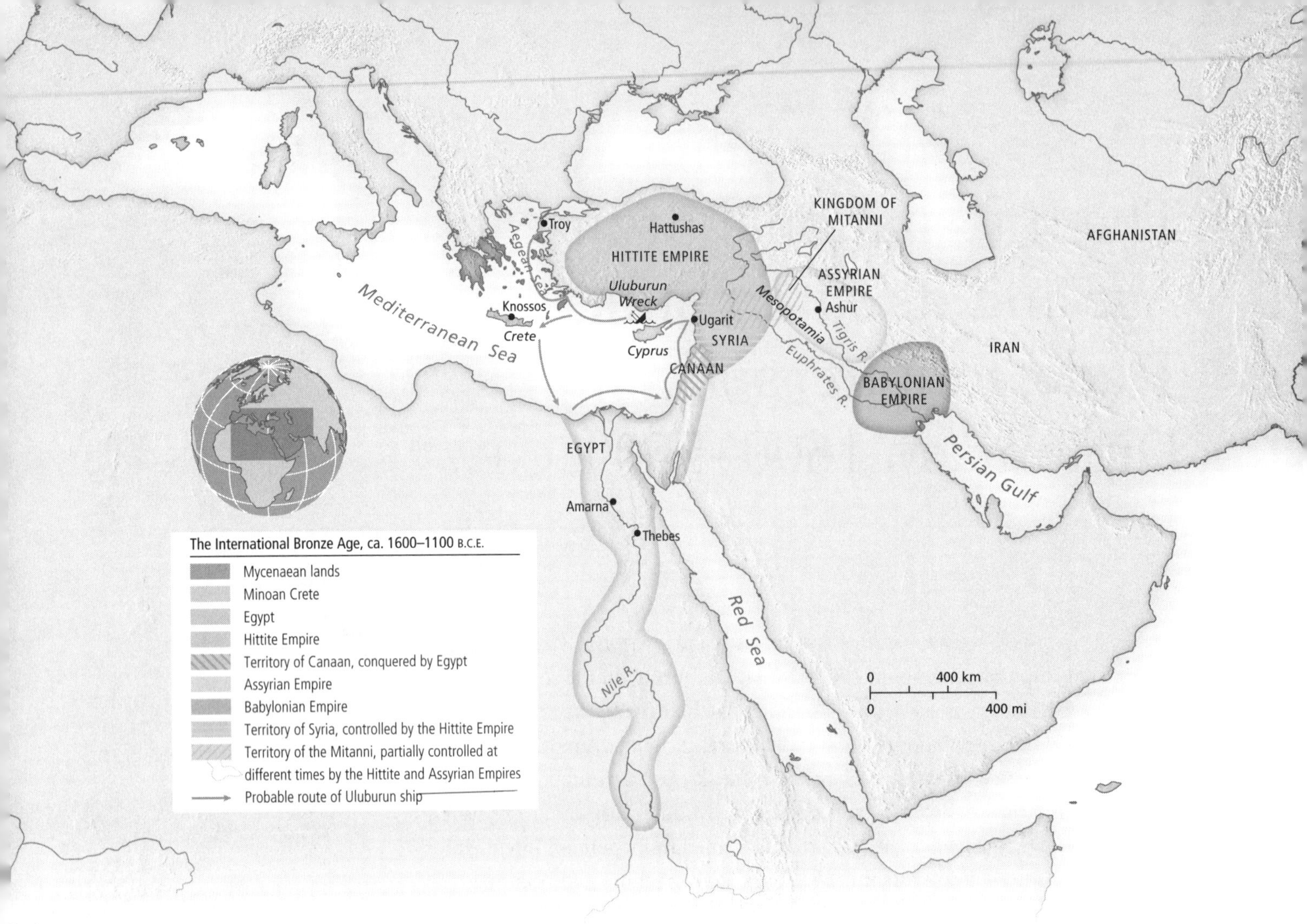

Map 2.1 The International Bronze Age, ca. 1600–1100 B.C.E.
For five hundred years, networks of commerce and diplomacy tied together the distinct cultures of Egypt, Greece, Anatolia, and the Middle East.

bronze technology among diverse peoples. By 1600 B.C.E., when peoples throughout the Middle East, Egypt, and Europe had mastered bronze making, the International Bronze Age began (see Map 2.1).

The new international trade in bronze provides the key to understanding how five separate regions in the Middle East, Africa, and Europe became linked in a large area of political and cultural influence and thus began to lay the foundations of Western civilization. The regions were the lands controlled by Egypt in northeast Africa and the Middle East, the territories ruled by the Hittite kingdom in Anatolia (modern Turkey), the Assyrian and Babylonian kingdoms in Mesopotamia, the maritime kingdoms of Minoan Crete and Mycenaean Greece in the eastern Mediterranean, and the small mercantile kingdoms of Troy and Ugarit, also situated in the eastern Mediterranean. The people in these different regions spoke different languages, worshiped different gods, and had different systems of government, but they were linked by trade and diplomacy, and they engaged in a series of commercial, technological, and cultural exchanges. Those exchanges formed the basis of what we now call the West.

These five regions depended on an international trade network to obtain the metals and other goods they needed for everyday life. Their rulers encouraged this trade because they needed bronze, mainly to develop new weapons, especially horse-drawn chariots, a new military technology. Chariot fighting was expensive, however, and therefore rulers constantly sought the acquisition of wealth and vital resources through trade and conquest.

The use of horse-drawn chariots and the continued quest for new sources of wealth to support them led to two major developments in international affairs. The first was the growth of empire—the expansion of the territories under the control of individual kingdoms. During the International Bronze Age rulers in Egypt, the Hittite kingdom, Assyria, and Babylonia used their superior military strength to build large, multiethnic empires. The growth of these empires became one of the main features of this historical period. The second development was the recognition that warfare, which these kingdoms had used to conquer foreign peoples, could interrupt trade and interfere with the successful management of a ruler's territories. Discovering the advantages of international cooperation for the first time, rulers during this period developed a system of diplomacy that produced long periods of peace—an unprecedented achievement. Trade was so important that royal families intermarried and exchanged precious gifts to maintain good international relations. That the Uluburun cargo ship could stop at so many ports and take on board merchandise from so many different kingdoms illustrates the benefit of these peaceful times.

The elaborate economic, diplomatic, and cultural networks of the International Bronze Age disintegrated about 1100 B.C.E. International trade in copper and tin broke down. Destructive raiders who had learned how to overcome chariot warriors destroyed the Hittite Empire as well as many smaller kingdoms. At the same time, Mycenaean power collapsed and the empires of Egypt and Mesopotamia went into a steep decline as well. After a period of slow recovery, however, powerful new empires emerged in Mesopotamia, while Phoenician civilization emerged in the Mediterranean. The Phoenicians, who were master mariners, took their culture to North Africa and Spain, creating a new civilization based on trade.

This chapter examines how the peoples of the International Bronze Age and the period immediately following its demise engaged in a series of commercial, technological, and cultural exchanges. To understand these changes we shall consider the following questions: (1) How did Egypt during the New Kingdom use warfare and diplomacy to develop an empire that reached from Nubia to Mesopotamia? (2) What were the political, religious, and cultural traditions of the Hittite Empire in Anatolia and the Assyrian and Babylonian Empires in Mesopotamia? (3) What were the characteristics of the Mediterranean civilizations of Minoan Crete, Mycenaean Greece, Ugarit, and Troy, and what roles did they play in international trade and politics? (4) What forces brought the International Bronze Age to a close and how did the Phoenicians, Assyrians, and Babylonians build new kingdoms and empires in its wake, generating new international economic, cultural, and political traditions?

The Egyptian Empire

A prosperous new phase of Egyptian history began when the Middle Kingdom ended about 1650 B.C.E. During the next 500-year period, Egyptians made use of a new military technology to create a vast multiethnic empire stretching from Africa to the Middle East. The term empire° identifies a kingdom or any other type of state that controls several foreign territories, either on the same continent or overseas. During this period Egyptian forces conquered Nubia in the south, and in Mesopotamia they marched as far east as the Euphrates River. Pharaohs combined military expansion with diplomacy and encouraged foreign trade, making Egypt a major force in international affairs.

THE HYKSOS AND THE REVOLUTION IN MILITARY TECHNOLOGY

Egyptian history changed course abruptly at the end of the Middle Kingdom when the Hyksos, a people from northern Palestine whose name meant "peoples of foreign lands," invaded Egypt and established a new regime in the northern Delta region. The Hyksos' rule had a lasting impact on Egyptian society in two ways.

First, through their ties with the Middle East, the Hyksos linked Egypt to the international network of commerce, technology, and diplomacy that was emerging in the International Bronze Age. The Hyksos maintained diplomatic and economic ties with kingdoms of Mesopotamia, Syria, and the Mediterranean. These connections encouraged cultural exchanges, such as when the Hyksos employed artists from Crete to paint vivid scenes on the walls of the royal palace at Avaris, their capital city.

Second, the Hyksos introduced an advanced military technology that was revolutionizing warfare throughout the Middle East, Anatolia, and Greece. The new military technology consisted of a chariot with lightweight wheels with bronze spokes drawn by a team of trained horses. Two young men wearing bronze chain-mail armor would ride into battle on each chariot, one driving the horses, the other shooting bronze-tipped arrows at the enemy. The archers used costly composite bows made of laminated layers of wood, horn, and sinew. It took between five and ten years for a composite bow to age properly, but they permitted archers to fire arrows as far as 200 yards—double or triple the range of simple wooden bows. This military technology enabled the Hyksos to conquer Egypt and later helped the Egyptians acquire a vast overseas empire.

Troops of trained charioteers and bowmen could easily outmaneuver the traditional massed infantry forces and inflict terrible casualties from a distance. Chariot squadrons would advance in a broad line with infantry marching behind them. When two armies with similar armament began a battle, the opposing lines of chariots would race toward each other, hoping to disable the enemy with dense arrow fire. Then they would wheel away in formation, and the infantrymen, also wearing bronze-plated armor and brandishing bronze swords and lances, would charge.

Chariot warfare reshaped the economic policies and foreign relations of Egypt and all the other kingdoms and empires of the International Bronze Age. To meet the enormous expenses of training and supplying armies of charioteers, rulers carefully organized domestic resources and tried to acquire more wealth through trade and conquest.

Administration and Government During the New Kingdom

About 1550 B.C.E. Pharaoh Ahmose I (r. ca. 1569–ca. 1545 B.C.E.) expelled the Hyksos from Egypt. Ahmose came from Thebes in southern Egypt, which had remained independent of Hyksos control, and he enjoyed the support of the majority of the Egyptian population. His mastery of the new military tactics enabled him to defeat the Hyksos and reunify Egypt under his command. Historians call the period of renewed Egyptian self-rule that began with Ahmose the New Kingdom (ca. 1550–1150 B.C.E.) During this period Egypt extended its territorial boundaries, acquiring lands in Asia and reaching the Euphrates River. Ahmose's new dynasty continued the highly centralized system of government that had been developed in the Middle Kingdom, adding a powerful new force: a permanent, or standing, army. For the first time in Egyptian history, a ruler could count on the readiness of highly trained regiments of charioteers and infantrymen to go to war whenever he wished. Troops would also remain as garrisons in conquered lands. The standing army extended the ruler's reach and influence abroad.

During the New Kingdom, Egypt's kings first took the title pharaoh, which means "great house"—or master of all Egyptians. Pharaohs exercised wide-ranging and unrivaled political power. Egyptians believed that the gods entrusted their safekeeping to the pharaoh's care and that he had the final authority in matters of government, law, and religion. As supreme commander of the military forces, he made all decisions about war and peace, and he supervised diplomatic ties with foreign nations. In return for the authority granted him by the gods, the pharaoh had the duty of maintaining peace and order in Egypt and bringing this order to the entire world. He did this by caring for the temples and cults of the gods, conquering Egypt's enemies, and ruling wisely.

In his role as supreme ruler, the pharaoh therefore served as a vital link between humanity and Heaven. All of his activities as pharaoh, whether protecting his people from foreigners, conquering enemies abroad, building huge temples in honor of the gods, governing his territories, or feeding his subjects, symbolized his fight against the forces of chaos on behalf of the gods. The total power of the pharaoh represented the divine will of Heaven at work on Earth.

As a consequence of its strong centralized system of government, Egypt during the New Kingdom developed a highly organized bureaucracy that helped the pharaoh maintain order. The chief minister of state and the highest official in the land was the vizier. As the pharaoh's chief executive officer the vizier superintended the administration of the entire kingdom, and he was responsible for guaranteeing that justice prevailed. Every year the vizier decided when to open the canal locks on the Nile, so that farmers' fields could be irrigated. He supervised the Egyptian treasury and the warehouses into which produce was paid as taxes. In addition to the vizier, four administrators chosen by the pharaoh directed the army, religious affairs, the pharaoh's properties, and internal administration.

During the New Kingdom, Egypt was divided into two major administrative regions. The southern region, called Upper Egypt, was governed from the city of Thebes, while Lower Egypt, in the north, was ruled from the city of Memphis. Regional administrators raised taxes and organized men to work on the pharaoh's building projects. Smaller cities were ruled by mayors who collected taxes and otherwise served as middlemen between the central gov-

Scribe Nebmertuf
Scribe Nebmertuf, who lived in Egypt about 1360 B.C.E., was a minor official who helped keep the tightly organized bureaucracy functioning. He writes on a scroll made of papyrus that he has unrolled in his lap. The baboon who watches him is the sacred animal of Thoth, the god of wisdom.

Tiles: Enemies of Egypt

These tiles found at the mortuary temple of Pharaoh Ramesses III were made around 1170 B.C.E. They depict Egypt's enemies with such great attention to details of clothing, hairstyle, and stereotyped physical features that we can know the ethnicity of the men. From left to right: a Libyan with tattooed arms, a Nubian with black skin, and a bearded Syrian. All wear handcuffs, a sign of their defeat and Egypt's triumph. Other figures in the series not shown here include a bedouin nomad and a Hittite.

ernment and the local population. Thousands of state officials labored in this complex administrative system. Called scribes, these literate officials maintained the careful records on which the bureaucracy depended.

Temples played an essential part in the government of Egypt. Many of the temples to the great gods, and the priests who managed them, acquired enormous wealth and influence because they possessed huge tracts of land. The temple of Amun at Karnak, for example, owned nearly one-quarter of all Egypt's grain fields and controlled a workforce of nearly 100,000 people. The high priests, whom the pharaoh appointed from among his most trusted advisers, had responsibility for building the tombs of the pharaoh and his family, the imperial granaries, and other public works. Priests also participated in the administration of imperial affairs. They managed the many thousands of peasants who labored in the vast estates attached to the temples, collecting taxes, organizing building projects, and administering justice.

MILITARY EXPANSION: BUILDING AN EMPIRE IN CANAAN AND NUBIA

During the New Kingdom, pharaohs conquered territories far beyond the borders of Egypt. The military power that came from chariot warfare technology, and the ability of the pharaoh to use the great wealth of the country to support a large army, made these conquests possible. A well-developed logistical system also contributed to Egypt's military strength. With food and supplies carefully prepared in advance by government administrators, the Egyptian army regularly waged war far from home. The army was efficient, highly mobile, and extremely well trained.

Egyptian attitudes toward non-Egyptians also encouraged the imperial expansion of the New Kingdom. Egyptians believed that the pharaoh should extend Egyptian power throughout the world. They divided the world into two groups: themselves (whom they referred to as "The People") and everyone else. Egyptians were people who lived in the Nile Valley and spoke Egyptian. The other peoples known to the Egyptians were the inhabitants of the Middle East (called Asians), Nubians, and Libyans. At the beginning of the New Kingdom, Egyptians considered the foreign people they encountered through trade and diplomacy inferior and naturally subordinate to themselves. They believed that forces of chaos resided in foreign lands where the pharaoh had not yet imposed his will. Thus it was the pharaoh's responsibility to crush all foreign peoples and bring order to the world. By the end of the New Kingdom, however, constant interaction with foreign peoples broadened the Egyptian worldview. By that time, for example, pharaohs treated foreign kings as equals and called them "brothers"—something not possible during earlier periods of Egypt's history.

In their drive to establish order in the world, Egyptian rulers in the New Kingdom clashed with kingdoms in Anatolia, Syria, and Mesopotamia, as we will see later in this chapter. Under the dynamic leadership of Thutmose I (r. 1504–1492 B.C.E.), the armies of Egypt conquered southern Palestine. A coalition of Syrian cities slowed further

JUSTICE IN HISTORY

Egyptian Tomb Robbers on Trial

In New Kingdom Egypt a council called a *kenbet,* composed of the local governor and temple priests, combined the functions of prosecutor, judge, and jury. There was no counsel for the defendants. At the village level people might bring lawsuits against one another at the *kenbet,* and women and men alike represented themselves at trial. Another court, the Great Kenbet, handled all cases of property and taxation affecting state revenues as well as all offenses against the pharaoh and the government. This court consisted of high officials of the government and was headed by the pharaoh's chief administrator, the vizier.

One of the most serious crimes in Egypt was robbing tombs. People accused of this crime were interrogated by the authorities, who routinely used beatings and torture to extract confessions. The Great Kenbet then delivered a verdict. Conviction of tomb robbing carried the death penalty. Lesser crimes not related to tomb robbing could result in confiscation of property, beatings, forced labor, and body mutilation.

The following document comes from the trial record of tomb robbers in the Great Tombs of the pharaohs in the Valley of the Kings.[1] These tombs were situated a few miles from the Nile River at Thebes, where most of the New Kingdom pharaohs and their families were buried. The trials were conducted over a period of several summer days during the reign of Ramesses IX (r. 1125–1107 B.C.E.). The vizier, assisted by the overseer of the granary and treasury and two royal stewards, conducted the proceedings, which were written on a papyrus scroll unearthed in 1872 C.E. The account shows how justice was carried out in the New Kingdom.

> *Examination. The herdsman Bukhaaf of the temple of Amun was brought. The Vizier said to him, "When you were about that business in which you engaged and the god caught you and brought and placed you in the hand of pharaoh, tell me all the men who were with you in the Great Tombs." Bukhaaf replied, "As for me, I am a field worker of the temple of Amun. The woman came to the place where I was and she said to me, 'some men have found something that can be sold for bread; let's go so you may eat it with them.'" [Bukhaaf gives some misleading testimony that does not deceive the Kenbet.] Bukhaaf was examined with the stick [i.e., beaten]. "Stop, I will tell," he said. The Vizier said to him, "Tell the story of your going to attack the Great and Noble Tombs." Bukhaaf said, "It was Pewer, a workman of the City of the Dead [the Tombs] who showed us the tomb of Queen Hebrezet." The Vizier and the others said to him, "In what condition was the tomb that you went to?" Bukhaaf said, "I found it already open." He was examined with the stick again. "Stop," he said, "I will tell." The Vizier said to him, "Tell what you did." He said, "I brought away the inner coffin of silver and a shroud of gold and silver together with the men who were with me. And we broke them up and divided them among ourselves."*
>
> *[Bukhaaf's punishment is not recorded, but it was in all likelihood death.]*
>
> *On the third day of the trial of thieves, a carpenter Thewenani was examined for a different robbery. He proclaimed his innocence and swore a great oath, "If I speak untruth may I be mutilated and sent to Ethiopia."*

Despite several beatings and torture, Thewenani would not confess, and the vizier let him off with the warning that if he were accused again, he would be sentenced to death. Later that day, Ese, the wife of the gardener Ker who had been implicated in stealing silver from the Great Tombs in still another case, was brought before the Kenbet. She swore an oath to be truthful or be mutilated and placed on a stake. She denied any connection with the robbery, but one of the officials at the trial asked her how she had suddenly gotten rich enough to buy several slaves. Her answer that she had saved the money from selling the produce of her garden did not convince the Kenbet, which brought in her slave to give testimony against her. Her fate is not recorded.

Why did Egyptian officials prosecute tomb robbers with such energy? They considered tomb robbing a serious crime for both religious and economic reasons. Egyptians were deeply concerned about the afterlife and stressed the proper treatment of the dead. They believed that when people died they were judged by the god Osiris. If they had lived good lives, their bodies would live again. The families of the deceased had the obligation to provide food and water at the graveside for the dead to eat. They also were required to remember the name of the dead. "Provide water for your father and mother who rest in the desert valley . . . Let the people know that you are doing it and then your son will do the same for you," advised one religious text.[2] In Egyptian eyes, robbing a tomb violated basic principles of religious behavior. It was a monstrous sacrilege.

The many gifts placed in a grave with the dead person were intended to make the deceased person's afterlife as comfortable as possible. Pharaohs and the wealthy elite of Egypt filled their tombs with luxury items of incalculable value—an irresistible lure for thieves. In addition to their profound desire to prevent sacrilege, Egyptian officials worried that plundering this treasure and putting it back into circulation would cause prices to fall and thereby derail the economy. From the point of view of Egyptian officials, tomb robbers deserved nothing less than death. Only this way would justice be served.

Questions of Justice

1. What values made tomb robbing "criminal" in Egypt during the New Kingdom? What does the crime reveal about the organization of Egyptian society?
2. What was the notion of justice that determined these trials and their outcome? What principles of justice are the judges trying to uphold?
3. To what extent do both the living and the dead play a part in this trial?

Taking It Further

Goelet, Ogden. "Tomb Robbery Papyri," in *The Oxford Encyclopedia of Ancient Egypt,* ed. Donald B. Redford, vol. 3, pp. 417–418. 2001. Provides the latest analysis of the documents relating to the trials of tomb robbers as well as further bibliography.

Kruchten, Jean-Marie. "Law," in *The Oxford Encyclopedia of Ancient Egypt,* ed. Donald B. Redford, vol. 2, pp. 277–282. 2001. An excellent overview of Egyptian law with helpful suggestions for further reading.

Judgment Day

Painted about 1285 B.C.E., this papyrus scroll shows the trial of a man called Hunefer on the day of judgment. The jackal-headed god Anubis leads Hunefer into the courtroom, where his heart is weighed against a feather on giant scales. Because the feather and the heart weigh the same, it means that the court decides that Hunefer has led a just life. The god of wisdom, Thoth, stands by the scale, records the result of the weighing, and leads Hunefer to the great god Osiris who judges and rules the dead. Hunefer can look forward to a peaceful eternity.

advance, but by the end of the reign of the great conqueror Thutmose III (r. 1458–1425 B.C.E.), Egypt had extended its control over all the lands between the Orontes River in Syria and the Euphrates in Mesopotamia. The western portion of this region, which today includes modern Lebanon, Israel, and parts of Jordan and Syria, was called Canaan.

The Egyptians conquered Canaan because of its great wealth. After Canaan had fallen under Egyptian control, a steady stream of caravans transported its natural resources and manufactured goods to Egypt. Fine Canaanite garments and tapestries, as well as grain, wine, opium, incense, honey, and olive oils were highly valued in Egypt. Canaan also provided many resources lacking in Egypt, such as timber and copper, which was used to create bronze for chariots and weapons. Silver came in large quantities from Jerusalem and nearby towns. Egyptian officials also demanded that the Canaanites supply horses, chariots, and highly trained charioteers as tribute.

Because Canaan was a trading center with ties to Mesopotamia and beyond, Egyptian merchants gained access to goods from distant lands not controlled by Egypt. Precious gems came from Afghanistan; incense for burning in temples came from Arabia; Cyprus, an island in the eastern Mediterranean Sea, was a main source of copper; and wines, luxury metalwork, textiles, oil, and expensive pottery came from Crete, another Mediterranean island. Syria provided cedar wood used for construction as well as other rare woods used to make luxury furniture and temple implements.

To maintain their grip on the rich resources of Canaan, the pharaohs chose a loyal and reliable leader in each Canaanite city to be the mayor. Like the mayors of Egyptian towns, these local officials swore an oath of allegiance to the pharaoh. Their sons were sent to Egypt to be hostages in exchange for their fathers' good behavior and to learn the ways of Egyptian culture. The mayors collected the heavy taxes that the central government required, and they administered the forced labor of the civilian population that was regularly demanded to build temples and maintain public buildings.

The New Kingdom also expanded its territorial grip southward, seizing the populous and prosperous African land known in antiquity as Nubia or Kush (modern Sudan). Nubia was extremely rich in gold and other natural resources, while trade routes from central and eastern Africa that converged in Nubia further augmented its wealth. In order to gain control of these riches, Egyptian forces conquered Nubia about 1500 B.C.E. and established an administration there that had a degree of self-rule (see Map 2.2).

An Egyptian governor, called the King's Son of Kush, ruled a vast region in the pharaoh's name and saw to its systematic economic exploitation. Egyptian control depended on the cooperation of Nubian princes, who organized local labor and guaranteed the regular delivery of tribute demanded by the pharaoh's agents. In return for this collaboration, the princes were permitted to govern their communities. As in Canaan, the pharaohs required local rulers to send their sons to Egypt to be educated. This practice ensured the loyalty of the boys' fathers. It also strengthened Egyptian control of Nubia, for when the

Map 2.2 Egypt in the New Kingdom

During the New Kingdom, Egyptians conquered Nubia, Canaan, and parts of the Middle East as far as the Euphrates River. They created a prosperous, multiethnic empire.

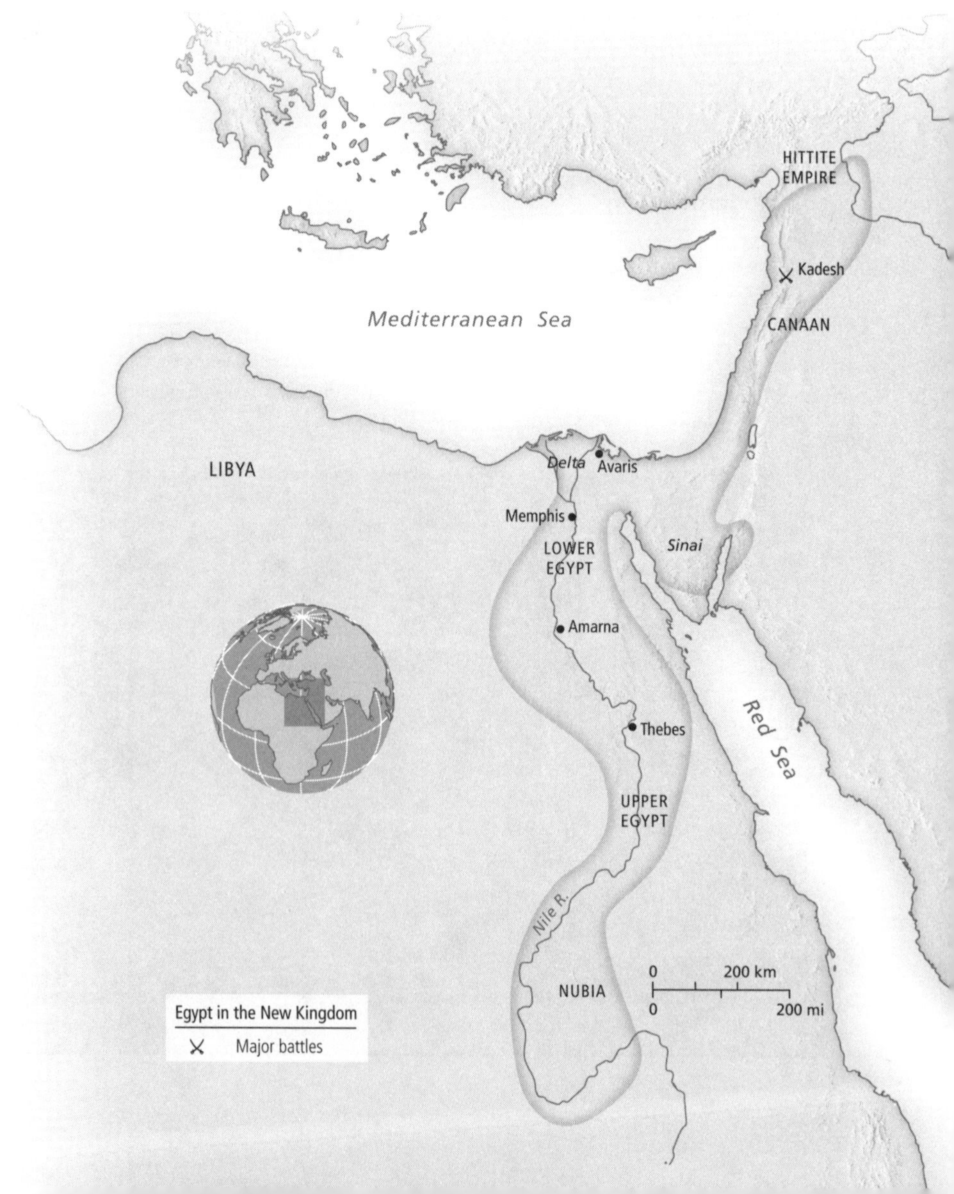

"Egyptianized" young men returned to Nubia to govern their communities after the death of their fathers, they brought with them a respect for Egyptian power and an appreciation for Egyptian culture.

Another strategy for maintaining the Nubians' allegiance was through worship of the pharaoh. In order to bring the presence of the pharaoh to the people of Nubia, the Egyptians built temples to their ruler and his ancestral gods in all the major commercial and garrison cities of the country. With the presence of the pharaoh all around them—and the threat of overwhelming force that it subtly implied—the people of Nubia would think twice before rebelling. They also were encouraged to participate in the worship of the pharaoh and the Egyptian gods.

To strengthen their grip over Nubia, pharaohs encouraged Egyptians to migrate to Nubia and establish communities along the Nile River. These Egyptian colonies increased the population of Nubia and exploited the fertile river lands for the benefit of the pharaoh.

Egypt gained enormous wealth from its empire in Nubia and Canaan. Conquest and centralized administration enabled the Egyptians to collect tribute and taxes from their subjects, and the resulting economic growth led to vigorous private commerce and many cultural encounters between Egyptians and other peoples. Even though Egyptians viewed the foreign peoples they ruled with contempt, they slowly absorbed many things from their subjects during the 400-year interaction. Egyptian speech, for example, adopted hundreds of Canaanite words, especially those pertaining to military affairs and the natural resources coveted by Egyptians. In addition, many fairy tales about exotic lands modeled on the Middle East made their way into Egyptian literature. Numerous gods of conquered peoples entered Egyptian life as well. For example, Baal and Astarte, who were worshiped widely in the Middle East, became popular Egyptian divinities. The cultural encounter between Egyptians and the people they conquered, therefore, resulted in an exchange of ideas and traditions, not just the imposition of the Egyptian culture on the people brought into their empire.

Hatshepsut as a Bearded Pharaoh

Although she was a woman, tradition required that Hatshepsut be depicted as a man.

PHARAOHS: THE SOURCE OF EGYPT'S SUCCESS

Egypt's success during the New Kingdom hinged in large part on the talents of its pharaohs. These rulers defined all aspects of Egyptian life, from empire building and trade to agriculture and worship. Several pharaohs left a particularly impressive mark during this era of Egyptian history.

Hatshepsut the Female Pharaoh and Thutmose III the Conqueror

One of the most remarkable rulers of the New Kingdom was Hatshepsut, the daughter of Thutmose I. Hatshepsut became co-ruler with her infant stepson Thutmose III when her husband, the pharaoh Thutmose II, died in 1479 B.C.E. Six years later, she seized power for herself, becoming the first female pharaoh.

Hatshepsut held power from 1479 to 1458 B.C.E., a period in which Egypt enjoyed great prosperity. With the aid of trusted advisers, Hatshepsut pursued policies of peace, though her armies waged war when necessary to secure Egypt's possessions in the Middle East. With Hatshepsut's encouragement, trade with the land of Punt (modern Somalia) flourished. Egyptians exchanged weapons, jewelry, and manufactured goods for ivory, gold, ebony, incense, myrrh, live animals, and exotic animal skins with merchants from Punt.

Because pharaohs had always been men, all of the images of kingly power were male, and all of the elaborate rituals of ruling presumed a male ruler. Hatshepsut very carefully adapted her image to these expectations. For example, in the inscriptions and paintings of the great funerary temple that she built in the holy valley of Deir el-Bahari near Thebes, Hatshepsut is represented as a man, the son of the god Amun-Re. In more private contexts, she referred to herself as a woman. Several decades after Hatshepsut's death, her name was systematically removed from monuments throughout Egypt, probably to inform the gods that Egypt had returned to "proper" male kingship.

Thutmose III (r. 1458–1425 B.C.E.) succeeded Hatshepsut and began a reign marked by military glory. When he ascended the throne, Egypt was in danger of losing its grip on Nubia, as well as Canaan and parts of Syria. Interfering in Egyptian affairs, the kingdom of Mittani in northern Syria stirred up revolts and rivalries among Egypt's subjects in the Middle East. In order to reassert Egyptian control, Thutmose led his armies into Canaan seventeen times during his reign. In one of his greatest victories at Megiddo (in modern Israel) Thutmose captured more than 900 war chariots from his enemies.

Thutmose restored Egyptian power as far as the Euphrates River in Mesopotamia. He also harshly suppressed revolts in Nubia. To maintain Egyptian authority throughout his empire, Thutmose established permanent garrisons in conquered territories, just as Ahmose had done when the territory had first been conquered. Thutmose closely supervised local government in the areas under Egyptian control. He also cultivated a triumphant military atmosphere at court that was quite different from that of Hatshepsut.

A man of high culture as well as a brilliant general, Thutmose wrote literary works and pursued an interest in science. From Syria he brought back samples of the region's flowers and plants and had them painted on temple walls. Under his influence, Egyptian artists perfected their ability to capture detail, movement, and emotion in painting and sculpture.

The Amarna Period: Religious Ferment and the Beginnings of Diplomacy

For more than a thousand years, Egyptians had worshiped the sun, Amun-Re, mightiest of all their deities. Pharaoh Amenhotep III (r. 1388–1351 B.C.E.) turned away from traditional Egyptian religion, however, believing that Amun-Re was not just the god of Egyptians but a universal deity who ruled all peoples. Amenhotep called the sun Aten and worshipped his physical form, the sun seen in the sky. He no longer recognized the other gods.

The pharaoh's son, Amenhotep IV (r. 1351–1334 B.C.E.), changed his own name to Akhenaten ("One useful to Aten") and took the revolutionary step of declaring that Aten was the only god. A contemporary hymn proclaimed, "O sole god unlike any other, you created the world according to your desire, while you were alone." Akhenaten attacked the worship of other gods, closed down many temples, and appropriated their wealth and lands for himself. He forbade the celebration of ancient public festivals to the other gods and even the mention of their names. His agents chiseled their names from monuments and buildings across the land.

Full of religious enthusiasm, Akhenaten and his queen, Nefertiti, abandoned the capital of Thebes and built a new city called Horizon of Aten in a valley in middle Egypt where no temples to other gods had ever stood. Because the modern name for this site is Tell el-Amarna, historians refer to this period of religious ferment as the Amarna Period. Left open to the sun, the city received the first rays of light as each day dawned. These rays touched the main temple of Aten through a natural break in the surrounding cliffs. Paintings and sculptures no longer depicted Aten in the traditional way, as a falcon-headed god, but instead represented the deity as a simple disc with radiating beams of light.

Akhenaten went too far in his enforcement of these regulations, losing the support of the general population as well as that of the priests who administered the temples of other gods. The people of Egypt were unwilling to abandon the many traditional gods who played such an important

A HYMN TO ATEN SUNG BY THE PHARAOH

The following Egyptian hymn was sung to Aten, the sun god, by the pharaoh. It describes a single god who created the universe:

Splendid you rise, O living Aten, eternal lord!
You are radiant, beauteous, mighty,
Your love is great, immense.
Your rays light up all faces,
Your bright hue gives life to hearts,
When you fill the Two Lands with your love.
August God who fashioned himself,
Who made every land, created what is in it,
All peoples, herds, and flocks,
All trees that grow from soil; they live when you dawn
for them,
You are mother and father of all that you made.
I am your son who serves you, who exalts your name,
Your power, your strength, are firm in my heart;
You are the living Aten whose image endures,
You have made the far sky to shine in it,
To observe all that you made. . . .

Source: From Miriam Lichtheim, *Ancient Egyptian Literature: The Old and Middle Kingdoms, Volume II.*

role their daily lives. Aten stood for light, love, and universal life, but Akhenaten's tight control of the government and suppression of all opposition to his rule made everyday existence dark during his reign.

In another deliberate break with tradition Akhenaten changed the standard representation of a pharaoh. Rather than a masculine figure with a taut body and highly symmetrical limbs, his statutes show him with an exaggerated stomach and hips and elongated face. Declaring that he was the mother as well as the father of his people, Akhenaten emphasized female traits in his statues.

These radical and abstract ideas did not survive Akhenaten. After his death, the royal court abandoned Horizon of Aten and returned to Memphis and then to Thebes. Akhenaten's religious beliefs do indicate, however, the cosmopolitan nature of New Kingdom Egypt. Taking into account the diverse people whom Egypt ruled, the religious thinkers around Akhenaten developed the idea of a single, transcendent god for all humanity.

The pharaohs of the Amarna Period immersed themselves as deeply in foreign policy as they did in religious innovation. Evidence of their diplomacy comes from an archive of documents discovered at Tell el-Amarna in Egypt in 1887 C.E. Written in Akkadian, the Mesopotamian language used for international communication, these letters show that Egyptian pharaohs were in regular contact with the rulers of neighboring peoples, such as the Hittites, Assyrians, Babylonians, and the leaders of much smaller city-states in the Middle East, as well as with their own officials in Canaan and Syria.

In their correspondence, the monarchs referred to themselves as "Great Kings" and addressed one another as "brother," despite their constant rivalry. By using these titles, the rulers recognized each other's authority and created a sense of international community. Though prepared for war, they preferred to cement their ties by arranging marriages among the royal families and exchanging lavish gifts. By these means they could guard their frontiers and protect the merchants who crisscrossed their territories.

Diplomacy did not always succeed. Ancient records describe murder, a failed marriage alliance, and the calamity that followed when ties between the Hittites and Egyptians broke down. When Pharaoh Tutankhamun died in 1333 B.C.E., his widow wrote to the Hittite king: ". . . My husband is dead. I have no son! I shall never take a servant of mine [that is, any Egyptian] and make him my husband. I have written to no other country. I have written only to you; so give me one son of yours . . . He will be my husband. In Egypt he will be king!"[3] No doubt delighted to extend Hittite influence, the Hittite monarch sent his fourth son, Prince Zannanza, to Egypt. On the journey, however, Zannanza was murdered, and the mystery of his death has never been solved. Furious at his son's death and seeking vengeance, the Hittite king invaded the Egyptian Empire in Syria, sacked several cities, and seized many thousands of

Amarna Altar Panel
Carved about 1340 B.C.E., this stone panel was found in an Egyptian home where it served as the focus of daily prayers. On the left, Akhenaten kisses his infant child. Facing him, his wife Nefertiti holds an older girl on her knee while resting another baby on her shoulder. The sun god Aten sends his rays down as a blessing to the entire royal family and so to all Egyptians. The oddly elongated heads and body shapes, especially of the pharaoh, typify a new way of depicting the royal family in the Amarna period.

prisoners. Although he soon withdrew his forces, tensions between the two empires continued to mount.

The mysterious murder of Prince Zannanza and the war that followed illustrate that open conflict among the empires remained a constant threat in the fourteenth century B.C.E. Nevertheless, for the first time in the ancient world, international relations among sovereign powers brought periods of peace and prosperity to different cultures over a huge area.

The Age of Ramesses

After Akhenaten's death, rule of Egypt passed through the hands of several men before Ramesses I took the throne in 1292 B.C.E. and established a new dynasty, the nineteenth in Egyptian history. The rulers in this dynasty used military force to control the provinces of Canaan, Syria, and Nubia, where revolts continually broke out. During their reign they confronted a further threat to Egyptian security on the northwestern frontier, where peoples from Libya called the Labu and the Meshwesh attempted unsuccessfully to enter the northern delta of the Nile.

The greatest king of the nineteenth dynasty was Ramesses II (r. 1279–1213 B.C.E.), who ruled for sixty-six years. A tireless builder of temples and monuments, he constructed a new imperial city, called City of Ramesses, in the eastern delta. Ramesses's greatest accomplishments, however, were in military action abroad.

Ramesses's efforts to restore Egyptian authority in Syria brought him into conflict with the king of the Hittites, Muwatallis, who wanted to conquer some of Egypt's possessions for himself. In 1274 B.C.E. the armies of Ramesses and Muwatallis clashed in a battle at the city of Kadesh on the Orontes River in northern Syria. At stake was the limit of expansion of both empires. Ramesses's goal was to smash Hittite power in Syria and regain the influence that Egypt had enjoyed during the great days of Thutmose III and his successors in the fifteenth and fourteenth centuries B.C.E. Muwatallis hoped to enlarge the Hittite sphere of influence by pushing south and taking more lands away from the Egyptian Empire.

The pharaoh struck first, leading his regiments north in two columns that converged on the Syrian city of Kadesh. A huge Hittite army, with perhaps 3,500 chariots and 37,000 infantry under the command of Muwatallis himself, caught the Egyptians by surprise. An attack of the Hittite chariots nearly destroyed Ramesses's forces, but in a last-minute counterattack led by the pharaoh himself, Egyptian troops rallied and pushed their enemy back across the Orontes. The battle ended in a stalemate, with heavy losses on both sides.

The Battle of Kadesh°, despite its indecisive outcome, produced a treaty between the two empires. Writing in Akkadian, the Egyptian and Hittite monarchs signed a treaty of friendship and cooperation in 1269 B.C.E. According to its terms, Ramesses recognized the new Hittite king Hattusili and formally abandoned Egyptian claims to the city of Kadesh and northern Syria. In return, the Hittite monarch acknowledged Egypt's right to control Canaan, establishing a boundary between the two states. The two powers also agreed to give one another aid and military assistance in case of invasion by a third party or in the event of internal rebellions. Plans for the Hittite king to visit Egypt did not materialize, but after further negotiations a dynastic marriage was arranged between a daughter of the Hittite king and Ramesses in 1256 B.C.E. A second Hittite woman entered the pharaoh's harem a few years later.

The Battle of Kadesh yielded nearly a century of peace between the Hittites and the Egyptians. During this period commerce flourished in the Near East, benefiting both realms. With peace established with the Hittites, Nubia pacified, and the Libyan border fortified, Egypt enjoyed many decades of prosperity under Ramesses II's rule. The Hittite king turned his attention to problems presented by the growing power of Assyria to his east. He also signed a treaty of alliance with the Kassite monarch of Babylonia in Mesopotamia. Rulers had discovered that thoughtful diplomacy offered far more benefits than warfare.

CHRONOLOGY

Egypt in the Bronze Age

1650–1550 B.C.E.	The Hyksos rule Egypt
1550 B.C.E.	Ahmose I expels Hyksos; New Kingdom begins
1479–1458 B.C.E.	The first female pharaoh, Hatshepsut, reigns
1458–1425 B.C.E.	Thutmose III reigns
1388–1351 B.C.E.	Amenhotep III reigns
1351–1334 B.C.E.	Amenhotep IV (Akhenaten) rules; Amarna period
1292 B.C.E.	Nineteenth Dynasty begins; Ramesses I reigns
1279–1213 B.C.E.	Ramesses II reigns
1274 B.C.E.	Egyptians and Hittites fight the Battle of Kadesh

WOMEN IN THE NEW KINGDOM

Under Egyptian law, women and men had complete equality in matters of property, business, and inheritance. In case of a divorce the wife's dowry (the wealth a woman brings to her husband in marriage) was returned to her and the couple's property divided. Women and men generally married within their own social class, and often within the same family occupations. For example, the daughter or sister of a shoemaker would likely marry a shoemaker. As a result, women frequently helped their husbands in the family business. They could earn on their own by weaving or selling garden produce.

Except for dynastic marriages in the royal family, Egyptian marriages were a private matter between two individuals and their families. The newlyweds celebrated their marriage with a party and the exchange of gifts. The union lasted as long as the husband and wife provided fidelity, love, and care for one another. Many elaborate marriage contracts, wills, and other financial documents that survive from the New Kingdom reveal careful planning for the welfare of family members and preserving family property through inheritance.

In the New Kingdom, women played an important role in religious worship. The wives of priests and officials formed musical groups called "Singers of Amun" that sang, clapped, and danced to the accompaniment of stringed instruments during religious rituals. These prestigious groups performed in communities throughout Egypt. Some women held priesthoods on their own. The most powerful was the "God's Wife of Amun." This priestess, often a member of the royal family, had administrative responsibilities as well as the obligation to perform religious rituals such as burning images of the god's enemies and summoning the god to meals.

The many female divinities prominent in Egyptian religion reflected Egyptian reverence for women. For example, Isis had fearsome powers as the protector of women and men against evil. She could cure the sick and revive the dead. Egyptians loved and feared her at the same time. Another goddess, Nut, was depicted as enveloping the entire Earth. At sunset Nut swallowed the sun and protected it in her body throughout the night until giving birth to it again in the morning, dramatizing the solar cycle with images of childbirth.

Egyptian families cherished their daughters as much as their sons, and women had a valued place in the household. In addition to preparing foods, weaving cloth, and caring for livestock and children, women arranged burials and worshiped at tombs to ensure an afterlife for departed parents and family members. In return they inherited a fair share of property from their parents.

The highly centralized government of the pharaohs created peaceful conditions that let Egypt prosper during the New Kingdom. Additional wealth came to Egypt through international commerce and from its empire in Canaan, Syria, and Nubia. Under the direction of talented and aggressive rulers, Egyptian imperial civilization reached its greatest height.

The Hittite, Assyrian, and Babylonian Empires

Egypt was only one of several large, highly centralized empires that developed during the International Bronze Age. Its main counterparts and rivals were the Hittite empire in Anatolia and the Assyrian and Babylonian empires in Mesopotamia.

THE GROWTH OF HITTITE POWER: CONQUEST AND DIVERSITY

By about 1650 B.C.E., the Hittites, who spoke an Indo-European language, had established control over the rich plateau of Anatolia (modern Turkey). Like the Egyptians, the warlike Hittites were among the first people to make use of the new chariot warfare technology. From their capital city at Hattushas, they not only maintained tight control over their subjects in Anatolia but also actively participated in long-distance commerce, established diplomatic ties with foreign states, and extended their power through military conquest.

Hittite imperial expansion was rooted in a long tradition of exploiting the resources of their neighbors. One early Hittite ruler, Hattusili I (ca. 1650–1620 B.C.E.), recorded his "manly deeds" in the following terms: ". . . three times I brought battle into the city gates of Hahha (a city to the south east of Hattushas). I destroyed Hahha, but its goods I took away and brought them to Hattushas, my city. Two complete four-wheeled carts were loaded with silver . . . I, the Great King . . . destroyed [Hassuwa and] Hahha and gave them over to fire totally, but their smoke I showed to the God of Storms . . . and the king of Hahha I yoked to the four-wheeled cart . . ."[4]

CHRONOLOGY

	The Hittites
CA. 1650 B.C.E.	The Hittite kingdom emerges
1380–1346 B.C.E.	Suppiluliuma I gains control of Syria
CA. 1300 B.C.E.	A Hittite king negotiates with a Mycenaean King about Millawanda
1274 B.C.E.	Egyptians and Hittites fight the Battle of Kadesh
CA. 1150 B.C.E.	The Hittite kingdom collapses

For two centuries Hittite power gradually expanded into northern Syria, Mesopotamia, and western Anatolia. About 1400 B.C.E. as they pushed southward, the Hittites became entangled in the quarrels of Syrian kingdoms over control of the trade routes to the Euphrates River. The kingdom of Mittani presented the chief obstacle to Hittite expansion into Syria. But under the rule of King Suppiluliuma I (ca. 1380–1346 B.C.E.) the Hittites crushed the kingdom of Mittani. This victory led to greater risks, for it brought the Hittites face to face with the Egyptian Empire, which stretched as far north as Palestine and the Euphrates. Within a century Hittite conflict with Egypt led to the Battle of Kadesh, as we saw earlier.

Expansion into western Anatolia brought Hittites into contact with the peoples of Greece and the Aegean Sea known as Mycenaeans. Some Mycenaeans established bases for piracy and trade on the western coast of Anatolia. Because the Hittites had no ships of their own, they were powerless to control these interlopers, who could always escape on their fast ships. Sometimes, however, Hittite kings were able to establish diplomatic ties with Mycenaean kings and thus create conditions of peace in which trade could flourish.

Cities played an important role in the Hittite imperial system because they functioned as administrative centers that gathered the resources of the countryside. Many of the cities had stone fortifications to guard royal residences and storehouses where the textiles, grains, and metals produced by the rural population were stored. From the carefully kept inventory tablets that have survived, historians know that the Hittites made great profits by trading these products to markets as far away as Cyprus and the Aegean, Syria, and Mesopotamia in return for metals and luxury goods.

As the Hittite Empire expanded, it grew increasingly multiethnic, absorbing many smaller kingdoms with their own languages and cultural traditions. The Hittites solved the thorny problem of administering this linguistically and culturally mixed empire by using Hittite, which was only one of many Indo-European languages spoken in Anatolia, as the official language of law and government. Nevertheless, the empire's cultural diversity and ties abroad forced the Hittites to keep records in other languages as well. An archive of more than 150,000 clay tablets unearthed by archaeologists at Hattushas in 1910 C.E. contains documents in seven languages in addition to Hittite, such as Akkadian and Luwian, the language possibly spoken at Troy. These tablets are written in cuneiform script, which the Hittites borrowed from nearby Mesopotamia, evidence of extensive cultural interaction with that region.

The Great King

Archaeologists have learned much about how the Hittite Empire functioned from the Hattushas archives. At the top of the Hittite Empire was the Great King, who ruled in the name of the supreme God of Storms. Like Egyptian rulers, the Great King owned the land of all his subjects, and he

Lion Gates at Imperial Palaces: Hattushas and Mycenae
On this monumental entrance gate to Hattushas above, the fortified capital of the Hittite Empire, massive stone lions flank the gate. Stone lions also guard the main entrance to the citadel of Mycenae in Greece (right). Lions symbolized royal strength in many kingdoms of the International Bronze Age. Their presence at fortress gates also suggests an international style of military architecture.

gave agricultural estates to the noblemen who served as his officials. In return they obeyed him and supplied the soldiers and charioteers he demanded for the army. The Great King also strengthened ties of allegiance throughout his empire by requiring his officials and subordinate monarchs to swear oaths of loyalty to the main Hittite gods. The Great King gave further unity to the empire by playing the role of chief priest of all the gods who were worshiped by the many different communities under his control.

Hittite kings worked hard to provide uniform justice throughout their realm for rich and poor, male and female alike. This proved a complex undertaking because the many different peoples who made up the Hittite Empire were permitted to follow their own customs and laws. Administering justice required close cooperation between subject peoples' local authorities and the Great King's legal officials.

Hittite Religion: "A Thousand Gods"

The Hittites spoke of their "thousand gods" because their religion drew from the empire's many subjects as well as from the neighboring people of Mesopotamia. The imperial government deliberately brought the statues of the gods of its subjects to Hattushas and built many temples for them in an effort to promote the unity of all the people under the Great King's rule.

The archive at Hattushas contained thousands of mythological and religious texts that reveal basic Hittite attitudes. Hittites believed that their gods were present in the form of their statues and that the gods wished to communicate with their human worshipers. Priests appointed by the Great King managed this "conversation" by making appropriate offerings to the deities at fixed intervals maintained in an elaborate calendar of festivals and holy days. The most important deity, Teshub, the God of Storms, presided over numerous gods, who controlled the heavens and involved themselves intimately in human affairs. According to Hittite belief, properly worshiped gods would protect the empire as well as any individuals who might pray to them privately. If a person sinned by violating standards of morality and piety set by the gods, such as committing murder or theft, breaking oaths, having sexual relations with certain animals, or neglecting the gods, the gods would punish that person as well as his or her entire family.

In addition to worshiping numerous gods, the Hittites relied heavily on magic to ward off evils, to stir up trouble for their enemies, and to gain the favor of certain gods. Hittites hired specialists to perform these magical rites, which often required the sacrifice of animals or humans, generally prisoners of war.

The Hittites believed in an afterlife in which the souls of the deceased continued their earthly occupations or lived in a huge palace ruled by the Goddess of Death in the Underworld, located far below the Earth's surface. Hittite rulers maintained a cult of dead kings in Hattushas, and it is likely that families worshiped their ancestors and made sacrifices to them as well.

The militaristic and deeply religious Hittite Empire grew strong from conquering and ruthlessly exploiting the resources of its subjects. As it expanded, it played a prominent role in the network of trade and communication of the International Bronze Age. Hittite kings maintained diplomatic ties with rulers in Syria, Egypt, Mycenaean lands, and Mesopotamia, and Hittite merchants traded with their counterparts in these same areas. These commercial interconnections fostered an era of unprecedented cultural and political exchange among great empires.

HITTITE MILITARY RITUALS

Religious rituals and magic played an important role in every aspect of Hittite life, including warfare. Hittite warriors believed that the gods were usually on their side in battle. They thought that if the gods saw them as impure, they would suffer defeat in combat. After a purification ritual, defeated Hittite soldiers could return to soldiering with renewed morale and vigor. The following document explains the ritual of purification that soldiers performed after a military defeat:

If our troops are defeated by the enemy, they perform the Far-Side-Of-The-River-Ritual. On the far side of the river, they cut in half a person, a billy goat, a puppy, and a piglet. Half of each they place on this side and half on that side (of the river). In front they build a gate of hawthorn. . . . Over the top they draw a rope. In front, on either side, they light a fire. The troops go through the middle. When they reach the river, they sprinkle them with water. Afterward they perform the Ritual-of-The-Battlefield for them in the usual way [and can return to battle].

Source: From Richard H. Beal, "Hittite Military Organization" in *Civilizations of the Ancient Near East 4V,* edited by Jack Sasson, Charles Scribner's Sons, © 1995 by Charles Scribner's Sons. Reprinted by permission of The Gale Group.

THE MESOPOTAMIAN EMPIRES

The kingdoms of Mesopotamia, which rivaled the Hittite Empire in wealth and power, had an equally vital place in the political, commercial, and cultural networks of the International Bronze Age. As we discussed in Chapter 1, highly organized agriculture and urbanism produced distinctive cultures in northern and southern Mesopotamia. The political scene in these regions changed as small cities were transformed into large kingdoms that included many peoples. Because of their size and diversity, these kingdoms, like those of the Egyptians and Hittites, are properly referred to as empires.

During this period, two powerful empires emerged in Mesopotamia: Babylonia in the south and Assyria in the north. Their rulers controlled the economic production of their subjects, and they maintained diplomatic ties with the Egyptians and Hittites. Groups of people called Hapiru also lived in Mesopotamia beyond the control of the Assyrian and Babylonian states. Their seminomadic way of life on the outskirts of settled communities offered an alternative to the tightly controlled, sedentary agricultural societies of Babylonia and Assyria.

The Kingdom of Babylonia: Prosperity Under Kassite Rule

By about 1600 B.C.E. people known as Kassites infiltrated Mesopotamia as raiders, soldiers, and laborers. Their language and precise place of origin are unknown, but by 1400 B.C.E. they had gradually gained control of most of southern Mesopotamia. For the next 250 years, until about 1150 B.C.E., Kassite monarchs maintained order and prosperity in Babylonia, establishing the longest-ruling dynasty in ancient Middle Eastern history.

During these centuries, Babylonia enjoyed a golden age. Kassite kings politically unified Babylonia's many cities through a highly centralized administration that closely controlled both urban centers and countryside. These skilled monarchs won the loyalty of individuals of all ranks and temple priesthoods by giving them tracts of land. The Kassite kings gained a reputation for fair rule and for that reason were popular with their subjects. The government spent lavishly on temples, public buildings, and projects such as canals throughout the kingdom. Bureaucrats kept careful track of revenues. From these resources the government supported a large number of soldiers, artisans, officials, and temple officials.

A minority within the population, the Kassites quickly assimilated into Babylonian culture. They adopted Akkadian, the language of Babylonia, and abandoned their original tongue in an effort to fit in. Under Kassite rule, Babylonia became renowned as a center of trade, culture, and learning.

Babylonia's reputation for learning was linked primarily to science, medicine, and literature, which flourished during this period. With encouragement from the Kassite kings, who wished to demonstrate their full integration into Babylonian society, scribes systematically copied the works of earlier Mesopotamian cultures to preserve their intellectual legacy. Treatises on omens, astrology, and medicine gathered an enormous body of knowledge. This learning passed to future generations, adding to the foundations of the Western tradition.

Owing to their learning and skill, especially with herbal remedies and magic, Babylonian doctors earned fame throughout the Middle East. Gula, the goddess of healing known as the Great Physician, was the divine patron of a religious center where doctors received their training. A hymn of praise to Gula gives a glimpse of medical practices of the age. "I am a physician, I can heal. I carry around all healing herbs. I drive away disease. I gird myself with the leather bag containing health-giving incantations. I carry around texts which bring recovery. I give cures to mankind."[5]

In literature, the Babylonian creation epic *Enuma Elish* tells the story of the origin of the world by Marduk, the god of Babylon and sole lord of the universe. The order that Marduk creates reflects the organized rule that the Kassite kings provided for Babylonia. Babylonian authors also wrote versions of the *Epic of Gilgamesh,* the Sumerian story about the establishment of civilization that we discussed in Chapter 1. These two great works were translated into many languages and entertained people throughout the Middle East for more than a thousand years.

The Kingdom of Assyria: Expansion and Trade

As we saw in Chapter 1, around 1350 B.C.E. the Assyrian kingdom in northern Mesopotamia recovered from more than a century of submission to the neighboring kingdom of Mittani in Syria. When Hittite armies crushed the Mittanians, the Assyrians took advantage of the confusion and reestablished their independence. They began to build a new empire by conquering neighboring peoples. Under the skillful rule of Ashur-Uballit (ca. 1365–1330 B.C.E.) the Assyrian kingdom began a new phase of expansion by grabbing some former Mittanian territories that were rich in grain.

Ashur-Uballit wanted Assyria to stand on equal footing with the Egyptian and Hittite Empires and to take part in the long-distance network of trade and diplomacy that characterized the International Bronze Age. As a letter found in Egypt reveals, he tried to win the favor of the pharaoh in Egypt

> *Thus speaks Ashur-Uballit, king of Assyria. May everything be well with you, your house, your land, your chariots and your troops. I am sending a messenger to you to visit you and to visit your country. Until now, my predecessors did not write; but today I am writing. I am sending you a beautiful chariot, two horses, and a bead of authentic lapis-lazuli [a valuable gemstone] as your greeting gift . . . My messenger will see how you are and how your country is, and then may he come back to me.*[6]

Ashur-Uballit and his successors understood the value of close diplomatic ties with Egypt and other great powers. They also knew that their own power depended on control of natural resources and trade routes, and so they were quite willing to go to war to safeguard their economic interests. To that end, Assyrian kings pushed westward, clashing with the Hittites over trade, metal ores, and timber. The Assyrians built a string of garrisons on their border with the Hittite kingdom and seized territories in northern Syria that had come under Hittite control.

Assyrian kings also competed with Babylonia for control of copper, tin, horses, and other prized natural resources in the hilly lands to Mesopotamia's north and east. The mighty ruler Tukulti-Ninurta I (r. 1244–1208 B.C.E.) led his armies to victory over the Babylonian state, and by the time of his death Assyria controlled all the lands extending from northern Syria to southern Iraq—the greatest reach Assyria would ever attain. Even though Babylonia would reassert its independence within the next twenty years, Assyria dominated Mesopotamian affairs for the next two centuries.

Assyrian power expanded again during the reign of Tiglath-Pileser I (r. 1114–1076 B.C.E.). This capable ruler waged wars against the seminomadic pastoral tribes living on his frontiers, threatening essential Assyrian trade routes. Assyria had become a major consumer of materials imported from abroad, such as timber, copper, cedar, ivory, and tin. In order to protect his sources of supply, Tiglath-Pileser led an expedition to the Mediterranean coast, where he established cordial relations with many trading cities such as Byblos that supplied many of these valued items.

Military victories allowed Assyrian monarchs to sponsor grand public works. Tukulti-Ninurta, for example, celebrated his successes by building a new royal city, called the Harbor of Tukulti-Ninurta, on the banks of the Tigris River. The new capital included a grand canal to facilitate trade, and boasted many palaces and temples decorated with colorful tiles. The chief temple, built in the form of a huge mud-brick ziggurat, honored the Assyrian god Ashur. Assyrian rulers also established many administrative centers throughout their lands from which they could control the wealth produced by their subjects.

The Hapiru: On the Edges of Settled Life

Although they had fierce armies and abundant wealth, the kingdoms of Babylonia and Assyria could not control the diverse peoples called Hapiru, or "landless peoples," who lived on the margins of their lands. Unlike the Kassites, who had settled in Babylonia and achieved political power, different groups of Hapiru maintained a seminomadic existence that was an alternative to life in the highly centralized, agriculture-based empires. They never achieved any political unity.

The Hapiru comprised peoples of diverse origins. Historians believe some were fugitives from economic exploitation by the centralized governments of the Mesopotamian kingdoms or refugees from the constant wars among them. Others were pastoral peoples who had never lived in cities or practiced agriculture. Regardless of their origin, the Hapiru demonstrate that there was room for unsettled peoples on the boundaries between the great empires. Some Hapiru raided urban communities and lived as bandits and occasionally as mercenaries. Others were enslaved and forced to labor on government building projects in Mesopotamia and as far away as Egypt.

At the end of the International Bronze Age, when the great Mesopotamian empires collapsed, the Hapiru nearly disappeared from the historical record. As we will see in the next chapter, however, one group of landless Hapiru entered the land of Canaan about 1100 B.C.E. Some historians believe that these wandering landless people were the ancestors of the people known in the Bible as Hebrews.

CHRONOLOGY

The Peoples of Mesopotamia

CA. 1400 B.C.E.	The Kassites gain control of Babylonia
1365–1330 B.C.E.	Ashur-Uballit renews Assyrian power
1244–1208 B.C.E.	Tukulti-Ninurta I conquers Babylonia; literature, science, and medicine flourish
1114–1076 B.C.E.	Assyrian king Tiglath-Pileser reigns
CA. 1200–1000 B.C.E.	Hapiru live on fringes of settled life
CA. 1000	Arameans invade Assyria

The Civilizations of the Mediterranean

During the International Bronze Age, two vigorous and distinctive civilizations developed in the eastern Mediterranean: the Minoan civilization of Crete (a large island south of Greece) and the Mycenaean civilization on mainland Greece. These were the first civilizations in Europe. Both developed from native peoples who had been in Crete and Greece since the Neolithic period. They prospered from agriculture and long-distance trade, rivaling the empires of Assyria and Babylonia in wealth and influence. The political history of these two civilizations has been forgotten, but the myths and legends of Greek civilization in later centuries preserve some memories of their achievements. Archaeologists have unearthed their palaces, tombs, and objects of everyday life, which provide glimpses into their civilizations.

Also situated on the eastern Mediterranean, and serving as buffer states between Egypt, Mycenaean Greece, and the

Hittite Empire, were several small coastal cities and kingdoms. These states participated in the brisk trade that developed in this region during the International Bronze Age. The two most prosperous of these states, the mercantile kingdoms of Ugarit and Troy, played a "middle-man" role in the trading and diplomatic networks that developed during these centuries.

MINOAN CRETE

About 2000 B.C.E. small urban communities on the island of Crete, which lies midway between Greece and Egypt in the Mediterranean Sea, began to import copper and tin from the eastern Mediterranean. Sir Arthur Evans, the British archaeologist who discovered the remains of the palaces and shrines of Bronze Age Crete in 1899 C.E., called their society Minoan, from the legendary Cretan king Minos in Greek mythology. Minoans raised livestock and cultivated grapes, olives, and cereals that were introduced to the island from the Middle East during the food-producing revolution. Protected from enemies by the surrounding sea, the population of Crete slowly grew in size and prosperity.

In the course of the second millennium B.C.E., the Minoans became highly skilled navigators. They developed a busy merchant navy that traded with Greece, Egypt, and the coastal communities of the eastern Mediterranean. Crete became a thriving center of long-distance trade. The Minoans imported metals, especially copper and tin to make bronze, and they exported textiles, jewelry, wine, and olive oil in beautifully painted ceramic pots. Their civilization was the most brilliant in the Mediterranean until the sixteenth century B.C.E., when it was surpassed by that of the Mycenaeans.

Palace Administration: Collecting and Redistributing Wealth

The Minoan economy revolved around four major urban administrative centers, called palaces, at Knossos, Phaistos, Mallia, and Zakros. A network of roads linked the palaces, suggesting highly centralized political authority. Minoan rulers collected agricultural produce from farmers in the countryside and stored it in the palaces. Palace administrators told farmers how much to grow and collected the produce from them, then gave back sufficient food for their

The Palace of Minos at Knossos, Crete

This detailed reconstruction of the palace of a Minoan king at Knossos, Crete, is based on archaeological excavations. In one of the rooms adjacent to the central court, the royal family and palace officials worshiped the Snake Goddess (see illustration on page xxx).

subsistence. Palace officials also controlled the specialized artists who produced crafts, such as delicately painted pottery, jewelry, and fabrics, that were traded abroad.

Archaeologists believe that the three-acre palace complex at Knossos was the most important in Crete. At its center stood a courtyard surrounded by hundreds of rooms intended as living quarters for the governing and religious elite, administrative headquarters, shrines for religious worship, and warehouses for storing crops and wine in huge clay jars. Archaeologists estimate that the warehouses at Knossos could hold more than a quarter of a million gallons of wine or olive oil. Some rooms functioned as workshops for weaving, pottery manufacture, and metalwork. These warehouses show the Minoan rulers' tight control over the production of wealth on Crete.

The Minoan elites lived in great luxury in palaces connected to warehouses. Built with carefully fitted blocks of smooth limestone cut to a standard unit of measure, with beams of wood and columns wider with flared tops, the palaces had several stories—Knossos sported five. Vivid frescoes (plaster painted while it is still wet) of sea creatures, flowers, court officials and acrobats in bright garments, and scenes of daily life adorned their walls. The residents enjoyed indoor plumbing and running water, comforts that most people in the West would not enjoy until the nineteenth century C.E. The palaces had no fortifications, suggesting that the Minoans felt quite safe on their island.

Like other monarchs, Minoan rulers carefully kept precise records of their wealth and possessions on clay tablets. Accountants recorded long lists of the livestock, produce, raw materials, and merchandise brought to the palace warehouses, as well as the amounts given back to the community. They also kept track of land holdings, debts, and payments made to the palace. These administrators used a form of writing known as Linear A, a simplified hieroglyphic script that developed on Crete around 1700 B.C.E., probably influenced by Egyptian writing. Linguists have not entirely deciphered the script. Minoan mercantile documents found in ports along the eastern coast of the Mediterranean (the Levant) as well as on Crete reveal the international reach of Minoan travel and commerce.

Minoan merchants and artists cultivated extensive commercial links abroad, especially throughout the eastern Mediterranean. For example, archaeologists have excavated Minoan trading posts on the islands of the central Aegean Sea, on the island of Rhodes, and in other locations along the eastern Mediterranean coast. The artists produced beautiful jewelry of precious metals and stones, painted sophisticated designs of sea creatures on vases, and carved delicate figures in ivory, gold, and a deep blue gemstone called lapis lazuli° obtained from the Middle East. Minoan merchants sold their wares on the Greek mainland, and Minoan delegations brought rich gifts to the courts of Egyptian pharaohs. Exporting these luxury goods to eager foreign buyers made the Minoans extremely rich.

CHRONOLOGY

Minoan Crete and Mycenaean Greece

CA. 6000 B.C.E.	First settlements on Crete
CA. 3000 B.C.E.	Minoans begin trading with the Levant
CA. 2300 B.C.E.	Bronze technology enters Aegean region
CA. 2000 B.C.E.	First palaces are built on Crete
CA. 1700 B.C.E.	Linear A script develops (still undeciphered)
CA. 1600 B.C.E.	Mycenaean civilization emerges on Greek mainland; shaft graves constructed at Mycenae
CA. 1450 B.C.E.	First palaces built at Mycenae; Linear B script develops
CA. 1400 B.C.E.	Mycenaean cities fortified
CA. 1375 B.C.E.	Mycenaeans control Crete and eastern sea routes
CA. 1200 B.C.E.	Raiders of Land and Sea appear
CA. 1150 B.C.E.	Mycenaean palaces and towns destroyed on mainland, Cyprus, and coast of Asia Minor

Some Minoan artists traveled abroad to work for wealthy patrons. Frescoes painted by artists from Crete have been found in the Hyksos capital of Avaris in the Egyptian delta and at sites in modern Israel and Syria. Historians believe that these painters might have accompanied Minoan princesses who married foreign leaders to cement diplomatic relations. These clues suggest the elaborate commercial ties that developed in the eastern Mediterranean during the International Bronze Age.

The Mystery of Minoan Religion

The many frescoes and ritual artifacts unearthed from Bronze Age Crete provide archaeologists with a tantalizing but incomplete glimpse of Minoan religious observance. Minoans set aside rooms in their houses as shrines where they worshiped the gods and offered sacrifices. Religious rituals took place in the countryside as well. Worshipers brought offerings of swords, miniature axes, and figurines to more than twenty-five sacred caves in the mountains of Crete. On mountaintop sanctuaries people built bonfires into which they threw clay figurines of humans and animals. Archaeologists have found traces of human sacrifice at some sites, but their meaning remains unclear.

Snake Goddess
One of the most important divinities of Minoan civilization was the Snake Goddess. Here she (or her priestess) is captured in typical pose and dress: She grasps a snake in each outstretched hand and wears a tight-fitting, layered dress that exposes her breasts. A sacred bird perches on her head.

Historians believe that female divinities dominated Minoan religion. Minoans worshiped the powerful Mistress of Animals at some mountaintop shrines, and in their homes they prayed to a goddess whom they always depicted as holding a snake. Statues show this Snake Goddess (or her priestess) wearing a many-tiered skirt, with breasts exposed and snakes coiled around her outstretched arms. Minoans also worshiped the Goddess of Childbirth and a Dove Goddess, who was perhaps the goddess of love, as well as an assortment of demons and male gods.

Despite the rich array of artifacts and sites unearthed by archaeologists, we know very little about the basic beliefs of Minoan religion because no written texts that discuss them have been found. The beliefs of the Minoans remain a mystery.

The Collapse of Minoan Prosperity

Minoan prosperity and power came to a sudden and unexplained end around 1450 B.C.E., when all of the Cretan towns and palaces were destroyed except for Knossos, which fell about 1375 B.C.E. Excavations reveal that immediately after the destruction of the Minoan palaces, artifacts from mainland Greece appeared on Crete and throughout the Aegean. Goods from the Greek mainland, such as pottery painted with distinctive patterns and nautical images, weapons, and wine replaced Minoan products in Syria and the western Mediterranean. Graves on Crete began to contain Greek-style weapons and armor. Archaeologists do not know whether Mycenaean Greeks from the mainland caused the collapse of Minoan power or merely took advantage of it, but it is certain that invaders from Greece took control of Crete and its trade networks around this time. The international economy and the balance of maritime power in the eastern Mediterranean shifted from the island of Minoan Crete to the mainland of Mycenaean Greece.

MYCENAEAN GREECE

A German archaeologist, Heinrich Schliemann, first brought the Bronze Age civilization of mainland Greece to light in 1876 C.E. Determined to prove that the epic poems of the Greek poet Homer about the Trojan war were based in fact, Schliemann first dug at Troy (see next section) and then at the fortress of Mycenae, the home of the Greek king Agamemnon in Homer's *Iliad.* He made spectacular finds of golden treasures and sophisticated architecture at Mycenae, which archaeologists today believe was only one of perhaps six kingdoms on the Greek mainland.

The name *Mycenaean* refers to the kingdom of Mycenae, but since we do not know its ancient name or that of any of the other kingdoms of Greece, the term is also applied generally to the culture of Greece during the International Bronze Age. Historians believe that Mycenaean civilization lasted from around 1600 to 1100 B.C.E.

Mycenaean Civilization

Mycenaean civilization emerged among the native populations of the Peloponnese, the southern portion of Greece. The larger Mycenaean communities consisted of heavily fortified palaces with outlying agricultural lands. Historians do not know anything about the political organization of Mycenaean Greece, but the palace fortifications suggest that the rulers of different palaces frequently warred with one another and that there was no political unity in Greece. Extensive excavation also shows that the strongest fortresses stood at Mycenae, Tiryns, Pylos, Gla, and Thebes. Archaeologists assume that these fortified palaces represented different kingdoms, perhaps linked by alliances.

As on Crete, the Mycenaean palaces functioned as administrative centers of food collection, storage, and distribution. They also served as manufacturing centers that produced pottery, jewelry, tapestries, and other trade goods. Literate bureaucrats living in the palaces were essential in governing the Mycenaean kingdoms. These administrators kept a sharp eye on all aspects of economic production. Like their counterparts in Crete and the Middle East, they recorded long lists of livestock, slaves, farm produce, land holdings, taxes, and tribute taken from peasants and slaves. They also kept detailed records of imported and exported luxury goods and raw materials. The lists include foreign terms for many of the exotic objects found in the Uluburun shipwreck, further evidence of a flourishing international market (see Map 2.3).

By 1400 B.C.E. a uniform Mycenaean civilization had reached its apex throughout southern Greece and in Mycenaean settlements abroad. The similarity of pottery and other manufactured goods from Mycenaean sites in Greece and abroad prevents us from knowing which of the fortress kingdoms traded with a foreign land or campaigned on foreign shores.

Administrative records of the Mycenaean kings demonstrate that the Mycenaeans were Greeks. We know this because palace administrators recorded their lists on clay tablets in a script known as Linear B, which developed around 1450 B.C.E. A British scholar who deciphered Linear B in the early 1950s C.E. proved that it was an early form of the Greek language still spoken today. Moreover, even though the Linear B tablets contain only palace bookkeeping records and do not record literature or history, some of them included the names of gods, such as Poseidon, Zeus, Hera, and Hermes. Greeks worshiped these gods until Christianity took hold during the Roman Empire in the sixth century C.E.

Mycenaean kings controlled their realms in ways similar to those of their counterparts in Egypt and Anatolia. Kings stood at the top of the administrative hierarchy. They led their people in wartime, formed diplomatic alliances with other monarchs, and tried to become richer and more powerful through trade and conquest.

The Warrior Kingdom of Mycenae

The most influential kingdom in southern Greece during this period was located at Mycenae, where kings governed from a citadel looking down on a broad agricultural plain. This center of power, which lasted until around 1100 B.C.E., reveals much about in life in Bronze Age Greece. Thirty royal burials consisting of deep shafts arranged in two circles on the citadel and dating from 1600 to 1450 B.C.E. suggest a highly warlike people. The graves contain bronze swords, daggers, spearheads, and stone arrowheads and blades. The skeletons of the rulers buried in these graves stood nearly six feet tall, which made them tower over the general population. Apparently they enjoyed better nutrition than their subjects, whose graves reveal more diminutive skeletons. The many gold and silver drinking vessels and pieces of jewelry found in the graves further demonstrate that the Mycenaean leaders enjoyed tremendous luxury.

The rulers of Mycenae possessed enough wealth to construct beehive-shaped vaulted tombs, bigger than any other buildings previously built in the Mediterranean. More than fifty such tombs survive. One king's tomb had a diameter of nearly fifty feet, stood forty-three feet high, and was topped by a capstone weighing more than a hundred tons.

The Mycenaean kings also relied on aristocratic warriors, who enforced the monarchs' decisions and served as

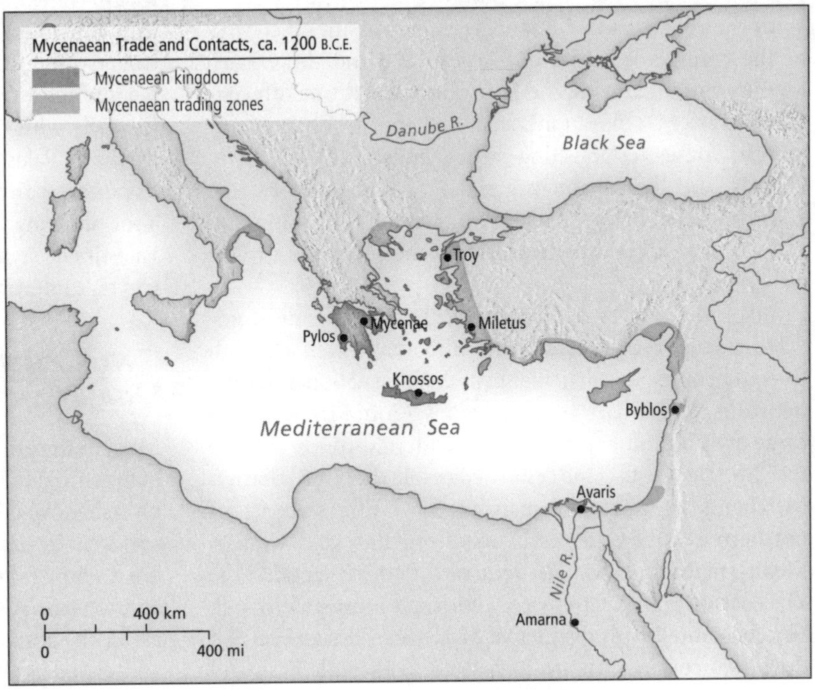

Map 2.3 Mycenaean Trade and Contacts
The Mycenaean Greeks traded extensively with communities throughout the eastern Mediterranean world, including Egypt, the coastal towns of Asia Minor, and Canaan. Sometimes their commerce was little more than raiding and piracy.

Mycenaean Decorated Pot
This Warrior Vase, dating to about 1200 B.C.E., shows a marching troop of infantrymen, an indication of the Mycenaeans' military activities throughout the eastern Mediterranean.

military officers during wartime. As in Egypt, Anatolia, and the Middle East, elite warriors used light, fast-moving chariots pulled by horses. They also took their favorite weapons of war with them to the grave, suggesting that they valued military prowess very highly.

Infantrymen ranked below the aristocrats in the military organization of the Mycenaean states. These soldiers followed the chariots into battle and engaged in hand-to-hand combat using spears and swords. The infantry was drawn from farmers who leased lands from aristocrats and kings. Aristocratic women with religious titles controlled some estates independently, and they may have supplied soldiers to the king's armies as well.

Overseas Trade and Settlement

The Mycenaeans took advantage of the peaceful conditions in the eastern Mediterranean that diplomatic ties between Egypt and the Hittite Empire had helped to create. With the collapse of Minoan Crete, they assumed control of the commerce across the Aegean Sea and the eastern Mediterranean. During the fourteenth and thirteenth centuries B.C.E., Mycenaean merchants extended Minoan commercial routes, establishing strong links with Egyptians, Hittites, and the inhabitants of Ugarit and other Middle Eastern coastal towns. During this time of expansion and commercial success, the treasuries of the Mycenaean rulers were filled.

Like other rulers of their time, the Mycenaeans cultivated extensive commercial and diplomatic contacts with foreign peoples. As participants in the international trading networks, they imported many goods. From Minoan Crete came artistic influences in stone- and goldworking. From the Middle East came knowledge of the war chariot. Merchants brought amber from the Baltic seacoast of northern Europe and metal ores from Italy and western Mediterranean lands. In return for these goods, the Mycenaeans traded tapestries, wine, and perfumed olive oil. Vessels painted with distinctive Mycenaean designs carried the liquid commodities to Egypt and the Middle East, and as far west as Spain and northern Italy.

Mycenaean rulers also forged diplomatic ties with Hittite and Egyptian monarchs. Ambassadors of Pharaoh Amenhotep III visited Crete and the Greek mainland, including Mycenae, where they presented ceremonial plaques bearing the pharaoh's name. Expensive gifts from Mycenaean rulers to pharaohs also have been discovered in Egypt. In the interest of maintaining good relations and brisk commerce, Egyptian and Mycenaean rulers avoided war with each other during this period.

Mycenaean relations with the Hittites were not quite so cordial. To extend and protect their trade routes, some Mycenaean Greeks settled on the coast of Asia Minor, a sphere of Hittite influence. There they engaged in trade, piracy, and warfare with surrounding communities. Hittite documents dating to the fourteenth century B.C.E. tell of meddling Mycenaean kings who slipped away to sea in their ships, out of the reach of landbound Hittite forces. The pottery of the Mycenaeans in these settlements shows that they shared the culture of the Greek mainland. Nevertheless, historians do not know how they were connected to the great palace-fortresses of the Greek mainland.

The Mycenaeans also coveted the copper mines on Cyprus, an island south of modern Turkey in the eastern Mediterranean Sea (*Cyprus* means "copper" in Greek). To gain control of the deposits of this prized ore, Mycenaean traders established numerous trading colonies on Cyprus beginning in the fourteenth century B.C.E. They traded extensively with the local inhabitants and with the peoples of Syria and Palestine. Archaeologists have found rich deposits of pottery painted in the styles of the Greek mainland, but also showing the influence of Cypriot, Syrian, and Palestinian styles, evidence of the varied cultural encounters that international trade facilitated.

Two Coastal Kingdoms: Ugarit and Troy

Many independent cities existed along the border regions between Egypt, Mycenaean Greece, and the Hittite Empire. Overshadowed by their more powerful neighbors, each city survived by acknowledging the superiority of one of the great empires and following its lead in trade, diplomacy, and warfare. A string of these small communities stretched along the seacoast from the Aegean Sea to the Gaza Strip and served as a buffer between the three major powers. The two most notable cities were Ugarit and Troy.

THE MILLAWANDA LETTER

About 1300 B.C.E., a Hittite king wrote the following letter to an unknown Mycenaean king, complaining of the behavior of a lesser ruler on the Aegean coast of Asia Minor who had defied the Hittite king's commands. It reveals the limitations placed on the Hittites by their lack of a navy.

The author's insistence on the formalities of diplomatic communication is striking. The letter indicates the significant role of international diplomatic relations among the great powers, but it leaves some questions unanswered: Was the Mycenaean kingdom of Ahhijawa on Rhodes, on Cyprus, or in Greece? What was the previous trouble over the city of Wilusa (another name for Troy)?

I have to complain of the insolent and treacherous conduct of . . . Tawagalawas. We came into contact in the land of Luqqa [in southwest Asia Minor]; and he offered to become a vassal of the Hittite Emperor . . . I order him, if he desires to become a vassal of mine, to make sure that no troops of his are to be found in Ijalanda [an unknown location] when I arrive there. And what do I find when I arrive at Ijalanda? The troops of Tawagalawas fighting on the side of my enemies. I defeat them, take many prisoners, devastate the district, scrupulously keeping the fortress of Atrija intact out of respect for my treaty with you. Now comes a Hittite subject, Pijamaradus, . . . who steals my 7000 prisoners, and makes off to your city Millawanda (Miletus). I command him to return to me: he disobeys. I write to you: you send a surly message, unaccompanied by gift or greeting. . . . So I go to fetch him. I enter your city Millawanda, for I have something to say to Pijamaradus, and it would be well that your subjects there should hear me say it. But my visit is not a success. I ask for Tawagalawas: he is not at home. I should like to see Pijamaradus: he has gone to sea. . . . Are you aware, and is it with your blessing, that Pijamaradus is going around saying that he intends to leave his wife and family, and incidentally my 7000 prisoners, under your protection, while he makes continual inroads into my territory? Kindly tell him either to settle down peacefully in your country, or to return to my country. Do not let him use Ahhijawa as a base for operations against me. You and I are friends. There has been no quarrel between us since we came to terms in the matter of Wilusa [Troy]: the trouble there was all my fault, and I promise you that it shall not happen again. As for my military occupation of your city Millawanda, please consider it a friendly visit. I am sorry that in the past you have had occasion to accuse me of being aggressive and of sending impolite messages: I was young then and carried away in the heat of action. I may add that I also have had harsh words from you, and I suggest that the fault may not lie with ourselves but with our messengers. Let us bring them to trial, cut off their heads, mutilate their bodies, and live henceforward in perfect friendship.

Source: From Denys L. Page, *History and the Homeric Iliad*,

Ugarit: A Mercantile Kingdom

Directly east of Cyprus on the Syrian coast lay the port city of Ugarit, which controlled a small but influential kingdom of about 2,000 square miles. Ugarit was one of several small kingdoms dotting the coast that grew wealthy from maritime trade and agriculture. Lying in the area known as Canaan, Ugarit shared Canaanite gods, customs, and social organization with other communities in the region.

Ugarit became a highly cultured city with international connections because of its rich natural resources. The fertile plain offered arable land for grape vines, olive trees, and grains, while the heavily forested surrounding hills provided timber for shipbuilding and construction. Perhaps Ugarit's greatest asset was a fine natural harbor that made the city a hub of international trade. Merchant ships like the one that sank at Uluburun sailed to Ugarit from Cyprus and the Aegean, the coast of western Anatolia, and Egypt. Caravans laden with goods arrived from Mesopotamia, the Hittite lands, and Canaan. People from all these places settled in Ugarit, whose population is estimated at 10,000 inhabitants. Another 25,000 people lived as farmers in the Ugarit countryside.

The city of Ugarit consisted of two major sections. An enormous, fortified palace occupying about 10,000 square yards dominated the city. It contained residential quarters with running water and sewage disposal facilities, administrative buildings, and imposing temples to the gods Baal and Dagan, who protected the city. In a second section of the city, wealthy inhabitants lived in spacious homes with elaborate family tombs under the floor of one room. In these spacious houses archaeologists have excavated numerous baked clay tablets containing legal, financial, literary, diplomatic, and religious texts written in Ugaritic, the local Semitic language. The tablets demonstrate the literacy of the Ugaritic elite. Young people studied their own language in school while also mastering foreign languages useful in trade and diplomacy. The tablets show an innovative alphabet. In it, each spoken sound was represented by just one letter or sign. This Ugaritic alphabet was the ancestor of all modern alphabets that follow the same principle of one sign per spoken sound.

The kings of Ugarit controlled a substantial military force in the form of an elite corps of 2,000 aristocratic charioteers. These warriors supplied their own horses, a sign of the city's enormous wealth. The rulers could also afford to hire battalions of mercenary troops from neighboring lands. Even with these forces, however, Ugarit was always overshadowed by mighty Egypt to the south and the combative Hittite Empire to the north. To maintain Ugarit's independence, the port city's rulers had to be clever diplomats. Archaeologists have unearthed records of treaties made between the kings of Ugarit and Hittite, Mitannian, Assyrian, and other rulers in the Middle East. These treaties show that Ugarit played a crucial role in international diplomacy.

Troy: A City of Legend

Troy, the best known and yet most mysterious of all Bronze Age cities, has captured the popular imagination for 3,000 years, but archaeology cannot explain the origins of the people who lived there, or even their language. Situated in northwest Asia Minor on a promontory overlooking a bay about six miles from the Aegean Sea, this city has become immortal as the site of the Trojan War in Homer's epic poems the *Iliad* and the *Odyssey*.

Composed about 750 B.C.E., these stories were legends, not history. Still, they formed part of an enduring oral tradition that began in the International Bronze Age. In some ways they reflect social conditions and perhaps even events that actually occurred. Archaeologists began excavating Troy, Mycenae, and other sites specifically to investigate the reliability of Homer's accounts. Today, however, historians appreciate Troy primarily as a city embedded in the intricate web of trade, diplomacy, and warfare that linked the societies of the International Bronze Age.

Archaeologists have unearthed numerous distinct layers of occupation and construction in Troy, as generations of inhabitants rebuilt their city from about 3000 to 1200 B.C.E. Around 1700 B.C.E. the inhabitants of Troy VI (meaning the sixth major layer of occupation) constructed huge gateways and a royal palace consisting of many roomy mansions. A fortified citadel, Troy VI was built with monumental blocks of masonry similar to that used by the Hittites and the Mycenaeans, suggesting that techniques of military engineering had spread among these kingdoms. Sandwiched between the Hittite Empire and the kingdoms of Mycenaean Greece, Troy retained its independence, though it probably remained under the shadow of the Hittite Empire.

The Trojans prospered in the fifteenth and fourteenth centuries B.C.E. by trading with Mycenaean Greeks, Hittites, Cypriots (from Cyprus), and merchants from Ugarit. They produced woolen fabrics and fine tapestries for export. They also won notice as breeders of fine horses, which warrior aristocrats used in chariot combat. The skipper of the

The "Death Mask of Agamemnon" This thin gold mask, about 11 inches long, was found at the citadel of Mycenae in the tomb of a ruler who died about 1550 B.C.E. Heinrich Schliemann, who excavated the tomb, mistakenly jumped to the conclusion that it was the death mask of King Agamemnon, who led the Greek forces during the Trojan War, as told in Homer's *Iliad*. Later archaeologists have discovered that this king died several centuries before the period that Homer described.

ship wrecked at Uluburun likely stopped at Troy during one of his many voyages.

Around 1270 B.C.E., an earthquake tumbled the mighty walls of Troy VI and the city went up in flames. The Trojans' prosperity and influence ended. Heinrich Schliemann, the first archaeologist to excavate Troy, erroneously concluded that Troy VI was the city destroyed by Mycenaean Greeks in Homer's *Iliad.* Later archaeologists proved that Greeks had nothing to do with the city's collapse.

The survivors of the earthquake rebuilt the city, which archaeologists have named Troy VIIa, on a very modest scale. Situated within the rubble of Troy VI's fortress walls, this new version of the city also fell to ruin about 1190 B.C.E. The presence of human bones in the debris suggest that warfare destroyed it. Most archaeologists believe that if there is even a kernel of truth in Homer's stories about the Greek destruction of Troy, it must lie in the violent end of Troy VIIa, not Troy VI.

We have no hope of reconstructing an accurate account of these events. Nevertheless, Hittite royal documents indicate that Mycenaeans raided the coastlands of Asia Minor in search of slaves and booty, and Linear B tablets from the Greek mainland list slaves captured on the Asia Minor coast. These records suggest that Troy VIIa may well have fallen prey to a Mycenaean attack. Some historians believe that in the centuries following Troy VIIa's destruction, the story of a Mycenaean raid slowly took on epic proportions as generations of Greek bards told and retold it. Older tales recounting the glory of Troy VI may have augmented the legend of the Trojan War.

CHRONOLOGY

Ugarit and Troy

CA. 1700–1270 B.C.E.	Troy VI flourishes; trades with Mycenaeans and Hittites
CA. 1700 B.C.E.	Ugarit emerges as important trading center
CA. 1270 B.C.E.	Troy VI falls
CA. 1270–1150 B.C.E.	Troy VIIa inhabited
CA. 1150 B.C.E.	Troy VIIa falls; Raiders of the Land and Sea burn Ugarit

The End of the International Bronze Age and Its Aftermath

The intricate diplomatic, cultural, and economic interconnections between Egypt, the Middle East, Anatolia, and Greece broke between 1200 and 1100 B.C.E. These formerly vibrant civilizations plummeted into a dark age, marked by invasions, migrations, and the collapse of stable governments. The era of prosperity and international cooperation came to an abrupt end.

THE RAIDERS OF THE LAND AND SEA

For Mycenaean Greece, warfare among the mainland's many competitive kingdoms probably began a chain of disasters. Some archaeologists argue that overpopulation and competition for resources may have sparked these struggles. These conflicts resulted in the breakdown of the palace-centered economic system about 1150 B.C.E. When the Mycenaean kingdoms collapsed, the economy disintegrated as well. Literacy disappeared because there was no need for scribes to learn Linear B and keep palace inventories. Trade and population declined rapidly, and many Greeks migrated to the coast of Asia Minor in search of new homes. Village life dragged on, though at an impoverished level. The Greek language and some religious beliefs survived, but the crafts, artistic styles, and architectural traditions of Mycenaean life were forgotten. Some memories of Mycenaean fighting on the coast of Asia Minor were preserved in distorted form in Greek legends of later centuries. These stories claimed that a wave of invaders from the north entered the Greek mainland at this time, but there is no archaeological evidence to support this assertion. In contrast to the brilliance of Mycenaean civilization, the poverty and hardship of the era that followed merit the name "dark age."

For the Hittite Empire, a deadly combination of economic decline and invasions early in the twelfth century B.C.E. triggered the government's collapse. The subject kingdoms in the western regions of the Hittite Empire began to rebel, and peasants fled their lands, perhaps due to droughts. The Hittites became ever more dependent on foreign sources of grain, forcing their rulers to import larger supplies from Egypt and Syria. Sometimes rebellions blocked these shipments, worsening the Hittites' plight.

When seaborne raiders invaded from the west, the Hittites, who had no navy of their own, made a desperate, defensive alliance with the kings of the maritime city of Ugarit. The combined effort of the allied war fleets and Hittite troops temporarily protected the empire's western flank, but by the first decade of the twelfth century B.C.E. an enemy force of uncertain origin stormed through the Hittite Empire and burned the capital city of Hattushas. With no effective leadership, Hittite power soon crumbled. Within just a few generations, the empire's glory was forgotten.

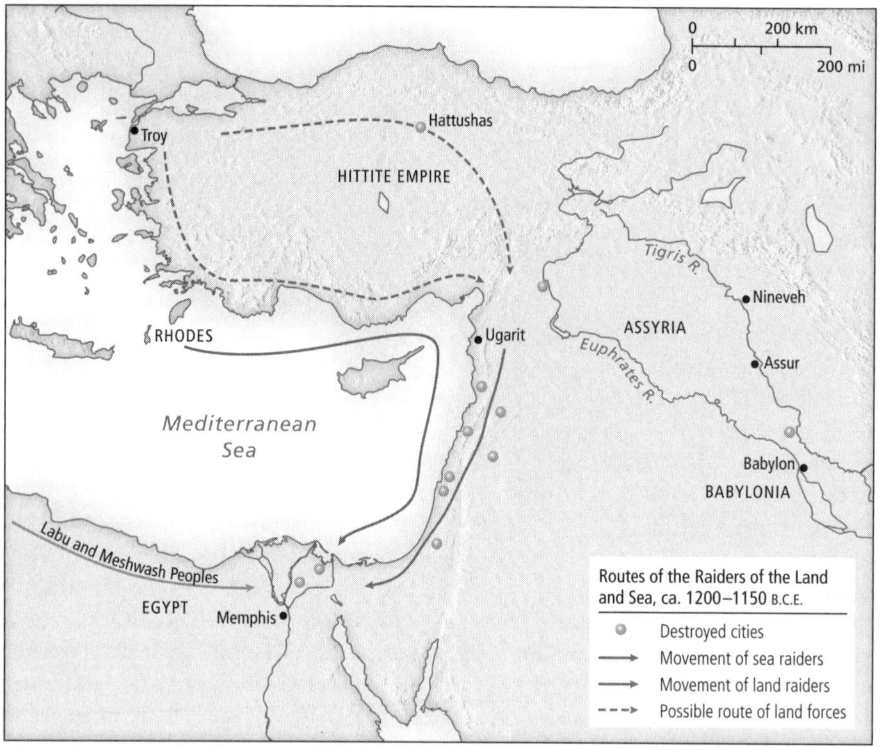

Map 2.4 Routes of the Raiders of the Land and Sea, ca. 1200–1150 B.C.E.
Migrating peoples, known as the Raiders of the Land and Sea, destroyed the network of commerce and diplomacy that had flourished during the International Bronze Age. Traveling along the eastern Mediterranean coast, these displaced peoples destroyed many kingdoms and cities before being stopped and dispersed by Egyptian forces.

The collapse of Hittite and Mycenaean power contributed to migrations throughout the eastern Mediterranean. People fled their homes in search of new lands to settle. Overcoming all resistance, these displaced groups plundered cities and brought destruction to the entire eastern Mediterranean as they moved south toward Egypt.

In Egyptian documents these people are referred to as Raiders of the Land and Sea°. They came from many places and there is no single explanation of what set them in motion (see Map 2.4). Earthquakes, plague, climate change, political instability, and economic decline likely spurred them to migrate. Some of the raiders came from the Aegean region and included Mycenaean Greeks. Others originated in Cyprus and the territories seeking to break free from Hittite control. Perhaps some came from the region of Troy. Still more originated in the Middle East. Although they included pirates and mercenaries, the raiders were not simply a coalition of violent bandits. They included migrating groups that traveled with their families and livestock in search of new lands.

Moving south through Syria and Palestine, the raiders destroyed Ugarit and other coastal cities that formerly had ties with the Hittites and Egyptians. "Now the ships of the enemy have come, and they have burned my cities in fire and have committed atrocities in my land!" lamented the last king of Ugarit in a letter to the ruler of Cyprus. Bound together in a loose confederation, the raiders moved further south toward Egypt in search of land and food.

Taking advantage of Egypt's preoccupation with the raiders, the Labu and Meshwesh people, who originated in Libya, invaded the Nile's western delta. Pharaoh Merenptah (r. 1213–1203 B.C.E.) stopped them after a long and bloody battle. Within twenty-five years the Labu and the Meshwesh entered the delta again, this time settling there. They allied themselves with the Raiders of the Land and Sea from the north, making common cause with groups who had participated in the destruction of the Hittite capital, as well as Ugarit and other cities on Cyprus and the Mediterranean coast. Ramesses III (r. 1185–1153 B.C.E.) overcame this coalition in battle, but the worst was yet to come. In 1177 B.C.E., another huge coalition of raiders from the north invaded Egypt territory. Ramesses defeated their land forces in a fierce battle in Palestine and then crushed their sea forces off the Nile delta. The pharaoh recorded his victory in a huge stone carving at Medinet Habu. The inscriptions on his mortuary temple gloat over his triumph:

> *The foreign lands made a convocation in their islands, bursting forth and scattering in the strife of the lands at one time; no land could stand before their arms, beginning with the Kingdom of the Hittites . . . They laid their hands on countries as far as the circuit of the earth trusting and confident: "Our plans will succeed! . . . Those who came upon the sea, the consuming flame faced them at the Nile mouths . . . they were dragged up, surrounded and cast down upon the shore, slaughtered in heaps from head to tail."*[7]

Egypt avoided destruction at the hands of the Raiders of the Land and Sea, but nevertheless slipped into a long economic and military decline. Within fifteen years of Ramesses III's death in 1153 B.C.E., the empire had lost control of Syria and Canaan. Groups of raiders settled on the Mediterranean coast and extended their power inland, where they destroyed the last of the Bronze Age cities by about 1100 B.C.E. In Egypt, drought, poor harvests, and inflation ruined the economy, while weak rulers struggled unsuccessfully to hold Egypt together. The bonds between Upper and Lower Egypt were severed, and the land of Egypt split once again into separate kingdoms.

Some raiders who escaped Egyptian troops spread across the Mediterranean. Some probably settled in Sicily, Sardinia, and Etruria. Others, the Peleset People, eventually settled on the coast of Canaan. These people are known to us as the Philistines, a name that survives in the modern word *Palestine.*

In Mesopotamia, the kingdoms of Babylonia and Assyria experienced an economic and political breakdown, though not as great as that of the Mycenaeans and Hittites. Historians are uncertain of the precise causes of the decline of these two great Mesopotamian powers. They attribute it primarily to invasions by Arameans, who were seminomadic peoples originating in Syria and areas to the west of Mesopotamia. The Arameans invaded Assyrian territories, destroying harvests and causing famines. They seized control of portions of the Assyrian kingdom and established their own rule. Assyrian monarchs retained authority over a much reduced kingdom. Babylonia, for its part, endured frequent invasions by different peoples from the Iranian plateau, called Elamites. Babylonia's leaders, too, lost power and political influence. The Assyrians and Babylonians nevertheless maintained their identity as distinct peoples throughout these troubled centuries.

After the International Bronze Age ended about 1100 B.C.E., the people of the Middle East from the Mediterranean coast to Mesopotamia gradually evolved into new and powerful kingdoms with distinctive cultures. Long-distance trade in tin and copper broke down but did not disappear. People began to rely on iron rather than bronze for making weapons and other tools because it existed in many sites throughout the Mediterranean and Middle East and so was cheaper to use. It took several centuries for iron to displace bronze as the preferred metal for weapons, and bronze continued to be used for many other purposes.

During this time, two regions acquired special importance: the eastern coast of the Mediterranean, where the Phoenicians developed a maritime culture built on the traditions of cities like Ugarit, and Mesopotamia, the land between the Tigris and Euphrates rivers, where the kingdoms of Assyria and Babylonia revived. (We will examine the Middle Eastern civilization of the Hebrews, which emerged in the aftermath of the International Bronze Age, in Chapter 3.)

THE PHOENICIANS: MERCHANTS OF THE MEDITERRANEAN

Two hundred years after the International Bronze Age drew to a close, a dynamic maritime civilization took shape in the cities that stretched along the eastern Mediterranean seaboard. These seafaring people, whom historians call Phoenicians, continued the commercial traditions of Ugarit and other small Bronze Age kingdoms. Historians do not know what Phoenicians called themselves, but they probably used the term Canaanites, as they spoke a Semitic Canaanite language. The name *Phoenician* apparently derives from a Greek word meaning "red," in reference to the valuable dark red dye extracted from murex shells that was essential to the Phoenician textile industry, a basic part of their commerce.

Phoenicians are known mainly as accomplished sailors and merchants. By 950 B.C.E. they established extensive trade and political connections with peoples of the Levant and spread their civilization into the Mediterranean world as far as North Africa, Italy, and Spain. The independent port cities of Byblos, Tyre, and Sidon were the main centers of Phoenician life and served as the original departure

CHRONOLOGY

The Aftermath of the International Bronze Age

1100–900 B.C.E.	Emergence of Phoenicians in eastern Mediterranean
950 B.C.E.	Phoenician trading voyages extend as far west as Spain; trading posts established in Spain, North Africa, and Sicily
800 B.C.E.	Tyrian traders found Carthage and voyage to Britain and West Africa; children sacrificed to gods in Phoenician communities
CA. 750 B.C.E.	Phoenician alphabet reaches Greece; Neo-Assyrian Empire emerges
730s B.C.E.	Phoenicians begin competing with Greek colonists in Sicily and Italy
721 B.C.E.	Assyria conquers Israel (Northern Kingdom)
603 B.C.E.	Assyrian Empire falls
612–539 B.C.E.	Neo-Babylonian Empire emerges; astronomers are active

points for movement to the western Mediterranean. Phoenicians did not, however, form a large, centralized state. Their cities, therefore, became vulnerable to attack and lost their independence in the fifth century B.C.E., but their strong mercantile and seafaring culture lasted into Roman times.

Economic Expansion

The search for metal ores, such as tin, copper, iron, silver, and gold, motivated Phoenician commerce. Merchants from Tyre led the rapid expansion of Phoenician trade westward into Mediterranean markets, where they created a large commercial empire by following old Minoan and Mycenaean trade routes of the International Bronze Age that had not been forgotten (see Map 2.5). Phoenician sailors were legendary for their skills in navigation and shipbuilding. Hundreds of their ships crisscrossed the Mediterranean and ventured into the Atlantic Ocean in search of trade. Phoenician metal prospectors located deposits of precious ores in North Africa, Spain, Italy, Britain, and France. They did business with the local inhabitants in these regions who had been working the mines for centuries. In this way Phoenician traders established economic connections with lands that would later become the center of Western civilization.

The enterprising Phoenicians also learned techniques of smelting metals (including iron) for weapons, tools, and jewelry that had been developing in European lands since the International Bronze Age, and they transmitted this knowledge to Middle Eastern peoples. In return, they brought back Middle Eastern and Egyptian artistic styles to western Mediterranean lands. These transactions in metal ores, manufactured goods, and timber occurred at the trading posts that Phoenician merchants established.

By 800 B.C.E., Carthage ("New City"), a colony from Tyre located on the northern coast of modern Tunisia, had become the chief Phoenician city in the west. For this reason, Phoenician culture in the western Mediterranean is often called Carthaginian. With its magnificent harbor and strategic location midway between the Levant and the

Map 2.5 Phoenician Expansion, ca. 600 B.C.E.

Several centuries after the collapse of the International Bronze Age, adventurous merchants from the eastern Mediterranean coast developed a commercial empire across the Mediterranean Sea. By 600 B.C.E. Carthage had become the chief Phoenician city in the western Mediterranean. It controlled the resources of North Africa and Spain.

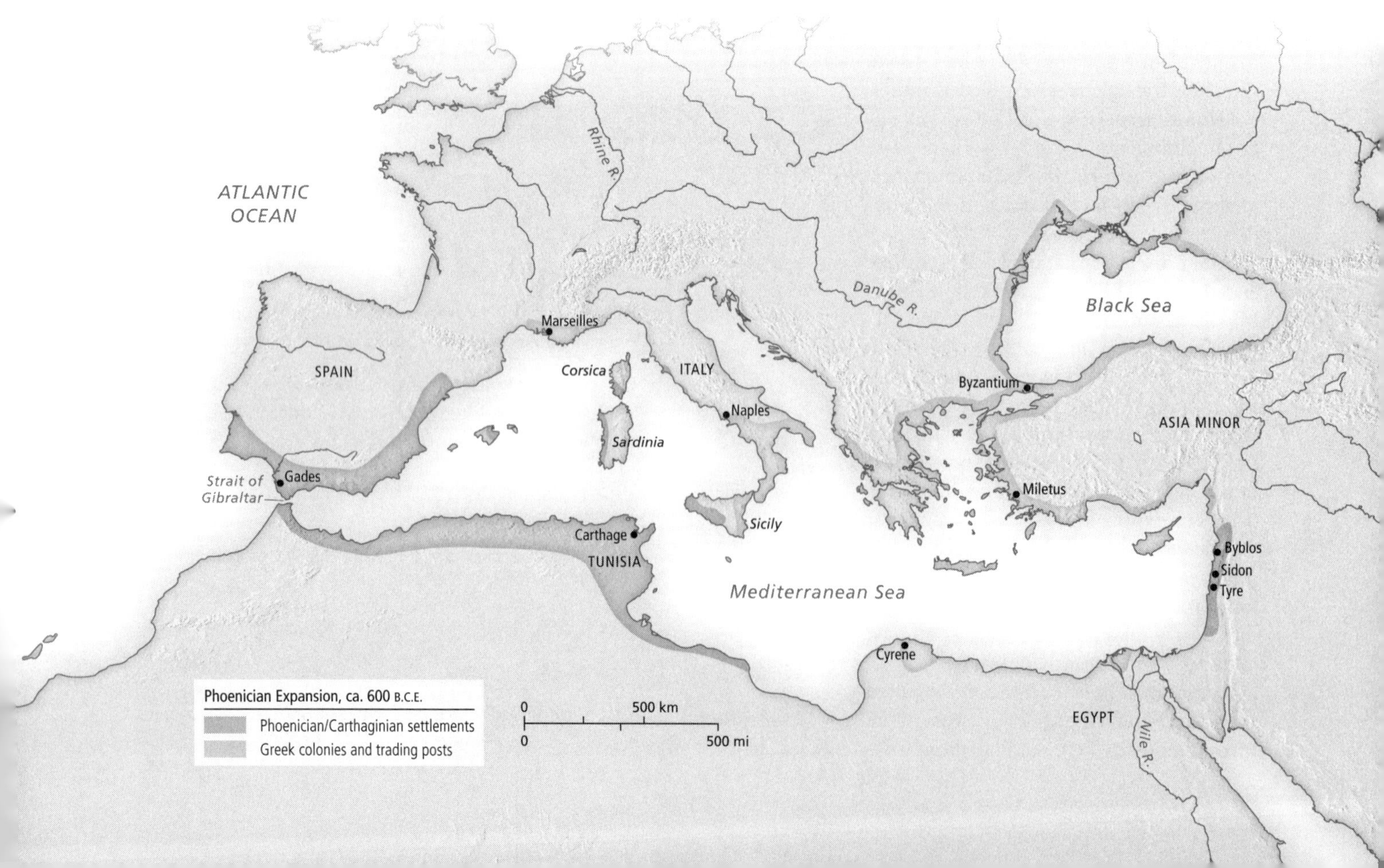

Phoenician Bowls

Customers from many different cultures admired the beautiful metal bowls with elaborate patterns made by skilled Phoenician craftworkers. The artists drew their inspiration from the traditions they encountered throughout the Mediterranean world, which they then used to create their own style. The silver bowl shown here was found in Cyprus. In the center is a common Egyptian motif, a king clubbing an enemy on the head.

straits of Gibraltar, Carthage controlled trade between the eastern and western Mediterranean. Its inhabitants developed a land-based empire on the North African coast and in Spain. Merchants from the city explored the Spanish deposits of tin, which was used as an alloy with other metals, and silver, which was prized for jewelry. Some merchants ventured as far north as Britain to exploit that country's rich tin deposits.

As we will see in Chapter 3, Phoenician and Greek merchants competed for trade in the western Mediterranean, but they controlled different spheres of influence. Phoenician colonies clung to the southern shore of the Mediterranean, while Greek colonies held the northern shore. Unlike the Greeks, who established their colonies on land taken by force from the local inhabitants, Phoenicians were more interested in trading than settling. Their approach to business facilitated good relations with the southern Mediterranean's native inhabitants, especially in Sicily and Italy.

Religion and Culture

Phoenician religion showed remarkable continuity through time and across the Mediterranean. Many of their gods and goddesses had also been worshiped by Middle Eastern peoples during the International Bronze Age. Even though the deities' names differed among many Phoenician cities, their roles as protectors and warriors remained the same. The chief gods were Baalat ("Lady of the Heavens") and her husband Baal ("Lord of the Heavens"), who represented the order of the natural world and protected the Phoenicians from danger. In one religious festival, celebrated throughout the Phoenician world every spring, worshipers burned a statue of the Lord of the Heavens on a ritual pyre to mark his annual death. After a sacred ritual marriage with the Lady of the Heavens he was reborn. This festival celebrated the rebirth of nature and the restoration of heavenly order. The idea of a god's death and resurrection during springtime was widely shared throughout the Mediterranean world, and eventually influenced later religions of the Greek and Roman world, including Christianity.

In the Carthaginian cities of the western Mediterranean, the Lady of the Heavens became associated with the practice of sacred prostitution. Within her temples, women fulfilled vows taken in the goddess's name and made themselves sexually available to male visitors. Every sexual union symbolized the fertility and regenerative power of the Lady of the Heavens. In addition, many parents killed their firstborn son as an offering to the Lord and Lady of the Heavens at moments of crisis or as an offering for the fulfillment of a personal vow. Child sacrifice continued at Carthage and other Carthaginian settlements, often secretly, as late as 200 C.E.

Because Phoenicians traveled so widely, they encountered many foreign gods and goddesses and often adopted some as their own. Some Egyptian divinities, such as Bes, the goddess of childbirth and protector of women and children, and Isis, who offered a special sense of security and comfort, became extremely popular among the Phoenicians, an indication of the close contact between Phoenician and Egyptian cultures. The religious interactions between the Phoenicians and other peoples throughout the Mediterranean world powerfully illustrate how cultural encounters can transmit influential ideas and beliefs.

The Phoenicians' most lasting cultural contribution to the peoples of the Mediterranean world was the alphabet, a system of writing based on that of Ugarit in which each letter represented a single sound. Thus the alphabet could be used to record the sounds of any language. The Phoenician alphabet spread throughout the Mediterranean world, where the Greeks and then the Romans adopted it. In this way it became the source of all alphabets and writing in the West.

MESOPOTAMIAN KINGDOMS: ASSYRIA AND BABYLON, 1050–550 B.C.E.

The decline of both Assyria and Babylonia at the end of the International Bronze Age did not result in their disappearance as kingdoms. Torn apart by invasions, they nevertheless managed to survive, and beginning in about 1050 B.C.E., Assyria and then Babylonia began to regain effective control over their territories, re-establish their commercial power, and reconquer neighboring lands.

Neo-Assyrian Imperialism

After 1000 B.C.E., the Assyrian kings slowly reasserted their dominance in northern Mesopotamia and overseas by regaining control of the trade routes that had made them rich in earlier centuries and by gradually reconquering old and new lands. In 745 B.C.E., Tiglath-Pileser III (r. 745–727 B.C.E.) ascended the Assyrian throne and ushered in a century of astonishing expansion. Historians call the realm he acquired the Neo-Assyrian Empire.

Because Tiglath-Pileser and his successors believed that Ashur, their chief god, had commanded them to expand their empire's borders, they went to war frequently. As a result, the Assyrians overran the peoples of Canaan (including the Israelites), Phoenicians, Babylonians, many Iranian peoples, and much of Egypt. They created the first empire to control the Tigris, Euphrates, and Nile River valleys, where civilization had first emerged two millennia before (see Map 2.6). By 500 B.C.E., Nineveh, the empire's capital city, boasted at least 500,000 inhabitants drawn from all of these regions.

Neo-Assyrian rulers, who called themselves "Kings of the Universe," developed a highly militarized empire. To terrify their victims and aid their conquests, they cultivated a reputation for extreme cruelty. Assyrian armies tortured, butchered, and enslaved the inhabitants of defeated cities. Then, after carting off everything of value, they burned the cities to the ground. They immediately spread the news of their atrocities to neighboring areas, which quickly and understandably surrendered.

As the Assyrians conquered more and more peoples, they faced problems that have troubled empires ever since: How can subject peoples be controlled and what degree of cultural independence should they be permitted to retain? Assyrian solutions were thoughtful yet violent. Assyrian rulers permitted their subjects to continue their traditions and religious practices without interference. If they rebelled against Assyrian authority, however, the army would crush them and deport entire populations to distant corners of the empire. Some Assyrian rulers depopulated entire regions, forcing perhaps as many as a million and a half people from their homes. Many deportees perished and others lost their cultural identity after years of assimilation.

Like their predecessors during the International Bronze Age, the Neo-Assyrian rulers grew wealthy from agriculture and trade. They also exploited their subjects more harshly than previously. Provincial administrators imposed crippling taxes and systematically drained away their subjects' resources. With these revenues, the kings could maintain armies of more than 100,000 men and supply them with iron weapons. At the same time, the government strengthened the economy by rebuilding cities, increasing the amount of land under cultivation, and building roads to improve trade and communications throughout the empire.

Ashurbanipal (r. 669–626 B.C.E.), the last strong ruler of the Neo-Assyrian empire, attempted to create a uniform culture throughout his vast realm. At his command, scholars collected subject people's written knowledge, translated it into Akkadian, and distributed copies on clay tablets throughout Assyrian lands. Ashurbanipal did not succeed in imposing a standardized culture on the empire, but he was the first monarch to try to organize the diverse cultural inheritance of his multiethnic empire. Many subsequent empires, such as those of the Hellenistic world (discussed in Chapter 4) and Rome (discussed in Chapter 5) gained stability by cultivating a dominant culture shared by the empires' elites.

Despite its prosperity and efficient administration, the Neo-Assyrian model of imperial rule failed to bring lasting unity to its peoples. Serious internal dynastic struggles and ineffective leadership after Ashurbanipal's death weakened the empire. Most destructive of all, subject peoples who had endured brutal treatment at the hands of Assyrian administrators nursed a bitter resentment and revolted as soon as possible. The most significant of these rebels was the Babylonian king Nabopolassar in southern Mesopotamia

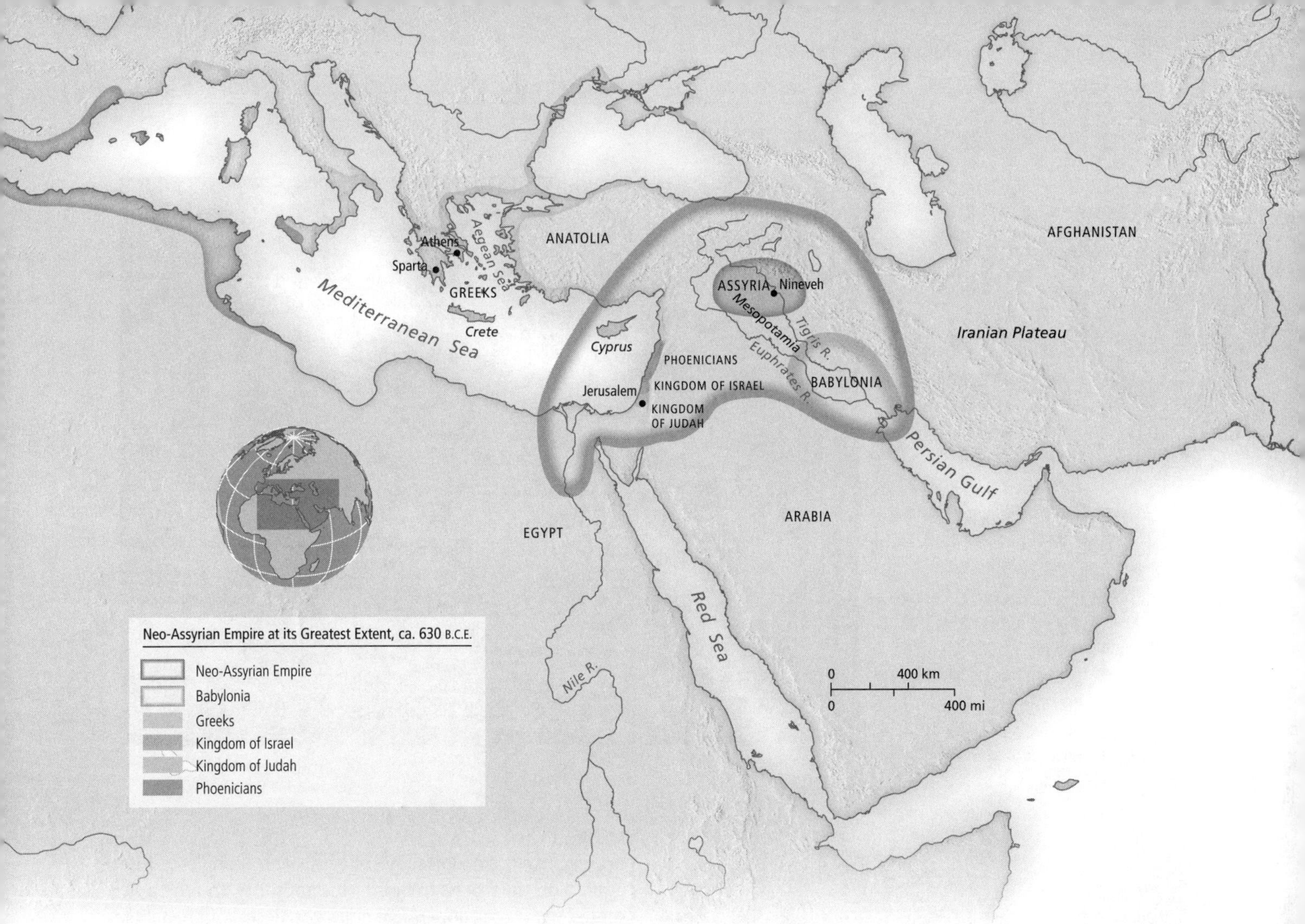

■ **Map 2.6 The Neo-Assyrian Empire at Its Greatest Extent, ca. 630 B.C.E.**
By 630 B.C.E., the Assyrians had recovered their strength and established the Neo-Assyrian Empire. This huge realm included Mesopotamia, the Israelite kingdoms, Phoenicia, and parts of Egypt.

(r. 625–605 B.C.E.). He allied himself with Iranian kings and began a successful revolt against Assyrian rule. By 603 B.C.E., the Assyrian Empire collapsed again.

The Neo-Babylonian Empire

After Nabopolassar acquired Assyrian territory, he built the Neo-Babylonian (or Chaldean) Empire into the most powerful in the Middle East, which lasted until 539 B.C.E. His son, the brilliant general Nebuchadnezzar II (r. 604–562 B.C.E.), conquered lands that had broken free when Assyrian rule collapsed (see Map 2.7). Babylonian armies seized Egypt, Syria, Phoenicia, and the kingdom of Judah, where they destroyed the city of Jerusalem and exiled many Jews to Babylon. (We will learn more about this exile in Chapter 3.)

With the wealth acquired from these conquests, Nebuchadnezzar made his capital city, Babylon, one of the most luxurious in the ancient world. A moat flooded with waters from the Euphrates River surrounded Babylon's eight miles of walls. The emperor also built the Ishtar Gate, which his artisans decorated with glazed, brightly colored tiles. The gate opened onto a grand avenue leading to the temple of Marduk, Babylon's greatest god. According to tradition, Nebuchadnezzar also built the "Hanging Gardens of Babylon" for a favorite wife who missed her mountainous homeland. Splendid flowers and plants cascaded down the slopes of a terraced hillside that from a distance seemed to float in the air. In ancient times, people considered the Hanging Gardens to be one of the great wonders of the world.

The Neo-Babylonian Empire comprised a constellation of wealthy cities in which life revolved around the uninterrupted worship of Marduk. At the center of each community stood a magnificent temple to the all-powerful god. Each city also had complex religious, political, and economic arrangements with the king. For example, the Babylonians considered proper worship essential for the prosperity of their communities. They looked to the king to provide the peaceful conditions in which they could worship their gods without interruption. The king, for his

Ishtar Gate

The magnificently tiled Ishtar Gate provided a dramatic entrance to Babylon, the capital city of the Neo-Babylonian Empire. Babylonian artists used brightly colored tiles to create complicated three-dimensional depictions of animals, including lions which represented royal power. The gate now rests in a museum in Berlin. An artist's reconstruction of the gate is also shown.

part, expected his subjects to obey his commands, and he counted on the priests to bolster his authority. In return he granted the most cooperative cities privileges and benefits, such as exemption from taxes. If city dwellers detected even a hint of weakness on the part of their ruler, they might revolt in search of a more effective king.

Religion not only gave the Babylonians a profound sense of spiritual security, it also expanded their scientific knowledge. Babylonians believed that the Earth and the sky were interrelated. In their view, proper interpretation of the celestial bodies through astronomy could help them understand the meaning of daily events as well as the will of the gods. Building on the Sumerians' mathematical and astronomical legacy, Babylonian astronomers patiently observed and recorded the movements of the stars, the planets, and the moon. They kept a continuous log of observations between 747 B.C.E. and 61 C.E., an astonishing achievement. Starting around 500 B.C.E., they had accumulated so much information about the movements of the planets and stars that they could perform complicated mathematical computations to predict eclipses of the moon and sun. They also calculated the first appearance of the new moon every month, which enabled them to devise a calendar. These astronomers' brilliant calculations, which Persians and Greeks would later adopt, have helped lay the foundation of Western science. From these able scientists, the West has inherited the names of many constellations, the zodiac, and many complex mathematical models of astronomical phenomena.

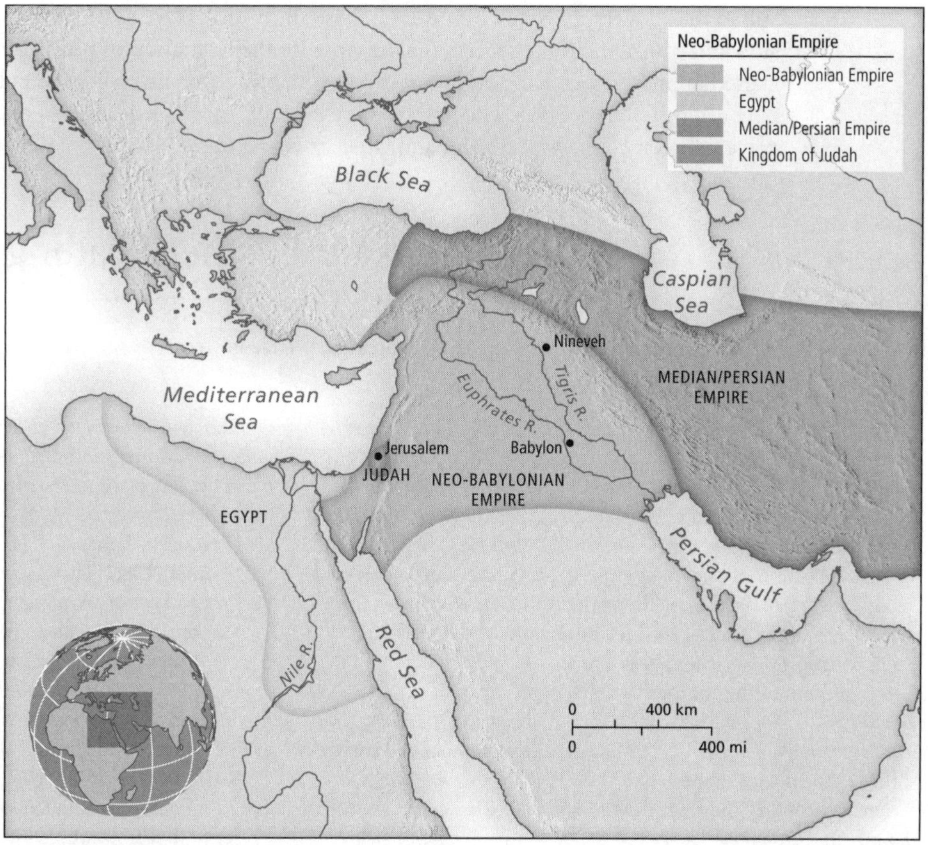

Map 2.7
The Neo-Babylonian Empire, ca. 580 B.C.E.
By ca. 580 B.C.E., the Neo-Babylonian Empire had replaced the Neo-Assyrian Empire as the dominant power in the Middle East.

CONCLUSION

The International Bronze Age and the Emergence of the West

The International Bronze Age marked an early but crucial phase in the formation of Western civilization. Within a large geographical area centered on the eastern Mediterranean but stretching far beyond its shores, an intricate network of political, commercial, and cultural ties was established among cities and kingdoms that had previously lived in relative isolation from each other. During the International Bronze Age this geographical area extended to Mesopotamia in the east, Nubia in the south, and Greece and Anatolia in the north. The forces that exposed the cultures of these areas to each other were the expansion of international trade, the development of a new military technology, the growth of large, multiethnic empires, and the establishment of diplomatic relations among rulers.

The encounters that took place among the peoples of these lands contributed to the emergence of Western civilization. Long before it was possible to identify what we now call the West, the exchange of commodities, the spread of religious ideas, the growth of common political traditions, the dissemination of scientific and technological techniques, and the borrowing of one language from another created a complex pattern of cultural diffusion over a vast geographical area.

During subsequent centuries the content of such cultural exchange would change, and the geographical area within which the exchanges took place would shift, first to the lands controlled by Persia, then to the Hellenistic world conquered by Alexander the Great, and later still to the sprawling Roman Empire. All these shifts took place as the result of imperial expansion and consolidation, a process that began with the formation of multiethnic empires discussed in this chapter. Each period of expansion, moreover, involved new cultural encounters between different peoples. The first of these periods, in which a series of encounters took place between Hebrews, Persians, and Greeks, will be the subject of the next chapter.

Suggestions for Further Reading

For a comprehensive list of suggested readings, please go to www.ablongman.com/levack/chapter2

Bryce, Trevor. *The Kingdom of the Hittites* 1998. The latest synthesis of Hittite history and culture.

Cline, Eric H., and Diane Harris-Cline, eds. *The Aegean and the Orient in the Second Millennium: Proceedings of the 50th Anniversary Symposium, Cincinnati, 18–20 April 1997, Aegaeum* 18. 1998. A collection of papers by experts providing state-of-the-art discussions of all aspects of the connections among Bronze Age civilizations of the eastern Mediterranean and Middle East.

Dickinson, Oliver. *The Aegean Bronze Age.* 1994. Now the standard treatment of the complex archaeological data.

Dothan, Trude, and Moshe Dothan. *People of the Sea: The Search for the Philistines.* 1992. A recent, highly popularized survey of the archaeological material.

Drews, Robert. *The End of the Bronze Age: Changes in Warfare and the Catastrophe ca. 1200 B.C.* 1993. A controversial but well-argued analysis that offers new solutions to the question of why the Bronze Age ended.

Fitton, J. Lesley. *The Discovery of the Greek Bronze Age.* 1996. A lucid and well-illustrated study of the archaeologists who brought the Greek Bronze Age to light in the nineteenth and early twentieth centuries.

Harding, A. F. *The Mycenaeans in Europe.* 1984. Exploration of the trade and cultural connections between Mycenaeans and the rest of Europe.

Hornung, Erik. *History of Ancient Egypt: An Introduction,* trans. David Lorton. 1999. A concise and lucid overview of Egyptian history and life.

Knapp, A. Bernard. *The History and Culture of Ancient Western Asia and Egypt.* 1988. A reliable archaeological and historical overview without excessive detail.

Kuhrt, Amelie. *The Ancient Middle East, ca. 3000–330 B.C.,* 2 vols. 1995. A magisterial, up-to-date overview, with excellent bibliography. The place to start for a continuous historical narrative of the region.

Macqueen, James G. *The Hittites and their Contemporaries in Asia Minor.* 1986. This account stresses the interconnections of Hittites and other peoples.

Markoe, Glenn. *Phoenicians.* 2000. The best and most up-to-date treatment of Phoenician society by a noted expert.

Page, Denys. *History and the Homeric Iliad.* 1959. An entertaining and provocative examination of the historical context of the events described in Homer's *Iliad.*

Redford, Donald B. *Egypt, Canaan and Israel in Ancient Times.* 1992. An excellent, detailed synthesis of textual and archaeological evidence that emphasizes interconnections among cultures.

Schulz, Regine, and Matthias Seidel, eds. *Egypt: The World of the Pharaohs.* 1999. A sumptuously illustrated collection of essays on all aspects of Egyptian society and life by leading experts.

Traill, David. *Schliemann of Troy: Treasure and Deceit.* 1995. A fascinating discussion of the motivations and methods of the archaeologist who discovered the Bronze Age.

Walker, Christopher, ed. *Astronomy Before the Telescope.* 1996. A fascinating collection of essays about astronomy in the premodern period, which makes clear Western civilization's enormous debt to the Babylonians.

Wood, Michael. *In Search of the Trojan War.* 1985. A valuable introductory discussion of the archaeological and historical problems of placing Homer's Trojan War in its Bronze Age context.

Notes

1. T. Eric Peet, *The Great Tomb Robberies of the Twentieth Egyptian Dynasty,* I–II, (Oxford, 1930) reprinted in one volume (Hildesheim, 1977). (Contains texts and translations of this and other trials.)
2. Regina Schulz and Matthias Seidel, eds., *Egypt: The World of the Pharaohs* (1998), p. 485.
3. Trevor Bryce, *The Kingdom of the Hittites* (1998), pp. 195–199.
4. A. Khurt, *The Ancient Middle East,* vol. I (1995), p. 242.
5. W. G. Lambert, "The Gula Hymn of Bullutsa-rabi," *Orientalia* n.s.36 (1967), p. 121.
6. Translated in Kuhrt, pp. 350–351.
7. Donald Redford, *Egypt, Canaan, and Israel in Ancient Times* (1992), 251, 256, with some changes.

CHAPTER

3

Building the Classical World: Hebrews, Persians, and Greeks, 1100–336 B.C.E.

IN THE SECOND HALF OF THE SIXTH CENTURY B.C.E., CYRUS THE GREAT, A PERSIAN king from southern Iran, created the largest empire the world had ever seen, with territories in Asia, the Middle East, Africa, and Europe. According to one of the many legends surrounding this celebrated ruler, Cyrus grew restless as a young man under the rule of another king. He summoned the Persian tribal leaders who owed him allegiance and instructed them to spend a day clearing land with sickles. When they finally stopped their backbreaking labor, he invited them to a magnificent banquet. After the men had devoured the last delicacy, Cyrus asked them which they enjoyed more, tasting the wonderful food or sweating in the fields. The chieftains shouted in unison that they preferred the wine and fine foods. Cyrus then proclaimed:

> *Men of Persia, follow me and I promise that you will enjoy this sort of luxury for he rest of your lives, but if you do not, your lives will be full of painful toil with no such rewards from your present masters.*[1]

Without hesitation the men joined Cyrus in his successful revolt. Under his able leadership the Persians conquered more than twenty-three different peoples in territories ranging from the eastern Mediterranean coast to Central Asia. Cyrus's successors added Egypt and parts of Greece and India to the Persian Empire. With its huge expanse and the stable government it provided to an enormous mix of cultures, Persia marked a turning point in the history of the ancient world.

This chapter examines the civilizations that developed during the six centuries that followed the collapse of the International Bronze Age around 1100 B.C.E. When long-distance trade in copper and tin broke down at that time, iron

Persian Art: Persian artists drew freely from the artistic traditions of their subject peoples. This illustration shows how they put their own stamp on the Babylonian art of ceramic tile. The tiles show two members of the elite imperial guard, known as the Immortals. The details of their uniforms appear in vivid color. Soldiers like these in Xerxes's army fell to the Greeks in the fifth century B.C.E.

became the preferred metal for making tools and weapons throughout the ancient world. As a result of the widespread use of iron, archaeologists refer to the new period as the Iron Age. Most historians, however, refer to the period that began after 1100 B.C.E. as the Classical Age because of the distinctive religious, political, and cultural innovations and transformations that resulted from Persian encounters with other peoples, particularly the Hebrews and Greeks.

For two centuries after Cyrus's death, the Persian empire prospered as its leaders methodically expanded their territory abroad and shrewdly managed their many subject peoples. The interaction of local cultures with Persian culture made an indelible impression on the history of the West. From their Assyrian and Babylonian subjects, the Persians inherited –and improved upon—a political legacy of ruling a multi-ethnic empire. They also benefited from a scientific legacy that stretched back to the Sumerians. The Persians' capacity to borrow and adapt the most useful features of other cultures strengthened their own highly organized and justly administered empire.

In addition to developing their own dynamic culture, the Persians made possible the spread of two highly influential ideas in the Western tradition, although they did not originally conceive of them. The first of these ideas was monotheism°, the belief in only one god. This concept originated with the Hebrews about 1000 B.C.E. During the Classical Age, the Hebrews came under Persian rule. As a consequence, Hebrew religion was transformed into Judaism under the blanket of Persian imperial administration. The idea of monotheism became the core principle of Judaism and Christianity. Followers of Islam also link their faith to the tradition of biblical monotheism.

The second idea was democracy°, the conviction that people should share equally in the government of their community, devise their own governing institutions, and select their own leaders. Originating in the Greek city-state of Athens in the sixth century B.C.E., democratic institutions helped the Athenians repel several Persian invasions in the fifth century B.C.E. When the Persian threat ended, democratic institutions in Athens flourished even more. Athenian victory over the Persians gave Athens the economic stability and security needed for their governmental institutions to become more democratic. Artists and thinkers flourished in Athens' creative atmosphere during the Classical Age. They established philosophical schools, where students learned to examine the validity of every assumption and to explain natural phenomena without referring to the gods. Drama became a powerful moral voice in Greek society, providing a mirror in which the audience could judge themselves and their community. In sculpture, architecture, and other arts, they created the distinctive Greek classical style, which influenced the Romans, and has continued to be a source of inspiration in Western civilization up to the present day.

In many respects, the Classical Age created the most lasting cultural foundations of the West, foundations built on Hebrew monotheism and ethics and Greek philosophy and arts—all against the backdrop of Persian imperial power.

To understand how the Classical Age came together from so many cultural elements, we will explore these questions: (1) What political and religious beliefs and institutions gave Hebrew civilization its unique character, and what consequences came of its interactions with the Assyrians, Babylonians, and Persians? (2) How did the Persian Empire bring these peoples of the Middle East together in a stable realm, and what elements of Persian religion and government have influenced Western thought? (3) How did Greek city-states develop in the framework of a larger world dominated by Persia? (4) What were the intellectual, social, and political innovations of Greece in the Classical Age?

Hebrew Civilization and Religion

One of the most influential civilizations in the West has been that of the Jews, a people who originated in the Middle East when the International Bronze Age came to an end. As we saw in Chapter 2, the Raiders of the Land and Sea destroyed many Canaanite cities around 1100 B.C.E. and caused great upheaval among the local populations. At about the same time, different groups of semi-nomadic pastoralists, called *Hapiru* ("landless people"), began to migrate into the hill country of Canaan, where they settled, herded their flocks, and began farming. Some historians think that this settlement was the origin of the biblical Hebrews, who gradually cohered into tribes and then kingdoms.

THE SETTLEMENT IN CANAAN

If these historians are correct, sometime around 1100 one small group of wandering Hapiru arrived in Canaan from Egypt, bringing with them the seeds of a powerful new religious belief. They gave allegiance to only one god. Belief in this deity gave them a strong sense of identity and distinguished them from the Canaanite peoples, who worshiped many gods. These followers of one god became known as Hebrews, then Israelites, and later Jews. Many centuries later, their traditions explained that a leader called Moses had led them from slavery in Egypt to freedom in Canaan, and that he had communicated God's law to them. Known today as the Ten Commandments, these laws forbid such acts as murder, theft, lying, and worshiping other gods, as apparently some Hebrews continued to do.

By absorbing new members and conquering other groups, a loose confederation of tribes gained control of most of Canaan during the eleventh century B.C.E. Impressed by the Hebrew victories, many Canaanites began to worship the Hebrew God and joined the Hebrew tribes. Gradually these various tribes came to believe that they all shared a common history and a common ancestor, Abraham, who had traveled to Canaan from his home in Mesopotamia long before Moses. According to biblical tradition, Abraham was the first person to worship only one god. For this reason, he is considered the first Hebrew monotheist and the ancestor of the Jews.

The Hebrew tribes built shrines to their God throughout Canaan. The most important religious site was the shrine in the town of Shiloh, where they celebrated their allegiance to their God and settled disputes about property, inheritance, and crime. They kept their most sacred object, the Ark of the Covenant, in this shrine. The Ark of the Covenant was a gold-covered box that reputedly contained a divine and mysterious power. Concealed from the sight of everyone but the priests who organized God's worship, the Ark symbolized the connection between God and his followers as well as the unity of all the Hebrew tribes.

The confederation of Hebrew tribes faced many enemies in Canaan. The most serious threat came from the Philistines, who were descendants of a group of Raiders of the land and Sea called the Peleset. They controlled the Mediterranean coastal plain in Canaan and pushed relentlessly at the Hebrews living in the inland hills. Around 1050 B.C.E., a Philistine army defeated the Hebrew tribes in battle, captured the ark of the Covenant, and destroyed Shiloh. According to traditions recorded in the Bible, the desperate Hebrews chose a king to give them stronger leadership, even though tribal tradition was hostile to the notion of kings. The tribes chose Saul to be the first king about 1020 B.C.E, and he retrieved the Ark from the Philistines. Some twenty years later, a popular warrior, in Saul's court named David succeeded Saul as king and reigned from approximately 1000 to 962 B.C.E.

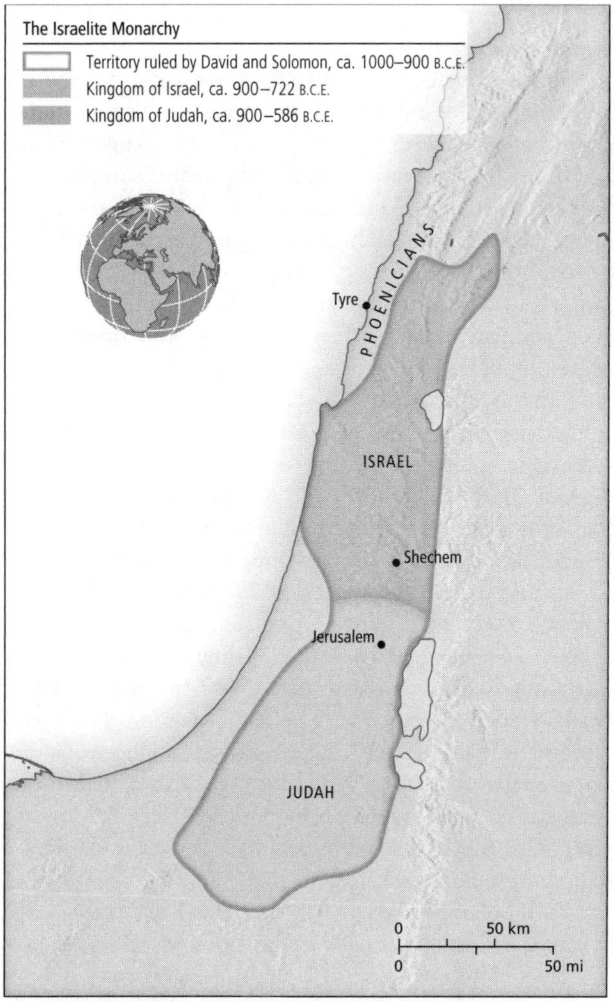

Map 3.1 The Iraelite Monarchy
The kingdom established by David (ca. 1000–962 B.C.E.) and expanded by his son Solomon (ca. 962–922 B.C.E.) unified the Hebrew tribes of Canaan. At Solomon's death, the realm divided into two smaller kingdoms. Assyrian armies destroyed the northern kingdom of Israel in 722 B.C.E., and Babylonian forces destroyed the southern kingdom of Judah in 587 B.C.E.

THE ISRAELITE KINGDOMS

David was a talented monarch. By establishing a strong alliance among the Hebrew tribes of northern and southern Canaan, he defeated the Philistines permanently and built a prosperous kingdom. Called the Israelite monarchy by historians, this kingdom lay sandwiched between the empires of Egypt and Mesopotamia. By imitating the government institutions of these neighboring states, David transformed the nature of Israelite society. He set up a centralized bureaucracy run by professional soldiers, administrators, and scribes. David established a census as the basis for tax collection and military conscription, and he created a royal court complete with a harem. Jerusalem, an old Canaanite city, served as the capital of his new kingdom. He moved the Ark of the Covenant from Shiloh to Jerusalem, bringing the worship of the Hebrew God under the control of the monarchy.

During the reign of David's son Solomon (ca. 962–922 B.C.E.), the kingdom of Israel enjoyed peace and prosperity. One of Solomon's greatest achievements was the construction of a grand temple in Jerusalem to serve as the house of God and a resting place for the Ark of the Covenant. Constructed with the technical assistance of architects and craftsmen from the neighboring Phoenician kingdom of Tyre and the forced labor of Solomon's subjects, the

Jerusalem temple became the focal point of religious worship in his kingdom.

Solomon pursued an ambitious foreign policy devoted to developing long-distance commerce. He controlled the major trade routes running from Egypt and Arabia to Syria, and under his supervision Israelite merchants prospered as middlemen in an expanding system of international commerce. Under his leadership, the kingdom enjoyed substantial control over the trade of horses sent south from Asia Minor and chariots sent north from Egypt. Solomon developed his own corps of charioteers to protect these trade routes from bandits.

With the assistance of Phoenician shipbuilders, Solomon constructed a merchant fleet for trade in the Red Sea. His merchants sailed as far south as Somalia, the portion of the African coast that touches the Arabian Sea, from where they brought jewels, gold, ivory, and other items of luxury. In addition, Solomon also developed overland trade with Arabia and established economic ties with the kingdom of Sabaea (Sheba) in Yemen. According to tradition, the Queen of Sheba visited Solomon, bringing delightful gifts including spices from east Asia. What Solomon's merchants traded in return is uncertain. Solomon developed diplomatic relations with Egypt, as well as the seafaring Phoenicians, and other kingdoms in Africa and Middle East. He married foreign princesses in order to cement diplomatic ties, and he permitted his wives to build shrines to gods of their homelands.

When Solomon died in 922 B.C.E., his heirs' inability to placate the northern Israelite tribes, which felt that Solomon had favored his own tribe of Judah at their expense, caused the Israelite kingdom to break into two parts. The kingdom of Israel, in the northern region of the former kingdom, established its capital at Shechem and remained reasonably stable in comparison to its southern rival. In the southern kingdom of Judah, Solomon's successors retained Jerusalem as its capital, but political stability remained elusive for them due to dynastic instability and quarrels among the leaders. Only for two brief periods did the kingdom of Judah enjoy stable government. Over the two centuries after 922 B.C.E., however, both of the two successor kingdoms struggled to survive under the shadow of the far more powerful neighboring empires of Assyria and Babylonia. During these tumultuous centuries, the gap between the rich and the poor in both kingdoms widened. The upper classes grew extremely wealthy from trade and the accumulation of land, which they acquired from the indebted poor. In their anguish the poor called out for social justice, a cry heard by the prophets.

The Hebrew Prophets

Rapacious kings, greedy aristocrats, and high taxes meant that more and more debt-ridden peasants lost their farms to rich landholders. The poor found champions in the Hebrew prophets, men who spoke out on behalf of the downtrodden with words they believed to be inspired by God. These social critics strongly censured what they saw as religious and moral decay among the landowners and kings, such as the worship of Canaanite gods, a practice that remained widespread. They urged the entire population toward moral reform and spiritual consciousness. The prophet Elijah, who lived in the ninth century B.C.E., proclaimed that kings should not break the laws with impunity but should conform to the same laws as everyone else. The principle that kings and rulers are not above the law remained as a basic political idea in what eventually became the West. In the next century, another champion of social justice named Amos mocked the irony and hypocrisy of the royal court's celebrating lavish religious ceremonies in God's name while the poor starved. Isaiah, a prophet who lived in Jerusalem, demanded that people attempt to establish a just society in order to avert divine punishment. He had no patience for religious observance empty of personal commitment. According to Isaiah, God said:

> *What need have I of all your sacrifices? . . . I am sated with burnt offerings of sacrificial rams . . . Incense in offensive to me. . . . though you pray at length, I will not listen. Your hands are stained with crime. Wash yourselves clean; Put your evil doings away from my sight. Cease to do evil; learn to do good; devote yourself to justice; aid the wronged. Uphold the rights of the orphan. Defend the cause of the widow. [Isaiah 1: 11–17]*

Preoccupied with internal problems, the Israelites failed to note the growing power of the neighboring Assyrian Empire As we saw in Chapter 2, Assyrian armies under the command of king Tiglath-Pileser conquered the Israelite kingdom. In 722 B.C.E. Eleven years later, when the Israelite ruler refused to pay tribute, the Assyrians destroyed the kingdom and deported nearly 30,000 Israelites to Mesopotamia, a standard Assyrian practice with defeated enemies. The deported people, known as the Lost Ten Tribes, forgot their cultural identity in their new homes and disappeared from the historical record. The Kingdom of Israel had come to an undignified end.

The kingdom of Judah, however, survived. By accepting the overlordship of the Assyrians and later the Babylonians, who had replaced the Assyrians as the dominant power in the Middle East by the late seventh century B.C.E., Judah escaped Israel's fate. After the destruction of the northern kingdom, a mood of religious reform spread throughout Judah. People began to believe that God had destroyed the kingdom of Israel in anger, though they disagreed about the causes of his rage and how to appease him.

To regain God's favor, some of Judah's leaders insisted on the absolute primacy of the temple in Jerusalem as the place for religious worship on the assumption that God disapproved of his followers worshiping him at many shrines instead of only one. By insisting on Jerusalem as the sole place of worship, the priests of Jerusalem increased their power. With the help of the king's soldiers, the temple priests in Jerusalem violently suppressed all other shrines to God scattered across the land. The consequence was greater uniformity of worship among the Hebrews and a centralized religious authority. These developments enhanced a sense of Hebrew identity.

Some Hebrew prophets, however, sought to appease God by countering this trend. They challenged the supremacy of the Jerusalem priests and emphasized the need for personal reform and the creation of a just society. One of these prophets was Jeremiah, who began preaching in 627 B.C.E. In the tradition of Isaiah, he placed little value on the strength of the temple priesthood's prayers on Judah's behalf. He predicted that God would cause the Babylonians to destroy Judah because its people were corrupt. Jeremiah's predictions proved correct. When Judah revolted against the Babylonians in 598 B.C.E., the Babylonian king Nebuchadnezzar sent a large army to put down the rebellion. The next year he captured Jerusalem and deported Judah's king and high priests to Babylonia. Ten years later, when another revolt broke out, Babylonian forces burned Jerusalem to the ground and demolished Solomon's temple, the spiritual and political center of the kingdom of Judah. Perhaps as many as 20,000 people were deported to Babylonia, an event historians call the Babylonian Exile°.

The Babylonian Exile

After the destruction of the Jerusalem temple in 587 B.C.E., the Hebrew exiles living in Babylon struggled to maintain their cultural and religious identity. But Babylonian culture influenced their religious practice. Babylonian astronomy contributed to the institution of a seven-day week (and perhaps sabbath worship on the seventh day). The Hebrews developed a calendar that adopted Babylonian names of months. The Babylonian month Nissanu is the same as the Hebrew month Nisan. Like the Babylonians, the Hebrew exiles structured their calendar around seasonal festivals. The exiles added their own new religious celebrations to the structure provided by the Babylonian calendar. The Hebrews observed a New Year's Day and a Day of Atonement in the autumn. In the spring they celebrated Passover, the commemoration of the departure of the Hebrews from Egypt under the leadership of Moses.

Sometime after the year 538 B.C.E., an anonymous author, referred to as Second Isaiah, comforted the dispirited Hebrews in Babylonia. Trying to find meaning in the destruction of the kingdoms of Israel and Judah, he explained that God's primary interest lay in the human spirit, not in earthly kingdoms. The God described by Second Isaiah was a truly universal God who alone governs all creation and shapes the lives of all the peoples of the world. This vision of a single universal God not bound by time or place was perhaps the greatest legacy of civilization.

Second Isaiah promised that God would return his people to Jerusalem and that Cyrus the Great King of Persia would serve as God's agent in this task. The reference to the Persian king demonstrates that Second Isaiah wrote sometime after 538 B.C.E., when Cyrus instituted a policy permitting all peoples exiled by the Babylonians return to their homelands (we will learn more about this policy shortly). Many of the Hebrew exiles in Babylonia returned to their old homes, now governed by Persia, and attempted to revive traditional religious life in Jerusalem.

The Second Temple and Jewish Religious Practice

Nearly two generations passed before the Hebrews, with Persian assistance, finished building a new temple in Jerusalem, called the Second Temple. In 458 B.C.E., with the authority of the Persian king, a leader called Ezra the Scribe began to organize and regulate religious practices. He instituted regular sabbath worship and began a program of teaching religious law to the population. For the next 500 years this restored temple worship would be the center of religious life. Historians call the Hebrews who lived after the completion of the Second Temple Jews. Henceforth, the people are known as Jews and their religion is called Judaism.

CHRONOLOGY

	The Israelite Kingdom
CA. 1250 B.C.E.	Traditional date of Hapiru Exodus from Egypt to Canaan
1100 B.C.E.	The International Bronze Age ends; Philistines arrive in Canaan
1000–922 B.C.E.	David and Solomon rule the Israelite kingdom
922 B.C.E.	The Israelite kingdom splits into Judah (southern kingdom) and Israel (northern kingdom)
CA. 800 B.C.E.	Prophets begin to preach moral reform
721 B.C.E.	Assyrians destroy northern kingdom (Israel)
587 B.C.E.	Babylonians defeat southern kingdom (Judah) and destroy Jerusalem and the Temple
538 B.C.E.	Cyrus of Persia permits Israelites to return to Palestine and rebuild Temple

Second Temple
This recreation of the Second Temple in Jerusalem is based on all current archaeological and literary evidence available. Smoke from a sacrifice can be seen rising from the altar in the center of the sanctuary.

Ezra and other religious thinkers believed that God had destroyed the kingdoms of Israel and Judah before the Babylonian Exile because the people had failed to observe religious law properly. For this reason, knowledge of the law (or Torah) through study and observance now became all-important for the preservation of the Jewish community and Jewish identity. In particular, the priesthood in Jerusalem, who controlled secular and religious affairs, insisted on very strict observance of laws concerning temple sacrifice and ritual. The priests also made decisions that determined the status of women in Jewish society. By deciding that descent through the mother determined Jewish identity, they gave women a crucial role within Judaism. Membership in the Jewish community depended on who your mother was, a situation that enhanced the status of Jewish wives.

Despite these reforms, the public role of women in organized worship grew quite restricted. Prior to the Babylonian exile, women participated in worship as priestesses, singers, and dancers. Canaanite religion gave a high status to female goddesses of fertility, and Israelite women sometimes participated in their cults as well. In the Second Temple period, however, the Jews worshipped only one male god and denied all other deities. Women could not enter the most sacred portions of the temple where the main sacrifices were performed, because according to religious law the blood of menstruation and childbirth made them ritually unclean. Many of these ancient attitudes regarding the place of women in religious and family life have survived to the present day, especially in the exclusion of women from the most sacred rituals and responsibilities in some kinds of Judaism and Christianity.

The Hebrew Bible

After the second temple was built in 515 B.C.E., the Hebrew Bible (called the Old Testament by Christians) slowly took the shape it has today. Like many other peoples in the ancient Middle East, the Hebrews believed that their God had chosen them to serve him. They believed that historical events described in the Bible illustrate and interpret that relationship. As a historical document, the Hebrew Bible provides a chronology of the world from the moment of its creation and gives an account of the early development of the Hebrew people. Drawn from a variety of oral and written sources, and composed many centuries after the events they describe, the biblical accounts condense and simplify a

TALES OF THE FLOOD

One of the most popular tales of the Classical age, a god destroys the earth in a great flood but permits some humans to survive on a boat and repopulate the earth once the waters had subsided. Here we see excerpts from three versions of the flood story composed by Babylonians, Hebrews, and Greeks. The similarities indicate encounters among these cultures through the oldest of pleasures: telling stories.

THE EPIC OF GILGAMESH: HOW THE GODS SHARED UT-NAPISHTI'S

[Everything I owned] I loaded aboard:
all the silver I owned I loaded aboard,
all the gold I owned I loaded abroad,
all the living creatures I had I loaded aboard.
I sent on board all my kith and kin,
the beasts of the field, the creatures of the wild, and
members of every skill and craft . . .
. . . . . . For six days and [seven] nights,
there blew the wind, the downpour,
the gale, the Deluge, it flattened land.
But the seventh day when it came,
the gale relented, the Deluge ended.
The ocean grew calm, that had thrashed like a woman in
labour,
the tempest grew still, the Deluge ended . . .
Enlil [a powerful god] came up inside the boat,
[and blessed Uta-napishti and his wife, saying:]
In the past Uta-napishti was a mortal man,
but now he and his wife shall become like us gods!

THE HEBREW BIBLE: NOAH'S STORY

Then the Lord said to Noah, "Go into the ark with all your household, for you alone have I found righteous before Me in this generation. Of every clean animal you shall take seven pairs, males and their mates, and of every animal that is not clean, two, a male and its mate. Of the birds of the sky, also . . . . . . For in seven days I will make it rain upon the earth, forty days and forty nights, and I will blot out from the earth all existence that I created. And Noah did just as the Lord commanded him. . . . And on the seventh day the waters of the Flood came upon the earth. . . .

GREEK MYTHOLOGY: DEUCALION'S STORY

In this Greek tale, King Deucalion survives because his father, the god Prometheus, warns him.

When Zeus, the king of the gods, decided to destroy humankind . . . Deucalion by the advice of Prometheus constructed a chest, and having stored it with provisions he embarked in it with Pyrrha, his wife. But Zeus, by pouring heavy rain from heaven flooded the greater part of Greece, so that all men were destroyed, except for a few who fled to high mountains in the neighborhood. . . . But Deucalion, floating in the chest over the sea for nine days and as many nights, drifted to Mount Parnassus, and there, when the rain ceased, he landed and sacrificed to Zeus . . . And Zeus . . . allowed Deucalion to choose whatever he wished, and he chose to create men. At the bidding of Zeus, he picked up stones and threw them over his head, and the stones became men, and the stones that Pyrrha threw became women. . . .

Sources: From *The Epic of Gilgamesh: The Babylonian Epic Poem and Other Texts in Akkadian and Sumerian,* translated by Andrew George (Allen Lane The Penguin Press, 1999). Translation copyright © 1999 by Andrew George. Reproduced by permission of Penguin Books Ltd.; from *Tanakh, A New Translation of The Holy Scriptures According to the Traditional Hebrew Text,* 1985, Exodus 7-8. Published by the Jewish Publication Society.; and Reprinted by permission of the publishers and the Trustees of the Loeb Classical Library from *Apollodorus: Volume I,* Loeb Classical Library Volume L 121, translated by J. G. Frazer, Cambridge, Mass.: Harvard University Press, 1921. The Loeb Classical Library ® is a registered trademark of the President and Fellows of Harvard College.

very complex process of migration, settlement, and religious development.

Many details in the Bible have been confirmed by non-Hebrew sources, but the Bible must be understood primarily as an expression of religious meaning through historical traditions of different sorts. It combines highly detailed narratives with folklore, prophecies, parables, stories, and poems. The Bible provided far more than the narration of events. It explains God's presence in human lives and establishes a moral vision of human existence. As a result no book has had more influence on the religious thought of the West.

For historians, the significance of the Hebrew Bible lies in the religious principles that its stories illustrate. The book describes a single God who protects the Earth and his chosen people, the Hebrews. Historical events demonstrate his concern for them, for he punishes and rewards his people in accordance with their actions. In the Hebrew Bible, events such as the restoration of the temple in Jerusalem by Cyrus, have significance in terms of a divine plan and the fulfillment of prophecy. As part of this divine plan, God expects his followers to follow a strict code of compassionate, ethical behavior, toward their fellow human beings. As a religious work the Hebrew Bible provides the basis of

Judaism. In conjunction with the New Testament, written in the first century C.E., it is the core text of Christianity. Muslims also recognize both the Hebrew and Christian texts as holy writings, superceded only by the Qur'an.

The Second Temple was built and the Hebrew Bible took shape under Persian rule. We turn now to see how the Persian Empire developed and gained control over the peoples of the Middle East.

Classical Persia: An Empire on Three Continents

Persian history began about 1400 B.C.E., when small groups of people started migrating with their herds and flocks into western Iran from areas north of the Caspian Sea. Over five centuries these settlers slowly coalesced into two closely related groups, the Medes and the Persians.

The Medes organized a loose confederation of tribes in western Iran and began to expand their territory. By about 900 B.C.E., they established mastery over the entire Iranian plateau, including the Persians. In 612 B.C.E., with the assistance of the Babylonians, the Medes conquered the Assyrians. Then they pushed into central Asia Minor (modern Turkey), Afghanistan, and possibly farther into central Asia. In the sixth century, Persia broke away from Medean rule under the leadership of Cyrus the Great (r. 550 B.C.E.–530 B.C.E.), and soon conquered the kingdom of the Medes. Under the guidance of this brilliant monarch and his successors, the Persians acquired a vast empire. They followed a monotheistic religion, Zoroastrianism, and governed their subjects with a combination of tolerance and firmness.

CYRUS THE GREAT AND PERSIAN EXPANSION

After ascending the Persian throne about 550 B.C.E., Cyrus embarked on a dazzling twenty-year career of conquering neighboring peoples. His military genius and organizational skills transformed the small kingdom near the Persian Gulf into a giant, multiethnic empire that stretched from India to the Mediterranean Sea. Cyrus's swift victory over the Medes put Persia at the center of the Middle East and thrust it into face-to-face encounters with a diverse array of peoples.

Cyrus expanded his empire beyond Persia in several stages. In 547 B.C.E. he conquered Asia Minor, where he first came into contact with Greeks living on the westernmost coast and islands, a region called Ionia. Cyrus conquered these Ionian Greek cities and installed loyal Greek administrators. Next he defeated the kingdom of Babylonia in 539 B.C.E., thus gaining control of the entire Mesopotamian region. After that he brought Afghanistan under his control and fortified it against the raids of the Scythian nomads, who posed a perpetual threat to the settled territories of Persia.

photo to come .324

Scythian Nomads
A Scythian nomad strings his bow. The Greek artist who made this bowl pays scrupulous attention to the details of the Scythian's clothing, including his leggings, peaked cap, and tunic.

With his borders expanded and secured, Cyrus turned his attention to the welfare of his Persian homeland. Dissatisfied with his capital city of Susa, he founded a spacious new capital city called Pasargadae. Builders, craftsmen, artists, and merchants flocked to it from Asia Minor, Egypt, Mesopotamia, and Greece. Inspired by Cyrus's brilliant leadership, these artisans turned the new capital into a cosmopolitan city of tremendous ethnic diversity.

After Cyrus died in 529 B.C.E. fighting against steppe nomads north of Persia, his son Cambyses II (r. 529–522 B.C.E.) continued his father's policy of expansion by subduing Egypt and the wealthy Phoenician port cities. The capture at Phoenicia gave the Persians a new strategic advantage. With control of Phoenician naval resources, the Persian Empire could reach overseas, in a way that the landlocked Hittites could not during the International Bronze Age. Phoenician fleets became an integral part of the Persia's invasion of Greece, as we will see later in this chapter. By the time of Cambyses' death in 522 B.C.E., Persia had become the mightiest empire in the world, with territorial possessions spanning Europe, Asia, the Middle East and Africa.

To ensure that they could easily communicate with their subjects, the Great Kings of Persia established an elaborate system of roads to link their provinces. Special officials maintained supply stations at regular intervals along these roads. The chief branch of this system, called the Royal Road, stretched between Asia Minor and the Persian homeland. Persian road building was an indication of the sophistication of the Great Kings in managing an empire. Along these roads flowed not just soldiers but merchants and goods, and with this trade subjects of the Persian Empire exchanged ideas as well.

A Government of Tolerance

The key to maintaining power of such a diverse population lay in the Persian government's treatment of its many ethnic groups. The highly centralized Persian government wielded absolute power, but it rejected the model of the Assyrian and Babylonian imperial system in favor of a more tolerant approach.

As we saw in the case of the Hebrews, Cyrus began a popular policy of allowing peoples exile by the Babylonians to return to their homelands. He proclaimed:

> *I am Cyrus, the king of the world. Marduk, the great god, rejoices at my pious acts . . . I gathered all their peoples and led them back to their abodes . . . and at the order of Marduk . . . I had all the gods [of exiled peoples] installed in their sanctuaries . . . May all the gods whom I have led back to their cities pray daily for the length of my days.*[2]

Map 3.2 The Persian Empire at Its Greatest Extent

The Persian Empire begun by Cyrus about 550 B.C.E. grew to include all of the Middle East as far as India, Egypt, and northern Greece. This multi-ethnic, multi-religious empire governed its many peoples firmly but tolerantly.

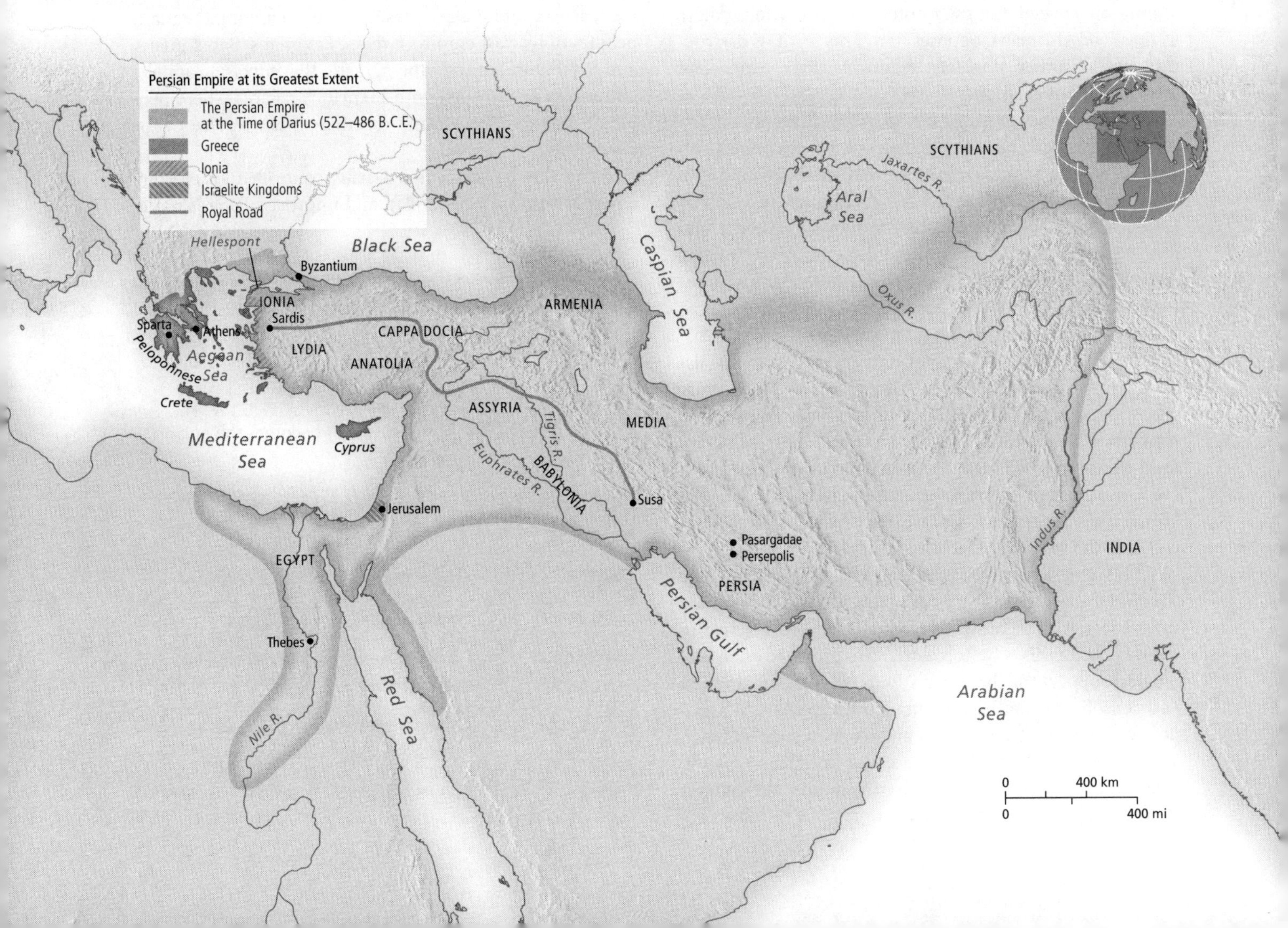

Subject peoples were permitted to worship freely if they acknowledged the political supremacy of the Great king. In this way the Persians won the loyalty and gratitude of their ethnically diverse subjects throughout the empire.

The firm but tolerant methods of governing developed by the Persian government provided a legacy of Western civilization. As we will see in Chapter 4, Greek rulers continue to permit subjects to worship as they wished in the Hellenistic period following Alexander the Great's conquest of Persia.

Zoroastrianism: An Imperial Religion

The Great Kings of Persia and the Persian people followed Zoroastrianism°, a monotheistic religion that still exists today. Its founder, the prophet Zoroaster, lived and preached between 1500 and 1200 B.C.E. His message spread widely throughout Iran for a thousand years before it became Persia's chief faith.

Persians transmitted Zoroaster teachings, known collectively as the *Avesta,* through oral tradition until scribes recorded them in the sixth century C.E. According to Zoroaster, Ahura Mazda (Lord Wisdom), the one and only God of all creation, is the cause of all good things in the universe. He represents wisdom, justice, and proper order among all created things. Another eternal being, Angra Mainyu (or Ahriman), opposes him. This spirit of destruction and disorder threatens Ahura Mazda's benevolent arrangement of creation.

In Zoroastrian belief, Ahura Mazda will eventually triumph in this struggle with the forces of evil, leaving all creation to enjoy a blissful eternity. Until then, the cosmic fight between Ahura Mazda's forces of light and Angra Mainyu's forces of darkness gives meaning to human existence and lays the foundation for a profoundly ethical way of life; Ahura Mazda requires humans to contribute to the well-being of the world. Everyone has the responsibility of choosing between right and wrong actions.

At the last Day of Judgment, sinners who have not listened to Ahura Mazda's instructions, for example, those succumbing to the "filth of intoxication," will suffer eternal torment in a deep pit of terrible darkness. Those who have lived ethical lives will be live eternally in a world purged of evil. In a period of transformation called "the Making Wonderful," the dead will be resurrected, and all will live together in the worship of Ahura Mazda.

The Great Kings of Persia believed themselves to be Ahura Mazda's earthly representatives. They committed their energies to fighting the forces of disorder active in their world. In this way, Zoroastrianism provided as an ideological support for the Persian Empire's wars of conquest and consolidation at home. The Great Kings lavishly supported the Zoroastrian church and its priests, called magi, and established the faith as the empire's official religion. They build grand temples with sacred fires throughout Persian lands. Because Zoroastrian worship at fire altars occurred wherever Persian power expressed itself, the religion became a reminder to subject peoples of an enduring imperial presence around them. Although the Persian Empire tolerated other religions, Zoroastrianism became the official religion that supported the emperor.

Zoroastrian beliefs have played an important role in shaping Western religious thought. The idea of a final judgment followed by an afterlife in heaven or hell became a central concept in Christianity and Islam. Likewise, the idea of a final combat between the Devil and God, followed by the judgment of humanity and the establishment of the kingdom of God on Earth, is still important in many Christian communities.

THE ACHAEMENID DYNASTY

In 522 B.C.E., a Persian nobleman, Darius, seized the throne by murdering one of the sons of Cyrus the Great, and initiated the Achaemenid dynasty. Named for a legendary ancestor, Achaemenes, the new dynasty inaugurated an epoch of territorial expansion and cultural activity that lasted until the Macedonian conqueror Alexander the Great overwhelmed Persia in 330 B.C.E.. Darius built a new capital city at Persepolis. Like Cyrus before him, Darius drew workmen, artists, and material resources from among the many peoples of his vast empire. Greeks, Egyptians, Babylonians, and Scythians, among others, made the imperial capital a glittering city crowded with luxurious palaces where people of many cultures came together in the service of the Great King.

From this power center, Darius controlled an efficient administration. He expanded and improved Persia's roads,

CHRONOLOGY

	Persia
550 B.C.E.	Cyrus begins Persian Empire; Zoroastrianism becomes the empire's religion
546 B.C.E.	The Persians conquer Asia Minor
539 B.C.E.	The Persians capture Babylon
530 B.C.E.	Cyrus dies fighting steppe nomads
525 B.C.E.	Persian troops conquer Egypt
522 B.C.E.	Darius chosen king; the Achaemenid dynasty begins
490 B.C.E.	Greeks stop invasion of Greece at Marathon
480–479 B.C.E.	Failure of Xerxes's invasion of Greece

set up a postal system, and standardized measures and coinage. He also reorganized Cyrus's system of provincial government, dividing the empire into twenty provinces called *satrapies.* Each province paid an annual sum to the central government based on its productivity. The provincial governors, Persian noblemen called *satraps,* collected these taxes and gathered military recruits. In addition, the provincial capitals imitated Persepolis, maintaining administrative archives and serving as local centers of tax collection and bureaucracy. As we will see in the next chapter, this system of administration served as a model for later empires, particularly that of Alexander the Great.

By 513 B.C.E. Darius I had greatly expanded his empire. On his northeastern frontier he annexed portions of India as far as the Indus River. He built a canal in Egypt that linked the Mediterranean and Red Seas. But his conquests on the northwestern frontier of the Persian Empire had the greatest impact on Western civilization because they brought Persia into direct contact with the Greeks. Eager to conquer Greece, Darius sent troops across the Hellespont, the channel of water that separates Europe from Asia, in order to establish military bases in the north of Greece. Such incursions along the Greek frontier were only a small part of Darius' grand imperial strategy, but to the Greeks, the growing Persian presence caused tremendous anxiety. The stage was now set for the confrontation between the Persians and the Greeks, a confrontation that demonstrated the limits of Persian imperialism.

Greece Rebuilds, 1100–479 B.C.E.

As we saw in Chapter 2, at the end of the International Bronze Age Greek civilization entered a period of bitter poverty and political instability. This period, known as the Dark Age, lasted until about 750 B.C.E., when the Archaic Age began. The Archaic Age was marked by economic growth at home and many Greek encounters with Phoenicians and Persians abroad. This period of revival set the stage for Greece's Classical Age, at time of great cultural achievement.

The Dark Ages (ca. 1100–750 B.C.E.)

Compared with the wealth and splendor of the Mycenaean communities, Greek life in the Dark Age was quite gloomy. Few new settlements were established on the mainland and urban life disappeared. Linear B writing dropped out of use entirely, and extensive maritime trade ended. A serious decline in agriculture led to a steep decrease in food production and population.

A slow economic recovery began in the Greek world about 850 B.C.E., for reasons that remain obscure. Because of the harsh living conditions on the mainland during the Dark Age, many Greeks had abandoned their homes and moved to a region called Ionia that encompassed the coasts and islands of western Asia Minor. Relatively isolated from other Greek communities, these pioneers developed their own distinctive Ionian variation of the Greek language. By 800 B.C.E. the Ionian Greeks were regularly interacting with the Phoenicians in the eastern Mediterranean. These seafarers forged a link between Greeks and the cultures of the Middle East that exerted a lasting impact on Greek society because it marked the end of Greek isolation (see map on page 00-00).

The Archaic Age (ca. 750–479 B.C.E.)

Between about 750 and 650 B.C.E., many fresh ideas poured into Greece from the Middle East through contact with the Phoenicians and other peoples. Historians call this exciting period the Archaic Age. Encounters with Middle Eastern poets, merchants, artisans, refugees, doctors, slaves, and spouses brought innovations to Greece: new words such as tyrant and gold; new economic practices such as the use of coinage and charging interest on loans, new myths and literary themes (such as the story of the flood; see document on page 00-00), new ritual procedures for sacrificing animals, new gods and goddesses (such as Dionysus, the god of wine), and new inventions of convenience (such as parasols to provide shade).

By far the most valuable import from the Phoenicians was the alphabet. As we saw in Chapter 2, the Phoenicians, who had been using an alphabet of twenty-two letters for at least three centuries, introduced the system to Greece sometime just before 750 B.C.E. The adoption of the alphabet was one of the developments that marked the beginning of the Archaic Age. Because an alphabet records sounds, not words, it can be adjusted easily for any language. Greeks quickly recognized the potential of the new tool, and quickly adopted it throughout their communities. Greeks learned to write and read, first for business purposes and then for pleasure. They began to record their oral traditions, legends, and songs. At the same time, they began to compose an entirely new literature and write down their laws.

Homer's Epic Poems

Two of the greatest works of epic literature ever composed, the *Iliad* and the *Odyssey,* were soon written down in the new alphabet. A Greek poet named Homer, who probably lived around 750 B.C.E. is credited with composing these poems, but they were certainly not his personal invention. The stories of the *Iliad* and the *Odyssey* drew from a large and widely recited cycle of tales about the legendary Trojan War that wandering poets had recited for centuries. The

Map 3.3 Greece in the Archaic and Classical Ages
During the Archaic and Classical Ages, Greek cities spread from Greece to the shores of the Black Sea and as far west as Italy and southern France. Never unified politically, these cities spoke Greek, worshiped the same gods, and shared a similar culture.

poets had elaborated upon the stories so much over time that all historical accuracy was lost. Nevertheless, many details in the poems, especially about weapons and armor no longer used in Homer's day, suggest that the earliest versions of the poems were first recited in the International Bronze Age and may be very loosely based on events of that time.

The body of poems of which the *Iliad* and the *Odyssey* were a part tells how an army of Greek warriors sailed to Troy, a wealthy city on the northwest coast of Asia Minor, to recover a beautiful Greek princess, Helen, who had been stolen by a Trojan prince. After ten years of savage fighting, the Greeks finally stormed Troy and won the war, though their greatest fighters had died in battle. When the surviving heroes returned home to Greece, they were met with treachery and bloodshed. One of the best known episodes of the Trojan saga (though Homer does not relate it) tells how the Greeks won their final victory by means of a ruse—the most famous deception in literature. The Greeks pretended to abandon their siege of Troy but left behind a hollow wooden horse filled with Greek soldiers. The Trojans dragged the horse into their city, only to permit the Greeks to climb out after dark and open the city gates for their companions. By the next morning, Troy was a smoking ruin.

The genius of Homer lay in his retelling of these old stories. He did not relate the entire saga of the Trojan war because he knew that his audiences were familiar with it. Instead, he selected certain episodes in which he emphasized aspects of human character and emotion in the midst of violent conflict in fresh ways. In the *Iliad*, for example, he describes how the hero Achilles, the mightiest of all the Greeks fighting at Troy, grows angry when his commander-in-chief Agamemnon steals his favorite concubine. In a rage, Achilles withdraws from the battle and returns to fight only to avenge his best friend who had been killed by

Hector, the mainstay of the Trojan defense. Achilles eventually slays Hector, but does not relinquish his fury until Hector's father, Priam, the king of Troy, begs him to return his son's corpse for proper burial. " Honor the Gods, Achilles, and take pity upon me, remembering your own father," implores King Priam, "Yet I am still more pitiful than he. I have endured more than any other mortal: I kiss the hand of the man who has killed my sons." Achilles relents and weeps, his humanity finally restored after so much killing. In Homer's hands, the story of Achilles's anger becomes a profound investigation into human alienation and redemption.

The *Odyssey* tells a different kind of story. The hero of this poem, the Greek king Odysseus, wants nothing more than to return to his wife after the fall of Troy. His trek takes ten years, full of suspenseful adventures as he sails about in the Mediterranean Sea. Odysseus's endless patience, relentless cunning, intellectual curiosity, and deep love for his family finally brings him home. Due to their very human strengths and weaknesses, Achilles and Odysseus are two of the most finely drawn characters in Western literature.

The Polis (City-State)

In addition to telling epic tales that glorified heroes of the past, Greeks in the Archaic Age experimented with new forms of social and political life. They developed a new style of community called the polis°, (plural *poleis,*) or city-state. A polis was a self-governing community that consisted of an urban center with a defensible hilltop called an acropolis° and all the surrounding lad farmed by citizens of the polis. Greek cities varied in size from a few square miles to several hundred. All contained similar institutions: an assembly in which the men of the community gathered to discuss and make decisions about public business; a council of male elders who offered advice on public matters; temples to gods who protected the polis and whose good will was necessary for the community's prosperity; and an open area in the center of town called an *agora,* which served as a market and a place for informal discussions.

Living in a polis provided an extremely strong sense of community. A person could be a citizen of only one polis, and every citizen was expected to place the communities interests above all other concerns. Even the women, who were citizens but not permitted to play a role in public life, felt powerful ties to their polis. While only citizens had full membership in a polis, enjoying the greatest responsibilities, every city had noncitizens from other communities. Some of these noncitizens had limited rights and obligations. Others were slaves, who had no rights at all.

Colonization and the Settlement of New Lands

A population boom during the Archaic Age forced Greeks to emigrate because the rocky soil of the mainland could not provide enough food. From about 750 to 550 B.C.E., cities such as Corinth and Megara on the mainland and Miletos in Ionia established more than 200 colonies overseas.

Greek emigrants traveled by boat to foreign shores. Many colonists settled on the Aegean coast north into the Black Sea region, which offered plentiful farmlands. The important settlement at Byzantium controlled access to the agricultural wealth of these Black Sea colonies. Greeks established many new cities in Sicily and southern Italy, as well as on the southern coast of France and the eastern coast of Spain. By 600 B.C.E. Greek had founded colonies in North Africa in the region of modern Libya and on the island of Cyprus and Crete. Greek merchants also set up a trading community on the Syrian coast and another in the Egyptian delta, with the pharaoh's permission.

New cities like Syracuse and Tarentum in Italy, Massilia (Marseilles) in France, and Neapolis (Naples) in Italy gave land-hungry settlers the opportunity to prosper through farming, manufacturing, and trade. The colonists obtained metal ores, timber, and slaves from the regions they settled and began growing wheat, olives, and wine for export. Manufacturers carried the goods to markets all over the Mediterranean. The overseas world of the Greeks prospered, and a vibrant Greek culture with common language, gods, and social institutions spread throughout the Mediterranean and into the Black Sea.

Although all of the Greek colonies maintained some formal religious ties with their mother city-states, or *metropoleis,* they were self-governing and independent. Some colonies failed, but others grew rich and populous enough to send out their own colonies. Because the Greek colonists seized territory by force and sometimes slaughtered the local inhabitants, relations with the people already living in these lands were often quite tense.

The Greek adoption of coinage spurred commercial activity among many Greek communities. Coinage first replaced barter as a medium of exchange in western Asia Minor about 600 B.C.E. as a form of portable wealth that could use to buy goods and services. Minted from precious metals and uniform weight, coins helped people standardize they value of goods, a development that revolutionized commerce. By 600 B.C.E. Greeks living in Ionia and on the Greek mainland began to mint their own coins. Each city-state used a distinctive emblem to mark its currency. When Athens became the dominant economic power in the Aegean during the second half of the fifth century B.C.E., Athenian coinage became the standard throughout the Greek world and beyond.

Greek colonization played a critical role in shaping Western civilization by creating wealthy centers of Greek culture along the Mediterranean's western coast. Sometimes overshadowed in the historical record by city-states of the Greek mainland, such as Athens, Sparta, and Corinth, the impressive new poleis spread Greek civilization, language, literature, religion, and art far beyond Greece itself. The

Athenian

(front)

(back)

Jewish Second Temple period

(front)

(back)

Athenian Coinage The coins made in Athens displayed the head of Athena on one side, and her sacred bird, the owl, on the other side. The coin shown an the top dates to the height of the Athenian Empire. On the bottom, another coin of similar weight and appearance is called a Jehud (from the old name of Judah). Minted near Jerusalem, it shows an owl and Hebrew writing. The similarities of these coins reveal the international influence of Athenian coinage and the importance of standard weights in long-distance trade.

colony of Syracuse in Sicily grew to be larger than any city in Greece. Greek communities deeply influenced local cultures and would make a tremendous impact on Etruscan and Roman civilization in Italy, as we will see in Chapter 4. Overseas colonies also prepared the way for the rapid explosion of Greek culture that followed the conquests of Alexander the Great.

Elite Athletic Competition in Greek Poleis

Athletic contests called panhellenic° games, because they drew participants from the entire Greek world, were a mainstay of aristocratic Greek culture in the Archaic Age. As many as 150 cities regularly offered aristocratic men the chance to win glory through competition in chariot racing, discus throwing, wrestling, foot racing and other field events. Through sports the Greeks found a common culture that allowed them to express their Greek identity and honor the gods at the same time.

The Olympic games, which originated in 776 B.C.E., carried the most prestige. Every four years Greek athletes from southern Italy to the Black Sea gathered in the sacred grove of Olympia in central Greece to take part in games dedicated to Zeus, the chief Greek god. The rules required the poleis to call truces to any wars, even if they were in the middle of battle, and allow safe passage to all athletes traveling to Olympia. There are records of the naming of champions at Olympia from 776 B.C.E to 217 C.E. The Roman emperor Theodosius I, who was a Christian, abolished the games in 393 C.E. because they involved the worship of Greek gods.

The Hoplite Revolution

The new wealth flowing through the panhellenic world transformed Greek life. For the first time, men who were not aristocrats could afford to purchase the weapons of war. Called hoplites°, these men had the means to own helmets, shields, swords, shin guards, and thrusting spears. Hoplites developed a completely different method of fighting. Rather than galloping into battle on horseback, the method preferred by aristocrats with their expensive mounts, or engaging in individual hand-to-hand combat to win personal glory, hosplites entered the battlefield as a phalanx°, fighting as a group that moved in unison. Standing shoulder to shoulder in rows eight men deep, each fighter relied on the man to his right to shield him while he struck forward with his sword or spear. If the line broke, the enemy could easily rout the soldiers. Thus the hoplites' success depended on intense training and, above all, cooperation.

Greeks glorified battling in this close-knit manner. Hoplite fighting generated a sense of pride and common purpose that had political consequences, as hoplites demanded a political voice in the communities for which they fought. Their growing confidence directly challenged aristocratic families who traditionally held tight control over community decision making. In many poleis, new political leaders arose to champion the cause of the hoplite citizenry. These political leaders were known as tyrants°, a word borrowed from the Middle East that originally did not have the negative connotation it carries today.

Tyrants typically came from the ruling classes, but they found their political support among the hoplites and the poor who felt otherwise left out of the political life of the community. When tyrants seized power in a polis, they served the interests of the community as a whole, not just the aristocrats. They promoted overseas trade, built harbors, protected farmers, and began public-works projects to employ citizen workers and to beautify their cities. They also cultivated alliances with other tyrants in other poleis to establish peace and prosperity. Most important, the tyrants' authority enabled a broad range of Greek citizens to participate in government for the first time.

But tyrannies contained a fatal flaw. Although the power of the tyrant was handed down from father to son, and successors rarely inherited their fathers' qualities of leadership. As a result, the tyrannies often became oppressive and unpopular, especially among the hoplites and poor who had supported the tyrants in the first place. Few of them lasted more than two generations.

Two of the most important poleis on the Greek mainland, Sparta and Athens, dealt with tyranny in radically opposing ways. As a result they created very different political and social systems for their citizens—Sparta the model for an authoritarian, military society, and Athens the model for democracy.

Sparta: A Militarized Society

Cut off from the rest of Greece by high mountain ranges to the west and north, Sparta dominated the Peloponnese, the southernmost part of Greece. Until about 700 B.C.E. Spartans lived very much like other Greeks except that their hoplite forces achieved political power without the aid of tyrants, whom they despised. Rapid expansion in the Peloponnese prompted Spartans to develop a highly militarized way of life among the Greeks. All political power rested with a corps of warrior hoplites that comprised the entire population of male citizens. The Spartan hoplites, who called themselves "the Equals," controlled all the polis's land and developed their time in military training.

The Spartan system gradually grew more elaborate in 700 B.C.E. when the Spartans conquered Messenia, a fertile region in the western Peloponnese. To maintain control over the Messenians, who vastly outnumbered them, the Spartans brutally reduced the Messenians to the status of helots°, a level barely higher than beasts of burden. Technically free, helots were nevertheless bound to the land and forced to farm. If a Spartan master sold the land to another Spartan, the helots stayed with the land. Helots paid half of their produce to their Spartan masters and could be murdered with impunity. Controlling the helots through terror became Spartas' preoccupation.

In Sparta's social hierarchy the free subjects of the Spartans stood one level above the helots. These individuals

TYRTAEUS, ELEGIES 6–7

During the mid-seventh century B.C.E., the Spartan poet Tyrtaeus wrote many poems glorifying warfare on behalf of the polis. Spartan troops sang his poems as they marched into combat. This poem explains how young men should seek glory and avoid and avoid shame by fighting in the front ranks.

It is a noble thing for a good man to die fighting in the front lines for his country;
but to abandon his city and fertile fields, to be reduced to poverty,
this is most grievous of all things, for then a man wanders from place to place
with his beloved mother and elderly father, his small children and lawful wife. . . .
And so, since a wanderer receives no recognition, neither honor nor respect nor mercy,
let us fight with all our might for this land, and die for our children,
never caring to spare our lives.
Stand together and fight, then, O young men; take no step in shameful flight.
Be not overcome by fear, but let the heart be great and strong in your breast,
never flinching when you face the enemy. . . .
So let every man bite his lip, and, with both feet firmly on the ground,
take his place for battle.

Source: From *Ancient Greece: Documentary Perspectives, Second Edition* by Stylianos V. Spyridakis and Bradley P. Nystrom.

included merchants, manufacturers, and other businessmen who lived in communities throughout Spartan territories. They paid taxes and served in the army when needed, but they were not Spartan citizens.

The male and female citizens of Sparta stood at the top of the social pyramid. They devoted themselves completely to a military way of life. The greatest responsibility of all Spartan citizens was to fulfill the needs of the polis. From early childhood, boys trained to become soldiers and girls trained to become the mothers of soldiers. Boys left home at seven years of age to live in barracks, where they mastered the skills of battle. They learned that their comrades-in-arms played a more important role in their lives than their own families. Young married Spartans were not permitted to live with their wives, but had to sneak away from their barracks at night to visit them.

Contempt for pain and hardship, blind obedience to orders, simplicity in word and deed, and unabashed courage were the chief Spartan virtues. Cowardice had no place in Sparta. Before sending their men to war, wives and mothers warned, "Come home with your shield—or on it!" Sparta's splendidly trained armies won a reputation as the most ferocious force in all of Greece.

After its conquest of Messenia, Sparta strengthened its presence further by organizing the Peloponnesian League, an informal alliance of most of the poleis in the Peloponnese. Spartans avoided wars far from home, but they and their allies joined with the Athenians and other Greeks in resisting Persia's aggression against Greece, as we will see shortly.

CHRONOLOGY

Greece Rebuilds

CA. 1100 B.C.E.	Mycenaean palaces collapse; Dark Age begins
900 B.C.E.	Greek population begins to grow; trade and settlements increase
776 B.C.E.	Traditional date of first Olympic Games
750–720 B.C.E.	Homer composes *Iliad* and the *Odyssey*
750 B.C.E.	City-states emerge, overseas colonization begins; Greeks adopt the alphabet from the Phoenicians
700–650 B.C.E.	Hoplite armor and tactics develop; Spartans conquer Messenia
670–500 B.C.E.	Tyrants rule many city-states
600 B.C.E.	Coins first minted in Lydia in Asia Minor; science and philosophy start in Ionia
594 B.C.E.	Solon reforms Athenian Constitution
560–514 B.C.E.	Peisistratus and sons become tyrants in Athens; Sparta dominant in Peloponnese
507 B.C.E.	Cleisthenes's democratic reforms unify Attica

Athens: Toward Democracy

Athens, the best known polis of ancient Greece, made an incalculably rich contribution to the political, philosophical, artistic, and literary traditions of Western Civilization. The first democracy in the ancient world, Athens developed principles of government that remain alive today. Athens's innovative form of government and the flowering of its intellectual life stemmed directly from its response to tyranny and Persian aggression.

In the eighth and seventh centuries B.C.E., the Athenians settled Attica, the territory surrounding their city, rather than sending colonists abroad. Athens gained more land and a greater population than any other polis. By the beginning of the sixth century, aristocrats controlled most of the wealth of Attica, and many of the Athenian peasants became heavily indebted to them, pledging their bodies as collateral on loans. They risked being sold into slavery abroad if they did not repay the debt.

With civil war between the debt-ridden peasantry and the aristocracy on the horizon, both segments of the population of Attica agreed to let Solon, an Athenian statesman known for his practical wisdom, reform the political system. In 594 B.C.E. Solon (ca. 650–570 B.C.E.) enacted several reforms that limited the authority of the aristocracy and enabled all male citizens to participate more fully in Athenian public life. These reforms created the institutions of public political life from which democracy eventually developed. Solon cancelled debts, eliminated debt-slavery, and raised enough funds to buy back enslaved Athenians. Then he took additional steps to give all Athenian men a greater voice in governing their city. Taking advantage of a rise in literacy, Solon directed scribes to record his new laws on wooden panels for the whole community to see. This diminished aristocratic control of the interpretation of Athenian law and ensured that the laws would be enforced fairly for all Athenian citizens, regardless of their status.

Solon next organized the population into four classes based on wealth. Only men in the two richest classes could hold the highest administrative office of *archon* and be elected to the highest court, traditionally a base of aristocratic authority. From the third class, Solon created the *boule,* a council of 400 men who prepared the agenda for the general citizen assembly. Men from the fourth and poorest class, who could not afford hoplite weapons, could vote in the citizen assembly, though they could not be elected to any office. Finally, men of any class could serve on a new court that Solon established. Women and slaves had no voice in government at all. These changes provided a temporary solution to Athens' problems.

After a generation of internal peace, Athenian aristocrats began to chafe at their loss of power and rebelled against Solon's system. In 561 B.C.E. a nobleman named Peisistratus (ca. 590–528 B.C.E.) seized power and ruled Athens as a tyrant. Like other tyrannies in Greece, Peisistratus's regime initially enjoyed widespread support. He sponsored building projects, supported religious festivals, encouraged trade and economic development, and supported the arts. He initiated a vigorous tradition of Athenian intellectual life by inviting artists and poets to come to Athens from all over Greece. His sons, however, abused their power, and jealous aristocrats assisted by Sparta toppled the family's rule in 510. Peisistratus's surviving son fled to Persia.

Two years later, the assembly selected a nobleman named Cleisthenes to reorganize Athens. By cleverly rearranging the basic political units of Attica, Cleisthenes unified Attica and made Athens the center of all important political activity. Building upon Solon's reforms, he set the basic institutions of democracy in place with a new council of 500 male citizens drawn from throughout Attica, which made decisions for the community. He ensured every male citizen a permanent voice in government, broke the power of aristocratic families, and set up the lasting fundamental structures of Athenian democracy. The strength of Cleisthenes's new system would be tested in the face of invasions by Persia in the fifth century.

THE PERSIAN WARS (490–479 B.C.E.)

Around 510 B.C.E. the Persian king Darius I conquered the Ionian Greek poleis. The Persians ruled their new subjects fairly, but the Greeks nevertheless revolted in 499 B.C.E. Ionian Greek rebels traveled to Sparta and Athens to ask for assistance against the Persians. The Spartans refused to send any troops when they learned how far away Ionia was. The Athenians, however, sent an expeditionary force that helped the rebels burn Sardis, a Persian provincial capital. The Persians crushed the rebellion in 494 B.C.E., but they did not forget Athens.

The Marathon Campaign

In 490 B.C.E., after four years of meticulous planning, a Persian army crossed the Aegean Sea in the ships of their Phoenician subjects. They landed at the beach of Marathon, some twenty-six miles from Athens. The vicinity around Marathon was the traditional stronghold of Peisistratus, the former Athenian tyrant. The Persians brought Peisistratus's son Hippias with them, planning to install him as the new tyrant of Athens.

To save their city, the Athenians marched to Marathon, and with the aid of troops from a neighboring polis (Spartan reinforcements arrived too late), the outnumbered Greek army overcame the better armed Persian forces. This surprising victory at Marathon demonstrated that a well-trained hoplite force could defeat a far more numerous foe. It also showed that Cleisthenes' democratic reforms had unified Attica so firmly that its citizens had no interest in helping the Persians restore tyranny. Democracy worked.

Athenian Naval Power and the Salamis Campaign

After Marathon, Athens embraced even more dramatic reforms. A new political leader named Themistocles persuaded his fellow citizens to spend the proceeds from a rich silver mine in Attica on a new navy and port. By 480 B.C.E. Athens possessed nearly 200 battleships, called triremes°. With three banks of oars manned by the poorest citizens of the polis, the triremes transformed Athens into a naval powerhouse. The entire male citizen body of Athens, not just the aristocrats and hoplites, could now be called to arms. The Athenian navy embodied Athenian democracy in action in which every male citizen had an obligation to defend his homeland.

The battle of Marathon dealt a shameful blow to the Persians' pride that they resolved to avenge, but a major revolt in Egypt and Darius's death in 486 B.C.E. prevented them from invading Greece again for nearly a decade. In 480 B.C.E., Xerxes I, the new Persian Great King, launched a massive invasion of Greece. He brought an overwhelming force of some 150,000 soldiers, a navy of nearly 700 mostly Phoenician vessels, and ample supplies. His troops crossed from Asia into Europe by means of a bridge of boats over the Hellespont, while the nave followed a parallel path by sea in order to supply the troops. They intended to smash Athens.

Terrified by the magnitude of the Persian army, fewer than 40 of the more than 700 Greek poleis joined the defensive coalition that had formed in anticipation of the invasion. Under the leadership of Sparta, the Greek allies planned to hold back the Persian land force in the north, while the Athenian navy sailed north to attack the invaders at sea. The Spartan king Leonidas, led the coalition. Under his command, a Greek force stopped the Persians at the pass of Thermopylae, until a traitor revealed an alternate path through the mountains. On the last day of the battle, Leonidas, his entire force of 300 valiant Spartans, and several thousand allies, died fighting.

Their sacrifice was not in vain. The disaster at Thermopylae gave the Athenians precious time to evacuate their city and to station their highly maneuverable fleet in the narrow straits of Salamis, just off the Athenian coast. In a stunning display of naval skill, the Athenian triremes defeated the Persian navy in a single day of heavy fighting. Xerxes withdrew most of his forces to Asia Minor, but left a large army in northern Greece.

Early in 479 B.C.E., a combined Greek army once again stopped the Persians at the battle of Plataea, north of Attica,

Warfare at Sea

In the classical world, a long rowed vessel with a bronze battering ram at the water line. The ship was propelled by 170 oarsmen. Invented in either Egypt or Phoenicia about 650 B.C.E., the trireme became the backbone of the Athenian fleet. Highly trained rowers could reach a speed of more than nine knots over short distances.

after a large contingent of Spartans led a decisive final charge. In the same year, the combined naval forces of Greece defeated the Persian navy off the Ionian coast. Without a single substantial military success, Xerxes gave up the attempt to conquer Greece and returned to Persia.

The Classical Age of Greece, 479–336 B.C.E.

The defeat of mighty Persia by a handful of Greek cities shocked the Mediterranean world. Xeres's failure did not seriously weaken Persian society, but it greatly strengthened the Greeks, not only by boosting their economy and by enhancing their own position in the Mediterranean but also for what we would now call their self-image. After the defeat of the Persians, the Greeks exhibited immense confidence in their ability to influence human events. The Greeks began to imagine a more optimistic view of the world, one in which people were not completely subject to the whims of the gods but could alter the course of their own lives. In the political realm, the emboldened Athenians created a powerful empire that made them the dominant power in the Greek world. During this time democratic institutions flourished in Athens. Yet the very success of Athens sowed the seeds of its demise. After alienating many of the other Greek poleis, Athens lost the long and bitter Peloponnesian War with Sparta.

The distinguishing feature of the Classical Age was its remarkable level of creativity, especially in drama, science, history writing, philosophy, and the visual arts. Despite the turmoil of the Persian and Peloponnesian Wars, Greek society remained rigidly hierarchic with strictly defined gender roles and a large class of slaves who performed much of the heavy labor. The structures of Greek society provided many male citizens with the leisure time for debating about public affairs in a democratic fashion, for attending plays, and for speculating about philosophical issues. The many deities of the Greek pantheon were the subject of much a Greek art and their worship the purpose of the Greek temples that established the Classical style, which was imitated throughout subsequent centuries. None of the Greek cities produced as many creative men as Athens, which makes its experience as an empire and a democracy particularly revealing.

THE RISE AND FALL OF THE ATHENIAN EMPIRE

With the Persian threat to Greece nearly eliminated, Athens began a period of rapid imperial expansion. This aggressive foreign policy backfired. It set off waves of discord among the other Greek city-states that led to war and the eventual collapse of the Athenian Empire.

From Defensive Alliance to Athenian Empire

After Thermopylae, the Greek defensive alliance went on the offensive to clear the Persians once and for all from the Ionian coast. The Spartans soon grew disillusioned with the effort and withdrew their troops, leaving Athenians in charge. In the winter of 478 B.C.E., Athens reorganized the alliance, creating the Delian League° named for the small island of Delos, where the members met. Athens contributed approximately 200 warships to continue attacks against Persians, while the other members supplied ships or funds to pay for them. The league ultimately gathered a naval force of 300 ships, and by 469 B.C.E. it drove the last Persians from the Aegean.

With the Persians ousted, several poleis tried to leave the league, but the Athenians forced them to remain. The Athenians were rapidly turning the Delian League into an Athenian Empire organized for their own benefit. In subsequent decades the Athenians established military garrisons and interfered in the political life of many cities of the league by imposing heavy taxes and establishing many rules and financial regulations. Several open revolts broke out, but no polis in the empire could overcome Athens's might. In 460 B.C.E. Athens sent approximately 4,000 men and 200 warships to assist in an Egyptian revolt against Persia, but Persian troops destroyed the entire expeditionary force. Sobered by this fiasco, the Athenians moved the treasury of the Delian League from Delos to Athens, claiming that they were protecting it from Persian retaliation. In fact, the Athenians spent the league treasury on public buildings in Athens, including the Parthenon. Athenian policy had become indifferent to the original purpose of the league, but the revenues generated by the league's exploitation simultaneously enabled democracy to flourish at home.

CHRONOLOGY

	Classical Greece
490 B.C.E.	Battle of Marathon; first Persian invasion stopped
480–478 B.C.E.	Xerxes invades Greece and is defeated
447 B.C.E.	Delian League formed; growth of Athenian democracy and imperialism
450s B.C.E.	Pericles ascendant in Athens; Herodotus writes his *Histories*
477–432 B.C.E.	Parthenon built in Athens; Sophists active
431–404 B.C.E.	Peloponnesian War; Thucydides writes his *History*
429 B.C.E.	Death of Pericles; Euripides and Sophocles active
415–413 B.C.E.	Athen's campaign in Sicily fails
404–403 B.C.E.	Sparta defeats Athens
339 B.C.E.	Trial and death of Socrates
339–347 B.C.E.	Plato writes *Dialogues* and founds Academy

Democracy in the Age of Pericles

The chief designer of the Athenian Empire was Pericles, an aristocrat who dominated Athenian politics from 461 B.C.E. until his death in 429 B.C.E. During the so-called "Age of Pericles," Athens's democracy at home and empire abroad reached their peak.

During the Age of Pericles, about 40,000 citizen men lived in Athens. Only male over age 18 could participate in the city's political life. Women, foreigners, slaves, and other imperial subjects had no voice in public life.

The representative council of 500 men established by Cleisthenes continued to administer public business. The citizen assembly met every ten days and probably never had more than 5,000 citizens in attendance, except for the most important occasions. The assembly made final decisions on issues of war, peace and public policy by majority vote. Because men gained political power through debate in the assembly, a politician's rhetorical skills played an all-important role in convincing voters.

Ten officials called *generals* were elected every year by popular vote to handle high affairs of state and to direct Athens's military forces. Generals typically were aristocrats who had proven their expertise. Pericles, for example, won reelected almost continually for more than twenty years.

A vast increase in public business multiplied the number of public administrators running the empire. By the middle of the fifth century, Athens had grown to some 1,500 officials in its bureaucracy. Now responsible for administrating the Delian League, boards of assessors determined the amount of money its members would pay. Many legal disputes arose among cities in the league, forcing Athens to increase the number of its courts. Because of the constant need for jurors and other office holders, Pericles began paying wages for public service, the first such policy in history. Jurors were chosen by lot, and trials

Map 3.4 The Peloponnesian War
During this long conflict that lasted from 431 to 404 B.C.E., the forces of Athens and its allies struggled with Sparta and its allies for control of mainland Greece. Though Sparta defeated the Athenian Empire, Athens survived as an influential force in Greek social, political, and economic life.

lasted no more than a day to expedite cases, save money, and prevent jury tampering.

Athenians took steps to ensure honesty in public affairs. Every official who spent public revenues had his account books examined at the beginning and at the end of his term of office. Citizens meeting in the assembly had regular opportunities to write down the name of any other citizen they disliked or distrusted on a broken piece of pottery called an *ostrakon.* If a sufficient number of citizens singled out the same person, he would be expelled from Athenian lands for ten years, though his property would remain intact for his return. This procedure, called ostracism°, provided a way to get rid of corrupt or overly ambitious politicians. A strong sense of shared identity and common purpose resulted from these democratic institutions and attracted men of all social classes to public service.

Additional reforms by Pericles gave women a more important role in Athenian society. Before 451 B.C.E., children born to Athenian men and their foreign wives attained full citizenship. Pericles' new law allowed citizenship only if both parents were Athenian citizens. As a result, Athenian citizen women took pride in giving birth to the polis's only legitimate citizens. Nevertheless, citizen women continued to be denied full freedom of action in public life.

Conflict with Sparta: The Peloponnesian War

Sparta and its allies felt threatened by growing Athenian power. Between 460 and 431 B.C.E., Athens and few allies fought intermittently with Sparta and the Peloponnesian League. War broke out between the two sides in 431 B.C.E., dragging on until 404 B.C.E. In the beginning of the conflict, called the Peloponnesian War, the Spartans repeatedly raided Attica in the hope of defeating Athenian forces in open battle.

Thanks to Athens's fortifications and the two parallel five-mile-long walls connecting the city to its main port of Piraeus, the Athenians endured the devastating Spartan invasions. Safe behind their fortifications, they relied on their navy to deliver foot and supplies from cities of the Athenian Empire that Spartan armies could not reach. The Athenians also launched attacks from the sea against Spartan territory almost at will. With the hope that their greater resources would sustain them until victory, the Athenians fought on. Although plague struck the overcrowded city in 430 B.C.E., killing almost one-third of the population including Pericles, Athens and Sparta continued to fight.

In 421 B.C.E., Spartan and Athenians generals agreed to a fifty-year truce, but a mere six years later war broke out again. The reckless policies of Alcibiades, an Athenian general, started a new round of warfare. A nephew of Pericles, Alcibiades lacked his uncle's wisdom. In 415 B.C.E. he persuaded the Athenians to send a large expeditionary force of 5,000 hoplites to invade Sicily and take its resources for the war effort. Just as the fleet was about to sail, Alcibiades's enemies accused him of profaning a religious festival, and he fled to Sparta. After two years of heavy fighting, the Athenian expedition ended in utter disaster. Syracusan soldiers captured every Athenian ship and either slaughtered the Athenian soldiers or sold them into slavery.

The Collapse of Athenian Power

The Peloponnesian war dragged on for another ten years, but Athens never fully recovered from the catastrophic loss of men and ships in Sicily. At the suggestion of Alcibiades, the Spartans established a permanent military base within sight of Athens, which enabled them to control Attica. When 20,000 slaves in the Athenian silver mines escaped to freedom under the Spartans, Athens lost its main source of revenue. The final blow came when Lysander, the Spartan commander-in-chief, obtained money from Persia to build a navy strong enough to challenge Athenian sea power. At the battle of Aegospotami on the Hellespont, Lysander's navy sank every Athenian ship. Athens surrendered in 404 B.C.E.

The victorious Spartan forces pulled down Athens's long walls stretching to Piraeus, but they refused to burn the city to the ground as some enemies of Athens demanded, because Athens had been Sparta's valiant ally in the Persian Wars. Instead, the Spartans set up an oligarchy°, or government by a few. Led by the "Thirty Tyrants," a violent and conservative political faction, the oligarchy soon earned the hatred of Athenian citizens. Within a year they overthrew the tyrants and restored democracy.

Sparta's victory did not bring peace to the Greek world. Following the defeat of the Athenian empire, the Spartans began a shortsighted attack on the Persian provinces in Asia Minor. Angered by Sparta's aggression, the Persians retaliated by financing Athens and other poleis to fight Sparta. Bitter war raged among the Greek poleis, but finally agents of the Persian Great King negotiated the King's Peace in 386 B.C.E. With this treaty the Persians promised not to interfere again in Greek affairs. In return the Greek cities of Asia Minor would remain under Persian control. The war-weary Greek states eagerly agreed. For the next two decades, the Greek city of Thebes dominated Greek affairs after defeating Sparta in 371 B.C.E., but wars among different poleis continued on a small scale. When not fighting other Greeks, many Greek hoplites fought as mercenaries for Persian kings in the period after the Peloponnesian War. These Greek soldiers learned that well-trained, highly disciplined hoplite troops were more than a match for the Persian army. In the next chapter we will see how the kingdom of Macedonia to the north of Greece benefited from this important lesson.

CLASSICAL GREECE

Amid the violence of the Classical Age, the Greek poleis developed a vibrant way of life, in which men and women had distinct roles to play, one that freed men for involvement in public affairs. Greek men and women lived very different lives, guided by strict rules of behavior. A hierarchy of gender roles determined individuals' access to public space, legal rights, and opportunities to work. In this emphatically patriarchal society, only men held positions of public authority, controlled wealth and inheritance, and enjoyed the right to participate in political life. Women were expected to engage in domestic activities, out of sight of non–family members. At the bottom of society were slaves of both genders, who had no rights at all.

Gender Roles

Greek women were expected to marry early in puberty, typically to men at least ten years older. Through marriage legal control of women passed from father to husband. In the case of divorce, which only men could instigate, the husband had to return his wife's dowry to her father. Greek houses were small and usually divided into two parts. In the brighter, front rooms husbands entertained their male friends at dinner and enjoyed active conversation and social interaction with other males. Wives spent the majority of their time in the more secluded portions of the home, supervising the household slaves, raising children, dealing with a mother-in-law, and weaving the family's clothing.

Greek men feared that their wives would commit adultery, which carried the risk of illegitimate offspring and implied that husbands could not control their possessions or access to their homes. Consequently, Greek men strictly monitored and closely controlled women's sexual activity. Because men considered females powerless to resist seduction, respectable women rarely ventured out in public without a chaperone. Slaves went to market and ran errands. To the typical Greek husband, the ideal wife stayed out of public sight, dutifully obeyed him, and was satisfied by sexual relations with him three times a month. She was not supposed to mind if he had relations with prostitutes or adolescent boys. Above all, she was expected to produce legitimate children, preferably sons, who would continue the family line and honorably serve the polis.

Greek Women

Male-dominated Greek communities kept women at the margins of society. (a) This Athenian vase of the fifth century B.C.E., reflects Greek men's view of a properly subordinate woman. In the image, the wife bids goodbye to her young husband, who is going off to war. Her place is at home, tending to chores until his return. (b) This vase depicts women as wild, drunken, potentially murderous followers of Dionysus, god of wine. (c) This vase portrays an Amazon, a mythological female warrior. Amazons embodied everything opposite of the Greek view of women. They fought in battle like men and ruled themselves.

photo to come

(b)

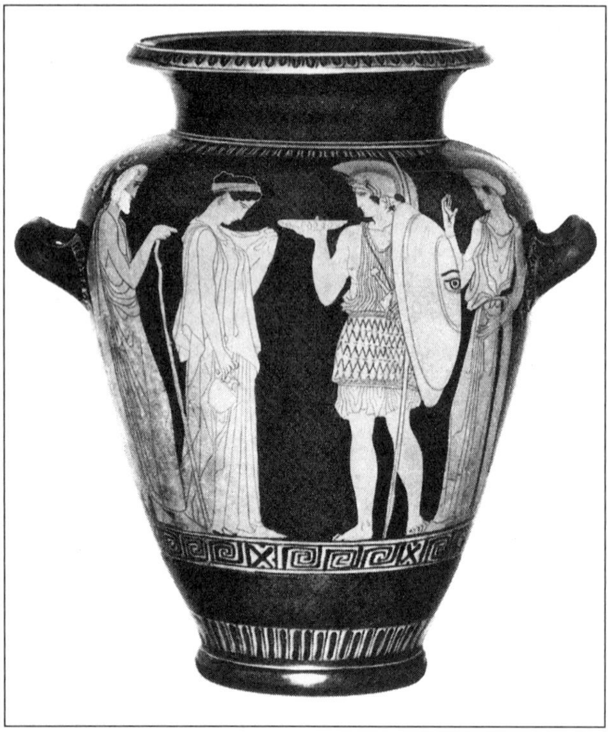

(a)

(c)

Women who worked outside the home did so primarily in three capacities: as vendors of farm produce or cloth in the marketplace, as priestesses, and as prostitutes. Female vendors in the marketplace came from the lower classes. Their skills in weaving cloth and making garments, as well as in growing vegetables in their gardens, gave them the opportunity to supplement the family income.

Priestesses served the temples of goddesses such as Hera in Argos and Athena in Athens. In classical Athens, more than forty publicly sponsored religious cults had female priests. These women gained high prestige as well as a respectable salary. Greeks believed that some women possessed a special spirituality that made them excellent mediums through divinities often spoke. Such women served as oracles, as in the temple of Apollo at Delphi. They attracted visitors from all over the Mediterranean world who wanted to discern the gods' wishes or learn what the future might bring.

Prostitutes lived in all Greek cities, but unlike priestesses, their profession was considered shameful. In Athens most prostitutes were slaves from abroad. Some women worked as elite courtesans called hetairai°. Because Greek men did not think it possible to have intellectual exchanges with their spouses, they hired hetairai to accompany them to social gatherings and to participate in stimulating conversations on about politics, philosophy, and the arts. Like ordinary prostitutes, hetairai also were expected to be sexually available for pay.

The most famous of all hetairai was Aspasia, who came to Athens from the Ionian city of Miletus. She became Pericles's companion and their son gained Athenian citizenship by special vote of the assembly. Aspasia participated fully in the circle of scientists, artists, and intellectuals who surrounded Pericles and made Athens "the school of Greece." According to legend, she taught rhetoric and regularly conversed with the philosopher Socrates. The Athenian orator Demosthenes famously summed up Greek attitudes toward women in this way: "We have hetairai for the sake of pleasure, regular prostitutes to care for our physical needs, and wives to bear legitimate children and be loyal custodians of our households."[3]

In classical Greece, where men considered women to be intellectually and emotionally inferior, many men believed that the best sort of friendship was found in make homosexual unions. Greek men frequently courted adolescent youths. The older man became a mentor and a good example for his younger lover. Some poleis institutionalized such relationships. In the city of Thebes, for example, the elite "Sacred Band" of 150 male couples led the city's hoplites into battle in the fourth century B.C.E. These men were considered the best warriors because they would not endure the shame of showing cowardice to their lovers. The Sacred Band could defeat even Spartan warriors.

photo to come .335

Male Homosexuality

This painted vase displays a common homoerotic scene, the courting of an unbearded youth by an older man. The youth holds a garland that suggests athletic victory.

Slavery: The Source of Greek Prosperity

Unlike free citizens of a polis, slaves were totally under the control of other people and had no political or legal rights. Masters could kill them without serious penalty and could demand sexual favors at any time. Slavery existed in every polis at every social level. The slave population expanded in the period after 600 B.C.E. as poleis prospered and demands for labor increased.

Most information about Greek slavery comes from Athens, which was the first major slave society that is well-documented. Between about 450 and 320 B.C.E the thriving polis had a total population of perhaps a quarter of a million people, one-third of whom were enslaved. The proportion of slaves to free persons was similar in other poleis. In the Archaic period (ca. 750–479 B.C.E) the Athenian aristocracy began to rely on slave labor to work their large landed estates. Most of these slaves had fallen into bondage for debt, but after Solon made the enslavement of Athenian citizens illegal in 594 B.C.E., the wealthy turned to sources outside Attica. Many slaves were captured during the Persian Wars, but most slaves were either the children of slaves or purchased on the thriving slave market on non-Greek peoples from around the Aegean.

Athenians and other Greeks relied on slaves to perform an enormous variety of tasks. The city of Athens owned slaves who served as a police force, as public executioners, as clerks in court, and in other public capacities. Most slaves, however, were privately owned. Some labored as highly skilled artisans and businessmen who lived apart from their owners but were required to pay them a high percentage of their profits. Every Greek household male and female slaves who performed menial tasks. Some rich landowners owned gangs of slaves who worked in the fields. Others rented slaves to the polis to labor in the silver mines, where they were worked to death under hideous conditions.

Slavery did not necessarily last until a person's death. A few slaves won their freedom through the generosity of their owners. Others saved enough money from their trades to buy their freedom. Freed slaves could not become citizens. Instead, they lived as resident foreigners in the polis of their former masters and often maintained close ties of loyalty and obligation with them.

Slavery was so widespread in Athens because it was extremely profitable. The Athenian political system evolved to permit and support the exploitation of noncitizen slaves to benefit the citizen class. The slaves were primarily responsible for the prosperity of Athens and gave the aristocrats the leisure to engage in intellectual pursuits and to create the rich culture tat became part of the core of Western civilization.

Religion and the Gods

Religion permeated Greek life. It provided a structured way for Greeks to interact with the deities who exercised considerable influence over their lives. Greeks worshiped many gods, whom they asked for favors and advice. Every city kept a calendar of religious observances established for certain days. Festivals marked phases in the agricultural year, such as the harvest or sowing seasons, and initiation ceremonies marked an individual's transition from childhood to adulthood.

Above all, Greeks gave their devotion to the gods who protected the city. For instance, during the annual Panathenaea festival in Athens the entire population, citizen and noncitizen alike, honored the city's patron goddess Athena with a grand procession and numerous sacrifices. Every fourth year, the celebration was expanded to include major athletic and musical competitions. In a joyous parade, the citizens would convey a robe embroidered with mythological scenes to the statue of Athena in her temple, called the Parthenon, or House of the Virgin Goddess that stood on the Acropolis hill in the center of the city.

Although every polis had its own set of religious practices, people throughout the Greek world shared many ideas about the gods. Like the Greek language, these common religious attitudes gave a common identity to Greeks. They also distinguished them from so-called barbarians who worshipped strange gods in ways Greeks considered uncivilized.

Most Greeks believed that immortal and enormously powerful gods and goddesses were all around them. These deities often embodied natural phenomena like the sun or moon, but Greeks attributed very human personalities and desires to them. Because these divine forces touched every aspect of daily life, human interactions with them were unavoidable and risky, for the gods could be as harmful as they were helpful to humans.

The Greeks believed that the twelve greatest gods inhabited Mount Olympus in the northern Greece as a large and quite dysfunctional family. Zeus was the father and king, Hera was his sister and wife; and Aphrodite the goddess of sex and love. The jealous clan also included Apollo, god of the sun, prophecy, and medicine; Ares, the god of war; and Athena, the goddess of wisdom. Greek mythology developed a set of stories about the Olympian gods that have passed into Western literature and art.

In addition to their home on Mount Olympus, the gods also maintained residences in cities. Temples served as the gods' living quarters. They displayed the wealth and piety of every polis, for Greek cities spared no expense to employ the finest architects and best materials available. Rows of carved marble columns surrounded the central room and supported the temple's roof. Sculptural decorations on the temple walls that told stories about the gods were brilliantly painted, but today they have been bleached white by the sun and weather. The gods' likeness, typically a very large statue, stood at the center of these rectangular marble structures, facing an altar in front of the building.

Worship at Greek temples consisted of offerings and sacrifices. Outside in the open air, the worshipers made offerings, perhaps a small offering of flowers, a pinch of incense,

The Acropolis and Parthenon

The Acropolis of Athens, with the Parthenon, stood as a symbol of Athenian imperial culture.

photo to come .338

Dragons and Serpents

Current archaeological research suggests that the dragons and serpents that appear in Greek mythology represent ancient attempts to explain dinosaur fossils. Greek vase painters illustrated these stories with such accuracy that paleontologists today can identify the dinosaur. This vase was painted about 550 B.C.E. It shows Hercules and Hesione fighting a sea monster. Scientists believe that the monster's head might have been modeled on the skull of *Samotherium,* a giant giraffe that lived about eight million years ago. Many fossils of this creature have been found in Greece and Turkey.

or a small grain cake. On especially important festivals Greek sacrifice live animals to their gods. Priests and priestesses supervised these rituals. The god inside the temple watched the priests prepare the sacrifice, hear the sacrificial animals bleat as their throats were slit, and listen to women howl as blood poured from the victims. Finally, the god smelled the aroma of burning meat as the victim was cooked over the flames. Satisfied, the god awaited the next sacrifice.

In addition, Greeks took pains to discern the future. They hired religious experts to analyze their dreams and to predict the future based on the examination of the internal organs of specially sacrificed birds. Greeks and non-Greeks alike traveled to consult the priestess of Apollo, the so-called Oracle of Delphi, at a shrine in central Greece. If the god chose to reply to a particular query, he spoke through the mouth of his oracle, a priestess who would lapse into a trance. Priests stood nearby to record and explain the oracle's utterances, which often could have more than one interpretation. When King Croesus of Lydia asked the oracle what would happen if he went to ware with Persians, Appolo told him that "a great kingdom will fall." Croesus never dreamed it would be his own.

INTELLECTUAL LIFE

In the Classical Age, Greeks investigated the natural world and explored the human condition with astonishing freshness and vigor. Their legacy in drama, science, philosophy, and the arts continued to inspire people in many subsequent periods of history. The term *Renaissance,* which is applied to several cultural movements in later periods, refers to attempts to recapture the intellectual vitality of the Greek Classical Age as well as that of the Romans.

Greek Drama

Greek men examined their society's values through public dramatic performances. Peisistratus, the tyrant of Athens, introduced plays around 550 B.C.E. Initially, plays were performed in annual festivals dedicated to Dionysus, the god of wine, and authors entered their plays for competition. Dramatic productions soon became a mainstay of Greek life. In their plays set in the mythical past, the playwrights explored issues relevant to contemporary society. Above all, Greeks who attended the plays (only men were allowed) could expect to be educated and entertained. Fewer than fifty plays from the Greek classical period have survived, but they remain among the most powerful examples of literature in the Western tradition.

In tragedies Athenian men watched stories about the terrible suffering underlying human society. In many of these plays an important aristocrat or ruler is destroyed by a fatal personal flaw beyond his or her ability to control. With an unflinching gaze, playwrights examined conflicts between violent passion and reason and between the laws of the gods and those of human communities. Their dramas depicted the terrible consequences of vengeance, the brutality of war, and the relationship of the individual to the polis. In the plays of the three great Athenian tragedians—Aeschylus, Sophocles, and Euripides—characters learn vital lessons through their suffering, and the audience learns it, too.

Aeschylus (525–456 B.C.E.) believed that the gods were just and that human suffering stemmed directly from human error. His most powerful works include a trilogy called the *Oresteia.* This collection of three plays expresses the notion that a polis can survive only when courts made up of citizens settle matters of murder, rather than leaving justice to family vendettas. The cycle of retaliation that tormented the family of King Agamemnon of Mycenae for generations finally ends when Athena and her citizens provide the hideous deities violent revenge an honorable resting place in Athens.

Another of his plays, called *The Persians,* put Athenians in a triumphal mood after the defeat of the Persians at Salamis and the subsequent withdrawal by the enemy from Greece. This play shows the tragic consequences of Xerxes's limitless arrogance and ambition. Aeschylus also makes a sharp distinction, for the first time in Greek literature, between Greek civilization and foreign barbarism. This contrast developed into a major theme in Greek thought, and it still is used to categorize cultures today.

In the plays of Sophocles (ca. 496–406 B.C.E.), humans are free to act, but they are trapped by their weaknesses, their history, and the will of the gods. In *Antigone,* a young woman buries her outlaw brother in accordance with divine principles but in defiance of her city's laws, knowing that she will be executed for her brave act. The misguided king who wrote the law and ordered her death realizes too late that a polis will prosper only if human and divine laws come into proper balance. In *Oedipus the King,* Oedipus unknowingly kills his father and marries his mother. When he learns what he has done, he understands that he was the one who committed the immoral acts.

Like Sophocles's works, the plays of Euripides (ca. 484–406 B.C.E.), portray humans struggling against their fates. In these works, the gods have no human feeling and are capable of bestial action against humans. Unlike other writers of his day, he showed remarkable sympathy for women, who often fall victim to war and male deceit in his plays. At the end of *The Trojan Women,* the despairing Trojan queen Hecuba stands amid the smoldering ruins of her vanquished city, lamenting the cruel life as a slave that awaits her: "Lead me, who walked soft-footed once in Troy, lead me a slave where earth falls sheer away by rocky edges, let me drop and die withered away with tears."[4]

In addition to the tragedies, Greeks delighted in irreverent comedies. Performances of comedy probably began in the seventh century B.C.E. as lewd sketches associated with Dionysus, the god of wine and fertility. The playwright Aristophanes of Athens (ca. 450–388 B.C.E.) proved a master at presenting comedy as social commentary. No person, god, or institution escaped his mockery. Although fully committed to Athenian democracy, Aristophanes had no patience for hypocritical politicians or self-important intellectuals. His comic plays are full of raunchy sex and allusions to the day's issues, containing withering sarcasm, silly puns, and outrageous insults. Audiences howled at the fun, but these plays always carried a thought-provoking message as well. *The Birds* is an apt example. In this satire, Aristophanes tells the story of two down-on-their-luck Athenians who flee the city looking for peace and quiet. On their trek they have to deal with an endless stream of Athenian bureaucrats and frauds whom Aristophanes mercilessly skewers. Finally the travelers seize powering the Kingdom of the Birds—and then transform it into a replica of Athens. This satire of Athenian imperialism shows Athenians helpless to avoid their own worst instincts.

GREEK VERSUS BARBARIAN

In the years following excerpt Hippocrates of Kos (d. ca. 400 B.C.E.), known as the Father of Medicine, explained the forms of government of the Near East and the character of the people, whom he calls Asiatics. Like other Greeks of his time, Hippocrates believed in the superiority of Greek civilization to that of all other peoples. In this passage, he explains that the climatic zones in which people live determine the equality of their culture.

The small variations of climate to which the Asiatics are subject, extremes of both heat and of cold being avoided, account for their mental flabbiness and cowardice . . . They are less warlike than Europeans and tamer of spirit, for they are not subject to those physical changes and the mental stimulation that sharpen tempers and induce recklessness and hot-headedness . . . Such things appear to me to be the cause of the feebleness of the Asiatic race, but a contributory cause also lies in their customs; for the greater part is under monarchical rule . . . Even if a man be born brave and of stout heart, his character is ruined by this form of government.

Source: From Paul Cartledge, *The Greeks: A Portrait of Self and Others,* Oxford University Press, 1993.

Scientific Thought in Ionia

Greek science began about 600 B.C.E. in the cities of Ionia, when a handful of men began to ask new questions about the natural world. Living on the border between Greek and Persian civilizations, these Greek thinkers encountered the still vigorous Babylonian scientific and mathematical traditions that still flourished in the Persian Empire. Inspired by these methods of carefully observing the natural world and systematically recording data, Greek thinkers started pulling away from traditional Greek explanations for natural phenomena.

They rejected old notions of gods who arbitrarily inflicted floods, earthquakes, and other disasters on humanity. Instead, they looked for general principles that could explain each natural phenomena. To these investigators, the natural world was orderly, knowable by means of careful inquiry, and therefore ultimately predictable. These scientists inquired about the physical composition of the natural world, tried to formulate the principles of why change occurs, and began to think about proving their theories logically.

Thales of Miletus (ca. 625–547 B.C.E.), the first of these investigators, theorized that the Earth was a disk floating on water. When the earth rocked in the water, he proposed, the motion caused earthquakes. Thales traveled to Egypt to study geometry and established the pyramids' height by calculating the length of their shadows. Perhaps influenced by Egyptian and Babylonian teachings, he believed that water gave rise to everything else. His greatest success an astronomer came when he predicted a solar eclipse in 585 B.C.E.

One of Thales's students, Anaximander (ca. 610–547 B.C.E.), wrote a pioneering essay about natural science called *On the Nature of Things.* Anaximander became the first Greek to make a map of the inhabited world. He also argued that the universe was rational and symmetrical. In his view, it consisted of Earth as a flat disk at its center, held in place by the perfect balance of the limitless space around it. Anaximander also believed that change occurred on Earth through the tension between opposites, such as hot versus cold and dry versus wet.

A third great thinkers from Miletus, Anaximenes (ca. 545–525 B.C.E.), suggested that air is the fundamental substance of the universe. Through different processes, air could become fire, wind, water, earth, or even stones. His conclusions, along with those of Thales and Anaximander, may seem odd and unsatisfactory today, but these men were pioneers of science exploration of the natural world. Their brave willingness to remove the gods from explanations of natural phenomena, and their efforts to provide arguments in defense of their theories, established the foundations of modern scientific inquiry and observation.

These Milesian thinkers sparked inquiry in other parts of the classical Greek world as well. Soon other investigators developed their own theories. Heraclitus of Ephesus (ca. 500 B.C.E.) argued that fire, not gods, provided the true origin of the world. Leucippus of Miletus (fifth century B.C.E.) and Democritus of Abdera (ca. 460–370 B.C.E.) proposed that the universe consisted entirely of an endless number of material atoms. Too small to be seen, these particles floated everywhere. When the atoms collided or stuck together, they produced the elements of the world we live in, including life itself. These atomists had no need for gods in their explanations of the natural world.

The Origins of Writing History

The Western tradition of writing history has its roots in the work of Herodotus (ca. 484–420 B.C.E.), who grew to adulthood in the Ionian city of Halicarnassus. Theis Greek author concerned himself with finding the general causes of human events, not natural phenomena. He called his work *Investigations* (the original Greek meaning of the word history), and he attempted to explain the Persian War. He believed this conflict deserved to be analyzed and remembered because it had been the greatest war ever fought. For Herodotus, "the war between the Greeks and the non-Greeks" was just one episode in an unending cycle of violence between East and West, between barbarian and civilized, between oppressed and free.

Gods appear in Herodotus's narrative, but do not play a causal role in events. Instead, he attempted to show that humans always act in accordance with the general principle of reciprocity; that is, people predictably respond in equal measure to what befalls them. He sketched the reciprocal violence between East and West in legends, such as that of the Trojan War, and then described the conquest of Lydia by the Persian Great King Cyrus in the sixth century. He tells how the Greeks became involved in Persian affairs and finally triumphed over Persian aggression.

Herodotus traveled widely. He frequently went to Athens, where he read portions of his analysis of the Persian War to appreciative audiences. His also made voyages to Egypt, Babylonia, and other foreign lands, gathering information about local religions and customs. Herodotus relished the differences among cultures, and his narrative brims with vivid descriptions of exotic habits in far-off lands.

Although he considered Greeks superior to other peoples, Herodotus raised basic questions about cultural encounters that are still engage us today. How can we judge whether one culture's customs are better than another's? Is it possible to evaluate a foreign culture on its own terms or are we doomed to view things through our own eyes and experiences only? Herodotus made description and analysis of foreign cultures an integral part of his "investigations." Today historians justly refer to him as the "Father of History."

Western civilization also owes an incalculable debt to Thucydides of Athens (d. ca. 400 B.C.E.), who further advanced the science of writing history. His brilliant *History of the Peloponnesian War* stands as perhaps the single most influential work of history in the Western tradition because it provides a model for analyzing the causes of human events and the outcomes of individual decisions. In it he combines meticulous attention to accuracy and detail with a broad moral vision. To Thucydides, the Peloponnesian War represented a profound tragedy. At one time under the wise leadership of Pericles, Athens epitomized all that was good about a human community. In this "school of Greece," culture flourished and creativity and political accomplishment had no limits. Unfortunately, Athenians, like all humans, possessed a fatal flaw, the unrelenting desire to posses more. Never satisfied, they followed unprincipled leaders after

The Classical Nude Male Figure

Classical Greek culture celebrated the human male body in literature and art. Men dominated polis life, and considered the male body the standard of human beauty. In the eyes of Greek men, males embodied the most admirable virtues; in the physical world the male body came closest to perfection. Greeks considered beauty an active force that "attracted the eyes like a magnet."[5] Throughout the Greek world, from the Black Sea to Spain, freestanding marble and bronze statues of men filled the public spaces of cities. By attracting viewer to their beauty, statues became a vibrant presence in public life, conveying these masculine values to the people who admired them.

As Greek society changed so did the statues. By considering how the statues of men changed over time, we can learn about the development of the Greek attitudes that lay behind them.

Egyptian statues originally inspired Greek sculptors. For more than a thousand years, Egyptians had made statues according to the same conventions. The rigidly symmetrical figure with one leg forward was best viewed from the front. In their sculptures, the forward leg was just simply made longer. Egyptian artists had no interest in exploring how the body moves or how its weight shifts (see an Egyptian male statue on p. 000).

Greeks sculptors first encountered Egyptian art about 650 B.C.E. Intrigued, they began to make statues of young men. Like their Egyptian models, these works tended to be stiff. As techniques for carving marble developed, Greek artists became fascinated with representing human anatomy more realistically.

For an Greek artist, how the body moves, how it relates to surrounding space, and how it evokes emotions became matters of intense interest. For these artists, a *kouros,* an adolescent male at the height of his physical perfection, served as the ideal subject. Carved from white marble, the Kouros from Attica shown here (see bottom) was made in Athens about 530 B.C.E. It depicts a young man stepping forward and putting his weight on his left foot, which causes his right heel to rise. His arms are held tightly at his side, and he stares straight ahead. Although the statue captures the shifting of weight in the man's stride, his muscles are too symmetrical to be lifelike, and his posture is quite rigid. This statue presents an idealized image of a perfect adolescent.

In the burst of creative excitement that followed victory over the Persians, Greek sculptors turned away from the rigid style that the *kouros* represents and energetically began exploring all the possibilities of rendering the human body in a more lifelike fashion. The ideal was an autonomous man, in control of his emotions and with a disciplined body, well-trained for combat and victory over others. Polyclitus of Argos, a sculptor who worked between about 460 and 410 B.C.E., created a bronze statue of a warrior, probably Achilles, that became the standard for masculine perfection and for precise representation of anatomy. Called the Spear-Carrier, or *Doryphoros,* this statue (top) was widely copied in antiquity, but the original has not survived. This Roman replica is proportioned according to Polyclitus's meticulous measuring of the ideal male figure. The Spear-Carrier's anatomy is accurately and purposefully depicted. The beautiful muscles indicate the self-discipline necessary for much physical training, and their power implies the force of male strength in warfare in defense of the polis. The Doryphoros is the perfect male citizen, balanced and controlled, yet poised to fight. ■

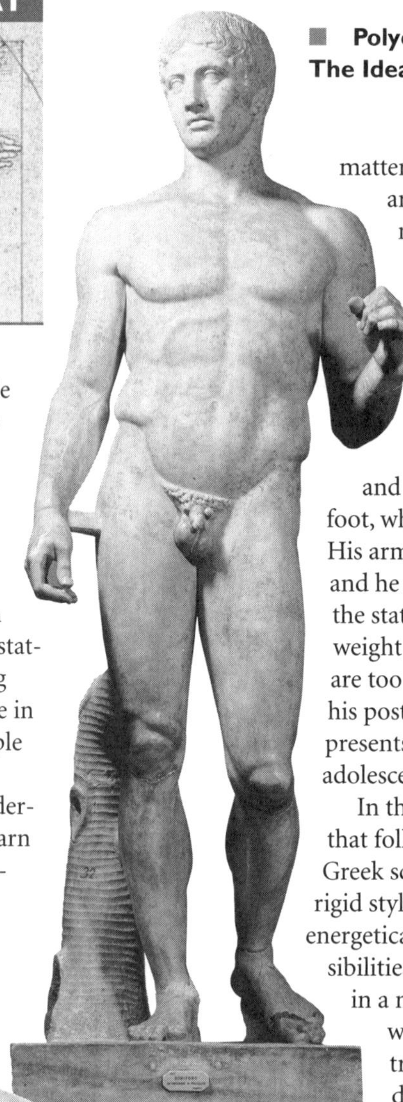

■ **Polyclitus's Spear-Carrier: The Ideal Man, ca. 430 B.C.E.**

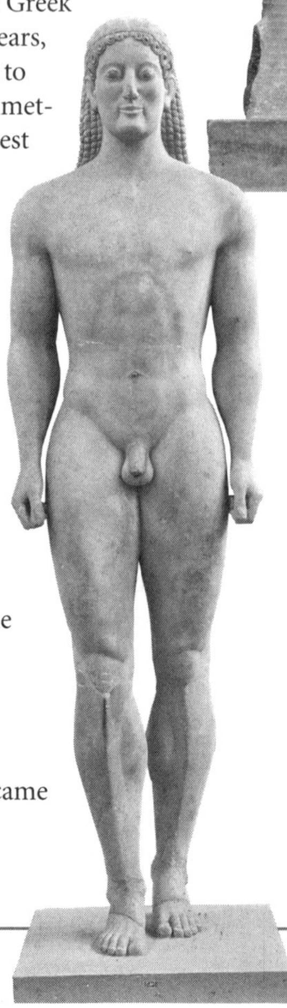

■ **The Ideal Youth, ca. 530 B.C.E.**

For Discussion

How does depicting the human body in Greek art reveal basic assumptions held by Greek culture?

Pericles' death, embarking on foolhardy adventures that eventually destroyed them.

In Thucydides's analysis, humans, not the gods, are entirely responsible for their own triumphs and defeats. As an analyst of the destructive impact of uncontrolled power on a society, Thucydides has no match. Even more than Herodotus, he set the standard for historical analysis in the West.

Nature Versus Customs and the Origins of Philosophical Thought

The Greeks believed that their communities could prosper only when governed by just political institutions and fair laws. They questioned whether the political and moral standards of the day were rooted in nature or whether humans had invented them a preserved them as customs. They wondered whether absolute standards that should guide the polis life or whether humans are the measure of all things. No one has answered these questions satisfactorily to this day, but one of the legacies of classical Greece is that they were asked at all.

During the fifth century B.C.E., a group of teachers known as sophists°, or wise men, traveled throughout the Greek-speaking world. They shared no common doctrines, and they taught everything from mathematics to political theory with the hope of instructing individuals in the best ways to lead better lives. The best-known among them was Protagoras (ca. 485–440 B.C.E.), who denied the existence of gods and absolute standards of truth. All human institutions, Protagoras argued, were created through human custom or law and not through nature. Thus, because truth is relative, an individual should be able to argue either side of an argument persuasively.

Socrates (469 B.C.E.–399 B.C.E.), an Athenian citizen, challenged the sophists' notion of there were no absolutes to guide human life. He spent his days trying to help his fellow Athenians understand the basic moral concepts that governed their lives by relentlessly asking them questions: Because Socrates wrote nothing himself, we know of his ideas chiefly through the accounts of his student Plato of Athens (ca. 428–347 B.C.E.), who made his teacher the central figure in his own philosophical essays.

Plato, established a center called the Academy in Athens for the purpose of teaching and discussion, and earned a towering reputation among the classic Greek philosophers. Like Socrates, he rejected the notion that truth and morality are relative concepts. Plato taught that absolute virtues such as goodness, justice, and beauty do exist, but on a higher level of reality than human existence. He called these eternal, unchanging absolutes Forms°. In fact, in Platonic thought, the Forms represent true reality. Like shadows that provide only an outline of an object, what we experience in daily life is merely an approximation of this true reality. Plato's theories about the existence of absolute truths and how humans can discover them continue to shape Western thought. In particular, Platonic thought emphasizes how the senses deceived us and how the truth is often hidden. Truth can be discovered only through careful, critical questioning rather than through observation of the physical world. As a result, platonic thought emphasizes the superiority of theory over scientific investigation.

According to Plato, humans can gain knowledge of the Forms. This is possible because we have souls that are small bits of a larger eternal Soul that enters our bodies at birth, bringing knowledge of the Forms with it. Our individual bits of Soul always seek to return to their source, but they must fight the constraints of the body and physical existence that stand in the way of their return. Mortals can aid the Soul in its struggle to overcome the material world by using reason to seek knowledge of the Forms. This rational quest for absolutes, Plato argued, is the particular responsibility of the philosopher, but all of us should do our best to embark on this search.

In his treatise *The Republic,* Plato described how people might construct an ideal community based on the principles he had described. In this ideal state, educated mean and women called the Guardians, would lead the polis because they were capable of comprehending the Forms. They would supervise the brave Auxiliaries who defended the city. At the bottom society were the Workers who produced the basic requirements of life. Workers were the least capable of abstract thought.

Plato and his student Aristotle (384–322 B.C.E.) stand as the two greatest thinkers of classic Greece. Aristotle founded his own school in Athens, called the Lyceum. Unlike his teacher, Aristotle did not envision the Forms as separate from matter. In his view, form and matter are completely bound together. For this reason, we can acquire knowledge of the Forms by carefully observing the world around us and classifying what we find. Following this theory, Aristotle rigorously investigated a huge range of subjects including animal and plant biology, mechanics, and physics. His many books made him the most influential natural scientist in the Western tradition before the modern period.

In his treatise *Politics,* Aristotle discussed the difference between Greeks and non-Greeks, whom he refers to collectively as "barbarians." He argued that barbarians are slaves by nature, while Greeks are free. Furthermore, Greeks were truly noble in every way, while barbarians were noble only in accordance with their own customs. Aristotle used this argument to justify Greek imperialism abroad; his notions of cultural superiority survive to this day as justifications for racism and imperialism.

The Arts: Sculpture, Painting, and Architecture

Like philosophers and dramatists during the Classical Age, Greek sculptors, architects, and painters pursued ideal beauty and truth. Classical artists believed the human body was beautiful and an appropriate subject of their attention.

JUSTICE IN HISTORY

The Trial and Execution of Socrates the Questioner

In 399 B.C.E. the people of Athens tried and executed Socrates, their fellow citizen, for not believing in Athenian gods, for introducing new gods, and for corrupting the city's young men. The charges were paradoxical, for Socrates had devoted his life to investigating how to live ethically and morally. Although Socrates could have escaped, he chose to die rather than betray his most fundamental beliefs. Socrates wrote nothing down, yet his ideas and the example that he set by his life and death make him one of the most influential figures in the history of Western thought.

Born in Athens in 469 B.C.E., Socrates fought bravely during the Peloponnesian War. Afterward he openly defied the antidemocratic Thirty Tyrants whom the Spartans had installed in Athens. Socrates did not seek a career in politics or business. Instead he spent his time thinking and talking, which earned him a reputation as an eccentric. His friends, however, loved and deeply respected Socrates.

Socrates did not give lectures. Instead, he questioned people who believed they knew the truth. By asking them such questions as What is justice? Beauty? Courage? What is the best way to lead a good life? Socrates revealed that they—and most people—do not truly understand their most basic assumptions. Socrates did not claim to know the answers, but he did believe in the relentless application of rational argument in the pursuit of answers. This style of questioning, known as the Socratic method, infuriated complacent men because it made them seem foolish. But Socrates's method delighted people interested in taking a hard look at their most cherished beliefs.

Socrates attracted many followers. His brightest student was the philosopher Plato, to whom Socrates was not only a mentor, but a hero. Plato wrote a number of *dialogues,* or dramatized conversations, in which Socrates appears as a questioner, pursuing the truth about an important topic. Four of his dialogues—*Euthyphro, Apology, Crito,* and *Phaedo,* involve Socrates's trial and death.

The trial began when three citizens named Lycon, Meletus, and Anytus accused Socrates before a jury of 501 men. The accusers charged Socrates with corrupting the youth of Athens, failing to believe in the gods, and introducing new gods to the city. Socrates spoke in his own defense, but instead of showing any remorse, he boldly defended his method of questioning. Annoyed by Socrates's stubbornness, the jury convicted him.

Athenian law permitted accusers as well as defendants to suggest alternative penalties. When the accusers asked for death, . Socrates responded with astonishing arrogance. He suggested instead that Athens pay him a reward for making the city a better place. Outraged by Socratres's behavior, the jury chose the death penalty by an even wider margin. Socrates accepted their verdict calmly.

While Socrates sat in prison waiting for his execution, a friend named Crito offered to help him escape. Socrates refused to flee. He told Crito that only a man who did not respect the law would break it, and that such a man would indeed be a corrupting influence on the young. Socrates pointed out that he had lived his life as an obedient Athenian citizen and would certainly not break the law now. Human laws may be imperfect, he admitted, but they permit a society to function. Private individuals should never disregard them. To the end he remained a loyal citizen.

On his final day, with his closest friends around him, Socrates drank a cup of poison and died bravely. Plato wrote, "This is the way our dear friend perished. It is fair to say that he was the bravest, the wisest, and the most honorable man of all those we have ever known." (*Phaedo* line 118)

Historians and philosophers have discussed Socrates's case since Plato's time. Were the accusations fair? What precisely was his crime? In the matter of corrupting Athens's youth, there is no doubt that at least two of his most fervent young followers, Alcibiades and Critias, had earned terrible reputations. Alcibiades had betrayed his city in the Peloponnesian War. Critias was one of the most violent of the Thirty Tyrants. Many Athenians suspected Socrates of influencing them, even though these men represented everything he opposed.

Charges of impiety were harder to substantiate, but Athenians took them

Socrates on Trial
Many sculptors made portraits of Socrates in the centuries after his death. Though Socrates was viewed as a hero who died for his beliefs, the sculptor did nothing to glamorize him in this portrait. Socrates was famous for the beauty of his thoughts—and the ugliness of his face.

seriously. His fellow citizens knew that Socrates always participated in Athenian religious life. But during his defense Socrates admitted that his views were not exactly the same as those of his prosecutors. His claim to have a divine *daimon* or "sign" who sat on his shoulder and gave him advice was eccentric though not actually sacrilegious. Many Athenians thought this daimon was a foreign god, and not Socrates's metaphor for his own mental processes.

The reasons for Socrates's prosecution lie much deeper than the official charges. His trial and execution emerged from an anti-intellectual backlash bred in the frustrations of Athens's defeat in the Peloponnesian War and in the Thirty Tyrants' rule. Even though Athenians had restored democracy, deep-seated resentments sealed Socrates's fate. In many societies throughout history, especially democratic ones like that of Athens that grant freedom to explore new ideas, people who fear change and creativity often strike out at artists, intellectuals, and innovators at times of stress. Athenians resented Socrates because he challenged them to think. He wanted them to live better lives, and they killed him. ■

Questions of Justice

1. What threat did Socrates' prosecutors imagine he presented to the community? Do you think they were right?
2. Under what circumstances can an individual benefit society by breaking its laws? Under what circumstances can an individual harm society by obeying its laws?

Taking It Further

Brickhouse, Thomas C., and Nicholas D. Smith. *Socrates on Trial.* 1989. A thorough analysis of Socrates's trial.

Stokes, Michael. *Plato: Apology, with Introduction, Translation, and Commentary.* 1997. The best translation, with important commentary.

They also valued the human capacity to represent in art the ideals of beauty, harmony, and proportion found in nature. Classical Greek men celebrated their ability to make rational judgments about what was beautiful and pleasing to the eye—and to create art that embodied those judgments.

To create a statue that was an image of physical perfection, sculptors copied the best features of several human models while ignoring their flaws. They strove to depict the muscles, movement, and balance of the human figure in a way that was both lifelike in its imitation of nature and yet idealized in the harmony and symmetry of the torso and limbs. The balance between realism and idealism has continually inspired artists in the Western tradition.

Greek painters explored movement of the human body as well as colors and the optical illusion of depth. The figures that they depicted on vases and on walls became increasingly lively and realistic as the Classical Age unfolded. Artists portrayed every sort of activity from religious worship to erotic fun, but regardless of the subject, they shared a similar goal; to create a lifelike depiction of the human figure.

In a similar effort to capture ideals of perfection, Greek architects designed their buildings, especially temples, to be symmetrical and proportional. They used mathematical ratios that they observed in nature to shape their designs. The buildings they created show a grace, balance, and harmony that have inspired architects for more than two millennia.

The temple of Athena in Athens called the Parthenon or "House of the Virgin Goddess," stands as the greatest triumph of classical Greek architecture. Built on the Acropolis of Athens, The temple symbolized Athens's imperial glory. Using funds appropriated from the Delian League, Athenians dedicated the huge temple to their divine protector between 447 and 432 B.C.E. The architects Ictinus and Callicrates achieved a superb example of structural harmony, perfectly balancing all the building's elements according to mathematical proportions copied from nature. For the Pathenon's sacred inner room, Phidias, a friend of Pericles, sculpted a statue of Athena made of gold and ivory over a wooden core and decorated it with gems and other precious metals. The temple also displayed an elaborate series of carved and brightly painted marble panels depicting the mythology of Athena. The Parthenon remained nearly intact until 1687 C.E., when powder kegs stored inside exploded, causing irreparable damage.

CONCLUSION
Classical Foundations of the West

During the Classical Age, which ended about 338 B.C.E, several of the elements of what would later be considered the cultural inheritance of the West came into being. These ancient peoples did not have a conception of "The West" as a cultural realm. What they did is to create things that have had a lasting influence. The legacy of the Hebrews has been their religious and ethical teachings, encapsulated in the Hebrew Bible.

The Persians supplied a model for an efficient empire that was inherited by later conquerors, most notably Alexander the Great and his followers. It also established a model for other imperial systems of the future, including the Roman Empire. By permitting forms of worship other than the official Zoroastrianism, the Persians limited dissent, and by allowing exiled peoples, such as the Hebrews, to return to their homes, they knitted together an efficient multiethnic, multireligious empire. Throughout that empire the older Middle Eastern traditions of science, mathematics, astronomy, and navigation (discussed in Chapter 2) passed on to the Greeks and then into the western Mediterranean, North African, and eventually Europe. Zoroastrian religious ideas of Heaven and Hell and the struggle between God and the Devil also found their way into other western religions, most notably Christianity.

the stumbling blocks for Persian imperial expansion to the West were the hoplite armies and fleets of the Greeks. When the Persians arrive don the shores of Greece, the institutions of the poleis were well established. However, the Greek victory strengthened those institutions and facilitated the further extension of Athenian democracy. Under the political and cultural leadership of Athens, Greek civilization thrived, producing the most lasting and characteristic artistic and philosophical contributions from the ancient world to the history of the West.

The Classical Age demonstrated that well-trained, highly disciplined Greek hoplite troops were more than a match for the Persian army. In the next chapter, we will see how the kingdom of Macedonia to the north of Greece also learned this important lesson. After conquering Greece, the Macedonians, led by Alexander the Great, overwhelmed the entire Persian Empire. Alexander's conquests inaugurated a new era in history, the Hellenistic Age, in which classical Greek civilization spread over an enormous region.

Suggestions for Further Reading

For a comprehensive list of suggested readings, please go to www.ablongman.com/levack/chapter3

Boardman, John. *Persia and the West: An Archaeological Investigation of the Genesis of Achaemenid Art.* 2000. A brilliantly illustrated study that stresses intercultural influences in every aspect of Persian Art.

Boyce, Mary. *A History of Zoroastrianism.* Vol. 2, 1975. This authoritative examination provides a masterful overview of the religion of the Persian Empire.

Burkert, Walter. *The Orientalizing Revolution: Near Eastern Influence on Greek Culture in the Early Archaic Age,* trans. Margaret Pinder and Walter Burkert. 1993. Explains how the Semitic East influenced the development of Greek society in the Archaic age.

Cohn, Norman. *Cosmos, Chaos, and the World to Come: The Ancient roots of Apocalyptic Faith.* 1993. Expert critical analysis of apocalyptic religions in the West, including Zoroastrianism, ancient Judaism, Christianity, and other faiths.

Finkelstein, Israel, and Neil Asher Silberman. *The Bible Unearthed: Archaelogy's New Vision of Ancient Israel and the Origin of the Sacred Texts.* 2001. An important archaeological interpretation that challenges the narrative of the Hebrew Bible and offers a reconsideration of biblical history.

Gottwald, Norman K. *The Hebrew Bible: A Socio-Literary Introduction.* 1985. Combines a close reading of the Hebrew Bible with the latest archaeological and historical evidence.

Just, Roger. *Women in Athenian Law and Life.* 1989. Provides an overview of the social context of women in Athens.

Kuhrt, Amélie. *The Ancient Near East, ca. 3000–330 B.C.* Vol 2. 1995. This rich and comprehensive bibliography is a remarkably concise and readable account of Persian history with excellent discussion of ancient textual evidence. Many important passages appear in fluent translation.

Lindberg, David C. *The Beginnings of Western Science: The European Scientific Tradition in Philosophical, Religious, and Institutional Context, 600 B.C. to A.D. 1450.* 1992. This highly readable study provides an exciting survey of the main developments in western science.

Markoe, Glenn. *Phoenicians.* 2000. The best and most up-to-date treatment of Phoenician society by a noted expert.

Murray, Oswyn. *Early Greece.* 1983. A brilliant study of all aspects of the emergence of Greek society between the Dark Ages and the end of the Persian Wars.

Osborne, Robin. *Greece in the Making, 1200–479 B.C.* 1996. An excellent narrative of the development of Greek society with special regard to the archaeological evidence.

Stewart, Andrew. *Art, Desire, and the Body in Ancient Greece.* 1997. A provocative study that examines Greek attitudes toward sexuality and art.

Walker, Christopher, ed. *Astronomy Before the Telescope,* 1996. A fascinating collection of essays about astronomy in the premodern period, which makes clear our enormous debt to the Bablonians.

Wieshöfer, Josef. *Ancient Persia from 550 B.C. to A.D. 650,* trans. Azizeh Azodi. 1996. A fresh and comprehensive overview of Persian cultural, social, and political history that relies on Persian evidence more heavily than biased Greek and Roman sources.

Notes

1. Based on Herodotus, *History,* vol. 1, trans. Rex Warner (2000), pp. 125–126.
2. James B. Pritchard, *Ancient Near Eastern Texts Relating to the Old testament.* 3rd edition with supplement (1969) pp. 315–316.
3. Demosthenes, *Orations,* 59.122.
4. From Euripides, *The Trojan Women.* Translated by Peter Levi in *The Oxford History of the Classical World,* eds. John Boardman, Jasper Griffith, and Oswyn Murray (1986), p. 169.
5. Andrew Stewart, *Art, Desire, and the Body in Ancient Greece* (Cambridge: Cambridge University Press, 1997, p. 19.

CHAPTER

4

The Hellenistic Age, 336–31 B.C.E.

Chapter Outline

- The Warlike Kingdom of Macedon
- Hellenistic Society and Culture
- Rome's Rise to Power
- Beginnings of the Roman Revolution

One evening after dinner in 193 B.C.E., at the palace of a Greek king in Asia Minor, two battle-hardened generals from different lands debated the identity of the greatest military commander of all time. Both generals came from aristocratic backgrounds. One had grown up in Rome, Italy; the other in Carthage, an imperial city on the coast of North Africa. They conversed in Greek, the language of diplomacy and culture that was used throughout the Mediterranean and the Middle East. The Carthaginian was Hannibal, a military genius who had led the armies of Carthage in a savage war against Rome between 218 and 201 B.C.E., and who now lived in exile. The Roman, who was visiting Asia Minor as part of a diplomatic mission, was Publius Cornelius Scipio Africanus. This equally brilliant general had defeated Hannibal and ended the bloodiest war in Rome's history. When Scipio asked Hannibal who he thought was the world's greatest general, Hannibal named the legendary Macedonian conqueror Alexander the Great. With a smile Scipio then asked his former foe, "What if *you* had defeated *me?*" "In that case," replied the Carthaginian in a flattering tone, "I would be the greatest general of them all."

This anecdote illuminates some fundamental elements of a period that historians call the Hellenistic Age. First, it reveals a cosmopolitan, Greek-based culture in which a Carthaginian general, whose native tongue was a Semitic language, and a Latin-speaking Roman aristocrat could easily communicate. Second, these two warriors shared knowledge of the history of Mediterranean lands, politics, and diplomatic etiquette. Most of all, both admired Alexander the Great, who had made their cosmopolitan world possible. Scipio, Hannibal, and doubtless their host sought to imitate the Macedonian king. Alexander and the

Celt and Wife: This dramatic statue epitomizes the mixing of cultures in the Hellenistic Age. The statue is a Roman copy in marble of a bronze original made at Pergamum in Asia Minor by a Greek sculptor. The artist tells the tragic story of a defeated Celt who has just killed his wife and is at the precise moment of taking his own life rather than be captured alive. In typically Hellenistic style, the artist combines anatomical accuracy with psychological agony.

civilization he had inaugurated had set the standard for success in the minds of men from very different cultural backgrounds.

The Hellenistic period began when Alexander (r. 336–323 B.C.E.) conquered the Persian Empire, extending Greek culture as far east as Afghanistan and India. Greeks called themselves *Hellenes,* and thus historians use the terms *Hellenism* and *Hellenistic* to describe the complex cosmopolitan civilization that developed in the wake of Alexander's conquests. This civilization offered a rich variety of goods, technologies, and ideas to anyone who knew or was willing to learn Greek. Just as people throughout the world today study English because it is the primary language used in high technology, global business, and international politics, Greek became the common tongue used in trade, politics, and intellectual life.

Political borders did not limit Hellenistic civilization. After Alexander died, the empire he had built fragmented into smaller kingdoms that often fought one another. Despite the instability and warfare, however, Hellenistic culture thrived within Alexander's successor kingdoms. It also spread far beyond the lands conquered by Alexander, mainly in the western Mediterranean, where it had a profound effect on the civilizations of North Africa, Europe, and especially Rome. Romans, Jews, Persians, Celts, Carthaginians, and other peoples all absorbed elements of Greek culture—its philosophy, religion, literature, and art. Hellenism gave a common language of science and learning to diverse peoples speaking different languages and worshiping different gods. Hellenism thus gave a cultural unity to a vast area stretching from Europe in the west to Afghanistan in the east. Large portions of this cultural realm ultimately became what historians call the West.

The spread of Hellenistic culture over this vast area involved a series of cultural exchanges. Greek culture offered great prestige and possessed a powerful intellectual appeal to non-Greek peoples, but it also posed a threat to their local, traditional identities. Instead of simply accepting Greek culture, these non-Greek peoples engaged in a process of cultural adaptation and synthesis. In this way Hellenism, which throughout this period remained open to outside influences, absorbed foreign scientific knowledge, religious ideas, and many other elements of culture. These elements then entered the mainstream of Hellenistic culture and were transmitted to the greater Hellenistic world. Some of the basic components of Western civilization originated in these cultural encounters between Greek and non-Greek peoples. These include the seven-day week, beliefs in Hell and Judgment Day, the study of astrology and astronomy, and technologies of metallurgy, agriculture, and navigation.

The Hellenistic era and the age of independent Hellenistic kingdoms came to a close in 31 B.C.E., when the Roman politician and military commander Octavian won sole control of the Mediterranean world, the Middle East, Egypt, and parts of Europe. This political development did not, however, put an end to the influence of Hellenistic culture. By forging a new, more resilient civilization in which Greeks, Romans, and many other peoples intermingled in peace, the Romans created their own version of Hellenism and introduced it to western Europe.

To understand the Hellenistic Age, this chapter will explore four questions: (1) How did Alexander the Great create an empire in which Greek civilization flourished in the midst of many diverse cultures? (2) What were the distinguishing features of Hellenistic society and culture, and what was the result of encounters between Greeks and non-Greeks? (3) How did the Roman Republic come to dominate the Mediterranean world during the Hellenistic Age, and how did Roman rule over the Hellenistic East affect Rome's development? (4) What political and social changes brought the Roman Republic to an end?

The Warlike Kingdom of Macedon

The Hellenistic Age had its roots in Macedon, a kingdom to the north of Greece that was rich in timber, grain, horses, and fighting men. Most Macedonians lived in scattered villages and made a living by engaging in small-scale farming, raiding their neighbors, and trading over short distances. Relentless warfare against wild Thracian and Illyrian tribesmen to the north and west kept Macedonians constantly ready for battle.

Macedonians spoke a dialect of Greek, but their customs and political organization differed from those of the urbanized Greek communities that lay to their south. Unlike democratic Athens, Macedon had a hereditary monarchy. Cutthroat struggles for ascendancy in the royal family trained Macedonian kings to select the best moment to deliver a lethal blow to any enemy. Maintaining centralized political control over their territory proved a constant problem for Macedon's kings because independent-minded nobles resented their rule. Only the army of free citizens could legitimize a king's reign. In return for their support, the soldiers demanded the spoils of war. As a result, Macedonian kings had to wage war continuously to obtain that booty and keep their precarious position on the throne.

Unity and Expansion Under King Philip

Throughout most of the classical period (ca. 700–335 B.C.E.), these fierce Macedonian highlanders knew little of city life and seemed like savages to sophisticated Greeks. When cities started to appear in Macedon in the fifth cen-

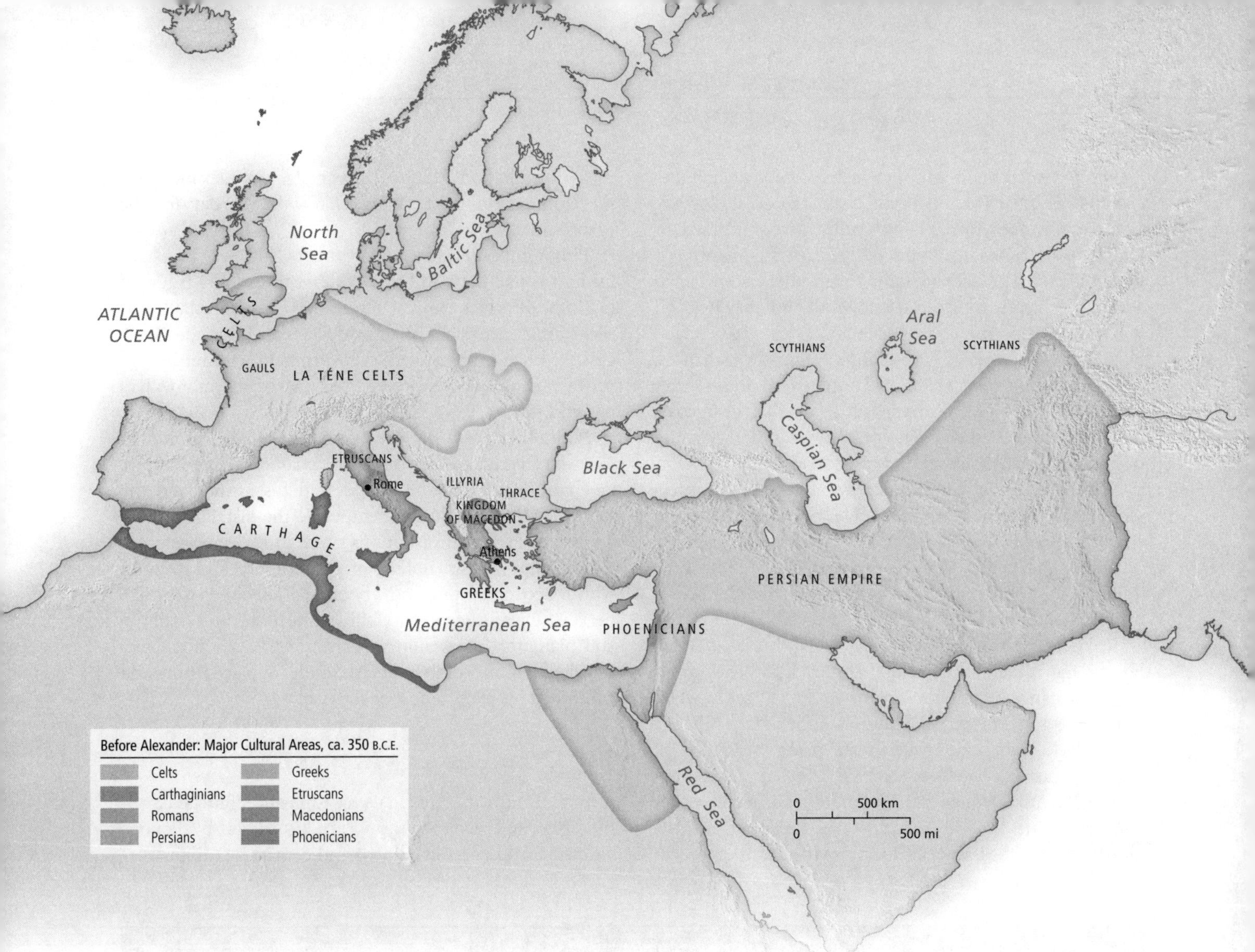

■ **Map 4.1 Before Alexander: Major Cultural Areas, ca. 350 B.C.E.**
During the Hellenistic Age, Greek culture influenced many cultures. This map shows the realms of the Persians, Celts, Romans, Carthaginians, and Phoenicians, whose societies would participate in the Hellenistic Age.

tury B.C.E., Macedonian aristocrats began to emulate the culture of classical Greece. The members of the royal family, for example, claimed the Greek hero Hercules as their ancestor. This move won them the right to compete in the Olympic Games, which were open only to Greeks. Macedonian aristocrats also offered rich stipends to Greek playwrights and scholars to lure them to their capital city of Pella.

In the political realm, however, Macedon shrewdly avoided Greek affairs. During the Persian Wars (490 B.C.E. and 480–479 B.C.E.), Macedonian kings pursued a cautious and profitable policy of friendship with the Persian invaders. During the convulsions of the Peloponnesian War (431–404 B.C.E.) and its turbulent aftermath, Macedon refrained from exploiting Athens, Sparta, and the other Greek cities as they bled to exhaustion. The lack of Greek entanglements, however, could not ease the tensions between kings and nobles. In 399 B.C.E., Macedon slipped into a forty-year period of anarchy. Just as Macedon was on the verge of disintegration, King Philip II (382–336 B.C.E.) stepped forward and transformed the Macedonian kingdom.

A ruthless opportunist with a gift for military organization, Philip consolidated his power by eliminating his rivals, killing many of them in battle. He unified the unruly nobles who controlled different regions of Macedon by demonstrating the advantages of cooperation under his leadership. As Philip led the nobles to victory after victory over hostile frontier tribes and shared his plunder with them and with the common soldiers, the Macedonians embraced his leadership (see Map 4.1).

Philip created a new army in which the nobles had a special role as cavalry armed with heavy lances. Called the Companions, they formed elite regiments bound to their king by oaths of loyalty. Philip reorganized the infantry, or foot soldiers, into military units called phalanxes. Armed with lances nearly fourteen feet long, the infantry held off the enemy while the cavalry galloped in to strike a fatal blow. This new strategy gave Philip's armies an enormous tactical advantage over traditional hoplite formations. After seizing the gold and silver mines of the north Aegean coast of Greece, Philip had ample funds to hire additional armies of mercenaries to augment his Macedonian troops.

With Macedon firmly under his control, its borders secure and his army eager for loot, Philip stood poised to strike at Greece. In 349 B.C.E. he seized several cities in northern and central Greece, inaugurating a decade of diplomacy, bribery, and threats as he maneuvered for power over the rest of the Greek *poleis.*

Recognizing that Philip represented a threat to Greek liberty, the brilliant Athenian orator Demosthenes organized resistance among the city-states. In 340 B.C.E., when Philip attempted to seize the Bosporus, the link to Athens's vital Black Sea trade routes, the *poleis* took action. Demosthenes delivered a series of blistering speeches against Philip known as "the Philippics" and assembled an alliance of cities. In 338 B.C.E., however, Philip crushed the allied armies at the battle of Chaeronea in central Greece. In this confrontation Philip's 18-year-old son Alexander led the Companions in a charge that won the day for the Macedonians.

Philip imposed Macedonian rule over Greece by establishing a coalition of Greek cities called the League of Corinth, of which he was the leader. He also established Macedonian garrisons at strategic sites and forbade Greek cities to change their form of government without his approval. For the Greek *poleis,* the age of autonomy had passed forever.

Philip next cast his eyes on the Persian Empire. In 337 B.C.E. he cloaked himself in the mantle of Greek culture and announced that he would lead his armies and the forces of Greece against the empire to the east. His reason? To avenge Persia's invasion of Greece in the previous century. Philip's shrewd linking of classical Greek civilization with Macedonian force now became a rallying cry for imperialist expansion under Philip's direction. But as Philip laid plans for his assault on Persia 336 B.C.E. an assassin murdered him. Philip's son Alexander replaced him and continued his plans to invade the east.

THE CONQUESTS OF ALEXANDER

A man of immense personal charisma and political craftiness, Alexander won the support of his soldiers by demonstrating fearlessness in combat and displaying military ge-

The Macedonian Phalanx

This reconstruction drawing shows the Macedonian phalanx advancing into battle. The soldiers hold long spears called sarissas. Men in the first rank level their sarissas at the enemy. The soldiers behind them will lower their spears in turn as they advance Calvary regiments of Companions wait for an opportunity to attack.

nius on the battlefield. He combined a predatory instinct for conquest and glory with utter ruthlessness in the pursuit of power. These traits proved to be the key to his success. By the time of his death, at the age of just 33, Alexander had won military victories as far east as India, creating a vast empire. Alexander's successes made him a legend during his lifetime, and millions of his subjects worshiped him as a god. Historians consider him a pivotal figure in the history of Western civilization because his conquests led to the dissemination of Hellenistic culture in lands that were to become important components of the West.

After brutally consolidating power in Macedonia and Greece following his father's death, Alexander launched an invasion of Persia. With only about 40,000 infantry and 5,000 cavalry, Alexander crossed the Hellespont—the narrow strait dividing Europe from Asia where the Black Sea meets the Aegean Sea—and marched into Persian territory in 334 B.C.E.. Darius III, the Great King of Persia who had ascended the throne two years earlier, proved no match for Alexander's tactical brilliance. The young Macedonian king won his first great victory in battle over Persian forces at the Granicus River, giving him control over Asia Minor with its rich Greek coastal cities and fleets. A few weeks later he marched into Syria, where he broke the main Persian army near the town of Issus. Just as he had done at the battle of the Granicus River, Alexander led the Macedonian cavalry's victorious charge into the teeth of the enemy. From this victory Alexander gained control of the entire eastern coast of the Mediterranean Sea and the Persian naval bases located there.

When the maritime city of Tyre succumbed to Alexander's siege in 332 B.C.E., Darius panicked and offered the young Macedonian his daughter and all of his empire west of the Euphrates River in return for peace. Alexander rejected the offer and marched into Egypt, where the inhabitants welcomed him as a liberator from their Persian masters. From Egypt he advanced into Mesopotamia, where he crushed Darius once again on the battlefield at Gaugamela near the Tigris River.

When Alexander entered Babylon in triumph he once again received an enthusiastic welcome as a liberator. From Babylon his forces ventured southeast to Persepolis, the Persian capital, which Alexander captured in January 330 B.C.E. He plundered the city and burned it to the ground. The enormous wealth he acquired from Persepolis paid for all of his military activities for the next dozen years and invigorated the entire Macedonian economy. Darius escaped the destruction of his capital but was soon murdered by his own nobles. The once-powerful Persian Empire lay in ruins.

Alexander had fulfilled his father's pledge to gain vengeance against Persia, but he had no intention of slowing down his march of conquest (see Map 4.2). He pushed past the tribesmen of the harsh Afghan mountain ranges to penetrate Central Asia. Then in 327 B.C.E. he entered the territory that is modern Pakistan through the Khyber Pass. There he defeated the Indian king, but then the tide of fortune slowly turned against him. He planned to cross the Indus River and advance into India, but his exhausted armies refused to follow. He had little choice but to begin a long and arduous return westward. Most of his soldiers died on the way, and Alexander himself suffered nearly fatal wounds. While recuperating at Babylon in 323 B.C.E., where he had begun to plan further conquests, Alexander succumbed to fever after a drinking bout. He had never lost a battle.

In strategic locations through the lands he had conquered, Alexander established cities as garrisons for his troops. More than a dozen of these cities received the name Alexandria in his honor. Thousands of Greeks migrated east to settle in the new cities to take advantage of the expanded economic opportunities for trade and farming. These Greek settlers became the cultural and political elite of the new cities.

Governing an empire of this size proved to be a difficult challenge. It was much easier for Alexander to conquer an enormous empire than to rule it. The Macedonian kingdom that he led was geared to seizing land and plundering cities. It was another task entirely to create the infrastructure and discipline necessary for ruling an immense territory that

CHRONOLOGY

Alexander the Great and the Greek East

359–336 B.C.E.	Philip II rules Macedon
338 B.C.E.	Philip II conquers Greece (Battle of Chaeronea)
336–323 B.C.E.	Alexander the Great reigns
334 B.C.E.	Battle of Granicus River fought
333 B.C.E.	Battle of Issus fought
331 B.C.E.	Battle of Gaugamela fought; Alexander founds Alexandria in Egypt
330 B.C.E.	Alexander destroys Persepolis, capital of Persia
327 B.C.E.	Alexander reaches India
323 B.C.E.	Alexander dies at Babylon
323–CA. 300 B.C.E.	Successors to Alexander establish kingdoms

had little linguistic or cultural unity. Alexander understood that he was no longer king of just Macedon. He recognized that the only model of rule suitable to such a diverse empire was that devised by his Persian predecessors: a Great King presiding over a hierarchy of nobles who governed Persian territory, and subject kings who ruled non-Persian regions.

Necessity thus forced Alexander to bring his Macedonian troops and his new Persian subjects together in an uneasy balance. To that end, Alexander persuaded his army to proclaim him "King of Asia"—that is, the new Great King. With his Companions he simply took over the government of the former Persian Empire from the top. He included a handful of loyal Persians in his administration by making them regional governors or satraps, while offering other Persians minor roles in his regime.

These practical steps promised to bring order to the empire. By adopting the elaborate Persian role of the Great King, Alexander demonstrated to his foreign subjects that his regime stood for security and continuity of orderly rule. His proud Macedonian soldiers, however, ultimately stymied his efforts. They refused to grovel before him as Persian royal ceremony dictated. And though Alexander may well have thought of himself as a god, they refused to worship him while he lived. Instead, they saw Alexander's recruitment of 30,000 Persian troops into their army as a threat to the traditional relationship between Macedonian soldiers and their king. They also resented the marriages with the daughters of Persian noblemen that Alexander forced upon them in order to unite Macedonians and Persians—although no Persian nobles received Greek wives. The Macedonian troops expected to keep all the spoils of victory for themselves. They wanted to be conquerors, not partners in a new government. They failed to understand that men of other cultures within the new empire might be equally loyal to Alexander and thus deserve a share of power and public honor. Alexander's charismatic personality held his conquests together, but his death destroyed any dreams of cooperation between Persians and Greeks.

Map 4.2 Macedon and the Conquests of Alexander the Great

Alexander led troops from his Macedonian homeland as far east as the Indus Valley. He defeated the Persian Empire and incorporated it into his kingdom. This map shows the route of Alexander's march of conquest and the sites of his most important victories.

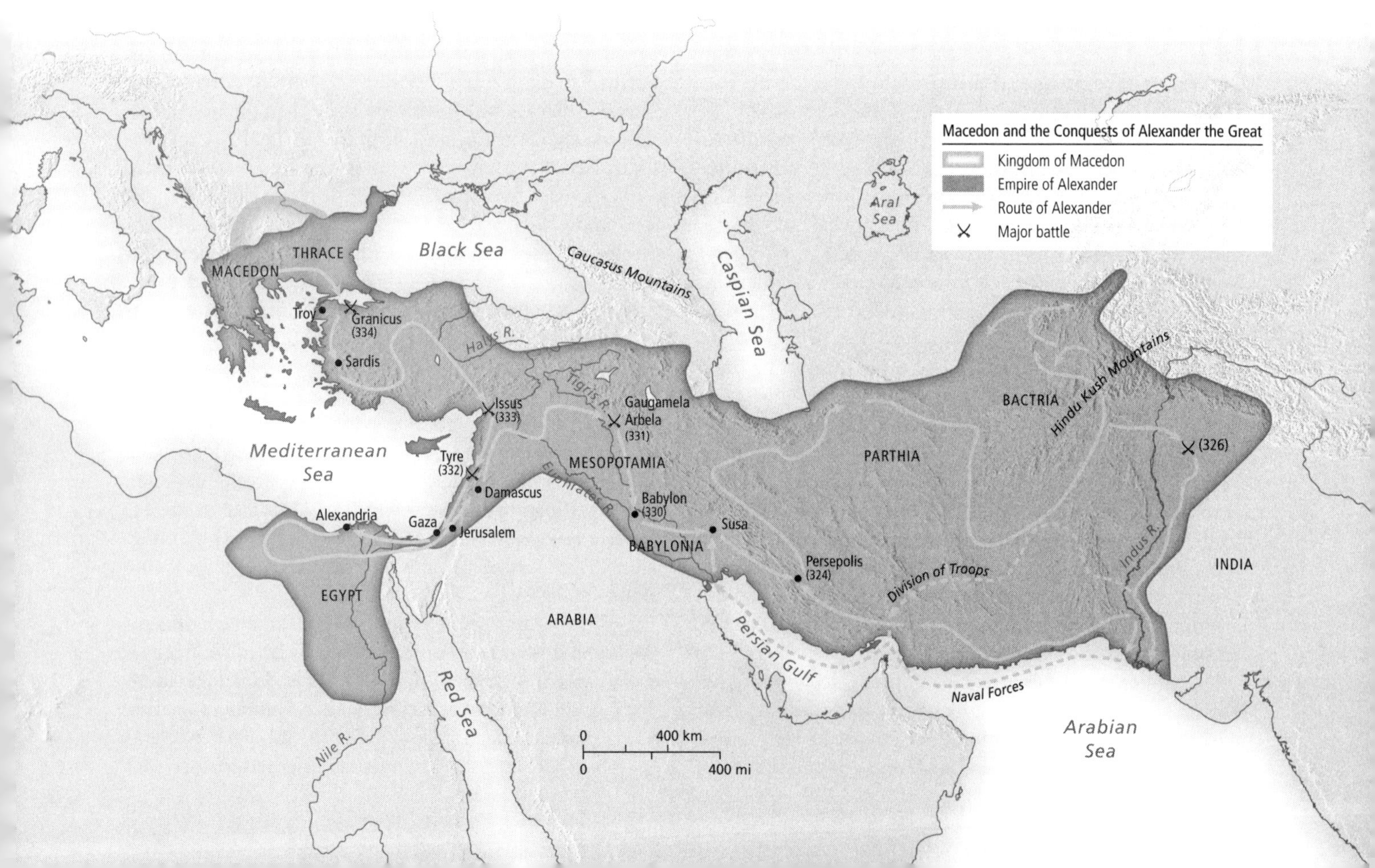

SUCCESSOR KINGDOMS: DISTRIBUTING THE SPOILS

Alexander left no adult heir, and the Macedonian nobles who served as his generals fought viciously among themselves for control of his conquered territory. Eventually these generals created a number of kingdoms out of lands Alexander had acquired (see Map 4.3). One general, Ptolemy, established the Ptolemaic dynasty in Egypt, which would last until 30 B.C.E. Antigonus "the One-Eyed" gained control of the Macedonian homeland and established the Antigonid dynasty, which survived until Rome defeated it in 167 B.C.E. The largest portion of Alexander's conquests, comprising the bulk of the old Persian Empire, fell to his general Seleucus. But in the mid-third century B.C.E., the Parthians, a people from northeastern Persia, shook off Seleucid rule and created a vigorous state. By 150 B.C.E. the Seleucids ruled only Syria.

Smaller kingdoms were also carved out of the areas Alexander had conquered. Bactria (in northern Afghanistan) came under the rule of a Greek-speaking government that would control it well into the second century B.C.E. In 303 B.C.E. the Indian king Chandragupta Maurya conquered the easternmost Indian territories and incorporated them into his own non-Greek kingdom in India. Another lesser successor kingdom emerged in Asia Minor. Centered on the city of Pergamum, a buffer between the Seleucid and Antigonid kingdoms, was ruled by the Attalid dynasty.

Following the example of Macedon itself, the Hellenistic successor states all acquired a monarchical form of government, in which a king ruled the with the support of the army and highly regimented bureaucracies. The members of the administrative hierarchy were all Greeks and Macedonians; indigenous people were not recruited into the ruling elite. Greek was the language of rule in the successor kingdoms. The talented queen Cleopatra (69–30 B.C.E.), who was the last descendant of Ptolemy to rule in Egypt, was the first of her line ever to speak Egyptian. Greek-speaking monarchs were nonetheless aware that they needed to cultivate the goodwill of their non-Greek-speaking subjects. As one monarch asked in a Hellenistic political dialogue, "How can I accommodate myself to all the different races in my kingdom?" A subject answered: "By adopting the appropriate attitude to each, making justice one's guide."

The king towered over Hellenistic society, holding authority over all his subjects and bearing ultimate responsibility for their welfare. Following the example of Alexander, Hellenistic monarchs earned legitimacy by leading their troops into wars of conquest. A king embodied the entire community that he ruled. He was at once the ruler, father, protector, savior, source of law, and god of all his subjects. His garb reinforced his elevated position—kings arrayed themselves in battle gear with a helmet or Macedonian sombrero, crowns, purple robes, scepters, and special seal rings. Monarchs earned the loyalty of their subjects and glorified their own rule by establishing cities, constructing public buildings, and rewarding their inner circle.

Ptolemaic King of Egypt
This golden seal is a masterpiece of the art of portraiture. It depicts Ptolemy, ruler of Egypt, as a pharaoh wearing a double crown, the age-old symbol of Egyptian monarchy. The seal demonstrates the integration of political symbols at the top of the political order.

Ptolemy II, who ruled in Egypt from 283 to 246 B.C.E., exemplifies these notions of Hellenistic kingship. Ptolemy expanded his dominions by conquering parts of Asia Minor and Syria from rival monarchs. He also expanded the bureaucracy, refined the taxation system, and funded many new military settlements. With his support, merchants established new trading posts on the Red Sea, where they engaged in commerce with merchants from India and other eastern lands. Ptolemy patronized the arts and sciences by building impressive research institutes and libraries. He transformed Egypt's capital city of Alexandria, founded by Alexander in Egypt in 331 B.C.E., into the leading center of Greek culture and learning in the Hellenistic world. To reinforce his authority and majesty, he encouraged his subjects to worship him as a god.

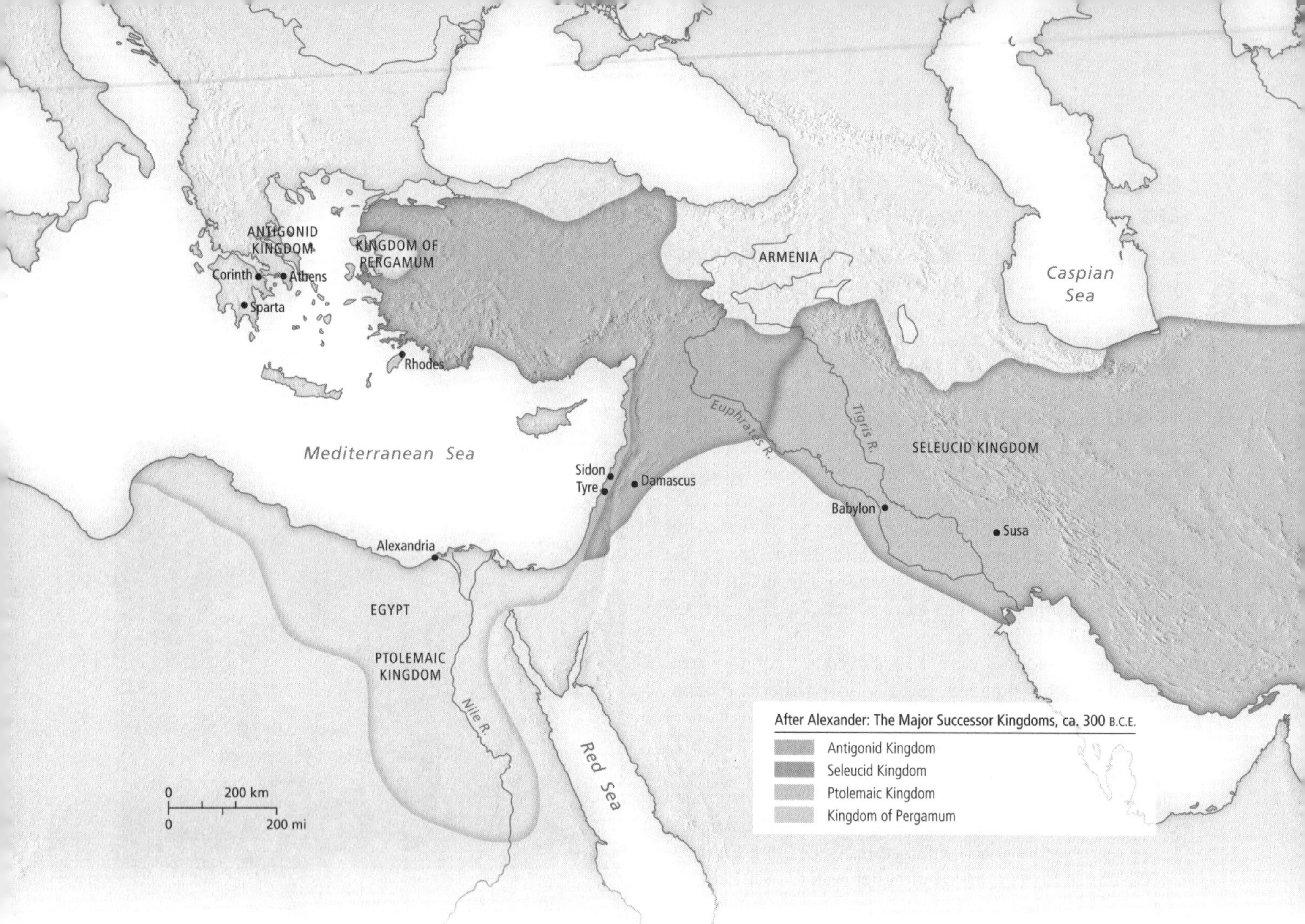

Map 4.3 After Alexander: Major Successor Kingdoms, ca. 300 B.C.E.
After Alexander's death, his generals quarreled and broke the empire into several smaller kingdoms.

This worship of Hellenistic monarchs drew from indigenous traditions throughout the Middle East, but in its Hellenistic form it had a political rather than a spiritual significance. People worshipped their kings as a spontaneous expression of gratitude for the protection and the peace that good government made possible. For example, when the Antigonid king Demetrius "the Besieger" captured Athens in 308 B.C.E., the pragmatic Athenians sang a song in honor of their new master: "The other gods either do not exist or are far off, either they do not hear, or they do not care; but you are here and we can see you, not in wood and stone but in living truth".[1] Deification legitimized a king's right to rule. In turn the ruler cult, in which monarchs were worshiped as gods, channeled all-important loyalty directly to the king.

In addition to the loyalty of their subjects, Hellenistic kings also depended on permanent professional armies to wage the military campaigns so essential to maintaining their authority and to defending their territories. Hellenistic kings fought wars over much larger territories than those that had led to squabbles among Greek city-states in previous centuries. The conquest of such territories required an increase in the size of field armies. The Athenian hoplites had numbered about 10,000 in the fifth century B.C.E., but in the Hellenistic Age kings routinely mustered armies of between 60,000 and 80,000 men. Many soldiers came from military colonies established by the kings. In return for land, the men of these Greek-speaking colonies were obliged to serve generation after generation in the king's army and to police the native, non-Greek populations.

Hellenistic Society and Culture

Chronic warfare among Hellenistic monarchs made political unity among the Hellenistic kingdoms impossible. Nevertheless, the social institutions and cultural orientation of Greek-speaking people in all these kingdoms gave them a unity that their monarchs could achieve.

CITIES: THE HEART OF HELLENISTIC LIFE

Alexander and his successors seized dozens of Greek city-states scattered across the eastern Mediterranean and founded dozens of new glittering urban communities in all the territories they conquered. Hellenistic cities were much more than garrisons put in place to enforce the conquerors' power. They continued traditions of learning, art, and architecture, as well as traditions of citizen participation in public life that had flourished in the classical *poleis.* Most important, people in cities throughout the Hellenistic world spoke a standard version of Greek called koine° that gave them a sense of common identity. Greek city life defined Hellenistic civilization.

On the surface, many of the institutions of the classical *poleis* remained the same: magistrates, councils, and popular assemblies ran the cities' affairs, and some form of democracy remained the ideal in local government. Yet beneath the surface, the *poleis* had undergone radical changes. Because kings wielded absolute power, once-independent cities such as Athens and Corinth lost their freedom to make peace or wage war. They now served as the bureaucratic centers that administered their rulers' huge kingdoms.

Hellenistic kings preferred to maintain the illusion of the cities' independence and rarely intervened in urban affairs, permitting considerable freedom in local government. Nonetheless, Hellenistic methods and those of classical Greece differed in one important way. Democracies had developed in Greece during the Archaic and Classical Ages to protect the interests of the poor as well as the rich. Now, in the Hellenistic Age, the wealthy dominated society and government while the condition of the poor deteriorated. Rich men appointed by the king controlled all the courts, held all the magistracies, and represented all the cities at the court of the kings, who in return showered these civic leaders with honors. Through land grants, tax immunities, and other favors, the monarchs developed networks of personal ties that bound civic leaders to them. In return, these urban elites did more than serve their king. They spent their vast fortunes on behalf of their cities, building magnificent temples, gymnasiums, and other structures for their fellow citizens.

Hellenistic kings and aristocrats spent fortunes turning their cities into showcases of art and design. Distinctive styles of building and ornamentation quickly spread from the east to Italy, Carthage, and Rome. Laying out streets on a grid plan became standard in the Mediterranean world, lending a sense of order to urban space. Stone theaters for plays and spectacles, council halls, and roofed colonnades called *stoas* sprang up everywhere, as did baths with heated pools and gymnasium complexes with sports facilities and classrooms.

In all the major Greek cities of the Hellenistic world, architects built on a monumental scale, integrating sculpture with surrounding buildings and the natural landscape. Temple precincts reveal designers' delight in sweeping

Greek Athletics and Culture
Athletic competition, such as wrestling, was a significant part of Greek culture. Every self-respecting Greek city had a gymnasium. Great cities like Pergamum might have half a dozen. More than just sports centers, gymnasiums served as centers of education and social life for Greek-speaking communities. In these clusters of colonnaded porticoes, wealthy young men of the city learned the basics of Greek literature, rhetoric, science, and music from teachers paid with public funds. For centuries gymnasiums produced leaders and carriers of Hellenistic culture. Here lies the paradox of Hellenism: At the same time that gymnasiums created a shared culture and sense of unity over an enormous geographical extent, they also established a sense of exclusivity and distance from people who did not speak Greek.

vistas across carefully planned terraces and grand stairways. Redefined by these features, the natural setting served as a backdrop for the temple and its processions and rituals.

The freestanding sculpture that decorated public spaces in Hellenistic cities took classical Greek forms in new directions. Turning away from representations of ideal perfection, Hellenistic artists delighted in exploring the movement of the human body and varieties of facial expression. Their subjects ranged from alluring love goddesses to drunks and haggard old boxers. Artists enjoyed portraying the play of fabrics across the human body to accentuate the contours of male and female flesh. Sometimes painted in bright colors, these statues explored human frailty and homeliness as often as they celebrated beauty and lofty emotions.

As we saw in Chapter 3, citizenship in the city-states of classical Greece was a carefully limited commodity that gave people a sense of identity, guaranteed desirable rights and privileges, and demanded certain responsibilities. The territories controlled by any city-state were relatively small, yet even Athens at the height of its empire never considered giving Athenian citizenship to all of the people it ruled outside Attica. In contrast, during the Hellenistic Age, large kingdoms containing many cities were the basic political unit. People were subjects of a king and citizens of their particular cities. To be sure, some philosophers played with the idea of a universal citizenship of all humankind, but there was no notion of a citizenship shared by all the people in one kingdom. Citizenship lost its political force because individual cities had lost their political autonomy. In a sharp break with earlier practice, important individuals sometimes gained the honor of citizenship in more than one city, something that Greeks in the Classical Age would have found inconceivable.

Hellenistic cities contained more diverse populations than had classical *poleis.* Alexandria, in Egypt, the largest and most cosmopolitan of Greek cities, boasted large communities of Macedonians, Greeks, Jews, Syrians, and Egyptians. Although these groups lived in different areas of town and often fought violently with one another, they all participated to varying degrees in the Hellenistic culture of the city. For example, Alexandrian Jews who spoke Greek translated the Hebrew Bible into Greek, a version called the Septuagint°, so that they could more easily read and understand it.

In some older cities such as Babylon and Jerusalem, deep-seated cultural and religious traditions prevented the complete penetration of Greek civilization. Many traditional customs and forms of religious worship, such as the Babylonian worship of the great god Marduk, continued untouched by the Greek way of life. Even the Greek language found limited use in local government. In Mesopotamian cities, for example, local administrators continued to use Aramaic, the local language. The leading families of these cities learned Greek, however, so they could communicate with the members of the king's government and gain political influence.

NEW OPPORTUNITIES FOR WOMEN

One measure of the status of women in a society is the amount of female infanticide permitted. Greek parents in the Classical Age routinely abandoned unwanted female babies, leaving them to die. In Hellenistic families, however, particularly those of the Ptolemaic nobility, baby girls were raised in greater numbers than before. Greek women in Egypt, as well as many other Hellenized lands, enjoyed full citizenship and held religious offices. Many owned land and property, paying taxes as men did, but they could enter into business contracts only of minimal value.

Women in the upper levels of Hellenistic society had the opportunity to wield considerably more power than was conceivable for aristocratic women in the classical Greek period. The wives of Hellenistic kings emerged as models of the new, more powerful Hellenistic woman. Inscriptions engraved in stone praise Hellenistic queens for demonstrating such traditional female virtues as piety and for producing sons. As public benefactors, these women built sanctuaries and public works, sponsored charioteers at the Olympic games, and provided dowries for poor brides. Queens sometimes exerted real authority, supporting and commanding armies. For example, in Egypt the Ptolemaic queen Arsinoë II (r. 276–270 B.C.E.), sister and wife of Ptolemy II of Egypt, directed the armies and navies of the Ptolemaic kingdom in their conquest of Phoenicia and much of the coast of Asia Minor. Egyptian sources refer to her as Pharaoh, a royal title usually reserved for men. The reverence paid to her was also related to the worship of the goddess Isis, with whom she was often identified.

To a lesser extent, opportunities for nonaristocratic Greek women also increased during the Hellenistic age. In Alexandria young women received education in dancing, music, rudimentary reading and writing, and scholarship and philosophy. Often the daughters of scholars became scholars in their own right. Although their work is lost, we know that women wrote about astronomy, musical theory, and literature, and many female poets competed for honors. A few Hellenistic women distinguished themselves as portrait painters, architects, and harpists. Despite these accomplishments, women still had fewer rights and opportunities than men, and they remained under the supervision of their male relatives. In Egypt a woman still could not travel overnight without her husband's permission.

HELLENISTIC LITERATURE, PHILOSOPHY, AND SCIENCE

The Hellenistic Age witnessed the continuation of some trends in classical Greek scholarship while promoting some striking innovations in literature, philosophy, and science.

Literature: Poetry and History Writing

Much Hellenistic literature has vanished, but some surviving works give a glimpse of creativity and originality, which often combined urbanity and thoughtful scholarship. Hellenistic poets turned to frivolous themes because the repressive political climate discouraged questioning of authority. Light comedy became immensely popular, especially in the hands of the playwright Menander of Athens (ca. 300 B.C.E.). This clever author delighted audiences with escapist, frothy tales of temporarily frustrated love and happy endings. These plays, known now as New Comedy, developed from the risqué satires of classical Athens. They featured vivid street language and a cast of stock characters: crotchety parents, naive young men and silly young women, tricky slaves, and wicked pimps.

Theocritus (ca. 300–ca. 260 B.C.E.), who came from Syracuse but wrote in Alexandria in the 270s B.C.E., invented a new genre called pastoral poetry. His verses described idyllic life in the countryside, but his coarse herdsmen reflect the sadness and tensions of city life. Of all the Hellenistic poets, Theocritus has had the most wide-ranging and enduring influence, providing a model for pastoral verse in Rome, Shakespeare's England, and even in nineteenth-century Russia. The other great poet from Alexandria, Callimachus (ca. 305–240 B.C.E.), combined playfulness with extraordinary learning in works ranging from *Collections of Wonders of the World* to his moving love poems, the *Elegies.* His poetry provides the best example of the erudite style known as Alexandrianism, which demonstrated a command of meter and language and which appealed more to the intellect than to the emotions.

Powerful Hellenistic monarchs influenced the writing of history. Kings wanted flattering accounts of their deeds, not the probing, critical independence of mind that Thucydides had offered in the classical period. Some writers resisted these pressures, however. Hieronymous of Cardia, a professional administrator who lived to age 104, described nearly three generations of political intrigue that followed Alexander's death. His conclusion? Fortune, not the efforts of mighty kings, determines the affairs of men.

HONORING A FAMOUS WOMAN POET

In the third century B.C.E., a distinguished female poet named Aristodama visited the city of Lamia in Thessaly, where she recited from her work. The Lamians enjoyed her performances so much that they made her a citizen of their town and gave her several honorific titles to show their appreciation. The remarkable inscription on a marble plaque from Lamia recording the town's decision to honor Lamia reveals that in the Hellenistic Age a person's citizenship was not confined to one city. It also shows the greater freedom and status available to women in the Hellenistic Age. It would have been almost unthinkable in Classical Greece for a woman to become a famous poet.

. . . Resolved by the city of the Lamians. Since Aristodama, daughter of Amyntas, a citizen of Smyrna in Ionia, epic poetess, while she was in our city gave several public recitations of her poems in which [our] ancestors were worthily commemorated and since the performance was done with great enthusiasm, she shall be a Special Friend of the city and a Benefactress, and she shall be given citizenship and the right to possess land and a house and the right of pasture and inviolability and security on land and sea in war and peace for herself and her descendants and their property for all time together with all other privileges that are given to other foreign guests and benefactors.

Source: From *The Hellenistic Age: From the Battle of Ipsos to the Death of Kleopatra VII,* edited and translated by Stanley M. Burstein. Copyright © 1985 by Cambridge University Press.

Philosophy: The Quest for Peace of Mind

The study of philosophy continued to flourish in the Hellenistic world. Plato's Academy and Aristotle's Lycaeum remained in operation in Athens, drawing intellectually curious men from around the Mediterranean. In this environment several new schools of philosophy arose. Three of them in particular—the Epicureans, the Stoics, and the Cynics—shared the common goal of overcoming what they called disturbance, thereby acquiring an inner tranquility or peace of mind. According to Xenocrates (d. 314 B.C.E.), the head of the Platonic Academy, the purpose of studying philosophy "is to allay what causes disturbance in life."

The first of these philosophical schools, the Epicureans°, was founded by Epicurus of Samos (341–271 B.C.E.). Known by its meeting place, the Garden, this school was open to women and slaves as well as free men. Because Epicurus believed that "the entire world lives in pain," he urged people to gain tranquility in their troubled souls through the rational choice of pleasure. The word *epicurean* today denotes a person of discriminating taste who takes pleasure in eating and drinking, but the pleasure Epicurus sought was intellectual, a perfect harmony of body and mind. To achieve this harmony Epicurus recommended a virtuous and simple life, characterized by plain living and withdrawal from the stressful world of politics and social competition. Epicurus also reassured his students that they should fear neither death nor the gods. There was no reason to fear death because the soul was material; hence there was no afterlife. Nor was there any reason to fear the gods, who lived in a happy condition far from Earth, unconcerned

THE HUMAN BODY IN HISTORY

Aphrodite of Melos: The Hellenistic Portrayal of the Perfect Female

Perhaps the best-known female statue surviving from antiquity is that of Aphrodite of Melos, popularly known as the Venus di Milo (her Italian name). Sculpted from marble in the second century B.C.E., the goddess is half-nude. She rests on her right foot and seems to step forward toward the viewer. Though her arms are missing today, originally one arm was probably raised to cover her breasts in a gesture of modesty. Her facial expression is serene. The garment draped loosely around her hips gave an artist the opportunity to explore the play of thin cloth over her thighs, expressing his delight in movement and physicality. Somewhat more sedate than other voluptuous representations of Aphrodite, the goddess of love, this statue portrays a male vision of a perfect woman, highly sexual but also charmingly modest.

Nude statues of Aphrodite meant to be erotic and provoke sexual feelings in men became popular in the Hellenistic Age as the result of changing male attitudes about women. Greek women in the Classical Age led secluded lives at home, with no role to play in warfare, politics, debate, or intellectual pursuits. Men appreciated women primarily as mothers and maintainers of the household, not as objects of sexual desire. Statues of women in the Classical Age generally presented them as heavily draped to protect their bodies from the stares of men. In this misogynistic environment, homoeroticism flourished, and men idealized young men as suitable objects of their love and sexual desire.

In the Hellenistic Age, Greek women achieved more social freedom. Although still excluded from politics, women won greater legal rights and participated more fully in activities outside the home. One consequence of women's changed status in the polis was that men began to appreciate them more fully as objects of sexual desire. Male intellectuals debated whether sex with young men or with young women was better for men, and male artists began portraying women as an erotic ideal. Men created nudes like Aphrodite of Melos for other men to enjoy. It is not known what Hellenistic women thought of these statues. ■

■ **Aphrodite of Melos**
Aphrodite, the goddess of sexual love, displayed the perfection of the female form. This marble statue found on the Greek island of Melos was carved in the second century B.C.E.

For Discussion

What does this work of art tell us about attitudes toward sexuality and the status of women in the Hellenistic Age?

Comedy Mosaic from Pompeii
Brilliant decorative mosaics have survived in great numbers from the Hellenistic world. Often derived from Greek paintings, which have entirely disappeared, these scenes give a vivid glimpse into everyday life. This mosaic is based on a scene from a comedy performed in a theater. We can almost hear the music as street entertainers play and dance in front of a rich man's house.

with human activity. With these fears assuaged, humans could find inner peace.

The main rival to Epicureanism was Stoicism°, the school established by Zeno of Citium (ca. 335–ca. 263 B.C.E.) at Athens in 300 B.C.E. Taking its name from the Stoa Poikile (the Painted Portico) where Zeno and his successors taught, Stoicism remained influential well into the time of the Roman Empire. Stoics believed that all human beings have an element of divinity in them and therefore participate in one single indissoluble cosmic process. They could find peace of mind by submitting to that cosmic order, which Stoics identified with nature or fate. Thus the word *stoic* today carries the meaning of a person who responds to pain or misfortune without showing passion or feeling. Stoics believed that wise men did not allow the vicissitudes of life to distract them. Rather than calling for withdrawal from the world, like the Epicureans, Stoicism encouraged people to participate actively in public life. Because Stoicism accepted the status quo, many kings and aristocrats embraced it. They wanted to believe that their success formed part of a cosmic, divine plan.

The members of the Cynic° school took a different approach to gaining peace of mind. Founded by Antisthenes (ca. 445–360 B.C.E.), a devoted follower of Socrates, the Cynic school taught that the key to happiness was the rejection of all needs and desires. To achieve this goal, Cynics rejected all pleasures and possessions, leading a life of asceticism. Diogenes (ca. 412–324 B.C.E.), the chief representative of the school, made his home in an empty barrel. Cynics manifested contempt for the customs and conventions of society, including wealth, social position, and prevailing standards of morality. One prominent Cynic, Crates of Thebes (ca. 328 B.C.E.), caused a public scandal when he did the unthinkable: He took his wife, the philosopher Hipparchia, out for a meal in public instead of leaving her at home where respectable women belonged. The word *cynic* today usually refers to a person who sneeringly denies the sincerity of human motives and actions. Some Cynics took the doctrine of Diogenes to extremes by satisfying, rather than denying, their simplest natural needs. Their behavior, which included public masturbation and defecation, repelled so many people that their philosophy failed to have a lasting impact.

Explaining the Natural World: Scientific Investigation

While Athens remained the hub of philosophy in the Hellenistic Age, the Ptolemaic kings made Alexandria the preeminent center of scientific learning. These monarchs sponsored scientific research and lectures on the natural world by professional scholars at an institution called the Museum. Nearby, the Library housed hundreds of thousands of texts that attempted to organize the knowledge of the world. In addition to summarizing the work of previous scholars, Hellenistic scientists sought to depict the world as it actually was. This emphasis on realism involved the rejection of some of the more speculative notions that had characterized classical Greek science.

In mathematics, Euclid (ca. 300 B.C.E.) produced a masterful synthesis of the knowledge of geometry in his great work, the *Elements,* which remained the standard geometry textbook until the twentieth century. Euclid demonstrated how one could attain knowledge by rational methods alone—by mathematical reasoning through the use of deductive proofs and theorems. Equally famous as a theorist and engineer was Archimedes of Syracuse (ca. 287–212 B.C.E.), who calculated the value of *pi* (the ratio of a circle's circumference to its diameter) and measured the diameter of the sun. A sophisticated mechanical engineer, Archimedes reputedly said: "Give me a fulcrum and I will move the world." Archimedes put his scientific knowledge to work in wartime. During the Roman siege of Syracuse in 212 B.C.E., he built a huge reflecting mirror that focused the bright Sicilian sun on Roman warships, burning holes in their decks.

Astronomy advanced as well during the Hellenistic Age. In their research, Hellenistic investigators borrowed from the long tradition of precisely recorded observation of the heavens that Babylonian and Egyptian scholars had established. This intersection of Middle Eastern and Greek astronomical work produced one of the richest new areas of knowledge in the Hellenistic world. For example, Heraclides of Pontus (ca. 390–310 B.C.E.) anticipated a heliocentric (sun-centered) theory of the universe when he observed that Venus and Mercury orbit the sun, not the Earth. Aristarchus of Samos (ca. 310–230 B.C.E.) established the idea that the planets revolve around the sun while spinning on their own axes. Eratosthenes of Cyrene (ca. 276–194 B.C.E.) made a calculation of the Earth's circumference that came within 200 miles of being accurate.

The sun-centered view never caught on because of fierce opposition from the followers of Aristotle, whose geocentric (Earth-centered) theories had become canonical. Instead, Hipparchus of Nicaea (ca. 146–127 B.C.E.), who produced the first catalogue of stars, insisted that the Earth was the center of the universe. The geocentric view of the universe prevailed until the sixteenth century C.E., when the Polish astronomer Nicholas Copernicus, who had read the work of Heraclides and Aristarchus, provided mathematical data to support the heliocentric theory. (See Chapter 16.)

Medical theory and research also flourished in the great Hellenistic cities. Diocles, a Greek doctor of the fourth century B.C.E. who combined theory and practice, wrote the first handbook on human anatomy and invented a spoon-like tool for removing arrowheads from the human body that physicians used on King Philip of Macedon. Doctors during this period believed that human behavior as well as disease were products of the interactions of fluids in the body, called humors. They argued about whether to categorize the humors as hot, cold, wet, and dry; as earth, water, fire, and air; or as blood, phlegm, yellow bile, and black bile. Praxagoras of Cos (late fourth century B.C.E.) argued that the body contained more than a dozen kinds of humors. He also studied the relation of the brain to the spinal cord. Other doctors, like Herophilus and Erasistratus, who lived in Alexandria in the fourth century B.C.E., systematically dissected human cadavers. They also may have practiced vivisection, operating on living subjects to study living organs. There is some evidence that with the king's permission they conducted experiments on condemned criminals who had not yet been executed, a practice that is outlawed today. Through dissection these physicians learned a great deal about the human nervous system, the structure of the eye, and reproductive physiology.

The Hellenistic medical tradition outlasted the Hellenistic Age and flourished in the Roman Empire. Galen (129–199 C.E.), the greatest doctor of antiquity, organized Hellenistic medical knowledge, producing accurate, realistic descriptions of human anatomy, and formulated a theory regarding the motion of the blood from the liver to the veins that was not replaced until William Harvey discovered the circulation of the blood in the seventeenth century (see Chapter 16). Galen's theories, like many other aspects of Hellenistic culture, had a profound impact on Western scholarship during the Middle Ages.

Encounters with Foreign Peoples

During the Hellenistic Age, Greeks encountered large numbers of foreign peoples, and the effects of these interactions laid some of the foundations of the West. The encounters took place when Greeks explored the unknown regions in Africa and Europe; when Hellenistic culture met with resistance from Babylonians, Egyptians, and Hebrews; and when Celtic peoples migrated to the boundaries of the Hellenistic world.

Exploring the Hellenistic World

A spirit of inquiry—combined with hunger for trade and profit—drove men to explore and map the unknown world during the Hellenistic Age (see Map 4.4). Explorers backed by monarchs ventured into the Caspian, Aral, and Red Seas. By the second century B.C.E., Greeks had established trading posts along the coasts of modern Eritrea and Somalia, where merchants bought goods, particularly ivory, transported from the interior of Africa. Hellenistic people also craved pepper, cinnamon, and other spices and luxury goods from India, but Arab middlemen made direct trade nearly impossible. One intrepid navigator named Eudoxus made an unsuccessful attempt to find a sea route to India by sailing down both the east and west coasts of Africa, but he never got farther than Morocco.

The most ambitious and successful of all Hellenistic explorers was Pytheas of Marseilles (ca. 310–306 B.C.E.). Setting out from the Greek city of Gades (the modern Spanish port of Cadiz), he sailed around Britain and reported the existence of either Iceland or Norway. He may even have reached the Vistula River in Poland. Throughout his journeys Pytheas contributed much to navigational knowledge by recording astronomical bearings and natural wonders such as the Northern Lights.

As these explorers expanded geographical horizons, Greeks developed a lively though condescending interest in the different peoples of the world. Greeks considered themselves culturally superior to non-Greek-speaking peoples, including Jews, Babylonians, Celts, steppe nomads, and sub-Saharan Africans who lived beyond the borders of Hellenistic kingdoms. Greeks considered all of these peoples inferior barbarians. Despite this prejudice, educated men and women throughout the Hellenistic world enjoyed reading accounts in Greek of foreign peoples' customs, myths, natural history, and forms of government.

Knowledge about different peoples often came from non-Greek intellectuals who translated their accounts into Greek. For example, Berosus, a Babylonian priest, wrote a history of his people that provided Greek readers with extensive astronomical knowledge as well. Manetho, an Egyptian priest, composed a history of his land. Hecataeus of Abdera, a Greek, wrote a popular history arguing that

Map 4.4 Hellenistic Trade and Exploration

During the Hellenistic Age, merchants traveled widely across the breadth of the Mediterranean and throughout the Near East. They sailed into the Persian Gulf and Indian Ocean on commercial ventures.

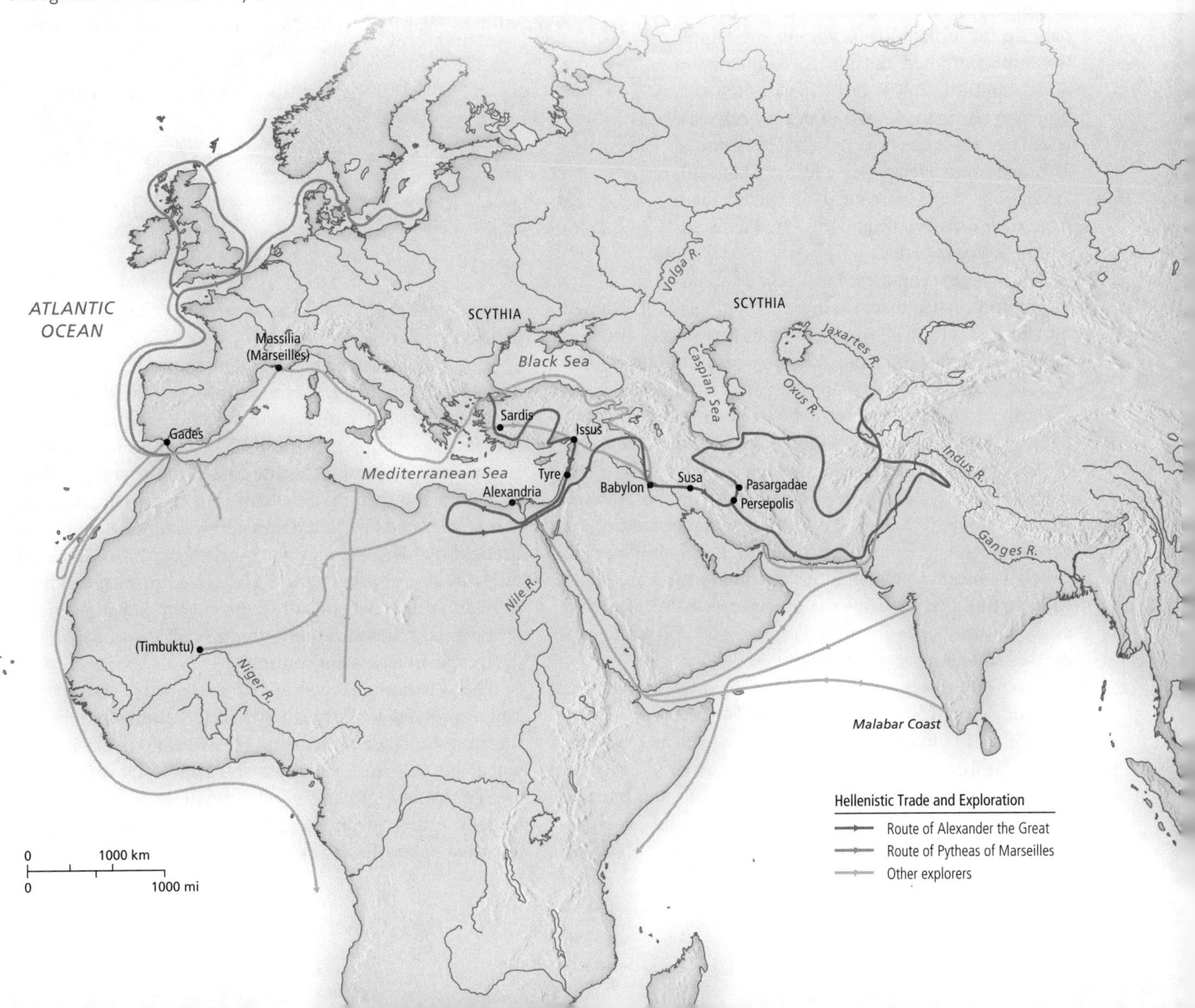

Egypt was the site of the origin of civilization. Most of what was known in the West about India until the Middle Ages derived from the reports of Megasthenes, a Seleucid diplomat. Information about the histories and belief systems of their neighbors entertained intellectuals and helped Hellenistic rulers govern their conquered peoples.

Resistance to Hellenistic Culture

Despite this curiosity among educated Greeks about foreign customs, a great barrier of mutual incomprehension and suspicious resentment separated Greeks and their subjects. Language was one such barrier. In most kingdoms, administrators conducted official business only in Greek. Few Greek settlers in the cities or even in far-flung, isolated military colonies ever bothered to learn the local languages, and only a small percentage of the local populations learned Greek. Many communities preferred to ignore their Greek rulers completely. In Babylonia, for example, age-old patterns of urban life centering on temple worship continued outside the influence of Greek culture. Some non-Greeks, however, hoped to rise in the service of their Greek masters. They made an effort to learn Greek and to assimilate into Hellenistic culture. Their collaboration with Greek rulers alienated them from their own people and provoked divisions within native societies.

CHRONOLOGY

Hellenistic Science and Philosophy

CA. 445–360 B.C.E.	Antisthenes founds the Cynic School at Athens
390–320 B.C.E.	Heraclides of Pontus notes that some planets orbit the sun
CA. 350 B.C.E.	First books on human anatomy are written
310–230 B.C.E.	Aristarchus of Samos establishes heliocentric theory
CA. 310–306 B.C.E.	Pytheas of Marseilles explores coasts of the North Sea
CA. 295 B.C.E.	Ptolemy I founds Museum and Library in Alexandria in Egypt; Menander of Athens writes New Comedy; Zeno of Cition teaches Stoicism at Athens; Euclid writes *Elements of Geometry*
287–212 B.C.E.	Archimedes of Syracuse works
276–194 B.C.E.	Eratosthenes of Cyrene calculates the Earth's circumference
CA. 147–127 B.C.E.	Hipparchus of Nicaea argues that the Earth is the center of the universe
140S B.C.E.	Polybius writes history of Rome's rise to world power
60S–40S B.C.E.	Cicero writes on rhetoric and philosophy at Rome
129–199 C.E.	Galen codifies Hellenistic medical knowledge

Many people conquered by the Greeks continued to practice their traditional religions. Still stunned by the loss of their empire, some aristocratic Persians found solace in practicing Zoroastrianism, the traditional Persian religion. Zoroastrianism teaches that the world is in the grip of an eternal struggle between the good forces of light, represented by the divine creator, Ahura Mazda, and the evil forces of darkness, represented by Angra Mainyu, the demonic destroyer. These Persians interpreted Alexander as Angra Mainyu's agent. In the aftermath of the Persian defeat an important religious text (composed in Greek, ironically) predicted that a military messiah would soon restore Persia's true religion and rulers. In Babylon a book known as the *Dynastic Prophecy* (ca. 300 B.C.E.) expressed similar hopes for Babylonians.

Resentful voices also rang out in Egypt. The *Demotic Chronicle* (ca. 250 B.C.E.) and *The Oracle of the Potter* (ca. 250 B.C.E.) maintained that the Ptolemies had brought the punishment of the gods to Egypt by displacing the pharaohs and interfering with religious customs. One day, the book assured readers, a mighty king would expel the conquerors. Not coincidentally, a series of open rebellions erupted in Egypt about the same time that these works gained popularity.

The Jewish response to Hellenism produced the best-known account of resistance, preserved in the Hebrew Bible as the First and Second Book of Maccabees. After Alexander's conquest of the Persian Empire in 333 B.C.E., Jerusalem and Jewish Palestine passed to the control of the Ptolemies and then the Seleucids. The Ptolemaic monarchs at first tolerated Jewish religion and welcomed the rapid assimilation of Jerusalem's priestly aristocracy into Greek culture. Under the rule of these Hellenized priests, a gymnasium and other elements of Greek culture first appeared in Jerusalem. At the same time traditional Jewish worship at the temple in Jerusalem continued.

The situation changed in 167 B.C.E., when the Seleucid king Antiochus IV Epiphanes tried to demonstrate his authority by further Hellenizing the city; when the Jews resisted, his soldiers desecrated the temple by introducing foreign worship there, an abomination in Jewish eyes. Initially, Antiochus intended to advertise his own strength, not to suppress Jewish practice, but his plan backfired. A family of Jewish priests, the Maccabees, began a religious war of liberation. They drove Antiochus's armies out of Palestine, purified the Temple in Jerusalem, and established an independent Jewish kingdom under their rulership. Later, when Jewish writers sought to explain their actions to the Greek-speaking Jews of Alexandria, they described their struggle in terms of resistance to Hellenism. However, the Maccabean dynasty that had led the victorious struggle against Hellenism soon adopted many Greek customs, causing deep rifts within Jewish society.

Celts on the Fringes of the Hellenistic World

In addition to the Greek culture that spread throughout the Mediterranean and Near East, Celtic civilization flourished in Europe during the Hellenistic Age. Celtic peoples emerged in continental Europe north of the Alps about 750 B.C.E. The Celts, who lived in tribes that were never politically unified on a large scale, shared common dialects, metal- and pottery-making techniques, and agricultural and home-building methods. They are the ancestors of many peoples of northern and central Europe today.

Through trade and war, Celts played an influential role on the northern margins of the Hellenistic world from Asia Minor to Spain. Trading routes were established as early as the eighth century B.C.E., but commerce was often interrupted by war. The military activities of Celtic tribes restricted the expansion of Hellenistic kingdoms, thereby pressuring them to strengthen their military capacities.

Archaeologists call the first Celtic civilization in central Europe Hallstatt culture, because of excavations in Hallstatt, Austria. Around 750 B.C.E., Hallstatt° Celts started to spread from their homeland into Italy, the Balkans, Ireland, Spain, and Asia Minor, conquering local peoples on the way. These people left no written records, so we know little of their political practices. The luxury goods and weapons left in their graves, however, indicate a stratified society led by a warrior elite. Hallstatt sites were heavily fortified, suggesting frequent warfare among communities. Men gained status through competitive exchange of gifts, raiding, and valor in battle. In southern France, Celts encountered Hellenistic civilization at the Greek city of Massilia (modern Marseilles). There they participated in lively trade along the Rhone River for Greek luxury goods, including wine and drinking goblets.

In the middle of the fifth century B.C.E. a new phase in Celtic civilization began, called La Tène° culture, which takes its name from a site in modern Switzerland. More weapons appeared in tombs than in the Halstatt period, indicating intensified warfare. La Tène Celts developed new centers of wealth and power, especially in the valleys of the Rhine and Danube Rivers. They also founded large,

A JEWISH MARTYR FOR A HELLENISTIC AUDIENCE

This excerpt from the narrative of II Maccabees in the Greek version of the Hebrew Bible tells the tragic tale of an old Jew who endured martyrdom for his refusal to compromise with Hellenistic life. Written for a Greek-speaking Jewish audience in Alexandria, the story is told with many allusions to the death of Socrates, demonstrating how Greek ideas had influenced even the enemies of Hellenism.

Eleazar, one of the foremost teachers of the Law, a man already advanced in years and of most noble appearance, had his mouth forced open, to make him eat a piece of pork. But he, resolving to die with honour rather than to live disgraced, walked of his own accord to the torture of the wheel. . . . The people supervising the ritual meal, forbidden by the law, because of the time for which they had known him, took him aside and privately urged him to have meat brought of a kind he could properly use, prepared by himself, and only pretend to eat the portions of sacrificial meat as prescribed by the king; this action would enable him to escape death, by availing himself of an act of kindness prompted by their long friendship. But having taken a noble decision worthy of his years and the dignity of his great age and the well-earned distinction of his grey hairs, worthy too of his impeccable conduct from boyhood and about all of the holy legislation established by God himself, he answered accordingly, telling them to send him at once to Hades. "Pretence, he said, does not befit our time of life. Many young people would suppose that Eleazar at the age of ninety had conformed to the foreigners' way of life and because I had played this part for the sake of a paltry brief spell of my life, might themselves be led astray on my account; I should only bring defilement and disgrace on my old age. Even though for the moment I avoid execution by man, I can never elude the grasp of the Almighty. Therefore if I am man enough to quit this life here and now, I shall have left the young a noble example of how to make a good death, eagerly and generously, for the venerable and holy laws." So saying he walked straight to the wheel . . .

Source: Excerpt from *The New Jerusalem Bible,* copyright © 1985 by Darton, Longman & Todd, Ltd. and Doubleday, a division of Random House, Inc. Reprinted by permission.

Celtic Warriors
These two Celtic statuettes of fighting men reveal the impact of Hellenistic art on native traditions. The first warrior, who stands stiffly and without a well-articulated anatomy, is the product of Celtic artistic traditions untouched by Greek art. The second figure shows the influence of Greek styles. He is well-balanced to throw a spear. His muscles are clearly understood and he turns convincingly in space.

photo to come .534

fortified settlements in these regions as well as in present-day France and England.

La Tène craftsmen benefited from new trade routes across the Alps to northern Italy, the home of Etruscan merchants and artisans. Etruscans traded bronze statuettes to the Celtic north, and they may have also introduced the two-wheeled fighting chariots found in aristocratic Celtic tombs. Greek styles in art reached the Celts through these Etruscan intermediaries, but Celtic artists developed their own distinctive style of metalwork and sculpture. Many Celtic communities began to use coinage, which they adopted from the Greeks.

For about a century relations between the Celtic and Mediterranean peoples centered on trade, but around 400 B.C.E. overpopulation in central Europe instigated massive migrations of Celtic tribes. Around 390 B.C.E. one migrating group of Celts sacked the city of Rome. Their invasion had an unexpected effect on Roman military technology: The Romans began to use the highly effective Celtic short sword, which became the standard weapon of the Roman legions.

This period of hostile migrations lasted until 200 B.C.E. Some Celts traveled to lands that are Slavic today (Slovakia and southern Poland), while others established new homes in the Po Valley in northern Italy, as well as Spain, Britain, and Ireland. Other groups of Celts invaded the Balkans, plundered Greece, and finally settled in Asia Minor, where they established a kingdom, called Galatia, known for the bravery and cruelty of its soldiers. These fighters played an important role as mercenaries in the constant wars among the Hellenistic successor kingdoms. Ultimately the Celts would be absorbed, together with the peoples in the Hellenistic kingdoms in the eastern Mediterranean, into the Roman Empire (see Map 4.5).

Rome's Rise to Power

From Rome's Capitoline Hill a tourist today can look down upon the Roman Forum and see a large field of broken monuments. These remains lie at the heart of what was once an enormous empire extending from northern England to Iraq, and from Morocco to the Black Sea. A few yards away on the western slope of the neighboring Palatine Hill, archaeologists have uncovered hut foundations from the city's earliest occupants in the tenth century B.C.E. How the Roman Empire emerged from this crude village above a swamp remains one of the most remarkable stories in the history of the West.

During the Hellenistic Age, Rome expanded from being a relatively small city-state with a republican form of government into a vast and powerful empire. As it conquered the peoples who ringed the Mediterranean—the Carthaginians, the Celts, and the Hellenistic kingdoms of Alexander's successors—Rome incorporated these newcomers into the political structure of the republic. Trying to govern these sprawling territories with institutions and social traditions suited for a city-state overwhelmed the Roman republic° and led to the establishment a new form of government, the Roman Empire, by the end of the first century B.C.E.

ROMAN ORIGINS AND ETRUSCAN INFLUENCES

Interaction with outsiders shaped the story of Rome from its very beginning. Resting on low but easily defensible hills covering a few hundred acres above the Tiber River, Rome lies at the intersection of north-south and east-west trade routes that had been used in Italy since the Neolithic Age. Romans used these same routes to develop a thriving commerce with other peoples, many of whom they eventually conquered and absorbed into their Roman polity.

Settlements began in Rome about 1000 B.C.E., but we know little about the lives of these first inhabitants. So small was the scale of village life that clusters of huts on the different hills may have constituted entirely different communities. What would one day be the Forum°—the place of assembly for judicial and other public business—was an undrained marsh, which villagers used as protection and burial grounds.

Control of the Tiber river crossing and trade allowed Rome to grow quickly. Excavated graves from the eighth century B.C.E. reveal that a wealthy elite or aristocracy had already emerged. Women evidently shared the benefits of increased prosperity. One grave contained a woman buried

Map 4.5 Celtic Expansion: Fifth to Third Century B.C.E.
During the Hellenistic Age, Celtic peoples migrated into many parts of Europe and Asia Minor. This map shows their routes.

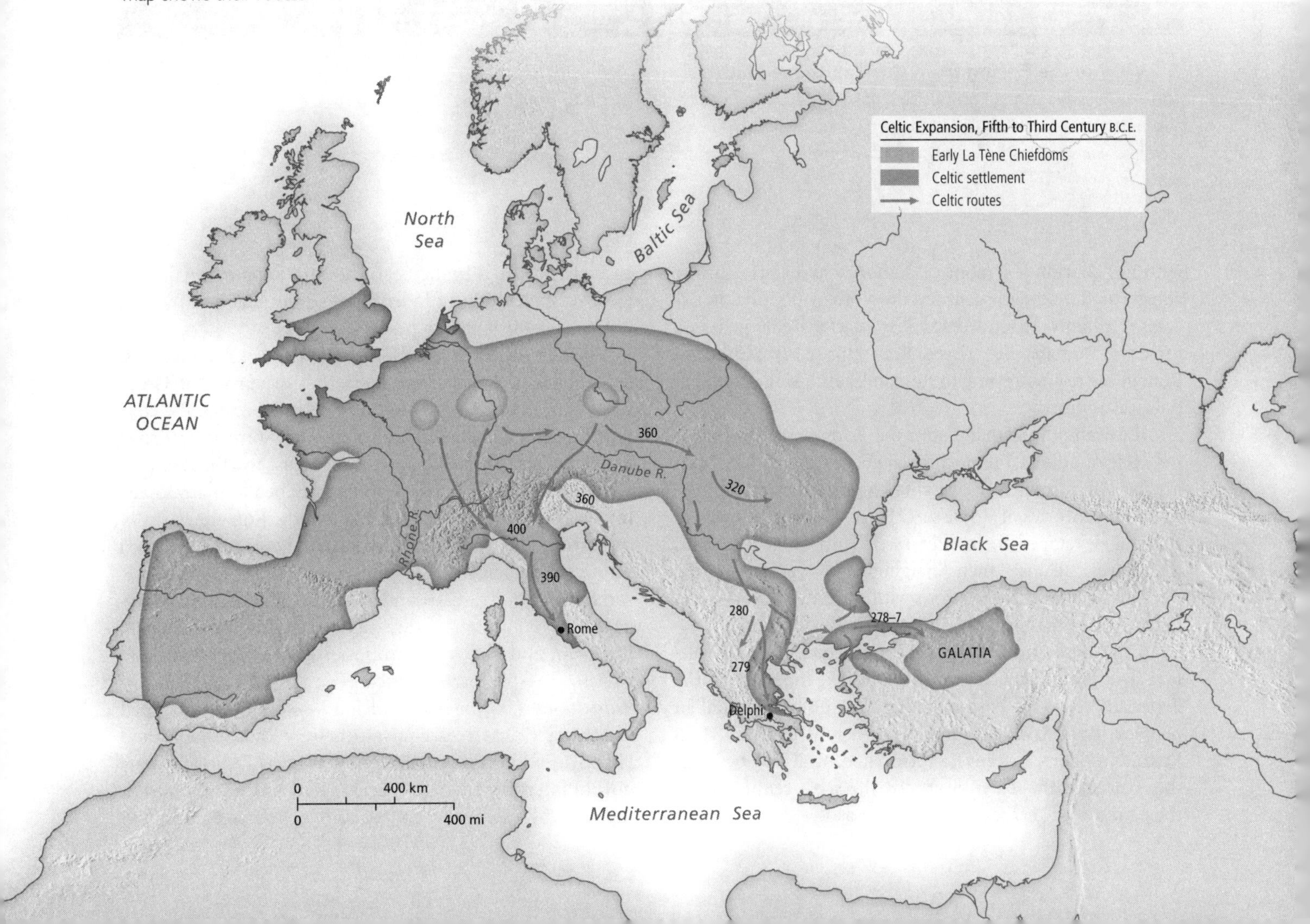

View of the Forum from the Capitoline Hill
This view down into the Forum valley was taken from the site of the Temple to Jupiter, Rome's mightiest god. All victory processions after a successful war would have ended at this temple, where sacrifices were made. Now tourists fill the remains of buildings from which Rome ruled an international empire.

with her chariot, a symbol of authority and status. In the course of the seventh century the Roman population increased rapidly. Extended families or clans emerged as a force in Roman life. Throughout this early period of Roman history, according to Roman legend, kings exercised political authority.

Historians think that Latin, the Roman language, was only one of at least 140 distinct languages and dialects spoken by Italy's frequently warring communities during the first four centuries of Rome's existence. During this period, Romans developed their military skills in order to defend themselves against their neighbors. Nevertheless, the Romans had amicable relations with some neighbors—particularly the Etruscans, who lived northwest of Rome.

In the sixth and seventh centuries B.C.E., Etruscan culture strongly influenced that of Rome. Like the Romans, the Etruscans° descended from indigenous prehistoric Italian peoples. By 800 B.C.E., they were firmly established in Etruria (modern Tuscany), a region in central Italy between the Arno and the Tiber rivers. By the sixth century B.C.E. they controlled territory as far south as the Bay of Naples and east to the Adriatic Sea. The Etruscans maintained a loose confederation of independent cities that often waged war against other Italian peoples.

Etruscans carried on a lively trade with Greek merchants, exchanging native iron ore and other resources for Greek vases and other luxury goods. Commerce became the conduit through which Etruscans and later Romans absorbed many aspects of Greek culture. The Etruscans, for example, adopted the Greek alphabet and subscribed to many Greek myths, which they later transmitted to the Romans.

During the sixth century B.C.E., the Etruscans ruled Rome, influencing its religion and temple architecture. Although the Etruscans and Romans spoke different languages, a common culture derived from native Italian, Etruscan, and Greek communities gradually evolved, especially in religious practice. The three main gods of Rome—Jupiter, Minerva, and Juno—were first worshiped in Etruria. (The Greek equivalents were Zeus, Athena, and Hera.) In addition, Romans learned from Etruscans seers how to interpret omens, especially how to learn the will of the gods by examining the entrails of sacrificed animals.

Etruscans also gave the Romans a distinctive temple architecture that differed from that of the Greeks. While people could walk around a Greek temple and see it from all sides, Etruscan and eventually Roman temples featured deep porches and were placed on a high platform at the back of a long sacred enclosure. This positioning directed the worshippers' attention to the god's temple and the altar in front of it rather than the building's placement in the landscape.

THE BEGINNINGS OF THE ROMAN STATE

By about 600 B.C.E. Romans had prospered sufficiently to drain the marsh that lay at the center of their city, which would be called the Forum. At the same time they began to construct temples and public buildings, including the first senate house, where the elders met to discuss community affairs. Under the rule of its kings, some of whom were of Etruscan origin, Rome became an important military power in Italy. Only free male inhabitants of the city who could afford their own weapons voted in the citizen assembly, which made public decisions with the advice of the senate. Poor men could fight but not vote. Thus began the struggle between rich and poor that would plague Roman life for centuries.

About 500 B.C.E., when Rome had become a powerful city, with perhaps as many as 35,000 inhabitants, the Romans put an end to kingship and began a new system of government that historians call the Roman Republic. According to legend, in 509 B.C.E. a courageous aristocrat named Brutus overthrew the tyrannical Etruscan king, Tarquin the Arrogant. After the coup, Roman aristocrats established several new institutions in place of the kingship that structured political life for 500 years. An assembly comprising Rome's male citizens, called the Centuriate Assembly because of the units of 100 into which the population was divided, managed the city's legislative, judicial, and administrative affairs. As in the Greek *poleis,* only men participated in battle and public life. Each year, the assembly elected two chief executives called consuls, who could apply the law but whose decisions could be appealed. As time went on, the assembly also selected additional officers to deal with legal and financial responsibilities. A body of elders, called the Senate, comprising about 300 Romans who had held administrative offices, advised the consuls, though they had no formal authority. Priests performed religious ceremonies on behalf of the city.

Hatred of kings, which became a staple of Roman political thought, prevented any one man from becoming too prominent. A relatively small group of influential families held real power within the political community, by both holding offices and working behind the scenes. This kind of government is known as an oligarchy°, or "the rule of the few."

To celebrate the replacement of monarchy with oligarchy, the people of Rome built a grand new temple to Jupiter on the Capitoline Hill, looking down on the Forum. Probably at the same time the Romans also established the community of Vestal Virgins as caretakers of the sacred fire and hearth in the Temple of Vesta, one of Rome's most ancient religious sites. In such ways the welfare of Rome became a shared public concern.

Tensions between the rich and the poor shaped political and social life at Rome in the first two centuries of the Republic. At the top of the social hierarchy stood the patricians°, aristocratic clans whose high status extended to the days of the kings. These men, including the legendary Brutus, had been responsible for toppling the monarchy. Because they monopolized the magistracies and the priesthoods, they occupied most of the seats in the Senate. Other rich landowners and senators with lesser pedigrees, as well as the prosperous farmers who made up the army's phalanxes, joined the patricians in resisting the plebeians°, the poorest segments of society. The plebeians demanded more political rights, such as a fair share of distributed public land and freedom from debt bondage. These efforts of poor Romans to acquire a political voice, called the Struggle of the Orders°, accelerated during the fifth century B.C.E., when Rome experienced a severe economic recession.

A victory in the plebeians' struggle came in 494 B.C.E., when they won the right to elect two tribunes each year as their spokesmen. Tribunes could veto magistrates' decisions and so block arbitrary judicial actions by the patricians. Then, in 471 B.C.E., a new Plebeian Assembly gave plebeians the opportunity to express their political views in a formal setting, although without the formal authority to enact actual legislation. About 450 B.C.E., the plebeians took another major step forward with the publication of the Law of the Twelve Tables. Until that time, Romans did not write down their laws, and aristocrats often arbitrarily interpreted and applied laws to the disadvantage of the poor. The plebeians pressed for codification and public display of the law to ensure that the rights of all free Romans would be recognized and respected. The Twelve Tables covered all aspects of life from the proper protection of women ("Women shall remain under the guardianship [of a man] even when they have reached legal adulthood") and debt bondage ("Unless he pays his debt or someone stands surety for him in court, bind him in a harness, or in chains . . .") to religious matters. Even when cruel, the law could now be applied uniformly.

The plebeians continued to make their presence felt in Roman life. In 445 B.C.E., a new law permitted marriage between plebeians and patricians. This enabled wealthy plebeians to marry into aristocratic families. A high point came in 367 B.C.E., when politicians agreed that one of each year's two consuls should come from the plebeian class. The plebeians now were fully integrated within the Roman government. Moreover, around the same time Romans limited the amount of public land that could be distributed to any

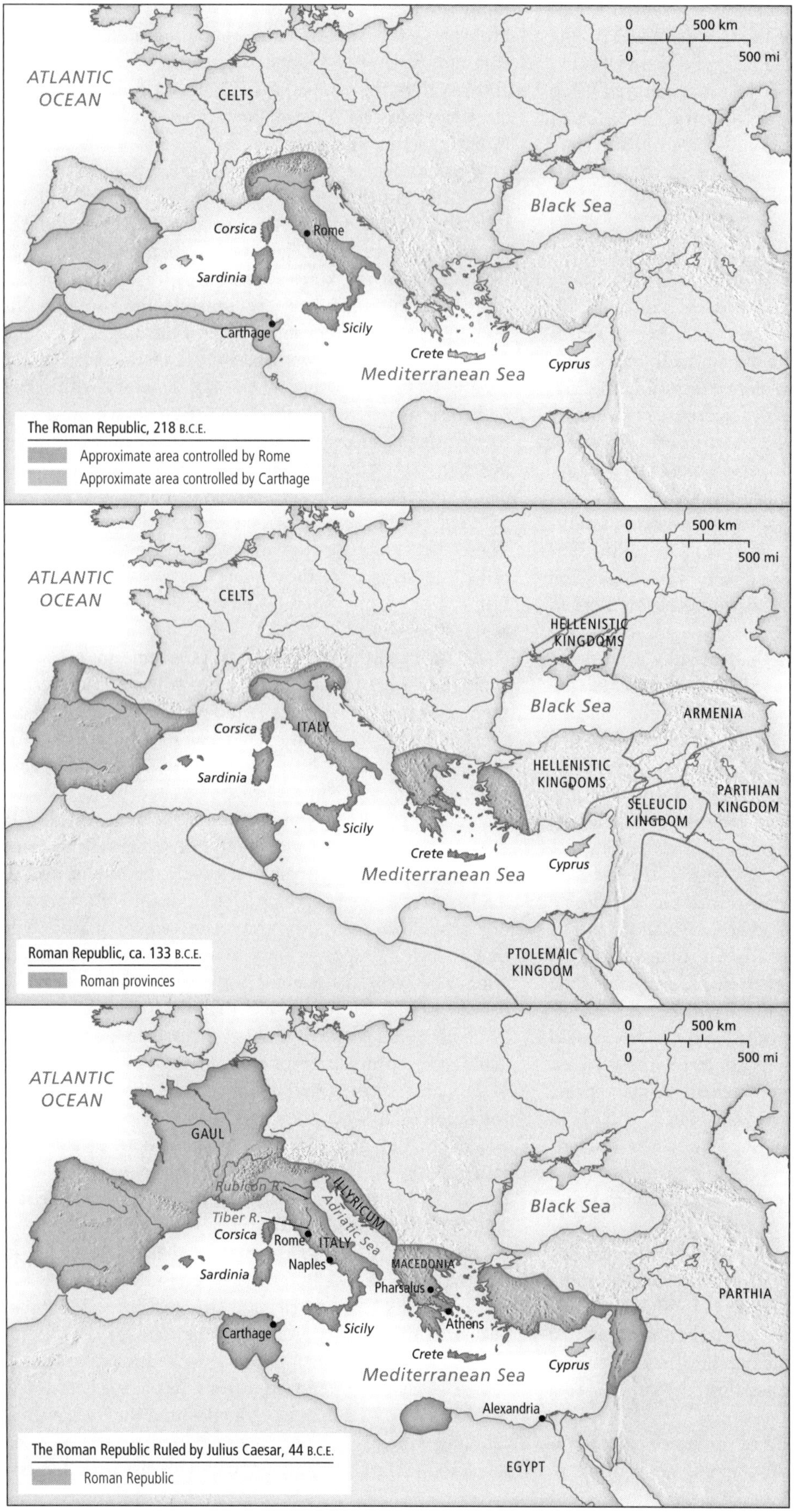

Map 4.6 The Roman Conquest of the Mediterranean During the Republic
Armies of the Roman Republic conquered the Mediterranean world during the Hellenistic Age, overcoming the Carthaginian Empire, the Hellenistic successor kingdoms, and many Celtic peoples in Spain and Gaul.

citizen. The new arrangement prevented aristocrats from seizing the lion's share of conquered territories and permitted poor citizen soldiers to receive a share of captured land. The last concession to the plebeians came in 287 B.C.E., when the decisions of the Plebeian Assembly became binding on the whole state. The plebeians acquired their political strength and full acceptance in the political arena by simple extortion: They threatened to leave the army if the aristocratic elite filed to meet their demands. Without the plebeians, who constituted the bulk of the Roman army, the Republic could not protect itself from invaders or conquer new lands.

At the same time a new underclass of slaves emerged as the result of military expansion in Italy. Poor Roman farmers eagerly settled in newly conquered territories. These farmers in turn served as soldiers in further wars of expansion in which Romans enslaved other conquered peoples. Thus a self-perpetuating cycle of conquest, settlement, and enslavement began to take shape, reaching full development after 200 B.C.E.

ROMAN TERRITORIAL EXPANSION

During the period of the Republic, Rome conquered and incorporated all of Italy, the vast Carthaginian Empire in northern Africa, and Spain, and many of the lands inhabited by Celtic people to the north and west of Italy (see Map 4.6). As a result of these conquests, the Roman state found it necessary to change the methods of government established in the fifth century B.C.E.

Winning Control of Italy

The new political and military institutions that developed in Rome enabled the Romans to conquer the entire Italian peninsula by 263 B.C.E. In the process the Romans learned the fundamental lessons necessary for ruling much larger territories abroad. Romans began to expand their realm by allying with neighboring cities in Italy. For centuries, Rome and the other Latin-speaking peoples of Latium (the region of central Italy where Rome was situated) had belonged to a loose coalition of cities called the Latin League. Citizens of these cities shared close commercial and legal ties and could intermarry without losing citizenship rights in their native cities. Most important, they forged close military alliances with one another.

In 493 B.C.E. Rome successfully led the Latin cities in battle against fierce hill tribes who coveted Latium's rich farmlands. From the success of this venture, Rome learned the value of political alliances with neighbors. Rome and its allies next confronted the Etruscans. In 396 B.C.E. they overcame the Etruscan city of Veii through a combination of military might and shrewd political maneuvering. From this experience, the Romans discovered the uses of careful diplomacy.

A temporary setback to Rome's expansion occurred in 386 B.C.E., when a raiding band of Celts from the Po Valley in the north of Italy defeated a Roman army and plundered the city of Rome before returning home. Only after a generation did Romans recover from this disaster and reassert their preeminence among their allies. Still, they had learned that tenacity and discipline enabled them to endure even a serious military reversal.

The next major step in Rome's expansion came in 338 B.C.E., when Roman troops smashed a three-year revolt of its Latin allies, who had come to resent Rome's overlordship. The peace settlement set the precedent for Rome's future expansion: Rome permitted defeated peoples to become citizens, giving them either partial or full citizenship depending on the treaty it struck with each community. The conquered allies were permitted to continue their own customs, and were not forced to pay tribute. Rome asked for only two things in return: loyalty and troops. All allied communities had to contribute soldiers to the Roman army in wartime. With the huge new pool of troops, Rome became the strongest power in Italy.

In return for their military service and support of Rome, the newly incorporated citizens, especially aristocrats from the allied communities, received a share of the profits of war. They also received the guarantee of Roman protection

CHRONOLOGY

Rome's Rise to Power

CA. 509 B.C.E.	Roman Republic is created
508 B.C.E.	Romans sign treaty with Carthage
494 B.C.E.	Tribunes of the Plebeians created
474 B.C.E.	Plebeian Assembly is created
451 B.C.E.	Twelve Tables of Law is published
387 B.C.E.	Celts sack Rome
287 B.C.E.	Laws of Plebeian Assembly become binding on all Romans
280 B.C.E.	Pyrrhus of Epirus is defeated
264–241 B.C.E.	First Punic War
218–201 B.C.E.	Second Punic War
215–167 B.C.E.	Wars with Macedona
148–146 B.C.E.	All of Macedon and Greece becomes a Roman province
67–62 B.C.E.	Pompey establishes Roman control over Asia Minor, Syria, and Palestine

from internal dissension or outside threats. Those communities not granted full Roman citizenship rights could hope to earn it if they served Roman interests faithfully. Some communities joined the Roman state willingly. Others, particularly the Samnites of south central Italy, resisted bitterly, but to no avail.

Romans continued their march through Italy, becoming embroiled in the affairs of Greek cities of the "toe" and "heel" of the boot-shaped Italian peninsula. Some of these Greek cities invited King Pyrrhus of Epirus, a Hellenistic adventurer, to wage war against Rome on their behalf. Pyrrhus invaded southern Italy with 25,000 men and twenty elephants. Though he defeated Roman armies in two great battles in 280 B.C.E., he lost nearly two-thirds of his own troops and withdrew from Italy. "Another victory like this and I'm finished for good!" he said to a comrade, giving rise to the expression "a Pyrrhic victory," which is a win so costly that it is ruinous. Without Pyrrhus's protection, the Greeks in southern Italy could not withstand Rome's legions, and by 263 B.C.E. Rome ruled all of Italy.

CHRONOLOGY

Imperial Carthage

CA. 850 B.C.E.	Phoenicians found Carthage
600s B.C.E.	Carthage expands in North Africa, Sardinia, southern Spain, and Sicily
508 B.C.E.	Carthage makes treaty with Rome
500–200 B.C.E.	Conflicts with Greeks in Sicily
264–241 B.C.E.	Carthage fights First Punic War against Rome
218–203 B.C.E.	Hannibal fights in Italy
218–201 B.C.E.	Carthage fights Second Punic War against Rome
202 B.C.E.	Battle of Zama; Hannibal is defeated near Carthage
149–146 B.C.E.	Carthage fights Third Punic War against Rome; end of Carthaginian Empire
146 B.C.E.	Destruction of the city of Carthage

The Struggle with Carthage

By the third century B.C.E., imperial Carthage dominated the western Mediterranean region. From the capital city of Carthage located on the north African coast near modern Tunis, Carthaginians held rich lands along the African coast from modern Algeria to Morocco, controlled the natural resources of southern Spain, and dominated the sea lanes of the entire region. Phoenician traders had founded Carthage in the eighth century B.C.E., and the city's energetic merchants carried on business with Greeks, Etruscans, Celts, and eventually Romans.

Hellenistic culture deeply affected Carthage as it did other Mediterranean and Middle Eastern cities. During the Classical Age, Carthaginian trade with the Greek cities in Sicily, and likely with Greek artisans in north Africa, introduced many elements of Greek culture to Carthage. For example, Carthaginians worshiped the Greek goddess of agriculture, Demeter, and her daughter, Kore (also called Persephone), in an elegant temple served by Carthaginian priests and priestesses. By the fourth century B.C.E. the Carthaginian Empire was playing an integral role in the economy of the Hellenistic world by exporting agricultural products, raw materials, metal goods, and pottery.

Rome and Carthage were old acquaintances. Eager for widespread recognition at the beginning of the Republic, Roman leaders signed a commercial treaty with Carthage. Several centuries of wary respect and increasing trade followed. In 264 B.C.E., just as Rome established power throughout the Italian peninsula, a complicated war between Greek cities in Sicily drew Rome and Carthage into conflict. When a Carthaginian fleet went to help a Greek city in Sicily, another city asked Rome for assistance in dislodging them. The aristocratic Senate refused, but the Plebeian Assembly, eager for the spoils of war, voted to intercede. Rome invaded Sicily, setting off the First Punic War, so called because the word Punic comes from the Latin word for Phoenician.

The First Punic War between Rome and Carthage for control of Sicily lasted from 264 to 241 B.C.E. During this time the Romans learned how to fight at sea, cutting off the Carthaginian supply lines to Sicily. In 241 B.C.E. Carthage signed a treaty in which it agreed to surrender Sicily and the surrounding islands and to pay a war indemnity over the course of a decade. Roman treachery, however, wrecked the agreement. While the Carthaginians struggled to suppress a revolt of mercenary soldiers, Rome seized Corsica and Sardinia, over which Carthage had lost effective control, and demanded larger reparations. Roman bad faith stoked Carthaginian hatred and desire for revenge.

War did not resume for another two decades. Under the able leadership of Hamilcar Barca (r. 238–229 B.C.E.), Carthage put its energy into developing resources in Spain, while Rome campaigned against Celts living in the Po Valley and fierce tribes on the Adriatic coast. During these years trade between Rome and Carthage continued, reaching new heights. Soon, however, the rapid growth of Carthaginian power in Spain led to renewed conflict with Rome. The Second Punic War (218–201 B.C.E.) erupted when Hamilcar's son, Hannibal, 25 years old and eager for vengeance, ignored a Roman warning and captured Saguntum, a Spanish town with which Rome had formal ties of friendship. In an imaginative and daring move, Hannibal then launched a surprise attack on Italy by crossing the Alps and invading from the north. With an army of nearly 25,000 men and eighteen elephants, he crushed the Roman armies sent against him. In the first major battle, at the Trebia River in the Po Valley, 20,000 Romans died. At Lake Trasimene in Etruria in 216 B.C.E., another 25,000 Romans fell. In the same year at Cannae, 50,000 men perished in Rome's worst defeat ever.

Despite these staggering losses, the Romans persevered and eventually defeated the Carthaginian general. They succeeded, first of all, because Hannibal lacked sufficient logistical support from Carthage to capitalize on his early victories and take the city of Rome. Second, most of Rome's allies in Italy proved loyal. They had often seen Romans prevail in the past and knew that the Romans took fierce revenge on disloyal friends. Thus the Roman policy of including and protecting allies paid off. A third reason for Hannibal's defeat was the indomitable Roman spirit. The Romans simply refused to stop fighting, even after suffering devastating causalities.

The turning point in the war came when Roman commanders devised a new strategy. After incurring so many defeats, the army dared not face Hannibal in open battle. Instead Fabius, the Roman commander in Italy, avoided open battle and used guerilla tactics to pin down Hannibal in Italy, thus earning the nickname "the Delayer," while Publius Cornelius Scipio Africanus, the Roman general introduced at the beginning of this chapter, took command of Roman forces in Spain. Within a few years he defeated Carthaginian forces there, cutting completely the thin lines of logistical support to Hannibal. In 204 B.C.E., Scipio led Roman legions into Africa, forcing Carthage to recall Hannibal from Italy in order to protect the city.

In one last effort Hannibal confronted Scipio on Carthaginian soil. At the battle of Zama near Carthage in 202 B.C.E., fortune finally deserted Hannibal. Scipio put an end to his string of victories, forcing him into exile. Hannibal had won every battle but his last. Though Scipio spared Hannibal's life and did not destroy Carthage, the peace treaty transferred all of Carthage's overseas territories to Roman control.

Because the war against Hannibal had claimed so many Roman lives, many vengeful Romans agitated for the total destruction of Carthage. In particular, the statesman Marcus Porcius Cato (234–149 B.C.E.), who ended every public utterance with the demand "Carthage must be destroyed!" goaded Romans to violate the peace treaty and resume war with its old adversary. The Third Punic War (149–146 B.C.E.) resulted in the destruction of Carthage. Survivors were enslaved, and the city was burned to the ground and plowed under with salt. Its territories were reorganized as the Roman provinces of Africa.

Conflict with the Celts

Celtic peoples in western Europe fiercely resisted Roman military expansion. After Carthaginian power ended in the Iberian peninsula (modern Spain and Portugal) following the Punic Wars, Romans struggled for more than a century to establish their control over the region's natural resources, particularly its metals and rich farmlands. Not until the reign of Augustus (31 B.C.E.–2 C.E.) did the Romans bring the Iberian peninsula under complete control. The constant fighting drained Rome's manpower and contributed to severe economic and political turmoil in the Republic during the second century B.C.E.

Relations with the Celts had not always been acrimonious. The Roman colonies along the Mediterranean coast that formed an administrative unit called "the Province" (modern Provence) traded peacefully and actively with their Gallic Celtic neighbors. By the late second century B.C.E., Rome had made military alliances with the Aedui, a Celtic tribe that lived further inland. Peace with the Celts, however, ended in 58 B.C.E., when the Roman general Julius Caesar invaded the part of Gaul that lies across the Alps. There he found numerous Celtic tribes with sophisticated political systems dominated by warrior aristocrats. After six years of bloody conquest and massacre, Caesar conquered Gaul, turning the region into several Roman provinces that within a century became an integral part of the Roman Empire.

From the sack of Rome by Celts in the fourth century B.C.E. to the incorporation of some Celtic lands into the Roman state at the end of the Republic, the Celts were a significant factor in Roman life. In his *History,* Polybius suggested that the constant threat of Celtic invasion contributed to the growth of Roman military force. The Roman Republic was geared for constant warfare, and the Celts frequently were the enemy. Thus the Celts shaped

CHRONOLOGY

The World of the Celts

CA. 400 B.C.E.	Celts expand from central Europe
CA. 390–386 B.C.E.	Celts invade Italy and plunder Rome
281 B.C.E.	Celts kill Macedonian king in battle
279 B.C.E.	Celts invade Greece
270s B.C.E.	Celts establish kingdom in Asia Minor
100s B.C.E.	Romans campaign against Celts in Spain
58–49 B.C.E.	Julius Caesar fights Celts in Gaul

Roman foreign policy as well as the Roman allocation of military resources.

ROME AND THE HELLENISTIC WORLD

By the end of the Punic Wars, Rome had become involved in the affairs of the vigorous Hellenistic kingdoms of the East. Initially reluctant to take direct control of these regions, Roman leaders gradually changed their policies. They assumed responsibility for maintaining order and gradually established absolute control over the entire eastern Mediterranean region.

The Macedonian Wars

Rome waged three wars against Macedon between 215 and 168 B.C.E. that resulted in mastery of Macedon and Greece. The First Macedonian War (215–205 B.C.E.) began when the Macedonian king, Philip V (221–179 B.C.E.), had made an alliance with Hannibal after the Roman defeat at the battle of Cannae. The results of the conflict were inconclusive.

Rome entered a second war with Macedon (205–197 B.C.E.) because Philip and the Seleucid king Antiochus III of Syria had agreed to split the eastern Mediterranean between them. The *poleis* of Greece begged Rome for help, and Rome responded by ordering Philip to cease meddling in Greek affairs. Philip refused, and Roman forces easily defeated him with the support of Greek cities. In 196 B.C.E. the Roman general Titus Quinctius Flamininus declared the cities of Greece free and withdrew his forces.

These cities were not truly free, however. Rome installed oligarchic governments on whose support the Romans could rely. These unpopular regimes perpetuated the class distinctions of Rome. When Antiochus III sent an army to Greece to free it of Roman control, Rome struck back again, defeating him in 189 B.C.E. Rome imposed heavy reparations but claimed no territory, preferring to protect the newly freed Greek cities of Asia Minor and Greece from a distance.

Rome's policy of control from a distance changed after a third war with Macedon (172–168 B.C.E.). A harsher attitude took hold in Rome when a new Macedonian king tried to supplant Rome as protector of Greece. After a smashing victory, Rome imposed crippling terms of surrender on Macedon. Rome chopped Macedon into four separate republics, and strictly forbade marriage and trade across the new borders. Roman troops ruthlessly stamped out all opposition, destroying seventy cities that objected to Rome's presence and selling 150,000 people into slavery.

When some Greek cities tried to pull away from Roman control and assert their independence, the heel of Rome came down hard. To set an example of the danger of resistance, the Roman commander Mummius burned the opulent city of Corinth to the ground and enslaved its inhabitants. For weeks, ships carrying booty and slaves from the fallen city docked in Italy.

The Encounter Between Greek and Roman Culture

Romans had interacted with Greek culture to some degree for centuries, first indirectly through Etruscan intermediaries, and then through direct contact with Greek communities in southern Italy and Sicily. During the second century B.C.E., when Rome acquired the eastern Mediterranean through its wars with Macedon, the pace of Hellenism's intellectual influence on Rome accelerated. In addition to fine statues and paintings, Greek ideas about literature, art, philosophy, rhetoric, and education poured into Rome after the Macedonian wars.

This Hellenistic legacy challenged many Roman assumptions about the world. But there was a paradox in the reaction of Roman aristocrats to Hellenism. Many noblemen in Rome felt threatened by the novelty of Hellenistic ideas. They preferred to maintain their conservative traditions of public life and thought. They also wanted to present to the world the image of a strong and independent Roman culture, untainted by traditions from other cultures. Thus during the second century B.C.E., Romans occasionally tried to expel Greek philosophers from their city because they worried that Greek culture might corrupt traditional Roman values. At the same time, many truly admired the sophistication of Greek political thought, art, and literature, and they wished to participate in the Hellenistic community.

Consequently many aristocrats learned Greek but refused to speak it while on official business in the East. While Latin remained the language spoken in the Senate house, senators hired Greek tutors to instruct their sons at home in philosophy, literature, science and the arts, and Greek intellectuals found a warm welcome with Rome's upper class. Cato the Censor, the senator who had insisted that Rome destroy Carthage, embodied the paradox of maintaining public distance from Greek culture while privately cherishing it. He cultivated an appearance of forthrightness and honesty, traditional Roman values that he claimed were threatened by Greek culture. He publicly denounced Greek oratory as unmanly, while drawing upon his deep knowledge of Greek rhetoric and literature to write his speeches praising Roman culture.

Before their exposure to the Hellenistic world in the second century B.C.E., Romans had little interest in literature. Their written efforts consisted mainly of inscriptions of laws and treaties on bronze plaques hung from the outer walls of public buildings. Families kept records of the funeral eulogies of their ancestors, while priests maintained simple lists of events and religious festivals. By ca. 240 B.C.E., Livius Andronicus, a former Greek slave, began to translate Greek dramas into Latin. In 220 B.C.E., a Roman senator, Quintus Fabius Pictor, wrote a history of Rome in the Greek language—the first major Roman prose work. In the next century, Polybius, Greek historian who stood watching with Scipio Aemilianus while Carthage burned, made a major contribution to the writing of Roman history. Taken to Rome from Greece as a hostage in the 160s B.C.E., Polybius came to realize the futility of opposing Roman force. His *History,* written in the analytical tradition of the Greek historian Thucydides, traces Rome's astounding rise to world dominance in a mere fifty-three years and includes moralizing attacks on the abuse of power.

Hellenistic culture also had a major impact on Roman drama. Two Roman playwrights, Plautus (ca. 250–184 B.C.E.) and Terence (ca. 190–159 B.C.E.), took their inspiration from Hellenistic New Comedy and injected some fun into Roman literature. Their surviving works offer entertaining glimpses into the pitfalls of everyday life while also reinforcing the aristocratic values of the rulers of Rome's vast new domains.

Many educated Romans found Greek philosophy extremely attractive. The theory of matter advanced by the Hellenistic philosopher Epicurus, whose ethical philosophy we have already discussed, gained wide acceptance among Romans. Epicurus believed that everything has a natural cause; that "nothing comes from nothing." Romans learned about Epicurus's theories of matter and the infinity of the universe from the poem *On the Nature of the Universe* by the Roman poet Lucretius (d. ca. 51 B.C.E.), who wrote in Latin. The Hellenistic ethical philosophy that held the greatest appeal to Romans was Stoicism, because it encouraged an active public life. Stoic emphasis on the mastery of human difficulties appealed to aristocratic Romans' sense of duty and dignity. The great Roman orator and politician Marcus Tullius Cicero, (106–43 B.C.E.) in particular combined Stoic ideas in a highly personal yet fully Roman way. He stressed moral behavior in political life while urging the attainment of a broad education. Cicero's high-minded devotion to the Republic won him the enmity of unscrupulous politicians, and he was murdered in 43 B.C.E. for his defense of Roman republican liberty.

Despite their openness to Greek philosophy, many members of the Roman ruling elite objected to foreign religious practices. In 186 B.C.E., for example, the Senate suppressed the popular orgiastic cult of the wine god Bacchus, not simply to protect public morals, as they claimed, but to demonstrate and extend their authority over religious worship. Nevertheless, at crucial moments Rome welcomed foreign gods. In 204 B.C.E., two years before the end of the war with Hannibal, the Senate imported the image of the nature goddess Cybele, called the Great Mother, to Rome in order to inspire and unify the city. The cult of Cybele

photo to come .540

Magna Mater

Romans worshipped The Great Mother after her cult was introduced in Rome during the Second Punic War against Hannibal. People had worshipped this goddess throughout the eastern Mediterranean since remote antiquity. This statue expresses her majestic power.

flourished in the Hellenistic kingdom of Pergamum, where devotees worshiped her in the form of an ancient and holy rock. A committee of leading citizens brought this sacred boulder to a new temple on the Palatine Hill amid wild rejoicing. When the ship carrying the rock got stuck in the Tiber River, legend has it that a noble lady, Claudia Quinta, towed the ship with her sash. Not only did Rome defeat Hannibal soon after the arrival of Cybele's sacred stone, but the move cemented Roman relations with Pergamum.

The massive infusion of Hellenistic art following the Macedonian wars inevitably affected public taste. The most prestigious works of art decorated public shrines and spaces throughout the city. Many treasures went to private collectors. Greek artists soon moved to Rome to enjoy the patronage of wealthy Romans. Although copyists made replicas of Greek masterpieces, distinctively Roman artistic styles also emerged, just as they did in rhetoric, literature, philosophy, and history writing. In portrait sculpture, especially, a style developed that unflinchingly depicted all the wrinkles of experience on a person's face. In this way the venerable Roman tradition of carving ancestral busts merged with Greek art.

In architecture, the magnificent temple of Fortune at Praeneste (first century B.C.E.), a town near Rome, combined Italian and Hellenistic concepts to produce the first great monument demonstrating a genuinely Greco-Roman style. By the end of the Republic, Romans had gained enough confidence to adopt the intellectual heritage of Greece and put it to their own ends without fear of seeming "too Greek."

LIFE IN THE ROMAN REPUBLIC

During the Hellenistic Age, Rome prospered from the acquisition of new territories. A small number of influential families dominated political life, sometimes making decisions about war from which they could win wealth and prestige. The Roman Republic remained strong because these ruling families took pains to limit the amount of power any one man or extended political family might attain.

Patrons and Clients

The ruling families of Rome established political networks that extended their influence through all levels of Roman society. These relationships depended on the traditional Roman institution of patrons and clients°. By exercising influence on behalf of a social subordinate, a powerful man (the patron) would bind that man (the client) to him in anticipation of future support. In this way complex webs of personal interdependency influenced the entire Roman social system. The patron-client system operated at every level of society, and it was customary for a man of influence to receive his clients on matters of business at his home the first thing in the morning. In a modest household the discussion might involve everyday business such as shipping fish, arranging a marriage, or making a loan. But in the mansion of a Roman aristocrat a patron might be more interested in forging a political alliance. When several patron-client groups joined forces, they became significant political factions under the leadership of one patron.

Pyramids of Wealth and Power

Like its political organization, Rome's social organization demonstrated a well-defined hierarchy. By the first century B.C.E., a new, elite class of political leaders had emerged in Rome, composed of both the old noble families and those families of plebeian origin who had been able to attain membership in the Senate through their service in the various public offices. The men of this leadership class dominated the Senate and formed the inner circle of government. From their ranks came most of the consuls. They set foreign and domestic policy, led armies to war, held the main magistracies, and siphoned off the lion's share of the Republic's resources.

Beneath this elite group came the equestrian class. Equestrians normally abstained from public office, but were often tied to political leaders by personal obligation. They were primarily businessmen who prospered from the financial opportunities that Rome's expansion provided. For example, during the Republic, equestrian businessmen could bid on contracts to collect taxes in different areas. The man awarded the contract was permitted to collect taxes—with few restraints on his methods. After paying the Senate the amount agreed upon in the contract, he could keep any other tax funds that he had gathered. Many equestrians accumulated fortunes in this way.

Next in rank came the plebeians, the mass of citizens who lived in Rome and throughout Italy. As we have seen, though protected by law with certain hard-won rights and offices, the Plebeian Assembly had gradually come under the control of plebeian politicians who were the clients of aristocratic patrons. These plebeian politicians and their patrons had little interest in the condition of the poor. This left the plebeians with no direct way to express their political will. The demands of army service kept many peasants away from their small farms for long periods of time. Rich investors took the opportunity to create huge estates by grabbing the bankrupt farms and replacing the free farmers with slaves captured in war. Sometimes impoverished plebeians became dependent tenant farmers on land they had once owned themselves. As a result, the citizen peasantry turned more and more to leaders who would protect them and give them land.

Rome's Italian allies had even fewer rights than the plebeians, despite their service in the Roman armies. Although millions of allies inhabited lands controlled by Rome, only a privileged few of the local elites received Roman citizenship. The rest could only hope for the goodwill of Roman officials.

At the bottom of the Roman hierarchy were slaves. By the first century B.C.E., about two million slaves captured in war or born in captivity lived in Italy and Sicily, amounting to about one-third of the population. Romans considered the slaves to be pieces of property, "talking tools," whom their owners could exploit at will. Freed slaves owed legal obligations to their former masters and were their clients. The brutal inequities of this system led to violence. The slave gangs who farmed vast estates in Sicily revolted first. In 135 B.C.E. they began an ill-fated struggle for freedom that lasted three years and involved more than 200,000 slaves.

Thirty years later another unsuccessful outburst began in southern Italy and Sicily because slave owners refused to comply with a senatorial decree to release any slaves who once had been free allies of Rome. Thirty thousand slaves took up arms between 104 and 101 B.C.E. The most destructive revolt occurred in Italy during the years from 74 to 71 B.C.E. An army of more than 100,000 slaves led by the Thracian gladiator Spartacus (gladiators were slaves who fought for public entertainment) battled eight Roman legions totaling about 50,000 men before being crushed by the superior Roman military organization.

The Roman Family

A Roman *familia* typically included not just the husband, wife, and unmarried children, but also their slaves and often freedmen and others who were dependent on the household. Legitimate marriages required the agreement of both husband and wife. Women usually married at puberty, and men did so in their twenties. Because few babies survived infancy, most families had only two or three children. Although Roman men could have only one wife at a time, men frequently cohabited with women to whom they were not married (concubines). Having a concubine was perfectly acceptable, but doing so was legal only if both parties involved had no living spouse.

The Roman family mirrored the patterns of authority and dependency found in the political arena. Just as a patron commanded the support of his clients regardless of their status in public life, so the male head of the household directed the destiny of all his subordinates within the *familia.* A man ruled his *familia* with full authority over the purse strings and all of his descendants until he died. The head of the family, or *paterfamilias,* held power of life and death over his wife, children, and slaves, though few men exercised this power. In reality, women and grown children often had a great deal of independence, and aristocratic women often exerted a strong influence in political life, though always from behind the scenes.

Upper-class Romans placed great value on the continuity of the family name, family traditions, and control of family property through the generations. For these reasons they often adopted males, even of adult age, to be heirs, especially if they had no legitimate sons of their own. Legitimate offspring always took the name of their father, and in case of divorce, which could be easily obtained, continued to live with him. Illegitimate offspring stayed with the mother.

With very few exceptions Roman women remained legally dependent on a male relative. In the most common form of marriage, a wife remained under the formal control of the *paterfamilias* to whom she belonged before her marriage—in most cases, her father. In practice this meant that the wife retained control of her own property and the inheritance she had received from her father. A husband in this sort of marriage would have to be careful to avoid the anger of his wife's father or brothers, and so he might be inclined to treat his wife more justly. Another form of marriage brought the wife under the full control of her husband after the wedding. She had to worship the family gods of her husband's household and accept his ancestors as her own. If her husband died, one of his male relatives became the woman's legal protector.

The stability of family life through the generations desired by free Romans was impossible for slaves to attain. Former female slaves (freedwomen) remained tied to their former masters with bonds of dependency and obligation. Roman law did not recognize marriage between slaves. Some Roman handbooks explaining how to use slaves to maximum advantage advocated letting slaves establish conjugal arrangements. Owners could shatter such alliances by selling the enslaved partners or their offspring.

Beginnings of the Roman Revolution

The inequalities of wealth and power in Roman society led to the disintegration of the Republic. The rapid acquisition of territories and enormous wealth overseas heightened those differences. Roman reformers' attempts to face the new economic realities met with fierce resistance from those who profited the most from imperial rule: politicians, governors, high military personnel, and businessmen. These men sought personal glory and political advantage even if it came at the Republic's expense. Their quest for political prominence through military adventure, coupled with deep-seated flaws of political institutions, eventually overwhelmed the Republic's political structure and brought about a revolution—a decisive, fundamental change in the political system.

The Gracchi

During the second century B.C.E., more and more citizen farmers in Italy lost their fields to powerful landholders, who replaced them with slaves on their estates. As a result, the slave population of Italy increased dramatically. Some members of the political elite feared the danger inherent in these developments. If citizen farmers failed to meet the property requirements for military service and pay for their own weapons, as they traditionally had done, Rome would lose its supply of recruits for its legions.

Two young brothers, Tiberius and Gaius Gracchus, attempted some reforms. Although their mother was an aristocrat (the daughter of Scipio Africanus), she had married a wealthy plebeian. Thus, the brothers were legally plebeian, and they sought influence through the tribunate, an office limited to plebeians. As a tribune, Tiberius Gracchus (162–133 B.C.E.) convinced the Plebeian Assembly to pass a bill limiting the amount of public land that one man could possess. The new law required that the excess land from wealthy landholders be redistributed in small lots to poor citizens. While the land redistribution was in progress, conservative senators ignited a firestorm of opposition to Tiberius Gracchus. He responded by running for a second term as tribune, which was a break with precedent. Fearing revolution, a clique of senators in 133 B.C.E. arranged for assassins to club Tiberius to death. Land redistribution did not cease, but a terrible precedent of public violence had been set.

A decade later, when Tiberius's brother Gaius Gracchus became tribune in 123 B.C.E., he turned his attention to the problem of extortion in the provinces. With no checks on their authority, many corrupt governors forced provincials to give them money, valuable goods, and crops. Gaius Gracchus attempted to stop these abuses. In an attempt to dilute the power of corrupt provincial administrators chosen from the Senate and to win the political support of equestrians in Rome, he permitted equestrian tax collectors to operate in the provinces and to serve on juries that tried extortion cases. Gaius also tried to speed up land redistribution. But when he attempted to give citizenship to Rome's Italian allies in order to protect them from having their land confiscated by Romans, he lost the support of the Roman people, who did not wish to share the benefits of citizenship with non-Romans. In 121 B.C.E. Gaius committed suicide rather than allow himself to be murdered by a mob sent by his senatorial foes.

The ruthless suppression of the Gracchi (the Latin plural form of Gracchus) and their supporters lit the fuse of political and social revolution at Rome. By attempting to effect change through the Plebeian Assembly, the Gracchi unwittingly paved the way for less scrupulous aristocrats to seek power by falsely claiming to represent the interests of the poor. The introduction of assassinations into the public debate signaled the end of political consensus among the oligarchy. Rivalry among the elite combined with the desperation of the poor in an explosive blend, with the army as the wild card. If an unscrupulous politician were to join forces with poverty-stricken soldiers, the Republic would be in peril.

Gaius Marius (157–86 B.C.E.) became the first Roman general to play this wild card. He rose to power when the angry Roman poor made him their champion. Despite his equestrian origins, this experienced general won the consulship in 107 B.C.E. A special law of the Plebeian Assembly put him in command of the legions fighting King Jugurtha in Numidia in North Africa, and he brought the war to a

THE RUINOUS EFFECTS OF CONQUEST

Roman conquests in Italy damaged the economy of newly captured rural areas. The following description by the Roman historian Appian describes the process of Roman settlement in newly taken territories in Italy, and the consequences of that settlement. The reforms of the Gracchi were intended to correct some of these problems.

The Romans, as they subdued the Italian peoples successively in war, seized a part of their lands and built towns there, or established their own colonies in already existing towns, using them as garrisons. Of the land thus acquired by war they assigned the cultivated part forthwith to settlers, or leased or sold it. Since they had no leisure as yet to allot the part which then lay desolated by war (this was generally the greater part), they proclaimed that in the meantime those who were willing to work it might do so for a share of the yearly crops—a tenth of the grain and a fifth of the fruit. From those who kept flocks, a tax was fixed for the animals, both oxen and small cattle. This they did in order to multiply the Italian race, which they considered to be the most laborious of peoples, so that that they might have plenty of allies at home. But the very opposite happened; for the rich, getting possession of the greater part of the undistributed lands, and being emboldened by the lapse of time to believe that they would never be dispossessed, and adding to their holding the small farms of their poor neighbors, partly by purchase and partly by force, came to cultivate vast tracts instead of single estates, using for this purpose slaves as laborers and herdsmen, lest free laborers be drawn from agriculture into the army. . . . Thus the governing class became enormously rich and number of slaves multiplied throughout the country, while the Italian peoples dwindled in numbers and strength . . .

Source: From *A History of Rome through the Fifth Century, Volume 1: The Republic*, edited by A. H. M. Jones, 1968.

quick and successful conclusion. Then in response to a new threat from Germanic tribes seeking to invade Italy, Marius trained a new army and trounced the invaders.

In organizing his army Marius made some radical changes. He eliminated the property requirement for enlistment, thereby opening the ranks to the very poorest citizens in the countryside and in Rome. These soldiers swore an oath of loyalty to their commander-in-chief, who in return promised them farms after a victorious campaign. Marius's reforms put generals in the crossfire of the long-running political struggle between the Senate and the Plebeian Assembly, the two groups authorized to allocate lands won in war.

Marius achieved great personal power, but he did not use it against the institutions of the Republic. When he left public life in old age, the Roman Republic lurched ahead to its next major crisis: a revolt of the Italian allies.

The Social War

In 90 B.C.E. Rome's loyal allies in Italy could no longer endure being treated as inferiors when it came to distribution of land and booty. They launched a revolt against Rome known as the Social War (from the Latin word *socii,* which means "allies"). The confederation of allies demanded not independence but participation in the Roman Republic. They wanted full citizenship rights because they had been partners in all of Rome's wars and thus felt entitled to share in the fruits of victory. The allies lost this war, but once they were defeated, Rome granted all their demands. All of Rome's Italian allies, consisting of the entire population of the peninsula, obtained Roman citizenship and quickly became a potent force in Roman political life. Their presence in the political arena tilted the political scales away from the wealthy in Rome toward the population of Italy in general.

The Social War in Italy stemmed in part from a war abroad. The aristocrat Lucius Cornelius Sulla (138–78 B.C.E.), consul in 88 B.C.E., was setting out with an army to put down a serious provincial revolt in Asia Minor when the Plebeian Assembly turned command of his troops over to Marius, whose military reforms had aided the poor. In response, Sulla marched from southern Italy to Rome and reestablished his control by placing his own supporters into positions of authority in the Senate, the Plebeian Assembly, and various administrative offices.

However, only a year later, when Sulla returned to Asia Minor to resume command of the war against King Mithradates of Pontus, Marius and the other consul, Cinna, won back political control of Rome. They declared Sulla an outlaw and slaughtered his supporters. When Sulla returned to Italy in 82 B.C.E., at the head of a triumphant and loyal army, he seized Rome after a battle in which about 60,000 Roman soldiers died, and then murdered 3,000 of his political opponents. The Senate named him dictator, which gave him complete power. With the support of the aristocratic Senate, whose power he hoped to restore, Sulla crippled the political power of the plebeians. In particular, he restricted the powers of tribunes to propose legislation because they had stirred up so much political instability for fifty years. After restoring the peace and the institutions of the state, Sulla surprised many people by resigning as dictator in 80 B.C.E. Like Marius, Sulla was unwilling to destroy the Republic's institutions for the sake of his own ambition. It was enough for him to have restored peace and the preeminence of the Senate. Nevertheless, he had set a precedent for using armies in political rivalries. In the next fifty years the Senate conspicuously failed to restrain private generals backed by public armies, thereby contributing to the collapse of the Republic.

The First Triumvirate

The Roman Republic's final downward spiral of social turmoil was provoked by three men: Pompey (Gnaeus Pompeius, 106–48 B.C.E.), Marcus Licinius Crassus (ca. 115–53 B.C.E.), and Gaius Julius Caesar (100–44 B.C.E.). Pompey, the general who suppressed a revolt in Spain, and Crassus, the wealthiest man in Rome who had been one of Sullas's lieutenants, joined forces to crush the slave revolt of Spartacus in 71 B.C.E. Backed by their armies, they then coerced the Senate into naming them consuls for 70 B.C.E.,

CHRONOLOGY

Social Conflict in Rome and Italy

133 B.C.E.	Tiberius Gracchus initiates reforms
123–122 B.C.E.	Gaius Gracchus initiates reforms
107 B.C.E.	Marius serves his first consulship
104–100 B.C.E.	Marius holds consecutive consulships
90–88 B.C.E.	Rome fights "Social War" with Italian allies
88 B.C.E.	Sulla takes Rome
82–79 B.C.E.	Sulla serves as dictator
77–71 B.C.E.	Pompey fights Celts in Spain
73–71 B.C.E.	Spartacus's slave revolt
70 B.C.E.	Cicero prosecutes Verres in court

JUSTICE IN HISTORY

A Corrupt Roman Governor Is Convicted of Extortion

Governors sent by the Roman Senate to rule the provinces wielded absolute power, which often corrupted them. One such man was Gaius Verres, who was convicted in 70 B.C.E. in a court in Rome for his flagrant abuse of power while governor of Sicily. The courtroom drama in which Verres was found guilty reveals one of the deepest flaws of the Roman Republic: the unprincipled exploitation of lands under Roman control. It also reveals one of Rome's greatest strengths: the presence of men of high ethical standards who believed in honest government and fair treatment of Roman subjects. The trial and its result reveals Republican Rome at its best and worst.

While governor from 73 to 71 B.C.E., Verres had looted Sicily with shocking thoroughness. In his pursuit of gold and Greek art, Verres tortured and sometimes killed Roman citizens. His outraged victims employed the young and ambitious lawyer Marcus Tullius Cicero (106–41 B.C.E.) to prosecute Verres. They could not have chosen a better advocate.

The prosecution of Verres marks the beginning of Cicero's illustrious career as one of the most active politicians and certainly the greatest orator of the Republic. Cicero also stands as one of the most influential political philosophers of Western civilization, one who hated the corruption of political life and opposed tyranny in any form. His many works have influenced political thinkers from antiquity to the present.

In the Roman Republic, only senators and equestrians between ages 30 and 60 could serve on juries for civil crimes like those committed by Verres. All adult male citizens had the right to bring a case to court, but women had less freedom to do so. After swearing oaths of good faith, accusers read the charges in the presence of the accused, who in turn agreed to accept the decision of the court.

When trials began, the prosecutor was expected to be present, but the accused could decline to attend. The prosecution and the defense both produced evidence, then cross-examined witnesses. Since a Roman lawyer could discuss any aspect of the defendant's personal or public life, character assassination became an important—and amusing—rhetorical tool.

After deliberating, the jury delivered its verdict and the judge gave the penalty required by law, generally fines or periods of exile. No provisions for appeal existed, but pardon could be obtained by a legislative act.

Cicero worked this system to his advantage in his prosecution of Verres. He nimbly quashed an attempt to delay the trial until 69 B.C.E., when the president of the court would be a crony of Verres. Then, with a combination of ringing oratory and irrefutable evidence of Verres's crimes, Cicero made his case. The following excerpt from his speech shows Cicero's mastery of persuasive rhetoric:

> *Judges: at this grave crisis in the history of our country, you have been offered a peculiarly desirable gift . . . For you have been given a unique chance to make your Senatorial Order less unpopular, and to set right the damaged reputation of these courts. A belief has taken root which is having a fatal effect on our nation—and which to us who are senators, in particular, threatens grave peril. This belief is on everyone's tongue, at Rome and even in foreign countries. It is this: that in these courts, with their present membership, even the worst criminal will never be convicted provided that he has money. . . . And at this very juncture Gaius Verres has been brought to trial. Here is a man whose life and actions the world has already condemned—yet whose enormous fortune, according to his own loudly expressed hopes, has already brought him acquittal! Pronounce a just and scrupulous verdict against Verres and you will keep the good name which ought always to be yours. . . . I spent fifty days on a careful investigation of the entire island of Sicily; I got to know every document, every wrong suffered either by a community or an individual. . . .*
>
> *For three long years he so thoroughly despoiled and pillaged the province that its restoration to its previous state is out of the question. . . . All the property that anyone in Sicily still has for his own today is merely what happened to escape the attention of this avaricious lecher, or survived*

his glutted appetites. . . . It was an appalling disgrace for our country.

. . . In the first stage of the trial, then, my charge is this. I accuse Gaius Verres of committing acts of lechery and brutality against the citizens and allies of Rome, and many crimes against God and man. I claim that he has illegally taken from Sicily sums amounting to forty million sesterces. By the witnesses and documents, public and private, which I am going to cite, I shall convince you that these charges are true.[2]

Republican Portrait of Cicero

This portrait of Cicero captures his uncompromising personality. The style of depicting every wrinkle conforms both to Hellenistic interest in psychological portraiture and traditional Roman directness. In the Republican period this type of portraiture was enormously popular.

Cicero's speech was persuasive and the jury found Verres guilty. Verres went into exile in Marseilles to avoid his sentence, but he did not avoid punishment altogether. Justice—relentless and ironic—caught up with him some years later during the civil wars that followed Julius Caesar's death. Mark Antony, who was also a connoisseur of other people's wealth, wanted Verres's art collection for himself and so put Verres's name on a death list to obtain it. The former governor of Sicily was murdered in 43 B.C.E.

In his prosecution of Verres, Cicero delivered more than an indictment of one corrupt man; for a brief moment he revealed some of the deepest, fatal flaws of the Roman Republic. The trial inspired some short-term reforms, but not until the reforms of the Emperor Augustus did the relationship between Roman administrators and provincial populations become more fair. ■

Questions of Justice

1. What does Verres's trial reveal about weaknesses in the Roman Republic?
2. Cicero's speech illustrates his disdain for corruption and tyranny. What are the tensions between personal morality and the requirements of governing a large empire?

Taking It Further

Rawson, Elizabeth. *Cicero, A Portrait.* 1975. This book gives a balanced account of Cicero's life.

Gruen, Erich S. *The Last Generation of the Roman Republic.* 1974. A magisterial analysis of the Republic's decline, with emphasis on legal affairs.

even though Pompey was legally too young and had not yet held the prerequisite junior offices.

During their consulship, Pompey and Crassus made modest changes to Sulla's reforms. They permitted the tribunes to propose laws again and let equestrians serve on juries. After their year in office they retired without making further demands. Pompey continued his military career. He received a special command in 67 B.C.E. to clear pirates from the Mediterranean in order to protect Roman trade. The following year Pompey crushed another rebellion in Asia Minor. He reorganized Asia Minor and territories in the Middle East, creating new provinces and more client kingdoms subservient to Rome.

When Pompey returned to Rome he asked the Senate to grant land to his victorious troops. The Senate, jealous of his success and afraid of the power he would gain as the patron of so many troops, would not comply. To gain land for his soldiers and have his political arrangements in Asia Minor and the Middle East ratified, Pompey made an alliance with two men even more ambitious and less scrupulous than he: his old ally Crassus and Gaius Julius Caesar, the ambitious descendant of an ancient patrician family. The three formed an informal alliance historians call the First Triumvirate°. With their influence now combined, no man or institution could oppose them. Caesar obtained the consulship in 59 B.C.E., despite the objections of many senators. By using illegal means that would return to haunt him, he directed the Senate to ratify Pompey's arrangements in the Middle East and Asia Minor and to grant land to his troops. He arranged for Crassus's clients, the equestrian tax collectors, to have their financial problems resolved at public expense.

As a reward for his efforts on behalf of the triumvirate, the perpetually debt-ridden Caesar arranged to receive the governorship of the Po Valley and the Illyrian coast for five years after his consulship ended. Later he extended that term for ten years. During this time, he planned to enrich himself at the expense of the provincials. As he set out for his governorship, he assumed command of Transalpine Gaul (northwest of the Alps) when its governor died. This put Caesar in a position to operate militarily in all of Gaul—and ultimately to conquer it.

JULIUS CAESAR AND THE END OF THE REPUBLIC

Caesar's determination to conquer Gaul lay in pursuing personal advantage. He knew that he would win glory, wealth, and prestige in Rome by conquering new lands, and so he promptly began a war (58–50 B.C.E.) against the Celtic tribes of Transalpine Gaul. A military genius, Caesar chronicled his ruthless tactics and military successes in his *Commentaries on the Gallic War*, as famous today for its elegant Latin as for its unflinching glimpse of Roman methods and justifications of conquest. In eight years Caesar conquered the area of modern France and Belgium, turning these territories into Roman provinces. He even briefly invaded Britain. His intrusion into Celtic lands led to their eventual Romanization. The French language developed from the Latin spoken by Roman soldiers. Similarly Spanish, Italian, Portuguese, and Romanian also derived from the tongue of Roman conquerors and are called "Romance" languages.

Meanwhile, the other members of the triumvirate, Crassus and Pompey, also sought military glory. The wealthy Crassus raised an army out of his own pocket, reputedly asserting, "If you can't afford to pay for an army, you shouldn't command it!" His attempt to conquer the Parthians, the successors to the Persian Empire, ended in disaster in 53 B.C.E. in Syria. The Parthians killed Crassus, destroyed his army, and captured the military insignia (metal eagles on staffs, called standards) that each legion proudly carried into battle. Pompey again assumed the governorship of Spain, but stayed in Rome while subordinates waged war there against Spain's Celtic inhabitants.

In Rome, a group of senators grew fearful of Caesar's power, ambitions, and arrogance. They appealed to Pompey for assistance, and he brought the armies loyal to him to the aid of the Senate against Caesar. The Senate then asked Caesar to lay down his command in Gaul and return to Rome. Caesar knew that if he complied with this request he would be indicted on charges of improper conduct or corruption as soon as he returned to Rome. Facing certain conviction, Caesar refused to return for a trial. In 49 B.C.E. he left Gaul and marched south with his loyal troops against the forces of the Senate in Rome. Recognizing the enormity of his gamble ("I've thrown the dice!" he said when he crossed the Rubicon River, the boundary of land under direct control of the Senate), he deliberately plunged Rome into civil war. Because of his victories in Gaul and his generosity to the people of Rome, Caesar could pose as the people's champion while seeking absolute power for himself. Intimidated by Caesar's forces and public support, Pompey hastily withdrew to Greece, but Caesar overtook and defeated him at Pharsalus, a town in Thessaly, in 48 B.C.E. When Pompey fled to Egypt high officials of the Ptolemaic pharaoh's court immediately murdered him to win Caesar's favor.

It took Caesar more than two years to crush remnants of senatorial resistance to his authority before he could return to Italy in 45 B.C.E. In 44 B.C.E., back in Rome, he had himself proclaimed dictator for life and assumed complete control over all aspects of government, flagrantly disregarding the precedents of the Republic. Because his plans did not reach fulfillment, Caesar's long-term goals for the Roman state remain unclear, but some version of Hellenistic monarchy seems to have been his plan.

Once in power, Caesar permanently ended the autonomy of the Senate. He enlarged the Senate from 600 (its size at the time of Sulla) to 900 men, and then filled it with his supporters. He also established military colonies in Spain, North Africa, and Gaul to provide land for his veterans and to secure those territories. He adjusted the chaotic Republican calendar by adding one day every leap year, creating a year of 365.25 days. The resulting "Julian" calendar lasted until the sixteenth century C.E. He regularized gold coinage and urban administration and planned a vast public library. At his death, plans for a major campaign against Parthia were underway, suggesting that conquest would have remained a basic feature of his rule.

Caesar seriously miscalculated by assuming he could win the support of his enemies by showing clemency to them and by making administrative changes that disregarded Republican precedent. These changes earned Caesar the resentment of traditionalist senators who failed to recognize that the Republic could never be restored. On March 15, 44 B.C.E., a group of idealistic senators, led by Cassius and Brutus, stabbed Caesar to death at a Senate meeting. The assassins claimed that they wanted to restore the Republic, but in reality they had only unleashed another brutal civil war.

Marcus Antonius (Mark Antony), who had been Caesar's right-hand man, stepped forward to oppose the conspirators. He was soon joined by Octavian, Caesar's grandnephew and legal heir. Though Octavian was only 19, he gained control of some of Caesar's legions and compelled the Senate to name him consul. Marcus Lepidus, commander of Caesar's cavalry, joined Mark Antony and Octavian to form the Second Triumvirate°. The new trio coerced the Senate into granting them power to rule Rome legally.

At the battle of Philippi, a town in Macedonia, in 42 B.C.E., forces of the Second Triumvirate crushed the army of the senators who had assassinated Caesar. But soon Antony, Octavian, and Lepidus began to struggle among themselves for absolute authority. Lepidus soon dropped out of the contest, while Antony and Octavian maneuvered for control of Rome. Reluctant to begin open warfare, they agreed to separate spheres of influence. Octavian took Italy and Rome's western provinces, while Antony took the eastern provinces.

In Egypt, Antony joined forces with Cleopatra VII, the last descendent of the Hellenistic monarch Ptolemy. Both stood to gain from this alliance: Antony would gain the resources of Egypt in his quest to gain complete power over the eastern provinces, while Cleopatra would strengthen her rule in Egypt. In response to this alliance, Octavian launched a vicious propaganda campaign. Posing as the conservative protector of Roman tradition, he accused Antony of surrendering Roman values and territory to an evil foreign seductress. The inevitable war broke out in 31 B.C.E. At the battle of Actium, in Greece, Octavian's troops defeated Antony and Cleopatra's land and naval forces. The couple fled to Alexandria, in Egypt, where they committed suicide a year later.

The 31-year-old Octavian now stood as absolute master of the Roman world. He had a clear vision of the problems that had destroyed the Republic, and from its ashes he planned to rebuild the Roman state. Under the leadership of Octavian, who came to be known as the emperor Augustus, Rome created a new political system, the Roman Empire, in which Octavian had unprecedented power over a vast geographical area.

The new world order that Octavian created brought an end to the Hellenistic Age. Rome now ruled all the lands that Alexander the Great had conquered, except for Persia and the territories farther to the east, and Hellenistic culture would now have to accommodate the realities of Roman rule. As we will see in the next chapter, Octavian succeeded where Alexander had failed: He created a world empire that had the infrastructure it needed to endure, and the peaceful conditions that enabled its culture to flourish and spread.

CHRONOLOGY

The Collapse of the Roman Republic

60 B.C.E.	The First Triumvirate is established
59–49 B.C.E.	Julius Caesar conquers northern and central Gaul
53 B.C.E.	Crassus is killed in the Parthian War
49 B.C.E.	Caesar crosses Rubicon River and begins civil war
48 B.C.E.	Battle of Pharsalus; Pompey is killed in Egypt
45 B.C.E.	Caesar wins civil war
47–44 B.C.E.	Caesar serves as dictator
44 B.C.E.	Caesar is murdered; civil war breaks out
43 B.C.E.	The Second Triumvirate is formed; Cicero is murdered
42 B.C.E.	Battle of Philippi; Caesar's assassins are defeated
31 B.C.E.	Octavian defeats Antony and Cleopatra and gains absolute power

CONCLUSION

Defining the West in the Hellenistic Age

During the Hellenistic Age the cultural and geographical boundaries of what would later be called the West began to take shape. These boundaries encompassed the regions where Hellenistic culture penetrated and had a lasting influence. The lands within the empire of Alexander the Great, all of which lay to the east of Greece and Egypt, formed the core of this cultural realm, but the Hellenistic world also extended westward across the Mediterranean, embracing the lands ruled by Carthage from North Africa to Spain. Hellenism also reached the edges of the lands inhabited by Celtic peoples. Most of all, Hellenistic culture left a distinctive mark on Roman civilization in Italy. In all these locations Greek culture interacted with those of the areas it penetrated, and the synthesis that resulted became one of the main foundations of Western civilization.

During the period of the Roman Empire, which will be the subject of the next chapter, a new blend of Hellenistic and Latin cultures, in which Hellenism was an important but not the dominant component, took shape. The geographical arena within which this culture flourished was that of the vast Roman Empire, covering a large part of Europe, North Africa, and the Middle East. The culture that characterized this empire gave a new definition to what we now call the West.

Suggestions for Further Reading

For a comprehensive list of suggested readings, please go to www.ablongman.com/levack/chapter4

Boardman, John, Jasper Griffin, and Oswyn Murray, eds. *Greece and the Hellenistic World, The Oxford History of the Classical World.* 1988. A synthesis of all aspects of Hellenistic life, with excellent illustrations and bibliography.

Cohn, Norman. *Cosmos, Chaos, and the World to Come: The Ancient Roots of Apocalyptic Faith.* 1993. This brilliant study explains the development of ideas about the end of the world in the cultures of the ancient world.

Cornell, T. J. *The Beginnings of Rome: Italy and Rome from the Bronze Age to the Punic Wars (ca. 1000–264 B.C.).* 1996. A synthesis of the latest evidence with many important new interpretations.

Crawford, Michael. *The Roman Republic,* 2nd ed. 1992. This overview by a leading scholar lays a strong foundation for further study.

Cunliffe, Barry. *The Ancient Celts.* 1997. This source analyzes the archaeological evidence for the Celtic Iron Age, with many illustrations and maps.

Cunliffe, Barry, ed. *The Oxford Illustrated Prehistory of Europe.* 1996. A collection of well-illustrated essays on the development of European cultures from the end of the Ice Age to the Classical period.

Gardner, Jane F. *Women in Roman Law and Society.* 1986. Explains the legal position of women in the Roman world.

Green, Peter. *Alexander to Actium: The Historical Evolution of the Hellenistic Age.* 1990. A vivid interpretation of the world created by Alexander until the victory of Augustus.

Gruen, Erich S. *The Hellenistic World and the Coming of Rome.* 1984. An extremely important study of how Rome entered the eastern Mediterranean world.

Kuhrt, Amélie, and Susan Sherwin-White, eds. *Hellenism in the East: The Interaction of Greek and Non-Greek Civilizations from Syria to Central Asia After Alexander.* 1987. These studies help us understand the complexities of the interaction of Greeks and non-Greeks in the Hellenistic world.

Pollitt, J. J. *Art in the Hellenistic Age.* 1986. A brilliant interpretation of the development of Hellenistic art.

Notes

1. Athenaios, 253 D; cited and translated in J. J. Pollitt, *Art in the Hellenistic Age* (1986), p. 271.

2. From *Cicero, Selected Works,* translated by Michael Grant. First published in 1960 by Penguin Books Ltd.

CHAPTER

5

Enclosing the West: The Early Roman Empire and Its Neighbors, 31 B.C.E.–235 C.E.

Chapter Outline

IN THE MIDDLE OF THE SECOND CENTURY C.E., AELIUS ARISTIDES, AN ARISTOCRATIC Greek writer who held Roman citizenship, visited Rome, where he gave a long public oration in honor of the imperial capital. His words reveal what the Roman Empire meant to a wealthy, highly educated man from Rome's eastern provinces: "Rome is to the whole world what an ordinary city is to its suburbs and surrounding countryside . . . you have given up the division of nation from nation . . . you have separated the human race into Roman and non-Romans."

Aristides' description of the empire as one grand city with a unified culture set off from the "barbarian" peoples in the world is an exaggeration. Nevertheless it points to the key element of the Romans' success—a willingness to share their culture with their subjects and to assimilate them into the political and social life of the empire. Aristides understood that Roman culture flourished primarily in cities, and he saw that Roman urban life was the mark of civilization. He dismissed with a contemptuous sniff those not fortunate enough to live as Romans. In Aristides's opinion, Rome's destiny was to bring civilization to the rest of the world. His satisfied view of the Roman Empire demonstrates how successfully Rome had created a sense of common purpose among its elite citizens.

During its first two and a half centuries of existence, the Roman Empire brought cultural unity and political stability to an astonishingly diverse area stretching from the Atlantic Ocean to the Persian Gulf. Imperial rule disseminated Roman culture throughout not only the Mediterranean region and the Middle East, but also northwestern Europe. Within imperial Rome's parameters—intellectual, religious, political, and geographic—the basic outlines of what we call the West today were drawn.

This chapter examines the Roman Empire at the height of its power (ca. 31 B.C.E.–235 C.E.). We will see how its encounters with far-flung subject populations helped shape its development. Autocratic and exploitative, the

Marcus Aurelius: This magnificent bronze statue shows the emperor Marcus Aurelius (r. 161–180) raising his right hand in a gesture of command, compelling the viewer to obey. A triumph of the art of bronze casting, this statue conveys the majesty of the Roman Empire.

Roman imperial system nonetheless provided the climate for rich developments in social, religious, and political life. Military force maintained the imperial system, but the peace and prosperity that accompanied Roman rule persuaded many subject peoples of its benefits. The new regime established a stable governing system that brought a nearly unbroken peace to the Mediterranean world for more than two centuries. Historians call this era the *Pax Romana*°, the Roman peace. In these centuries Roman culture slowly took root across western Europe, North Africa, and the Middle East, transforming the lives of local populations. In the eyes of millions of people during these years, Rome ceased to be an unfamiliar and predatory occupying power. They came to regard Rome as a "civilizing agent" that provided unity and common culture. But others, particularly the slaves whose labor fueled the Roman economy and the small farmers whose taxes supported the Roman state, experienced Rome as an oppressive ruler.

This chapter analyzes imperial Rome's constantly evolving political and cultural community as three concentric circles of power—the imperial center, the provinces, and the frontiers and beyond. The imperial center served as the site of the main agents of control—the emperor, the Roman senate, the chief legal and administrative institutions, and the army. In the second circle, provincial populations struggled with the challenges raised by the imposition of Roman culture and politics and in the process contributed to the construction of a new imperial culture. The outermost circle of the empire, its frontier and beyond, contained those peoples who lived outside the empire's formal boundaries, but who nonetheless interacted with Rome through trading and warfare. Throughout the chapter we will explore what it meant to be a Roman in each of these concentric circles. Four questions guide this exploration: (1) How did the Roman imperial system develop and what roles did the emperor, senate, army, and Rome itself play in this process? (2) How did provincial peoples assimilate to or resist Roman rule? (3) How did Romans interact with peoples living beyond the imperial borders? (4) What was the social and cultural response to the emergence and consolidation of empire?

The Imperial Center

After civil wars left the Roman Republic in ruins, a new political system emerged from its ashes. Rome continued to acquire and rule huge territories far from Italy. Its form of government, however, changed from a republic, in which members of an oligarchy competed for power that they shared by serving in elected offices, to an empire, in which one man, the emperor, held absolute power for life. Roman culture, with its strict social divisions and political structures, its distinctive forms of architecture and art, its shared intellectual and religious life, and its legal system defining the rights of citizens and subjects, was now securely anchored by an imperial system based on force. The city of Rome, the center of imperial operations, became the model for social life, political processes, and architectural styles throughout the empire. At the same time, Roman law united Roman citizens throughout the empire and distinguished them from conquered peoples, who kept their own laws and customs. After 212 C.E. all free people in the empire gained Roman citizenship, a sign of growing cultural unity: the Romanization of the diverse peoples under imperial rule (see Map 5.1).

IMPERIAL AUTHORITY: AUGUSTUS AND AFTER

As we saw in Chapter 4, Julius Caesar's heir, Octavian, destroyed the Republic while pretending to preserve it. Octavian wrenched the state from the spiral of civil war and claimed that he had restored normal life to the Republic. In his own eyes, as well as those of a people weary of bitter civil war, Octavian was the savior of Republican Rome. In public affairs, however, nothing could have been further from the truth. Behind a carefully crafted façade of restored Republican tradition, Octavian created a Roman version of a Hellenistic monarchy, like those of Alexander the Great's successors in the eastern Mediterranean. By neutralizing all of his political enemies in the Roman Senate; vanquishing his military rivals, such as Antony and Cleopatra; and establishing an iron grip on every visible mechanism of power, Octavian succeeded where Julius Caesar and the other less able Republican politicians had failed: He achieved total mastery of the political arena at Rome. No one successfully challenged his authority.

To mask his tyranny, Octavian never wore a crown and modestly referred to himself as *Princeps*, or First Citizen. He took several steps to create a political position in Rome that was all-powerful and at the same time unobtrusive. In 27 B.C.E., as he boasted in the official account of his reign, Octavian "transferred the Republic from his power into that of the Senate and the Roman people." This abdication was a carefully organized sham. In reality, he maintained absolute political control over Rome. Following his instructions, the powerless Senate showered honors upon him, including the title "Augustus." This invented title best illustrates the political cleverness of Rome's absolute master. "Augustus" implied a uniquely exalted, godlike authority in the community, but the word had no previous associations with kingship. Augustus "accepted" the Senate's plea to remain consul and agreed to exercise control over the frontier provinces where the most troops were stationed, including Spain, Gaul, and Syria. The senators rejoiced, calling Augustus "sole savior of the entire empire."

In 23 B.C.E. Augustus took further steps to establish his paramount position. He had held the consulship every year since the end of the civil war in 31 B.C.E., but he recognized that holding the power of a consul year after year was inconsistent with his claim to have restored the Republic. So, in 23 C.E. he renounced the consulship and shrewdly arranged for the Senate to grant him unprecedented power, but disguised by Republican trappings. He assumed the powers of a tribune, which included the right to conduct business in the Senate, the right to veto, and immunity from arrest and punishment. He could now legally intercede in all government activities and military affairs by virtue of "greater authority" granted to him by the Senate. Other generals continued to lead the legions into battle, but always in his name. Other magistrates continued to administer the state in accordance with the traditional responsibilities of their office, but no one was chosen without his approval.

Augustus selected or approved all his provincial governors. He assumed direct control over particularly rich provinces, such as Egypt, and those, like Germany, that required a strong military presence to ward off invaders and control the recently conquered population. The Roman Senate maintained authority over peaceful provinces like Greece and Sicily. Yet even in these provinces, Augustus intervened whenever he wished.

Later rulers, accepting the trappings of monarchy more openly than Augustus, abandoned the fiction of the "Princeps" and used the title *imperator*, or emperor. Despite this change, the imperial system established by Augustus long survived his death, even when the throne was occupied by brutal men such as Caligula (r. 37–41 C.E.), who tried to have his favorite horse elected to the Senate, or Nero (r. 54–68 C.E.), who murdered both his wife and his mother.

Map 5.1 The Roman Empire at Its Greatest Extent
The Roman Empire reached its greatest extent during the reign of Trajan (98–117 C.E.). Stretching from the north of Britain to the Euphrates River, the empire brought together hundreds of distinct ethnic groups.

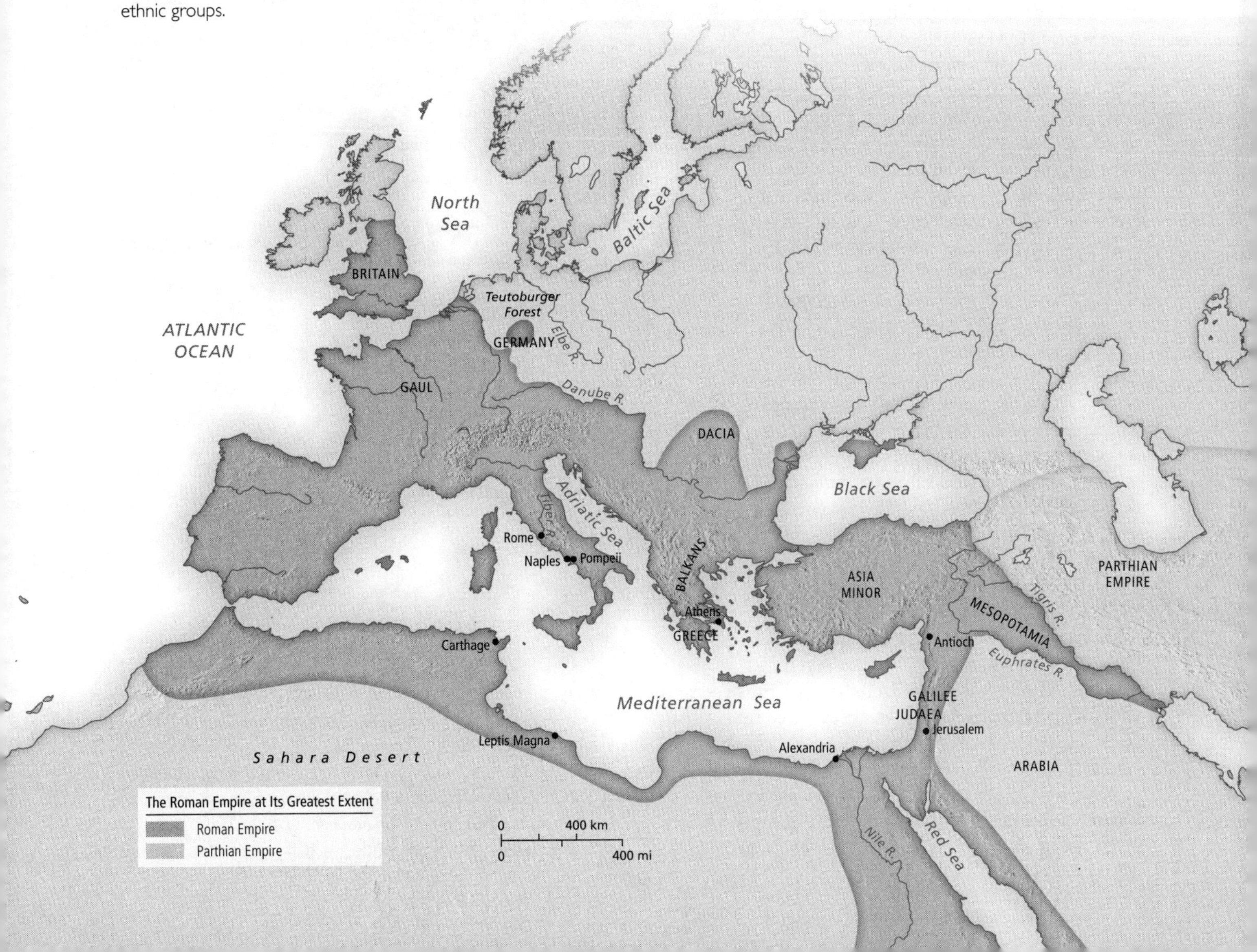

The Problem of Succession

Augustus, following the example of the Hellenistic world, hoped to establish a hereditary monarchy, in which power passed down through his family. When he died in 14 C.E., his stepson Tiberius (r. 14–37 C.E.) took control of the empire without opposition. A hereditary monarchy was now firmly in place. Some senators muttered occasionally about restoring the Republic, but this remained an idle—and very dangerous—dream. Neither the army nor the people would have supported a Senate-led anti-imperial rebellion.

The hereditary principle remained unchallenged for centuries, in part because it staved off the instability that would have come with open competition for the throne. In the dynasty inaugurated by Augustus, which is known as the Julio-Claudian dynasty and which lasted almost 100 years, every ruler came from Augustus's extended family. But when Nero, the last of Augustus's family line, committed suicide in 68 C.E. he left no heirs and so there were no obvious successors to the throne. Civil war broke out among four contenders.

During this "Year of the Four Emperors," Rome learned what the historian Tacitus later called the "secret of empire"—that troops far from the imperial city could choose emperors. Four different emperors took the throne in quick succession, as different Roman armies competed to put their commanders on the throne. The winner of this contest, the general Titus Flavius Vespasianus, or Vespasian (r. 69–79 C.E.), after breaking the back of a great Jewish rebellion that raged from 66–70 C.E., moved to seize power when he learned of Nero's death. Vespasian carefully consulted with other Roman commanders to obtain their support for his royal ambitions before embarking for Italy. By the end of 69 C.E. he had defeated his rivals and became the first emperor who did not come from the Roman nobility. Born into the equestrian class, he built his reputation on his military prowess.

The Flavian dynasty that Vespasian established lasted twenty-five years until the death of his last son, Domitian (r. 81–96 C.E.). A conscientious and able monarch, Domitian nevertheless ruled with an openly autocratic style. He executed many aristocratic senators, creating a reign of terror among Rome's elite. Fittingly, a group of senators murdered him.

To avoid the chaos of another succession crisis, the Senate cooperated with the army in choosing a new emperor, the elderly Nerva (r. 96–98 C.E.). They hoped that this elderly, highly respected man who had no sons would ensure a smooth transition to the next regime, and so he did. Under pressure from the restless military establishment, Nerva adopted the vigorous and experienced general Trajan (r. 98–117 C.E.) as his son and heir. He thus inaugurated the era historians call the Antonine Age. For almost a century, Rome enjoyed competent rule, to a large degree because

CHRONOLOGY

Emperors of Rome

27 B.C.E.–14 C.E.	Augustus	JULIO-CLAUDIAN DYNASTY
14–37 C.E.	Tiberius	
37–41 C.E.	Caligula	
41–54 C.E.	Claudius	
54–69 C.E.	Nero	
68–69 C.E.	Galba	
69 C.E.	Otho	
69 C.E.	Vitellius	
69–79 C.E.	Vespasian	FLAVIAN DYNASTY
79–81 C.E.	Titus	
81–96 C.E.	Domitian	
96–98 C.E.	Nerva	
98–117 C.E.	Trajan	
117–138 C.E.	Hadrian	
138–161 C.E.	Antoninus Pius	ANTONINE DYNASTY
161–180 C.E.	Marcus Aurelius	
161–169 C.E.	Lucius Verus	
180–192 C.E.	Commodus	
193 C.E.	Pertinax	
193 C.E.	Didius Julianus	
193–211 C.E.	Septimius Severus	SEVERAN DYNASTY
211–217 C.E.	Caracalla	
211–212 C.E.	Geta	
217–218 C.E.	Macrinus	
218–222 C.E.	Elagabalus	
222–235 C.E.	Severus Alexander	

Nerva's practice of adopting highly qualified successors continued. After Trajan adopted Hadrian (r. 117–138 C.E.), Hadrian in turn adopted Antoninus Pius (r. 138–161 C.E.). Antoninus adopted Marcus Aurelius (r. 161–180 C.E.) to succeed him. Historians consider the Antonine age a high point of Roman peace and prosperity. The Roman historian Tacitus, who survived Domitian's tyranny to live during Nerva's and Trajan's reigns, praised these latter emperors for establishing "the rare happiness of times, when we may think what we please, and express what we think."

But yet again the murder of an emperor brought an end to peace. Marcus Aurelius unfortunately abandoned the custom of picking a highly qualified successor, and instead was followed to the throne by his incompetent, cruel, and eventually insane son Commodus (r. 180–192 C.E.). In 192 C.E., several senators arranged to have Commodus strangled, triggering another civil war.

A senator from North Africa, Septimius Severus, emerged victorious from this conflict and assumed the imperial throne in 193 C.E. Fluent in Latin, Greek, and Punic, the Phoenician language still widely spoken in North Africa, Septimius Severus exemplified the ascent of provincial aristocrats to the highest levels of the empire. The Severan dynasty he established lasted until 235 C.E. Septimius Severus could afford to ignore the Senate because he was popular with the army—he raised its pay for the first time in more than 100 years. But when the last emperor of his dynasty, Severus Alexander (r. 222–235 C.E.), attempted to negotiate with the German tribes in 235 C.E. by offering them bribes, his own troops killed him because they wanted the cash for themselves. Once again, the murder of an emperor provoked civil war. Fifty years of political and economic crises followed the end of the Severan dynasty. As we will see in the next chapter, the imperial structure that emerged after this time of crisis differed significantly from the Augustan model.

The Emperor's Role: The Nature of Imperial Power

Under the Augustan imperial system, four main responsibilities defined the emperor's role. First, the emperor both protected and expanded imperial territory. Only the emperor determined foreign policy and made treaties with other nations. Only the emperor waged war—both defensive wars to protect the empire from its enemies and aggressive campaigns of conquest. Generals fighting under Augustus's orders conquered huge tracts of Spain, Germany, and the Balkans. The emperor Trajan won great glory by conquering the rich Dacian kingdom north of the Danube River between 101 and 106 C.E. Other emperors smashed internal revolts or fought long border wars. From Augustus's reign onward, the northern frontier with Germany was particularly troublesome. Marcus Aurelius had to pawn palace treasures to finance campaigns against confederations of Germanic tribes.

The emperor's second responsibility was to administer justice and to provide good government throughout his dominions. In theory all citizens could appeal to the emperor directly for justice. In addition, the emperor and his staff responded to questions on points of law and administration from provincial governors and other officials who ruled in the emperor's name. Emperors provided emergency relief after natural disasters, looked after the roads and infrastructure of the empire, and financed public buildings in cities in all the provinces.

The emperor's third responsibility stemmed from his religious role. As *Pontifex Maximus,* or High Priest, the emperor supervised the public worship of the great gods of Rome, particularly Jupiter, as well as the goddess Roma as his deified imperial ancestors. Emperors and subjects alike believed that in order to fulfill Rome's destiny to rule the world, they must make regular sacrifices to the gods.

Finally, the emperor gradually became a symbol of unity for all the peoples of the empire. He embodied the empire and served as the focal point around which all life in the empire revolved. Inevitably, the emperor seemed more than human, even worthy of worship, for he was the guarantor of peace, prosperity, and victory for Rome, and he had infinitely more power than anyone else alive.

CHRONOLOGY

	Political and Military Events
31 B.C.E.	Octavian defeats Mark Antony and controls Mediterranean world
27 B.C.E.	Octavian adopts the name Augustus
9 C.E.	Varus and three legions are defeated; Romans abandon Germany
63 C.E.	Revolt of Boudica crushed in Britain
66-70 C.E.	Jewish Revolt; Jerusalem destroyed
69 C.E.	"Year of the Four Emperors"
113–117 C.E.	Trajan conquers Mesopotamia and Dacia; Rome at greatest extent
120s C.E.	Hadrian's Wall built in Britain
168–175 C.E.	Marcus Aurelius fights Marcomanni and other tribes
212 C.E.	Antonine Constitution grants Roman citizenship to all free inhabitants of the empire
235 C.E.	Fifty years of political turmoil begin

Aqueducts: The Pont du Gard
This graceful aqueduct, now known as the Pont du Gard, was built about 14 C.E. to carry water to the city of Nimes, in the south of France, from its surrounding hills. Romans were highly sophisticated hydraulic engineers, and waterworks like this aqueduct were a common feature of all the large cities of the empire.

Worship of the emperor began with Augustus. He was reluctant to call himself a god because Roman tradition opposed such an idea, but he permitted his spirit to be worshiped in a paternal way, as a sort of *paterfamilias* or head of a universal family of peoples of the empire. He also referred to himself as the "son of a god"—in this case Julius Caesar, whom the Senate had declared divine. After Augustus, imperial worship became more pronounced, although only a few emperors, such as Domitian, emphasized their divinity during their lifetimes. Most were content to be worshiped after death, assuming that the Senate would declare them gods after their funerals. On his deathbed, Vespasian managed to joke, "I guess I'm becoming a god now."

In Rome's eastern provinces such as Egypt and Syria, where people for thousands of years had considered their kings divine, the worship of the emperor spread quickly. Each city's official calendar marked the emperor's day of accession to the throne. Soon, cities across the empire worshiped the emperor on special occasions through games, speeches, sacrifices, and free public feasts in which people ate the flesh of the animals sacrificed in the emperor's honor. Within magnificent temples, priests conducted elaborate public rituals to venerate the emperor.

This cult of the emperor provided a focus of allegiance for the diverse peoples of the empire and so served as a unifying force. Although most people would never see their ruler, he was in their prayers and their public spaces every day. In addition to encouraging worship or veneration in public ceremonies throughout the empire, emperors made their presence felt by building and restoring roads, temples, harbors, aqueducts, and fortifications. These public works demonstrated the emperor's unparalleled patronage and concern for the public welfare. In turn, local leaders emulated his generosity in their own cities.

Other elements of material culture also made the imperial presence real for the emperor's subjects. Coins, for example, provided a glimpse of the emperor's face and a phrase that characterized some aspect of his reign. Slogans such as "Restorer of the World," "Concord with the Gods," and "The Best Ruler—Sustenance for Italy" brought the ruler's message into every person's pocket. Statues of the emperor served a similar purpose. (One statue of an emperor found in Carthage had a removable head, so that when a new ruler ascended the throne, the town leaders could save money by replacing only the head.) In his own portraits, Augustus tended toward the conventions of classical Greek portraiture that presented him as remote and ageless. On the other hand, most emperors were willing to place fairly realistic portraits of their faces on their coins and statues.

Emperors also used military and sporting victories to make their presence felt throughout the empire. In the Republic, conquest had brought wealth and glory to its many generals. In contrast, in the new imperial system, only

Augustus: A Commanding Presence
This imposing statue of Augustus dating to 19 B.C.E. depicts him as a warrior making a gesture of command. His face is ageless, the carving on his armor celebrates peace and prosperity, and his posture is balanced and forceful.

the emperor could take credit for victory in war. Imperial propaganda described the emperor as eternally triumphant. Sporting events, too, glorified the emperor. At the Circus Maximus in Rome, a chariot racetrack where a quarter of a million people could gather to cheer their favorite charioteer, as well as in racetracks throughout the empire, victory in every race belonged symbolically to the emperor.

The Agents of Control

The emperor stood at the heart of the imperial system devised by Augustus. But the imperial center also included other agents of control. The Roman Senate continued to play a significant administrative role in the new system. As it grew to represent not just the aristocracy of the city of Rome, but a new ruling elite drawn from the provinces, the Senate solidified new networks of power and communications that tied the imperial center to its outlying regions. The army, too, constituted an important element of the imperial center. It not only conquered new territories and ensured the emperor's rule throughout the empire, it also served as a Romanizing force, bringing Roman cultural and political practices to distant regions.

The Roman Senate: A Loss of Autonomy

In the imperial system fashioned by Augustus, the Senate continued to function, but with a more restricted role. To maintain the illusion that he had saved rather than destroyed the Republic, Augustus took pains to show respect for the Senate. He allowed its members to compete among themselves for promotion and honor in his service. He permitted the old Republican offices such as tribune and consul to remain in place, and encouraged ambitious men in Rome to compete for them. Augustus also emphasized integrity in the service of the state and sent able senators to govern provinces, thereby reducing corruption. In these ways the basic machinery of government inherited from the Republic continued to operate—but in conformity with the emperor's wishes. In the new imperial system, the emperor, not the Senate, controlled military, financial, and diplomatic policy. Free political debate was silenced. Because he wanted to avoid the ruthless competition for power that had destroyed the Republic, Augustus eliminated his opponents and filled the Senate with loyal supporters.

At the same time, Augustus both restructured the Senate and revised its political role. He trimmed the number of senators to a manageable 600 men, a number that remained standard for several centuries. He recruited able men from the ranks of the equestrians and so ensured that nonaristocrats entered the Senate in greater numbers. He also gave the Senate legislative powers that had once belonged to the popular assemblies—but he retained the right to veto any legislation for himself. Deprived of its autonomy, the Senate became a legislative arm of imperial rule.

Augustus and the emperors who followed him allowed the Senate to exist because they needed a pool of skilled administrators to manage the empire's day-to-day affairs. Senators served as provincial governors, army commanders, judges, and financial officers. They managed the water and grain supplies of the city of Rome, and some of them served on the emperor's advisory council. In return for their cooperation, emperors let senators bear responsibility and earn honor in public service. As a result, aristocratic senators learned to serve the empire faithfully even if they disliked the emperor.

Emperors often brought new men into the Senate from the provinces as a reward for their support, with the belief that Rome grew strong through admitting the best of its provincials to the highest levels of government. Broadening Senate membership in this way enabled more and more of the Romanized elites of the empire to feel they had a stake in the imperial enterprise. Participation in the Senate at Rome was the ultimate reward for a provincial citizen. Some Roman-born senators, however, balked at such inclusiveness. The emperor Claudius (r. 41–54 C.E.) caused considerable dismay among the snobbish Roman senators when he admitted a few new members from Gaul. Nevertheless, the numbers of provincials in the Roman

Senate increased in the first two centuries. By the end of the third century C.E. more than half of Rome's senators came from outside of Italy.

The Roman Army: Conquest and Coercion

Like the Senate, the Roman army was a crucial component of the imperial center. Soldiers enforced peace in the provinces, defended the borders, and conquered new lands to win glory for the emperor. The emperor, in turn, relied on the army's support to remain in power. The army could make or break an emperor—something that every ruler understood. Without the army's support, Augustus would never have succeeded in transforming the Republic into his imperial system. In 41 C.E., after the death of Caligula, soldiers of the palace guard dragged the lame, stammering Claudius from behind a curtain and forced him to take the throne, as a means of ensuring imperial continuity—and their own livelihoods. When Vespasian took the throne in 69 C.E. with the support of his troops, no one in Rome, least of all the emperors, could doubt the power of the army to influence political affairs. After 235 C.E., many emperors, including Aurelian (r. 270–275 C.E.) and Diocletian (r. 284–305 C.E.), rose through the ranks and became emperor due to the support of their fellow soldiers.

Augustus created a highly efficient professional army that would be the bulwark of the empire for nearly two and a half centuries. His first step was to reduce the army from 60 to 28 legions, so that the troops now totaled 150,000 citizens. (Trajan later added two more legions.) This force included the elite Praetorian Guard, which consisted of one and a half legions stationed in Rome to serve as a ceremonial escort for the emperor, maintain order in the city, and enforce the emperor's will throughout Italy. The strength of the army was augmented by subject peoples who had not been granted citizenship, the prerequisite for service in the legions. These subjects served as auxiliary troops. The combined legions and auxiliaries brought the military strength of the Roman army to 300,000 men.

Legionnaires enlisted for twenty-five years but only about half survived this term of service. Short life expectancy rather than death in battle kept the figure low, although regular rations and medical care may have helped soldiers live longer than civilians. A soldier with special skills, such as literacy, could rise through the ranks to have significant responsibilities and perhaps become an officer. For those who survived their period of enlistment, Augustus established military colonies in Italy and the provinces of Africa, Spain, and Asia. He rewarded more than 100,000 veterans with grants of land in return for their military service. Later emperors continued the same practice.

■ **Oplontis**

Painted on the wall of a private villa at the foot of Mount Vesuvius, near Naples, Italy, this vividly colored fresco imitated the interior architecture of a palace. When Mount Vesuvius exploded in 79 C.E., hot ash enveloped the building and preserved the painting.

THE CITY OF ROME

At the center of the imperial system stood the city of Rome. This urban hub was a monument to the power of the ruling elite and celebrated the paramount authority of the emperor. Augustus boasted that he had found Rome built of brick and left it built of marble. Though an exaggeration, this claim nevertheless reveals the effect of monarchy on Rome's urban fabric. Every emperor wanted to leave his mark on the city of Rome as a testimony to his generosity and power. As Rome grew, it became the model for cities throughout the empire. Its public spaces and buildings provided a stage for the acting out of basic principles of imperial rule (see Map 5.2).

The center of political and public life in the city of Rome was the Forum, an area filled with many imposing buildings—administrative headquarters such as the treasury and

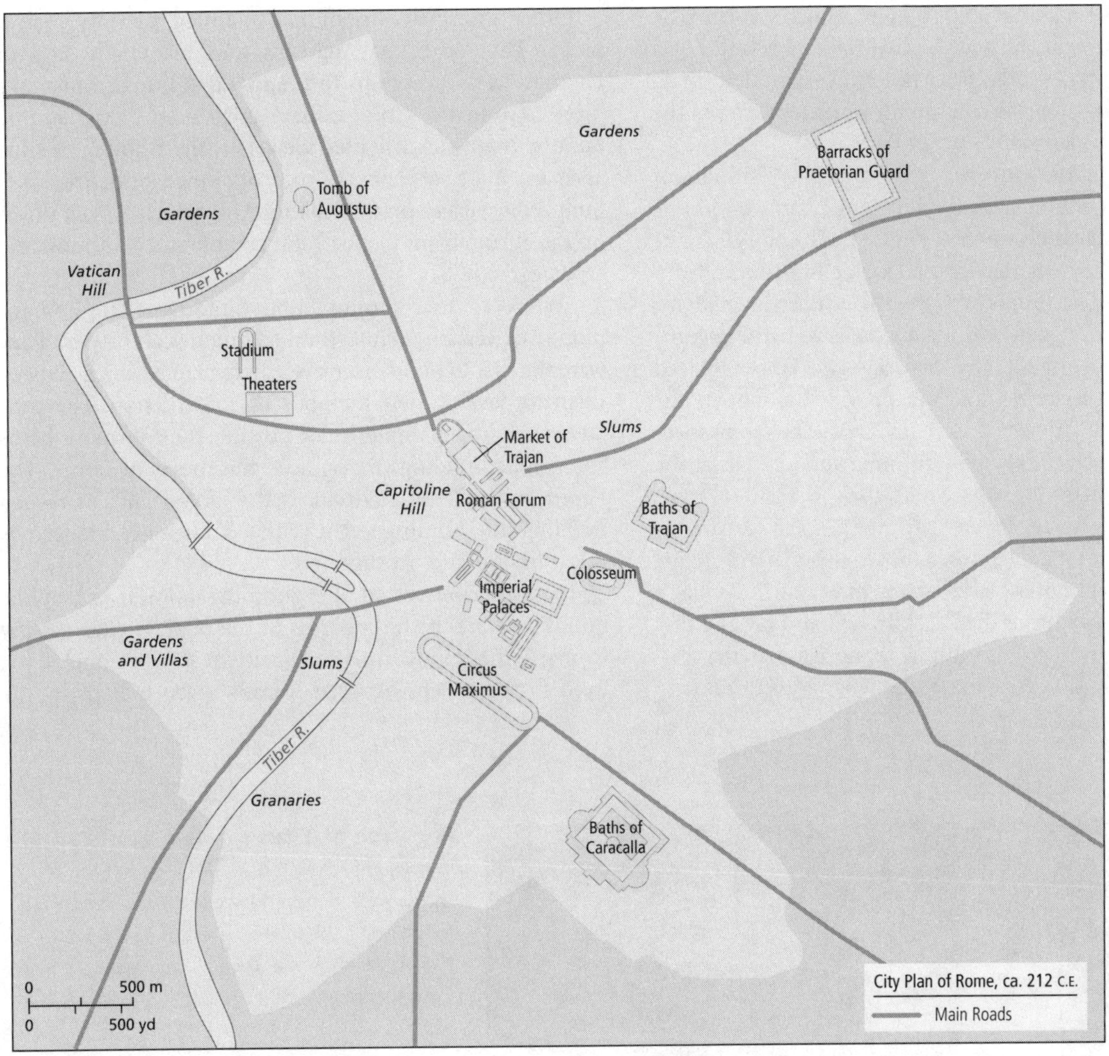

■ **Map 5.2 The City of Rome**
This diagram shows the main public buildings of the imperial capital. Most cities elsewhere in the empire imitated this urban this plan.

records office, law courts, and the Senate House. An altar to the goddess Victory stood in the Senate, where generals took oaths of allegiance to the emperor before marching to war. Roman laws were inscribed on gleaming bronze tablets and placed on the outer walls of these buildings, testimony to the principles of justice and order that formed the framework of the Roman state. Basilicas, a kind of colonnaded hall in which Romans conducted public business ranging from finance to law courts, crowded against the sides of the Forum. Because public and religious life were intertwined, the Forum also contained many grand temples of the gods who controlled Rome's destiny. For example, the goddess Concordia, who represented political agreement among Romans, had a gleaming shrine. Jupiter, Rome's chief god, had a huge marble temple on the Capitoline Hill looking down on the Forum. The Forum lay at the physical center of Rome—just as the political power it represented lay at the center of the imperial system and just as the laws so visibly displayed marked the center of Roman citizenship.

The Forum particularly highlighted the emperor's power within the imperial system. Emperors built huge arches in the Roman forum to celebrate their triumphs. After a victorious military campaign, emperors would parade through the Forum on the Sacred Way, pass under the arches, and finish at the temple of Jupiter. Delighted crowds would see defeated kings pass by in chains and marvel at huge floats piled high with loot. In the victory parade, slaves carried huge paintings that depicted important battles and other scenes of the war. Each emperor from Augustus through Trajan built a new marble forum adjacent to the original Forum in the center of Rome. These new forums met the need for additional space to conduct administrative and legal business as the empire grew. Trajan's Forum, by far the biggest, included huge libraries of Greek and Latin texts, a multistoried marketplace not unlike a modern mall, shops, and a huge marble column on which was carved the story of Trajan's victorious Dacian Wars.

The might of the emperor was on display throughout the city of Rome. Emperors spent gigantic sums on public waterworks and entertainment. They built colossal bathhouses and aqueducts that carried water into Rome from outlying hills. The emperor Caracalla was renowned for constructing the biggest and most expensive bathing complex. The Colosseum, built by Vespasian and Titus, replaced Nero's private pleasure pond and provided a spot in the very heart of the city where as many as 50,000 happy spectators could watch the slaughter of men and animals at the emperor's expense. Romans could also go to the Circus Maximus to see horse-drawn chariots compete for victory under the emperor's auspices. Emperors built and maintained theaters, libraries, parks, and markets for the public's enjoyment. The camp of the Praetorian Guard lay at a discreet distance from the Forum, a reminder that the emperor could summon crippling force to suppress dissent.

Other impressive monuments dotted the city's landscape. The tombs of Augustus and his family and of Hadrian were exceptions to the rule that burials must take place beyond the city's walls. A great map of the empire built by Augustus delighted viewers while at the same time asserting imperial claims to control of the world. Emperors built their palaces on the Palatine Hill, which looked down on the Forum from the east, and great men's mansions covered nearby hills.

To erect these monumental buildings, the Romans pioneered certain architectural techniques and styles. They were the first to build extensively in concrete, which allowed them to develop new methods of construction. The concrete vault, for example, made possible the enormous baths and public buildings that graced the streets of Rome. The Pantheon, built by Hadrian, is the largest ancient roofed building still standing today. With a diameter of 142 feet, its dome has no interior supports.

In stark contrast to the gleaming homes and public buildings were the filthy slums of the poor. Unlike wealthy Romans, the impoverished majority of Rome's inhabitants lived in the valleys between Rome's seven hills or by the

Arch of Titus

This triumphal arch built at the end of the first century C.E. honors the recently deceased Titus for crushing the Jewish revolt of 66–70 C.E. Marble reliefs inside the arch represent the loot from the Temple of Jerusalem in the triumphal parade.

Baths of Caracalla
This gigantic bath complex built by Caracalla in 212–216 C.E. covers more than fifty acres in central Rome. It contained numerous pools heated to different temperatures, exercise grounds, and rooms for reading and relaxation. With walls covered in colored marble, statues, and works of art prominently displayed, the baths were a visual treat for the public. The building's structure demonstrates Roman architectural planning and hydraulic engineering at their finest. One of the bathing pools has been converted to a stage where today full productions of the opera *Aida* are performed—with a parade of elephants!

Tiber River, where they crowded into apartment buildings up to six stories high. Each building contained several apartments, consisting of small rooms without plumbing, fireplaces, or proper ventilation. Lacking proper foundations, apartment buildings often collapsed and could easily become firetraps. Unlike the Forum, then, these slums reveal the poverty rather than the splendor of Rome.

Life in the Roman Provinces: Assimilation and Resistance

Beyond the city of Rome and the imperial center lay the second concentric circle of power, the Roman Empire's provinces. In these diverse regions some people assimilated readily to Roman ways, while others fiercely resisted. Unlike the Greeks of the Classical Age, Romans in the imperial era were willing to include their subjects in the political and cultural life of the empire. Anyone could adopt the practices of Roman daily life, while formal grants of Roman citizenship gave many people the legal rights and privileges that Roman citizens enjoyed.

The Roman way of life manifested itself most noticeably in cities. Modeling themselves on the imperial capital, provincial cities became "little Romes." They served the empire's purposes by funneling wealth from its massive hinterland into imperial coffers. As Roman culture came to predominate in urban centers, however, the division between city and countryside widened. Provincial urban elites benefited from government that was more efficient and orderly than it had been during the Republic. In contrast, rural inhabitants, who formed the majority of the empire's population, faced economic exploitation and threats to their traditional ways of life. Social unrest always boiled beneath the surface of the Roman peace. Yet of the many revolts against Roman authority, only one ever succeeded. Roman military efficiency kept most subject peoples in check, but so, too, did the more positive aspects of Roman rule. Many provincial people came to think of themselves as Roman, with both the Roman army and the Roman law serving as significant unifying forces.

CONQUEST AND ADMINISTRATION

Augustus brought peace to Rome and its provinces, but he kept up the wars of conquest that had fueled Rome's economy. Like the generals of the Republic and the Hellenistic kings, Augustus set out to conquer as much land as possible in order to win glory and demonstrate his power. During his reign large portions of Germany and the Danube River basin came under Roman rule. His successors continued to add new lands to the empire. Claudius brought Britain into the Roman fold in 43 C.E., and by 117 C.E. Trajan had conquered Dacia (modern Romania), Mesopotamia, and parts of Arabia bordering the Red Sea. At this point the empire reached its greatest territorial extent. Trajan's successor, Hadrian, abandoned Mesopotamia because it was too expensive to control. Instead of conquest and expansion, Hadrian focused on consolidation. He organized Rome's frontier with a series of carefully planned fortifications, in-

PLACES OF ENCOUNTER

The Colosseum

It mattered where you sat to enjoy the carnage at the Colosseum. When the 50,000 spectators filed to their seats in this huge shaded arena, they witnessed more than just the spilling of blood. Laid out around them was the order of Roman society and the distribution of power within it.

All of Rome came together in the Colosseum, and everyone was seated according to rank. The rich and famous did not mingle with the poor and insignificant members of society. The emperor and his entourage lounged in a private, gilded enclosure. Special seating was set aside for senators, equestrians, Vestal Virgins (an elite group of female priests), and male religious officials, who wore the ceremonial garb appropriate to their rank. Civilians in togas in the bottom tiers were separated from soldiers in uniform. Bachelors sat apart from married men. Schoolboys and their tutors had a separate block. Farthest from the field of action sat women, the poorest men, and unimportant foreigners. These seating arrangements made everyone who attended the games acutely aware of their social status.

Outside the building prostitutes and food vendors hawked their wares. Inside the elaborate basement below the killing floor of the arena prowled caged animals and men waiting their turn to fight and die. The whole world seemed to take part, for the contests pitted beasts from distant Africa and Asia against each other—and against men from every Roman province and lands beyond. The crowds cheered while exotic animals fed on human blood. In one year of Trajan's reign, 11,000 animals perished: rhinos battled bulls; tigers fought lions; elephants, giraffes, bears, deer, boars, panthers, crocodiles, and hippos delighted the crowd by dying. The toll of human life was also enormous. Common slaves, convicted criminals, and prisoners of war were routinely butchered in the Colosseum. In addition, highly trained slaves called gladiators fought to the death. Gladiators epitomized the glory of gaining victory over death through discipline, bravery, and submission. Considered sexy and glamorous, they became favorites of the crowd—while they lived. In one celebration alone, 5,000 pairs of gladiators fought in games given by Trajan to commemorate the end of the Dacian War in 107 C.E. Fewer gladiators fought regularly in arenas throughout the Empire.

Although the emperor was expected to accept the verdict of the spectators, a vestige of ancient days when the people of Rome still had a voice, he himself (or the officiating magistrate) made the final decision about whether to spare a defeated gladiator. The emperor's power to decide on life and death delivered an unmistakable message to the whole community: Just as individuals might struggle for survival over hostile fortune in their own lives, so the all-powerful and beneficent emperor brought safety and order to a violent world.

Despite the popularity of gladiatorial combats and wild animal fights, in 325 C.E. the emperor Constantine suppressed the games in accordance with Christian sensibilities.

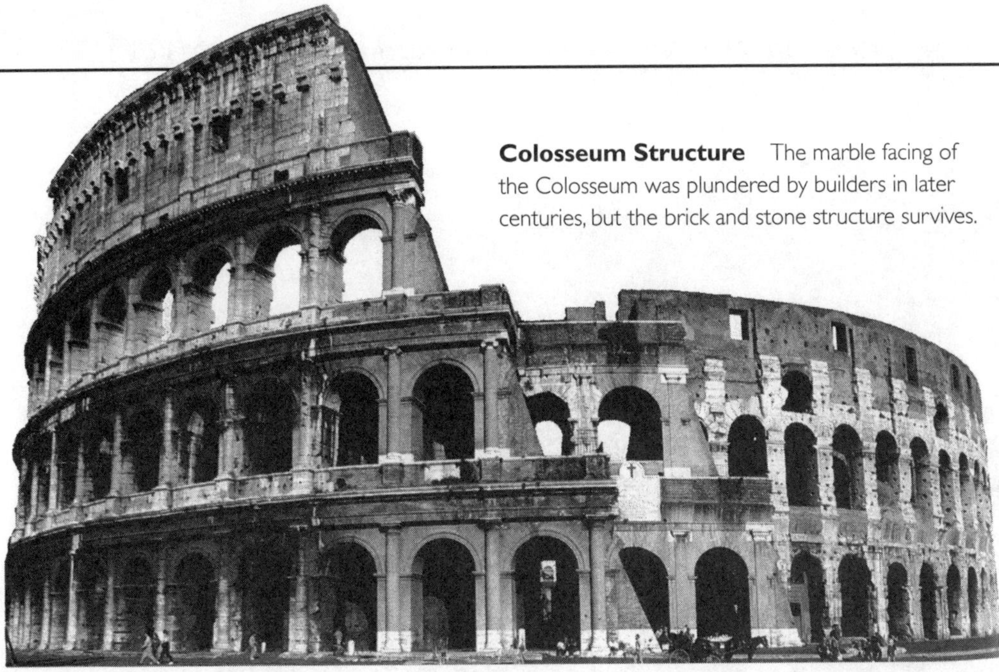

Colosseum Structure The marble facing of the Colosseum was plundered by builders in later centuries, but the brick and stone structure survives.

photo
to come .646

The Colossus of Nero This gilt bronze statue from Nero's palace, over which the Colosseum was built, may have given the amphitheater its name.

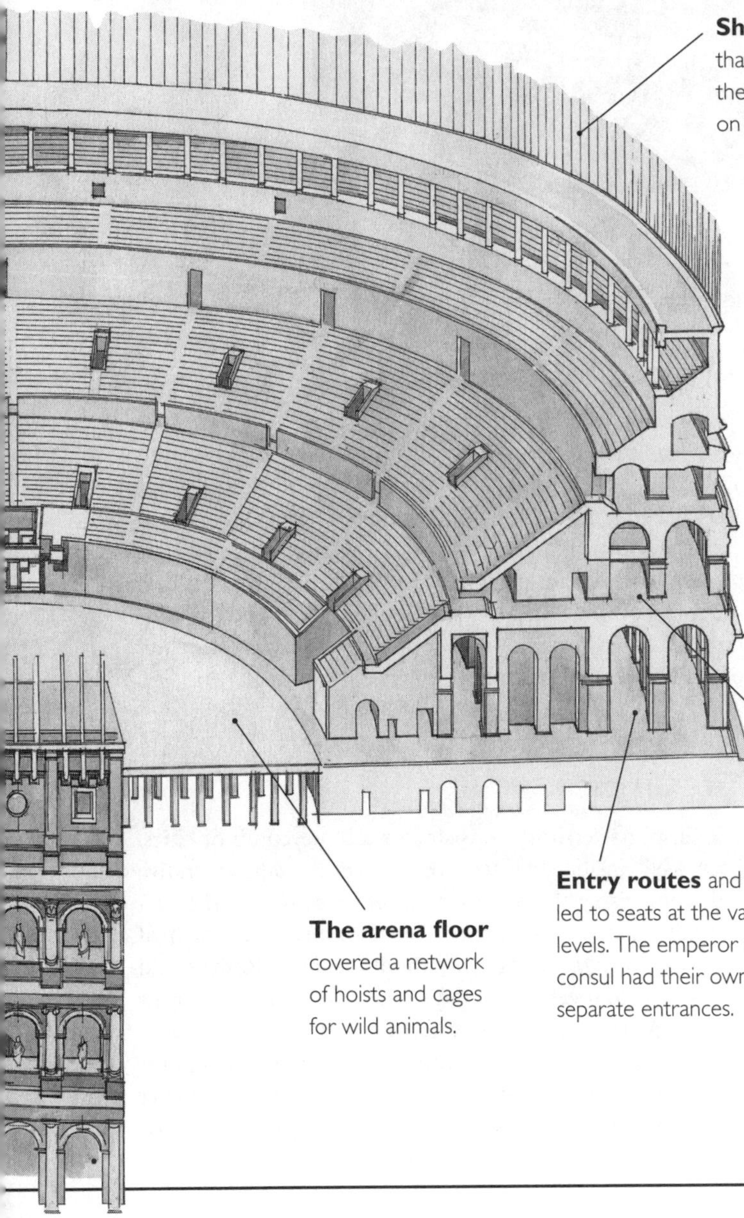

Shade A huge sailcloth awning that sheltered spectators from the sun was supported by poles on the upper story.

The arena floor covered a network of hoists and cages for wild animals.

Entry routes and stairs led to seats at the various levels. The emperor and consul had their own, separate entrances.

Internal Corridors These allowed the large and often unruly crowd to move freely and be seated quickly.

For Discussion

What is the relation between public entertainment and social status? How do public entertainment and sports still reveal social status?

Hadrian's Wall

This massive fortification epitomizes the second-century-C.E. military concept of the fortified frontier. Stretched across northern Britain, it separated the Roman provinces to its south from the "barbarians" to the north.

cluding the renowned wall that still crosses the north of Britain and bears his name.

One of the chief accomplishments of the Augustan state was establishing a well-managed and prosperous provincial system that lasted until the late third century C.E. Conquered lands were quickly organized into provinces. A governor ruled over each province and orchestrated the flow of slaves, timber, metals, horses, spices, and other treasures back to Rome. Although the Roman Empire at its height had about 50 million inhabitants, only a few thousand men participated directly in imperial administration in the provinces. Most administrative work was performed at the local level by city councilors of the empire, who in turn were loosely supervised by imperial governors and their staffs. The governors' responsibilities included protecting the frontiers, collecting taxes, administering justice, and suppressing rebellions.

This structure of government gave rise to an administrative-military class that drew its members from both the senatorial and the equestrian orders. In the service of the emperor, these men enjoyed splendid careers, climbing the ladder of success through appointments in different provinces. As a group, they provided a cadre of officials with empire-wide experience. Gnaeus Julius Agricola is an apt example. The father-in-law of the historian Tacitus, Agricola had a brilliant military career under the Flavian emperors. During his five years as governor of Britain, he brought that distant province firmly under Roman control. Agricola epitomized loyalty to the state, experience in military affairs, and a thoughtful approach to drawing the elites of defeated enemies into the imperial way of life.

THE CITIES

The empire's territory consisted of a honeycomb of cities. Each "cell" in the structure constituted one administrative unit comprising the main urban center as well as the surrounding lands and villages. The Romans called each of these cells a *civitas*°, or city. Without the cities, Rome could not have held together the huge territories conquered by its armies. As centers for tax collection and law courts, cities were the locations where the imperial administrators interacted with provincial aristocrats, who had influence over the local population. Through cities, the empire's vast territories were linked to the imperial center.

More than a thousand cities dotted the imperial map, connected by more than 40,000 miles of roads (see Map 5.3). In regions where Roman urban traditions were little-known, the Romans created new urban centers. Cities such as Lugdunum (Lyons) in France or Eburacum (York) in Britain were created in the first years of conquest as centers of Roman culture and authority. In contrast, in regions throughout the Mediterranean where urban culture had deep roots, provincial cities such as Athens or Jerusalem had long been centers of learning or religion. Some urban hubs, such as Carthage and Alexandria, teemed with several hundred thousand people. In these immense provincial cities, governors and their staffs represented the Roman order in grand fashion.

In their physical layout and architecture, these provincial cities modeled themselves on the imperial capital. Each had gladiator arenas; bathhouses; a forum; a council house; and temples to its gods, to Rome, and to the emperor. Worship of the emperor linked these new communities to the larger imperial system.

All cities governed themselves. A city council modeled on the Roman Senate presided over each city's affairs. Only a handful of the community's wealthiest men served in the city council and held the various magistracies and priesthoods. Council membership passed from father to son. Wealthy women held no administrative office and had no role in public decision making, though they presided as priestesses in civic religious observances. The male citizens of each city voted on local issues and elected town officials.

City councilors had many responsibilities, which they viewed as great honors. The imperial government could rely on city councils to control the agricultural resources of the surrounding farmlands, thus reducing the need for a top-heavy imperial bureaucracy. City councils managed the grain supply, arranged for army recruitment, supervised the marketplaces, administered justice in local law courts, and most important of all, collected taxes for the central government. Councilors paid out of their own pockets for the upkeep of public works, aqueducts, and baths. They also funded religious festivals and celebrations of the imperial cult. In addition, they sponsored gladiatorial games, wild-beast slaughters, chariot races, and other forms of public amusement. This system of making private donations for the public good permitted aristocrats to compete for recognition and public offices in ways that benefited the city and its people. As provincial officials performed their public responsibilities on behalf of their hometowns, they imitated the efforts of that greatest patron of all, the emperor himself. The city councilors were the "mouthpiece of Rome."

When Romans took over the lands of others and organized provinces during the era of the Republic they did not try to impose a uniform legal and administrative system. Once a victorious general ended a war of conquest, he established the terms of peace with Rome's new subjects in legal charters, city by city, tribe by tribe. These separate arrangements collectively were called the Law of the Province. This system continued during the imperial era. When a governor assumed command of his province, he issued an edict stating the legal terms of his rule and describing the structure of his administration. Although they were under no obligation, subsequent governors generally accepted the arrangements of their predecessors. This provided a certain smoothness of transition, but it also meant that different provinces might experience Roman government in quite different ways.

AGRICOLA THE GENERAL

The historian Tacitus wrote a biography of his father-in-law, the general and administrator Gnaeus Julius Agricola (49–93 C.E.). Agricola had a glittering military career under the Flavian emperors. As commander-in-chief of Roman forces in Britain from 78 to 83 C.E., he subdued most of the island and advanced deep into Scotland. Agricola encouraged urbanization and Mediterranean customs such as public bathing and chariot racing. In the following selection, Tacitus considers the implications of deliberate "Romanization."

The following winter passed without disturbance, and was employed in salutary measures. For, to accustom to rest and repose through the charms of luxury a population scattered and barbarous and therefore inclined to war, Agricola gave private encouragement and public aid to the building of temples, courts of justice and dwelling houses, praising the energetic and reproving the indolent. Thus an honourable rivalry took the place of compulsion. He likewise provided a liberal education for the sons of the chiefs, and showed such a preference for the natural powers of the Britons over the industry of the Gauls that they who lately disdained the tongue of Rome now coveted its eloquence. Hence, too, a liking sprang up for our style of dress and the toga became fashionable. Step by step they were led to things which dispose to vice, the lounge, the bath, the elegant banquet. All this in their ignorance they called civilization, when it was but a part of their servitude.

Source: From Tacitus, "Agricola 21" in *Complete Works of Tacitus*, edited by Moses Hadas, translated by Alfred John Church and William Jackson Brodribb, (New York: The Modern Library, 1942).

THE COUNTRYSIDE

The wealth that enabled aristocratic men throughout the empire to gain an education, enter public service, and pay for public buildings, festivals, and games came from agriculture. Control of the countryside was the key to the prosperity of the imperial system. The wealthiest men owned the most land. Landholdings, however, varied greatly in size and distribution. The emperor was the greatest property owner, controlling millions of acres of land throughout the empire. Augustus, for example, personally owned the entire province of Egypt. Like Augustus, wealthy Roman investors owned properties in many different areas, some bridging entire continents. Some of these landed magnates chose to enter a life of public service either in Rome or in their home cities. Others preferred to enjoy the benefits of their enormous wealth away from the risks of political life.

At the bottom of the pyramid toiled the peasants, who lived in the countryside and performed the agricultural labor that made local landowners rich. The circumstances of peasant life varied greatly throughout the empire. Some peasants owned small farms sufficient to maintain their families, perhaps with the assistance of seasonal wage laborers or a few slaves. Others rented their lands from landlords to whom they owed payment in the form of produce, money, or labor. Degrees of dependency on landlords var-

Map 5.3 Major Cities and Roads of the Roman Empire
Thousands of miles of roads linked the cities of the Roman Empire. Used primarily as military highways, the roads also helped merchants travel with their wares. When they crossed imperial frontiers, merchants traded with many peoples eager for Roman goods, especially wine and luxury objects.

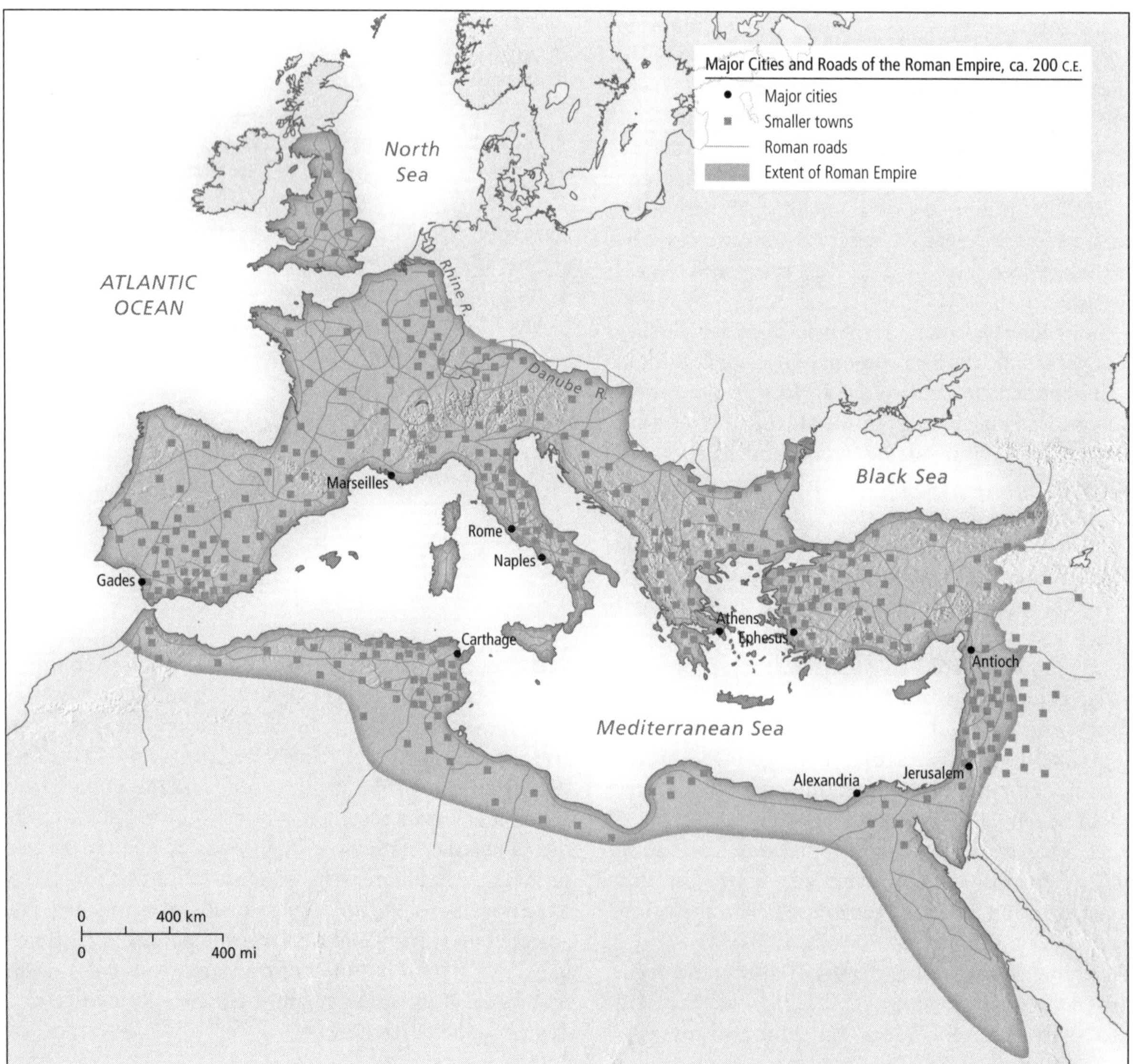

ied as well. Extremely fierce penalties for inability to pay rents ranged from enslavement to other forms of bondage.

All landowning peasants faced one prevalent threat—the possibility that a more powerful landowner might seize their fields by force. When this happened, peasants had little hope of getting their land back. The imperial system favored the property rights of the wealthy and worked to the disadvantage of the rural poor. Cities gobbled up the peasants' crops; government officials extorted taxes from them; and landlords and soldiers bullied them. Rabbi Hanina ben Hama, who lived in Palestine about 240 C.E., stated bluntly that the empire established cities "in order to impose upon the people forced labor, extortion and oppression." In addition to this relentless exploitation, the specters of famine, natural disasters, and debt constantly threatened the peasants' very survival.

Despite these hardships, the peasantry during the empire's first three centuries managed to produce enough surplus crops to maintain the imperial system, especially the army with its ravenous demands for supplies and foods. Indeed, agricultural productivity during this era was remarkable, considering the low yields of farms, the difficulty and expense of transportation (it was less expensive to ship a load of grain all the way across the Mediterranean Sea than to send it 100 miles overland), and the rudimentary farming technology of the time. Some historians estimate that Europe did not see a comparable level of agricultural productivity again until the seventeenth century.

Food staples in the Mediterranean region included olives, grains, and wines, while in more northern regions butter replaced oil and beer substituted for wine. Large flocks of sheep and herds of cattle provided necessary wool and leather. Farmers did not export their produce over long distances; the vast Roman road network was developed to move troops, not crops. But if famine struck, relief supplies could be obtained quickly from fields a few days' transport away—provided the political organization existed to make the arrangements.

Terrain and climate as much as investment and local farming custom determined the methods of agricultural exploitation. In Sicily and parts of southern Italy, chain gangs of slaves predominated, working on vast estates. Migrant workers labored in the olive groves of North Africa, while seasonal movement of grazing animals predominated in hilly regions of Italy and the Balkans. In Egypt, the annual flooding of the Nile determined the rhythms of agricultural life and made the Nile Valley one of the empire's chief producers of grain.

REVOLTS AGAINST ROME

Conquest by Roman armies could be a long and brutal ordeal. After the shock of military defeat and surrender to Roman generals came the imposition of the administrative structures of Roman rule and the mechanisms of economic exploitation. Not surprisingly, resentment simmered among conquered peoples. Revolts against Roman authority often followed soon after a subject people's initial defeat, while freedom was still a living memory. The stories of several revolts illustrate that subject peoples rarely adjusted smoothly to Roman rule, and that with only one exception, Roman force proved overwhelming.

Arminius and the Revolt in Germany

In 9 C.E. Arminius, chieftain of a Germanic tribe called the Cherusci, led the only successful revolt against Roman rule. As a young man serving in an auxiliary regiment in the Roman army, Arminius earned Roman citizenship, learned to speak Latin, and gained the rank of equestrian. Arminius seemed to be a real friend of Rome, but the Cherusci had a history of belligerence and resistance. Arminius's tribal ties proved stronger than his loyalty to the empire. The Romans underestimated the pugnacity of their new Germanic subjects and sent the wrong man, Lucius Varus, to be their governor. Varus was a peacetime administrator, not a general. His previous experience in Syria and North Africa had not prepared him for the challenges he encountered east of the Rhine River. He imposed economic exploitation and taxation—the hallmarks of the Roman peace—upon the Cherusci too quickly. Not used to a monetary economy, debt, and foreign control, the Germanic tribe rose in revolt—led by Arminius.

Arminius lured the unsuspecting Varus into a trap in the Teutoberg Forest, slaughtering Varus and three entire Roman legions. A relief army under the command of the future emperor Tiberius contained the disaster, but nevertheless, when Augustus died in 14 C.E., all of Rome's legions were on the west side of the Rhine. No emperor ever again attempted to conquer Germany. One lasting result of Arminius's successful revolt is the linguistic distinction that still cuts across Europe. Whereas French and Italian derive from Latin, German does not because the tribes living between the Rhine and Elbe Rivers managed to throw off the Roman yoke in 9 C.E.

Boudica's Revolt in Britain

Fifty years after Arminius's victory, another major uprising broke out in Britain, led by Boudica, the queen of the people known as the Iceni. The revolt had a long, complex history. In the decades following the initial conquest of the island by the emperor Claudius in 43 C.E., the Romans consolidated their power by playing favorites among the local tribes. They also encouraged those tribes not under Roman control to ally themselves with Rome as client states. Under King Prasutagus, the Iceni were one of these client states that supplied troops to the Roman army in return for Roman protection. Before King Prasutagus died in

60 C.E., he named the Roman emperor his co-heir with his wife, Boudica, and his daughters. Within a few years the emperor Nero pushed Boudica aside and incorporated the kingdom of the Iceni directly into the Roman state. Emboldened by their new dominance over the Iceni, the agents of the tyrannical Roman governor abused Boudica and raped her daughters.

The queen then led her forces into open rebellion. With the aid of several neighboring tribes who also resented the Roman presence in Britain, Boudica destroyed a legion and leveled several cities, including Camulodunum, a major imperial cult center with a temple dedicated to Rome and the emperor. Resistance ended quickly after Roman force routed Boudica's troops and the queen took her own life.

The Britons learned that resistance to Rome was futile. The Romans learned a lesson as well: Subject peoples should be treated more justly. The next Roman governor of Britain adopted more lenient administrative policies.

The Revolt of Julius Civilis in Gaul

Like Arminius, Julius Civilis was a Germanic tribal leader who had served in the Roman army. Julius Civilis was both a Roman citizen and a prince of his tribe, the Batavi. Like the Iceni in Britain, the Batavi had supplied troops but not tribute to Rome for several decades. Civilis was serving as a commander of Roman auxiliary troops in Gaul when civil war broke out in Rome in 69 C.E. following Nero's death. Quick to seize an opportunity, Julius Civilis led an army—consisting not only of Batavians but also men from several unconquered German tribes and some restless Gallic tribes—against Roman legionary bases depleted by the civil war.

Despite his career in Roman military service and his involvement in provincial politics, Civilis presented himself to his Batavian followers in religious terms, with native-style oaths of allegiance sworn in a sacred grove. He also maintained close ties with a Batavian prophet, who may have predicted that Civilis would lead his people to freedom. But unlike the revolt of Arminius, the revolt of Civilis came to an end when the new emperor Vespasian brought stability back to the frontier through a combination of diplomacy and swift military action.

Jewish Revolts

Augustus had created the province of Judaea and annexed it to the Empire in 6 C.E. With Roman rule came mediocre governors and heavy taxation that caused Judaea's economy to decline. Famines and banditry became common, and political discontent mounted among the Jews. Open rebellion almost broke out when the emperor Caligula (r. 37–41 C.E.) ordered that his statue be placed in the Temple in Jerusalem, an unthinkable sacrilege for the Jews. Only his death in 41 C.E. prevented the beginning of war between Rome and the Jews of Judaea.

Under Roman rule, a significant divide opened up within the Jewish community. The Jewish priestly caste grew to appreciate many aspects of Hellenistic culture, and the landed elite benefited directly from Roman rule. Ordinary Jews, however, suffered from high taxation and viewed their leaders as collaborators with an occupying and godless power. These Jews gave their loyalty and respect to the scribes, men of learning who devoted their lives to copying religious texts and interpreting the Bible. These learned and religious men had little stake in preserving Roman rule.

Sixty years of Roman mismanagement combined with a desire for independence sparked a massive revolt in Judaea in 66 C.E. Jews stopped offering sacrifices for the emperor's health and formed their own government. They appointed regional military commanders, chose a leader by lot, abolished debt, and issued their own coinage imprinted with

GALEN THE PHYSICIAN

Galen, the greatest physician of the imperial age, described in vivid terms how peasants in the countryside often were very close to starvation.

As soon as summer was over, those who live in the cities, in accordance with their universal practice of collecting a sufficient supply of grain to last a whole year, took from the fields all the wheat, with the barley, beans and lentils, and left to the rustics only those annual products which are called pulses and leguminous fruits; they even took away a good part of these to the city. So the people in the countryside, after consuming during the winter what had been left, were compelled to use unhealthy forms of nourishment. Through the spring they ate twigs and shoots of trees, bulbs and roots of unwholesome plants, and they made unsparing use of what are called wild vegetables, whatever they could get hold of, until they were surfeited; they ate them after boiling them whole like green grasses, of which they had not tasted before even as an experiment. I myself in person saw some of them at the end of spring and almost all at the beginning summer afflicted with numerous ulcers covering their skin and inflamed tumours, others from spreading boils, others had an eruption resembling . . . leprosy.

Source: From Galen, translated by G. E. M. de Ste. Croix in *The Class Struggle in the Ancient Greek World.* Copyright © 1981 by G. E. M. de Ste. Croix. Reprinted by permission of Duckworth Publishers.

messages of freedom. Internal political conflicts within the Jewish community, however, weakened the rebellion and proved as fatal to their cause as the might of Roman legions. In 70 C.E. imperial forces captured Jerusalem, destroyed the Temple, and enslaved an estimated two million people. The victorious generals were Vespasian and his son Titus, both of whom later became emperors.

Despite their overwhelming defeat in 70 C.E., Jewish communities continued to resist Rome. During Trajan's reign, minor revolts broke out in the eastern Mediterranean (115–118 C.E.). Revolts erupted again in 132–135 C.E., prompted by Hadrian's attempt to forbid the Jewish ritual circumcision of male infants. This latter revolt was led by Simon Bar Kochba, or "Son of the Star," who claimed to be the messiah, a leader who would end foreign oppression and inaugurate a new era for the Jewish nation. Other rebellions occurred under the emperors Antoninus Pius (r. 138–161 C.E.) and Septimius Severus (r. 193–211 C.E.). The last major Jewish uprising occurred in Palestine in the fourth century C.E. All of these revolts failed.

Several conclusions may be drawn from these instances of resistance. In each of the western revolts, the Romans overestimated their ability to pacify subject peoples soon after conquering them. Even a tribal leader's service in the Roman auxiliary forces did not blunt tribal identity and allegiance. The rebel leaders appealed to their fellow tribesmen in traditional rather than in Roman terms. It required more than one generation after conquest for tribal elites to embrace the imperial system.

In the case of the Jewish revolt of 66–70 C.E., the Romans misunderstood the nature of leadership and loyalty in Judea's Jewish society. The Romans allied themselves with members of the Jewish elite, whom the majority of Jews distrusted and refused to follow. The continuation of Jewish opposition to Roman rule demonstrates that a population with a strong sense of religious identity rooted in a set of sacred texts could resist—and survive—the overwhelming power of Rome. Rebels in western Europe lacked this focus. Within a few generations these unsuccessful rebels assimilated fully into Roman society. The Jews never did so.

FORCES OF ROMANIZATION

Two very different institutions worked as Romanizing forces in the provinces of the empire. The first, the army, proved vital in not only establishing the geographic limits of the empire but also in transmitting Roman culture within those limits. The second, Roman law, helped erode the local loyalties and traditions of the diverse provincial peoples and so furthered this process of creating a Roman imperial culture.

The Roman Army

More than any other institution, the army mirrored the growth of the Roman Empire from a diverse collection of conquests to a well-organized state with a common culture. The army was a significant force of Romanization° throughout the imperial era. During the Republic, soldiers tended to be drawn from the city of Rome and surrounding regions—a natural consequence of the fact that Roman soldiers were required to be Roman citizens. In the course of the first two and a half centuries of imperial rule, however, the number of troops from Italy steadily diminished as territories under Roman rule increased. After 212 C.E., when all free men and women within imperial borders gained citizenship, the army drew recruits from all the provinces.

Army bases in far-flung regions provided the first taste of Roman culture and language to provincial peoples. The army introduced provincial recruits to the Latin language, Roman religion, social organization, and values. Oaths of loyalty bound soldiers to the emperor and Rome, neither of which most legionnaires would ever see. Latin, the language of command and army administration, provided another common bond to men whose mother tongues reflected the empire's ethnic diversity. Many inscriptions on soldiers' tombstones reveal that a simplified version of Latin developed in the army. (This language became the ancestor of French, Spanish, and other Romance languages.)

Roman soldiers who settled in the provinces also served as a Romanizing force. Soldiers could not legally marry during their military service because Romans believed that family obligations reduced troops' willingness to be stationed far from home. Many men reared families anyway with local women. Septimius Severus pragmatically abandoned the restriction against marriage in the army at the end of the second century C.E. At retirement, most soldiers stayed near the bases in which they had been stationed. Many towns arose full of former military personnel and their friends, families, and small businesses. These towns helped transmit Roman culture and values to provincial peoples.

The imperial army maintained a very high degree of organization, discipline, and training—characteristics on which Romans prided themselves. Each of the legions with a contingent of auxiliary troops was stationed as a permanent garrison in a province with an elaborate logistical infrastructure to provide weapons, food, and housing. Legions had a standard chain of command to organize officers and men. The architecture of camps and fortification, as well as weapons, armor, and tactics, followed the same conventions across the empire, thus reinforcing the army's role as a Romanizing force. Generals and staff officers often had postings in different provinces during their careers, so there developed a strong sense of shared enterprise in the command structure as well as a common body of knowledge about how the army worked from the inside.

Romans knew that strict military discipline distinguished their soldiery from disorganized "barbarians." Military punishments were notoriously ferocious. For example, if a soldier fell asleep during sentry duty, his barrackmates were required to beat him to death. But tight discipline and vigorous training did produce highly professional fighters. To keep in fighting trim, troops constantly drilled in weaponry, camp building, and battle formations.

The army also confronted Romans with new cultural ideas. Some provincial troops seemed exotic to Roman eyes. For example, sun-worshipping legionnaires from Syria stationed in Rome raised eyebrows by saluting their god at dawn. Soldiers from the Rhine who felt uncomfortable in the noonday heat of Rome once baffled onlookers by drinking water from the Tiber, which everyone in Rome knew was contaminated.

Roman Citizenship and Law

Roman law, like the Roman army, constituted a strong force for Romanization. In the early days of the empire, Roman law set Romans apart from the bulk of the empire's peoples, who followed their own laws. For example, Jews could live according to Jewish law or Athenians by Athenian law, as long as they paid their taxes to the emperor and did not cause trouble. If a Jew or an Athenian held Roman citizenship, however, he or she could also enjoy the rights and benefits of Roman law. A Roman citizen possessed crucial legally defined rights, including the guarantee of freedom from enslavement. Male citizens had the right to compete for public magistracies, vote in public assemblies, serve in the legions, and make an appeal in a criminal trial. As the Roman Empire expanded during the first and second centuries C.E., conditions of peace and prosperity encouraged the spread of both Roman-style cities and Roman citizenship, and thus the dominance of Roman law. In this way, Roman law tied the vast empire together. No matter where they lived in the empire, Roman citizens took pride in their centuries-old legal tradition, and in their rights of citizenship.

Then, in 212 C.E., Emperor Aurelius Antoninus (r. 211–217 C.E.), nicknamed Caracalla, issued what became known as the Antonine Decree°. This ruling was a milestone because it granted citizenship to all free men and women within the empire, presumably to increase the tax base. By formally eliminating the distinction between Roman conquerors and subject peoples, the Antonine Decree enabled Roman law to embrace the entire population. This legal uniformity further strengthened provincial loyalty to Rome. Provincial allegiances to their own traditions and laws that had coexisted with Roman imperial law for centuries began to diminish.

Roman law distinguished between civil law and criminal law. Civil law dealt with all aspects of family life, property and inheritance, slavery, and citizenship. It also dealt with legal procedure, trial, appeal, and the settling of disputes. Civil law, therefore, defined relations among different classes of Roman society and enabled courts to judge disputes among citizens. Criminal law addressed theft, homicide, sexual crimes, treason, and offenses against the government. These distinctions between civil and criminal law created by the Romans have become standard in the legal systems of nations that are part of Western civilization.

The significance of Roman law extended beyond the imperial age. One of the most important aspects of Roman law was the development of the concept of the "law of nature." This concept stemmed from Stoicism, with its ideal of an underlying rational order to all things. From this Stoic assumption of rational order the idea developed: that certain principles of justice are part of nature itself. Ideally, at least, laws of human societies should conform to the law of nature. Hence the Romans developed the idea that codes of law, although the product of particular societies and circumstances, were based on universally applicable principles. This idea would become a foundation of Western civilization. Building on this Roman idea, later thinkers would insist that all human beings had inalienable rights and that all individuals should be treated as equals under the law.

Equality under the law did not, however, exist in the Roman imperial age. Roman citizens had more rights than noncitizens. In the first century C.E. the vast differences in wealth that divided citizens took on legal significance. The wealthy upper class, generally called *honestiores,* and the poor, called *humiliores,* acquired different legal rights, especially in criminal law. For example, *honestiores* convicted of crimes were spared the most gruesome punishments, such as being crucified or being thrown to wild animals in the arena.

Responsibility for making laws shifted as the Republic gave way to the empire. During the Republic the Senate gave advice on legal matters to magistrates or citizen assemblies that had official authority to issue laws. During the empire these lawmaking procedures changed, as the control of law shifted into the emperor's hands. Whether the emperor was issuing a decree on his own initiative, making a general policy in response to an inquiry from a provincial administrator, or making a technical ruling on a point of law in consultation with legal experts on his staff, his decisions had the same status as any law issued by a citizen assembly during the Republic. The idea that the emperor was above the law and that his wishes had the force of law was widely accepted by the early third century C.E.

Legal experts also played a critical part in the evolution of Roman law. In the Republic these legal experts had been aristocratic, independent scholars, entrusted with the task of understanding and interpreting the law. They served as an invaluable resource to the practice of law. Their methods of interpretation made it possible to apply the law to new circumstances as the precedents they established became the basis for future law.

During the empire, legal experts lost their independence but continued their work in imperial service. Combining legal scholarship, teaching, and administrative careers, the legal experts of the Roman Empire collected and analyzed earlier laws and the opinions of their predecessors. Papinian, Paul, and Ulpian, who lived in the early third century C.E., were the greatest of these specialists. They wrote hundreds of books of commentary that shaped the interpretation of Roman law for centuries. Their opinions, collected and organized during the reign of Justinian in the sixth century C.E., were passed on to the lawyers of medieval and Renaissance Europe. Roman law remains the foundation of Italian, French, and Spanish legal traditions today, as well as the legal system of the state of Louisiana.

The Frontier and Beyond

The third concentric circle of the Roman world consisted of the frontier—the outermost boundaries of the empire, and beyond. In this section we will see how boundaries and border zones took shape on the edges of the empire and how cultural distinctions emerged between "civilized" Romans and "barbarians" living across the borders. Some contacts between the two groups, such as trade with sub-Saharan Africa, India, and China, only temporarily affected the empire. Other encounters with foreign peoples, such as the Parthians in the Middle East and the Germanic peoples living north of the Danube and Rhine Rivers, profoundly influenced Rome and the shaping of the West.

FRONTIER ZONES: CIVILIZATION AND BARBARIANS

By the early second century C.E., the empire's northern border was marked by regularly spaced military bases and fortresses. Armed naval forces patrolled the Rhine and Danube, and the great wall of Hadrian stretched across the north of Britain. In the East, another line of military defenses extended from the Black Sea to the Nile. In North Africa as well, a perimeter of fortifications marked the limits of cultivable land along the empire's southernmost edge. This demarcation of the empire's edges and the gradual emergence of the idea of perimeter defense reveals much about the evolution of the imperial government, as well as the spread of Roman culture and ideas about empire.

As in so many other areas, the Augustan regime provided the catalyst. After 9 C.E., when three of his best legions perished in the revolt of Arminius in Germany, Augustus realized that the empire lacked the resources to expand indefinitely. Augustus put a stop to unlimited imperial expansion, but Jupiter's promise that Romans would have empire without limits, as described by Virgil (70–19 B.C.E.) in the *Aeneid*, (ca. 26–19 B.C.E.) nevertheless remained an official conceit.

Only as the pace of conquest slowed and as the empire absorbed the client kingdoms on the fringes of the empire did imperial policies change. By the end of the first century C.E., emperors turned their attention to consolidating conquests systematically and developing fortified lines of defense across areas that lacked rivers or other natural obstacles. As we have seen, the contrasting policies of Trajan and Hadrian illustrate this shift. Trajan saw himself as an old-fashioned conqueror, seizing lands as far as his legions could push. His troops conquered Dacia (modern Romania) and Mesopotamia. Trajan's successor Hadrian looked at the empire differently. Hadrian abandoned the conquests that he thought Rome could not maintain, and then he secured the frontier with a strong line of border defenses.

The borders established by Roman forces in the initial phase of conquest were intended to control newly conquered peoples and to protect against enemies beyond Rome's borders. After conquest Roman armies remained in place as occupying forces. The Romans spoke a different language than that of their subjects, worshiped different gods, and enforced strange and unwelcome rules. The tension between Roman armies and provincial populations never entirely went away, but gradually the conquered peoples became Romanized. As the occupying Roman forces settled in and raised families with local women, defeated peoples started to assimilate into Roman culture. They adopted Roman customs and language, and provincial elites began to enter Roman politics. Romanization transformed the provinces from occupied zones where shattered communities obeyed foreign masters to well-integrated territories in which Roman culture flourished.

Natural boundaries such as the Rhine and Danube Rivers, and humanmade ones, such as Hadrian's Wall in the north of Britain, separated the Roman Empire from its unconquered neighbors. For the Romans, these boundaries symbolized a cultural division between civilization and barbarism. In the Romans' view, all peoples who did not live under Roman rule were barbarians and therefore hostile. As a result, the most important borders separated Romanized provinces from lands beyond the limits of Roman control. Emperors systematically and heavily fortified these lines of political and cultural demarcation. Romans used this distinction to help define their place in the world and to justify their conquest and absorption of other peoples. Despite the resources spent on maintaining these borders, they remained highly permeable. These borders represented the limits of Roman authority, but they could not prevent non-Romans from entering the empire altogether.

ROME AND THE PARTHIAN EMPIRE

Although the Roman Empire dominated a huge expanse of territory, it did have one formidable rival: the Parthian Empire (Parthia) to the east. This realm stretched from the Euphrates River to the Indus River (covering modern Iraq, Iran, and Pakistan). Unlike the poorly organized and politically unstable Celtic and Germanic tribes the Romans confronted in western Europe, the Parthian Empire was highly structured and enormously powerful. It replaced the successor states of Alexander the Great in Iran in the mid-third century B.C.E. The Parthian Empire ended in 224 C.E., when another Iranian dynasty, the Sasanian, rose to power.

The structure of the highly stratified Parthian society included a king and warrior aristocracy; a middle range of doctors, artisans, and traders; and a large class of peasants. In addition Parthia contained many subject peoples with their own cultures, such as Babylonians, Jews, and Armenians. Unlike Rome, Parthia did not permit subject peoples and internal minorities to enter the ruling elite. The Parthian Empire did tolerate practice of various religions, although Zoroastrianism was the main religion of the Parthian state.

The Romans knew the Parthians as fierce warriors. Parthia's specially bred battle horses, which were famous as far away as China, made heavily armed Parthian cavalrymen and their archers worthy opponents of Rome's legions. Glory-seeking Roman generals of the late Republic found Parthia an attractive but dangerous target. Marcus Licinius Crassus (the associate of Julius Caesar and Pompey in the First Triumvirate) invaded the Parthian Empire, but died there in battle in 53 B.C.E. Most of his troops perished as well, but a few survivors may have ended their days in central Asia fighting as mercenaries for the emperor of China, who maintained ties with the Parthian emperor. After defeating his rivals in 45 B.C.E., Julius Caesar was preparing another invasion of Parthia, but he was assassinated before the attack could begin.

Augustus inaugurated a new Roman policy toward Parthia, just as he initiated changes in so many other aspects of Roman rule. He avenged Crassus's death and regained Roman honor through diplomatic means. Like Augustus, most Roman emperors preferred diplomacy to open conflict with Parthia because they knew they could not conquer and assimilate such a vast territory. Trajan, however, proved an exception. He conquered the Parthian provinces of Armenia and Mesopotamia in ambitious campaigns in 115–116 C.E., when Parthia was weakened by civil war. But Trajan's triumph proved short-lived. His successor, Hadrian, abandoned these conquests because he knew that they overextended Rome's resources.

The most important result of the rivalry between Parthia and Rome was the exchange of ideas and technology between their peoples. Romans highly prized Parthian steel and leather, as well as the exotic spices traded through Parthia from even farther east. The Romans also adopted some military technology and tactics from Parthia, particularly the use of heavily armed cavalry. By the fourth century C.E. these units constituted the core of Roman military might.

There was also an erratic exchange of nonmilitary technological expertise between the two empires. From the Parthians, the Romans learned new techniques of irrigating fields. In turn, Roman hydraulic engineers and masons went to Persia to help construct a great dam for the Parthian king. *Via,* the Latin word for "paved road," entered the Persian language, an indication that other Roman specialists worked in Parthia as well.

Religious ideas also flowed in both directions. Many people in the Roman Empire studied Parthian astrology and magic, while Jewish scholars in the Roman Empire maintained close ties with the Jewish academies in the Parthian province of Babylonia. It was Christianity, however, that was the most directly influenced by this religious interchange between the Parthians and the Romans. The Persian Mani (216–276 C.E.), founder of a religion called Manichaeism, preached that an eternal conflict between forces of light and darkness caused good and evil to intermingle. God's soul had become trapped in matter, and Jesus, the son of God, had come to Earth to retrieve God's soul. Mani taught that all those who followed him and turned their back on earthly possessions would be redeemed. These ideas deeply influenced some Christians in the Roman Empire. Small Christian communities also appeared in Parthia during the imperial period.

ROMAN ENCOUNTERS WITH GERMANIC PEOPLES

The peoples living north of the Rhine and Danube Rivers, not the Parthians, posed the greatest threat to Rome during the first two and a half centuries C.E. Called "Germans" by the Romans, these peoples never used that term among themselves or thought of themselves as one group. Numbering in the tens of millions, most of them spoke their own dialects and did not understand the language of other tribes. Lacking political unity, different Germanic peoples constantly grouped and regrouped, taking new names and following new leaders. Led by aristocratic warriors, they often fought bitterly among themselves. Occasionally for short periods of time they formed loose confederations under the leadership of charismatic warlords in order to defend themselves from Roman aggression or to invade the empire themselves. For example, the Marcomanni, meaning "men of the borderlands," constituted one of these hostile confederations during the reign of Marcus Aurelius. Seeking land and booty, this confederation of many armed groups attacked the Roman Empire with more than a hundred thousand men. Only after fourteen years of brutal war did Marcus Aurelius crush them.

In the early years of Augustus's reign, Roman legions conquered large portions of what is now called Germany between the Rhine and the Elbe Rivers. Arminius's successful revolt in 9 C.E. drove out the Romans, however, and Roman civilization never took root in Germany. The Rhine and Danube Rivers became the symbolic boundary between Romans and their northern enemies. Most of Rome's legions were stationed along this boundary to defend against attacks from their northern neighbors. Tribes along the northern border sometimes fragmented into pro- and anti-Roman factions. Romans supported kings who would favor their cause by fighting Rome's enemies beyond the borders and supplying troops to the auxiliary regiments of the Roman army.

During long periods of peace, the people on either side of the border had the opportunity to interact with one another through military service and trade. Through extensive trade with Roman merchants, mostly Italians and Syrians, many Germanic aristocrats developed a taste for Mediterranean luxuries, including wine and jewelry. By the second century C.E. some chose to live in Roman-style villas in imitation of Roman aristocrats. Many Germanic men gained exposure to Roman civilization when they served in the Roman army as auxiliary troops. As members of the Roman army, they fought wherever they were sent in the empire, even if that meant warfare with other Germanic tribes to the north. Discharged after the standard twenty-five years of service, many of these men returned to their homes with Roman money in their purses, a smattering of Latin, and knowledge of the riches and power of the Roman Empire.

By the end of the second century C.E. the weight of different peoples pressing on Rome's northern borders began to crack the imperial defenses. With the end of the Severan dynasty in 235 C.E., the empire entered a period of unrelieved disasters that lasted nearly fifty years. Invading groups from north of the Rhine and Danube Rivers pushed into the empire as far south as central Italy in search of plunder and land on which to settle. The Romans ultimately marshaled the military resources to repel the invaders and restore the empire's security late in the third century C.E. As we will see in the next chapter, however, the restored Roman Empire differed radically from the system Augustus inaugurated.

ROMAN ENCOUNTERS WITH ASIANS AND AFRICANS

More than 3,000 forbidding miles separated the empires of Rome and Han China, but commerce brought them together. China produced silk, the luxurious textile coveted in the West. Merchants risked great dangers to bring silk and other luxury goods westward from China in their caravans. Chinese documents from the first century C.E. mention Chinese ambassadors sent to Rome who reached as far as the Persian Gulf. Emperor Marcus Aurelius sent ambassadors to China in 166 C.E., but the two empires never established formal ties.

India came to the attention of the Hellenistic world and later to Rome through the campaigns of Alexander the Great. For centuries the Indian subcontinent inspired Greek fantasy writers, who were intrigued by rumors of enormous wealth, exotic animals, and very different social customs in the Indian subcontinent brought back to the Hellenistic world by traders and travelers. In the first and second centuries C.E. India also played a crucial role in the silk trade as the main depot for silk coming from China on its way to Rome.

Indian trade with merchants coming from the Roman Empire, particularly from Alexandria, was brisk and highly profitable in the first several centuries C.E. Trade routes linked the Mediterranean basin, the East African coast, the Persian Gulf, and the Red Sea with India's western Malabar coast, as well as with lands across the Bay of Bengal in Southeast Asia and China. One Roman account from the first century C.E., *Voyage Around the Red Sea,* written by an unknown author, describes a vast international commercial network.

Roman demand for spices (especially pepper) and luxury items from the Far East meant that Roman trading networks extended as far as Java in East Asia. In the first century C.E., Pliny the Elder griped, "And by the lowest

Wineship

Found in Germany, this energetic but unsophisticated sculpture of the second century C.E. depicts wine merchants hurrying their cargo to thirsty customers somewhere on the Rhine River. Because grapes could not be cultivated in this northern region, wine was a luxury there. Common people drank beer.

reckoning India, China, and the Arabian Peninsula take from our Empire many thousands of pounds of gold every year—that is the sum which our luxuries and our women cost us." Pliny's concern was not unfounded: Archaeologists have discovered thousands of Roman coins in India and even in Thailand, evidence of commerce's extensive reach. Only the rise of Islam in the seventh century C.E. would disconnect Rome and Mediterranean lands from this far-reaching Asian trade network.

In addition to trading with China and India, Romans did some exploring in sub-Saharan Africa. Roman coins found deep in the interior of Africa suggest that they may have had commercial dealings with peoples there as well. To the Romans, however, "Africa" was one of their provinces bordering the Mediterranean Sea—the region we know as North Africa today—not the vast continent that lay to the south, beyond the Sahara Desert. Only in the European Middle Ages would the name Africa come to stand for the entire land mass of the continent.

The Romans knew little about sub-Saharan Africa. In 146 B.C.E., the Roman general Scipio sent the historian Polybius on an expedition down the west coast of Africa. Polybius's expedition got as far as Senegal and a place Scipio called Crocodile River. In the first century C.E., a Roman military expedition that marched south from a base in North Africa in pursuit of some raiders may have reached Chad. One hundred years later, an intrepid Roman officer named Julius Maternus traveled south for four months, reaching a place "where the rhinoceroses gather." He emerged in the Sudan, where he found the Nile and returned home.

The Romans used the word *Aethiopians* ("the People with Burned Faces") to refer to the peoples who lived south of the Sahara desert. Most of their knowledge of these peoples came from the Egyptians, who regularly traded with peoples living in the extreme south of the Nile River valley. From the Egyptians they learned of a place of fabulous wealth and exotic creatures. It would take many centuries, however, before European peoples viewed Africa as anything other than a fantasyland.

Society and Culture in the Imperial Age

The same central theme that characterized Roman politics after Augustus also characterized Roman society in the imperial age—the illusion of continuity with the Republic, masking fundamental change. The social pyramid described in Chapter 4 remained intact—aristocrats at the top, followed by equestrians, plebeians and peasants, freedmen, and slaves. Important changes, however, occurred within the pyramid, as imperial rule altered social and economic relationships. The shift from republic to empire also had a profound influence on Roman culture and religious belief. In their works, writers, poets, and historians explored the ambivalence of life under stable but autocratic rule. At the same time, the spread of religious cults promising salvation hinted that many people under Roman rule found life less than stable, and looked outside the political sphere for safety. Christianity, which emerged during the Augustan era, possessed a special appeal to those classes of society that benefitted the least from imperial governance.

The Upper and Lower Classes

In the Roman Empire, aristocrats continued to stand at the top of the social pyramid, enjoying the greatest wealth, power, and prestige. Roman emperors recognized three social groups, or orders, as having aristocratic status. The first order, the senators of Rome, occupied a place of honor at the very top of the social pyramid. Augustus attempted to rebuild the Roman Senate and boost its morale after the civil war by recruiting new members and dismissing men whom he considered of low moral character. The Roman Senate was not a hereditary aristocracy, but Augustus encouraged the sons of senators to follow in their fathers' footsteps, and he offered financial incentives to senators to have children and perpetuate their family line. Despite these efforts, most of the oldest Roman senatorial families died out by the end of the first century C.E., due to death in war, failure to protect heirs, and falling victim to political intrigues. With the approval of the emperor, new aristocratic families emerged to take their place and serve in the Senate. These senators came from Roman families that had grown in wealth and prestige through service to the emperor. Many new senators also stemmed from the provinces and came to Rome to be in the Senate and serve as imperial officials. All senators, and their descendants for three generations, had the right to wear a broad purple stripe on their togas (formal clothing) as a badge of honor.

Below the senators stood the equestrian order, which was much larger than the senatorial order. Like senators, equestrians had to possess high birth and wealth—but to a lesser degree. The equestrian order flourished in the imperial age. Many equestrians continued to follow business careers as they had during the Republic, but the expansion of the Republic provided them with new opportunities for public service. Equestrians staffed the diplomatic, fiscal, and military services. Many served in the Roman Senate. They constituted an increasing percentage of Rome's senators in the first centuries of the empire.

The third aristocratic order consisted of the city councilors who served in the councils of every Roman city throughout the provinces. Like senators and equestrians, they were expected to be wealthy, of respectable birth, and of good moral character. In many cities, the sons of freedmen (men who had once been slaves) were permitted to be city councilors.

These three aristocratic orders represented only a tiny fraction of the empire's population. Below them came the plebeians—Rome's poor but free underclass of citizens. Though not included in political life, plebeians living throughout the empire benefited in some ways from imperial rule. In the city of Rome, for example, they received a daily allotment of free grain. (Approximately half of Rome's population of one million depended on the daily gifts of grain.) With little incentive to work and deprived of the rights and responsibilities of political participation, the plebeians enjoyed much leisure time. By the first century C.E., Romans had approximately 100 days designated as holidays. The plebeians demanded a steady diet of bloody entertainment, such as the gladiatorial combats in the Colosseum and the chariot races in the Circus Maximus. Thus plebeian life in the city of Rome was degraded into "bread and circuses": free grain and free entertainment.

In the city of Rome, the plebeians needed bread and circuses to compensate not only for their loss of political power but also for their poor living conditions. Crowded into vile tenement slums with little light and no plumbing, the poor lived in misery. The streets flowed with human and animal excrement and other sewage. Vultures picked at the refuse dumped outside butcher shops. Fire was a constant threat, and the Tiber flooded frequently. The urban poor had no access to education or political power. Disease kept the birth rate and life expectancy very low. Probably more than a quarter of all infants died within their first five years, and a third of those who survived were dead by age 10. The average Roman man died at age 45, and the average woman at age 34.

Poor people lived in similarly wretched conditions in every Roman city—but without the free distributions of grain. They relied on local aristocrats to provide food in times of emergency and to provide public entertainments. Plebeians in the countryside made their living primarily by farming, and they provided the bulk of troops in the Roman army.

SLAVES AND FREEDMEN

Slavery was one of the harshest facts of life in the Roman Empire. Slaves made up a huge percentage of Roman society, at the very bottom of the social order. Of the city of Rome's approximately one million inhabitants, an estimated 400,000 were slaves during the early empire. When Augustus took control of Rome, slaves constituted 35 to 40 percent of the total population of Italy.

Everyone accepted that humans could be reduced to property. Millions of slaves inhabited the empire, holding the lowest possible status in a society in which social and legal status meant everything. No Roman citizen ever objected to slavery as an institution. Some high-minded Stoic philosophers, who noted the common humanity of slaves and owners, did criticize slavery, but only because they feared its corrupting effect on the masters. They had no concern for the condition of the slaves themselves. Later Christian writers living within the empire stressed that slaves should obey their masters "with fear and trembling."

The victims of a brisk international trade in humans, most slaves entered the empire through conquest. Others were enslaved from birth, having been born of a slave mother. There was never a shortage of slaves, and sometimes after a successful military campaign, such as Trajan's defeat of the Dacians in 106 C.E., the market was glutted.

Ownership of slaves conveyed a person's status. The emperor himself owned tens of thousands of slaves who labored on his estates throughout the empire. Rich men, too, possessed them in huge numbers. Even poor artisans and teachers might hold one or two. Former slaves who had gained their freedom (freedmen) also owned slaves. Slaves were permitted to earn money, with the result that even some slaves owned slaves.

Slaves used for domestic service or in commerce and crafts were the lucky ones. Many slaves worked on the great plantations, or latifundia°, as part of large slave gangs. The absentee owners cared little for the welfare of these slaves. Latifundia slaves often labored in chains and slept in underground prisons. The slaves sent to work in the mines experienced even worse conditions. For them, only a wretched death lay ahead. Female slaves were spared the horrors of working in the fields and mines, but they were valued far less than were male slaves.

Dehumanized by their enslavement and stripped of their identity when taken from family and home, slaves lived in fear of their masters, who could abuse them physically or sexually with impunity. Violence lay at the heart of this institution, for ultimate control of slaves rested on force. In 61 C.E. when Pedanius Secundus, the chief administrator of the city of Rome, was killed by one of his slaves, all the other 400 slaves in his household were executed in accordance with Roman custom, on the assumption that some of them surely must have known the killer's intention. The Senate affirmed this decision as the right thing to do. Romans, in common with the Greeks and other ancient peoples, believed that the only way to compel a slave to tell the truth was through torture. Thus, any testimony provided by a slave in court was valid only if it was extracted by torture. Galen, the great physician, did recommend that owners not beat their slaves, but only because of its medical benefits to the owners: "If a man adheres to the practice of never striking any of his slaves with his hand, he will be less likely to succumb to a fit of anger later on. . . . I have criticized many of my friends when I saw how they had bruised their hands by hitting their slaves on the mouth." In the face of such brutality, slaves had few options. Slaves could try to escape, but if caught were branded on the forehead. Slave revolts never succeeded.

Despite their utter lack of freedom, many slaves formed emotional and sexual relationships with one another. Epitaphs on graves demonstrate that they used conventional terms of affection and marriage bonds such as husband and wife, although Roman law did not recognize these informal slave marriages. Some slave owners permitted slave marriages because they understood that slaves with families would be less likely to rebel. Complete submissiveness and the goodwill of their masters were necessary to hold a slave family together.

Slavery was not, however, necessarily a permanent condition. Slaves might obtain their freedom through manumission. Through this carefully regulated legal procedure, a master granted freedom to a slave as a reward for faithful service or docile behavior, or even out of genuine affection. Of course manumission worked to the best interests of the owner: The merest hope of manumission kept most slaves docile. Moreover, Roman law established limits to manumission. No more than 100 slaves could be freed at the death of an owner, and the slave had to be at least 30 years old and the owner at least 25.

Despite these restrictions, the freedmen constituted an important class in Roman society. Freedmen made up only about 5 percent of Rome's population, but their enterprise and ambition marked them as some of the more successful members of Roman society. Many former slaves worked in business or as skilled laborers, teachers, and doctors. Unlike in other ancient societies, freedmen rid themselves of the taint of slavery in only one generation. A freed slave had only partial citizen rights, but his or her children became full Roman citizens, who could freely marry other citizens. The historian Tacitus records a remark made in a senatorial debate about this phenomenon: "Not without good reason had our ancestors, in distinguishing the position of the different orders, thrown freedom open to all." Tacitus noted that some senators and many equestrians could point to ex-slaves among their ancestors.

Slavery remained a part of Mediterranean economic and social life until the early Middle Ages, but in the second century C.E. the role of slaves in the economy began to diminish. As Roman emperors concentrated on consolidating rather than expanding the borders of the empire, the supply of slaves dwindled, and the cost of slaves rose. Thus, slave owning may have become less economically viable.

WOMEN IN THE ROMAN EMPIRE

Women in the senatorial and equestrian ranks possessed far more freedom than was usual in the ancient world. By 250 C.E., the form of marriage by which a woman passed from the control of her father to that of her husband had almost entirely died out. Women remained, at least theoretically, under the control of their father or legal guardian. In practice, this form of marriage gave a woman more freedom, in large part because her husband no longer controlled her dowry. Some women used this freedom to move more into the public view, taking part in banquets, attending the gladiatorial battles at the Colosseum and the races at the Circus Maximus, and even presiding over literary salons. Many women were educated in the liberal arts and lived a cultivated lifestyle. Their surviving portraits (carved in stone) reveal a restrained physical elegance. The portraits of several wives and daughters of emperors even appeared on coins.

As these coins suggest, at the highest level of society some women possessed real political power, though expressed behind the scenes. Livia, married to Augustus for fifty-two years, possessed a great deal of influence during his reign and worked actively to ensure the succession of her son Tiberius. The emperor Hadrian may have received his throne in part because of the influence of his cousin Trajan's wife, Plotina. At Plotina's funeral, Hadrian admitted, "She often made requests of me, and I never once refused her." The empress Julia Domna survived her husband Septimius Severus to become an important political power during the reign of her son Caracalla.

Although literary evidence demonstrates that many aristocratic Roman men cherished their daughters, the practice of female infanticide remained common throughout Roman society. In addition, some children born outside marriage, and those born deformed or ill, were regularly exposed—left on a pile of garbage or by the roadside. Not all the exposed children died. Sometimes they were rescued and raised as slaves by ordinary people. In other cases, slave dealers picked up the abandoned babies and sold them.

LITERATURE AND EMPIRE

As in the Republic, in the empire Roman writers continued to look to Greek Hellenistic culture for their models. But the presence of the empire itself influenced Roman writers. No author could avoid the political facts of life, whether he cynically ignored them, enthusiastically embraced them, or cautiously probed their limits. The presence of imperial autocracy, as well as Rome's expanding might, affected literary production in different ways.

Writers during the reign of Augustus embodied the tensions and uncertainties of living in a society that had exchanged freedom for stability. Livy (59 B.C.E.–12 C.E.) wrote a massive history of Rome, called *From the Foundation of the City,* that traced Rome from its origins until his own time. Though less than a fifth of this work survives, we see that Livy presented Rome's rise to world mastery as a series of instructive moral and patriotic lessons. He showed how

Rome grew to world power through vanquishing many enemies. Although proud of Rome's greatness, Livy also believed that with power came decadence. He expressed the hope that Augustus would restore Rome's glory and put an end to what he perceived as its moral and political decline.

The tragic career of Ovid (43 B.C.E.–17 C.E.) demonstrates the risks of offending an emperor. Ovid's brilliant love elegies had made him the darling of Rome. But in 8 C.E., his erotic poem "The Art of Love," along with an obscure scandal involving Augustus's family, earned him the hostility of the prudish emperor. Augustus exiled Ovid to a squalid village on the Black Sea, where he died in sorrow.

The poet Horace (65–8 B.C.E.), son of a wealthy freedman, walked a more careful path. He avoided political entanglements and maintained close ties to Augustus. His poetry on public themes praised Augustus for bringing peace and the hope of a moral life to the world. Throughout his work, Horace urged serene appreciation of life's transient joys. In his most famous verse (*Odes* I.11.6ff) he sings, "Be wise, taste the wine, and since our time is brief, be moderate in your aspirations. Even as we speak, greedy life slips away from us. Grasp each day (*carpe diem*) and do not pin your hopes on tomorrow."

Virgil stands as the greatest of the Roman poets. Drawing on Hellenistic poetic forms, Virgil wrote of the wisdom, safety, and serenity found in an idealized country life—with the terrible uncertainties of civil war providing a silent backdrop. At Augustus' request Virgil composed the *Aeneid*°, an epic poem that legitimized and celebrated the emperor's reign. Ostensibly the poem was about the mythic foundation of the Roman state by the hero Aeneas, a Trojan prince fleeing the destruction of his native city by the Greeks. But through a series of cinematic "flash-forwards," Virgil presented the entire history of the Roman people as culminating in the reign of Augustus. In the *Aeneid,* the emperor brings to completion the nearly unendurable efforts of his Trojan ancestor.

Although the *Aeneid* praises Augustus, Virgil was not just a propagandist for the imperial regime. Virgil remained his own man throughout his lifetime, praising those aspects of peace and fulfillment of duty that he genuinely valued, but nevertheless questioning the costs of warfare and the demands of empire on human beings. Virgil subtly investigated the effects of warfare and public duty on individual character. In the *Aeneid* Virgil's hero Aeneas was deeply tempted by his love for the Carthaginian queen Dido to abandon his mission of founding Rome. But Aeneas overcame his private desire in favor of the destiny of Rome. He willingly abandoned Dido to continue his divinely inspired mission. At the end of the poem, Aeneas stands victorious—but a psychological ruin. He had given everything to his duty. Virgil makes his readers wonder about the costs of such utter public service. If any writer understood the promise and the threat of the imperial system, it was Virgil.

Seneca (ca. 4 B.C.E.–41 C.E.), who combined philosophical interests with literary skill, accepted the imperial system. His integrity and rhetorical brilliance earned him the unenviable task of being Nero's tutor when the emperor was still an impressionable 12-year-old boy. For eight years Seneca guided Nero, and the empire enjoyed good government. As Nero matured, however, he found other, less decent advisers. Appalled by his student's descent into corruption, Seneca plotted to kill Nero. When he was caught, he killed himself.

In the Middle Ages Seneca's works were so highly regarded that many people believed he had exchanged letters with the Christian Paul of Tarsus. Stoic beliefs deeply influenced Seneca's writing. He intended his writings to give sound advice to rulers. Seneca courageously acknowledged how hard it was to control one's human weaknesses and live a truly moral life.

Other writers analyzed the imperial system differently. Practitioners of the art of public speaking (rhetoric) had to grapple with new realities during the imperial age. The new autocratic government made free political debate impossible. Nevertheless, opportunities for public speech still abounded: Law cases still had to be tried in court, and emperors had to be bathed in praise at regular intervals. Thus, rhetoric blossomed in the new imperial world. Quintilian (ca. 35–ca. 90 C.E.) exemplifies the new kind of imperial rhetorician. He rose to prominence in Rome as a teacher and speaker, becoming the tutor in the royal household of the emperor Domitian. His masterpiece, *Training in Oratory,* calls for clarity and balance in speaking. It also rather wistfully suggests that an orator might guide the Senate and the state, as Quintilian's model Cicero had done during the days of the Republic.

The historian and rhetorician Tacitus (ca. 56–ca. 118 C.E.) took a more realistic approach than Quintilian. In his *Dialogue on Orators* he argued—correctly—that political autocracy had killed true oratory, reducing it to mere public entertainment and ceremonial flourishes. Sardonic and terse, Tacitus's historical accounts covering the first century of the Augustan age displayed a deep understanding of human psychological reaction to the harsh political realities of early imperial tyranny. Although Tacitus's career flourished under the tyrannical Domitian, he hated political oppression and he never abandoned his love for the best of Roman ideals. In the *Agricola,* his biography of his father-in-law, Tacitus affirmed that good men could serve their country honorably, even under bad rulers. The *Agricola* thus inadvertently revealed an important accomplishment of Augustus's imperial system: It had tamed the competitive energies of Rome's aristocrats, transforming them into an efficient governing class.

Eager to contemplate the cultural superiority of the Roman Empire over other peoples, Rome's ruling elite took a strong interest in the habits of non-Romans. In his

Geography, Strabo (64 B.C.E.–ca. 25 C.E.), a native Greek and a Roman citizen, wrote a detailed account of the many peoples ruled by Rome, stressing how Roman civilization could change foreign cultures for the better. He suggested that Rome's rulers and administrators should "bring together cities and peoples into a single Empire and political management." Drawing on Hellenistic and Greek traditions of writing about foreign cultures, Strabo placed the Roman Empire at the center of the inhabited world.

In addition to geography, other forms of scientific writing made great strides in the early centuries of the Roman Empire. Claudius Ptolemy of Alexandria maintained the high standards of the Hellenistic science tradition that continued to flourish under Roman rule. Writing in the second half of the second century C.E. (historians cannot be precise about the dates of his life or death), Ptolemy composed definitive works in many fields. Using the division of spheres into units of 60 first developed by the Sumerians and perfected by the Babylonians, Ptolemy's *Almagest* proved the theories and tables necessary to compute the positions of the sun, the moon, and five known planets. He accepted the Greek theory that the sun revolves around the Earth. Western astronomers used his maps of the heavens for nearly 1,500 years. His *Geography* gave readings in longitude and latitude and provided information for drawing a world map, which remained the basis of cartography until the sixteenth century. Translated from Greek into Arabic, Ptolemy's books became standard in the medieval Islamic world. Eventually they were translated into Latin and so passed back into use in western Europe during the Middle Ages.

RELIGIOUS LIFE

Religious expression in the Roman Empire took many forms. The imperial government made no effort to impose uniform belief, so subject peoples freely worshiped many gods and maintained their traditional religious rituals. Within many religious cultures, trends that first appeared in the Hellenistic Age continued, but important new changes emerged during the imperial era. Judaism was transformed during this period. At the same time, an entirely new religion, Christianity, emerged from Jewish roots. This new faith grew to become the dominant religion in the empire by 400 C.E. and eventually suppressed polytheistic religions.

Polytheism in the Empire

Syncretism°, the practice of equating two gods and fusing their cults, was a common feature of imperial religious life. Like many other Mediterranean peoples, the Romans often identified a foreign god with their own deities. For example, Julius Caesar described the Gallic god of commerce as Mercury, because Mercury served the same function in Roman religion. Romans did not care that other people throughout the empire might worship Jupiter or Juno or any other Roman god in different ways, or might give the gods different attributes. Syncretism, then, helped unify the diverse peoples and regions under Roman rule. Through syncretism, shared religious experiences spread across the empire.

Roman religious practice was a public, not private, phenomenon. Imperial subjects worshiped the emperor and Rome, the protectors of the entire empire. In addition, each city in the empire had its own gods, whom people imagined as dwelling within the temples dedicated to them. Worshipers gathered in front of the temples to offer sacrifices at altars located in front of the shrines. On religious holidays, thousands of city dwellers participated in parades and feasted at the great banquets that followed the sacrifice of many specially selected animals at temple altars. Particularly elaborate celebrations even attracted pilgrims and visitors from afar.

The gods worshiped in specific cities and at specific holy sites generally were of great antiquity. Gods such as Athena in Athens or Jupiter in Rome were as old as the town itself. People believed that these gods would protect and benefit their communities if the residents made the proper sacrifices. Although a deity might be associated with a similar god in another town, its worship in each city had a unique quality, deeply intertwined with the history and architecture of the town itself. For example, Hercules protected many places, but his temple in each town was connected to a different local myth about him.

Some religious cults transcended their places of origin and spread widely, particularly among slaves, freedmen, and the urban poor who felt lost in the sprawl of the empire's big cities. As we have seen, large numbers of the urban poor had no stake in the success of the Roman system. The anonymity of life in big cities for the poor contributed to the spread of religions that offered a measure of identity and community and a kind of salvation as well. Religions that promised victory over death or liberation from the abuses and pain of daily existence possessed a wide appeal and spread quickly across the empire. The goddess Isis, for example, who originated in Egypt, offered freedom from the arbitrary abuses of fate to her many followers throughout the empire. Her cult particularly attracted women. Because she was often depicted holding her baby son Horus, she represented the universal mother. In his work *The Golden Ass,* the Roman writer Apuleius (ca. 125–ca. 170 C.E.) describes the goddess's protective power. Full of eroticism and magic, the work tells the story of Lucius, a carefree young Romeo, who is turned into a miserable donkey when caught spying on a gorgeous witch. After many comic misadventures in which Lucius learns how uncertain fate can be, Isis restores him

Mummy Wrapping from Egypt
This painted linen cloth was wrapped around a mummy in an Egyptian burial during the second century C.E. It shows the Egyptian god Osiris (on the left) and the jackal-headed god Anubis (on the right). Between them is the deceased man, dressed in Roman clothing. His portrait has been carefully painted and added separately. This wrapping and portrait show the continuity of ancient Egyptian religion during Roman imperial rule.

to human form. In gratitude, Lucius joins her religion and becomes her priest.

Another popular religion that promised salvation to its initiates was that of Mithras, a sun god. Artists depicted Mithras slaying a bull, an archetypal sacrifice that his followers reenacted in secret ceremonies. Limited to men, worship of Mithras took place in underground chambers in which small groups held banquets, recited sacred lessons about the celestial journey of the soul after death, and made sacrifices to the god in imitation of his killing of the bull. Because this religion stressed both physical courage and performance of duty, it particularly attracted soldiers and administrators.

The most important religion of an eastern god whose worship spread throughout the Roman Empire was that of the Unconquered Sun. Originating in Syria, this deity came to be associated with Apollo and Helios, two Greco-Roman sun gods. When Elagabalus, the high priest of the Syrian sun god (El-Gabal), became Roman emperor (r. 218–222 C.E.), he built a huge temple dedicated to his god in Rome, and designated December 25 as a special day of worship to the deity. Within fifty years, the Unconquered Sun became the chief god of imperial and official worship. Only the rise of Christianity would displace the worship of the Unconquered Sun.

Gnosticism, which originated in the Hellenistic Age, continued its influence in the Roman Empire, affecting Judaism, Christianity, and many polytheistic religions. Gnostics believed that the material world of daily life is incompatible with the supreme god. They thought that sparks of divinity (sometimes considered the human soul) are imprisoned within the body. Only a redeemer sent from the supreme god could release these divine sparks.

The Origins of Rabbinic Judaism

Following the Roman devastation of Judaea and the destruction of the Temple in Jerusalem in 70 C.E., Judaism began to take the shape it has today. Since priests could no longer make sacrifices at the Temple and provide a focus for Jewish worship, a new kind of community-based religious life began to develop among Jews in Judaea and other lands. Rabbis replaced priests in the roles of religious instructors and community guides. Unlike the priests who had served as intermediaries between the community and God by offering prayers and animal sacrifices on the people's behalf, the rabbis had no sacred function. *Rabbi,* a Hebrew term of respect meaning "my master," was the term that Jews applied to teachers. Men with legal training, rabbis interpreted and taught the Jewish law contained in the Torah, the first five books of the Hebrew Bible. Rabbis placed tremendous importance upon studying the Torah. "It is the unlearned who bring trouble into the world," said Rabbi Judah the Prince, a Jewish scholar of the late second century C.E.

Rabbis became more important after the failed Jewish revolt against Rome (66–70 C.E.). According to Jewish tradition, a rabbi named Johannon ben Zakkai, who had opposed the revolt, was smuggled out of Jerusalem around 68 C.E. Johannon ben Zakkai gained permission from the Romans to establish an academy at Jamnia in Judaea, where men might study and interpret Jewish law. Judaea remained a center of rabbinic teaching until the Bar Kochba revolt of 132–135 C.E. In the aftermath of this bloodily suppressed rebellion in which more than half a million Jews were killed, the emperor Hadrian built a new city on the site of ruined Jerusalem and barred Jews from admission all but one day a year. Galilee (a region to the north of Jerusalem)

Dura Europus

Located on the Euphrates River, the town of Dura Europus was on the eastern frontier of the Roman Empire, and had a large and prosperous Jewish community i the third century C.E. The walls of the community's synagogue were painted with many scenes illustrating stories from the Hebrew Bible.

and the coastal city of Caesarea then became important rabbinic centers. Historians have found little evidence that rabbis taught elsewhere in the Roman Empire for many centuries afterward.

By 200 C.E., synagogues emerged as communal centers that served many functions for Jews. In these buildings rabbis studied Jewish law and passed judgment on disputes. Members of the community gathered there to celebrate sacred meals on the Sabbath and to hear the Jewish law read aloud and explained. Gradually synagogues developed into centers where the Jewish community would pray together.

The greatest product of the rabbinic academies was the Mishnah, a collection of legal opinions, legal decisions, and homilies to explain the law to unlearned people. Jewish teachers had begun accumulating this material in Hellenistic times, but it was completed around the year 220 C.E. In their desire to prepare a manageable body of material for reference and teaching, rabbis undertook a task not unlike that of the Roman jurists. But unlike Roman compilations, which drew from written texts, the Mishnah drew largely from oral law that had been memorized and transmitted through many generations.

Compiled by Rabbi Judah the Prince and his school, the Mishnah consists of sixty-three books, each dealing with a particular aspect of law, ranging from matters of ritual purity to calendrical issues to civil and criminal law. Because legal opinions are attributed to the rabbi who gave the original judgment, we can trace the development of Jewish law in the first and second centuries C.E. Among the many moral principles stressed by the Mishnah, saving life was paramount. According to the Mishnah, no person could save his or her own life by causing another's death, and no person could be sacrificed for the welfare of the community. Moreover, to save a life, any person could break any Jewish religious law, except those forbidding idolatry, adultery, incest, or murder. In Jewish thought, saving one life symbolized saving humanity. A radical idea slowly emerged from this principle: Since all humans are made in God's image, they should all have equal rights. This idea contributed to the gradual decline of slave holding among Jews.

In addition to the rabbis who led individual Jewish communities, an official called the Patriarch represented the Jews as a whole to the emperor. The Romans appointed the Patriarch and gave him the highest political authority in Jewish affairs in the empire. The Patriarch's responsibilities included collecting taxes for Rome and choosing judges for Jewish courts. The Romans gave the Patriarch the rank of senator, as the representative of all the Jews in the empire. This arrangement, a clear example of how Roman authorities let local populations manage their own laws, continued until Christianity became the official religion of the empire in the fifth century C.E. Christian emperors then began persecuting Jews and limiting their participation in public life.

The Emergence of Christianity

So far in this chapter we have considered the interaction of the Roman government with communities that had existed for many centuries. The emergence of Christianity, however, forced the Romans to deal with an entirely new community within the empire. Christians had a new sense of shared identity, a new sense of history, and a new perception of the Roman system. Christianity gradually became the most widespread religion in the Roman Empire, and within 400 years of the death of its founder became the official religion of the empire.

The founder of Christianity was a Jew named Yeshua ben Yosef, known today as Jesus of Nazareth (ca. 4 B.C.E.–ca. 30 C.E.). Born to a poor couple in Galilee during the reign of Augustus, Jesus grew to manhood in the Jewish community. Around age 30 he began to travel through Palestine with a band of followers, urging men and women to repent their sins because God would soon come to rule the Kingdom of Heaven on Earth. Jesus probably believed himself to be the messiah whose death would inaugurate a new age and a new covenant with God. By means of this covenant, God's earthly kingdom would begin and all humanity would be freed from sin, death, and the power of the Devil.

Jesus was a holy man and a healer. Like other contemporary Jewish teachers, he insisted that having the right intent in carrying out God's law mattered more than conforming to the outward performance of the law. When asked what the greatest commandment is, Jesus replied, "You must love the Lord your God with all your heart, with all your soul, and with all your mind. This is the greatest and the first commandment. The second resembles it: You must love your neighbor as yourself. On these two commandments hang the whole Law." (Matthew 22:37–39)

In 30 C.E. Jesus entered Jerusalem to preach his message. The Roman authorities arrested and tried him as a revolutionary. They executed Jesus by crucifixion, the usual Roman death penalty for noncitizens. Jesus' followers, however, insisted that he lived. They believed that he rose from the dead three days after being executed, and that forty days later he entered heaven to be united with God. His followers came to believe that Jesus was the Son of God, and that he had died on the cross as part of a divine plan. In Christian theology, Jesus' brutal death at the hands of the Romans became a loving sacrifice: Jesus took the punishment for sin due to all human beings. Christians, then, regarded Jesus as their savior, as the God whose intervention in human history guaranteed them eternal life.

Jesus recorded none of his ideas in writing, but his followers transmitted his teachings orally for several decades after his death before beginning to write them down. By about 120 C.E. they had compiled an authoritative body of texts that recorded Jesus' life and words, which Christians call the New Testament. Much early writing about Jesus was not included in the New Testament, but enough of this material survives to show that many different interpretations of Jesus, his death, and his message existed even during his lifetime.

For many decades after Jesus' death, his followers still thought of themselves as Jews. The word *Christian* (which comes from the Greek word *Christos,* meaning "the anointed one" or "messiah") was first used in the Syrian city of Antioch in the second half of the first century C.E. Christianity drew much from Judaism. For example, both faiths believe that that there is only one God, with whom contact is direct and immediate, that this God has a plan for his people on Earth, and that he wishes them to live by a moral and ethical code elaborated in his law.

Christianity diverges from Judaism in several ways. Unlike Jews, Christians have a strong sense of mission. Proselytizing (preaching to nonbelievers in order to convert them) became a central activity for followers of the new faith. As we have seen, the destruction of the Jerusalem Temple in 70 C.E. forced Jews to abandon ritual sacrifice. By contrast, Christians created a priesthood to maintain the sacrament of the Eucharist (Holy Communion), a ritual that recalls Jesus' death on the cross in order to fulfill Jesus' instructions: "Jesus . . . broke some bread, and he said, 'this is my body, which is for you; do this as a memorial of me.' And in the same way, with the cup after supper, saying, 'Whenever you eat this bread, then, and drink this cup, you are proclaiming the Lord's death until he comes.'" (1Corinthians 11:23–26) In this ritual, the Christian tastes bread and wine, representing the flesh and blood of Jesus. The Christian is thus united to God through Jesus. At the same time, this tasting of the Eucharist reminds the Christian of Jesus' sacrifice to ensure his or her salvation.

Christians and Jews further disagree about how to interpret texts that both communities consider fundamental. For example, Christians hold that Jesus' teachings (contained in the New Testament) build on the teachings of the Hebrew Bible, which they called the Old Testament. Consequently, they interpret the Hebrew Bible solely in light of Christianity. For example, Christians believe that the prophetic writings of the Hebrew Bible predict Jesus' birth, death, and resurrection. They also believe that baptism, the ritual that signals an individual's membership in the Christian community, replaces circumcision as a sign of God's promise to his people. Thus, unlike Judaism, Christianity does not require male circumcision for its adherents.

For all their fundamental differences of belief, Christianity and Judaism share some characteristics that distinguish them from other religions of antiquity. First, both Christianity and Judaism combine a statement of belief with a social ethic. Their ethical systems, which they believe stems from divine revelation, are embodied in values that strengthen the religious community. In antiquity Christians and Jews married within their own communities and both protected the underprivileged in their communities—widows, orphans, and the poor. Second, both religious communities had an internal organization that did not depend on Rome. Their leaders (bishops for Christians and rabbis for Jews) gave judgments based on law that was separate from the Roman justice system. Finally, both Judaism and Christianity were monotheistic. To the Romans, who believed in many gods, this monotheism was the strangest aspect of the two faiths. Worshiping only one god made no sense to Romans, with their tradition of making sacrifices to many gods.

JUSTICE IN HISTORY

The Trial of Jesus in Historical Perspective

In 30 C.E. Roman authorities in Jerusalem tried and executed a Jewish teacher known today as Jesus of Nazareth or Jesus Christ, whose teachings lie at the foundation of Christianity, the faith of hundreds of millions of people in the world today. Although an insignificant event at the time, the trial of Jesus and its interpretation made a profound impact on Western civilization. We can learn much about the West by understanding the ways in which the trial has been interpreted through the ages.

Information about Jesus' trial comes from the New Testament books of Matthew, Mark, Luke, and John. These narratives, called the Gospels, were written thirty to sixty years after Jesus' death. They relate that during three years of teaching and miraculous healing, Jesus earned the resentment of some Jewish religious leaders by disregarding aspects of Jewish religious law. According to the Gospels, when Jesus entered the Temple precinct in Jerusalem, he started a riot by overturning the tables of money changers who served pilgrims and by denouncing the hypocrisy of the priestly elite, who then conspired to kill him. The priests paid one of Jesus' followers to reveal his whereabouts, arrested him on either the night before or the night of the Passover feast, and tried him immediately before the Sanhedrin, the highest Jewish court, which met that same night in the house of the Jewish high priest. The Gospels say that the Sanhedrin found Jesus guilty of blasphemy for claiming to be the Messiah and the Son of God. Lacking the authority to put Jesus to death, the Jewish leaders brought Jesus before Pontius Pilate, the Roman governor, and demanded that he execute Jesus. Pilate was reluctant to do so, but the priests persuaded him by insisting that Jesus threatened the emperor's authority with his claim to be King of the Jews. Pilate's soldiers crucified Jesus—a terrible punishment in which the condemned person was tied or nailed to a wooden cross and left to die. According to the Gospel accounts, however, the real blame for Jesus' death rests with the Jews, who had demanded his execution. In all four Gospel accounts, Jewish crowds in Jerusalem reject Jesus and cry out, "Crucify him!" to a reluctant Pontius Pilate.

The Gospel narratives, however, do not correspond to what historians know about the conduct of trials by Jewish authorities or Roman administrators. For example, the Sanhedrin could not hold trials at night; it never met in the house of the High Priest, only in the Hall of Justice in the Temple precinct; and it never met on a Jewish feast day or the night before a feast. The most important difference, however, is that according to Jewish law it was not a crime to claim to be the messiah. Originating in ceremonies of anointing kings, the word *messiah* had many interpretations as a kingly figure of power—but not as a god.

If Jesus had not committed a crime under Jewish law by claiming to be the messiah, what then was his offense? Jesus had committed a very dangerous act by denouncing the priests in Jerusalem. These men, especially the High Priest himself, owed their positions of power to the Roman overlords and were responsible for maintaining order. These Jewish elites saw Jesus as an agitator who posed a threat to their authority.

For this reason Jesus was first brought before the Sanhedrin, the Jewish court permitted by the Romans to deal with affairs within the Jewish community. The Romans had appointed all seventy-one members of the court, including Caiaphas, the high priest who led it. These court members knew that if they could not control Jesus, the Romans would certainly replace them. The Sanhedrin could not punish Jesus under Jewish law, but it could send him before Roman magistrates on a charge that the Romans would not hesitate to prosecute—stirring up rebellion.

Jesus' popularity with the common people and the riot in the Temple precinct would have been enough to arouse Roman suspicion. It is also likely that the Roman authorities did not understand the concept of messiah or how Jesus understood the term. Any uncertainty in Pontius Pilate's mind about Jesus' claims would quickly have led to a death sentence. Roman officials usually responded to real or imagined threats to the political order by crucifixion. In the eyes of Pontius Pilate, a cautious magistrate, Jesus constituted a

The Scales of Justice
This coin shows the goddess Aequitas who represents the idea of fairness in Roman justice.

threat to public order, and so deserved execution.

Why, then, do the Gospels shift the blame for Jesus' death from Pontius Pilate and place it on the Jewish community as whole? The Gospel narratives began to be written down in an atmosphere of growing hostility and suspicion between Jews and Christians. After Roman armies destroyed the Jerusalem Temple in the Jewish rebellion of 66–70 C.E., Christians wanted to disassociate themselves from Jews in Roman eyes, hoping to persuade Roman authorities to think of them not as rebels but rather as followers of a lawful religion. The Gospels link the death of Jesus in 30 C.E. and the destruction of the Temple in 70 C.E., by saying that Jesus predicted the Temple's destruction. These accounts interpret both events from a post–70 C.E. perspective. They present Jesus' death as willed by Jewish leaders, and they suggest that the Roman officials in fact did not want to kill him. According to the Gospels, the destruction of the Temple was punishment for the Jews who had caused Jesus' death.

This interpretation of Jesus' trial and execution helped poison Christian–Jewish relations for two millennia. From the first century C.E. through the twentieth, the Christian community blamed Jews for Jesus' crucifixion. ■

Questions of Justice

1. What does the trial of Jesus show about Roman provincial administration?
2. From the point of view of a member of the Sanhedrin, why was the execution of Jesus justifiable?

Taking It Further

Crossan, John Dominic. *Who Killed Jesus: Exposing the Roots of Anti-Semitism in the Gospel Story of the Death of Jesus.* 1997. A highly engaging investigation.

Johnson, Luke Timothy, John Dominic Crossan, and Werner H. Kelber. *The Jesus Controversy.* 1999. Three experts discuss the problems of finding who Jesus "really was."

Sherwin-White, A. N. *Roman Society and Roman Law in the New Testament.* 1963. A leading Roman historian puts the New Testament in its Roman context.

The Spread of Christianity

Christianity drew many of its first converts from socially marginalized groups, such as women, noncitizens, and slaves. Indeed, Jesus' message was revolutionary in the way it overturned conventional boundaries of class, gender, and ethnicity. The writings of Paul of Tarsus° (d. ca. 65 C.E.) in the New Testament illustrate this perspective. Paul became the most effective early Christian missionary. He preached to non-Jewish audiences that Jesus had inaugurated a new age in human history, and that the end of the current age was imminent. Paul encouraged a communal life in which all followers of Jesus were equal in the eyes of God. As he wrote to a small Christian community in Galatia in Asia Minor, "For in Christ Jesus . . . there is no longer Jew or Greek, there is no longer slave or free, there is no longer male or female; for all of you are one in Christ Jesus." Paul therefore urged the entry of gentiles (non-Jews) into the Christian community, believing that Jesus' teachings would one day unify the entire human race.

Christianity continued to attract the poor and outcast, but by the middle of the second century C.E., an important change occurred within the ranks of Christian adherents. Many new converts to the faith were men and women who had already been educated in Greek philosophy. They began to analyze and understand Christianity in the terms with which they were familiar: the abstract ideas of the Hellenistic philosophical tradition. Rather than dismiss the philosopher Plato, for example, they argued that his ideas about the supremacy of the soul and what it meant to lead a good life anticipated the teachings of Jesus. Because it eventually led to Christianity's assimilation of much of classical culture, this encounter between Christians and the intelligentsia of the Mediterranean world transformed the Christian faith. As Christians explained their faith to educated gentiles in the language of traditional philosophical education, they won even more converts. They developed methods of analyzing biblical texts drawn from philosophy and rhetoric. The language of Christianity and Greek and Latin intellectual life fused.

Much of this development centered on the works of a group of Christian writers, whom historians call Apologists°. The Apologists publicly defended their faith to learned non-Christian audiences (just as Socrates had defended his beliefs in Plato's *Apology*—hence the name *Apologists.*) In the process, they helped shape the Christian response to the challenges of Hellenist philosophy and cosmology. One of the most important of the Apologists, Justin Martyr (ca. 100–165 C.E.), sought to make Christianity comprehensible to other intellectuals like himself who had not grown up as Christians. Justin insisted that Christian beliefs accorded with rational thought. He interpreted Christianity as the culmination of intellectual developments that had begun in the classical past. For example, he believed that Plato had anticipated some Christian truths, such as the existence of a single, transcendent God.

CHRONOLOGY

	Cultural and Religious Events
59–12 B.C.E.	Livy writes *History of Rome*
70–19 B.C.E.	Virgil writes poetry, completes *Aeneid*
65–8 B.C.E.	Horace writes poetry
43 B.C.E.–17 C.E.	Ovid writes poetry
4 B.C.E.–30 C.E.	Life of Jesus of Nazareth
4 B.C.E.–41 C.E.	Seneca writes works of Stoic philosophy
CA. 35–90 C.E.	Quintilian writes about rhetoric
CA. 56–CA. 118 C.E.	Tacitus writes about recent Roman history
CA. 100 C.E.	New Testament completed
CA. 100–165 C.E.	Justin Martyr explains Christianity
125–170 C.E.	Apuleius writes *The Golden Ass*
CA. 160–240 C.E.	Tertullian defends Christianity and criticizes Rome
184–255 C.E.	Origen writes about the theory and practice of Christianity

Justin Martyr's embrace of Greek philosophy was typical of Apologist thought. Another Apologist, Clement of Alexandria (ca. 150–216 C.E.), wrote that the study of Greek philosophy could prepare a Christian to understand Jesus' teachings. Origen (ca. 184–255 C.E.), the most profound thinker among the Apologists, was as much a classical scholar as a churchman. A talented editor and commentator on biblical texts, he also made significant contributions to Christian theology. He and Clement laid the groundwork for the integration of classical Greek philosophy and culture with Christianity. This complex step was of unparalleled importance in the development of Western civilization because it not only enhanced the appeal of Christianity among educated believers but also ensured the transmission of many Greek philosophical ideas to what would become Western culture.

The Apologists faced stiff opposition from within the Christian community because many churchmen viewed classical learning with deep suspicion. Tertullian (ca. 160–240 C.E.), Origen's influential contemporary, argued forcefully for the separation of Christianity from the learning and culture of the non-Christian world. He worried that the mingling of religious cults so common in his day might corrupt Christianity. Tertullian summed up his opposition to classical culture: "What has Athens to do with Jerusalem? What is there in common between the philosopher and the Christian? . . . After the Gospel we have no need for further research." Christians like Tertullian mistrusted the power of the human intellect and stressed the need to remain focused on the divine revelation of the Christian Scriptures. Yet Tertullian could not stop the integration of Christianity with classical learning. By the third century C.E. Christians could no longer ignore the Mediterranean world in which they lived.

And that world could no longer ignore them. Many of Christianity's core concepts, such as its ideas about personal salvation, the equality of individual men and women before God, and the redemption of humanity from sin, distinguished it from the empire's polytheistic faiths. Perhaps the greatest difference between polytheists and Christians, however, was Christianity's intolerance of other people's forms of worship. Christians referred to all polytheist forms of worship collectively as "paganism" and tried to convert pagans to Christianity.

Through their proselytizing and their hostility to other forms of religious expression, Christians gained enemies. Their close community life meant they kept to themselves; this failure to engage in the public life of Roman culture won them suspicion. As a result, Christians sometimes endured persecution, though the danger in these early years was never as severe as later Christian writers claimed. Claudius expelled Christians from Rome, and in 64 C.E., the Roman emperor Nero blamed Christians for a destructive fire that consumed central Rome. (Popular legend blamed him, equally wrongly). Hundreds of Christians died in the arena before cheering crowds.

By the second half of the first century C.E., many Roman officials perceived Christians as potential enemies of the state because they refused to join in the worship of the emperor. Christians who refused to renounce their religious beliefs were sometimes executed. During an inspection tour in Asia Minor for the emperor Trajan in 112 C.E., the lawyer Pliny interrogated people suspected of being Christians. Pliny tried to follow proper legal procedure and to avoid unwarranted harassment of the suspects, but he did execute anyone found guilty of being a Christian. Christians believed that these victims of religious persecution had died gloriously and called them martyrs, or witnesses for their faith. Tertullian chided his Roman persecutors, "We multiply whenever we are mown down by you; the blood of Christians is [like] seed."

In their vision of all humanity united under a single God and their desire to suppress other forms of religious expression, Christians were truly revolutionary. Christians eventually succeeded in displacing all polytheist religions within the Roman Empire. Although polytheism still exists in many parts of the world today, it is virtually absent from the West. As a consequence, the Western world has lost touch with a fundamental part of how many peoples understood—or still understand—the world.

CONCLUSION
Rome Shapes the West

The map of the Roman Empire outlined the heart of the regions included in the West today. Rome was the means by which cultural and political ideas developed in Mediterranean societies and spread into Europe. This quilt of lands and peoples was acquired mostly by conquest. An autocratic government held the pieces together. Although Roman authorities permitted no dissent in the provinces, they allowed provincial peoples to become Roman. Being Roman meant that one had specific legal rights of citizenship, not that one belonged to a particular race or ethnic group. Thus, in addition to expanding the boundaries of the empire and patrolling its borders, the Roman army brought a version of Roman society to subject peoples. Provincial cities became "little Romes." By imitating Roman styles of architecture and urban life, the cities, too, helped spread Roman civilization. Moreover, the elites of these cities helped funnel the resources of the countryside into the emperor's coffers, and so sustain the imperial system.

For two and a half centuries the *Pax Romana* inaugurated by Augustus fostered a remarkable degree of cultural uniformity within the empire's boundaries. Rome's civilization, including its legal system, its development of cities, and its literary and artistic legacy, made it the foundation of Western civilization as we know it today. The legal precedents established by Roman jurists remain valid in much of Europe. Latin and Greek literature of the early Roman Empire has entertained, instructed, and inspired readers in the West for nearly 2,000 years. Until very recently all educated people in the West could read Latin and Greek, and looked to the works of the Romans for their model in prose style. Many of our public buildings and memorial sculptures continue to adhere to the artistic and architectural models first outlined in Rome. Perhaps most important, the monotheism of Judaism, adapted and developed by Christianity, has been a prominent force in shaping Western ideals and attitudes.

A debilitating combination of economic weakness, civil war, and invasions by northern peoples would almost destroy the Roman Empire in the third century C.E. How the Roman Empire recovered and was transformed in the process is the story of the next chapter.

Suggestions for Further Reading

For a comprehensive list of suggested readings, please go to www.ablongman.com/levack/chapter5

Beard, Mary, John North, and Simon Price. *Religions of Rome.* 1995. The first volume contains essays on polytheist religions, and the second contains translated ancient sources.

Gardner, Jane F. *Women in Roman Law and Society.* 1987. Discusses issues pertaining to women in Rome.

Garnsey, Peter, and Richard Saller. *The Roman Empire: Economy, Society, and Culture.* 1987. Stresses the economic and social foundations of the Roman Empire.

Hornblower, Simon, and Antony Spawforth, eds. *The Oxford Classical Dictionary,* 3rd ed. 1996. This encyclopedia treats all aspects of Roman culture and history.

Markus, Robert. *Christianity in the Roman World.* 1974. An excellent study of the growth of Christianity.

Romm, James. *The Edges of the Earth in Ancient Thought: Geography, Exploration, and Fiction.* 1992. An exciting introduction to the Roman understanding of real and imaginary peoples.

Talbert, Richard, ed. *The Barrington Atlas of the Classical World.* 2000. This atlas contains the best maps available.

Webster, Graham. *The Roman Imperial Army,* 3rd ed. 1985. Discusses military organization and life in the empire.

Wiedemann, Thomas. *Emperors and Gladiators.* 1992. An important study of the ideology and practice of gladiatorial combat.

Wolfram, Herwig. *The Roman Empire and Its Germanic Peoples.* 1997. Examines the interrelation of Romans and Germans over several centuries.

Woolf, Greg. *Becoming Roman: The Origins of Provincial Civilization in Gaul.* 1998. The best recent study of Romanization.

[illegible]

CHAPTER

6

Late Antiquity: The Age of New Boundaries, 250–600

Chapter Outline

- Crisis and Recovery in the Third Century
- Christianizing the Empire
- New Christian Communities and Identities
- The Breakup of the Roman Empire

During the last week of August in 410, an event occurred that stunned the Roman world. A small army of landless warriors—no more than a few thousand men—led by their king Alaric forced their way into the city of Rome and plundered it for three days. For more than a year Alaric had been threatening the city in an attempt to extort gold and land for his people. When his attempts at extortion failed, he resorted to attacking the great city of Rome. Because Alaric's followers—the Visigoths—were Christian, they spared Rome's churches and took care not to violate nuns. But that left plenty of booty—gold, silver, and silks—for them to cart away.

For these migrating warriors and the families, who had first invaded the Roman Empire from their homelands in southern Russia thirty years earlier, pillaging the most opulent city in the Mediterranean world was a pleasant interlude in a long struggle to secure a permanent home. But for the Romans, the looting of Rome was an unfathomable disaster. They could scarcely believe that their capital city, the gleaming symbol of world rule, had fallen to an army made up of people they regarded as barbarian. "If Rome is sacked, what can be safe?" lamented the churchman Jerome when he heard the news in far-off Jerusalem. His remark captures the outrage and astonishment felt by Roman citizens everywhere, Christian and non-Christian alike, who believed that their empire was divinely protected and would last forever.

To understand how the Visigoths managed to sack Rome, we must examine late antiquity, the period between about 250 and 600, which bridged the classical world and the Middle Ages. During this critical era in the development of Western civilization, the Roman Empire underwent radical transformation.

Vienna Genesis: Written in silver ink on purple-died parchment, this sumptuous manuscript of the first book of the Bible was created in the sixth century, probably for a member of the imperial court in Constantinople. Though the illustration tells a biblical story, certain details reflect conditions in late antiquity such as fortified cities and the growing importance of camels in travel and commerce. The seated, semi-nude female in the lower left is derived from polytheist religion. She personifies the stream from which the more modestly dressed woman gathers water.

After its recovery from a half century of near-fatal civil war, foreign invasion, and economic crisis, Rome experienced a hundred years of political reform and economic revival. Yet by the middle of the fifth century, the political unity of the Mediterranean world had come to an end. The Roman Empire collapsed in western Europe. In its place, new Germanic kingdoms developed in Italy, Gaul, Britain, Spain, and North Africa. These kingdoms would serve as the foundation of western medieval Europe.

In contrast, the Roman Empire in the east managed to hold together and prospered. Rome's eastern provinces formed the nucleus of what historians call the Byzantine Empire, based in the city of Constantinople (modern Istanbul in Turkey). Until their empire fell to the Turks in 1453, the inhabitants of this eastern realm considered themselves Romans. The Byzantine Empire served as the most important cultural center in Europe throughout the Middle Ages. In both Byzantium (where Roman political administration was maintained) and the new kingdoms of the West (where it was not) Rome's cultural legacy continued, although in very different ways.

The late antique era witnessed not only the collapse of the Roman Empire in the West but also the emergence of Christianity as the dominant religion throughout the imperial realm. From there it spread beyond the imperial borders, bringing new notions of civilization to the people of Europe, North Africa, and the Middle East. In this era one did not have to be Roman to be Christian, but it was necessary to be Christian to be civilized. New cultural boundary lines divided Christian communities from Jews and polytheists, and as we will see in Chapter 7, the followers of another emerging faith, Islam.

To explore this complex age of consolidation, transformation, and cultural transmission, we will consider the following questions: (1) How did the Roman Empire successfully reorganize following the instability of the third century? (2) How did Christianity become the dominant religion in the Roman Empire, and what impact did it exert on Roman society? (3) How did Christianity enable the transformation of communities, religious experience, and intellectual traditions inside and outside the empire? (4) How and why did the Roman Empire in the West disintegrate?

Crisis and Recovery in the Third Century

In the years between 235 and 284, the Roman Empire staggered under waves of political and economic turmoil. Rival generals competed for the throne, chronic civil war shook the empire's very foundation, and invaders hungry for land and plunder broke through the weakened imperial borders. The economy collapsed and the imperial administration broke down. But in 284, a new emperor seized power and halted the process of decline, shoring up the empire with both drastic administrative and social reforms and religious persecution.

The Breakdown of the Imperial Government

In 135, the assassination of Emperor Alexander Severus, the last member of the Severan dynasty, sent the imperial administration into a tailspin. Military coup followed military coup as ruthless generals with nicknames like "Sword-in-Hand" competed for the throne. In the latter half of this century, not one of more than four dozen emperors and would-be emperors died a natural death. Gallienus clung to the throne longest; his reign lasted fifteen years (253–268). Most emperors held power for only a few months. Preoccupied with merely staying on the throne, they neglected the empire's borders, leaving them vulnerable to attack.

This situation had dire consequences for the empire. Foreign invaders attacked both eastern and western provinces throughout late antiquity. To the Romans' deep

The Walls of Rome
The emperor Aurelian built a twelve-mile circuit of walls around Rome in the 370s to protect the city from Germanic invaders. Twenty feet high and twelve feet thick, the walls had eighteen major gates. The Gate of Saint Sebastian, seen here, had additional towers added in later years. That Rome should need protective walls would have been unthinkable during the early empire.

Subjugation of Valerian

Persian kings built their tombs in a cliff six miles north of Persepolis, the old Persian capital. Here at Naqsh-i Rustam, a carving depicts the Great King Shapur I (239–272) on horseback holding the arm of his prisoner, the Roman emperor Valerian. The previous Roman emperor, Philip (known as "the Arab"), kneels in supplication.. Shapur bragged about his accomplishments: When I first came to rule, the Roman emperor Gordian gathered an army from the whole empire of the Romans, Goths, and Germans and came to Mesopotamia against my empire. . . . and we annihilated the Roman army. Then the Romans proclaimed Philip the new emperor . . . and he came to plead with me, and he paid 500,000 gold pieces as ransom and became our tributary . . . And when I marched against Carrhae and Edessa [Roman cities in Syria], the Emperor Valerian advanced against us . . . We fought a great battle . . . and I captured the emperor Valerian myself with my own hands."

shame, Emperor Valerian was captured in battle by the Great King of Persia in 260. Warbands from across the Rhine River reached as far south as Italy, forcing the emperor Aurelian to build a great wall around the city of Rome in 270. Many other cities across the empire constructed similar defenses. The Roman military system and the Roman economy buckled under the pressure of invasions and civil war. Inflation spun out of control and coins lost their value. The government paid soldiers in produce and supplies rather than cash. Not surprisingly, resentment boiled among the troops.

The seat of power now shifted from Rome to provincial cities. Unlike their predecessors, the soldier-emperors of this era, who came mostly from frontier provinces, had little time to cultivate the support of the Roman Senate. Instead, they held court in cities close to the embattled frontiers. Towns far from Rome, such as York in Britain or Trier in Gaul, had long functioned as military bases and supply distribution centers. Now they served as imperial capitals whenever the emperor resided there.

With the emperor on the move and the Senate far from imperial control, political power fragmented. This political decentralization weakened the empire further. Some cities and provinces took advantage of the weakened government to try to break away from Roman control. In the early 260s and 270s a large portion of Gaul known as the Gallic Empire briefly established independence. A few years later, Zenobia, the queen of Palmyra (r. 267–272), a city in Syria that had grown wealthy from the caravan trade, rebelled against Rome, and a bitter war ensued. The emperor Aurelian's troops finally crushed Palmyra in 272 and led Zenobia in chains through the streets of Rome in a triumphal procession. Such triumphs, however, were few and far between in these years.

The Restoration of Imperial Government

Fortunately for the Romans, Diocletian (r. 284–305) stepped in to rescue the empire from total ruin near the end of the third century. Diocletian launched a succession of military, administrative, and economic reforms that had far reaching consequences. Not since the reign of Augustus had the Roman Empire been so fundamentally transformed.

Diocletian's Reforms

After ruling alone for nine years, Diocletian recognized that the enormous responsibilities of imperial rule overburdened a single ruler, and so he took the dramatic step of dividing the empire into two parts. In 286 he chose a co-ruler, Maximian, to govern the western half of the empire, while he continued to rule in the east. Maximian maintained a separate administrative system and his own army. Then, in 293, Diocletian and Maximian subdivided their territories by appointing two junior-level emperors. These junior rulers administered their territories in the eastern and western parts of the empire with their own bureaucracies and armies.

Through this system of government called the Tetrarchy°, Diocletian hoped not only to make the imperial government more efficient, but also to put an end to the bloody cycle of imperial assassinations. Although he had gained the throne by murdering his predecessor, he knew that the empire's survival depended on a reliable succession strategy. To that end, Diocletian dictated that the junior emperors were to step into the senior emperors' place when they retired. Then they themselves were to select two new talented and reliable men to be junior emperors and their eventual replacements. Thus supreme power was to be handed down from capable ruler to capable ruler, and the constant cycle of assassinations and civil wars was to be broken.

Diocletian sought to enhance imperial authority by heightening the grandeur of the emperor's office. He used the title *dominus,* or lord, more freely than any emperor before him. Everything that had to do with the emperor was referred to as sacred or divine. During public ceremonies he arrayed himself in gorgeous robes of purple silk. He required his officials to prostrate themselves before him and kiss the hem of his gown before they spoke to him. Diocletian as well as his fellow tetrarchs claimed that specific gods had singled them out for glory and victory.

■ **The Tetrarchs**
Stolen by crusaders from its original site near Constantinople, this statue of the tetrarchs now is built into a wall of cathedral of San Marco in Venice. To depict their solidarity and readiness for war, the tetrarchs are presented as fierce soldiers in military uniform, holding their swords with one hand and clasping their colleague's shoulder with the other. Each pair of figures shows one junior emperor and one senior emperor, who has more worry lines in his forehead as a sign of his greater responsibilities.

Jupiter was Diocletian's special protector, while Mars (the god of war) and Hercules guarded other tetrarchs. By insisting on his own divinity and emphasizing his special ties to the mightiest god of Rome, Diocletian set himself apart from the rest of the imperial court. Increasingly, the imperial palaces resembled the court of the Great Kings of Persia. Even the geographical location of the center of power shifted eastward, with Diocletian residing for much of his early rule in the city of Nicomedia (in modern Turkey), strategically located at the point where Asia meets Europe.

To restore Roman military power that had been weakened during the crises of earlier decades, Diocletian reorganized the Roman army. He nearly doubled its size to about 400,000 men. In order to protect the empire from invaders, he stationed these troops along the borders of the empire and built military roads from Britain in the west to the Euphrates River in the east. At the same time, Diocletian sought to reduce the army's involvement in political affairs. Although he was a soldier himself, he recognized that the army had played a disruptive role in earlier decades by constantly engaging in civil wars. He reduced the size of each legion in order to limit its commander's power as well as to increase its maneuverability. He placed the legions under new, loyal commanders. With these military reforms effected, Diocletian was able to secure the empires's borders once again and suppress internal revolts.

Reorganizing the army was only one part of Diocletian's vision of reform. To restore efficient government, he also embarked upon a thorough reorganization of the empire's administrative system. He redrew the map of the realm, drastically reducing the size of provinces and setting up separate civilian and military bureaucracies within each. These changes further reduced the risk of rebellion by limiting the power of any single civilian official. This administrative overhaul resulted in a significant expansion of the numbers of bureaucrats and military commanders.

Maintaining the bloated civilian and military apparatus created by the Tetrarchy demanded full utilization of the empire's financial resources as well as far-reaching economic reforms—particularly in an era of rampant inflation. To halt the decrease of the purchasing power of money, Diocletian attempted—none too successfully—to freeze wages and prices by imperial decree. He also increased taxes and endeavored to make tax collection more effective through the establishment of a regular—and deeply resented—census to register all taxpayers. The new tax system generated enough revenues to fund the now enormous machinery of government.

This tax system was, however, riddled with loopholes and inequities. Senators, army officers, and other influential citizens were undertaxed or not taxed at all, and rich landowners often used bribery and force to fend off imperial tax collectors. Consequently the greatest burden fell on those least able to bear it: the peasants. In hopes of increasing economic productivity, Diocletian's administrators used the census to enforce laws that required peasants and craftsmen to remain at their work by insisting that they not move from the place at which they were registered. During the late antique era, then, the gap between rich and poor continued to grow. Fewer rich men controlled more of the empire's land and the wealth it generated than ever before. The emperor himself was the wealthiest of all, adding to his possessions through confiscation of lands owned by cities and private individuals.

Diocletian did nothing to address the widening social and economic division in his empire; instead, he attempted to reinforce the cultural unity of the empire through religious persecution. In 303, he and his junior emperor Galerius initiated an attack on Christians that is now known as the Great Persecution°. The two emperors believed that failure to worship the traditional Roman gods had angered the deities and brought hardship to the empire. In the interest of unity, these rulers tried to destroy Christianity in the eastern part of the empire, which was under their rule. Diocletian and Galerius forbade Christians to assemble for worship and ordered the destruction of all churches and sacred books. Several thousand women and men refused to cooperate and were executed.

Unintended Consequences

Diocletian's reforms stabilized and preserved the Roman Empire. They also, however, had three crucial although largely unintended consequences. First, urban life in the west deteriorated under the impact of his reforms. As we saw in Chapter 5, cities played an essential role in imperial Rome's economic and cultural life. The vitality of urban life was one of the characteristics that allowed Romans to see themselves as "civilized." In the late antique era, that vitality began to diminish. Cities did continue to serve as local centers of tax collection, helping to link the provinces to the imperial government, and the number of Roman cities remained stable, but the increasingly centralized and costly bureaucracy put new pressures on urban areas. Emperors confiscated most civic lands and revenues, resulting in a reduction of funds to spend on civic life—games, public buildings, and maintenance of the urban infrastructure.

Furthermore, the city councilors, who had the responsibility of raising the tax revenues required by the central government, were frustrated. They knew that failure to provide the imperial government with the sums it demanded could lead to public flogging with lead-tipped whips—a punishment as humiliating as it was painful. Understandably, the idea of holding civic office, which most men had considered a great honor, began to lose its appeal. Because a position in the imperial bureaucracy granted immunity from service in city government, with its crushing fiscal obligations (not to mention its risk of public flogging), many ambitious men turned to the imperial bureaucracy to win the honors, status, and power that used to come with positions in the city government. Meanwhile, both the wealth and even the numbers of city aristocrats, the traditional leaders and patrons of their communities, dwindled.

One result of this shift in power away from the traditional urban aristocracy was a deterioration in the fabric of urban life. The inscriptions in marble attached to public buildings reveal a gradual decline in public spending by all but the very wealthiest citizens. As civic monuments and public buildings decayed, restoration and repair rather than new building became the order of the day in cities throughout the empire.

The second unintended consequence of Diocletian's reforms, then, was an acceleration in the long-term decentralization and fragmentation of economic and political power within the western provinces of the empire. As some men grew richer and more powerful, poor people turned to them for protection against other landowners and ruthless imperial tax collectors. In return for this protection, peasants gave their wealthy patrons the ownership of the farms on which they continued to work. These peasants (called *coloni*) lost the right to leave their farms and move elsewhere. Coloni had to perform labor for their landlords and had only limited control of their own possessions, although they could not be evicted and were still considered free Roman citizens.

The imperial government supported this form of near-slavery because it benefited the biggest landholders—including the emperor—who needed a stable workforce tied to the land to make agriculture as profitable as possible. The coloni system also promised the emperor a reliable source of tax revenues. But over time, landowners began to develop private armies to protect their vast country estates and the peasants who labored on them. This usurpation of the role of the central government weakened the authority of the emperor and his administration in the western provinces. In contrast, the eastern provinces of the empire remained prosperous into the sixth century. Private estates grew in size, but the imperial administrators in Constantinople maintained tight control of the economy.

The final unintended consequence of Diocletian's reforms, then, is that under Diocletian the center of gravity within the empire shifted decisively to the east, where the empire's wealth and political might were increasingly concentrated. Diocletian's own style of ruling contributed to this process. He not only delegated the government of the western (and by implication less important) provinces to his co-emperor, Maximian, he also lived for much of his reign in the east.

Map 6.1 The Roman Empire in Late Antiquity

Following the reforms of Diocletian, the Roman Empire enjoyed a century of stable government, with the same borders as in earlier centuries.

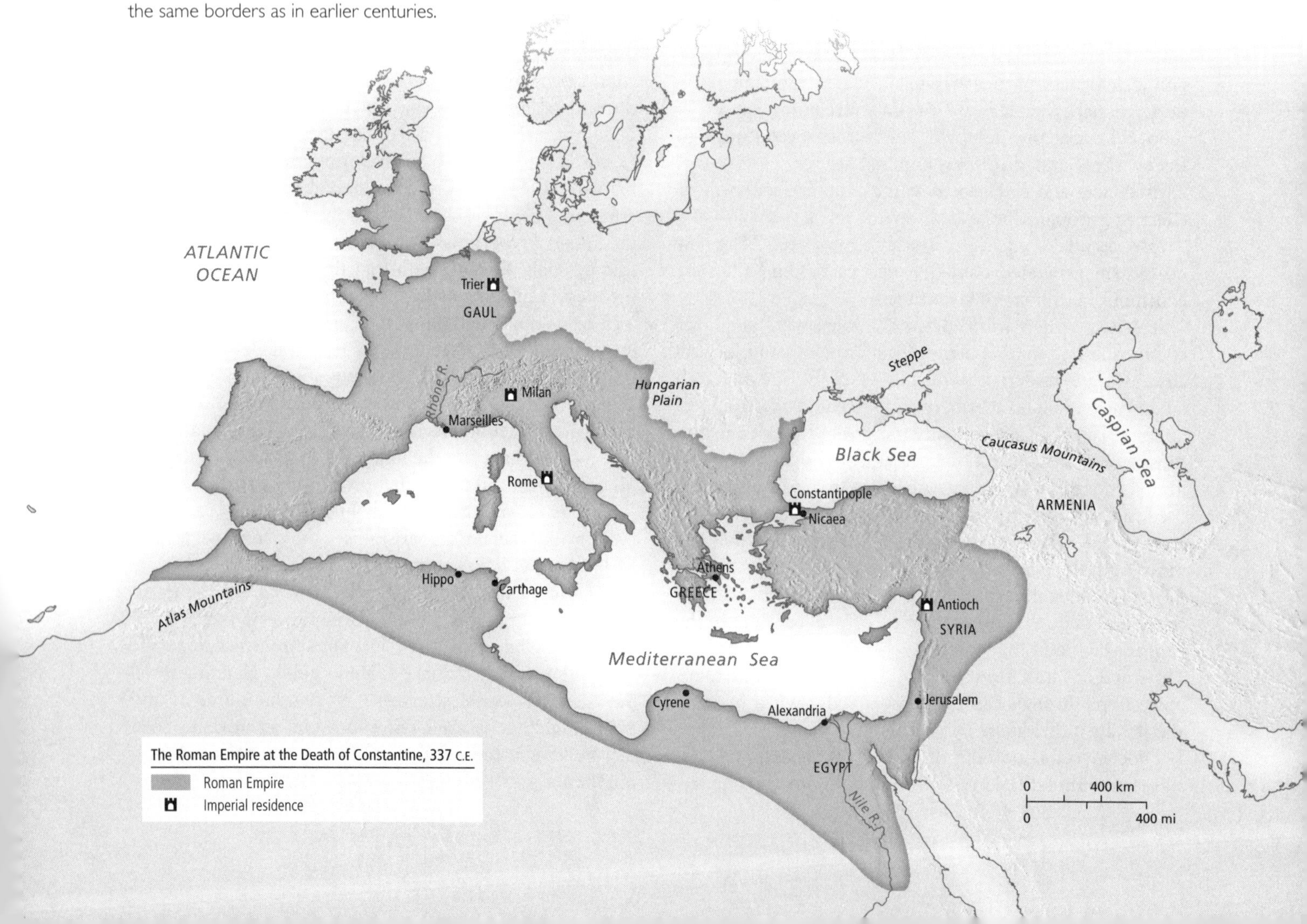

Free Grain for the City of Rome
This carving from the Arch of Constantine in Rome, built in 312, shows citizens lining up to receive grain allotments from imperial officials. Bureaucrats, shown in little offices above the heads of the citizens, check the eligibility lists. In the panel's center, the emperor sits on a throne surrounded by his staff.

Christianizing the Empire

When Diveletian died, he left the empire stronger militarily, administratively, and economically than it had been for nearly a century. The steps he had taken to confine the growing power of Christianity, however, turned out to be a failure. The new faith gathered momentum despite all the efforts of polytheist emperors. Eventually, it captured the imagination of a pious young Roman who would become the empire's first Christian emperor.

Constantine: First Christian Emperor

In 305, Diocletian stepped down from the imperial throne and insisted that his co-emperor in the west, Maximian, retire as well. Diocletian expected a peaceful succession to occur. It did, but just barely. The two junior emperors, Galerius and Constantius, took Diocletian's and Maximian's places. But just one year later, Constantius died in Britain. Abandoning the principles of the tetrarchy, the troops stationed in Britain proclaimed Constantius's son, Constantine (r. 306–337), to be his replacement. The ambitious young general set out to claim sole rule of the Roman Empire. In 312 he smashed the army of Maxentius, his last rival in the west, at the battle of the Milvian Bridge over the Tiber River at Rome. Twelve years later he defeated Licinius, the tetrarch ruling in the east. Constantine then joined the empire together with himself as absolute ruler. Thus both the division of the empire and the system of succession that Diocletian implemented barely outlasted his rule.

In other ways, however, Constantine continued along Diocletian's reformist path. For example, under Constantine the empire's eastern and western sectors retained separate administrations. To overcome the dangers of decentralization Constantine installed new officials called praetorian prefects in each sector. These rulers were directly accountable to the emperor. He also retained Diocletian's emphasis on a large field army, but ensured that heavily armored cavalry troops were trained for rapid deployment to trouble spots.

Moreover, Constantine, like Diocletian, did little to ease the economic burden weighing down the peasants and poor townsfolk. The imperial bureaucracy remained immense, the army remained huge, and so taxes remained high. But to reinforce the economic structures of the empire, Constantine undertook to reform the coinage system. He recognized that the existing coins had become so debased they were effectively worthless, so he created a unique gold coin—the solidus. (Seventy-two solidi equaled one pound of gold.) The creation of the solidus stabilized the economy by restoring the value of currency. The new coin ended the devastating inflationary spiral that had contributed so much to the political and social turmoil of the third century. The solidus remained the standard coin in the Mediterranean world for 800 years.

Constantine followed the path of military emperors in the third century C.E. by founding new capital cities as seats of his power. To glorify his name and monarchy, Constantine founded Constantinople, the "City of Constantine," on the site of the Greek city Byzantium in 324. (Today Constantinople is the city of Istanbul in Turkey.) Constantine's choice of location reveals a shrewd eye for strategy. The city lay at the juncture of two military roads that linked Europe and Asia and controlled access to the Black Sea. From this convenient spot the emperor could monitor the vast resources of the empire's eastern provinces. Like Diocletian, Constantine recognized that the wealth and power of the empire now lay in the east.

But unlike Diocletian, Constantine embraced the new religion of Christianity. Most emperors had associated themselves with a divine protector; Constantine chose the sun god Apollo as his first divine companion. During the night before the pivotal battle at the Milvian Bridge in 312, however, Constantine experienced a new revelation, which he interpreted as a sign from the Christian God. After triumphing in battle, Constantine attributed his success to Christ's favor, and he became a devout Christian. Later in his reign, writers described Constantine's victory as a miracle. It was not all that unusual for an emperor of antiquity to embrace a new god. But because monotheistic Christianity would not acknowledge rival gods or alternative forms of worship, Constantine's conversion had far-reaching effects. Constantine did not convert his realm to Christianity or forbid polytheist worship. He did, however, obtain the gold for his new solidus coin by looting the treasures that had been stored for centuries in polytheistic temples. He also encouraged widespread practice of his new faith and he lavished funds on church buildings. Now yoked to the imperial office, Christianity very quickly gained strength across the empire and became a potent challenger to traditional modes of worship.

The growth of Constantine's new city of Constantinople paralleled the growth of Christianity. Constantine did not intend to establish an exclusively Christian city as an alternative to Rome. He built no more than three churches and left the city's many temples to older gods intact. Within a generation, however, Constantinople became a Christian center, and the traces of polytheism in the city disappeared. Constantinople continued to grow in size and splendor, as palaces, monuments, churches, bathhouses, public buildings, and colonnaded streets appeared on a scale befitting the New Rome, as Constantinople came to be known. Constantine's capital also became a fortified city. In response to the threat of attack by Vandal pirates, the emperor Theodosius II erected massive defensive walls around the city in 413. In future centuries these fortifications would protect the city—and indeed, the empire—from ruin on several occasions. With a new Senate formed on the model of the Senate of the city of Rome, a steady supply of grain from Egypt to feed the capital's inhabitants, and plenty of opportunities for trade, Constantinople attracted inhabitants from all over the empire. The city rapidly grew in size, reaching perhaps several hundred thousand inhabitants by the early sixth century.

In addition to serving as an administrative center and an imperial capital, Constantinople came to symbolize the kingdom of heaven in the minds of Christians. As God ruled from his throne in the court of Heaven, so the emperor ruled in Constantinople. The emperor, whom God had chosen to rule, thus provided the essential link between the celestial and earthly kingdoms. With one Roman law wedded to one orthodox faith for all its subjects and led by an emperor who was God's representative on Earth, Constantinople became the center of a monotheistic empire.

THE SPREAD OF CHRISTIANITY

Backed by Rome's emperors, Christianity spread rapidly throughout the empire during the fourth century. With imperial support, church leaders transformed the face of cities by building churches and leading attacks on the institutions and temples of polytheist worship.

The Rise of the Bishops

As Christianity spread, it grew more complex in its internal organization. Shortly after Paul of Tarsus (ca. 5–67) had established much of the theological grounding of the new religion, a distinction developed between the laity—the ordinary worshipers—and the priests—the leaders who led the worship and administered the central rituals, or sacraments. Much of the early growth of the Christian community occurred in cities and so it is perhaps not surprising that as this community developed its own administrative structures and leadership hierarchy, it patterned itself along the lines of the imperial urban administration. Just as an imperial official directed each city's political affairs, so each city's Christian community came to be led by a bishop who in turn had a staff of priests and administrators, much as the empire's officers had civil servants. Moreover, just as a provincial governor controlled the political affairs of all of the cities and rural regions in his province, so the bishop of the main city of a province held authority over the other bishops and priests in the province. This main or head bishop came to be called a *metropolitan* in the east, an *archbishop* in the west. Through this hierarchy of archbishops/metropolitans, bishops, and priests, the scattered Christian communities were linked into what emerged as the Christian Church.

With its sophisticated administrative structure, the Church grew quickly and bishops emerged as important powers in their cities. A bishop's main task was to supervise the religious life of his *see*, which comprised not only the city itself but also its surrounding agricultural regions. Thus a central task of each bishop was to explain Christian principles and teach the Bible to these communities. But bishops soon became far more than simply religious teachers. As the Church grew wealthy from the massive donations of emperors like Constantine and the humbler offerings of pious women and men throughout the empire, bishops often used these resources to help the poor. They cared for the general welfare of orphans, widows, sick people, prisoners, and travelers. When famine struck southern Gaul in the fifth century, the bishop of Lyons sent so much food from his church estates that the Rhône and Saône Rivers as well as all the roads to the south were jammed with grain transports.

The Church's bishops soon became entangled in secular politics as Constantine incorporated them into the imperial government by permitting them to act as judges in civil actions. Litigants could choose to be tried before a bishop rather than a secular judge. The decisions of a bishop had the same legal authority as those made by civil judges and could not be appealed. Using the rhetorical skills they had learned in Roman schools, bishops were also the advocates of their cities before provincial governors or the imperial court. In many ways they usurped the role of the traditional urban aristocracy. For example, when the people of Antioch in Syria rioted and smashed a statue of the emperor, it was the local bishop, not a local aristocrat, who intervened with the emperor to prevent imperial troops from massacring the city's people.

Bishops also administered the financial affairs of their communities. Some sees remained poor, but the churches in the largest cities accumulated phenomenal wealth through donations of land and money received from the faithful. Sometimes bishops used this money for political purposes. In an attempt to win influence and political support, Cyril, bishop of Alexandria from 412 to 444, spent 2,500 pounds of gold on general expenses and bribes to court official and other clergymen during just one visit to Constantinople. In contrast, British bishops going to a Church conference in 359 could do so only with financial assistance from the government.

By 400 Rome had become the most important see in western Europe, and the bishop of Rome was called the "pope"—the papa or father of the other western bishops. By the middle of the fifth century the emperor formally recognized the pope's claim to have preeminence and the right of appeal over other bishops. A number of factors explain why the office of the bishop of Rome evolved into the papacy°. Together with Jerusalem, Rome was a site of key symbolic importance to Christians. Both the Apostle Peter, the first among Jesus's disciples, and Paul of Tarsus, the traveling teacher who took a leading role in spreading Christianity beyond its Jewish origins, died as martyrs in Rome, and popular Christian tradition held that Peter himself established the Roman bishopric. Thus all Roman bishops were believed to have inherited the authority of St. Peter.

This tradition received support from a conversation between Jesus and Peter recorded in the Gospel of Matthew. Punning on Peter's name, Jesus told him, "You are Peter [*petrus*] and upon this rock [*petram*] I will build my church, and the gates of Hell shall not avail against it. And I will give to you the keys of the kingdom of heaven." Early Christians interpreted these words to mean that Jesus had given Peter special authority, including the power to absolve a sinner's guilt, and that the Church was to be led by those who inherited Peter's position. What came to be called the doctrine of the Petrine Succession declared that just as Peter was specially anointed by Jesus, so subsequent bishops in Rome (the popes) were anointed with special, God-given powers.

In this way the pope became the chief bishop of the Christian world. They claimed that Rome took precedence over four other cities that also claimed that their bishops were spiritually descended from Jesus' apostles. In order of precedence after Rome, these cities were Constantinople, Alexandria in Egypt, Antioch in Syria, and Jerusalem in Palestine. These sees' bishops, also claimed to be legal kings of J's apostles. These bishops called patriarchs, held the greatest authority in the Church and often quarreled bitterly over matters of faith and politics. They did not accept papal authority, which contributed to tensions among Christian communities in the eastern and western parts of the empire.

Through these changes, the Church began functioning almost as an administrative arm of the government, although it still had its own internal organization. Indeed, when Roman rule collapsed in western Europe in the fifth century, the Church survived the crisis and stepped in to fill the vacuum of public leadership.

Christianity and the City of Rome

As Christianity spread, new church buildings transformed the appearance of Roman cities. Constantine set an example of public and private spending on churches, hospitals, and monastic communities that conformed to Christian values, and so construction of traditional buildings such as temples, bathhouses, and buildings for public entertainments such as circuses gradually declined. In addition, Christian festivals, processions, and holidays gradually replaced traditional celebrations. These developments can be seen in all the cities of the empire, but the Christianization of Rome during the fourth century offers especially vivid examples.

The first churches in Rome were built to honor Christian martyrs of earlier centuries. Because Roman custom forbade burials within city walls, martyrs had been buried outside the walls of Rome. One of the great churches that Constantine built in Rome was called "Saint Paul Outside the Walls." This imposing structure marked the burial spot of Paul of Tarsus. Constantine also financed the construction of another grand church on the presumed site of Peter's martyrdom and burial, in an obscure cemetery on what was called the Vatican hill, just outside Rome's northwest wall and across the Tiber River. St. Peter's Church was an enormous structure, with five aisles punctuated with marble columns. Its altar rested over Peter's grave. (Today the papal cathedral of Saint Peter stands on that same spot, in the heart of the Vatican, the city of the pope.) The construction of these churches signaled that Jesus' disciples Peter and Paul had replaced Rome's mythical founders Romulus and Remus as the city's sacred patrons. In other places, too, Christian saints took the place of traditional gods and heroes as protectors of city life.

Although Rome became a vital center of Christianity, the city's inhabitants did not adopt the Christian faith overnight. Throughout the fourth century, the huge temples and shrines of the old gods clustered in Rome's center continued to attract many worshipers, including influential senators. Church authorities hesitated to close these time-honored precincts because they did not have legal authority to do so. Even after imperial laws in 391 and392 forbade polytheist worship, sacrifices, and other religious rites, temples stood empty for a long time, for Christians believed that demons inhabited them. At the prompting of Rome's bishops, other public buildings that originally had had no religious connotations were turned into churches.

With the proliferation of new Christian houses of worship in Rome and other cities came new religious festivals and rituals. Christians marked the anniversaries of the martyrdom of saints on the calendar. Sometimes a Christian holiday (a holy day) competed with a non-Christian holiday. For example, Rome's churchmen designated December 25 as the birthday of Christ to challenge the popular festival of the Unconquered Sun, which fell on the same day. Other Christian holidays also aimed to draw worshipers away from the rites of older gods. By the early sixth century the Church had filled the calendar with many days devoted to Christian ceremonies. Christmas and Easter (which commemorates Jesus' death and resurrection) as well as days for worshiping specific martyrs supplanted traditional Roman holidays. These festivals thus changed the patterns of urban community life throughout the empire. Not all of the traditional Roman holidays disappeared, however. Those that Christians considered harmless continued to be observed as civic holidays. These included New Year's Day, the birthdays of the emperors, and the days that celebrated the founding of Rome and Constantinople.

One additional development in the Christian shaping of time was the use of the letters A.D. as a dating convention. A.D. stands for *anno domini,* or "in the year of our Lord," referring to the year of Jesus' birth. Today it is the standard dating convention used around the world. It began in 531, when Dionysius Exiguus, a monk in Rome, established a simple system for determining the date of Easter every year. He began his calendar with the birth of Jesus in the year 1 (zero was unknown in Europe at this time), and started counting from there. Although he was probably a few years off in his determination of the year of Jesus' birth, his system slowly came into general use by the tenth century. In modern secular societies, many people prefer not to use A.D. because of its association with Christianity. Instead, they use C.E.—meaning "in the Common Era"—to designate years (as is done in this textbook). In both systems, however, the year 1 still refers to Jesus' birth, and thus the calendar remains linked to Christianity regardless of what dating convention is used.

A Female Priest

This foot-high ivory panel shows a female priest making a sacrifice at an altar to an unnamed god or goddess. "Symmachorum" means "of the family of the Symmachi," an aristocratic Roman clan some members of which defended the old gods in the face of Christianity. This elegant plaque commemorates some now-forgotten event in the family's life.

Old Gods Under Attack

Many people today identify themselves as members of a religious community—as Christians, Buddhists, Jews, or Muslims. For the most part these faiths are mutually exclusive—there are no Muslim Catholics, for example. In late antiquity, however, before Christianity became the dominant religion in the Roman Empire, people prayed to gods of all sorts. Different deities met different needs, and the worship of one did not preclude worship of another. Some divinities—such as Isis, who promised life after death—had elaborate cults throughout the empire. The empire's great gods—Jupiter, Juno, and Minerva—had temples in cities everywhere, and were formally worshiped on state occasions. And in the countryside a variety of deities protected laborers and ensured fertility of plants, animals, and the farmers themselves.

To Christians, this diverse range of religious expression was intolerable. They labeled all polytheistic worship with the derogatory term paganism° and made a determined effort to eradicate it. Christians attacked polytheism on two fronts: public practice and private belief.

After converting to Christianity in 312, Constantine ordered the end of the persecution of Christians. Although Christianity did not become the "official" religion of the empire for nearly a century, tolerance for non-Christian beliefs and practices began to fade. In the fourth century, imperial laws forbade sacrificing animals on the altars outside of the old gods' temples. Constantine's son, Constantius II (r. 337-361), ordered the Altar of Victory removed from the Senate House in Rome. Since Augustus's reign, generals had sworn oaths of allegiance to the emperor at this altar before marching to battle. State funding for polytheistic worship gradually stopped. Instead of temples, emperors built churches with money collected from the taxpayers.

During the fourth century bishops and monks, often in collusion with local administrators, led attacks on polytheist shrines and holy places. For example, in 392 the bishop and parishioners of Alexandria destroyed the city's Temple of Serapis, known for its huge size, its magnificent architecture, and the devotion of the local community to it. Similar clashes erupted in many cities across the empire. Libanius, an aristocrat from Antioch, complained to Emperor Theodosius in 390 about the destruction caused by gangs of zealous monks: "This black-robed tribe . . . hasten to attack the temples with sticks and stones and bars of iron, and in some cases, disdaining these, with hands and feet. Then utter desolation follows, with the stripping of roofs, demolition of walls, the tearing down of statues and the overthrow of altars, and the priests must either keep quiet or die."[1]

One emperor tried to restore traditional religion. Julian the Apostate (r. 360–363), who had been raised as a Christian in Constantine's court, rejected Christianity and tried to reinstate the old religions when he came to the throne. But his death during a campaign against Persia eliminated any hope for a restoration of pre-Christian ways. Emboldened by this turn of events, an increasingly zealous Church establishment attacked polytheism with renewed vigor. Theodosius I (r. 379–395) and his grandson Theodosius II (r. 402–450) forbade all forms of polytheistic worship, and non-Christian practice lost the protection of the law.

The attack on polytheism intensified. Because polytheism was not a single, organized religion, it offered no systematic opposition to government-supported Christian attacks. The most vocal opponents to this Christianization of the empire lived in Rome. In sharp contrast to the pious court at Constantinople, the conservative aristocracy of the city of Rome clung hard to the old gods. In 384, their spokesman unsuccessfully begged the emperor for tolerance. Quintus Aurelius Symmachus, a highly respectable nobleman who had pleaded unsuccessfully for the return of the Altar of Victory, argued that Rome's greatness had resulted from the observance of ancient rites. His pleas fell on deaf ears. By the middle of the fifth century the aristocracy of the city of Rome had accepted Christianity.

Humble people also struggled to maintain ancient forms of worship. Sometimes they brawled with monks to preserve the shrines of the gods their families had worshiped for generations. But with the empire's resources pitted against them, they could not resist for long. People began to join Christian communities, though often without fully understanding what the religion required of them. Surviving records of sermons reveal that church leaders preached for centuries afterward against the surprising persistence of "pagan" habits among their congregants. Priests repeatedly explained the risks to salvation that lurked in age-old festivals, bawdy public entertainments, and even regular bathing, which was considered a sensual pleasure.

Eventually, this priestly diligence paid off. The pace of conversion accelerated in the fifth and sixth centuries. Emperor Justinian (r. 527–565) helped things along by sponsoring programs of forced conversion in the countryside of Asia Minor, where tens of thousands of his subjects still followed ancient ways. But eradicating polytheism in the Roman Empire meant far more than the substitution of one religion for another. Polytheism lay at the heart of every community, influencing every activity, every habit of social life, in the pre-Christian world. To replace the worship of the old gods required a true revolution in social and intellectual life.

New Christian Communities and Identities

The spread of Christianity produced new kinds of identities based on faith and language. Christianity solidified community loyalties and allegiances by providing a shared belief system and new opportunities for participation in religious culture. But at the same time, Christianity opened up new divisions and gave rise to new hostilities. Certain new groups were respected and revered; others found themselves marginalized or persecuted. As Christians debated how to interpret the doctrines of their faith, sharp divisions emerged among them. Because Christians spoke Greek, Latin, Coptic Syriac, Armenian, and other languages, different religious interpretations and rituals sometimes took hold, creating distinct communities. As a result, new religious zones identified with different spoken languages and different interpretations of Christian texts appeared within the empire.

THE CREATION OF NEW COMMUNITIES

Christianity fostered the growth of large-scale communities of faith by providing a well-defined set of beliefs and values. These core principles had to be integrated with daily life and older ways of thinking. Thus Christianity required followers to study and interpret the Bible—the religion's core sacred text. The religion also demanded allegiance to the one God and a complex set of doctrines, and it dictated a distinctive lifestyle. Weaving these elements into daily life resulted in a strong sense of Christian identity and common purpose. This new Christian identity compete with and at times replaced older identities linked to Roman citizenship or shaped by regional or urban loyalties.

Christian Doctrine and Heresy

The Old and New Testaments gave a focal point to Christian worship, and their interpretation shaped Christian communities. Every week the priest read to parishioners from these sacred texts. As Christian communities developed, interpretation of that faith by its followers became all-important. The Church decided what interpretations of the Bible were correct, and expected all members of the community to accept these doctrines. In this way, Christian teaching contrasted sharply with secular (nonreligious) education in the Roman Empire, which was intended only for the urban elite. Christian teaching was meant for all. It required all people to live their lives based on a shared interpretation of the Bible and the meaning of Jesus' life, death, and resurrection.

But the Church soon ran into difficulties over interpretation of the texts, as Church leaders disagreed about the meaning of many biblical passages. Councils of bishops met frequently to try to resolve doctrinal differences and produce statements of the faith that all parties could accept. Two theological questions generated particularly tense discussion and drove wedges between several groups—the nature of the Trinity, and the nature of Jesus Christ.

Christians were monotheists: They believed that one God created and governed Heaven and Earth. This monotheistic foundation, however, undergirded a complex theological system in which the one God was understood to have three aspects or "persons," each fully and absolutely God—God the Father, God the Son, and God the Holy Spirit—or the Holy Trinity. Such a complex theology generated endless debates. Church leaders argued about the precise relation of the three persons to one another and within the Trinity. Were the Son and the Holy Spirit of the same essence as the Father? Were they equally divine? Did the Father exist before the Son?

These debates over the Trinity were intimately connected to the second issue of contention with the early Church—the question of the nature of Jesus. At one extreme, some Christian scholars believed that Jesus was entirely divine and had no human nature. This emphasis on Jesus' divinity made his death on the cross and his resurrection irrelevant—God could not suffer and die. It also severed the links between Jesus and his human followers by emphasizing that Jesus was entirely "transcendent" or "other," entirely beyond human comprehension or human limitations. At the other extreme, some Christians taught that Jesus was entirely human and not at all divine—thus challenging one of the core aspects of both the Christian belief in the Trinity and the Christian understanding of Jesus' mission on earth.

The questions of the nature of the Trinity and the nature of Jesus erupted in the first great Christian controversy of late antiquity: the dispute between the Arians and the Athanasians. The Arians followed Arius of Alexandera, a priest who used Greek philosophy to argue that the idea that Jesus, God the Son, was both fully divine and fully human was illogical. Arians argued that God the Father created Jesus and so Jesus could not be equal to or of the same essence as God the Father. The Athanasians, followers of the Bishop Athanasius of Alexandria (293–373), were horrified by what they saw as the Arians' attempt to degrade Jesus' divinity. They argued that Christian truths were beyond human logic, and that Jesus was fully God, equal to and of the same substance as God the Father, yet fully human.

The Arian-Athanasian dispute resulted in perhaps the most influential of the many church meetings held in late antiquity—the Council of Nicaea. In 325, Emperor Constantine summoned the bishops to Nicaea, a town near Constantinople, to reach a decision about the relationship among the divine members of the Holy Trinity. The bishops produced the Nicene Creed, which is still recited in Christian worship today. The creed states that God the Son—Jesus Christ—is identical in nature and essence to God the Father. In other words, the Athanasians won. More than a century later, the Council of Chalcedon of 451 drove the point home: The assembled bishops agreed that Jesus was both fully human and fully divine, and that these two natures were entirely distinct.

The Nicene Creed and the decisions of the Council of Chalcedon became the correct, or orthodox°, interpretation of Christian teaching because they had the support of most bishops and the imperial court. Still, some bishops and other religious leaders continued to debate conflicting interpretations of the Bible, and many ordinary Christians continued to hold beliefs that clashed with those defined as orthodox. People who held the orthodox point of view considered such alternative doctrines to be false beliefs, or heresies°, and they labeled their supporters *heretics.*

Communities of Faith and Language

The doctrinal differences between orthodox and unorthodox Christian groups created and helped cement different communal and ethnic identities in late antiquity. Several geographic zones of Christians emerged that held different interpretations of Christian doctrine. They produced

Bibles, sermons, and religious ceremonies in their native languages. A central zone based in Constantinople and including North Africa, Gaul, Italy, and the Balkans contained Christians called Chalcedonians°, or orthodox. (In the Latin-speaking western provinces they were also called Catholics). These believers followed the decision of the Council of Chalcedon in 451 that defined Christ's divine and human natures as equal but entirely distinct. In late antiquity, the emperors in Constantinople and the popes in Rome—as well as the bulk of the population of the Roman empire—were Chalcedonian Christians.

In the eastern regions of the empire most of the Christians were Monophysites° who did not accept the teaching of the Council of Chalcedon. They believed that Jesus Christ had only one nature rather than two. Three separate Monophysite communities had developed by the end of late antiquity. The first was in Armenia, a region in the Caucasus mountains of eastern Asia Minor. Around 300, Armenia became the first kingdom in the world to accept Christianity. The religion gave the Armenians a new sense of ethnic solidarity. A century later a translation of the Bible into Armenian fostered the development of a rich Christian literature among Armenia's clans. After the Council of Chalcedon, the Armenian church accepted the doctrines of Monophysite Christianity, which it still follows today.

Another Monophysite community arose in Egypt, among the native Egyptian speakers called Copts. Like the Armenians, the Copts accepted Monophysite Christianity after the Council of Chalcedon and developed a rich Christian culture expressed in the Egyptian language. They wrote their native tongue in Greek letters adopted during the Hellenistic Age, when their land was ruled by Greek speakers. Christianity took root in Egypt during the first century, and a Coptic Bible, completed in late antiquity, solidified a Coptic community that has survived to the present day.

In the Middle East, Christianity helped forge a vibrant new collective identity among the inhabitants of Syria. These Christians spoke Syriac, a Semitic language spoken by many cultures within the region. The Syriac Bible probably appeared in the second century. As was the case with Armenian and Coptic peoples, a vast literature of biblical interpretation, sermons, commentaries, and church documents slowly arose, forming the basis of a new Syriac-speaking Christian culture. Monophysite Christianity flourished among the Christians of Syria. In the sixth century the Syriac church developed its own hierarchy of priests and bishops independent of the Chalcedonian church in Constantinople. Monophysite beliefs kept the Syriac Church at odds with the emperor and his Chalcedonian followers.

In addition to the Chalcedonian and Monophysite regions, a third zone of Christians existed in late antiquity comprised of Arian Christians. As described above, Arians° believed that Jesus was not equal to or of the same essence as God the Father. Most of the people who followed Arian Christianity were the Goths and other Germanic settlers who seized political control of Rome's western provinces in the fifth century. The Goths had converted to Christianity in the fourth century, when they still lived north of the Danube River and in southern Russia. A Gothic priest named Ulfila created a Gothic alphabet and used it to translate the Bible and spread the faith. When the settlers who followed Arian Christianity entered the Roman empire, their faith kept them from marrying Roman Christians who followed Chalcedonian Christianity. In this way, the Arians' faith helped define their community in the face of the much larger Roman populations whom they ruled.

In all of these three zones, variations of the Christian faith expressed in different languages formed the seedbed of ethnic traditions, some of which survive to the present day, such as the Armenians, Copts, and Syriac- and Greek-speaking Orthodox Christians. But at the same time, the spread of Christianity weakened other local groupings. As language-based Christian communities spread inside and outside the empire, many local dialects and languages disappeared. Throughout most of western Europe the Celtic languages began to fade away during late antiquity. In the east the old languages of Asia Minor were gone by the end of the sixth century. Only those languages in which Christian thinking found textual expression survived.

In western Europe, Latin was the language of Christian literature and church ritual. About 410, the churchman Jerome finished a new Latin translation of the Bible, which replaced earlier Latin versions. This translation, called the Vulgate Bible, became the standard Bible in European churches for many centuries.

The Church's use of Latin kept the door open for the transmission of all Latin texts into a world defined by Christianity. This ensured the survival of Roman legal, scientific, and literary traditions, even after Roman rule had evaporated in western Europe. Latin also forged a common bond among different political communities of the empire's western sector. Latin served as an international language among the ruling elites in western Europe, even though they spoke different languages in their daily lives. Thus, church-based Latin served as a powerful unifying and stabilizing influence. The Latin language combined with Christianity to spur the development of Christendom°—many peoples and kingdoms in western Europe united by their common religion and shared language of worship and intellectual life.

In the eastern Mediterranean, Christianity had a different voice. There a Greek-based Church developed. Greek was the language of imperial rule and common culture in that region, and Greek became the language of the eastern Christian Church. In addition to the New Testament, which had been originally written in Greek, eastern Christians used a Greek version of the Hebrew Bible called the

The Ascetic Alternative

The idea that the human body, with all its physical needs, stands in the way of spiritual progress had long existed in the ancient Mediterranean world. Over the centuries, it has become deeply rooted in Western culture. As we saw in Chapter 3, in the fifth century B.C.E. Plato had argued that human souls are only bits of the great Soul that dwells in an unchanging celestial realm far above our earthly world. These bits of soul reside only temporarily in the human body during a person's life. By pursuing the philosophical life people might overcome the constraints of the human body and the material world and free these bits of soul to return to their source. Living a philosophical life meant combining a rigorous intellectual pursuit of knowledge with a disregard for physical needs. Greek and Roman philosophers following Plato dreamed of freeing their souls to ascend to a higher realm.

Christian ascetics took a different direction. They sought to suppress their physical needs to the extent that God might enter their souls and work through them. Making contact with God required constant preparation, as one might prepare for an athletic competition. For this reason Christian ascetics strived to deny the physical self all its manifestations. Many relied on deprivation, going without food and sleep. They would also punish their bodies through self-flagellation. Still others rejected human contact, living in uncomfortable places such atop a pillar or at the bottom of a dry well. All ascetics struggled to abstain from sex and to reject social standards of cleanliness, which they viewed as mere vanity.

Christian ascetic practice could also take subtler forms than physical abuse. Some followers rejected their families and communities, spurned all knowledge except for the content of the Christian Bible, and even denied the significance of the passage of time by insisting that each day was a new beginning. In all of these ways ascetics freed themselves from the practices that ordered and gave meaning to everyday life. In monasteries and nunneries men and women submitted to the absolute rule of abbots and abbesses in their quest to suppress individual aspirations.

Winning the endless battles against the desires of the self and the lures of the Devil made ascetics holy in the eyes of their fellow Christians. And once an ascetic achieved communion with God, that divine presence within the ascetic radiated a curative power. Uniquely situated on the border between the divine and the human, holy ascetics sometimes channeled their power to the benefit of the human community by performing healing miracles and mediating disputes.

The ascetic movement revealed a profound shift in ideas about the body, the accessibility of divinity, and the nature of sexuality. From the ascetic perspective, the human body ceased to be a beautiful gift to be glorified in statuary and song. Instead it became an obstacle to spiritual communion with the Almighty. An ascetic life was not just a suppression of sexual desires but a victory over them. For Christians, following an ascetic life was not a cowardly flight from the problems of the world. Rather, it represented a courageous encounter with personal demons and the evils of society. Through ascetic discipline, men and women challenged their physical existence and the basic values of the everyday Mediterranean world in new ways. ■

■ **Symeon the Pillar Saint**
The fifth-century ascetic saint Symeon lived atop a pillar in Syria. Crowds gathered to watch him perform holy acts of bodily mortification and to ask his advice and blessing. In this silver plaque Symeon is threatened by the Devil, who has taken the form of a serpent. Symeon, who wears the robes of a monk, resists with the help of a holy text that he holds on his lap. The conch shell above his head symbolizes his sainthood.

For Discussion

How did their religious beliefs affect the ways that Christians understood their bodies in late antiquity? What do these changed beliefs about the human body and sexuality tell us about late antique society?

Septuagint, which Greek-speaking Jews had prepared in Alexandria in the second century B.C.E. for their own community. The Septuagint combined with the Greek New Testament to become the authoritative Christian Bible throughout Rome's eastern provinces.

The Monastic Movement

Near the end of the third century, then, a new Christian spiritual movement took root in the Roman Empire. Known today as asceticism°, it both challenged the emerging connection between the political and religious hierarchies and rejected the growing wealth of the Church. Asceticism called for Christians to subordinate their physical needs and temporal desires to a quest for spiritual union with God.

The founder of the ascetic movement was Antony, an Egyptian Christian. Around 280 Antony sold all his property and walked away from his crowded village near the Nile into the desert in search of spiritual union with God. A few decades later, Bishop Athanasius composed a biography, the *Life of Antony,* telling how Antony overcame all the temptations the Devil could conjure up, from voluptuous naked women to opportunities for power and fame. Vividly describing the struggle between asceticism ("the discipline") and the demonic lures of everyday life ("the household"), Athanasius's work became one of the most influential books in Western literature. It captured the spiritual yearnings of many thousands of men and women, inspiring them to imitate Antony by following "the discipline" to seek spiritual communion with God. Within a century asceticism began to spread across the Mediterranean world. The desert, so accessible to Antony in Egypt, became a metaphor for any rough, isolated place where a person could pursue the quest for God. Across Europe the devout headed into their own versions of the desert, to find the God they so desperately desired.

Ascetic discipline required harsh and often violent mortification of the body. Some ascetics engaged in self-flagellation (whipping themselves), going without food and sleep, and living in the most uncomfortable places they could find, such as on a lonely, barren island or at the bottom of a dry well. Other ascetics lived as anchorites, individuals who struggled alone in their search for experience with God.

Over time, some believers sought to construct communities of the like-minded, both to offer assistance to individuals seeking unity with God and to regulate the practice of ascetic disciplines. The result was the monastic movement°. In the eastern church, Basil of Caesarea (ca. 330–379) set up one of the first monasteries, a community of monks. Basil had begun his quest for God as a hermit, but he came to repudiate the more extreme ascetic practices. Through his writings, he encouraged monks to discipline their souls through productive labor and voluntary poverty rather than through long bouts of self-flagellation or other physical tortures. He also insisted that monks should devote the greater part of their day to religious contemplation and prayer. In the monasteries, which sometimes held a thousand or more adherents, the monks typically shared meals and worship but engaged in ascetic discipline and prayer alone.

Monasticism spread first throughout the East, and then made its way into western Europe. Western monasticism was codified by Benedict (ca. 480–ca. 547), whose Latin *Rule* became the rulebook for almost all western monastic orders. Benedict founded a monastery on Monte Cassino near Naples in 529. Like Basil, Benedict emphasized voluntary poverty and a life devoted to prayer. Benedict, however, placed a greater stress on labor. Fearing that an idle monk was an easily tempted monk, Benedict sought to ensure that his monks kept busy. He therefore ordered that all monks perform physical labor for parts of every day. In societies still bearing the marks of the Greco-Roman contempt for manual labor, Benedict's orders were quite radical.

Monasticism, Women, and Sexuality

The monastic movement's impact on women was ambiguous. Both asceticism and monasticism certainly opened new avenues for female spirituality. In monastic communities, men and women lived separately to reduce sexual temptation, but within the confines of these communities, gender was irrelevant. It was just one more difficult physical boundary to cross over on the path to finding God. By joining monastic communities and leaving the routines of daily life behind, women could gain independence from the obligations of male-dominated society. In all the lands where Christianity was followed, ascetic women created communities of their own. They lived as celibate sisterhoods of nuns, dedicated to spiritual quest and service to God. Perhaps not surprisingly, church leaders approved of this lifestyle for women.

Some wives or daughters of wealthy and powerful families rejected traditional expectations to be wives and mothers by founding monastic communities. Such women wielded an authority and influence that would not have been available to them otherwise. For example, Melania the Younger (383–439), the daughter of a wealthy Roman senatorial family, decided to sell her vast estates and spend the proceeds in religious pursuits. When the Roman Senate objected to the breaking up of Melania's family estates, Melania successfully appealed to the empress, who interceded with the legal authorities to enable her to dispose of her property. (Melania's slaves also objected, because they did not want to be sold separately to raise cash for her religious projects, but Melania ignored them.) Melania spent her fortune on building monasteries in the Holy Land of Palestine. Most women lacked the financial resources to make such dramatic gestures, but they could imitate Melania's accomplishment on a modest scale, crafting a new kind of religious life over which they exercised control.

But monasticism also reinforced the hold of negative ideas about women and sexuality in the Church. Male ascetics preached and practiced sexual abstinence as an important self-denying discipline. In ascetic thought, women were linked to the corrupt world of the flesh against which the Christian must exercise unceasing vigilance. The ascetic retreat into the desert or monastery was a flight from temptation, and that meant a flight from women. As ascetic ideas gained in prominence, celibacy became a Christian ideal, with sexual relations within the confines of marriage viewed as distinctly second-best.

The increasingly negative view of women within Christian thought is apparent in the writings of churchmen of the late antique era. Christian writers branded women as disobedient, sexually promiscuous, innately sinful, and naturally inferior to men. They interpreted Genesis, the first book of the Bible, to mean that women bore a special curse. In their reading of the Genesis account, Eve, the first woman, seduced Adam, the first man. For this reason late antique Christians blamed Eve—and women collectively—for humanity's expulsion from the Garden of Eden and for all the woes human beings had suffered ever since. Ambrose, the influential bishop of Milan from 373 to 397, wrote, "Since a woman is not the image of God, a woman ought to veil her head, to show herself subject. And since falsehood began through her, she ought to have this sign, that her head be not free, but covered with a veil."[2] Yet, at the same time, Christians also believed that God would save the souls of women as well as men, and they honored Mary for her role in bringing Jesus, and therefore salvation, into the world. In many ways women occupied a position in the Christian religious imagination comparable to that held by Jews: They were considered guilty as a group of a terrible deed, yet they were accepted as a necessary part of God's plan for humanity. For these reasons Christian women never achieved full equality with men in daily life during late antiquity.

A Greek Zodiac in a Synagogue
In late antiquity, Jews living in Palestine sometimes decorated their synagogues with mosaic floors depicting the zodiac. Although these mosaics appeared in synagogues and often contained Hebrew writing, the scenes and style of the mosaics were typical of Greek and Roman art. This blending demonstrates that members of the Jewish congregation also participated in the general non-Jewish culture of the province.

Jews in a Christian World

Until Christianity became the official religion of the Roman Empire, Jews had been simply one group of people among hundreds who lived under Roman rule. Although polytheist Romans considered Jews eccentric because they worshiped only one god and refused to make statues of him, they still respected the antiquity of the Jewish people's faith. Throughout the empire, Jews had enjoyed full citizenship rights and appeared in all professions and at all levels of society.

Christianity erased all this. According to Christian belief, Jews had been the chosen people of God until the appearance of Jesus, who displaced them from their place in God's plan. Christians criticized Jews for failing to accept that Jesus' teachings had supplanted those of the Hebrew Bible, and blamed them collectively for Jesus' crucifixion. As Christians saw it, the Diaspora (the dispersion of Jews around the world after the destruction of Jerusalem by the Roman army in 70) was God's way of punishing the Jews.

With the advance of Christianity within the empire, the Jewish position worsened. Beginning in the fourth century, Roman laws began to discriminate against Jews, forbidding them to marry Christians, own Christian slaves, or accept converts into their faith. Church leaders sometimes forced entire communities of Jews to convert to Christianity on pain of death. A notable exception to this downward spiral was that Jews still retained the right to remain members of city senates. Although organized resistance among scattered Jewish communities was impossible, many Jews refused to accept the deepening oppression. Their resistance ranged from acts of violence against Jews who had converted to Christianity to armed revolt against Roman authorities.

Despite their marginal position in the empire, Jews did retain some security because most emperors honored traditional obligations to protect all their subjects. Roman emperors repeatedly issued laws forbidding the destruction of synagogues. They permitted Jews to worship on the sabbath, and excused them from performing public or private business on that day, as Jewish law required. Zealous bishops often objected to such fair treatment of Jews, and some especially zealous bishops goaded Christians into attacking synagogues. For example, in 388 the bishop of Callinicum, a town on the Euphrates River, destroyed the local synagogue with the assistance of his Christian congregation. When the emperor Theodosius I tried to punish the guilty citizens, Bishop Ambrose of Milan wrote a long letter stiffly rebuking the emperor: "Will you give the Jews this triumph over the Church of God, this victory over the people of Christ?" asked Ambrose. The emperor backed down, and the Christians of Callinicum went unpunished.

In 429, Roman officials abolished the office of Jewish Patriarch. The Roman emperors had long recognized the Patriarch as leader of the Jews throughout the empire, and had given the Patriarch certain legal and administrative duties. With the office abolished, the Roman treasury now collected for itself the special taxes that had been paid by Jews for the Patriarch's administration. The end of the Patriarch shows that Jesus had lost their status as an ethnic community in the eyes of the empire.

Individual Jewish communities continued to administer their own affairs under the leadership of rabbis—men who served as teachers and interpreters of Jewish law. With the completion of the Mishnah° (the final organization and transcription of Jewish oral law) by the end of the third century and the production of the Jerusalem and Babylonian Talmuds° (commentaries on the law) by the end of the fourth and fifth centuries, rabbis and their courts now dominated Jewish community life. These learned men established academies of legal study in Roman Palestine and Persian Babylonia, where they produced authoritative interpretations of law that guided everyday Jewish life.

Although some Jewish women served as leaders of synagogues in late antiquity, in general rabbinic Judaism legitimized the subordination of women in Jewish society. Jewish women did not benefit from the education at the Jewish academies. Excluded from the formal process of interpreting the Bible, Jewish women did not acquire highly prized religious knowledge. Instead, men expected them to conform to traditional roles as daughters, wives, and mothers, much as women in other religious communities were expected to do.

ACCESS TO HOLINESS: CHRISTIAN PILGRIMS

Christianity not only created new communities and condemned others, it also offered new avenues of participation in religious culture. In late antiquity, Christians of all social ranks took to the road, which they called going on a pilgrimage°. Their goal was to visit sacred places, especially places where sacred objects, known as relics°, were housed. They believed these relics were inherently holy because they were physical objects associated with saints and martyrs, or with Jesus himself. The most highly valued relics were the bones from the skeleton of the venerated person. Christians believed that contact with such relics could cure them of an illness, heighten their spiritual awareness, or improve their lives.

The mortal remains of Christian martyrs provided the first relics and the first objects of veneration for pilgrims, but after persecution of Christians ceased in 312, believers resorted to the bodies of great bishops and ascetic monks and nuns. From the fourth century onward, Christians regularly dug up saintly skeletons, chopped them up, and distributed the pieces to churches. The more important the holy person, the fiercer the competition for the bones and other objects associated with him or her. Churches in the largest cities of the empire, such as Rome, Constantinople, Alexandria, and Jerusalem, acquired fine collections. For example, the robe of the Virgin Mary, the mother of Jesus, was kept in a church in Constantinople. Residents of the city believed that the Virgin's robe drove away enemies when it was carried in procession along the city's battlements.

Emperors and important bishops acquired the greatest and most powerful relics of all—those that had reportedly touched Jesus himself. These included the crown of thorns he wore when crucified, the cross on which he died, and the nails that fastened him to the wood. Relics reminded Christians that Jesus' own death was symbolically repeated in the martyrdom of his followers. For this reason church altars where followers celebrated the Eucharist, the rite in which bread and wine are offered as Jesus' body and blood in memory of his death, were built over the graves or relics of martyrs.

Traveling to touch a relic was the primary motive for going on a pilgrimage, but there were other reasons. Palestine became a frequent destination of Christian pilgrims because it contained the greatest number of sacred sites and relics associated with events described in the Bible and particularly with Jesus' life and death. Between the fourth and seventh centuries, thousands of earnest Christian pilgrims from the Mediterranean and Middle Eastern worlds flocked to Palestine to visit holy sites and pray for divine assistance and forgiveness for their sins. Helena, the mother of Emperor Constantine, made pilgrimage fashionable. In the early fourth century she visited Jerusalem, where she reportedly found remnants of the cross on which Jesus was crucified, as well as many of the sites pertaining to Jesus' life.

Inspired by his mother's journey, Constantine funded the construction of lavish shrines and monasteries at these sites, as well as guest houses for pilgrims. Practically overnight Palestine was transformed from a provincial backwater to the spiritual focus of the Christian world. Religious men and women—rich and poor, old and young, sick and healthy—streamed to Palestine and Jerusalem. There they joined processions that made their way from holy place to holy place. At each site clergymen permitted them to view and sometimes kiss or touch holy relics. On the most important holidays, such as Easter, priests held special ceremonies at the different sites of Jesus' last day on earth—at the Mount of Olives where he was arrested by Roman soldiers, at the place of his trial, at the hill of his crucifixion, and at his tomb, called the Holy Sepulchre.

Palestine did not have a monopoly on holy places, however. Pilgrims traveled to places throughout the Roman world wherever saints had lived and died and where their relics rested. Their pilgrimages contributed to the growth of a Christian view of the world in several ways. Because pilgrimage was a holy enterprise, Christian communities gave hospitality and lodging to religious travelers. This fostered a shared sense of Christian community among people from many lands. Christians envisioned a Christian "map" dominated by spiritually significant places. Travel guides that explained this "spiritual geography" became popular among pilgrims. Most of all, pilgrims who returned home enriched in their faith and perhaps cured in mind or spirit inspired their home communities with news of a growing Christian world directly linked to the Bible lands they heard about in church.

CHRISTIAN INTELLECTUAL LIFE

In late antiquity, many Christians actively participated in the empire's intellectual life. Highly educated in Christian learning as well as the traditional studies of the Roman elite, writers examined the meaning of Christian life in the context of classical literature, philosophy, and the study of history.

Early Christian Hostility to Classical Learning

In Roman schools, the sons of wealthy families, as well as some poor boys with ambition and talent, studied the poets, dramatists, philosophers, and rhetoricians of the classical Greek, Hellenistic, and Roman periods. By late antiquity this curriculum, known today as classical learning, had become formalized into seven liberal arts: grammar, logical argument, and rhetoric (collectively called the Trivium); and geometry, arithmetic, astronomy and music (the Quadrivium). Law and medicine were taught separately, for those who aspired to those professions. This education prepared students for careers in the imperial bureaucracy and various other fields. Equally important, it provided aristocratic men with a common cultural bond—a shared version of history, a value system that legitimized their exercise of power, an appreciation of the benefits of city life, and a common understanding of how the universe functioned. No other institution before the rise of Christianity, not even the army, exerted such a powerful influence on the minds of the men who controlled Rome's destiny.

But classical learning and the educational system that kept it alive posed a challenge to Christian educators. Specifically, how should Christians reconcile classical teachings with the doctrines of their faith, particularly when the two conflicted? Did the classics of Greco-Roman literature constitute a threat to Christianity? Could Christians learn anything of value from pagan cultures? Should educated men turn their backs on classical learning in order to avoid being corrupted by it?

During the first three centuries after Jesus' death, when Christians were marginalized and at times persecuted in Roman society, many church leaders strongly criticized classical learning. Churchmen argued that the wisdom of pagan intellectuals was false wisdom, that it distracted the Christian from what was truly important—contemplation of Jesus Christ and the eternal salvation he offered—and therefore that it corrupted young Christians.

The Reconciliation of Christianity and the Classics

After Constantine's conversion in 312, however, the Church became an increasingly influential voice in the empire and classical learning no longer seemed as dangerous to Christians. Many church leaders now came from the empire's urban elite, where they had benefited from classical learning. Christian officials grudgingly approved secular education as churchmen recognized that the traditional curriculum still had practical value. Training in classical rhetoric, grammar, and literature became an integral part of upper-class Christian life. By the fifth century most Christians accepted traditional schooling as a useful if vaguely risky enterprise. As Basil the Great (ca. 330–379), bishop of Caesarea in Cappadocia (in modern Turkey), explained to young men about to embark on their studies, classical learning had both benefits and dangers: "It is sufficiently proved that this pagan learning is not without use to the soul . . . It is necessary . . . to watch incessantly in guarding our souls, lest that, charmed by the attraction of the words, we receive in our ignorance some bad impressions and with the honey introduce into our bosoms poisonous fluids."[3]

Influential churchmen, writing in Greek and Latin, now drew freely from classical texts and methods of discussion, even though they considered the Christian scriptures the sole source of truth. The career of Augustine

(354–430) shows how a classical education could serve Christian purposes. Born to parents of modest means, Augustine attended traditional Roman schools as a youth. His talent and schooling and prepared him for a high position in public life. After his conversion to Christianity, Augustine became an influential bishop in the city of Hippo Regius in North Africa. Using his episcopal office as a platform from which to launch his attacks on polytheism and heresy and to define all aspects of the Christian faith, Augustine displayed a sincere respect for certain aspects of Roman cultural and intellectual accomplishments—especially rhetoric and history—but he always believed Christianity was superior. For Augustine, the last enemy of all true Christians was "antiquity, mothers of all evils"—the source of false beliefs.

Like Augustine, Cassiodorus (ca. 490–ca. 585), an Italian statesman in the court of Ostragothic rulers of Italy, regarded classical learning as an intellectual inheritance of high value. Cassiodorus was appalled by the waning of the traditional classical educational system in the chaotic final days of the Roman Empire in the west. In response, he founded a monastery at Vivarium in the south of Italy, to which he retired at the end of his political career. Eager to preserve the liberal arts, Cassiodorus instructed his monks to copy classical literature in the monastery's library. "Let the task of the ancients be our task,"[4] he told them.

As the example of Cassiodorus shows, in the western Roman Empire, monasticism played a central role in preserving classical learning and thus allowing its integration into Christian culture in later centuries. Much of the responsibility for the preservation of the classical intellectual tradition lay with the monasteries founded by Benedict of Nursia (ca. 480–547). This group of monks, called the Benedictine order, established many monasteries throughout western Europe, modeled on the monastery of Mobe Cassino near Naples, Italy, that Benedict established. They followed Benedict's guidebook called the *Rule* that spelled out the duties of the monks and nuns. Benedict himself was wary of classical teaching, but he wanted the monks and nuns under his supervision to be able to read religious books. At least basic education, then, had to become part of monastic life. Benedictine monasteries were providing an education not only to their inhabitants but also to any eager scholar from the surrounding communities. The Benedictine definition of "manual labor" expanded to include the copying of ancient manuscripts and Benedictine monasteries developed significant libraries. As monasteries that followed Benedict's *Rule* spread throughout Europe, they served as centers of education and also succeeded in preserving much Latin literature.

Traditional schooling flourished throughout the empire as long as cities could afford to pay for teachers. In most of the towns in western Europe, schools gradually disappeared in the course of the fifth century as a result of the Germanic invasions. With the exception of a few major urban centers, such as Carthage in North Africa, where traditional Roman schooling continued after the establishment of the Vandal kingdom, cities no longer had the funds to pay for teachers. Classical education all but disappeared from urban life by the end of the fifth century. In the eastern half of the empire, classical learning lasted well into the sixth century as a basic part of elite education. Traditional education declined in Byzantium not because of decline in wealth but because of the growing influence of Christianity on daily life. After the emperor Justinian (r. 527–565) forbade non-Christians to teach, the number of schools declined. By the end of the seventh century, traditional schools of grammar and rhetoric had disappeared. The Psalter (the collection of Psalms in the Bible) became the primer for reading, and religious literature supplanted classical works. But as we will see in Chapter 7, classical learning revived in Byzantium after the seventh century.

Neoplatonism and Christianity

Greek and Roman philosophy continued to be enormously influential in late antiquity. One branch of this tradition, called neoplatonism° originated with Plotinus (205–270), a non-Christian. His teachings greatly influenced Christianity, an example of how classical and Christian thought intertwined in late antiquity. Plotinus, who taught in the city of Rome, traced his intellectual roots primarily to the works of Plato (ca.429–327 B.C.E.). He also drew ideas from Aristotle (384–322 B.C.E.) and various Stoic philosophers (third century B.C.E.), as well as the writings of their followers. In a series of essays called the *Enneads,* Plotinus applied Plato's views to the issues addressed in ancient philosophy, including ethical behavior, the physical structure of the cosmos, and the nature of perception, consciousness, and memory. He also turned Neoplatonism in religious directions, arguing that all things that exist, whether intangible ideas or matter, originate in a single force called the One. Iamblichus (ca. 245–ca. 325) and other Neoplatonist teachers established a school curriculum based on Plotinus' teachings.

According to Neoplatonists, the One has no physical existence; it is eternal and unchanging. The One is separated from the world of matter and physical change in which humans live by three descending grades of reality: the World Mind, the World Soul, and finally Nature. The World Mind contains the Forms that Plato described (see Chapter 3) and holds them all together as pure knowledge. The World Soul produces time and space. Nature is the lowest of these creative principles, consisting of things that come into being, change, and go out of existence. In Neoplatonic thinking, the human soul is a microcosm of these three levels of reality. The human soul "fell" from the One into the world of Nature and into the human body, thereby losing its connection with the One. But the human soul can be redeemed. Humans have the potential to reunite their souls with the One by overcoming their passions and physical desires. Many Neoplatonists believed that by gaining the help of the gods through magical rites (called theurgy) and by studying divine revelations, the human soul can reconnect with the One and fulfill its fullest potential.

With its emphasis on the fall and return of the soul to the One, Neoplatonism appealed to many Christians. For them, the One was God, and the Bible provided the divine revelations that could lead to the salvation of the human soul and reunification with God. The churchmen Gregory of Nyssa in the Greek East and Augustine in the Latin West were only two of the many churchmen who incorporated Neoplatonism into their own works in the later fourth century. Yet Christian and non-Christian Neoplatonists soon argued over such issues as whether the identity of "the One" could be equated with the Christian God and whether the use of theurgy constituted a pagan practice. In 529 the emperor Justinian closed Plato's Academy in Athens and forbade non-Christians to teach philosophy.

The impact of Neoplatonism on Christian theology remained profound. Neoplatonic thought helped to shape the Christian doctrine of the immortality of the human soul; it also reinforced the ascetic ideal. Thus, contempt for the material, temporal world and the physical body took deep root in Christian culture.

Christianity's View of the Empire in History

Christianity not only influenced the way people saw themselves in relation to philosophy and faith, it also shaped their view of the Roman Empire's role in human history. Eusebius, the bishop of Caesarea in Palestine from 313 to 339 and an advisor to Constantine, developed a theory of history that linked the development of the Roman Empire to a divine plan for humanity's salvation. Like other Christians before him, Eusebius believed that the Bible described the main events of human history, such as the creation of the first man and woman, God's revelation of his law to the Hebrews, and the appearance of Jesus. Events still to come, according to Eusebius, included the appearance of the Antichrist, who would inaugurate a brutal reign of evil on Earth, the return of Jesus, the overthrow of the Antichrist, and the End of Days, when God would judge all human beings, reward the pious, and punish the wicked.

Eusebius added the Roman Empire to this historical plan. He argued that God had sent Jesus to Earth at a divinely appointed place and time—during the reign of the emperor Augustus and thus at a time when much of the known world had been united under imperial rule. The Pax Romana, according to Eusebius, provided the perfect, indeed the divinely ordained, conditions for the rapid spread of Christian teaching and the rapid growth of the Christian Church. In Eusebius's view, Constantine's conversion to Christianity marked the next step in God's plan. With one world empire now united under the one true religion, it would be the emperor's job to bring this religion to all of humankind. This triumphal vision of history struck a powerful chord among the empire's Christian elite. It gave Rome a crucial role to play in human destiny. It also enabled aristocrats to justify their traditional roles as political leaders.

But by the fifth century, Romans found Eusebius's triumphalism less satisfying as troubling questions surfaced. As we saw in the chapter introduction, in 410 the Visigoths plundered the city of Rome itself. This epic event challenged Christians' confidence in Eusebius's vision. Did Rome really have a special role in God's divine plan for humanity? If God favored Rome, as Eusebius explained, why had he allowed Visigoths to humiliate the great city? Was God punishing Romans because they had not eradicated paganism?

Such questions prompted Augustine to reexamine conventional notions about Rome's place in the world. In his book *The City of God,* Completed in 423, Augustine developed a new interpretation of history. Though Augustine admired the Romans for their many virtues, he concluded

CHRONOLOGY

Christianity, Polytheism, and Judaism

CA. 280	Antony goes into the Egyptian desert
CA. 300	Armenia becomes the first Christian kingdom
303	Great Persecution of Christians
306–337	Reign of Constantine the Great
312	Constantine converts to Christianity
325	Council of Nicaea writes then icene Creed
360–363	Julian the Apostate reigns
391	Polytheist worship forbidden by Roman law
396–430	Augustine is Bishop of Hippo
CA. 400	Jerusalem Talmud completed
410	Jerome completes Latin translation of Hebrew Bible (Vulgate)
429	End of Jewish Patriarchate
451	Council of Chalcedon
CA. 500	Babylonian Talmud finished
529	Academy in Athens closed; non-Christians forbidden to teach; Benedict founds monastery at Monte Cassino in Italy
534	Benedict writes *Rule* for monastic life

that Rome played no significant role in salvation history and that the sack of Rome had no special meaning for Christians. Augustine's theory disconnected Christian ideas of human destiny from the fate of the Roman Empire. In his view, the Roman Empire was just one among many that had existed and that would exist before Jesus' return. According to Augustine, the only dates humanity should view as spiritually significant were Jesus' time on Earth and the End of Days sometime in the future. The significance of all events in between remained known only to God.

Augustine's theory proved quite timely. Within a few years of his death the Vandals seized North Africa and the Roman Empire lost control of all of its provinces in western Europe. Augustine thus gave Roman Christians a new perspective with which to view this loss: Rome had contributed to world civilization and to the growth of the Christian Church, but now Christianity would grow on its own without the support of Roman emperors.

Other churchmen explained the collapse of Roman power in western Europe differently. Salvian, a clergyman from the south of France who found himself living in a new Germanic kingdom in the first half of the fifth century, believed that Romans deserved to lose their empire in the west because of their sinful lives and oppressive social order. The Visigoths, while less sophisticated than Romans, were nevertheless purer at heart—better Christians despite their heretical Arian views. Salvian's views demonstrate that for many devout Christians, Roman civilization had come to the end of the road. It was time to build a new, Christian world.

The Breakup of the Roman Empire

During the fifth century, the Roman Empire split into two parts: the Latin-speaking provinces in western Europe, and the largely Greek- and Syriac-speaking provinces in the east. As the Roman government lost control of its western domains, independent Germanic kingdoms emerged there. The eastern provinces remained under the control of the Roman emperor, whose capital city was not Rome, but Constantinople. In this section we will discuss the breakup of the empire and explore its consequences.

THE FALL OF ROME'S WESTERN PROVINCES

Why did Roman rule remain strong in the eastern Mediterranean while collapsing in western Europe? This is one of the most hotly debated subjects in European history. Most Christians of the time attributed the collapse of Roman rule to God's anger at the stubborn persistence of polytheist worship. Polytheists, for their part, blamed Christians for destroying the temples of the gods who had protected Rome so well in the past. In later centuries, the explanations varied. Edward Gibbon, an eighteenth-century writer whose *Decline and Fall of the Roman Empire* has influenced all historians of Rome and remains one of the most widely read history books of all time, criticized the Catholic Church for diverting able men away from public service and into religious life. Other historians attributed Rome's collapse in the west to enormous waves of savage barbarian invasions. The reason the Romans lost their western provinces is, unfortunately, more complicated and less dramatic than any of these one-dimensional explanations.

Invasions from the North

During the first century, the Romans established the northern limits of their empire on the European continent along the Rhine and Danube Rivers. From that time forward, Roman generals and emperors withstood attacks of many different northern tribes looking for plunder and new lands. The Roman legions parried their attacks, maintaining a relatively stable northern frontier through not only military might and but also diplomacy. Since the time of Augustus, Roman emperors had made treaties with newcomers, permitting them to settle on Roman lands. The empire had always been able to absorb the settlers. Why did this state of affairs break down in late antiquity—to the degree that the Romans lost their western provinces? The rather undramatic answer is that the end of Roman rule in western Europe came in a haphazard and gradual fashion as the cumulative result of unwise decisions, weak leadership, and military failure.

In the fourth century, the sudden appearance in southern Russia of the Huns, a fierce nomadic people from central Asia, set in motion a series of events that helped bring about the eventual collapse of Roman rule in western Europe. Unlike the settled farmers who lived in Europe, the Huns were highly mobile nomads who herded their flocks over the plains (or *steppes*) that stretched from southern Russia to central Asia. Able to travel vast distances very quickly on their rugged horses, the Huns had earned a reputation for ferocity in battle. Always living under the specter of starvation, they lusted after the great riches and easy lifestyles they observed in the urbanized empires of Rome and Persia.

In 376, in what is now south Russia, an army of Huns drove a group of Visigoths from their farmlands. The refugees gained permission from the Roman emperor Valens to cross the Danube and settle in the Balkans in return for supplying troops to the Roman army. In the past, Roman rulers had frequently made this sort of arrangement with newcomers eager to settle in the empire. The Roman officials in charge of this resettlement, however, flagrantly exploited the refugees by charging them exorbitant fees for food and supplies. The situation grew so unendurable that in 378 the Visigoths revolted. At the battle of Adrianople in Thrace they killed Valens and an entire Roman army

The Visigoths' successful rebellion wounded the empire, but not fatally. Rome's response to the disaster, however, sowed the seeds for a serious loss of imperial power in the west. The new emperor, Theodosius the Great (r. 379–395), permitted the Visigothic military units to serve in the Roman army under their own Visigothic commanders. As Theodosius and the rest of Rome would unhappily discover, this precedent of letting independent military forces of dubious loyalty operate freely within the empire was a terrible mistake. The consequences of Theodosius's poor judgment became all too clear in the mid-390s when Alaric, the Visigoths' king, attacked and plundered Roman cities in the Balkans and Greece. In 401 Alaric invaded Italy, but was driven out. Seven years later the Visigoths appeared again at the walls of Rome and extorted a huge payment of gold and the precious spice pepper from the angry but powerless Senate.

Alaric's success only expanded his ambitions. In 409 he returned to the city of Rome and ordered that parts of northern Italy and the western coast of the Balkans be turned over to him. When the Senate refused, Alaric and his men sacked the city. Disbelieving senators and citizens alike could only watch as the Visigoths rampaged through their streets. Ironically, Alaric died soon after his triumph. To keep his burial place secret, his followers diverted the Busento River in Italy, buried their fallen leader and all his loot, and then executed the grave diggers. Finally, they returned the river to its original course. The exact location of Alaric's grave remains a mystery to this day, awaiting an archaeologist's spade.

The Visigoths' sack of Rome not only dealt a psychological blow to the empire's inhabitants, it also led indirectly to the loss of many of Rome's western provinces. To fight Alaric, the Roman general Stilicho had withdrawn legions from the empire's northwestern defenses, leaving the Rhine frontier vulnerable. In December 406, the Rhine River froze, enabling an array of migrating Germanic tribes to enter the empire with little opposition from Roman forces. In the aftermath of the invasions of the winter of 406–407, the military situation in the western provinces became chaotic.

In Britain, Rome abandoned its control entirely after an ambitious general, styling himself Constantine III, led Britain's last legions across the English Channel in an unsuccessful attempt to seize the imperial throne. This action left Britain defenseless, vulnerable to groups of Saxons al-

THE HUNS, MONSTROUS INVADERS

Shortly after the Huns rode in from the steppelands of central Asia and drove the Visigoths into the Roman Empire in the 370s, a Roman historian wrote this description of the event. His picture of the Huns, though filled with misconceptions and error, reveals the fear that the nomadic tribesmen inspired in the settled communities of the Mediterranean world. By describing the ways in which he views the Huns as uncivilized, the writer provides a good picture of Roman ideas of civilization.

The people of the Huns . . . exceed every degree of savagery. Since the cheeks of the children are deeply furrowed with steel knives from their very birth, in order that the growth of hair, when it appears at the proper time, may be checked by the wrinkled scars, they grow old without beards and without any beauty, like eunuchs. They all have compact, strong limbs and thick necks, and are so monstrously ugly and misshapen, that one might take them for two-legged beasts . . . They are so hardy that they have no need of fire or of savory food, but eat the roots of wild plants and the half-raw flesh of any kind of animal whatever, which they put between their thighs and the backs of their horses, and thus warm it a little. They are never protected by any buildings, but they avoid these like tombs . . . They are almost glued to their horses . . . They are subject to no royal restraint, but they are content with the disorderly government of their important men, and led by them they force their way through every obstacle. . . . You would not hesitate to call them the most terrible of warriors, because they fight from a distance with missiles having sharp bone . . . joined to the shafts . . . then they gallop over the intervening spaces and fight hand to hand with swords, regardless of their own lives . . . No one in their country ever plows a field. . . . They are all without fixed abode, without hearth, or law, or settled mode of life . . . Like unreasoning beasts they are utterly ignorant of the difference between right and wrong, they are deceitful and ambiguous in speech, never bound by any reverence for religion . . . They burn with an infinite thirst for gold . . .

Source: Reprinted by permission of the publishers and the Trustees of the Loeb Classical Library from *Ammianus Marcellinus, Volume III,* Loeb Classical Library Volume LCL 331, translated by John C. Rolfe, Cambridge, Mass.: Harvard University Press, 1939. The Loeb Classical Library ® is a registered trademark of the President and Fellows of Harvard College.

Stilicho and His Family Between 395 and 408 the general Stilicho ruled the western half of the empire as the regent for Honorius, the son of Theodosius I. Though his father was a Vandal, Stilicho was completely loyal to Rome. Carved in traditional Roman style, these ivory panels show Stilicho dressed in Vandal clothing, accompanied by his wife and son.

ready settled on British soil. Originally from the shores of the North Sea near modern Denmark, the Saxons had been fighting in Britain as allies of Roman forces. Now they turned on their former partners and attacked Roman-held Britain. The desperate inhabitants begged for help from the emperor Honorius. According to one contemporary, in 410 the beleaguered ruler merely told the Britons to fend for themselves.

Elsewhere the chaos continued. Small bands of marauding tribes such as Alans, Burgundians, and Sueves roamed through Gaul, while the Vandals and their allies raided their way through Spain. For over a decade, the various invaders tried to secure territory for themselves within the imperial borders by force. Vastly outnumbered by the provincial populations, they survived by plundering the countryside.

Although the invading bands were small, the imperial government in the west no longer possessed the administrative capacity to marshal its military resources and push the invaders out. Instead, it turned to diplomacy, offering the invaders a place within the Roman Empire. In Gaul, for example, the treaty of 418 granted the Visigoths a home in Aquitania (a region of southwestern Gaul). According to the treaty, the Visigoths received lands on which to settle permanently, something they had sought for nearly two generations and in return they would pay taxes, and would fight under Rome's banner to combat peasant rebels and other invading tribes. Within a generation, however, the Visigoths shook off their subordinate status to Rome. Refusing to pay taxes to Roman officials or send troops to fight in Roman armies, they established a kingdom of their own in Gaul by 450. A similar process of encroachment and settlement took place elsewhere in the western provinces. In 429 the Vandals moved on from Spain to North Africa where they soon established an independent kingdom. In 439 they seized Carthage and made it their capital.

Thus encroaching bands of Germanic peoples established independent kingdoms in the regions of Britain, Gaul, Spain, and North Africa through a gradual process. The empire was not invaded by overwhelming numbers of savage or barbaric invaders. In fact, their numbers were puny compared to the millions of Roman provincials they pitted themselves against. And although the Germans plundered and pillaged, they could not hold on to imperial

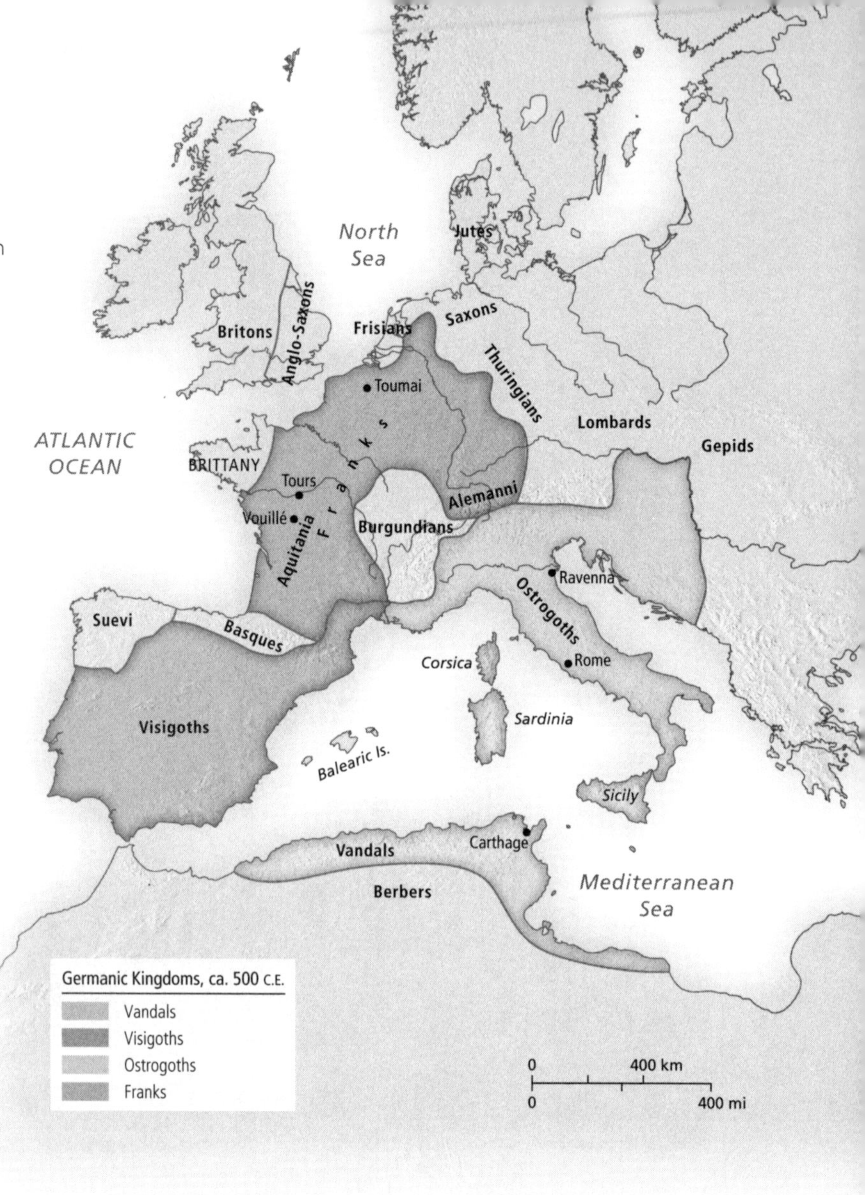

Map 6.2 Germanic Kingdoms, ca. 525
In little more than a century after their entry into the Roman Empire, different Germanic peoples had established several powerful kingdoms in western Europe.

lands and settle there without the active cooperation of Roman administrators. But once they put down roots, they steadily consolidated their strength and established rule on their own. By then, Roman authorities lacked both the organization and the strength to defeat them.

Even though most of the western provinces had fallen to invaders by 450, the Romans managed to hold on to Italy for a short while longer. The city of Rome remained the home of the Senate, while the emperor of the western provinces resided in Ravenna, a town on Italy's northeast coast. Military strongmen, however, held the real power in Italy, although they were formally subordinate to the emperor. These soldiers were usually not Romans by birth, but they adopted Roman culture and fought for Rome's advantage. But in 476 one of these strongmen, a Germanic general named Odovacar, ended the charade of obedience to the emperor. He deposed the last emperor in the west, a boy named Romulus Augustulus. Odovacar then assumed full power over the Italian peninsula, naming himself king of Italy. For many historians the year 476 symbolizes the end of the Roman Empire in the west. But in actuality, 476 is a date of little significance. The Romans' control of their western provinces had all but slipped away decades earlier.

The Empire of Attila

The Huns who had driven the Visigoths into the Balkans and sparked the series of events that led to Rome's loss of its western provinces continued to advance on Europe as late antiquity came to a close. By 400 they had carved out a powerful kingdom on the great plain of Hungary, where they could graze their horses and flocks. Throughout the first half of the fifth century the Huns remained a violent and disruptive presence on the European continent, relentlessly raiding the Balkans and western Europe. They forced conquered peoples to fight under Hunnic banners.

By 445, a charismatic and ruthless conqueror emerged as the sole leader of the Hunnic tribes and their allies. Named Attila, this terrifying warrior began to expand the Huns' empire from southern Russia to France. This move brought him face to face with the Roman Empire in the east. To their surprise, Roman diplomats from Constantinople who visited Attila's court found the Hunnic king to be a sophisticated bargainer as well as an able administrator. Attila, they discovered, included chieftains of subject peoples among his trusted assistants. The diplomats also found Roman merchants and craftsmen who had been attracted to Attila's camp, where they enjoyed freedom from oppressive Roman taxation and corrupt Roman officials.

Yet the Hunnic ruler had a shockingly brutal side as well. From his base of operations on the Hungarian plain, Attila hammered the Balkan provinces and forced the Roman emperor in Constantinople to pay him tribute in gold every year. In 450, when a new emperor refused to submit any longer to Attila's extortion, the Hun set a chilling example by turning westward and invading Gaul with an immense army. The savagery of his attack and the fear he inspired earned him the title "the Scourge of God."

The next year, the tide began to turn against Attila. A force of Visigoths (who still hated the Huns for having dri-

A ROMAN ARISTOCRAT LEARNS GOTHIC

Sidonius Apollinaris was a Roman aristocrat who lived in Gaul in the fifth century when Germanic kingdoms replaced Roman imperial rule. In this letter, he gently teases a Roman friend, Syagrius, who has been trying to find a place in the new power structure in the kingdom established in southern Gaul by the Burgundians, a Germanic tribe. Syagrius served as a legal advisor at the Burgundian court, where separate legal systems were enforced for Burgundians and Romans. Syagrius was one of a long succession of Romans who kept Roman culture and law working for several generations after the empire fell in the west—but he had to learn a new language:

Sidonius sends greetings to his friend, Syagrius:

You are the great-grandson of a consul . . . and you are descended from a poet . . . and the culture of his descendants has not declined one bit from his standard . . . I am therefore inexpressibly amazed that you have quickly acquired a knowledge of the German tongue with such ease. And yet I remember that your boyhood had a good schooling in liberal studies and I know for certain that you often declaimed with spirit and eloquence before your professor of oratory. This being so, please tell me how you have managed to absorb so swiftly into your inner being the exact sounds of an alien race, so that now after reading Vergil under the schoolmaster's cane and toiling and working through the rich fluency of . . . Cicero, you burst forth like a young falcon from an old nest. You have no idea what amusement it gives me, and others too, when I hear that in your presence the barbarian is afraid to perpetrate a barbarism in his own language. The bent elders of the Germans are astounded at you when you translate letters, and they adopt you as umpire and arbitrator in their mutual dealings . . . Only one thing remains, most clever of men: continue with undiminished zeal, even in your hours of ease, to devote some attention to reading; and like the man of refinement that you are, observe a just balance between the two languages: retain your grasp of Latin, lest you be laughed at, and practice the other, in order to have the laugh on them. Farewell.

Source: Reprinted by permission of the publishers and Trustees of the Loeb Classical Library from *Sidonius Poems and Letters, Volume II,* Loeb Classical Library Volume LCL 420, translated by W. B. Anderson, Cambridge, Mass.: Harvard University Press, 1935. The Loeb Classical Library ® is a registered trademark of the President and Fellows of Harvard College.

ven them from their homelands in south Russian nearly a century earlier) joined with Romans and other allies from the Germanic kingdoms in western Europe. This allied force stopped Attila's advance in a battle at the Catalaunian Fields in central Gaul in 451. The following year the tenacious warrior launched a new attack on Italy but failed to take the city of Rome, perhaps because his army was weakened by disease.

Soon after the ill-fated invasion of Italy, Attila died while in bed with a young bride. His sons divided the Hunnic Empire among themselves, but the realm could not endure without its great leader. Soon the Huns' subject peoples rebelled against their oppressors and reclaimed their independence. The mighty empire of the Huns fragmented and disappeared. Within a century another nomadic people, the Avars, would replace the Huns as the biggest menace to the Roman Empire and its successor kingdoms. The Huns seem to have made no material or intellectual contribution to Western civilization. But they did leave a cultural legacy. As a common enemy of the peoples of the settled Mediterranean world, they embedded in Western culture a frightening memory of bloodthirsty steppe peoples who attacked from the east.

Cultural Encounters After the End of Roman Rule

By the mid-fifth century, when the fighting between their Germanic invaders and the Romans stopped, the two sides had to learn to live with one another. The Germanic rulers possessed military power but were vastly outnumbered by the Romans. For example, only 40,000 Vandals controlled North Africa, which had a population of several million Romans. And although the Romans had no military power, they dominated urban life and agricultural production. Both sides faced unique challenges. The newcomers had the special problem of staying separate from the population they ruled. The Romans in turn had to adapt traditions of urban life and education to the new realities of life under Germanic masters.

Of course, Roman culture did not abruptly come to an end with the last vestiges of Roman rule. It remained a vital presence in most regions, but it took different forms in the various lands now ruled by Germanic leaders. In Britain, Roman culture perhaps fared the worst. Little of it survived into later ages. Yet legends hint at a fierce resistance against the invaders. The stories about King Arthur that have captivated English-speaking audiences since the Middle Ages are

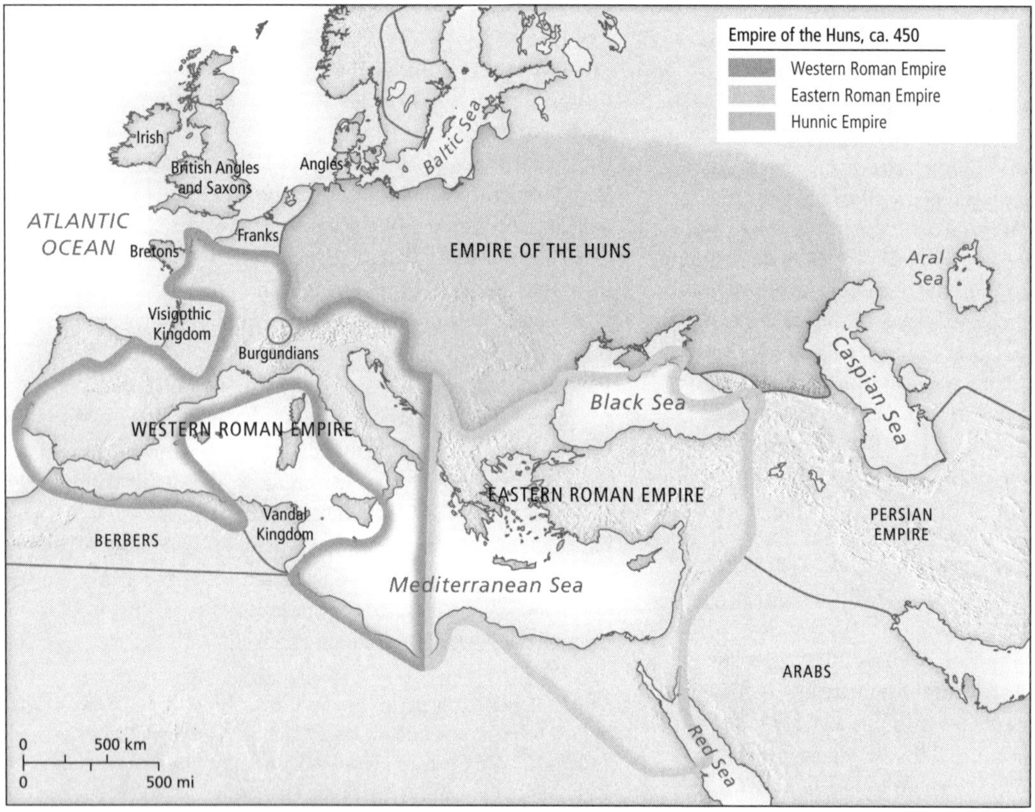

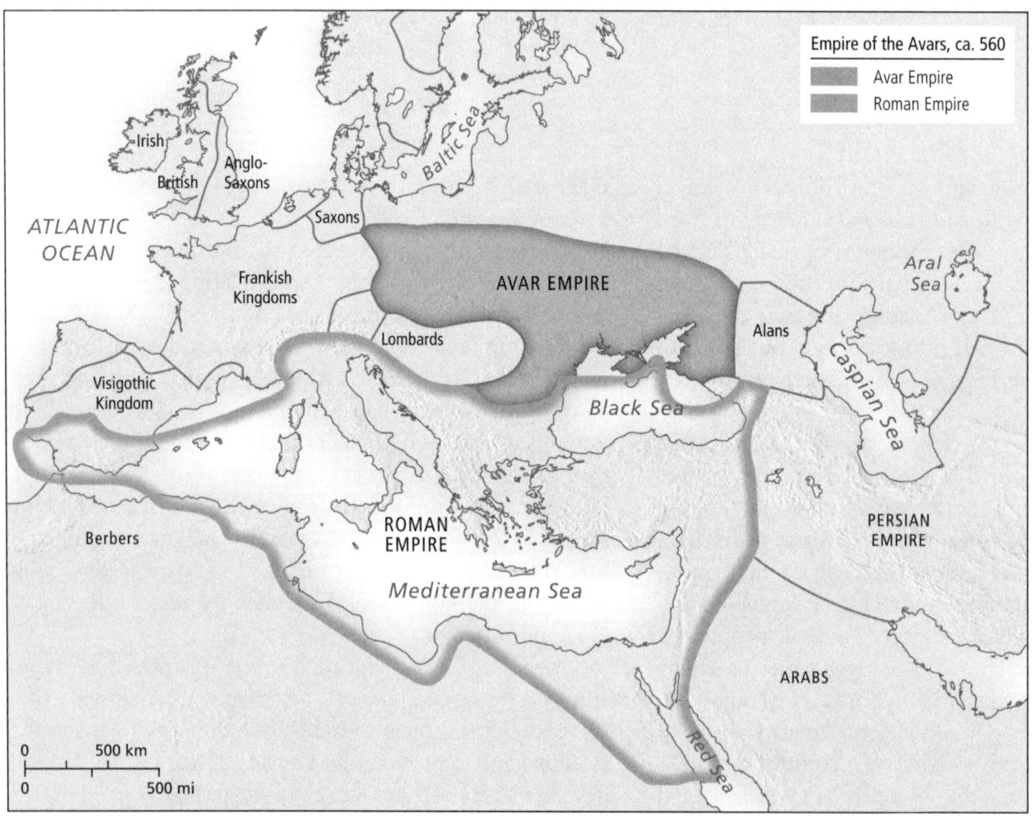

■ **Map 6.3 Nomad Empires**

During late antiquity, the Huns and later the Avars established powerful empires based on the Hungarian plain. These fierce horsemen terrified the settled peoples of the Roman world.

based on memories of valiant resistance to the Saxon invaders in the mid-fifth century.

In Gaul, North Africa, Italy, and Spain, the new settlers were Christian, which softened the shock of their presence. They followed Arian Christianity, however, a creed that viewed Jesus Christ as subordinate to God the Father. The Romans, on the other hand, followed orthodox Christianity and thus saw the invaders as heretics. Although this religious difference caused considerable friction between the two peoples, it also worked to their mutual advantage. Roman law forbade intermarriage between orthodox and Arian Christians, so the settlers remained a distinct minority in their new domains. This enabled them to maintain a separate Arian clergy and separate churches and hence a distinct identity in the midst of the vastly superior numbers of Roman provincials they ruled.

Confident in their position of power, the newcomers easily slipped into the role of military protectors of the Roman provincials they now ruled. For example, Vandal forces fought against Berber nomads from the foothills of the Atlas Mountains who tried to raid North Africa's fertile farmlands. To many Roman peasants, the new masters provided a welcome alternative to the callous imperial officials who had exploited them for so long. Salvian of Marseilles, a churchman who wrote in southern Gaul in the mid-fifth century, described the situation:

> *The Roman poor are despoiled, the widows groan, the orphans are tread underfoot, so much so that many of them . . . flee to the enemy . . . Although these Romans differ in religion and language from the barbarians to whom they flee, and differ from them in respect to filthiness of body and clothing, nevertheless . . . they prefer to bear among the barbarians a worship unlike their own rather than rampant injustice among the Romans. They prefer to live as freemen under an outward form of captivity than as captives under an appearance of liberty.*[5]

Of all the former empire's western provinces, Italy prospered the most under Germanic rule, particularly under the long reign of Theodoric the Ostrogothic (r. 493–526). In 493 Theodoric left the Balkans for Italy at the suggestion of the Roman emperor in Constantinople. The emperor told Theodoric that he could rule Italy if he was able to capture it from Odovacar, who was currently ruling there. The crafty emperor calculated that if Odovacar defeated Theodoric, the situation in Italy would remain unchanged, but a menace would be gone from the Balkins. If Theodoric won, the Balkans would be safe and there would be another barbarian ruling Italy. Either way he had little to lose and much to gain. Theodoric accepted the challenge and murdered Odovacar in Italy. Once on the throne of Italy, Theodoric took care to affirm his support for the Roman Empire and to acknowledge the emperor's superior status. In politics, Theodoric sought to create an atmosphere of mutual respect between Ostrogoths and Romans by maintaining two separate administrations—one for his Ostrogoths, the other for the Romans—so that both communities could manage their own affairs under his supervision. He also included aristocratic Romans among his closest advisers and most trusted administrators. Even in his religious policies Theodoric pursued mutual tolerance. As an Arian Christian, Theodoric supported a separate clergy, but he also maintained excellent ties with the pope, leader of the orthodox Roman Christians. Theodoric united Visigothic kingdoms in Spain and Gaul with his own in Italy, ultimately wielding great influence throughout western Europe. Under his rule Italy prospered, and the communities of Ostrogoths and Romans lived together amicably.

Throughout the western provinces, however, links to the Roman Empire in the east began to weaken. Most of the invaders had brought with them their traditional practice of pledging fidelity and obedience to a local chieftain, and this tradition began to eat away at loyalty to the far-off Roman emperor in Constantinople. By pledging themselves to a Germanic king, men gained a place in the "tribe" of their new chieftain. Many of these soldiers had served in units of the Roman army under their own officers, but now they looked to their king—not to the emperor—to provide gifts and the opportunities to win prestige, honor, and land. Thus service to the empire gradually gave way to oaths of loyalty to local chieftains. Over time, new warrior-based

CHRONOLOGY

Roman Empire, East and West

235–284	Crisis in Roman government
284	Diocletian begins imperial reforms
293	Tetrarchy established
312	Constantine wins control of western empire
330	Constantinople dedicated
378	Battle of Adrianople; Visigoths invade empire
406	Vandals and other tribes cross the Rhine
410	Romans withdraw from Britain; Visigoths plunder Rome
418	Visigoths settle in Gaul
429–439	Vandals take North Africa
434–453	Attila rules the Hunnic Empire
476	Romulus Augustulus, last western emperor, deposed
493–526	Theodoric the Ostrogoth rules Italy

aristocracies took shape in which landowning noblemen forged ties of personal loyalty to their local king.

Some deeply rooted Roman ways remained, however. Except for in Britain, where the language spoken by the Saxon invaders and their Angle allies took hold and began developing into the English spoken today, the settlers quickly learned the tongues of the provincials they ruled. Within several centuries these Latin-based "Romance" (based on the Roman speech) languages grew into the early versions of Italian, Spanish, and French. Latin continued as the language of literacy, and the settlers borrowed heavily from Roman literary forms. Writing in Latin, they produced histories of their tribal kingdoms in imitation of Roman historians. They also developed law codes composed in Latin influenced by Roman models.

The Cathedral of Holy Wisdom (Haghia Sophia)
When Justinian entered his newly completed cathedral of Holy Wisdom (Haghia Sophia) in Constantinople, he boasted, "Solomon, I have outdone you!" He meant that his church was bigger than the Jerusalem Temple built by the biblical King Solomon. For centuries Haghia Sophia was the largest building in Europe. In 1453 the church became a mosque. Today it is a public museum.

THE BIRTH OF BYZANTIUM

The Roman Empire endured in the eastern Mediterranean without interruption in late antiquity, despite the profound alterations wrought by Christianity and Rome's loss of the western provinces. Constantinople, the imperial city founded by Constantine in 324, became the center of a remodeled empire that over several centuries acquired both Christian and Roman characteristics. Historians have named this realm the Byzantine Empire, or Byzantium, although the inhabitants of the realm continued to think of themselves as Romans for a thousand years.

Christianity and Law Under Justinian

The most important amalgamation of Christian and Roman traditions took place during the reign of the emperor Justinian (r. 527–565). Born in the Balkans, Justinian was the last native Latin-speaking emperor. When his uncle became emperor in 518, Justinian was the real power behind the throne. He combined a powerful intellect, an unshakable Christian faith, and a driving ambition to reform the empire. He defied convention by marrying Theodora, a strong-willed former actress, and including her in imperial decision making once he took control of the empire in 527.

Justinian inaugurated a number of changes that highlighted his role as a Christian emperor. First of all, he emphasized the position of the emperor at the center of society in explicitly Christian terms. He was the first emperor to use the title "Beloved of Christ" and he amplified the emperor's role in Church affairs. Justinian considered it his duty as emperor to enforce uniform religious belief throughout his domain. By bullying clergymen and writing his own works on doctrinal matters he tried to usurp the bishops' control of the definition of orthodox Christianity. Justinian considered it his duty as emperor to enforce uniform religious beliefs throughout his domain. He ruthlessly purged non-Christians and heretical Christians from public life so that only men who were orthodox Christians could now hold government offices. In addition, Justinian directed Christian priests to force the conversion of surviving pockets of polytheists to orthodox Christianity.

Justinian attempted to create a Christian society by using Roman law coupled with military force. Unlike rulers of Rome's early empire, who permitted subject peoples to maintain their own customary laws, Justinian suppressed local laws throughout his realm. He envisioned all of his subjects obeying only Roman law—law that he defined and that God approved. (Justinian was sure that if God did not approve of his legislative changes, God would not allow him to continue as emperor.) Justinian believed that by spending orthodox Christianity throughout the empire he was spreading civilization.

Thus, in his God-given mission as emperor-legislator, Justinian reformed Roman law. In an effort to simplify the vast body of civil law, he ordered his lawyers to sort through all the laws that had accumulated over the centuries and determine which of them should still be enforced. This monumental effort, which was completed in 534, is known as the *Code of Justinian.* His lawyers also prepared a handbook of basic Roman law for law students, called the *Institutes,* as well as the *Digest,* a collection and summary of several centuries' worth of commentary on Roman law by legal experts. Justinian then banned any additional commentary on the law, naming himself as the only interpreter of existing laws and the sole source of new laws. While the *Code, Digest,* and *Institutes* were composed in Latin, the traditional legal language of Rome, Justinian's new legislation, called the *Novels,* was issued in Greek, the common language of the eastern empire. Collectively, this legal work is called the Corpus of Civil Law°. Roman law passed down to later generations primarily through this compilation. At the end of the eleventh century, scholars in Italy discovered manuscripts of Justinian's legal works in church libraries, and interest in Roman law began to revive. The *Digest* became the most influential legal text in medieval Europe. Thus the *Corpus* became a pillar of Latin-speaking European civilization.

Reconquering the Provinces in the West

Once he had reorganized Byzantium's legal system, Justinian turned his attention to Rome's fallen western provinces. He wanted to reestablish imperial control over Rome's western provinces, now ruled by Germanic kings. Between 533 and 554 Justinian's armies snatched back North Africa from the Vandals, seized Sicily and Italy from the Ostrogoths, and won parts of Spain from the Visigoths. With the empire nearly restored to its former glory, Justinian's plan was to impose his version of Christian orthodoxy upon the Arian Christian Vandals and Ostrogoths still living in his western domains. He would also force them to live under his version of Roman law and government.

In 533, Justinian sent a fleet of 10,000 men and 5,000 cavalry under the command of his general Belisarius to attack the Vandal kingdom in North Africa. The Vandal kingdom fell quickly, and within a year Belisarius celebrated his triumph in Constantinople. Encouraged by this easy victory, Justinian set his sights on Italy, where the Ostrogothic ruling family was embroiled in political infighting. But this time Justinian had underestimated his opponents. The Ostrogoths, who had won the support of the Roman population in Italy, mounted a fierce resistance to Belisarius's invasion in 536. Justinian, for his part, did not trust his own general and failed to support him with adequate funds and soldiers. Bitter fighting between Justinian's troops and the Ostrogothic armies dragged on

AN EMPRESS REFUSES TO PANIC

As Justinian's wife, Theodora exerted a strong influence at court and throughout the empire. Early in his reign, Justinian was almost driven from the throne in an urban riot called the Nika Revolt. When the emperor and his advisers were frantically discussing whether they should flee from Constantinople, Theodora's proud remarks persuaded her husband not to give up. His soldiers bolted the gates to the Hippodrome, where the protesters had gathered, and slaughtered at least 30,000 of them. The revolt ended.

As to the belief that a woman ought not to be daring among men or to assert herself boldly among those who are holding back from fear, I consider that the present crisis most certainly does not permit us to discuss whether the matter should be regarded in this or in some other way. For in the case of those whose interests have come into the greatest danger nothing else seems best except to settle the issue immediately before them in the best possible way. My opinion then is that at the present time, above all others, is inopportune for flight, even though it bring safety. For while it is impossible for a man who has seen the light also not to die, for one who has been emperor it is unendurable to be a fugitive. May I never be separated from this purple [the color of the imperial robes], and may I not live that day on which those who meet me shall not address me as mistress. If now it is your wish to save yourself, O Emperor, there is no difficulty. For we have much money, and there is the sea, here are the boats. However consider whether it will not come about that after you have been saved that you would gladly exchange that safety for death. For as for myself, I approve a certain ancient saying that royal robes are a good burial shroud.

Source: Reprinted by permission of the publishers and the Trustees of the Loeb Classical Library from *Procopius, Volume I,* Loeb Classical Library Volume LCL 48, translated by H. B. Dewing, Cambridge, Mass.: Harvard University Press, 1914. The Loeb Classical Library ® is a registered trademark of the President and Fellows of Harvard College.

JUSTICE IN HISTORY

Two Martyrdoms: Culture and Religion on Trial

Between the reigns of Diocletian (r. 284–305) and Justinian (r. 527–565) the status of Christians changed dramatically. Christians went from being a religious minority persecuted by the imperial government to a majority that persecuted non-Christians with the Roman government's backing. But one thing did not change during this period. Whether polytheist or Christian, Roman emperors used force to compel their subjects to believe and worship in prescribed ways and so, they hoped, keep the empire in the gods' good graces. To ensure religious conformity, emperors used the Roman judicial system. A comparison of the trials of a Christian soldier named Julius in 303, and Phocas, an aristocrat in Constantinople accused of paganism in 529 and 545, illustrates the objectives and methods of Roman government.

In 303 officials arrested a veteran soldier named Julius and brought him before the prefect Maximus. The following excerpt comes from a description of the trial[6]:

> *"Who is this?" asked Maximus. One of the staff replied: "This is a Christian who will not obey the laws." "What is your name?" asked the prefect. "Julius," was the reply. "Well, what say you, Julius?" asked the prefect. "Are these allegations true?" "Yes, they are," said Julius. "I am indeed a Christian. I do not deny that I am precisely what I am." "You are surely aware," said the prefect, "of the emperors' edicts which order you to sacrifice to the gods?" "I am aware of them," answered Julius. "I am indeed a Christian and cannot do what you want; for I must not lose sight of my living and true God." . . . "If you think it a sin," answered the prefect Maximus, "let me take the blame. I am the one who is forcing you, so that you may not give impression of having consented voluntarily. Afterwards you can go home in peace, you will pick up your ten-year bonus, and no one will ever trouble you again. . . . If you do not respect the imperial decrees and offer sacrifice, I am going to cut your head off." "That is a good plan," answered Julius, "Only I beg . . . that you execute your plan and pass sentence on me so that my prayers may be answered. . . . I have chosen death for now so that I might live with the saints forever." The prefect Maximus then delivered the sentence as follows: "Whereas Julius has refused to obey the imperial edicts, he is sentenced to death."*

After Constantine's conversion to Christianity in 312, persecution of Christians stopped, and Christian officials began to attack polytheism with the government's support. The emperor Justinian (r. 527–565) severely enforced laws against polytheists, executing anyone who sacrificed animals to non-Christian gods. During Justinian's reign, the imperial government launched three major persecutions of polytheists. In the first episode of persecution in 528–529, one year after Justinian ascended to the throne, a handful of government officials were charged with the crime of worshiping pagan gods. One of these men was Phocas the Patrician, a distinguished lawyer who held the post of Praetorian Prefect. Phocas was cleared of charges and released, but in 545–546, during the second wave of persecution, he was among the doctors, teachers, lawyers, and officials arrested and convicted. Rather than undergo the humiliation of public execution, Phocas committed suicide. Justinian ordered that his body be buried in a ditch like an animal, without prayer or ceremony of any sort. Phocas thus missed the third purge of 562, when polytheists were arrested throughout the empire, paraded in public, imprisoned, tried, and sentenced. Zealous crowds threw thousands of non-Christian books into bonfires in the empire's cities.

Why did the government use such a heavy hand in persecuting polytheists during Justinian's reign? Men like Phocas who were attacked as pagans were highly educated in the traditional learning of the Greco-Roman world. Indeed, it was this learning that was really on trial. Phocas and other victims had a deep commitment to traditional Roman culture; their "paganism" was not the furtive worship of old gods like Zeus or Apollo. Rather, Phocas was considered a pagan because he was loyal to classical philosophy, literature, and rhetoric, without any Christian overlay or interpretation. In Justinian's eyes, this sort of classical learning had no place in a Christian empire.

■ **Justinian**

This mid-sixth-century ivory panel depicts the emperor Justinian in a standard pose of Roman emperors. He rides a horse, while beneath his feet subject barbarians in native clothing bring offerings of gold and ivory. An angel of victory hovers next to the emperor, and another supports his foot. An attendant carries a statue adorned with a wreath of victory. At the top is a representation of Jesus holding a cross and making a gesture of blessing. The panel sends the message that Justinian rules the world with the approval and support of God.

Questions of Justice

1. How did the change from polytheism to Christianity alter the ways in which the Roman government understood religious persecution in late antiquity?
2. What did justice mean to the author of the trial of Julius the veteran soldier?

Taking It Further

Helgeland, John. *Christians in the Military: The Early Experience.* 1985. An introduction to the persecutions of Christians in the Roman army and their depiction in Christian literature.

Maas, Michael. *John Lydus and the Roman Past: Antiquarianism and Politics in the Age of Justinian.* 1992. This book explains how Justinian's policies about religion also involved an encounter with the empire's classical heritage.

for two decades. Justinian's armies eventually wrestled Italy back under imperial control, but the long-term effects of the protracted reconquest had disastrous consequences for Justinian's empire. The many years of fighting devastated Italy's cities and countryside. Between pouring precious financial resources into the Italy campaign and maintaining his grip on North Africa, Justinian was draining his empire's resources dry.

One of the reasons Justinian's reconquest of Italy took decades was the impact of the bubonic plague. The plague struck the empire in 542 and spread throughout Justinian's realm, migrating swiftly to Italy, North Africa, and Gaul. The first onslaught took the lives of perhaps half the population of Constantinople—about a quarter of a million people. An estimated one-third of the entire population of Byzantium's inhabitants succumbed to the dreaded disease. With the empire's population devastated by the plague, Justinian's army could not recruit the large number of soldiers it needed to fight on several fronts; the protracted battle for Italy was the result. But the plague's impact extended far beyond slowing Justinian's military adventures. Farms lay deserted and city populations shriveled. More than any other single factor, the bubonic plague weakened the Roman Empire and contributed to the eventual collapse of Mediterranean unity in the mid-seventh century.

After Justinian's death, Byzantine emperors would never again attempt to reestablish control over the entire Mediterranean world. Instead, they focused their attention on matters of more pressing interest closer to home. Justinian's ill-fated reconquests did, however, leave a mark on religious affairs in Mediterranean lands. The bishops of North Africa and Italy had deeply resented Justinian's attempts to Meddle in doctrinal matters. As a result a bitter division arose between Christian churches in the eastern and western Mediterranean—a chasm that would endure for centuries.

The Struggle with Persia

Although Justinian's greatest military successes—and religious failures—were in the western Mediterranean, his most dangerous enemy was the Persian Empire on his eastern flank. This huge, multi-ethnic empire, under the rule of the Sasanian dynasty (r. ca. 220–633), had been Rome's main rival throughout late antiquity. The tension stemmed chiefly from competition over Armenia, which was a source of excellent troops, and Syria, which possessed enormous wealth. From the time that Emperor Julian died in combat against Persia in 363, emperors at Constantinople kept up their guard against this eastern threat. Though wars were frequent, neither side could win permanent superiority over the other.

Justinian fought several brutal wars with Persia. The emperor gave top priority to the struggle on his eastern frontier by supplying more than half of the Byzantine troops, led by his best generals. He also provided more financial resources to the struggle in the east than to the wars of reconquest in the west. Chosroes I, the aggressive and ambitious Great King of Persia, proved to be a worthy adversary for Justinian. Chosroes often invaded the Byzantine Empire, causing great damage. In 540, for example, he sacked Antioch, the wealthiest city in Syria. Because war with Persia was extraordinarily expensive, Justinian made peace by paying thousands of pounds of gold to the Persian monarch in order to bring the fighting to a close. Even this great cost was less than continuing to fight every year. By the time of Justinian's death, the two superpowers had established an uneasy coexistence, but the basic animosity between them remained unresolved. For the next half century, Justinian's successors engaged in intermittent bitter warfare with the Persian rulers. This protracted struggle between Byzantium and Persia demonstrates how the Byzantines' most important enemies lay to the east. Fighting to regain

Map 6.4 The Byzantine Empire at the Death of Justinian

When Justinian died in 565, the territories of Italy, North Africa, and part of Spain that had been lost in the fifth century were restored, temporarily, to imperial rule.

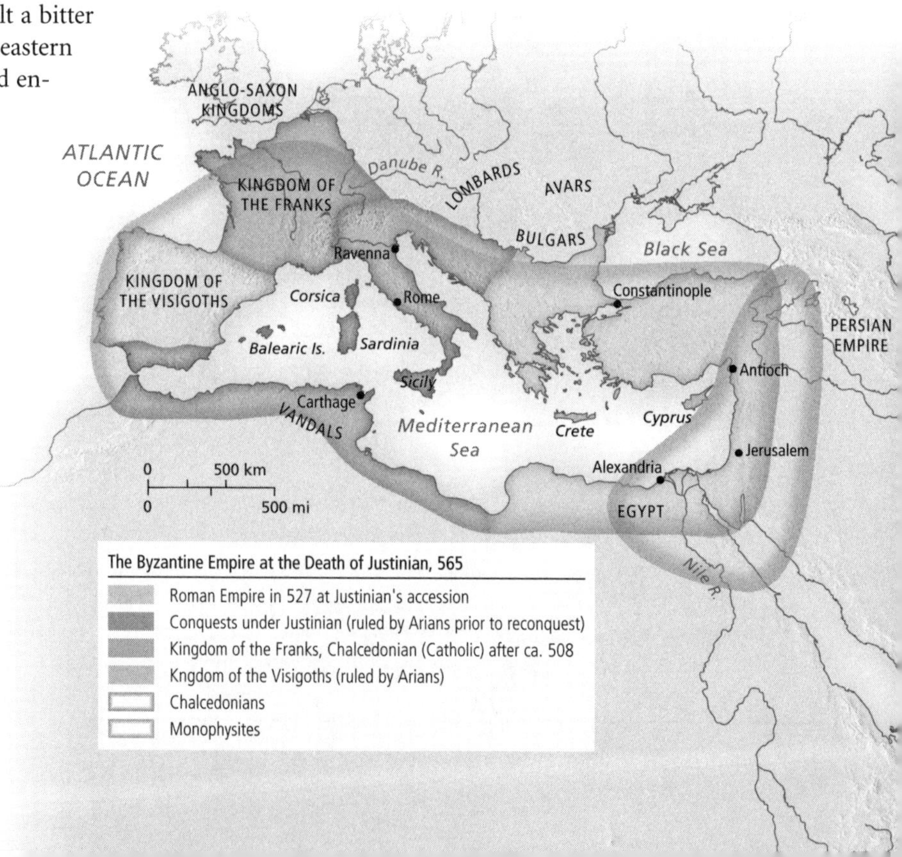

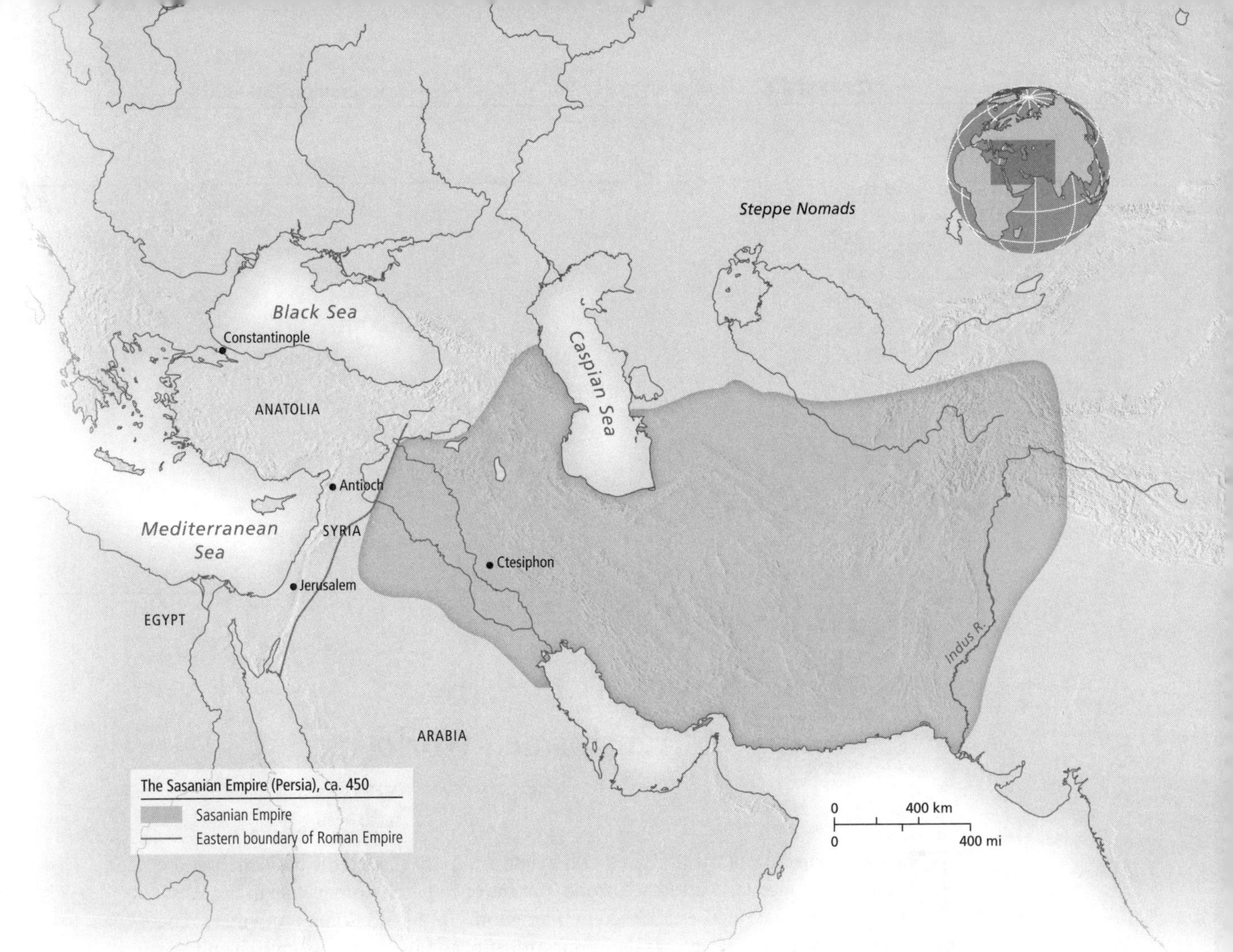

Map 6.5 The Persian Empire under the Sasanian Dynasty
Under the dynamic Sasanian dynasty, the Persian Empire fought many wars with Rome. The Persian Empire had equivalent resources to Rome.

provinces in the west brought glory, but war with Persia was a matter of life and death for the Byzantine Empire.

By fighting expensive wars on the eastern and western flanks of his empire, Justinian hastened the disintegration of Byzantine imperial rule. The overextension of resources ensured that Byzantium could not maintain lasting control of the western Mediterranean region. When new invaders descended on Italy and the Balkans in the late sixth century, the empire would not have the strength to resist them. The drain of resources on the Persian front helped weaken Byzantium as well. If Justinian had been less ambitious, it is likely that the Byzantine Empire could have withstood the attack of Muslim armies in the seventh centuries and retained control of provinces in North Africa, Egypt, and Syria. Nevertheless, Justinian succeeded in creating a Christian-Roman society, united under one God, one emperor, and one law. On the basis of the unified culture created by Justinian, the Byzantine Empire would survive for nearly a millennium—though on a smaller scale.

CHRONOLOGY

The Reign of Justinian and After

429	Plato's Academy in Athens closed
527–565	Reign of Justinian
532	Nika Revolt in Constantinople
527–533	Law Code of Justinian
534	Justinian's reconquest of North Africa
534–561	Reconquest of Italy
542	Plague strikes empire

Persian Coins and the Religion of Zoroaster

This silver Persian coin depicts the Sasanian Great King Ohrmazd II (302–309). He wears an elaborate crown. On the coin's other side two Zoroastrian priests tend a fire altar. Zoroastrianism was the state religion of the Persian Empire in late antiquity.

photo to come .587

CONCLUSION

A Transformed World

The transformation of the Roman world in late antiquity created the basic map of the West as we understand it today. Europe split into two parts. Roman rule in the West collapsed. Germanic rulers established new kingdoms in the old Roman provinces. These kingdoms spoke Romance languages derived from Latin, and used Latin in church and law. In the eastern Mediterranean, the Roman Empire developed in new ways. Christian and Roman civilization merged to create the vibrant Byzantine civilization.

When Islam emerged as a powerful religious and political entity at the end of the late antique period, as we will see in the next chapter, its adherents were by definition excluded from the European community of Christian believers. As a result, the North African, Middle Eastern, and Balkan lands that Islamic conquerors seized from the Byzantine Empire lost their place in the roster of "Western" communities, while those lands not conquered by Islam became the bastion of a civilization that defined itself as Western, European, and Christian.

Suggestions for Further Reading

For a comprehensive list of suggested readings, please go to www.ablongman.com/levack/chapter6

Bowersock, G. W. *Hellenism in Late Antiquity.* 1990. Explains the important role of traditional Greek culture in shaping late antiquity.

Bowersock, G. W., Peter Brown, and Oleg Grabar, eds. *Late Antiquity: A Guide to the Postclassical World.* 1999. An indispensable handbook containing synthetic essays and shorter encyclopedia entries.

Brown, Peter. *The Cult of the Saints: Its Rise and Function in Late Antiquity.* 1981. A brilliant and highly influential study.

Brown, Peter. *The Rise of Western Christendom: Triumph and Diversity.* 1996. An influential and highly accessible survey.

Brown, Peter. *The World of Late Antiquity.* 1971. A classic treatment of the period.

Cameron, Averil. *The Later Roman Empire.* 1993. *The Mediterranean World in Late Antiquity.* 1997. Excellent textbooks with bibliography and maps.

Clark, Gillian. *Women in Late Antiquity: Pagan and Christian Life-Styles.* 1993. The starting point of modern discussion, lucid and reliable.

Harries, Jill. *Law and Empire in Late Antiquity.* 1999. Explores the presence and practice of law in Roman society.

Lee, A. D. *Information and Frontiers: Roman Foreign Relations in Late Antiquity.* 1993. An exciting and original investigation.

Maas, Michael. *Readings in Late Antiquity: A Sourcebook.* 2000. Hundreds of ancient sources in translation illustrating all aspects of late antiquity.

Markus, Robert. *The End of Ancient Christianity.* 1995. Excellent introduction to the transformation of Christianity in late antiquity.

Rich, John, ed. *The City in Late Antiquity.* 1992. Important studies of changes in late antique urbanism.

Thompson, E. A. *The Huns,* rev. Peter Heather. 1996. The best introduction to major issues.

Notes

1. Libanius, *On the Temples,* in A. F. Norman, *Libanius: Selected Works* (1977), 107–109.
2. Ambrose, *Commentary on Paul's First Letter to the Corinthians,* trans. Karl Frederick Morrison, *Rome and the City of God* (1964), 46–47
3. Nigel G. Wilson, ed, *Saint Basil on the Value of Greek Literature* (1975).
4. Marcia L. Colish, *Medieval Foundations of the Western Intellectual Tradition* (1997), p. 49.
5. Salvian, *On the Government of God,* trans. Jeremiah O'Sullivan, *Fathers of the Church: The Writings of Salvian the Presbyter* (1947), 132–137, with some slight changes.
6. John Helgeland, Christians in the Military: The Early Experience (1985), p. 64–65.

CHAPTER

7

Byzantium, Islam, and the Latin West: The Foundations of Medieval Europe, 550–750

Chapter Outline

- Byzantium: The Survival of the Roman Empire
- The New World of Islam
- The Beginnings of Latin Christendom

One gray day in central Germany in 740, an English monk named Boniface swung his axe at an enormous oak tree. This was the sacred Oak of Thor, where German men and women had prayed for centuries to one of their mightiest gods. Some local Christians cheered and applauded the monk. But an angry crowd of men and women gathered as well, cursing Boniface for attacking their sacred tree. Then something extraordinary occurred. Though Boniface had only taken one small chop, the entire tree came crashing down, split neatly into four parts. Boniface's biographer, a monk named Willibald, explained the strange event as God's judgment against "pagan" worshipers. In Willibald's account of the incident, the hostile crowd was so impressed by the miracle that they immediately embraced Christianity. As the news spread, more and more Germans accepted the faith, and Boniface's fame grew. According to Willibald, "The sound of Boniface's name was heard through the greater part of Europe. From the land of Britain, a great host of monks came to him—readers, and writers, and men trained in other skills."[1]

Whether or not the miracle at the Oak of Thor actually occurred, Boniface, a skilled diplomat who cooperated closely with the pope in Rome, played a leading role in spreading Christianity among the peoples of northern Europe. The Christian missionaries who traveled to lands far beyond the Mediterranean world brought Latin books and established monasteries, where a few men and women learned to read and write. Through Christianity and the literacy that spread from these monastic centers, the monks established unbreakable ties to Roman learning and the late antique world.

But Boniface was not Roman. He was English, a descendant of the Anglo-Saxon invaders who took control of much of Britain after the Roman legions

Theodolinda's Gospel Book: Pope Gregory the Great gave a valuable copy of the Gospels to the Lombard queen Theodolinda when her son was christened in 603. Jewels, enamels, and Roman cameos decorated the book's covers. By giving lavish gifts to the polytheist rulers of Germanic states, Gregory hoped to encourage their conversion to Christianity.

abandoned it in the early fourth century. Boniface's England (as southern Britain is called after the Anglo-Saxon settlements) was just one of the former Roman provinces in western Europe in which Germanic and Roman cultures had mixed. In Spain, Italy, France, and North Africa as well, the new settlers grafted their societies onto a still-living Roman stalk. The intermingling of these cultures produced Christian kingdoms on a Roman foundation. Historians refer to these kingdoms collectively as Latin Christendom.

The Latin Christendom that came to dominate western Europe was only one of three major civilizations that emerged on the ruins of the late antique Roman world and that constituted the West during this period. A second major cultural force was taking shape as Boniface chopped down the Oak of Thor. This was the Byzantine Empire, which consisted of the eastern provinces of the Roman Empire. Roman rule continued uninterrupted in the Byzantine Empire, and its citizens continued to call themselves Roman. But because their capital was Constantinople, a city previously known as Byzantion, historians today refer to the inhabitants of the empire as Byzantines. By the time of Boniface the Byzantine Empire, also known as Byzantium, had dramatically shrunk in size and endured many hardships, especially in its wars with the Islamic Empire. But in the process Byzantium developed a vibrant Christian culture that spread through the Balkans and influenced eastern Europe and eventually Russia. As the dominant Christian power in the eastern Mediterranean, Byzantium played a significant role in Western political and cultural life for a thousand years as a vigorous, militaristic empire; as a center of learning and as the most important intermediary between the peoples of western Europe and the Middle East.

During this same period, another religion—Islam—shook the foundations of the late antique world, creating a third major civilization. In the century after the death of its founder, the prophet Muhammad, in 632, Islam's followers burst from their home in Arabia to conquer an empire stretching from Spain to central Asia. Muslims (believers in Islam) rejected Christianity and did not adopt Roman law. Nevertheless they absorbed some Roman institutions of imperial government, which played a fundamental role in shaping their empire.

We consider all three of these medieval civilizations—Latin Christendom, Byzantium, and Islam—parts of Western civilization because they emerged in the Middle East and Europe, the core lands where civilization began. Moreover, all three drew from Rome's cultural, administrative, and religious legacy, although in different ways. Finally, these civilizations all centered on monotheistic religions that shared basic beliefs about God and the origin of their faiths. However, because each of these medieval civilizations defined itself as an exclusive community of faith, cultural and political boundaries developed between them that are still visible today. Byzantium and Latin Christendom grew apart, and Islam gained an adversarial status in Christian eyes that continues in the minds of some people to this day.

These three civilizations transformed the world of late antiquity. Historians call the new era they inaugurated the Middle Ages (550–1450), or the West's medieval period. To understand the impact of this era, we will explore three questions in this chapter: (1) How did the Roman Empire's eastern provinces evolve into the Byzantine Empire? (2) How did Islam develop in Arabia, and how did its followers create a vast empire so quickly? (3) How did Latin Christendom—the new kingdoms of western Europe—build on Rome's legal and governmental legacies and how did Christianity spread in these new kingdoms?

Byzantium: The Survival of the Roman Empire

The emperor Justinian (r. 527–565) tried to restore the glory of the Roman Empire by reconquering Roman provinces in North Africa, Italy, and part of Spain from Germanic rulers who had established kingdoms in these territories in the fifth century. When Justinian died, his realm extended from southern Spain to the Persian frontier. As we saw in Chapter 6, it was an empire in which many of the institutions and traditions of the late antique Roman state, such as the imperial bureaucracy and provincial organization, still functioned. Despite these continuities with the Roman Empire of earlier centuries, Justinian brought profound changes to his empire. By insisting that his subjects follow Orthodox Christianity and by eradicating the last traces of polytheist worship, he gave religious unity and strength to his empire. By emphasizing the role of Christianity in every aspect of his government, education, and other aspects of daily life, he made classical culture a part of Christian life. Because of these profound changes in imperial life that Justinian's reign inaugurated, historians refer to the Roman Empire during his reign and afterwards as the Byzantine Empire. After Justinian's death in 565, the Byzantine empire began losing territory to enemies who surrounded the empire on all sides. The economy changed due to the loss of rich territories to Islamic conquerors. In response, emperors reorganized Byzantium for military purposes. Several important Roman institutions remained from late antiquity, however: the emperor with his imperial bureaucracy, the army, and the Orthodox Church. These institutions gave strength to the Byzantine empire and helped it endure many challenges.

AN EMBATTLED EMPIRE

By 750, the Byzantine Empire was reduced to a much smaller regional power struggling for survival against many enemies. Italy fell to Lombard invaders. Avars and Slavs seized the Balkans. The worst threat came from the Muslim armies that conquered Egypt, North Africa, and Syria, the empire's richest territories. As the Byzantines struggled to recover from these catastrophic losses, their fragile empire began to change.

The Balkan Front: Avars, Slavs, and Bulgars

The Avars were a nomadic people with a bone-chilling reputation for cruelty and ferocity in warfare who first appeared on the steppes north of the Black Sea in the sixth century. Based in the plains of present-day Hungary, the Avars' territory extended into central Europe. These tenacious warriors posed a constant menace to the new kingdoms taking shape in Italy and France as well as Byzantium.

Like the Huns in the fifth century, the Avars created an empire by forcing conquered peoples to serve in their armies. Some of the peoples were Slavs. Between about 400 and 600, Slavic societies had formed from an blending of many cultures and ethnic groups, including Dacians, Goths, and Sarmatians. The Slavic communities that developed in eastern Europe between the Baltic Sea and the Balkans lay outside Byzantium's borders. Thus, they knew little of Roman models of politics, administration, agriculture and social organization. Their Avar conquerors ruled by brute force, and most Slavs could not win back their independence. A few Slavic communities managed to overthrow Avar rule, however. In the middle of the seventh

Map 7.1 The Byzantine Empire, ca. 600

By 600 the Byzantine Empire consisted of Anatolia, Greece, part of the Balkans, Syria, Egypt, and some territories in North Africa and Spain. The Persian empire remained its greatest enemy.

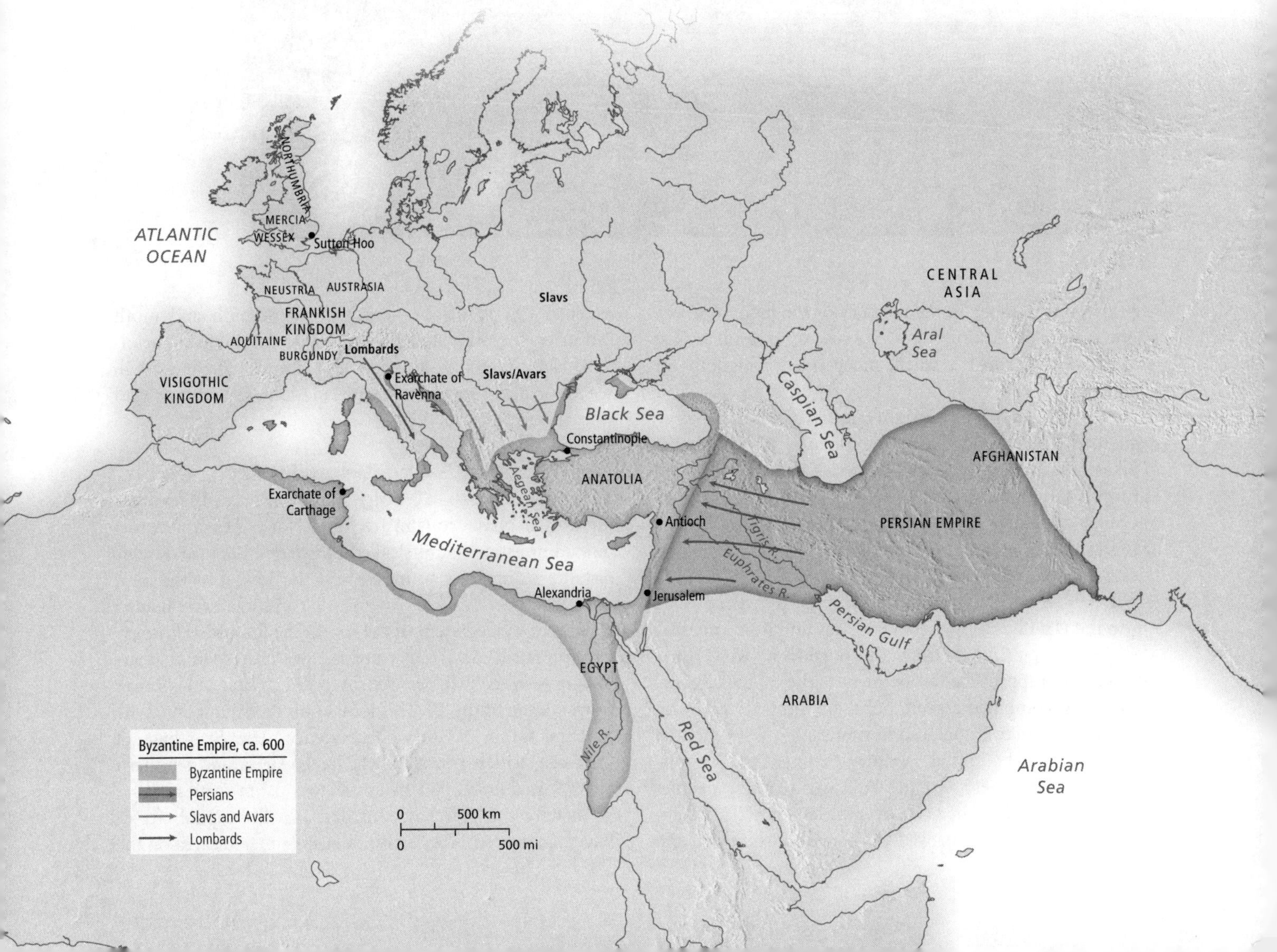

(a)

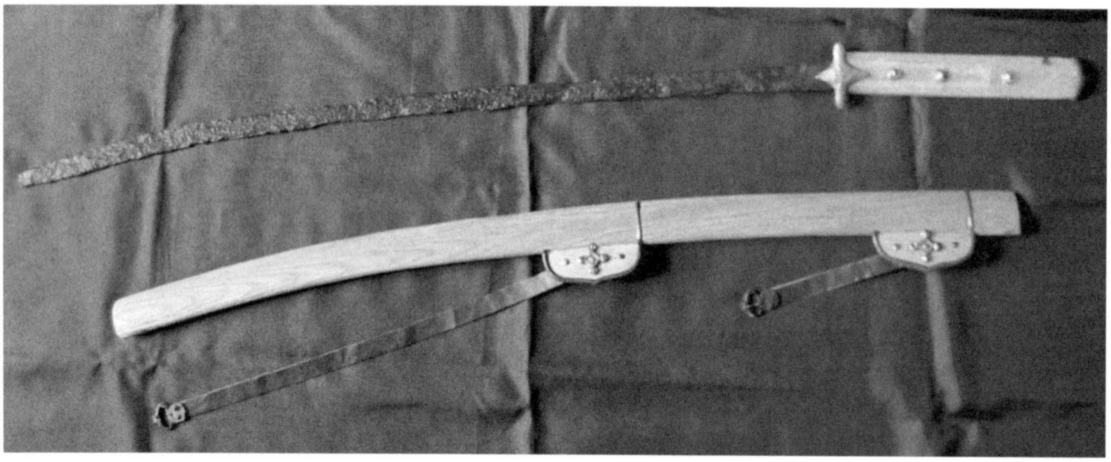

(b)

Avar Stirrups Supported the Weight of Heavily Armed Cavalry

Originally a nomadic people from central Asia, the Avars settled in Hungary and created an empire in central Europe. They depended on their heavily armed cavalry in battle. Byzantine military writers carefully studied Avar cavalry tactics and maneuvers. This pair of iron stirrups (a) gave an Avar rider extra striking power with a slashing saber (b).

century, for example, in the territory of the modern Czech Republic, the Slavic king Samo led a successful revolt against the Avars and ruled a small, independent kingdom for nearly forty years.

In the second half of the sixth century, bands of Slavs began to migrate south across the Danube River into the Balkans, searching for new homes. Collaborating with groups of marauding Avars, the Slavs settled in sparsely populated frontier lands in the northern Balkans. As the Slavs pushed south, many Byzantines fled their cities, abandoning them to the invaders.

By 600, Slavic groups had seized most Byzantine lands from the Danube to Greece. In 626, Slav and Avar forces attacked Constantinople from the northwest, while their Persian allies approached from the east. The capital city survived their combined assault, but the Byzantines never reasserted control over their old territories.

Farther north, in the territory between the Danube River, the Black Sea, and the Balkans, nomadic peoples called Bulgars established rule over the largely Slavic inhabitants. The Bulgars destroyed old Roman cities there and expelled Christians. Between the late seventh and ninth centuries, the Slavs and Bulgars merged into an independent Slavic-speaking kingdom called Bulgaria. As we will see in the next chapter, this new kingdom frequently waged war with Byzantium.

The Italian and North African Fronts

At the end of the sixth century, Byzantine emperors reorganized their possessions in Italy and North Africa into two new administrative units called *exarchates.* Because of their distance from Constantinople and the weight of the local problems they confronted, the two exarchates remained somewhat independent of the rest of the Byzantine Empire. Governors called exarchs ruled the exarchates, holding authority over civilian as well as military affairs—a break from Roman tradition. This joint command augmented the exarch's authority and independence. The Exarchate of Carthage, which consisted of North Africa and southern Spain, lasted until 698 when it fell to Muslim armies.

In Italy, the exarchate was based in the capital city of Ravenna, located in an easily defensible marshy area on the northeastern coast. The Exarchate of Ravenna consisted of Byzantine possessions in Italy and Sicily, including the city of Rome, where the support of the pope was important for implementing Byzantine policies. After the Lombard invasion in the late sixth century, the Exarchs of Ravenna struggled to maintain control of Italy. The Lombards eventually captured Ravenna and put an end to the exarchate in 751.

The Persian Front

Ruled by the Sasanian dynasty, Persia continued to threaten Byzantium after Justinian's death. The two powers fought intermittently for the rest of the sixth century. In 602 the struggle entered a new and final phase when the Persian king Chosroes II launched a series of devastating attacks against Byzantium. In 614 he seized Antioch, the richest Roman city in Syria. Then he captured Jerusalem, the holiest Christian city in the Byzantine Empire, and stole the holiest relic in the Christian world: a fragment of the cross on which Jesus reportedly had been crucified.

Motivated by a desire to avenge these losses and regain the holy relics, the Byzantine emperor Heraclius (r. 610–641) devoted his life to crushing the Persians once and for all. This resourceful and tenacious emperor spent most of his reign locked in a life-and-death struggle against Persia. In 622 Heraclius took a huge gamble. Leaving Constantinople in the hands of its capable patriarch Sergius, he led the Byzantine army deep into Persian territory, where he campaigned for years at a time. Believing that Constantinople now lay vulnerable due to the emperor's absence, the Persians made an alliance with the Avars in 626 and attacked the Byzantine capital. The city's massive walls thwarted their assault. After two more years of desperate fighting, Heraclius finally defeated Chosroes on Persian territory.

When Heraclius defeated the Persian emperor, he recovered the fragment of Jesus' cross that had been stolen from Jerusalem. When the Byzantine emperor returned the cherished relic to Jerusalem, he won a spiritual as well as a military and political triumph. Writers of the day described his struggle with Persia as a victory of Christianity. Heraclius announced his victory to the inhabitants of Constantinople with these words: "Let all the earth raise a cry to God . . . and let all we Christians, praising and glorifying, give thanks to the one God, rejoicing with great joy in his holy name, for fallen is the arrogant Chosroes, opponent of God." Despite the rejoicing, Heraclius's victory over Persia had exacted a huge toll. It left the Byzantines (and the Persians) too exhausted to resist the sudden onslaught of a new enemy, the Muslim Arab armies.

The Islamic Front

A ferocious new enemy challenged Byzantium from the east after the defeat of the Persian emperor—the armies of Islam. After the establishment of the Islamic caliphate in the

LEVA.8336.603
photo to come

David Plate

Nine silver plates made in Constantinople about 630 illustrate scenes from the career of the biblical King David. The largest plate (about 20 inches in diameter) shows David battling the giant Goliath. Though the subject matter is biblical, the style of representing clothing, human bodies, and spatial relationships comes directly from the Classical tradition. The artist may have intended to show a connection between the warrior king of the Bible and the emperor Heraclius, who defeated the mighty Persian emperor Chosroes II.

FAILURE OF COMMUNICATION BETWEEN EMPEROR AND CALIPH

The Byzantine emperor Leo III (r. 717–741) corresponded with the Caliph Umar II (r. 717–720). This letter from Leo demonstrates the importance of religious beliefs in defining relations between the two empires. Leo's letter sarcastically criticizes Muslim beliefs and refuses to address Umar by his Muslim religious title "Chief of the Believers." There would be little progress in the mutual understanding of Muslims and Christians for the next thousand years.

Emperor Flavianus Leo, the Servant of Jesus Christ . . . to Umar, the Chief of the Saracens:

What exact reply can I make to all the arguments you advance against me? . . . As a matter of fact, nothing would induce us to discuss with you our doctrines, since our Lord and Master Himself (Jesus Christ) has bidden us refrain from exposing our unique and divine doctrine before heretics, for fear it be turned into ridicule, and least of all before those to whom the predictions of the Prophets of the Bible and the testimony of the Apostles are as something strange. This is the rule we preserve towards others. It is true that we have several times written to you, and shall write to you again as necessity demands, but it has always been about mundane affairs, never about affairs divine. Still, Holy Writ bids us reply to those who question us and maintain silence before those who do not. You call "the Way of God" these devastating raids which bring death and captivity to all peoples. Behold your religion and its recompence. Behold your glory, you who pretend to live an angelic life. As for us, instructed in and convinced of the marvelous mystery of our redemption, we hope, after our resurrection, to enjoy the celestial kingdom, so we are submissive to the doctrines of the Gospel, and wait humbly for a happiness such that "eyes have never seen it, nor ears ever heard it, but which God has prepared for those who love Him" (I Cor. II,9). We do not hope to find there springs of wine, honey or milk. We do not expect to enjoy there commerce with women who remain forever virgin, and to have children by them, for we put no faith in such silly tales engendered by extreme ignorance and by paganism. May such dreams, such fables remain distant from us. "The kingdom of God consisteth not in eating and drinking" (Rom.XIV.17), as saith the Holy Spirit, "but in justice," and "at the resurrection men will not marry women, nor women men, but they shall be as the angels" (Matt. XXII,30). For you who are given up to carnal vices, and who have never been known to limit the same, you who prefer your pleasures to any good, it is precisely for that reason that you consider the celestial realm of no account if it is not peopled with women.

Source: From A. Jeffrey, "Gevond's Text of the Correspondence between Umar II and Leo III," *Harvard Theological Review*, (Cambridge, MA, 1944), vol. 37, pp. 281, 328-330.

630s, Islamic armies in search of booty attacked the Byzantine Empire every year from the east, raiding deep into Anatolia (modern Turkey) and sometimes threatening Constantinople itself. In 636, the formidable enemy crushed a Byzantine army at the battle of the Yarmuk River, forcing the Byzantines to abandon the wealthy province of Syria. A few years later Arab troops seized Egypt from Byzantine hands. Encouraged by their victories, an enormous Arab force of more than 100,000 men and 1,800 ships besieged Constantinople itself between 716 and 718. The attack failed completely because of the courage of the defenders, the strength of Constantinople's walls, and logistical problems among the Arabs. Some Byzantines claimed that the Virgin Mary had helped defend their capital.

Undismayed by their failure to capture Constantinople, Arab troops soon resumed their annual raids into Byzantine territory, defeating every Byzantine army that opposed them. Finally, in 740, Emperor Leo III (r. 717–741) won the Byzantine Empire's first important victory over the Muslim armies at the battle of Akroinon in western Asia Minor. Exhausted Byzantine troops could not go on the offensive, but they had slowed Arab momentum against their empire.

EMPEROR, ARMY, AND CHURCH

Despite assaults from so many directions, three institutions enabled the Byzantine Empire to survive the turmoil of its times: the emperor who set policies and safeguarded his subjects' welfare; the army that defended the realm's frontiers; and the Christian Church, which provided spiritual guidance.

Imperial Administration and Economy

Based in the capital city of Constantinople, the emperor stood at the very center of Byzantine society. His authority, which his people believed had been granted by God, reached to every corner of the empire. This supreme ruler governed with the assistance of a large bureaucracy that he tightly controlled. In this hierarchical bureaucracy different clothing indicated different levels of importance. Only the emperor or members of his household, for example, could wear the color purple, a symbol of royalty. High dignitaries wore silk garments of different colors encrusted with jewels; the higher the official, the more gems he was permitted to display. Courtiers lined up in elaborate processions in order of their importance, as indicated by the color of their clothing and shoes.

Men fortunate enough to obtain a job in the imperial government acquired considerable wealth and influence. For this reason leading provincial families sent their sons to Constantinople in search of positions in the imperial hierarchy. Through this method of recruitment Constantinople remained in close touch with the outlying regions of the empire. However, many men obtained their positions by bribing court officials who worked for the emperor. This practice produced corruption throughout the system as officials gave jobs to men on the basis of bribes rather than talent.

From his position at the head of this elaborate hierarchy, the emperor controlled Byzantium's economy. When Justinian died, the imperial taxation system that Constantine had established in the early fourth century still generated the funds that kept the imperial system working. Imperial officials also minted coins, enriching many cities and spurring a flourishing cash-based economy.

By the end of the seventh century, however, when the rich provinces of Egypt and Syria and the wealthy cities of Alexandria, Antioch, Jerusalem, and many others had fallen to the Arabs, the Byzantine economy stumbled. Thousands of refugees from lands conquered by Muslims streamed into the empire and strained its dwindling resources. In conquered provinces, Muslim rulers monopolized Middle Eastern trade revenues and prevented Byzantine merchants from participating in long-distance commerce. Cut off from foreign markets, Byzantines stopped manufacturing goods for export. As the economy shriveled, Byzantines stopped building new homes and churches. By 750, the standard of living in most Byzantine cities steeply declined.

The Military System

Byzantine society was organized in constant preparation for war. Emperors relied on their armies to protect Constantinople, the nerve center of the shrinking Byzantine state, and defend against invaders. By about 650, emperors abandoned the late antique system of provinces and reorganized their forces in Asia Minor into four military districts called themes, each with its own army and administration commanded by a general chosen by the emperor. The theme's armies developed strong traditions of local identity and prided themselves on their expert military skills a legacy the Byzantine Empire inherited from Rome. These military forces remained strong enough to keep the empire from collapsing in spite of devastating losses to Islamic armies throughout the seventh century.

By 750 the themes developed considerable independence from Constantinople and were the basis of further reorganization of the agricultural economy and procedures for recruitment. Soldiers and sailors who were once paid in cash from the emperor's tax revenues now were granted land on which to support themselves. Fighting men had to provide their own weapons from their income as farmers.

Even with reorganized defenses, Constantinople could not be protected without naval power. During the seventh and eighth centuries, the Byzantine fleet successfully kept Arab forces at bay through the use of "Greek Fire," a kind of napalm hurled against enemy ships to ignite them. Muslims soon learned how to use "Greek Fire," but the Byzantines used it more effectively in battle.

The Church and Religious Life

Most Byzantines identified themselves as Orthodox Christians, meaning that they followed the kind of Christianity practiced by the emperor and the court in Constantinople. They accepted the doctrines established by the Council of Chalcedon in 451 that defined Christ's human and divine natures as being united in one divine "person" without any separation, division, or change. This distinguished Byzantine Christians from other Christian communities that interpreted the nature of Christ differently, as we saw in Chapter 6. Constantinople boasted so many churches and sacred relics that by 600 Byzantines had begun to think of it as a holy city, protected by God and under the special care of the Virgin Mary, Jesus' human mother. Churchmen taught that Constantinople was a "New Jerusalem" that would be at the center of events at the end of days when God would bring history to an end and judge humanity.

Like the empire itself, the Byzantine clergy had a hierarchical organization. The Patriarch (or chief bishop) of Constantinople led the Orthodox Church, administering several thousand clergymen in the capital and directing church affairs throughout the empire. Emperors generally controlled the Patriarchs, and often they worked closely together, serving Byzantium's spiritual needs. The Patriarch helped impose religious unity throughout Byzantium by controlling the network of bishops

Christ on Byzantine Coins: An Emperor's Piety
Coins often indicate beliefs important to the society that minted them. The emperor Justinian II (685–695) introduced a new kind of coin that for the first time depicted the head of Christ. The emperor moved his own image holding a cross to the back of the coin, a statement of his subordination to Christ.

LEVA.8336.600
photo to come

Continuity in Portraits of God from Polytheism to Christianity

This fine icon of Christ Pantokrator (Lord of All) is located in the monastery of Saint Catherine at Mount Sinai in Egypt. Painted in the last decades of the seventh century, it portrays Christ's face in the same style that we can see on coins of the period. (See the illustration on page xxx.) The icon demonstrates the highest level of Roman painting techniques. With its long hair and beard, Christ's portrait echoes ancient representations of Zeus, chief of the old Greek gods. We can see similarities between the portrait and this marble head of Zeus from the fourth century B.C.E.

based in cities. As leaders of urban religious life, bishops supervised the veneration of the saints' relics stored in each city's churches. Byzantines believed that the relics protected each community, as the pagan gods had done in the pre-Christian past. Bishops often came from the city's elite, and they continued the centuries-old Mediterranean tradition of leadership and decision making on the local level.

Many cities also had monasteries, which played a significant role in the empire's daily life. Most important, men and women went to separate monasteries to live a spiritual life, praying for their salvation and that of other people. People in need of assistance, such as orphans, the elderly, battered wives, and the physically and mentally ill, found refuge and assistance in many monasteries. Monks and nuns regularly distributed food and clothing to the needy outside the monastery walls. Generous donors gave lavishly to monasteries to fund these activities, and many monasteries grew extremely wealthy through these gifts. Some monks championed the use of images of Jesus, the Virgin Mary, and the saints as means of reaching God.

As the Islamic Empire absorbed groups whom the Orthodox Christian Byzantines considered heretical, such as Monophysite Christians living in Syria and Egypt, Byzantium's population became almost entirely Orthodox. The resulting unity of faith and culture helped hold the empire together during its darkest hours in the seventh century.

During the seventh and eighth centuries, the traditional Roman educational system gave way to Christian instruction. As we saw in Chapter 6, by about 600, city leaders had stopped paying schoolmasters to offer traditional instruction because they lacked funds. Pious Christians also developed a deep suspicion of classical learning, with its references to ancient gods and customs frowned on by the Church. People now learned how to read by studying the Bible, not the classics of Greek antiquity. Knowledge of classical literature and science disappeared everywhere except in Constantinople, and even there the academic community was tiny. Byzantines nearly forgot the history and knowledge of classical antiquity. For example, many Byzantines thought that the marble statues from earlier centuries adorning their cities were sinister demons.

During the seventh century, most Byzantines could neither read nor write. Only a few people obtained an education in law, literature, mathematics, or philosophy. Use of Latin disappeared except among those scribes who communicated with the kingdoms of western Europe. No more than a handful of Byzantines could write the elegant Greek that had been the language of learning for nearly 2,000 years.

Icons and the Iconoclastic Controversy

As the Muslims and other enemies tore at the empire, Byzantines wondered why God was punishing them so severely. Their only answer was that somehow they were failing God. Convinced that only appeasing God could save them, Emperor Leo III (r. 717–741) took action. First he forcibly converted communities of Jews to Christianity in order to make a uniformly Christian empire. Second, he challenged the use of icons°, the images of God and saints found everywhere in Byzantine worship.

Byzantine theologians understood icons as vehicles through which the divine presence could make itself accessible to believers. Churchmen cautioned that God or saints do not actually reside within the icons, and so believers should not worship the images themselves. Rather, they should consider icons as doorways to a spiritual world, enabling believers to encounter a holy presence. Thus Byzantines treated icons with great love and respect.

The first Christians refused to make images of Christ and other holy individuals. They had two reasons for banning such representations. First, the Hebrew Bible forbids creating any representations of God. Second, they thought that Christians might start to worship their images in the same way that polytheists worshiped statues in their temples. "When images are put up, the customs of the pagans do the rest," wrote one church leader in the fourth century.

Despite such warnings, Christians responded to the beautiful polytheist statues and images that filled the cities in which they lived. Christian sculptors and painters started to create a uniquely Christian art that combined religious beliefs with the styles and techniques of classical art. After Constantine converted to Christianity in 312 and put an end to the persecution of Christians, this new art flourished. Artists routinely portrayed Christ and the saints in churches. During the sixth and seventh centuries Byzantines used religious images with greater zeal than ever before. By 600, for example, the emperor placed a large image of Christ above the Bronze Gate, the main entrance to the imperial palace in Constantinople. Smaller paintings became intensely popular in churches and in people's homes.

Some Byzantine religious thinkers in the eighth century advised Emperor Leo that icon veneration should be halted because too many people thought icons were divine themselves. Following their advice, Leo decided to forbid use of icons, but public resistance forced him to move very carefully. For example, when he ordered workers to remove the image of Christ from the Bronze Gate at the imperial palace in 726, the people of the city rioted. Four years later, Leo forbade the presence and veneration of holy images (except for crucifixes) throughout the empire on his own authority as the ruler chosen by God. The prohibition and destruction of icons, known as iconoclasm° (image breaking), sparked a bitter controversy that divided Byzantine society until 842.

Leo's iconoclasm backfired because the veneration of icons was such a vital part of popular religious life. He found it difficult to enforce iconoclasm outside Constantinople. For example, especially in Greece and southern Italy, revolts sometimes broke out when imperial messengers arrived

CHRONOLOGY

The Byzantine World

527–565	Reign of Justinian I
542	Bubonic plague spreads through Mediterranean
568	Lombards invade Italy
610	Heraclius arrives from Carthage and begins reign
614–616	Persians take Jerusalem and Egypt
624	Heraclius campaigns in Transcaucasus
626	Avars and Persians besiege Constantinople
630	Heraclius defeats Persian king and restores True Cross to Jerusalem
636	Byzantines lose Battle of Yarmuk: Arabs take Syria and Jerusalem
642	Muslims take Egypt
698	Muslims take Carthage
716–718	Muslims besiege Constantinople
740	Byzantines defeat Arabs at Akroinos
751	Lombards conquer Ravenna and end the Exarchate of Italy

LEVA.8336.601
photo to come

An Icon that Survived Iconoclasm: St. Peter in the Monastery at Mount Sinai
This image of St. Peter, painted sometime during the sixth century, is in the Monastery of St. Catherine on Mount Sinai in Egypt. Because Egypt was in Muslim hands when the Iconoclastic Controversy broke out, this image survived.

with orders to destroy images. The iconoclastic controversy affected international politics as well. Outraged by the emperor's prohibition of icons, the pope excommunicated Leo. In retaliation the emperor deprived the pope of political authority over southern Italy, Sicily, and Illyricum (the Balkan coast of the Adriatic Sea). The Roman popes never forgave the emperor for this slight. This conflict contributed to a growing rift between Greek Orthodox and Latin Christianity.

After years of turmoil, two Byzantine empresses who sympathized with their subjects' religious convictions restored icons to churches. In 797, the empress Irene called a general church council that reversed Leo's ruling. After a brief renewal of iconoclasm, in 843 the empress Theodora introduced a religious ceremony for commemorating images, which Orthodox Christians still celebrate annually. Icons remain an integral part of Orthodox worship today.

The New World of Islam

The Muslim armies that battered Byzantium created a thriving civilization that transformed the Mediterranean world. Today more than one billion Muslims around the globe adhere to Islam, playing a significant role in world affairs. This rapidly growing faith has left an indelible stamp not only on the West but also on the rest of the world.

Islam originated in the early seventh century among the inhabitants of the Arabian peninsula. Like Christianity 600 years earlier, the new religion's emergence surprised the settled communities of the Middle Eastern and Mediterranean worlds. Through conquest and expansion, Muslims created a single Islamic Empire stretching from Spain to central Asia by 750. In this section we will examine Islam's roots and impact on neighboring emires, and the imperial realm created by the Arab peoples.

ARABS BEFORE ISLAM

Before the emergence of Islam, Arabs were tribal people from the Arabian peninsula and the Middle East who spoke Arabic, a semitic language related to Hebrew, Aramaic, and Akkadian. Despite their shared language, Arab communities took different forms. Those living in the interior of the Arabian peninsula led a nomadic life herding camels. On the edges of the desert they raised goats and sheep. In south Arabia, they farmed and lived in towns. These communities, however, were not unified into a single state.

Arabs have a long history in the Middle East. They were first mentioned in the Hebrew Bible about 1000 B.C.E., and Middle Eastern, Greek, and Roman historical records continued to describe them for 1,500 years as raiders of settled communities, but never as serious military threats. The Arabs became more dangerous to their enemies after 300 B.C.E. because of a military innovation. They developed a new kind of saddle that let them ride the one-humped Arabian camel with greater comfort and efficiency in battle. Up to this time it took two men to use a camel in warfare, one to hold the reins and the other to hold the weapons. The new saddle let one rider grasp the camel's reins with

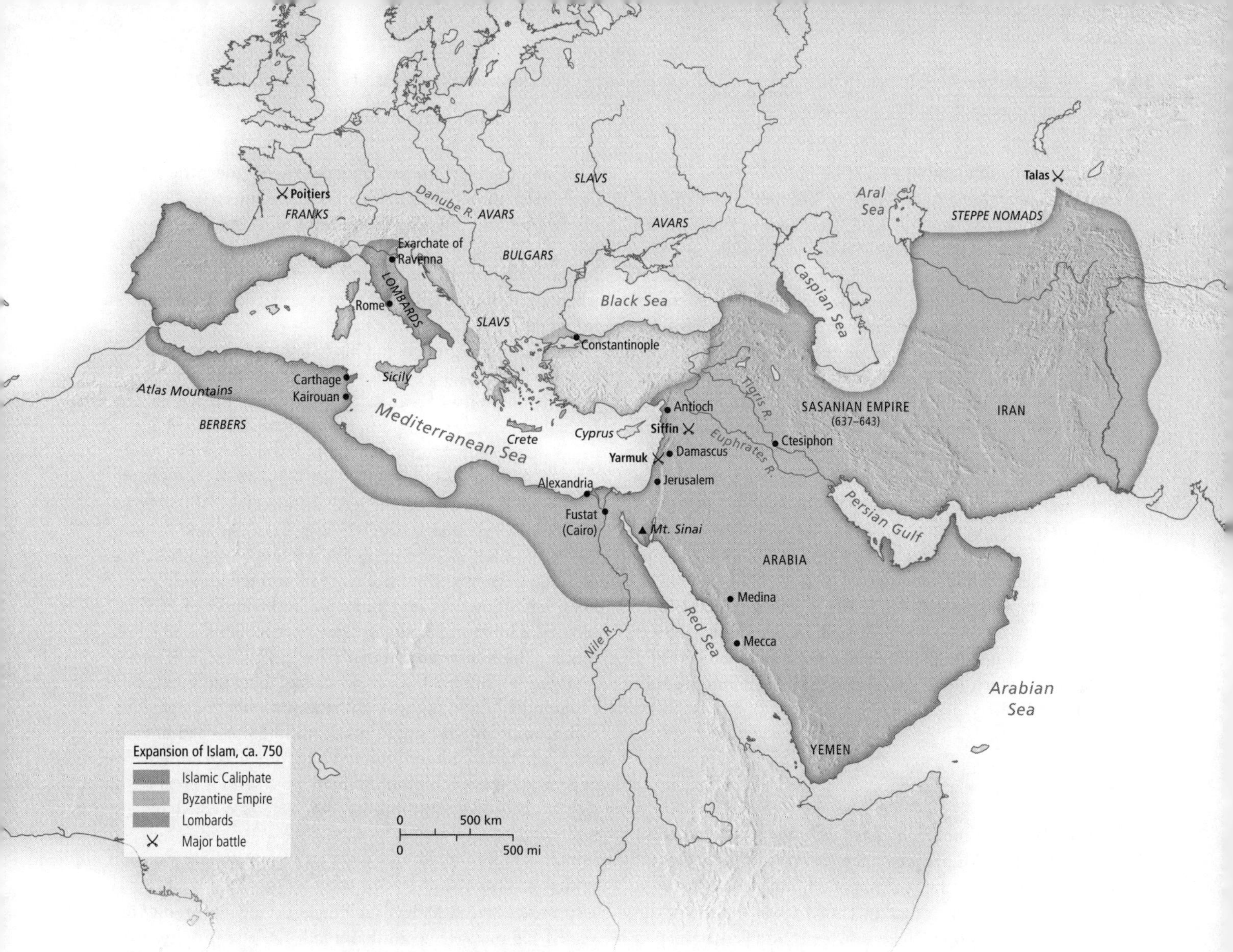

Map 7.2 The Umayyad Caliphate, ca. 750

By ca. 750 the Umayyad Caliphate had reached its greatest extent. It provided political unity to territories stretching from Central Asia to Spain. Islam became the dominant religion in this vast empire.

one hand while slashing downward at enemy troops with a sword in his other hand. Warriors on camels could attack with speed and crushing force. As a result of this innovation, Arab military power developed rapidly.

Military strength combined with trade in luxury goods made some Arab communities wealthy and powerful. By the first century B.C.E. Arabs had seized control of Petra, a merchant city in modern Jordan that controlled the incense trade. Merchants brought this precious, fragrant spice ituals across the Arabian peninsula from ports on the Red Sea and the Persian Gulf to Petra, where it was sold to other merchants from throughout the Middle East and the Mediterranean region. Petra also received merchandise such as ivory and gold from Egyptian traders. Other Arab cities such as Mecca and Medina, located on the western coast of the Arabian peninsula, also flourished due to long-distance caravan trade. Their merchants traded throughout the Middle East, sailed to India, and had extensive contacts with eastern Africa. At the same time, Arabs in north Arabia bred sturdier camels that could endure the harsh, arid terrain of central Asia. This enabled Arab merchants to travel to China along the silk route.

Most Arab communities organized themselves into tribes, each of which claimed descent from a common male ancestor. There was no formal government holding each tribe together. The chiefs who led their tribes did so by personal prestige and by the common consent of the tribesmen. Arab tribes protected the lives and property of all their members. Arabs constantly feuded with one another, killing the men and stealing the herds and women of other tribes. Honor required retribution for every grievance, and so cycles of violence often lasted for generations.

An injury to any member of a tribe obliged fellow tribesmen to seek either vengeance or compensation. Some feuding men chose to settle their grievances through mediation. If both parties agreed, mediators would set fair terms of compensation.

Before the rise of Islam in the seventh century, most Arabs worshiped many gods, including natural objects such as the sun and certain rocks or trees. Some Arabs worshipped only a single deity. Unlike their Egyptian and Greco-Roman neighbors, however, they did not erect huge temples to these deities. Through their encounters with Jews, Christians, and Zoroastrians in Syria, Palestine, Mesopotamia and Arabia, Arabs also learned about different sorts of monotheism, especially as revealed in sacred texts such as the Bible and the Avesta. Large Jewish communities existed in the cities of western Arabia as well as in Yemen, the southwest corner of the Arabian peninsula. Christianity had spread on Arabia's southern coast, and small groups of Zoroastrians lived in eastern Arabia. Arabs developed ideas about heaven and hell, about the individual judgment of the human soul after death, and about divinely inspired prophecy.

THE RISE OF ISLAM

Islam is based on the teachings of the prophet Muhammad (ca. 570–632). Muhammad was born in the powerful Quraysh tribe in the cosmopolitan and wealthy west Arabian trading city of Mecca. This city was the site of the Kaaba, a sacred stone where polytheist Arabs worshipped various deities. As a young man Muhammad married a widowed businesswoman, Khadija, and worked as a caravan merchant. In this profession he earned a reputation as a skilled arbitrator of disputes. When he was meditating in solitude at about age 40, an angel appeared before him, saying, "Muhammad, I am Gabriel and you are the Messenger of God. Recite!" The angel gave him a message to convey to the people of Mecca. Muhammad's message was a call to the Arabs to worship the one true God (the god of Abraham) and to warn of the fires of hell if they failed to answer that call. Muhammad continued to receive these revelations for the rest of his life. They were written down as the Qur'an (meaning "recitation"), the holy book of Islam. Though Muhammad won some followers among friends and family, the people of Mecca initially did not accept his monotheist message.

In 622, Muhammad and his followers moved from Mecca to Medina, a city 200 miles to the north. Aware of Muhammad's skill as a mediator, several feuding tribes in Medina had invited him to settle their long-lasting disputes. Muhammad's emigration to Medina, known as the *Hijra*, is the starting date of the Muslim calendar. The event marks a historical turning point in the development of Islam. For the first time Muhammad and his followers lived as an independent community. As the prophet of God, Muhammad strictly regulated the internal affairs of his new community and its relations with outsiders, creating a society that was political as well as religious. At the center of this Islamic community lay the mosque°, the place where his followers gathered to pray and hear Muhammad's teachings.

Initially, Muhammad and his followers enjoyed good relations with the Jews in Medina. He and his followers even followed some Jewish rituals. Like Jews, they turned toward Jerusalem while praying. But because the Jewish tribes refused to accept Muhammad's political authority, even though he did not demand that they convert, violence broke out. Muhammad changed the direction of prayer to Mecca and expelled a tribe of Jews from Medina in 625. Two years later Muhammad's followers massacred the men of another Jewish tribe, enslaving its women and children. With Jewish opposition eliminated and control of Medina secured, Muhammad and an army of his followers attacked Mecca, which surrendered in 630.

Using a combination of force and negotiating skills , Muhammad drew many Arab tribes into his new religious community. By the time of his death in 632 he had unified most of Arabia under Islam. Muhammad harnessed the enormous energy of the Arabian population, creating a tightly controlled community that was electrified by his teachings.

Islam as Revealed by Muhammad

Islam teaches that Alah (which means "God" in Arabic) revealed his message to Muhammad, the last prophet in a line that included Abraham, Moses, David, all pivotal biblical figures in the Jewish tradition who transmitted divine instruction to humanity, and Jesus Christ, whom Muslims accept as a prophet but not the son of God. Muslims claimed Abraham as their ancestor because he was the father of Ishmael, whom they consider to be the father of the Arab peoples.

Muhammad taught his followers five basic principles called the Pillars of Islam°. *Islam* means "submission," and by performing these acts of faith Muslims demonstrate submission to the will of God. First, all Muslims must acknowledge that there is only one God and that Muhammad is his prophet. Second, they must state this belief in prayer five times a day. On Fridays the noon prayers must be recited in the company of other believers. Muslims may say their prayers anywhere. Third, Muslims must fast between sunrise and sunset during Ramadan, the ninth month of the Muslim calendar. Fourth, Muslims must give generous donations of money and food to the needy in their community. Islam expects its followers to be kind to one another, especially to orphans and widows, and to work for the good of the entire Islamic community. Fifth, Muslims must make a pilgrimage to Mecca at least once in their lives if it is possible.

The Kaaba in Mecca
In pre-Islamic times, Arabs worshiped a large, black stone at the Kaaba shrine in the center of Mecca. When Muhammad established Islam in Mecca in 629, he rejected the polytheist past and transformed the Kaaba into the holiest place in the Islamic world, revered as the House of God. Muslim teachers interpreted polytheist rituals that continued under Islam, such as walking around the Kaaba seven times, as symbols of the Muslim believer's entry into God's presence. Muslims from all over the world make pilgrimages to the Kaaba. These journeys foster a sense of shared religious identity among them, no matter where their homelands lie.

As the focus of prayer and pilgrimage, Mecca quickly became the center of the Muslim world. Muhammad affirmed Mecca's special role in Islam with these words: "Announce the Pilgrimage to the people. They will come to you on foot and riding along distant roads on lean and slender beasts, in order to reach the place of advantage (the Kaaba) for them, and to pronounce the name of God on appointed days over cattle he has given them as food; then eat the food and feed the needy and the poor." (Qur'an 22:26) With the spread of Islam to Persia, Asia, and parts of Europe in the seventh century, Muslims from many different lands encountered one another in Mecca, developing a shared Islamic identity.

The Qur'an contains many examples of proper behavior for the community to follow, and Muslims look to the prophet Muhammad's example as a guide. Muhammad taught his followers to struggle for the good of the community morally, spiritually, intellectually, and when necessary by force of arms. This combined effort is called *jihad.* Often translated as "holy war," *jihad* is a commitment to confront a community's problems through the teachings of a moral faith.

The Islamic Community After Muhammad

Muhammad had demonstrated a remarkable talent for leadership during his lifetime, but he did not choose anyone to succeed him. His death in 632 caused a profound crisis among his followers. Would the Islamic community stay united under a single new leader or break up into smaller groups? After many deliberations, the leaders of the community chose the prophet's father-in-law, Abu Bakr, to lead them. Abu Bakr (r. 632–634) became the first caliph, or successor to Muhammad. The form of Islamic government that evolved under his leadership is called the caliphate°.

Most Muslims supported Abu Bakr wholeheartedly, but some opposed him. One group claimed that Muhammad's son-in-law and cousin, Ali, should have become the first caliph instead. Called the Shi'a (party) of Ali, this group developed into one of Islam's major sects, the Shiites. Other Arab tribes rejected not only Abu Bakr's succession, but Islam itself. They rebelled, claiming that their membership in the Islamic community had been valid only when Muhammad was alive. Abu Bakr crushed these forces in a struggle called the Wars of Apostasy (a word meaning renunciation of a previous faith). By the time of his death in 634, Abu Bakr had brought most of Arabia back under his control. In the course of these wars, he created a highly trained Muslim army eager to spread the faith and gain additional wealth and power. The rich Persian and Byzantine Empires became an irresistible target.

Attacks on the Byzantine and Persian Empires

Under the leadership of the second caliph, Umar (r. 634–644), Muslim forces moved north from the Arabian peninsula and invaded Byzantine and Persian territory. As we saw earlier, they seized Syria in 636. The next year they crushed the main Persian army and captured the Persian capital city, Ctesiphon. Within just a decade Islamic troops

JUSTICE IN HISTORY

"Judgment Belongs to God Alone": The Battle and Arbitration at Siffin

On a spring day in 657, two Muslim armies confronted each other at Siffin, a village on the Euphrates River in Mesopotamia. The armies were commanded by men who had been rivals for a long time, the Caliph Ali (r. 656–661) and Muawiya, the governor of Syria. Their rivalry stemmed from Muawiya's refusal to accept Ali's authority as caliph. The Battle of Siffin became a defining moment in the development of the Islamic state. Basic Islamic ideas about divine judgment were put to the test, leading to passionate debate about how God makes his judgment known to Muslims.

Ali had taken power after the assassination of his predecessor, Caliph Uthman, in 656. The murder went unpunished, but many people considered Ali responsible because when he became caliph he appointed officials known to have taken part in the murder and because he had never disavowed the crime. Uthman belonged to the influential Umayyad clan, and his supporters and family felt an obligation to avenge their kinsman's death. Chief among Ali's opponents was Muawiya, a leading member of the Umayyad clan. Muawiya maintained a strong army and powerful support in Syria.

The immediate provocation of the confrontation between Muawiya and Ali was Uthman's murder, but the men's quarrel also stemmed from tensions about status and membership in the Muslim community. The earliest converts to Islam and their descendants believed that their association with Muhammad entitled them to greater status than the many new non-Arab converts to the religion, most of whom supported Ali. Resenting Ali's popularity among the newer members of the Islamic community, the early converts supported Muawiya. Further support for Muawiya came from many tribal leaders who opposed the caliph's growing authority.

The new converts to Islam also had complaints. In their view, the earliest Muslims, including the Umayyad clan, unfairly enjoyed a privileged position in the Islamic community even though all Muslims were supposed to be treated equally.

When Ali and Muawiya confronted each other at Siffin, they hesitated to fight because many of their soldiers felt strongly that Muslims should not shed the blood of other Muslims. As one of Ali's followers said, "It is one of the worst wrongs and most terrible trials that we should be sent against our own people and they against us. . . . Yet, if we do not assist our community and act faithfully toward our leader, we deny our faith, and if we do that, we abandon our honor and extinguish our fire."[2] So for three months, the armies engaged in only occasional skirmishes.

Finally, in July 657, real fighting broke out. Ali encouraged his men with these words, "Be steadfast! May God's spirit descend on you, and may God make you firm with conviction so that he who is put to flight knows that he displeases his God . . . "

The furious battle came to a sudden halt in July when Muawiya's soldiers held up pages of the Qur'an on the ends of their spears and appealed for arbitration. When Ali's men saw this symbolic gesture, they stopped fighting and demanded that their leader settle his differences with Muawiya peacefully through arbitration.

Mediation of conflicts by third-party arbitrators frequently occurred among Arab tribes. Muhammad himself had earned renown as a skilled mediator before Islam was revealed to him. However, the arbitration between Ali and Muawiya failed to resolve the conflict. The two men and their armies separated without having reached an agreement. Ali continued to rule as caliph for six more years, but his authority declined rapidly because many Arabs interpreted his willingness to go to arbitration as a sign of weakness. In 661 Ali was assassinated.

In contrast, Muawiya's power grew after the battle of Siffin. He openly claimed the caliphate for himself and began making deals with the tribal leaders for their support in order to form his own coalition. After Ali's assassination, Muawiya became caliph.

The fact that the arbitration at Siffin occurred at all had long-lasting consequences. Most important, a small but influential Muslim faction emerged when the two leaders first confronted one another. They objected to Ali's initial agreement to arbitration, arguing that God was the only true arbitrator. They believed that Ali should

■ **Title to come**
Caption to come

pull out of the arbitration and submit to God's judgment, which they believed could be known only through battle. These Muslims wanted to fight Muawiya in order to find out what God wanted. This splinter group became known as the Kharijites or "seceders." The Kharijites expressed their view in the phrase "Judgment belongs to God alone."

The Kharijites went one step further in their beliefs. They declared not only that Ali was wrong to accept human arbitration, but that he and his supporters should no longer be considered Muslims. In their view, Ali and his supporters had committed an unpardonable grave sin by accepting arbitration. The Kharijites claimed that they were the only true Muslims. Small in numbers, they established several independent communities in the Islamic Empire and turned their back on Islamic society. They lived as bandits until the tenth century, when they disappeared from the historical record.

Other Muslims who disagreed with the Kharijites proclaimed that neither the Kharijites nor any other human being could know whether sinners were still Muslims in the eyes of God. In their opinion, believers would discover God's judgment on these matters only at the End of Days, when God will judge all humanity. ■

Questions of Justice

1. During this formative period of the Islamic Empire, how did different Arab groups explain how god makes his justice known to humans.
2. How did these ideas influence their beliefs about arbitration and authority?

Taking It Further

W. M. Watt. *The Formative Period of Islamic Thought.* 1973. This account discusses the formation of sects and political groups in early Islamic history.

The Dome of the Rock in Jerusalem
The Dome of the Rock, an eight-sided building with a gilded dome, dominates Jerusalem's skyline. Completed in 692 on the Temple Mount (the site of the Jewish Temple destroyed by the Romans in 69), the building encloses a rock projecting from the floor. Scholars disagree about the structure's original purpose. A Muslim of the tenth century thought that it had been built as a statement of Islam's triumph at the heart of the holiest Christian city. During the sixteenth century the story began to circulate that when Muhammad ascended to heaven at night his winged horse took one leap from Mecca to the rock and then sprang skyward. The artists who completed the dome's interior mosaics probably came from Constantinople, the only place where art of such high quality was being produced. The mosaic patterns also draw from contemporary styles in the Mediterranean world and Persia.

had conquered Egypt, Syria, and all of Persia as far east as India. Meanwhile, Muslim navies, manned by subject Egyptian and Syrian sailors and Arab troops, seized Cyprus, raided in the eastern Mediterranean, and defeated a large Byzantine fleet. Muslim armies were racing across North Africa without serious opposition when civil war broke out in 655 and temporarily halted their advance.

Two groups struggled for control of the caliphate in this civil war, which lasted for six years. On one side were Muhammad's son-in-law Ali, who had become caliph in 656, and his supporters. On the other side was the wealthy Umayyad family who opposed him. In 661 they arranged Ali's assassination and took control of the caliphate, establishing a new dynasty that would last until 750. They established Damascus in Syria as their new capital city, which shifted Islam's power center away from Mecca.

The Umayyad Caliphate

The Umayyad dynasty produced brilliant administrators and generals. At the end of the civil war in 661, these talented leaders consolidated their control of conquered territories and established peaceful conditions in the empire. Then they resumed wars of conquest to spread the Islamic state's political sovereignty and to gain wealth.

Conquests

As we saw in Chapter 5, the Romans distinguished themselves from "uncivilized barbarians" who had not yet come under Roman rule. In a similar fashion, the Umayyads viewed the world as consisting of two parts: the "House of Islam," which contained the territories under their political control, and the "House of War," which included all non-Muslim lands, which they hoped to conquer. By 700, Muslim armies had rolled west across North Africa as far as the Atlantic Ocean in order to conquer non-Muslim lands.

Eleven years later, they invaded Spain and overthrew the Visigothic kingdom in just one battle. From Spain they attacked France, but in 732, Charles Martel "the Hammer," king of the warlike Franks, stopped their advance into Europe at the battle of Poitiers. After their defeat, the Umayyad armies retreated to their territories in Spain.

Umayyad caliphs attempted to conquer the Christian kingdom of Nubia south of Egypt to gain its gold and spread Islam. The Nubians successfully repelled the Muslim invaders, however, and in 661 a lasting peace treaty was signed between the Umayyad caliphate and Nubian kingdoms. This treaty was unique, because the Nubians belonged to the "House of War," which meant that they were enemies still to be conquered.

While struggling with the Nubians, Umayyad armies continued to strike at the Byzantine Empire. After seizing Egypt and Syria, they made regular attacks on the Byzantine territories, sometimes reaching as far as Constantinople, which remained protected by its massive walls. After the last formidable land and sea attacks failed in 717, Umayyad armies made no further attempt to conquer the Byzantine Empire. They did, however, continue to plunder Byzantine Anatolia (in modern Turkey) every year to gain booty.

Umayyad armies moved eastward with equal speed and success. They reached the territories of modern Pakistan and India and even penetrated central Asia, where they captured the caravan city of Samarkand in 710. During the Umayyad caliphate, this city served as a commercial hub on the trade route to China. In 751, just after the death of the last Umayyad caliph, Muslim armies defeated Chinese troops of the expansionist Chinese Tang dynasty at the battle of Talas beyond the Jaxartes River. Despite their victory, the Muslims decided to halt their expansion and did not advance further into Chinese-controlled areas in central Asia. One unexpected consequence of this encounter was the introduction of paper from China into the Islamic world, from where it spread into Europe 500 years later.

Like the battle of Poitiers, which marked the limit of the Umayyads' expansion into western Europe, the battle of Talas marked the limit of Muslim military expansion into central Asia. For the next four centuries, these borders would define the Islamic world. Within a century the Umayyads built an empire that reached from southern France to Central Asia and India. Never again would the entire world of Islam be united under one government.

Governing the Islamic Empire

Drawing heavily on the administrative systems of the Byzantine and Persian provinces they had conquered, the Umayyads developed a highly centralized and autocratic regime that changed the political character of the Muslim community. The first Umayyad caliph, Muawiya (r. 661–680), established a hereditary monarchy to ensure orderly succession of power. This was a major change in the caliphate. Unlike the first four caliphs who ruled by virtue of their prestige (as did Arab tribal chiefs), the Umayyads made the caliphate an authoritarian institution. Because of this, the soldiers protested that the Umayyads had turned "God's servants into slaves," corrupted the faith and seized the property of God. A second civil war broke out (683–692), and the Umayyads emerged victorious.

In order to control their vast empire, Umayyad rulers developed a new administrative system. They designed new provinces that replaced old Roman and Persian administrative units. In addition, the Umayyads developed a professional bureaucracy based in the capital of Damascus to meet their expanding financial needs and to ensure that the taxes collected in the provinces came to the central treasury. Most of the administrators were local officials who had served the Roman Persian empires. Many of them were non-Muslims, but a large number also converted to Islam. They provided significant administrative continuity between the caliphate and the empires that it conquered.

The Umayyads used the Arabic language to unify their empire. Arabic gradually replaced the languages of the conquered peoples. Only in Iran did Persian survive as a widely spoken language, and even there Arabic served as the language of government. In the Umayyad caliphate, the Arabic language functioned as Latin had done in the Roman Empire: It provided a common language for diverse subject peoples. By 800 Arabic had become the essential language of administration and international commerce in lands from Morocco to central Asia.

Settlements and Cities

The rapid expansion of Islam created problems for Umayyad rulers eager to consolidate their power. Arab armies had conquered enormous territories, but were only a small minority among the huge non-Muslim populations whose great wealth and manpower resources they controlled. Umayyad policy was to establish garrison cities in conquered lands to hold down the more numerous local populations. Just as Greek colonists followed in the footsteps of Alexander the Great in the fourth century B.C.E., Arab settlers from the Arabian peninsula migrated to newly conquered lands in great numbers. They established themselves first in the garrison towns where government officials were based, and then they became a significant presence in major cities, such as Alexandria, Jerusalem, and Antioch. Some immigrants were nomadic tribes that adopted a settled way of life for the first time. Others were farmers from the highlands of Yemen, who brought sophisticated irrigation systems and agricultural traditions to their new homes. Arab migrations to cities ended many old Arab traditions of nomadic life.

In addition to settling in existing cities, Arabs founded many new ones. In Egypt they built Fustat, which would later become Cairo. In North Africa, they established Kairouan in Tunisia. In Mesopotamia they created Basra, an important port city, as well as Kufa on the Euphrates River. Though built on a smaller scale than the major urban centers of the Roman and Persian Empires, most new Arab cities drew from Hellenistic town planning. They had a square shape, walls with gates on all four sides, towers, and a central plaza. In the heart of all of these cities, Umayyad caliphs built a mosque to emphasize the central role of Islam in community life and to celebrate their own authority. The magnificent mosques in Damascus, Jerusalem, and other cities were intended to surpass the grand Christian churches in prestige.

Urban life continued in the Byzantine cities such as Jerusalem, Antioch, and Alexandria that Muslim armies conquered, but with significant changes, especially in urban street patterns. Winding, narrow streets in which camels could easily maneuver replaced the long, straight, wide streets appropriate for wagons that typified Hellenistic and Roman cities. Wheeled vehicles gradually disappeared from use. Especially in markets, the old, wide streets and sidewalks filled up with small shops, and pedestrians walked through narrow alleys behind the shops.

Patterns of daily activity also changed under Muslim rule. With Islam now dominating public life, cities ceased to carry Greco-Roman culture. Theaters fell out of use because there was no Arabic tradition of publicly performed drama and comedy. The exercise fields, sports buildings, libraries, and schools associated with public baths and gymnasiums in the Classical Age also fell out of use, though people continued to enjoy bathhouses with heated pools.

Revenues once earmarked for gymnasiums and other public buildings now went to local mosques. These centers of Islamic urban culture replaced the forums and agoras of the Roman and Greek world as the chief public space for men. Mosque schools provided education for the community. Muslims gathered at mosques for public festivals and, of course, for religious worship. In their capacity as administrative centers, mosques provided courtooms, assembly halls, and treasuries for the community. Judges, tax collectors, bureaucrats, and emissaries from the caliph conducted their affairs in the mosque precinct.

During the Umayyad caliphate, many Muslim farmers and craftsworkers lived in prosperous villages. Many of these small communities stood on the vast estates of rich landowners who controlled the workers' labor. The caliphate also sponsored huge land reclamation projects on the edges of the desert in Syria and Mesopotamia. Officials of the imperial government drew revenues directly from the villages that sprang up in these new farmlands.

Becoming Muslims

Islam sharply defined the differences between Muslims and their ethnically diverse subjects. The conquerors understood themselves as a community of faith. Only individuals who converted to Islam could gain full participation in the Islamic community. Their ethnicity did not matter. Therefore Muslims defined their new subjects by their religions, something Egyptians, Assyrians, Persians, Greeks, or Romans had never done. The Qur'an states that "there is no compulsion in religion," meaning that monotheists (Jews, Christian, and Zoroastrians) cannot be forced to convert to Islam. Muslims viewed polytheists differently. Polytheists had the choice of conversion to the Muslim faith or dying.

Throughout the Umayyad period, the number of Muslims grew slowly, reaching perhaps only 10 percent of the total population. Many Christians, Jews, and Zoroastrians willingly converted to the new religion. Other converts were slaves in the households of their Muslim owners. Still others were villagers who migrated to garrison cities and converted in the hope of sharing in the spoils of conquest—and avoiding the taxes demanded of non-Muslims. Their eagerness to convert threatened the tax base, and many Muslim officials refused to acknowledge their conversion and sent them home.

Conversion to Islam increased as Muslim armies fought their way across North Africa. In the huge area that stretches from Egypt to the Atlantic Ocean, the Muslims conquered many distinct polytheist ethnic groups whom the Arab conquerors collectively called Berbers. Faced with the choice of conversion or death, huge numbers of Berbers joined the victorious Muslim armies. Islam unified the Berber populations and brought them into a wider Islamic world. With the aid of these troops, Islamic power spread even more quickly across North Africa and into Spain.

Peoples of the Book

How do empires handle minorities? Do they have the same privileges and obligations as their rulers? Can they freely enter into the society of their masters? In previous chapters we have seen how the Assyrians, Persians, Hellenistic Greeks, and Romans answered these questions. Though their solutions differed, none of these great empires considered the religions of their subjects when deciding their place in society.

By distinguishing their subjects on religious, not ethnic grounds, the Umayyad caliphate took a different approach to governing their subject peoples. Jews, Christians, and Zoroastrians constituted the main religions among conquered peoples. Islamic law called them "Peoples of the Book" because each of these religious communities had a sacred book. They had lower status than Muslims, and they had to pay extra taxes, but they were free to practice their religion. Islamic law forbade their persecution or forcible conversion. For this reason, large communities of Christians, Jews, and Zoroastrians lived peacefully under Muslim rule.

Several Christian communities, separated by old controversies about doctrinal issues, coexisted within the Islamic Empire, since the caliphate was indifferent to which Christian doctrine they followed. Followers of the Chalcedonian Orthodox church changed the language of prayer from Greek to Syriac and then to Arabic. Though these Christians had no direct ties with Constantinople, they followed the Byzantine emperors' Chalcedonian Orthodoxy. Thus their church was called the Melkite, or Royal, church. The Melkite church continues to be the largest Christian community in Muslim lands in the Middle East today. Another Christian church, called the Jacobite church, was formed by Monophysite Christians in the late sixth century, as we saw in Chapter 6. Its Bible and prayers are in Syriac. The Nestorian church, comprising of Christians who emphasized Jesus' humanity rather than the combination of his humanity and divinity, also flourished under Muslim rule in Persia, Syria, and northern Arabia. Nestorians also established communities in India, central Asia, and China. The variety of Christian communities in the caliphate was greater than in Byzantium and Latin Christendom.

Jewish communities also flourished throughout Umayyad lands, notably in Spain and Mesopotamia. Jews found their subordinate but protected status under Islam preferable to the open persecution they suffered in many Christian kingdoms. In Persia, Zoroastrian communities fared less well. As they were slowly forced into remote regions of central Iran, their numbers gradually dwindled. In the tenth century, many Zoroastrians migrated to India, where they are known today as Farsis, a word that means "Persians."

Commercial Encounters

The economic system of the Muslim world changed under Umayyad rule. From the time of the first conquests, rev-

THE PACT OF UMAR: ISLAM ENCOUNTERS THE GREAT FAITHS OF THE ANCIENT MIDDLE EAST

Islam recognized Christians, Jews, and Zoroastrians as fellow "Peoples of the Book," because they were monotheists and because their religions were based on holy texts. The Pact of Umar, *issued by the Caliph Umar I (r. 643–644), introduced the idea that Muslim authorities would protect them, though with restrictions. This letter was sent by the Christians of Syria to Umar I, spelling out the restrictions they accepted.*

When Umar . . . may God be pleased with him, accorded a peace to the Christians in Syria, we wrote to him as follows:

In the name of God, the Merciful and Compassionate.

This is a letter to the servant of God Umar, Commander of the Faithful, from the Christians of such-and-such a city. When you came against us, we asked you for safe-conduct for ourselves, our descendants, our property, and the people of our community, and we undertook the following obligations toward you:

We shall not build, in our cities or in their neighborhood, new monasteries, churches, convents, or monks' cells, nor shall we repair, by day or night, such of them as fall in ruins or are situated in the quarters of the Muslims.

We shall not give shelter in our churches or in our dwellings to any spy, nor hide him from the Muslims.

We shall not teach the Qur'an to our children.

We shall not manifest our religion publicly nor convert anyone to it.

We shall not prevent any of our kin from entering Islam if they wish it.

We shall show respect toward the Muslims, and we shall rise from our seats when they wish to sit.

We shall not seek to resemble the Muslims by imitating any of their garments, the headgear, the turban, footwear, or the parting of the hair.

We shall not mount our saddles, nor shall we gird swords nor bear any kind of arms nor carry them on our persons.

We shall not engrave Arabic inscriptions on our seals.

We shall not sell fermented drinks.

We shall not display our crosses or our books in the roads or markets of the Muslims. We shall only use clappers in our churches very softly. We shall not raise our voices in our church services or in the presence of Muslims, nor shall we raise our voices when following our dead (in funeral processions). We shall not show lights on any of the roads of the Muslims or in their markets. We shall not bury our dead near the Muslims.

We shall not take slaves who have been allotted to the Muslims.

We shall not build houses overtopping the houses of the Muslims.

We accept these conditions for ourselves and for the people of our community, and in return we receive safe-conduct.

If we in any way violate these undertakings for which we ourselves stand surety, we forfeit our covenant, and we become liable to the penalties for contumacy [resistance to authority] and sedition.

Source: From Bernard Lewis, ed., *Islam: From the Prophet Muhammad to the Capture of Constantinople, Vol. II: Religion and Society.* Originally published by Harper & Row, 1974.

enues derived primarily from the huge amounts of gold and silver taken in war, taxes, and contributions made by Muslims to support widows and orphans. To increase their revenues further, Umayyad rulers introduced a land tax for Muslim landowners, in imitation of Byzantine and Persian systems of taxation. Even the proud Arab tribesmen, for whom paying taxes was a humiliation because it implied subordination to a greater authority, had to pay taxes, though not as much as non-Muslims. With land tax revenues Umayyad caliphs could afford to establish a standing professional army. This further reduced the fighting role of individual Arab tribes. It also enabled caliphs to cement their authority more firmly.

Long-distance overland trade rapidly expanded due to the peaceful conditions in Umayyad lands. Although merchants could travel safely from Morocco to Central Asia and earn great sums, such long-distance expeditions were expensive. Merchants had to invest considerable sums of money to cover the costs of a trading expedition in the hopes of making a profit at the end of the journey. The Qur'an approves of mercantile trading, and Islamic law permitted letters of credit, loans, and other financial instruments that made commerce over huge distances possible long before they were known in Europe.

Umayyad rulers further stimulated international commerce by creating a new currency that imitated Persian and Roman coinage The Persian silver *drahm* (a word derived from the Greek *drachma*) inspired the Umayyad *dirham,* which became the standard coin throughout the caliphate by the 780s. Muslim merchants, as well as businessmen as far away as western Europe, Scandinavia, and Russia, used silver *dirhams* to pay for goods. For gold coinage the Umayyads minted the *dinar* (a word derived from a Roman coin, the *denarius*). Like the *dirham,* the *dinar* also became

Islamic coin

(front)

(back)

Byzantine prototype

(back)

(back)

Designing Muslim Coins: The Encounter with Persian and Roman Prototypes

In the early years of the Umayyad state, caliphs experimented with the design of Islamic coins. Because Arabs had no tradition of minting coins, they borrowed freely from the images they saw on Persian and Byzantine coins. Then they made the necessary adjustments to change Christian or Persian symbols to Islamic ones. For example, Caliph Yazid I (680–683) used a Persian coin showing the late Sasanian emperor Chosroes I (590–628) on the front and a Zoroastrian fire altar on the back (a). Only the stamp on the back that says "year one of Yazid" indicates that this is an Islamic coin. On a *dinar* of Abd al-Malik (685–705) (b), the artist changed the Byzantine emperor Heraclius and his heirs, who carry globes with small crosses, to the caliph and his heirs, holding globes without crosses. On the coin's reverse side, Muhammad's scepter replaced the Christian cross. By the end of his reign, Abd al-Malik did away with images altogether and decorated his coins entirely with written quotations from the Qur'an. This coin (c) says "There is no God but God, and Muhammad is his messenger, whom he sent with guidance and the religion of truth to make it supreme over all others whether the polytheists like it or not."

a standard coin in the caliphate as well as in distant lands. Merchants could depend on the value of this currency wherever they did business.

Camels played a significant role in the expanding Islamic economy because they made long-distance trade extremely profitable. Merchants had used domesticated camels throughout the Arabian peninsula for many centuries, but the caliphate's huge size and peaceful conditions brought new opportunities for long-distance camel-borne trade. Camels can carry heavy cargoes through harsh terrain for long periods, and they require little water. Because these "ships of the desert" do not need paved roads, caravan routes did not have to stick to Roman road systems. New trade routes suited for camels developed from Morocco to Central Asia. Camel-based commerce proved so successful that between 700 and 1500, paved roads, as well as the carts and wagons that traveled on them, nearly disappeared. Furthermore, because of long-distance camel caravans, the Mediterranean Sea, the great superhighway of the Roman Empire, lost its primary place in international trade. The revenues earned from the camel caravans helped make the Umayyad caliphate extremely rich.

In addition to supporting long-distance overland trade by camel caravans, Umayyad caliphs also developed maritime trade. The Egyptian city of Alexandria became the chief Mediterranean naval base for Arab commercial shipping . The Syrian port cities of Acre and Tyre also contributed to maritime shipping in the eastern Mediterranean region. The Umayyads maintained peaceful conditions in the Persian Gulf and the Indian Ocean. Arab merchants sailed past Zanzibar and India to Canton in southern China, following sea routes established by Persian navigators. Arab traders also sailed down the coast of East Africa to obtain slaves and natural resources brought from the interior. In later centuries Muslim navigators reached Malaysia, Indochina, and eventually Indonesia and the Philippines.

By 850, Muslims in cities throughout the caliphate could buy many exotic luxuries. These goods included panther skins, rubies, and coconuts from India; paper, silk, fine ceramics, eunuchs (castrated men), slaves, and marble workers from China; hawks from North Africa; Egyptian papyrus; and furs and sugar cane from Central Asia. People could also buy less-expensive fabrics and manufactured items crafted locally.

Arab traders also brought back valuable ideas and scientific knowledge from the peoples encountered through trade in the East. Many Arabic nautical terms derive from Persian, and late in the eighth century scholars translated Persian and Indian astronomical works into Arabic, the beginning of an explosion of scientific knowledge in the Islamic world.

Throughout the formative period of Islam and the Umayyad caliphate, Muslims took firm hold of territories stretching from North Africa to Central Asia, creating a single political realm there for the first time in history. The inhabitants of the entire Arabian peninsula, with their trade connections to Africa and Asia, for the first time joined the peoples of the Middle East and the Mediterranean in an intricate system of commerce and government. These new commercial networks affected the economy of the Mediterranean world and Europe, making a deep impact on Europe's development. By replacing Roman civilization in North Africa and the Middle East, Muslims introduced a new monotheistic religion to the Mediterranean world.

CHRONOLOGY

The New World of Islam

CA. 570	Muhammad born in Mecca
622	Muhammad flees to Medina (the Hijra)
632	Muhammad dies in Medina
633–640	Muslims conquer Syria, Palestine, and Mesopotamia
642	Byzantines abandon Alexandria; Muslims conquer Egypt
651	Muslims conquer Persia; text of the Qur'an established
661	Caliph Ali is assassinated
661–750	Umayyad dynasty rules from Damascus
CA .691–692	Dome of the Rock built in Jerusalem
706–715	Great Mosque of Damascus built
710	Muslim army reaches the Indus River in India
711	Muslims conquer Spain
732	Charles Martel defeats Muslims at Poitiers
751	Abbasid dynasty begins; muslim armies defeat Chinese forces at Talas in central Asia

The Birth of Latin Christendom

By 750, several new kingdoms had emerged in the lands that used to constitute the western part of the Roman Empire. The Lombards ruled in Italy; the Visigoths in Spain; and the Franks in modern-day France, Germany, and the Netherlands. Various Anglo-Saxon kings controlled most of England. These territories were not politically united as they had been under the Roman Empire. Though their populations were quite diverse ethnically and linguistically, they shared certain social and religious characteristics. They had enough in common that historians refer to these kingdoms collectively as Latin Christendom.

Germanic Kingdoms on Roman Foundations

Historians describe these new kingdoms of Christendom as Germanic because the peoples who established them spoke languages related to modern German. And although most of these kingdoms borrowed from Roman law while establishing government institutions, they maintained their own cultural identity and relied on German methods of rule. For example, in the new kingdoms kinship obligations to a particular clan of blood relatives rather than citizenship, as in the Roman Empire, defined a person's place in society and his or her relationship to rulers. In the Germanic kingdoms personal loyalty rather than legal rights unified society.

Christianity became the dominant religion in the kingdoms, providing another powerful unifying force. Indeed, the faith united the disparate regions, as these realms' rulers followed the same form of Christianity as their subjects.

Map 7.3 Europe, ca. 750

By ca. 750 the kingdom of the Franks had become the dominant power in western Europe. The Umayyad Caliphate controlled Spain, and the Lombard kingdom governed most of Italy. The Byzantine Empire held power in Greece, as well as its core lands in Asia Minor.

The Germanic settlers and remaining Romans merged quickly through intermarriage. The particular kind of Christianity that spread into these kingdoms was Latin Christianity or Catholicism, in which Latin served as the language of worship, learning, and diplomacy.

Anglo-Saxon England

Roman civilization collapsed more completely in Britain during the fifth century than it did on the European continent, largely because of Britain's long distance from Rome and the small number of Romans who had settled there. About 400, the Roman economic and administrative infrastructure of Britain fell apart, and the last Roman legions left the island to fight on the continent. Raiders from the coast of the North Sea called Angles and Saxons (historians refer to them as Anglo-Saxons) took advantage of Britain's weakened defenses and began to invade. In their light, fast ships, they began to probe the island's southeast coast, pillaging the small villages they found there and establishing permanent settlements of their own. Many Roman Britons fled to Brittany on the northern coast of modern France, and others retreated to Cornwall, southern Scotland, and Wales.

The economic situation in Britain continued to deteriorate. By 420 coinage had fallen out of use on the island, and barter became the sole means of exchange. By 450, cities either shrank to very small villages or lay abandoned. A century later, fortified villas in the countryside—the last vestige of Roman life—had disappeared.

Christian worship also evaporated in southeast England, though temporarily, around this time due to the settlement of the polytheist Anglo-Saxons. Christianity hung on, however, in Wales, Cornwall, and southern Scotland. Due to the efforts of missionaries from Italy, Gaul, and Ireland, by 750 Christianity had re-emerged and become deeply embedded in Anglo-Saxon culture.

Because the small bands of Anglo-Saxon settlers fought as often among themselves as they did with the Roman Britons, the island remained fragmented politically during the first few centuries of the invaders' rule. But by 750, three warring kingdoms managed to seize enough land to coalesce and dominate England: Mercia, Wessex, and Northumbria.

Because Roman culture had virtually disappeared in these areas, Roman legal traditions did not influence Anglo-Saxon law. Moreover, Roman and Anglo-Saxon societies did not merge as they did in Spain, Italy, and Gaul. We can see evidence of this in the English language, which derives primarily from the Germanic languages spoken by the Anglo-Saxon settlers of Britain. In contrast, the Romance (or Roman-based) languages of Spanish, Italian, and French developed from Latin spoken in Rome's former provinces on the continent where Roman civilization was more deeply rooted. In Wales, which the Anglo-Saxons did not conquer, the Welsh language shows a combination of Latin and the region's older Celtic tongues.

LEVA.8336.609
photo to come

Sutton Hoo: A King Proclaims His Power
Around 625, the Anglo-Saxon ruler of a kingdom in eastern England was buried in his raiding ship under a massive mound at Sutton Hoo. This method of burial is entirely Germanic. An extremely rich array of military equipment, jewelry, and coins accompanied this monarch into the next world. These treasures illustrate the wealth and long-distance connections of his dynasty. The king's magnificent iron helmet (a) with face mask and decorations in gold, silver, and precious stones is based on Roman ceremonial helmets of the late empire, but is in keeping with the armor of Anglo-Saxon warrior kings.

The Franks: A Dual Heritage

The encounter between Roman and Frankish cultures from the third to the seventh century produced the largest and most powerful state in western Europe, the kingdom of the Franks. Yet the Franks had modest origins. In the third century a number of small tribes living in what is now the Netherlands and the northwestern part of Germany organized themselves into a loose confederation. According to Roman records, Frankish warbands launched destructive attacks on northern Gaul (now northern France) and raided Spain and North Africa during the second half of the third century. The armies of the Roman emperor Constantine finally brought the Franks under control in the early fourth century. After that those Franks who lived beyond Roman borders did not dare to attack Rome, and those Franks living within the empire served faithfully as soldiers in the Roman army. These men retained dual identities, remaining both Frankish and Roman. As a third century soldier's gravestone proudly states: "I am a Frank, a Roman citizen, and an armed soldier."[2] Several Franks even became important Roman generals.

But in the course of the fifth century, as Roman imperial control of western Europe disintegrated, Frankish power grew. One group among the Franks, called Salians, gradually gained preeminence among the Frankish people. The Salians' leading family called themselves Merovingians because they claimed descent from a legendary warrior named Merovech. A crafty Merovingian war chief named Childeric ruled the Franks from about 460 until his death in 482.

During his long reign, Childeric set the stage for the rapid consolidation and expansion of Frankish power. Childeric gave Frankish warriors the opportunity to participate in campaigns to seize control of Gaul, rewarding them handsomely with loot. But the complex political situation in Gaul posed a problem for the Merovingian leader. After Roman imperial government collapsed throughout most of Gaul by the 420s, some independent groups of Romans continued to fight for control of territory against Huns, Visigoths, and other peoples who had settled there. In a few places Roman churchmen and aristocrats managed to hold on to some authority. Although Childeric was not Christian, he cooperated with these Romans in an effort to win their support and consolidate his power in northern Gaul, and the result was a stronger kingdom than any other in western Europe during this troubled period.

With the support of loyal Frankish soldiers, Childeric laid the foundation for the Merovingian kingdom. His energetic and ruthless son Clovis (r. 481–511) made the Franks the leading power in western Europe. Clovis aggressively expanded his father's power base through conquest of Gaul and neighboring territories. He also murdered many of his relatives and other Frankish chieftains whom he considered rivals. In 486 he overcame the last Roman stronghold in northern Gaul and stood as the most powerful ruler in western Europe.

Clovis's wife, Clotild, followed Latin or Catholic Christianity, the religion followed by most of the inhabitants of the former Roman Empire in western Europe. Historians refer to this version of Christianity as Latin Christianity because its followers used a Latin Bible, performed church services in Latin, and were native Latin speakers. Catholic Christianity, like the Greek-based Orthodox Christianity in the Byzantine Empire, teaches the full equality of the Father, the Son, and the Holy Spirit in the Trinity. In contrast to Catholic Christianity in the western provinces was the Arian Christianity practiced by the Germanic kings and their subjects, who had established new kingdoms in western Europe during the fifth century. Arians believed that Christ was divine, but inferior to God the Father in rank, authority, and glory.

The theological distinction between Catholic and Arian Christians in western Europe was a crucial political issue that divided the Roman and Germanic populations. Around 500, perhaps influenced by his wife's beliefs, the polytheist Clovis converted to Catholic Christianity. About 3,000 warriors, the core of his army, joined their king in this change to the new faith. Clovis had practical reasons to convert as well. He intended to attack the Visigothic kingdom in southern Gaul. The Visigoths followed Arian Christianity, but their subjects, the Roman inhabitants of the region, followed Catholic Christianity. By converting to Catholicism, Clovis won the support of the Visigoths' subjects. With their help Clovis and his Frankish army crushed the Visigothic king Alaric II at the battle of Vouillé in the summer of 507, forcing him to retreat to Visigothic territories in Spain. Clovis now controlled almost all of Gaul as far as Spain.

Clovis also conquered other Germanic peoples as well. His armies overran the kingdom of the Thuringians to the east of his homeland. They also defeated the Alemanni, who lived in what are now Switzerland and southwest Germany. In order to consolidate his authority in these varied lands, Clovis needed recognition from both the emperor in Constantinople and the Roman Church in Gaul. He shrewdly achieved both. After defeating Alaric II, the Merovingian ruler won the Gallic clergy's support by donating much of the booty from his victory to the church of the most important saint in Gaul, Martin of Tours. Clovis then earned the recognition of the Byzantine emperor by formally acknowledging his authority. At the pageant when Clovis brought the treasure to Martin's church, ambassadors of the Byzantine emperor made him an honorary consul. Wearing a Roman military uniform, Clovis celebrated a Roman-style victory parade in which he scattered gold coins to the crowd. For the next three centuries, Merovingian kings followed Catholic Christianity and received similar honors from Byzantine emperors.

The Frankish kingdom thrived under several able monarchs in the sixth and seventh centuries. Continuing their father's expansionist policies, Clovis's sons conquered the Burgundian kingdom in 534 and acquired Provence (the southern coast of Gaul) two years later. They also carved out a foothold in northern Italy.

Despite these successes, the Merovingian dynasty gradually grew weak as a result of conflicts among kings, their quarrelsome sons, and independent-minded aristocrats. As a result of these squabbles, Clovis's kingdom split into three separate realms: Neustria in the west; Austrasia, which included lands east of the Rhine River as well as in Gaul; and

ENCOUNTERING CHRISTIANITY: THE COURTESY AND CONVERSION OF KING ETHELBERT OF KENT

When Pope Gregory the Great sent missionaries to England in 597, King Ethelbert of Kent treated them with kindness. In this passage, the English historian Bede (ca. 673–735) presents the point of view of the unconverted English as well as the missionaries' piety.

Reassured by the encouragement of the blessed father Gregory, Augustine and his fellow-servants of Christ resumed their work in the word of God, and arrived in Britain. The King of Kent at this time was the powerful King Ethelbert. To the east of Kent lies the large island of Thanet. It was here that God's servant Augustine landed with companions, who are said to have been forty in number. At the direction of blessed Pope Gregory, they had brought interpreters from among the Franks, and they sent these to Ethelbert, saying that they came from Rome bearing very glad news, which infallibly assured all who would receive it of eternal joy in heaven, and an everlasting kingdom with the living and true God. On receiving this message, the king ordered them to remain in the island where they had landed, and gave directions that they were to be provided with all necessaries until he should decide what action to take. For he had already heard of the Christian religion, having a Christian wife of the Frankish royal house . . . After some days, the king came to the island, and sitting down in the open air, summoned Augustine and his companions. But he took precautions that they should not approach him in a house, for he held an ancient superstition that if they were practisers of magical arts, they might have opportunity to deceive and master him. But the monks were endowed with power from God, not the Devil, and approached the king carrying a silver cross as their standard, and the likeness of our Lord and Saviour painted on a board. . . . And when, at the king's command, Augustine had sat down and preached the word of life to the king and his court, the king said: "Your words and promises are fair indeed, abut they are new and strange to us, and I cannot accept them and abandon the age-old beliefs of the whole English nation. But since you have travelled far, and I can see that you are sincere in your desire to instruct us in what you believe to be true and excellent, we will not harm you. We will receive you hospitably, and take care to supply you with all that you need; nor will we forbid you to preach and win any people you can to your religion."

Source: From *A History of the English Church and People* by Bede, translated by Leo Sherley-Price, revised by R. E. Latham (Penguin Classics 1955, Revised edition 1968.)

Burgundy in the south. Rulers of these independent kingdoms issued their own law codes, collected taxes from their subjects—and quarreled bitterly with one another. As they went their separate ways politically, striking linguistic differences emerged. For example, in Neustria, the people spoke an early form of French, while in Austrasia they spoke a German language. These communities stood as the foundations of medieval France and Germany.

Though Merovingian kings still ruled in Neustria, Austrasia, and Burgundy, they had become so ineffectual that real power passed to the official in charge of the royal household called the "Mayor of the Palace." One of these mayors, Charles Martel "the Hammer" (r. 714–741), established his personal power by regaining control over regions that had slipped away from Merovingian rule, and by defeating an invading Muslim army at Poitiers in 732. Martel's son, Pepin the Short (r. 751–768), dethroned the last of the Merovingian monarchs and in 751 made himself king of the Franks. As we will see in Chapter 8, the new royal house established by Charles Martel, called the Carolingian dynasty, initiated the most glorious period in Frankish history.

Visigoths in Spain

In contrast to the Frankish kings who after Clovis accepted Catholic Christianity, during the sixth century the Visigothic kings, who controlled southern Gaul and most of Spain, adhered to Arian Christianity. These kings attempted to force Arian conversion on the indigenous population. In southern Gaul, where much of the population accepted the Roman Church, forced conversion to Arianism caused hostility toward the Visigoths. When the Frankish king Clovis invaded southern Gaul in 507, many Catholics welcomed him and provided the Franks with military assistance. As a consequence of defeat, the Visigoth kings retreated to Spain, where they concentrated on unifying the people through the spread of Arianism and the acceptance of Roman law, which influenced the Visigoth law codes.

By 600, Visigoth kings ruled over most of the Spanish peninsula and had even managed to drive the last Byzantine forces from its southern coast. Under the Visigoths Spain thrived. From its vast, rich estates surpluses of grain, olive oil, and leather were exported by international merchants, including a substantial community of Jews as well as Greeks and even Syrians. By taxing this trade the Visigoth kings filled their treasuries with gold and became the envy of their neighbors.

Despite their best efforts the Visigoth kings failed to enforce Arianism on the population, and when King Reccared (r. 586–601) himself converted to Catholicism, most of the population followed. The kings began to imitate the Byzantine emperors with the elaborate court ceremonies of Constantinople and used frequent Church councils as assemblies that enforced their will. Thus, the key to their success was the ability to employ the spiritual authority of the Church to enhance the secular authority of the king. However, King Reccared's conversion was accompanied by growing intolerance for minority religions and even more ardent attempts to create religious unity through forced conversions. The principal victims of these conversion campaigns were the Jews, who were ordered to be baptized or leave the kingdom in 613. The forced conversion of the Jews was never carried out, but it created distrust and opposition among them that weakened the kingdom. The autocratic instincts of the Visigoth kings also alienated many of the substantial landowners who were easily lured by the promise of alternative kings.

In 711 invading armies of Muslims from North Africa vanquished the last Visigothic king. As a result, Spain became part of the Umayyad Caliphate. The Jews, in particular, welcomed the Muslim conquerors because Islam granted them a measure of religious toleration they had not experienced under the Visigoths. Many Christians from the upper classes converted to Islam to preserve the property and offices of authority. Some survivors of the Visigoth kingdoms held on in the northwest of Spain, where they managed to keep Christianity alive.

Lombards in Italy

Between 568 and 774, a people known as the Lombards controlled most of northern and central Italy. These Germanic men and women lived in the area of modern Germany during the first five centuries. They called themselves *Langobardi*, or "Long Beards," from which the name *Lombard* derives. In the first part of the sixth century under their ruler Waccho, Lombards established a kingdom in the area of modern Hungary. As we have seen, Justinian's wars and a devastating plague drained the Byzantine Empire's strength. Without imperial troops to defend Italy, the peninsula became vulnerable to invasion. The Lombard king Alboin (ca. 565–572) took advantage of the situation and invaded Italy in 568. Alboin's army contained soldiers of different ethnic backgrounds. In addition to Lombards, his forces included smaller bands of Goths, Avars, Saxons, and other non-Romans. Some were Arian Christians; others were Catholic Christians. Still others practiced polytheism. Alboin's highly diverse army indicated his ability to attract followers but also implied a lack of common purpose among them other than the opportunity to pillage. That lack of common purpose meant that Alboin lacked the ability to build a strong, lasting kingdom.

The Romans living in Italy put up a feeble resistance. Within three years Alboin controlled all of northern Italy, Tuscany, and parts of southern Italy in the region of Spoleto, near Naples. Yet until 700, the Lombard kings proved weak. Throughout their lands real power lay in the hands of semi-independent dukes based in heavily populated urban centers such as Benevento and Spoleto. These dukes gradually expanded their possessions within Italy, jockeying among themselves for land and power. After 700, the Lombard kings reasserted their authority by developing a royal bureaucracy of judges and legal officials, compensating somewhat for the weaknesses of the Lombard system evident in the initial conquest. The new infrastructure enabled them to overshadow the dukes' local authority.

Despite the Lombard kings' newfound strength, they still faced two formidable external enemies. The most dangerous of these were the Byzantine forces who remained in the Exarchate of Ravenna. These soldiers hoped to crush the Lombards and regain control of Italy in the name of the Byzantine emperors. Again and again they battled with Lombards in an attempt to crush their kingdom, but their efforts proved futile. In 751 the Lombard ruler Aistulf defeated the Exarchate of Ravenna. The Franks posed the second threat to the Lombards. These hardy warriors marched into Italy several times during the seventh century, trying to crush the Lombards and seize their lands. Sometimes they joined with Byzantine forces from the Exarchate of Ravenna. During other attacks, the Franks had the backing of the popes in Rome, who resented the Lombards' power. Despite their diplomatic and military efforts, however, the Franks failed to achieve their goals of conquest. The Lombards always drove them out of Italy.

The tide of battle soon turned against the Lombards. In the middle of the eighth century, internal political disputes once again tore at the kingdom. The Lombards' diplomatic relations with the papacy and their uneasy standoff with the Franks deteriorated. As we will see in Chapter 8, the Frankish king Charlemagne, responding to a call for assistance from Pope Leo III, invaded Italy and crushed the Lombards in 774.

The Growth of the Papacy

In theory, the Byzantine emperors still controlled the city of Rome and its surrounding lands during this violent time. However, strapped for cash and troops, these distant rulers proved unequal to the task of defending the city from internal or external threats. In the resulting power vacuum, the popes stepped in to manage local affairs and became, in effect, princes who ruled over a significant part of Italy.

Gregory the Great (r. 590–604) stands out as the most powerful of these popes. The pragmatic Gregory realized that Rome could no longer count on Byzantium for protection. The Roman Church's future, he concluded, lay with the Frankish kingdoms in western Europe instead. Through clever diplomacy, Gregory successfully cultivated the goodwill of the Christian communities of western Europe by offering religious sanction to the authority of friendly kings. He negotiated skillfully with his Lombard, Frankish, and Byzantine neighbors to gain their support and establish the authority of the Roman church. He also encouraged Christian missionaries to spread the faith in England and Germany. In addition, he took steps to train educated clergymen for future generations, in this way securing Christianity's future in western Europe.

Gregory had set the stage for a dramatic increase in papal power. As his successors' authority expanded over the next few centuries, relations between Rome and the Byzantine emperors slowly soured. By the early eighth century the popes abandoned the fiction that they were still subject to the Byzantines and sought protection from the Frankish kings. The popes established political independence during the period but remained dependent on the Franks for military assistance when necessary.

DIFFERENT KINGDOMS, SHARED TRADITIONS

With the exception of England, where Anglo-Saxon invaders drove out the Roman population, the leaders of the new Germanic kingdoms faced a similar problem: how should the Germanic minority govern subject peoples who vastly outnumbered them. These rulers found a solution to this problem by blending Roman and Germanic traditions. For example, the kings served as administrators of the civil order in the style of the Roman emperor, issuing laws and managing a bureaucracy. They also served as war leaders in the Germanic tradition, leading their men into battle in search of glory and booty. As the Germanic kings defined new roles for themselves, they discovered that Christianity could bind all their subjects together into one community of believers. The merging of Roman and Germanic traditions could also be traced in the law, which eventually erased the distinctions between Romans and Germans, and in the ability of women to own property, a right far more common among the Romans than the Germans.

Civil Authority: The Roman Legacy

In imitation of Roman practice, the monarchs of Latin Christendom designated themselves the source of all law and believed that they ruled with God's approval. Kings controlled all appointments to civil, military, and religious office. Accompanied by troops and administrative assistants, they also traveled throughout their lands to dispense justice, collect taxes, and enforce royal authority.

Frankish Gaul provides an apt example of how these monarchs adopted preexisting Roman institutions. When Clovis conquered the Visigoths in Gaul, he inherited the nearly intact Roman infrastructure and administrative system that had survived the collapse of Roman imperial authority. Merovingian kings (as well as Visigoth and Lombard rulers in Spain and Italy) gladly maintained parts of the preexisting system—and the officials who ran them. For instance, Frankish kings relied on the bishops and counts in each region to deal with local problems. Because Roman aristocrats were literate and had experience in Roman administration on the local level, they often served as counts. Based in cities, these officials presided in local law courts, collected revenues, and raised troops for the king's army. Most bishops also stemmed from the Roman aristocracy. In addition to performing their religious responsibilities, bishops aided their king by providing for the poor, ransoming hostages who had been captured by enemy warriors from other kingdoms, and bringing social and legal injustices to the monarch's attention. Finally, the kings used dukes, most of whom were Franks, to served as local military commanders and community patrons.

War Leaders and *Wergild*: The Germanic Legacy

The kingdoms of Latin Christendom developed from war bands led by chieftains. By rewarding brave warriors with land and loot taken in war, as well as with revenues skimmed from subject peoples, chieftains created political communities of loyal men and their families, called clans or kin groups°. Though these followers sometimes came from diverse backgrounds, they all owed military service to the clan chiefs. Because leadership in Germanic society was hereditary, networks of loyalty and kinship expanded through the generations.

Though the principle of loyalty to a superior defined life in these Germanic communities, many men ignored this principle in the pursuit of their own interests. Rivalries among warriors unwilling to follow their chieftain and among power-hungry men who competed for the kingship within the royal families often led to bloody struggles that weakened the political fabric of the kingdoms. Frankish leaders proved particularly vicious in their quest for power, thinking nothing of betrayal and assassination of their rivals. Despite the bloodshed and brutal competition for power, the various political communities gradually evolved into distinct ethnic groups led by a king, such as the Lombards and the Franks. These ethnic groups developed a sense of shared history, kinship, and culture. The coalescence of these kingdoms resulted from the Germanic settlers' pride in their new homelands as well as from their allegiance to their monarchs who governed them fairly at home and who protected them from foreign enemies.

The new Germanic kingdoms had highly hierarchical societies geared for warfare. Kinship-based clans stood as the most basic unit of Germanic society. The clan consisted of all the households and blood relations loyal to the clan chief, a warrior who protected them and spoke on their behalf before the king on matters of justice. Clan chieftains in turn swore oaths of loyalty to their kings and agreed to fight for him in wars against other kingdoms. The clan leaders formed an aristocracy among the Germanic peoples. Like the Roman elites before them, the royal house and the clan-based aristocracy consisted of rich men and women who controlled huge estates. The new Germanic aristocrats intermarried with the pre-existing Roman elites of wealthy landholders, thus maintaining control of most of the land. These people stood at the very top of the social order, winning the loyalty of their followers by giving them gifts and parcels of land. Under the weight of this new upper class, the majority of the population, the ordinary farmers and artisans, slipped into a deepening dependence on these nobles. Eventually, ordinary farmers merged with the Roman peasantry. Most peasants could not enter into legal transactions in their own name, and they had few protections and privileges under the law. Even so, they were better off than the slaves who toiled at society's very lowest depths. Valued simply as property, these men, women, and children had virtually no rights in the eyes of the law.

Though this social hierarchy showed some similarities to societies in earlier Roman times, the new kingdoms' various social groups were defined by law in a fundamentally different way. Unlike Roman law, which defined people by citizenship rights and obligations, the laws of the new kingdoms defined people by their wergild°. A Germanic concept, *wergild* referred to what an individual was worth in case he or she suffered some grievance at the hands of another. If someone injured or murdered someone else, *wergild* was the amount of compensation in gold that the wrongdoer's family had to pay to the victim's family.

In the wergild system, every person had a price that depended on social status. For example, among the Lombards service to the king increased a free man's worth—his *wergild* was higher. In the Frankish kingdom, if a freeborn woman of childbearing age was murdered, the killer's family had to pay 600 pieces of gold. Two-thirds of that sum went to the victim's family. The king received the rest. Noble women and men had higher *wergild* than peasants, while slaves and women past childbearing age were worth very little.

If proper *wergild* was not paid, the injured party's kin group felt obligated to gain vengeance for their loss. The desire for revenge and compensation frequently led to vicious feuding. In order to minimize the bloodletting that could sometimes drag on for generations after a crime had been committed, representatives of the king or a local aristocrat urged families to accept *wergild.*

Unity Through Law and Christianity

Within the kingdoms of Latin Christendom, rulers achieved unity by merging Germanic and Roman legal principles and by accepting Roman Christianity (Catholicism). Religious diversity among the peoples in their kingdoms made this unity difficult to establish. As we saw in Chapter 6, many of the tribes that invaded the Roman Empire during the fifth century practiced Arian Christianity. They kept themselves apart from the Latin or Catholic Christians by force of law. For example, they declared marriage between Arian and Catholic Christians illegal.

These barriers began to collapse when some Germanic kings converted to the Catholic Christianity of their Roman subjects. Some converted for reasons of personal belief, or because their wives were Catholic. Others decided to become Catholic to gain wider political support. For instance, when Clovis converted to Catholic Christianity about 500 and drove the Arian Visigoths into Spain, laws against intermarriage in Gaul disappeared. More and more Franks and Romans began to marry one another, blending the two formerly separate communities into one and reinforcing the strength of Catholicism. Similarly in 587, when the Visigothic king Reccared converted from Arianism to Catholicism, he made Catholic Christianity the official religion of Spain. Soon Visigoths and Romans began to intermarry legally. In Italy, the Lombards had become Catholic by about 650 and they, too, began to marry Romans. By 750, all of the western European kingdoms had become Catholic.

Germanic kings adopted Roman Catholic Christianity, but they had no intention of abandoning their own Germanic law, which differed from Roman law on many issues, especially relating to the family and property. Instead, they offered their Roman subjects the opportunity to turn their back on Roman law, which still governed their lives, in favor of living under the Germanic law that governed the king. Clovis's *Law Code* or *Salic Law,* published sometime between 508 and 511, illustrates this development. The *Law Code* applied to Franks and to any other non-Roman peoples in his realm who chose to live according to Frankish law. Because the Romans dwelling in the Frankish kingdom technically still followed the laws of Byzantium, Clovis did not presume to legislate for them. Romans could follow their own law if they wished, or they could follow his laws and become Franks.

Permitting his subjects to switch to Frankish law helped Clovis strengthen his kingdom. It fostered a shared sense of Frankish identity throughout his kingdom. Eventually the Frankish king's policies eroded distinctions among Romans, Franks, and other ethnic groups within his realm. By 750, most Romans had chosen to abandon their legal identity as Romans and live according to Frankish law, and the distinction between Roman and Frank lost all meaning.

A similar process occurred in other Germanic kingdoms. The Lombards slowly mixed with the Romans living in Italy. By 750 their law, which originally protected only Lombards, now applied to all the Catholic inhabitants of Italy. In Spain, the Roman and Visigothic populations merged once the religious barriers came down. In 654 the Visigothic king Recceswinth abolished the separate Roman law entirely and brought his entire population under Visigothic law. As in the Frankish and Lombard kingdoms, this unification of two peoples under one law happened without protest, a sign that various groups had blended politically, religiously, and culturally.

Women and Property

Roman law influenced more than just local administration in Latin Christendom. It also prompted Germanic rulers to reconsider the question of women's right to inherit land. In the Roman Empire, women had inherited land without difficulty. Indeed, perhaps as much as 25 percent of the land in the entire realm had been owned by women. In many Germanic societies, however, men could inherit land and property far more easily than women. Attitudes about female inheritance began to shift when the Germanic settlers established their homes in previously Roman provinces—and began to marry Roman women who owned property.

By comparing the law codes of the new kingdoms over time, historians have detected the impact of Roman customs on Germanic inheritance laws. By the late eighth century women in Frankish Gaul, Lombard Italy, and Visigothic Spain could inherit land, though often under the restriction that they must eventually pass it on to their sons. Germanic rulers adopted the custom of female inheritance because it enabled the new settlers to keep within their own families the property that their Roman wives had inherited and brought to the marriage. Despite these limitations, the new laws transformed women's lives. A woman who received an inheritance of land could live more independently, support herself if her husband died, and have a say in the community's decisions.

The Spread of Catholic Christianity in the New Kingdoms of Western Europe

As Catholic Christianity slowly spread through the new kingdoms, churchmen decided that they had a moral responsibility to convert all the people of the world to their faith. They sent out missionaries to explain the religion to nonbelievers and challenge the worship of polytheist gods. Their hard work paid off. By 750 everyone living in the new kingdoms except Jews had become Catholic Christians.

Meanwhile, Bishops based in cities directed people's spiritual lives, instilling the moral and social conventions of Christianity through sermons delivered in church. Monks such as Boniface traveled from their home monasteries in

■ Map 7.4 Spread of Latin Christianity in Northern Europe

By ca. 750 Catholicism had spread throughout western Europe. Travelling monks converted many polytheists to Christianity. They established monasteries that served as centers of education and places where Latin literature was copied and preserved. Because Latin was the language of worship and education throughout these lands, historians refer to Christianity in western Europe as Latin Christianity. This term distinguishes western Europe from Byzantine lands in the eastern Mediterranean, where Greek served as the main language of worship and education.

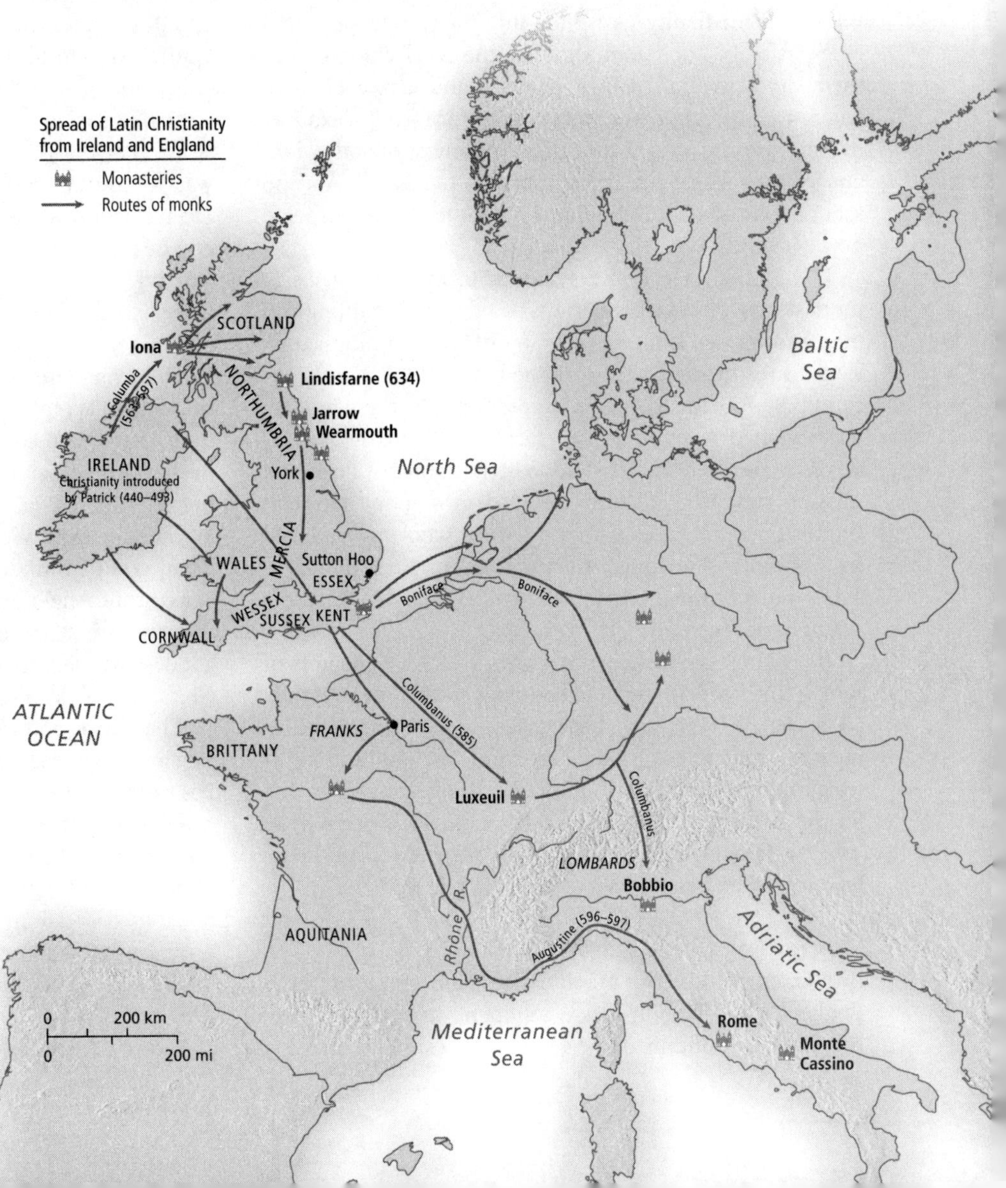

Ireland, England, and Gaul to spread the faith into Germany and other areas. Monasteries became centers of intellectual life, and monks replaced urban aristocrats as the keepers of books and learning.

Converting the Irish

Though the Romans had conquered most of Britain during the imperial period, they never attempted to bring Ireland into their empire. Thus the island off England's west coast had had only minimal contact with Christianity. This changed after 432. According to a pious legend, at some point in the early 400s, Irish slavers stole a young boy named Patrick (ca. 410–ca. 492) from his Christian family in England and transported him to Ireland, where they sold him into bondage. Patrick learned Irish during his years in captivity. He managed to escape to Britain, where he eventually became a bishop. In 432 Patrick returned to Ireland as a missionary. There, he converted thousands of polytheist worshipers by preaching Catholic Christianity.

But Ireland was still a rural place. Patrick and his fellow missionaries wondered how to Christianize the Irish without a Roman urban foundation to build on. Elsewhere in the West Christianity spread out into the countryside from cities, with bishops administering the local church from their city cathedrals. However, the island lacked cities in which to build churches and housing for bishops. No one living in Ireland knew Latin, Greek, or any of the other languages into which the Bible had been translated. And no schools existed where churchmen might teach the Gospel to new converts.

Irish churchmen found solutions to these problems in monasteries, places where priests could receive training and men and women from the surrounding communities could learn to read Latin and absorb the basics of Christian education. By 750, the Irish scholars produced by these monasteries gained a reputation in their own lands as well as across western Europe. Irish monasteries sent out dozens of missionaries, who in turn founded new monasteries in England, France, and Germany. Irish scholars produced magnificently illustrated manuscripts in their libraries. These books brought Irish art to all the lands where the missionaries traveled.

Irish monasteries sometimes grew rich from the gifts of money and property provided by kings and other pious folk. Such centers, especially those that became bishops' headquarters, acquired substantial economic and political influence in their local communities by settling disputes, caring for the sick, and employing local laborers. Having proved its value in Ireland, the monastery system spread from the island to England and then to the European continent.

Converting the Anglo-Saxons

By 600, numerous Irish missionaries had begun to travel to England and the European continent to establish new monasteries. Columbanus (543–615), for example, founded several monasteries on the Irish model in the kingdom of Burgundy. The most notable among these were the monastery of Luxeuil in the Rhone River valley, and Bobbio in northern Italy. These centers inspired the founding of many additional nunneries and monasteries in northern Gaul. From there Catholicism spread east of the Rhine River, into lands where the religion had not yet penetrated.

Irish missionaries also expanded their monastic network in their own land. Columba (521–597), for instance, founded several new monasteries in Ireland as well as one on the island of Iona, Scotland's western coast. From this thriving community missionaries began to bring Catholicism to the men and women of Scotland. The offshoot monastery of Lindisfarne in northern England also became a dynamic center of learning and missionary activity. During the seventh century, missionaries based there carried Christianity to many other parts of England. They also began converting the people of Frisia on the North Sea, in the area of the modern Netherlands.

Irish monks who went to Anglo-Saxon England sometimes found themselves working side by side with monks sent from Rome by Pope Gregory the Great (r. 590–604) and his successors. Gregory believed that the Catholic Church should fill the void left by the collapse of Roman government. By filling this void, Catholics could forge a Christian society throughout Europe. But Gregory understood that the first step in creating that new community was to convert as many people as possible to the faith. Deep learning about the religion could come later. To that end he instructed missionaries to permit local variations in worship and to accommodate harmless vestiges of pre-Christian worship practices. "Don't tear down their temples," Gregory advised; "put a cross on the roofs!"

Following Gregory's pragmatic suggestion, missionaries in England accepted certain Anglo-Saxon calendar conventions that stemmed from polytheist worship. For example, in the Anglo-Saxon calendar, the weekdays took their names from old gods: Tuesday derived from Tiw, a war god; Wednesday from Woden, king of the gods; Thursday from Thor, god of thunder; and Friday from Freya, goddess of agriculture. Anglo-Saxon deities eventually found their way into the Christian calendar as well. Eostre, for example, a goddess whose festival came in April, gave her name to the Christian holiday Easter.

The Irish and Roman monks working throughout England disagreed strongly about proper Catholic practice. For instance, they argued over how to perform baptism, the ritual of anointing someone with water to admit him or her into the Christian community. They bickered about how monks should shave the tops of their heads to show their religious dedication, and they squabbled about the correct means of calculating the date of Easter. These disputes threatened to create deep divisions among England's Christians. The overall conflict finally found resolution in 664 in the Anglo-Saxon kingdom of Northumbria, where

photo to come .612

photo to come .688

A Mixture of Cultural Traditions in Anglo-Saxon England
This box , which is about 10 inches long, 6 inches high, and 8 inches wide, was carved from whalebone early in the first half of the eighth century in England. The style continues the Roman art of ivory carving, but the writing on the box is Anglo-Saxon. The box depicts scenes from Roman, Jewish, Christian, and Germanic traditions. Images on different sides include Romulus and Remus (the twin founders of Rome) , the Adoration of the Magi (wise men who worshiped the infant Jesus in his manger crib), the Roman capture of Jerusalem in 70, and Weland, a magical artisan from Germanic mythology. Used to hold precious objects at a monastery, this box illustrates the broad range of cultural interests and the rich intellectual life that thrived at these religious centers in England. The box captures encounters among Christianity, Anglo-Saxon culture, and the legacy of classical antiquity.

monastic life flourished. At a council of monks and royal advisers called the Synod of Whitby, the Northumbrian monarch commanded that the Roman version of Catholicism would prevail in his kingdom. His decision eventually was accepted throughout England.

Monastic Intellectual Life

The missionaries from Rome were members of the vigorous monastic movement initiated by Benedict of Nursia (ca. 480–547) from his monastery at Monte Cassino in Italy (see Chapter 6). These monks followed Benedict's *Rule,* a guidebook for the management of monastic life and spirituality. In the *Rule* Benedict had written that individual monks should live temperate lives devoted to spiritual contemplation, communal prayer, and manual labor. So that their contemplations might not depart from the path of truth, monks must also seek guidance in the Bible, in the writings of the renowned theologians, and in works of spiritual edification. For Benedict, contemplative reading constituted a fundamental part of monastic life. Thus, monks had to be literate in Latin. They needed training in the Latin classics, which required books.

Medieval monasteries set aside at least two rooms—the scriptorium° and the library—to meet the growing demand for books. In the scriptorium, scribes laboriously copied Latin and Greek manuscripts letter by letter and word by word, often without understanding what they were copying. But copying manuscripts was an act of religious devotion, so the monks persevered. Monastery libraries were small in comparison to the public libraries of fourth-century Rome—but the volumes were cherished and carefully controlled. Because books were precious possessions, these libraries set forth strict rules for their use. Some librarians chained books to tables to prevent theft. Others pronounced a curse against anyone who failed to return a borrowed book. Nevertheless, librarians also generously lent books to other monasteries to copy.

Monks preferred to read Christian texts with a spiritual message, so these books were the most frequently copied. In many monasteries, however, monks preserved non-Christian texts. By doing so, they kept knowledge of Latin and classical learning alive. Indeed, every surviving work by an author of the Classical Age was copied and passed on by monks in the sixth and seventh centuries. In addition to Christian works, monks also studied the writings of Latin poets such as Vergil and Juvenal, scientists such as Pliny the Elder, and philosophers such as Boethius and Cicero, as well as the works of grammarians, mathematicians, scientists, and physicians from the ancient world. Without the monasteries and scriptoria, we would know almost nothing about the literature of the classical world today.

Sometimes classical works survived merely by accident. Because parchment, the specially prepared sheepskin on which writers copied their manuscripts, was expensive, many monks scrubbed old manuscripts clean and reused them to copy religious texts. By studying these reused parchment sheets, called palimpsests°, modern scholars have succeeded in reclaiming vital classical texts that otherwise would have been lost forever. Cicero's treatise *On the Republic,* which has influenced many political thinkers including the writers of the U.S. Constitution, is one example. This work survived only because in the seventh century at the monastery of Bobbio in northern Italy, a monk erased Cicero's text and copied an interpretation of the Psalms by Augustine onto the parchment. Modern scholars can read Cicero's words below Augustine's.

Monks did far more than merely copy ancient texts, however. Some wrote original books of their own. At the English monastery at Jarrow, for example, Bede (d. 735) became the most distinguished scholar in eighth-century Europe. He wrote many books, including the *History of the English Church and People.* This work provides an invaluable source of information about the early Anglo-Saxon kingdoms.

Monks carried books with them when they embarked on missionary journeys. They also acquired new books during their travels. For instance, Benedict Biscop, the founder of the monasteries of Wearmouth (674) and Jarrow (682) in England, made six trips to Italy. Each time he brought back crates of books on all subjects, including works written by classical authors whom a handful of monks studied with interest. Other Anglo-Saxon missionaries transported this literary heritage to the monasteries they founded in Germany during the eighth century. As monks avidly read, copied, wrote, and transported books of all sorts, knowledge and intellectual discourse flourished in the monasteries.

Monks shared their expanding knowledge with Christians outside the monastery walls. They established schools at monasteries where boys (and in some places girls) could learn to read and write. Most of the very few literate people who lived between 550 and 750 gained their education at monastery schools. The men trained in these schools played an important role in society as officials and bureaucrats. Their skills in reading and writing were necessary for keeping records and writing business and diplomatic letters.

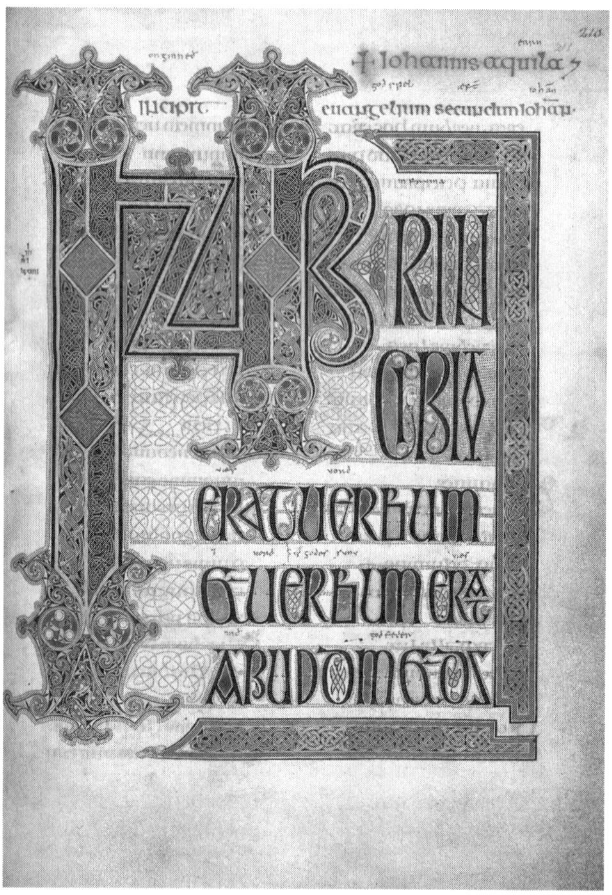

The Lindisfarne Gospels

Eadfrith, a monk and later bishop of the Lindisfarne monastery in England, completed the writing and Illustration of this Gospel book by 698 to honor a saint whose relics had come to the altar that year. A monk wrote an Anglo-Saxon translation of the book between the lines of Latin sometime during the tenth century. The artist painted soft, bright colors into elaborate interconnected designs that characterize Celtic art, showing continuity of Celtic artistic traditions through the Roman and early medieval periods. The page shown here is the first page of the Gospel of John and was the most complicated of Eadfrith's designs.

Jews in a Christian World

For Jews during this era, quality of life varied in the different western European kingdoms. Jews continued to work in every profession, own land, serve in the army, and engage in trade. Most of the time monarchs protected the Jewish minorities living in their kingdoms. Thus many Jews prospered in the Frankish, Visigothic, and Lombard realms (no Jews lived in England during this period). At times, theological curiosity led to intellectual encounters between Jews and Christians. In Lombard Italy, for example, Jews and Christians sometimes engaged in public debates about their religious beliefs.

Yet churchmen still blamed Jews collectively for Jesus' death. Consequently, Jews sometimes suffered severe discrimination at the hands of Christian rulers. For example, in Visigothic Spain, kings passed new laws attempting to force Jews to convert to Christianity or endure terrible penalties, including torture, exile, and enslavement.

Leading churchmen in the western kingdoms also developed theological reasons for wanting Jews to convert to Christianity. Pope Gregory urged conversion because he believed that Christ would return to Earth only when Jews embraced Christianity. Nevertheless, Gregory advocated the use of persuasion and kindness to encourage conversion, rather than force or terror. On numerous occasions he intervened to stop Christians from committing violence against Jews. Other Christian writers, such as the Isidore of Seville (in Spain), further developed the idea that Jews had a place in Christian society because of their role in bringing about Christ's return and then the Day of Judgment. Highly ambivalent, Christians both persecuted and protected Jews. They permitted Jews to live in their midst, but granted them fewer rights than Christians had. Violence against Jews might flare up suddenly, yet its perpetrators neither applied it systematically nor sustained it for very long.

CHRONOLOGY

The Beginnings of Latin Christendom

482–511	Clovis reigns; Frankish kingdom divided at his death
CA. 525	Benedict founds monastery at Monte Cassino
520s–560s	Slavs penetrate Balkans
542	Bubonic plague strikes Mediterranean
554	Justinian's armies defeat Ostrogoths in Italy
568	Lombards invade Italy
582	Avars enter Balkans
587	Visigothic king of Spain converts to Catholicism; Columbanus travels to Gaul from Ireland
597	Augustine of Canterbury begins conversions in England
672	Lombards accept Catholicism
727–743	Lombards attack Byzantine holdings in Italy
732	Charles Martel defeats Muslims at Poitiers
751	Pepin overthrows last Merovingian king; Exarchate of Italy Falls to Lombards

CONCLUSION

Three Cultural Realms

The death of the Byzantine emperor Justinian I in 565 marked the last time the territory spanning from Spain to Carthage to Constantinople would be united under one imperial ruler. The Persian Empire still menaced Byzantium's eastern frontier, and except for Italy and some coastal areas of Spain, western Europe was now ruled by Germanic kings. During the next two centuries western Europe, the Mediterranean world, and the Middle East as far as India and central Asia were utterly reconfigured politically and culturally. By ca. 750, three new realms had come into sharp focus: the Christian Byzantine Empire based at Constantinople; the vast Umayyad caliphate created by Muhammad's Islamic followers; and Latin Christendom in western Europe, which was fragmented politically but united by Catholic Christianity. Each of these regions was a community of uncompromising religious faith. The cultural foundations they established as well as the bitter divisions that emerged among them are still shaping the West today.

These three cultural realms of the West each borrowed from the heritage of ancient Rome, especially its network of cities, which survived most completely in the Mediterranean and the Middle East. They were each influenced by the religious traditions of antiquity, especially the emphasis on monotheism in Judaism. They each adapted parts of Roman law but reshaped it to suit changing needs and new cultural influences. The heritage of Rome remained strongest in Byzantium. Indeed, the Byzantines continued to call themselves Romans. But during the sixth to eighth centuries these three cultural realms came to be distinguished by the language that dominated intellectual life and by the forms of monotheism practiced. In Byzantium the Greek language and Orthodox Christianity with its distinctively elaborate ceremonies defined the culture. In the Umayyad Caliphate a similar function was performed by the Arabic language and the five pillars of Islam. In western Europe, many languages were spoken but Latin became the universal language of Catholicism and government. None of these cultural realms, however, had yet achieved the level of uniformity and monolithic authority they would achieve during the subsequent centuries of the Middle Ages.

The year 750 saw the end of the Umayyad caliphate and the limit of Muslim expansion in western Europe and central Asia. After that the Byzantine Empire struggled for survival. In the Latin West, the Merovingian dynasty lost control of the Frankish kingdom. In the next chapter we will see how the Carolingian dynasty that succeeded the Merovingians led the Franks to predominance in western Europe. We will also discover how the Abbasid caliphate inaugurated a new, rich period in Islamic life, and how Byzantium began to reassert itself politically and culturally.

Suggestions For Further Reading

For a comprehensive list of suggested readings, please go to www.ablongman.com/levack/chapter7

Bowersock, Glen, Peter Brown, and Oleg Grabar, eds. *Late Antiquity: A Guide to the Post-Classical World.* 1999. Interpretive essays combined with encyclopedia entries make this a starting point for current discussion.

Brown, Peter. *The Rise of Western Christendom: Triumph and Diversity A.D. 200–1000.* 2001. A brilliant interpretation of the development of Christianity in its social context.

Brown, Thomas S. *Gentlemen and Officers: Imperial Administration and Aristocratic Power in Byzantine Italy, A.D. 554–800.* 1984. The basic study of Byzantine rule in Italy between Justinian and Charlemagne.

Bulliet, Richard W. *The Camel and the Wheel.* 1990. A fascinating investigation of the importance of the camel in history.

Cohen, Jeremy. *Living Letters of the Law: Ideas of the Jew in Medieval Christianity.* 1999. A masterful investigation of early medieval Judaism.

Cook, Michael. *Muhammad.* 1996. A short, incisive account of Muhammad's life that questions the traditional picture.

Cormack, Robin. *Writing in Gold: Byzantine Society and Its Icons.* 1985. An expert discussion of icons in the Byzantine world.

Crone, Patricia, and Michael Cook. *Hagarism: The Making of the Islamic World.* 1977. A challenging new view of the origins of Islam.

Donner, Fred M. *The Early Islamic Conquests.* 1981. Discusses the first phases of Islamic expansion.

Geary, Patrick J. *The Peoples of Europe in the Early Middle Ages.* 2002. Discusses the emergence of the new kingdoms of Europe, stressing the incorporation of Roman elements.

Hourani, George. *Arab Seafaring in the Indian Ocean in Ancient and Early Medieval Times.* 1995. The standard discussion of Arab maritime activity.

Robinson, Francis, ed. *The Cambridge Illustrated History of the Islamic World.* 1977. Many excellent and well-illustrated articles that will be useful for beginners.

Strayer, Joseph B., ed. *Dictionary of the Middle Ages.* 1986. An indispensable reference work.

Treadgold, Warren. *A History of the Byzantine State and Society.* 1997. A reliable narrative of Byzantine history.

Webster, Leslie and Michelle Brown, eds. *The Transformation of the Roman World, A.D. 400–900.* 1997. A well-illustrated synthesis with maps and bibliography.

Wickham, Chris. *Early Medieval Italy: Central Government and Local Society, 400–1000.* 1981. Examines the economic and social transformation of Italy.

Notes

1. Willibald, *The Life of Boniface,* in *Anglo-Saxon Saints and Heroes* trans. Clinton Albertson (1967) 308–310.
2. Al-Tabari, *The History of Al-Tabari. vol. XVII. The First Civil War,* trans. and annotated by G. R. Hawting (1985), 50.
3. Kent Rigsby, *Zeitschrift für Papyrologie and Epigraphie* 126 (1999) 175–176.

CHAPTER 8

Empires and Borderlands: The Early Middle Ages, 750–1050

IN 860 FIERCE RUS TRIBESMEN ABOARD A FLEET OF SLEEK DRAGON SHIPS RAIDED THE villages along the shores of the Black Sea and then stomped up to the gates of Constantinople, ready for pillage and rape. Completely taken by surprise, the Byzantines were gripped with panic. The Byzantine patriarch Photius called upon the people to repent of their sins to avoid God's wrath, and when the Rus unexpectedly broke camp and departed, it was interpreted as an act of divine intervention.

Throughout the tenth century, the barbarian Rus tribes mounted sporadic raids and invasions on civilized Byzantine cities, particularly Constantinople, the largest city in the Western world. The Byzantines clearly considered the Rus as little more than savages, prone to the worst kinds of violence, and tried to keep them under control while in Constantinople by signing treaties. The treaties stipulated that no more than fifty Rus could enter the city at one time, all must be unarmed, and they all had to leave by autumn. In exchange for civilized behavior, however, the Rus received during their stay free baths, food, provisions for a month, and equipment for their return. The Rus inhabited the river valleys of present-day Ukraine and Russia in eastern Europe. After spending the winters collecting tribute from the Slavic tribes, the Rus set off in their boats, risking dangerous rapids and waterfalls on the Dnieper River and ambush from hostile tribes, to reach the Black Sea and the splendid emporium of the world, Constantinople, which they called simply the "Great City."

Accustomed to the rough life of long winter treks, grubby little villages, and constant danger, the Rus were dazzled by the sight of the Great City, with its half a million inhabitants, the gilded cupolas of its churches, the marble palaces of

Chapter Outline

- The Carolingians
- Invasions and Recovery in the Latin West
- Byzantium and Eastern Europe
- The Dynamism of Islam

Reliquary Bust of Charlemagne, from ca. 1350: This bust was made more than 500 years after the death of Charlemagne, which means it is unlikely to be an accurate portrait of him. Medieval portraits, however, were not intended to represent the individuals as they actually looked but to represent their status or spiritual qualities. The majesty of this work, which housed some of the bones of Charlemagne, encouraged veneration of the great ruler considered a saint by many during the Middle Ages.

the aristocrats and emperor, the cavernous wharves and warehouses of its merchants, and the twelve miles of fortifications and walls that protected the city. The people of Constantinople were equally astonished by the sight of the Rus merchants—sun-worn, fur-clad, and armed to the teeth—whom they met with fascination and no little fear. The usual purpose of these repeated visitations was trade. The merchants of Constantinople traded Byzantine and Chinese silks, Persian glass, Arabian silver (highly prized by the Rus), and Indian spices for honey, wax, slaves, and musty bales of furs from Scandinavia and what is now northern Russia.

In the merchant stalls of Constantinople, traders from many cultures met, haggled, and came to know something of one another. None perhaps were more unlike each other than the rough Rus and the refined Byzantines, but their mutual desires for profit kept them in a persistent, if tentative, embrace. These repeated interactions among very different peoples who traded, competed, and fought with one another offer clues for understanding the medieval world, also known as the Middle Ages.

The term *Middle Ages* refers to the period between the ancient and modern civilizations, that is from ca. 550 to 1500. The culture of that period rested on the foundations of three great civilizations: the Latin-Christian kingdoms of western Europe; the Greek Christianity of Byzantium; and the Arabic-speaking Islamic caliphates of the Middle East, North Africa, and Spain. The dynamic interactions among these three civilizations, distinguished by religion and language, lay at the heart of medieval culture. But the great civilizations also encountered barbarian peoples outside Christian and Islamic civilization—traders, raiders, and nomads from the North and East.

During the Early Middle Ages, the period from ca. 750 to 1050, the Latin, Greek, and Islamic kingdoms and empires began to form a distinctively Western civilization, but there were vast borderlands between them and at the frontiers with barbarian peoples that escaped Western domination and cultural influence. In this crucial phase in forming Western civilization, expansive empires made possible greater political cohesion that brought together ethnically and linguistically diverse peoples under obedience to an emperor, or caliph in the case of the Islamic empires. The empires enforced or encouraged uniformity of religion, spread a common language among the ruling elite, and instituted systematic principles for governing. The most important innovation from this period was that a distinctive Latin Christian or Roman Catholic culture began to emerge in western Europe. The Carolingian empire, which lasted from 800 to 843 and controlled much of western Europe, re-established the Roman Empire in the West for the first time in more than 300 years and sponsored a revival of interest in antiquity called the Carolingian Renaissance. The Carolingian empire's collapse was followed by a period of anarchy as Europe faced wave after wave of hostile invaders. Only during the late tenth and eleventh centuries did the kingdoms of western Europe become strong enough to resist the invaders and to convert many of them to Roman Catholicism. At the same time the strength of the Byzantine empire was sapped by invaders and internal strife, but it too revived and experienced a remarkable Renaissance under the Macedonian dynasty (867–1056). The most energetic of the three civilizations during this period was certainly Islam, which threatened militarily both the Latin Christian kingdoms and Byzantium, supported important philosophical and scientific work, and produced a thriving economy.

It was during the period from 750 to 1050 that the first signs appeared of a shift in the balance of military and cultural power away from Byzantium and the Islamic states toward the kingdoms of western Europe. The principal task of this and the following chapter is to trace how that happened. This chapter will address four questions: (1) How did the Carolingian empire contribute to establishing a distinctive western European culture? (2) After the collapse of the Carolingian empire, how did the Western kingdoms consolidate in the core of the European continent and how did Roman Catholicism spread to its periphery? (3) Why did Byzantium revive after a series of invasions and then decline? (4) What were the sources of dynamism and weakness within the Islamic states?

The Carolingians

Among the successor kingdoms to the Roman Empire in the West, as we saw in Chapter 7, none was more powerful militarily than the kingdom of the Franks, which encompassed much of the ancient Roman province of Gaul. The Merovingian dynasty ruled the kingdom of the Franks during the sixth and seventh centuries. But the Merovingian dynasty was plagued by factions, royal assassinations, and do-nothing kings. The Merovingians were so weak that real power passed to the "mayor of the palace," the official in charge of the royal household. In 751 one of these mayors, Pepin the Short (ca. 714–768), deposed the last of the Merovingian kings and made himself king of the Franks. Pepin inaugurated the Carolingian dynasty, which vastly expanded the political and cultural reach of the Franks to encompass much of western Europe.

Both the weak Merovingians and the strong Carolingians illustrated how the problem of succession from one king to another destabilized early medieval monarchies. The kingdom was considered the private property of the royal family, and according to Frankish custom, a father was obliged to divide his estates among his legitimate sons. As a result, whenever a king of the Franks died, the kingdom was divided up. When Pepin died in 768, the kingdom was divided between his sons, Charlemagne and Carloman. When Carloman died suddenly in 771, Charlemagne ignored the inheritance rights of Carloman's sons and may even have had them killed, making himself the sole ruler of the Franks.

THE LEADERSHIP OF CHARLEMAGNE

Charlemagne's (r. 768–814) ruthlessness with his own nephews epitomized the crafty leadership that made him the mightiest ruler in western Europe and gave him the nickname of Charles the Great. One of his court poets labeled him "The King Father of Europe"; no monarch in European history has enjoyed such posthumous fame.

An unusually tall and imposing figure, Charlemagne was a superb athlete and swimmer, a lover of jokes and high living, but also a deeply pious Christian. As Pepin's eldest son, he had frequently accompanied the army during his father's campaigns, and these youthful experiences gave him an unbending will and a fighting spirit.

During his reign, Charlemagne engaged in almost constant warfare, especially against polytheistic tribes that when defeated were usually compelled to accept Christianity. He went to war some eighteen times against the Germanic tribe the Saxons, whose forced conversion only encouraged future rebellions. The causes for Charlemagne's persistent warfare were complex. He believed he had an obligation to spread Christianity. He also needed to control his borders from incursions by hostile tribes. Perhaps most important, however, was his need to satisfy his followers, especially the members of the aristocracy, by providing them with opportunities for plunder and new lands. As a result of these wars, he established a network of subservient kingdoms that owed tribute to the Frankish empire (see Map 8.1).

Map 8.1 Carolingian Empire

Charlemagne's conquests were the greatest military achievement of the Early Middle Ages. The Carolingian armies successfully reunified all western European territories of the ancient Roman Empire except for southern Italy, Spain, and Britain. However, the empire was fragile due to Frankish inheritance laws that required all legitimate sons to inherit lands from their father. By the time of Charlemagne's grandsons the empire began to divide.

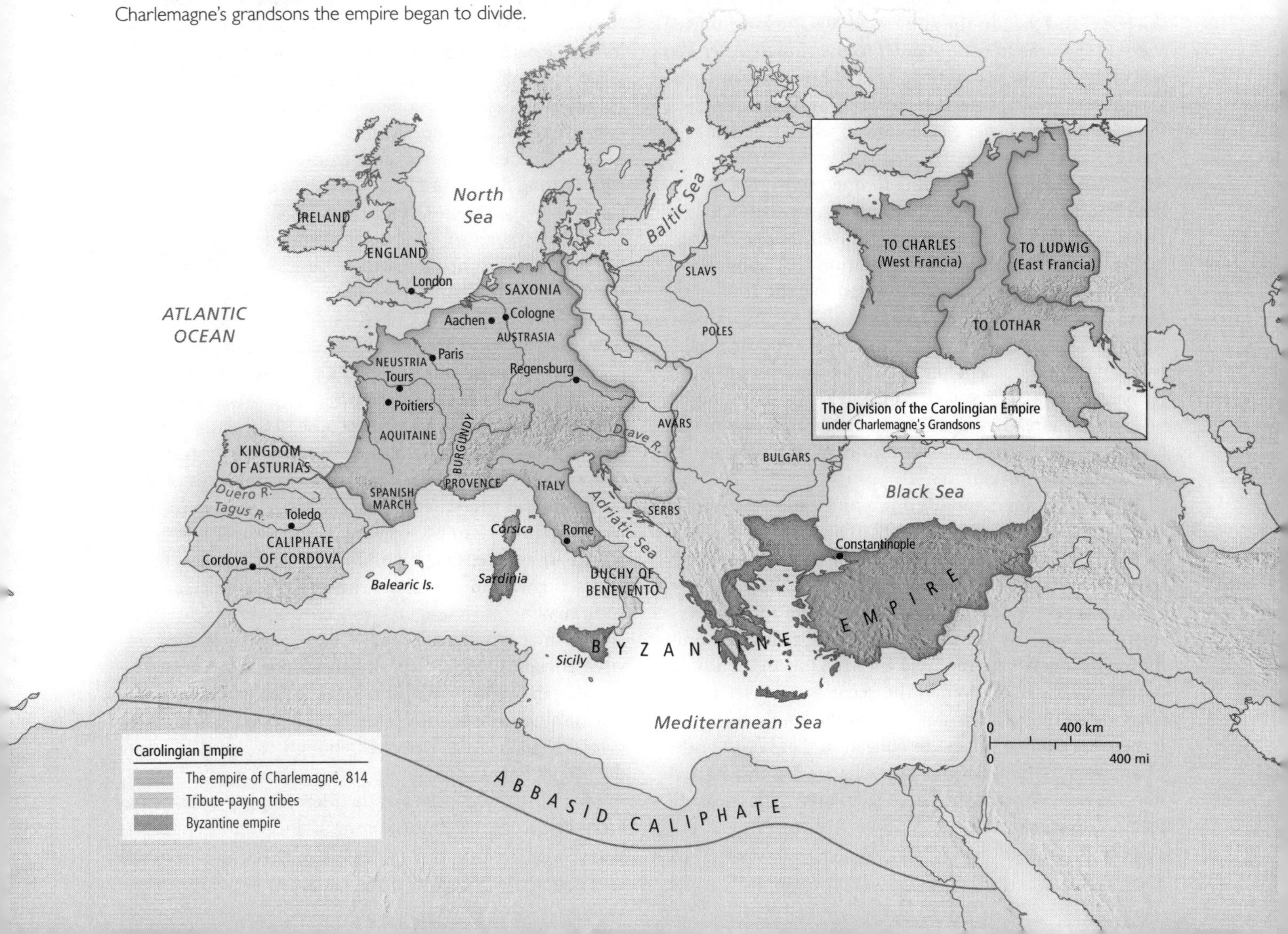

The extraordinary expansion of the Frankish empire represented a significant departure from the small, loosely governed kingdoms that had prevailed in the wake of the collapse of the Roman Empire. Charlemagne's empire covered all of western Europe except for southern Italy, Spain, and the British Isles. His military ambitions had brought the Franks into direct confrontation with other cultures—the polytheistic German tribes, Scandinavians, and Slavs; the Orthodox Christians of Byzantium; and the Muslims in Spain. These confrontations were usually hostile and violent, characterized as they were by the imposition of Frankish rule and faith.

Coronation of Charlemagne as Emperor

Charlemagne's coronation as Roman emperor at the hands of Pope Leo III (r. 795–816) conferred extraordinary authority on the Frankish kingdom. In 799 Pope Leo found himself embroiled in a vicious dispute with a faction of Roman nobles who accused him of adultery and lying. Kidnapped on the streets of Rome, he barely escaped having his tongue and eyes cut out before he was rescued by some of his attendants. Charlemagne put together a commission of prominent churchmen and nobles to conduct a judicial inquiry into the charges against the pope, and then in the autumn of 800 the king himself set out for Rome to restore order to the church. After Leo was cleared of the accusations against him, on Christmas Day 800 in front of a large crowd at St. Peter's Basilica, Pope Leo presided over a ceremony in which Charlemagne was crowned emperor. Historians have debated exactly what happened, but according to one report, the assembled throng acclaimed Charlemagne as Augustus and emperor, and the pope prostrated himself before the new emperor in a public demonstration of submission. Charlemagne's biographer later stated that the coronation came as a surprise to the king, but that seems unlikely. Charlemagne may have wished to make it appear that he was reluctant to accept the crown because he knew the coronation was certain to antagonize Constantinople, where there already was a Roman emperor. Nevertheless, Charlemagne became the first Roman emperor in the West since the fifth century.

The coronation exemplified two of the most prominent characteristics of the Carolingians. The first was the conscious imitation of the ancient Roman Empire, especially the late Roman Christian empire of Constantine. Charlemagne's conquests approximated the former territory of the western Roman Empire, and the churches built during his reign were modeled after the fourth- and fifth-century basilicas of Rome. The second characteristic of Carolingian rule was the obligation of the Frankish kings to protect the Roman popes, an obligation that began under Charlemagne's father Pepin. In exchange for this protection, the popes offered the Carolingian monarchs the legitimacy of divine sanction.

The imperial title bestowed on Charlemagne tremendous prestige and tremendous risk. With the imperial crown came the rulership of northern Italy and theoretical superiority over all other rulers in the West. But it made dangerous enemies of the Byzantine emperors. They had been calling themselves Roman emperors since the fourth century and justly claimed to be the true heirs of the legal authority of the ancient Roman Empire. To them Charlemagne was nothing more than a usurper of the imperial crown. In their minds the pope had no right to crown anyone emperor. Instead of reuniting the eastern and western halves of the ancient Roman Empire, the coronation of Charlemagne drove them further apart.

Carolingian Rulership

Even under the discerning and strong rulership of Charlemagne, the Carolingian empire never enjoyed the assets that had united the ancient Roman Empire for so many centuries. The Carolingians lacked a standing army and navy, professional civil servants, properly maintained roads, regular communications, and a money economy. There was not even a capital city in which Charlemagne could show off his power and establish a governmental bureaucracy, a stark contrast with the splendid Byzantine capital of Constantinople. From Christmas to Easter and sometimes longer, Charlemagne wintered in one of the imperial palaces, usually in the Frankish heartland. In the summer he and his court traveled about, camping out or living as guests in the castles of friendly lords, where he dispensed justice, decided disputes, and enforced obedience to his rule. During these summer travels he frequently conducted campaigns against the Saxon tribes.

Such a system of government depended more on personal than institutional forms of rule. Personal loyalty to the Carolingian monarch, expressed in an oath of allegiance, provided the strongest bonds unifying the realm, but betrayals were frequent. The Carolingian system required a monarch with outstanding personal abilities and unflagging energy, such as Charlemagne possessed, but a weak monarch threatened the collapse of the entire empire. Until the reign of Charlemagne, royal commands had been delivered orally, and there were few written records of what decisions had been made. Charlemagne's decrees (capitularies) gradually came to be written out. Although first presented in a hodgepodge fashion that combined different issues, the written capitularies began to strengthen and institutionalize governmental procedures through written aids to memory. In addition, Charlemagne's leading adviser, Alcuin, insisted that all official communications be stated in the appropriate Latin form, which would help prevent falsification because only the educated members of Charlemagne's court were well enough educated to know the proper forms.

One of the weaknesses of the Merovingian dynasty had been the decentralization of power, as local dukes appropriated royal resources and public functions for themselves. To combat this weakness, Charlemagne followed his father's lead in reorganizing government around territorial units called counties°, each administered by a count. The counts were rewarded with lands from the king and sent to areas where they had no family ties to serve as a combined provincial governor, judge, military commander, and representative of the king. To check on the counts, traveling circuit inspectors reviewed the counts' activities on a regular basis and remedied abuses of office. On the frontiers of their sprawling kingdom, the Franks established special territories called marches°, which were ruled by margraves with extended powers necessary to defend vulnerable borders.

In many respects, however, the Church provided the most vital foundations for the Carolingian system of rulership. During the last years of the ancient Roman Empire, the administration of the Church was organized around the office of the bishop. By the late seventh century this system had almost completely collapsed, as many bishoprics were left vacant or were occupied by royal favorites and relatives who lacked qualifications for church office. Because Carolingian monarchs took responsibility for the welfare of Christianity, they took charge of the appointment of bishops and reorganized church administration into a strict hierarchy of archbishops who supervised bishops who, in turn, supervised parish priests. Pepin and Charlemagne also revitalized the monasteries and endowed new ones, which provided the royal court with trained personnel—scribes, advisers, and spiritual assistants. Most laymen of the time were illiterate, so monks and priests wrote the emperor's letters for him, kept government records, composed histories, and promoted education—all essential for Carolingian rule.

Copying Manuscripts
This manuscript illumination of the Ascension from the Sacramentary of Archbishop Drogo of Metz, ca. 842, reveals the pious care that went into the copying of manuscripts during the Carolingian period. The faded letters around the illumination are examples of the Carolingian minuscule writing style.

The Carolingian Renaissance

In addition to organizing efficient political administration, Charlemagne sought to make the royal court an intellectual center. He gathered around him prominent scholars from throughout the realm and other countries. Under Charlemagne's patronage, these scholars were responsible for the flowering of culture that is called the Carolingian Renaissance.

The Carolingian Renaissance° ("rebirth") was one of a series of revivals of interest in ancient Greek and Latin literature. Charlemagne understood that both governmental efficiency and the propagation of the Christian faith required the intensive study of Latin, which was the language of the law, learning, and the Church. The Latin of everyday speech had evolved considerably since antiquity. During Charlemagne's time, spoken Latin had already been transformed into early versions of the Romance languages of Spanish, Italian, and French. Distressed that the poor Latin of many clergymen meant they misunderstood the Bible, Charlemagne ordered that all prospective priests undergo a rigorous education and recommended the liberal application of physical punishment if a pupil was slow in his lessons.

Charlemagne's patronage was crucial for the Carolingian Renaissance, which took place in the monasteries and the imperial court. Many of the heads of the monastic writing rooms wrote literary works of their own, including poetry and theology. The Carolingian scholars developed a beautiful new style of handwriting called the Carolingian minuscule, in which each letter was carefully and clearly formed. Texts collected by Carolingian librarians provided the foundation for the laws of the Church (called canon law) and codified the liturgy, which consisted of the prayers offered, texts read, and chants sung on each day of the year.

As we saw in Chapter 7, monastic scribes helped preserve ancient Latin literature. During the Carolingian period, the copying and studying of ancient Latin texts intensified. Much of what has survived of classical Latin learning, including the works of some seventy ancient authors, was preserved by Carolingian scribes. Some 8,000 Carolingian manuscripts still exist, a small portion of the total number known to have been produced.

The brighter young clerics and some promising laymen required instruction more advanced than the typical monastery could provide; to meet this need, Charlemagne established a school in his palace in Aachen. To staff his school and to serve as advisers, Charlemagne sought the best talent from within and outside the empire. Grammarians, historians, geographers, and astronomers from Ireland, England, Italy, Germany, and Spain flocked to Charlemagne's call.

The man most fully responsible for the Carolingian Renaissance was the English poet and cleric Alcuin of York (ca. 732–804), whom Charlemagne invited to head the palace school. Charlemagne himself joined his sons, his friends, and his friends' sons as a student, and under Alcuin's guidance the court became a lively center of discussion and exchange of knowledge. They debated issues such as the existence or nonexistence of Hell, the meaning of solar eclipses, and the nature of the Holy Trinity. After fifteen years at court, Alcuin became the abbot of the monastery of St. Martin at Tours, where he expanded the library and produced a number of works on education, theology, and philosophy.

A brilliant young monk named Einhard (ca. 770–840) who studied in the palace school quickly became a trusted friend and adviser to Charlemagne. Based on twenty-three years of service to Charlemagne and research in royal documents, Einhard wrote the *Life of Charlemagne* (830–833), which describes Charlemagne's family, foreign policy, conquests, administration, and personal attributes. In Einhard's vivid Latin prose, Charlemagne comes alive as a great leader, a lover of hunting and fighting, who unlike his rough companions possessed a towering sense of responsibility for the welfare of his subjects and the salvation of their souls. In Einhard's biography, Charlemagne appears as an idealist, the first Christian prince in medieval Europe to imagine that his role was not just to acquire more possessions but to better humankind.

Charlemagne's rule and reputation has had lasting significance for western Europe. Around 776 an Anglo-Saxon monk referred to the vast new kingdom of the Franks as the Kingdom of Europe, reviving the Roman geographical term *Europa.* Thanks to the Carolingians, Europe became more than a geographical expression. It became the geographical center of a new civilization that supplanted the Roman civilization of the Mediterranean and transformed the culture of the West.

THE DIVISION OF WESTERN EUROPE

None of Charlemagne's successors possessed his personal skills, and without a permanent institutional basis for administration, the empire was vulnerable to fragmentation and disorder. When Charlemagne died in 814, the imperial crown passed to his only surviving son, Louis the Pious (r. 814–840). Louis's most serious problem was dividing the empire among his own three sons, as required by Frankish inheritance laws. Disputes among Louis's sons led to civil war, even before the death of their father, and while they were fighting the administration of the empire was neglected.

After years of fighting, the three sons—Charles the Bald (d. 877), Lothair (d. 855), and Louis the German (d. 876)—negotiated the Treaty of Verdun, which divided the Frankish kingdom. Charles the Bald received the western part of the territories, the kingdom of West Francia. Louis the German received the eastern portion, the kingdom of East Francia. Lothair obtained the imperial title as well as the central portion of the kingdom, the "Middle Kingdom," which extended from Rome to the North Sea. In succeeding generations, the laws of inheritance created further fragmentation of these kingdoms, and during the ninth and tenth centuries the descendants of Charlemagne died out or lost control of their lands. By 987 none were left.

The Carolingian empire lasted only a few generations. Carolingian military power, however, had been formidable, providing within the Frankish lands an unusual period of security from hostile enemies, measured by the fact that few settlements were fortified. After the empire's collapse virtually every surviving community in western Europe required fortifications, represented by castles and town walls. Post-Carolingian Europe became fragmented as local aristocrats stepped into the vacuum created by the demise of the Carolingians—and it became vulnerable, as raiders plundered and invaders carved out land for themselves.

CHRONOLOGY

The Carolingian Dynasty

751	Pepin the Short deposes last Merovingian king
800	Charlemagne crowned emperor in Rome
843	Treaty of Verdun divides Frankish kingdom
987	Death of the last Carolingian king

Invasions and Recovery in the Latin West

Despite Charlemagne's campaigns of conquest and conversion, the spread of Christianity throughout western Europe remained uneven and incomplete. By 900, Roman Catholicism was limited to a few regions that constituted the heartland of western Europe—the

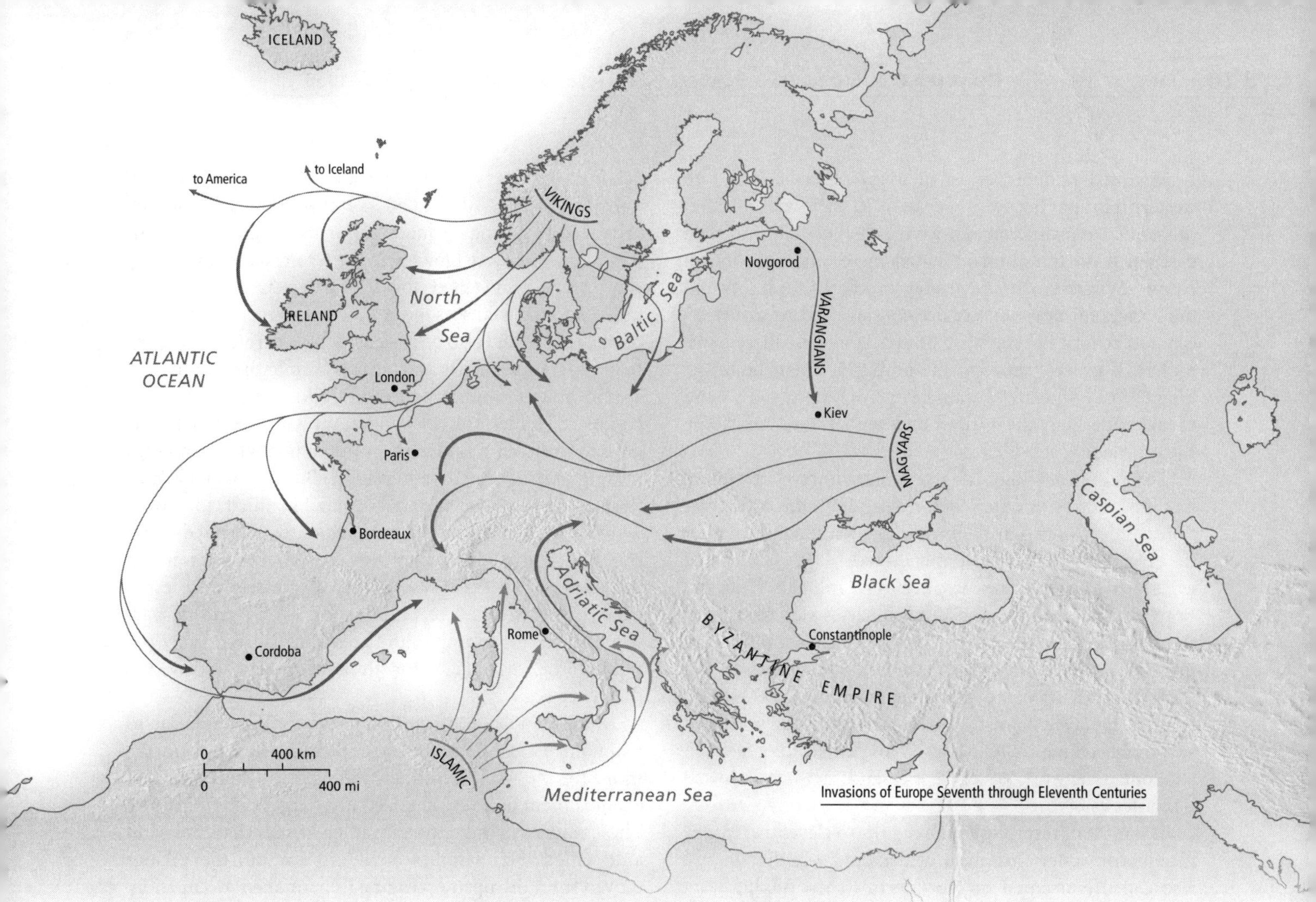

Map 8.2 Invasions of Europe, Seventh through Eleventh Centuries
Especially after the division of the Carolingian empire, Europe came under severe pressure from invading Viking bands from Scandinavia. The effects of the Viking invasions were felt most gravely in the British Isles and northern France. From the East came the Magyars, who eventually settled in the vast Hungarian plain. From the South there were persistent raids and conquests from various Islamic states, some of which established a rich Muslim civilization in Europe.

Frankish lands, Italy, parts of Germany that had been under Carolingian rule, the British Isles, and a fringe in Spain. During the ninth and tenth centuries, hostile polytheistic tribes raided deep into the tightly packed Christian core of western Europe (see Map 8.2). Despite these attacks Christianity survived, and many of the polytheist tribes eventually accepted the Christian faith. These conversions were not always the consequence of Christian victories in battle, as had been the case during late antiquity and the Carolingian period. More frequently they resulted from organized missionary efforts by monks and bishops.

The Polytheist Invaders of the Latin West

Some of the raiders during the eighth to eleventh centuries plundered what they could from the Christian settlements of the West and returned home. Others seized lands, settled down, and established new principalities. The two groups who took advantage of the weakness of the Latin West most often during this period were the Magyars and Vikings. The original homeland of the Magyars, later known as the Hungarians, was in the central Asian steppes. Gradually driven by other nomads to the western edge of the steppes, the Magyars began to penetrate Europe in the late ninth century. By 896 they had crossed en masse into the middle of the Danube river basin, occupying sparsely settled lands that were easily conquered. The grassy plains of this basin had long attracted nomads, including the Huns and Avars before them, and like other nomads, the Magyars were accomplished horsemen. Once established, the Magyar tribes divided the vast plain among themselves and pushed at the borders of the neighboring Slavic and German principalities.

Mounted raiding parties of Magyars ranged far into western Europe. Between 898 and 920 they sacked settlements in the prosperous Po River valley of Italy and then descended on the remnant kingdoms of the Carolingian empire. Wherever they went they plundered for booty and took slaves for domestic service or sale. The kings of western and central Europe were powerless against these fierce raiders, who were unstoppable until 955 when the Saxon king Otto I (who later became emperor) destroyed a band of marauders on their way home with booty. After 955, Magyar raiding subsided.

The definitive end of Magyar forays, however, may have had less to do with Otto's victory than with the consolidation of the Hungarian plain into its own kingdom under the Árpád dynasty, named after Árpád (d. 907), who had led seven Magyar tribes in their migration to Hungary. Both Orthodox and Catholic missionaries vied to convert the Magyars, but because of an alliance with German monarchs, the Árpáds accepted Roman Catholicism. On Christmas Day 1000, the Árpád king Stephen I (r. 997–1038) received the insignia of royalty directly from the pope and was crowned king. To help convert his people, King Stephen laid out a network of bishoprics and lavishly endowed monasteries.

The most devastating of the eighth- to eleventh-century invaders of western European settlements were the Vikings, also called Norsemen or Northmen. (These Viking warriors were ethnically related to the Rus who harassed Constantinople at the same time.) During this period, Danish, Norwegian, and Swedish Viking warriors sailed on long-distance raiding expeditions from their homes in Scandinavia. Every spring the long Viking dragon ships sailed forth, each carrying 50 to 100 warriors avid for loot. Propelled by a single square sail or by oarsmen when the winds failed or were blowing in the wrong direction, Viking ships were unmatched for seaworthiness and regularly sailed into the wild seas of the North Atlantic. The shallow-draft vessels could also be rowed up the lazy rivers of Europe to plunder monasteries and villages far into the interior.

The causes for the enormous Viking onslaught were complex. Higher annual temperatures in the North may have stimulated a spurt in population that encouraged raiding and eventually emigration. But the primary motive seems to have been an insatiable thirst for silver, which was deemed the essential standard of social distinction in Scandinavian society. As a result, monasteries and cathedrals with their silver liturgical vessels were especially prized sources of plunder for Viking raiding parties. In 793, for example, the great English monastery at Lindesfarne was pillaged for silver and largely destroyed in the process.

By the middle of the ninth century, the Vikings began to maintain winter quarters in the British Isles and on the shores of the weak Carolingian kingdoms—locations that enabled them to house and feed ever-larger raiding parties. These raiders soon became invading armies that took land and settled their families on it. As a result, the Vikings moved from disruptive pillaging to permanent occupation, which created a lasting influence in Europe. In western Europe amid the ruins of the Carolingian empire, Viking settlements on the Seine River formed the beginnings of the duchy of Normandy ("Northman land"), whose soldiers

A Norman Ship, Possibly Based on a Viking Design, Used in the Invasion of England in 1066

Note the single sail, the horses and warriors in the hold of the ship, and the tiller, which was mounted on the starboard side toward the stern of the ship. Stern-mounted rudders, which gave the helmsman much greater control of the direction of the ship, were gradually introduced during the twelfth century.

would conquer during the eleventh century England, Sicily, and much of southern Italy.

The most long-lasting influence of the Vikings outside of Scandinavia was in the British Isles and North Atlantic. In 865 a great Viking army conquered large parts of northeastern England, creating a loosely organized network of territories known as the Danelaw. The Danish and Norse conquests in the British Isles left deep cultural residues in local dialects, geographical names, personal names, social structure, and literature. The most enduring example in Old English, the earliest form of spoken and written English, remains the epic of *Beowulf*, which recounts the exploits of a great Scandinavian adventurer in combat with the monster Grendel, Grendel's mother, and a fiery dragon.

In the North Atlantic, Vikings undertook long voyages into the unknown across cold rough seas. Beginning about 870, settlers poured into unsettled Iceland. Using Iceland as a base, they ventured farther asea and established new colonies in Greenland. In Iceland the adventures of these Viking warriors, explorers, and settlers were celebrated in poetry and sagas. The sagas of Erik the Red and the Greenlanders recount hazardous voyages to the coasts of Canada. In 930 the fiercely independent Icelanders founded a national parliament, the *althing*, an institution at which disputes were adjudicated through legal procedures rather than combat.

After the mid-ninth century, the kings of Scandinavia (Norway, Denmark, and Sweden) began to assert control over the bands of raiders who had constituted the vanguard of the Viking invasions. By the end of the tenth century, the great age of Viking raiding by small parties ended. The Scandinavian kings established a firm hold over the settled population and converted to Christianity, bringing their subjects with them into the new faith. Henceforth, the descendants of the Viking raiders settled down to become peaceable farmers and shepherds.

AN OATH OF VOLUNTARY SUBMISSION TO A LORD

Many men who found themselves in desperate circumstances became vassals in order to feed themselves and to find protection from someone richer and stronger. This voluntary oath of obedience reflects the origins of the relationship of dominance and submission between lords and vassals. In the eighth century a destitute man addressed a certain "magnificent lord" as follows:

Inasmuch as it is known to all and sundry that I lack the wherewithal to feed and clothe myself, I have asked of your pity, and your goodwill has granted to me permission to deliver and commend myself into your authority and protection . . . in return you have undertaken to aid and sustain me in food and clothing, while I have undertaken to serve you and deserve well of you as far as lies in my power. And for as long as I shall live, I am bound to serve you and respect you as a free man ought, and during my lifetime I have not the right to withdraw from your authority and protection, but must, on the contrary for the remainder of my days remain under it.

And in virtue of this action, if one of us wishes to alter the terms of the agreement, he can do so after paying a fine of ten solidi to the other. But the agreement itself shall remain in force. Whence it has seemed good to us that we should both draw up and confirm two documents of the same tenor, and this they have done.

Source: This example of a voluntary oath of obedience comes from Tours, in the eighth century.

THE RULERS IN THE LATIN WEST

As a consequence of the disintegration of the Carolingian order and the subsequent invasions, people during the ninth and tenth centuries began to seek protection from local warlords who assumed responsibilities once invested in royal authorities.

Lords and Vassals

The society of warlords derived from Germanic military traditions in which a great chief attracted followers who fought alongside him. The relationship was voluntary and egalitarian. By the eighth century, however, the chief had become a lord° who dominated others, and his dependents were known as vassals°.

The bond of loyalty between lord and vassal was formalized by an oath. In the Carolingian period the vassal proved his loyalty to the lord by performing an act of homage, which made the vassal the "man" of the lord. The act of homage was a ritual in which the kneeling vassal placed his clasped hands between the hands of the lord and made a verbal declaration of intent, usually something such as, "Sir, I become your man." In return for the vassal's homage or fealty, as it came to be called, the lord swore to protect the vassal. The oath established a personal relationship in which the lord reciprocated the vassal's loyalty and willingness to obey the lord with protection and in some cases with a land grant called a fief°. Lords frequently called upon their vassals for military assistance to resist invaders or to fight with other lords. The fief supplied the vassal with an income to cover the expenses of armor and weapons and of raising and feeding horses, all of which were necessary to be an effective mounted soldier, known by the twelfth century as a knight°. This connection between lord-vassal relations and the holding of a fief is called feudalism°.

JUSTICE IN HISTORY

Revealing the Truth: Oaths and Ordeals

No participant in a lawsuit or criminal trial today would dream of entering the courtroom without an accompanying pile of documents to prove the case. In modern society we trust written over oral evidence because we are aware of how easily memories can be distorted. In an early medieval court, however, the participants usually arrived with nothing more than their own sworn testimony and personal reputations to support their cause. Papers alleging to prove one thing or another meant little in a largely illiterate society. Unable to read and perhaps aware that the few who could read might deceive them, most people trusted what they had personally seen and heard. Count Berthold of Hamm expressed the opinion of many when, after being presented with documents opposing his claim to a piece of land, he "laughed at the documents, saying that since anyone's pen could write what they liked, he ought not to lose his rights over it."

To settle disputes, medieval courts put much more faith in confession or in eyewitness testimony than in documents. In 1124 Pope Calixtus II pronounced that "we put greater faith in the oral testimony of living witnesses than in the written word."

Under normal trial procedures, a man would give his oath that what he was saying was true. If he was an established and respected member of the community, he would also have a number of "oath-witnesses" testify for his reliability, although not to the truth or falsehood of his evidence. The court would also hear from witnesses in the case. This system worked well enough when two local men, known in the community, were at odds. But what happened when there was a trial involving a person who had a bad reputation, was a known liar, or was a stranger? What would happen in a case with no witnesses?

In these instances, medieval courts sometimes turned to trial by ordeal to settle the matter. The judicial ordeal was used only as a last resort, as a German law code of 1220 declared: "It is not right to use the ordeal in any case, except that the truth may be known in no other way." The wide range of situations and people handed over to the ordeal makes clear that in the eyes of the medieval courts, the ordeal was a fallback method when all else failed to reveal the truth.

What was a trial by ordeal? There were several types. The most common was trial by fire. The accused would plunge his or her arm into a cauldron of boiling water to retrieve a coin or a jewel, or alternately would pick up a red-hot iron and walk nine paces. A variation of this method was to walk over hot coals or red-hot ploughshares. After the accused suffered this ordeal, his or her hand or foot would be bound for three days and then examined. If the wound was healing "cleanly," meaning without infection, the accused was declared innocent. If not, he or she was adjudged guilty. Another common form of the ordeal was immersion in cold water, or "swimming," made famous in later centuries by its use in witch trials. The accused would be thrown into a river or lake. If the water "rejected" her and she floated, then she was guilty. If the water "embraced" her and she sank, then she was innocent. The obvious complication that a sinking person, even though innocent, may have also been a drowning person did not seem to deter use of trial by water.

The ordeal was especially widespread in judging crimes such as heresy and adultery and in assigning paternity. In 1218, Inga of Varteig carried the hot iron to prove that her son, born out of wedlock, was the son of deceased King Hakon III, which if true would change the line of succession in Norway. The ordeal was also used to decide much more pedestrian matters. In 1090, Gautier of Meigné claimed a plot of land from the monks of Saint Auban at Angers, arguing that he had traded a horse in return for the property. He too carried the iron to prove his claim.

The belief that an ordeal could effectively reveal guilt or innocence in a judicial matter was based on the widespread conviction that God constantly and actively intervened in earthly affairs and that his judgment could be seen immediately. To focus God's attention on a specific issue, the participants performed the ordeal in a ritual manner. A priest was usually present to invoke God's power and to bless the implements employed in the ordeal. In one typical formula, the priest asked God "to bless and sanctify this fiery iron, which is used in the just examination of doubtful issues." Priests would also inform the accused, "If you are innocent of this charge . . . you may confidently receive this iron in your hand and the Lord, the just judge, will free you." The ritual element of the judicial ordeal emphasized the judgment of God over the judgment of men.

During the eleventh and twelfth centuries, the use of the ordeal waned. The recovery of Roman law, the rise of literacy and written documents in society at large, and a greater belief in the power of human justice to settle disputes all contributed to the gradual replacement of the ordeal with the jury trial or the use of torture to elicit a confession from the accused. In England the common law began to entrust the determination of the truth to a jury of peers who listened to and evaluated all the testimony. The jury system valued the opinions of members of the community over the reliability of the ordeal to reveal God's judgment. These changes mark a shift in medieval society toward a growing belief in the power of secular society to organize and police itself, leaving divine justice to the afterlife. But the most crucial shift came from within the Church itself, which felt its spiritual mission compromised by the involvement of priests in supervising ordeals. In 1215 the Fourth Lateran Council forbade priests from participating, and their absence made it impossible for the ordeal to continue as a formal legal procedure. ■

■ **Trial by Ordeal**

In this twelfth-century miniature, a woman or man is being subjected to submersion in cold water as a way to test the veracity of her or his testimony. The accused is bound hand and foot. If the accused sank, innocence was declared. If the accused floated, guilty was the judgment.

Questions of Justice

1. Why would it have been so crucial during this troubled period to have a decisive verdict even in cases when the evidence of guilt was unknown or inconclusive?
2. Why was someone's reputation in the community so significant for determining the truth in a medieval trial? How do reputations play a role in trials today?
3. What do oaths and the trial by ordeal reveal about the relationship between human and divine justice during the Middle Ages?

Taking It Further

Bartlett, Robert. *Trial by Fire and Water: The Medieval Judicial Ordeal.* 1986. Associates the spread of the trial by ordeal with the expansion of Christianity. The best study of the ordeal.

van Caenegen, R. C. *An Historical Introduction to Private Law.* 1992. A basic narrative from late antiquity to the nineteenth century that traces the evolution of early medieval trial procedures.

During the ninth and tenth centuries, the lords often became the only effective rulers in a particular locality. After the collapse of public authority during the invasions and the dissolution of the Carolingian empire, lordship implied political and legal jurisdiction over the inhabitants of the land. These lords came to exercise many of the powers of the state, such as adjudicating disputes over property or inheritance and punishing thieves and murderers. The rendering of justice represented the most elementary attribute of government, and in the absence of a formal legal system and systematic record keeping, local lords rendered a rough and ready justice. The personal loyalties of those involved in a dispute were crucial for determining the outcome. Those well-connected to the lord, especially those who were his vassals, were always better off than those who were outsiders or had fallen into his disfavor. In a society in which personal ties meant everything, the truth of conflicting testimonies was often determined by the public reputations and personal connections of those who testified. When the reputations of disputants or an alleged criminal could not determine whom to believe, lords acting as judges relied on oaths and ordeals to determine the truth.

The mixture of personal lord-vassal obligations, property rights conveyed by the fief, and legal jurisdiction over communities caused endless complications. The king's vassals were also lords of their own vassals, who in turn were lords over lesser vassals down to the level of simple knight. In theory such a system created a hierarchy of authority that descended down from the king, but reality was never that simple. In France, for example, many of the great lords enjoyed as much land as the king, which made it very difficult for the king to force them to enact his will. Many vassals held different fiefs from different lords, which created a confusion of loyalties, especially when two lords of the same vassal went to war against one another.

Women could inherit fiefs and own property of their own, although they could not perform military services. They often managed royal and aristocratic property when men were absent or dead, made decisions about how property would be divided up among heirs, and functioned as lords when receiving the homage of male vassals. The lineage and accomplishments of prominent ladies enhanced their husbands' social prestige. A number of aristocratic families traced their descent from the female line, if it was more prestigious than the male line, and named their children after the wife's illustrious ancestors.

Lord-vassal relationships infiltrated many medieval social institutions and practices. Since most vassals owed military service to their lords, medieval armies were at least partially composed of vassal-knights who were obliged to fight for their lord for a certain number of days (often forty) per year. Vassals were required to provide their lord with other kinds of support as well. When summoned, they had to appear at the lord's court to offer advice or sit in judgment of other vassals who were their peers. When the lord traveled, his vassal was obliged to provide food and shelter in the vassal's castle, sometimes for a large entourage of family and retainers who accompanied the lord. Vassals were obliged to pay their lord certain fees on special occasions, such as the marriage of the lord's daughter. If the lord was captured in battle, his vassals had to pay the ransom.

The Western European Kingdoms After the Carolingians

At a time when the bonds between lords and vassals were the only form of protection from invaders and marauders, lordship was a stronger social institution than the vague obligations all subjects owed to their kings. To rule effectively, a king was obliged to be a strong lord, in effect to be-

Otto III

The Emperor Otto III is represented here in a form usually reserved for Christ. The emperor sits on a throne, is surrounded by a mandorla (lines surrounding his body in the shape of an almond), and reaches out to the four evangelists—Matthew, Mark, Luke, and John—who are signified by the winged figures of an eagle, lion, bull, and man. The hand of God reaches down from the heavens to crown Otto. The idea of divine sanction of kingship could not be more graphic.

come the lord of all the other lords, who in turn would discipline their own vassals. Achieving this difficult goal took several steps. First, the king had to establish a firm hand over his own lands, the royal domain. With the domain supplying food, materiel, and fighting men, the king could attempt the second step—establishing control over lords who lived outside the royal domain. To hold sway over these independent-minded lords, kings sometimes employed force but frequently offered lucrative rewards by giving out royal prerogatives to loyal lords. These prerogatives included the rights to receive fines in courts of law, to collect taxes, and to perform other governmental functions. As a result, some medieval kingdoms, such as France and England, began to combine in the hands of the same people the personal authority of lordship with the legal authority of the king, creating feudal kingship.

The final step in the process of establishing royal authority was to emphasize the sacred character of kingship. With the assistance of the clergy, kings emulated the great Christian emperors of Rome, Constantine and Justinian. Medieval kings became quasi priests who demanded obedience from their subjects because kings represented the majesty of God on earth. The institution of sacred kingship gave kings an additional weapon for persuading the nobles to recognize the king's superiority over them.

Under the influence of ancient Roman ideas of rulership, some kings began to envision their kingdoms as something grander than private property. As the Germanic king and later emperor Conrad II (r. 1024–1039) put it, "If the king is dead the kingdom remains, just as the ship remains even if the helmsman falls overboard."[1] The idea slowly began to take hold that the kingdom had an eternal existence separate from the mortal person of the king and that it was superior to its component parts—its provinces, tribes, lords, families, bishoprics, and cities. This profound idea reached its fullest theoretical expression many centuries later. Promoting the sacred and eternal character of kingship required monarchs to patronize priests, monks, writers, and artists who could formulate and express these ideas.

The kingdoms of East and West Francia, which arose out of the remnants of the Carolingian empire, produced kings who attempted to expand the power of the monarchy and enhance the idea of kingship. East Francia largely consisted of Germanic tribes, each governed by a Frankish official called a duke. During the tenth century, several of these dukes became powerful lords, but they had to rule from the saddle, constantly on the road—being seen, making judgments, suppressing revolts, punishing disloyal vassals, and rewarding loyal ones.

After 919 the dukes of Saxony were elected the kings of East Francia, establishing the foundations for the Saxon dynasty. With few lands of their own, the Saxon kings maintained their power by acquiring other duchies and controlling appointments to high church offices, which went to family members or loyal followers. The greatest of the Saxon kings, Otto I the Great (936–973), combined deep Christian piety with formidable military ability. More than any other tenth-century king, he supported the foundation of missionary bishoprics in polytheist Slavic and Scandinavian lands, thereby pushing the boundaries of Christianity beyond what they had been under Charlemagne. Otto launched a major expedition to Italy, where he reestablished order in anarchic Rome, deposed one pope, and nominated another. As a consequence of his intervention in Italy, the new pope crowned him emperor in 962, reviving the Roman Empire in the West, as Charlemagne had done earlier. Otto and his successors in the Saxon dynasty attempted to rule a more restricted version of the western empire than had Charlemagne. By the 1030s the German Empire consisted of most of the Germanic duchies, north-central Italy, and Burgundy. In later centuries these regions collectively came to be called the Holy Roman Empire.

As had been the case under Charlemagne, effective rulership in the new German Empire included the patronage of learned men and women who enhanced the reputation of the monarch. Otto and his able brother Bruno, the archbishop of Cologne, initiated a cultural revival, the Ottonian Renaissance°, which centered around the imperial court. Learned Irish and English monks, Greek philosophers from Byzantium, and Italian scholars found positions there. Among the many intellectuals patronized by Otto, the most notable was Liutprand of Cremona (ca. 920–ca. 972), a vivid writer whose unabashed histories reflected the passions of the troubled times. For example, his history of contemporary Europe vilified his enemies and was aptly titled *Revenge*.

CHRONOLOGY

The Western European Kingdoms Emerge

787	First recorded raid by the Danes in Anglo-Saxon England
843–911	Carolingian dynasty in East Francia
843–987	Carolingian dynasty in West Francia
919–1024	Saxon or Ottonian dynasty
955	Otto I defeats Magyars
962	Otto crowned emperor in Rome
987–1328	Capetian dynasty in France
1066	William the Conqueror defeats last Anglo-Saxon king

Like East Francia, West Francia included many groups with separate ethnic and linguistic identities, but the kingdom had been Christianized much longer because it had been part of the Roman Empire. Thus West Francia, although highly fragmented, possessed the potential for greater unity by using Christianity to champion the authority of the king.

Strengthening the monarchy became the crucial goal of the Capetian dynasty, which succeeded the last of the Carolingian kings. Hugh Capet (r. 987–996) was elevated king of West Francia in an elaborate coronation ceremony in which the prayers of the archbishop of Reims offered divine sanction to the new dynasty. The involvement of the archbishop established an important precedent for the French monarchy: From this point on, the monarchy and the church hierarchy were closely entwined. From this mutually beneficial relationship, the king received ecclesiastical and spiritual support while the upper clergy gained royal protection and patronage. The term *France* at first applied only to Capet's feudal domain, a small but rich region around Paris, but through the persistence of the Capetians West Francia became so unified that the name France came to refer to the entire kingdom.

The Capetians were especially successful in soliciting homage and services from the great lords of the land—despite some initial resistance. Hugh and his successors distinguished themselves from other lords by emphasizing that unlike other lords, kings were appointed by God. Shortly after his own coronation, Hugh had his son crowned—a strategy that ensured the succession of the Capetian family. Hugh's son, Robert II, the Pious (r. 996–1031), was apparently the first to perform the king's touch, the reputed power of the king to cure certain skin diseases. The royal coronation cult and the king's touch established the reputation of French kings as miracle workers.

Anglo-Saxon England had never been part of the Carolingian empire, but because it was Christian, England shared in the culture of the Latin West. England suffered extensive damage at the hands of the Vikings. After England was almost overwhelmed by a Danish invasion during the winter of 878–879, Alfred the Great (r. 871–899) finally defeated the Danes as spring approached. As king of only Wessex (not of all England), Alfred consolidated his authority and issued a new law code. Alfred's able successors cooperated with the nobility more effectively than the monarchs in either East or West Francia and built a broad base of support in the local units of government, the hundreds and shires. The Anglo-Saxon monarchy also enjoyed the support of the Church, which provided it with skilled servants and spiritual authorization.

During the late ninth and tenth centuries, Anglo-Saxon England experienced a cultural revival under royal patronage. King Alfred proclaimed that the Viking invasions had been God's punishment for the neglect of learning, without which God's will could not be known. Alfred accordingly promoted the study of Latin. He also desired that all men of wealth learn to read the language of the English people. Under Alfred a highly sophisticated literature in Europe appeared in Old English. This literature included poems, sermons, commentaries on the Bible, and translations of important Latin works. The masterpiece of this era was a history called the *Anglo-Saxon Chronicle.* It was begun during Alfred's reign but maintained over several generations.

During the late tenth and early eleventh centuries, England was weakened by a series of Viking raids and a succession of feeble kings. In 1066 William, the duke of Normandy and a descendant of Vikings who had settled in the north of France, defeated King Harold, the last Anglo-Saxon king. William seized the English throne. William the Conqueror opened a new era in which English affairs

A Medieval Windmill
The peasant on the left is carrying a sack of grain for milling. The entire mill was built on a pivot so that it could be rotated to catch the wind.

A Heavy *Carruca* Plow
At the center of the two-wheeled plow is a sturdy timber from which the coulter projects just in front of the plowshare, which is hidden by the earth.

became deeply intertwined with those of the duchy of Normandy and the kingdom of France.

THE COMMON PEOPLE

After the end of the invasions of the ninth and tenth centuries, the population of western Europe recovered dramatically. Technological innovations created the agricultural revolution° that increased the supply of food. With more food available, people were better nourished than they had been in more than 500 years. As a result of more and better food, the population began to grow. In the seventh century all of Europe was home to only about 14 million inhabitants. Much of the land cultivated in the ancient world had reverted to wild forests, simply because there were not enough people left to farm it due to the deaths from plague and the barbarian invasions. By 1300 the population had exploded to 74 million. From the seventh to the fourteenth centuries, then, the population grew many times over, perhaps as much as 500 percent. The most dramatic signs of population growth began after the year 1000.

The Medieval Agricultural Revolution

At the beginning of the eleventh century, the vast majority of people lived in small villages or isolated farmsteads. Peasants literally scratched out a living from a small area of cleared land around the village by employing a light scratch plow that barely turned over the soil. The farms produced mostly grain, which was consumed as bread, porridge, and ale or beer. Vegetables were rare, meat and fish uncommon. Over the course of the century , the productivity of the land was greatly enhanced by a number of innovations that came into widespread use.

The invention of new labor-saving devices ushered in the power revolution. This development, which occurred in the tenth to twelfth centuries, harnessed the first new sources of power since the domestication of oxen and the invention of the ship in the ancient world. There would not be a technological discovery of similar magnitude until the development of steam power in the eighteenth century. Perhaps the most notable innovation was the exploitation of nonanimal sources of power from water and wind. The water mill was invented in late Roman times, but it came into widespread use only in the tenth and eleventh centuries. Water mills were first used to grind grain but were gradually adapted to a wide variety of tasks, including turning saws to mill timber. By the end of the twelfth century windmills also began to appear, which were used for similar purposes.

As important as the harnessing of water and wind power was the enhanced ability to use animal power. Knights began to breed large, powerful war-horses. They equipped their horses with metal armor and stirrups, which kept knights on their horses, and metal horseshoes (until then, horses' hooves had been bound in cloth), which gave horses better footing and traction. Improvements in this period also included a new type of horse collar, which increased the animal's pulling power. Earlier collars fit tightly around a horse's neck, which choked the animal if it pulled too great a weight. The new collar transferred the pressure points from the throat to the shoulders. Originally devised to make horses more effective at fighting, the collar was adapted to make both horses and oxen more efficient farm draft animals. With enhanced animal pulling power, farmers could plow the damp, heavy clay soils of northern Europe much more efficiently.

The centerpiece of the agricultural revolution was the heavy plow, which replaced the widely used Mediterranean scratch plow. Developed for light, sandy soils that were easily broken up, the scratch plow was barely able to dig into the poorly drained soils of the northern European plain.

The heavy plow had several distinctive advantages. It cut through and lifted the soil, aerating it and bringing to the surface minerals vital for plant growth. It created a furrow that channeled drainage, preventing the fields from

Twelfth-Century Village

Aerial photograph of the village of West Whelpington North (England), which was settled in the twelfth century but whose inhabitants died out during the Black Death of the fourteenth century (see Chapter 10). Outlines of the individual families' farm gardens can be seen in the left center. On the lower right are the ridges and furrows of the elongated fields required by the use of the heavy plow.

being flooded by the frequent rains of northern Europe. The heavy plow was very cumbersome, however. It required six or eight horses or oxen to pull it, and no single peasant family in the tenth or eleventh century was able to afford that many draft animals. Farmers had to pool their animals to create plow teams, a practice that required mutual planning and cooperation. A two-wheeled heavy plow pulled by a team of eight oxen was difficult to turn, which meant it was best to continue plowing in a straight line for as long as possible. Thus, the heavy plow required peasants to cooperate further in redesigning their fields—from compact square fields, which had been cross-plowed with the older scratch plow, to long narrow fields that minimized the number of turns and provided a headland at the end to permit the draft team to make a wide turn. The new plow created the elongated fields that were distinctive to northern Europe.

The necessity to replenish the soil meant that half the arable land lay fallow while the other half was planted with crops. The fields would be reversed in the following year. In northern Europe farm animals were allowed to graze in the fallow field, what was called the open field, leaving their manure to recondition its soil. This practice, the two-field system, was gradually supplanted by the three-field system. In the three-field system one field was planted in the fall with grain; one was planted in the spring with beans, peas, or lentils; and one lay fallow. Both fall and spring plantings were harvested in the summer, after which all the fields shifted. The open three-field system produced extraordinary advantages: the amount of land under cultivation was increased from one-half to two-thirds; beans planted in the spring rotation returned nitrogen to the soil; and the crop rotation combined with animal manure reduced soil exhaustion from excessive grain planting.

This shift to a three-field system had a significant effect on society. First, villagers learned to cooperate—by pooling draft animals for plow teams, by redesigning and elongating their fields, by coordinating the three-field rotation of crops, and by timing the harvest schedule. To accomplish these cooperative ventures, they created village councils and developed habits of collective decision making that were essential for stable community life. Second, the system produced not only more food, but better food. Beans and other vegetables grown in the spring planting were rich in proteins. Slaughtering cattle for meat was still out of the question for peasants, but a plate of beans had a nutritional value similar to that of beef.

Manors and Serfs

The medieval agricultural economy bound landlords and peasants together in a unit of management called the manor. A manor referred to the holding of a single lord and the community of farmers who worked it. A single village might be divided up to serve several small manors, or a large manor might draw from several villages. Some lords possessed several manors and traveled from one to another throughout the year. The lord of the manor usually had his own large house or stone castle and served as the presiding judge of the community. The lord's manor court was the only form of law that rural people knew. The lord typically appointed the priest of the parish church and was responsible for enforcing church attendance and maintaining the church buildings. The parish priest worked land loaned to him by the lord in exchange for his religious services to the village and manor.

Unlike in the ancient world, in which slaves performed most of the heavy farm work, slaves seldom worked on farms during the Middle Ages. A much more common status was that of serf. Unlike slaves, serfs° were not owned, but they were tied to a specific manor, which they could not leave. They had certain legal rights denied slaves, such as the right to a certain portion of what they produced, but they were obliged to subject themselves to the lord's will. In theory, at least, the relationship between the lord and his serfs was reciprocal. The lord supplied the land, sometimes tools and seed, and protection from invaders and bandits. In return serfs supplied the labor necessary to work the land. Serfs were most common in England and northern France.

There were also free peasants who worked as independent farmers and owned their land outright. Free peasants appeared in Scandinavia, northern Germany, southern France, Switzerland, and northern Italy. In many villages of Europe free peasants could be found scattered among larger communities of serfs.

At the bottom of rural society were the numerous impoverished cottagers who farmed smaller plots of land than serfs or free peasants but who did not have the right to pass the land down to succeeding generations as serfs and free peasants did. Even serfdom, which was onerous, was preferable to being a cottager or completely landless; at least serfdom provided peasants with the means to feed themselves and their families.

The most important social units on a medieval manor were families who worked the land together, each member performing tasks suitable to their abilities, strength, and age. The rigors of medieval farm labor did not permit a fastidious division of labor between women and men. Women did not usually drive the heavy plow, but they toiled at other physically demanding tasks. The life of one young girl—documented because she later achieved sainthood as Saint Alpaix—was probably typical. From age 12, Alpaix worked with her father in the fields, carrying heavy baskets of manure and sheep dung to fertilize the garden. When her arms became exhausted, she was harnessed to a sledge by a rope so that she could drag manure to the fields. During the critical harvest times, women and children worked alongside men from dawn to dusk. Young girls typically worked as gleaners, picking up the stalks and kernels that the male harvesters dropped or left behind, and girls were responsible for weeding and cleaning the fields. Before the use of water mills and windmills, women ground the grain by hand.

The fundamental fact of life on a medieval farm was the necessity of unremitting toil for women, men, girls, and boys. Even during the dormant winter months, no one stayed idle for long because of the need to make and repair farm tools, and to spin, weave, sew, brew, and bake.

The Growth of Cities

Before the eleventh century the vast majority of people in Europe lived in rural villages or perhaps small market towns of a few thousand people. The cities that survived from the ancient world remained small, except in the Mediterranean. Constantinople was by far the largest city, with a population in the hundreds of thousands. The vibrant Islamic cities of Spain were the largest in the West, and it was said that more people could fit into the mosque of Córdoba than lived in Rome. When the population began to grow as a consequence of the agricultural revolution, immigrants swelled the market towns into cities and repopulated the few cities that had survived from antiquity.

The newly thriving cities proved to be troublesome for the lords, bishops, and kings who usually had legal authority over them. As the population grew and the merchant classes became rich, city dwellers attempted to throw off their rulers to establish self-rule or, at least, substantial autonomy for their city. In the cities of north-central Italy, for example, the prominent townsmen began to chafe at the violent authority the rural lords held over them. The lords taxed or even stole the wealth that the townsmen earned through manufacturing and trade. The lords made life unsafe and unbearable, fighting among themselves and robbing from the humble inhabitants of the cities. To counter the power of the lords, townsmen formed sworn defensive associations called communes°, which quickly became the effective government of the towns. The communes evolved into city-states, which were self-governing cities that became small states by seizing control of the surrounding countryside. Perhaps as many as a hundred or more cities in north-central Italy formed communes after 1070.

Outside Italy the movement for urban liberty was strongest in southern France, the Christian parts of Spain, and the Netherlands. Kings fiercely resisted attempts to establish urban autonomy. Especially in northern Europe, urban liberty was often extracted at a high price. Townsmen bought their freedom by agreeing to pay higher taxes to kings, who were always desperate for cash. London, which had been an old Roman city and began to thrive again by the end of the eleventh century, gained urban rights in a piecemeal fashion from several kings.

As a result of the population explosion after the year 1000, growing cities became one of the defining features of medieval life. Most of these cities were modest in size—numbering in the tens of thousands rather than hundreds of thousands—but they became important as centers of trade and manufacturing and the source for new ideas.

The Spread and Reform of Christianity in the Latin West

As the core of the Latin West became politically stronger and economically more prosperous during the tenth and eleventh centuries, Christianity spread among the previously polytheistic tribes in northern and eastern Europe. Through conversion, Roman Catholicism became the dominant religion in Europe and came to distinguish itself more firmly from the Orthodox Christianity of Byzantium. Catholicism and Orthodoxy gradually grew apart during the Middle Ages, primarily over theological differences and

A Silver Crucifix from Birka, Sweden, ca. 900
The Viking fascination with silver was exploited by early missionaries, who had local silversmiths adapt the symbolism of Christianity to traditional Scandinavian art forms. Such objects assisted in the conversion of the Swedes.

disputes about the ultimate authority in the Church. For most Christians, however, the crucial differences were over liturgy and language. The liturgy° consists of the forms of worship—prayers, chants, and rituals. In the Middle Ages there was a great deal of variety in the Christian liturgy, and a number of languages were used, but followers of the Roman church gradually came to identify themselves with the Latin language and the Latin liturgy. As a result, the diverse peoples of medieval western Europe began to be called the "Latin people," although they spoke many different languages. The term *Latin* came to represent more than a language or liturgy; during the Middle Ages it became a religious and even cultural identity.

Conversions

Among the polytheistic tribes on the northern and eastern frontiers of the Latin West in Scandinavia, the Baltic Sea region, and parts of eastern Europe, the first Christian conversions usually took place when a king or chieftain accepted Christianity, and his subjects were expected to follow. Teaching Christian principles and forms of worship required much more time and effort, of course. Missionary monks usually arrived after a king's conversion, but these monks tended to take a tolerant attitude about variations in the liturgy. Because most Christians were isolated from one another, new converts tended to practice their own local forms of worship and belief. Missionaries and Christian princes discovered that the most effective way to combat this localizing tendency was to found bishoprics. The bishopric was a territorial unit (called the *diocese*), presided over by an official (called the *bishop*), who was responsible for enforcing correct worship, combating the vestiges of polytheism and false Christian beliefs (known as *heresy*), and disciplining immorality. Especially among the illiterate, formerly polytheist tribes in northern and eastern Europe, the foundation of bishoprics created cultural centers of considerable prestige that attracted members of the upper classes. Those educated under the supervision of these new bishops became influential servants to the ruling families, further enhancing the stature of Christian culture.

In eastern Europe both Byzantine Greek and Catholic Latin forms of Christianity spread. From the middle of the tenth century along the eastern frontiers of Germany, a line of newly established Catholic bishoprics became the base for the conversion of the polytheist Slavic tribes. Over a period of about sixty years, these German bishoprics pushed the Latin form of Christianity deep into east-central Europe. This effort ensured that the Poles, Bohemians (Czechs), and Magyars (Hungarians) looked to the West and the pope for their cultural models and religious leadership. These peoples remain overwhelmingly Catholic to this day.

The first bishoprics in Scandinavia were also established in the last half of the tenth century. Whereas Germans were primarily responsible for the spread of Catholicism among the Slavs, it was English missionaries who evangelized Scandinavia. Denmark had the first completely organized church in Scandinavia, represented by the establishment of nine bishoprics by 1060. The diffusion into Sweden, Norway, and Iceland came later after the strong kingdoms developed in those countries and a pro-Christian dynasty could assist the spread of the new religion. Christian conversion especially benefited women through the abandonment of polygamous marriages, common among the polytheist peoples. As a result, aristocratic women played an important role in helping convert their peoples to Christianity. That role gave them a lasting influence in the churches of the newly converted lands, both as founders and patrons of convents and as writers on religious subjects. By the end of the fourteenth century organized polytheistic worship had disappeared.

The Power of the Saints

Saints are holy persons whose moral perfection gives them a special relationship with the sacred. Ordinary Christians venerated saints to gain access to supernatural powers, protection, and intercession with God. A saintly intercessor was someone who could be trusted to obtain God's favor. In many places the newly converted simply transformed polytheistic deities into saints, a process that greatly facilitated the adoption of Christianity.

The relationship between Christian believers and the saints was profoundly intimate and intertwined with many aspects of life: Christian children were named after saints who became their special protectors; every church was dedicated to a saint; every town and city adopted a patron saint. And even entire peoples cherished a patron saint; for example, the Irish adopted Saint Patrick, who supposedly brought Christianity to the island.

A city gained protection from a patron saint by obtaining the saint's corpse or skeleton or part of the skeleton or some object associated with the saint. These body parts and material objects, called relics°, served as contacts between Earth and Heaven and were verified by miracles. The belief in the miraculous powers of relics created an enormous demand for them in the thriving medieval cities. But because the remains of the martyrs and early saints of the church were spread across the Middle East and Mediterranean from Jerusalem to Rome, relics first had to be discovered and transferred from where they were buried to new homes in the churches of the growing western European cities. The demand created a thriving market in saints' bones and body parts. They were bought or stolen, and there was ample room for fraud in passing off unauthentic bones to gullible buyers.

Possessing relics was also important for establishing the legitimacy of political authority. For example, the ruler of the city of Venice, the doge, claimed to possess the relics of Saint Mark, one of the four evangelists who wrote the gospels of the New Testament. Based on their possession of these prestigious relics, the Venetians argued that God had authorized the city's liberty from outside interference. They used this argument against their one-time imperial masters in Constantinople, against the Carolingians who attempted to conquer the thriving city, against bishops from the mainland who claimed authority over Venice's churches, and eventually even against the pope when he attempted to control the Venetian church. The great basilica of Saint Mark in Venice became a pilgrimage shrine visited by Catholics from all over Europe on their way to the Holy Land. Each pilgrim learned of Venice's intimate association with Saint Mark from the magnificent mosaics that adorned the basilica's ceilings and walls.

The Task of Church Reform

As Christianity expanded, its spiritual mission suffered from its success in the violent and materialistic world of secular affairs. The immense wealth of the Church made it prone to corruption. Many Roman popes who had benefited from the wealth of the Church were reluctant to promote reforms. Even those who wanted to eliminate corruption were slow to assemble the administrative machinery necessary to enforce their will across the unruly lands of Latin Christianity.

As we saw in Chapter 7, Pope Gregory the Great (r. 590–604) served as the moral guidepost of the western Church during his tenure. But after Gregory the papacy gradually fell into a degraded moral state. Popes were caught in a web of scandal spun by the ambitious aristocratic families of Rome that involved the theft of church property, sexual intrigue, and even murder. During the tenth century the Crescentii family became the virtual dictators of papal administration, were rumored to have murdered popes who got in their way, and set members of their own clan on the papal throne. The slow but determined

Mosaics in the Basilica of Saint Mark in Venice
Pilgrims learned of Venice's intimate association with Saint Mark from the magnificent mosaics that adorned the basilica's ceilings and walls. This scene shows a miracle that occurred after Saint Mark's body was lost during a fire in the basilica. After the leaders of Venice spent days in prayer, shown on the left, Saint Mark revealed himself by opening a door in a column, shown at the far right. In between these two scenes, those who witnessed the miracle turn to one another in amazement.

progress of the popes from this low point to regain their prominence as moral reformers is one of the most remarkable achievements of the eleventh century.

The movement for reform, however, did not begin with the popes. The idea and energy for the reform of the Church came out of the monasteries. Monks thought the best way to clean up corruption in the Church would be to improve the morals of individuals. If men conducted themselves with a sense of moral responsibility, the whole institution of the Church could be purified. The model for self-improvement was that provided by monks themselves, who set an example for the rest of the Church and for society at large. The most influential of the reform-minded monasteries was that of Cluny° in Burgundy, which was established in 910. Cluny itself became the center of a far-reaching reform movement that was sustained in more than 1,500 Cluniac monasteries.

From the very beginning Cluny was exceptional, for several reasons. First, its aristocratic founder offered the monastery as a gift to the pope. As a result, it was directly connected to Rome and completely independent from local political pressures, which were so often the source of corruption. The Rome connection positioned Cluniacs to assist in reforming the papacy itself. Second, the various abbots who headed Cluny over the years closely coordinated reform activities of the various monasteries in the Cluniac system. Some of these abbots were men of exceptional ability and learning who had a European-wide reputation for their moral stature. Third, Cluny regulated the life of monks much more closely than did other monasteries, so the monks there were models of devotion. To the Cluniacs moral purity required as complete a renunciation of the benefits of the material world as possible and a commitment to stimulating spiritual experiences. Cluniac purity was symbolized by the elegantly simple liturgy in which the text of the mass and other prayers were sung by the monks themselves. The beauty of the music enhanced the spiritual experience, and its simplicity clarified rather than obscured the meaning of the words. The Cluniac liturgy spread to the far corners of Europe.

The success of Cluny and other reformed monasteries provided the base from which reform spread beyond the isolated world of monks to the rest of the Church. The first candidates for reform were parish priests and bishops. Called the *secular clergy* (in Latin *saeculum,* meaning "secular") because they lived in the secular world, they differed from the regular clergy (in Latin *regula,* those who followed a "rule") who lived in monasteries apart from the world. The lives of many secular clergy differed little from their lay neighbors. (*Laypeople* or *the laity* referred to all Christians who had not taken religious vows to become a priest, monk, or nun.) In contrast to celibate monks, who were sexually chaste, many priests kept concubines or were married and tried to bequeath church property to their children. The Catholic Church had repeatedly forbidden priests to marry, but the prohibitions had been ineffective until Cluniac reform stressed the ideal of the sexually pure priest. During the eleventh century Catholic bishops, church councils, and reformist popes began to insist on a celibate clergy, a movement that differentiated the Catholic from the Orthodox Church, in which priests could marry.

The other objective of the clerical reform movement was the elimination of the corrupt practices of simony and lay investiture. Simony° was the practice of buying and selling church offices. Lay investiture° took place when nobles, kings, or emperors actually installed churchmen and gave them their symbols of office ("invested" them). Through this practice, the powerful laity dominated the clergy. Many nobles conceived of church offices as a form of vassalage and expected to be able to name their own candidates as priests and bishops in exchange for protecting the Church. The reformers saw as sinful any form of lay authority over the Church—whether that of the local lord or the emperor himself. The movement to eradicate simony and lay investiture contradicted the Carolingian ideal that obligated the emperor to oversee the Church. Now the reformers wanted the emperor and all other lords to keep their hands off. As a result of this controversy, the most troublesome issue of the eleventh century became establishing the boundaries between temporal and spiritual authorities.

Byzantium and Eastern Europe

In late antiquity Constantinople and Rome had been the capitals of the two halves of the Roman Empire. Once joined in a common Christian culture, eastern and western Christians had grown so far apart that by the late ninth century they began to constitute separate civilizations. There were still cultural exchanges among them as merchants, pilgrims, and scholars crossed back and forth, but the two civilizations had ceased to understand one another. They held different opinions about religious matters, such as the dating of Easter, the rituals of the liturgy, the role of images in worship, and the authority of the bishop in Rome, whom Orthodox Christians refused to recognize as pope. To Orthodox Christians, the pope was just one bishop among many Christian bishops. As the popes found protection from the Frankish kings and Carolingian emperors during the eighth and ninth centuries, their ties with the Byzantine emperor loosened. After the imperial coronation of Charlemagne, the eastern (Byzantine) and the western (Carolingian and later German) emperors became rival claimants to the authority of ancient Rome.

The East and West also spoke different languages. In the East, Greek was the language of most of the population, and Latin had been largely forgotten by the end of the sixth century. In the West, Latin or local dialects of Latin prevailed; except in southern Italy and Sicily, only a tiny few knew some Greek.

Eastern Europe, especially the Balkan peninsula, constituted a borderland between the rival Greek and Latin forms of Christianity. The two civilizations competed for converts and allies to their respective sides, and the struggle between the two has left permanent scars in the cultural divisions of the region.

BYZANTIUM

Like the West, the Byzantine empire suffered from a long period of instability provoked by wave after wave of invaders. During the eighth and early ninth centuries Byzantium was prey to a series of invasions by Muslim armies and by the Bulgars, who were a confederation of several groups of nomads from the steppes of central Asia. Resisting these invaders sapped the strength of the empire and its emperors. As we saw in Chapter 7, the iconoclastic controversy magnified internal dissension within Byzantium. When Emperor Leo III (r. 717–741) forbade religious images, except for crucifixes, he provoked rebellions and riots throughout the empire, especially among the laity, for whom the veneration of images was a vital part of spiritual life. During this troubled period, the pope in Rome excommunicated Emperor Leo and turned away from the Byzantine emperors to accept the protection of the Frankish kings, Pepin the Short and Charlemagne, a move that shifted the attention of the papacy toward the West.

The Macedonian Dynasty

Byzantium's weakness in the face of external enemies and its persistent internal dissension ceased during the Macedonian dynasty (867–1056), a line of emperors that lasted six generations. Byzantine emperors were elected, but after Basil I (r. 867–886) murdered his way to the throne he kept his family in power by naming his sons co-emperors and making imperial elections a mere formality. Under the Macedonian emperors, Byzantine armies took the field against the Arabs, and a missionary effort converted the Bulgars, the Russians, and many of the Slavic tribes.

Byzantium and Islam had been engaged in a life-and-death struggle since the seventh century. From the middle of the ninth century to the late tenth century, Byzantine armies and fleets fought Muslim armies on several fronts. In the East the Byzantines pushed into Syria and Palestine almost to Jerusalem. A large portion of the Mesopotamian river valley fell into their hands. They annexed the kingdom of Georgia and part of Armenia. In the Mediterranean the Byzantines retook the island of Cyprus and kept the Muslims from southern Italy, although they were unable to prevent Muslim conquests of Crete and Sicily, which became thriving centers of Muslim culture.

Whereas on the eastern borders the only option against the Muslims was a military one, in the polytheistic Balkans missionary efforts helped create new alliances. By conversion the Byzantines brought the southern Slavs and the Bulgars into their sphere of influence. The Bulgars, however, proved to be inconstant allies, and on several occasions threatened Constantinople itself.

Byzantine Manuscript

In this ninth-century Byzantine manuscript the figure with a pole is shown whiting out an image of Christ.

As we saw at the beginning of this chapter, the Rus also threatened Constantinople by sailing down the Dneiper River from Kiev to the Black Sea. After resisting a series of assaults from the Rus, the Byzantines sought to break down their hostility through diplomatic contacts and trade. Through conversions among members of the ruling families, Byzantine missionaries spread Christianity and Greek culture, making the Rus less isolated and more open to Byzantine influence. By the end of the tenth century the Rus had converted en masse and accepted the subordination of their church to the patriarch of Constantinople. As a result the Rus remained culturally connected to Byzantium, a connection that helped determine the forms of worship within Russian Orthodoxy.

During the seventh century, the settlement of the Slavic tribes between Byzantium and the western European kingdoms had widened the separation between the Greek and Latin worlds. The Byzantine success at converting the Slavs magnified a growing bitterness with Catholic Christians. For their part, the Byzantines under the Macedonian dynasty took heart from their military successes and assumed it was only a matter of time before the West returned to obedience to the one true emperor in Constantinople. Needless to say, Latin Christians did not accept the Byzantine vision of an empire in which they played a subordinate role, and relations between East and West soured during the tenth and eleventh centuries. Especially after the Saxon king Otto I was crowned emperor in 962, the Macedonian dynasty was hostile to the Latins. Visiting western ambassadors were treated with scorn and a superior attitude that precluded cooperation between Orthodox and Catholic Christians, especially against their common Muslim foes.

Under the Macedonian dynasty, the economy of Constantinople thrived. Home to more than half a million people by the tenth century, the city became a great marketplace where goods from as far away as China and the British Isles were exchanged. It was also the center for the production of luxury goods, especially silk cloth and brocades, which were traded throughout Europe, Asia, and northern Africa. During this period aristocratic families, the Church, and monasteries became immensely rich, and devoted themselves to embellishing the city with magnificent buildings, mosaics, and icons, creating the Macedonian Renaissance°.

The settlement of the iconoclastic controversy in 842 by Empress Theodora released great creative energies by defining the religious dogmas of Orthodoxy and creating unity within the Byzantine Church. Some of those energies went into missionary work, but the educated classes of courtiers, churchmen, monks, and scholars also produced a remarkable body of work. The most original work was spiritual in nature, embodied in sermons, theological scholarship, and especially hymns, but thanks to generous imperial patronage Constantinople also became a center for philosophical study, even if much of the work was derivative and unoriginal.

The patriarch Photius (ca. 810–ca. 893) became the most eminent scholar in the history of Byzantium. He maintained a huge library, which became a major center for the study of ancient Greek literature based on the rare manuscripts Photius had collected. Photius was the author of several important works, including the *Library*, an encyclopedic compendium of classical, late antique, and early Byzantine writers in both theology and secular literatures. By summarizing and analyzing these writers, Photius pioneered the book review, and his summaries remain especially vital because many of these books have been lost since his time. In addition to writing, Photius was deeply involved in church politics. Elected patriarch while still a layman, he was twice deposed from office due to the shifts of political winds in Constantinople. A bitter critic of the Catholics, Photius is often blamed for widening the gap between the two churches.

The quasi-sacred office of the emperor came to be magnified in elaborate court ceremonies under the Macedonian dynasty. The historian Emperor Constantine VII Porphyrogenetus (r. 912–959) wrote *On the Administration of the Empire*, an important source for Byzantine history. He also wrote the *Book of Ceremonies*, which became a model for royal ceremony throughout the Christian world and was adapted in kingdoms across Europe from Spain to Russia. The accumulation of ancient manuscripts and the compilations of ancient philosophy created an important cultural link between the medieval and the ancient worlds. In these accomplishments the Macedonian Renaissance surpassed the Carolingian Renaissance in the West.

CHRONOLOGY

Byzantium

CA. 810–CA. 893	Life of Photius, patriarch of Constantinople
867–1056	Macedonian dynasty
1025	Death of Basil II, emperor
1071	Loss of Bari and southern Italy; Seljuk Turks defeat Byzantine army at the Battle of Manzikert

Instability and Decline

Despite the achievements of the Macedonians, new threats loomed on the horizon. Under the Macedonian emperors, Byzantium had never been completely free from the external threat of invasions. The extent to which the empire succeeded in meeting these threats had depended on two factors—the political stability guaranteed by the Macedonian dynasty, and the organization and recruitment of the army through the military districts of the themes.

Emperor Basil II died in 1025 and left no direct heirs, but members of his family continued to rule until 1056, largely because of the general assumption that the peace and prosperity of the empire depended on the dynasty. Basil's successors, however, were not the strong leaders that had distinguished the earlier Macedonian dynasty. Administration of the empire was highly centralized, with a tangled bureaucracy that supervised everything from diplomatic ceremony to the training of lowly craftsmen. Without energetic leadership, the Byzantine bureaucracy quickly degenerated into routine and failed to respond to new challenges.

The success in checking invasions of the early Macedonian emperors had been largely the result of Byzantium's superior military capacities, guaranteed by the systematic organization of the army and navy and the strength of the economy. As we saw in Chapter 7, the military districts of the themes had originally been created as buffer territories against Muslims in Anatolia. Over time the four original themes were subdivided and new ones added until by the end of the eleventh century there were thirty-eight themes. The military strength of the empire depended on the theme system in which free, tax-paying soldier-farmers lived in villages under the supervision of a military commander who was also civil administrator. These soldier-farmers usually fought in their own districts, which meant they were defending their homes and families, and they provided a formidable bulwark against invaders.

By the eleventh century the independence of these soldier-farmers was threatened by deteriorating economic conditions. The emperor controlled virtually all industry and trade, which meant that the only profitable form of investment for aristocrats was to buy land. Every time a crop failed or a drought or famine struck, starving soldier-farmers in the themes were forced to surrender their land and their independence to one of the prosperous aristocrats who offered them food. As the great landowners acquired more land, the small farmers who were the backbone of the army began to disappear or lose their freedom. Because only free landholders could perform military service, the concentration of land in the hands of a few was disastrous for the army. After the death of Basil II, none of his successors was able to control these land-grabbing aristocrats, and the army began to decay.

After 1025 Byzantium faced formidable new enemies. In the West the Normans, who were distant descendants of Viking settlers, advanced on southern Italy and Sicily, crushing Byzantine power in Italy forever. The Normans, however, preserved a great deal of Byzantine culture in these regions, even as the Byzantine empire became a distant memory. Official documents were issued in Latin, Greek, and Arabic, and the Norman princes acted as patrons of the Greek monasteries. Greek continued to be spoken in southern Italy for many centuries as remnants of Byzantine civilization survived alongside other languages and cultures.

In the East Byzantium faced an even more dangerous enemy. In 1071, the Seljuk Turks captured the Byzantine emperor himself at the battle of Manzikert in Turkish-held Armenia. The Seljuks advanced across Asia Minor and threatened the very survival of Byzantium. The situation looked bleak indeed, and over the succeeding centuries, western European armies and the Turks ate away at Byzantium until its final collapse in 1453.

Borderlands in Eastern Europe

In much of the Balkan peninsula during the seventh through ninth centuries, the dissolution of Byzantine power created a power vacuum among peoples who were Christians and still considered themselves subjects of the Roman Empire. The peninsula was also home to substantial numbers of the more recently arrived polytheist Slavic and Bulgar peoples who had never been subject to Rome. During the ninth through eleventh centuries, most of these tribes converted to one or another form of Christianity, and the patterns of those conversions have had lasting consequences to this day. The religious dividing line between those who adhered to Roman Catholicism and those who followed Orthodox rites cut directly through Slavic Europe.

The various Slavic tribes in eastern Europe were extremely fragmented politically. The intricate distribution of ethnic and linguistic groups made this region more diverse than western Europe and complicated state building there.

Map 8.3 The Expanding States of Eastern and Northern Europe
Eastern Europe during the Early Middle Ages was home to a very diverse population of tribes and fledgling states. Within this diversity the states of Bulgaria, Kievan Rus, and Poland emerged by the beginning of the eleventh century.

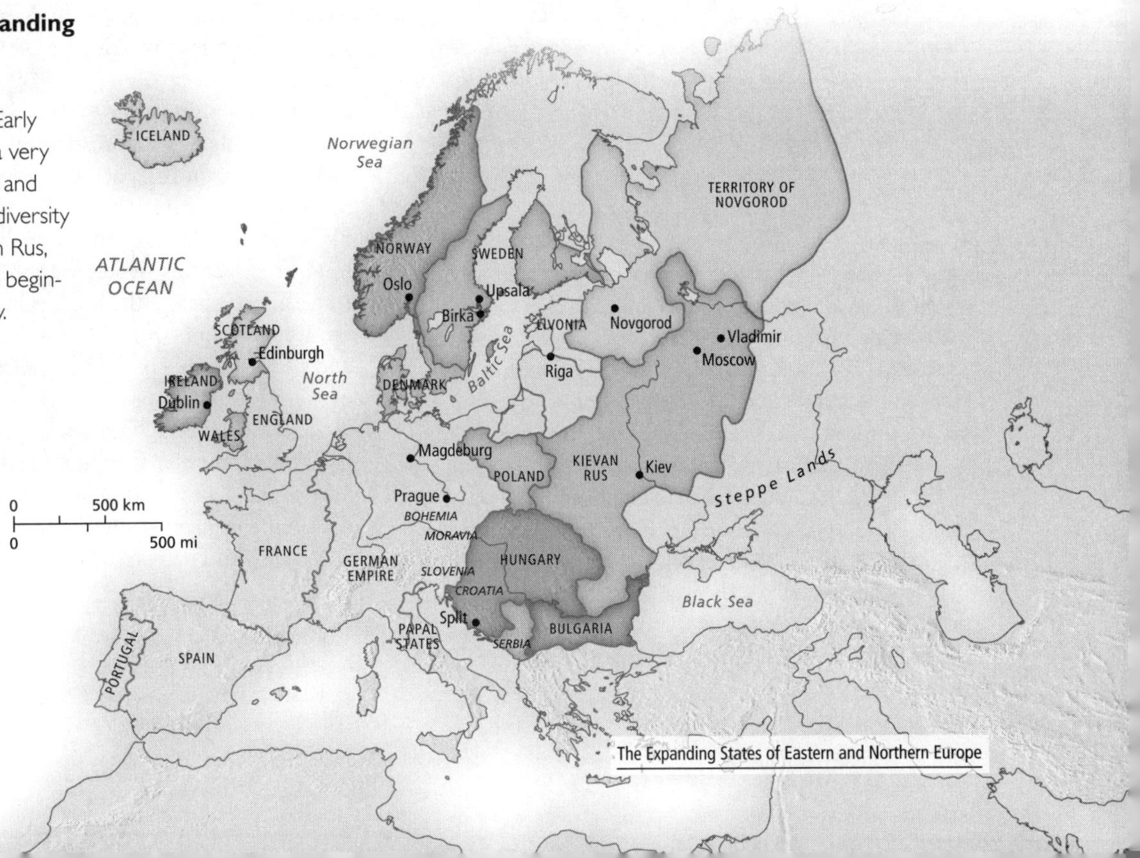

Throughout this region, tribal loyalties had long dominated society and prevented sophisticated political development. But by about 1000 the new kingdoms of Bulgaria, Kievan Rus, and Poland began to solidify as certain dominant families made dynastic claims to rule over clusters of tribes (see Map 8.3). Bulgaria and Kievan Rus became bastions of Orthodox Christianity, Poland of Roman Catholicism.

Even before it accepted Christianity, Bulgaria began to expand at the expense of the Byzantine empire. In 811, after annihilating the Byzantine army, the Bulgarian Khan (the head of a confederation of clans) Krum (r. 808–814) had the Byzantine emperor murdered and lined his skull with silver in order to turn the rival's head into a drinking cup. With this symbolic act of debasement, the Bulgarians gained a fierce reputation as enemies of Christianity. In 865, however, Khan Boris I (r. 852–889) accepted Orthodox Christianity from Byzantium. His conversion illustrates the politics of the period. During the ninth century Christianity had acquired a powerful allure among the polytheistic tribes, not the least because so-called pagans were considered by Christian rulers as legitimate objects of aggression, and their acceptance of Christianity opened the possibility for diplomatic ties and alliances. For Boris, therefore, conversion was a way to ward off Byzantine aggression. For some four years, Boris brilliantly negotiated with Rome, Constantinople, and German missionaries, all of whom sought to convert the Bulgars. In the end Boris got what he wanted—a Bulgarian Church that recognized the ultimate authority of the patriarch of Constantinople but was essentially autonomous.

The autonomy of the Bulgarian Church was further guaranteed later in the ninth century by the adoption of a Slavic rather than Latin or Greek liturgy. This was made possible by the missionary work in neighboring Moravia of Saint Cyril (ca. 826–869) and his brother Saint Methodius (815–885), who had invented an alphabet to write the Slavic language. They translated a church liturgy into a version of the Slavic language, now known as Old Church Slavonic. The acceptance of the Slavonic liturgy gradually led the ethnically and linguistically mixed peoples of Bulgaria to identify with Slavic culture and language. From a string of monasteries established by the Bulgarians, the Old Church Slavonic liturgy spread among the Serbs, Romanians, and Russians, creating cultural ties among these widespread peoples that have survived to the present.

Despite their conversion to Orthodox Christianity, the Bulgarians remained military rivals of Byzantium. A foolhardy Bulgarian attempt to capture impregnable

AN ARAB TRAVELER DESCRIBES THE RUS

During the years 921–922 the Arab Ibn Fadlan was a member of a diplomatic mission sent from Baghdad to the Bulgars on the Volga River. Along the way, Ibn Fadlan encountered the Rus at a camp and trading post. In his description of them, which remains the most celebrated account of the Viking Rus, he betrayed a fascination with their exotic appearance and customs. He identified Rus culture in terms of dress and rituals.

I have seen the Rus as they came on their merchant journeys and encamped by the Atil (Volga river). I have never seen more perfect physical specimens, tall as date palms, blond and ruddy; they wear neither tunics nor caftans, but the men wear a garment which covers one side of the body and leaves a hand free. Each man has an axe, a sword, and a knife, and keeps each by him at all times. . . . Each woman wears on either breast a box of iron, silver, copper, or gold; the value of the box indicates the wealth of the husband. Each box has a ring from which depends a knife. The women wear neck-rings of gold and silver . . . Their most prized ornaments are green glass beads . . . They string them as necklaces for their women.

. . .

When they have come from their land and anchored on, or tied up at the shore of, the Volga, which is a great river, they build big houses of wood on the shore, each holding ten to twenty persons more or less. Each man has a couch on which he sits. With them are pretty slave girls destined for sale to merchants.

. . .

When the ships come to this mooring place, everybody goes ashore with bread, meat, onions, milk and *nabid* [an intoxicating drink, perhaps beer] and betakes himself to a long upright piece of wood that has a face like a man's and is surrounded by little figures [idols], behind which are long stakes in the ground. The Rus prostrates himself before the big carving and says, "O my Lord, I have come from a far land and have with me such and such a number of girls and such and such a number of sables," and he proceeds to enumerate all his other wares. Then he says, "I have brought you these gifts," and lays down what he has brought with him, and continues, "I wish that you would send me a merchant with many dinars and *dirhems* [coins], who will buy from me whatever I wish and will not dispute anything I say."

Source: Excerpts from H. M. Smyser, "Ibn Fadlan's Account of the Rus with Some Commentary and Some Allusions to Beowulf" in *Frunciplegius: Medieval and Linguistic Studies in Honor of Francis Peabody Magoun, Jr.*, eds. Jess B. Bessinger, Jr. and Robert P. Creed, 1965. Reprinted by permission of New York University Press.

Constantinople, safe behind its massive circuit of walls, provoked a formidable military reaction. By 1018 Bulgaria had lost its independence and was reincorporated into the Byzantine empire.

Like the Bulgars, the Rus eventually adopted a Slavic language and Slavic customs. The Rus commanded the river routes from the Baltic to the Black and Caspian Seas. They established a headquarters at Kiev on the Dnieper River and extended their domination over the local Slav tribes by collecting tribute. From among the merchant-warriors of the Rus arose the forebears of the princes of Kiev, who by the end of the tenth century ruled a vast forest domain through a loose collective of principalities. The term *Rus* (later *Russian*) came to be applied to all the lands ruled by the princes of Kiev.

The zenith of Kievan Rus was under Vladimir the Great (r. 980–1015) and his son Iaroslav the Wise (r. 1019–1054). A ruthless fighter, Vladimir consolidated into a single state the provinces of Kiev and Novgorod, a city in the far north that had grown rich from the fur trade. A polytheist by birth, Vladimir had seven wives and took part in human sacrifices. However, when offered a military alliance with Byzantium in 987, he abandoned his other wives, married the Byzantine emperor's sister, and accepted conversion to Orthodox Christianity. He then forced the inhabitants of Kiev and Novgorod to be baptized and had their idols cast into the rivers. The Byzantine Church established administrative control over the Rus Church by appointing an Orthodox archbishop for Kiev. The liturgy was in Old Church Slavonic, which provided a written language and the stimulus for the literature, art, and music at the foundations of Russian culture.

The religious and political connection between the Rus and Byzantium influenced the course of Russian history; it also limited the eastward spread of Roman Catholicism. Iaroslav helped establish a bulwark of Orthodox culture throughout the Kievan state by collecting books, employing scribes to translate Greek religious books into Old Slavonic, and founding new churches and monasteries.

Unlike Bulgaria and Kievan Rus, Poland favored Roman Catholicism, an association that helped create strong cultural ties to western Europe. The Slavic Poles inhabited a flat plain of forested land with small clearings for farming. First exposed to missionaries tied to Saint Methodius, Poland resisted Christianity until Prince Mieszko (ca. 960–992) created the most powerful of the Slav states and accepted Christianity in 966. To solve the problem of German religious and political interference in his lands, Mieszko subordinated his country to the Roman pope with the Donation of Poland (c. 991). Thus began Poland's long and special relationship with the papacy.

Mieszko's successor, Boleslaw the Brave (992–1025), expanded his territories through conquest, making Poland one of the largest European kingdoms. He guaranteed the independence of the Polish church from German ecclesiastical control by obtaining the pope's approval for a Polish archdiocese, and within a few years a string of bishoprics were set up across Poland. In 1000 the German emperor recognized the independence of Poland. In 1025 the pope gave Boleslaw a royal crown, making him the equal of any monarch in Europe. Boleslaw's immediate successors, however, allowed the central authority of the government to slip away into the hands of the local nobility and even lost the title of king.

By the eleventh century the three great Christian kingdoms of eastern Europe had been established, but Bulgaria, Kievan Rus, and Poland rested on shaky foundations. All three were subject to dissolution whenever a succession crisis or a weak king opened the door for the nobility to seize power. Bulgaria and Kiev became bastions of Old Slavonic Orthodoxy. Poland had become the principal Catholic state among the Slavs.

The Dynamism of Islam

The principal reason for the rapid spread of the religion of the prophet Muhammad was the capacity of his message to unify many diverse communities in Arabia. Especially during its early centuries, Islam disseminated Muhammad's message by both force and persuasion. Islamic rule quickly spread from Arabia into Persia, Egypt, Palestine, Syria, and beyond. In the early years of the Islamic empire, the majority of conquered peoples—who were Jews, Christians, and Zoroastrians—did not become Muslims. Instead, they agreed to accept Islamic political control and to pay a poll tax in exchange for the right to continue to practice their religion. Only later did many of these people convert to Islam, often to avoid paying higher taxes.

One of the Islamic Empire's continuing problems was how to sustain political unity over time. The fundamental problem arose from disagreements about succession. After Muhammad's death in 632, the ruler of the Islamic state was called the caliph°. The first cracks in the unity of Islam broke open over the proper succession to the caliphate. To this day the principal sectarian divisions within Islam between the Shi'ites and the Sunnis derive from conflicts over succession that emerged after the death of Muhammad.

As we saw in Chapter 7, after the assassination of Muhammad's son-in-law Ali, the caliphate fell under the control of the Umayyad clan, who governed a vast Islamic Empire between 661 and 750. The Umayyads, however, were never firmly in control of the entire Islamic world and faced a series of rebellions, especially from the Shi'ites, the followers of Ali, and the Abbasid clan, who were descendants of Muhammad's uncle. These two groups—the Shi'ites and the Abbasids—were briefly allied in mutual hostility to the Umayyads. However, after the last Umayyad caliph died in a battle in 750, the Abbasids seized the caliphate and Shi'ite support for the Abbasids collapsed. Abbasid victory made permanent the split within Islam between the minority Shi'ites and the majority Sunni. While the Shi'ites and Sunni both considered the caliphate a hereditary office restricted to members of Muhammad's clan, the Quraysh, the Shi'ites believed that only direct descendants of Muhammad through his daughter Fatima and son-in-law Ali should rule the Islamic community. The Sunni, in contrast, devised a more flexible theory of succession that allowed them to accept the Abbasid caliphs and in later generations even foreign caliphs. The caliphate developed into an office that combined some governmental and some religious responsibilities.

Once they had secured the caliphate, the Abbasids engaged in a campaign to exterminate the entire Umayyad family. The only Umayyad to escape their extermination order, Abd ar-Rahman I (r. 756–788), fled to Spain where he founded what would later become the Umayyad caliphate of Córdoba. In the tenth century the Fatimids established the Shi'ite caliphate in North Africa, which claimed direct succession from Muhammad's daughter, Fatima, and opposed both the Abbasids and the Umayyads of Spain. From this time on, the Muslim world split apart into rival caliphates.

THE ABBASID CALIPHATE

The Abbasid caliphate (750–945) quickly altered the character of the Muslim world. In 762–763 a new capital was established in Baghdad. In this new location, the Abbasids were exposed to the ceremonial and administrative traditions of Persia, which helped expand the intellectual horizons of the caliphs, their courtiers, and bureaucrats. The Abbasid caliphate continued to be dominated by Arabs, and Arabic remained the language of the court. Nevertheless, the Abbasids considered all Muslims equals, whether Arabs or not. This belief fostered a distinctive Islamic civilization that fused ideas and practices derived from Arabic, Persian, Byzantine, and Syrian cultures. Despite opposition from purists, the Abbasids married non-Arabs and recruited Turks, Slavs, and other non-Muslims to serve as palace guards.

The Abbasid caliphs expanded their control over society, but they were far from despots. The caliph was first and foremost an emir—that is, the commander of a professional army. He was also responsible for internal security, which meant suppressing rebellions, supervising officials, and making sure taxes were honestly collected. But the caliph did not become involved in other public institutions, such as the mosques, hospitals, and schools. The principal exception was the office of market inspector, through which the caliph guaranteed fair business practices. In this commitment to the integrity of markets and trade, the Islamic caliphate was considerably more advanced than either Byzantium or the Latin states.

The period of Abbasid greatness lasted about a century (754–861), and its eclectic nature is reflected in its literature. The famous *Arabian Nights,* stories written down for the Caliph Harun al-Rashid (r. 786–809), were based on Hellenistic, Jewish, Indian, and Arab legends. The *Arabian Nights* and the rich tradition of Arabic poetry, which often recounted tales of thwarted love, in turn influenced Western Christian poetry of courtly love. Caliph Harun al-Rashid began the grand project of translating into Arabic the literature of ancient Greece, as well as texts from Syria, India, and Persia.

Philosophical and scientific inquiry thrived under Caliph al-Mamun (r. 813–833), who had an astronomical observatory built in Baghdad and who appreciated the work of al-Kindi (who died sometime after 870), the first outstanding Islamic philosopher. Al-Kindi grappled with questions specific to Islam but also with the works of Aristotle and problems in astrology, medicine, optics, arithmetic, cooking, and metallurgy—topics that made him well known outside the Islamic world. The work of the Arabic translators in the ninth and tenth centuries created a crucial cultural link between the ancient and medieval worlds. The Muslims supplied Arabic translations of ancient Greek texts to a later generation of Jews and Christians in Spain, who translated them into Latin. These secondhand and third-hand Latin translations of ancient philosophy and science became the core of the university curriculum in western Europe during the twelfth century.

Abbasid political power ceased in 945 when a clan of rough tribesmen from northwestern Iran seized Baghdad. The Abbasid caliphs remained figureheads, and there were occasional attempts to reinvigorate the caliphate, but its greatness as a ruling institution had ceased. However, the caliphate remained a vital symbol of Islamic unity and survived as formal institution, at least, for another 300 years.

ISLAMIC CIVILIZATION IN EUROPE

During the eighth and ninth centuries the Muslim armies chipped away at Christian territories in Europe. Unlike their fellow Muslims in the Middle East and North Africa, most of the Muslims in Europe conducted themselves more as raiders than conquerors. They plundered and pillaged but did not stay long and did not attempt a mass conversion of Christians to Islam. The effects of these raids cannot be underestimated, however. The populations of many Mediterranean cities were vulnerable and began to disappear as urban life became impossible. The only hope for survival was to disperse into the countryside, where families could live off the land and find protection with one of the many local lords who built castles for defense. Thus the Muslim raids contributed to the decline of cities along

A HUMBLE CHRISTIAN MONK MEETS THE CALIPH OF CÓRDOBA

In 953 the German emperor Otto I sent the abbot John of Gorze on a diplomatic mission to the court of Abd al-Rahman III, the caliph of Córdoba, in order to enlist his help in stamping out piracy in the western Mediterranean. Unfortunately for John, because the letters he carried from the emperor were overtly hostile to Islam, he was put under house arrest for three years. The caliph also could not understand the commitment to poverty and filth required of a Christian monk and interpreted John's refusal to dress elegantly as a calculated slight. However, John's pious sincerity eventually changed the caliph's mind. In recognition of the power of John's convictions, the caliph extended him a sign of exceptional respect by allowing him to kiss the royal hand.

John, released from almost three years of cloistered seclusion, was ordered to appear in the royal presence. When he was told by the messengers to make himself presentable to royalty by cutting his hair, washing his body, and putting on clean clothes, he refused, lest they should tell the caliph that he had changed in his essential being beneath a mere change of clothes. The caliph then sent John ten pounds in coin, so that he might purchase clothing to put on and be decent in the royal eyes, for it was not right for people to be presented in slovenly dress. John could not at first decide whether to accept the money, but eventually he reasoned that it would be better spent for the relief of the poor, and sent thanks for the caliph's generosity and for the solicitude he had deigned to show him. The monk added in his reply: "I do not despise royal gifts, but it is not permitted for a monk to wear anything other than his usual habit, nor indeed could I put on any garment of a color other than black." When this was reported to the caliph, he remarked: "In this reply I perceive his unyielding firmness of mind. Even if he comes dressed in a sack, I will most gladly receive him." . . .

When John arrived at the dais where the caliph was seated alone—almost like a godhead accessible to none or to very few—he saw everything draped with rare coverings, and floor-tiles stretching evenly to the walls. The caliph himself reclined upon a most richly ornate couch. As John came into his presence, the caliph stretched out a hand to be kissed. The hand-kissing not being customarily granted to any of his own people or to foreigners, and never to persons of low and middling mark, the caliph none the less gave John his hand to kiss.

Source: From Colin Smith, *Christians and Moors in Spain, Volume 1,* (Aris and Phillips, 1988).

the coastlines of the Christian Mediterranean. These cities revived only when Muslim raids tapered off in the eleventh century, allowing for the growth of cities discussed earlier.

The significant exceptions to the pattern of raiding were in Sicily and Spain. Muslim farmers and merchants began to settle in Sicily. Between 703 and 1060, large numbers of Arabs migrated there from North Africa, and Islam spread among the general population even though pockets of Christianity remained. In Spain, Muslim conquests in the early eighth century brought all of the peninsula into the orbit of Islam except for the mountains and coastal regions of the extreme north.

Sicily and Spain became the principal borderlands through which Arabic learning and science filtered into Catholic Europe. These borderlands became zones of particularly intense cultural interaction, where several languages were spoken and different faiths were practiced. Although small, Muslim Sicily and Spain were among the most dynamic places in Europe during the eighth to early eleventh centuries. Certainly no Christian city in western Europe could rival Córdoba, and even within the Muslim world, which enjoyed many splendid cities, only Córdoba was comparable to Baghdad. A German nun visiting Córdoba in Muslim Spain during the tenth century thought the city embodied "the majesty and adornment of the world, the wondrous capital . . . radiating in affluence of all earthly blessings."[2] During the tenth century the caliphate of Córdoba became the most important intellectual capital in western Europe, renowned for the learning of both its Muslim and Jewish scholars. Córdoba's fame derived from the extensive authority and magnificent building projects encouraged by the caliph Abd al-Rahman III (r. 912–961) and his three successors.

With an ethnically mixed population of more than 100,000, Córdoba boasted 700 mosques, 3,000 public baths, 5,000 silk looms, and 70 libraries. The caliph alone possessed a library housing more than 400,000 volumes. The streets of the city were paved and illuminated at night, the best houses enjoyed indoor plumbing, and the rich enjoyed country villas as vacation retreats. (In contrast, the city of Rome did not erect street lamps for another thousand years.) Besides the great mosque, which was one of the most famous religious monuments in Islam, the architectural centerpiece of the city was Madinat az-Zahra, a colossal 400-room palace that Abd al-Rahman III built for his favorite concubine, Zahra. Adorned with marble and semiprecious stones from Constantinople, the palace took twenty years to build and housed 13,000 household

■ **Mosque of Córdoba**

The great mosque was one of the wonders of the world during the tenth century. Since Islam prohibited the depiction of the human body, mosques were embellished with geometrical forms and quotations from the Koran. The repetition of multiple arches is echoed by the indentations on each arch, creating an intricate pattern that changes as the viewer moves about in the space.

servants in addition to the diplomats and courtiers who attended the caliph.

The lasting influence of the golden age of Córdoba can be found in the legacy of the poets, scientists, physicians, astronomers, and architects who thrived under the caliphs' patronage. Despite some tensions among Muslims and Jews, many of the prominent intellectuals in the caliphs' court were Jews. Hasdai ibn Shaprut (915–970) was a courtier who became famous for his medical skills, in particular his antidotes for poisons. In the caliphs' court the demand for his cures was strong, because several princes had fallen victim to conspiracies hatched in the palace harem or had been poisoned by a lover. The trust that Hasdai gained from his medical skills led to political appointments to deal with sensitive customs and diplomatic disputes. Both Muslim and Christian rulers considered Jews like Hasdai politically neutral, making them prized as diplomatic envoys. The Jew Samuel ibn Nagrela (993–1055) astonishingly rose to the position of vizier (prime minister) of the neighboring Muslim kingdom of Granada. An able Hebrew poet, biblical commentator, and philosopher, Samuel was also an effective commander of Muslim armies. His brilliant career reflected the value Muslims placed on learning and skill.

During the early eleventh century, the caliphate of Córdoba splintered into numerous small states. The disunity of the Muslim world provided opportunities for the stubborn little Christian states to push against the frontiers of their opulent Muslim neighbors. The kingdom of Navarre under Sancho I (r. 1000–1035) was the first to achieve dramatic success against Muslims. After Sancho's death the division of his conquests created the three kingdoms of Navarre, Aragon, and Castile. During the reign of Alfonso VI (r. 1072–1109), Castile became the dominant military power on the peninsula. Forcing Muslims to pay tribute to him to finance further wars and gathering assistance from French knights eager for plunder and French monks ardent for converts, Alfonso launched a massive campaign known as the Spanish Reconquest that led to the capture of Toledo in 1085. Once the center of Spanish Christianity before the Muslim conquests, Toledo provided Alfonso with a glorious prize that made him famous throughout Christian Europe (see Map 8.4).

The loss of Toledo so shocked the Muslim states that they invited into Spain a sect of warriors called the Almoravids from northern Africa. The Almoravids defeated Alfonso VI and temporarily halted the Spanish Reconquest in 1086. The halt of active warfare against the Muslims provided the young Christian kingdoms time to mature by establishing the basic institutions of government. After the time of Alfonso VI, the Reconquest was seldom more than an occasional rallying cry to justify particular acts of aggression, and a few surviving remnants of Muslim power managed to hang on in Spain for another 400 years.

CHRONOLOGY

Islamic Civilization

661–750	Umayyad caliphate
703–1060	Arab occupation of Sicily
750–945	Abbasid caliphate
756–1031	Umayyad dynasty of Córdoba
AFTER 870	Death of al-Kindi
1085	Capture of Toledo from Muslims

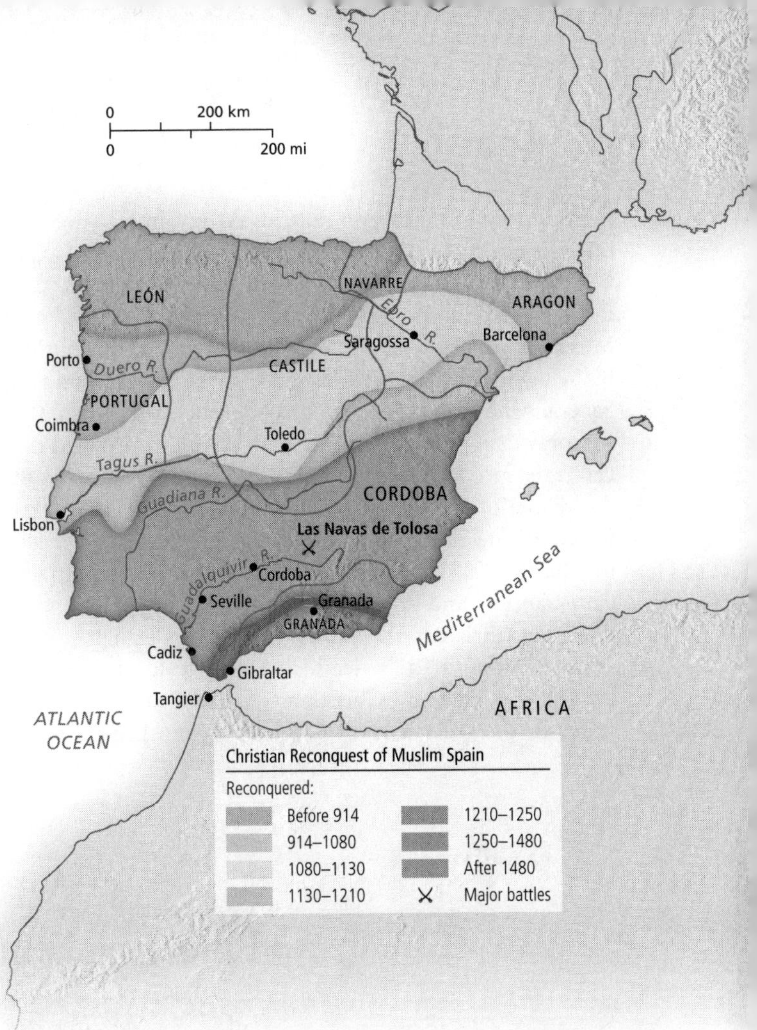

■ **Map 8.4 Reconquest of Muslim Spain**

The Spanish Reconquest refers to the numerous military campaigns by the Christian kingdoms of northern Spain to capture the Muslim-controlled cities and kingdoms of southern Spain. This long, intermittent struggle began with the capture of Toledo in 1085 and lasted until Granada fell to Christian armies in 1492.

Legends of the Borderlands

From the late eighth to the eleventh centuries, Muslim and Christian armies grappled in innumerable violent engagements. The border regions between their respective lands became militarized through building of fortresses and castles, assignment of territory to lords and generals willing to defend the borders, and settlement by soldier-farmers who served as infantrymen when required. The borderlands, however, were more than just places of conflict. During times of peace, Christians and Muslims traded with and even married one another, and in the confused loyalties typical of the times, soldiers and generals from both faiths frequently switched sides. One of the lasting fruits of these borderland societies were legends of great heroes. These legends began as stories recited in verse to entertain the aristocrats whose ancestors had fought in the borderlands, and several of these oral legends were eventually refashioned into epic poems that became extremely popular and much imitated. There were French, Byzantine, and Spanish versions of borderland epics, each strongly influencing language and culture.

The Song of Roland, an Old French epic poem that dates from around 1100, tells a story about the Battle of Roncesvalles, which took place in 778. The actual historical battle had been a minor skirmish between the soldiers of Charlemagne returning from a campaign in Spain against Basques who massacred the rear guard of the Frankish army in revenge for Charlemagne's brutal destruction of their homes. *The Song of Roland,* however, transforms this sordid episode into a great epic battle. It replaces the Basques with Muslims—the recurring enemies of the Christian Franks—and explores the psychology of family betrayal, a personality clash among friends, and the folly of heedless courage. In the climax of the poem, the hero Roland, seeking renown for his valor, rejects his companion Oliver's advice to blow a horn to alert Charlemagne of a Muslim attack. The battle is hopeless, and when the horn is finally sounded it is too late to save Roland or Oliver. For those who heard and cherished the poem, the disagreement between the prudent Oliver and the reckless Roland expressed the complicated values of bravery and loyalty, the most important values in medieval French society. In this poem the borderland conflicts between Christians and Muslims became a primal source for medieval aristocratic culture.

The epic tenth-century Greek poem *Digenes Akritas* describes the heroic feats of soldiers during the late eighth century on the eastern frontier of the empire, where Byzantine and Arab populations both fought and cooperated in a complex symbiosis. The father of the hero of the poem was an Arab soldier who abducted the daughter of a Byzantine general, married her, and converted to Christianity. The son of this mixed marriage was Digenes ("two-blooded"), a man of two peoples and two religions, who became a border fighter. This greatest Byzantine hero, who lived between two cultures, was the poetic embodiment of the engagement between Byzantium and Islam at a time when the former seemed clearly in the ascendant. Like *The Song of Roland* for the French, the legends surrounding *Digenes Akritas* had a profound influence on Greek literature. Later writers referred to it and retold its stories again and again.

In the border wars of eleventh-century Spain, the most effective soldier was Rodrigo Díaz de Vivar (ca. 1043–1099), known to history as El Cid (from the Arabic word for "lord"). Fighting for Alfonso VI, the king of Castile, El Cid was the most famous figure of the Spanish Reconquest. He is remembered in legend as a heroic Christian knight fighting for God; however, El Cid did not in fact live out this role during his life. After a quarrel with Alfonso, El Cid went over to the Muslim side. For nearly ten years, this most prestigious of the Christian warriors defended the Muslim king of Saragossa. During this period of fighting his fellow Christians, El Cid added to his reputation as a general who had never suffered defeat. Even when the Almoravids invaded from North Africa and threatened the very existence of Christian Spain, El Cid did not come to the rescue of the Christian kingdoms. Instead he undertook a private adventure to carve out a kingdom for himself in Muslim Valencia. Under El Cid the city was partially Christianized and Christian immigrants began to move there, but Christian rule did not survive his death.

Soon after El Cid's death and despite his inconstant loyalty to Castile and Christianity, he was elevated to the status of the great hero of Christian Spain. Legend soon supplanted historical truth. The popularity of the twelfth-century epic poem *The Poem of My Cid* transformed this cruel, vindictive, and utterly self-interested man into a model of Christian virtue and self-sacrificing loyalty.

Similar to the western American frontier, the medieval borderlands created legends of heroism and epic struggles. The borderlands were a wild frontier into which desperate men fled to hide or to make opportunities for themselves. Like Digenes Akritas, many were the products of mixed ancestry because of Christian and Muslim abductions and marriages. The borderlands produced a class of professional warriors, such as El Cid, who took advantage of the perpetual conflicts of the Christian and Muslim kingdoms to enrich themselves and their followers. The meeting of Christians and Muslims that took place there stimulated medieval poetry and the values of knightly valor that characterized the Middles Ages.

CONCLUSION

An Emerging Unity in the Latin West

The most lasting legacy of the Early Middle Ages was the distinction between western and eastern Europe, established by the patterns of conversion to Christianity. Slavs in eastern Europe, such as the Poles, who were converted to Catholicism looked to Rome as a source for inspiration and eventually considered themselves part of the West. Those who converted to Orthodox Christianity, such as the Bulgarians and Russians, remained Europeans certainly but came to see themselves as culturally distinct from their Western counterparts. The southern border of Christian Europe was defined by the presence of the Islamic caliphates, which remained in a state of semipermanent enmity with the Christian kingdoms. The only groups to move freely between these hostile camps were soldiers of fortune in the borderlands and Jewish merchants whose trading interests pulled them across frontiers.

During this same period, however, a tentative unity began to emerge among western European Christians, just as Byzantium fell into decline and Islam divided among competing caliphates. That ephemeral unity was born in the hero worship of Charlemagne and the resurrection of the Roman Empire in the West, symbolized by his coronation in Rome. The collapse of the Carolingian empire created the basis for the European kingdoms that dominated the political order of Europe for most of the subsequent millennium. These new kingdoms were each quite distinctive, and yet they shared a heritage from ancient Rome and the Carolingians that emphasized the power of the law on the one hand and the intimate relationship between royal and ecclesiastical authority on the other. The most distinguishing mark of western Europe became the practice of Roman Catholicism, identifiable by the use of the Latin language and the celebration of the church liturgy in Latin.

By about 1050, three social institutions had emerged that became characteristic of Latin medieval society for the next 400 years or more. The first was the system of personal loyalties associated with lordship and vassalage. All medieval kings were obliged to build their monarchies upon the social foundations of lordship, which provided the only cohesive force available. The second institution was the agricultural economy built on manors, which took advantage of the productive capacities of the agricultural revolution and guaranteed a steady supply of agricultural labor through the institution of serfdom. The third institution distinctive to Latin medieval society was the demographic revival of cities, a development that energized western Europe, in particular, with economic vigor and with the idea of a community's freedom from external tyranny.

By the end of the eleventh century, emerging western Europe had recovered sufficiently from the many destructive invaders and had built new political and ecclesiastical institutions that enabled it to assert itself on a broader stage. The first move was sensational: The leaders of the Roman Church declared their intention to achieve what the Byzantines had failed to do—recapture Jerusalem from Islam. As we shall see in the next chapter, with the beginning of the Crusades, western Europeans began an aggressive engagement outside of their own continent.

Suggestions for Further Reading

For a comprehensive list of suggested readings, please go to www.ablongman.com/levack/chapter8

Bartlett, Robert. *The Making of Europe: Conquest, Colonization and Cultural Change: 950–1350.* 1993. The best, and often greatly stimulating, analysis of how Latin Christianity spread in post-Carolingian Europe.

Fletcher, Richard. *Moorish Spain.* 1992. Highly readable.

Franklin, Simon, and Jonathan Shepard. *The Emergence of Rus: 750–1200.* 1996. The standard text for this period.

Gimpel, Jean. *The Medieval Machine: The Industrial Revolution of the Middle Ages.* 1976. A short, lucid account of the power and agricultural revolutions.

Hollister, C. Warren. *Medieval Europe: A Short History.* 1997. This concise, crisply written text presents the development of Europe during the Middle Ages by charting its progression from a primitive rural society, sparsely settled and impoverished, to a powerful and distinctive civilization.

Jones, Gwyn. *A History of the Vikings.* 2001. A comprehensive, highly readable analysis.

McKitterick, Rosamond. *The Early Middle Ages.* 2001. The best up-to-date survey for the period 400–1000. It is composed of separate essays by leading specialists.

Reuter, Timothy. *Germany in the Early Middle Ages, c. 800–1056.* 1991. A lucid explanation of the complexities of German history in this period.

Reynolds, Susan. *Fiefs and Vassals: The Medieval Evidence Reinterpreted.* 1994. The most important reexamination of the feudalism problem.

Riché, Pierre. *The Carolingians: A Family Who Forged Europe.* 1993. Translated from the 1983 French edition, this book traces the rise, fall, and revival of the Carolingian dynasty, and shows how it molded the shape of a post-Roman Europe that still prevails today. This is basically a family history, but the family dominated Europe for more than two centuries.

Stenton, Frank M. *Anglo-Saxon England.* 2001. This classic history covers the period ca. 550–1087 and traces the development of English society from the oldest Anglo-Saxon laws and kings to the extension of private lordship.

Treadgold, Warren T. *A Concise History of Byzantium.* 2001. The best short survey.

Notes

1. Quoted in Edward Peters, *Europe and the Middle Ages* (1989), 158.
2. Quoted in Jane S. Gerber, *The Jews of Spain: A History of the Sephardic Experience* (1992), 28.

CHAPTER

9

The West Asserts Itself: The High Middle Ages, 1050–1300

Chapter Outline

OUSAMA, A TWELFTH-CENTURY ARAB NOBLEMAN, MADE A BUSINESS TRIP TO Jerusalem, which at the time was occupied by Christian crusaders. To fulfill the obligation of his Muslim faith to pray daily, Ousama went to the Al-Aksa mosque, the oldest Muslim shrine in Jerusalem. He was struck by the contrast between those crusaders who had resided in Jerusalem for some time and had an understanding of Islam and those who had just arrived and "show themselves more inhuman." Some of the old-timers had even befriended him and made certain he had a place to pray. But the newcomers were far from friendly. He reported, "One day I went into [the mosque] and glorified Allah. I was engrossed in my praying when one of the Franks [as Muslims called all western Europeans] rushed at me, seized me and turned my face to the East, saying, 'That is how to pray!'" At that time Christians were supposed to pray facing the rising sun in the East. Muslims pray facing Mecca to the south of Jerusalem. On two occasions the Templars, members of a Christian military order who guarded the mosque, had to expel the zealous Frank from the mosque so Ousama could return to his prayers. The Templars apologized to Ousama, saying, "He is a stranger who has only recently arrived from Frankish lands. He has never seen anyone praying without turning to the East."

An uneasy familiarity developed among the Christians and Muslims in Jerusalem during this period. It was possible for an Arab such as Ousama to describe the Templars as his "friends," and they in turn protected him from the intolerance of the newly arrived Europeans. This peculiar mixture of friendliness and intolerance cut both ways. Muslims were shocked by what they perceived as the impiety of Christians. Ousama recounted another scene he witnessed when a descendant of Muhammad visited the Dome of the Rock, the place from which it was believed that Muhammad had ascended to heaven but which crusaders had transformed into a Christian church. A Templar came up to him and asked if he would like to see God as a child. When the Muslim answered "yes," the

Gothic Architecture: Interior view of stained-glass windows in Sainte-Chapelle, upper chapel, interior toward east, Paris.

Frankish knight displayed a painting of the Virgin Mary with the Christ child on her lap. The Muslims were shocked at the Christian's idolatry of referring to an image as God. "May Allah raise himself high above those who speak such impious things!"[1] Ousama exclaimed.

Throughout the Middle Ages, Muslims and Christians mixed mutual curiosity with militant hostility. Their tentative appreciation of each other was undermined by grotesque misunderstandings. The complexity of the relationship became especially clear in spiritual centers such as the mosques and churches of Jerusalem.

The cultural exchanges and clashes among the Catholic West, the Orthodox East, and the Muslim South were punctuated by the battles of the Crusades. Based on the efforts of the knights who fought in the Crusades and European merchants, the Catholic West began to assert itself both militarily and economically in Byzantium and in the Muslim world. As a result, western Europeans more sharply distinguished themselves from the Orthodox and Muslim worlds. The West became more exclusively Latin and Catholic. Westerners began to see themselves as culturally and religiously superior in comparison to their eastern and southern neighbors.

The consolidation of a distinctive Western identity and the projection of Western power outside Europe for the first time was made possible by internal developments within Europe. A number of vigorous kings created political stability in the West by consolidating their authority through financial and judicial bureaucracies. The most effective of these kings used a variety of strategies to force the most dangerous element in society, the landed aristocrats, to serve the royal interest. At the same time, the West experienced a period of creative ferment unequaled since antiquity. The Roman Catholic Church played a central role in encouraging intellectual and artistic activity, but there was also a flourishing literature in the languages of the common people—the vernaculars, such as French, German, and Italian.

During the twelfth and thirteenth centuries western Europe, in particular, was profoundly transformed. To understand this transformation, this chapter will address several fundamental questions: (1) What were the causes and consequences of the Crusades? (2) How did the Catholic Church consolidate its hold over the Latin West? (3) How did the western European monarchies strengthen themselves? (4) What made western European culture distinctive?

The West in the East: The Crusades

On a chilly November day in 1095 in a bare field outside of Clermont, France, Pope Urban II (r. 1088–1099) delivered a landmark sermon to the assembled French clergy and laypeople eager to hear the pope. In stirring words Urban recalled that Muslims in the East were persecuting Christians and that the holy places in Palestine had been ransacked. He called upon the knights "to take up the cross" to defend their fellow Christians in distress.

Urban's appeal for a Crusade was stunningly successful. When he finished speaking, the crowd chanted back, "God wills it." The news of Urban's call for a holy war in the East spread like wildfire, and all across France and the western part of the German Empire knights prepared for the journey to Jerusalem. Unexpectedly and probably contrary to the pope's intentions, the poor and dispossessed also became enthused about an armed pilgrimage to the Holy Land. The zealous Peter the Hermit (ca. 1050–1115) preached the Crusade among the poor and homeless and gathered a huge unequipped, undisciplined army, which left for Jerusalem well in advance of the knights. The army was annihilated along the way.

Urban's call for a Crusade gave powerful religious sanction to the western Christian military expeditions against Islam. Between 1095 and 1291, there were eight major Crusades and many smaller-scale expeditions (see Map 9.1).

The Origins of Holy War

The original impulse for the Crusades° was the perceived threat that Muslim armies posed to Christian peoples, pilgrims, and holy places in the eastern Mediterranean. By the middle of the eleventh century the Seljuk Turks, who had converted to Islam, were putting pressure on the Byzantine empire. In 1071 the Seljuks defeated the Byzantine army at Manzikert; their victory opened all of Asia Minor to Muslim occupation. Pope Urban's appeal for a Crusade in 1095 came in response to a request for military assistance from the Byzantine emperor Alexius Comnenus, who probably thought he would get yet another band of Western mercenaries to help him reconquer Byzantine territory lost to the Seljuks. Instead, he got something utterly unprecedented, a massive volunteer army of perhaps 100,000 soldiers devoted less to assisting their Byzantine Christian brethren than to wresting Jerusalem from Muslim hands.

To people in the eleventh century, the very idea of Jerusalem had a mystical allure. Enhancing this allure was a widespread confusion between the actual earthly city of Jerusalem in Palestine, where Jesus had been crucified more than a millennium before, and the fantastic heavenly city of Jerusalem with walls of dazzling precious stones as promised in the Bible (Revelation, 21:10ff). Many of the crusaders probably could not distinguish between the earthly and the heavenly cities and thought that when they abandoned their homes for Jerusalem, they were marching directly to Paradise. The promise of an eternal reward was reinforced by a special offer Pope Urban made in his famous sermon at Clermont to remit all penance for sin for those who went on the Crusade. Moreover, a penitential pilgrimage to a holy site such as Jerusalem provided a sinner with a pardon for capital crimes such as murder.

There was a significant difference between a pilgrim and a crusader, however. A pilgrim was always unarmed. A crusader carried weapons and was willing not just to defend other pilgrims from attack but to launch an assault on those he considered heathens. The innovation of the Crusades was to create the idea of armed pilgrims who received special rewards from the Church. The merger of a spiritual calling and military action was strongest in the knightly orders. The Templars, Hospitallers, and Teutonic Knights were soldiers who took monastic vows of poverty, chastity, and obedience. But rather than isolating themselves to pray in a monastery, they went forth, sword in hand, to conquer for Christ. These knightly orders exercised considerable political influence in Europe and amassed great wealth.

In the minds of crusader-knights, greed probably jostled with fervent piety. Growing population pressures and the spread of primogeniture (passing landed estates onto the eldest male heir) left younger sons with little to anticipate at home and much to hope for by seeking their fortunes in the Crusades.

Nevertheless, crusaders testified to the sense of community they enjoyed by participating in "the common enterprise of all Christians." The crusader Fulcher of Chartres was especially captivated by the unity displayed by crusaders from so many different countries: "Who has ever heard of speakers of so many languages in one army . . . If Breton or a German wished to ask me something, I was utterly without words to reply. But although we were divided by language, we seemed to be like brothers in the love of God and like near neighbors of one mind."[2] For many crusaders the exhilarating experience of brotherhood in the love of God seemed to be a sufficient motive.

CRUSADING WARFARE

The crusaders' enthusiasm for getting to Jerusalem diverted the knights from providing any direct help to the Byzantine emperor as originally planned. Instead the crusaders landed

Map 9.1 The Major Crusades

During the first three Crusades, Christian armies and fleets from western Europe attacked Muslim strongholds and fortresses in the Middle East in an attempt to capture and hold Jerusalem. The Fourth Crusade never arrived in the Middle East, as it was diverted to besiege Constantinople.

in the Middle East and struck out to capture Jerusalem itself from the Muslims. In achieving this goal, the First Crusade (1095–1099) was strikingly successful.

Several factors had weakened Muslim solidarity in the Middle East and the ability to resist the Crusaders. First, the onslaught of the Seljuk Turks threatened the Arab states that controlled access to Jerusalem as much as Byzantium. When the crusaders arrived, these states had already been weakened from fighting the Turks. Second, Muslims were divided internally. There were theological divisions between Sunnite and Shi'ite Muslims that prevented the Muslim caliphs from uniting against the Christians.

In 1099, after a little more than a month's siege, the crusaders scaled the walls of Jerusalem and slaughtered thousands of Muslims and Jews. The Christian triumph led to the establishment of the Latin principalities, which were devoted to maintaining a Western foothold in the Holy Land. The Latin principalities included all of the territory in contemporary Lebanon, Israel, and Palestine.

The subsequent crusades never achieved the success of the first. In 1144 Muslims captured the northernmost Latin principality, the county of Edessa—a warning to Westerners of the fragility of a defensive system that relied on a few scattered fortresses strung along a thin strip of coastline. In response to the loss of Edessa, Christians launched the Second Crusade. The ambitious offensive on several fronts failed so disastrously that the crusader movement lost credibility in the eyes of many. In 1187, the sultan of Egypt and Syria, Saladin (1137–1193), recaptured Jerusalem for Islam. In response to this dispiriting loss, the Third Crusade (1189–1193) assembled the most spectacular army of European chivalry ever seen, led by Europe's three most powerful kings: German Emperor Frederick Barbarossa, Philip Augustus of France, and Richard the Lion-Heart of England. After Frederick drowned wading in

CHRONOLOGY

The Crusades

1071	Battle of Manzikert; Seljuk Turks defeat the Byzantine emperor
1095	Council of Clermont; Urban II calls First Crusade
1096–1099	First Crusade
1099	Christians capture Jerusalem
1147–1149	Second Crusade
1189–1192	Third Crusade, led by Emperor Frederick Barbarossa (who drowned), King Richard the Lion-Heart of England, and King Philip II of France
1202–1204	Fourth Crusade, culminates in capture of Constantinople by Western crusaders
1208–1213	Albigensian Crusade

Krak des Chavaliers
This crusader castle survives in northern Syria in what was once the County of Edessa, a Latin Christian principality constructed to defend the Holy Land. The word *krak* derives from an Arabic word meaning "strong fort."

Byzantine Defense Against Islam
This Greek manuscript depicts the Byzantines defending themselves against a Muslim army. Dangerously weakened by the Fourth Crusade, Byzantium found itself unable to resist Muslim military pressure.

a river en route and Philip went home, Richard the Lion-Heart negotiated a truce with Saladin.

The Fourth Crusade proved the most disastrous. In 1199, Pope Innocent III called for yet another Crusade to recapture Jerusalem, but the Frankish knights and Venetian sailors who provided transportation allowed themselves to be diverted from that mission. In 1204 in an attempt to assist an exiled candidate for the throne of the Byzantine empire, the crusaders and the Venetians besieged and captured the Byzantine capital Constantinople. The Westerners divided up the empire among themselves, set up a Latin regime that lasted until 1261, and forgot about their sacred obligation to reconquer Jerusalem. The Fourth Crusade dangerously weakened the Byzantine empire by making it a prize for Western adventurers and opened the path to its eventual destruction. None of the four subsequent Crusades achieved lasting success, even though they continued to preoccupy Westerners until 1291.

THE SIGNIFICANCE OF THE CRUSADES

Despite the capture of Jerusalem during the First Crusade, the crusaders could not maintain control of the city and for more than a century wasted enormous efforts on what proved to be a futile enterprise. Neither did any of the Latin principalities in the Middle East survive for very long. The crusaders who resided in these principalities were obliged to learn how to live and trade with their Muslim neighbors, but few of them learned Arabic or took seriously Muslim learning. The strongest Islamic cultural and intellectual influences on Christian Europe came through Sicily and Spain rather than via returning crusaders. Perhaps the deepest irony of the Crusades was the extent to which they destabilized the Byzantine empire, thus weakening the West's only Christian ally so that it became an easy target for Muslim conquest.

The most important immediate consequence of the Crusades was not the tenuous Western possession of the Holy Land but the expansion of trade and economic contacts the expeditions facilitated. No one profited more from the Crusades than the Italian cities that provided transportation and supplies to the crusading armies. During the Crusades, Genoa, Pisa, and Venice were transformed from small ports of regional significance into hubs of international trade. Genoa and Venice established their own colonial outposts in the eastern Mediterranean, and both vied to monopolize the rich commerce of Byzantium. The new trade controlled by these cities included luxury goods, such as silk, Persian carpets, medicine, and spices, all expensive, exotic consumer goods found in the bazaars of the Middle East. Profits from this trade helped galvanize the economy of western Europe, leading to an era of exuberant economic growth during the twelfth and thirteenth centuries.

The Consolidation of Roman Catholicism

The late eleventh through thirteenth centuries witnessed one of the greatest periods of religious vitality in the history of Roman Catholicism. Manifest by the rise of new religious orders, remarkable intellectual creativity, and the final triumphant battle with the surviving polytheistic tribes of northern and eastern Europe, the religious vitality of the era was due in no small part to the effective leadership of a series of able popes. They gave the Church the benefits of the most advanced, centralized government in Europe. However, the papacy's successful intervention in worldly affairs helped undermine its spiritual authority, opening the way to the degradation of the papacy in the fourteenth century.

THE POPE BECOMES A MONARCH

Religious vitality required unity within the Church. The most important step in building unity was to define what it meant to be a Catholic. Catholics began to define themselves in two ways. First, the Church insisted on conformity in rites. Rites consisted of the forms of public worship called the liturgy, which included certain prescribed prayers and chants, usually in Latin. Uniform rites meant that Catholics could hear the Mass celebrated in essentially the same way everywhere from Poland to Portugal, Iceland to Croatia. Conformity of worship created a cultural unity that transcended differences in language and ethnicity. When Catholics from far-flung locales encountered one another, they shared something meaningful to them all because of the uniformity of the rites. The second thing that defined a Catholic was obedience to the pope. Ritual uniformity and obedience to the pope were closely interrelated because both the ritual and the pope were Roman. There were many bishops in Christianity, but as one monk put it, "Rome is . . . the head of the world."

The task of the medieval popes was to make this theoretical claim to authority real—in short, to make the papacy a religious monarchy. In the last half of the eleventh century under a series of dynamic reformers, the papacy firmly reasserted itself as the head of the Roman Catholic world. Among the reformers who gathered in Rome was Hildebrand (ca. 1020–1085), one of the most remarkable figures in the history of the Church, a man considered saintly by his admirers, and considered an ambitious, self-serving megalomaniac by many others. From 1055 to 1073 during the pontificates of some four popes, Hildebrand became the power behind the throne, helping enact wide-ranging reforms that enforced uniformity of worship and establishing the rules for electing new popes by the college of cardinals. In 1073 Hildebrand was himself elected pope and took the name Gregory VII (r. 1073–1085).

Gregory's greatness lay in his leadership over the internal reform of the Church. Every year he held a church council in Rome where he decreed against simony (the buying and selling of church offices) and priests who married and attempted to bequeath church property to their children. Gregory centralized authority over the Church itself by sending out papal legates, representatives who delivered orders to local bishops, and attempted to free it from external influence by asserting the superiority of the pope over all other authorities. Gregory's theory of papal supremacy led him into direct conflict with the German Emperor Henry IV (r. 1056–1106). The issue was lay investiture, the power of kings and emperors to pick their own candidates for ecclesiastical offices, especially bishoprics. As we saw in Chapter 8, during the eighth and ninth centuries weak popes relied on the Carolingian kings and emperors to name suitable candidates for these offices in order to keep them out of the hands of local aristocrats. At stake was not only power and authority, but also the income from the enormous amount of property controlled by the Church, which the emperor was in the best position to protect. During the eleventh century, Gregory VII and other reform-minded popes sought to regain control of this property. Without the ability to name his own candidates as bishops, Gregory recognized that his whole campaign for church reform would falter. When Pope Gregory tried to negotiate with the emperor over the appointment of the bishop of Milan, Henry was defiant, ordering Gregory to resign the papacy in a letter with the notorious salutation, "Henry, King not by usurpation, but by the pious ordination of God to Hildebrand now not Pope but false monk."

Gregory struck back in an escalating confrontation now known as the Investiture Controversy°. He deposed Henry from the imperial throne and excommunicated him. Excommunication° prohibited the sinner from participating in the sacraments and forbade any social contact whatsoever with the surrounding community. People caught talking to an excommunicated person or writing a letter or even offering a drink of water could themselves be excommunicated. Excommunication was a form of social death, a dire punishment indeed, especially if the excommunicated person was a king. Both sides marshaled arguments from scripture and history, but the excommunication was effective. Henry's friends started to abandon him, rebellion broke out in Germany, and the most powerful German lords called for a meeting to elect a new emperor. Backed into a corner, Henry plotted a clever counterstroke.

Early in the winter of 1077 Pope Gregory set out to cross the Alps to meet with the German lords. When Gregory reached the Alpine passes, however, he learned that Emperor Henry was on his way to Italy. In fear of what the emperor would do, Gregory retreated to the castle of Canossa, where he expected to be attacked. Henry surprised Gregory, however, by arriving not with an army but as a supplicant asking the pope to hear his confession. As a priest Gregory could hardly refuse to hear the confession of a penitent sinner, but he nevertheless attempted to humiliate Henry by making him wait for three days, kneeling in the snow outside the castle. Henry's presentation of himself as a penitent sinner posed a dilemma for Gregory. The German lords were waiting for Gregory to appear in his capacity as the chief justice of Christendom to judge Henry, but Henry himself was asking the pope to act in his capacity as priest to grant absolution for sin. The priest in Gregory won out over the judge, and he absolved Henry.

Even after the deaths of Gregory and Henry, the Investiture Controversy continued to poison relations between the popes and emperors until the Concordat of Worms in 1122 resolved the issue in a formal treaty. The emperor retained the right to nominate high churchmen, but in a concession to the papacy, the emperor lost the ceremonial privileges of investiture that conveyed spiritual authority. Without the ceremony of investiture, no bishop could exercise his office. By refusing to invest unsuitable

Map 9.2 Universal Monarchy of Pope Innocent III
Besides his direct control of the Papal States in central Italy, Pope Innocent III made vassals of many of the kings of Catholic Europe. These feudal ties provided a legal foundation for his claim to be the highest authority in Christian Europe.

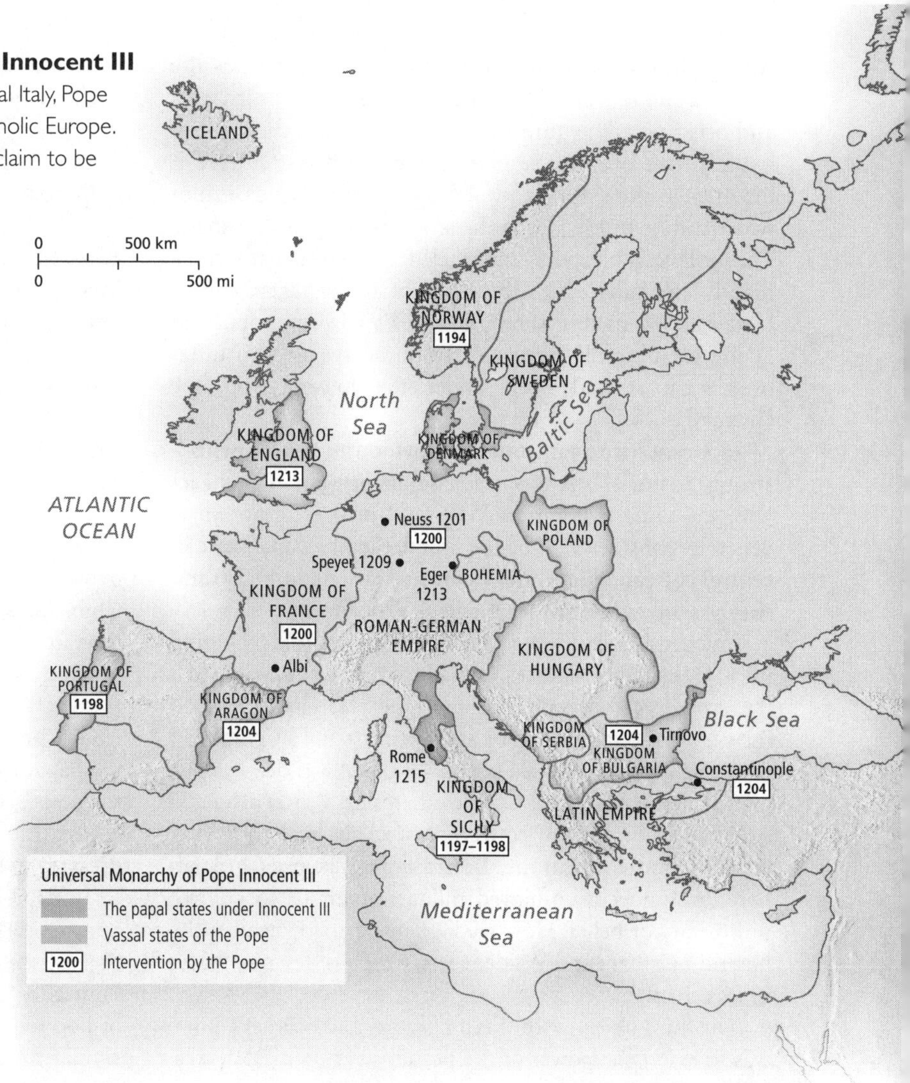

nominees, the popes had the last word. Gregory VII's vision of papal supremacy over all kings and emperors persevered.

How the Popes Ruled

The most lasting accomplishment of the popes during the twelfth and thirteenth centuries derived less from dramatic confrontations with emperors than from the humdrum routine of the law. Beginning with Gregory VII, the papacy became the supreme court of the Catholic world by claiming authority over a vast range of issues. To justify these claims, Gregory and his assistants conducted a massive research campaign among old laws and treatises. These were organized into a body of legal texts called canon law°.

Canon law came to encompass many kinds of cases, including all those involving the clergy, disputes about church property, and donations to the Church. The law of the Church also touched on many of the most vital concerns of the laity—all those who were not priests, monks, or nuns—including annulling marriages, legitimating bastards, prosecuting bigamy, protecting widows and orphans, and resolving inheritance disputes. Most of the cases originated in the courts of the bishops, but the bishops' decisions could be appealed to the pope and cardinals sitting together in the papal consistory. The consistory could make exceptions from the letter of the law, called dispensations, giving it considerable power over kings and aristocrats who wanted to marry a cousin, divorce a wife, legitimate a bastard, or annul a will. By the middle of the twelfth century, Rome was awash with legal business. The functions of the canon law courts became so important that those who were elected popes were no longer monks but trained canon lawyers, men very capable in the ways of the world.

The pope also presided over the curia°, the administrative bureaucracy of the Church. The cardinals served as ministers in the papal administration and were sent off to foreign princes and cities as ambassadors, or legates. Because large amounts of revenue were flowing into the coffers of the Church, Rome became the financial capital of the West.

In addition to its legal, administrative, and financial authority, the papacy also made use of two powerful spiritual weapons against the disobedient. Any Christian who refused to repent of a sin could be excommunicated, as the Emperor Henry IV had been. The second spiritual weapon was the interdict°, which usually applied to a whole city or kingdom whose ruler had displeased the pope. During an interdict, the sacraments were not celebrated, and the churches closed their doors, creating panic among the faithful who could not baptize their children or bury their dead. The interdict, which encouraged a public outcry, could be a very effective weapon for undermining the political support of any monarch who ran afoul of the pope.

The Pinnacle of the Medieval Papacy: Pope Innocent III

The most capable of the medieval popes was Innocent III (r. 1198–1216). Only 37 when elected, Innocent was tough-minded and the ideal candidate to bolster the papal monarchy, because of both his extensive family connections in Italy and Germany and his training in theology and canon law (see Map 9.2). Innocent possessed a clear-sighted concept of the papal monarchy. To him the pope was the overlord and moral guide of the Christian community, with authority over the entire world. He recognized the right of kings to rule over the secular sphere, but he considered it his duty to prevent and punish sin, a duty that gave him wide latitude to meddle in the affairs of kings and princes. The indefatigable pope pummeled the world with commands and advice, which were not to be taken lightly. Under Innocent, the sheer volume of correspondence to Spain, for example, increased by some twenty-five times over what it had been under the hyperactive Pope Gregory VII.

Innocent's first task was to provide the papacy with a strong territorial base of support so that the popes could act with the same freedom as kings and princes. Innocent is generally considered to be the founder of the Papal State in central Italy, an independent state that lasted until 1870 and survives today in a tiny fragment as Vatican City.

Innocent's second task was keeping alive the crusading ideal. He called the Fourth Crusade, which went awry when the crusaders attacked Constantinople. He also expanded the very idea of crusading by attempting to use a Crusade to eradicate heretics within Europe. Innocent was deeply concerned about the spread of new heresies, which attracted enormous numbers of converts, especially in the growing cities of southern Europe. By crusading against Christian heretics, Innocent employed military methods to enforce uniformity of belief. He waged a fierce crusade against the heretical Cathars and Waldensians, which is described later in this chapter.

The third objective of this ambitious and energetic pope was to assert the power of the papacy over political affairs. Innocent managed the election of Emperor Frederick II; he also assumed the right to veto imperial elections. He excommunicated King Philip II of France to force him to take back an unwanted wife. And he placed England under the interdict to compel King John to cede his kingdom to the papacy and receive it back as a fief, a transaction that made the king of England the vassal of the pope. Using whatever means necessary, he made papal vassals of the rulers of Aragon, Bulgaria, Denmark, Hungary, Poland, Portugal, and Serbia. Through these manipulations of the feudal law of vassalage, Innocent brought the papacy to its closest approximation of a universal Christian monarchy.

Innocent's fourth and greatest accomplishment was to codify the rites of the liturgy and to define the dogmas of the faith. This monumental task was the achievement of the Fourth Lateran Council, held in Rome in 1215. This council, attended by more than 400 bishops, 800 abbots, and the ambassadors of the monarchs of Catholic Europe, issued decrees that reinforced the celebration of the sacraments as the centerpiece of Christian life. They included rules to educate the clergy, define their qualifications, and govern elections of bishops. The council condemned heretical beliefs, and it called yet another Crusade. It became the guidepost that has governed many aspects of Catholic practice, especially with regard to the sacraments. It did more than any other council to fulfill the goal of uniformity of rites in Catholicism, and its influence survives to this day.

The Troubled Legacy of the Papal Monarchy

Innocent was a crafty, intelligent man who in single-minded fashion pursued the greater good of the Church as he saw it. His policies, however, had ruinous results in the hands of his less able successors. Their blunders undermined the pope's spiritual mission, especially when they attempted to influence the fate of the kingdom of Sicily, which lay on the southern border of the Papal State. Innocent's successors went beyond defending the Papal State and embroiled all Italy in a series of bloody civil wars between the Guelfs, who supported the popes, and the Ghibellines, who opposed them. The pope's position as a monarch superior to all others collapsed under the weight of immense folly and hypocrisy during the pontificate of Boniface VIII (r. 1294–1303). His personal faults, which included breathtaking vanity and rudeness, did little to help the papacy's blemished reputation. Widely believed to be a religious skeptic addicted to amulets and magic, Boniface enjoyed the company of riotous companions and loved to dress up in the regalia of an emperor.

In 1302 Boniface promulgated the most extreme theoretical assertion of papal superiority over lay rulers. Behind the statement was a specific dispute with King Philip IV of France (r. 1285–1314), who was attempting to try a French bishop for treason. The larger issue behind the dispute was similar to the Investiture Controversy of the eleventh century, but this time no one paid much attention to the pope. The loss of papal moral authority had taken its toll. In the heat of the confrontation, King Philip accused Pope Boniface of heresy, one of the few sins of which he was not guilty, and sent his agents to arrest the pope. They forced their way into his rooms at the papal palace of Anagni in

CHRONOLOGY

The Papal Monarchy

1073–1085	Reign of Pope Gregory VII
1075–1122	The Investiture Controversy
1095	Council of Clermont; Urban calls First Crusade
1198–1216	Reign of Pope Innocent III
1215	Fourth Lateran Council
1294–1303	Reign of Pope Boniface VIII

1303 where they found the 70-year-old Boniface in bed. Traumatized by the arrest and the threats of violence against him, the old man died shortly after he was released. With Boniface the papal monarchy died as well. It took more than a century for the popes to recover their independence from French influence and longer still to recapture their dignity.

Fontenay Abbey, a Cistercian House Founded in Burgundy in 1118
The austere simplicity of the architecture is typical of the Cistercian style.

DISCOVERING GOD IN THE WORLD

Even before the First Crusade, Catholic Europe began to experience an unprecedented spiritual awakening. The eleventh-century papal campaign to reform the morals of the clergy helped make priests more respectable. As a consequence, many laypeople who had previously been Christians in name only began to attend church services and to show genuine enthusiasm for the Church. Others were drawn to dedicating their lives to religion. In England, for example, the number of monks increased tenfold from the late eleventh century to 1200. The most vital indication of spiritual renewal was the success of new religious orders, which satisfied a widespread yearning to discover the hand of God in the world.

The New Religious Orders

By the eleventh century many men attracted to the religious life found the Benedictines too lax in their discipline and the Cluniacs too worldly with their elaborate liturgy and decorated churches. In 1098 a small group of Benedictine monks removed themselves to an isolated wasteland to establish the Cistercian Order. The Cistercians practiced a very strict discipline. They ate only enough to stay alive. Each monk possessed only one robe. Unlike other orders that required monks to attend frequent and lengthy services, the Cistercians spent more time in private prayer and manual labor. Their churches were bare of all decoration. Under the brilliant leadership of Bernard of Clairvaux (1090–1153), the Cistercians grew rapidly, as many men disillusioned with the sinful and materialistic society around them joined the new order. Bernard's asceticism led him to seek refuge from the affairs of the world, but he was also a religious reformer and activist, engaged with the important issues of his time. He even helped settle a disputed papal election and preached a crusade.

The Cistercians established their new monasteries in isolated, uninhabited places where they cleared forests and worked the land so that they could live in complete isolation from the troubled affairs of the world. Their hard work had an ironic result. By bringing new lands under the plow and by employing the latest technological innovations, such as water mills, many of the Cistercian monasteries produced more than was needed for the monks, and the sale of excess produce made the Cistercians very rich. The economic success of the Cistercians helped them expand even more rapidly. In their first century, the Cistercians built more than 500 new monasteries, many in places previously untouched by Western monasticism. Numerous colonies of Cistercian monks moved into northeastern Europe in areas recently converted to Catholicism. English Cistercians moved into Norway, Germans into Poland. There were also foundations in Greece and Syria, both bastions of Eastern Orthodoxy. The rapid Cistercian push beyond the frontiers of Catholic Europe helped disseminate the culture of Catholic Christianity through educating the local elites and attracting members of the aristocracy to join the Cistercians.

More than a century after the foundation of the Cistercians in France, two religious figures from Spain and Italy formulated a new kind of religious order composed of mendicant friars°. Instead of working in a monastery to feed themselves as did the Cistercians, friars ("brothers") wandered from city to city and throughout the countryside begging for alms (*mendicare* means "to beg", hence *mendicant*). Unlike monks who remained in a cloister, friars tried to help ordinary laypeople with their problems by preaching and administering to the sick and poor.

The Spaniard Dominic (1170–1221) founded the Dominican Order to convert Muslims and Jews and to combat heresy among Christians, especially the Albigensians, against whom he began his preaching mission while traveling through southern France. The ever-perceptive Pope Innocent III recognized Dominic's talents while he was visiting Rome and gave his new order provisional approval. Dominic believed the task of conversion could be achieved through persuasion and argument. To hone the Dominicans' persuasive skills, they created the first multigrade, comprehensive educational system. It connected schools located in individual friaries with more advanced regional schools that offered specialized training in languages, philosophy, and especially theology. Most Dominican friars never studied at a university but enjoyed, nevertheless, a highly sophisticated education that made them exceptionally influential in European intellectual life. Famed for their preaching skills, Dominicans were equally successful moving the illiterate masses and debating sophisticated opponents.

From the beginning, the Dominican order synthesized the contemplative life of the monastery and the active ministry of preaching to laypeople. Perhaps Dominic's greatest skill was as an innovative organizer. In contrast to traditional monastic orders, the Dominican order was organized like an army. Each province was under the supervision of a master general, and each Dominican was ready to travel wherever needed to preach and convert.

The Franciscan Order enjoyed a similar success. The Italian Francis of Assisi (1182–1226) was less an organizer than an intensely spiritual man and a visionary. The son of a prosperous merchant, Francis as a young man rebelled against the selfishness of his father's materialistic world. In a famous episode, he stripped naked in the town square as a symbol of his rejection of all possessions. Dressed in rags, he begged for food, preached repentance in the streets, and ministered to outcasts and lepers. Without training as a priest or license as a preacher, Francis at first seemed like a devout eccentric or even a dangerous heretic, but his rigorous imitation of Jesus began to attract like-minded followers. In 1210 Francis and his ragged brothers showed up in the opulent papal court of Innocent III seeking approval of a new religious order. A lesser man than Innocent would have sent the strange band packing or thrown them in prison as a danger to established society, but Innocent was impressed by Francis's sincerity and his willingness to profess obedience to the pope. Innocent's provisional approval of the Franciscans was a brilliant stroke, in that it gave the papacy a way to manage the widespread enthusiasm for a life of spirituality and purity.

Deeply influenced by Francis, Clare of Assisi (1194–1253) founded a parallel order for women, the Poor Clares. Like the Franciscans, she and her followers enjoyed the "privilege of perfect poverty," which forbade the ownership of any property even by the community itself. Clare devoted herself to penitential prayer, which was said to have twice saved the town of Assisi from besieging armies.

Both the Dominican and Franciscan Orders spread rapidly. Whereas the successful Cistercians had founded 500 new houses in their first century, the Franciscans established more than 1,400 in their first hundred years. Liberated from the obligation to live in a monastery, the mendicant friars traveled wherever the pope ordered them, making them effective agents of the papal monarchy. They preached Crusades. They pacified the poor. They converted heretics and non-Christians through their inspiring preaching revivals. Even more effectively than the Cistercians before them, they established Catholic colonies along the frontiers of the West and beyond. They became missionary scouts looking for opportunities to disseminate Christian culture. In 1254 the Great Khan in Mongolia sponsored a debate on the principal religions of the world. There, many thousands of miles from Catholic Europe, was a Franciscan friar ready to debate the learned men representing Islam, Buddhism, and Confucianism.

THE SONG OF BROTHER SUN

Francis of Assisi is known as a nature mystic, which means he celebrated God's creation through a love of nature. In one of the most renowned celebrations of nature ever written, "The Song of Brother Sun," Francis transforms the inanimate forces of nature into his spiritual brothers and sisters.

Be praised, my Lord, with all Your creatures,
Especially Sir Brother Sun,
By whom You give us the light of day!
And he is beautiful and radiant with great splendor.
Of You, Most High, he is a symbol!
Be praised, my Lord, for Sister Moon and the Stars!
In the sky You formed them bright and lovely and fair.
Be praised, my Lord, for Brother Wind
And for the Air and cloudy and clear and all Weather,
By which You give sustenance to Your creatures!
Be praised, my Lord, for Sister Water,
Who is very useful and humble and lovely and chaste!
Be praised, my Lord, for Brother Fire,
By whom You give us light at night,
And he is beautiful and merry and mighty and strong!
Be praised, my Lord, for our Sister Mother Earth,
Who sustains and governs us,
And produces fruits with colorful flowers and leaves!

Source: From *The Little Flowers of St. Francis* by St. Francis of Assisi, translated by Raphael Brown, copyright ©1958 by Beverly Brown. Used by permission of Doubleday, a division of Random House, Inc.

The Flowering of Religious Sensibilities

During the twelfth and thirteenth centuries the widespread enthusiasm for religion exalted spiritual creativity. Experimentation pushed Christian piety in new directions, not just for aristocratic men, who dominated the Church hierarchy and the monasteries, but for women and laypeople of all classes.

Catholic worship concentrated on the celebration of the Eucharist° (Holy Communion or the Lord's Supper). The Eucharist, which was the crucial ritual moment during the Mass, celebrated Jesus' last meal with his apostles. The Eucharistic rite consecrated wafers of bread and a chalice of wine as the body and blood of Christ. After the consecration, the celebrating priest distributed to the congregation the bread, called the host. Drinking from the chalice, however, was a special privilege of the priesthood. More than anything else, belief in the miraculous change from bread to flesh and wine to blood, along with the sacrament of baptism, distinguished Christian believers from others. The Fourth Lateran Council in 1215 obligated all Christians to partake of the Eucharist:

> All the faithful of both sexes shall after they have reached the age of discretion faithfully confess all their sins at least once a year to their own priest, and perform to the best of their ability the penance imposed, receiving reverently, at least at Easter, the sacrament of the Eucharist, unless perchance at the advice of their own priest they may for a good reason abstain for a time from its reception; otherwise they shall be cut off from the Church during life, and deprived of Christian burial in death.[3]

This statement in its stark simplicity defined the core obligation of all medieval Catholics. As simple as it was as a ritual observance, belief in the Eucharistic miracle presented a vexing and complex theological problem—why the host still looked, tasted, and smelled like bread rather than flesh, and why the blood in the chalice still seemed to be wine rather than blood. After the Fourth Lateran Council, Catholics solved this problem with the doctrine of transubstantiation°. The doctrine rested on a distinction between the outward appearances of the object, which the five senses can perceive, and the substance of an object, which they cannot perceive. When the priest spoke the words of consecration during the Mass, the bread and wine were changed into the flesh and blood of Christ in substance ("transubstantiated") but not in outward appearances. Thus, the substance of the Eucharist literally became God's body, but the senses of taste, smell, and sight perceived it as bread.

Veneration of the Eucharist enabled the faithful to identify with Christ because believers considered the consecrated Eucharistic wafer to be Christ himself. By eating the host, they had literally ingested Christ, making his body part of their bodies. Eucharistic veneration became enormously popular in the thirteenth century and the climax of dazzling ritual performance. Priests enhanced the effect of the miracle by dramatically elevating the host at the moment of consecration, holding it in upraised hands. Altar screens had special peepholes so that many people could gawk at the elevation, and the faithful would rush from altar to altar or church to church to witness a succession of host elevations.

St. Francis of Assisi Asks Pope Innocent III for a License to Preach

The drama of the meeting between the simple brothers shown kneeling, presenting their rule to the pope, and the sumptuous prelates of the curia is captured by the greatest of all medieval painters, Giotto. This fresco was painted in the Franciscan church in Assisi shortly before 1300.

■ **Mary, the Model of Charity**
Etienne Chevalier, the minister of finance to the king of France, is shown here adoring the Virgin Mary, who is suckling the Christ child.

During the twelfth and thirteenth centuries public veneration of saints also began to undergo a subtle shift of emphasis, away from the cults of the local patron saints toward more universal figures such as Jesus and the Virgin Mary. The patron saints had functioned almost like the family deities of antiquity who served the particular interests of individuals and communities, but the papal monarchy encouraged uniform rites that were universal throughout Catholicism.

Christians had always honored the Virgin Mary, but beginning in the twelfth century her immense popularity provided Catholics with a positive female image that contradicted the traditional misogyny and mistrust associated with Eve. Clerics and monks had long depicted women as deceitful and lustful in luring men to their moral ruin. In contrast, the veneration of the Virgin Mary promoted the image of a loving mother who would intervene with her son on behalf of sinners at the Last Judgment. Theologians still taught that the woman Eve had brought sin into the world, but the woman Mary offered help in escaping the consequences of sin.

The popularity of Mary was evident everywhere. Most of the new cathedrals in the burgeoning cities of Europe were dedicated to her. She became the favorite example of preachers as a model for women, and numerous miracles were attributed to her. Part of her appeal derived from her image as the ideal mother with the bouncing Christ child on her knee. Countless paintings and sculptures of the Madonna and child adorned the churches of Europe, and Mary's tender humanity stimulated artists to find new ways to evoke human emotions. Mary became the center of a renewed interest in the family and the Christian value of love within the family.

Mary became a model with whom women could identify, presenting a positive image of femininity. In images of her suckling the Christ child, she became the perfect embodiment of the virtue of charity, the willingness to give without any expectation of reward. Through the image of the nursing Virgin Mary, the ability to nurture became associated not just with Mary but with Christ himself. In contrast to the early Christian saints who were predominantly martyrs and missionaries, during the twelfth and thirteenth centuries saints exhibited sanctity more through nurturing others, especially by feeding the poor and healing the sick. Nurturing was associated with women, and many more women became saints during this period than during the entire first millennium of Christianity. In 1100 fewer than 10 percent of all the saints were female. By 1300 the percentage had increased to 24 percent. During the fifteenth century about 30 percent were women. Far from a feminist

THE HUMAN BODY IN HISTORY

A Tale of Two Marys

Medieval thinking about women began with the fundamental dichotomy between Eve, the symbol of women as they are, and Mary, the ideal to which all women strived. These two female archetypes classified women by what they did or did not do with their bodies. Eve brought sin and sex into the world through her disobedience to God. Mary, the Virgin Mother, kept her body inviolate.

Into the gap between the two natures of women emerged Mary Magdalen, a repentant prostitute whose veneration reached a pinnacle in the twelfth century. The medieval image of Magdalen was a composite figure, based on confusion among several different women in the New Testament. In contrast to the perpetually virginal ideal of Mary, the mother of Christ, Magdalen offered the possibility of redemption to all women. The clerical discussion of the natures of these two Marys—the Virgin Mary and Mary Magdalen—reveals a complex and changing medieval discussion about the nature of women. This discussion was pursued through a theoretical examination of women's bodies and their sexuality.

The precise significance of Mary's virginity long preoccupied Christian thinkers. Two of the Gospels simply assert that Mary had not known a man before she became pregnant with the Christ child. Later Christian thinkers extended this idea to assert that she remained a virgin after the birth of Jesus and even that she miraculously managed to preserve her virginity "before, during, and after delivery" of the infant. By discussing her as a virgin who gave birth and still remained a virgin, these Christian thinkers relegated Mary to a heavenly realm where the physical facts of real women's lives did not apply.

Geoffroy of Vendôme (d. 1132), a cleric educated in a cathedral school, drew an astonishing conclusion from these speculations about Mary's reproductive anatomy:

> *Virtuous Mary gave birth to Christ, and in Christ she gave birth to Christians. Hence the mother of Christ is the mother of all Christians. If the mother of Christ is the mother of all Christians, then clearly Christ and Christians are brothers. Not only is Christ the brother of all Christians, he is also the father of all men and primarily of Christians. From which it follows that Christ is the Virgin's father and husband as well as her son.*[4]

Geoffroy collapsed all male family relationships into one: the lineage of father, husband, and son merges with the equality of brotherhood among all Christians. What is most remarkable about Geoffroy's way of thinking is that this great Christian drama takes place within the confines of a mother's womb, invisible to sight yet so mysteriously open to speculative examination. The problem with this way of thinking was that its implications were not merely theoretical. Geoffroy and other priests were pastors who offered practical advice to real women. The model of the Virgin Mary left them with only one avenue for giving advice: They recommended that women remain lifelong virgins, which was rather impractical advice for the vast majority of women who were married.

Mary Magdalen's life provided an alternative, more practical model to follow. Known in the early Church, her veneration spread after the abbey at Vézelay, Burgundy, changed its dedication from the Virgin Mary to Mary Magdalen in 1095 and began to flourish as a pilgrimage site. Throughout France, "Madeleine" became a popular name for girls. In 1105 Geoffroy of Vendôme assembled most of the known and presumed information about her in a sermon, "In Honor of the Blessed Mary Magdalen." All writers agreed she had been a prostitute. Some insisted she had been afflicted by insatiable lust. But she had redeemed herself. By confessing her sins, she saved herself, and Christ forgave her. Thus, a woman whose body had once been corrupted saved not only herself but through her example brought others to repentance. If Magdalen could achieve redemption from her degraded state, did she not offer hope to all women? This medieval understanding of human redemption was worked out through a discussion of woman's reproduction and sexuality. ■

■ **Mary Magdalen** The repentant prostitute, Mary Magdalen, represented the possibility of redemption for all sinners.

For Discussion

What did the medieval depiction of the two Marys reveal about the way people thought about women, sexuality, and moral worth?

religion, Catholicism nevertheless developed a sacred female principle and offered an ideal woman for veneration much more prominently than did Judaism or Islam.

Many Christians became attracted to mysticism, the attempt to achieve union of the self with God. To the mystic, complete understanding of the divine was spiritual, not intellectual, an understanding best achieved through asceticism, the repudiation of material and bodily comforts. Both men and women were mystics, but women concentrated on the more extreme forms of asceticism. For example, some women allowed themselves to be walled up in dark chambers to achieve perfect seclusion from the world and avoid distractions from their mystical pursuits. Others had themselves whipped, wore painful scratching clothing, starved themselves in a form of holy anorexia, or claimed to survive with the Eucharist as their only food. Female mystics, such as Juliana of Norwich (1342–ca. 1416), envisioned a holy family in which God the Father was almighty but the Mother was all wisdom. Some female mystics believed that Christ had a female body because he was the perfect nurturer, and they ecstatically contemplated spiritual union with him.

Saints and mystics were exceptional people, however. Most Christians contented themselves with the sacraments, especially baptism, penance, and the Eucharist; perhaps a pilgrimage to a saint's shrine; and a final attempt for salvation by making a pious gift to the Church on their deathbed. The benevolent process of discovering God also stimulated a related malevolent process of attempting to detect the influence of the Devil in the world. To eradicate the Devil's influence, Christians made some people the outcasts of Western society.

CHRONOLOGY

Medieval Religious Developments

1098	Founding of Cistercian Order
1221	Death of Dominic
1226	Death of Francis of Assisi
1208–1213	Albigensian Crusade
1215	Fourth Lateran Council promulgates dogma of transubstantiation

CREATING THE OUTCASTS OF EUROPE

As churchmen and kings sought to enforce religious unity and moral reform during the twelfth and thirteenth centuries, they were disturbed by peoples who did not seem to fit into official notions of Christian society. Some of these people, such as lepers and male homosexuals, were physically or socially different; others, such as heretics and Jews, actively rejected church authority. The Church began a dramatic wave of persecutions, including campaigns to convert, control, or suppress these minorities, who were made social outcasts.

The Heretics: Cathars and Waldensians

In its efforts to defend the faith, the Church during the first half of the thirteenth century began to authorize bishops and other clerics to conduct inquisitions (formal inquiries) into specific instances of heresy or perceived heresy. The so-called heretics tended to be faithful people who sought a form of religion purer than the Church provided. During the thirteenth and early fourteenth centuries, inquisitions and systematic persecutions targeted the Cathars and Waldensians.

The Cathars were especially strong in northern Italy and southern France. Heavily concentrated around the French town of Albi, the Cathars were also known as Albigensians. They departed from Catholic doctrine, which held that God created the Earth, because they believed that an evil force had created all matter. To purify themselves, an elite few—known as "perfects"—rejected their own bodies as corrupt matter, refused to marry and procreate, and in extreme cases gradually starved themselves. These purified perfects provided a dramatic contrast to the worldly Catholic clergy. For many, Catharism became a form of protest against the wealth and power of the Church. By the 1150s the Cathars had organized their own churches, performed their own rituals, and even elected their own bishops. Where they became deeply rooted, as in the south of France, they practiced their faith openly and publicly mocked Catholics.

The Waldensians were the followers of Peter Waldo (died ca. 1184), a merchant of Lyons, France, who had abandoned all his possessions and taken a vow of poverty. Desiring to imitate the life of Jesus and live in simple purity, the Waldensians preached and translated the Gospels from the Latin into their own language so that common people could read and understand it. The Waldensians created an alternative church that became immensely popular in southern France, Rhineland Germany, and northern Italy.

Catholic authorities were unremittingly hostile to the Cathars and Waldensians. They declared heretics liable to the same legal penalties as those guilty of treason, which authorized the political authorities to proceed against them. In 1208 Pope Innocent III called the Albigensian Crusade, the first of several holy wars launched against heretics in the south of France. To eradicate the remaining Cathars and Waldensians, several kings and popes initiated inquisitions. By the middle of the thirteenth century the Cathars had been exterminated except for a few isolated pockets in the mountains, which were systematically mopped up by later inquisitors. The Waldensians were nearly wiped out by inquisitorial campaigns, but a few scattered groups have managed to survive to this day, mostly by retreating to the relative safety of the high Alps.

Systematic Persecution of the Jews

Before the Crusades, Christians and Jews had lived in relative harmony in Europe. In fact, during the Carolingian period the Frankish kings and emperors had protected Jewish communities from the occasional hostility of bishops who sought to expel them. The Crusades fomented increased violence against Jews, however. Discrimination and assaults against Jews soon became far more common than ever before. In 1182 Jews were expelled from France and allowed to return only under dire financial penalties. In England the monarchy discriminated against the Jews, opening the way for the massacre and mass suicide of the entire Jewish community of York in 1190. The 1215 decrees of the Fourth Lateran Council, which were the centerpiece of Innocent III's pontificate, attempted to regulate the activities of the Jews of Europe. These decrees prohibited Jews from holding public offices and required them to wear distinctive dress.

Christians justified their persecution of Jews during the twelfth and thirteenth centuries in two ways. First, they depicted Jews as the enemies of Christ. This bias was based on the belief that Jews were members of a conspiratorial organization devoted to the destruction of Christianity. Second, jurists began to consider Jews as royal serfs because they lived in a Christian kingdom at the king's sufferance. By classifying Jews as serfs, the law deprived them of the rights of private property. As the jurist Bracton put it, "The Jew can have nothing of his own, for whatever he acquires he acquires not for himself but for the king; for the Jews live not for themselves but for others and so they acquire not for themselves but for others."[8] This precept, which was promulgated in Spain, England, and the German Empire, justified the repeated royal confiscations of Jewish property. Especially when faced with a fiscal shortfall, kings were inclined to solve their financial problems by expropriating the property of the Jewish community.

"The Living Dead": Lepers

The widespread presence of lepers produced dramatically conflicting emotions in medieval Europe. Leprosy (Hansen's disease), which destroys the blood vessels, skin tissues, and ligaments of its victims, creating grotesque disfigurements and bone deformations, was greatly feared. Leviticus 13:45–46 says of the leper, "he is unclean: he shall dwell alone." Following these biblical precepts, many communities during the twelfth century established leper houses to segregate victims of leprosy and other disfiguring or repellent diseases. Lepers' separation from the world made them objects of admiration for some pious Christians. To wash the sores and kiss the lesions of lepers constituted a charitable act of special merit, especially for pious women.

Some medieval thinkers equated lepers with heretics and Jews. A monk was reported to have shouted to a heretical preacher, "you too are a leper, scarred by heresy, excluded from communion by the judgment of the priest, according

Burning of Heretics During the Early Thirteenth Century

These were followers of Amalric of Bène, whose body was dug up and burned in 1210. King Philip II of France supervises the burning.

JUSTICE IN HISTORY

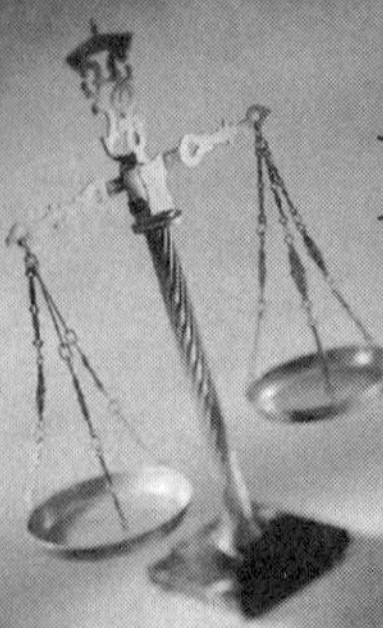

Inquiring into Heresy: The Inquisition in Montaillou

In 1208 Pope Innocent III issued a call for a Crusade against the Cathars or Albigensians. Fighting on behalf of French King Philip II, Simon de Montfort decisively defeated the pro-Cathar barons of southern France at Muret in 1213. Catharism retreated to the mountains, where it was kept alive by a clandestine network of adherents. The obliteration of these stubborn remnants required methods more subtle than the blunt instrument of a Crusade. It required the techniques of inquisitors adept at interrogation and investigation.

Against the Cathar underground, the inquisition conducted its business through a combination of denunciations, exhaustive interrogations of witnesses and suspects, and confessions. Because its avowed purpose was to root out doctrinal error and to reconcile heretics to the Church, eliciting confessions was the preferred technique. But confessed heretics could not receive absolution until they informed on their friends and associates.

One of the last and most extensively documented inquisition cases against Catharism took place in Montaillou, a village in the Pyrenees Mountains, near the border of modern-day France and Spain. The Montaillou inquisition began in 1308, a century after the launch of the Albigensian Crusade and long after the heyday of Catharism. However, the detailed records of the inquisitors provide a revealing glimpse into Catharism and its suppression as well as the procedures of the inquisition. The first to investigate Montaillou was Geoffrey d'Ablis, the inquisitor of Carcassone. In 1308 he had every resident over age 12 seized and imprisoned. After the investigation, the villagers suffered the full range of inquisitorial penalties for their Cathar faith. Some were burned at the stake or sentenced to life in prison. Many who were allowed to return to Montaillou were forced to wear a yellow cross, the symbol of a heretic, sewn to the outside of their garments.

Unfortunately for these survivors, Montaillou was investigated again from 1318 to 1325 by the most fearsome inquisitor of the age, Jacques Fournier, who was later elected Pope Benedict XII. Known as an efficient, rigorous opponent of heresy, Fournier forced virtually all the surviving adults in Montaillou to appear before his tribunal. When the scrupulous Fournier took up a case, his inquiries were notoriously lengthy and rigorous. Both witnesses and defendants spoke of his tenacity, skill, and close attention to detail in conducting interrogations. If Fournier and his assistants could not uncover evidence through interrogation and confession, they did not hesitate to employ informers and spies to obtain the necessary information. When Pierre Maury, a shepherd who had been sought by the inquisitors for many years, returned to the village for a visit, an old friend received him with caution: "When we saw you again we felt both joy and fear. Joy, because it was a long time since we had seen you. Fear, because I was afraid lest the Inquisition had captured you up there: if they had they would have made you confess everything and come back among us as a spy in order to bring about my capture."[5]

Fournier's success in Montaillou depended on his ability to play local factions against each other by encouraging members of one clan to denounce the members of another. Fournier's persistence even turned family members against one another. The clearest example of this convoluted play of local alliances and animosities, family ties, religious belief, and self-interest is the case of Montaillou's wealthiest family, the Clergues.

Bernard Clergue was the count's local representative, which made him a kind of sheriff, and his brother Pierre was the parish priest. Together they represented both the secular and religious arms of the inquisition in Montaillou. In his youth, Pierre had Cathar sympathies, and he reportedly had kept a heretical book or calendar in his home. Nevertheless, at some time before 1308, he and Bernard betrayed the local Cathars to the inquisition. In the proceedings that followed, they had the power to either protect or expose their neighbors and family members. When one of his relatives was summoned to appear before the inquisition, Bernard warned her to "say you fell off the ladder in your house; pretend you have broken bones everywhere. Otherwise it's prison for you."[6] Pierre relentlessly used his influence for

Heretics Besiege the Church

In this fifteenth-century painting the Church is symbolized by a castle, which is defended by the pope and bishops. Many of the heretics attacking the Church wear blindfolds, which symbolized their inability to see the truth.

his own and his family's benefit. A notorious womanizer, Pierre frightened women into sleeping with him by threatening to denounce them to the inquisition. Those he personally testified against were primarily from other prominent Montaillou families who represented a challenge to the Clergues' power. As one resident bitterly testified, "the priest himself cause[s] many inhabitants of Montaillou to be summoned by the Lord Inquisitor of Carcassone. It is high time the people of the priest's house were thrust as deep in prison as the other inhabitants of Montaillou."[7]

Despite the Clergues' attempted misuse of the inquisitorial investigation for their own purposes, the inquisitor Fournier persevered according to his own standards of evidence. In 1320 he finally had Pierre Clergue arrested as a heretic. The sly priest died in prison.

Questions of Justice

1. How did the methods of the inquisition help create outcasts from Catholic society? How did these methods help consolidate Catholic identity?
2. The trial of the people of Montaillou focused on differences of belief. How did the inquisition trial make these differences more apparent both to Cathars and Catholics?
3. The primary function of the inquisition was to investigate what people believed. In this sense the inquisition differed from secular criminal courts that investigated alleged criminal actions. What kinds of evidence would reveal what people believed as opposed to what people had done?

Taking It Further

Lambert, Malcolm. *The Cathars.* 1998. The best place to investigate the Cathar movement in the full sweep of its troubled history.

Le Roy Ladurie, Emmanuel. *Montaillou: The Promised Land of Error,* trans. Barbara Bray. 1978. The best-selling and fascinating account of life in a Cathar village based on the records of Fournier's inquisition.

Moore, R. I. *The Formation of a Persecuting Society: Power and Deviance in Western Europe, 950–1250.* 1987. Places the harassment of heretics in the broader context of medieval persecutions.

CRUSADERS MASSACRE THE JEWS OF RHINELAND GERMANY

On May 25, 1096, a restless crusading army attacked the Jews living in the city of Mainz, one of the great Rhineland cities on the route to the Holy Land. The Jews had taken refuge in the courtyard of the archbishop's palace, where, surrounded by heavily armed soldiers, they were given a stark choice—convert to Christianity or die. Most chose to hold fast to their faith and accept death. A Hebrew narrative recounts how a mother realizing that her children were about to be captured by the crusaders killed them herself.

There was a notable lady, Rachel the daughter of Rabbi Isaac [son of Rabbi] Asher. She said to her companions: "I have four children. On them as well have no mercy, lest these uncircumcised come and seize them and they remain in their pseudo-faith. With them as well you must sanctify the Holy Name." One of her companions came and took the knife. When she [Rachel] saw the knife, she cried loudly and bitterly. She beat her face, crying and saying: "Where is your steadfast love, O Lord?" She took Isaac, her small son—indeed he was very lovely—and slaughtered him. She had said to her companions: "Wait! Do not slaughter Isaac before Aaron." But the lad Aaron, when he saw that his brother had been slaughtered, cried out: "Mother, Mother, do not slaughter me!" He then went and hid himself under a bureau. She took her two daughters, Bella and Matrona, and sacrificed them to the Lord God of Hosts, who commanded us not to abandon pure awe of him and to remain loyal to him. When the saintly one finished sacrificing her three children before our Creator, she then lifted her voice and called out to her son: "Aaron, Aaron, where are you? I shall not have pity on you either." She pulled him by the leg from under the bureau, where he had hidden, and sacrificed him before the sublime and exalted God. She then put them under her two sleeves, two on one side and two on the other, near her heart. [The soldiers] convulsed near her, until the crusaders seized the chamber. They found her sitting and mourning them. They said to her: "Show us the money which you have under your sleeves." When they saw the slaughtered children, they smote her and killed her.

Source: From *The Jews and the Crusaders*, translated from the Hebrew by Shlomo Eidelberg. Published by The University of Wisconsin Press, 1977. Reprinted by permission of the author.

to the law, bare-headed, with ragged clothing, your body covered by an infected and filthy garment." In 1321 rumors alleged that a conspiracy between lepers and Jews had poisoned the wells in France. Heretics, lepers, and Jews became interchangeable co-conspirators in league with the Devil to destroy Christianity. As the assumed common enemy, they all became subject to persecution.

The Invention of Sexual Crimes

The Christian disapproval of men who engaged in sexual relations with other men derived from a medieval interpretation of the biblical condemnation of the Sodomites, the people of the city of Sodom and its sister cities. Ezekiel 16:49 states, "This was the guilt of your sister Sodom: she and her daughters had pride, excess of food, and prosperous ease, but did not aid the poor and needy." According to this passage, the sin of the people of Sodom was the failure to be charitable; sexual behavior was not mentioned. In fact, during the first millennium of Christianity, there was no particular concern about homosexuality. Christian theologians advocated chastity for everyone and did not consider homosexual relations between men to be any more sinful than any other form of sexual behavior.

During the eleventh century, however, the sin of Sodom came to be associated with homosexual relations, prompted perhaps by reports of forced child prostitution in Muslim lands. The first church legislation against the practice came in 1179. The reasons for this dramatic shift of opinion—from tolerating such behavior to treating it as criminal—are obscure, but the language of the time paired sodomy with leprosy. Male sodomites began to be persecuted, and by 1300 most governments had made male sodomy punishable by death, in many statutes death by burning. In the process of creating new outcasts, however, female homosexuals were never mentioned. It appears that the male authors of penal legislation could not imagine that erotic relationships between women were even possible.

By the thirteenth century, heretics, Jews, lepers, and male sodomites were identified as outcasts and subjected to legal discrimination, persecution, violence, and—in the case of heretics—even extermination. The so-called cleansing of Christian Europe of its outcasts was a particularly violent example of the use of power by the dominant society over certain minority groups within it. One of the ways medieval Catholic society became unified was by ostracizing certain groups of people from within its midst. The cleansing of Christian Europe was a tragedy for its victims, but it gave both church and government officials a greater sense of unity and control.

Strengthening the Center of the West

During the twelfth and thirteenth centuries, Catholic western Europe became the supreme political and economic power in the Christian world, eclipsing Byzantium—an achievement that made it a potent rival to the Islamic states. One reason was heightened political unity. The kings of France and England, in particular, achieved unprecedented power over their own dominions. A second reason was economic. From the city-states in Italy to the cities of the Hanseatic League on the shores of the Baltic Sea, Europe was bound together by an extensive trading network controlled by sophisticated merchants. As a result, by the thirteenth century Europeans enjoyed a high level of prosperity.

THE MONARCHIES OF WESTERN EUROPE

The three forms of government during the Middle Ages were empires, city-states, and monarchies. The best example of an empire was Byzantium, a potentially formidable military power, but too diverse and far flung to maintain the loyalty of its subjects. During the twelfth century the threads that held the Byzantine empire together began to fray. The other empire at the time was the German Empire, which boasted some impressive monarchs but lacked unity and thus never achieved its potential as the dominant power in Europe. Italian city-states, such as Venice, Milan, Florence, Pisa, and Genoa, thrived as the engines of economic innovation and vitality, but they were vulnerable to foreign conquest and frequently enfeebled by internal rivalries and feuds. In contrast to overextended empires and underdefended city-states, the western European monarchies gathered the military resources and created the bureaucratic structures necessary to surpass all other forms of government. These kingdoms created the foundations of the modern nation states, which remain to this day the dominant forms of government around the globe. What happened in France and England during the twelfth and thirteenth centuries, therefore, represents one of the most important and lasting contributions of the West to world history.

During the High Middle Ages, France and England began to exhibit the fundamental characteristics of modern states. Several developments explain how these states strengthened themselves. First, they formed political units that persisted. That is, these units had borders that survived despite changes in rulers and dynasties. Second, they developed lasting, impersonal institutions that managed finances and administration. That is, they created bureaucracies. Third, they established a system for resolving disputes and rendering justice in which the final authority was the king. That is, they established the principle of sovereignty. Fourth, the medieval monarchies resolved that the fundamental loyalty of subjects should be to the laws of the state, a loyalty greater than the obligations of a vassal to a lord or even a son to a father. Stable borders, permanent bureaucracies, sovereignty, and the rule of law—these were the foundations on which France and England established strong states in the twelfth and thirteenth centuries (see Map 9.3).

Expansion of Power: France

For the French kings, the pressing task was to unify their hodge-podge kingdom. Through most of the twelfth century the only part of France the kings ruled directly was the royal domain, the Ile-de-France, an area roughly the size of Vermont but with the fertile soil of Illinois. Over the rest of the kingdom, the king of France was merely the overlord with vague obligations from his vassals, one of whom, the king of England, directly controlled more French territory than he did. Upon these unpromising foundations, the twelfth- and thirteenth-century French monarchs built the most powerful kingdom in Europe and one of the most unified. The kings of France achieved unity through military conquests and shrewd administrative reforms.

France was blessed with a continuous succession of kings who ruled for long periods of time, produced male heirs, and avoided succession disputes. In the turbulent Middle Ages, dynastic continuity was a key ingredient in building loyalty and avoiding chaos. The vigorous Philip I (r. 1060–1108) initiated a succession of extremely effective kings. Unpopular with the clergy because of his alleged adultery, he took charge of his own domain, where he countermanded the arbitrary justice of local lords by extending royal justice. By focusing his attention on establishing himself as the undisputed lord of his own domain, Philip provided his descendants with a powerful lordship upon which they built the French monarchy.

Louis VI, the Fat (r. 1108–1137), secured complete control of the Ile-de-France, thus providing the dynasty with a dependable income from the region's abundant farms and the thriving trade of Paris. He shoved aside the great barons who had dominated the royal administration and replaced them with career bureaucrats who were loyal only to the king. The most prominent of these was the highly talented Suger, a lower-class priest who had been Louis's tutor and served the king as a statesman of vision.

Louis's grandson, Philip II Augustus (r. 1180–1223), lacked education but proved himself a shrewd realist who outmaneuvered his vassal, the English King John, to recover much of western France for himself. To administer his domain and newly acquired lands, Philip introduced new royal officials, the *baillis*, who were paid professionals and often trained in Roman law. Directly responsible to the king, they had full administrative, judicial, and military powers in their districts. Philip tolerated considerable regional diversity, but the *baillis* laid the foundation for a bureaucracy that centralized French government. Many historians consider Philip Augustus the most important figure in establishing the unity of the French state.

The medieval French king who came closest to exemplifying the moral ideals of kingship was Louis IX (r. 1226–1270), who was canonized Saint Louis in 1297 for his exemplary piety and reputation for justice. A tall imposing figure, Louis was blessed with impeccable manners and a chivalrous nature. Prompted by an ardent desire to lead a Crusade to the Holy Land, he sought to strengthen the kingdom so that it could operate and survive in his absence. He introduced a system of judicial appeals that expanded royal justice and investigated the honesty of the *baillis.*

The reputation of the monarchy so carefully burnished by Louis IX suffered during the reign of his grandson, Philip IV, the Fair (r. 1285–1314)—known for his ruthless use of power. Philip greatly expanded the king's authority and also managed to bring the Church under his personal control, making the French clergy largely exempt from papal supervision. To pay for his frequent wars, Philip expelled the Jews after stripping them of their lands and goods, and then turned against the rich Order of the Knights Templar, a crusader order that had amassed a fortune as the papal banker and creditor of Philip. He confiscated the Templars' lands and tortured the knights to extort confessions to various crimes in a perverse campaign to discredit them. Philip was perhaps most effective in finding new ways to increase taxation. Under Philip, royal revenues grew tenfold from what they had been in the saintly reign of Louis IX.

Map 9.3 Western European Kingdoms in the Late Twelfth Century
The kings of England occupied Ireland as well as much of western France. France itself was consolidated around the Ile-de-France, the area around Paris. The kingdoms of Germany, Bohemia, Burgundy, and Italy were ruled by the German emperors.

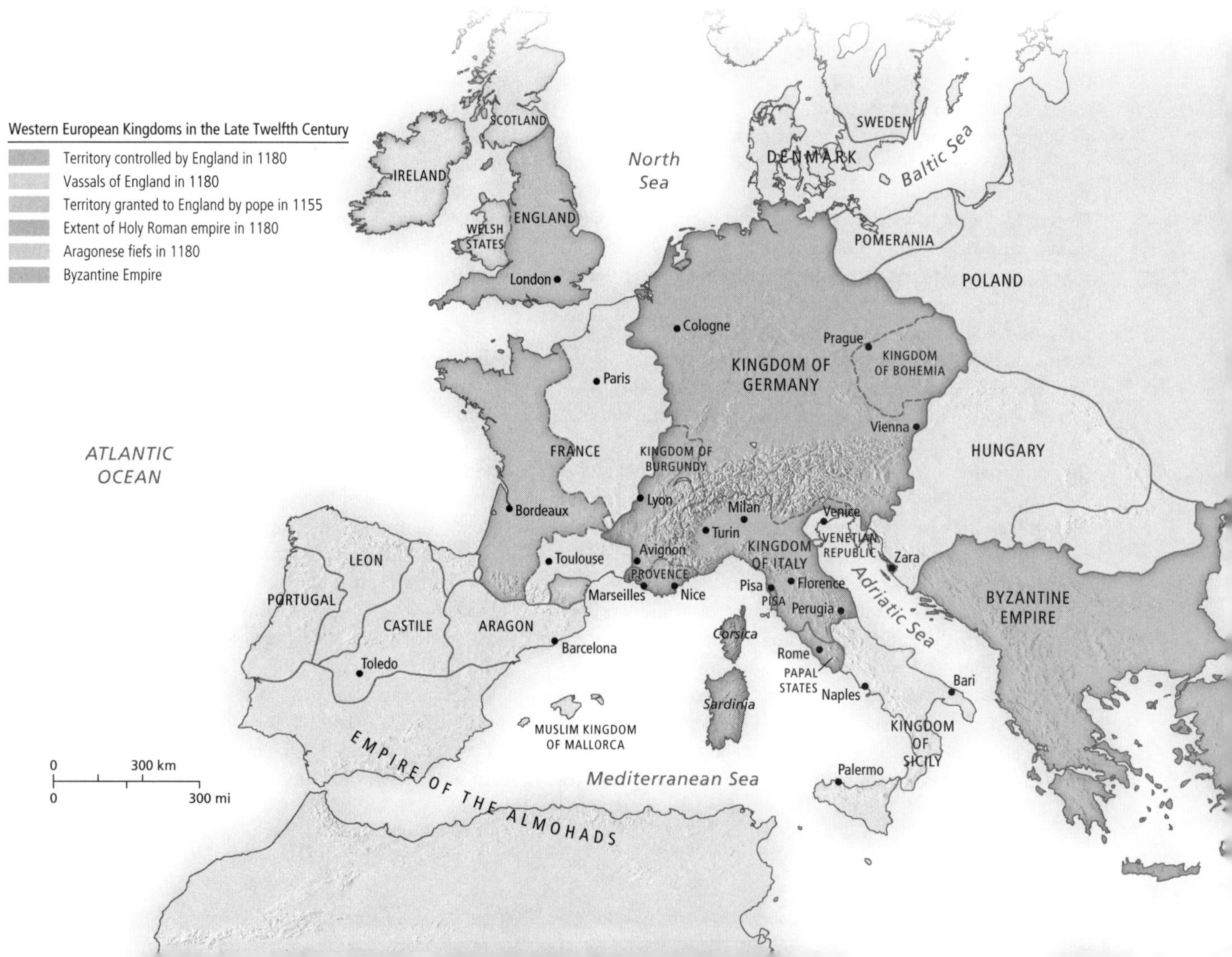

The Fertile Medieval Countryside
During the month of June everyone in the village participated in the wheat harvest. The men cut the grain while the women raked it. In the background is one of the Great Palaces of the Dukes of Burgundy.

Lord of All Lords: The King of England

When the Norman William I, the Conqueror (r. 1066–1087), seized England in 1066, he claimed that as the conqueror he possessed all the land. The new king kept about one-fifth of the land under his personal rule and parceled out the rest to the loyal nobles, monasteries, and the churches. This policy ensured that every bit of England was held as a fief, directly or indirectly, from the king, a principle of lordship enforced by an oath of loyalty to the crown required of all vassals. About 180 great lords from among the Norman aristocracy held land directly from the king, and hundreds of lesser nobles were vassals of these great lords. William accomplished what other kings only dreamed about: He had truly made himself the lord of all lords. William's hierarchy of nobles transformed the nature of the English monarchy, giving the Norman kings far greater authority over England than any of the earlier Anglo-Saxon kings had enjoyed and creating a more unified realm than any kingdom on the continent.

The legacy of the conquest provided William's successors with a decided advantage in centralizing the monarchy. Nevertheless, the system required the close personal attention of the king. King Henry II (r. 1154–1189) proved himself an indefatigable administrator and calculating realist who made England the best-governed kingdom in Europe at the time. Reacting to the anarchy that prevailed when he ascended to the throne, he strengthened the government of England and extended English authority—with varying degrees of success—over Ireland, Wales, and Scotland.

The greatest innovations of Henry's rule were judicial. His use of sheriffs to enforce the royal will produced the legends of Robin Hood, the bandit who resisted the nasty sheriff of Nottingham on behalf of the poor. But in reality the sheriffs probably did more good than evil in protecting the weak against the powerful. In attempting to reduce the jurisdiction of the nobles, Henry made it possible for almost anyone to obtain a writ that moved a case to a royal court. To make justice more available to those who could not travel to Westminster, just outside of London where the royal court usually sat, Henry introduced a system of itinerant circuit court° judges who visited every shire in the land four times a year. When this judge arrived, the sheriff was required to assemble a group of men familiar with local affairs to report the major crimes that had been committed since the judge's last visit. These assemblies were the origins of the grand jury° system, which persists to this day as the means for indicting someone for a crime.

For disputes over the possession of land, sheriffs assembled a group of twelve local men who testified under oath about the claims of the plaintiffs, and the judge made his decision on the basis of their testimony. These assemblies were the beginning of trial by jury°. The system was later extended to criminal cases and remains the basis for rendering legal verdicts in common-law countries, including Britain, the United States, and Canada.

With his usual directness, Henry tackled the special legal privileges of the clergy, the thorn in the side of medieval kings everywhere. According to canon law, priests could be tried only in church courts, which were notoriously easygoing in punishing even murderers with a simple penance. Moreover, these verdicts—however trivial—could be appealed to Rome, a process that could delay justice for years. Henry wanted to subject priests who had committed crimes to the jurisdiction of the royal courts in order to establish a universal justice that applied to everyone in the realm, a principle fiercely opposed by Thomas Becket, the archbishop of Canterbury. When four knights—believing they were acting on the king's wishes—murdered Becket before the altar of Canterbury cathedral, the public was outraged and Henry's attempts to subject the Church to royal justice were ruined. Becket was soon canonized and revered as England's most famous saint.

The royal powers assembled by Henry met strong reaction under King John (r. 1199–1216). In 1204 John lost to King Philip II of France the Duchy of Normandy, which had been one of the foundations of English royal power since William the Conqueror. After the French defeated King John at the Battle of Bouvines in 1214, the barons of England grew tired of being asked to pay for wars the king lost. In 1215 some English barons forced John to sign Magna Carta° ("great charter," in reference to its size), in which the king pledged to respect the traditional feudal privileges of the nobility, towns, and clergy. Contrary to widespread belief, Magna Carta had nothing to do with asserting the liberty of the common people or guaranteeing universal rights. It addressed only the privileges of a select few rather than the rights of the many. Subsequent kings, however, swore to uphold it, thereby accepting the fundamental principle that even the king was obliged to respect the law. After Magna Carta the lord of all lords became less so.

English government boasted two important innovations under King Edward I (r. 1272–1307). The first was the foundation of the English Parliament (from the French "talking together"). Edward called together the clergy, barons, knights, and townsmen in Parliament in order to raise large sums of money for his foreign wars. The members of Parliament had little choice but to comply with the king's demands, and all they received in return was Edward's explanation of what he was going to do with their money. The English Parliament differed from similar assemblies on the continent in that it more often included representatives of the "commons." The commons consisted of townsmen and prosperous farmers who lacked titles of nobility but whom the king summoned because he needed their money. The second governmental innovation during Edward's reign consisted of an extensive body of legal reforms. Edward curtailed the power of the local courts, which were dominated by rural landlords and aristocrats. And he began to issue statutes that applied to the entire kingdom. Under Edward, lawyers began to practice at the Inns of Court in London, where they transformed customary legal practices into the common law that still survives as the foundation of Anglo-American law.

A Divided Regime: The German Empire

The German Empire, heir to the old Carolingian kingdom of East Francia, suffered from the division between its principal component parts in Germany and northern Italy. Germany itself was an ill-defined region, subdivided by deep ethnic diversity and powerful dukes who ruled their lands with a spirit of fierce independence. As a result, emperors could not rule Germany directly but only by demanding homage from the dukes who became imperial vassals. These feudal bonds were fragile substitutes for the kinds of monarchic institutions that evolved in France and England. An effective emperor could call upon the dukes to help him crush rivals, but he could neither dictate to his vassals nor claim vacant fiefs for the crown, as in France and England. The emperor's best asset was the force of his personality and his willingness to engage in a perpetual show of force to prevent rebellion. In northern Italy, the other part of the emperor's dominion, he did not even enjoy these extensive ties of vassalage and could rely only on vague legal rights granted by the imperial title and his ability to keep an army on the scene.

The century between the election of Frederick I (r. 1152–1190), known as Barbarossa or "red-beard," and the death of his grandson Frederick II (r. 1212–1250) represented the great age of the medieval German Empire, a period of relative stability preceded and followed by disastrous phases of anarchy and civil war. Both of these Hohenstaufen emperors, however, faced hostility from the popes whose own monarchic pretensions clashed with imperial rule in Italy.

Barbarossa projected enormous personal charisma that helped him awe recalcitrant vassals. He became a careful student of the imperial dignities encoded in Roman law, surrounded himself with experts in that law, and considered himself the heir of the great emperors Constantine, Justinian, and Charlemagne. He even managed to have Charlemagne canonized a saint.

Barbarossa's lofty ambitions contrasted with the flimsy base of his support. His own ancestral lands were in Swabia, an impoverished region barely capable of subsistence let alone supporting Frederick's imperial adventures. To set himself on a firmer financial footing, Frederick launched a series of expeditions across the Alps to subdue the enormously wealthy Italian cities that were technically part of his realm, even though they acted as if they were independent. The campaign proved a disaster. It galvanized papal

CHRONOLOGY

Strengthening the Center of the West

1170	Murder of Thomas Becket
1176	Battle of Legnano; Lombard League defeats Emperor Frederick I Barbarossa
1214	Battle of Bouvines; Philip II of France allied to Emperor Frederick II defeats John of England and his allies
1215	Magna Carta
1231	Constitutions of Melfi

opposition to him and forced the Italian city-states to put aside their rivalries to form an anti-imperial coalition, the Lombard League. At the Battle of Legnano in 1176 the League decisively defeated the German imperial army, forcing Barbarossa to recognize the autonomy of the city-states.

Barbarossa's young grandson, Frederick II, turned the traditional policy of the German emperors upside down. Instead of residing in Germany and attempting to influence Italian affairs from afar, Frederick, who loved the warm climate and engaging society of the South, lived in Sicily and left Germany alone.

Frederick has long enjoyed a remarkable historical reputation as the "wonder of the world," the most cosmopolitan monarch of the Middle Ages, who laid out grand plans for a united Italy embodied in the Constitutions of Melfi, which he put forth in 1231 (see Map 9.4). Through them, he proposed to rule through a professional imperial bureaucracy, to employ itinerant inspectors to check corruption, and to introduce uniform statutes based on Roman law. In effect, he sought a level of uniformity similar to what France and England had achieved during this period, and he was probably subject to similar influences derived from ancient Roman political theory and law. However, the popes' enduring antagonism to these plans and Frederick's own despotic tendencies undermined these ambitious and potentially fruitful reforms. He cut himself off from honest advice by declaring it an act of sacrilege even to discuss, let alone question, any of his decisions. He so overtaxed southern Italy and Sicily that these lands, which were once the richest in Italy, became an economic backwater. And his abandonment of Germany to its feuding princes prevented the centralization and implementation of legal reforms that took place in France and England.

After Frederick II's death, his successors lost their hold on both Italy and Germany. During the nearly constant warfare and turmoil of the late thirteenth century, the exceedingly inappropriate name of "Holy Roman Empire" came into general use for the German Empire. The term suggested a universal empire ordained by God and descended from ancient Rome, but the lofty claims embedded in the name found no basis in the crude reality of the rebellious, disunited lands of Germany and Italy.

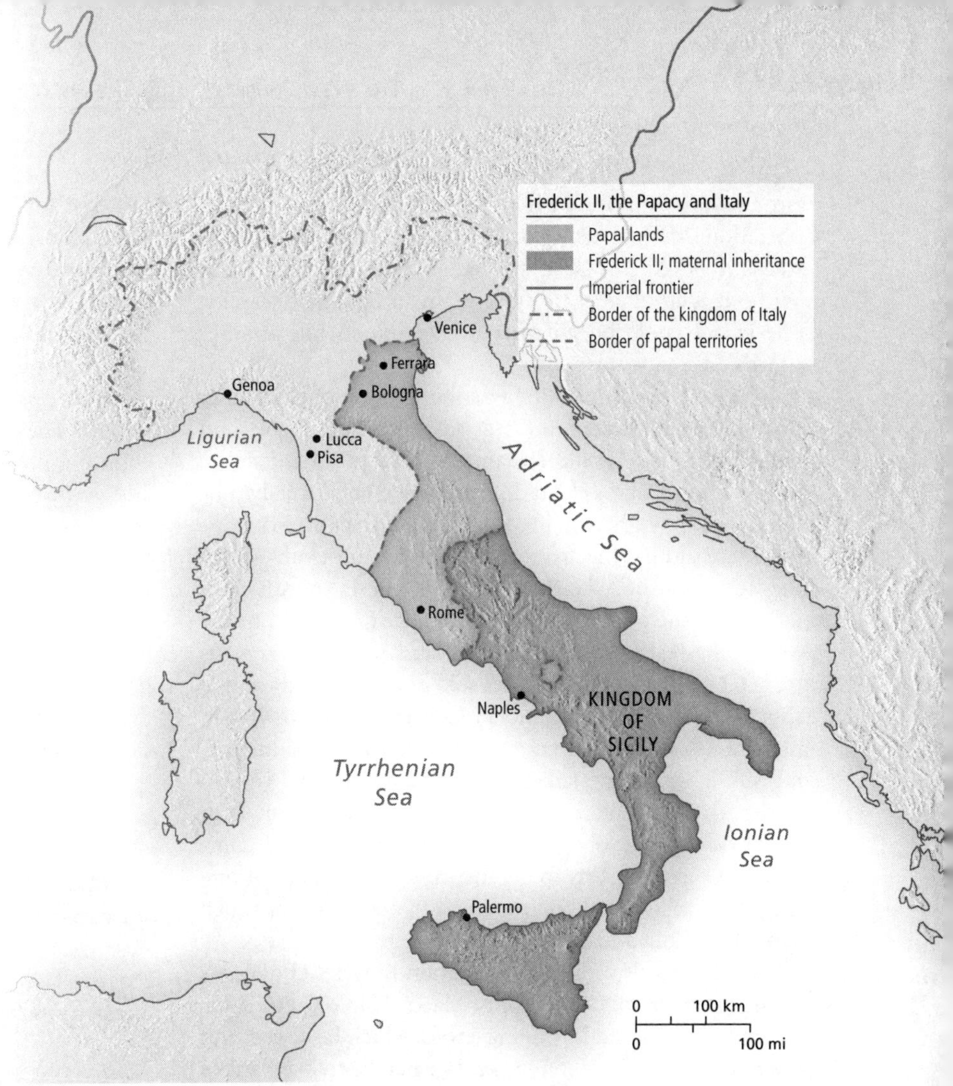

■ **Map 9.4 The Empire and the Papacy in Italy**
During the reign of Emperor Frederick II, the kingdom of Sicily became the most potent power in Italy and presented a challenge to the papacy. After Frederick's death, the peninsula suffered from a long series of wars as rival claimants attempted to replace him in Sicily and the popes attempted to control events.

The Economic Boom Years

The kingdoms of the medieval West thrived on an economic base of unprecedented prosperity. What made possible the twelfth- and thirteenth-century economic boom? As we saw in Chapter 8, the agricultural and power revolutions of the eleventh century certainly provided the necessary foundations, but three other factors also proved crucial.

First, there were advances in transportation networks. Trade in grain, woolen cloth, and other bulk goods depended on the use of relatively cheap water transportation for hauling goods. Where there were neither seaports nor navigable rivers, goods had to be hauled cross-country by pack train, a very expensive enterprise. To address the problem and to facilitate transportation and trade, new roads and bridges were built, and old Roman roads that had been neglected for a thousand years were repaired. These improvements, however, were unevenly distributed, leaving large parts of Europe without any effective form of transportation. Many roads were little more than deeply rutted tracks, blocked in places by bogs of mud or fallen trees. Without a cheap way to move grain to places of scarcity, one village could be suffering from famine while another nearby enjoyed a surplus.

The most lucrative trade was the international trade in luxury goods. Because these goods were lightweight and high-priced, they could sustain the cost of long-distance transportation across land. Italian merchants virtually monopolized the European luxury trade. The Genoese distributed rare alum—the fixing agent for dyeing cloth—from the west coast of Asia Minor to the entire European cloth industry. Venetians and Genoese imported cotton from the Middle East. Raw silk, transported aboard camel caravans from China and Turkestan, was sold at trading posts on the shores of the Black Sea and in Constantinople to Italian merchants who earned enormous profits selling shimmering silk fabric to the ladies and gentlemen of the western European aristocracy. The silk trade was quite small in quantity, but it was of great value to international commerce because silk was so highly prized. One ounce of fine Chinese black silk sold on the London market for as much as a highly skilled mason would earn in a week's labor.

Rubies, pearls, coral, and diamonds were also easily transported for fantastic profits. Marco Polo of Venice, for example, specialized in trading jewels, which he sewed into the linings of his clothing for safety when he trekked across Asia from Venice to China and back. During the thirteenth century, he was only one of many, as countless European merchants crisscrossed the caravan routes of Asia and north Africa. Italian merchant fleets sailed the Mediterranean, but transportation from the European ports in the Mediterranean to northern Europe still employed costly pack trains traversing the Alpine passes north. By the end of the thirteenth century, however, first Genoese and then other Italian fleets ventured beyond the Straits of Gibraltar into the stormy Atlantic, dramatically improving transportation between northern and southern Europe.

Even the bulk commodities the Italians brought from the East were valuable enough to sustain the high transportation costs. Known by the generic term "spices," these included hundreds of exotic items: True spices such as pepper, sugar, cloves, nutmeg, ginger, saffron, mace, and cinnamon were used to enhance the otherwise boring, bland medieval cuisine; indigo and madder were used for dyes; and medicinal herbs including opiates were used as pain relievers. The profits from spices generated most of the capital in European financial markets.

The second factor responsible for the economic boom of the twelfth and thirteenth centuries was the creation of new business techniques that long-distance trade necessitated—for example, money. Coins had virtually disappeared in the West for nearly 400 years during the Early Middle Ages, when most people lived self-sufficiently on manors and bartered for what they could not produce for themselves. The expansion of trade and new markets, however, required a moneyed economy. By the thirteenth century Venice and Florence were minting their own gold coins, which became the medium for exchange across much of Europe.

Merchants engaged in long-distance trade began to develop the essential business tools of capitalism during this period. They created business partnerships, uniform accounting practices, merchants' courts to enforce contracts and resolve disputes, letters of credit (used like modern traveler's checks), bank deposits and loans, and even insurance policies. The Italian cities established primary schools to train merchants' sons to write business letters and keep accounts—a sign of the growing professional character of business. Two centuries earlier an international merchant had been an itinerant peddler who led pack trains over dusty and muddy tracks to customers in small villages and castles. But by the end of the thirteenth century an interna-

Map 9.5 European Fairs and Trade Routes
Trade routes crisscrossed the Mediterranean Sea and hugged the Atlantic Ocean, North Sea, and Baltic Sea coastlines. Land routes converged in central France at the Champagne fairs. Other trade routes led to the large market cities in Germany and Flanders.

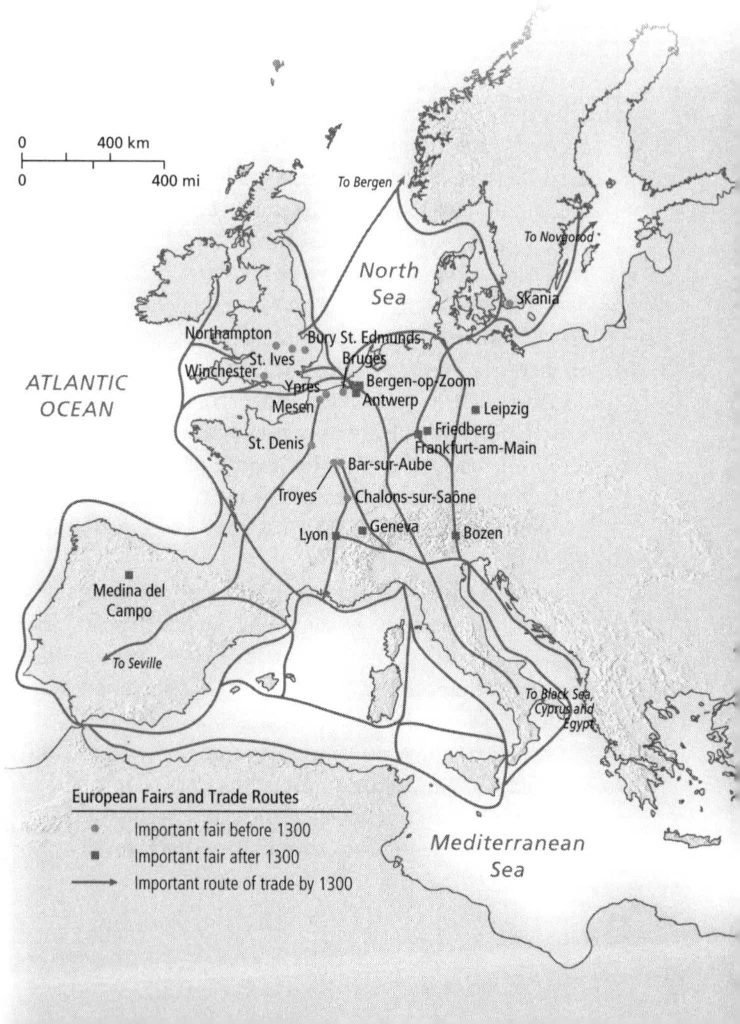

tional merchant could stay at home behind a desk, writing letters to business partners and ship captains and enjoying the profits from his labors in the bustling atmosphere of a thriving city.

At the center of the European market were the Champagne fairs in France, where merchants from northern and southern Europe met every summer to bargain and haggle (see Map 9.5). The Italians exchanged their spices for English raw wool, Dutch woolen cloth, German furs and linens, and Spanish leather. From the Champagne fairs, prosperity spread into previously wild parts of Europe. Cities along the German rivers and the Baltic coast thrived through the trade of raw materials such as timber and iron, livestock, salt fish, and hides. The most prominent of the North German towns was Lübeck, which became the center of a loose trade association of cities in Germany and the Baltic coast known as the Hanseatic League. Never achieving the level of a unified government, the league nonetheless provided its members mutual security and trading monopolies—necessary because of the weakness of the German imperial government.

The third factor in the economic prosperity of the period was cities. Cities both facilitated the commercial boom and were the primary beneficiaries of it. All across Europe, especially in Flanders, the Netherlands, and north-central Italy, cities exploded in size. Exact population figures are hard to come by, but there is ample evidence of stunning growth. Between 1160 and 1300 Ghent had to expand its city walls five times to accommodate all its inhabitants. During the thirteenth century the population of Florence grew by an estimated 640 percent.

Urban civilization, one of the major achievements of the Middle Ages, was an outgrowth of commerce. And from urban civilization came other achievements. All the cities built a large new cathedral to flaunt their accumulated wealth and to honor God. New educational institutions, especially universities, trained the sons of the urban, commercial elite in the professions. However, these merchants who commanded the booming urban economy were not necessarily society's heroes. The populace at large viewed them with deep ambivalence, despite the immeasurable ways in which they enriched society. The landed aristocrats treated merchants with withering disdain even when forced to borrow money from them and to tax them to finance grandiose expenditures. Many merchants themselves were ambivalent about trade and aspired to retire as soon as they could afford to buy land and take up life as a country gentleman.

Churchmen worried about the morality of making profits. Church councils condemned usury—the lending of money for interest—even though papal finances depended on it. Theologians promulgated the idea of a "just price," the idea that there should be a fixed price for any particular commodity. The just price was anathema to hardheaded merchants who were committed to the laws of supply and demand. Part of the ambivalence toward trade and merchants came from an inequity in all market-based economies, even the primitive one of the Middle Ages—the rewards of the market were unevenly distributed, both socially and geographically. The prosperous merchants were the most visible signs of puzzling social changes, but they were also the dynamic force that made possible the intellectual and artistic flowering of the High Middle Ages.

Medieval Culture: The Search for Understanding

Cultural encounters during the High Middle Ages took many forms. Some were direct exchanges, as when Christians and Muslims in crusader Jerusalem discovered their different ways of praying. Other encounters were more indirect, as when medieval thinkers read the books of ancient philosophers and so were confronted with the thinkers of a more sophisticated culture. During the twelfth and thirteenth centuries, this second kind of encounter, based on the renewed availability of works of classical Greek philosophy, opened creative possibilities, especially in theology. The Greek philosophers had been dead for nearly 1,500 years, but the medieval thinkers who discovered ancient philosophy experienced profound cultural shock. First Muslim and then Jewish and Christian writers struggled to reconcile the rational approach of Aristotle and other Greek philosophers with the faith demanded by Islam, Judaism, and Christianity. Some suffered from a crisis of faith. Others confronted the challenge presented by ancient philosophy and attempted to reconcile reason and faith by creating new philosophical systems.

The medieval intellectual engagement with new ideas spread in many directions. Lawyers began to look back to ancient Roman law for guidance about how to settle disputes, adjudicate crimes, and create governmental institutions. Muslim influences reinvigorated the Christian understanding of the sciences. Themes found in Persian love poetry, which were echoed in Arabic poems, found their way into the Christian notion of courtly love. Catholic western Europe experienced a cultural flowering through the spread of education, the growing sophistication of Latin learning, and the invention of the university. Distinctively Western forms developed in literature, music, drama, and above all the Romanesque and Gothic architecture of Europe's great cathedrals.

The city of Paris was the breeding ground for much of the most creative activity. The dynamism of Paris attracted thinkers and artists from all over Europe. Thirteenth-century Paris represented the cultural pinnacle of the High Middle Ages, comparable to Athens in the fifth century B.C.E. or Florence in the fifteenth century.

REVIVAL OF LEARNING

The magnitude of the educational revolution in medieval western Europe is clear from simple statistics. In 1050 less than 1 percent of the population of western Europe could read, and most of these literate people were priests who knew just enough Latin to read the offices of the liturgy. Four hundred years later, as many as 40 percent of men and a smaller percentage of women were literate in the cities of western Europe. Europeans had embraced learning on a massive scale even before inexpensive printed books became available in the late fifteenth century. In fact, the printing revolution of the fifteenth century was not so much the stimulus for new learning as a response to the escalating demand for more books. How did this demand come about?

In 1050 education was available only in monasteries and cathedral schools, and the curriculum was very basic, usually only reading and writing. These two kinds of schools had different educational missions. Monastic education trained monks to read the books available in their libraries as an aid to contemplating the mysteries of the next world. In contrast, the cathedral schools, which trained members of the ecclesiastical hierarchy, emphasized the practical skills of rational analysis that would help future priests, bishops, and royal advisers solve the problems of this world.

By 1100 the number of cathedral schools had grown significantly and the curriculum expanded to include the study of the ancient Roman masters, Cicero and Virgil, who became models for clear Latin composition. These schools met the demand for trained officials from various sources—the thriving cities, the growing church bureaucracy, and the infant bureaucracies of the Western kingdoms. As the number of schools expanded, they became less exclusively devoted to religious training and began to provide a practical education for laymen. But the Church was still the dominant force.

Scholasticism: A Christian Philosophy

The cathedral schools, in addition to teaching Latin grammar, recognized a growing need for training in logic as well. Refuting heresies required precise logical arguments. Anselm of Canterbury (ca. 1033–1109), for example, employed strict logic in an attempt to prove the existence of God. He began with the question of how the mind conceived ideas. He could not imagine ideas coming from nothing, arguing that they must have some basis in reality. Did not the very presence of the idea of God in the mind, Anselm concluded, demonstrate that God must exist? Intrigued by such arguments, students began to seek more advanced instruction than that provided by the standard curriculum. They tended to gather around popular lecturers in the cathedral schools where they were trained in scholasticism, which emphasized the critical methods of reasoning, pioneered by Anselm.

Scholasticism° literally means "of the schools," but the term also refers to a broad philosophical and theological movement that dominated medieval thought. In this broader sense, scholasticism refers to the use of logic learned from Aristotle to interpret the meaning of the Bible and the writings of the Church Fathers, who created Christian theology in its first centuries. Books were scarce in the cathedral schools because the only means of duplication before the invention of the printing press was hand copying onto expensive sheepskin parchment. So the principal method of teaching and learning was the lecture. Teachers read out loud texts in Latin verbatim, and students were obliged to memorize what they heard. In the classroom the lecturer would recite a short passage, present the comments of other authorities on it, and draw his own conclusions. He would then move onto another brief passage and repeat the process. Students heard the same lectures over and over again until they had thoroughly memorized the text under discussion. In addition to lectures, scholastics engaged in disputations. Participants in a disputation presented oral arguments for or against a particular thesis, a process called dialectical reasoning. Disputants were evaluated on their ability to investigate through logic the truth of a thesis. Disputations required several skills—verbal facility, a prodigious memory so that apt citations could be made, and the ability to think quickly. The process we know today as debate originated with these medieval disputations. Lectures and disputations became the core activities of the scholastics, who considered all subjects, however sacred, as appropriate for dialectical reasoning.

None of the scholastic teachers was more popular than the acerbic, witty, and daring Peter Abelard (1079–1142). Students from all over Europe flocked to hear Abelard's lectures at the cathedral school of Paris. Peter Abelard's clever criticisms of the ideas of other thinkers brought him hoards of delighted students. In *Sic et Non* ("Yes and No"), Abelard boldly examined some of the foundations of Christian truth. Employing the dialectical reasoning of a disputation, he presented both sides of 150 theological problems discussed by the Church Fathers. He left the conclusions open in order to challenge his students and readers to think further, but his intention seems to have been less to undermine accepted biblical truths than to point out how apparent disagreements among the experts masked a deeper level of agreement about Christian truth.

Universities: Organizing Learning

From the cathedral schools arose the first universities. The University of Paris evolved from the cathedral school where Abelard once taught. The universities were, at first, little more than guilds (trade associations), organized by either students or teachers to protect their interests. As members

A Lecture in a Medieval University
Some of the students are sleeping and others are chatting with their neighbors. The most earnest students are sitting in the front row. Some things never change.

of a guild, students bargained with their professors and townspeople as would other tradesmen over costs and established minimum standards of instruction. The guild of the law students at Bologna received a charter in 1158, which probably made it the first university. Some of the early universities were professional schools, such as the medical faculty at Salerno, but true to their origins as cathedral schools, most emphasized theology over other subjects.

The medieval universities formulated the basic educational practices that are still in place today. They established a curriculum, examined students, conferred degrees, and conducted graduation ceremonies. Students and teachers wore distinctive robes, which are still worn at graduation ceremonies. Teachers were clergymen—that is, they "professed" religion—hence the title of professor for a university instructor. In their first years students pursued the liberal arts curriculum, which consisted of the *trivium* (grammar, rhetoric, and logic) and the *quadrivium* (arithmetic, geometry, astronomy, and music). This curriculum is forerunner of the arts and sciences faculties and distribution requirements in modern universities. Medieval university students devoted many years to rigorous study and rote memorization. Completion of a professional doctorate in law, medicine, or theology typically required more than ten years.

Medieval universities did not admit women, in part because women were barred from the priesthood and most university students were training to become priests. (Women did not attend universities until the nineteenth century.) There was also a widespread fear of learned women who might think on their own. The few women who did receive advanced educations had to rely on a private tutor.

The Ancients: Renaissance of the Twelfth Century

The scholastics' integration of Greek philosophy with Christian theology represents a key facet of the Twelfth-Century Renaissance°, a revival of interest in the ancients comparable in importance to the Carolingian Renaissance of the ninth century and the Italian Renaissance of the fifteenth. During Peter Abelard's lifetime, very few western Europeans knew Greek, the language of ancient philosophy, and only a few works of the Greeks were available in Latin translations. Between about 1140 and 1260 this cultural isolation dramatically changed.

A flood of new Latin translations of the Greek classics came from Sicily and Spain, where Christians had close contacts with Muslims and Jews. Muslim philosophers had translated into Arabic the Greek philosophical and scientific classics, which were readily available in the Middle East and North Africa. These Arabic translations were then translated into Latin, often by Jewish scholars who knew both languages. Later a few Catholic scholars traveled to Byzantium, where they learned enough Greek to make even better translations from the originals.

As they encountered the philosophy of the ancients, Muslim, Jewish, and Christian thinkers faced profoundly disturbing problems. The principles of faith revealed in the Qur'an of Islam and the Hebrew and Christian Bibles were not easily reconciled with the philosophical method of reasoning found in Greek works, especially those by Aristotle. These religious thinkers recognized the obvious superiority of Greek thought over their own. They worried that the power of philosophical reasoning undermined religious truth. As men of faith they challenged themselves to demonstrate that philosophy did not contradict religious teaching, and some of them went even further to employ philosophical reasoning to demonstrate the truth of religion. However, they always faced opposition within their own religious faiths, especially from people who thought philosophical reason was an impediment to religious faith.

The first Muslim thinker to confront the questions raised by Greek philosophy, such as how to prove the existence of God or account for the creation of the world, was Avicenna (980–1037), an Iranian physician. His commentaries on Aristotle deeply influenced the Catholic scholastics, who quoted him extensively. Avicenna attempted a rational proof of the existence of God based on the "necessary existent." Without God nothing exists; therefore, if we exist, so must God. Following Avicenna's lead, Al-Ghazali (1058–1111) taught the ancient Greek philosophers to Muslim students. But from the daunting task of reconciling philosophy and religion he suffered a nervous breakdown, which forced him to abandon lecturing temporarily and turn to religious mysticism. After this experience, he wrote *The Incoherence of the Philosophers,* in which he argued that religious truth was more accessible through mystical experience than through rational and systematic analysis.

The most powerful answer to Al-Ghazali's critique of philosophy came from Averroës (1126–1198), who rose to become the chief judge of Córdoba, Spain, and an adviser to the caliph. In *The Incoherence of the Incoherence* (1179–1180), Averroës argued that the aim of philosophy is to explain the true, inner meaning of religious revelations. This inner meaning, however, should not be disclosed to the unlettered masses, who must be told only the simple, literal stories and metaphors of Scripture. Although lively and persuasive, Averroës's defense of philosophy failed to revive philosophical speculation within Islam. Philosophy and science within Islam, once far superior to that of the Catholic world, went into a steep decline as mysticism and rote learning were favored over rational debate. Averroës received a more sympathetic hearing among Jews and Catholics than among Muslims.

Within Judaism, many had attempted unsuccessfully a reconciliation of Greek philosophy with Hebrew law and scripture. Success was achieved by a contemporary of Averroës, also from Córdoba—the Jewish philosopher, jurist, and physician Moses Maimonides (1135–1204). His most important work in religious philosophy was *The Guide for the Perplexed* (ca. 1191), which synthesized Greek philosophy, science, and Judaism. Widely read in Arabic, Hebrew, and Latin versions, the book stimulated both Jewish and Christian philosophy. Maimonides's efforts, like those of Averroës, distressed many of his fellow Jews. Maimonides's tomb was desecrated, but as controversy abated he came to be recognized as a pillar of Jewish thought.

For medieval Catholic philosophers, one of the most difficult tasks was reconciling the biblical account of the divine creation with Aristotle's teaching that the universe was eternal. Even in this early clash between science and religion, creationism was the sticking point. Following the lead established by Avicenna, Averroës, and Maimonides, the great project of the scholastics became to demonstrate the fundamental harmony between Christian faith and the philosophical knowledge of the ancients.

The most effective resolution of this problem was found in the work of Thomas Aquinas (1225–1274), whose philosophy is called Thomism°. A Dominican friar, Thomas spent most of his career developing a school system for the Dominicans in Italy, but he also spent two short periods teaching at the University of Paris. The temperamental opposite of the fiery Abelard, Thomas avoided distracting controversies and academic disputes to concentrate on his two great summaries of human knowledge— the *Summary of the Catholic Faith against the Gentiles* (1261) and the *Summary of Theology* (1265–1274). In both of these massive scholastic works, reason fully confirmed Christian faith. Encyclopedias of knowledge, they rigorously examined whole fields through dialectical reasoning. Thomas's method was to pose a question derived from the Bible—such as "Whether woman was made from man?"—and then draw on the accumulated thought of the past to suggest answers, raise critical objections to the answers, refute the objections, and reach a conclusion. Then he proceeded to the next question, "Whether [woman was made] of man's rib?"

Building upon the works of Averroës, Thomas solved the problem of reconciling philosophy and religion by drawing a distinction between *natural truth* and *revealed truth.* For Thomas, natural truth meant the kinds of things anyone can know through the operation of human reason; revealed truth referred to the things that can be known only through revelation, such as the Trinity and the incarnation of Christ. Thomas argued that these two kinds of truths could not possibly contradict one another because both came from God. Apparent contradictions could be accommodated by an understanding of a higher truth. On the issue of creation, for example, Thomas argued that Aristotle's understanding of the eternal universe was inferior to the higher revealed truth of the Bible that God created the universe in seven days.

The most influential of the scholastic thinkers, Thomas asserted that to achieve religious truth one should start with faith and then use reason to reach conclusions. He was the first to understand theology systematically in this way, and in doing so he raised a storm of opposition among Christians who were threatened by philosophical reason. Like the work of Avicenna and Maimonides before him, Aquinas's writings were at first prohibited by the theological faculties in universities. Nevertheless, his method remains crucial for Catholic theology to this day.

Just as scholastic theologians looked to ancient Greek philosophy as a guide to reason, jurists revived ancient Roman law, especially at the universities of Bologna and

Pavia in Italy. In the law faculties, students were required to learn the legal work of the Emperor Justinian—the text of the *Body of the Civil Law,* together with the commentaries on it. The systematic approach of Roman law provided a way to make the legal system less arbitrary for judges, lawyers, bureaucrats, and advisers to kings and popes. Laws had long consisted of a contradictory mess of municipal regulations, Germanic customs, and feudal precepts. Under Roman law, judges were obliged to justify their verdicts according to prescribed standards of evidence and procedure. The revival of Roman law in the twelfth century made possible the legal system that still guides most of continental Europe.

EPIC VIOLENCE AND COURTLY LOVE

In addition to the developments in philosophy, theology, and the law, the Twelfth-Century Renaissance included a remarkable literary output in the vernacular languages, the tongues spoken in everyday life. The great heroic epics, most of which were adapted from oral tradition or composed between 1050 and 1150, were in English, German, Celtic, Slavonic, Nordic, Icelandic, French, and Spanish. These epics, often repeated from memory as popular entertainment, recounted adventure stories about medieval warriors. They were manly stories that celebrated the beauty and terror of battle and glorified cracked skulls and brutal death: "Now Roland feels that he is at death's door; Out of his ears the brain is running forth." Women hardly appear at all in these epics, except as backdrops to the battles among men or as battered wives. As we saw in Chapter 8, *The Digenes Akritas* in Greek, *The Poem of El Cid* in Spanish, and *The Song of Roland* in French became national epics that formed the literary roots of the modern vernacular literatures.

By the end of the twelfth century, however, a new vernacular literature appeared, created by poets called troubadours°. Unlike the creators of national epics, the troubadour poets included women as well as men, and their literature reflected an entirely new sensibility about the relationships between men and women. The troubadours wrote poems of love, meant to be sung to music; their literary movement is called courtly love°. They composed in Provençal, one of the languages of southern France, and the first audience for their poems was in the courts of southern France. These graciously elegant poems clearly show influences from Arabic love poetry and especially from Muslim mystical literature in which the soul, depicted as feminine, seeks her masculine God/lover. The troubadours secularized this theme of religious union by portraying the ennobling possibilities of the love between a woman and a man. In so doing, they introduced the idea of romantic love, one of the most powerful concepts in all of Western history, an ideal that still dominates popular culture to this day. It is especially remarkable that romantic love between the sexes, which we now assume to be so natural, is a cultural invention, one that can be dated from the twelfth century.

THE LOVE OF TRISTAN AND ISEULT

In Gottfried von Strassburg's thirteenth-century romance of Tristan and Iseult, love is a powerful, irresistible, ennobling force. At first the two lovers struggle to resist temptation and to doubt the other's love, but they find themselves unable to keep away from one another. His resistance is motivated by a sense of "faith and honor," hers by "maiden shame," but love triumphs and the two consummate their relationship.

Now, when the man and the maid, Tristan and Iseult, had drunk of the potion, Love, who never resteth but besetteth all hearts, crept softly into the hearts of the twain [the two], and ere [before] they were aware of it had she planted her banner on conquest therein, and brought them under her rule. They were one and undivided who but now were twain and at enmity. . . . But one heart had they—her grief was his sadness, his sadness her grief. Both were one in love and sorrow, and yet both would hide it in shame and doubt. She felt same of her love, and the like did he. She doubted of his love, and he of hers. For though both their hearts were blindly bent to one will, yet was the chance and the beginning heavy to them, and both alike would hide their desire.

When Tristan felt the pangs of love, then he bethought him straightway of his faith and honor, and would fain have set himself free. . . . So would he turn his heart, fighting against his own will, and desiring against his own desire. . . . Yet ever the more he looked into his heart the more he found that therein was nought but Love—and Iseult.

Even so was it with the maiden: she was as a bird that is snared with lime. . . . Love drew her heart towards him, and shame drove her eyes away. Thus Love and maiden shame strove together till Iseult wearied of the fruitless strife, and did as many have done before her—vanquished, she yielded herself body and soul to the man, and to Love.

Source: From *The Love of Tristan and Iseult* by Gottfried von Strassburg, thirteenth century.

An innovative aspect of the courtly love poems of the troubadours was their idealization of women. The male troubadours, such as Chrétien de Troyes (1135–1183), placed women on a pedestal and treated men as the "love vassals" of beloved women to whom they owed loyalty and service. Female troubadours, such as Marie de France (dates unknown), did not place women on a pedestal but idealized emotionally honest and open relationships between lovers. Unlike the epics in which women were brutalized, the troubadours typically saw women as holding power over men or acting as their equals. From southern France, courtly love spread to Germany and elsewhere throughout Europe. Many of the German poems were romances, reinterpreting the stories of the epics to conform to the values of courtly love. The courtly love ideal, though often satirized as hopelessly unrealistic, has persisted across the centuries in innumerable popular revivals.

Romanesque Cathedral Architecture
The rounded arches, the massive columns, the barrel vaults in the ceilings, and the small windows were characteristic of the Romanesque style. The pointed arch over the apse is a later Gothic addition.

The Center of Medieval Culture: The Great Cathedrals

When tourists visit a European city today, they usually want to see the town's cathedral. Most of these imposing structures were built between 1050 and 1300 and symbolize the soaring ambitions and imaginations of their largely unknown builders. During the great medieval building boom, old churches, which were often perfectly adequate but out of style, were ripped down. In their place hundreds of new cathedrals and thousands of other churches were erected, sparing no expense and reflecting the latest experimental techniques in architectural engineering and artistic fashion. These buildings became multimedia centers for the arts—incorporating architecture, sculpture, stained glass, and painting in their structure and providing a setting for the performance of music and drama.

Architecture: The Romanesque and Gothic Styles

The Romanesque° style spread throughout western Europe during the eleventh century and the first half of the twelfth century because the master masons who understood sophisticated stone construction techniques traveled from one building site to another, bringing with them a uniform style. The principal innovation of the Romanesque was the arched stone roofs, which were more aesthetically pleasing and less vulnerable to fire than the flat roofs they replaced. The rounded arches of these stone roofs were called barrel vaults because they looked like the inside of a barrel. Romanesque churches employed transepts, which fashioned the church into the shape of a cross if viewed from above, the vantage point of God. The intersection of the transept with the nave of the church required a cross vault, a construction that demanded considerable expertise. The high stone vaults of Romanesque churches and cathedrals required the support of massive stone pillars and thick walls. As a result, windows were small slits that imitated the slit windows of castles. Romanesque churches had a dark, yet cozy appearance, which was sometimes enlivened by painted walls or sculpture.

The religious experience of worshiping in a Romanesque cathedral had an intimate, almost familiar quality to it. The worshiper was enveloped by a comforting space, surrounded by family and neighbors, and close to deceased relatives buried beneath the pavement or in tombs that lined the walls. Romanesque churches and cathedrals were the first architectural expression of the new and growing medieval cities, proud and wealthy places. In such a building, God became a fellow townsman, an associate in the grand new project of making cities habitable and comfortable.

More than a century after the urban revival began, during the late twelfth and thirteenth centuries, the Gothic° style replaced the Romanesque. The innovation of this style was the ribbed vault and pointed arches, which superseded the barrel vault of the Romanesque. These narrow pointed arches drew the viewer's eye upward toward God and gave the building the appearance of weightlessness that symbolized the Christian's uplifting reach for heaven. The neighborly solidity of the Romanesque style was abandoned for an effect that stimulated a mystical appreciation of God's utter otherness, the supreme divinity far above mortal men and women. The Gothic style also introduced the innovation of the flying buttress, an arched construction on the outside of the walls that redistributed the weight of the roof. This innovation allowed for thin walls, which were pierced by windows much bigger than was possible with Romanesque construction techniques.

The result was stunning. The stone work of a Gothic cathedral became a skeleton to support massive expanses of stained glass, transforming the interior spaces into a mystical haven from the outside world. At different times of the day, the multicolored windows converted sunlight into an ever-changing light show that offered sparkling hints of the secret truths of God's creation. See, for example, the image on page 000. The light that passed through these windows symbolized the light of God. The windows themselves contained scenes that were an encyclopedia of medieval knowledge and lore. In addition to Bible stories and the lives of saints, these windows depicted common people at their trades, animals, plants, and natural wonders. These windows celebrated not only the promise of salvation but all the wonders of God's creation. They drew worshipers out of the busy city in which they lived and worked toward the perfect realm of the divine.

The first Gothic church was built at the abbey of St. Denis, outside Paris, under the direction of the abbot Suger. From northern France the style spread all across Europe. In France, Germany, Italy, Spain, and England, cities made enormous financial sacrifices to construct new Gothic cathedrals during the economic boom years of the thirteenth century. Gothic cathedrals expressed civic pride as well as Christian piety, and cities vied to build taller and taller cathedrals with ever more daringly thin walls. The French city of Beauvais pushed beyond reasonable limits by building its cathedral so high that it collapsed. Because costs were so high, many cathedrals remained unfinished, but even the incomplete ones became vital symbols of local identity.

Flying Buttresses of Chartres Cathedral
The flying buttress did more than hold up the thin walls of Gothic cathedrals. The buttress created an almost lace-like appearance on the outside of the building, magnifying the sense of mystery evoked by the style.

Interior of a Gothic Cathedral
Narrow columns and the pointed arches characterized the Gothic style.

Music and Drama: Reaching God's Ear and the Christian's Soul

The churches and cathedrals were devoted to the celebration of the Latin liturgy, which at the time was a chanted form of prayer. Because the function of chant was worship, music was one of the most exquisite expressions of medieval religious life. The liturgical chant that survives from the Middle Ages can still be sung today because the Benedictine monk Guido of Arezzo (ca. 990–1050) devised a system of musical notation, which forms the basis for modern Western musical notation. In Guido's time, chant was primarily plainchant°, a straightforward melody sung with simple harmony by a choir to accompany the recitation of the text of the liturgy. The simple clarity of plainchant matched the solid familiarity of the Romanesque style in church architecture.

In the Paris cathedral around 1170, however, musical experiments led to an important new breakthrough. Instead of using a simple plainchant melody to sing the liturgy, the simultaneous singing of two melodies was employed. This new form was called polyphony°, the singing of two or more independent melodies at the same time. Polyphony represented a major innovation in music by creating an enchanting sound to echo throughout the vast stone chambers of Gothic cathedrals, a musical form of praise that enhanced the mystical experience of worship.

In addition to its advances in architecture and music, Paris became the center for innovation in liturgical drama. Some time during the twelfth century, portions of the liturgy began to be acted out in short Latin plays, usually inside the church. These rudimentary plays were soon translated into the vernacular language so that everyone in the congregation could understand them. As they became more popular, the performances moved outside in front of the church. The function of these liturgical dramas was to educate as well as to worship. The priests who put on the plays wanted to teach Christian stories and provide moral examples to the young and to the uneducated laity. From these early liturgical plays arose the Western dramatic tradition that evolved into the secular theater of Shakespeare and the ubiquitous dramas of modern television and film.

CONCLUSION
Asserting Western Culture

During the twelfth and thirteenth centuries, western Europe matured into its own self-confident identity. The common culture of Catholic Christianity spread into the most distant corners of Europe by converting the remaining adherents of polytheistic religion. Through penal laws, discrimination, and extermination, heretical groups within Europe were systematically transformed into outcasts or eradicated altogether. The processes of creating outcasts within Europe and defining what it meant to be a Catholic accompanied the external assertion of Latin power. The West looked both inward and outward as it measured itself, defined itself, and promoted itself. The most dramatic outward assertion of Western identity was the series of Crusades, when European power was extended outside the continent for the first time since the fall of the Roman Empire in the West.

Less a semibarbarian backwater than it had been even in the time of Charlemagne, western Europe cultivated modes of thought that revealed an almost limitless capacity for creative renewal and critical self-examination. That capacity, first evident during the Twelfth-Century Renaissance, is what has most distinguished the West ever since. Part of the reason for this creative capacity rested in the cultivation of critical methods of thinking, codified in scholasticism. No medieval thinker followed these critical methods consistently, and they repeatedly caused alarm among the more intellectually timid. However, this tendency to question basic assumptions is among the greatest achievements of Western civilization. The process evident in the ancient philosophers emerged again in the medieval scholastics. The university system, which was based on teaching methods of critical inquiry, differed from the educational institutions in other cultures, such as Byzantium or Islam, that were devoted to passing on received knowledge. This distinctive critical spirit connects the cultures of the ancient, medieval, and modern West.

Suggestions For Further Reading

For a comprehensive list of suggested readings, please go to www.ablongman.com/levack/chapter9

Bony, Jean. *French Gothic Architecture of the Twelfth and Thirteenth Centuries.* 1983. With many beautiful illustrations, this is a good way to begin an investigation of these magnificent buildings.

Colish, Marcia L. *Medieval Foundations of the Western Intellectual Tradition, 400–1400.* 1997. The best general study.

Keen, Maurice. *Chivalry.* 1984. Readable and balanced in its coverage of this sometimes misunderstood phenomenon.

Keen, Maurice, ed. *Medieval Warfare: A History.* 1999. Lucid specialist studies of aspects of medieval warfare.

Lambert, Malcolm. *Medieval Heresy: Popular Movements from the Gregorian Reform to the Reformation.* 2nd ed. 1992. The best general study of heresy.

Lawrence, C. H. *The Friars: The Impact of the Early Mendicant Movement on Western Society.* 1994. The best general study of the influence of Dominicans and Franciscans.

Moore, R. I. *The Formation of a Persecuting Society: Power and Deviance in Western Europe, 950–1250.* 1987. A brilliant analysis of how Europe became a persecuting society.

Morris, Colin. *The Papal Monarchy: The Western Church from 1050 to 1250.* 1989. A thorough study that should be the beginning point for further investigation of the many fascinating figures in the medieval Church.

Mundy, John H. *Europe in the High Middle Ages, 1150–1309.* 3rd ed. 1999. A comprehensive introduction to the period.

Peters, Edward. *Europe and the Middle Ages.* 1989. An excellent general survey.

Riley-Smith, Jonathan Simon Christopher. *The Crusades: A Short History.* 1987. Exactly what the title says.

Strayer, Joseph R. *On the Medieval Origins of the Modern State.* 1970. Still the best short analysis.

Notes

1. *The Autobiography of Ousama (1995–1188),* trans. G. R. Potter, in Brian Tierney, ed., *The Middle Ages,* Vol. 1: *Sources of Medieval History,* 3rd. ed. (1978), 162.
2. Fulcher of Chartres, *Historia Hierosolymitana,* ed. Heinrich Hagenmeyer (1913), 202–203.
3. Edward Peters, *Heresy and Authority in the Middle Ages* (1980), 177.
4. Cited in Jacques Dalarun, "The Clerical Gaze," in Christiane Klapisch-Zuber, ed., *A History of Women in the West,* Vol. 2: *Silences of the Middle Ages* (1992), 27.
5. Cited in Emmanuel Le Roy Ladurie, *Montaillou: Promised Land of Error,* trans. Barbara Bray (1978), 130.
6. Ibid., 56.
7. Ibid., 63.
8. A. F. Pollock and F. W. Maitland, *The History of English Law,* Vol. 1 (1895), 468.

non essent registrantes que non
et futuris ministrantes que per

CHAPTER

10

The West in Crisis: The Later Middle Ages, 1300–1450

THE STORY WE ARE ABOUT TO TELL IS NOT A PLEASANT ONE, BUT IT SPEAKS TO the extraordinary scope of human experiences that occurred in Europe in the fourteenth and early fifteenth centuries. The fourteenth century dawned with a chill. In 1303 and then again during 1306–1307, the Baltic Sea froze over. No one had ever heard of that happening before, and the freezings foretold worse disasters. The cold spread beyond its normal winter season, arriving earlier in the autumn and staying later into the summer. Then it started to rain and did not let up. The Caspian Sea began to rise, flooding villages along its shores. In the summer of 1314 all across Europe, crops rotted in sodden fields. The meager harvest came late, precipitating a surge in prices for farm produce and forcing King Edward II of England to impose price controls. But capping prices did not grow more food.

In 1315 the situation got worse. In England during that year, the price of wheat rose 800 percent. Preachers compared the ceaseless rains to the great flood in the Bible, and floods did come, overwhelming dikes in the Netherlands and England, washing away entire towns in Germany, turning fields into lakes in France. Everywhere crops failed.

And then things got much worse. Torrential rains fell again in 1316, and for the third straight year the crops failed, creating the most severe famine in recorded European history. The effects were most dramatic in the far North. In Scandinavia agriculture almost disappeared, in Iceland peasants abandoned farming and turned to fishing and herding sheep, and in Greenland the European settlers began to die out. Already malnourished, the people of Europe became susceptible to disease and starvation. Desperate people resorted to desperate options. They ate cats, rats, insects, reptiles, animal dung, and tree leaves. Stories spread that some ate their own children. In Poland the starving were said to cut down criminals from the gallows for food.

Chapter Outline

- A Time of Death
- A Cold Wind from the East
- Economic Depression and Social Turmoil
- A Troubled Church and the Demand for Religious Comfort
- An Age of Continuous Warfare
- The Culture of Loss

A Time of Death: Burying plague victims of Tournai, 1349. The fourteenth and early fifteenth centuries were a time of famine, war, and plague.

By the 1340s, nearly all of Europe was in an endless cycle of disease and famine. Then came the deadliest epidemic in European history, the Black Death, which killed at least one-third of the total population. The economy collapsed. Trade disappeared. Industry shriveled. Hopeless peasants and urban workers revolted against their masters, demanding relief for their families. Neither church nor state could provide it. The popes left the dangerous streets of Rome for Avignon, France, where they became the puppets of the kings of France and were obliged to extort money to survive. The two great medieval kingdoms of France and England became locked in an interminable struggle that depleted royal treasuries and wasted the aristocracy in a series of clashes that historians call the Hundred Years' War. European culture became obsessed with death.

Of all the frightening elements of these disasters, perhaps most frightening was that their causes were hidden or completely unknowable given the technology and medical understanding of the time. In many respects, the West was held captive by the climate, economic forces that no one completely understood, and microbes that would not be identified for another 550 years. During the twelfth and thirteenth centuries the West had asserted itself against Islam through the Crusades and spread Catholic Christianity to the far corners of Europe. During the fourteenth and early fifteenth centuries, however, the West drew into itself due to war, plague, and conflicts with the Mongol and Ottoman Empires. Western European contact with Russia became more intermittent, and the Byzantine Empire, once the bastion of Orthodox Christianity, fell to the Muslim armies of the Ottomans.

This chapter explores the multiple, interlocking crises of the fourteenth and fifteenth centuries. It addresses six questions: (1) What caused the deaths of so many Europeans? (2) How did forces outside Europe, in particular the Mongol and Ottoman Empires, affect conditions in the West? (3) How did disturbances in the rudimentary global economy of the Middle Ages precipitate almost complete financial collapse and widespread social discontent in Europe? (4) Why did the church fail to provide leadership and spiritual guidance during these difficult times? (5) How did incessant warfare transform the most powerful medieval states? (6) How did European culture offer explanations and solace for the otherwise inexplicable calamities of the times?

A Time of Death

Because of demographic research, we know a great deal about life and death during the fourteenth century. The magnitude of Europe's demographic crisis is evident from the raw numbers. In 1300 the population of Europe was about 74 million—roughly 15 percent of its current population. Population size can be an elementary measure of the success of a subsistence economy to keep people alive, and by this measure Europe had been very successful up to about 1300. It had approximately doubled its population over the previous three hundred years. After the 1340s, however, Europe's ability to sustain its population evaporated. Population fell to just 52 million.

The raw numbers hardly touch the magnitude of human suffering, however, which fell disproportionately on the poor, the very young, and the old. Death by starvation and disease became the fate of uncomprehending millions. The demographic crisis of the fourteenth century was the greatest natural disaster in Western civilization since the epidemics of antiquity. How did it happen?

MASS STARVATION

Widespread famine began during the decade of 1310–1320. During the famines in 1315 and 1316 alone, more than 10 percent of Europe's population probably died. One eyewitness described bands of people as thin as skeletons in 1315:

> *We saw a large number of both sexes, not only from nearby places but from places as much as five leagues away, barefooted, and many even, except the women, in a completely nude condition, with their priests coming together in procession at the church of the holy martyrs, and they devoutly carried bodies of the saints and other relics to be adored.*[1]

A crisis in agriculture produced the famines.

As we saw in Chapter 8, the agricultural revolution of the eleventh century had made available more food and more nutritious food, triggering the growth of the population during the Middle Ages. During the twelfth and thirteenth centuries, vast tracks of virgin forests were cleared for farming, especially in eastern Europe. By the thirteenth century this region resembled the American frontier during the nineteenth century, as settlers flocked in, staked out farms, and established new towns. The additional land under the plow created an escape valve for population growth by preventing large numbers of people from going hungry. But by the fourteenth century no more virgin land was available for clearing, which meant that an ever-growing population tried to survive on a fixed amount of farming land. Because of the limitations of medieval agriculture, the ability of farmers to produce food could not keep up with unchecked population growth.

The imbalance between food production and population set off a dreadful cycle of famine and disease. Insufficient food resulted in either malnutrition or starvation. Those who suffered from prolonged malnutrition were particularly susceptible to epidemic diseases, such as typhus, cholera, and dysentery. By 1300, children of the poor faced the probability of extreme hunger once or twice during the course of their expected lifespan of thirty to thirty-five years. In Pistoia, Italy, priests kept the *Book of the*

Dead, which recorded the pattern: famine in 1313, famine in 1328–1329, famine and epidemic in 1339–1340 that killed one-quarter of the population, famine in 1346, famine and epidemic in 1347, and then the killing hammer blow—the Black Death in 1348 (see Map 10.1).

The Black Death

In the spring of 1348 the Black Death arrived in Europe with brutal force. In the lovely hilltop city of Siena, Italy, all industry stopped, carters refused to bring produce and cooking oil in from the countryside, and on June 2 the daily records of the city council and civil courts abruptly ended, as if the city fathers and judges had all died or rushed home in panic. A local chronicler, Agnolo di Tura, wrote down his memories of those terrible days:

> *Father abandoned child, wife husband, one brother another; for this illness seemed to strike through the breath and sight. And so they died. And none could be found to bury the dead for money or friendship. Members of a household brought their dead to a ditch as best they could, without priest, without divine offices. Nor did the [death] bell sound. And in many places in Siena great pits were dug and piled deep with the multitude of dead. . . . And I, Agnolo di Tura, called the Fat, buried my five children with my own hands. And there were also those who were so sparsely covered with earth that the dogs dragged them forth and devoured many bodies throughout the city.*[2]

During the summer of 1348 more than half of the Sienese died. The construction of Siena's great cathedral, planned to be the largest in the world, stopped and was never resumed due to a lack of workers. In fact, Siena, once among the most prosperous cities in Europe, never fully recovered and lost its economic preeminence to other cities.

Experts still dispute the cause of the Black Death, but most consider the bubonic plague° the most likely culprit. The bubonic plague can appear in two forms. In the classic form it is usually transmitted to humans by a flea that has bitten a rodent infected with the *Pasteurella pestis* bacillus, usually a rat. The infected flea then bites a human victim. The infection enters the bloodstream, causing inflamed swellings called buboes (hence, "bubonic" plague) in the glands of the groin or armpit, internal bleeding, and discoloration of the skin, which suggested the name "Black Death." The symptoms of bubonic plague were

■ Map 10.1 Spread of the Black Death
After the Black Death first appeared in the ports of Italy in 1348, it spread relentlessly throughout most of Europe, killing at least 20 million people in Europe alone.

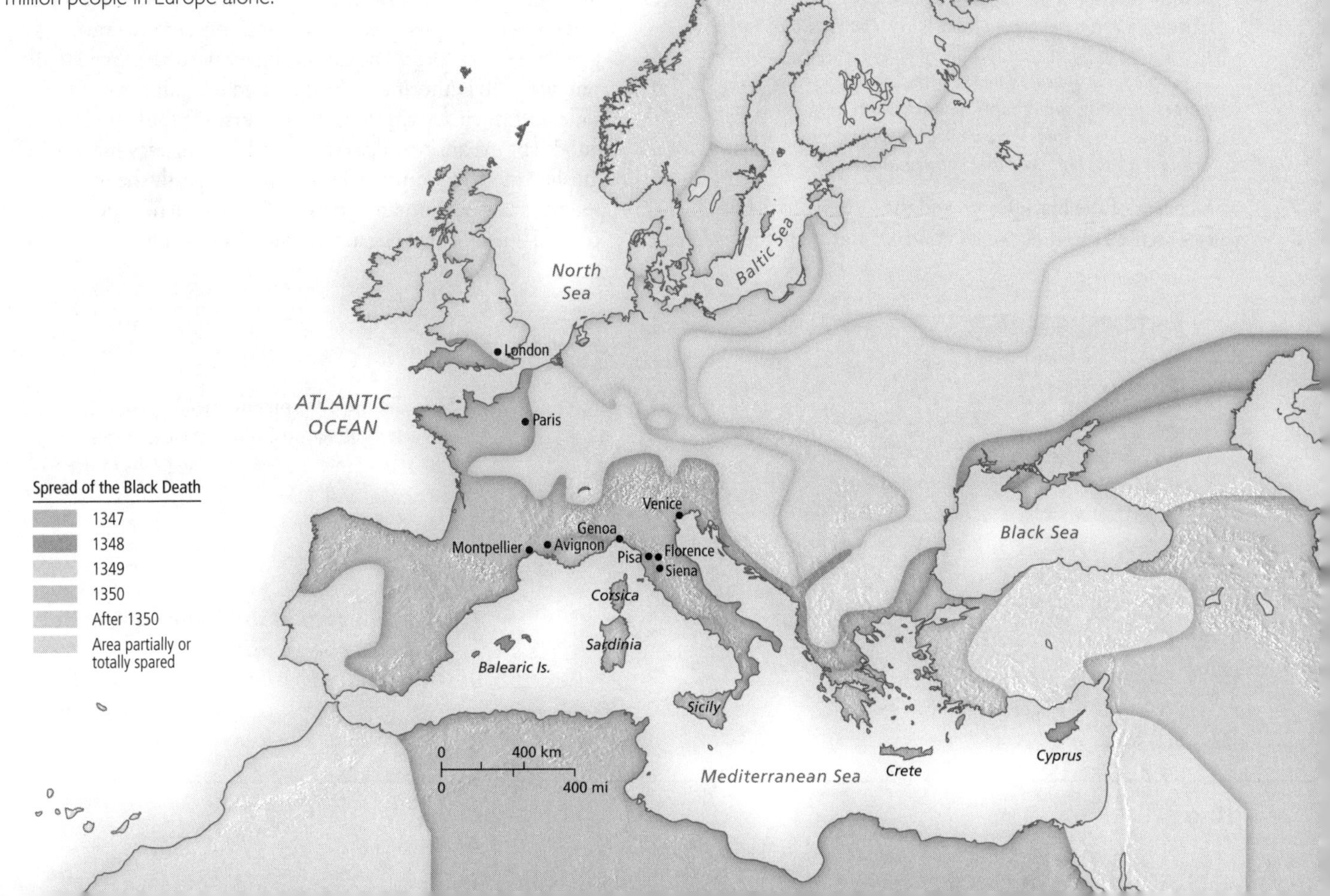

THE HUMAN BODY IN HISTORY

The Black Death: The Signs of Disease

Infectious diseases are invisible. They are carried by viruses or bacteria that infect the body, but until the invention of the microscope and the development of epidemiology in the nineteenth century the disease itself could not be directly observed. Diseases manifest themselves indirectly through symptoms: fevers, cold sweats, pain, coughing, vomiting, diarrhea, paleness, glandular swellings, skin lesions, and rashes. Through these symptoms, the disease leaves a distinctive sign on the body.

No disease left more distinctive and disturbing signs on the body than the bubonic plague. In the introduction to *The Decameron*, Giovanni Boccaccio described what he had witnessed of the symptoms:

> *In the year 1348 after the fruitful incarnation of the Son of God, that most beautiful of Italian cities, noble Florence, was attacked by deadly plague. . . . The symptoms. . . began both in men and women with certain swellings in the groin or under the armpit. They grew to the size of a small apple or an egg, more or less, and were vulgarly called tumors. In a short space of time these tumors spread from the two parts named [to] all over the body. Soon after this the symptoms changed and black or purple spots appeared on the arms or thighs or any other part of the body, sometimes a few large ones, sometimes many little ones. These spots were a certain sign of death, just as the original tumor had been and still remained.*[3]

The fear of the Black Death and the inability to discern its causes focused the attention of contemporaries on the bodies of the sick, and when someone fell ill there was intense concern to determine whether the signs of plague were present. As a result, almost any discoloration of the skin or glandular swellings could be interpreted as a sign of the presence of plague, and other diseases, such as smallpox, could be readily confused with plague. Physicians and surgeons, of course, were the experts in reading the signs of the body for disease. As victims and their distraught families soon discovered, however, physicians did not really know what the glandular swellings and discolorations of the skin meant. Boccaccio reported that "No doctor's advice, no medicine could overcome or alleviate this disease. . . . Either the disease was such that no treatment was possible or the doctors were so ignorant that they did not know what caused it, and consequently could not administer the proper remedy."[4] As it quickly became evident that very few recovered, respect for the medical profession declined.

Upon the advice of physicians, governmental authorities tried to stop the contagion by placing the houses of the sick and sometimes entire neighborhoods under quarantine when plague was suspected. Within the councils of city governments, greater attention began to be paid to the poor, largely because their bodies were more likely to manifest deformities and skin problems because of malnutrition and poor living conditions. The bodies of the poor became subject to systematic regulation. In general, the poor were much more likely to be quarantined than the rich. The deformed might even be driven out of town. Cities established hospitals to segregate the most wretched of the poor, and health officials set up border guards to prevent poor vagabonds from entering towns. To maintain quarantines and bury the dead, a public health bureaucracy was created, complete with its own staff physicians, grave diggers, and police force. The extraordinary powers granted to the public health authorities helped expand the authority of the state over its citizens in the name of pursuing the common good. The expansion of governmental bureaucracy that distinguished modern from medieval states was partly the result of the need to keep human bodies under surveillance and control—a need that began with the Black Death. ■

For Discussion

How did the government's need to control the Black Death contribute to the expansion of the state? How did it reveal the limits of the power of the state?

■ Allegory of the Dance of Death
During the plague years paintings such as these two panels depicted the fact that Death did not discriminate. Death could arrive at any time and take anyone.

The Triumph of Death
A detail from Francesco Traini's fresco *The Triumph of Death,* in the Camposanto, Pisa, ca. 1350. Frescoes such as this reflect the horror of the Black Death.

exceptionally disgusting, according to one quite typical contemporary description: "all the matter which exuded from their bodies let off an unbearable stench; sweat, excrement, spittle, breath, so fetid as to be overpowering; urine turbid, thick, black or red. . . ."[5]

The second form of plague was the pneumonic type, which infected the lungs and spread by coughing and sneezing. Either form could be lethal, but the complex epidemiology of bubonic plague meant that the first form could not be transmitted directly from one person to another. After being infected, however, many victims probably developed pneumonia as a secondary symptom, which then spread quickly to others. As one contemporary physician put it, one person could seemingly infect the entire world. In some cases, the doctor caught the illness and died before the patient did. The visitations of the bubonic plague in the twentieth century, which have been observed by physicians trained in modern medicine, provide some idea of mortality rates: Between 30 and 90 percent of those who received the bacillus through a flea bite died, but 100 percent of those who contracted pneumonic plague died, on average a mere 1.8 days after contracting it. Most historians think something similar to this must have happened in 1348, but the disease was so mysterious that some historians think the real culprit has not yet been found.

Two summers before the plague's appearance in Europe, sailors returning from the East had told stories about a terrible pestilence in China and India. Entire regions of India, they said, were littered with corpses with no survivors to bury them. But the vague information that arrived in European seaports in 1346 caused no particular alarm. Asia was far away and the source of stories so baffling that most people could hardly credit them. No one knew that the plague bacillus was already on its way to Europe.

With the galley slaves dying at their oars, Genoese ships first brought the disease to ports in Italy, and by the spring of 1348 the Black Death began to spread throughout the Italian peninsula. Ironically, the very network of shipping that had connected the Mediterranean with northern European waters and propelled the great economic boom of the Middle Ages spread the deadly disease. By summer the pestilence had traveled as far north as Paris; by the end of the year it had crossed the English Channel, following William the Conqueror's old route from Normandy to England. From Italy the Black Death passed through the rugged Alpine passes into Switzerland and Hungary. In 1349 the relentless surge continued, passing from France into the Netherlands and from England to Scotland, Ireland, and Norway, where a ghost ship of dead men and live rats swarming among bales of wool ran aground near Bergen. From Norway the deadly disease migrated to Sweden, Denmark, Prussia, Iceland, and Greenland. By 1351 it had arrived in Russia.

Modern estimates indicate that during the late 1340s and early 1350s from India to Iceland, about one-third of the population perished. In Europe this would have meant that about twenty million people died, with the deaths usually clustered in a matter of a few weeks or months after the disease first appeared in a particular locale. The death toll, however, varied erratically from place to place, ranging from about 20 to 90 percent. So great was the toll that entire villages were depopulated or abandoned. In Avignon 400 died daily, in Pisa 500, in Paris 800. Paris lost half its population, Florence as much as four-fifths, and Venice two-thirds. Living in enclosed spaces, monks and nuns were especially hard hit. All the Franciscans of Carcassonne and Marseille in France died. In Montpellier, France, only 7 of the 140 Dominicans survived. In isolated Kilkenny, Ireland, Brother John Clyn found himself left alone among his dead brothers, and he began to write a diary of what he had witnessed because he was afraid he might be the last person left alive in the world.

Civic and religious leaders had neither the knowledge nor the power to prevent or contain the disease. Following the biblical passages that prescribed ostracizing lepers, governments began to treat plague victims as temporary lepers and quarantined them for forty days. Because such measures were ineffective, the plague kept coming back. In the Mediterranean basin where the many port cities formed a network of contagion, the plague reappeared between 1348 and 1721 in one port or another about every fifteen to twenty years. Some of the later outbreaks were just as lethal as the initial 1348 catastrophe. Florence lost half its population in 1400; Venice lost a third in 1575–1577 and a third again in 1630–1631. Half a million people died in northern Spain from an epidemic in 1596–1602. Less exposed than the Mediterranean, northern Europe suffered less and saw the last of the dread disease in the Great Plague of London of 1665.

Modern research has suggested that the homeland of the *Pasteurella pestis* bacillus is an extremely isolated area in Central Asia, from which the plague spread during the fourteenth century. It is evident that the fate of the West was largely in the hands of unknown forces that ensnared Eurasia from China to Iceland in a unified biological web. The strongest strands in that web were those of merchant traders and armies who were responsible for accidentally disseminating microbes. During the Later Middle Ages, no army was as important for the fate of Europe as the mounted warriors of the distant Mongol tribes, whose relentless conquests drove them from Outer Mongolia across central Asia toward Europe.

A Cold Wind from the East

The Mongols and Turks were nomadic peoples from central Asia. Closely related culturally but speaking different languages, these peoples exerted an extraordinary influence on world history despite a rather small population. Map 10.2 shows the place of origin of the Mongols and Turks and where they spread across a wide belt of open, relatively flat land stretching from the Yellow Sea between China and the Korean peninsula to the Baltic Sea and the Danube River basin in Europe. Virtually unwooded and interrupted only by a few easily traversed mountain ranges, the broad Eurasian plain has been the great migration highway of world history from prehistoric times to the medieval caravans and the modern trans-Siberian railway.

As the Mongols and Turks charged westward out of central Asia on their fast ponies, they put pressure on the kingdoms of the West. Mongol armies hobbled Russia, and Turks conquered Constantinople. As a consequence the potential Orthodox allies in the East of the Catholic Christian West were weakened or eliminated. Under the Ottomans, adherents to Islam were reinserted into the West, this time in the Balkans. In contrast to the era of the Crusades in the twelfth century, Catholic Europe found itself on the defensive against a powerful Muslim foe.

The Mongol Invasions

Whereas the Europeans became successful sailors because of their extensive coastlines and close proximity to the sea, the Mongols became roving horsemen because they needed to migrate several times a year in search of grass and water for their ponies and livestock. They also became highly skilled warriors because they competed persistently with other tribes for access to the grasslands.

In roughly fifty years (1206–1258), the Mongols transformed themselves from a collection of disunited tribes with a vague ethnic affinity to create the most extensive empire in the history of the world. The epic rise of the previously obscure Mongols was the work of a Mongol chief who succeeded in uniting the various quarreling tribes and transforming them into a world power. In 1206 he was proclaimed Genghis Khan (ca. 1162–1227) ("Very Mighty King"), the supreme ruler over all the Mongols. Genghis broke through the Great Wall of China, destroyed the Jin

CHRONOLOGY

The Mongols

1206–1227	Reign of Genghis Khan
1206–1258	Mongol armies advance undefeated across Eurasia
1241	Mongols defeat Poles, Germans, and Hungarians
1257–1294	Reign of Kubilai Khan in China
1260	Defeat in Syria of Mongols by Mamluks of Egypt
1369–1405	Reign of Tamerlane, Khan of Chagatay
1380–1489	Russians drive out Mongols
1462–1505	Tsar Ivan III unifies Russia and defeats Mongols

(Chin) empire in northern China, and occupied Beijing. His cavalry swept across Asia as far as Azerbaijan, Georgia, northern Persia, and Russia. Eventually, Mongol armies conquered territories that stretched from Korea to Hungary and from the Arctic Ocean to the Arabian Sea. They even attempted seaborne expeditions to overpower Japan, which ended in disaster, and Java, which they were only able to hold temporarily. These failures indicated that Mongol strength was in their army rather than their navy.

The Mongol success was accomplished through a highly disciplined military organization, tactics that relied on extremely mobile cavalry forces, and a sophisticated intelligence network. During the Russian campaign in the winter of 1223, the Mongol cavalry moved with lightning speed across frozen rivers to accomplish the only successful winter invasion of Russia in history. Although the Russian forces outnumbered the Mongol armies and had superior armor, they were crushed in every encounter with the Mongols.

The Mongol armies employed clever tactics. First they unnerved enemy soldiers with a hail of arrows. Then the Mongols would appear to retreat, only to draw the enemy into false confidence before the Mongol horsemen delivered a deadly final blow. European chroniclers at the time tried to explain their many defeats at the hands of the Mongols by reporting that the Mongol "hordes" had overwhelming numbers, but evidence clearly shows that their victories were the result not of superior numbers but of superior discipline and the sophistication of the Mongol intelligence network.

Map 10.2 The Mongol Empire, 1206–1405

The Mongols and Turks were nomadic peoples who spread out across Asia and Europe from their homeland in the region of Mongolia. The Mongol armies eventually conquered vast territories from Korea to the borders of Hungary and from the Arctic Ocean to the Arabian Sea.

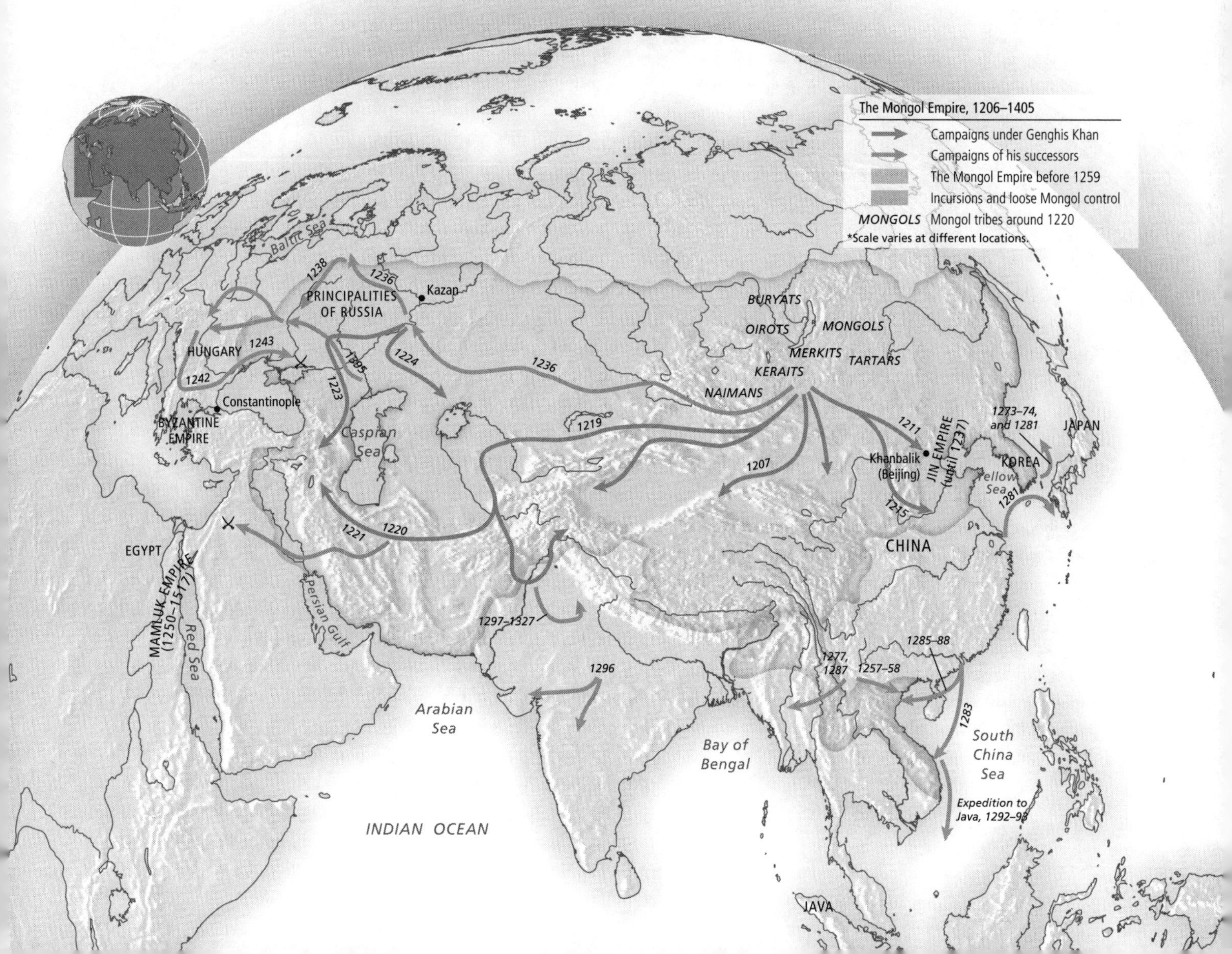

The Mongol invasions completely altered the composition of Asia and much of eastern Europe—economically, politically, and ethnically. Once they had conquered new territories, they established the Mongol Peace by reopening the caravan routes across Asia, which had been closed for a thousand years, making trans-Eurasian trade possible and merchants safe from robbers. The most famous of the many who traversed this route were the Venetian merchants from the Polo family, including Marco Polo, who arrived at the court of the Great Khan in China in 1275. Marco Polo's book about his travels offers a vivid and often remarkably perceptive account of the Mongol Empire during the Mongol Peace. It also illustrates better than any other source the cultural engagement of the Christian West with the Mongol East during the late thirteenth century, an encounter in which both sides demonstrated an abiding fascination with the other's religion and social mores.

Mongol power climaxed in 1260. In that year the Mongols suffered a crushing defeat in Syria at the hands of the Mamluk rulers of Egypt, an event that ended the Mongol reputation for invincibility. Conflicts and succession disputes among the various Mongol tribes made them vulnerable to rivals and to rebellion from their unhappy subjects. The Mongol Empire did not disappear overnight, but its various successor kingdoms never recaptured the dynamic unity forged by Genghis Khan. During the fourteenth century the Mongol Peace came to an end.

In the wake of these upheavals, a warrior of Mongol descent known as Tamerlane (r. 1369–1405) created an army composed of Mongols, Turks, and Persians, which challenged the established Mongol khanates. Tamerlane's conquests rivaled those of Genghis Khan, but with very different results. His armies pillaged the rich cities that supplied the caravan routes. Thus, in his attempt to monopolize the lucrative trans-Eurasian trade, Tamerlane largely destroyed it. The collapse of the Mongol Peace broke the thread of commerce across Eurasia and stimulated the European search for alternative routes to China that ultimately resulted in the voyages of Christopher Columbus in 1492.

THE RISE OF THE OTTOMAN TURKS

The Mongol armies were never very large, so the Mongols had always augmented their numbers with Turkish tribes. The result was that outside of Mongolia, Turks gradually absorbed the Mongols. Turkish replaced Mongolian as the dominant language, and the Turks took over the govern-

MARCO POLO AND TIBETAN RELIGION

In his travels to China, Marco Polo recorded numerous observations of the Mongol Empire. Polo was a merchant who spent more than two decades in Asia, but after he returned to his hometown of Venice, he was captured in battle by the Genoese, the enemies of the Venetians. While languishing in prison he dictated an account of his travels. His report of what he saw in Mongol China seemed so improbable to his contemporaries that his book was dubbed the "Million," from the seemingly million lies it contained. Modern historians, however, have established that Polo's observations were mostly accurate. He was particularly impressed by the influence of a class of astrologers and enchanters on the Mongol ruler Kubilai Khan. Called the Bakhshi, *they were members of the Great Khan's court who came from Tibet and Kashmir.*

Let me tell you of a strange thing which I had forgotten. You must know that, when the Great Khan was staying in his palace and the weather was rainy or cloudy, he had wise astrologers and enchanters who by their skill and their enchantments would dispel all the clouds and the bad weather from above the palace so that, while bad weather continued all around, the weather above the palace was fine. The wise men who do this are called Tibetans and Kashmiris; these are two races of men who practise idolatry. They know more of diabolic arts and enchantments than any other men. They do what they do by the arts of the Devil; but they make others believe that they do it by great holiness and by the work of God. For this reason they go about filthy and begrimed, with no regard for their own decency or for the persons who behold them; they keep the dirt on their faces, never wash or comb, but always remain in a state of squalor. . . .

Here is another remarkable fact about these enchanters, or *Bakhshi* as they are called. I assure you that, when the Great Khan is seated in his high hall at his table, which is raised more than eight cubits above the floor, and the cups are on the floor of the hall, a good ten paces distant from the table, and are full of wine and milk and other pleasant drinks, these *Bakhshi* contrive by their enchantment and their art that the full cups rise up of their own accord from the floor on which they have been standing and come to the Great Khan without anyone touching them. And this they do in the sight of 10,000 men. What I have told you is the plain truth without a word of falsehood. And those who are skilled in necromancy [magic] will confirm that it is perfectly feasible.

Source: From *The Travels of Marco Polo*, translated by Ronald Latham (Penguin Classics, 1958), 109–110 and 157–158.

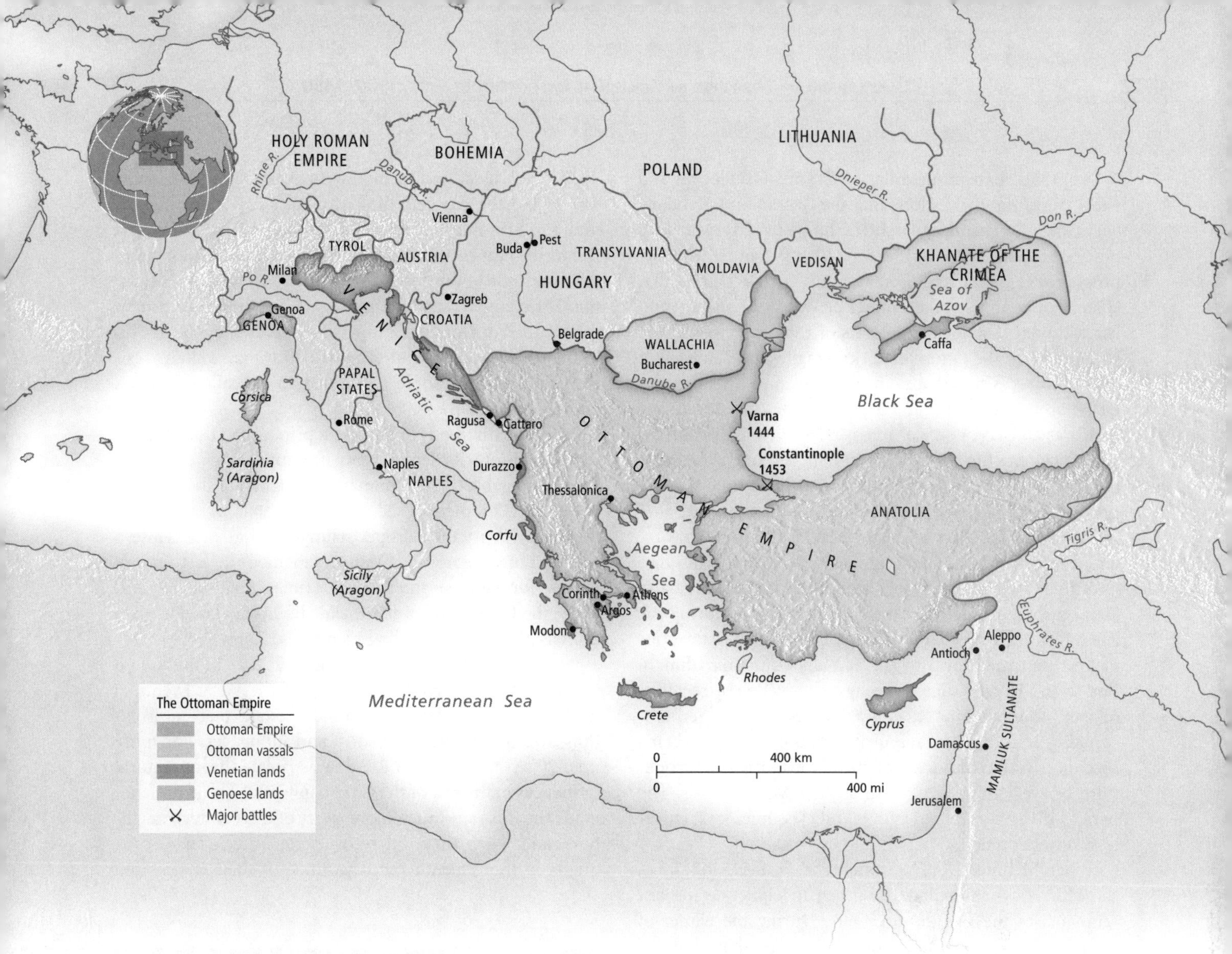

■ **Map 10.3 The Ottoman Empire**
The Ottoman state expanded from a small principality in Anatolia, which is south of the Black Sea. From there the Ottomans spread eastward into Kurdistan and Armenia. In the west they captured all of Greece and much of the Balkan peninsula.

ment of the central Asian empires that had been scraped together by the Mongol conquests. In contrast to the Mongols, many of whom remained Buddhists, the Turks became Muslims and created an exceptionally dynamic, expansionist society of their own (see Map 10.3).

Among the Turkish peoples, the most successful state builders were the Ottomans. Named for Osman I (d. 1326), who brought it to prominence, the Ottoman dynasty endured for more than six hundred years, until 1924. The nucleus of the Ottoman state was a small principality in Anatolia (a portion of present-day Turkey), which in the early fourteenth century began to expand at the expense of its weaker neighbors, including the Byzantine Empire. The Ottoman state was built not on national, linguistic, or ethnic unity, but on a purely dynastic network of personal and military loyalties to the Ottoman prince, called the sultan. Thus the vitality of the empire depended on the energy of the individual sultans. The Ottomans thought of themselves as *ghazis*, warriors for Islam devoted to destroying polytheists, including Christians. (To Muslims the Christian belief in the Trinity and veneration of numerous saints demonstrated that Christians were not true monotheists.) During the fourteenth century, incessant Ottoman guerrilla actions gradually chipped away at the Byzantine frontier.

The Byzantine Empire in the middle of the thirteenth century was emerging from a period of domination by Frankish knights and Venetian merchants who had conquered Constantinople during the Fourth Crusade in 1204. In 1261, the Byzantine Emperor Michael VIII Palaeologus (r. 1260–1282) recaptured the great city. The revived Byzantine Empire, however, was a pale vestige of what it once had been, and the Palaeologi emperors desperately sought military assistance from western Europe to defend themselves from the Ottomans. Dependent on mercenary armies and divided by civil wars, the Byzantines offered only pathetic resistance to the all-conquering Ottomans.

From their base in Anatolia, the Ottomans raided far and wide, launching pirate fleets into the Aegean and gradually encircling Constantinople after they crossed over into Europe in 1308. By 1402 Ottoman territory had grown forty times greater than it had been a century earlier. During that century of conquests, the frontier between Christianity and Islam shifted. The former subjects of the Byzantines in the Balkans fell to the Ottoman Turks. Fragile Serbia, a bastion of Orthodox Christianity in the Balkans, broke under Ottoman pressure. First unified in the late twelfth century, Serbia established political independence from Byzantium and autonomy for the Serbian church. Although the Serbs had taken control over a number of former Byzantine provinces, they fell to the invincible Ottomans at the Battle of Kosovo in 1389. Lamenting the Battle of Kosovo has remained the bedrock of Serbian national identity to this day.

Serbia's western neighbors, the kingdoms of Bosnia and Herzegovina, deflated under Ottoman pressure during the late fifteenth century. Unlike Serbia, where most of the population remained loyal to the Serbian Orthodox Church, Bosnia and Herzegovina had long been divided by religious schisms. The dominant, educated classes were Serbian-speaking Muslims; the subjugated peasants, also Serbian-speaking, were Orthodox Christians who turned over one-third of everything they raised to their Muslim lords. The parallel divisions along religious and class lines long enfeebled Bosnian unity.

When Mehmed II, "The Conqueror" (r. 1451–1481), became the Ottoman sultan, he began to obliterate the last remnants of the Byzantine Empire. During the winter of 1451–1452, the sultan ordered the encirclement of Constantinople, a city that had once been the largest in the world but now was reduced from perhaps a million people to fewer than 50,000. The Ottoman siege strategy was to bombard Constantinople into submission with daily rounds from enormous cannons. The largest was a monster cannon, twenty-nine feet long, that could shoot 1,200-pound stones. It required a crew of 200 soldiers and sixty oxen to handle it, and each firing generated so much heat that it took hours to cool off before it could be fired again. The siege was a gargantuan task because the walls of Constantinople, which had been built, repaired, and improved over a period of a thousand years, were formidable. However, the new weapon of gunpowder artillery had rendered city walls a military anachronism. Brought from China by the Mongols, gunpowder had gradually revolutionized warfare, and breaching city walls in sieges was merely a matter of time as long as the heavy metal cannons could be dragged into position. Quarrels among the Christians also hampered the defense of the walls. Toward the end, the Byzantine emperor was forced to melt down church treasures so "that from them coins should be struck and given to the soldiers, the sappers and the builders, who selfishly cared so little for the public welfare that they were refusing to go to their work unless they were first paid."[6]

The final assault came in May 1453 and lasted less than a day. When the city fell, the Ottoman army spent the day plundering, raping, and enslaving the populace. The last Byzantine emperor, Constantine XI, was never found amid the multitude of the dead. The fall of Constantinople ended the Christian Byzantine Empire, the continuous remnant of the ancient Roman Empire. But the idea of Rome was not so easily snuffed out. The first Ottoman sultans resident in Constantinople continued to be called "Roman emperors."

Although the western European princes had done little to save Byzantium, its demise was a profound shock, rendering them vulnerable to the Ottoman onslaught. For the next 200 years the Ottomans used Constantinople as a base to threaten Christian Europe. Hungary and the eastern Mediterranean empire of Venice remained the last lines of defense for the West, and at various times in succeeding centuries the Ottomans launched expeditions against the great capitals of Europe, including Vienna and Rome.

Hundreds of years of attacks by the Mongol and Ottoman Empires redrew the map of the West. Events in western Europe did not and could not take place in isolation from the eastern pressures and influences. For more than 200 years Christian Russia was isolated from cultural influences in the rest of the Christian world. The experience made the Russians much more aware of their eastern neighbors, and when they did recover from the Mongol conquests in the fifteenth century, much of their energy and

CHRONOLOGY

The Conquests of the Ottoman Turks

1281–1326	Reign of Osman I
1308	Ottoman Empire advances into Europe
1366	Bulgaria conquered
1389	Battle of Kosovo; Prince Lazar of Serbia slain; Serbia becomes vassal state of the Ottomans
1451–1481	Reign of Mehmed II, "The Conqueror"
1453	Fall of Constantinople and death of last Byzantine emperor
1459	Serbia definitively incorporated into the Ottoman Empire
1463	Bosnia conquered
1483	Herzegovina conquered
1499	Montenegro conquered

military might was directed toward expanding eastward into the void left by the collapse of the Mongol Empire. The Ottoman conquests also created a lasting Muslim presence within the borders of Europe, especially in Bosnia and Albania. In succeeding centuries Christian Europe and the Muslim Ottoman Empire would be locked in a deadly competitive embrace, but they also benefited from innumerable cultural exchanges and regular trade. Hostility between the two sides was recurrent but never inevitable and was broken by long periods of peaceful engagement. In fact, the Christian kingdoms of western Europe went to war far more often with one another than with the Turks.

Economic Depression and Social Turmoil

Adding insult to injury in this time of famine, plague, and conquest, the West began to suffer a major economic depression during the fourteenth century. The economic boom fueled by the agricultural revolution and the revitalization of European cities during the eleventh century and the commercial prosperity of the twelfth and thirteenth centuries petered out in the fourteenth. The causes of this economic catastrophe were complex, but the consequences were obvious. Businesses went bust, banks collapsed, guilds were in turmoil, and workers rebelled.

The Collapse of International Trade and Banking

The Mongol Peace during the thirteenth century had stimulated vast, lucrative trade in exotic luxury items between Europe and Asia. When the Mongol Empire began to break up in the fourteenth century, the trade routes were cut off or displaced. Later in the century, Tamerlane's forcible channeling of the caravan trade through his own territory created a narrow trade corridor with outlets on the coast of the Middle East. Rulers along this path, such as the Mamluks in Egypt, took advantage of the situation to levy heavy tolls on trade, raising the price of goods beyond what the market could bear. As a result, trade dwindled. Alternative routes would have taken merchants through Constantinople, but Ottoman pressure on Byzantium endangered these routes.

The financial infrastructure of medieval Europe was tied to international trade in luxury goods. The successful, entrepreneurial Italian merchants who dominated the luxury trade deposited their enormous profits in Italian banks. The Italian bankers lent money to the aristocracy and royalty of northern Europe to finance the purchases of exotic luxuries and to fight wars. The whole system was mutually reinforcing, but it was very fragile. With the disruption of supply sources for luxury goods, the financial networks of Europe collapsed, precipitating a major and lasting depression.

For most of the thirteenth century the Italian city of Siena had been one of the principal banking centers of the world, the equivalent of New York or Tokyo today. In 1298, however, panic caused a run on its largest bank, which failed. Soon the lesser Sienese banks were forced to close, and the entire city fell into a deep economic depression. Siena never recovered its economic stature and is a major tourist attraction today simply because it is largely unchanged from the time when the banks went broke.

In nearby Florence, several local banks took advantage of Siena's collapse and became even bigger than the Sienese banks had been. Through these banks, the coinage of Florence, the florin, became the common currency of Europe. By 1346, however, all of these banks crashed due to a series of bad loans to several kings of Europe. With the bank crash, virtually all sources of credit dried up all across Europe. At the same time, wars between France and England deprived their aristocracies of the money to buy luxuries from the Italian merchants whose deposits had been the principal source of capital for the banks. With disruptions in the supply of Asian luxury goods, a catastrophic loss of capital by Italian bankers, and a decline in demand for luxuries in France and England, Europe entered a major depression.

Rebellions from Below

The luxury trade that brought exotic items from Asia to Europe represented only half of the economic equation. The other half was the raw materials and manufactured goods that Europeans sold in exchange, principally woolen cloth. The production of woolen cloth depended on a highly sophisticated economic system that connected shepherds in England, the Netherlands, and Spain with woolen cloth manufacturers in cities. The manufacture of cloth and other commodities was organized by guilds. The collapse of the luxury trade reduced the demand for the goods produced by the guilds, depriving guildsmen and urban workers of employment. The situation must have seemed ironic. Workers knew that the population decline from famine and pestilence had created a labor shortage, which according to the elementary laws of supply and demand should have produced higher wages for the workers who survived. However, wages stagnated because of the decline in business. Royal and local governments made matters worse by trying to control wages and raise taxes in a period of declining revenues. Frustrated and enraged, workers rebelled.

An Economy of Monopolies: Guilds

Central to the political and economic control of medieval cities were the guilds°. Because of their importance, guilds were at the center of the economic collapse of the fourteenth century and the turmoil that accompanied it. Guilds were professional associations devoted to protecting the special interests of a particular trade or craft and to monopolizing production and trade in the goods the guild produced. There were two dominant types of guilds. The first type, merchant guilds, attempted to monopolize the local market for a particular commodity. There were spice guilds, fruit and vegetable guilds, and apothecary guilds. The second type, craft guilds, regulated the manufacturing processes of artisans, such as carpenters, bricklayers, woolen-cloth manufacturers, glass blowers, and painters. These guilds were dominated by master craftsmen, who were the bosses of their own shops. Working for wages in these shops were the journeymen, who knew the craft but could not yet afford to open their own shops. Under the masters and journeymen were apprentices, who worked usually without pay for a specific number of years to learn the trade.

Guild regulations governed virtually all aspects of guildsmens' lives. In fact, until a youth passed from apprenticeship to become a journeyman, he could not marry or own property of his own. Craft guilds functioned like a modern professional association by guaranteeing that producers met certain standards of training and competence before they could practice a trade. Like merchant guilds, they also regulated competition and prices in an attempt to protect the masters' local monopoly in the craft.

In many cities the guilds expanded far beyond the economic regulation of trade and manufacturing to become the backbone of urban society and politics. The masters of the guilds constituted part of the urban elite, and guild membership was often a prerequisite for holding public office. The guilds unified the economic and political control of medieval cities; one of the obligations of city government was to protect the interests of the guildsmen, who in turn helped stabilize the economy through their influence in city hall. The guilds were often at the center of a city's social life as well, countering the anonymity of city life by offering fellowship and a sense of belonging. Medieval festivals were often organized by the guilds, whose members engaged in sports competitions with other guilds. In Nuremberg, for example, the butchers' guild organized and financed the elaborate carnival festivities that absorbed the energies of the entire city for days on end. In many places guilds supplied the actors for the Corpus Christi plays that acted out stories from the Bible or the lives of the saints for the entertainment and edification of their fellow citizens. In

WORKER REBELLIONS IN FLANDERS AND FRANCE

A Florentine businessman, Buonaccorso Pitti, who had witnessed the Ciompi revolt in Florence in 1378, found himself in Paris when the Maillotins *revolt broke out. Like his contemporaries, he concluded that the violence in Bruges and Ghent was somehow connected to the outbreak of violence in Rouen and Paris. This was a reasonable assumption, because the count of Flanders and the French royal court had many intimate ties. Thus, rebellion in one place had political implications elsewhere. Here is what Pitti reported.*

In 1381 the people of Ghent rebelled against their overlord, the count of Flanders, who was the father of the duchess of Burgundy. They marched in great numbers to Bruges, took the city, deposed the Count, robbed and killed all his officers, and dealt in the same way with all the other Flemish towns which fell into their hands. Their leader was Philip van Artevelde. As the number of Flemings rebelling against their overlords increased, they sent secret embassies to the populace of Paris and Rouen, urging them to do the like with their own lords, and promising them aid and succor in this undertaking. Accordingly, these two cities rebelled against the King of France. The first insurrection was that of the Paris mob, and was sparked off by a costermonger [someone who sells produce from a cart] who, when an official tried to levy a tax on the fruit and vegetables he was selling, began to roar "Down with the *gabelle* [a food tax]." At this cry the whole populace rose, ran to the tax-collectors' houses and robbed and murdered them. Then, since the mob was unarmed, one of their number led them to the Chatelet where Bertrand du Guesclin, a former High Constable, had stored 3000 lead-tipped cudgels in preparation for a battle which was to have been fought against the English. The rabble used axes to break their way into the tower where these cudgels or mallets (in French, *maillets*) were kept and, arming themselves, set forth in all directions to rob the houses of the King's representatives and in many cases to murder them. The. . . men of substance who in French are called *bourgeois*, fearing lest the mob (who were later called *Maillotins* and were of much the same kidney [nature] as the *Ciompi* in Florence) might rob them too, took arms and managed to subdue them. They then proceeded to take government into their own hands, and together with the *Maillotins*, continued the war against their royal lords.

Source: Reprinted by permission of Waveland Press, Inc. from Gene Brucker, ed., *Two Memoirs of Renaissance Florence: The Diaries of Buonaccorso Pitti and Gregorio Dati*, translated by Julia Martines. (Prospect Heights, IL; Waveland Press, Inc., 1967, reissued 1991)

Florence the church of the guildsmen became a display case for works of sculpture by the city's most prominent artists, each work sponsored by a specific guild. The guilds endowed magnificent chapels and provided funeral insurance for their members and welfare for the injured and widows of masters.

When the economy declined during the fourteenth century, the urban guilds became lightning rods for mounting social tension. Guild monopolies produced considerable conflict, provoking anger among those who were blocked from joining guilds and thus excluded from the economic and political benefits available to guild members, and among young journeymen who earned low wages. These tensions exploded into dangerous revolts.

Slaughter of Peasants
The slaughter of the peasant rebels during the Jacquerie on the bridge at Meaux.

"Long Live the People, Long Live Liberty"

Economic pressures erupted into rebellion most dramatically among woolen-cloth workers in the urban centers in Italy, the Netherlands, and France. The most famous revolt involved the Ciompi, the laborers in the woolen-cloth industry of Florence, Italy, where guilds were a powerful force in city government. The Ciompi, who performed the heaviest jobs such as carting and the most noxious tasks such as dyeing, had not been allowed to have their own guild and were therefore deprived of the political and economic rights of guild membership. Fueling the Ciompi's frustration was the fact that by the middle of the fourteenth century woolen-cloth production in Florence dropped by two-thirds, leaving many workers unemployed. In 1378 the desperate Ciompi rebelled. A crowd chanting, "Long live the people, long live liberty," broke into the houses of prominent citizens, released political prisoners from the city jails, and sacked the rich convents that housed the pampered daughters of the wealthy. Over the course of a few months, the rebels managed to force their way onto the city council, where they demanded tax and economic reforms and the right to form their own guild. The Ciompi revolt is one of the earliest cases of workers demanding political rights. The disenfranchised workers did not want to eliminate the guilds' monopoly on political power; they merely wanted a guild of their own so that they could join the regime. That was not to be, however. After a few weeks of success, the Ciompi were divided and defeated.

Shortly after the Ciompi revolt faded, troubles broke out in the woolen-cloth centers of Ghent and Bruges in Flanders and in Paris and Rouen in France. In these cases, however, the revolt spread beyond woolen-cloth workers to voice the more generalized grievances of urban workers. In Ghent and Bruges the weavers attempted to wrest control of their cities from the local leaders who dominated politics and the economy. In Paris and Rouen in 1380, social unrest erupted in resistance to high taxes and attacks by the poor on the rich. The pinnacle of the violence involved the *Maillotins* ("people who fight with mallets") in Paris during March 1382, when the houses of tax collectors were sacked and the inhabitants murdered. Although the violence in Flanders and France was precipitated by local issues, such as control of the town council and taxes, both cases were symptomatic of the widespread social conflicts that followed in the wake of the great depression of the fourteenth century that profoundly affected the crucial woolen-cloth industry.

Like urban workers, many rural peasants also rebelled during the troubled fourteenth century. In France in 1358 a peasant revolt broke out that came to be called the *Jacquerie*, a term derived from "Jacques Bonhomme" ("James Goodfellow"), the traditional name for the typical peasant. Jacquerie became synonymous with extreme, seemingly mindless violence. Filled with hatred for the aristocracy, the peasants indulged in pillaging, murder, and rape, but they offered no plan for an alternative social system or even for their own participation in the political order, so their movement had no lasting effects. They were quickly defeated by a force of nobles.

Unlike the French Jacquerie, the peasants who revolted in England in 1381 had a clear political vision for an alternative society, a fact that makes their revolt far more significant. In England the rebels' motives stemmed from the frustration of rising expectations that were never realized. The peasants believed that the labor shortage caused by the Black Death should have improved their condition, but the exact opposite was happening. Landlords clung to the old system that defined peasants as serfs who were tied to the land and unable to bargain for the price of their labor. Although the English peasants were probably better off than their fathers and grandfathers had been, their expectations of an even better life were blocked by the land-holding aristocracy. The clashing interests of the peasants and the aristocrats needed only a spark to ignite a conflagration. That spark came from the Poll Tax controversy.

The traditional means of raising revenue in England had been a levy on the more well-to-do landowners, who were taxed according to the size and value of their holdings. In 1381, however, the crown attempted to levy a Poll Tax, which taxed with little concern for the ability of each person to pay. The Poll Tax, in effect, shifted the burden of taxation to a lower social level, and the peasants bitterly resented it. As agents came to collect the Poll Tax in June 1381, riots broke out throughout eastern England, and rioters burned local tax records. The rebels briefly occupied London, where they lynched the lord chancellor and treasurer of the kingdom. The rebels demanded lower rents, higher wages, and the abolition of serfdom—all typical peasant demands—but to these they added a class-based argument against the aristocracy. They had been influenced by popular preachers who told them that in the Garden of Eden there had been no aristocracy. Following these preachers, the English rebels imagined a classless society, a utopian vision of an alternative to medieval society that was entirely structured around distinctive classes.

The 15-year-old English king, Richard II (r. 1377–1399), promised the rebels that their demands would be met. Satisfied that they had gotten what they wanted, including the abolition of serfdom, the peasants disbanded. The king then rescinded his promises and ordered that the peasant leaders be hunted down and executed. Thus, the greatest peasant rebellion in English history ended with broken promises and no tangible achievements.

None of the worker or peasant revolts of the fourteenth century met with lasting success. The universal failure of lower-class rebellion was due, in part, to the lack of any clear alternative to the existing economic and political system. The Ciompi wanted to join the existing guild system. The weavers of Ghent and Bruges were as much competing with one another as rebelling against the Flanders establishment. The extreme violence of the Jacquerie frightened away potential allies. Only the English rebels had precise revolutionary demands, but they were betrayed by King Richard.

CHRONOLOGY

Economic Depression and Social Turmoil

1298	Collapse of Sienese banks
1310–1320	Famines begin
1342–1346	Collapse of Florentine banks
1348	Arrival of Black Death in Europe
1358	Jacquerie revolt in France
1378	Ciompi revolt in Florence
1379–1385	Urban revolts in Flanders and France
1381	Peasants revolt in England

A Troubled Church and the Demand for Religious Comfort

In reaction to the suffering and widespread death during the fourteenth century, many people naturally turned to religion for spiritual consolation and for explanations of what had gone wrong. But the spiritual authority of the Church was so dangerously weakened during this period that it failed to satisfy the popular craving for solace. The moral leadership that had made the papacy such a powerful force for reform during the eleventh through thirteenth centuries was completely lacking in the fourteenth. Many laypeople gave up looking to the pope for guidance and found their own means of religious expression, making the Later Middle Ages one of the most religiously creative epochs in Christian history. Some of the new religious movements, especially in England and Bohemia, veered onto the dangerous shoals of heresy, breaking the fragile unity of the Church.

THE BABYLONIAN CAPTIVITY OF THE CHURCH AND THE GREAT SCHISM

Faced with anarchy in the streets of Rome as local aristocrats engaged in incessant feuding, a succession of seven consecutive popes chose to reside in the relative calm of Avignon, France. This period of voluntary papal exile is known as the Babylonian Captivity of the Church° (1305–1378), a biblical reference recalling the captivity of the Jews in Babylonia (587–539 B.C.E.). The popes' subservience to the kings of France during this period dangerously politicized the papacy, destroying its ability to rise above the petty squabbles of the European princes.

The loss of revenues from papal lands in Italy lured several popes into questionable financial schemes, which included accepting kickbacks from appointees to church offices, taking bribes for judicial decisions, and selling indulgences°. Indulgences were certificates that allowed penitents to atone for their sins and reduce their time in purgatory by paying money.

When Pope Urban VI (r. 1378–1389) was elevated to the papacy in 1378 and announced his intention to reside in Rome, a group of disgruntled French cardinals returned to Avignon and elected a rival French pope. The Church was then divided over allegiance to Italian and French claimants to the papal throne, a period called the Great Schism° (1378–1417). Toward the end of the schism there were actually four rival popes. Some of these antipopes completely lacked spiritual qualities. The most infamous was Baldassare Cossa, whom a faction of cardinals elected Pope John XXIII (r. 1410–1415) because he had been an effective commander of the papal troops. The cardinals who supported rival popes charged Pope John with the crimes of piracy, murder, rape, sodomy, and incest—charges without much substance—but the publication of the allegations further undermined the moral reputation of the papacy.

Urban VI's decision to return the papacy to Rome and end the Babylonian Captivity of the Church resulted from an intense demand for his presence in Italy. The reason was the growing influence of a young woman mystic. Catherine Benincasa (1347–1380), better known as St. Catherine of Siena, demonstrated her mystic tendencies at an early age by locking herself in a room of her parents' house for a year to devote herself to prayer and fasting. She soon became famous for her holiness and severe asceticism, which during the troubled times of the Babylonian Captivity gave her a powerful moral authority. She went to Avignon, and although the pope ignored her, she attracted the attention of others in the papal court. Catherine became the most important advocate for encouraging the return of the pope from Avignon to Rome and launching a new crusade against the Muslims. She helped Pope Urban VI reorganize the Church after he returned to Rome, and she sent out letters and pleas to the kings and queens of Europe to gain support for him during the schism. Although illiterate, Catherine produced an influential body of letters, prayers, and treatises by dictating to others. At a time when all of the great powers of Europe were failing to provide leadership, the void was filled by a young woman with a strong sense of moral mission.

The Great Schism created the need for a mechanism to sort out the competing claims of rival popes. That need led

The Government of the Church

Concern for the compromised authority of the Church during the Babylonian Captivity preoccupied churchmen everywhere. This elaborate allegory, *The Government of the Church*, was commissioned for the most important Dominican church in Florence, Santa Maria Novella, and painted by Andrea da Firenze in the Spanish Chapel, 1366–1368. The allegory demonstrates how the pope is assisted by the Dominicans, who fought heresy through preaching.

to the Conciliar Movement°. The conciliarists argued that a general meeting or council of the bishops of the Church had authority over the pope, it could be called to order by a king, and it could pass judgment on a standing pope or order a conclave to elect a new one. Several general councils were held during the early fifteenth century to resolve the schism and initiate reforms. The Council of Constance (1414–1417) finally succeeded in restoring unity to the Church and also in formally asserting the principle that a general council is superior to the pope and should be called frequently. The Council of Basel (1431–1449) approved a series of necessary reforms, although these were never implemented due to the hostility to conciliarism by Pope Eugene IV (r. 1431–1447). The failure of even the timid reforms of the Council of Basel opened the way for the more radical rejection of papal authority during the Protestant Reformation of the sixteenth century. The Conciliar Movement, however, was not a complete failure because it provided a model for how reform could take place. This model would later become central to the Catholic Reformation and the foundation of modern Catholicism (see Chapter 13).

CHRONOLOGY

Troubles in the Church

1305–1378	Babylonian Captivity of the Church; popes reside in Avignon
1320–1384	John Wycliffe
1347–1380	St. Catherine of Siena
1369–1415	Jan Hus
1378–1417	Great Schism; more than one pope
1414–1417	Council of Constance
1431–1449	Council of Basel
CA. 1441	*Imitation of Christ*

THE SEARCH FOR RELIGIOUS ALTERNATIVES

The popes' loss of moral authority during the Babylonian Captivity and the Great Schism opened the way for a remarkable variety of reformers, mystics, and preachers, who appealed to lay believers crying out for a direct experience of God and a return to the message of the original apostles of Christ. Some of these movements were heretical, but the weakened papacy was unable to control them, as it had successfully done during the thirteenth century crusade against the Albigensians.

Protests Against the Papacy: New Heresies

For most Christians during the fourteenth century, religious life consisted of witnessing or participating in the seven sacraments, which were formal rituals celebrated by duly consecrated priests usually within the confines of churches. After baptism, which was universally performed on infants, the most common sacraments for lay adults were penance and communion. Both of these sacraments emphasized the power of the clergy over the laity and therefore were potential sources for resentment. The sacrament of penance required the layperson to confess his or her sins to a priest, who then prescribed certain penalties to satisfy the sin. At communion, it was believed, the priest changed the substance of an unleavened wafer of bread, called the Eucharist, into the body of Christ and a cup of wine into his blood, a miraculous process called transubstantiation. Priest and lay recipients of communion both ate the wafer, but the cup was reserved for the priest alone. More than anything else, the reservation of the cup for priests profoundly symbolized the privileges of the clergy. Since medieval Catholicism was primarily a sacramental religion, reformers and heretics tended to concentrate their criticism on sacramental rituals, especially of their spiritual value compared to other kinds of worship such as prayer.

The most serious discontent about the authority of the popes, the privileges of the clergy, and the efficacy of the sacraments appeared in England and Bohemia (a region in the modern Czech Republic). An Oxford professor, John Wycliffe (1320–1384), criticized the power and wealth of the clergy, played down the moral value of the sacraments, and exalted the benefits of preaching, which promoted a sense of personal responsibility. During the Great Schism, Wycliffe rejected the authority of the rival popes and asserted instead the absolute authority of the Bible, which he wanted to make available to the laity in English rather than in Latin, which only priests understood.

Wycliffe's ideas found their most sympathetic audience outside England among a group of reformist professors at the University of Prague in Bohemia where Professor Jan Hus (1369–1415) regularly preached to a large popular following. Hus's most revolutionary act was to offer the cup of consecrated communion wine to the laity, thus symbolically diminishing the special status of the clergy. When Hus also preached against indulgences, which he said converted the sacrament of penance into a cash transaction, Pope John XXIII excommunicated him. Hus attended the Council of Constance to defend his ideas. Despite a safe-conduct from the Holy Roman emperor (whose jurisdiction included Bohemia and Constance) that made him immune from arrest, he was imprisoned, his writings were condemned, and he was burned alive as a heretic.

Imitating Christ: The Modern Devotion

In the climate of religious turmoil of the fourteenth and fifteenth centuries, many sincere Christians sought deeper spiritual solace than the institutionalized Church could provide. By stressing individual piety, ethical behavior, and intense religious education, a movement called the Modern Devotion° became highly influential. Promoted by the Brothers of the Common Life, a religious order established in the Netherlands, the Modern Devotion was especially popular throughout northern Europe. In the houses for the Brothers, clerics and laity lived together without monastic vows, shared household tasks, joined in regular prayers, and engaged in religious studies. (A similar structure was devised for women.) The lay brothers continued their occupations in the outside world, thus influencing their neighbors through their pious example. The houses established schools that prepared boys for church careers through constant prayer and rigorous training in Latin. Many of the leading figures behind the Protestant Reformation in the sixteenth century had attended schools run by the Brothers of the Common Life.

The Modern Devotion was also spread by the best-seller of the late fifteenth century, the *Imitation of Christ*, written in 1441 by a Common Life brother, probably Thomas à Kempis. By emphasizing frequent private prayer and moral introspection, the *Imitation* provided a spiritual manual to guide laypeople in the path toward spiritual renewal that had traditionally been reserved for monks and nuns. There was nothing especially reformist or antisacramental about the *Imitation of Christ*, which emphasized the need for regular confession and communion. However, its popularity helped prepare the way for a broad-based reform of the Church by turning the walls of the monastery inside out, spilling out a large number of lay believers who were dedicated to becoming living examples of moral purity for their neighbors.

The moral and financial degradation of the papacy during the fourteenth and early fifteenth centuries was countered by a remarkable spiritual awakening among the laity, manifest in the Modern Devotion. As a result, throughout Europe laypeople began to take more responsibility, not only for their own salvation, but for the spiritual and material welfare of their entire community and of the Church itself. These pious people founded hospitals for the sick and dying, orphanages for abandoned children, and confraternities that engaged in a wide range of charitable good works—from providing dowries for poor women to accompanying condemned criminals to the gallows.

An Age of Continuous Warfare

Western Europe was further weakened during the fourteenth century by prolonged war between its two largest and previously most stable kingdoms, England and France. The Hundred Years' War° (1337–1453) was a struggle over England's attempts to assert its claims to territories in France. The prolonged conflict drained resources from the aristocracies of both kingdoms, deepening the economic depression and making it last longer. The Hundred Years' War sowed the seeds of a military revolution that by the sixteenth century transformed the kingdoms of western Europe. Monarchies, ruled by relatively weak kings and strong aristocracies, evolved into modern states, ruled by strong monarchs who usurped many of the traditional privileges of the aristocracy in order to centralize authority and strengthen military prowess.

The Fragility of Monarchies

The most dangerous threat to the kings of France and England during the fourteenth and fifteenth centuries came less from worker and peasant rebellions than from members of the aristocracy, who were fiercely protective of their

Royal Justice
English kings were preoccupied with extending their prerogatives over the judiciary as a way to express royal power. Despite the corruption of the many lower courts, the Court of the King's Bench attempted to assert a level of uniform procedures and royal control of justice.

jurisdictional privileges over their lands. The privilege of jurisdiction allowed aristocrats to act as judges for crimes committed in their territories, a privilege that was a crucial source of their power. In both kingdoms, royal officials asserted the legal principle that aristocratic jurisdictions originated with the crown and were subordinate to it. The problem behind this controversy was inherent in the system of rule in France and England—overlapping, conflicting, and sometimes contradictory jurisdictions and loyalties produced by many generations of inheritance. The system bred strife and limited the power of the monarch. Thus the Hundred Years' War was both a conflict between two kingdoms and a series of civil wars between aristocratic factions and imperiled monarchs.

Medieval monarchies depended on the king to maintain stability. Despite the remarkable legal reforms and bureaucratic centralization of monarchies in England and France during the twelfth and thirteenth centuries (see Chapter 9), weak or incompetent kings were all too common during the fourteenth. Weak kings created a perilous situation made worse by disputed successions. The career of Edward II (r. 1307–1327) of England illustrates the peril. Edward was unable to control the vital judicial and financial sinews of royal power. He continued the policy of his father, Edward I, by introducing resident justices of the peace who had replaced the inadequate system of itinerant judges who traveled from village to village to hear cases. In theory, these justices of the peace should have prevented the abuses of justice typical of aristocratic jurisdictions, but even though they were royal officials who answered to the king, most of those appointed were also local landowners who were deeply implicated in many of the disputes that came before them. As a result, justice in England became notoriously corrupt and the cause of discontent. Edward II was so incompetent to deal with the consequences of corrupted justice that he provoked a civil war in which his own queen joined his aristocratic enemies to depose him.

The French monarchy was no better. In fact, the French king was in an even weaker constitutional position than the English monarch. In France the king had effective jurisdiction over only a small part of his realm. Many of the duchies and counties of France were quasi-independent principalities, paying only nominal allegiance to the king, whose will was ignored with impunity. In these regions the administration of justice, the collection of taxes, and the recruitment of soldiers all remained in the hands of local lords. To explain why he needed to raise taxes, Philip IV, "The Fair" (r. 1285–1314), created a representative assembly, the Estates General, which met for the first time in 1302, but he still had to negotiate with each region and town individually to collect the taxes. Given the difficulty of raising taxes, the French kings resorted to makeshift solutions that hurt the economy, such as confiscating the property of vulnerable Jewish and Italian merchants and debasing the coinage to increase the value of scarce silver. Such a system made France especially vulnerable.

THE HUNDRED YEARS' WAR

The Hundred Years' War revealed the fragility of the medieval monarchies. The initial cause of the war involved disputes over the duchy of Aquitaine. The king of England also held the title of duke of Aquitaine, who was a vassal of the French crown, which meant that the English kings technically owed military assistance to the French kings whenever they asked for it. A long succession of English kings had reluctantly paid homage as dukes of Aquitaine to the king of France, but the unusual status of the duchy was a continuing source of contention.

The second cause of the war derived from a succession crisis over the French crown. When King Charles IV died in 1328, his closest surviving relative was none other than the archenemy of France, Edward III (r. 1327–1377), king of England. To the barons of France, the possibility of Edward's succession to the throne was unthinkable, and they excluded him because his relation to the French royal family was through his mother. Instead the barons elected to the throne a member of the Valois family, King Philip VI (r. 1328–1350), and at first Edward reluctantly accepted the decision. However, when Philip started to hear judicial appeals from the duchy of Aquitaine, Edward changed his mind. He claimed the title of king of

Siege Warfare
English soldiers pillaging and burning a French town.

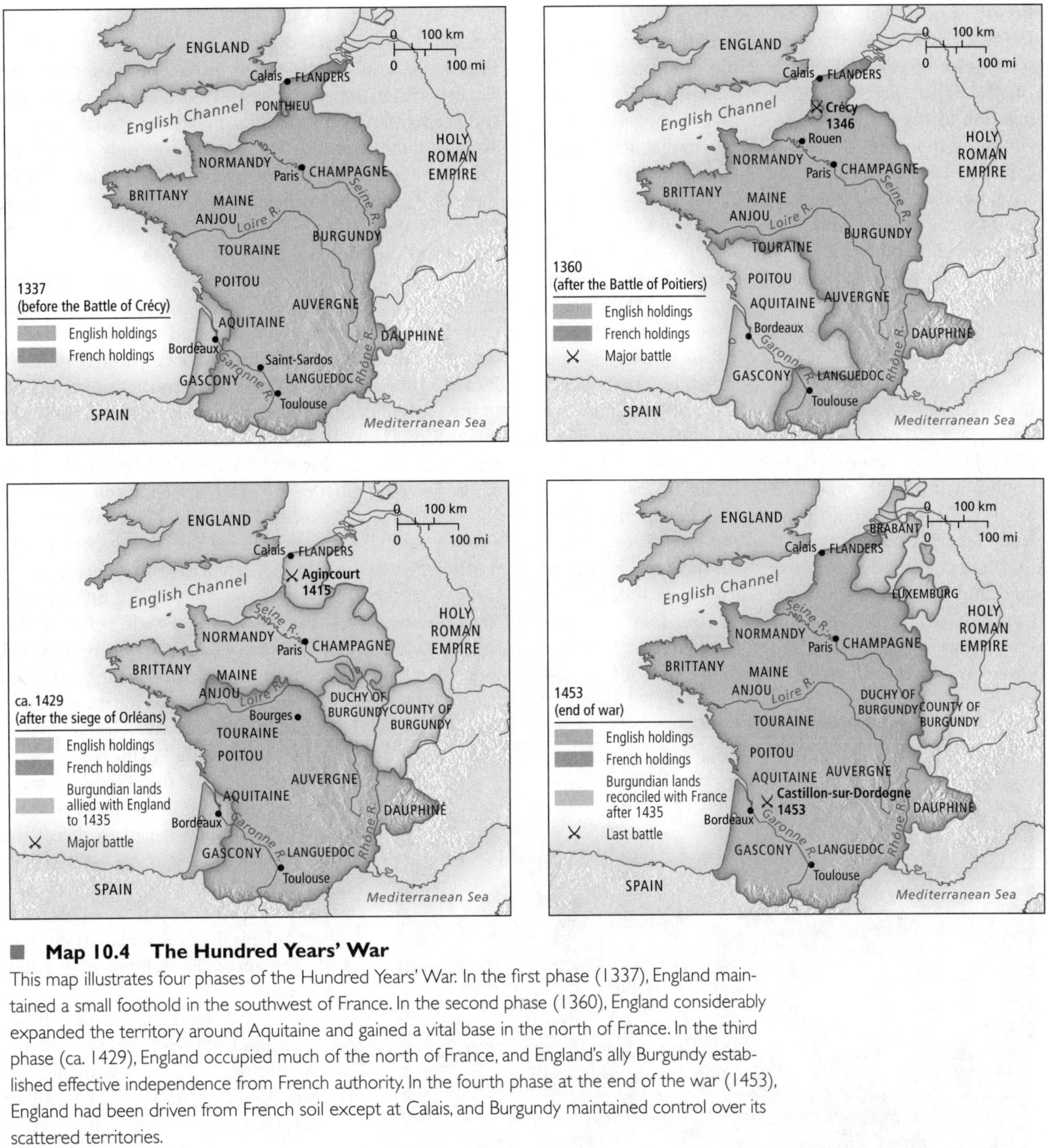

Map 10.4 The Hundred Years' War

This map illustrates four phases of the Hundred Years' War. In the first phase (1337), England maintained a small foothold in the southwest of France. In the second phase (1360), England considerably expanded the territory around Aquitaine and gained a vital base in the north of France. In the third phase (ca. 1429), England occupied much of the north of France, and England's ally Burgundy established effective independence from French authority. In the fourth phase at the end of the war (1453), England had been driven from French soil except at Calais, and Burgundy maintained control over its scattered territories.

France for himself, sparking the beginning of more than a century of warfare (see Map 10.4).

The Hundred Years' War was not a continuous formal war but a series of occasional pitched battles, punctuated by long truces and periods of general exhaustion. The term *Hundred Years' War* was invented by nineteenth-century historians to describe a prolonged time of troubles between the two countries that lasted from 1337 to 1453. In terms of its potential for warfare, France, far richer and with three times the population, held the advantage over sparsely populated England. In nearly every battle the French outnumbered the English, but the English were usually victorious because of superior discipline and the ability of their longbows to break up cavalry charges. As a rule, the English avoided open battle, preferring raids, sieges of isolated castles, and capturing French knights for ransom. For many Englishmen the objective in fighting in France was to get rich by looting. And because all the fighting took place on French soil, France suffered extensive destruction and significant civilian casualties from repeated English raids.

From English Victories to French Salvation

In the early phases of the war, the English enjoyed a stunning series of victories. At the Battle of Sluys in 1340, a small English fleet of 150 ships carrying the English invasion forces ran into a French blockade of more than 200 ships. In the heavy hand-to-hand combat, the English captured 166 French ships and killed some 20,000 men, so many that it was later said, "If fish could talk, they would speak French." At Crécy in 1346, the English longbowmen shot thousands of arrows "like thunderbolts" into the flanks of the charging French knights, killing men and horses in shocking numbers. The French knights mounted one disorderly, hopeless charge after another, until the piles of dead blocked further charges. Though wounded, King Philip escaped, leaving 3,000 of his men dead on the field, including 1,500 knights. The aristocracy of France was decimated. At Poitiers in 1356, King John of France (r. 1350–1364) encircled 6,000 English with a vastly superior royal army of 15,000, but—as at Crécy—the English archers broke up the overly hasty French cavalry charge, and the English counterassault crushed the French. Two thousand French knights died and another 2,000 were captured, including King John himself. With its king imprisoned in England, France was forced to pay a huge ransom and grant formal sovereignty over a third of France to the king of England.

The Battle of Sluys

At the Battle of Sluys, ships lined up side by side to enable fierce hand-to-hand combat. Even in these close quarters, longbows were brought into play, giving the English a lethal advantage.

At Agincourt in 1415, King Henry V (r. 1413–1422) and England's disease-racked army of 6,000 were cut off by a French force of about 20,000. In the ensuing battle the English archers repelled a hasty French cavalry charge and the fleeing, terrified horses trampled the French men-at-arms as they advanced. The English lost only a few hundred, but the French suffered nearly 10,000 casualties. After Agincourt, the French never again dared challenge King Henry in open battle, and were forced to recognize him as the heir to the French throne. By 1420 the English victory appeared complete. Now with the responsibility of ruling rather than conquering France, the English could no longer rely on their old strategy of mounted raiding and had to hold the French cities, which proved exceedingly difficult. By 1422, however, Henry V was dead, leaving two claimants to the French throne. The English asserted the rights of the infant King Henry VI of England, son of King Henry V, the victor at Agincourt. Most of the French defended the claim of the Dauphin Charles, the only surviving son of the late King Charles VI of France. The Hundred Years' War entered a new phase with factions of the French aristocracy supporting the two rivals in a bloody series of engagements.

By 1429 the English were on the verge of final victory. They occupied Paris and Rheims, and their army was besieging Orleans. The Dauphin Charles was penniless and indecisive. Even his own mother denied his legitimacy as king. At this point a 17-year-old illiterate peasant from Burgundy, Joan of Arc [Jeanne d'Arc, 1412?–1431], following "divine voices," went to Orleans to lead the French armies. Under her inspiration Orleans was relieved, French forces began to defeat the English, much of the occupied territory was regained, and the Dauphin was crowned King Charles VII (r. 1429–1461) in the cathedral of Rheims. After Joan failed to recapture Paris, however, her successes ceased.

Charles VII reorganized the French army and gradually chipped away at the English holdings in France, eventually taking away Aquitaine in 1453. The English lost all their possessions in France except Calais, which was finally surrendered in 1558. There was no peace treaty, just a fading away of war in France, especially after England stumbled into civil war—the War of the Roses (1455–1485).

The Hundred Years' War in Perspective

The Hundred Years' War had broad consequences. First, nearly continuous warfare between the two most powerful kingdoms in the West exacerbated other conflicts as well. Scotland, the German princes, Aragon, Castile, and most importantly Burgundy were drawn into the conflict at various stages, making the English-French brawl a European-wide war at certain stages. The squabble between France and England made it much more difficult to settle the Great Schism that split the Church during the same period. Second, the war devastated France, which eventually regained control of most of its territory but still suffered the most from the fighting. During the century of the war, the population dropped by half, due to the ravages of combat, pillage, and plague. Agriculture languished after the repeated English mounted raids that destroyed crops and sacked peasant villages. Third, the deaths of so many nobles and destruction of their fortunes diminished the international luxury trade; merchants and banks as far away as Italy went broke; and the Flemish woolen industry was disrupted, causing further economic damage. Finally, the war helped make England more English. Before the war the Plantagenet dynasty in England was more French than English. The monarchs possessed extensive territories in France and were embroiled in French affairs. English aristocrats also had business in France, spoke French, and married their French cousins. After 1450 the English abandoned the many French connections that had stretched across the English Channel since William the Conqueror sailed from Normandy to England in 1066. Henceforth, the English upper classes cultivated English rather than French language and culture.

English Archers

English archers practicing the longbow. Note that the unpulled bows are the height of a man.

THE MILITARY REVOLUTION

The "military revolution," whose effects first became evident during the Hundred Years' War, refers to changes in warfare that marked the transition from the late medieval to the early modern state. The heavily armored mounted knights, who had dominated European warfare and society since the Carolingian period, were gradually supplanted by foot soldiers as the most effective fighting unit in battle. Infantry units were composed of men who fought on foot in disciplined ranks, which allowed them to break up cavalry charges by concentrating firepower in deadly volleys. Infantry soldiers could fight on a greater variety of terrains than mounted knights, who needed even ground and plenty of space for their horses to maneuver. The effectiveness of infantry units made battles more ferocious but also more decisive, which was why governments favored them. Infantry, however, put new requirements on the governments that recruited them. Armies now demanded large numbers of well-drilled foot soldiers who could move in disciplined ranks around a battlefield. Recruiting, training, and drilling soldiers made armies much more complex organizations than they had been, and officers needed to possess a wide range of management skills. Governments faced added expenses as they needed to arrange and pay for the logistical support necessary to feed and transport those large numbers. The creation of the highly centralized modern state resulted in part from the necessity to maintain a large army in which infantry played the crucial role.

CHRONOLOGY

An Age of Continuous Warfare

1285–1314	Reign of Philip IV, "The Fair," of France
1307–1327	Reign of Edward II of England
1327–1377	Reign of Edward III of England
1328–1350	Reign of Philip VI of France
1337–1453	Hundred Years' War
1340	Battle of Sluys
1346	Battle of Crécy
1356	Battle of Poitiers
1377–1399	Reign of Richard II of England
1399–1413	Reign of Henry IV of England
1412?–1431	Life of Joan of Arc
1413–1422	Reign of Henry V of England
1415	Battle of Agincourt
1422–1461	Reign of Charles VII of France
1455–1485	War of the Roses in England

JUSTICE IN HISTORY

The Trial of Joan of Arc

After only fifteen months as the inspiration of the French army, Joan of Arc fell into the hands of the English, who brought her to trial for witchcraft. The English needed to stage a kind of show trial to demonstrate to their own demoralized forces that Joan's remarkable victories had been the result not of military superiority but rather of witchcraft. In the English trial, conducted at Rouen in 1431, Joan testified that her mission to save France was in response to voices she heard that commanded her to wear men's clothing. On the basis of this evidence of a confused or double gender identity, the ecclesiastical tribunal declared her a witch and a relapsed heretic. The court sentenced her to be burned at the stake.

Political motivations governed the 1431 English trial for witchcraft, but Joan's testimony provides some clues to her own identity conflicts. One of the most compelling questions arising from the trial is why the English tried Joan as a heretic in a church court rather than in a military one as a prisoner of war. The answer can be found in the two pieces of evidence against Joan that ultimately resulted in her condemnation: the spiritual "voices" she claimed to hear and her cross-dressing in men's clothing.

From the beginning of her emergence onto the political scene, Joan's voices intrigued all who came into contact with her. Joan claimed that she was guided by the voices of St. Catherine, St. Margaret, and the Archangel Michael. To Joan, these voices had the authority of divine commands. The problem the English judges faced was to demonstrate that the voices came not from God but from the Devil. If they could prove that, then they had evidence of witchcraft and sorcery. Following standard inquisitorial guidelines, the judges knew that authentic messages from God would always conform to church dogma. Any deviation from official doctrines would constitute evidence of demonic influence. Thus, during Joan's trial the judges demanded that she make theological distinctions that were alien to her. When they wanted to know if the voices were those of angels or saints, Joan seemed perplexed and responded, "This voice comes from God. . . I am more afraid of failing the voices by saying what is displeasing to them than answering you."[7] The judges kept pushing, asking if the saints or angels had heads, eyes, and hair. Exasperated, Joan simply replied, "I have told you often enough, believe me if you will."

The judges reformulated Joan's words to reflect their own rigid scholastic categories and concluded that her "veneration of the saints seems to partake of idolatry and to proceed from a pact made with devils. These are less divine revelations than lies invented by Joan, suggested or shown to her by the demon in illusive apparitions, in order to mock at her imagination while she meddled with things that are beyond her and superior to the faculty of her condition."[8] In other words, Joan was just too naive and uneducated to have authentic visions. But the English judges were on dangerous ground because during the previous fifty years there had been a number of notable female mystics, including the illiterate St. Catherine of Siena and St. Bridget of Sweden, whose visions had been accepted as authentic by the pope. The English could not take the chance that they were executing a real saint. They had to prove Joan was a witch by showing that her visions were theologically unsound. But that they could not do.

If they could not convict her for bad theology, the English needed evidence for superstitious practices. In an attempt to do that, they drew up seventy charges against her. Many of these consisted of allegations of performing magic, such as chanting spells, visiting a magical tree at night, and invoking demons. They attempted to prove bad behavior by insinuating that a young man had refused to marry her on account of her immoral life. They asserted that her godmother was a notorious witch who had taught her sorcery. None of these ploys worked, however, because Joan consistently denied these charges. She did, however, admit to one allegation: she cross-dressed as a man.

Some of the charges against her and many of the questions she was asked concerned how she dressed:

> *The said Joan put off and entirely abandoned women's clothes, with her hair cropped short and round in the fashion of young men, she wore shirt, breeches, doublet, with hose joined together, long and fastened to the said doublet by twenty points, long leggings laced on the outside, a short mantle reaching to the knee, or thereabouts, a close-cut cap, tight-fitting boots or buskins, long spurs, sword, dagger, breastplate, lance and other arms in the style of a man-at-arms.*[9]

The judges explained to her that "according to canon law and the Holy Scriptures" a woman dressing as a man or a man as a woman is "an abomination before God."[10] She replied simply

■ **Joan of Arc**

Joan of Arc appears before King Charles VII and his council. In this miniature taken from a chronicle of the period, Joan appears dressed in full armor and sword in the lower right corner. The label next to her knee reads, "La Pucelle," which means "The Young Girl." There are no contemporary portraits of Joan, and this image is clearly a generalized one of a young woman in armor rather than a portrait taken from the real Joan.

and consistently that "everything that I have done, I did by command of the voices" and that wearing male dress "would be for the great good of France."[11] When they asked her to put on a woman's dress in order to take the Eucharist on Easter Sunday, she refused, saying the miracle of the Eucharist did not depend on whether she wore a man's or a woman's clothing. On many occasions she had been asked to put on a woman's dress and refused. "And as for womanly duties, she said there were enough other women to do them."[12]

After a long imprisonment and psychological pressure from her inquisitors, Joan confessed to charges of witchcraft, signed a recantation of her heresy, and agreed to put on a dress. She was sentenced to life imprisonment on bread and water. Why did she confess? Some historians have argued that she was tricked into confessing because the inquisitors really wanted to execute her but could not do so unless she was a *relapsed* heretic. To be relapsed she had to confess and then somehow return to her heretical ways. If that was the inquisitors' intention, Joan soon obliged them. After a few days in prison, Joan threw off the women's clothes she had been given and resumed dressing as a man. As a witness put it, "The said Catherine and Margaret [instructed] this woman in the name of God to take and wear a man's clothes, and she had worn them and still wears them, stubbornly obeying the said command, to such an extent that this woman had declared she would rather die than relinquish these clothes."[13]

Joan was willing to be burned at the stake rather than dress as a woman. Why? Historians will never know for sure, but dressing as a man may have been necessary for her to fulfill her role as a military leader. The men who followed her into battle and trusted her voices accepted the necessity of this mutation of gender. In her military career, Joan had adopted the masculine qualities of chivalry: bravery, steadfastness, loyalty, and a willingness to accept pain and death. She made herself believable by dressing as a knight. A number of soldiers who had served with her testified that although they knew Joan was a woman, they had never felt any sexual desire for her, which suggests that she seemed androgynous to them. It was precisely Joan's gender ambiguity that the inquisitors found a dangerous sign of Satan's hand. And it was Joan's refusal to abandon her ambiguous gender identity that provided the inquisitors with the evidence they needed.

Joan's condemnation was much more than another example of men's attempt to control women. The inquisitors needed evidence of demonic influence, which to their minds Joan's transgressive gender behavior supplied. Joan's confused gender identity threatened the whole system of neat hierarchical distinctions upon which scholastic theology rested. To the theologians, everything in God's creation had its own proper place and anyone who changed his or her divinely ordained position in society presented a direct affront to God.

The English verdict and Joan's tragic fate greatly wounded French pride. In 1456 the French clergy reopened her case in a posthumous trial that sought to rehabilitate her in the eyes of the church. To these churchmen, she was an authentic visionary and a saint who listened to a direct command from God. To the French people ever since, she has become a national symbol of pride and of French unity against a foreign invader. In our own time, Joan has been characterized as many things—a saint, a madwoman, a female warrior, a woman exercising power in a male world, and a woman openly transgressing gender categories by dressing in men's clothes. ■

Questions of Justice

1. How did Joan's claim that she heard voices help her find her own voice and mission in life? Did she have any other way of finding her own voice and mission?
2. What motivated Joan? From our distant perspective, can we know her motivations?
3. In these ecclesiastical trials, what kinds of evidence were presented? What were the prosecutors trying to achieve by employing these kinds of evidence?

Taking It Further

Joan of Arc. *In Her Own Words*, trans. Willard Trask. 1996. The record of what Joan reputedly said at her trials.

Warner, Marina. *Joan of Arc: The Image of Female Heroism*. 1981. A highly readable feminist reading of the Joan of Arc story.

Infantry used a variety of weapons. The English demonstrated the effectiveness of longbowmen during the Hundred Years' War. Capable of shooting at a much more rapid rate than the French crossbowmen, the English longbowmen at Agincourt protected themselves behind a hurriedly erected stockade of stakes and rained a shower of deadly arrows on the French cavalry to break up charges. In the narrow battlefield, which was wedged between two forests, the French cavalry had insufficient room to maneuver, and when some of them dismounted to create more room, their heavy armor made them easy to topple over and spear through the underarm seam in their armor. Some infantry units deployed ranks of pikemen who created an impenetrable wall of sharp spikes.

The military revolution of the fourteenth and fifteenth centuries also introduced gunpowder to European warfare. Arriving from China with the Mongol invasions, gunpowder was first used in the West in artillery. Beginning in the 1320s huge wrought-iron cannons were used to shoot stone or iron against fortifications during sieges. By the early sixteenth century bronze muzzle-loading cannons were used in field battles. With the introduction during the late fifteenth century of the first handgun and the harquebus (a matchlock shoulder gun), properly drilled and disciplined infantrymen could deliver very destructive firepower. Gun shot pierced plate armor, whereas arrows bounced off. The slow rate of fire of these guns, however, necessitated carefully planned battle tactics. Around 1500 the Spanish introduced mixed infantry formations that pursued "shock" and "shot" tactics. Spanish pikemen provided the shock, which was quickly followed up by gun shot or missile fire. Spanish infantry formations were capable of defeating cavalry even in the open field without defensive fortifications, an unprecedented feat. By the end of the fifteenth century, trained infantry were necessary in every army.

The chivalric aristocrats, who made up the heavily armored cavalry forces and whose fighting ability justified their social privileges, tried to adapt to the changes by improving plate armor, employing longer lances, and drilling their horses for greater maneuverability. They were successful enough and retained enough political influence that heavy cavalry remained necessary in the professional armies that began to appear in the fifteenth century. However, the military revolution precipitated a major shift in European society as well as in battlefield tactics. The successful states were those that created the financial base and bureaucratic structures necessary to put into the field a well-trained professional army composed of infantry units and artillery. Armies now required officers who were capable of drilling infantry or understanding the science of warfare in order to serve as an artillery officer. The traditional landed aristocrats, accustomed to commanding armored knights, found that noble lineage was not as important as technical skills and talents.

The Culture of Loss

To the influential Dutch historian Johan Huizinga the culture of fourteenth- and fifteenth-century northern Europe conveyed a passionate intensity of life:

When the world was half a thousand years younger all events had much sharper outlines than now. The distance between sadness

Calamaties Stimulate Creative Literature
During the fourteenth and fifteenth centuries death was ever present, but some creative people responded by advocating social change. Here Christine De Pisan presents a copy of her poems to Isabeau of Bavaria, the wife of King Charles VI of France. Christine championed the cause of women in literary work.

and joy, between good and bad fortune, seemed to be much greater than for us; every experience had that degree of directness and absoluteness that joy and sadness still have in the mind of a child.[14]

This childlike, passionate intensity of life, according to Huizinga, derived from the omnipresence of violence and death. Suffering and death became a common theme in the arts, and strangely the subject matter for jokes, fancy-dress masquerades, and wild dances. The preoccupation with death revealed an anxious attachment to fleeting life.

This widespread anxiety had many manifestations. Some people sought escape from the terror. Aristocrats indulged in a beautiful fantasy life of gallant knights and beautiful ladies. Others went on long penitential pilgrimages to the shrines of saints or to the Holy Land. During the fourteenth century the tribulations of the pilgrim's travels became a metaphor for the journey of life itself, stimulating creative literature. Still others tried to find someone to blame for calamities. When no other explanation could be found, alleged witches became handy scapegoats. The search for scapegoats also focused on minority groups, especially Jews and Muslims.

Tomb Effigy of a Knight
This effigy above the tomb of Jean d'Alluy shows the deceased as if he were serenely sleeping, still dressed in the armor of his worldly profession.

Reminders of Death

In no other period of Western civilization has the idea of death constituted such a pervasive cultural theme as during the fourteenth and fifteenth centuries. The religious justification for this preoccupation was the Reminder of Death, a theme in a contemporary book of moral guidance advising the reader that "when he goes to bed, he should imagine not that he is putting himself to bed, but that others are laying him in his grave."[15] Reminders of Death became the everyday theme of preachers, and popular woodcuts represented death in simple but disturbing images. These representations emphasized the transitory nature of life, admonishing that every created thing perishes. The Reminder of Death tried to encourage ethical behavior in this life by showing that in everyone's future was neither riches, nor fame, nor love, nor pleasure, but only the decay of death.

The most macabre Reminder of Death was the Dance of Death. First appearing in a poem of 1376, the Dance of Death evolved into a street play, performed to illustrate sermons that called for repentance. It also appeared in church murals, depicting a procession led by a skeleton that included representatives of the social orders, from children and peasants to pope and emperor. All were being led to their inevitable deaths. At the Church of the Innocents in Paris, the mural depicting the Dance of Death is accompanied by an inscription that reads:

Advance, see yourselves in us, dead, naked, rotten and stinking. So will you be. . . . To live without thinking of this risks damnation. . . . Power, honor, riches are nothing; at the hour of death only good works count. . . . Everyone should think at least once a day of his loathsome end [in order to escape] the dreadful pain of hell without end which is unspeakable.[16]

In earlier centuries, tombs had depicted death as serene: On top of the tomb was an effigy of the deceased, dressed in the finest clothes with hands piously folded and eyes open to the promise of eternal life. In contrast, during the fourteenth century tomb effigies began to depict putrefying bodies or naked skeletons, symbols of the futility of human status and achievements. These tombs were disturbingly graphic Reminders of Death. Likewise, poems spoke of the putrid smell of rotting flesh, the livid color of plague victims, the cold touch of the dead. Preachers loved to personalize death. They would point to the most beautiful young woman in the congregation and describe how she would look while rotting in the grave, how worms would crawl through the empty sockets that once held her alluring eyes.

In reminding people of the need to repent their sins in the face of their inevitable deaths, no sin was more condemned than pride, the high opinion of one's own qualities and conduct. In contrast to modern times, when pride

Decomposing Cadaver
The tomb effigy of Jean de Lagrange.

is often understood as a virtue, late medieval moralists saw pride as an affront to God, a rejection of God's will that humanity should concentrate on spiritual rather than worldly things. Pride, in fact, was often discussed as the ultimate source of all the other deadly sins: lust, gluttony, avarice, sloth, wrath, and covetousness. The theme was encapsulated by the inscription on the tomb of a cardinal who died in 1402: "So, miserable one, what cause for pride?"[17]

Late medieval society was completely frank about the unpleasant process of dying, unlike modern societies that hide the dying in hospitals and segregate mourning to funeral homes. Dying was a public event, almost a theatrical performance. The last rites of the Catholic Church and the Art of Dying served to assist souls in their final test before God and to separate the departed from their kin. According to the Art of Dying, which was prescribed in numerous advice books and illustrations, the sick or injured person should die in bed, surrounded by a room full of people, including children. It was believed that a dying person watched a supernatural spectacle visible to him or her alone as the heavenly host fought with Satan and his demon minions for the soul. The Art of Dying compared the deathbed contest to a horrific game of chess in which the Devil did all he could to trap the dying person into a checkmate just at the moment of death. In the best of circumstances, a priest arrived in time to hear a confession, offer words of consolation, encourage the dying individual to forgive his or her enemies and redress any wrongs, and perform the last rites.

ILLUSIONS OF A NOBLE LIFE

Eventually death arrived for everyone, peasant and noble alike, a fact that the Reminders of Death were designed to keep foremost in the minds of all Christians. Some people, especially among the nobility, sought to ignore this funda-

Nobles Hunting
Nobles hunting deer with their ladies riding pillion. Hunts such as this one would have been a typical recreation of the dukes of Burgundy and their courtiers.

mental truth through escapist fantasies. These fantasies shielded nobles not only from the inevitability of death but also from all the other perils of the age—the worker and peasant rebellions, the economic depression that depleted their wealth, and the military revolution that challenged their monopoly on soldierly valor. As a result, the fantasy world of chivalry intensified. As discussed in Chapter 9, chivalric values among aristocratic knights and ladies emphasized honorable behavior and refined manners. During the Later Middle Ages, nobles indulged in chivalric escapism and idealized their class as the remedy for evil times. They thought God had placed them on earth to purify the world. Chivalry was an aesthetic ideal, a fantasy world of grace and beauty, that aspired to become an ethical ideal, a model for achieving virtue.

Much of the attraction of chivalry derived from its fanciful vision of the virtues of the ascetic life, the life that practices severe self-discipline and abstains from physical pleasures. The ideal medieval knight was as much a self-denying ascetic as the ideal medieval monk. The highest expression of the chivalric ideal was the knight-errant, a warrior who roamed in search of adventure. He was poor and free of ties to home and family, a man who lived a life of perfect freedom but whose virtue led him to do the right thing. In reality most knights were hardly ascetics but rich, propertied men who were completely involved in the world and who indulged in all of its pleasures.

The ideal of the ascetic knight-errant was pursued in an elaborately developed dream culture that occupied much of the time and cultural energy of the aristocracy. The French nobleman Philippe de Mézières (ca. 1327–1405), whose chivalric imagination knew no bounds, dreamed of establishing a new order of knights, the Order of the Passion, whose members would be spiritually removed from worldly affairs and devoted to reconquering the Holy Land. He drew up a plan for the order, but it never became a reality. He imagined that the knights in the Order of the Passion would peacefully end all wars among Christians and bind themselves together in a great crusade against the Mongols, Jews, Turks, and other Muslims. In reality, no serious crusade had been mounted since the failure of the Eighth Crusade in 1270. But several kings did found new crusading orders, which aristocrats joined with unbridled enthusiasm—the Order of the Garter in England, the Order of the Stars and Order of St. Michael in France, and the most fantastic of all, the Order of the Golden Fleece in Burgundy. Members of these orders indulged in extravagant acts of self-deprivation—for example, wearing fur coats in summer but refusing to wear a coat, hat, or gloves in freezing temperatures. They loved to take vows: One knight swore he would not sleep in a bed on Sundays until he had fought the Muslims; another took an oath that he would keep his right arm bare of any armor during battle with the Turks. None of these would-be crusaders came close to fighting Turks.

A Sumptuous Aristocratic Banquet

An aristocratic banquet with scenes of fighting in the background. Dining was the principal occasion at which nobles displayed refined manners showing their commitment to the beautiful life.

Many vows were taken in the name of ladies, revealing that the chivalric ideal also included a heavy dose of erotic desire. Besides ascetic self-denial, the most persistent chivalric fantasy was the motif of the young hero who liberates a virgin, either from a dragon or from a rioting mob of peasants. The myth of the noble knight suffering to save his beloved was the product of the male imagination, revealing how men wished to be admired in the eyes of women, but the myth has had a profound and lasting influence on Western culture.

The dream world of the noble life especially animated the duchy of Burgundy, a quasi-independent principality that paid nominal allegiance to the French king. Burgundy set the chivalric standards for all of Europe during the fifteenth century. Famous for his lavish life style, Duke Philip the Good (r. 1419–1467) was a notorious rake who seduced numerous noble ladies and produced many illegitimate children, but he also epitomized the ideals of chivalry in his love of horses, hunting, and court ceremonies. He was also an extravagant patron of the arts, which made him famous throughout Europe. Musicians, manuscript illuminators, painters, tapestry makers, and historians thrived with his support and made Burgundy the center of European aristocratic fashion.

The dukes of Burgundy sustained their power through their personal ties to the nobility and elites of the cities of their dominions. They were constantly on the move, visiting palaces, castles, and towns. They created a kind of theater state, staging elaborate entry ceremonies to the towns they visited; celebrating with fantastic splendor every event in the ducal family, such as marriages and births; entertaining the nobles with tournaments and the people with elaborate processions; and guaranteeing the loyalty of the nobles by inviting them to join the Order of the Golden Fleece, which occupied its members by training for a crusade.

Peasants and a Ducal Castle in Burgundy
Peasants sowing wheat and shearing sheep in the rich agricultural region that made possible the expensive court life of the duchy of Burgundy. One of the many great castles of the dukes appears in the background.

PILGRIMS OF THE IMAGINATION

During the Middle Ages, a pilgrimage offered a religiously sanctioned form of escape from the omnipresent suffering and peril. Pious Christians could go on a pilgrimage to the Holy Land, Rome, or the shrine of a saint, such as Santiago de Compostela in Spain or Canterbury in England. The usual motive for a pilgrimage was to fulfill a vow or promise made to God, or to obtain an indulgence, which exempted the pilgrim from some of the time spent in punishment in Purgatory after death. The pilgrimage became the instrument for spiritual liberation and escape from difficulties. As a result, going on a pilgrimage became a compelling model for creative literature, especially during the fourteenth century. Not all of these great works of literature were fictional pilgrimages, but many evoked the pilgrim's impulse to find a refuge from the difficulties of daily life or to find solace in the promise of a better life to come.

Dante Alighieri and *The Divine Comedy*

In *The Divine Comedy* the Italian poet from Florence, Dante Alighieri (1265–1321), imagined the most fantastic pilgrimage ever attempted, a journey through Hell, Purgatory, and Paradise. A work of astounding originality, *The Divine Comedy* remains the greatest masterpiece of medieval literature. Little is known about Dante's early life except that somehow he acquired an encyclopedic education that gave him expertise in Greek philosophy, scholastic theology (the application of logic to the understanding of Christianity; see Chapter 9), Latin literature, and the newly fashionable poetic forms in Provençal, the language of southern France. Dante was involved in the dangerous politics of Florence, which led to his exile under pain of death if he ever returned. During his exile Dante wandered for years, suffering grievously the loss of his home: "bitter is the taste of another man's bread and . . . heavy the way up and down another man's stair" (*Paradiso*, canto 17). While in exile, Dante sustained himself by writing his great poetic vision of human destiny and God's plan for redemption.

In the poem Dante himself travels into the Christian version of the afterlife, but the poetic journey displays numerous non-Christian influences. The passage through Hell, for example, derived from a long Muslim poem reconstructing Mohammed's *miraj*, a night journey to Jerusalem and ascent to heaven. Dante's poem can be read on many levels—personal, historical, spiritual, moral, theological—as it recounts an allegorical pilgrimage to visit the souls of the departed. Dante connects his personal suffering with

DANTE DESCRIBES HELL

In The Divine Comedy, *Dante imagined a series of circles in Hell into which were cast those guilty of a certain class of sin. In the eighth circle Dante and his guide Virgil came upon those guilty of fraud. They suffered for all eternity in the depths of stinking, filthy caverns in the ground. Dante and Virgil followed a path through Hell, and at this point the path led to a series of arches that spanned over the caverns.*

Here we heard people whine in the next chasm,
and knock and thump themselves with open palms,
and blubber through their snouts as if in a spasm.

Steaming from that pit, a vapor rose
over the banks, crusting them with a slime
that sickened my eyes and hammered at my nose.

That chasm sinks so deep we could not sight
its bottom anywhere until we climbed
along the rock arch to its greatest height.

Once there, I peered down; and I saw long lines
of people in a river of excrement
that seemed the overflow of the world's latrines.

I saw among the felons of that pit
one wraith who might or might not have been tonsured—
one could not tell, he was so smeared with shit.

He bellowed: "You there, why do you stare at me
more than at all the others in this stew?"
And I to him: "Because if memory

serves me, I knew you when your hair was dry.
You are Alessio Interminelli da Lucca.
That's why I pick you from this filthy fry."

And he then, beating himself on his clown's head:
"Down to this have the flatteries I sold
the living sunk me here among the dead."

And my Guide prompted then: "Lean forward a bit
and look beyond them, there—do you see that one
scratching herself with dungy nails, the strumpet

who fidgets to her feet, then to a crouch?
It is the whore Thais . . .

the historical problems of Italy, the warnings of the dead who had sinned in life, and the promise of rewards to those who had been virtuous. Dante's trip, initially guided by the Latin poet Virgil, the epitome of ancient wisdom, starts in Hell. While traveling deeper into its harsh depths, Dante is warned of the harmful values of this world by meeting a cast of sinful characters who inhabit the world of the damned. In Purgatory his guide becomes Beatrice, Dante's deceased beloved, who stands for the Christian virtues. In this section of the poem, he begins the painful process of spiritual rehabilitation where he comes to accept the Christian image of life as a pilgrimage. In Paradise he achieves spiritual fulfillment by speaking with figures from the past who have defied death.

The lasting appeal of this long, complex, and difficult poem is a wonder. Underlying the appeal of *The Divine Comedy* is perhaps its optimism, which expresses Dante's own cure to his depressing condition as an exile. The power of Dante's poetry established the form of the modern Italian language. Even in translation the images and stories can intrigue and fascinate.

Giovanni Boccaccio and *The Decameron*

Like Dante, Giovanni Boccaccio (1313–1375) was a Florentine. He grew up in a prosperous merchant banking family that was bankrupted during the Florentine financial crisis of the 1340s. Losing the shelter of economic and social privilege, Boccaccio's life became one of poverty and endless adversity. In the freedom from business responsibilities created by enforced poverty, Boccaccio turned to writing tales of chivalry and love, which were immediately very popular and had lasting influence on other writers.

After witnessing the ravages of the Black Death in Florence in 1348 and 1349, Boccaccio turned to polishing his masterpiece, *The Decameron*, a collection of 100 humorous, satirical, majestic, and sometimes pornographic stories. The book begins with a somber description of the social chaos created by the plague and tells how ten young people (seven women and three men) escaped the plague in Florence for a refuge in the country. *The Decameron* is less a story of a pilgrimage than the depiction of a refuge, but it is no less an escape from the cruel realities of the world. In their luxurious fantasy world of the country, each of the ten tells a story every night for ten nights. Displaying an open-minded attitude toward human weaknesses, *The Decameron* represents Boccaccio's initial response to the Black Death. Believing there was no future other than death, Boccaccio responded with a celebration of life in stories full of heroism, romance, unhappy love, wit, trickery, sexual license, and laughter. Although *The Decameron* was often read as escapist fantasy literature designed to lift the gloom of events, it was also a literary masterpiece that created a vivid, swift moving narrative.

Geoffrey Chaucer and *The Canterbury Tales*

Boccaccio profoundly influenced Geoffrey Chaucer (ca. 1342–1400), the most outstanding English poet prior to Shakespeare. As a courtier and diplomat, Chaucer was a trusted adviser to three successive English kings. But he is best known for his literary output, including *The Canterbury Tales*, which exhibit some of the same earthy humor and tolerance for human folly as *The Decameron*.

In *The Canterbury Tales* a group of some thirty pilgrims tell stories as they travel on horseback to the shrine at Canterbury. By employing the pilgrimage as a framing device for telling the stories, Chaucer was able to bring together a collection of people from across the social spectrum, including a wife, indulgence hawker, miller, town magistrate, clerk, landowner, lawyer, merchant, knight, abbess, and monk. The variety of characters who told the tales allowed Chaucer to experiment with many kinds of literary forms, from a chivalric romance to a sermon. The pilgrimage combined the considerations of religious morality with the fun of a spring vacation more concerned with the pleasures of this world than preparing for the next, which was the avowed purpose of going on a pilgrimage. In this intertwining of the worldly and the spiritual, Chaucer brought the abstract principles of Christian morality down to a level of common understanding.

Margery Kempe and the Autobiographical Pilgrimage

As the daughter of a town mayor, Margery Kempe (1373–1440) was destined for a comfortable life as a middle-class wife in provincial England. After her first child was born, however, she experienced a bout of depression during which she had a vision of Christ. Her failure in the brewery business (women dominated brewing in the Middle Ages) led to more visions and the calling to a spiritual life. As a married woman she could not become a nun, which would have been the normal course for a woman with her spiritual inclinations. Instead, she accepted her marital duties and bore fourteen children.

At the age of about 40 she persuaded her husband to join her in a mutual vow of chastity and embarked on her own religious vocation. Always a bit of an eccentric, Kempe became a fervent vegetarian at a time when meat was scarce but highly desired. She also developed an insatiable wanderlust, undertaking a series of pilgrimages to Jerusalem, Rome, Germany, Norway, Spain, and numerous places in England. On these pilgrimages she sought out mystics and recluses for their spiritual advice. Her own devotions took the form of loud weeping and crying, which alienated many people who feared she might be a heretic or a madwoman. Toward the end of her life she dictated an account of her difficult dealings with her husband, her spells of madness, her ecstatic visions, and her widespread travels as a pilgrim. For Kempe the actual experience of undertaking pilgrimages made it possible for her to examine the course of her own life, which she understood as a spiritual pilgrimage. Her *Book* (1436) was the earliest autobiography in English.

Christine De Pisan and Early Feminism

The work of the poet Christine De Pisan (1364–1430) was neither escapist like Giovanni Boccaccio's nor a spiritual pilgrimage like Margery Kempe's but a thoughtful and passionate commentary on the tumultuous issues of her day. At age 15 Christine married a notary of King Charles V of France, but by age 25 she was a widow with three young children. In order to support her family, she turned to writing and relied on the patronage of the royalty and wealthy aristocrats of France, Burgundy, Germany, and England, even though she continued to live in Paris.

Christine De Pisan was an early feminist who championed the cause of women in a male-dominated society that was often overtly hostile to them. Following the fashion of the times, she invented a new chivalric order, the Order of the Rose, whose members took a vow to defend the honor of women. She wrote a defense of women for a male readership and an allegorical autobiography. But she is most famous for the two books she wrote for women readers, *The Book of the City of Ladies* and *The Book of Three Virtues* (both about 1407). In these she recounted tales of the heroism and virtue of women and offered moral instruction for women in different social roles. In 1415 she retired to a convent where in the last year of her life she wrote a masterpiece of ecstatic lyricism that celebrated the early victories of Joan of Arc. Pisan's book turned the martyred Joan into a feminist heroine.

DEFINING CULTURAL BOUNDARIES

During the Later Middle Ages, systematic discrimination against certain ethnic and religious groups increased markedly in Europe. As European society enforced ever-higher levels of religious uniformity, intolerance spread in the ethnically mixed societies of the European periphery. Intolerance was marked in three especially troubled areas: Spain with its mixture of Muslim, Jewish, and Christian cultures; the German borderlands in east-central Europe, where Germans mingled with Slavs; and Ireland and Wales, where Celts came under the domination of the English. Within the heartland of Europe were other areas of clashing cultures—for example, Switzerland where the folk culture of peasants and shepherds living in the isolated mountains collided with the intense Christian religiosity of the cities.

During the eleventh and twelfth centuries, ethnic diversity had been more widely accepted. A Hungarian cleric wrote in an undated work from this period, "As immigrants come from various lands, so they bring with them various languages and customs, various skills and forms of armament, which adorn and glorify the royal household and quell the pride of external powers. A kingdom of one race and custom is weak and fragile."[18] By the fourteenth and fifteenth centuries, however, this optimistic celebration of diversity had faded. Ethnic discrimination and residential segregation created the first ghettos for ethnic and religious minorities.

Spain: Religious Communities in Tension

The Iberian peninsula was home to thriving communities of Muslims, Jews, and Christians. Since the eleventh century the aggressive northern Christian kingdoms of Castile and Aragon had engaged in a protracted program of Reconquest (*Reconquista*) against the Muslim states of the peninsula. By 1248 the Reconquest was largely completed, with only a small Muslim enclave in Granada holding out until 1492. The Spanish Reconquest placed former enemies in close proximity to one another. Hostilities between Christians and Muslims ranged from active warfare to tense stalemate, with Jews working as cultural intermediaries between the two larger communities.

During the twelfth and thirteenth centuries Muslims, called the Mudejars, who capitulated to the conquering Christians, received guarantees that they could continue to practice their own religion and laws. During the fourteenth century, however, Christian kings gradually reneged on these promises. In 1301 the king of Castile decreed that the testimony of any two Christian witnesses could convict a Jew or Muslim, notwithstanding any previously granted privileges that allowed them to be tried in their own courts. The Arabic language began to disappear in Spain as the Mudejars suffered discrimination on many levels. By the sixteenth century, the practice of Islam became illegal, and the Spanish state adopted a systematic policy to destroy Mudejar culture by prohibiting Muslim dress, customs, and marriage practices.

The Jews also began to feel the pain of organized, official discrimination. Christian preachers accused Jews of poisonings, stealing Christian babies, and cannibalism. When the Black Death arrived in 1348, the Jews of Aragon were accused of having poisoned the wells, even though Jews were dying just like Christians. Beginning in 1378, a Catholic prelate in Seville, Ferrant Martínez, commenced an anti-Jewish preaching campaign by calling for the destruction of all twenty-three of the city's synagogues, the confinement of Jews to a ghetto, the dislodging of all Jews from public positions, and the prohibition of any social contact between Christians and Jews. His campaign led to an attack on the Jews of Seville in 1391. Violence spread to other cities throughout the peninsula and the nearby Balearic Islands. Jews were given a stark choice: conversion or death. After a year of mob violence, about 100,000 Jews had been murdered and an equal number had gone into hiding or fled to more tolerant Muslim countries. The 1391 pogroms led to the first significant forced conversions of Jews in Spain. A century later in 1492, on the heels of the final Christian victory of the Reconquest, all remaining Jews in Spain were compelled to either leave or convert.

German and Celtic Borderlands: Ethnic Communities in Tension

Other regions with diverse populations also witnessed discrimination and its brutal consequences. During the population boom of the twelfth and thirteenth centuries, German-speaking immigrants had established colonial towns in the Baltic and penetrated eastward, creating isolated pockets of German culture in Bohemia, Poland, and Hungary. During the fourteenth and fifteenth centuries, the bias of native populations against the colonizing Germans was manifest in various ways. One Czech prince offered 100 silver marks to anyone who brought him 100 German noses. The German settlers exhibited a similar intolerance of the natives. The Teutonic Knights, who had been the vanguard of the German migrations in the Baltic, began to require German ancestry for membership. In German-speaking towns along the colonized borderlands of east-central Europe, city councils and guilds began to restrict by ethnicity the qualification for holding certain offices or joining a guild. The most famous example was the "German Paragraph" in guild statutes, which required candidates for admission to a guild to prove German descent. As the statutes of a bakers' guild put it, "Whoever wishes to be a member must bring proof to the councillors and the guildsmen that he is born of legitimate, upright German folk." Others required members to be "of German blood and tongue," as if language were a matter of biological inheritance.[19] German guildsmen were also forbidden to marry non-Germans.

A similar process of exclusion occurred in the Celtic fringe of the British Isles. In Ireland the ruling English promulgated laws that attempted to protect the cultural identity of the English colonists. The English prohibited native Irish from citizenship in town or guild membership. The Statutes of Kilkenny of 1366 attempted to legislate ethnic purity: They prohibited intermarriage between English and Irish; they required English colonists to speak English, use English names, wear English clothes, and ride horses in the English way; and they forbade the English to play Irish games or listen to Irish music. The aggressive legislation of the English in Ireland was essentially defensive. The tiny English community was attempting to prevent its absorption into the majority culture. A similar pattern appeared in Wales, where the lines dividing the Welsh and English communities hardened during the fourteenth century.

Enemies Within

The Black Death and its aftermath transformed many segments of Europe into a persecuting society. The year 1348 represented a watershed; in the period that followed, vague biases and dislikes sharpened into systematic violence against minorities. The plague sparked assaults against lepers, people with handicaps and physical deformities, beggars, vagabonds, foreigners, priests, pilgrims, Muslims, and Jews. Anyone who looked strange, dressed differently, spoke with an accent, practiced a minority religion, or did not fit in was vulnerable to becoming a scapegoat for the miseries of others. Minorities took the blame for calamities that could not be otherwise explained.

Violence against minorities occurred in many places, but it was most systematic in German-speaking lands. Between November 1348 and August 1350, violence against Jews occurred in more than eighty German towns. Like the allegations in Aragon, the fear that Jews poisoned the wells led to massacres in German lands even *before* plague had arrived in these communities. The frequent occurrence of violence on Sundays or feast days suggests that preachers consciously or unconsciously encouraged the rioting mobs.

The troubles caused by the Great Schism (1378–1417, when there was more than one pope) also contributed to a heightened sensitivity to cultural differences. During the Council of Basel (1431–1449), German bishops and theologians in attendance began to exchange information about cases of alleged witchcraft they had heard about in the nearby Swiss Alps. What these learned priests and friars thought of as witchcraft was probably nothing more than harmless folk magic, but to them the strange details of peasant behavior seemed evidence of a vast Satanic conspiracy to destroy Christianity. For most of its history, the Catholic Church had denied that witchcraft existed, but the terrible events of the fourteenth century cried out for explanation. In 1484 Pope Innocent VIII changed official Catholic policy by calling upon two Dominican professors of theology to examine the alleged spread of witchcraft in Germany. As a guide to witch hunters, they wrote a detailed handbook on witchcraft, *The Hammer of Witches*, which went through twenty-eight editions between 1486 and 1600, evidence of its enormous success and influence.

The Hammer of Witches codified the folklore of the Alpine peasants as the basis for witchcraft practices. The book condemned as heretics those who disbelieved in the power of witches and established legal procedures for the prosecution of witches. It sanctioned torture as the most effective means for obtaining confessions, and it established much lower standards of evidence than in other kinds of cases. As an anthology of mythical stories about the activities of supposed witches, *The Hammer* summed up the worst of prevailing attitudes about women: "all witchcraft comes from carnal lust, which in women is insatiable." As we shall see in Chapter 14, most witchcraft persecutions came later in the sixteenth and seventeenth centuries, but the publication of *The Hammer of Witches* represented the culmination of the frenzied search to find enemies within European society, which was quickened by the events of the fourteenth and fifteenth centuries. With the dissemination of the idea of the reality of witchcraft, virtually anyone could be hauled before a court on charges of maintaining a secret liaison with Satan.

ANTI-GERMAN BIAS

The language of intolerance tends to borrow from a very limited repertoire of negative stereotypes. As a result, biased ideas have little if any relationship to reality. In this tract from fourteenth-century Bohemia, the Czech author applied to the hated German minority the very same stereotypes that Germans used against Jews. The author asserts that God had singled out the Germans to be a slave race, but they had usurped land and wealth of others. This tract called on Czechs to launch an anti-German pogrom.

The wise man should observe and the prudent man consider how this crafty and deceitful race has intruded itself into the most fertile prebends [church lands], the best fiefs [noble lands], the richest possessions, even into the prince's council. . . the sons of this race enter into the lands of others. . . . thus they plunder and devastate all lands; thus enriched they begin to oppress their neighbors and rebel against the princes and their other proper lords. Thus did Judas and Pilate behave. No one with any experience doubts that the Germans are wolves in the flock, flies in the food, serpents in the lap, whores in the house. . . .

It would be profitable, just and customary if the bear stayed in the wood, the fox in his den, the fish in water and the German in Germany. The world was healthy when the Germans were placed as a target for the arrow—in one place eyes were torn out, in another they were hung up by the foot, in one place they were thrown outside the walls, in another they gave their nose as a toll payment, in one place they were killed peremptorily in the sight of the princes, in another they were forced to eat their own ears, in one place they were punished one way and in another in a different way.

Source: From "De Theutonicis bonum dictamen" as quoted in Robert Bartlett, *The Making of Europe: Conquest, Colonization and Cultural Change, 950–1350*. Copyright 1993 by Robert Bartlett. Reprinted by permission of Princeton University Press.

CONCLUSION
Looking Inward

Unlike the more dynamic, outward-looking thirteenth century, Europeans during the fourteenth and early fifteenth centuries turned their attention inward to their own communities and their own problems. Europe faced one calamity after another, each crisis compounding the misery. In the process the identity of the West became more defensive and the fragility of Christianity itself was laid bare. The process of changing Western identities can be seen in two ways. First, as a result of the Western encounters with the Mongol and Ottoman Empires, the political and religious frontiers of the West shifted. These two empires redrew the map of the West by ending the Christian Byzantine Empire and by leaving Christian Russia on the margins of the West. With the Mongol invasions, the eastward spread of Christianity into Asia ended. The Ottoman conquests left a lasting Muslim influence inside eastern Europe, particularly in Bosnia and Albania. Peoples who were predominantly Christian and whose political institutions were a heritage of the ancient Roman Empire now survived under the domination of Asiatic empires and in a tenuous relationship with the rest of the Christian West. Most of the new subjects of these empires remained Christian, but their Mongol and Ottoman masters destroyed their political autonomy. The Ottoman Empire remained hostile to and frequently at war with the Christian West for more than 200 years.

Second, in western Europe people reinforced their identity as Christians and became more self-conscious of the country in which they lived. At the same time Christian civilization was becoming eclipsed in parts of eastern Europe, however, it revived in the Iberian peninsula where the Muslim population, once the most extensive in the West, suffered discrimination and defeat. The northern Spanish kingdoms, for example, began to unify their subjects around a militant form of Christianity that was overtly hostile to Muslims and Jews. In many places in the West, religious and ethnic discrimination against minorities increased. A stronger sense of self-identification by country can be most dramatically seen in France and England as a consequence of the Hundred Years' War. The French rallied around a saintly national heroine, Joan of Arc. After dropping claims to France after the Hundred Years' War, the English aristocracy stopped speaking French and adopting the customs of the French court. They became less international and more English. The Western countries became more self-consciously characterized by an attitude of "us" versus "them."

Except for the very visible military conquests of the Mongols and the Ottomans, the causes of most of the calamities of the fourteenth century were invisible or unknown. No one recognized a climate change or understood the dynamics of the population crisis. No one could see the plague bacillus. No one grasped the role of the Mongol Empire in the world economy or the causes for the collapse of banking and trade. Unable to distinguish how these forces were changing their lives, western Europeans only witnessed their consequences. In the face of these calamities, European culture became obsessed with death and with finding scapegoats to blame for events that could not be otherwise explained. However, calamity also bred creativity, manifest in the passionate intensity of life. The search for answers to the question, "Why did this happen to us?" produced a new spiritual sensibility and a rich literature. Following the travails of the fourteenth century, moreover, there arose in the fifteenth a new, more optimistic cultural movement—the Renaissance. Gloom and doom was not the only response to troubles. During the Renaissance some people began to search for new answers to human problems in a fashion that would transform the West anew.

Suggestions for Further Reading

For a comprehensive list of suggested readings, please go to www.ablongman.com/levack/chapter10

Duby, Georges. *France in the Middle Ages, 987–1460: From Hugh Capet to Joan of Arc.* 1991. Traces the emergence of the French state.

Gordon, Bruce, and Peter Marshall, eds. *The Place of the Dead: Death and Remembrance in Late Medieval and Early Modern Europe.* 2000. A collection of essays that shows how the placing of the dead in society was an important activity that engendered considerable conflict and negotiation.

Herlihy, David. *The Black Death and the Transformation of the West.* 1997. A pithy, readable analysis of the epidemiological and historical issues surrounding the Black Death.

Holmes, George. *Europe: Hierarchy and Revolt, 1320–1450.* 1975. Excellent examination of rebellions.

Huizinga, Johan. *The Autumn of the Middle Ages*, trans. Rodney J. Payton and Urlich Mammitzsch. 1996. A new translation of the classic study of France and the Low Countries during the fourteenth and fifteenth century. Dated and perhaps too pessimistic, Huizinga's lucid prose and broad vision still make this an engaging reading experience.

Imber, Colin. *The Ottoman Empire, 1300–1481.* 1990. The basic work that establishes a chronology for the early Ottomans.

Lambert, Malcolm. *Medieval Heresy: Popular Movements from the Gregorian Reform to the Reformation.* 1992. Excellent general study of the Hussite and Lollard movements.

Le Roy Ladurie, Emmanuel. *Times of Feast, Times of Famine: A History of Climate since the Year 1000*, trans. Barbara Bray. 1971. The book that introduced the idea of the Little Ice Age and promoted the study of the influence of climate on history.

Lynch, Joseph H. *The Medieval Church: A Brief History.* 1992. A pithy, elegant survey of ecclesiastical institutions and developments.

Morgan, David O. *The Mongols.* 1986. Best introduction to Mongol history.

Nirenberg, David. *Communities of Violence: Persecution of Minorities in the Middle Ages.* 1996. An important analysis of the persecution of minorities that is deeply rooted in Spanish evidence.

Sumption, Jonathan. *The Hundred Years' War: Trial by Battle.* 1991. First volume goes only to 1347. When it is completed it will be the best comprehensive study.

Swanson, R. N. *Religion and Devotion in Europe, c. 1215–c. 1515.* 1995. The best up-to-date textbook account of late medieval religious practice.

Notes

1. Quoted in Emmanuel Le Roy Ladurie, *Times of Feast, Times of Famine: A History of Climate since the Year 1000*, trans. Barbara Bray (1971), 47.
2. Quoted in William Bowsky, "The Impact of the Black Death," in Anthony Molho, ed., *Social and Economic Foundations of the Italian Renaissance* (1969), 92.
3. Giovanni Boccaccio, *The Decameron*, trans. Richard Aldington (1962), 30.
4. Ibid.
5. Cited in Philip Ziegler, *The Black Death* (1969), 20.
6. Quoted in Mark C. Bartusis, *The Late Byzantine Army: Arms and Society, 1204–1453* (1992), 133.
7. Trial record as quoted in Marina Warner, *Joan of Arc* (1981), 122.
8. Ibid., 127.
9. Ibid., 143.
10. *The Trial of Joan of Arc*, trans. W. S. Scott (1956), 134.
11. Ibid., 106.
12. Ibid., 135.
13. Warner, *Joan of Arc*, 145.
14. Johan Huizinga, *The Autumn of the Middle Ages*, trans. Rodney J. Payton and Ulrich Mammitzsch (1996), 1.
15. Ibid., 156.
16. Quoted in Barbara W. Tuchman, *A Distant Mirror: The Calamitous 14th Century* (1978), 505–506. Translation has been slightly modified by the authors.
17. Ibid., 506
18. *Libellus de institutione morum*, ed. J. Balogh, *Scriptores rerum Hungaricarum 2* (1938), 625. Quoted in Robert Bartlett, trans., *The Making of Europe: Conquest, Colonization and Cultural Change 950–1350* (1993), 239.
19. *Codex diplomaticus Brandenburgensis*, ed. Adolph Friedrich Riedel (41 vols., 1838–1869), 365–367. Cited in Bartlett, *The Making of Europe*, 238.

CHAPTER 11

The Italian Renaissance and Beyond: The Politics of Culture, 1350–1550

Chapter Outline

- The Cradle of the Renaissance: The Italian City-States
- The Influence of Ancient Culture
- Antiquity and Nature in the Arts
- The Early Modern European State System

For fifteen years Niccolò Machiavelli worked as a diplomat and political adviser, a man always at the center of the action in his hometown of Florence. But in 1512 there was a change of regimes in the city-state of Florence. Distrusted by the new rulers and suspected of involvement in an assassination plot, he was abruptly fired from his job, imprisoned, tortured, and finally ordered to stay out of town. Exiled to his suburban farm, impoverished, and utterly miserable, Machiavelli survived by selling lumber from his wood lot to his former colleagues, who regularly cheated him. To help feed his family he snared birds; to entertain himself he played cards in a local inn with the innkeeper, a butcher, a miller, and two bakers. As he put it, "caught this way among these lice I wipe the mold from my brain [by playing cards] and release my feeling of being ill-treated by Fate."

In the evenings, however, Machiavelli transformed himself into an entirely different person. He entered his study, removed his mud-splattered clothes, and put on the elegant robes he had once worn as a government official. And then, "dressed in a more appropriate manner I enter into the ancient courts of ancient men and am welcomed by them kindly." Machiavelli was actually reading the works of the ancient Greek and Latin historians, but he described his evening reading as a conversation: He asked the ancients about the reasons for their actions, and in reading their books he found answers. For four hours, "I feel no boredom, I dismiss every affliction, I no longer fear poverty nor do I tremble at the thought of death: I become completely part of them."[1]

Machiavelli's evening conversations with the long-dead ancients perfectly expressed the sensibility of the Italian Renaissance. This wretched man, disillusioned with his own times and bored by his empty-headed neighbors, found in the ancients the stimulating companions he could not find in life. For him the

The Birth of Venus: Sandro Botticelli's depiction of the birth of the ancient goddess of love exemplifies the Renaissance fascination with the culture of antiquity.

ancient past was more alive than the present. And in this sense Machiavelli was very much a Renaissance man, because feeling part of antiquity is what the Renaissance is all about. For those who were captivated by it, the ancient past and the examples of leadership and beauty it offered seemed to be a cure for the ills of a decidedly troubled time.

As we saw in Chapter 10, during the fourteenth and fifteenth centuries Europeans experienced a prevailing sense of loss, a morbid preoccupation with death, and a widespread pessimism about the human capacity for good. Yet in Florence during this same period a cultural movement began to express a more optimistic view of life. We now call that movement the Renaissance. The new optimism emerged from the desire to improve the human condition during times of trouble, and that desire was first manifest in the intellectually free environment of the independent city-states of Italy. Machiavelli—despite the bleak circumstances of his later life—was one of the Renaissance thinkers who thought the world could be improved. He strongly believed that human virtue derived from a blend of learning and political action, and in this respect he differed from the medieval writers who thought the contemplative life of the monk was the highest calling to which a man could aspire. The Renaissance was born and developed because the political structures of the Italian city-states encouraged cultural experimentation and fostered the idea that society could be reengineered according to the principles that made ancient Greece and Rome great.

The word Renaissance°, which means "rebirth," is a term historians invented to describe a movement that sought to imitate and understand the culture of antiquity. The fundamental Renaissance principle was the need to keep everything in balance and proportion, an aesthetic ideal derived from ancient literature. In political theory, this meant building a stable society upon the foundations of well-balanced individuals who conformed to a rigorous code of conduct. In the arts it meant searching for the underlying harmonies in nature, which typically meant employing geometry and the mathematics of proportion in drawing, painting, sculpting, and designing buildings. Renaissance artists thought geometry unlocked the secrets of nature and revealed the hidden hand of God in creation.

As we have seen in Chapters 8 and 9, the Italian Renaissance was not the first time the West experienced a revival of ancient learning and thought. In the Carolingian Renaissance of the ninth century, members of the Emperor Charlemagne's court reinvigorated education in Latin. And the European-wide Renaissance of the twelfth century led to the foundation of the universities, the reintroduction of Roman law, and the spread of scholastic philosophy and theology. The Renaissance considered in this chapter refers to a diffuse cultural movement that occurred at different times in different regions, and as a result its dates are very approximate. Most historians date the movement from about 1350 to 1550.

The Renaissance helped refashion the concept of Western civilization. From the fifth to the fourteenth centuries, the West identified itself primarily through conformity to Roman Catholicism, which meant the celebration of uniform religious rituals in Latin and obedience to the pope. The Renaissance added a new element to this identity. Although by no means anti-Christian, Renaissance thinkers began to think of themselves as the heirs of pre-Christian cultures—Hebrew, Greek, and Roman. In this sense, they began to imagine a Western civilization that was more than just Christian.

Through reading the texts and viewing the works of art of the long-dead ancients, people during the Renaissance gained historical and visual perspective on their own world and cultivated a critical attitude. To understand what was distinctive about their insights, this chapter will address four questions. (1) In what ways did the political and social climate peculiar to the Italian city-states help create Renaissance culture? (2) How did Renaissance thinkers create historical perspective and devise methods of criticism for interpreting texts? (3) How did various attempts to imitate antiquity in the arts alter perceptions of nature? (4) How did the monarchies of western Europe gather the strength to become more assertive and more effective?

The Cradle of the Renaissance: The Italian City-States

In comparison with the rest of Europe and other world civilizations, Renaissance Italy was distinguished by the large number and political autonomy of its thriving city-states. The Netherlands and parts of the Rhine Valley were as thoroughly urbanized, but only in Italy did cities have so much political power. The evolution of the Italian city-states can be encapsulated into two distinct phases.

The first phase in the evolution of the Italian city-states occurred during the eleventh and twelfth centuries. As we saw in Chapter 8, during this period about one hundred Italian towns became independent republics, also known as communes, and developed the laws and institutions of self-government. The male citizens of these tiny republics gathered on a regular basis in the town square to debate important issues such as assessing new taxes, improving the city walls, or going to war. To conduct the day-to-day business of government, they elected city officials from among themselves.

The governmental practices of these city-states produced the political theory of republicanism°, which described a state in which government officials were elected by the people or a portion of the people. The Renaissance theory of republicanism was first articulated by Marsilius of Padua (1270–1342) in *The Defender of the Peace,* a book that relied on the precedents established by the ancient Roman republic as a source of theory for the Italian Renaissance republics. Marsilius recognized two kinds of government—principalities and republics. Principalities relied upon the descending principle that political authority came directly from God and trickled down through kings and princes to the rest of humanity. According to this principle, the responsibility of government was to enforce God's laws. Marsilius, however, rejected the idea that the task of the political world was to express the will of God. His ascending principle of republicanism suggested that laws derive not from God but from the will of the people, who freely choose their own form of government and who are equally free to change it. In Marsilius's theory, citizens regularly expressed their will through voting. The first phase in the evolution of the Italian city-states established the institutions of self-government, the procedures for electing officials, and the theory of republicanism.

In the second phase of evolution, which occurred during the fourteenth century, most city-states abandoned or lost their republican institutions and came to be ruled by princes. The reasons for the transformation of these republics into principalities were related to the economic and demographic turmoil created by the international economic collapse and the Black Death. Two of the largest republics, however, did not go through this second phase and survived without losing their liberty to a prince. The Renaissance began in these two city-states, Florence and Venice (see Map 11.1). Their survival as republics, which made them exceptions to the rule by the fifteenth century, helps explain the origins of the Renaissance.

THE RENAISSANCE REPUBLICS: FLORENCE AND VENICE

In an age of despotic princes, Florence and Venice were keenly aware of how different they were from other cities, and they feared they might suffer the same fate as their neighbors if they did not defend their republican institutions and liberty. In keeping alive the traditions of republican self-government, these two cities created an environment of competition and freedom that stimulated creative ingenuity. Although neither of these cities were democracies, nor were they particularly egalitarian, they were certainly more open to new ideas than cities ruled by princes. In both Florence and Venice, citizens prized discussion and debate, the skills necessary for success in business and politics. By contrast, in the principalities all cultural activity tended to revolve around and express the tastes of the prince, who monopolized much of the wealth. In Florence and Venice a few great families called the *patriciate* controlled most of the property, but these patricians competed among themselves to gain recognition and fame by patronizing great artists and scholars. This patronage by wealthy men and women made the Renaissance possible. And because the tastes of these patricians dictated what writers and artists could do, understanding who they were helps explain Renaissance culture.

Florence Under the Medici

The greatest patron during the early Renaissance was the fabulously rich Florentine banker Cosimo de' Medici (1389–1464). Based on his financial power, Cosimo effectively took control of the Florentine republic in 1434, ushering in a period of unprecedented domestic peace and

Map 11.1 Northern Italy in the Mid-Fifteenth Century

During the Renaissance the largest city-states, such as Milan, Venice, and Florence, gained control of the surrounding countryside and smaller cities in the vicinity, establishing regional territorial states. Only Venice and Florence remained republics. Milan and Savoy were ruled by dukes. The Gonzaga family ruled Mantua and the Este Modena and Ferrara. The states of the Church were ruled by the pope in Rome.

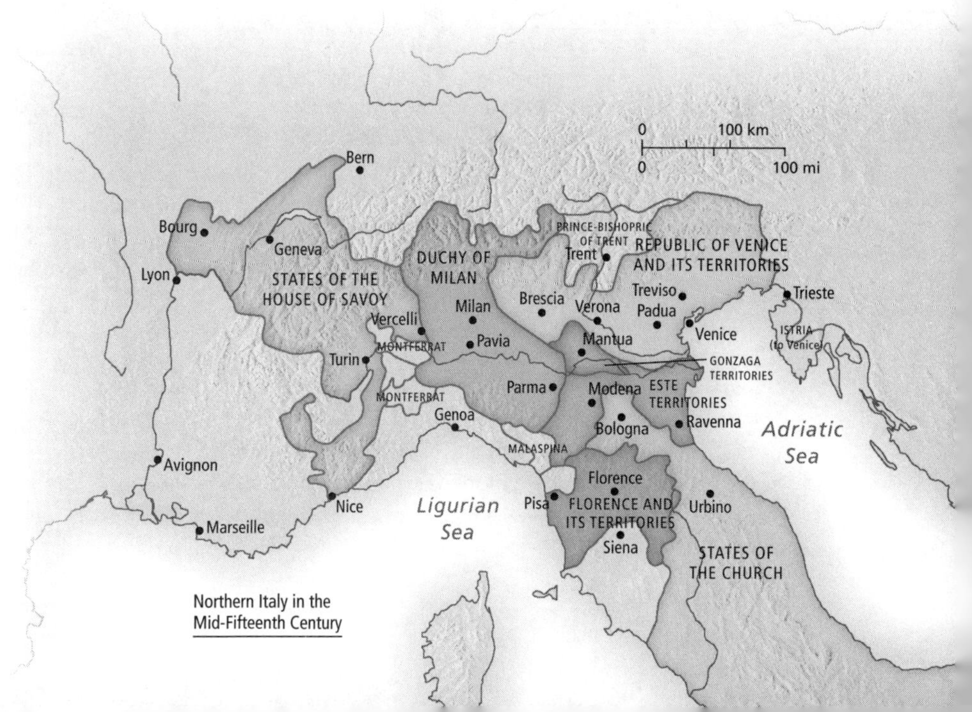

artistic splendor called the Medicean Age (1434–1494). Cosimo's style of rule was exceedingly clever. Instead of making himself a prince, which the citizens of Florence would have opposed, he managed the policies of the republic from behind the scenes. He seldom held public office, but he made himself the center of Florentine affairs through shrewd negotiating, the quiet fixing of elections, and the generous distribution of bribes, gifts, and jobs. Cosimo's behind-the-scenes rule illustrated a fundamental value of Renaissance culture—the desire to maintain appearances. In this case, the appearance of the Florentine republic was saved, even as the reality of Florentine liberty was subverted.

Cosimo's brilliant patronage of intellectuals and artists mirrored a similar ambition to maintain appearances. It helped make Cosimo appear a pious, generous man who modeled himself after the great statesmen of the ancient Roman republic. Cosimo appreciated intelligence and merit wherever he found it. He frequented the discussions of prominent scholars, some of whom became his lasting friends. Intrigued by what he learned from them, he personally financed the search for and acquisition of manuscripts of ancient Latin and Greek literature and philosophy for new libraries he helped establish. In return for his financial support, many Florentine scholars dedicated their works to Cosimo. He took particular interest in the revival of the ancient Greek philosopher Plato, and he set up the neo-Platonic philosopher Marsilio Ficino (1433–1499) with a house and steady income.

Cosimo's most significant patronage of the arts clustered in the neighborhood where he lived. He rebuilt the nearby monastery of San Marco. He personally selected Fra Angelico, a monk, to paint the austere yet deeply emotive frescoes throughout the monastery. As the centerpiece of his neighborhood beautification plans, Cosimo built for his own family a magnificent new palace, which he filled with innumerable objects of beauty and exquisite paintings.

Cosimo's artistic patronage helped create the image of a man who was an open-handed and benevolent godfather for his community. Since Cosimo had not been elected to rule Florence, his political influence was illegitimate and he needed to find a way to create a proper image that would justify his power. To do that he decorated the private chapel in his palace with frescoes that depicted him accompanying the magi, the wise men or kings who brought gifts to the baby Jesus. Thus, Cosimo made himself appear similar to those ancient kings who first recognized the divinity of Christ. By having himself depicted with the magi, Cosimo created an image that helped justify the fact that he controlled elections and dictated policies.

Cosimo's grandson Lorenzo the Magnificent (r. 1469–1492) expanded the family's dominance in Florentine politics through what has been called "veiled lordship." Lorenzo never took the title of prince but behaved very much like

COSIMO DE' MEDICI'S REPUTATION

Among the common genres of writing during the Renaissance were short biographies of illustrious men and women. Vespasiano da Bisticci's Lives of Illustrious Men *imitated the model of ancient biographies and was based on Vespasiano's personal recollections of many of his subjects. The owner of a bookshop that for many years served as a meeting place for learned men in Florence, Vespasiano knew and admired Cosimo de' Medici. In this example, Vespasiano recalls Cosimo's own views about his role as a patron.*

I once heard Cosimo say that the great mistake of his life was that he did not begin to spend his wealth ten years earlier; because, knowing well the disposition of his fellow-citizens, he was sure that, in the lapse of fifty years, no memory would remain of his personality or of his house save the few buildings he might have built. He went on, "I know that after my death my children will be in worse situation than those of any other Florentine who has died for many years past; moreover, I know I shall not wear the crown of laurel [a reference to an ancient sign of honor] more than any other citizen." He spoke like this because he knew the difficulty of ruling a state as he had ruled Florence, through the opposition of influential citizens who had rated themselves his equals in former times. He acted privately with the greatest discretion in order to safeguard himself, and whenever he sought to achieve something he tried to let it appear that the matter had been set in motion by someone else and thus he escaped envy and unpopularity. His manner was admirable; he never spoke ill of anyone, and it angered him greatly to hear slander spoken by others. He was kind and patient to all who sought a word with him: he was more a man of deeds than of words: he always did what he promised, and when this had been done he sent a message to let the petitioner know that his wishes had been granted. His replies were brief and sometimes obscure, so that they might be made to bear a double meaning.

Source: From Vespaniano, *Renaissance Princes, Popes, and Prelates,* translated by William George and Emily Waters, Harper Torchbooks, 1963. First English translation published by George Routledge & Sons, Ltd., London, 1926.

one by intervening publicly in the affairs of the state. In contrast to his grandfather's commitment to public patronage, Lorenzo's interest in the arts concentrated on building private villas, collecting precious gems, and commissioning small bronze statues, the kinds of things that gave him private pleasure rather than a public reputation. A fine poet and an intellectual companion of the most renowned scholars of his age, Lorenzo created a lasting reputation as a well-rounded, accomplished Renaissance man, but his princely style of rule, which ignored the republican sensibilities of the Florentines, created discontent and undermined public support for the Medicis. There were several conspiracies against him; during an attempted assassination of Lorenzo, his brother Giuliano was killed.

During the fifteenth century Florence became the first society that dedicated itself to the production and appreciation of what we now call Renaissance culture. As a republic on the perilous edge of financial survival, Florence had surrendered the behind-the-scenes rule to the Medici family, who supported a movement in philosophy and the arts that, as we shall see, imitated and celebrated the heritage of pre-Christian antiquity, especially the culture of Greece and Rome.

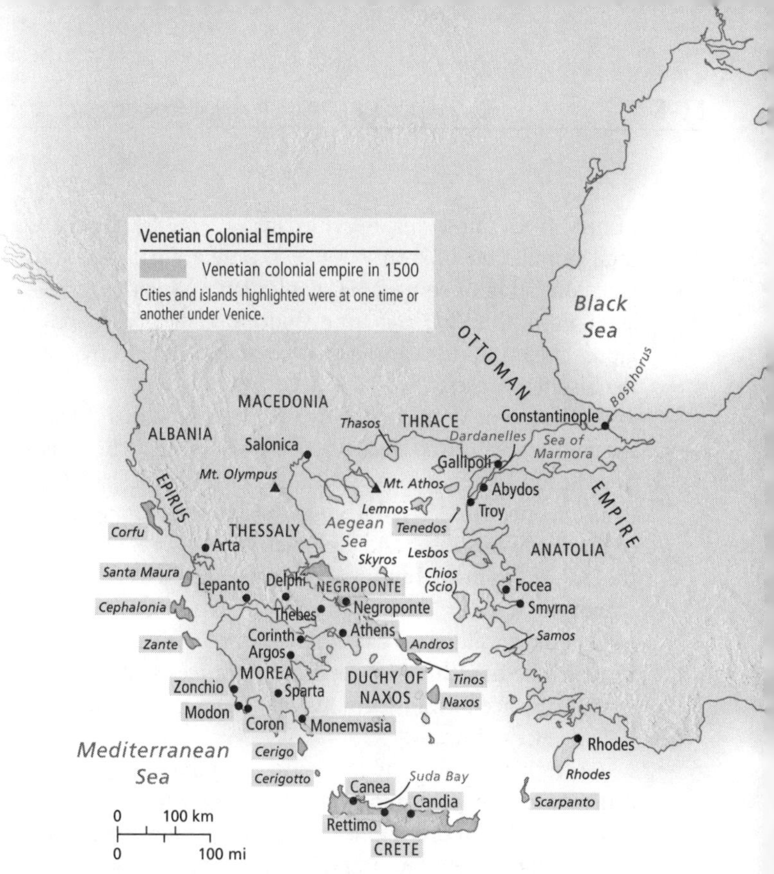

Map 11.2 Venetian Colonial Empire
The Venetian colonies included the Greek-speaking islands in the Adriatic and a number of important islands in the Aegean. These colonies were threatened by the Ottoman Empire with its capital in Constantinople.

Venice, the Cosmopolitan Republic

Venice resembled Florence in that it survived into the Renaissance period with its republican institutions intact, but it was far more politically stable. Situated in the midst of a vast lagoon, Venice's streets consisted of broad channels in which great seagoing merchant ships were moored and small canals choked with private gondolas for local transportation. To protect their fragile city from flooding, the Venetians recognized that they had to cooperate among themselves, and thus the imperative for survival helped create a republic that became a model of stability and ecological awareness. The Venetians, for example, created the world's first environmental regulatory agencies, which were responsible for hydrological projects, such as dikes and dredging canals, and for forestry management to prevent soil erosion and the consequent silting up of the lagoon.

Venice was among the first European powers to have colonies abroad. To guarantee its merchant ships access to the eastern Mediterranean and Constantinople, Venice conquered a series of ports, including a significant number in Greece (see Map 11.2). Its involvement in international trade and governing distant colonies made Venice unusually cosmopolitan. Many Venetian merchants spent years living abroad and some settled in the colonies. Moreover, people from all over Europe flocked to the city of Venice—Germans, Turks, Armenians, Albanians, Greeks, Slovenes, Croats, and Jews—each creating their own neighborhood communities and institutions. Venetian households owned Russian, Asian, Turkish, and African slaves, all of whom contributed to the remarkable diversity of the city.

Of the many foreign groups in Venice, the most influential were the Greeks. Venice had long maintained close commercial and cultural ties with the Greek world. Its churches were modeled after the huge basilicas of Constantinople, and many Venetian merchants spoke Greek. After the fall of the Byzantine empire to the Ottoman Turks in 1453, many Greek Christian refugees found a new home in Venice and other Italian cities, including influential scholars who helped reintroduce Greek philosophy and literature to an eager Italian readership. One of these scholars was John Bessarion (1403–1472), a Byzantine archbishop who compiled a magnificent library of Greek manuscripts that he bequeathed to the republic of Venice. Venice also became the leading center in western Europe for the publication of Greek books, printing the important texts in Greek philosophy and science, and making them widely available for the first time in western Europe.

The defining characteristic of Venetian government was its social stability, a trait that made it the envy of other more troubled cities and the source of imitation by republican-minded reformers throughout Europe. Whereas the Florentine republic was notoriously unstable and subject to quiet subversion by the Medicis, Venice boasted a largely unchanging republican constitution that lasted from 1297 to 1797. Thus Venice is the longest-surviving republic in history. It was, however, a very exclusive republic. Out of a total population of nearly 150,000, only a small political elite consisting of some 2,500 nobles enjoyed voting privileges. From this elite and from Venice's many wealthy religious institutions came the resources to patronize Renaissance artists.

At the top of Venetian society was the *doge*, a member of the nobility who was elected to the job for life. The most notable Renaissance doge was Andrea Gritti (r. 1523–1538), whose reputation derived from his brilliant early career as a military administrator and diplomat. Gritti sometimes bent the laws in his favor, but he never manipulated elections or managed Venice's affairs as completely as Cosimo de' Medici did in Florence a century before. Like the Medicis, however, he used his own financial resources and his personal influence to transform his city into a major center of Renaissance culture.

Gritti hired some of the most prominent European artists, musicians, and poets to come to Venice. These included Pietro Aretino (1492–1556), the greatest master of satire of the sixteenth century, and the architect and sculptor Jacopo Sansovino (1486–1570). As official architect of the city, Sansovino transformed its appearance with his sculptures, palaces, and churches that imitated the styles of classical Greece and Rome. One of his most notable buildings is the Marciana Library, which was begun in 1537 to house Bessarion's collection of Greek manuscripts.

Artistic and scholarly creativity in Florence and Venice thrived on the competition among many different patrons. Neither the Medicis in Florence nor Gritti in Venice entirely dominated the cultural scene. Artistic patronage in these republics mirrored the dynamic political life that engaged many people. The diversity of patronage gave extensive employment to painters, sculptors, and architects, thereby attracting the best artists to these two cities. Later sections of the chapter will examine the works they produced.

Federico da Montefeltro as the Ideal Prince
The papal tiara in the upper left alludes to the pope's authorization of his title as duke. Federico is shown studying a book while dressed in armor, reflecting his two sides as scholar and soldier. His dynastic ambitions are represented by the presence of his son and potential successor standing at his feet.

PRINCES AND COURTIERS

Although the Renaissance began in the relative freedom of republics, such as Florence, it soon spread to principalities, those states ruled by one man, the prince. In contrast to the multiple sources of support for the arts and learning in the republics, patronage in the principalities was more constricted, confined to the prince and members of his court. The terms *lord* and *prince* refer to rulers who possessed formal aristocratic titles, such as the Marquis of Mantua, the Duke of Milan, or the King of Naples. Most Renaissance princes came from local aristocratic families who seized control of the government by force. Some, however, had been soldiers of fortune who had held on to a city as a spoil of war or had even overthrown a government that had once employed them to defend the city. Regardless of how a prince originally obtained power, his goal was to establish a dynasty, that is, to guarantee the rights of his descendants to continue to rule the city. Some dynasties—such as that of the D'Este family, which ruled Ferrara from 1240 to 1597—were well established and quite popular.

The Ideal Prince, the Ideal Princess

Federico II da Montefeltro (1422–1482), Duke of Urbino, succeeded in achieving the lasting fame and glorious reputation that so many princes craved. Although he was illegitimate, his father gave him the best possible education by sending him to study at the most fashionable school in Italy and to apprentice as a soldier under the most renowned mercenary captain. In Renaissance Italy, an illegitimate boy could not inherit his father's property. Thus he usually had two career options: He could become a priest to obtain a living from the church, or he could become a mercenary and take his chances at war. Federico became a mercenary. From among the peasants of the duchy he recruited an army, which he hired out to the highest bidder. He soon earned a European-wide reputation for his many victories and enriched the duchy with the income from mercenary contracts and plunder. When his half-brother was assassinated in 1444, Federico became the ruler of Urbino, and by 1474 he obtained from the pope the title of duke. Federico epitomized the ideal Renaissance prince—a father figure to his subjects, astute diplomat, brilliant soldier, generous patron, avid collector, and man of learning. This was a prince who combined the insights of contemplative study with active involvement in the affairs of the world.

Federico's rule was paternalistic. He was concerned for the welfare of his subjects and personally listened to their complaints and adjudicated their disputes. His military adventures tripled the size of his duchy. Conquests brought the prosperity that financed his expensive building projects and his collection of Latin manuscripts. Federico's personal library surpassed that of any contemporary university library in Europe, and his wide-ranging reading interests showed his openness to the latest developments in learning. Federico's greatest achievement, however, was the building of a vast palace. At one stage the project was supervised by the architect Luciano Laurana (ca. 1420–1479), but it was Federico who clearly deserves most of the credit for what remains the single best example of Renaissance architectural ideals in a palace. Because of Federico, the small mountainous duchy of Urbino acquired a cultural importance far greater than its size warranted.

The best candidate for the ideal princess was Isabella d'Este (1474–1539), the Marchioness of Mantua. Such was her fame as a patron that she was known during her lifetime as "the first lady of the world." Enjoying an education that was exceptional for a girl in the fifteenth century, she grew up in the court at Ferrara, where she was surrounded by famous painters and poets and where she cultivated foreign ambassadors and leading intellectuals of the time. Such was her fame that her own clothing designs established the fashion for all of Europe. But her influence went far beyond that. When her husband was absent and after his death, she ruled Mantua by herself, earning a reputation for her just decisions and witty charm. She gained renown for her ability as a tenacious negotiator and behind-the-scenes diplomat. An avid reader and collector, she personally knew virtually all the great artists and writers of her age. Her influence spread far beyond Mantua, in part through her voluminous correspondence, which is estimated to include some 12,000 letters.

The Ideal Courtier

Just as the Renaissance republics developed a code of conduct for citizens, so the principalities created a model for the ideal courtier. A courtier was a man or woman who lived in or regularly visited the palace of a prince. Courtiers helped the prince's household function by performing all kinds of services, such as taking care of the family's wardrobe, managing servants, educating children, providing entertainment, keeping accounts, administering estates,

Courtiers Waiting on a Princely Family

The man at the far right is posing in a nonchalant manner. Members of the prince's family on the left congregate around him as he conducts business from the throne, which is just a chair with a dog resting underneath. In this scene the prince confers with a messenger who has brought him a letter.

going on diplomatic missions, and fighting battles. To best serve the princely family in whatever was needed, a courtier needed to cultivate a wide range of skills. Men trained in horsemanship, sword play, and all kinds of sports, which were useful for keeping in shape for war. Women learned to draw, dance, play musical instruments, and engage in witty conversation. Both men and women needed to be adept at foreign languages so that they could converse with visitors and diplomats. Men and some women in the courts knew Latin and Greek, which was the foundation of a formal education. The stability and efficiency of the princely states depended on the abilities of the courtiers, who performed many of the functions that elected officials did in the republics. It was also extremely important to prevent conflicts among the courtiers; otherwise the peace of the state would be compromised. The most influential guide to how a courtier should behave was *The Book of the Courtier* (1528) by the cultivated diplomat, Baldassare Castiglione (1478–1529). Underlying the behavior and conversation of the ideal courtier described in this book were two general principles that governed all civilized manners—nonchalance and ease:

> *I have found quite a universal rule which . . . seems to me valid above all others, and in all human affairs whether in word or deed: and that is to avoid affectation in every way possible as though it were some very rough and dangerous reef; and (to pronounce a new word perhaps) to practice in all things a certain nonchalance, so as to conceal all art and make whatever is done or said appear to be without effort and almost without any thought about it. . . .*
>
> *Therefore we may call that art true art which does not seem to be art; nor must one be more careful of anything than of concealing it, because if it is discovered, this robs a man of all credit and causes him to be held in slight esteem.*[2]

In other words, nonchalance is the ability to do something that requires considerable training and effort while making it appear to be natural and without effort. The need to maintain appearances, which we first saw in the disguised rulership of Cosimo de' Medici in Florence, became one of the distinguishing traits of Italian Renaissance culture. According to Castiglione, all human action and communication should be moderate and balanced, creating the effect of ease. In effect, *The Book of the Courtier* translated the ideals of harmony and proportion so admired in Renaissance culture into a plan for human comportment. By using courtly manners, human beings governed the movements of the body according to an almost mathematical ideal of proportion.

Through *The Book of the Courtier* and its many imitators, the Renaissance ideal of courtly manners began to be widely disseminated during the sixteenth century. Written in a lucid Italian that made for lively reading, the book was translated into Latin, English, French, and Spanish and widely plagiarized, imitated, and absorbed into the literature of Europe. By studying these books, any young man or woman of talent and ambition could aspire to act and speak like a great aristocrat. The courtly ideal was completely accessible to anyone who could read, and many of its precepts were incorporated into the educational curriculum.

CHRONOLOGY

The Cradle of the Renaissance: The Italian City-States

AFTER 1070	Founding of first city republics or communes
1270–1342	Marsilius of Padua, author of *The Defender of the Peace*
1434–1464	Rule of Cosimo de' Medici in Florence
1444–1482	Rule of Federico II da Montefeltro, Duke of Urbino
1469–1492	Rule of Lorenzo, the Magnificent, de' Medici in Florence
1474–1539	Life of Isabella d'Este, Marchioness of Mantua
1492–1503	Pontificate of Alexander VI
1508	Baldassare Castiglione begins writing *The Book of the Courtier*
1503–1513	Pontificate of Julius II
1513–1521	Pontificate of Leo X
1523–1538	Rule of Andrea Gritti, Doge of Venice

The Papal Prince

The Renaissance popes were the heads of the Church; they also had jurisdiction over the Papal State in central Italy. Thus they combined the roles of priest and prince. The Papal State was supposed to supply the pope with the income to run the affairs of the Church, but as we saw in Chapter 10, during the period when the popes left Rome and resided in Avignon (France) and during the Great Schism of 1305–1418, the popes lost control of the Papal State. After 1418 the popes saw that they had two main tasks—first, to regain the revenues of the Papal State; second, to restore the city of Rome, which had become a neglected ruin. To collect the taxes and revenues due them, many popes were obliged to use military force to bring the rebellious lords and cities into obedience. The popes also engaged in squabbles with the neighboring states that had taken advantage of the weakness of the papacy during the schism.

These military and diplomatic adventures thrust the popes into some very nasty quarrels—a situation that undermined the popes' ability to provide moral leadership. Pope Alexander VI (r. 1492–1503) financed his son Cesare Borgia's attempts to carve out a principality for himself along the northern fringe of the Papal State. He also married off his daughter, Lucrezia Borgia, in succession to several different Italian princes who were useful allies in the pope's military ambitions. The members of the Borgia family made many enemies who accused them of all kinds of evil deeds, including the poisoning of one of Lucrezia's husbands, brother-sister and father-daughter incest, and conducting orgies in the Vatican. Even though many of these allegations were false or exaggerated, the reputation of the papacy suffered. Alexander's successor, Pope Julius II (r. 1503–1513), continued to pursue military advantage in the Papal State. He took his princely role so seriously that he donned armor, personally led troops during the siege of Bologna, and rather presumptuously rewarded himself with a triumphal procession, an honor that had been granted in ancient Rome to victorious generals such as Julius Caesar.

Many of the Renaissance popes were embarrassed by the squalor of the city of Rome, an unfit place to serve as the capital of the Church. By the late fifteenth century a number of popes were ambitious to create a capital they felt worthy for Christendom. The most clear-sighted of the builders of Rome was Pope Leo X (r. 1513–1521), the second son of Lorenzo the Magnificent. Educated by the circle of scholars who surrounded the Medicis, Leo was destined for a clerical career at a young age. He received a doctorate in canon law and was made a cardinal at age seventeen. During Leo's pontificate, Rome was transformed into one of the centers of Renaissance culture. Leo transformed the University of Rome into a distinguished institution through the appointment of famous professors. For his own private secretaries he chose famous intellectuals. Leo's ambition can best be measured in his project to rebuild Saint Peter's Basilica as the largest church in the world. He tore down the old Basilica, which had been a major pilgrimage destination for more than a thousand years, and planned the great church that still dominates Rome today.

THE CONTRADICTIONS OF THE PATRIARCHAL FAMILY

The contradiction between the theory of the patriarchal family and realities of family life produced much of the creative energy of the Italian Renaissance. When theory dramatically departed from actual experience, many people began to distrust the theory and seek alternative ways of looking at society and the world. That is what happened in Renaissance Italy.

Advice books on family management, such as Leon Battista Alberti's *Four Books on the Family* (written in the 1430s), were popular and influential. Such books propounded the theory that husbands and fathers ruled. They were the sources of social order and discipline, and not just within the family but of all of society. Groups of male relatives were responsible for rectifying injuries and especially for avenging any assault on a family member. Nearly all marriages were arranged by fathers or male guardians who sought beneficial financial and political alliances with other families, a situation that gave older men an advantage in the marriage market, as they were usually better off financially than younger ones. As a result, husbands tended to be much older than wives. In Florence in 1427, for example, the typical first marriage was between a 30-year-old man and an 18-year-old woman. Husbands were encouraged to treat their spouses with a kindly but distant paternalism. All women were supposed to be kept under strict male supervision, and the only honorable role for an unmarried woman was as a nun.

However, the reality of family life often departed from theory. A number of factors explain the disparity. First, a variety of circumstances made family life insecure and the very survival of families tenuous—death from epidemic diseases, especially plague, and separations due to marital strife, which were common enough even though divorce was not possible. Second, the wide age gap between husbands and wives meant that husbands were likely to die long before their wives, and thus many women became widows at a relatively young age with children still to raise. Third, many men, especially international merchants and migrant workers, were away from their families for long periods of time. Regardless of the patriarchal assertion that fathers should be in control, in reality they were often absent or dead.

The contradiction between the theory of patriarchy and the fragile reality of family life had far-reaching consequences. Unlike the strong hand fathers were supposed to wield over their families, most were remote figures who had little direct influence. Mothers who were supposed to be modest, obedient to their husbands, and invisible to the outside world not only had to raise children alone but often had to manage their dead or absent husband's business and political affairs. By necessity, many resilient, strong, and active women were deeply involved in the management of worldly affairs, and mothers had much more direct influence on children than fathers. Despite the theory of patriarchy, the families of Renaissance Italy were in fact matriarchies in which mothers ruled.

The contractions of family life became one of the most discussed problems in the Renaissance. Making fun of impotent old husbands married to beautiful but unfulfilled young wives became a major theme in comic drama. Given the demographic ravages of the plague, concern for the care of babies preoccupied preachers, while the many Renaissance paintings in which little cherubs seem to fall from the sky manifested a deep and widespread craving for healthy children. A widespread anxiety produced by the contradictions of family life and by the tenuous hold many

JUSTICE IN HISTORY

Vendetta as Private Justice

During the fourteenth and fifteenth centuries, the official justice provided by the law courts competed with the private justice of revenge. Private justice was based on the principle of retaliation. When someone was murdered or assaulted, it became the obligation of the victim's closest male relatives to avenge the injury by harming the perpetrator or one of his relatives to a similar degree. A son was obliged to avenge the death of his father, a brother the injury of his brother. Given the weakness of most governments, the only effective justice was often private justice or, as the Italians called it, *vendetta.* As the most significant source of disorder during the Renaissance, vendetta was a practice that all governments struggled to eradicate.

One of the attributes that distinguished an act of private justice from a simple violent crime was that avengers committed their acts openly and even bragged about what they had done. A criminal covered his tracks. An avenger did not. Therefore, the violence of an act of revenge was carried out in public so there would be witnesses, and often it was performed in a highly symbolic way in order to humiliate the victim as much as possible.

In Renaissance Italy private justice took many forms, but always such acts sought to do more than create another victim. They sought to deliver a message. After a period of disorder in 1342, the Florentines granted extraordinary judicial powers to a soldier of fortune, Walter of Brienne, known as the Duke of Athens. But Walter offended many Florentines by arresting and executing members of prominent families. In September of that year a crowd led by these families besieged the government palace and captured the duke's most hated henchmen, the "conservator" and his son. Even though the conservator had been the highest judge of Florence, the Florentines repudiated his authority by obtaining revenge. An eyewitness reported what happened next:

> *The son was pushed out in front, and they cut him up and dismembered him. This done, they shoved out the conservator himself and did the same to him. Some carried a piece of him on a lance or sword throughout the city, and there were those so cruel, so bestial in their anger, and full of such hatred that they ate the raw flesh.*[3]

This story of revenge in the most sophisticated city in Europe on the eve of the Renaissance illustrates the brutality of private justice, especially the need to make a public example of the victim.

Another account from nearly 200 years later tells of the murder of Antonio Savorgnan, a nobleman from Friuli who had killed a number of his enemies the previous year. Rather than attempting to have Antonio arrested as they could have, the murderers avenged their dead relatives through private justice. One eyewitness recounted that Antonio was attacked while leaving church, and then, "It was by divine miracle that Antonio Savorgnan was wounded: his head opened, he fell down, and he never spoke another word. But before he died, a giant dog came there and ate all his brains, and one cannot possibly deny that his brains were eaten."[4] This time a dog did the avengers' work for them. Perhaps the strangest detail in both of these accounts is that the writers wanted readers to believe that the victim had been eaten, either by humans or by a dog. Why was this an important message to get across?

The eating of a victim was one way avengers signaled that they were killing as an act of private justice. In both of the killings just described, the killers were retaliating for the murder of one of their close relatives and symbolically announcing to others that the attack was not an unjustifiable crime but a legitimate act of revenge. To convey that message, avengers could not ambush their opponent in the dark of night but were obliged to confront him openly in broad daylight before witnesses. There had to be the appearance, at least, of a fair fight. Murderers symbolized their revenge in several ways: They butchered the corpse as if it were the prey of a hunt or fed the remains to hunting dogs or even ate it themselves in what appeared to be a frenzy of revenge.

One of the major objectives of any government, whether a tiny city-state or a great monarchy, was to substitute public justice for private justice; but the persistence of tradition was strong. During the sixteenth century as governments sought to control violence and as the Renaissance values of moderation spread, a different kind of private justice appeared—the duel.

Private Justice
A man wearing a breastplate and hiding a drawn sword behind his back grabs the collar of his enemy before assaulting him. To enact honorable revenge the attacker could not stab his enemy in the back but had to give him a chance in a fair fight.

Traditionally, the duel had been a means of solving disputes among medieval knights, but during the sixteenth century duels became much more common, even among men who had never been soldiers. Dueling required potential combatants to conform to an elaborate set of rules: The legitimate causes for a challenge to a duel were few, the combatants had to recognize each other as honorable men, the actual fight took place only after extensive preparations, judges who were experts on honor had to serve as witnesses, and the combatants had to swear to accept the outcome and abstain from fighting one another in the future.

The very complexity of the rules of dueling limited the violence of private justice, and that meant that fewer fights actually took place. Dueling, in effect, civilized private justice. Although dueling was always against the law, princes tended to wink at duels because they kept conflicts among their own courtiers under control. At the same time, governments became far less tolerant of other forms of private justice, especially among the lower classes. They attempted to abolish feuds and vendettas and insisted that all disputes be submitted to the courts. ■

Questions of Justice

1. How did the persistence of private justice present a challenge to an emerging state?
2. How would a person in the Renaissance likely defend himself against the charge that a crime had been committed through an act of private justice?

Taking It Further

Muir, Edward. *Mad Blood Stirring: Vendetta in Renaissance Italy.* 1998. A study of the most extensive and long-lasting vendetta in Renaissance Italy. It traces the evolution of vendetta violence into dueling.

Weinstein, Donald. *The Captain's Concubine: Love, Honor, and Violence in Renaissance Tuscany.* 2000. A delightfully engaging account of an ambush and fight among two nobles over a woman who was the concubine of the father of one of the fighters and the lover of the other. It reveals the disturbing relationship between love and violence in Renaissance society.

An Old Man and His Grandson

In Renaissance Italy, children barely knew their fathers and seldom their grandfathers, who were distant figures. This portrait of an old man with his grandson visually expresses the ideal of patriarchy, which was the emotional bond between different generations. In fact, it is known that this little boy never knew his grandfather, who died years before he was born. Just as the painting idealizes the loving relationship between a grandfather and grandson who never knew each other, it is also realistic by depicting the grandfather's deformed nose. This combination of idealizing an emotional state while depicting the human body realistically is typical of the Renaissance style.

families had on survival stimulated the distinctive family theme in the culture of Renaissance Italy.

The Influence of Ancient Culture

The need in Renaissance Italy to provide effective models for how citizens, courtiers, and families should behave stimulated a reexamination of ancient culture. The civilizations of ancient Greece and Rome had long fascinated the educated classes in the West. In Italy where most cities were built around or on top of the ruins of the ancient past, the seduction of antiquity was particularly pronounced. During the fourteenth and fifteenth centuries many Italian thinkers and artists attempted to foster a rebirth of ancient cultures. At first they merely attempted to imitate the Latin style of the best Roman writers. Then scholars tried to do the same thing with Greek, stimulated in part by direct contact with Greek-speaking refugees from Byzantium. Artists trekked to Rome to fill their notebooks with sketches of ancient ruins, sculptures, and medallions. Wealthy collectors hoarded manuscripts of ancient philosophy, built libraries to house them, bought up every piece of ancient sculpture they could find, and dug up ruins to find more antiquities to adorn their palaces. Patrons demanded that artists produce new works that imitated the styles of the ancients and that displayed a similar concern for rendering natural forms. Especially prized were lifelike representations of the human body.

Patrons, artists, and scholars during the Renaissance not only appreciated the achievements of the past but began to understand the enormous cultural distance between themselves and the ancients. That insight made their perspective historical. They also developed techniques of literary analysis to determine when a particular text had been written and to differentiate authentic texts from ones that had been corrupted by the mistakes of copyists. That ability made their perspective critical.

PETRARCH AND THE ILLUSTRIOUS ANCIENTS

The founder of the historical critical perspective that characterized the Renaissance was Francesco Petrarca (1304–1374), known in English as Petrarch. In contrast to the medieval thinkers who admired the ancients and treated their words as repositories of eternal wisdom, Petrarch discovered that the ancients were mere men much like himself. More than anything else, that insight might distinguish what was new about the Italian Renaissance, and Petrarch was the first to explore its implications.

Petrarch's early fame came from his poetry, in both his native Italian and in Latin. In an attempt to improve his Latin style, Petrarch engaged in a detailed study of the best ancient Roman writers and searched to find old manuscripts that were the least corrupted by copyists. In that search he was always watching for anything by the Roman orator Cicero (106–43 B.C.E.), who was the Latinist most revered for literary style. In 1345 Petrarch briefly visited Verona to see what he could find in the library of a local monastery. While thumbing through the dusty volumes, he excitedly happened upon a previously unknown collection of letters Cicero had written to his friend Atticus.

As Petrarch began to read the letters, however, he suffered a profound shock. Cicero had a reputation as the greatest sage of the Romans, a model of good Latin style, of philosophical sophistication, and most of all of high ethical standards. But in the letters Petrarch found not sage moral advice but gossip, rumors, and crude political calculations. Cicero looked like a scheming politician, a man of crass ambition rather than grand philosophical wisdom. Although Petrarch could never forgive Cicero for being less than what he had avowed in his philosophical writings, he had discovered the human Cicero rather than just the idealized Cicero, a man so human you could imagine having a conversation with him.

And having a conversation was precisely what Petrarch set out to do. Cicero, however, had been dead for 1,388 years. So Petrarch wrote a letter to Cicero's ghost. Adopting Cicero's own elegant Latin style, Petrarch lambasted the Roman for going against the moral advice he had given others. Petrarch quoted Cicero back to Cicero, asking him how he could be such a hypocrite.

> *Your letters I sought for long and diligently; and finally, where I least expected it, I found them. At once I read them, over and over, with the utmost eagerness. And as I read I seemed to hear your bodily voice, O Marcus Tullius [Cicero's given names], saying many things, uttering many lamentations, ranging through many phases of thought and feeling. I long had known how excellent a guide you have proved for others; at last I was to learn what sort of guidance you gave yourself. . . . Now it is your turn to be the listener.*[5]

Petrarch went on to lecture Cicero for his false dealings, his corruption, and his moral failures. The point of the exercise of writing a letter to a dead man was to compare the ideals Cicero had avowed in his philosophical work and the reality he seemed to have lived. Making comparisons is one of the elementary techniques of a critical method, and it became the hallmark of Petrarch's mode of analysis. Petrarch's letter reduced the stature of the ancients a bit, making them less like gods and more like other men who made mistakes and told lies. Petrarch ended this remarkable, unprecedented letter with a specific date, given in both the Roman and Christian ways, and a description of Verona's location in a way an ancient Roman would understand—as if he were making it possible for Cicero to find and answer him. This concern for historical precision typified the aspect that was most revolutionary about Petrarch's approach. No longer a repository of timeless truths, the ancient world became a specific time and place, which Petrarch perceived to be at a great distance from himself. The ancients had ceased to be godlike; they had become historical figures. After his letter to Cicero, Petrarch wrote a series of letters to other illustrious ancients in which he revealed the human qualities and shortcomings of each.

Petrarch developed his critical methods by editing classical texts, including parts of Livy's history of Rome, which was written about the time of Jesus. Petrarch compared different manuscript versions of Livy's work in an attempt to establish exactly the original words, a method very different from the medieval scribe's temptation to alter or improve a text as he saw fit. Petrarch strived to get the words right because he wanted to understand exactly what Livy had meant, a method now called the philological approach. Philology° is the comparative study of language, devoted to understanding the meaning of a word in a particular historical context. Petrarch's philology demonstrated that words do not have fixed meanings but take on different meanings depending on who is using them and when they were written. It was obvious to Petrarch, for example, that the word *virtue* had meant something quite different to the polytheist Livy than it did to Petrarch's contemporaries, who understood virtue in Christian terms. A concern for philology gave Petrarch access to the individuality of a writer. In the particularity of words, Petrarch discovered the particularity of actual individuals who lived and wrote many centuries before.

An interest in the meaning of words led Petrarch to study the rhetoric° of language. Rhetoric refers to the art of persuasive or emotive speaking and writing. From his studies of rhetoric, Petrarch became less confident about the ability of language to represent truth than he was about its capacity to motivate readers and listeners to action. He came to think that rhetoric was superior to philosophy because he preferred a good man over a wise one, and rhetoric offered examples worthy of emulation rather than abstract principles subject to debate. Petrarch wanted people to behave morally, not just talk or write about morality. And he believed that the most efficient way to inspire his readers to do the right thing was to write moving rhetoric.

THE HUMANISTS: THE LATIN POINT OF VIEW

Those who followed Petrarch's approach to the classical authors were the Renaissance humanists°. The Renaissance humanists studied Latin and sometimes Greek texts on grammar, rhetoric, poetry, history, and ethics. (The term *humanist* in the Renaissance meant something very different from what it means today—someone concerned with human welfare and dignity.) The humanists sought to resurrect a form of Latin that had been dead for more than a thousand years and was distinct from the living Latin used by the Church, law courts, and universities—which they thought was mediocre compared to ancient Latin. In this effort, humanists acquired a difficult but functional skill that opened a wide variety of employment opportunities to them and gave them great public influence. They worked as schoolmasters, secretaries, bureaucrats, official court or civic historians, and ambassadors. Many other humanists were wealthy men who did not need a job but were fascinated with the rhetorical capabilities of the new learning to persuade other people to do what they wanted them to do.

Because humanists could be found on different sides of almost all important questions of the day, the significance of their work lies less in what they said than in how they said it. They wrote about practically everything: painting

A HUMANIST LAMENTS THE RUINS OF ROME

In 1430 the distinguished humanist Poggio Bracciolini (1380–1459) was working in Rome as a papal secretary. In this account he describes his and a friend's response to seeing the ruins of the once-great city of Rome. Poggio's lament and those of other humanists stimulated popes to commit themselves to the rebuilding of the city, but the enthusiasm to return Rome to its ancient splendor had some unfortunate side effects. Many of the building materials for the new Rome were pillaged from the ruins of the old Rome. As a result, much of the destruction of the ancient city of Rome occurred during the Renaissance.

Not long ago, after Pope Martin left Rome shortly before his death for a farewell visit to the Tuscan countryside, and when Antonio Lusco, a very distinguished man, and I were free of business and public duties, we used to contemplate the desert places of the city with wonder in our hearts as we reflected on the former greatness of the broken buildings and the vast ruins of the ancient city, and again on the truly prodigious and astounding fall of its great empire and the deplorable inconstancy of fortune. And once when we had climbed the Capitoline hill, and Antonio, who was a little weary from riding, wanted to rest, we dismounted from our horses and sat down together within the very enclosures of the Tarpeian ruins, behind the great marble threshold of its very doors, as I believe, and the numerous broken columns lying here and there, whence a view of a large part of the city opens out.

Here, after he had looked about for some time, sighing and as if struck dumb, Antonio declared, "Oh, Poggio, how remote are these ruins from the Capitol that our Vergil celebrated: 'Golden now, once bristling with thorn bushes.' How justly one can transpose this verse and say: 'Golden once, now rough with thorns and overgrown with briars.'

pictures, designing buildings, planting crops, draining swamps, raising children, managing a household, and educating women. They debated the nature of human liberty, the virtues of famous men, the vices of infamous ones, the meaning of Egyptian hieroglyphics, and the cosmology of the universe.

How did the humanists' use of Latin words and grammar influence the understanding of this vast range of subjects? Their approach was entirely literary. When they wanted to design a building, they read ancient books on architecture instead of consulting masons and builders. By studying the ancients, humanists organized experience into new categories that changed people's perceptions of themselves, the society they lived in, and the universe they inhabited. Humanist writing revealed what might be called the *Latin point of view.* Each language organizes experience according to the needs of the people who speak it, and all languages make arbitrary distinctions, dividing up the world into different categories. People who have studied a foreign language have run across these arbitrary distinctions when they learned that some expressions can never be translated exactly.

The humanists' recovery of the Latin point of view contributed new words, new sentence patterns, and new rhetorical models that often altered their own perceptions in very subtle ways. For example, when a fifteenth-century humanist examined what the ancient Romans had written about painting, he found the phrase *ars et ingenium*. *Ars* referred to skills that can be learned by following established rules and adhering to models provided by the best painters. Thus, the ability of a painter to draw a straight line, to mix colors properly, and to identify a saint with the correct symbol are examples of *ars* or what we would call craftsmanship. The meaning of *ingenium* was more difficult to pin down, however. It referred to the inventive capacity of the painter, to his ingenuity. The humanists discovered that the ancients had made a distinction between the craftsmanship and the ingenuity of a painter. As a result, when humanists and their pupils looked at paintings, they began to make the same distinction and began to admire the genius of artists whose work showed ingenuity as well as craftsmanship. Ingenuity came to refer to the ability of the painter to arrange his figures in a novel way, to employ unusual colors, or to create emotionally exciting effects that conveyed piety, sorrow, or joy as the subject demanded. So widespread was the influence of the humanists that the most ingenious artists demanded higher prices and became the most sought after. In this way, creative innovation was encouraged in the arts, but it all started very simply with the introduction of new words into the Latin vocabulary of the people who paid for paintings. A similar process of establishing new categories altered every subject the humanists touched.

The humanist movement spread rapidly during the fifteenth century. Leonardo Bruni (ca. 1370–1444), who became the chancellor of Florence (the head of the government's bureaucracy), employed humanist techniques to defend the republican institutions and values of the city. Bruni's defense of republican government is called civic humanism°. He argued that the truly ethical man should devote himself to active service to his city rather than to passive contemplation in scholarly retreat or monastic seclusion. Thus Bruni formulated the ethic of responsible citizenship that remains today as necessary to sustain a free society. Given the supreme value Christianity had long placed on the passive contemplation of divine truth, Bruni's assertion that active public service constituted an even higher vocation was radical indeed.

Lorenzo Valla (1407–1457) employed philological criticism to undermine papal claims to authority over secular rulers, such as the princes and republics of Italy. He did so by proving that a famous document, the Donation of Constantine, was a forgery. The Donation recorded that during the fourth century the Emperor Constantine had transferred his imperial authority in Italy to the pope, and although Renaissance popes could not get what they wanted just by citing this document, it was part of the legal arsenal popes used against secular rulers. Valla demonstrated that the Donation had actually been forged in the ninth century, a work of detection that showed how the historical analysis of documents could be immensely useful for resolving contemporary political disputes. The controversy between defenders and enemies of the papacy that followed Valla's discovery stimulated the demand for humanist learning because it became clear that humanist methods were necessary for political debate and propaganda.

The intellectual curiosity of the humanists led them to master many fields of endeavor. This breadth of accomplishment contributed to the ideal of the "Renaissance Man," a person who sought excellence in everything he did. No one came closer to this ideal than Leon Battista Alberti (1404–1472). As a young man, Alberti wrote Latin comedies and satirical works that drew on Greek and Roman models, but as he matured he tackled more serious subjects. Although he was a bachelor and thus knew nothing firsthand about marriage, he drew upon the ancient writers to create the most influential Renaissance book on the family, which included sections on relations between husbands and wives, raising children, and estate management. He composed the first grammar of the Italian language. He dabbled in mathematics and wrote on painting, law, the duties of bishops, love, horsemanship, dogs, agriculture, and flies. He mapped the city of Rome and wrote the most important fifteenth-century work on the theory and practice of architecture. His interest in architecture, moreover, was not just theoretical. In the last decades of his life, he dedicated much of his spare time to architectural projects that included restoring an ancient church in Rome, designing Renaissance façades for medieval churches, and building a palace for his most important patron. One of his last projects was the first significant work for making and deciphering secret codes in the West.

The humanists guaranteed their lasting influence through their innovations in the educational curriculum. The objective of humanist education was to create well-rounded male pupils (girls were not usually accepted in humanist schools) who were not specialists or professionals, such as the theologians, lawyers, and physicians trained in universities, but critical thinkers who could tackle any problems that life presented. It was a curriculum well suited for the active life of civic leaders, courtiers, princes, and churchmen. The influence of the humanist curriculum persists in the general-education requirements of modern universities, which require students, now of both sexes, to obtain intellectual breadth before they specialize in narrow professional training.

Historians have identified a few female humanists from the Renaissance. Because they were so unusual, learned humanist women were often ridiculed. Jealous men accused the humanist Isotta Nogarola (1418–1466) of promiscuity and incest, and other women insulted her in public. A famous male schoolmaster said that Isotta was too feminine in her writings and should learn how to find "a man within the woman."[6] Laura Cereta (1475–1506), who knew Greek as well as Latin and was adept at mathematics, answered the scorn of a male critic with rhetorical insult worthy of Petrarch himself:

> *I would have been silent, believe me, if that savage old enmity of yours had attacked me alone. . . . But I cannot tolerate your having attacked my entire sex. For this reason my thirsty soul seeks revenge, my sleeping pen is aroused to literary struggle, raging anger stirs mental passions long chained by silence. With just cause I am moved to demonstrate how great a reputation for learning and virtue women have won by their inborn excellence, manifested in every age as knowledge, the [purveyor] of honor. Certain, indeed, and legitimate is our possession of this inheritance, come to us from a long eternity of ages past.*[7]

These few humanist women can be seen as among the first feminists. They advocated female equality and female education but also urged women to take control of their own lives. Nogarola answered her critics in a typical humanist fashion by reinterpreting the past. Thinking at this time suggested that all women were the daughters of Eve, who in her weakness had submitted to the temptation of the serpent, which led to the exile of humanity from the Garden of Eden. Nogarola pointed out that Eve had been no weaker than Adam, who also ate of the forbidden fruit, and therefore women should not be blamed for the Fall from God's grace. Cereta was the most optimistic of the women humanists. She maintained that if women paid as much attention to learning as they did to their appearances, they would achieve equality. Despite the efforts of Cereta and other female humanists, progress in women's education was extremely slow. The universities remained closed to talented women. The first woman to earn a degree from a university did so in 1678, and it took another two hundred years before very many others could follow her example.

Through the influence of the humanists, the Latin point of view permeated Renaissance culture. They educated generations of wealthy young gentlemen whose appreciation of antiquity led them to pay to collect manuscripts of ancient literature, philosophy, and science. These patrons were also responsible for encouraging artists to imitate the ancients. What began as a narrow literary movement became the stimulus to see human society and nature through entirely new eyes. As we shall see in Chapter 13, some humanists, especially in northern Europe, applied these techniques with revolutionary results to the study of the Bible and the sources of Christianity.

Understanding Nature: Moving Beyond the Science of the Ancients

The humanists' initial concern was to emulate the language of the ancients. Most of them preferred to spend time reading a book rather than observing the world around them. In fact, their methods were ill-suited to understanding nature, and when they wanted to explain some natural phenomenon such as the movement of blood through the body or the apparent movements of the planets and stars, they looked to ancient authorities for answers rather than to nature itself. The Renaissance humanists' most prominent contributions to science consisted of recovering classical texts and translating the work of ancient Greek scientists into the more widely understood Latin. This is in contrast to the scientific method with which we are familiar today, in which we form a hypothesis and then determine whether it is correct by observing the natural world as directly as possible. In contrast, Renaissance scientists searched for ancient texts about nature, and then debated about which ancient author had been correct.

These translated texts broadened the discussion of two subjects crucial to the scientific revolution of the late sixteenth and seventeenth centuries—astronomy and anatomy. In 1543 the Polish humanist Nicolaus Copernicus (1473–1543) resolved the complications in the cosmological system of the second-century astronomer Ptolemy. Whereas Ptolemy's writings had placed the earth at the center of the universe, Copernicus cited other ancient writers who put the sun in the center. Thus the first breakthrough in theoretical astronomy was achieved not by making new observations but by comparing ancient texts. Nothing was proven, however, until Galileo Galilei (1564–1642) turned his telescope to the heavens in 1610 to observe the stars through his own eyes rather than through an ancient text.

Andreas Vesalius (1514–1564) built upon recently published studies in anatomy from ancient Greece to write a survey of human anatomy, *On the Fabric of the Human Body* (1543), a book that encouraged dissection and anatomical observations. With Vesalius, anatomy moved away from relying exclusively on the authority of ancient books to encouraging medical students and physicians to examine the human body with their own eyes. Building upon Vesalius's work, Gabriele Falloppio (ca. 1523–1562) made many original observations of muscles, nerves, kidneys, bones, and most famously the "Fallopian tubes," which he described for the first time. By the late sixteenth century, astronomy and anatomy had surpassed what the ancients had known.

Besides recovering ancient scientific texts, the most important Renaissance contributions to science came secondhand from developments in the visual arts and technology. A number of Florentine artists experimented during the early fifteenth century with the application of mathematics to the preliminary design of paintings. The goal was to make paintings more accurately represent reality by creating the visual illusion of the third dimension of depth on a two-dimensional rectangular surface, a technique known as linear perspective (see next section). These artists contributed to a more refined understanding of how the eye perceives objects, and their understanding of how the eye worked led to experiments with glass lenses. A more thorough knowledge of optics made possible the invention of the telescope and microscope.

Of all the developments in the fifteenth century, however, none matched the long-term significance of a pair of rather simple inventions—cheap manufactured paper and the printing press. Paper made from rags created an inex-

CHRONOLOGY

The Influence of Ancient Culture

106–43 B.C.E.	Marcus Tullius Cicero, Latin rhetorician
1304–1374	Francesco Petrarca (Petrarch), first humanist
CA. 1370–1444	Leonardo Bruni, chancellor of Florence
1404–1472	Leon Battista Alberti, humanist and architect
1407–1457	Lorenzo Valla, humanist
1418–1466	Isotta Nogarola, first female humanist
CA. 1454	Johann Gutenberg begins printing books
1473–1543	Nicholaus Copernicus, humanist and cosmological theorist
1475–1506	Laura Cereta, humanist
1514–1564	Andreas Vesalius, writer on anatomy
CA. 1523–1562	Gabriele Falloppio, conducted anatomical dissections
1564–1642	Galileo Galilei, astronomer

pensive alternative to sheepskins, which had been the preferred medium for medieval scribes. And just as paper replaced sheepskin, the printing press replaced the scribe. Several Dutch and German craftsmen had experimented with printing during the 1440s, but credit for the essential innovation of movable metal type has traditionally been accredited to Johann Gutenberg (ca. 1398–1468) of Mainz in the 1450s. German immigrants brought printing to Italy, which rapidly became the publishing center of Europe, largely because it boasted a large, literate urban population who bought books.

Scientific books accounted for only about 10 percent of the titles of the first printed books, but the significance of printing for science was greater than the sales figures would indicate. In addition to making ancient scientific texts more readily available, print meant that new discoveries and new ideas reached a wider audience, duplication of scientific investigation could be avoided, illustrations were standardized, and scientists built upon each other's work. With the invention of the printing press, scientific work became closely intertwined with publishing, so that published scientific work advanced science, and scientific work that was not published went largely unnoticed. It is revealing that Leonardo da Vinci (1452–1519), the greatest Renaissance observer of nature, contributed nothing to science because he failed to publish his findings. The fundamental principle of modern science and, in fact, of all modern scholarship is that research must be made available to everyone through publication.

Antiquity and Nature in the Arts

More than any other age in Western history, the Italian Renaissance is identified with the visual arts. The unprecedented clusters of brilliant artists active in a handful of Italian cities during the fifteenth and sixteenth centuries overshadow any other contribution of Renaissance culture. Under the influence of the humanists, Renaissance artists began to imitate the sculpture, architecture, and painting of the ancients. At first they concerned themselves with merely copying ancient styles and poses. But soon they attempted a more sophisticated form of imitation. They wanted to understand the principles that made it possible for the artists from classical Greece and Rome to make their figures so lifelike. That led them to observe more directly nature itself, especially the anatomy of the human body. Renaissance art was driven by the passionate desire of artists and their patrons both to imitate ancient models and to imitate nature. These twin desires produced a certain creative tension in their work because the ancients, whose works of art often depicted gods and goddesses, had idealized and improved upon what they observed in nature. Renaissance artists sought to depict simultaneously the ideal and the real—an impossible goal, but one that sparked remarkable creativity.

All of the Renaissance arts displayed the mark of patrons, those discriminating and wealthy people who controlled the city-states and who had been educated in humanist schools. Until the end of the sixteenth century, all painters, sculptors, and even poets worked for a patron. An individual patron would commission a particular work of art, such as an altar painting, portrait bust, or palace. The patron and artist would agree to the terms of the work through a contract, which might spell out in considerable detail exactly what the artist was to do, what kinds of materials he was to use, how much they could cost, how much he was allowed to rely on assistants, how much he had to do himself, and even how he was to arrange figures. The same sort of contract was used when work was commissioned by a group—for example, a guild, lay religious society (called a confraternity), convent, or government. Michelangelo Buonarroti (1475–1564) sculpted *David*, which has become the most famous work of Renaissance art, to fulfill a contract that had been debated in a committee meeting. Regardless of their talent or ingenuity, artists were never free agents who could do whatever they wanted.

Another kind of patron supported the career of an artist for an extended period of time. Princes, in particular, liked to take on an artist, give him a regular salary and perhaps even some official title, in exchange for having him perform whatever duties the prince deemed necessary. In this kind of an arrangement, Duke Lodovico Sforza (1451–1508) brought Leonardo da Vinci to Milan, where Leonardo painted a portrait of the duke's mistress, devised plans for a giant equestrian statue of the duke's father, designed stage sets and carnival pageants, painted the interior decorations of the castle, and did engineering work. The artist Cosmè Tura (active ca. 1450–1495) probably spent more time painting furniture than canvases for the Duke of Ferrara.

Most patrons supported the arts in order to enhance their own prestige and power. Some, such as Pope Julius II (r. 1503–1513), had exceptional influence on the work of artists. He persuaded the very reluctant Michelangelo, who saw himself as a sculptor, to become a painter in order to decorate the ceiling of the Sistine Chapel.

SCULPTURE, ARCHITECTURE, AND PAINTING: THE NATURAL AND THE IDEAL

Just as humanists recaptured antiquity by collecting, translating, and analyzing the writings of classical authors, so Renaissance artists made drawings of surviving classical medals, sculpture, and architecture. Collected in sketch books, these drawings often served as pattern books from which the apprentices in artists' workshops learned how to draw. Because artists believed that the classical world enjoyed an artistic tradition vastly superior to their own, these sketches became valuable models from which other artists could learn. Two of the most influential Florentine artists, the architect Filippo Brunelleschi (1377–1446) and the sculptor Donatello (1386–1466), may have gone to Rome together as young men to sketch the ancient monuments. No Roman paintings survived into the fifteenth century (Pompeii, which proved to have a treasure trove of Roman art buried under layers of volcanic ash, had not yet been excavated), and no Renaissance artist ever saw a Greek building, so the only examples of ancient art to copy were the ruins of Roman buildings and a few surviving Roman statues. As a result, architecture and sculpture led the way in the imitation of ancient art, but Renaissance artists imposed their own sensibilities on the ancients as much as they imitated them.

The Renaissance style evolved in Florence during the first few decades of the fifteenth century. In 1401 the 24-year-old Brunelleschi entered a competition to design bronze relief panels for the north doors of the Baptistery. He narrowly lost to the even younger Lorenzo Ghiberti (1378–1455). Look at the illustrations on this page. The rules of the competition required both artists to fit their relief panels within a fancy decorative frame in the Gothic style, which had been in fashion for nearly 300 years. However, both competition relief panels seem constrained by the curves and angles of the frame. For example, some of the figures in the Brunelleschi panel project outside it as if trying to escape the restraints of the style. Ghiberti's relief shows the two characteristic elements of the early Renaissance style: The head of Isaac is modeled after a classical Roman sculpture, and the figures and horse on the left are depicted as realistically as possible. In these elements, Ghiberti was imitating both antiquity and nature.

Ghiberti worked on the north doors for twenty-one years and won such renown as a result that when he finished he was immediately offered a new commission to complete panels for the east portal. These doors, begun in 1425, took twenty-seven years to finish. In the east doors,

The Competition Panels of the Sacrifice of Isaac

These two panels were the finalists in a competition to design the cast bronze doors on the north side of the Baptistery in Florence. Each demonstrates a bold new design that attempted to capture the emotional trauma of the exact moment when an angel arrests Abraham's arm from sacrificing his son Isaac (Genesis 22:1–12). Both artists went on to be closely associated with the new style of the Renaissance. The panel on the left, by Filippo Brunelleschi, lost to the one on the right, by Lorenzo Ghiberti. Notice how the Ghiberti relief better conveys the drama of the scene by projecting the elbow of Abraham's upraised arm outward toward the viewer. As a result the viewer's line of sight follows the line of the arm and knife directly toward Isaac's throat.

Linear Perspective
In these panels Ghiberti broke out of the Gothic frame that had inhibited him in the panels on the north doors. Now he was free to explore the full potential of the newly discovered principles of linear perspective.

Ghiberti substituted a simple square frame for the Gothic frame of the north doors, thereby liberating his composition. In the illustration above, which also depicts the biblical story of Isaac, the squares in the pavement set up an underlying geometry to the scene. The background architecture of rounded arches and crisp-angled columns in the classical style creates the illusion of depth in the relief. This illusion is achieved through linear perspective, that is, the use of geometrical principles to depict a three-dimensional space on a flat, two-dimensional surface. The rigorous geometry of the composition provided the additional benefit of allowing Ghiberti to divide up the space to depict several different scenes within one panel. In the panels of the east doors, he created the definitive Renaissance interpretation of the ancient principles of the harmony produced by geometry. Michelangelo later remarked that the doors were fit to serve as the "gates of paradise."

After failing to win the competition for the Baptistery doors, Brunelleschi turned to architecture. In his own time, Brunelleschi was considered to have revived ancient Roman principles, but it is evident now that he was less a student of antiquity than an astutely original thinker. In his buildings he employed a proportional system of design that is best seen in his masterpiece, the Pazzi Chapel. He began with a basic geometric unit represented by each of the small rectangles clustered in groups of four on the upper third of the façade of the chapel. The height of each of these was approximately the height of an average man. All the other dimensions of the building were multiples of these basic rectangles. Thus, the building was formed from the proportions of a human being. Brunelleschi employed what he saw as the natural dimensions of humanity and transformed them into principles of architectural geometry. The result was a stunning impression of harmony in all the spaces of the building.

Later sculptors and architects built upon the innovations of Ghiberti and Brunelleschi. Florence became renowned for its tradition of sculpture, producing the two greatest Renaissance masters of the art, Donatello and Michelangelo. In their representations of the human form, both of these sculptors demonstrated the Renaissance preoccupation with the relationship between the ideal and the natural.

Conceptions of both the ideal and the natural are evident in the work of the most important painter of the early Florentine Renaissance, Masaccio (1401–ca. 1428), who worked in fresco. Fresco, a common form of decoration in

The Geometry of Renaissance Architecture

Filippo Brunelleschi designed the Pazzi Chapel in Florence to match the geometrical proportions of the human body.

churches, was the technique of applying paint to wet plaster on a wall. In his great fresco cycle for the Brancacci chapel painted in the 1420s, Masaccio depicted street scenes from Florence complete with portraits of actual people, including himself. These were examples of naturalism. On some other figures—Jesus, St. Peter, and St. John—he placed heads copied from ancient sculptures of gods. These were examples of idealized beauty, which were especially suitable for saints. In Masaccio's frescoes, both realistic and idealized figures appeared in the same work. The realistic figures helped viewers identify with the subject of the picture by allowing them to recognize people they actually knew. The idealized figures represented the saintly, whose superior moral qualities made them appear different from average people.

Masaccio developed the technical means for employing linear perspective in painting. To achieve the effect of perspective, he organized the entire composition around the position he assumed a viewer would take while looking at the picture. Once he established the point of view, he composed the picture to direct the viewer's gaze through the pictorial space. In *The Tribute Money*, he drew the spectator's eye to the head of Jesus, who is the figure in the middle pointing with his right hand. In addition, Masaccio recognized that the human eye perceives an object when light shines on it to create lighted surfaces and shadows. He used this understanding in creating a

Combining Natural and Idealized Representations

In this detail of a fresco of Christ and his Apostles, Masaccio mixed naturalism and idealized beauty. The figure on the right with his back turned to the viewer is a tax collector, who is depicted as a normal human being. The head of the fourth figure to the left of him, who represents one of the apostles, was copied from an ancient statue that represents ancient ideals of beauty.

THE HUMAN BODY IN HISTORY

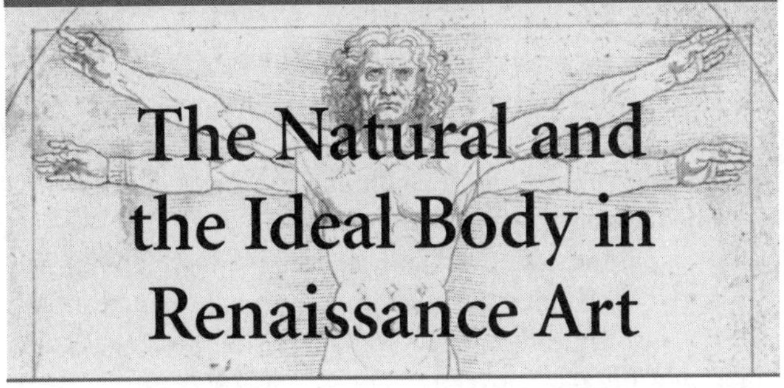

The Natural and the Ideal Body in Renaissance Art

During the Italian Renaissance artists depicted the human body, especially the nude body, with a greater sensitivity to anatomy than at any time since antiquity. In attempting to portray the human body, Renaissance sculptors and painters explored two possible approaches. Should they attempt to imitate nature by depicting human bodies as they really appear, or should they improve upon nature by representing human bodies in an idealized way?

The Florentine sculptor Donatello (1386–1466) was the master of the first approach, the naturalistic representation of the human body. His major achievement was solving the difficult technical problem of creating a freestanding life-size statue of a human being that looked as if the person depicted were standing in a natural way. In his solution, called *contraposto,* one leg of the human form is kept straight and the other is slightly bent, with the hips slanting in the opposite direction from the slant of the shoulders. One contemporary described Donatello's statues as so lively that they appeared to move. Following Donatello's lead, Florentine sculptors dedicated themselves to "the return to nature," the attempt to make inanimate works of art imitate not just ancient sculpture, but nature itself.

During the later Renaissance, Michelangelo Buonarroti (1475–1564) perfected the second approach by idealizing the human body. He did not want just to imitate nature, he wanted to surpass nature. His figures, such as his famous *David,* often seemed super-human. In creating figures such as this, he brought the Renaissance preoccupation with antiquity full circle because many classical sculptors had intended to achieve the same effect. After all, most of their work was for polytheist temples, and by improving on nature they wanted to create images of the perfect bodies of the gods.

With Michelangelo, Western art entered an entirely new phase. He advanced art from the simple goal of imitating classical motifs and observing nature to a more grandiose goal of improving on the ancients and on nature. According to Michelangelo, since nature alone never achieved perfection, great art can be even more powerful than nature itself. ■

■ **The Naturalistic Body**
In the *contraposto* pose of Donatello's David, the weight of the figure is carried on one leg of the human form, which appears straight and taut while the other seems relaxed and slightly bent.

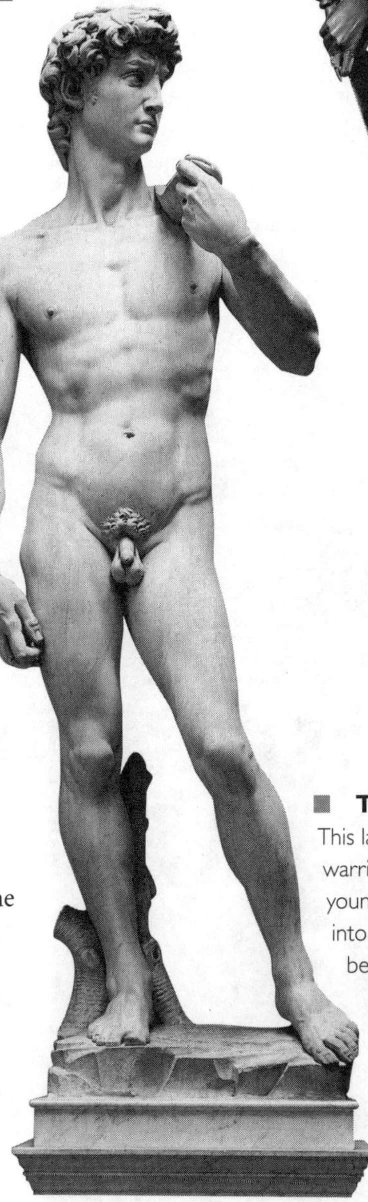

■ **The Idealized Body**
This larger-than-life figure of the biblical warrior King David transformed the young boy who slew the giant Goliath into a kind of superman whose physical bearing was greater than any normal man. Michelangelo altered the proportions of a natural man, making the head and hands significantly larger than normal. In its original placement on a staircase in a large open square, the statue towered above viewers.

For Discussion

How might the Renaissance humanist concerns for imitation produce both the artistic conceptions of naturalism and idealized beauty?

painting technique called *chiaroscuro* ("light and shade"). There is a single source of light in the painting coming from the same direction as the light in the room. That light defines figures and objects in the painting through the play of light and shadow. The strokes of Masaccio's paintbrush tried to duplicate the way natural light plays upon surfaces.

The techniques developed by Masaccio came to complete fulfillment in the career of Leonardo da Vinci (1452–1519). So compelling was Leonardo's curiosity and desire to tackle new problems that many of his paintings remained unfinished. He was a restless experimenter, never settling on simple solutions. Because of experiments Leonardo made with paint, his *Last Supper* fresco in Milan has seriously deteriorated. His mature works, such as *Mona Lisa*, completely reconciled the technical problems of representing human figures with realistic accuracy and the spiritual goal of evoking deep emotions. Unlike some of his predecessors, who grouped figures in a painting as if they were statues, Leonardo managed to make his figures appear to interact and communicate with one another.

Depicting Human Emotions in Art
In this painting the maternal feelings of two mothers, Mary the mother of Jesus and St. Anne the mother of Mary, become the dominant message of the work. Leonardo da Vinci successfully united naturalism and idealism: The Virgin Mary is both a human mother who loves her fidgeting little boy and the perfectly beautiful eternal Mother who represents the love of God.

The technique of painting with oils achieved new levels among painters in the Netherlands and in Flanders (in present-day Belgium, but at the time a province in the Duchy of Burgundy). By carefully layering numerous coats of tinted oil glazes over the surface of the painting, these painters created a luminous surface that gave the illusion of depth. The use of glazes enabled painters to blend brush strokes in a way that made them virtually imperceptible. As a result Flemish and Dutch painters excelled in painting meticulous details, such as the textures of textiles, the reflections of gems, and the features of distant landscapes. Jan van Eyck (ca. 1395–1441) was the most famous Flemish painter. He worked as a court painter for the Duke of Burgundy, for whom he undertook many kinds of projects including decorating his palaces and designing stage sets and ornaments for festivals. His oil paintings were so famous that he was much praised by the Italian humanists, and numerous Italian patrons, including the Medicis, bought his works.

Most humanist theorists of painting linked artistic creativity with masculinity. By the sixteenth century, however, these theorists were proved wrong, as a number of female painters rose to prominence. The most notable was Sofonisba Anguissola (ca. 1532–1625). Born into an aristocratic family in Cremona, Italy, she received a humanist education along with her five sisters and brother. Because she was a woman, she was prohibited from studying anatomy or drawing male models. As a result she specialized in portraits, often of members of her family, and self-portraits. She developed a distinctive style of depicting animated faces. Her example inspired other aristocratic women to take up painting.

MUSIC OF THE EMOTIONS

Renaissance humanists' fascination with the visual arts of the ancients led them to assume that composers should imitate ancient music. But in attempting to turn humanist theories about music into real music, fifteenth-century composers faced a formidable problem—no one had the slightest clue what ancient Greek music actually sounded like. As a result, musical innovations lagged behind the other arts until the late sixteenth century, when a musical Renaissance finally took hold.

During the fourteenth and fifteenth centuries the principal composers came from France and the Netherlands. The greatest of them, Josquin de Prez (ca. 1440–1521), was born and trained in the Netherlands and later found patrons in Milan, Rome, and Ferrara. His finest talent as a composer consisted of his ability to enhance musically the meaning of lyrics. In contrast to Josquin's sensitivity to matching music

Northern Renaissance Art
In this mid-fifteenth century Flemish painting, the use of oil paint and glazes made it possible to convey the shimmering surfaces of the metal and gold in this goldsmith's shop. Shown in the mirror, which is leaning on the counter to the right, are a couple looking through a window into the shop. They are in the exact position of the viewers of the picture, and placing them in the mirror was a way to draw viewers into the scene.

and lyric, most other composers relied on stereotypical rhythmic patterns and a simple melodic line that had no connection to the text. In fact, almost any lyric could be sung to the same music.

Recognizing that the music of their time did not measure up to what ancient writers had reported about the emotional intensity of their music, several prominent musician-humanists conducted extensive discussions about how to combine music and words in a way that would create a fuller aesthetic and emotional experience. The initial consequence of these discussions was the Renaissance madrigal, a type of song in which the music closely followed a poetic lyric to accentuate the shades of textual meaning. For example, when the text described a happy mood, the music would rise up the scale. A somber text would be lower-pitched. When the lyric described agitation or fear, the rhythm would quicken in imitation of the heart beating faster.

The most important consequence of the discussions about the need for a richer musical experience was the invention of opera° during the final decades of the sixteenth century. A group of humanist thinkers called the *Camerata* thought the power of ancient Greek music could be recovered by writing continuous music to accompany a full drama. The drama was performed as a kind of speech-song with the range of pitch and rhythms closely following those of natural speech. Singers were accompanied by a small ensemble of musicians. The first operas composed in this vein were by Jacopo Peri (1561–1633) and Giulio Caccini (ca. 1550–1618), and were performed in Florence at the Grand Duke's court around 1600. These lengthy, bloated works attracted little attention among audiences, and opera likely would have sunk under its own weight had it not been for Claudio Monteverdi (1567–1643), who discovered its dramatic and lyrical potential. His sumptuous productions employed large ensembles of singers and instrumentalists, punctuated speech-song with arias (long sung solos) and dances, and included magnificent stage machines that simulated earthquakes, fires, and battles. Under Monteverdi's masterful hand, opera became the first complete multimedia art form. Arias from his productions became popular hits sung on every street corner, and opera moved from being a private amusement for princely courtiers to mass entertainment. The first public opera house opened in Venice in 1637. By the end of the seventeenth century, Venice boasted seventeen opera houses for a population of only 140,000. With the rise of opera houses and theaters for plays, the close bond between patrons and artists began to break down. Until then, artists were bound by the wishes of patrons. Now they began to serve the much larger marketplace for popular entertainment.

CHRONOLOGY

Antiquity and Nature in the Arts

1377–1446	Filippo Brunelleschi, Florentine sculptor and architect
1378–1455	Lorenzo Ghiberti, Florentine sculptor who created the "Gates of Paradise"
1386–1466	Donatello, Florentine sculptor
CA. 1395–1441	Jan van Eyck, Flemish painter
1401–CA. 1428	Masaccio, Florentine fresco painter
CA. 1440–1521	Josquin de Prez, composer
1452–1519	Leonardo da Vinci, Florentine painter and inventor
1475–1564	Michelangelo Buonarroti, Florentine sculptor, painter, architect, poet
CA. 1532–1625	Sofonisba Anguissola, painter
1567–1643	Claudio Monteverdi, opera composer

The Early Modern European State System

The civic independence that had made the Italian Renaissance possible was profoundly challenged during the Italian Wars (1494–1530). During these wars France, Spain, and the Holy Roman Empire attempted to carve up the peninsula for themselves, and the Italian city-states were thrown into turmoil. By 1530 the Italian city-states, with the exception of Venice, had lost their independence to the triumphant king of Spain. The surrender of the rich city-states of Italy was the first and most prominent sign of a major transformation in the European system of states. The age of city-states was over because they could never muster the level of materiel and manpower necessary to put and keep a large army in the field. Only the large monarchies of the West could do that. The Italian Wars revealed the outlines of the early modern European state system, which was built on the power of large countries that had been brought under control by their own kings. These kings amassed an unprecedented level of resources that not only crushed Italy but made possible, as we shall see in Chapter 12, the European domination of much of the globe through establishment of colonies in the Americas, Asia, and eventually Africa.

MONARCHIES: THE FOUNDATION OF THE STATE SYSTEM

During the last half of the fifteenth century, the monarchies of western Europe began to show signs of recovery from the turmoil of the fourteenth century, which had been marked by famine, plague, revolts, and continuous warfare. France and England ended the Hundred Years' War, which had bled both kingdoms of men and resources during the century before 1453. England escaped from its civil war, the War of the Roses, in 1485. The kingdoms of Castile and Aragon joined in 1479 to create the new kingdom of Spain, which in 1492 completed the reconquest of territories from the Muslims that had been underway since the eleventh century. The Holy Roman Empire, which became allied to Spain through marriage, pursued a grand new vision for unifying the diverse principalities of Germany.

The early modern European state system was the consequence of five developments. First, governments established standing armies. As a result of the military revolution that brought large numbers of infantrymen to the field of battle and gunpowder cannons to besiege cities and castles, governments were obliged to modernize their armies or face defeat. Since the ninth century, kings had relied on feudal levies, in which soldiers were recruited to fulfill their personal obligation to a lord, but by the late fifteenth century governments began to organize standing armies. These armies enjoyed high levels of professionalism and skill, but they were very expensive to maintain because the soldiers had to be regularly paid. Moreover, the new artillery was costly, and improvements in the effectiveness of artillery bombardments necessitated extensive improvements in the walls of castles, fortresses, and cities. As a result, kings were desperate for new revenues.

The need for revenues led to the second development, the systematic expansion of taxation. Every European state struggled with the problem of taxation. The need to tax efficiently produced the beginnings of a bureaucracy of tax assessors and collectors in many states.

People naturally resisted the burden of new taxes, and monarchs naturally responded to the resistance. This tension led to the third development. Monarchs attempted to weaken the institutional seats of resistance by abolishing the tax-exempt privileges of local communities and ignoring regional assemblies and parliaments that were supposed to approve new taxes. During the twelfth and thirteenth centuries, effective government was local government, and kings seldom had the power to interfere in the affairs of towns and regions. During the fifteenth century, however, kings everywhere attempted to eliminate or erode the independence of towns and regional parliaments in order to raise taxes more effectively and to express the royal will throughout the realm.

The fourth development, closely linked to the third, can be seen in monarchs' attempts to constrain the independence of the aristocracy and the Church. In virtually every kingdom, the most significant threats to the power of the king were the powerful aristocrats. In England a civil war among aristocrats almost tore the kingdom apart. Kings everywhere struggled to co-opt or force submission from these aristocrats. Likewise, the autonomy of the Church threatened monarchial authority, and most monarchs took measures to oblige churchmen to act as agents of government policy.

The fifth development in the evolution of the European state system was the institution of resident ambassadors. During the Italian Wars, the kings of Europe began to exchange permanent, resident ambassadors who were responsible for informing their sovereign about conditions in the host country and representing the interests of their country abroad. Resident ambassadors became the linchpins in a sophisticated information network that provided intelligence about the intentions and capabilities of other kings, princes, and cities. These ambassadors typically enjoyed a humanist education, which helped them adapt to many strange and unpredictable situations, understand foreign languages, negotiate effectively, and speak persuasively. Ambassadors cultivated courtly manners, which smoothed over personal conflicts. For the development of the new state system, gathering reliable information became just as important as maintaining armies and collecting taxes.

France: Consolidating Power and Cultivating Renaissance Values

With the largest territory in western Europe and a population of more than 16 million, France had the potential to become the most powerful state in Europe if the king could figure out how to take advantage of the kingdom's size and resources. By 1453 the Hundred Years' War between France and England had come to an end. With the inspiration of Joan of Arc and with the reform of royal finances by the merchant-banker Jacques Coeur, King Charles VII (r. 1422–1461) expelled the English and regained control of his kingdom. Under Charles, France created its first professional army. Equally important, during the Hundred Years' War the Pragmatic Sanction of Bourges° (1438) guaranteed the virtual autonomy of the French Church from papal control, giving the French king unparalleled opportunities to interfere in religious affairs and to exploit Church revenues for government purposes.

Louis XI (r. 1461–1483), called the "Spider King" because of his fondness for secret intrigue, took up the challenge of consolidating power over the great nobles of his kingdom, who thwarted his state building and threatened his throne. When Louis came to power, the Duchy of Brittany was virtually independent; one great aristocrat, René of Anjou, controlled more territory and was richer than the king himself; and, most dangerous of all, the dukes of Burgundy had carved out their own splendid principality, which celebrated extravagant forms of courtly ritual and threatened to eclipse the prestige of France itself.

Against these powerful rivals, Louis turned to an equally powerful new weapon—the *taille*. During the final years of the Hundred Years War, in order to support the army, the Estates General (France's parliament) granted the king the *taille*, the right to collect an annual direct tax. After the war, the tax continued and Louis turned it into a permanent source of revenue for himself and his successors. Armed with the financial resources of the *taille*, Louis took on his most rebellious vassal, Charles the Bold, the Duke of Burgundy, and in 1477 professional Swiss infantrymen in the pay of Louis defeated the plumed knights of Burgundy. Charles was killed in battle, and only his daughter Mary's hurried marriage to the Habsburg Archduke Maximilian bought the protection Burgundy needed from the Holy Roman Empire and prevented France from seizing all of the duchy.

The monarch most responsible for the spread of Renaissance culture in France was Francis I (r. 1515–1547), a sportsman and warrior who thrilled to the frenzy of battle. Much of his early career was devoted to pursuing French interests in the Italian Wars, until he was captured in battle in 1525 in Italy. Thereafter he focused more on patronizing Italian artists and humanists at his court and importing Italian Renaissance styles. He had the first Renaissance-style chateau built in the Loire Valley and hired artists, including Leonardo da Vinci. As a result of Francis's patronage, Italy was no longer the exclusive center of Renaissance culture.

Spain: Unification by Marriage

In the early fifteenth century the Iberian peninsula was a diverse place, lacking political unity. It was home to several different kingdoms—Portugal, Castile, Navarre, and Aragon, which were all Christian, and Granada, which was Muslim. Each kingdom had its own laws, political institutions, customs, and languages. Unlike France, the Christian kingdoms of medieval Iberia were poor, underpopulated, and preoccupied with the reconquest, the attempt to drive the Muslims from the peninsula. There was little reason to assume that this region would become one of the greatest powers in Europe, the rival of France.

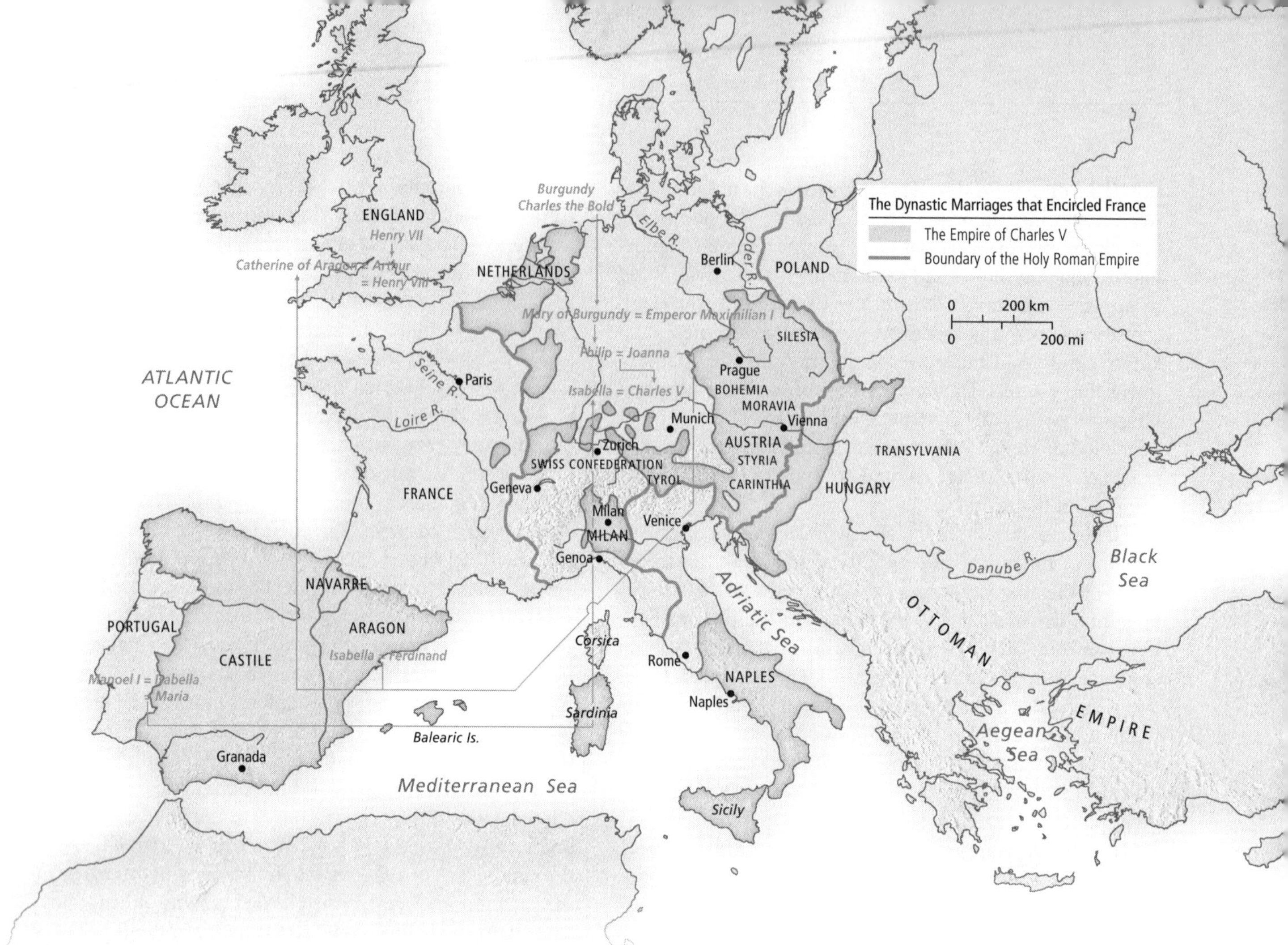

Map 11.3 Dynastic Marriages That Encircled France
Through skillfully arranging the marriages of their sons and daughters, Ferdinand of Aragon and Isabella of Castile managed to completely surround the rival kingdom of France with a network of alliances.

That rise to power began with a wedding. In 1469 Isabella, who later would become Queen of Castile (r. 1474–1504), married Ferdinand, who later would be King of Aragon (r. 1479–1516). The objective of this arranged marriage was to solidify an alliance between the two kingdoms, not to unify them, but in 1479 Castile and Aragon were combined into the kingdom of Spain. Of the two, Castile was the larger, with a population of perhaps six million, and the richer because of the government-supported sheep-raising industry called the *Mesta.* Aragon had less than a million people and was a hybrid of three very distinct regions that had nothing in common except that they shared the same king. Together Isabella and Ferdinand, each still ruling their own kingdoms, at least partially subdued the rebellious aristocracy and built up a bureaucracy of well-educated middle-class lawyers and priests to manage the administration of the government.

The Christian kings of Iberia had long aspired to making the entire peninsula Christian. In 1492 the armies of Isabella and Ferdinand defeated the last remaining Iberian Muslim kingdom of Granada. While celebrating the victory over Islam, the monarchs made two momentous decisions. The first was to rid Spain of Jews as well as Muslims. Isabella and Ferdinand decreed that within six months all Jews must either convert to Christianity or leave. To enforce conformity to Christianity among the converted Jews who did not leave, the king and queen authorized an ecclesiastical tribunal, the Spanish Inquisition, to investigate the sincerity of conversions. The second decision was Isabella's alone. She financed a voyage by a Genoese sea captain, Christopher Columbus, to sail west into the Atlantic in an attempt to reach India and China. Isabella's intention seems to have been to outflank the Muslim kingdoms of the Middle East and find allies in Asia. As we shall see in the next chapter, Columbus's voyage had consequences more far-reaching than Isabella's intentions, adding to the crown of Castile immense lands in the Americas.

Despite the diversity of their kingdoms, Isabella and Ferdinand made Spain a great power. The clever dynastic marriages they arranged for their children allowed Spain to encircle rival France and established the framework for the diplomatic relations among European states for the next century and a half (see Map 11.3). Their eldest daughter and, after her death, her sister were married to the king of Portugal. Their son and another daughter, Joanna, married offspring of Mary of Burgundy and the Emperor Maximilian I of the Holy Roman Empire. Joanna's marriage produced a son, Charles V, who amassed extraordinary power. He succeeded to the Habsburg lands of Burgundy, inherited the crowns of Castile and Aragon (r. 1516–1556), was elected Holy Roman Emperor (r. 1519–1558), ruled over the Spanish conquests in Italy, and was the Emperor of the Indies, which included all of Spanish Central and South America. This was the greatest accumulation of territories by a European ruler since Charlemagne. The encirclement of France was completed with the wedding of Isabella and Ferdinand's daughter Catherine of Aragon to the Prince of Wales and after his death to his brother, King Henry VIII (r. 1509–1547) of England.

The Holy Roman Empire: The Costs of Decentralization

Like Spain, the Holy Roman Empire saw powerful France as its most dangerous enemy. And when the French king's invasion of Italy initiated the Italian Wars, it launched a struggle that pitted the empire and Spain against France for the next 200 years. Members of the Habsburg family had been elected to the throne of the Holy Roman Empire since 1438. As we have seen, Emperor Maximilian I (r. 1493–1519) wed Mary, the daughter of Charles the Bold of Burgundy, and although they were not able to preserve all of Burgundy from the French, they did keep substantial parts, including the extremely rich Netherlands.

In an era of coolly calculating monarchs, Maximilian cut an odd figure. Like his father-in-law, Charles the Bold, he loved chivalry and enjoyed nothing more than to play the role of a knight leading his men into battle. The problem was that he was not very good in that role. His military adventures led to a series of disasters, often at the hands of the rough Swiss mercenaries who were experts in using the pike (a long pole with a metal spearhead) to cut up aristocratic cavalrymen and who passionately hated everything about the autocratic Habsburgs who had once ruled their lands. Maximilian also came under the influence of Italian Renaissance culture and imagined himself another Caesar with a special mission to reconquer Italy for the Holy Roman Empire. The French invasion of Italy in 1494 drew him into the quagmire of Italian affairs as he attempted to counter French influence there. His erratic military policies, however, could not quite keep pace with these imperial ambitions.

Maximilian's inability to execute a consistent military policy in Italy was a consequence of the highly decentralized nature of the empire. Unlike the other European monarchs who inherited their thrones at the death of their predecessors, the emperor was selected by seven electors, who even after an election exercised considerable independent power. The German part of the Holy Roman Empire, home to 15 to 20 million people, was composed of some 300 sovereign and quasi-sovereign principalities and free cities (legally exempt from direct imperial rule). Besides the emperor, only a few institutions served to unify the empire. Most important was the imperial diet, an assembly that included the seven electors, other princes, and representatives of the imperial free cities. The imperial diet was established during the fifteenth century to control the relentless feuding among the German princes, but it often became instead a forum for resisting the emperor.

Maximilian's reign produced some limited reforms. These included a moratorium on feuds, a Supreme Court to impose ancient Roman law throughout Germany, a graduated property and income tax, and eventually an imperial council to exercise executive functions in the absence of the emperor. In practice, however, these institutions worked only to the degree that the emperor and German princes cooperated. The empire remained a fractured, dissent-ridden jumble with no real unity. Compared to the centralizing monarchies in France, Spain, and England, or even to the better managed among the Italian city-states such as tiny Venice, which recurrently defeated Maximilian in battle, the empire under Maximilian was little more than a glorious-sounding name.

England: From Civil War to Stability Under the Tudors

At the end of the Hundred Years' War in 1453, the English crown was defeated. Thousands of disbanded mercenaries were let loose in England and enlisted with one quarreling side or the other in feuds among aristocratic families. The mercenaries brought to England the evil habits of pillage, murder, and violence they had previously practiced in the wars with France. King Henry VI (r. 1422–1461) suffered from bouts of madness that made him unfit to rule and unable to control the disorder. Under the tensions caused by defeat and revolt, the royal family fractured into the two houses of Lancaster and York, which fought a vicious civil war, now known as the Wars of the Roses (1455–1485) from the red and white roses used to identify members of the two opposing sides.

After decades of bloody conflict, the cynical but able Richard III (r. 1483–1485) usurped the throne from his twelve-year-old nephew Edward V and had Edward and his brother imprisoned in the Tower of London, where they were murdered, perhaps on Richard's orders. Richard's apparent cruelty and his scandalous intent to marry Edward's young sister, now heir to the throne, precipitated open defections against him. When Henry Tudor challenged Richard, many nobles flocked to Henry's banner. At the

Battle of Bosworth Field (1485), Richard was slain and his crown discovered on the field of battle. His naked corpse was dragged off and buried in an unmarked grave.

When Henry Tudor became King Henry VII (r. 1485–1509), there was little reason to believe that exhausted England could again become a major force in European events. It took years of patient effort for Henry to become safe on his own throne. He revived the Court of Star Chamber as an instrument of royal will to punish unruly nobles who had long bribed and intimidated their way out of trouble with the courts. Because the king's own handpicked councilors served as judges, Henry could guarantee that the court system became more equitable and obedient to his wishes. Henry confiscated the lands of the rebellious lords, thereby increasing his own income, and he prohibited all private armies except those that served his interests. By managing his administration efficiently, eliminating unnecessary expenses, and staying out of war, Henry governed without the need to call on Parliament for increased revenues.

England was still a backward country and, with fewer than three million people, a fraction of the size of France. By nourishing an alliance with newly unified Spain, Henry was able to bring England back into European affairs. When his son Henry VIII succeeded to the throne, the Tudor dynasty was more secure than any of its predecessors and England more stable than it had ever been before. As we shall see in Chapter 14, by the reign of Henry VII's granddaughter, Elizabeth I (r. 1558–1603), England could boast of a splendid Renaissance court and a fleet that would make it a world power.

CHRONOLOGY

The Early Modern European State System

1422–1461	Reign of Charles VII of France
1455–1485	Wars of the Roses in England
1461–1483	Reign of Louis XI of France
1474–1504	Reign of Isabella of Castile
1479–1516	Reign of Ferdinand of Aragon
1479	Unification of Spain
1483–1485	Reign of Richard III of England
1485–1509	Reign of Henry VII of England
1492	Conquest of Granada; expulsion of the Jews from Spain; voyage of Christopher Columbus
1493–1519	Reign of Maximilian I, Holy Roman Emperor
1494–1530	The Italian Wars
1515–1547	Reign of Francis I of France
1515–1556	Reign of Charles I, King of Spain, who also became Charles V, Holy Roman Emperor (1519–1558)

THE ORIGINS OF MODERN HISTORICAL AND POLITICAL THOUGHT

The revival of the monarchies of western Europe and the loss of the independence of the Italian city-states forced a rethinking of politics. As in so many other fields, the Florentines led the way. In an attempt to understand their own troubled city-state, they analyzed politics by making historical comparisons between one kind of government and another and by carefully observing current events. Two crucial figures in these developments, Francesco Guicciardini and Niccolò Machiavelli, had both served Florence as diplomats, an experience that was crucial in forming their views.

History: The Search for Causes

During the fifteenth century there were two kinds of historians. The first kind were chroniclers who kept records of the important events in their city or principality. The chroniclers recorded a great deal of factual information in the simple form of one-occurrence-after-another. In so doing they established chronologies, which meant they arranged history according to a sequence of dates. But they lacked any sense of how one event caused another, and they failed to interpret the meaning and consequences of the decisions leaders and other people had made.

The second kind of historians were humanists. Petrarch established that the fundamental principle for writing humanist history was to maintain historical distance—the sense that the past was past and had to be reconstructed in its own terms. The most dangerous historical error in writing history became anachronism, that is, imposing present sensibilities and understandings on the past. Before the Renaissance the most common version of anachronism was for historians to interpret pre-Christian history in the light of Christian understandings of God's plan for humanity. In contrast to that approach, humanist historians attempted to offer explanations for why things had happened in human terms. When they interpreted past events, they tried to respect the limitations people had faced. For example, they understood that the moral code of the Roman orator and senator Cicero, who died two generations before Jesus was born, derived from Greek philosophy and Roman ethics rather than a premonition of Christianity. The humanists' interest in rhetoric, however, led them to make moral judgments about the past in an attempt to encourage morality among their readers. Thus, they were prone to pull especially compelling examples of good or bad conduct out of the historical context in which it had taken place and to compare it with other examples. For example, they might compare the behavior of the citizens in fifth-century B.C.E. Athens with the actions of citizens in fifteenth-century Florence.

The shock of the Italian Wars that began in 1494 stimulated a quest for understanding the causes of Italy's fall and prompted a new kind of history writing. The first person to write a successful history in the new vein was Francesco Guicciardini (1483–1540). Born to a well-placed Florentine family, educated in a humanist school, and experienced as a diplomat, governor, and adviser to the Medicis, Guicciardini combined literary skill and practical political experience. Besides collecting information about contemporary events, Guicciardini kept a record of how his own thoughts and values evolved in response to what he observed. One of the hallmarks of his work was that as he analyzed the motives of others, he engaged in self-scrutiny and self-criticism.

From this habit of criticizing himself and others, Guicciardini developed a strong interpretive framework for his histories. His masterpiece, *The History of Italy* (1536–1540), was the first account of events that occurred across the entire Italian peninsula. In many respects, this book originated the idea that Italy is more than just a geographical term and has had a common historical experience. Like the humanist historians, Guicciardini saw human causes for historical events rather than the hidden hand of God, but he refined the understanding of causation through his psychological insights. He suggested, for example, that emotions mattered more than rational calculation and noted that nothing ever turns out quite as anticipated.

FRANCESCO GUICCIARDINI ON THE CHARACTER OF LODOVICO SFORZA

Guicciardini filled The History of Italy *with many insightful accounts of the leaders of the various European states during the Italian Wars. Here he analyzes the character and psychology of Lodovico Sforza, who rose to be duke of Milan after the death of his nephew in suspicious circumstances. Taken prisoner in 1500 after a defeat in battle, Lodovico spent the last ten years of his life in a French prison.*

Thus within a narrow prison were enclosed the thoughts and ambitions of one whose ideas earlier could scarcely be contained within the limits of all Italy—a prince certainly most excellent in eloquence, in skill and many other qualities of mind and nature, and worthy of obtaining a name for mildness and clemency if the infamy come upon him as a result of his nephew's death had not blemished that reputation. But on the other hand he was vain, and his mind full of ambitious, restless thoughts, and he violated his promises and his pledges; always presuming so much on the basis of his own knowledge that being highly offended whenever the prudence and counsels of others were praised, he convinced himself that he could turn everyone's ideas in whatever direction he pleased by means of his own industry and manipulations.

Source: From Guicciardini, Francesco; *The History of Italy*, translated by Sidney Alexander.

Political Thought: Considering the End Result

Guicciardini's contemporary and Florentine compatriot Niccolò Machiavelli (1469–1527) also wrote histories, but he is best known as a political theorist. Trained as a humanist, he lacked the personal wealth and family connections that allowed Guicciardini to move as a matter of birthright in high social and political circles. As we saw in the story that opened this chapter, Machiavelli had worked as a diplomat and military official but had been exiled for complicity in a plot against the Medici family, who had retaken Florence in 1512. While in exile he wrote a book of advice for the Medicis in the vain hope that they would give him back his job. They probably never read his little book, *The Prince* (1513), but it became a classic in political thought. In it he encouraged rulers to understand the underlying principles of political power, which differed from the personal morality expected of those who were not rulers. He thought it was important for a prince to appear to be a moral person, but Machiavelli pointed out that the successful prince might sometimes be obliged to be immoral in order to protect the interests of the state. How would the prince know when this might be the case?

Machiavelli's answer was that "necessity" forced political decisions to go against normal morality. The prince "must consider the end result," which meant that his highest obligation was preserving the very existence of the state, which had been entrusted to him and which provided security for all citizens of the state. This obligation was higher even than his obligation to religion.

Machiavelli's *The Prince* has sometimes been considered a blueprint for tyrants. However, as his more learned and serious work, *The Discourses of the First Decade of Livy* (1516–1519), makes clear, Machiavelli himself preferred a free republic over a despotic princely government. In some ways, *The Discourses* is an even more radical work than *The Prince* because it suggests that class conflict is the source of political liberty: "In every republic there are two different inclinations: that of the people and that of the upper class, and . . . all the laws which are made in favor of liberty are born of the conflict between the two."[8] In this passage, Machiavelli suggested that political turmoil was not necessarily a bad thing, because it was by provoking conflict that the lower classes prevented the upper classes from acting like tyrants.

In all his works, Machiavelli sought to understand the dynamics behind political events. To do this, he theorized that human events were the product of the interaction between two forces. One force was fortune, a term derived from the name of the ancient Roman goddess Fortuna. Fortune stood for all things beyond human control and could be equated with luck or chance. Machiavelli depicted fortune as extremely powerful, like an irresistible flood that swept all before it or the headstrong goddess who determined the fate of men. Fortune controlled perhaps half of all human events. The problem with fortune was its changeability and unpredictability: "since Fortune changes and men remain set in their ways, men will succeed when the two are in harmony and fail when they are not in accord." How could a ruler or even a simple citizen put himself in harmony with fortune and predict its shifts? The answer could be found in the characteristics of the second force, virtue, which he understood as deriving from the Roman concept of *virtus,* literally "manliness." The best description of virtue could be found in the code expected of an ancient Roman warrior: strength, loyalty, and courage. If a man possessed these traits he was most likely to be able to confront the unpredictable. As Machiavelli put it, "I am certainly convinced of this: that it is better to be impetuous than cautious."[9] The man possessing virtue, therefore, looked for opportunities to take control of events before they took control of him. In that way he put himself in harmony with Fortune.

Through Guicciardini's analysis of human motivations and Machiavelli's attempt to discover the hidden forces behind events, history and political thought moved in a new direction. The key to understanding history and politics was in the details of human events. To Guicciardini these details provided clues to the psychology of leaders. To Machiavelli they revealed the hidden mechanisms of chance and planning that governed not just political decisions but all human events.

CONCLUSION
The Politics of Culture

The Renaissance began simply enough as an attempt to imitate the Latin style of the best ancient Latin authors and orators. Within a generation, however, humanists and artists pushed this narrowly technical literary project into a full-scale attempt to refashion human society on the model of ancient cultures. Reading about the ancients and looking at their works of art provoked comparisons with contemporary Renaissance society. The result was the development of a critical approach to the past and present. The critical approach was accompanied by an enhanced historical sensibility, which transformed the idea of the West from one defined primarily by religious identification with Christianity to one forged by a common historical experience.

During the sixteenth century, western Europeans absorbed the critical-historical methods of the Renaissance and turned them in new directions. As we shall see in the next chapter, Spanish and Portuguese sailors encountered previously unknown cultures in the Americas and only vaguely known ones in Africa and Asia. Because of the Renaissance, those who thought and wrote about these strange new cultures did so with the perspective of antiquity in mind. As we shall see in Chapter 13, in northern Europe the critical historical methods of the humanists were used to better understand the historical sources of Christianity, especially the Bible. With that development, Christianity began to take on new shades of meaning, and many thoughtful Christians attempted to make the practices of the church conform more closely to the Bible. The humanist approach to religion led down a path that permanently divided Christians into contending camps over the interpretation of Scripture, breaking apart the hard-won unity of the Roman Catholic West.

Suggestions for Further Reading

For a comprehensive list of suggested readings, please go to www.ablongman.com/levack/chapter11

Baxandall, Michael. *Painting and Experience in Fifteenth Century Italy: A Primer in the Social History of Pictorial Style.* 1988. A fascinating study of how the daily social experiences of Florentine bankers and churchgoers influenced how these individuals saw Renaissance paintings and how painters responded to the viewers' experience. One of the best books on Italian painting.

Brown, Howard M. *Music in the Renaissance.* 1976. Dated but still the best general study of Renaissance music.

Brown, Patricia Fortini. *Art and Life in Renaissance Venice.* 1997. A delightful study about how art fit into the daily lives and homes of the Venetian upper classes.

Brucker, Gene. *Florence: The Golden Age, 1138–1737.* 1998. A brilliant, beautifully illustrated history by the most prominent American historian of Florence.

Burke, Peter. *The Italian Renaissance.* 1999. A concise and readable synthesis of the most recent research.

Hale, J. R. *Renaissance Europe, 1480–1520.* 2000. A witty, engaging, and enlightening study of Europe during the formation of the early modern state system. Strong on establishing the material and social limitations of Renaissance society.

King, Margaret L. *Women of the Renaissance.* 1991. The best general study of women in Renaissance Europe. It is especially strong on female intellectuals and women's education.

Kohl, Benjamin G., and Alison Andrews Smith, eds. *Major Problems in the History of the Italian Renaissance.* 1995. A useful collection of articles and short studies of major historical problems in the study of the Renaissance.

Martines, Lauro. *Power and Imagination: City-States in Renaissance Italy.* 1988. An excellent general survey that is strong on class conflicts and patronage.

Nauert, Jr., Charles G. *Humanism and the Culture of Renaissance Europe.* 1995. The best survey of humanism for students new to the subject. It is clear and comprehensive.

Skinner, Quentin. *Machiavelli: A Very Short Introduction.* 2000. This is the place to begin in the study of Machiavelli. Always clear and precise, this is a beautiful little book.

Stephens, John. *The Italian Renaissance: The Origins of Intellectual and Artistic Change before the Reformation.* 1990. A stimulating analysis of how cultural change took place.

Vasari, Giorgio. *The Lives of the Artists.* 1998. Written by a sixteenth-century Florentine who was himself a prominent artist, this series of artistic biographies captures the spirit of Renaissance society.

Notes

1. *The Portable Machiavelli,* trans. and ed. Peter Bondanella and Mark Musa (1979), 67–69.
2. Baldesar Castiglione, *The Book of the Courtier,* trans. Charles S. Singleton (1959), 43.
3. Giovanni Villani, *Cronica,* vol. 7 (1823), p. 52. Translation by the authors.
4. Agostino di Colloredo, "Chroniche friulane, 1508–18," *Pagine friulane* 2 (1889), 6. Translation by the authors.
5. Francesco Petrarca, "Letter to the Shade of Cicero," in Kenneth R. Bartlett, ed., *The Civilization of the Italian Renaissance: A Sourcebook* (1992), 31.
6. Quoted in Margaret L. King, *Women of the Renaissance* (1991), 197.
7. "Laura Cereta to Bibulus Sempronius: Defense of the Liberal Instruction of Women," in Margaret King and Alfred Rabil, eds., *Her Immaculate Hand: Selected Words by and about the Women Humanists of Quattrocento Italy* (1983), 82.
8. *The Portable Machiavelli,* trans. and ed. Peter Bondanella and Mark Musa (1979), 183.
9. Ibid., 161–162.

CHAPTER

12

The West and the World: The Significance of Global Encounters, 1450–1650

Chapter Outline

- Europeans in Africa
- Europeans in the Americas
- Europeans in Asia
- The Beginnings of the Global System

On a hot October day in 1492, Christopher Columbus and his men, dressed in heavy armor, clanked onto the beach of an island in the Bahamas. The captain and his crew had been at sea sailing west from the Canary Islands for some five weeks, propelled by winds they thought would take them straight to Asia. As the ships under Columbus's command vainly searched among the islands of the Caribbean for the rich ports of Asia, Columbus thought he must be in India and thus called the natives he met "Indians." At another point he thought he might be among the Mongols of central Asia, which he described in his journal as the "people of the Great Khan." Both of Columbus's guesses about his location were incorrect, but they have left a revealing linguistic legacy in terms still in use: "Indians" for the native Americans, and both "cannibals" and "Caribbean" from Columbus's inconsistent spellings of Khan. Columbus believed that the people he called the Cannibals or Caribs ate human flesh. But he got that information—also incorrect—from their enemies. Thus began one of the most lasting misunderstandings from Columbus's first voyage.

Historians know very little about the natives' first thoughts of the arrival of their foreign visitors, but we know that the effects of the arrival were catastrophic. Within a few generations the Caribs nearly disappeared, replaced by African slaves who worked the plantations of European masters.

Western civilization by the end of the fifteenth century hardly seemed on the verge of encircling the globe with outposts and colonies. Its kingdoms had barely been able to reorganize themselves sufficiently for self-defense, let alone world exploration and foreign conquest. The Venetian and Genoese colonies in the Mediterranean were retreating from the advancing Ottoman Turks, who would

The Encounter of Three Cultures: On this wooden bottle painted in the Incan style about 1650, an African drummer leads a procession, followed by a Spanish trumpeter, and an Incan official. The mixing of cultures that occurred after the arrival of the Spanish and Portuguese is what distinguished the Americas from other civilizations.

continue to occupy the Balkans for at least four more centuries. The Ottoman threat was so great that all of southern Europe was on the defensive. And the hostilities had blocked the traditional trade routes to Asia, which had stimulated the great medieval economic expansion of Europe. Scandinavian voyages to North America had ceased in the fourteenth century, and the isolated Western outpost of Christianity in Greenland vanished under the onslaught of advancing ice by the middle of the fifteenth. In comparison with the Ottoman Empire or Ming China, Europe's puny, impoverished states seemed more prone to quarreling among themselves than to seeking expanded horizons.

Nevertheless, by 1500 Europeans could be found fighting and trading in Africa, the Americas, and Asia. A mere fifty years later, Europeans had destroyed the two greatest civilizations in the Americas, had begun the forced migration of Africans to the Americas through the slave trade, and had opened trading posts throughout South and East Asia.

Before 1500 the West, identified by its languages, religion, agricultural technology, literature, folklore, music, art, and common intellectual tradition that stretched back to pre-Christian antiquity, was largely confined to Europe and the Middle East. After 1500 the wandering Europeans began to export Western culture to the rest of the world.

Especially after large numbers of European settlers moved to the Americas, the culture and technology of western Europe began to spread around the globe. After the sixteenth century, European culture could be found in many distant lands, and western European languages and forms of Christianity were adopted by or forced upon other peoples. The West was now more of an idea than a place, a certain kind of culture that thrived in many different environments. The process was not all one-way, however: Western Europeans came under the influence of the far-flung cultures they visited, transforming Europe into the most cosmopolitan corner of the Earth. The European voyages integrated the globe biologically and economically. Microbes, animals, and plants that had once been isolated were now transported throughout the world. Because the Europeans possessed the ships for transport and the guns for coercion, they became the dominant players in international trade, even in places thousands of miles from the European homeland.

To understand the European encounters with the world during the fifteenth and sixteenth centuries, this chapter will address four central questions: (1) Why did the European incursions into sub-Saharan Africa lead to the vast migration of Africans to the Americas as slaves? (2) How did the arrival of Europeans in the Americas transform native cultures and life? (3) Why was the European encounter with Asian civilizations far less disruptive than those in Africa and the Americas? (4) How was the world tied together in a global biological and economic system?

Europeans in Africa

Geographers of the ancient world, writing in Greek and Latin, had accumulated a substantial knowledge about all of North Africa, but they were almost completely ignorant of the region south of the Sahara desert. Medieval writers remained equally ill-informed, reporting that sub-Saharan Africa was populated by man-eaters, "great giants of twenty-eight foot long . . . and they eat more gladly man's flesh than any other flesh" and Amazons, warrior women who cut off one breast to facilitate archery.

In reality, the interior of sub-Saharan Africa had been governed for centuries by highly developed kingdoms and boasted numerous wealthy cities. By the fifteenth century, Muslim contacts with sub-Saharan Africa made it clear that the region was a rich source of gold and slaves. In search of these, Europeans, especially the Portuguese, began to swarm down the west coast of Africa. Enabled by new developments in ship technology, the Europeans were capable of making long sea voyages. European settlers founded colonies in the Atlantic islands off the west coast of Africa, establishing precedents for colonies that would later be installed in the Americas.

Sub-Saharan Africa Before the Europeans Arrived

During the Middle Ages a number of kingdoms that emulated ancient Egyptian forms of rulership arose south of the Sahara desert. Some kingdoms boasted large cities and consisted of as many as a million inhabitants who were subjects of strongly centralized regimes. The kingdoms were administered by public officials who could be transferred, demoted, or promoted according to the king's will in a bureaucratic system that paralleled what the European states had achieved.

For Europeans, the principal attraction to Africa were reports of its rich deposits of gold. These reports came from the Muslim kingdom of Mali, a landlocked empire between the Upper Senegal and Niger Rivers, to the north of the Guinea coast. The source of Mali's wealth was its monopoly of the gold caravans that carried the coveted metal from the fabled city of Timbuktu across the Sahara to the gold-greedy Mediterranean. The king of Mali, known as the Mansa, never owned the gold mines, the location of which was a closely kept secret, but he controlled the gold market. The gold from the mines went to the Mansa, whose agents traded it in distant lands for luxury goods. The Mansa's power rested on his cavalry, which by the middle of the fourteenth century had spread the rule of Mali from the Gambia and lower Senegal Rivers in the West through the Niger valley to South.

■ **Timbuktu, Mali**

This drawing was made by a nineteenth-century French explorer, René-Auguste Caillié, but it illustrates the city that had been built during the fourteenth century by the Mansa Musa. Built from the proceeds of the gold trade, Timbuktu became a major center of Islamic learning and was only one of several great Malian cities that arose during the fourteenth century.

The wealth of the Mansa became legendary after Mansa Musa (r. 1312–1337) conducted a spectacular pilgrimage to the Muslim holy city of Mecca in 1324. Mansa Musa made a magnificently opulent impression. A gold bird sat above the parasol that shaded him from the sun, and he carried a gilded staff, wore a gold skull cap, strung a gold quiver over his shoulder, and affixed a gold scabbard to his waist. The pilgrimage took more than a year, and Mansa Musa was so generous that his trip was remembered for centuries in Egypt, where he stayed for three months. He gave out so much gold that Egypt suffered a disastrous inflation of prices. Traveling with as many as a hundred camels, each loaded with 300 pounds of gold, the Mansa gave whole ingots of gold to officials along the way and to religious shrines he visited.

By 1400, however, the kingdom of Mali was in decline. Internal power struggles had split apart the once-vast empire. In 1482, when the Portuguese founded a gold-trading post at Elmina, some sixty miles west of the mouth of the Volta, they had to negotiate with a ruler called the Karamansa, whose title echoed the past glories of the Mansa of Mali but whose power was a mere shadow of what the rulers of Mali exercised during the fourteenth century (see Map 12.1).

Influenced by Mali, the forest kingdoms of Guinea were built on a prosperous urban society and extensive trading networks. Benin was a particularly great city, which European travelers compared favorably with the principal European cities of the time. The towns of Guinea held regular markets, similar to the periodic fairs of Europe, and carefully scheduled them so they would not compete with each other. The staples of the long-distance trade routes in this region were high-value luxury goods, especially imported cloth, kola nuts (a mild stimulant popular in Muslim countries), metalwork such as cutlasses, ivory, and of course gold. For money, African traders used cowrie shells, brought all the way from the Indian Ocean.

Unlike the kingdoms of the western sub-Sahara, which tended to be Muslim, mountainous Ethiopia was predominantly Christian. In fact, Europeans saw Ethiopians as potential allies against Islam. The Roman Catholic pope sent a delegation to Ethiopia in 1316, and Ethiopian embassies

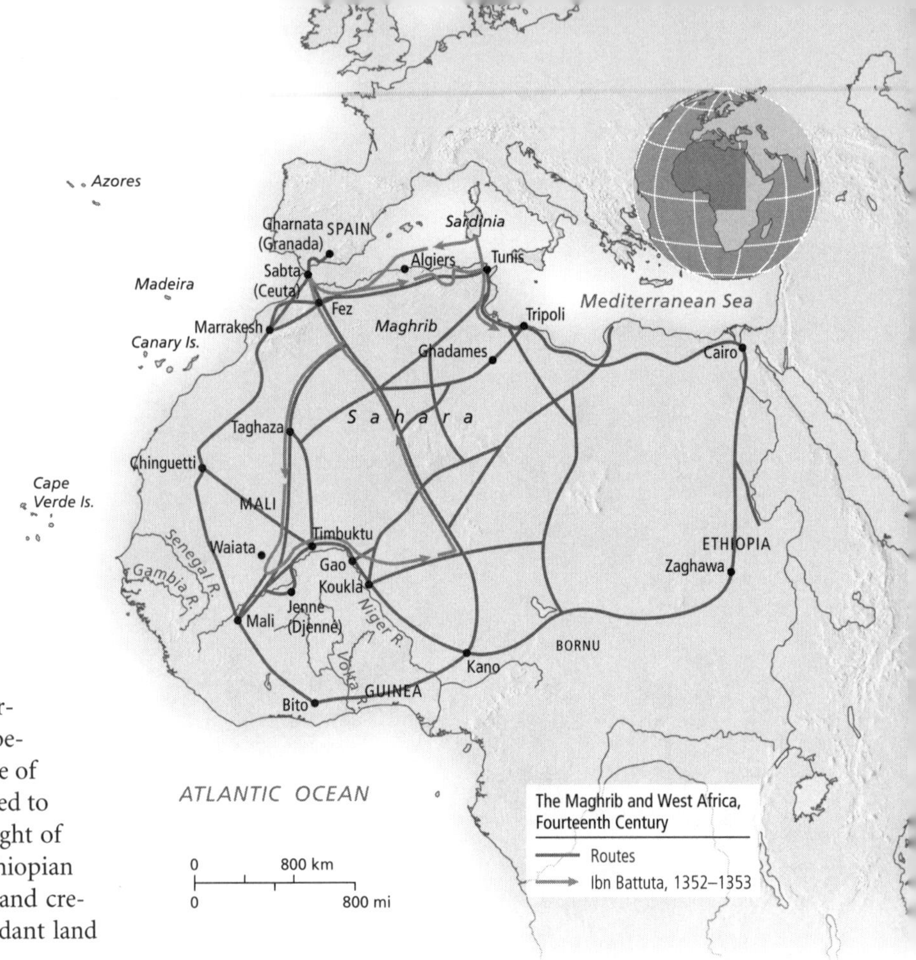

■ **Map 12.1 The Maghrib and West Africa, Fourteenth Century**
Long before the arrival of the Portuguese via sea routes, caravans of camels crisscrossed the Sahara desert during the fourteenth century, linking the sources of gold in Mali with the Maghrib (the coast of northwest Africa) and the seaports of the Mediterranean. The greatest medieval Arabic traveller, Ibn Battuta (1304–1368/69) crossed the Sahara and spent more than a year in Mali. He left the most extensive account of medieval West Africa.

occasionally appeared in Italy and Portugal during the fifteenth century. Diplomatic contacts between Rome and Ethiopia intensified at the time of the Council of Florence in 1439, which attempted to unify Christianity in defense against the onslaught of the Muslim Ottoman Turks. Learned Ethiopian churchmen became known in western Europe and created the impression that Ethiopia was an abundant land peopled by pious Christians.

Conditions during the later Middle Ages tended to confirm this image of Ethiopia. Threatened by Muslim invaders in 1270, the Ethiopian kingdom created a powerful army, rumors of which tantalized European Christians who sought allies against Islam. As the armies expanded Ethiopian power to the south and east, missionaries proselytized among the conquered peoples and helped unify the kingdom. Ethiopian expansion greatly enriched the kingdom through the control of trade in ivory, gold, slaves, and civet, a highly prized musky perfume. Portuguese visitors were duly impressed by the splendor of the emperor of Ethiopia, the Negus, who traveled with 2,000 attendants and 50,000 mules to carry provisions and tents.

By the early sixteenth century, the Ethiopian kingdom had become overextended. In the 1520s and 1530s Muslims attacked deep into the Ethiopian heartland, raiding and burning the wealthy Ethiopian monasteries. The raids severely weakened the power of the Negus. By destroying relics and religious images, the Muslims eradicated much of the great artistic heritage of Ethiopia. Ethiopia survived with the help of a Portuguese expeditionary force, but it was hobbled by competing Christian warlords and a weak central power, and it never regained its previous strength.

During the fifteenth and sixteenth centuries when European contacts with the sub-Sahara dramatically expanded, the once-strong kingdoms were either in decline or engaged in protracted struggles with regional rivals. The Europeans arrived at precisely the moment when they could take advantage of the weaknesses produced by internal African conflicts.

European Voyages Along the African Coast

Although sub-Saharan Africa represented something of a mystery to Europeans, merchants from Italy, Catalonia, Castile, and Portugal had long shown interest in the ports of the Maghreb, the collective name for the present-day regions of Morocco, Algeria, and Tunisia on the Mediterranean coast of North Africa. There they brought wool and woolen textiles, wine, dye stuffs, and clandestine items such as weapons, which they traded for various commodities, most significantly gold. Since at least the mid-thirteenth century, the Maghreb had been famous as the northern terminus of the gold caravans from Mali. In the thirteenth and fourteenth centuries, European traders obtained gold in the Maghreb in exchange for silver mined in Europe. They then resold the gold in the ports along the northern shore of the Mediterranean for more silver than they had originally paid to buy the gold. With the handsome silver profits made in the gold trade, merchants provided a steady supply that encouraged the general adoption of gold coinage throughout much of southern Europe. Gold was highly prized in Europe largely because it was rare in comparison to silver, and by the laws of supply and demand the commodity that is scarce is more valuable.

To gain more direct access to the sources of gold, European traders occasionally crossed the Sahara with the camel caravans—the "ships of the desert." For example, the

Florentine merchant Benedetto Dei told of traveling in 1470 as far as Timbuktu, where he saw many examples of European textiles on the local market. The efficient camel caravans created a vast trading network that stretched from Mali and Morocco in the west of Africa into central Asia, completely bypassing the Mediterranean. But Europeans had little hope of regularly using the "sea of sand" routes across North Africa because of the hostility of Muslim inhabitants who were wary about foreign interlopers, especially Christian ones.

The alternative for Europeans was to outflank the Muslims by crossing the sea of water. As early as the thirteenth century, European voyagers ventured down the west coast of Africa into uncharted waters. In 1291 the Vivaldi brothers left Genoa with the goal of circumnavigating Africa to reach the Indies. But their galleys were adapted to the relatively calm waters of the Mediterranean and were ill-suited for the voyage. Such ships, which required large crews of oarsmen, were easily swamped in the heavy seas of the Atlantic, and the long coastline of West Africa lacked protective harbors for refuge from storms. The Vivaldi expedition disappeared without a trace.

New Maritime Technology

The disadvantages of Mediterranean galleys were surmounted during the fifteenth century through changes in the technology of ocean sailing. The Iberian peninsula (the land of present-day Portugal and Spain), situated between the Mediterranean and the Atlantic, was uniquely located to develop a hybrid ship that combined features of Mediterranean and Atlantic types. The initial impulse for developing the shipping technology was to facilitate trade between the Mediterranean and northern Europe via the Atlantic. The resulting changes, however, also made possible much more ambitious voyages into the unknown southern regions.

The Iberians modified the cog design, the dominant ship in the Atlantic, by adding extra masts and creating a new kind of rigging that combined the square sails of Atlantic ships, suitable for sailing in the same direction as the wind was blowing, with the triangular "lateen" sails of Mediterranean galleys, which permitted sailing into the wind. The result was a ship that could sail in a variety of winds, carry large cargoes, be managed by a small crew, and be defended by guns mounted in the castle superstructure. These hybrid three-mast ships, called caravels°, appeared about 1450, and for the next 200 years Europeans sailed ships of this same basic design on long ocean voyages to the very ends of the Earth.

Also assisting European navigators were other technological innovations, the fruit of late medieval Mediterranean seafaring. The compass provided an approximate indicator of direction, and the astrolabe and naked-eye celestial navigation made it possible to estimate latitudes.

An Early Caravel
The caravel was typical of the hybrid ship developed during the fifteenth century on the Iberian peninsula.

Books of sailing directions, called portolanos°, included charts and descriptions of ports and recorded the location of dangerous shoals and safe harbors for future voyages. The advances in maritime technology made it possible for Europeans motivated by economic need and religious fervor to sail wherever they wanted.

New Colonialism

During the fifteenth century, European colonialism departed somewhat from the patterns of the past. Mediterranean colonies established during the Crusades of the twelfth and thirteenth centuries had relied on native inhabitants to produce commodities that could be expropriated by the colonizers. These were either aristocratic colonies in which a few warriors occupied castles to dominate the native population or mercantile colonies built around a trading post for foreign merchants.

As Europeans ventured into the Atlantic more frequently and expanded their contacts with sub-Saharan Africa, they established new patterns of colonization. In search of fertile lands for agriculture, Castile and Portugal founded colonies in the Canary Islands, the Madeira archipelago, the Azores,

■ **Oceangoing Ship**
This is a Flemish version of the three-mast ship, square-rigged on the foremast and mainmast, lateen-rigged on the mizzenmast. Versions of this ship carried Europeans throughout the world.

and the Cape Verde Islands. The climate of these islands was similar to the Mediterranean and invited the cultivation of typical Mediterranean crops, such as grains and sugar cane, but the islands lacked a native labor force. When Europeans arrived, the Canaries were seriously underpopulated and the other islands were uninhabited. In response to the labor shortage, two new types of colonies emerged, both of which were later introduced into the Americas.

The first new type of colony during this period was the settler colony°. The settler colony derived from the medieval, feudal model of government, in which a private person obtained a license from a king to seize an island or some part of an island. The king supplied financial support and legal authority for the expedition. In return the settler promised to recognize the king as his lord and occasionally to pay a fee after the settlement was successful. The kings of Castile and Portugal issued such licenses for the exploitation of Atlantic islands. The actual expeditions to colonize these islands were private enterprises, and adventurers from various parts of Europe vied for a license from any king who would grant them one. For example, the first European settlement in the Canary Islands was led by a Norman knight, Jean de Béthencourt, who could not obtain sufficient support from the king of France and thus switched loyalties to the king of Castile.

After the arrival of the Europeans, all the natives of the Canaries, called the Guanches, died off, creating the need for settler families from Europe to till the land and maintain the Castilian claim on the islands. These peasants and artisans, rather than living like islanders and adapting to the native culture, imposed their own culture. They brought with them their traditional family structures, customs, language, religion, seeds, livestock, and patterns of cultivation. Wherever settler colonies were found, whether in the Atlantic islands or the Americas, which the Europeans called the New World, they Europeanized the landscape and remade the lands they cultivated in the image of the Old World.

The second new type of colony was the plantation colony°. Until the occupation of the Cape Verde Islands in the 1460s, the Atlantic island colonies had relied on European settlers for labor. However, the Cape Verdes attracted few immigrants because of the rigors of the tropical climate, and yet the islands seemed especially well-suited for growing the lucrative sugar cane crop. The few permanent European colonists there tended to be exiled criminals, who had no choice but to stay, and the Cape Verdes became a haven for lawless ruffians who were disinclined to work. Because there was no indigenous population to exploit on the Cape Verdes, the few European colonizers began to look elsewhere for laborers and voyaged to the African coast where they bought slaves who had been captured from inland villages. These slaves worked as agricultural laborers in the Cape Verdes sugar cane fields. Thus, in the Cape Verdes began the tragic conjunction between African slavery and the European demand for sugar. When sugar began to replace honey as the sweetener of choice for Europeans, the almost insatiable demand was supplied by sugar cultivated by slaves in plantation colonies, first in the Atlantic islands and later in the West Indies and American mainland. Over the next 300 years, this pattern for plantation colonies was repeated for other valuable agricultural commodities, such as indigo for dyes, coffee, and cotton, which were grown to sell in European markets. The first loop of what would eventually become a global trading circuit was now completed.

The Portuguese in Africa

The first European voyages along the African coast during the fifteenth century were launched by the Portuguese. The sponsor of these voyages was Prince Henry the Navigator (1394–1460). As governor of Algarve, the southernmost province of Portugal, Henry established a headquarters at

Sagres and financed numerous exploratory voyages. Driven by the quest for fame and a profound faith in astrology, Henry had two objectives above all else: In order to enhance his reputation, he wanted to steal the Canary Islands from his archrival, the king of Castile; and to reward the men who sailed his ships, he desperately needed to get his hands on more gold.

The first Portuguese expeditions along the African coast were prompted by Henry's desire to capture the Canaries. He tried armed force, negotiations with the inhabitants, and entreaties to the pope, all with no success. He even purchased phony titles to the Canaries in a transparent attempt to fool the Castilians that he was really the lord of the islands. In the mid-1450s, however, Henry's disappointment over the Canaries subsided as it became evident that gold from Mali could be obtained further south from bases near the Senegal and Gambia rivers. Although the many voyages of Henry's sailors did not fulfill his dreams of conquest and enormous riches, he and other members of his family did help colonize Madeira and the Azores, and as a source of sugar, Madeira became a valuable colony (see Map 12.2).

CHRONOLOGY

Europeans in Africa

1270	Beginnings of the Ethiopian kingdom
1316	Papal delegation sent to Ethiopia
1324	Pilgrimage to Mecca by Mansa Musa of Mali
1394–1460	Life of Prince Henry the Navigator of Portugal
1450s	Appearance of new European ship designs, the caravel
CA. 1450	European slave trade in Africa begins
1460s	Occupation of Cape Verde Islands
1482	Portuguese gold-trading post founded at Elmina
1520s–1530s	Muslim attacks against Ethiopian kingdom

Map 12.2 Europeans in the World, Fifteenth and Sixteenth Centuries

During the fifteenth and sixteenth centuries European sailors opened sea lanes for commerce across the Atlantic, Pacific, and Indian Oceans. Dates indicate first arrival of Europeans.

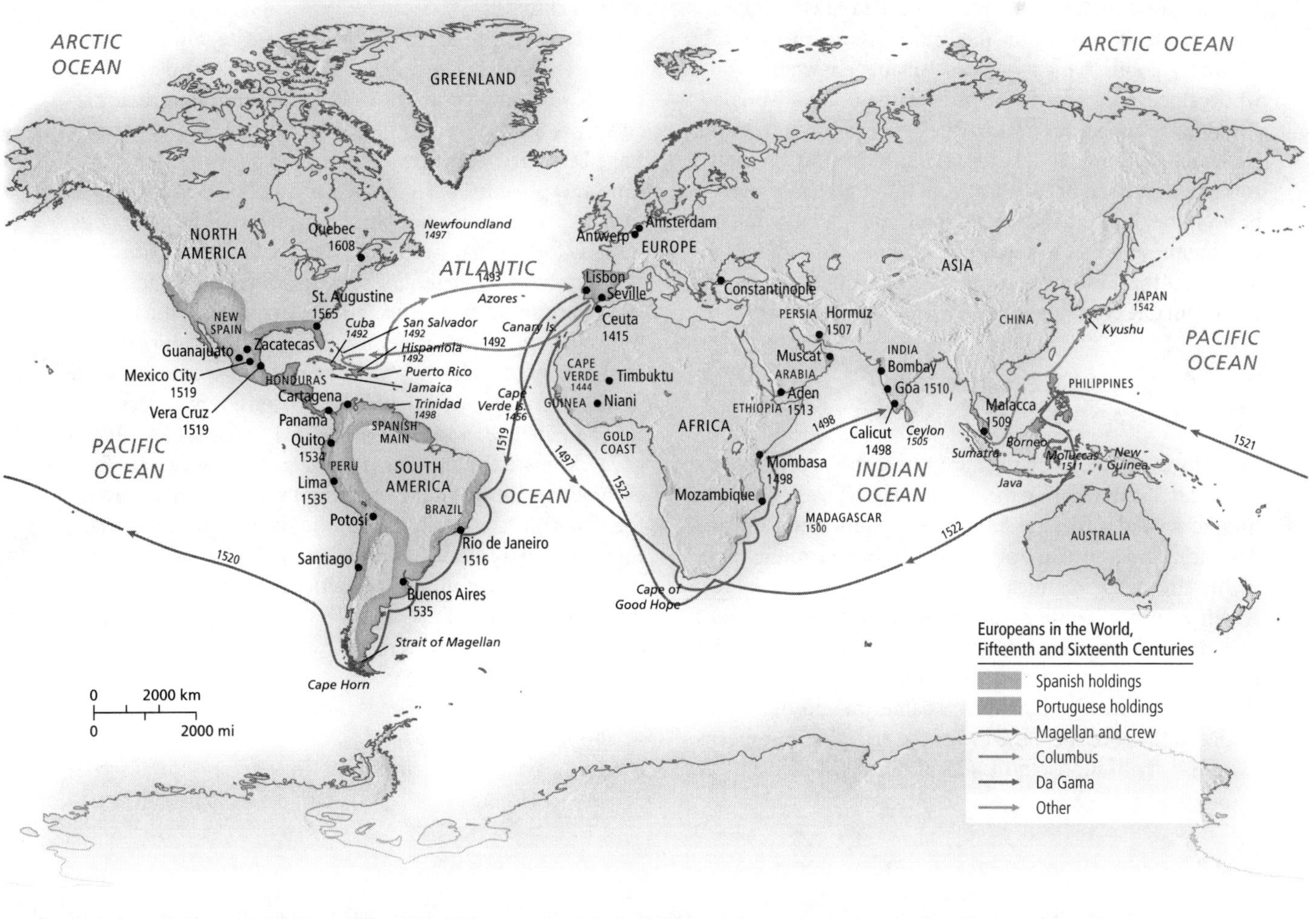

After Henry's death, Portuguese exploration of the African coast accelerated. In only six years, a private merchant of Lisbon commissioned voyages that added 2,000 miles of coastline that was known to the Portuguese. In 1482 the exploration policy that had been a loose and haphazard enterprise under private contractors was transformed. That year the Portuguese royal house took control of trade with Africa; they required that all sailings be authorized and all cargoes inventoried, and they built a permanent fortress at Elmina near the mouth of the Volta River. At Elmina, Portuguese traders found local sources of gold and opportunities to obtain more upriver. Rather than establishing new settler or plantation colonies, the Portuguese on the African coast relied on trading posts that supplied gold, ivory, pepper, and slaves.

Europeans in the Americas

Like the Europeans who sailed along the African coast, the first European voyagers to the Americas coveted gold and an alternative route to India and China. The European impulse to reach Asia by sailing west came from the fact that the Ottoman Empire, which was pushing into the Mediterranean after the conquest of Constantinople in 1453, blocked the traditional trade routes through the Middle East and across the Black and Red Seas. Europeans relied on Asian sources for medicines, spices, and all kinds of luxury goods, which were unavailable elsewhere. Those who gained access to the source of these lucrative goods could make enormous profits. The desire to profit from this trade impelled men to take great risks to find an alternative route to East Asia. In the short run, the Americas proved to be an impediment to achieving these goals because the two continents stood in the way of getting to Asia. But in the long run, the European voyages to the Americas brought unimaginable consequences.

The Americas Before the Conquistadores

Prior to their contact with Europeans, the peoples of the Americas displayed remarkable cultural variety. Nomadic hunters spread across the sub-Arctic regions, western North America, and the Amazon jungles, while farming settlements prevailed in much of South America and eastern North America. Some of these North American cultures, such as the Anasazi and Iroquois, developed highly sophisticated forms of political organization, but none matched the advanced civilizations of Mesoamerica and the central Andes to the south. On the eve of the arrival of Europeans, two great civilizations, the Aztecs of central Mexico and the Incas of highland Peru, had built extensive empires that dominated their neighbors.

The Mexican Empire of the Aztecs

Mesoamerica (the region we know today as Mexico and Central America) had been the home of a series of highly urbanized, politically centralized cultures: the Mayans (300–900), the Toltecs (900–1325), and finally the Aztecs (1325 to the Spanish conquest in 1522). The Aztecs found safety from incessant warfare with neighboring tribes on an island in Lake Texcoco, where they established the city of Tenochtitlán, now Mexico City. From their base at Tenochtitlán the Aztecs followed a brilliantly successful policy of divide and conquer, first allying with powerful neighbors to attack weaker groups, then turning against former allies.

The Aztec king, Montezuma I (r. 1440–1469), consolidated an empire that stretched across most of central Mexico. In order to provide food for his people during a severe famine between 1450 and 1454, Montezuma first conquered the breadbasket of Mexico, the rich coastal region of the Totonacs. In repeated attacks, swarms of Aztec troops took city after city, captured the local chief whenever possible, burned the temple, and extorted tribute payments from the population. With the riches gained from conquest, Montezuma transformed Tenochtitlán from a dusty town of mud houses to a great imperial capital built of stone with a grand botanical garden that displayed plants taken from various climates.

The Aztecs excelled in the perpetual state of war that had long been the dominant fact of life in Mexico, and as a result they attributed great religious value to war. From their predecessors they inherited the concept of the "flowery war," a staged occurrence when states agreed to a predetermined time and place for a battle, the only objective of which was to take prisoners for temple sacrifice. Sustaining the gods' hunger for human sacrifices became the most notorious feature of Aztec religion. The Aztecs attributed their military successes to their tribal god, Huitzilpochti, the giver of light and all things necessary for life, but Huitzilpochti could be nourished only with human blood, creating the need among the Aztec faithful to acquire human captives.

The rituals of sacrifice permeated Aztec society. It has been estimated that some 10,000 victims were sacrificed each year, with the number rising to 50,000 on the eve of the Spanish conquest. From the very first encounters, Europeans have been baffled by the paradox of Aztec culture. Despite their apparent practice of human sacrifice, the Aztecs displayed refined manners, a sensitivity to beauty, and a highly developed religion.

The Incan Empire of the Andes

At about the same time the Aztecs were thriving in Mexico, the Incas expanded their empire in Peru and developed a

The Aztec Rite of Human Sacrifice
Human victims had their hearts cut out by a priest at the top of the stairs to a temple.

comprehensive imperial ideal. Whereas the Aztecs created a loosely linked empire based on tribute payments, the Incas employed a more direct form of rulership. As they pushed out from their base in the south Andes during the fifteenth century, they imposed on conquered peoples their own form of economic organization, their culture, and their religion.

The first Incan emperor, Pachacuti Inca Yupanqui (r. 1438–1471), founded the empire around 1438 when he spread Incan rule beyond the valley of Cuzco. By the end of the fifteenth century, the Incas had begun to integrate by force the distinctive cultures of the various conquered regions. In this way, they created a mountain empire 200 miles wide and 2,000 miles long, stretching from modern-day Chile to Ecuador and comprising a population of about ten million. From his capital at Cuzco, the Incan emperor lived in luxury and established an elaborately hierarchic political structure. His authority was carried through layers of aristocrats down to officials who were responsible for every ten families in every village. These families supplied food and tribute for the empire, worked on roads and bridges, and served in the army. State-owned warehouses of food guaranteed the peasants freedom from starvation and provided for the sick and elderly.

Emperor Huayna Capac (r. 1493–1525) founded a second capital further south at Quito, established to decentralize the overextended empire, but at his death a bitter civil war broke out between the northern and southern halves of the empire, led respectively by his rival sons. This war weakened Incan unity on the eve of the Spanish conquest.

The Incas were impressive in creating a strong imperial administration, and as rulers they were as severe as the Aztecs. Huayna Capac slaughtered some 20,000 recalcitrant Caranqui and poisoned Lake Yahuar-Cocha with their corpses. After conquering a region, the Incas would kill the native population or remove them to a secure area and replace the inhabitants with loyal colonists. During the early sixteenth century, for example, Huayna Capac brought in 14,000 colonists from all over the empire to settle the Cochabamba valley. A superb network of roads and bridges covered more than 18,000 miles and made it possible to communicate with relays of runners who could cover as much as 140 miles a day. Troops could also be quickly dispatched to trouble spots via these roads. Despite this well-organized imperial system, the Incan Empire became overly centralized and decisions could only be made by the emperor himself, a fatal flaw that, as we shall see, allowed the Spanish invaders to crush it very quickly.

THE MISSION OF THE EUROPEAN VOYAGERS

The European arrival in the Americas was the result of a mistake promoted by Christopher Columbus's (1451–1506) stubborn sense of mission. Born in Genoa to an artisan family, Columbus followed the destiny of so many of his compatriots by becoming a sailor. "From my earliest

Christopher Columbus
A portrait of the navigator.

youth," he reported late in life, "I went to sea and I have remained at sea until this day. It has occupied me for more than forty years. Wherever men have sailed, I too have sailed." Of his skills as a navigator and seaman there can be no doubt, but his personality remains an enigma that has allowed a wide variety of interpretations. Historians once depicted Columbus as a practical-minded experimenter, who was opposed by ignorant fools, but now he is understood as a more complex figure whose defining characteristic was his religious devotion. Columbus believed that he had been predestined to fulfill biblical prophecies. If he could reach China, he could outflank the Ottoman Turks and recapture Jerusalem from the Muslims who had held it since 1187, an achievement that would usher in the Second Coming of Christ. In trying to convince Queen Isabella of Castile to finance his mission to voyage to China by sailing west, he later admitted that to make his case he ignored navigational data and, instead, relied "entirely on holy, sacred Scripture and certain prophetic texts by certain saintly persons, who by divine revelation have had something to say on this matter."[1]

It had long been recognized that it was theoretically possible to reach China, Columbus's goal, by sailing west. Most educated people, and certainly all those influenced by the Renaissance humanists, agreed the world was round. The problem was not a theoretical one about the shape of the Earth but a practical one about getting around it. During Columbus's life the most widely accepted authority on the circumference of the Earth was the ancient Greek geographer Ptolemy, who had estimated that the distance across the Atlantic Ocean from Europe to Asia was more than 10,000 miles. The practical problem was that no ship in Columbus's day could hope to sail that far without landfalls along the way for finding provisions and making repairs. In fact, Ptolemy had underestimated the size of the Earth by 25 percent, but Columbus decided that Ptolemy had overestimated the distance. Columbus also imagined that the wealthy island of Japan lay farther east of the Asian continent than it actually does, thus further minimizing the distance of the voyage. When he first presented his project for sailing west to Asia, King John II of Portugal consulted a committee of experts who quite correctly pointed out how seriously Columbus had miscalculated the distance. Skilled navigator that he was, Columbus was no geographer. His extremely inaccurate estimate of how close China was seems to have been more the result of wishful thinking and religious fervor than geographical expertise. King John's rejection led Columbus to seek patronage elsewhere. Columbus applied to Queen Isabella of newly unified Spain, whose own advisers at first recommended against the voyage for the same reasons the Portuguese experts had rejected his plan. When the Spanish defeated the Muslim kingdom of Granada in 1492, which completed the Christian reconquest of the Iberian peninsula, Isabella succumbed to the religious enthusiasm of the moment and relented. She offered Columbus a commission for the voyage in the hope that it would ensure a final Christian victory over Islam.

On August 3, 1492, Columbus set sail with three small ships—the Niña, Pinta, and Santa Maria—and a crew of some ninety men and boys. After refitting in the Canary Islands, the modest convoy entered unknown waters guided only by Columbus's faith in finding China, which was, in fact, many thousands of miles farther west than he thought it would be. At two in the morning on the moonlit night of October 12, a lookout spied land, probably Watling Island in the Bahamas.

In all, Columbus made four voyages across the Atlantic (1492, 1493, 1498, 1502), exploring the Caribbean Islands, the coast of Central America, and part of the coast of South America. He never abandoned the belief that he had arrived in Asia. His four voyages were filled with adventures. On the third voyage, he was arrested by the newly appointed Spanish governor of Hispaniola on false charges and sent home in chains for trial; on the fourth he was marooned for nearly a year on Jamaica after worms weakened the timbers of his ships. He garnered considerable wealth in gold found on his voyages, but he never received the titles and offices that Queen Isabella had promised him before his first voyage.

Soon after Columbus returned to Spain from his first voyage, the Spanish monarchs who had sponsored him tried to obtain a monopoly to explore the western Atlantic. They applied to Pope Alexander VI, who was himself a Spaniard and sympathetic to their request. In an effort to give the Spanish a firm legal monopoly to the lands across the Atlantic, the pope confirmed in 1493 the right of Spanish sailors to explore all lands to the west as long as they did not infringe upon the rights of another Christian ruler. Since all involved still thought Columbus had arrived in China, the obvious other Christian ruler was the king of Portugal, whose sailors had already pushed far enough south down the African coast to realize that they could eventually reach China by sailing east. The pope ordered a line of demarcation drawn along a north-south line 100 leagues (about 300 miles) west of the Azores and Cape Verde Islands. Spain received all lands to the west of the line; Portugal obtained the lands to the east. This line of demarcation seemed to limit the Portuguese to Africa, which alarmed them and led to direct negotiations between the Portuguese and the Spaniards. The result of the negotiations was the Treaty of Tordesillas in 1494, which moved the line of demarcation to 370 leagues (about 1,110 miles) west of the Cape Verde Islands, a decision that granted to Portugal all of Africa, India, and Brazil.

Despite Columbus's persistent faith that he had found a route to the East Indies, other voyagers began to suspect, even before Columbus's death, that he had not found Asia at all and that other routes had to be explored. Another Italian, the Florentine Amerigo Vespucci (1454–1512), met Columbus, helped him prepare for the third voyage, and later made at least two voyages of his own across the Atlantic. From his voyages, Vespucci recognized something of the immensity of the South American continent and was the first to use the term "New World." Because he used the term and because the account of his voyages got into print before Columbus's, Vespucci's given name, Amerigo, came to be attached to the New World rather than Columbus's. By the 1520s, Europeans had explored the Americas extensively enough to recognize that the New World was nowhere near India or China.

After the Treaty of Tordesillas, explorers followed two distinct strategies for finding a sea route to East Asia. The Portuguese continued to pursue routes to the south and east around Africa. Between 1487 and 1488, Bartholomew Dias (ca. 1450–1500) reached the Cape of Good Hope at the southern tip of the African continent. This discovery made it evident that passage to India could be achieved by sailing south, rounding the tip of Africa, and crossing the Indian Ocean. Political and financial problems in Portugal prevented a followup to Dias's voyage for ten years, however. Between 1497 and 1499, Vasco da Gama (ca. 1460–1524) finally succeeded in sailing from Lisbon to India around the Cape of Good Hope. This celebrated voyage included a great looping westward course far out into the Atlantic to escape the doldrums, an area in the ocean where the

COLUMBUS'S CHRISTIAN MISSION

One of the most common features of Christopher Columbus's writings is the prevalence of Christian images and themes. Expectations of Christian salvation and the second coming of Christ motivated Columbus in his attempts to reach Asia by sailing west. The Introduction to the journal of his first voyage offers a glimpse of Columbus's militant Christianity. It depicts the stirring moment of Christian triumph when the Muslim king of Grenada surrendered to Ferdinand and Isabella in 1492.

I saw your Highnesses' banners victoriously raised on the towers of the Alhambra, the citadel of that city [of Grenada], and the Moorish king come out of the city gates and kiss the hands of your Highnesses [Ferdinand and Isabella] . . . And later in that same month, on the grounds of information I had given your royal Highnesses concerning the lands of India and a prince who is called the Great Khan—which means in Spanish 'King of Kings'—and of his and his ancestors' frequent and vain applications to Rome for men learned in the holy faith who should instruct them in it, your Highnesses decided to send me, Christopher Columbus, to see these parts of India and the princes and peoples of those lands and consider the best means for their conversion. For, by the neglect of the Popes to send instructors, many nations had fallen to idolatory and adopted doctrines of perdition, and your Highnesses as Catholic princes and devoted propagators of the holy Christian faith have always been enemies of the sect of Mahomet and of all idolatries and heresies.

Your Highnesses ordained that I should not go eastward by land in the usual manner but by the western way which no one about whom we have positive information has ever followed. Therefore having expelled all the Jews from your dominions in that same month of January, your Highnesses commanded me to go with an adequate fleet to those parts of India.

Source: From *The Four Voyages of Christopher Columbus,* translated by J. M. Cohen (London: Penguin Classics, 1969).

winds died. As a consequence of the route opened by da Gama, the Portuguese were the first Europeans to establish trading posts in Asia. They reached the Malabar coast of India in 1498 and soon found their way to the Spice Islands and China. By the middle of the sixteenth century, the Portuguese had assembled a string of more than fifty trading posts° and forts from Sofala on the east coast of Africa to Nagasaki in Japan.

The second strategy for reaching Asia consisted of Spanish attempts to pursue Columbus's proposed route west. The problem faced by those sailing under the Spanish flag was to find a way around the barrier presented by the American continents. A Portuguese sailor named Ferdinand Magellan (ca. 1480–1521), who had previously sailed to Asia aboard Portuguese ships, persuaded the king of Spain to sponsor a voyage to Asia sailing west around South America. That venture (1519–1522), which began under Magellan's command, passed through the strait named after him at the tip of South America and crossed the Pacific in a voyage of extreme hardship as his men suffered from thirst and hunger and died of scurvy. Magellan himself was killed by natives in the Philippines. After three years at sea, 18 survivors from the original 240 in Magellan's fleet reached Seville, having sailed around the world for the first time. Contemporaries immediately recognized the epic significance of the voyage, but the route opened by Magellan was too long and arduous for the Spanish to employ as a reliable alternative to the Portuguese route around Africa.

In the course of three centuries (about 1480–1780), European navigators linked the previously isolated routes of seaborne commerce, opened all the seas of the world to trade, and encountered many of the cultures and peoples of the world. For the first hundred years or so, the Portuguese and Spanish effectively maintained a monopoly over these trade routes, but gradually English, Dutch, and French sailors made their way all around the globe. In the Americas, inadvertently made known to Europeans by Christopher Columbus, the Spanish immediately began settlements and attempted to subdue the indigenous populations.

THE DIFFICULT LIFE OF SAILORS

During the expedition begun by Magellan, which completed the first circumnavigation of the globe, Antonio Pigafetta (ca. 1491–ca. 1536) kept a journal. The passage across the Pacific Ocean was especially difficult as food and water ran out. Sailors became so desperate that they ate sawdust from planks. The following entry is typical.

They sailed out from this strait [Strait of Magellan] into the Pacific Sea on the 28th of November in the year 1520, and they were three months and twenty days without eating anything [i.e., fresh food], and they ate biscuit, and when there was no more of that they ate the crumbs which were full of maggots and smelled strongly of mouse urine. They drank yellow water, already several days putrid. And they ate some of the hides that were on the largest shroud to keep it from breaking and that were very much toughened by the sun, rain and winds. And they softened them in the sea for four or five days, and then they put them in a pot over the fire and ate them and also much sawdust. A mouse would bring half a ducat or a ducat. The gums of some of the men swelled over their upper and lower teeth, so that they could not eat and so died. And nineteen men died from that sickness.

Source: From Antonio Pigafetta, *The Voyage of Magellan*, translated by Paula Spurlin Paige. Copyright © 1969 by The William J. Clements Library.

THE FALL OF THE AZTEC AND INCAN EMPIRES

Soon after the seafaring captains, such as Columbus and Magellan, came the conquistadores°, Spanish adventurers, usually from impoverished minor noble families. The conquistadores sought fortune and royal recognition through explorations and conquests of indigenous peoples. Spain was a poor land with few opportunities for advancement, a bleak situation that made the lands of the New World a powerful lure to many men seeking a fortune. Embroiled in almost continuous warfare in Europe, the Spanish crown was also perennially strapped for cash, which meant the king of Spain was highly motivated to encourage profitable foreign conquests. Many of the conquistadores launched their own expeditions with little or no legal authority, hoping to acquire sufficient riches to impress the king to give them official sanction for additional conquests. Those who did acquire legal authority from the crown received the privilege to conquer new lands in the name of the king of Spain and to keep a portion of those territories for themselves. In return they were obliged to turn over to the king one fifth—the "royal fifth"—of everything of value they acquired, an obligation enforced by a notary sent along with the conquistadores to keep a record of everything valuable that was found. The conquistadores also extended Spanish sovereignty over new lands and opened the way for missionaries to bring millions, at least nominally, into the Christian fold.

All conquistadores were required to read a document, called the requerimiento°, to the natives before making war on them. The document briefly explained the principles of Christianity and commanded the natives to accept them immediately along with the authority of the pope and the sovereignty of the king of Spain. If the natives refused, they were warned that they would be forced through war to sub-

Spanish Conquistadores Land on an Island in the New World
The armored Spaniards are met by the naked inhabitants who offer them jewels and gold. As one of their first acts, the Spaniards erect a cross, symbolizing the Christian conquest of the New World.

ject themselves "to the yoke and obedience of the Church and of Their Highnesses. We shall take you and your wives and your children, and shall make slaves of them, and as such shall sell and dispose of them as Their Highnesses may command. And we shall take your goods, and shall do you all the mischief and damage that we can."[2] The *requerimiento* revealed the conflicting motives behind the Spanish conquest. On the one hand, the Spanish were sincerely interested in converting the natives to Christianity. On the other, the conquistadores were trying to let themselves off the hook over the immorality of their actions by suggesting that the natives had brought the attack on themselves by refusing to obey the Spanish king.

Hernán Cortés and the Conquest of Mexico

Among the first and most successful of the conquistadores was Hernán Cortés (1485–1547). Cortés arrived on the Yucatán peninsula of present-day Mexico in February 1519, beginning a conquest that culminated in the collapse of the Aztec Empire and the Spanish colonization of Mexico. He followed a policy of divide and conquer with the natives, making alliances with peoples who hated the Aztecs and then using their warriors on the front lines of his battles where they absorbed most of the losses. If after a reading of the *requerimiento* the native chieftains did not immediately surrender, Cortés's men attacked them, breaking through their lines on horses, which the natives had never seen before.

After a number of bloody battles, Cortés set off with some 450 Spanish troops, 15 horses, and 4,000 native allies to conquer the great capital of the Aztec Empire, Tenochtitlán, a city of at least 300,000 and defended by thousands of warriors. As Cortés approached, Montezuma II was slow to set up a strong defense, because he suspected Cortés might be the white god, Quetzalcoatl, who according to prophecies would arrive one day from the east. The result was disastrous for the Aztecs. Montezuma knew his reign was doomed unless he could gain the assistance of other gods to drive Quetzalcoatl away. Thus, rather than an ardent military campaign, the king's defense primarily took the form of ritual sacrifices, which failed. Cortés captured Montezuma, who continued to rule for several months as a puppet of the conquistadores. The city revolted, however, killing Montezuma and driving out the Spanish. Cortés then gathered new troops and additional allies, built ships for use on the lake that surrounded Tenochtitlán, and besieged the city. By the time Tenochtitlán finally surrendered, the shiny jewel that had

Cortés Meets Montezuma in Tenochtitlán
The figure on the right is the native woman who served as Cortés's translator, a position often occupied by native women who served as mediators between the indigenous and Spanish cultures.

Spaniards Attacking Tenochtitlán, 1519
Notice how the Spaniards had placed cannons on the bows of these small ships, which were built to sail on the lake.

WHAT MONTEZUMA BELIEVED ABOUT THE SPANISH

After Cortés arrived in Tenochtitlán, he had an interview with Montezuma, the Aztec emperor. The following letter to the Emperor Charles V includes a speech Montezuma supposedly gave to Cortés in which the Aztec emperor surrendered authority to the Spanish because he assumed that Charles was an ancient ruler the Aztecs believed would return from the east. Just as Columbus was inspired by Christian prophecies to sail into the unknown, Montezuma was encouraged by Aztec prophecies to accept Cortés's invasion as a fulfillment of a religious obligation.

Long time have we been informed by the writings of our ancestors that neither myself nor any of those who inhabit this land are natives of it, but rather strangers who have come to it from foreign parts. We likewise know that from those parts our nation was led by a certain lord (to whom all were subject), and who then went back to his native land, where he remained so long delaying his return that at his coming those whom he had left had married the women of the land and had many children by them and had built themselves cities in which they lived, so that they would in no wise return to their own land nor acknowledge him as lord; upon which he left them. And we have always believed that among his descendants one would surely come to subject this land and us as rightful vassals. Now seeing the regions from which you [i.e., Cortés] say you come, which is from where the sun rises, and the news you tell of this great king and ruler [Emperor Charles V] who sent you hither, we believe and hold it certain that he is our natural lord: especially in that you say he has long had knowledge of us. Wherefore be certain that we will obey you and hold you as lord in place of that great lord of whom you speak, in which service there shall be neither slackness nor deceit: and throughout all the land, that is to say all that I rule, you may command anything you desire, and it shall be obeyed and done, and all that we have is at your will and pleasure. And since you are at your own land and house, rejoice and take your leisure from the fatigues of your journey and the battles you have fought; for I am well informed of all those that you have been forced to engage in on your way here. . . .

Source: From Hernán Cortés, "The Second Letter to Emperor Charles V" from Anthony Pagden, ed., *Letters from Mexico.*

so impressed the Spanish when they first glimpsed it from the surrounding mountains lay in smoldering ruins.

By 1522 Cortés controlled a territory in New Spain—as Mexico was renamed—larger than Old Spain itself. Aztec culture and its religion of human sacrifice disappeared as Franciscan friars arrived to evangelize the surviving population.

Francisco Pizarro and the Conquest of Peru

Like other conquistadores, Francisco Pizarro (ca. 1478–1541) was poor, but he bore the additional social liabilities of illegitimacy and illiteracy. With no prospects at home, Pizarro found his way to Panama where he accompanied Vasco Núñez de Balboa (1475–1519) on an expedition in 1513 across the Isthmus of Panama during which Europeans got their first look at the Pacific Ocean.

In 1531 Pizarro left Panama with a small expedition of some 180 men and 30 horses. His goal was to conquer Peru, known to be a land rich with gold. He gathered additional recruits along the way. He sailed to northern Peru and sent out spies who discovered that the Incan emperor, Atahuallpa, could be found in the highland city of Cajamarca. When Pizarro and his forces arrived there, the central square was empty, but Atahuallpa was encamped nearby with a large army. Pizarro treacherously invited Atahuallpa to come for a parlay, but instead took him captive. The news of the capture plunged the overly centralized Incan Empire into a crisis because no one dared take action without the emperor's orders. In an attempt to satisfy the Spaniards' hunger for gold and to win his freedom, Atahuallpa had a room filled with gold and silver for the conquistadores, but the treasure merely stimulated their appetite for more. In July 1533 Pizarro executed the emperor, and by the following November he had captured the demoralized Incan capital of Cuzco.

The conquest of Peru vastly increased the size of the Spanish Empire and began to satisfy the craving for gold that had impelled Columbus and the conquistadores in the first place. Through the collection of the royal fifth, gold and silver flowed into the royal coffers in Spain. The discovery in 1545 of the fabulous Peruvian silver mine of Potosí (in what is now in southern Bolivia) coincided with the introduction of the mercury amalgamation process that separated silver from ore. Mercury amalgamation enabled the Spaniards to replace surface gathering of silver ore with tunneling for ore, a procedure that led to greatly elevated yields of precious metals. For a century the silver of Peru helped provide otherwise impoverished Spain with the resources to become the most powerful kingdom in Europe.

The Ransom of a King
The Incas fill a room with gold objects to ransom Atahualpa.

SPANISH AMERICA: THE TRANSPLANTING OF A EUROPEAN CULTURE

With the defeat of the Aztec and Incan empires, the process of transplanting Spanish society to the Americas began in earnest. The arrival of Europeans was a catastrophe for most native peoples, some of whom—in the Caribbean, northern Argentina, and central Chile—completely disappeared through the ravages of conquest and disease. Whereas Spanish became the language of government and education, some native traditions survived and a mixed-blood immigrant and native population called *mestizos* gradually appeared. Through this process, Spanish America became the first lasting outpost of Western civilization outside of Europe.

The basic form of economic and social organization in Spanish America was the encomienda° system, which was created as an instrument to exploit native labor. An encomienda was a royal grant awarded for military or other services that gave the conquistadores and their successors the right to gather tribute from the Indians in a defined area. In return, the encomendero (the receiver of the royal grant and native tribute) was theoretically obliged to protect the natives and teach them the rudiments of the Christian faith. Because the encomiendas were very large, only a small number of Spanish settlers were actually encomenderos. In greater Peru, which included modern Peru, Ecuador, and Bolivia, there were never more than 500 encomenderos. By the seventeenth century these encomiendas had evolved to become great landed estates called haciendas°.

There were only a few prosperous encomenderos, but the stories about those who rose from rags to riches in the New World were so compelling that during the sixteenth century alone more than 200,000 Spaniards migrated there. They came from every part of the Iberian peninsula, from every class except the peasantry, and they practiced a wide variety of trades. There were nobles, notaries, lawyers, priests, physicians, merchants, artisans, and sailors; there were also vagabonds prone to crime and rebellion. In effect, these immigrants duplicated Spanish Catholic society in the New World, complete with its class divisions and tensions, except that the native population or African slaves substituted for the peasants as agricultural workers. Included among the immigrants were an unknown number of Jews who hid their faith and who escaped the rigors of the Spanish Inquisition by removing themselves to the Americas where they were less likely to suffer persecution.

For a long time the colonies suffered from a shortage of Spanish women. Only one in ten of Spanish immigrants were women. Although native Americans were usually excluded from Spanish society, many native women who were the mistresses and even wives of Spaniards partially assimilated to European culture and helped pass it on to their offspring. These native women learned Spanish and were converted to Christianity, but because of their origins they could mediate between the dominant Spanish and the subordinate native population. These women knew both languages, which made them valuable interpreters, and were familiar with both cultures, which enabled them to explain native customs to the Spanish. The progeny of European men and Indian women constituted the mestizo population.

Wherever they went in the Americas, the Spaniards brought African slaves with them. Most of the slaves remembered little about their original African cultures, however, because many had been born in Spain, the Caribbean, or the Cape Verde Islands, and Spanish had become their native language. At every stage from initial explorations to the building of new cities, Africans participated in helping make the Americas Spanish. In 1533, while Pizarro held the Incan emperor captive at Cajamarca, he sent to Cuzco an advance party of five men, including a black man who was entrusted to bring back a huge fortune in gold and silver. Unlike in the West Indies and the coastal regions where they became plantation workers, blacks in the interior of South America often fought and worked as partners with the Spanish, not as full equals but as necessary auxiliaries for and beneficiaries of the conquest.

The king of Spain was represented in the Americas by the two viceroys, who were the highest colonial officials. One in Mexico City governed the West Indies, the mainland north of Panama, Venezuela, and the Philippines; the other in Lima, Peru, had authority over all of Spanish South America, excluding Venezuela. However, the vast territory of Spanish America and the enormous cultural diversity within it precluded any rigorous centralized control either from Spain or from the viceregal capitals.

In Spanish America the church was a more effective presence than the state. Driven by the same religious fervor as Columbus, Catholic missionaries trekked into the farthest reaches of Spanish America, converting the native populations to Christianity with much more success than in Africa or Asia. Greed had enticed the conquistadores, but an ardent desire to spread the gospel of Christianity spurred the missionaries. As heirs to the long Christian struggle against Islam and, in particular, the reconquest of the Iberian peninsula from the Muslims, the missionaries found in the Americas an exceptional opportunity to expand Christianity. The most zealous missionaries were members of religious orders—Franciscans, Dominicans, and Jesuits—who were distinguished from the parish priests by their autonomy and special training for missionary work. Instead of answering to a bishop who had authority over a defined region, members of religious orders were organized like an army, followed the commands of the head of their order in Rome, and were willing to travel anywhere in the world. In fact, the head of the Society of Jesus, the official name of the Jesuits, was called a general.

The Spanish colonization of South America meant that missionaries did not have to contend with the opposition of local governments, as they did in Africa and Asia. Church officials generally assumed that it took ten years for the transition to a settled Christian society, a policy that meant that Christianity arrived in two stages. First, members of a religious order evangelized the population by learning the native language, then preaching and teaching in it. They also introduced the celebration of the Catholic sacraments. Once churches were built and Christianity was accepted by the local elite, the missionaries moved on to be replaced, in the second stage, by parish priests who expected to stay in one place for their entire lives. In the border regions, evangelizing never ceased and members of the missionary orders stayed on until the end of colonial times. In California, New Mexico, and Texas, missions formed outposts of Spanish society in regions that were otherwise often lawless borderlands. In Paraguay, the members of the Jesuit Order gathered the Guaraní peoples into *reductions*, highly disciplined and closed communities where the natives were subjected to a rigorous regime of labor and prayer, and even the most minute details of their daily lives were regulated.

PORTUGUESE BRAZIL: THE TENUOUS COLONY

In 1500 Pedro Cabral sighted the Brazilian coast, claiming it for Portugal under the Treaty of Tordesillas. While the Spaniards busied themselves with the conquest of Mexico and Peru, the Portuguese largely ignored Brazil, which lacked any obvious source of gold or temptingly rich civilizations to conquer. Instead, the Portuguese concentrated on developing their lucrative empire in Asia.

Brazil became a haven for pirates and castaways, especially French. In 1532 the Portuguese crown finally answered the French threat by devising a plan for Portuguese settlement and government of Brazil. Brazil was divided into fifteen captaincies, which were passed out to court favorites as compensation for services rendered or just to get them out of the way. The captains turned out to be tyrannical, incompetent, or absent, and they so completely failed to govern effectively that in 1549 the crown was forced to appoint a governor general and to establish a capital city at Salvador in eastern Brazil.

The impetus for the further colonization of Brazil was the growing European demand for sugar. The Brazilian climate was perfectly suited for cultivating sugar cane. Between 1575 and 1600, Brazil became the Western world's leading producer of sugar, luring thousands of poor young men from Portugal and the Azores who took native women as wives, thereby producing a distinctive mestizo population. In the coastal regions, the land was cleared for vast sugar cane plantations. Sugar cane production required back-breaking, dangerous labor to weed and especially to cut the cane. To work the plantations the Portuguese attempted to enslave the Tupí-Guaraní natives, but European diseases soon killed off this population.

The Portuguese increasingly looked to Africans to perform the hard labor they were unwilling to do themselves.

JUSTICE IN HISTORY

The Difficulties of a Transatlantic Marriage

In 1557 Francisco Noguerol de Ulloa, a Spanish conquistador who had fought in Peru, returned home to Spain. During his nearly two decades in the New World, he had amassed a sizable fortune and earned a great reputation for himself. He expected to enjoy his wealth and fame in a peaceful retirement, but instead almost immediately upon his return he was arrested on the charge of bigamy. During his long stay in Peru, he had neither seen nor heard from the Spanish woman he had married before he left, and when his sisters wrote to him that she had died he thought he was free to marry again. So he did. But when he returned to Spain, his first wife, Dona Beatriz, who was alive and well, heard about his second marriage and filed suit against him for bigamy.

The chance to escape Beatriz had impelled Francisco across the Atlantic in the first place. Many Spanish conquistadores were trying to flee troubles at home, such as a bad marriage. Francisco had married Beatriz under pressure from his widowed mother for the usual reasons parents forced their children into arranged marriages. Beatriz came with a large dowry and provided useful alliances for Francisco's mother and sisters, who felt vulnerable because of Francisco's father's untimely death.

But the marriage was a failure from the beginning. According to Francisco, they had never slept together, and in the eyes of the Church, at least, an unconsummated marriage was not a real marriage. Certainly Francisco and Beatriz never lived together, and she bore him no children. However, his lack of affection for his wife did not prevent him from accepting large payments for her dowry or from writing to his in-laws to ask for money when in his early years abroad he ran into difficulties in Peru. Even a letter of consolation on the death of his wife's sister included a request for more money. Francisco may never have had an affectionate or sexual relationship with Beatriz, but he certainly had a financial one.

Peru eventually rewarded Francisco with a great fortune. For his military prowess and devotion to the Spanish crown, he was granted one of the largest and most productive encomiendas in Peru, a vast tract of land that included the labor of thousands of Incas and a retinue of personal slaves, including a harem of female domestics. Once the false news of Beatriz's death spread throughout Peru, Francisco came to be regarded as the most eligible bachelor in the entire colony. Although many women were eager to become his wife, Francisco did not remarry for years after the news of his first wife's death.

Francisco's second wife, Dona Catalina, shared at least two attributes with his first wife: wealth and social prominence. Born into a respectable Castilian family, she was herself the widow of one of the most powerful Spaniards in Peru. She controlled her own vast fortune in property and other assets, which meant that she could bring a substantial dowry to her new husband. Her reputation as a woman of modesty and virtue was impeccable; she also possessed one vital asset that Beatriz apparently lacked—great beauty. Catalina was known as the "crown jewel of all the women of those parts." It is no wonder that Francisco chose her as his new wife. This time he consummated the marriage.

This case reveals much about the nature of marriage in imperial Spain, and the relative power of men and women in Spanish and colonial society. Marriage was the union of two families, not just two people. Social standing counted for more than affection in the choice of a spouse. Francisco, in fact, had to defend himself against the charge that he had fallen in love with Catalina and had, therefore, abandoned Beatriz so that he could marry Catalina. Love was not an acceptable reason for marriage, let alone an acceptable reason for leaving one marriage for another. In his trial and subsequent litigation, he never claimed to love his new wife and in fact denied that he knew her well at all before the wedding. As an honorable and respectable widow, she had lived a secluded life that would have made it impossible for Francisco to have had much contact with her at all, or so he said.

To escape Beatriz, Francisco had to prove that the marriage had never been a real marriage. To this end, he and his lawyers highlighted the fact that he had never consummated his first marriage, a fact that would have automatically invalidated it as a legal marriage according to the canon law of the Church. To keep Francisco as her husband, Beatriz had to prove that they had had sex together at least once. Francisco's belief that Beatriz was dead had no legal bearing on the case because she was not.

Despite Francisco's arguments that the marriage had never been valid, the judges initially decided in favor of Beatriz. Francisco was sentenced to pay a heavy fine to Beatriz, to serve time in jail, and to separate from his second wife, whom he was forbidden to ever see again. Perhaps most galling of all, he was obliged to resume marital relations with Beatriz, with whom he had certainly never lived before. Beatriz won the case largely because of the legal protection women enjoyed in sixteenth-century Spain. Husbands had obligations toward their wives that the courts consistently enforced.

One of the most important protections women had was the dowry itself. A man could enjoy the income from his wife's dowry, but legally she still had certain claims to it. If he died before she did—which was quite likely given the difference in age between men and women at first marriage—she had a claim on his estate to have the entire sum of her dowry restored to her, not to his family or his heirs but only to her. Beatriz supplied the court with extensive evidence of receipts for dowry payments, signed by Francisco himself. The judges respected the legal protections for women and would not allow Francisco to squander the dowry or relegate it entirely for himself. Francisco's repeated requests to his in-laws for more money made him look like an opportunistic fortune hunter rather than a valuable family ally. The court's judgment in favor of Beatriz had less to do with the emotions of love than the defense of the dowry system and its role in maintaining social stability.

Catalina did not accept lightly the loss of the man she considered her husband. She needed to protect her own dowry from Beatriz's claims. Catalina filed a countersuit to assert that much of Francisco's assets were profits earned from her own dowry, which could not, therefore, be transferred to Beatriz. Catalina was fighting not just for her dowry but for her good name and her marriage, and the courts eventually found a way to recognize the rights of both women—Beatriz to her dowry portion and Catalina to her honorable marriage to Francisco.

In the end, it was the women who resolved the legal struggle that surrounded Francisco. For both women, the courts and the dowry system served as a powerful form of protection for their financial well-being and their honor. Despite the overwhelming authority of men in Spanish society, women were not passive pawns. They found ways to assert control over their own lives. It is revealing that the distance between the Old and New Worlds had little bearing on the status of or legal protections for these women. Far from becoming a lawless frontier, early colonial Peru was for Spaniards at least, an extension of Spanish society. ■

■ **A Spanish Couple**
Francisco Noguerol de Ulloa and Catalina would have dressed much like this aristocratic couple out for a stroll.

Questions of Justice

1. How would you have resolved the conflicting claims of Beatriz and Catalina?
2. What does this case tell us about the nature of marriage in early modern Spain?

Taking It Further

Cook, Alexandra Parma, and Noble David Cook. *Good Faith and Truthful Ignorance: A Case of Transatlantic Bigamy.* 1991. A detailed study of the Noguerol de Ulloa case.

As a result, the Brazilian demand for slaves intensified the Portuguese presence in West Africa and the African presence in Brazil. In the search for ever more slaves, Portuguese slave buyers enlarged their area of operations in Africa south to Angola, where in 1575 they founded a trading post. This post became the embarkation point for slave traders who sailed directly to Brazil and sold slaves in exchange for low-grade Brazilian tobacco, which they exchanged for more slaves when they returned to Angola.

As in Spanish America, Portuguese authorities felt responsible for converting the natives to Christianity. In Brazil, the Jesuits took the lead during the last half of the sixteenth century by establishing a school for the training of missionaries on the site of the present city of São Paulo. São Paulo became the headquarters for the "Apostle of Brazil," José de Anchieta, who worked among the indigenous peoples. In the seventeenth century, Father Antonio Vieira established a string of missions in the Amazon valley. Once converted, natives were resettled into villages called aldeias°, which were similar to Spanish missions. The Jesuits attempted to protect the natives against the white colonists who wanted to enslave them, creating a lasting conflict between the Jesuit fathers and local landowners. Both Jesuits and colonists appealed to the king to settle their dispute; finally the king gave the Jesuits complete responsibility for all Indians in aldeias but allowed colonists to enslave Indians who had not been converted or who were captured in war. The Portuguese connected Christian conversion with settlement in aldeias, which meant that any unsettled native was, by definition, a heathen. Nevertheless, these restrictions on enslaving Indians created a perceived labor shortage and further stimulated the demand for African slaves.

More rural, more African, and less centrally governed than Spanish America, Brazil during its colonial history remained a plantation economy in which the few dominant white European landowners were vastly outnumbered by their African slaves. In certain areas a racially mixed population created its own vibrantly hybrid culture that combined native, African, and European elements, especially in the eclectic religious life that combined Catholic with polytheistic forms of worship. Although Brazil occupied nearly half of the South American continent, until the twentieth century most of the vast interior was unexplored by Europeans and unsettled except by the small native population.

North America: The Land of Lesser Interest

Compared with Central and South America, North America outside of Mexico held little attraction for Europeans during the sixteenth century. European experience in North America consisted of a number of exploratory missions and several failed attempts at colonization. By 1600, when hundreds of thousands of Europeans and Africans had settled in the Caribbean, Central and South America, the only European settlements in North America (except for New Spain) consisted of a tiny Spanish garrison at St. Augustine, Florida, a doomed Spanish colony on the upper Rio Grande in New Mexico, and a few marooned Frenchmen on Sable Island far off the coast of Nova Scotia. Even by 1700, when English, French, and Spanish colonies were finally thriving in North America, they still played a very minor role in the global picture of European economic interests.

At first the principal attraction of North America was the cod fisheries in the waters off Newfoundland, which every spring lured ships from England, France, Spain, and Portugal and which may have been frequented by Europeans even before Columbus. An Italian captain in the employ of England, John Cabot (ca. 1450–ca. 1498), landed in North America in 1497 and established the basis for an English claim in the New World, but after he disappeared on a return trip the following year no one else bothered to follow up on the claim. Occasionally, fishermen dropped anchor at the harbors at St. John's, Newfoundland, and came to know the coasts of Maine and the Gulf of St. Lawrence. In 1521 some Portuguese families founded a settlement on Nova Scotia, but they soon disappeared.

The second attraction of North America lay in the vain hope of a Northwest Passage to China and India through or around the continent to the North. After Magellan's voyage (1519–1522), the Spanish knew how to sail around South America, but they preferred overland transportation from Vera Cruz, Mexico, to reach the Pacific coast at Acapulco, which became an embarkation port for Spanish trade with Asia. In 1524 the French king sent the Italian Giovanni da Verrazano (ca. 1485–1528) to find a passage around North America, which resulted in the first geographical description of the coast from North Carolina to Newfoundland. Following up on Verrazano's voyage, Jacques Cartier (1491–1557) discovered the St. Lawrence River in 1534. Hard winters defeated two French attempts to found a colony in the St. Lawrence Valley between 1541 and 1543. The English explored further north in a series of voyages that led to the discovery of Hudson Bay, which was thought for some time to be part of the Pacific Ocean. Only in 1616 did William Baffin (ca. 1584–1622) determine that there was no ice-free passage around North America.

In the competition over North America, the English arrived late, devoting themselves at first to preying on Spanish shipping rather than building their own colonies. During most of the sixteenth century England was considerably less well prepared than Spain or Portugal to sustain a campaign of conquest and colonization in the Americas. At this time the English monarchy had a fragile hold on power, its naval fleet was tiny, and it lacked the financial backing for risky expeditions. In contrast to the great convoys of Spanish and Portuguese ships that plied the Atlantic, the English were represented by a few "privateers," which was a polite word for pirates. These men sought quick, easy profits rather than the rigors of settling and pacifying the country. John Hawkins, the most famous of the early English privateers, and his nephew, Francis Drake (ca. 1543–1596) specialized in harassing the Spanish fleet, both to steal the gold and silver that was being transported back to Spain and to sustain an intermittent war against England's most powerful enemy.

During the reign of Queen Elizabeth I (r. 1558–1603), English efforts finally turned to establishing colonies in the Americas. Two prominent courtiers, Humphrey Gilbert and his stepbrother, Walter Raleigh, sponsored a series of voyages intended to establish an English colony called Virginia in honor of Elizabeth, "The Virgin Queen." The shift of English interest from piracy to colonization was made possible by Elizabeth's success in strengthening the monarchy, building up the fleet, and encouraging investments in New World colonies. In 1585 the first English colonists in the Americas landed on Roanoke Island off the coast of North Carolina, but they were so poorly prepared that their attempt and a second one in 1587 failed. The inexperienced and naive English settlers did not even make provisions for planting crops.

The successful English colonies came a generation later. Learning from past mistakes, the colonists of Jamestown in Virginia, who landed in 1607, brought seeds for planting, built fortifications for protection, and established a successful form of self-government. From these modest beginnings, the English gradually established vast plantations along the rivers of Virginia. There they raised tobacco to supply the new European habit of smoking, which had been picked up from native Americans. In 1620 religious refugees from England settled in Massachusetts Bay, but in contrast to Central and South America, most of North America by 1650 remained only marginally touched by Europeans.

CHRONOLOGY

Europeans in the Americas

CA. 1438	Founding of Incan empire in Peru by Pachacuti Inca Yupanqui
1440–1469	Reign of Montezuma I of the Aztec empire
1492–1493	First two voyages of Christopher Columbus
1497	John Cabot lands in North America
1498	Third voyage of Columbus
1500	Cabral sights Brazil
1502	Fourth voyage of Columbus
1519–1522	Spanish conquer Mexico
1524	Giovanni da Verrazano explores North American coast for France
1534	Jacques Cartier discovers St. Lawrence River
1549	Portuguese establish a governor-general at Salvador, Brazil
1585	English establish colony on Roanoke Island, North Carolina
1607	English establish colony at Jamestown, Virginia
1616	William Baffin fails to discover Northwest Passage around North America
1620	English establish colony at Massachusetts Bay

Europeans in Asia

India, the Malay peninsula, Indonesia, the Spice Islands, and China were the ultimate goal of the European explorers during the fifteenth and sixteenth centuries. They were eventually reached by many routes—by the Portuguese sailing around Africa, by the Spanish sailing around South America, and by the Russians trekking across the vastness of Siberia. Trade between Europe and Asia was very lucrative. Europeans were especially dependent on Asian sources for luxury goods such as silk, spices for cooking and preserving food, and medicines for pain relief and healing.

ASIA BEFORE THE EUROPEAN EMPIRES

As we saw in Chapter 10, after the collapse of the Mongol Empire in the fourteenth century, direct access for European merchants to China and the Indian Ocean was blocked. Plague, political unrest, and Muslim hostility to Christians reduced trade to a mere trickle of what it had been. The elaborate trade networks that had helped drive the expansion of the economy of the West during the thirteenth century were in disarray.

The greatest potential rival to the Europeans who sought access to Asian trade was Ming China (1368–1644), a highly advanced civilization with maritime technology and organizational capability to launch exploratory voyages far superior to Europe's. Even before the Portuguese began their slow progress down the west coast of Africa, the Chinese organized a series of huge maritime expeditions into the

Indian Ocean that reached far down the east coast of Africa. Between 1405 and 1433 the Chinese established diplomatic contacts and demanded tribute in dozens of kingdoms in India and Africa. The size and ambition of these fleets far surpassed anything that sailed from Europe at this time, and the massive crews of as many as 27,500 men (compared to Columbus's crew of 90) included a complement of scholars to communicate with foreign kings and highly skilled technicians to make repairs to the fleet. The Chinese fleets took trade goods, such as silk, tea, and porcelains, and brought back to China strange animals, hostage kings, and possible trade items. After nearly thirty years of searching the Indian Ocean ports, the Ming emperors concluded that China already possessed all the goods that were available abroad, that China was indeed the center of civilization, and that further investments in oceangoing expeditions were unwarranted.

The European and Chinese voyages of the fifteenth century differed in their objectives and in the motives of the governments that sponsored them. The Europeans were mostly privateers seeking personal profit or captains who enjoyed official government backing in return for a portion of the profits. The economic motive behind the European voyages made them self-sustaining because the Europeans sailed only to places where they could make money. In contrast, the imperial Chinese expeditions were only partially motivated by the desire for economic gain. The official purpose of the Chinese voyages was to learn about the world, and once the Chinese found out what they wanted, they ceased the official voyages. Chinese merchant traders continued to ply the seas on their own, however, and when the Europeans arrived in East Asia, they simply inserted themselves into this already developed Chinese-dominated trade network.

In contrast to the trade in Africa and America, Europeans failed to monopolize trade in Asia. The Europeans were just one among many trading groups, some working under government sponsorship, such as the Portuguese, and others working alone, such as the Chinese.

The Trading Post Empires

In 1497–1499 Vasco da Gama opened the most promising route for the Portuguese around Africa to South and East Asia. But the sailing distances were long, limiting the number of people who could be transported to Asia, and the Asian empires were well equipped to defend themselves against European conquest. As a result, European engagement with Asia was slight for some 300 years. Because Europeans lacked the support system provided by colonial conquest, few Europeans settled in Asia, and even missionary work proved much more difficult than in the Americas.

Unlike Brazil, where the Portuguese established colonial plantations, in Asia they established trading posts or factories along the coasts of India, China, and the Spice Islands. When the Portuguese first arrived at a good location for a trading post—one that had a safe harbor and easy access to the hinterland—they built a fort and forced, bribed, or tricked the local political authority, usually a chieftain, to cede the land around the post to Portugal. The agents sent to trade in Asia were called factors and their trading posts were called factories. But they were not factories in the modern sense of sites for manufacturing; they were safe places where merchants could trade and store their merchandise. The factors lived in the factories with a few other Portuguese traders, a small detachment of troops, and servants recruited from the local population. Nowhere did Portuguese authority extend very far into the hinterland. The traditional political structures of local chieftains remained, and the local elites usually went along with the arrangement because they profited by reselling European wares, such as cloth, guns, knives, and many kinds of cheap gadgets. The factors acquired silks, gold, silver, raw cotton, pepper, spices, and medicines. Some of these outposts of the Portuguese Empire survived until late in the twentieth century, but their roots remained exceedingly shallow. Even in places such as East Timor, an island off Southeast Asia, and Macao on the south China coast, which were Portuguese outposts for more than four centuries, only a small native elite ever learned the Portuguese language or adapted to European culture.

The Portuguese and later other Europeans were motivated to establish colonies in Asia primarily by commercial considerations. Consider the search for the spice nutmeg, which illustrates something of the enticement of the Asia trade. In an account published in 1510, an Italian traveler, Ludovico di Varthema, described for the first time in a European language nutmeg trees, which he found growing in the Banda Islands, a small archipelago some thousand miles east of Java. These were the only places in the world where nutmeg grew. Besides adding flavor to foods, nutmeg was believed to possess powers to cure all kinds of diseases and to induce a hallucinatory euphoria. The demand for nutmeg was so great and the supply so limited that exporting it yielded enormous profits. At one time, nutmeg was the most valuable commodity in the world after gold and silver. In the early seventeenth century the markup on a pound of nutmeg transported from the Banda Islands to Europe was 60,000 percent. It is no wonder European traders were willing to risk their lives on long, dangerous sea voyages to obtain nutmeg and other spices.

In return for raw materials such as nutmeg, European merchants typically traded manufactured goods, and they made every effort to ensure that other European powers were excluded from competing in this trade. Given the high profit potential, there was a great temptation to break a European rival's trading monopoly on a rare commodity such as nutmeg. Crucial to enforcing the system was a network of factories and a strong navy, which was primarily used against other European and occasionally Muslim interlopers. Through the trading post empires, commercial rivalries among European states extended abroad to Asia. Competition over these trading posts foreshadowed the beginnings of a global economy dominated by Europeans. It also demonstrated the Europeans' propensity to transform European wars into world wars.

In addition to trade, the Portuguese and other European powers sought to spread Christianity among the local populations. Franciscan, Dominican, and later Jesuit missionaries preached to the indigenous peoples. To accomplish conversions, they tried persuasion, because without the backing of a full-scale conquest as in the Americas, resorting to force was usually not an option. The missionaries frequently drew the ire of local rulers, who viewed the converts as traitors—a situation that led to the persecution of some of the new Christians. To accomplish their task of conversion, Christian missionaries had to learn the native languages and something of the native culture and religion. In this effort, the Jesuits were particularly dedicated; they sent members of their order to the Chinese imperial court, where they lived incognito for decades, although they made few converts. Jesuits also traveled to Japan, where they established an outpost of Christianity at Nagasaki. With the exception of the Spanish Philippines, which was nominally converted to Catholicism by 1600, Christian missionaries were far less successful than in the Americas. Perhaps one million Asians outside the Philippines had been converted during this period, but many of these conversions did not last. Christians were most successful in converting Buddhists and least effective among Muslims, who almost never abandoned their faith.

By the end of the sixteenth century, Portuguese and Spanish shipping in Asian waters faced recurrent harassment from the English, French, and Dutch. The Dutch drove the Portuguese from their possessions in Ceylon, India, and the Spice Islands, except for East Timor. But none of these sixteenth-century European empires was particularly effective at imposing European culture on Asia in a way comparable with the Americas. In the Spanish Philippines, for example, few natives spoke Spanish, and there were fewer than 5,000 Spanish inhabitants as late as 1850. European states competed among themselves for trade and tried to enforce monopolies, but the Europeans remained peripheral to Asian culture until the late eighteenth and early nineteenth centuries, when the British expanded their power in India and colonized Australia and New Zealand.

The expansion of the Russian Empire into Asia depended not on naval power but on cross-country expeditions. The heartland of the Russian Empire was Muscovy, the area around Moscow, but the empire would eventually spread from the Baltic Sea to the Pacific Ocean. After 1552 Russians began to push across the Ural mountains into Siberia, lured by the trade in exotic furs, which were in great demand among the upper classes of northern Europe, both to keep warm and as fashion statements. The Russians' search for furs was equivalent to the Spanish search for gold; like gold, fur attracted adventurous and desperate men. Following the navigable rivers and building strategic forts along the way, expeditions collected furs locally and then advanced deeper into the frozen wilds of Siberia. Several of the great aristocratic families of Russia acquired enormous wealth from the Siberian fur trade, which was so lucrative that Russian trappers kept pushing farther and farther east. In this quest for furs, expeditions reached the Pacific coast in 1649, by which time Russia had established a network of trading posts over all of northern Asia.

The significance of the European trading post empires lies less in the influence of Europe on Asia than in the influence of Asia on Europe. Asian products from spices and opium to silk cloth and oriental rugs became commonplace items in middle- and upper-class European households. European collectors became fascinated with Chinese porcelains, lacquered boxes, and screen paintings. At the same time, Asians began to visit Europe, a tradition begun when four Japanese converts to Christianity arrived in Lisbon in 1586 and made a celebrated tour of Europe.

CHRONOLOGY

Europeans in Asia

1487–1488	Bartholomew Dias reaches Cape of Good Hope
1497–1499	Da Gama reaches India via Cape of Good Hope
1498	Portuguese reach Malabar coast of India
1514	Portuguese reach China
1519–1522	Magellan's crew circumnavigate the globe

The Beginnings of the Global System

As a result of the European voyages of the fifteenth and sixteenth centuries, a network of cultural, biological, and economic connections formed along intercontinental trading routes. These connections created a global system that has been sustained ever since. Today's global economy, based on the Internet, air transportation, and free trade, operates much more efficiently and quickly than its predecessors, but it is merely an extension and elaboration of a system that first appeared on a global scale during the sixteenth century. For many thousands of years, Europe, northern Africa, and Asia had been in contact with each other, but the system that took form during the sixteenth century began to encompass most of the globe, including sub-Saharan Africa and the Americas. Unlike earlier international trading systems that linked Europe and Asia, the new global system was dominated by Europeans. They turned large parts of the Americas into plantations that used African slave labor to grow crops for European consumers. This system transformed human society by bringing into contact elements that had previously been separate and isolated—regional cultures, biological systems, and local economies.

The Columbian Exchange

The most dramatic changes were at first produced by the trade of peoples, plants, animals, microbes, and ideas between the Old and New Worlds—a process known as the Columbian Exchange°. For the native Americans, the importation of Europeans, Africans, and microbes had devastating consequences—threatening indigenous religions, making native technology irrelevant, disrupting social life, and destroying millions of lives. For Europeans, the discovery of previously unknown civilizations profoundly shook their own understanding of human geography and history. Neither the ancient philosophers nor the Bible, which was understood to be a history of humankind since the creation of the world, had provided a hint about the peoples of the Americas.

The Slave Trade

All of the ancient civilizations had been slave societies with as many as one-third of the population in bondage. During the Middle Ages a small number of slaves were employed as domestic servants and concubines in the Christian cities of the Mediterranean, and in Muslim countries large numbers of slaves were found in harems, used as laborers, and even trained as soldiers. Many of the slaves in Christian cities were Muslims, and many slaves in Muslim countries were Christians, because both religions considered it legitimate to enslave members of the opposing faith. In the wars between Christians and Muslims, captives were habitually enslaved or held for ransom. Large-scale transportation of black Africans began during the ninth and tenth centuries, when Muslim traders took tens of thousands from the island of Zanzibar off the east coast of Africa to lower Iraq, where they performed the heavy labor of draining swamps and cutting sugar cane. Slavery was also widespread in Islamic West Africa. Mali depended heavily on slave labor, and in Muslim Ghana slaves constituted about one-third of the population. Thus the institution of slavery was well established in Africa long before the beginning of the transatlantic slave trade dominated by Europeans.

The slave trade flourished only when and where it was profitable. The necessary conditions for profitability were a strong demand for labor-intensive agricultural commodities, a perceived shortage of local labor, a supply of people who could be captured elsewhere, and a moral and legal climate that permitted slavery. These conditions, which came together for Europeans during the colonization of the Cape Verde Islands, were all present in the late fifteenth and sixteenth centuries. The growing population of Europe developed a taste for exotic products such as sugar, tobacco, coffee, and indigo dye. The European colonizers who sought to supply the demand for these goods needed agricultural workers, first for the colonies in the Atlantic islands and then for plantations in the Americas. In the Americas, European diseases decimated the indigenous population, creating a labor shortage. Europeans also found it difficult to enslave the native peoples, who knew the territory and could easily escape.

The flourishing demand for labor was supplied by the population of Africa. Once Europeans started to buy up slaves in the coastal trading posts, enterprising African chieftains sent slave-hunting expeditions into the interior. As a consequence, the slave-trading states of the Guinea coast gained power at the expense of their neighbors and spread the unwelcome web of the slave trade deep into the African interior. The slave hunters sold captives to the Europeans for transportation across the Atlantic. Following the Portuguese in the trade came the Dutch, English, French, and Danes, who eventually established their own trading posts to obtain slaves.

In addition to the economic incentive for slavery, both Christianity and Islam provided a moral justification and legal protection for it. Enslaving others was considered legitimate punishment for unbelievers. Of all the Western religions, only Judaism demonstrated a consistent moral resistance to the slave trade because Jewish identity depended heavily on remembering the biblical account of the enslavement of the ancient Hebrews in Egypt. Notable exceptions were the few Jewish plantation owners in Surinam, who did use slave labor. The problem for Christian and Muslim slavers was that when a slave converted to Christianity or Islam, the pretext for enslavement disappeared. To solve this problem, Christians created a new rationalization by connecting slavery to race. As the African slave trade expanded during the seventeenth and eighteenth centuries, Europeans began to associate slavery with "blackness," which was considered inferior to "whiteness." Among Muslims, the justification for enslavement remained a religious one, and when a slave converted to Islam he or she was, at least theoretically, supposed to be freed.

During the 400 years of the transatlantic slave trade (ca. 1450–1870), more than ten million Africans were transported to the Americas, the result of which was that large slices of the Americas were transformed into outposts of sub-Saharan African cultures. Blacks came to outnumber

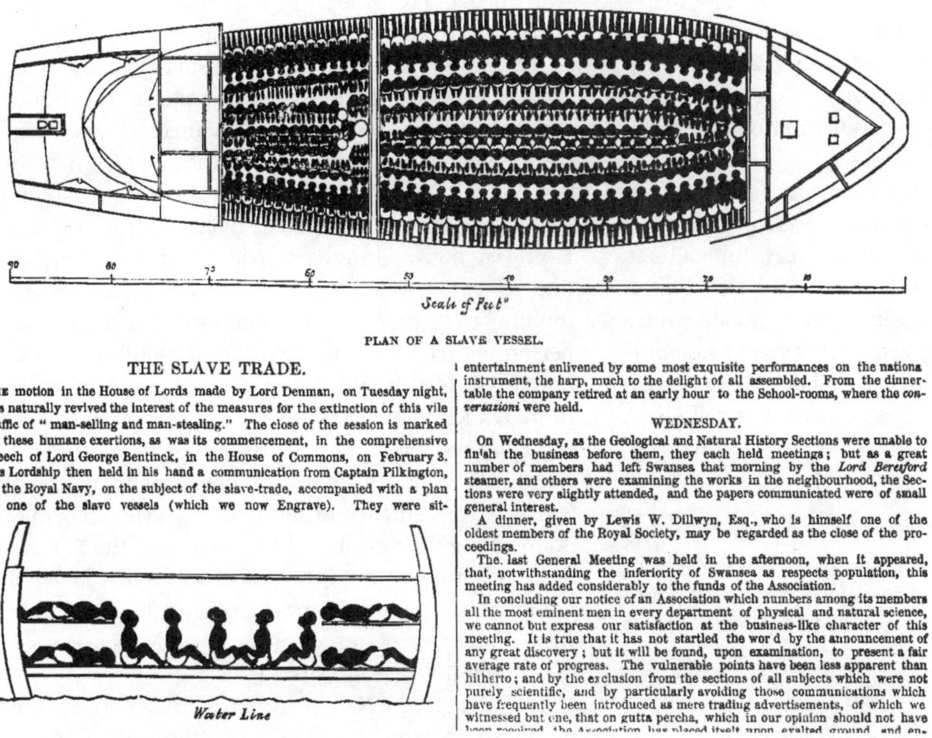

PLAN OF A SLAVE VESSEL.

THE SLAVE TRADE.

THE motion in the House of Lords made by Lord Denman, on Tuesday night, has naturally revived the interest of the measures for the extinction of this vile traffic of "man-selling and man-stealing." The close of the session is marked by these humane exertions, as was its commencement, in the comprehensive speech of Lord George Bentinck, in the House of Commons, on February 3. His Lordship then held in his hand a communication from Captain Pilkington, of the Royal Navy, on the subject of the slave-trade, accompanied with a plan of one of the slave vessels (which we now Engrave). They were sit-

entertainment enlivened by some most exquisite performances on the nationa instrument, the harp, much to the delight of all assembled. From the dinner-table the company retired at an early hour to the School-rooms, where the *conversazioni* were held.

WEDNESDAY.

On Wednesday, as the Geological and Natural History Sections were unable to finish the business before them, they each held meetings; but as a great number of members had left Swansea that morning by the *Lord Beresford* steamer, and others were examining the works in the neighbourhood, the Sections were very slightly attended, and the papers communicated were of small general interest.

A dinner, given by Lewis W. Dillwyn, Esq., who is himself one of the oldest members of the Royal Society, may be regarded as the close of the proceedings.

The last General Meeting was held in the afternoon, when it appeared, that, notwithstanding the inferiority of Swansea as respects population, this meeting has added considerably to the funds of the Association.

In concluding our notice of an Association which numbers among its members all the most eminent men in every department of physical and natural science, we cannot but express our satisfaction at the business-like character of this meeting. It is true that it has not startled the wor d by the announcement of any great discovery; but it will be found, upon examination, to present a fair average rate of progress. The vulnerable points have been less apparent than hitherto; and by the exclusion from the sections of all subjects which were not purely scientific, and by particularly avoiding those communications which have frequently been introduced as mere trading advertisements, of which we witnessed but one, that on gutta percha, which in our opinion should not have

The Middle Passage

The human cargo of slaves were packed together for the long voyage from a slave-trading post in Africa to the plantation colonies of the Americas.

the native Americans and constituted the majority of the colonial population in most of the Caribbean, and broad parts of coastal Central America, Venezuela, Guyana, and Brazil. Much of the male population of Angola was transported directly to Brazil, a forced migration that resulted in a dramatic excess of females over males in the most heavily depopulated areas of Angola. In the process, Portuguese Brazil became the single largest recipient of African slaves. It was the destination of some 3.6 million Africans—nearly ten times the number brought to all of English-speaking North America.

The slave ships that sailed the infamous Middle Passage across the Atlantic were so unhealthy, with humans "stacked like books on a shelf," that a significant portion of the human cargo died en route. The physical and psychological burdens that slavery placed on its victims can scarcely be imagined, in large part because few slaves were ever allowed to learn to read and write, and thus direct records of their experiences are rare. It is certain, however, that slaves were subjected to unhealthy living conditions, back-breaking work, and demoralization. The plantations of the New World mixed together Africans from different cultures and language groups, making it difficult for slaves to build the solidarity necessary to rebel successfully. In a few places, runaways established their own self-governing communities, such as the Saramakas of Surinam or the Cimarrón republic in Peru, but most found escape impossible because they had no place to go and certainly no way to return to their homeland. Despite these crushing hardships, and even within the harsh confines of white-owned plantations, black slaves created their own institutions, family structures, and cultures.

Biological Exchanges

Europeans certainly perpetuated atrocities in the New World, but the intentional genocide of whole peoples was exceedingly rare. Except for the first colonizers of the Canary Islands, even the most vicious colonizers wanted to enslave or exploit the natives, not destroy them. Nevertheless, the introduction of new diseases to the Americas and the disruption of traditional economies led to a form of unintentional genocide that resulted in the deaths of millions. The European, Asian, and African continents, on the one hand, and the Americas, on the other, had been isolated from each other for so long that they had become two biologically distinct worlds. After the voyages of

Christopher Columbus they were rejoined in ways that—for good or for ill—made them more alike culturally and, especially, biologically. As one historian has put it, the "trend toward biological homogeneity is one of the most important aspects of the history of life on this planet since the retreat of the continental glaciers."[3]

How did a few thousand Europeans so easily conquer the civilizations of the Americas, which were populated by millions of people? After all, the Aztecs, Incas, Tupinambas, and others put up a stubborn resistance to the conquistadores, and yet the Europeans triumphed time after time. The answer: epidemics. Along with their sense of superiority, the conquistadores' most effective allies were the invisible microbes of Old World diseases, such as smallpox. A native of the Yucatán peninsula recalled the better days before the conquest:

> *There was then no sickness; they had no aching bones; they had then no high fever; they had then no smallpox; they had then no burning chest; they had then no abdominal pain; they had then no consumption; they had then no headache. At that time the course of humanity was orderly. The foreigners made it otherwise when they arrived here.*[4]

Nearly every chronicler of the New World conquests was stunned by the toll that epidemic disease had on the natives soon after their initial contact with Europeans. Between 1520 and 1600, Mexico suffered fourteen major epidemics, and Peru suffered seventeen. By the 1580s the populations of the Caribbean islands, the Antilles, and the lowlands of Mexico and Peru had almost completely died off. Historians estimate the deaths in the tens of millions. The preconquest population of Mexico, which has been estimated at about 19 million, dropped in eighty years to 2.5 million. Even the infrequent contacts between European fishermen and fur traders with natives on the coast of what is now Canada led to rapid depopulation.

The most deadly culprit was smallpox, but measles, typhus, scarlet fever, and chicken pox also contributed to the devastation. All of these were dangerous and even life-threatening to Europeans and Africans, but from exposure, people of the Old World had either died young or survived the illness with a resistance to infection from the disease. However, native Americans had never been exposed to these diseases, and as a population completely lacked immunities to them. As a result, all it took was for one infected person to arrive from the Old World to kill off many millions in the New World. After Cortés's men were first driven from Tenochtitlán, a Dominican friar reported that a new ally appeared: "When the Christians were exhausted from war, God saw fit to send the Indians smallpox, and there was a great pestilence in the city. . . ."[5] The epidemic undoubtedly impaired the fighting ability of the Aztecs. The Spaniards' immunity to the very diseases that killed off so many Indians reinforced the impression that the Europeans were favored agents of the gods or gods themselves. As a Mayan put it, "we were born to die."[6]

In exchange, the New World gave the Old World syphilis, or at least contemporary Europeans thought so. Historians and epidemiologists have long debated what they call the Columbian question° about the origins of syphilis. Some argue that syphilis or a venereal disease that might be classified as its ancestor came back from the New World with Columbus's sailors; others assert that syphilis was widespread in the Old World long before 1492. We still do not know the answer to the Columbian question, but it is true that after about 1492 there were epidemic outbreaks of sexually transmitted diseases, leading many to assume an American origin.

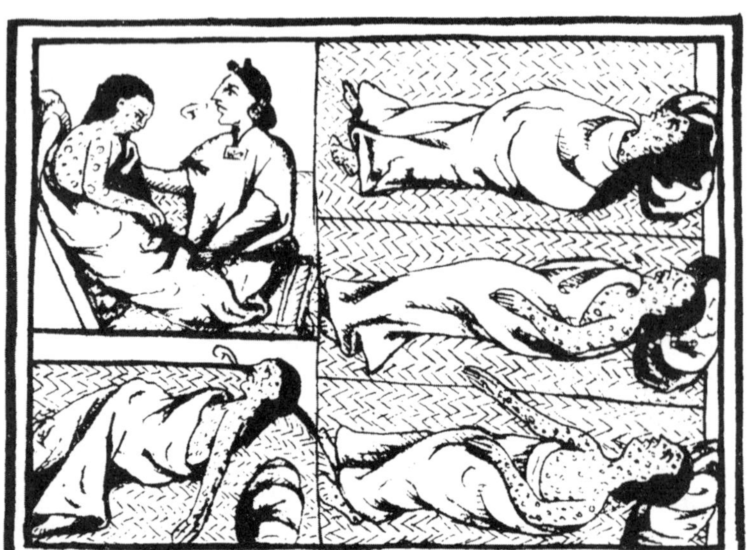

The Columbian Exchange
Aztecs fell victim to smallpox epidemics during the sixteenth century.

The exchange of other forms of life was less obviously disastrous. Following the Europeans came a flood of European animals and plants. With the conquistadores came pigs, cattle, goats, sheep, donkeys, and horses—all previously unknown in the New World. Pigs that escaped from the first Spanish ships to land in Florida were the ancestors of the ubiquitous wild razorback pigs of the southern United States. Vast areas of Mexico and Peru depopulated of humans were repopulated with enormous herds of sheep. The cattle herded by the present-day gauchos of Argentina derive from Iberian stock. The characteristic Latin American burro came from Europe as did the horse, which came to be so prized by the plains Indians of North America. Sheep, cattle, and horses, in particular, completely changed the way of life of the native American peoples.

From Europe came the lucrative plantation crops of sugar, cotton, rice, and indigo, crops that required a large supply of field hands. European varieties of wheat, grapes, and olives soon appeared as major crops in Mexico and elsewhere. In exchange, the Americas offered new crops to the Old World such as tobacco, cocoa, paprika, American cotton, pumpkins, beans, maize (corn), and potatoes. European peasant farmers discovered that maize and the potato provided an attractive substitute for wheat. In many places, the potato replaced wheat as the staple in the diet of the poor. By yielding more calories per acre than wheat or virtually any other traditional grain, the potato made it possible to support more people on a given amount of land. With the spread of the potato as a food source, European populations began to increase rapidly, a trend that created population pressures, which in turn stimulated additional European migrations to the Americas.

The Problem of Cultural Diversity

Before Columbus sailed west, Europeans possessed two systems of thought that seemed to explain everything to them—the Aristotelian and the Christian. The ancient Greek philosopher Aristotle and his followers provided a systematic explanation of geography and cosmology based on what they knew of the world. They had named the continents, described their peoples, and estimated the size of the globe. Particularly in the European universities, Aristotle was still considered practically infallible, the primary source of all human knowledge. But Aristotle had not even imagined the Americas, and that fact raised the possibility that he was wrong on other matters as well. He knew nothing of the llama, the potato, or syphilis—common knowledge to even the most ignorant conquistador. Aristotle had assumed that the heat of the equatorial zone was so great that no one could live there, but the Spanish had found great civilizations thriving astride the equator. In 1570, when Joseph de Acosta felt a chill in the tropics on his way to America, he observed, "what could I else do then but laugh at Aristotle's Meteors and his Philosophy."[7] Travelers to the New World began to realize that the ancients had not known half the truth about the world.

For Christians and Jews, the Bible remained the unchallenged authority on the origins of the whole world, but the New World created numerous problems for biblical interpretation. The book of Genesis told of the creation and the great flood, which had destroyed all people and all animals except those saved in Noah's ark. The New World brought into question that vision of a single creation and cleansing flood simply because it could not explain why the plants and animals of the Americas were so different. If the only animals on Earth were those Noah preserved, then why were they different on the two sides of the Earth? About the New World a French writer asked, "How falls it out that the nations of the world, coming all of one father, Noah, do vary so much from one another, both in body and mind?"[8] Thinkers argued either that there must have been more than one creation or that the great flood must have covered only Palestine rather than the entire Earth. However, these solutions tacitly recognized that a literal reading of the words of Scripture could not produce a satisfactory account of the history of the world.

The greatest conceptual challenge to Christian Europe were the New World peoples themselves. If these people were not the children of God's Creation, then how did they get there? If they were God's children, then why were they so different from Europeans? In the terms available to sixteenth-century thinkers, there were three possible ways to answer these questions. One was to assume that the native Americans were subhumans, demons, or some strange form of animal life. This answer was the most convenient one to those who sought to exploit the natives. Often with little or no foundation, these Europeans believed that the natives practiced devil worship, incest, sexual promiscuity, polygamy, sodomy, and cannibalism—all signs of their demonic nature. If not demons, the natives must be unnatural beasts: wild men, dog men, or satyrs. In this extreme form of European belief, the natives did not even possess a human soul and were neither capable of converting to Christianity nor worthy of human rights. Most European thinkers insisted that the natives must be descendants of Adam and Eve, and thus they possessed souls, could be redeemed, and were subject to divine law. But even among otherwise intelligent thinkers, some of the subhuman prejudice survived. The English philosopher Francis Bacon (1561–1626), who did not wallow in the common intolerance of his day, shared the view that as naked cannibals, Indians had defaced humanity.

A second answer to why the peoples of the New World were so different sprung from a belief that the natives were complete innocents. The native peoples lived in a kind of earthly paradise, unspoiled by the corruption of European society. Some of the early English explorers of Virginia found the natives "most gentle, loving and faithful, void of any guile or treason," and one missionary found them "all the more children of God owing to their very lack of capacity and skill."[9] A tiny number of unconventional theological thinkers hypothesized that the native Americans had been created before the Hebrews as reported in the Bible, and, therefore, had not been subject to the Fall of Man and still lived in the earthly paradise. The English humanist Thomas More (1478–1535) located his Utopia, an imagined ideal community, in the New World to demonstrate how corrupt the social institutions of the Old World had become.

The most influential spokesman during the sixteenth century for this idea of native innocence was the powerful advocate of human rights Bartholomew de Las Casas (1474–1566), the bishop of arid, impoverished Chiapas in Mexico. Throughout his career, Las Casas forcefully argued against the enslavement and ill treatment of the native Americans, which was chronicled in his most important published work, *The Brief Relation of the Destruction of the West Indies* (1542). Through Las Casas's influence, Spanish royal policy toward the Indians became more peaceful and sympathetic. As beneficent as he was toward the natives, however, Las Casas did not accept native culture as in any way equal or superior to European. He merely saw the natives as innocents who needed to be guided rather than forced to accept Christianity and who did not deserve to be slaves. He did not, however, bother to make the same argument on behalf of black Africans.

The third response to the question of how to explain the "differentness" of New World peoples neither dehumanized them nor assumed them innocent but simply recognized their differences as the natural consequence of human diversity. Advocates of this position proposed some form of cultural toleration. The inconvenient facts of the New World brought to the forefront the inadequacy of traditional moral standards for judging the behavior of other people. Deciding whether a particular people were bad or good raised questions about the criteria for making such judgments, and these questions introduced the principle of cultural relativism. Cultural relativism° recognized that many (but not necessarily all) standards of judgment are specific to particular cultures rather than the fixed truths established by natural or divine law. In our own society, cultural relativists attempt to understand why other people think and act the way they do before they judge them. Such an approach can be traced to a small group of sixteenth-century European thinkers who tried to make sense of the new discoveries. Perplexed by the cultural diversity he had observed in the New World, Peter Martyr D'Anghiera (1457–1526), a pious priest and astute historian of Spanish explorations, noted that different peoples made judgments on the basis of different criteria: "the Ethiopian thinks the black color to be fairer than the white, and the white man thinks otherwise. . . . The bearded man supposes he is more comely than he that wants a beard. As appetite therefore moves, not as reason persuades, men run into these vanities, and every province is ruled by its own sense. . . ."[10] What others thought fundamental moral truths, Martyr considered manifestations of superficial cultural differences.

The most eloquent voice for cultural toleration during the sixteenth century was Michel de Montaigne (1533–1592), the brilliant French essayist. After a career as a hard-working public official, he retired at age 38 to his estate to a life of study and contemplation. Among his many interests, he especially loved to read about travels to the New World. His essay "On Cannibals" pointed to the hypocrisy of Christians who condemned the alleged cannibalism of the native Americans but justified the torture and murder of other Christians over some minor theological dispute. Montaigne argued that a truly ethical, truly Christian person was not a rigid follower of biblical laws but was capable of understanding and tolerating cultural differences. The discovery in the New World that non-Christians could lead moral lives, love their families, practice humility and charity, and benefit from highly developed religious institutions shook the complacent sense of European superiority.

The Capitalist Global Economy

During the sixteenth century a truly global economy began to take shape as a consequence of the European encounters with the rest of the world. As the Europeans sailed the oceans of the world in search of profits, they pioneered a new form of economic organization—agrarian capitalism°. In agrarian capitalism Europeans organized the production of certain kinds of commercial crops, such as sugar, tobacco, and indigo, which were raised for sale to an expanding population in Europe. With land expropriated from native peoples in the Atlantic islands, the Americas, and parts of Asia, European capitalists began to raise commercial crops on an unprecedented scale. Unlike other forms of capitalism, which relied on workers who were paid a wage, agrarian capitalism relied on slave labor, mostly provided by transplanted Africans.

Agrarian capitalism depended on the creation of European empires—the settler colonies, plantation colonies, and trading post empires of the Portuguese, Spanish, Dutch, French, English, and Russians. These empires, however, were very different from those of the ancient world, medieval Europe, preconquest Americas, and Asia. In ancient Rome, medieval Byzantium, and early modern China, for example, imperial governments promoted monopolies and inhibited free access to the market and thus stymied the development of capitalism. These empires produced economic stagnation instead of growth. But in the European global empires of the sixteenth century, the organization of trade and the division of labor took place outside the authority of any one state, a fact that made it impossible for a single imperial government to monopolize completely economic resources. It was the competition among imperialist states, rather than control by a single powerful empire, that was new.

The creation of the European empires during the sixteenth century made it possible for capitalists to maximize their profits through regional specialization. Western Europe became the *core* of the global economy, the center of a complex variety of economic activities and institutions—banking, insurance, trade companies, gun manufacture, shipbuilding, and the production of cloth. In Europe agriculture was more and more devoted exclusively to producing food, and the labor supply was free—neither serfs, as had been the case in the Middle Ages, nor slaves, as was the case in parts of the Americas. The distant colonies, especially in Spanish and Portuguese America, became the *periphery* devoted to raising single cash crops, such as sugar, tobacco, cotton, coffee, or indigo for dyes. Agriculture in the periphery was produced on large estates by slaves.

The capitalist global economy has steadily and relentlessly expanded throughout the world since the sixteenth century. Much of the subsequent history of Western civilization can be understood only in terms of the triumph of capitalism and the economic integration of a world dominated by Westerners. The capitalist global economy has yielded many benefits in enhancing the material well-being of the middle classes of the West, increasing the available food supply of the world, and stimulating technological innovation. But there have been costs. Since the sixteenth century, the gap between rich and poor individuals and rich and poor countries has widened, and societies on the agrarian periphery have found it enormously difficult to break out of their disadvantaged position in the world economy.

CONCLUSION
The Significance of the Global Encounters

The world was forever changed by the European voyages from about 1450 to 1650. The significance of these encounters lay not so much in the Europeans' geographical discoveries as in the scale of permanent contact these voyages made possible among previously isolated peoples of the world. Europeans had been to the Americas before Columbus, and the Chinese had earlier engaged in long-distance voyages of reconnaissance as far as the east coast of Africa. But none of these early voyages had created a lasting economic system or lasting cultural contacts. The European voyages of the fifteenth and sixteenth centuries did.

As a result of the Portuguese slaving enterprises on the coast of West and Central Africa, millions of Africans were uprooted, transported in chains to a strange land, and forced to toil in subhuman conditions on plantations. There they grew crops for the increasingly affluent European consumers and generated profits often used to buy more slaves in Africa, parts of which became depopulated in the process. In Europe until the nineteenth century, every cup of coffee, every puff of tobacco, every sugar candy, and every cotton dress of indigo blue came from the sweat of a black slave.

Many of the native Americans lost their lives, their land, and their way of life as a result of European encounters. The most isolated of them retained their languages and religion, but other groups were assimilated to the point of nearly complete cultural loss. Everywhere in the Americas, native peoples suffered from the invasion of Old World microbes even more than from the invasion of Old World conquerors. The destruction of the Aztec and Incan empires were certainly the most dramatic, but everywhere native peoples struggled to adapt to an invasion of foreign beings from a foreign world.

Asia was far less altered by contact with Europeans. The most thorough Asian conquest—the Russians in Siberia—was of the least populated region of the entire Asian continent. European civilization remained on the cultural periphery of Asia. But European access to Asian luxury goods remained a crucial component in the expanding global economy that became one of the first fruits of European capitalism.

Coming to terms with the variety of world cultures became a persistent and absorbing problem in Western civilization. Most Europeans retained confidence in the inherent superiority of their civilization, but the realities of the world began to chip away at that confidence, and economic globalization profoundly altered Western civilization itself. Westerners began to confront the problem of understanding "other" cultures and in so doing changed themselves. The West came to mean less a place in Europe than a certain kind of culture that was exported throughout the world through conversion to Christianity, the acquisition of Western languages, and the spread of Western technology.

Suggestions for Further Reading

For a comprehensive list of suggested readings, please go to www.ablongman.com/levack/chapter12

Chaudhuri, K. N. *Trade and Civilization in the Indian Ocean: An Economic History from the Rise of Islam to 1750.* 1985. Arguing for the long-term unity of trade routes, the book lays out the importance of Asian merchants to maritime trade networks from the South China Sea to the Mediterranean.

Clendinnen, Inga. *Aztecs: An Interpretation.* 1991. A provocative, sometimes disturbing book that directly confronts the implications of human sacrifice and cannibalism among the Aztecs and offers an explanation for it by analyzing Aztec religion.

Crosby, Jr., Alfred W. *The Columbian Exchange: Biological and Cultural Consequences of 1492.* 1973. The most significant study on the implications of the biological exchanges for the cultural history of both the Old and New Worlds. It has the benefit of being an exciting book to read.

Curtin, Philip D. *African History: From Earliest Times to Independence.* 1995. An excellent survey by one of the most distinguished comparative historians.

Elvin, Mark. *The Pattern of the Chinese Past: A Social and Economic Interpretation.* 1973. An excellent overview of Chinese history that covers Chinese responses to Western encounters.

Fernández-Armesto, Felipe. *Before Columbus: Exploration and Colonization from the Mediterranean to the Atlantic, 1229–1492.* 1987. Engagingly written and original in scope, this is the best single account of early European colonization efforts.

Fernández-Armesto, Felipe. *Columbus.* 1991. The 500th anniversary of Columbus's voyage in 1492 provoked a wide-ranging reappraisal of his motives and career. This pithy, engaging book is by far the most convincing in revising Columbus's image, but it deflated much of the Columbus myth and caused considerable controversy.

Oliver, Roland. *The African Experience from Olduvai Gorge to the 21st Century.* 2000. A highly readable general survey.

Pagden, Anthony. *European Encounters with the New World: From Renaissance to Romanticism.* 1993. A fascinating examination of how Europeans interpreted their encounters with America.

Parry, J. H. *The Age of Reconnaissance.* 1982. An analysis of European shipping technology and the causes behind European explorations. It covers all the major voyages.

Parry, J. H. *The Spanish Seaborne Empire.* 1990. The standard study on the subject. It brings together an enormous range of material and presents it clearly and cogently.

Phillips, Jr., William D., and Carla Rahn Phillips. *The Worlds of Christopher Columbus.* 1992. A balanced analysis of Columbus's attempts to find financing for his voyage that pays equal attention to his personal ambition, Christian zeal, and navigational skills.

Notes

1. Christopher Columbus, quoted in Felipe Fernández-Armesto, *Columbus* (1991), 154.
2. Sir Arthur Helps, *The Spanish Conquest in America,* vol. 1 (1900), 1, 264–267.
3. Alfred W. Crosby, Jr., *The Columbian Exchange: Biological and Cultural Consequences of 1492* (1972), 3.
4. *The Book of Chilam Balam of Chumayel,* ed. and trans. Ralph L. Roy (1933), 83.
5. *The Conquistadores: First-Person Accounts of the Conquest of Mexico,* ed. and trans. Patricia de Fuentes (1963), 159.
6. *The Annals of the Cakchiquels and Title of the Lords of Totnicapán,* trans. Adrian Recinos, Dioniscio José Chonay, and Delia Goetz (1953), 116.
7. Ibid., 9.
8. Quoted in Margaret T. Hodgen, *Early Anthropology in the Sixteenth and Seventeenth Centuries* (1964), 207. Spelling has been modernized.
9. Ibid., 369.
10. Ibid., 373–374. Spelling and syntax have been modernized.

1500
Albertus Durerus Noricu
ipsum me propriis sic effin
gebam coloribus aetatis
anno XXVIII.

CHAPTER 13

The Reformation of Religion, 1500–1560

On October 31, 1517, an obscure monk-turned-university-professor nailed on the door of the cathedral in Wittenberg, Germany, an announcement containing ninety-five theses or debating propositions. Professor Martin Luther had no hint of the ramifications of this simple act—as common then as posting an announcement for a lecture or concert on a university bulletin board now. But Luther's seemingly harmless deed would spark a revolution. Within weeks all Germany was ablaze over what was widely seen as Luther's daring attack on the pope. Within a few short years Wittenberg became the European center for a movement to reform the Church. As the pope and high churchmen resisted the call for reform, much of Germany and eventually most of northern Europe and Britain broke away from the Catholic Church in a movement called the Protestant Reformation, which dominated European affairs from 1517 until 1555.

Martin Luther was successful because he expressed in print what many felt in their hearts—that the Church was failing in its most fundamental obligation to help Christians achieve salvation. In contrast, many Catholics considered the Protestants dangerous heretics who offended God with their errors. The division between Protestants and Catholics split the West into two distinctive religious cultures. The result was that the hard-won unity of the West, which had been achieved during the Middle Ages through the expansion of Christianity to the most distant corners of the European continent, was lost. Catholics and Protestants continued to share a great deal of the Christian tradition, but two fateful issues divided them: the Latin liturgy and obedience to the pope. After the Reformation of the sixteenth century, the common Christian culture was permanently severed by the Protestants' abandonment of Latin in the liturgy and their refusal to accept the authority of the pope.

The Imitation of Christ: In Albrecht Dürer's self-portrait at age 28, he literally shows himself imitating Christ's appearance. The initials AD are prominently displayed in the upper left-hand corner. They stand for Albrecht Dürer but also for *anno domini,* "the year of our Lord."

Chapter Outline

Throughout western Europe, countries officially became either Catholic or Protestant—a situation that enforced obedience to the official faith through the police powers of the state and caused considerable suffering among adherents to unofficial religions. The fundamental conflict during the Reformation was about religion, but religion can never be entirely separated from politics or society. The competition among the kingdoms and the social tensions within the cities of central and northern Europe magnified the religious controversies, making the Reformation a broad cultural movement that seeped into all aspects of life.

This chapter will explore the Reformation controversies by addressing five central questions: (1) What caused the religious rebellion that began in German-speaking lands and spread to much of northern Europe? (2) How did the Lutheran Reformation create a new kind of religious culture? (3) How and why did Protestant denominations multiply to such an extent in northern Europe and Britain? (4) How did the Catholic Church respond to the unprecedented threat to its dominance of religious authority in the West? (5) How did the religious turmoil of the sixteenth century transform the role of the visual arts and music in public life?

Causes of the Reformation

The Protestant Reformation was the culmination of nearly 200 years of turmoil within the Church. As we saw in Chapter 10, during the fourteenth and fifteenth centuries the Church was especially hampered by the contradiction between its divine mission and its obligations in this world. On the one hand, the Church taught that its mission was otherworldly, as the source of spiritual solace and the guide to eternal salvation. On the other hand, the Church was thoroughly of this world. It owned vast amounts of property, maintained a far-reaching judicial bureaucracy to enforce canon (Church) law, and was headed by the pope, who was also the territorial prince of the Papal State in central Italy. Whereas from the eleventh to the thirteenth centuries the popes had been the source of moral reform and spiritual renewal in the Church, by the fifteenth century they had become part of the problem. The problem was not so much that they had become corrupt but that they were unable to respond effectively to the demands of ordinary people who were increasingly concerned with their own salvation and the effective government of their communities.

Three developments, in particular, contributed to the demand for religious reform: the search for the freedom of private religious expression; the print revolution; and the Northern Renaissance interest in the Bible and sources of Christianity.

The Search for Spiritual and Fiscal Freedom

A series of events during the fourteenth century had weakened the authority of the popes and driven the Church to the point of splitting apart, more for political than theological reasons (see Chapter 10). Between 1305 and 1378 seven popes in a row abandoned Rome, which was plagued by dangerous feuds among its aristocratic families, and chose to reside in the relative calm of Avignon, France. The period came to be called the Babylonian Captivity of the Church, a pejorative term that reflected the opinion that the popes had become subservient to the kings of France. The loss of revenues from the Papal State in Italy forced the financial advisers of the popes into various shady financial schemes, which undermined the moral reputation of the papacy. The Babylonian Captivity was followed by an equally contentious period between 1378 and 1417, the Great Schism, when the Church was divided over allegiance to rival Italian and French popes, and eventually to three and four competing popes.

The degradation of the papacy during the Babylonian Captivity and the Great Schism led to the Conciliar Movement, an attempt by a group of bishops to solve the schism and to liberate the Church from the abuses of papal authority. The conciliarists argued that at a general meeting or council (hence, "conciliar"), the Church bishops would have authority over the pope and could depose him and arrange for the election of a new pope. Accordingly, the Council of Constance (1414–1417) ended the Great Schism, and the Council of Basel (1431–1449) voted for reforms. But the reforms were never implemented because of the uncompromising attitude of Pope Eugeneus IV (1431–1447). The failure of the moderate reforms of the Council of Basel opened the way for the more radical rejection of papal authority during the Protestant Reformation of the sixteenth century.

While the papacy's moral authority precipitously declined, lay Christians were drawn to new forms of worship. Particularly influential were the Modern Devotion, which was promoted by the Brothers of the Common Life, and the *Imitation of Christ,* written by a Common Life brother about 1441. By emphasizing frequent private prayer and moral introspection, the *Imitation* provided a kind of spiritual manual that helped laypeople follow the same path toward spiritual renewal that traditionally had been reserved for monks and nuns. The goal was to imitate Christ so thoroughly that Christ entered the believer's soul. For example, the 1500 self-portrait of Albrecht Dürer (1471–1528), a work influenced by the Modern Devotion, portrayed the artist as if he were Christ himself.

The religious fervor that drew many Christians to such profound forms of religious expression led them to question the moral authority of the papacy. They began to see the pope as a thieving foreigner who extorted money that could be better spent locally. German communities, in particular, protested against the financial demands and the questionable practices of the pope and higher clergy. Some bishops neglected their duties regarding the spiritual guidance of their flock. Some never resided in their dioceses (the district under the bishop's care), knew nothing of the problems of their people, and were concerned only with retaining their incomes and lavish living standards. Living amid the pleasures of Rome, these high clergymen were in no position to discipline parish priests, some of whom also ignored their moral responsibilities by living openly with concubines and even selling the sacraments. Although immorality of this sort was probably not widespread, a few notorious examples bred enormous resentment among the laity.

In an effort to assert control over the church in their own communities, city officials known as magistrates attempted to stem the financial drain and end clerical abuses. They restricted the amount of property ecclesiastical institutions could own, tried to tax the clergy, made priests subject to the town's courts of law, and eliminated the churchmen's exemption from burdensome duties, such as serving in the town militia or providing labor for public works. On the eve of the Reformation—especially in the cities of Germany and the Netherlands—magistrates had already begun to assert local control over the church, a tendency that prepared the way for the Protestants' efforts. For many laypeople, the overriding desire was to obtain greater spiritual and fiscal freedom from the Church.

THE PRINT REVOLUTION

Until the mid-fifteenth century, the only way in the West to reproduce any kind of text—a short business record or a long philosophical book—was to copy it laboriously by hand. As medieval scribes made copies on parchment, however, they often introduced errors or "improved" the original text as they saw fit. Thus, two different copies of the same text could read differently. Parchment books were also very expensive; a book as long as the Bible might require the skins of 300 sheep to make the parchment sheets and hundreds of hours of labor to copy the text. The high cost meant that books were limited to churchmen and to the very rich. Few Christians ever actually read the Bible simply because Bibles—like all books—were so rare.

Two fifteenth-century inventions revolutionized the availability of books. First, movable metal type was introduced around 1450, and after that time printed books first began to appear. Perhaps the very first was a Bible printed by Johannes Gutenberg in Mainz, Germany. Equally important, cheap manufactured paper replaced expensive sheepskins. These two developments reduced the cost of books to a level that made them available even to artisans of modest incomes.

Der Buchdrucker.

The Printer
This woodcut depicts the new printing press. The verse that accompanied the woodcut celebrated the skills of the printer and the new art of printing.

The demand for inexpensive printed books was astounding. During the first forty years of print, more books were produced than had been copied by scribes during the previous thousand years. By 1500, presses in more than 200 cities and towns had printed six million books. Half of the titles were on religious subjects, and because the publishing industry (then as now) produced only what people wanted to buy, the predominance of religion is a telling indication of what was on the minds of the reading public.

The buyers of printed books included, of course, the traditionally literate classes of university students, churchmen, professionals, and aristocratic intellectuals. Remarkably, however, there was also an enormous demand among people for whom books had previously been an unimaginable luxury. During the fourteenth and fifteenth centuries literacy rates had steadily risen and the power of literate culture was strongly felt even by those who could not write. For example, an illiterate farmer near Siena, Italy, had someone else keep a farming diary for him because he recognized that a written record would give him greater power over his own affairs. Literacy rates varied enormously across Europe. They were highest in the cities, especially in northern Italy, Germany, and the Netherlands. In the rural areas, literacy was still rare, probably limited to the village priest, the notary, and perhaps the local nobility. Everywhere men were more often literate than women. However, the knowledge of what was in books spread widely beyond the literate few. The reason was that reading for most people in the fifteenth and sixteenth centuries was an oral, public activity rather than a silent, private one. In parish churches, taverns, and private houses the literate read books out loud to others for their entertainment and edification.

The expansion of the university system during this period also created more demand for books. Between 1300 and 1500 the number of European universities grew from twenty to seventy. The universities also developed a new way of reading. During the fifteenth century the Sorbonne in Paris and Oxford University decreed that libraries were to be quiet places, an indication of the spread of silent reading among the most highly educated classes. Compared to the tradition of reading aloud, silent reading was faster and more private. The silent reader learned more quickly and also decided independently the meaning of what had been read. Once many cheap books were available to the silent readers among the best educated, the interpretation of texts, especially the notoriously difficult text of the Bible, could no longer be easily regulated.

Would the Reformation have succeeded without the print revolution? It is impossible to imagine that it could have. Print culture radically changed how information was disseminated and gave people new ways to interpret their experiences. Between 1517 and 1520, Martin Luther wrote some thirty tracts, mostly in a riveting colloquial German; 300,000 copies were printed and distributed throughout Europe. No other author's ideas had ever spread so fast to so many.

The Northern Renaissance and the Christian Humanists

As we saw in Chapter 11, the humanists were writers devoted to rediscovering the lost works of antiquity and imitating the style of the best Greek and Latin authors of the ancient world. As the humanists examined these ancient texts, they developed the study of philology, of how the meanings of words change over time. These endeavors stimulated a new kind of approach to the sources of Christianity. The humanist Lorenzo Valla (ca. 1407–1457), for example, evaluated the historical sources of papal authority, including the Donation of Constantine—a document that provided the legal justification for the Papal State and papal assertions of supreme authority in Italy. Because the Donation of Constantine used words that were not current during the time when it was supposedly written, Valla argued that it was a forgery. He went on to question the accuracy of the Vulgate, the Latin translation of the Bible accepted by the Church.

The humanists who specialized in subjecting the Bible to philological study are called the Christian humanists°. In examining the sources of Christianity, their goal was not to criticize Christianity or the Church but to understand the precise meaning of its founding texts, especially the Bible and the writings of the Church fathers, who wrote in Greek and Latin and commented on the Bible during the early centuries of Christianity. The Christian humanists sought to correct what they saw as mistakes in interpreting Christian doctrine. They believed that the path to personal morality and to Church reform lay in imitating "the primitive church," which meant the practices of Christianity at the time of Jesus and the apostles. Most of the Christian humanists came from northern Europe. They constituted the most influential wing of the Northern Renaissance, a movement that built on the foundations of the Italian Renaissance. Through their efforts, the foundations of Christianity came under intense scrutiny during the early sixteenth century.

Desiderius Erasmus
This portrait showing the great humanist writing was painted by Hans Holbein the Younger in 1523.

By far the most influential of the Christian humanists was a Dutchman, Desiderius Erasmus (ca. 1469–1536). To remedy the evils of the world, Erasmus became an ardent advocate of education, especially for future priests, whom he wanted to learn "the philosophy of Christ." As a guide to that philosophy, he published an annotated text of the Greek New Testament, which he opened with the optimistic preface: "If the Gospel were truly preached, the Christian people would be spared many wars." He later translated the Greek New Testament into a new Latin version. His critical studies were the basis of many translations of the Hebrew and Greek Bible into vernacular languages, including the popular English translation, the King James Bible.

Exploiting the potential of the relatively new printing industry, Erasmus became the most inspiring moral critic of his times. During times of war he eloquently called for peace; he published a practical manual for helping children develop a sense of morality; and he laid out easy-to-follow guidelines for spiritual renewal in the *Handbook for the Militant Christian.* He was most popular for his biting criticisms of the Church that revealed a genuine spiritual sorrow shared by many of his readers:

> *I could see that the common body of Christians was corrupt not only in its affections but in its ideas. I pondered on the fact that those who profess themselves pastors and doctors for the most part misuse these titles, which belong to Christ, for their own advantage. . . . Is there any religious man who does not see with sorrow that this generation is far the most corrupt there has ever been?*[1]

Albrecht Dürer, *The Knight, Death, and the Devil*
This engraving of 1513 illustrates Erasmus's *Handbook for the Militant Christian* by depicting a knight steadfastly advancing through a frightening landscape. A figure of death holds an hourglass, indicating that his time on Earth is limited. A devil follows behind him threateningly. His valiant horse and loyal dog represent the virtues that a pious Christian must acquire.

Erasmus's penchant for moral criticism reached the level of high satire in his masterpiece, *The Praise of Folly* (1514). In it he attacked theologians preoccupied by silly questions, such as how many angels could dance on the head of a pin; he lampooned corrupt priests who took money from dying men to read the last rites; he ridiculed gullible pilgrims who bought phony relics as tourist souvenirs; and he parodied the vanity of monks who thought the color of their robes more important than helping the poor. He saved some of his most biting sarcasm for the monks by pointing out "their filthiness, their ignorance, their bawdiness, and their insolence."[2]

Despite these criticisms Erasmus refused to abandon Catholicism and engaged in a very public conflict with Luther and the Protestants. He thought the militants on both sides were driven more by egotism than by Christian humility. In the combative age of the Reformation, Erasmus stood virtually alone as a voice of peace and moderation, and like many nonviolent men since that time, he was deeply hated. His lasting fame, however, rests on his perceptive philological analysis of the Bible and other early Christian texts. But he was also an eloquent popularizer, someone who demonstrated to a large public how individuals could apply to their daily lives previously obscure trends in humanist learning and how a better understanding of the Bible could purify faith and combat corruption within the Church.

Erasmus's friend, the Englishman Thomas More (1478–1535), is best known for his book, *Utopia* (1516). More's little book established the genre of utopian fiction, which describes imaginary, idealized worlds. It depicted a fantasy island in the New World, "Utopia," which in Greek

THOMAS MORE'S ARGUMENT AGAINST CAPITAL PUNISHMENT

In sixteenth-century England, there were literally hundreds of offenses, including simple theft, that could lead to capital punishment. Among the many aspects of contemporary society that Thomas More criticized in Utopia *(1516), capital punishment especially offended him because it was so clearly prohibited in the Bible. More combined moral precepts derived from Scripture and reasoned argument, a combination that is especially characteristic of the Christian humanists. Thomas More was himself a victim of capital punishment, executed by the courts of King Henry VIII.*

God said, "Thou shalt not kill"—does the theft of a little money make it quite all right for us to do so? If it's said that this commandment applies only to illegal killing, what's to prevent human beings from similarly agreeing among themselves to legalize certain types of rape, adultery, or perjury? Considering that God has forbidden us even to kill ourselves, can we really believe that purely human arrangements for the regulation of mutual slaughter are enough, without any divine authority, to exempt executioners from the sixth commandment? Isn't that rather like saying that this particular commandment has no more validity than human laws allow it?—in which case the principle can be extended indefinitely, until in all spheres of life human beings decide just how far God's commandments may conveniently be observed.

. . .

Well, those are my objections on moral grounds. From a practical point of view, surely it's obvious that to punish thieves and murderers in precisely the same way is not only absurd but also highly dangerous for the public. If a thief knows that a conviction for murder will get him into no more trouble than a conviction for theft, he's naturally impelled to kill the person that he'd otherwise merely have robbed. It's no worse to him if he's caught, and it gives him a better chance of not being caught, and of concealing the crime altogether by eliminating the only witness. So in our efforts to terrorize thieves we're actually encouraging them to murder innocent people.

Source: From *Utopia,* by Thomas More, translated by Paul Turner (Penguin Classics, 1961).

means "nowhere." Utopia was inhabited by monotheists who, although not Christians, intuitively understood pure religion, lived a highly regulated life, and shared their property in common. Utopia represented More's understanding of what a society based on the primitive church might look like. In particular he took the idea of abolishing all private property from Scripture, which states that the believers in Christ "were of one heart and soul, and no one claimed private ownership of any possessions, but everything they owned was held in common" (Acts 4:32). More shared some of Erasmus's ideas about the critical study of Scripture and a purer Church, but unlike Erasmus he was no pacifist. In his capacity as chancellor of England, he ruthlessly persecuted Protestants.

Erasmus and More remained loyal Catholics, and, as we shall see in the discussion of the English Reformation, More even sacrificed his own life to the faith. Nevertheless, their work helped popularize some of the principles that came to be associated with the Protestant reformers. To them, the test for the legitimacy of any religious practice was twofold: First, could it be found in the Bible; second, did it promote moral behavior? The Christian humanists' preoccupation with textual criticism focused attention on the sources of Christianity, and some were profoundly shaken by the deep disparity they perceived between the Christianity of the New Testament and the state of the Church in their own time.

The Lutheran Reformation

The Protestant Reformation began with the protests of Martin Luther against the pope and certain Church practices. Like Erasmus and More, Luther used the Bible as the litmus test of what the Church should do. If a practice could not be found in the Bible, Luther thought, then it should not be considered Christian. But unlike Erasmus and More, he also introduced theological innovations that made compromise with the papacy impossible.

Luther and his followers would not have succeeded without the support of the local political authorities, who had their own grievances against the pope and the Holy Roman Emperor. The Lutheran Reformation first spread in Germany with the assistance and encouragement of those local authorities: the town magistrates and the territorial princes. Luther's ideas had a magnetic appeal to a wide spectrum of the population, especially women and peasants. When the peasants understood that Luther's ideas about the freedom of the Christian also meant economic freedom, they revolted against their feudal lords. The violence of that revolt forced Luther to retreat and to back the forces of order, the lords and princes. In so doing he made it clear that the Reformation was not to be a social revolution but a religious reform. Lutheranism would not threaten the established political order. Under the sponsorship of princes and kings, Lutheranism spread from Germany into Scandinavia.

MARTIN LUTHER AND THE BREAK WITH ROME

Martin Luther (1483–1546) suffered a grim childhood and uneasy relationship with his father, a miner who wanted his son to become a lawyer. During a break from the University of Erfurt where he was studying law, Luther was thrown from his horse in a storm and nearly died. That frightening experience impelled him to become a monk, a decision that infuriated his father because it meant young Luther abandoned a promising professional career. By becoming a monk, Luther replaced the control of his father with obedience to his superiors in the Augustinian Order. They sent him back to the University of Erfurt for advanced study in theology and then transferred him from the lovely garden city of Erfurt to Wittenberg in Saxony, a scruffy town "on the edge of beyond," as Luther described it. At Wittenberg Luther began to teach at an undistinguished university, far from the intellectual action. Instead of lamenting his isolation, Luther brought the world to his university by making it the center of the religious reform movement.

As a monk, Luther had been haunted by a deep lack of self-worth: "In the monastery, I did not think about women, or gold, or goods, but my heart trembled, and doubted how God could be gracious to me. Then I fell away from faith, and let myself think nothing less than that I had come under the Wrath of God, whom I must reconcile with my good works."[3] Obsessed by the fear that no amount of charitable good works, prayers, or religious ceremonies would compensate for God's contempt of him, Luther suffered from anxiety attacks and prolonged periods of depression. He understood his psychic turmoil and shaky faith as any monk would—the temptations of the Devil, who was a very powerful figure in Luther's life.

Over a number of years, while preparing and revising his university lectures on St. Paul, Luther gradually worked out a solution to his own spiritual crisis by reexamining the theology of penance. The sacrament of penance provided a way to confess sins and receive absolution for them. If a penitent had lied, for example, he could seek forgiveness for the sin by feeling sorry about it, confessing it to a priest, and receiving a penalty, usually a specified number of prayers. Penance took care of only those penalties the Church could inflict on sinners; God's punishment for sins would take place in Purgatory (a place of temporary suffering for dead souls) and at the Last Judgment. But Catholic theology held that penance in this world would reduce punishment in the next. In wrestling with the concept of penance, Luther long meditated on the meaning of a difficult passage in St. Paul's Epistle to the Romans (1:17): "The just shall live by faith." Luther came to understand this passage to mean that eternal salvation came not from performing the religious good works of penance but as a gift from God. That gift was called "grace" and was completely unmerited. In other words, corrupt humans were incapable of earning eternal salvation, but God in his love for humanity promised to give it to a select few, the "Elect." Luther called this process of receiving God's grace "justification by faith alone°," because the ability to have faith in Christ was a sign that one was among the Elect.

Luther's emphasis on justification by faith alone left no room for human free will in obtaining salvation, because Luther believed that faith could come only from God's grace. This did not mean that God controlled every human action, but it did mean that humans could not will to do good. They needed God's help. Those blessed with God's grace would naturally perform good works. This way of thinking about God's grace had a long tradition going back to St. Augustine, the Church father whose work profoundly influenced Luther's own thought. In the turmoil of the Reformation, however, Luther's interpretation of St. Augustine separated Lutheran from Catholic theology. The issue of free will became one of the most crucial differences between Protestants and Catholics.

For Luther this seemingly bleak doctrine of denying the human will to do good was tremendously liberating. He no longer had to worry whether he was doing enough to please God or could muster enough energy to fight the Devil. All he had to do was trust in God's grace. After this breakthrough, Luther reported that "I felt myself to be born anew, and to enter through open gates into paradise itself. From here, the whole face of the Scriptures was altered."[4]

The Ninety-Five Theses

In 1517 Luther became embroiled in a controversy that led to the separation of him and his followers from the Roman Catholic Church. In order to finance the building of a new St. Peter's Basilica in Rome, Pope Leo X had issued a special new indulgence. An indulgence was a particular form of penance whereby a sinner could remove years of punishment in Purgatory after death by performing a good work here on Earth. For example, pilgrims to Rome or Jerusalem were often in search of indulgences, which were concrete measures of the value of their penances. Indulgences formed one of the most intimate bonds between the Church and the laity because they offered a means for the forgiveness of specific sins.

During the fourteenth century popes in need of ready cash had begun to sell indulgences. But Pope Leo's new indulgence went far beyond the promise of earlier indulgences by offering a one-time-only opportunity to escape penalties for all sins. Moreover, the special indulgence could apply not only to the purchaser but to the dead already in Purgatory. The new indulgence immediately made all other indulgences worthless because it removed all penalties for sin whereas others removed only some of them.

Frederick the Wise, the Elector of Saxony (a princely title indicating that he was one of those who elected the emperors of the Holy Roman Empire) and the patron of Martin Luther's university, prohibited the sale of Pope Leo's special indulgence in Electoral Saxony, but it was sold just a few miles away from Wittenberg, across the border in the domain of Archbishop Albrecht of Mainz. Albrecht needed the revenues that the sale of indulgences would bring because he was in debt. He had borrowed enormous sums to bribe Pope Leo to allow him to hold simultaneously three ecclesiastical offices—a practice that was against Church law. To help Albrecht repay his debts, the pope allowed Albrecht to keep half of the revenue from the indulgence sale in his territories. Wittenbergers began to trek over the border to Albrecht's lands to listen to the sales pitch from the shameless indulgence hawker, the Dominican John Tetzel (1470–1519). Tetzel staged an ecclesiastical version of a carnival barker's act in which he harangued the crowd about their dead parents who could be immediately released from the flames of Purgatory for the sacrifice of a few coins. He allegedly ended his sermons with the notorious jingle,

> *As soon as gold in the basin rings,*
> *Right then the soul to heaven springs.*[5]

Some of the Wittenbergers who heard Tetzel asked Martin Luther for his advice about buying the indulgence. Luther responded less as a pastor offering comforting advice to his flock than as a university professor keen for debate. He prepared in Latin ninety-five theses—arguments or talking points—about indulgences that he announced he was willing to defend in an academic disputation. Luther had a few copies printed and posted one on the door of Wittenberg Cathedral. The Ninety-Five Theses were hardly revolutionary in themselves. They argued a simple point that salvation could not be bought and sold, a proposition that was sound, conservative theology; and they explicitly accepted the authority of the pope even as they set limits on that authority. On that point, Luther was merely following what the Church councils of the fifteenth century had decreed. Luther's tone was moderate. He simply suggested that Pope Leo may have been misled in issuing the new indulgence. No one showed up to debate Luther, but someone translated the Ninety-Five Theses into German and printed them, and within a few weeks, a previously unknown professor from an obscure university was the talk of the German lands.

The Dominicans counterattacked. Tetzel himself drew up opposing theses, which provoked a public clamor that Luther had tried to avoid. In 1519 at Leipzig before a raucous crowd of university students, Luther finally debated the theses and more with John Eck, a professor from the University of Ingolstadt. When Eck cleverly backed him into a logical corner, Luther refused to retreat; he insisted that the Bible was the sole guide to human conscience, and he questioned the authority of both popes and councils. This was the very teaching for which earlier heretics had been burned at the stake. At this point Luther had no choice but to abandon his allegiance to the Church to which he had dedicated his life. By this time, Luther also had a large following in Wittenberg and beyond. The core of this group, who called themselves "evangelicals," were university students, younger humanists, and the well-educated, reform-minded priests and monks.

The Path to the Diet of Worms

In the wake of the Leipzig debate, Luther launched an inflammatory pamphlet campaign. Some pamphlets were first written in Latin, for learned readers, but all soon became available in Luther's acerbic German prose, which delighted readers. *Freedom of a Christian* (1520) argued that the Church's emphasis on good works had distracted Christians from the only source of salvation—faith. It proclaimed the revolutionary doctrine of the "priesthood of all believers°," which reasoned that all those of pure faith were themselves priests, a doctrine that undermined the authority of the Catholic clergy over the laity. The most inspirational pamphlet, *To the Christian Nobility of the German Nation* (1520), called upon the German princes to reform the Church and to defend Germany from exploitation by the corrupt Italians who ran the Church in Rome. When Pope Leo ordered Luther to retract his writings, he responded with a defiant demonstration in which he and his students burned the pope's decree and all of the university library's books of Church law. The die was cast.

The pope demanded that Luther be arrested, but the Elector Frederick answered by defending Luther. Frederick refused to make the arrest without first giving Luther a hearing at the Imperial Diet (parliament), which was set to meet at the town of Worms in 1521. Assembled at the Diet of Worms were haughty princes, grave bishops, and the resplendent young Emperor Charles V (r. 1519–1558), who was presiding over his first Imperial Diet. The emperor ordered Luther to disavow his writings, but Luther refused to do so. For several days the diet was in an uproar, divided by friends and foes of Luther's doctrines. Just before he was to be condemned by the emperor, Luther disappeared, and rumors flew that he had been assassinated. For days no one knew the truth. Frederick the Wise had kidnapped Luther for his own safety and hidden him in the castle at Wartburg, where for nearly a year he labored in quiet seclusion translating the New Testament into German.

The Lutheran Reformation in the Cities and Principalities

Luther had escaped arrest and execution at the hands of the emperor, but he could not manage to control his own followers and allies. The Reformation quickly became a vast, sprawling movement far beyond the control of any individual, even in Luther's own Wittenberg. One of the characteristics of the Protestant Reformation was that once reform-

MARTIN LUTHER'S POWERS OF PERSUASION

Part of Martin Luther's appeal derived from his polemical style. The Freedom of a Christian *(1520) was probably Luther's last serious attempt to reconcile himself with Pope Leo X. In the open letter to Pope Leo that introduces the tract, Luther asserts that he is criticizing corrupt advisers in the papal curia rather than the pope himself, but Luther's language seems more designed to embolden his own followers than to persuade the pope.*

Living among the monsters of this age with whom I am now for the third year waging war, I am compelled occasionally to look up to you, Leo, most blessed father, and to think of you. Indeed, since you are occasionally regarded as the sole cause of my warfare, I cannot help thinking of you. To be sure, the undeserved raging of your godless flatterers against me has compelled me to appeal from your see [officials] to a future council [of all the bishops of the Church], despite the decrees of your predecessors Pius and Julius, who with a foolish tyranny forbade such an appeal.

. . .

I have truly despised your see, the Roman Curia, which, however, neither you nor anyone else can deny is more corrupt than any Babylon or Sodom [places condemned for sinfulness in the Bible] ever was, and which, as far as I can see, is characterized by a completely depraved, hopeless, and notorious godlessness. I have been thoroughly incensed over the fact that good Christians are mocked in your name and under the cloak of the Roman church. I have resisted and will continue to resist your see as long as the spirit of faith lives in me.

. . .

I never intended to attack the Roman Curia or to raise any controversy concerning it. But when I saw all efforts to save it were hopeless, I despised it, gave it a bill of divorce, and said, "let the evildoer still do evil, and the filthy still be filthy" [Revelations 22:11]. Then I turned to the quiet and peaceful study of the Holy Scriptures so that I might be helpful to my brothers around me. When I had made some progress in these studies, Satan opened his eyes and then filled his servant Johann Eck, a notable enemy of Christ, with an insatiable lust for glory and thus aroused him to drag me unawares to a debate, seizing me by means of one little word which I had let slip concerning the primacy of the Roman church. Then that boastful braggart, frothing and gnashing his teeth, declared that he would risk everything for the glory of God and the honor of the Apostolic See. Puffed up with the prospect of abusing your authority, he looked forward with great confidence to a victory over me. . . . When the debate ended badly for the sophist, an unbelievable madness overcame the man, for he believed that it was his fault alone which was responsible for my disclosing all the infamy of Rome.

Source: Excerpt from *Luther's Works, vol. 31, Career of the Reformer: I*, edited by Harold J. Grimm (Philadelphia: Muhlenberg Press, 1957). Translated by W. A. Lambert and revised by Harold J. Grimm.

ers rejected the supreme authority of the papacy, even minor differences about forms of worship or biblical interpretation led to division within the movement and eventually to the formation of separate churches.

In its early phases the Reformation spread most rapidly among the educated urban classes. During the sixteenth century, fifty of the sixty-five German imperial cities, at one time or another, officially accepted the Protestant Reformation. Besides these large imperial cities, most of the 200 smaller German towns with a population of more than 1,000 experienced some form of the Protestant movement. During the 1520s and 1530s, the magistrates of these towns took command of the Reformation movement by seizing control of the local churches. The magistrates implemented Luther's reform of worship, disciplined the clergy, and stopped the drain of revenues to irresponsible bishops and the distant pope.

The German princes of the Holy Roman Empire had their own reasons to resent the Church. They wanted to appoint their own nominees to ecclesiastical offices and to diminish the legal privileges of the clergy. During the 1520s Luther's enormous popularity gave many German princes the opportunity they had been waiting for. Despite his steadfast Catholicism, Emperor Charles V was in no position to resist their demands. During most of his reign, Charles faced a two-front war—against France and against the Ottoman Turks. Charles could ill afford additional trouble with the German princes because he desperately needed their military assistance. At the Imperial Diet of Speyer in 1526, Charles granted the princes territorial sovereignty in religion by allowing them to decide whether they would enforce the imperial edict of the Diet of Worms against Luther and his followers. To preserve the empire from external enemies, Charles was forced to allow its internal division along religious lines.

The Appeal of the Reformation to Women

Reformist theology had particular appeal to women. In the early days of the movement, women felt that Luther's description of "the priesthood of all believers" meant that women as well as men could participate fully in the religious life of the Church. Women understood Luther's phrase "the freedom of a Christian" as freeing them from the restrictive roles that had traditionally kept them silent and at home. Moreover, Luther and the other major reformers saw positive religious value in the role of wife and mother. Abandoning the Catholic Church's view that celibate monks and nuns were morally superior to married people, Luther declared marriage holy and set an example by taking a wife, the ex-nun Katherine von Bora. The wives of the reformers often became partners in the Reformation, taking particular responsibility for organizing charities and administering to the poor.

In the early phases of the Reformation, women preached and published on religious matters. These women demanded to be heard in churches and delivered inspiring sermons. They asked that their writings be accepted as authentic products of the Holy Spirit. In some cases, female rulers brought their entire land over to the Reformation. Elisabeth of Brunswick-Calenburg reformed the local church and invited Protestant preachers into her lands. In Germany the noblewoman Argula von Grumbach argued that even though St. Paul had warned that women should be silent in church, she felt driven by the word of God to profess her faith publicly. Marie Dentière, a former abbess of a French convent who joined the Reformation cause, asked, "Do we have two Gospels, one for men and the other for women? . . . For we [women] ought not, any more than men, hide and bury within the earth that which God has . . . revealed to us women?"[6]

Most women were soon disappointed. Women's preaching and writing threatened the male religious and political authorities. The authorities ordered Argula von Grumbach's husband to make her stop writing. Other women who defended the Reformation were silenced by the reformers themselves, and women who spoke up in church were widely condemned. In some places laws were passed that prohibited groups of women from discussing religious questions. In England, noblewomen were even prevented from reading the Bible aloud to others. One kind of writing could not be controlled, however—the private diary. The Protestant imperative to discover the workings of faith within oneself helped promote writing private diaries. The practice spread rapidly with Protestantism, and many women used diaries as an outlet for personal expression and a way to develop a sense of their own personal identities.

The few women who were able to speak and act openly in public were either from the upper classes or the wives of prominent reformers. No man could silence Marguerite of Navarre and her daughter Jeanne d'Albret, who used their authority as queens to promote the Reformation. A body of religious literature developed that held up as models more humble women such as Katherine Zell, the wife of one of Strasbourg's reformers.

For most women participation in the Reformation was confined to the domestic sphere, where they instructed children, quietly read the Bible, and led prayer circles. Protestant authorities also allowed divorce, which was prohibited by Catholic Church law. However, the reform leaders were quite reluctant to grant women the same rights as their husbands in obtaining a divorce. During the early years of the Reformation, there were many marriages in which one spouse followed the old faith and the other the new. But if the woman converted and her husband did not, the Protestant reformers counseled that she obey her husband even if he forced her to act contrary to God's will. She could pray for his conversion but could not leave or divorce him. Most women were forced to remain married regard-

The Destruction of a Monastery During the Peasants' Revolt

Engravings such as this one depicted the violence of the peasants' revolt and helped galvanize Catholic support against the peasants.

less of their feelings. A few exceptional women left their husbands anyway and continued to proclaim their religious convictions to the world. One such woman, Anne Askew from England, was tortured and executed for her beliefs.

The German Peasants' Revolt

The Reformation also appealed to many peasants interested in purified religion and local control of the church. The peasants of Wendelstein, a typical South German village, had been complaining about the conduct of its priests for some time. In 1523, they hired a "Christian teacher" and told him in no uncertain terms: "We will not recognize you as a lord, but only as a servant of the community. We will command you, not you us, and we order you to preach the gospel and the word of God purely, clearly, and truthfully—without any human teachings—faithfully and conscientiously."[7] These villagers understood the Reformation to mean that they could take control of their local church and demand responsible conduct from the minister they hired. However, other peasants understood the Reformation as licensing radical social reforms as well.

In June 1524 a seemingly minor event sparked a revolt of peasants in many parts of Germany. When an aristocratic lady demanded that the peasants in her village abandon their grain harvest to gather snails for her, they rebelled and set her castle on fire. Over the next two years, the rebellion spread as peasants rose up against their feudal lords to demand the adoption of Lutheran reforms in the Church, a reduction of feudal privileges, the abolition of serfdom, and the self-government of their communities. Their rebellion was the largest and best organized peasant movement to that point in European history, a measure of the powerful effect of the Protestant reform message. Like the Reformation, the revolt was the culmination of a long period of discontent, but unlike the Reformation, it was a tragic failure.

These peasants were doing exactly what they thought Luther had advocated when he wrote about the "freedom of the Christian." They interpreted his words to mean complete social as well as religious freedom. However, Luther had not meant anything of the sort. To him the freedom of the Christian referred to inner, spiritual freedom, not liberation from economic or political bondage. Instead of supporting the rebellion begun in his name, Luther and nearly all the other reformers backed the feudal lords and condemned in uncompromising terms the violence of the peasant armies. In *Against the Thieving, Murderous Hordes of Peasants* (1525), Luther expressed his own fear of the lower classes and revealed that despite his acid-tongued attacks on the pope, he was fundamentally a conservative thinker who was committed to law and order. He urged that the peasants be hunted down and killed like rabid dogs. And so they were. Between 70,000 and 100,000 peasants died, a slaughter far greater than the Roman persecutions of the early Christians. To the peasants, Luther's conservative position on social and economic issues felt like betrayal, but it enabled the Lutheran Reformation to retain the support of the princes, which was essential for its survival.

CHRONOLOGY

The Lutheran Reformation

1517	Luther posts the 95 Theses
1519	Luther debates Johann Eck at Leipzig; election of Charles V as Holy Roman Emperor
1521	Diet of Worms
1524–1525	German peasants revolt
1531	Formation of the Schmalkaldic League
1555	The Religious Peace of Augsburg

Lutheran Success

Soon after the crushing of the Peasants' Revolt, the Lutheran Reformation faced a renewed threat from its Catholic opponents. In 1530 Emperor Charles V bluntly commanded all Lutherans to return to the Catholic fold or face arrest. Enraged, the Lutherans refused to comply. The following year the Protestant princes formed a military alliance, the Schmalkaldic League, against the emperor. Renewed trouble with France and the Turks prevented a military confrontation between the League and the emperor for fifteen years, giving the Lutherans enough breathing space to put the Reformation on a firmer basis by creating new institutions to govern the churches in Germany. In place of the Catholic bishops, Lutherans established regional consistories (boards of clerics) to supervise the new Protestant churches. Educational reforms introduced a humanist curriculum, established schools for girls, and organized religious instruction for the laity. In the meantime Lutheranism spread beyond Germany into Scandinavia.

After freeing himself yet again from foreign wars and failing to effect a compromise solution in Germany, Charles V turned his armies against the Protestants. However, in 1552 the Protestant armies defeated in battle the Catholic forces of the emperor, and Charles was forced to relent. In 1555 the Religious Peace of Augsburg° established the principle of *cuius regio, eius religio,* which means "he who rules determines the religion of the land." Protestant princes were permitted to retain all church lands seized before 1552 and to enforce Protestant worship, but Catholic princes were also allowed to enforce Catholic worship in their territories. Those who disagreed with the religion of their ruler would not be tolerated; their only option was to emigrate elsewhere. With the Peace of Augsburg the religious division of

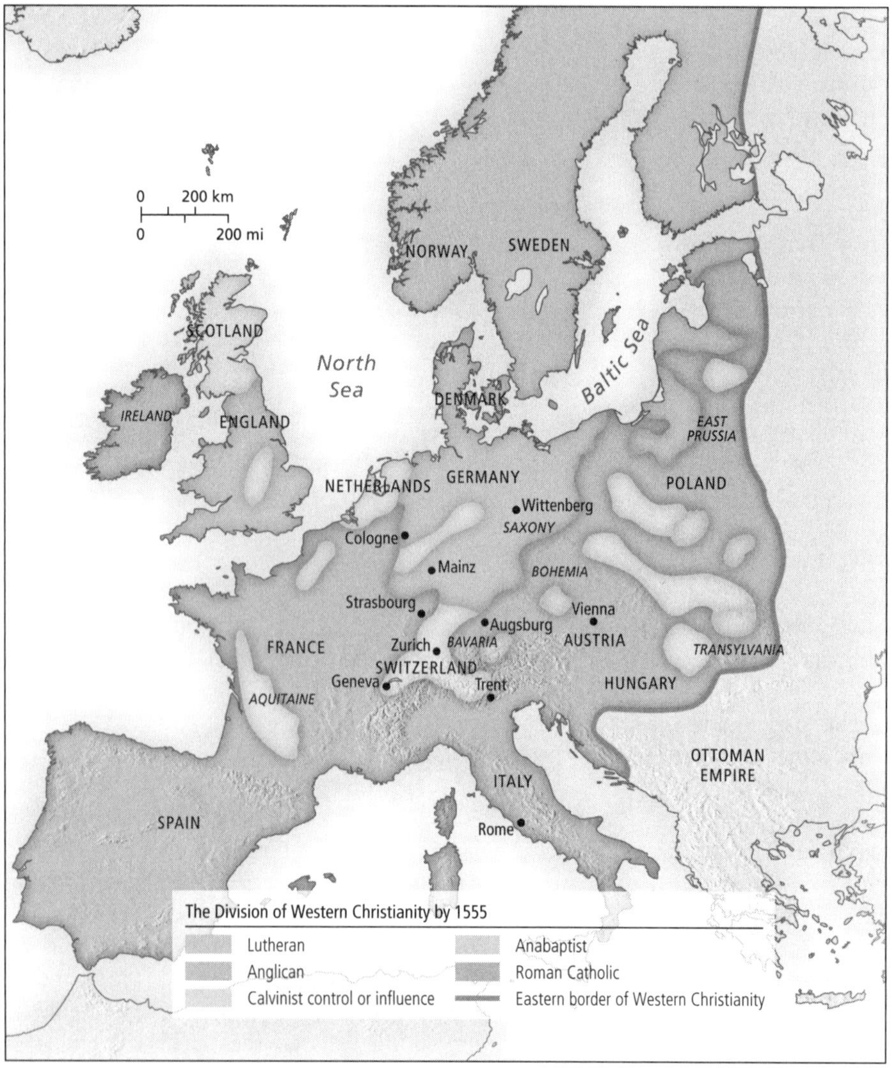

Map 13.1 The Division of Western Christianity by 1555

The West, which had been culturally unified by Christianity for more than a thousand years, split apart during the sixteenth century. These religious divisions persist to this day.

the Holy Roman Empire became permanent, and the legal foundations were in place for the development of the two distinctive religious cultures—Protestant and Catholic.

The following year, Emperor Charles, worn out from ceaseless warfare, the anxieties of holding his vast territories together, and nearly forty years of trying to stamp out Protestantism, abdicated and retired to a monastery where he died in 1558.

The Diversity of Protestantism

The term *Protestant* originally applied only to those followers of Luther who *protested* the decisions of the Imperial Diet of Speyer in 1529, but the term came to describe much more than that small group. It designated all western European Christians who refused to accept the authority of the pope. Protestantism encompassed innumerable churches and sects. Many of these have survived since the Reformation; some disappeared in the violence of the sixteenth century; others have sprung up since, especially in North America, where Protestantism has thrived.

The varieties of Protestantism can be divided into two types. The first type was the product of the Magisterial Reformation°, which refers to the churches that received official government sanction. These included the Lutheran churches in Germany and Scandinavia; the Reformed and Calvinist churches in Switzerland, Scotland, the Netherlands, and a few places in Germany; and the Anglican church in England. The second type was the product of the Radical Reformation° and includes the movements that failed to gain official recognition and were at best tolerated, at worst persecuted. This strict division into Magisterial and Radical Protestantism broke down in eastern Europe, where the states were too weak to enforce religious conformity. In eastern Europe religious variety prevailed over rigid conformity, at least for the sixteenth century (see Map 13.1).

THE REFORMATION IN SWITZERLAND

The governmental independence of Switzerland meant that local authorities could cooperate with the reformers without opposition from the emperor, as was the case in Germany. The Swiss Confederation bound together thirteen fiercely proud regions, called cantons, which had established their independence from the Habsburg dynasty of the Holy Roman Empire (see Map 13.2). Except for the leading cities of Bern, Basel, and Zürich, Switzerland remained an impoverished land of peasants who could not fully support themselves from the barren mountainous land. To supplement their meager incomes, young Swiss men fought as mercenaries in foreign armies, often those of the pope. Each spring, mercenary captains recruited able-bodied Swiss men from the mountain villages. The Swiss men left the women behind to tend the animals and farms. By summer, the villages were emptied of all men except the old and invalid. Each fall at the end of the fighting season, the survivors of that season's campaign trudged home, always bringing bad news to a fresh group of widows. The strain created by the mercenary's life stimulated the desire for sweeping reforms in Switzerland.

Zwingli's Zürich

Ulrich Zwingli (1484–1531) had served as a chaplain with the Swiss mercenaries serving the pope in Italy. In 1520, after being named the People's Priest of Zürich, Zwingli criticized his superior bishop for recruiting local young men to die in the papal armies. That same year he began to call for reform of the Church, advocating the abolition of the Roman Catholic mass, the marriage of priests, and the closing of monasteries. One of the novel features of Zwingli's reform was the strict emphasis on preaching the Word of Scripture during Church services, in contrast to the emphasis on ritual in the traditional Catholic liturgy. He ordered the removal of all paintings and statues from churches because they were too powerful a distraction from concentrating on the preaching. Zwingli was certainly influenced by the writings of Erasmus, but he denied that Luther had any effect on him at all. The Zwinglian Reformation began independently of the Lutheran Reformation and created a separate reform center from which initiatives spread throughout Switzerland, southern Germany, and England.

Two features distinguished the Zwinglian from the Lutheran Reformation. One was Zwingli's desire to involve reformed ministers in governmental decisions. In Lutheran Germany, church and state supported each other, but they remained legally separate, and the prince alone had the authority to determine the religion of the land. In Zürich, the moral Christian and the good citizen were one and the same, and Zwingli worked with the magistrates of the city council, who step-by-step legalized the Reformation and enforced conformity through its police powers. For Luther, the crucial task of the Christian was private, an introspective examination of the soul. For Zwingli the task of the Christian was public, an outward demonstration of conformity to the community's standards of morality.

Luther and Zwingli also differed in their understanding of the nature of the Eucharist, the sacrament that reenacted Christ's Last Supper with his apostles. Luther believed that Christ's body was spiritually present in the communion bread. "You will receive," as he put it, "as much as you believe you receive."[8] This emphasis on the inner, spiritual state of the believer was very characteristic of Luther's introspective piety. In contrast to Luther, Zwingli could not accept the idea of Almighty God making himself present in a humble piece of bread. To Zwingli the Eucharistic bread was just a symbol that stood for the body of Christ. The problem with the symbolic interpretation of the Eucharist was that the various reformers could not agree with Zwingli on exactly what the Eucharist symbolized. As early as 1524, it became evident that each reformer was committed to a different interpretation, and these different interpretations became the basis for different Protestant churches.

In 1529 Count Philip of Hesse (1504–1567) tried to forge a military alliance between the Protestants of Germany and Switzerland against the Catholics. The theological disputes over the Eucharist blocked full cooperation, however. Philip brought together Luther, Zwingli, and the other principal reformers for a formal discussion at the new Protestant university of Marburg. But Luther adamantly refused to compromise and shrugged off Zwingli's tearful pleas for cooperation. The failure of the Marburg Colloquy marked the permanent rupture of the Reformation movement.

Calvin's Geneva

In the next generation the momentum of the Reformation shifted to Geneva, Switzerland, under the leadership of John Calvin (1509–1564). Calvinism was closely associated with French-speaking Geneva's long struggle for independence from the Duke of Savoy and with the Genevan magistrates' attempts to build a holy community that was independent of the dictates of the Catholic bishop of the city. But Calvinism spread far beyond its Swiss home, becoming the dominant form of Protestantism in France, the Netherlands, Scotland, and New England. Zealous adherents to Calvinism insisted that society itself must be reformed so that people could say and do in public what they truly believed in private. Calvinists despised all forms of hypocrisy and valued personal sincerity, even at the cost of martyrdom.

Trained as a lawyer and exiled from his home in France in 1533 for his reformist views, Calvin spent several years wandering, searching for a quiet retreat and collaborating with other reformers. He eventually settled in Geneva, where he spent the rest of his life transforming the town into the City of God. The linchpin of the Genevan reform was the close cooperation between the magistrates of the city council and the clergy in enforcing the moral discipline of the citizens. To achieve this goal, Calvin convinced the magistrates in 1555 to grant the clergy the right to excommunicate sinners as well as those who disagreed in the slightest way with Calvinist theology. And in the Calvinist construction, excommunication meant more than banishment from church. Excommunicated people were completely shunned; no one could talk to them, including members of their own family; they effectively lost their property and ability to conduct business. Excommunication became a form of exile. The financial and psychological consequences of excommunication were deeply feared because the excommunicated were, in effect, socially dead.

Calvin's theology extended the insights of Luther and Zwingli to their logical conclusion. This pattern was most obvious in his understanding of justification by faith. Luther had argued that the Christian could not earn salvation through good works and that faith came only from God. Calvin reasoned that if an all-knowing, all-powerful God knew everything in advance and caused everything to happen, then the salvation of any individual was predetermined or, as Calvin put it, "predestined." Calvin's doctrine of predestination° was not new. In fact, it had long been discussed among Christian theologians. But for Calvin two considerations made it crucial. First was Calvin's certainty that God was above any influence from humanity. The "majesty of God," as Calvin put it, was the principle from which everything else followed. Second, Calvin and other preachers had noticed that in a congregation attending a sermon, only a few listened and paid attention to what was preached, while the vast majority seemed unable or unwilling to understand. The reason for this disparity seemed to be that only the Elect could truly follow God's Word. The Elect were known only to God, but Calvin's theology encouraged the converted to feel the assurance of salvation and to accept a "calling" from God to perform his will on earth. God's calling° gave Calvinists a powerful sense of personal direction, which committed them to a life of moral activity, whether as preacher, wife, or shoemaker.

Calvin erected an elegant theological edifice, the *Institutes of the Christian Religion,* first published in six chapters in 1535 but constantly revised and expanded until it reached eighty chapters in the definitive 1559 edition. Calvin the lawyer wrote a tightly argued and reasoned work, like a trial attorney preparing a case. In Calvin's theology the parts fit neatly together like a vast, intricate puzzle. Calvin's

Map 13.2 The Swiss Confederation

Switzerland bound together thirteen fiercely proud regions, called cantons, three of which established their independence in 1291 from the Habsburg dynasty of the Holy Roman Empire.

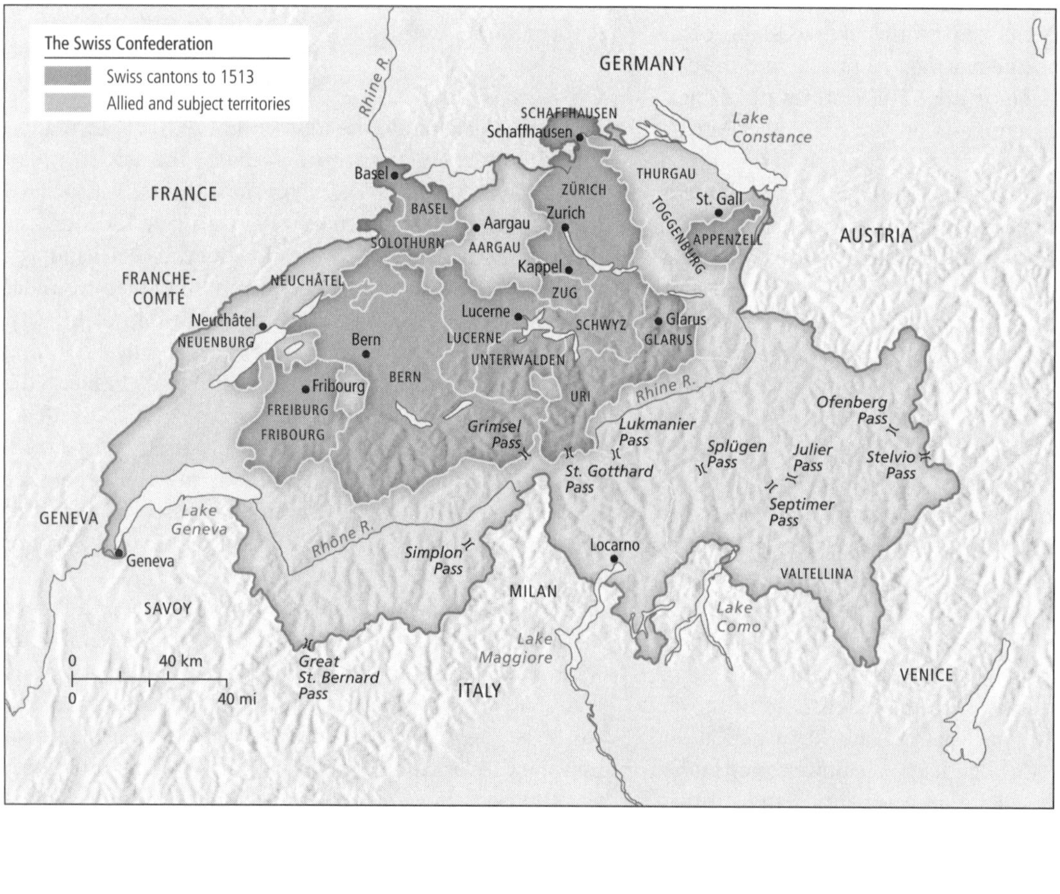

work aspired to be a comprehensive reformed theology that would convince through reasoned deliberation.

Given its emphasis on building a holy community, Calvinism helped transform the nuclear family into a social unit for training and disciplining children, a family in which women had a vital educational function that in turn encouraged women's literacy. Calvinist communities also began to allow divorce for women who had been abused by their husbands. Calvinist women and men were both disciplined and liberated—disciplined to avoid physical and material pleasures, liberated from the necessity to do good works but guided by God's grace to do them anyway.

THE REFORMATION IN BRITAIN

Great Britain, as the island kingdom is known today, did not exist in the sixteenth century. The Tudor dynasty, which began in 1485 with Henry VII (see Chapter 11), ruled over England, Wales, and Ireland, but Scotland was still a separate kingdom with its own monarch and church institutions. These countries had distinctive political traditions, culture, and language, and as a result their Reformation experiences differed considerably. The Tudors imposed the Reformation as a matter of royal policy, and they were mostly successful in England and Wales. But they hardly made a dent in the religious culture of Ireland, which was a remarkable exception to the European pattern of conformity to the religion of the ruler. There the vast majority of the population were Catholics, a faith different from that of their Protestant monarch. Scotland, also an exception to the rule, wholeheartedly accepted the Protestant Reformation against the will of its Catholic queen and most of the clergy.

The Tudors and the English Reformation

In 1527 the rotund, self-absorbed, but crafty King Henry VIII (r. 1509–1547) announced that he had come to the pious conclusion that he had gravely sinned by marrying his brother's widow, Catherine of Aragon. By this time the couple had been married for many years, their only living child was the princess Mary, and at age 42 Catherine was unlikely to give birth to more children. Henry let it be known that he wanted a son, mostly to secure the English throne for the Tudor dynasty. He also had his eye on a beauty of the court, the ravishing Anne Boleyn, who was less than half Catherine's age. In the past popes had usually been cooperative when a powerful king needed an annulment, but Pope Clement VII (r. 1523–1534) was in no position to oblige Henry. At the time of the marriage, the papal curia had issued a dispensation for Henry to marry his brother's widow, a practice that is prohibited in the Bible. In effect, Henry was asking the papacy to admit it had made a mistake. In addition, at the moment when Henry's petition for divorce arrived, Clement was under the control of Catherine's nephew, the Emperor Charles V, whose armies had recently captured and sacked the city of Rome. In 1531 Henry gave up trying to obtain papal approval and definitively separated from Catherine. Some eighteen months later he secretly married Anne Boleyn. England's compliant Archbishop Thomas Cranmer (1489–1556) pronounced the marriage to Catherine void and the one to Anne valid. But the marriage to Anne did not last. When she began to displease him, Henry had her arrested, charged with incest with her brother and adultery with other men. She was convicted and beheaded.

The English separation from the Roman Catholic Church, which took place in 1534 through Acts of Supremacy and Succession, has often been understood as a by-product of Henry's capricious lust and the plots of his brilliant minister, Thomas Cromwell (ca. 1485–1540). It is certainly true that Henry's desire to rid himself of Catherine led him to reject papal authority and to establish himself as the head of the Church of England. It is also certainly true that Henry was an inconstant husband: Of his six wives, two were divorced and two beheaded. However, the English Reformation cannot be explained simply as the consequence of royal whim or the machinations of a single minister.

The English Reformation began as a declaration of royal independence from papal supervision rather than an attempt to reform the practices of the Church. Under Henry VIII the English Reformation could be described as Catholicism without the pope. The concept of royal supremacy established control over the Church by granting to the king supervising authority over liturgical rituals and religious doctrines. Thomas Cromwell, who worked out the practical details for parliamentary legislation, was himself a Protestant, and no doubt his religious views emboldened him to reject papal authority. But the principal theorist of royal supremacy was a Catholic, Thomas Starkey (ca. 1499–1538). A sojourn in Italy had acquainted Starkey with Italian Renaissance political theory, which emphasized concepts of civic liberty—as we saw in Chapter 11. In fact, even many English Catholics found the change acceptable as long as it meant only abandoning submission to the pope in distant Rome. Those who opposed cutting the connection to Rome suffered for their opposition, however. Bishop John Fisher (ca. 1469–1535) and Sir Thomas More, the humanist author of *Utopia* and former chancellor of England, were both executed for their refusal to go along with the king's decision.

With this display of despotic power, Henry seized personal control of the English church, closed the monasteries, and confiscated their lands. He redistributed the monastic lands to the nobility in an effort to purchase their support. Henry's officials briefly flirted with some Protestant reforms, but theological innovations were largely avoided. The Reformation of Henry VIII was more significant for consolidating the dynastic power of the Tudors than for initiating wide-ranging religious reform.

JUSTICE IN HISTORY

The Trial of Anne Boleyn: The Dynastic Crime

Anne Boleyn, the first of Henry VIII's wives to be executed, was beheaded in the Tower of London's courtyard in May 1536, just a few hundred feet from the hall in which she had celebrated her coronation three years earlier. She had been tried by a court of peers and unanimously convicted of high treason. The evidence against her was for adultery, but the alleged adultery of a queen was considered treason because it put in question the paternity of potential heirs to the throne. Queen Anne insisted on her innocence until the end, but her final address to the crowd did not protest her execution. Instead, she said, "According to the law and by the law I am judged to die, and therefore I will speak nothing against it."[9] To twenty-first century observers, Anne seems to accept her unjust fate passively. To sixteenth-century observers, however, she died "boldly," and her refusal to admit guilt and to accept the law was one of the best indicators of her innocence.

To understand Anne Boleyn's scaffold statement, it is necessary to look at the idea of a "fair trial" in sixteenth-century England. She was condemned for high treason because of her supposed adultery with five men, including her own brother. But her supposed lovers were in other places when the adulteries were alleged to take place—evidence that casts doubt on their truth. She was unable to present this evidence, which today would serve as an alibi for the defendant, because she heard the charges against her for the first time at the actual trial. The queen enjoyed no counsel for the defense, had no opportunity to call witnesses on her own behalf, and had no protection against self-incrimination. Because she was the queen of England, her trial was unusual, but these procedures were standard in the sixteenth century.

It was widely known that the king wished her death, but because her trial followed the accepted legal procedures, it was considered a fair trial by the standards of the sixteenth century. When Anne married Henry, who had recently divorced Catherine of Aragon, Anne's most important role was to provide the king with a male heir. Anne soon gave birth to a daughter, Elizabeth, but she then suffered two miscarriages. Some historians argue that Henry wanted to get rid of Anne in favor of her younger rival, Jane Seymour, but others have suggested that because the fetus of Anne's second miscarriage was deformed, she was suspected of witchcraft. Henry himself stated that he had been seduced by witchcraft, which was why God had not permitted him to have a son. He considered the marriage null and void because Anne's witchery had coerced him into the liaison. As far as Henry was concerned, Anne's failure to bear him a son was evidence of some sort of wrongdoing on her part. It remained only to construct a case against her.

The king and his prosecutors assembled a large number of statements about Anne's infidelity, which shocked observers of the trial. John Husee wrote, "I think verily, if all the books and chronicles . . . which against woman hath been penned, contrived, and written since Adam and Eve, those same were, I think, verily nothing in comparison of that which hath been done and committed by Anne the Queen." James Spelman commented, "All the evidence was of bawdery and lechery, so that there was no such whore in all the realm."[10]

The quantity and offensive nature of the evidence was part of a propaganda campaign Henry orchestrated to convince the members of the nobility and the English people that Anne's execution was justified.

Despite the careful orchestration of the trial, the preponderance of the evidence, and the procedures that denied her systematic defense, Anne Boleyn managed to convince a number of observers that she was innocent. Charles Wriothesley recounted, "She made so wise and discreet answers to all things laid against her, excusing herself through her words so clearly as though she had never been faulty to the same."[11] Most telling was the opinion of Chapuys, the ambassador of Emperor Charles V to Henry's court. Chapuys had previously been hostile to Anne, but he considered the whole trial a sham. After the jury returned a guilty verdict, Anne herself shrewdly observed, "I believe you have reasons . . . upon which you have condemned me: but they must be other than those that have been produced in court."[12]

■ **Portrait Sketch of Anne Boleyn**
This portrait of Anne Boleyn may be by Hans Holbein the Younger. It was probably painted while Anne was queen of England.

The trial of Anne Boleyn was a classic example of the triumph of judicial form over the substance of evidence. Since Henry and the prosecutors had followed the proper trial procedures, they believed they were above reproach on legal grounds. Anne had been justly condemned even if the evidence against her had been faked. ■

Questions of Justice

1. Assuming that the evidence against Anne was false, why was her alleged treason defined as adultery rather than something else, such as witchcraft or heresy?
2. Explain Anne's reasoning behind the statement she made on the scaffold.
3. Characterize the relationship between Henry's continuing marital problems and the course of the English Reformation.

Taking It Further

Guy, John. *Tudor England.* 1990. Taking account of recent scholarship, this is the best general history of the period. It includes illuminating portraits of the principal figures.

Warnicke, Retha M. *The Rise and Fall of Anne Boleyn: Family Politics at the Court of Henry VIII.* 1991. Based on a careful examination of all the available evidence, Warnicke shows how the trial was a consequence of Henry VIII's desire to preserve his dynasty.

Under Henry's three children who succeeded him to the throne, the official religion of England gyrated wildly. Only ten years old when he followed his father to the throne, King Edward VI (r. 1547–1553) was the pawn of his Protestant protectors, some of whom pushed for a more thorough Protestant Reformation in England than Henry had espoused. After Edward's premature death, his half-sister, Queen Mary I (r. 1553–1558), daughter of Henry VIII and Catherine of Aragon, attempted to bring England back to obedience to the pope. Her unpopular marriage to the king of Spain and her failure to retain the support of the nobility, who were the foundation of Tudor government, damaged the Catholic cause in England.

Mary's successor and half-sister, Elizabeth Tudor, the daughter of Anne Boleyn, was an entirely different sort. Queen Elizabeth I (r. 1558–1603), raised as a Protestant, kept her enemies off balance and her quarrelsome subjects firmly in hand with her tremendous charisma and shrewd political judgments. Elizabeth became one of the most successful monarchs to ever reign anywhere, as Chapter 14 will demonstrate. Without the considerable talents of Elizabeth, England could easily have fallen into civil war over religion—as the Holy Roman Empire and France did and as England itself did some forty years after her death.

Between 1559 and 1563, Elizabeth repealed the Catholic legislation of Mary and promulgated her own moderately Protestant laws, collectively known as the Elizabethan Settlement, which established the Church of England (Episcopalian in the United States). Her principal adviser, William Cecil (1520–1598), implemented the details of the reform through reasonable debate and compromise rather than by insisting on doctrinal purity and rigid conformity. The touchstone of the Elizabethan Settlement was the Thirty-Nine Articles (finally approved by Parliament in 1571), which articulated a moderate version of Protestantism. It retained the ecclesiastical hierarchy of bishops as well as an essentially Catholic liturgy translated into English. This "middle way" between Roman Catholicism and militant Calvinism was ably defended by Richard Hooker (1553–1600), whose *Laws of Ecclesiastical Polity* emphasized how the law as promulgated by the royal government manifested the divine order.

The Church of England under Elizabeth permitted a wide latitude of beliefs, but it did not tolerate "recusants," those who as a matter of principle refused to attend Church of England services. These were mostly Catholics, who set up a secret network of priests to serve their sacramental needs and whom the government considered dangerous agents of foreign powers. Many others were militant Protestants who thought the Elizabethan Settlement did not go far enough in reforming religion. The most vocal and influential of the Protestant dissenters were the Puritans, who were influenced by Calvinism and demanded a church purified of what they thought were remnants of Roman Catholicism. As Chapter 15 will show, the hostility of the Puritans would eventually lead to civil war.

Scotland: The Citadel of Calvinism

While England groped its way toward moderate Protestantism, neighboring Scotland became one of the most thoroughly Calvinist countries in Europe. In 1560 the parliament of Scotland, with encouragement from Queen Elizabeth of England, overthrew Roman Catholicism against the will of Mary Stuart, Queen of Scots (1542–1587). The wife of the French king, Francis II, Mary was absent in France during the crucial early phases of the Reformation and returned to Scotland only after her husband's death in 1561. Despite her Catholicism, Mary proved remarkably conciliatory toward the Protestants by putting royal funds at the disposal of the new Reformed Kirk (Church) of Scotland. But the Scottish Calvinists never trusted her, and their mistrust would bring about her doom.

The Scots Confession of 1560, written by a panel of six reformers, established the new church. John Knox (ca. 1514–1572) breathed a strongly Calvinist air into the church through his many polemical writings and the official liturgy he composed in 1564, the *Book of Common Order.* Knox emphasized faith and individual Christian conscience over ecclesiastical authority, a priority that discouraged compromise among the Scots. Instead of the episcopal structure in England, which granted bishops the authority over doctrine and discipline, the Scots Kirk established a Presbyterian form of organization, which gave organizational authority to the pastors and elders of the congregations, all of whom had equal rank. As a result the Presbyterian congregations were more independent and subject to local variations than the episcopal structure allowed in the Anglican Church.

THE RADICAL REFORMATION

As we have seen, the magisterial reformers in Germany, Switzerland, England, and Scotland managed to obtain official sanction for their religious reforms, often at the cost of some compromise with governmental authorities. As a result, they were challenged by radicals from among their own followers who demanded faster, more thorough reform. In most places the radicals represented a small minority, perhaps never more than 2 percent of all Protestants. But their significance outstripped their small numbers, in part because they forced the magisterial reformers to respond to their arguments and because their enemies attempted to eradicate them through extreme violence.

The radicals can be divided into three categories: Anabaptists, who attempted to construct a holy community on the basis of literal readings of the Bible; Spiritualists, who abandoned all forms of organized religion to allow individuals to follow the inner voice of the Holy Spirit; and

Unitarians, who advocated a rational and tolerant religion that emphasized ethical behavior over ceremonies.

Anabaptists: The Holy Community

For Anabaptists, the Bible was a blueprint for reforming not just the church but all of society. Because the Bible reported that Jesus was an adult when he was baptized, the Anabaptists rejected infant baptism and adopted adult baptism (Anabaptism° means to rebaptize). An adult, they believed, could accept baptism as an act of faith, unlike an oblivious infant. Adult baptism allowed the creation of a pure church that included only the converted faithful, isolated from the sinfulness of the world. Anabaptists sought to obey only God and completely rejected all established religious and political authorities; they required adherents to refuse to serve in government offices, swear oaths, pay taxes, or fight in armies. Anabaptists sought to live in highly disciplined "holy communities," which excommunicated errant members and practiced simple services based on scriptural readings. Because the Anabaptist communities consisted largely of uneducated peasants, artisans, and miners, a dimension of economic radicalism colored the Anabaptist movement. For example, some Anabaptist radicals advocated the elimination of all private property and the sharing of wealth. On the position of women, however, Anabaptists were staunchly conservative, denying women any public role in religious affairs and insisting that they remain under the strict control of their fathers and husbands. Because the Anabaptists promoted such a radical reorganization of society along biblical lines, they provoked a violent reaction. In Zürich the city council decreed that the appropriate punishment was for all Anabaptists to be drowned in the local river where they had been rebaptizing themselves. By 1529 it became a capital offense in the Holy Roman Empire to be rebaptized, and during the sixteenth century perhaps as many as 5,000 Anabaptists were executed for the offense, a persecution that tended to fragment the Anabaptists into isolated, secretive rural communities.

During a brief period in 1534 and 1535, Anabaptists managed to seize control of the city of Münster in northern Germany. An immigrant Dutch tailor, John of Leiden, set up a despotic regime in Münster that punished with death any sin, even gossiping or complaining. John of Leiden introduced polygamy and collective ownership of property. John set an example by taking sixteen wives, one of whom he beheaded for talking back, stomping on her body in front of the other frightened wives. As the besieging armies closed in, John forced his followers to crown him king and worship him. After his capture, John was subjected to an excruciating torture, and as a warning to others his corpse was displayed for many years hanging in an iron cage.

"God opened the eyes of the governments by the revolt at Münster," as the Protestant reformer Heinrich Bullinger put it, "and thereafter no one would trust even those Anabaptists who claimed to be innocent."[13] The surviving Anabaptists abandoned the radicalism of the Münster community, embracing pacifism and nonviolent resistance. A Dutchman, Menno Simons (1496–1561), tirelessly traveled about the Netherlands and Germany, providing solace and guidance to the isolated survivors of the Münster disaster. His followers, the Mennonites, preserved the noblest features of the Anabaptist tradition of quiet resistance to persecution. Under Mennonite influence, Thomas Helwys founded the first Baptist church in England in 1612. As the leader of the English Baptists, Helwys wrote an unprecedented appeal for the absolute freedom of religion. In it he defended the religious rights of Jews, Muslims, and even atheists as well as all varieties of Christians. He was almost immediately put in prison, where he died.

The most significant measure of the influence of the Anabaptists is the fact that largest number of Protestants in the United States are Baptists. The modern Baptist movement has lost the social radicalism of its Anabaptist forbearers and now accepts the legitimacy of private property. Most Baptists have also forsaken pacifism, but during the civil rights movement of the 1950s and 1960s, it was a Baptist preacher, Dr. Martin Luther King, Jr., who reintroduced the principle of nonviolent resistance to persecution.

Spiritualists: The Holy Individual

Whereas the Anabaptists radicalized the Swiss Reformation's emphasis on building a godly community, the Spiritualists° radicalized Luther's commitment to personal introspection. Perhaps the greatest Spiritualist was the aristocratic Caspar Schwenckfeld (1490–1561), who was a friend of Luther's until he broke with the reformer over what he considered the weak spirituality of established Lutheranism. Schwenckfeld believed that depraved humanity was incapable of casting off the bonds of sin, which only a supernatural act of God could achieve. This separation from sinfulness was revealed through an intense conversion experience, after which the believer gained spiritual illumination. Schwenckfeld called this illumination the "inner Word," which he understood as a living form of the Scriptures written directly on the believer's soul by the hand of God. Schwenckfeld also prized the "outer Word," that is, the Scriptures, but he found the emotional experience of the inner Word more powerful than the intellectual experience that came from reading the Bible. Spiritualists reflected an inner peace evident in their calm physical appearance, lack of anxiety, and mastery of bodily appetites—a state Schwenckfeld called the "castle of peace."

The most prominent example of the Spiritualist tendency in the English-speaking world is the Quakers, who first appeared in England a century after the Lutheran Reformation. The Quakers, or Society of Friends, interpreted the priesthood of all believers to mean that God's spirit, which they called the Light of Christ, was given equally to all men and women. This belief led them to abandon entirely a separately ordained ministry and to replace organized worship with meetings in which any man, woman, or child could speak, read Scripture, pray, or sing, as the spirit moved them. The Quakers' belief in the sacredness of all human beings also inclined them toward pacifism and egalitarianism.

In no other religious tradition have women played such a prominent role for so long. From the very beginning of the movement, female Friends were prominent in preaching the Quaker gospel. In Quaker marriages, wives were completely equal to their husbands—at least in religious matters. Quakers long played a prominent role in various social reform movements as well. In the eighteenth century, they were the first to campaign for the abolition of slavery; in the nineteenth century, Quaker women were prominent in the movement to establish women's rights; and in the twentieth century they led antiwar movements and the campaign for nuclear disarmament.

Unitarians: A Rationalist Approach

Distinctive to Christian theology—in comparison to other monotheistic religions, such as Judaism and Islam—is the doctrine of the Trinity, which posits that the one God has three identities—God the Father, God the Son, and God the Holy Spirit. The doctrine of the Trinity made it possible for Christians to believe that God the Son "took on flesh" in what is called the "incarnation." At a particular moment in history, God became the human being Jesus Christ. The doctrine of the Trinity was officially established as Christian dogma at the Council of Nicea in 325, in response to the Arian heresy, which had denied Christ's divinity. The universal acceptance of the Trinity among Christians changed in the middle of the sixteenth century with the emergence of numerous radical sects that rejected the divinity of Christ. They were called Arians, Socinians, Anti-Trinitarians, or Unitarians°. The Italian Faustus Socinus (1539–1604) taught a rationalist interpretation of the Scriptures and argued that Jesus was a divinely inspired man, not God-become-man. Socinus's followers thus rejected the doctrine of the Trinity, which they found contrary to simple common sense and without support in Scripture. This dual emphasis remains central to Unitarianism—the specific rejection of Trinitarian doctrine and the general emphasis on rationality.

Catholics and magisterial Protestants alike were extremely hostile to Unitarians, who tended to be well-educated humanists and men of letters. Unitarian views thrived in advanced intellectual circles in northern Italy and eastern Europe, but the most famous critic of the Trinity was the brilliant, if eccentric, Spaniard Michael Servetus (1511–1553). Trained as a physician and widely read in the literature of the occult, Servetus published influential Anti-Trinitarian works and daringly sent his provocative works to the major Protestant reformers. Based on a tip from the Protestants in Geneva, the Catholic inquisitor-general in Lyons, France, arrested Servetus, but he escaped from prison during his trial. While passing through Protestant Geneva on his way to refuge in Italy, he was recognized while attending a church service and again imprisoned. Although no law in Geneva allowed capital punishment, Servetus was convicted of heresy and burned alive.

The Anabaptists and Unitarians shared some early connections and similarities, but the two groups soon parted ways. Both Anabaptists and Unitarians followed the logic of their own beliefs and were unwilling to compromise with other Protestants. Anabaptists remained dogmatic and committed to a very narrow interpretation of Scripture. Unitarians were far stronger intellectually, and in eastern Europe they attracted support from the powerful. Much more open to debate, Unitarians became influential advocates for religious toleration, which they found in eastern Europe.

THE FREE WORLD OF EASTERN EUROPE

During the sixteenth century eastern Europe offered a measure of religious freedom and toleration unknown elsewhere in Europe. As a result, eastern Europe was open to considerable religious experimentation and attracted refugees from the oppressive princes of western Europe, none of whom tolerated more than one religion in their territories. Such religious toleration was made possible by the relative weakness of the monarchs in Bohemia, Hungary, Transylvania, and especially Poland-Lithuania, where the great land-owning aristocrats exercised nearly complete freedom on their estates. All of these kingdoms had Catholic monarchs, but the Reformation radicalized the aristocrats who dominated the parliaments, enabling Protestantism to take hold even against the wishes of the monarch.

As we have seen, in Bohemia (now in the Czech Republic), the Hussite movement in the fourteenth century had rejected papal authority and some of the sacramental authority of the priesthood long before the Protestant Reformation. After the Lutherans and Calvinists attracted adherents in Bohemia, the few surviving old Hussites and the new Protestants formed an alliance in 1575, which made common cause against the Catholics. In addition to this formal alliance, substantial numbers of Anabaptists found refuge from persecution in Bohemia and lived in complete freedom on the estates of tolerant landlords who were desperate for settlers to farm their lands.

The religious diversity of Hungary was also remarkable by the standards of the time. By the end of the sixteenth century, much of Hungary's diverse population had accepted some form of Protestantism. Among the German-speaking city dwellers and the Hungarian peasants in western Hungary, Lutheranism prevailed, whereas in eastern Hungary Calvinism was dominant.

No other country was as tolerant of religious diversity as Transylvania (now in Romania), largely because of the weak monarchy, which could not have enforced religious uniformity even if the king had wanted to do so. In Transylvania, Unitarianism took hold more firmly than anywhere else. In 1572 the tolerant ruler Prince István Báthory (r. 1571–1586) granted the Unitarians complete legal equality to establish their own churches along with Catholics, Lutherans, and Calvinists—the only place in Europe where equality of religions was achieved. Transylvania was also home to significant communities of Jews, Armenian Christians, and Orthodox Christians.

The sixteenth century was the golden age of the Polish-Lithuanian Commonwealth, which was by far the largest state in Europe. It escaped both the Ottoman invasions and the religious wars that plagued the Holy Roman Empire. From the Lutheran cities in the German-speaking north to the vast open plains of Great Poland, where Calvinism took hold among the independent-minded nobility, religious lines often had been drawn along ethnic or class divisions. When Sigismund August (r. 1548–1572) became king, he declared, "I am not king of men's conscience," and inaugurated extensive toleration of Protestant churches, even while the vast majority of peasants remained loyal to Orthodoxy or Catholicism. Fleeing persecution in other countries, various Anabaptist groups and Unitarians found refuge in Poland. This extensive religious diversity in Poland was later snuffed out during the Counter Reformation.

CHRONOLOGY

The Diversity of Protestantism

1520	Zwingli declared the People's Priest in Zürich
1529	Marburg Colloquy
1534	Parliament in England passes the Acts of Supremacy and Succession
1534–1535	Anabaptist control of Münster, Germany
1535	Execution of John Fisher and Thomas More; first edition of John Calvin's *Institutes of the Christian Religion*
1541	Calvin introduces the Reformation in Geneva
1559–1563	The Elizabethan Settlement of the Anglican Church
1560	Scots Confession

The Catholic and Counter Reformations

The terms Catholic Reformation and Counter Reformation refer to two distinct movements that profoundly revitalized the Catholic Church and established an institutional and doctrinal framework that persisted into the late twentieth century. The Catholic Reformation° was a series of efforts to purify the Church; they were not necessarily a reaction to the Protestant Reformation but evolved out of late medieval spirituality, driven by many of the same impulses that stimulated the Protestants. The most important of these efforts was the creation of new religious orders, especially the Society of Jesus, whose members are known as the Jesuits. The Counter Reformation° was a response to the Protestant Reformation and embraced defensive and offensive actions against Protestantism. The Counter Reformation propagandized Catholic doctrine, disciplined clergy and laity, and repressed heresy. The Counter Reformation established the Holy Office of the Inquisition, promulgated the *Index of Prohibited Books,* and implemented the decrees of the Council of Trent (1545–1563).

Whereas the Catholic Reformation came from the religious enthusiasm that welled up from the laity and lower clergy, the popes were primarily responsible for the Counter Reformation, which had a strongly international character. Counter Reformation Catholicism retained Latin, in contrast to Protestantism, which conducted services in vernacular languages such as German or English. The success of the Counter Reformation tended to obliterate differences in religious culture from one Catholic country to another, creating greater uniformity in Catholic practice and doctrine than had been the case in the medieval period. The international spread of the Counter Reformation was a source of tremendous strength in revitalizing the Church and in creating a distinctively Catholic culture. For 400 years after the Counter Reformation, Catholics who found themselves in a foreign land could experience something very familiar merely by attending a mass, spoken or chanted in the ancient Latin of the Church.

The Religious Orders in the Catholic Reformation

The most dramatic and effective manifestation of the Catholic Reformation was the founding of new religious orders. These orders exhibited a religious vitality that had little to do with the Protestant threat. In fact, none of the new orders began near the centers of Protestantism, such as Germany. Italy, which remained strongly Catholic, produced the largest number of new orders, followed by Spain and France. All of the new orders remained committed to a very traditional Catholic theology, but they differed from the prayerful isolation of the traditional monastic orders by their commitment to an active ministry in the world.

Jesuits: The Soldiers of God

By far the most influential new order was the Society of Jesus. In 1534 a group of seven students at the University of Paris took a vow to go on a pilgrimage to Jerusalem after graduation. They were an international lot—a Portuguese, a Savoyard, an Aragonese, two Basques, and two Castilians. When the original seven plus some French companions gathered in Venice to take ship to Palestine, they found their way blocked by a war, a turn of events that led them to place themselves at the disposal of the pope. This loosely organized group of kindred spirits became the core of a new order. In 1540 they officially organized the Society of Jesus and elected Ignatius Loyola (1491–1556) the first General of the Society.

The dynamic personality and intense spirituality of Loyola gave the new order its distinctive commitment to moral action in the world. Loyola began his career as a courtier to King Ferdinand of Aragon and a soldier. In 1521 during a French attack on the Spanish garrison at Pamplona, Loyola's leg was shattered by a cannonball. Driven by vanity to keep his leg from looking deformed, he insisted on having his leg rebroken and reset several times despite the excruciating pain of the procedure. During the boredom of his convalescence, he turned to reading a life of Christ and the lives of the saints. From these he discovered tales of heroism superior to anything he had read of medieval knights. These revelations converted Loyola to Christ. Loyola's background as a courtier and soldier deeply influenced his religiosity. The Society of Jesus that he helped found preserved some of the better values Loyola had acquired as a courtier-soldier—social refinement, loyalty to authority, sense of duty, and high-minded chivalry.

Loyola's most impressive personal contribution to religious literature was the *Spiritual Exercises* (1548), which became the foundation of Jesuit practice. The *Spiritual Exercises* have been republished in more than 5,000 editions in hundreds of languages. The *Exercises* prescribe a month-long retreat devoted to a series of meditations in which the participant mentally re-experiences the spiritual life, physical death, and miraculous resurrection of Christ. Much of the power of the *Exercises* derives from the systematic employment of each of the five senses to produce a defined emotional, spiritual, and even physical response. Participants in the *Exercises* seem to hear the blasphemous cries of the soldiers at Christ's crucifixion, feel the terrible agony of His suffering on the cross, and experience the blinding illumination of His resurrection from the dead. Those who participated in the *Exercises* considered the experience life-transforming. These participants usually made a steadfast commitment to serve the Church.

The Jesuits distinguished themselves from other religious orders by extending their personal spirituality to minister to others. They did not wear clerical clothing, and on foreign missions or in dangerous situations they lived incognito for years. Jesuits became famous for their loyalty to the pope, and some took a special fourth vow (in addition to the three traditional vows of poverty, chastity, and obedience) to go on a mission if the pope requested it.

In Europe the Jesuit college system transformed the culture of the Catholic elite. These popular colleges provided free tuition to the poor, but they mostly attracted the sons of the aristocrats and the wealthy who absorbed from the Jesuit instructors the values of Renaissance humanism and the Catholic Reformation. Jesuit colleges were the equivalent of high schools, but some grew into universities or colleges within universities. By 1615 there were 372 Jesuit colleges in Europe; the system also spread to the major cities of the Americas. With the success of these colleges, education gradually replaced missionary work as the most important Jesuit activity.

The Jesuit order grew rapidly. At Loyola's death in 1556 there were about a thousand Jesuits, but by 1700 there were nearly 20,000, and many young men who wished to join had to be turned away because there were insufficient funds to train them. The influence of the Jesuits was even greater than their numbers would indicate, however. Besides their success in education, which shaped the values of the upper classes and guided intellectual life throughout Catholic Europe, Jesuits often served as the personal confessors to powerful figures, including several kings of France and Holy Roman emperors. By giving private advice on spiritual matters, confessors had many opportunities to influence royal policy, an influence the Jesuits were not shy to exercise.

Women's Orders: In But Not of the World

Creating a ministry that was active in the world was much more difficult for the female orders than for the Jesuits and the other male orders. Women who sought to reinvigorate old orders or found new ones faced hostility from ecclesiastical and civic authorities, who thought women had to be protected by either a husband or the cloister wall. Women in convents were supposed to be entirely separated from the world, "as if they were dead," but this principle was at odds with the desires of many devout women who wanted to help make the world a better place.

The cloistering of women was a highly controversial issue during the sixteenth century. Because it was cheaper to place a daughter in a convent than to provide her with a dowry for marriage, about one-third of the women of aristocratic families in Catholic countries found themselves in convents rather than on the marriage market. In some places, such as Venice during the late sixteenth century, more than three-quarters of the noblewomen were cloistered. In many convents, aristocratic women lived much as they would have lived in secular society, enjoying private apartments, servants, regular visits with relatives, musical entertainments, and even vacations. Many of these women felt like involuntary inmates living in a "Convent Hell," to quote the title of Arcangela Tarabotti's famous exposé of the nun's life (1654). The dreary experience of these reluctant nuns, however, contrasted with the genuine enthusiasm for convent life of many other women who were caught up in the religious enthusiasm of the Catholic Reformation.

The first task of those who were ardently religious was to reform convent life. The most famous model was provided by St. Teresa of Avila (1515-1582), who wrote a strict new rule for the long-established Carmelites, requiring mortifications of the flesh and complete withdrawal from the world. St. Teresa described her own mystical experiences in her *Autobiography* (1611) and in the *Interior Castle* (1588), a compelling masterpiece in the literature of mysticism. St. Teresa advocated a very cautious brand of mysticism, which was checked by regular confession and skepticism about extreme acts of self-deprivation. For example, she recognized that a nun who fell into an apparent rapture after extensive fasting was probably just having hallucinations from the hunger.

The Catholic convents of the sixteenth century presented many contradictions. On the one hand, they housed some women who had no special religious vocation, who did not want to be locked away from family and friends, and who suffered from the stifling boredom of living without apparent purpose. On the other hand, many women who willingly chose the religious life thrived in a community of women, were liberated from the rigors of childbearing, and were freed from direct male supervision. These women could devote themselves to cultivating musical or literary talents to a degree that would have been impossible in the outside world. Nuns created their own distinctly female culture, producing a number of learned women and social reformers, who had considerable influence in the arts, education, and charitable work such as nursing.

Paul III, The First Counter Reformation Pope

Despite the Protestant threat, which was fully evident by 1519, the Church was slow to initiate its own reforms because of resistance among bishops and cardinals of the Church hierarchy who worried that reform would threaten their income. More than twenty years after Luther's defiant stand at the Diet of Worms in 1521, Pope Paul III (r. 1534–1549) finally launched a systematic counterattack. As a member of the powerful Farnese family who had long treated church offices as their private property, Paul seemed an unlikely reformer. But more than any other pope, Paul understood the necessity to respond to the political winds of change. It was Pope Paul, for example, who formally approved the Jesuits and began to employ them as missionary soldiers for the Church.

In 1541, in an attempt to resolve the dangerous religious disputes provoked by the Lutherans, Paul sent a representative to a discussion between Catholic and Protestant theologians held in conjunction with the Imperial Diet of Regensburg. Despite the best efforts of the pope's reform-minded representative, the meeting failed, making it stunningly clear how wide the gap had become between Protestant and Catholic theology. The failure of Regensburg shifted Pope Paul's efforts from a plan of hesitant accommodation to a defensive strategy devoted to building a Catholic bulwark against Protestant ideas.

In 1542 on the advice of an archconservative faction of cardinals, Paul III reorganized the Roman Inquisition, called the Holy Office. The function of the Inquisition was to inquire into the beliefs of all Catholics primarily to discover indications of heresies such as those of the Protestants. Jews, for example, were exempt from its authority, although Jews who had converted or been forced to convert to Christianity did fall under the jurisdiction of the Inquisition. There had been other inquisitions, but most had been local or national. The Spanish Inquisition was controlled by the Spanish monarchs, for example. In contrast, the Holy Office came under the direct control of the pope and cardinals and termed itself the Universal Roman Inquisition. Its effective authority did not reach beyond northern and central Italy, but it set the tone for the entire Counter Reformation Church and created a climate of caution, if not fear, especially among intellectuals.

The Inquisition immediately began to crack down on suspected heretics. One of the first victims was Bernardino Ochino (1487–1563), the most popular preacher in Rome and the Minister General of the Capuchin order. When summoned to answer questions before the Holy Office, he

CHRONOLOGY

The Catholic and Counter Reformations

1534–1549	Pontificate of Pope Paul III
1535	Founding of the Ursulines
1540	Founding of the Society of Jesus
1542	Reorganization of the Roman Inquisition or Holy Office
1545–1563	Meetings of the Council of Trent
1548	*Spiritual Exercises* of Ignatius Loyola
1549	*Index of Forbidden Books*

THE HUMAN BODY IN HISTORY

The Ecstasy of St. Teresa of Avila: The Body and the Soul

St. Teresa of Avila (1515–1582) eloquently expressed the intimate connection between physical and spiritual experiences that was a common feature of Catholic mysticism. She was a Spanish Carmelite nun whose accounts of her own mystical experiences made her a model for other nuns throughout the world. Filled with religious ardor, she devoted herself to an ascetic regime of self-deprivations so intense that she fell ill and suffered paralysis.

Often afflicted by an intense pain in her side, Teresa reported that an angel had stuck a lance tipped with fire into her heart. This "seraphic vision," which became the subject of Gianlorenzo Bernini's famous sculpture in Santa Maria della Vittoria in Rome (1645–1652), epitomized the Catholic Reformation sensibility of understanding spiritual states through physical feelings. In St. Teresa's case, her extreme bodily deprivations, paralysis, and intense pain conditioned how she experienced the spiritual side of her nature. Many have seen an erotic character to the vision, which may be true, but the vision best demonstrates a profound psychological awareness that bodily and spiritual sensations cannot be precisely distinguished. As St. Teresa put it, "it is not bodily pain, but spiritual, though the body has a share in it—indeed, a great share." She described the paralysis of her soul and her body as interconnected: "The soul is unable to do either this or anything else. The entire body contracts and neither arm nor foot can be moved." She then described, in remarkably graphic terms, her repeated vision:

> *It pleased the Lord that I should sometimes see the following vision. I would see beside me, on my left hand, an angel in bodily form—a type of vision which I am not in the habit of seeing, except very rarely. . . . I pleased the Lord that I should see this angel in the following way. He was not tall, but short, and very beautiful, his face so aflame that he appeared to be one of the highest types of angel who seem to be all afire. . . . In his hands I saw a long golden spear and at the end of the iron tip I seemed to see a point of fire. With this he seemed to pierce my heart several times so that it penetrated to my entrails. When he drew it out, I thought he was drawing them out with it and he left me completely afire with a great love for God. The pain was so sharp that it made me utter several moans; and so excessive was the sweetness caused me by this intense pain that one can never wish to lose it, nor will one's soul be content with anything less than God. . . . So sweet are the colloquies of love which pass between the soul and God that if anyone thinks I am lying I beseech God, in His goodness, to give him the same experience.*[14]

Visions such as this one were difficult to interpret. Exactly what was going on in those sweet colloquies between St. Teresa's soul and God? St. Teresa associated these visions with intense physical pain, as if she had to suffer in order to receive divine illumination, which she described as a sweet conversation between her soul and God. Her sensibility about the necessary relationship between physical pain and spiritual experiences was especially pronounced among sixteenth-century Catholics. Pain and suffering were understood as a form of penance, and thus the body could play a positive and redemptive role in enabling spirituality. The best way to transcend this world was in bodily pain, because through pain the Christian escaped the temptations of the flesh and renounced the attractions of the world. ■

For Discussion

How was pain understood to have religious value? What was happening around St. Teresa that might explain her preoccupation with pain?

■ **The Ecstasy of St. Teresa**
In this sculpture St. Teresa lies suspended in air in a swoon induced by a vision. An angel is about to pierce her side with an arrow.

fled to Geneva. His defection to Calvin's Geneva caused an enormous sensation and fueled the clamor for more intense repression. Any form of criticism of the Church within earshot of an informant of the Inquisition became very dangerous. The Inquisition could subject defendants to lengthy interrogations and stiff penalties, including prison sentences and even execution in exceptional cases.

A second effort to stop the spread of Protestant and other ideas deemed heretical led to the first *Index of Forbidden Books,* drawn up in 1549 in Venice, the capital of the publishing industry in Italy. The *Index* censored or banned many books that the Church considered detrimental to the faith and the authority of the Church. Most affected by the strictures were books about theology and philosophy, but books of moral guidance were also prohibited or butchered by the censors, such as the works of Erasmus, and classics of literature, such as Giovanni Boccaccio's *The Decameron.* The official papal *Index* of 1559 even prohibited translations of the Bible into vernacular languages such as Italian. It remained possible to buy certain heretical theological books "under the counter," much as people today find ways to obtain illegal drugs, but possessing such books could be dangerous if agents of the Inquisition conducted a raid.

THE COUNCIL OF TRENT

By far the most significant of Pope Paul III's contributions to the Counter Reformation was his call for a general council of the Church, which began to meet in 1545 in Trent on the border between Italy and Germany. The Council of Trent launched a new direction for the Catholic Church that guided it for the next 400 years.

Between 1545 and 1563 the council met under the auspices of three different popes in three separate sessions, with long intervals of as much as ten years between sessions. The objective of these sessions was to find a way to respond to the Protestant criticisms of the Church, to reassert the authority of the pope, and to launch reforms that would guarantee a well-educated and honest clergy. The decrees of the Council of Trent, which had the force of legislation for the entire Church, defied the Protestants by refusing to yield any ground on the traditional doctrines of the Church. The decrees confirmed the efficacy of all seven of the traditional sacraments, the reality of Purgatory, and the spiritual value of indulgences.

The prelates at Trent were more reluctant in announcing reforms that would apply to themselves; although they ordered bishops to reside in their dioceses or regions, they left a large loophole for the pope to grant exemptions. They decreed that every diocese should have a seminary to train priests, providing a practical solution to the problem of clerical ignorance.

The Council of Trent represented a dramatic reassertion of the authority of the papacy, the bishops, and the priesthood. The actual implementation of the decrees varied considerably from country to country and from diocese to diocese, however. The model for enforcing the decrees was Archbishop Carlo Borromeo (archbishop, 1565–1584) of Milan. His energetic visitations of his diocese and attention to administrative detail became an example for others. Despite the hopes of some of the participants in the council, it had no effect whatsoever in luring Protestants back into the Catholic fold.

The Reformation in the Arts

Most of the paintings, sculptures, and musical compositions created before and during the sixteenth century were destined for churches or had some kind of religious function. But with the tensions brought about during the Reformation, one of the major issues dividing Protestants and Catholics was defining the proper role of the arts in Christian worship. Except among the most radical Protestants, who entirely rejected any role for the arts in religious worship, the difference between the two was more one of degree than of kind. Catholics considered religious images and religious music, properly regulated, vital for devotion. Protestants, however, were uneasy about religious art because they worried about confining divine truths within any kind of visual representation.

PROTESTANT ICONOCLASM

Protestants sometimes initiated reform by vandalizing churches through acts of iconoclasm, the removing, breaking, or defacing of religious statues, paintings, and symbols such as crucifixes. The destruction of religious works of art more often than not took place even when the reformers themselves discouraged or denounced it. Nevertheless, in town after town in the thrall of reform enthusiasm, laypeople destroyed religious art, including some of the greatest masterpieces of the Middle Ages and Renaissance. Their violence against property was seldom matched by violence against people. Protestant mobs were much more likely to rip down an altar painting than to attack a priest.

Three factors likely explain iconoclasm. One was that people feared the power of such images. Guillaume Farel, the reformer of Geneva before Calvin, told how his parents had taken him as a child to the shrine of the Holy Cross at Tallard. A priest stationed at the shrine told the pilgrims that the Cross shook violently during storms. What Farel remembered most about the Cross was his fear, reinforced by the apprehension of his parents. The implication was that images possessed great powers that could be used both to protect and to destroy. The problem with religious images, therefore, was not that they were a form of idolatry

Iconoclasm in the Netherlands
This engraving shows statues being hauled down by the men on the left of the church pulling ropes. Note that one statue is already lying on the ground. On the right side of the church, men are breaking the stained glass windows with clubs.

but that they were perceived to be too powerful and potentially dangerous.

A second reason for iconoclasm was that religious images devoured financial resources that could be better spent on the poor. Ulrich Zwingli was especially articulate on this point. He hoped that the assets devoted to paying for paintings and statues could be transformed into "food of the poor." In this sense iconoclasm was part of a pious project to redirect the energy of Christians toward solving the social problems of the community. Great paintings were given to hospitals to serve as fuel, and crucifixes were sold as lumber with the proceeds going to the indigent.

Many reformers spoke of a third concern about images. They worried that a church filled with works of art distracted worshipers from paying attention to the Word of Scripture. They found the meaning of images too ambiguous, too subject to misinterpretation. Instead they wanted to ensure that their preaching provided the interpretation of Scripture. In effect, they wanted to substitute the Word of God for the image of God. In many reformed Dutch churches, for example, the walls were stripped bare of images and whitewashed. Passages of scripture were then painted on the walls in place of the images.

Although skeptical of the role of images in churches, propagandists for the Reformation had no such reservation about woodcuts and engravings, which could be reproduced in multiple copies and cheaply sold to thousands of people. These images, the visual by-product of the printing revolution, promoted the Reformation to the masses in a simple graphic way by lampooning the pope and ridiculing the wealth of the clergy. These images were the prototype for modern political cartoons. Also popular were portraits of the reformers. Many a pious Lutheran household replaced an image of the Madonna with an engraving of Martin Luther and his wife, Katherine von Bora.

Counter Reformation Art

The Catholic Church retained a strong commitment to the religious value of the arts. However, the Counter Reformation recognized that abuses had taken place in works of art that depicted events that did not appear in Scripture and placed artists under much closer surveillance than before. Artists were enjoined to avoid representing impieties of any sort and to use their art to teach correct doctrine and to move believers to true piety. Religious art had to convey a message simply, directly, and in terms that unlettered viewers could understand. The best Counter Reformation art employed dramatic theatrical effects in lighting and the arrangement of figures to represent deep emotional and spiritual experiences. Through contemplating these pictures, viewers were supposed to create similar experiences within themselves. In this sense an aesthetic and a spiritual appreciation of art were inseparable.

The Council of Trent forced a reevaluation of previous trends in the arts and a number of existing works of art.

The Italian Renaissance, in particular, had glorified the human body, often represented in the nude. In earlier generations churchmen and even popes had not objected to the display of naked figures in churches and chapels, but after the Council of Trent many influential ecclesiastics disapproved this practice in the strongest terms. Michelangelo's *The Last Judgment,* a fresco painted in the Sistine Chapel in the Vatican in Rome between 1534 and 1541, came under severe attack the year after the last session of Trent. The polemical *Dialogue on the Errors of Painters* criticized Michelangelo for subordinating the representation of Christian truths to his own stylistic interests in the human nude. Genitals and bare breasts in *The Last Judgment* were painted over, disfiguring one of the greatest masterpieces of the Renaissance. The crude overpainting was not removed until the fresco was cleaned during the 1990s.

Anti-Catholic Propaganda

This woodcut, titled *I am the Pope,* satirizes the papacy by depicting Pope Alexander VI as a monster. Alexander was infamous for allegedly conducting orgies in the Vatican. This kind of visual propaganda was an effective way to undermine support for the papacy.

Everywhere in Catholic Europe, offending body parts were painted over. In the Catholic parts of the Netherlands, paintings and statues deemed indecent were even destroyed, in an odd echo of Protestant iconoclasm. In Venice the Inquisition got involved. In a celebrated inquiry in 1573, the inquisitor dragged in the painter, Paolo Veronese, to answer why he put into a painting of the Last Supper various figures that did not appear in the Bible. The inquisitor noticed a figure dressed like a German and badgered Veronese with the allegation that this might indicate Lutheran sympathies. Ordered to change the painting, Veronese quietly changed its title instead.

Since artists' livelihoods depended on the patronage of aristocrats and high ecclesiastical officials, most quickly fell into line with the new requirements. Artistic rebels were unknown in the late sixteenth-century Catholic world. In 1577 the pope founded a new academy in Rome to create guidelines for artists in promoting Christianity, and the Jesuits proved very influential in defining a new path for artists. Many prominent artists across Europe enthusiastically embraced the Counter Reformation. Some became friends of Jesuits, undertook commissions for Jesuits, and practiced the *Spiritual Exercises,* thereby suffusing a Jesuit sensibility throughout Catholic culture.

SACRED MUSIC: PRAISING GOD

The Protestants' concern that the Word of God be intelligible to ordinary believers also influenced their attitude toward music. Luther, in particular, recognized the power of music to move the souls of the congregation. In the Lutheran mass he retained much of the traditional chant, but he translated the words into German and encouraged congregational singing so that believers sang the text themselves rather than passively listened to a choir. A number of new hymns were composed for the Lutheran service, some by Luther himself. One of the lasting masterpieces of the Reformation is Luther's great hymn, "A Mighty Fortress Is Our God." The Lutheran hymnbook laid the foundations for the magnificent tradition of Protestant church music that culminated in the compositions of Johann Sebastian Bach (1685–1750).

Zwingli, less certain about the value of music, banished organs from churches because he thought they obscured the clarity of the biblical text. Some radicals eliminated all music from churches, creating an austere form of worship practiced in houses or bare chapels, in which nothing was allowed to distract from the preaching of God's Word and the direct influence of the Holy Spirit. In these radical sects, the intimate connection between Western Christianity and the arts, which had been so pronounced for centuries, came to an abrupt end. Radical Protestants such as Anabaptists left a lasting legacy of hostility toward creative artists.

The Last Judgment
The figure with the raised hand in the upper center is Christ. On his right sits the Virgin Mary. Both figures were painted over with clothing to hide their nudity.

The Council of Trent spent more than a year debating the reform of sacred music. The Council decreed that the purpose of liturgical music was to encourage a sense of worship in the congregation. This meant that unlike Protestant music, which appealed to the laity by employing folk tunes, Catholic composers should not borrow from secular music, but like the Protestants, the style of composition must allow for the words to be clearly heard. The Catholics did not follow the Protestant emphasis on congregational singing and rejected virtuoso vocal or instrumental displays. Catholic liturgical performances consisted only of the organ either accompanying voices or playing solos.

The new music of the Catholic Reformation remained firmly rooted in the innovations of Renaissance music and consisted of compositions for various forms of the Latin mass. The most important Catholic composer of church music in the later sixteenth century was Giovanni Pierluigi da Palestrina (ca. 1525–1594). Palestrina spent most of his career in Rome, where he worked as an organist and choir master. His more than 100 masses demonstrated to the often skeptical prelates, who wanted to abolish all elaborate compositions, that music could reflect the meaning of the words while not obscuring their audibility. Palestrina amplified the sumptuous effects of the unaccompanied choir, employing a exotic mixture of harmonic and melodic purity, carefully controlled dissonance, and a sensuous sound. For many generations his music served as the model for Catholic composers.

The Inquisition Criticizes a Work of Art

This painting was originally intended to represent the Last Supper when Christ introduced the mass to his apostles. Because there are many figures in it who are not mentioned in the biblical account and the supper appears as if it were a Renaissance banquet, the artist, Paolo Veronese, was obliged to answer questions from the Inquisition. Ordered to remove the offending figures, Veronese instead changed the name of the painting to depict the less theologically controversial supper in the house of Levi.

THE INQUISITION INTERROGATES PAOLO VERONESE

In 1572 the prominent painter Paolo Veronese was called before the Inquisition in the city of Venice to answer questions about a painting of the Last Supper that he had created for the refectory of the friars of Santi Giovanni e Paolo. Paintings of the Last Supper were particularly sensitive during the controversies of the Reformation because Catholics believed Christ had instituted the mass at the Last Supper.

[The inquisitor] said to him, "Who do you think was really present at that supper?"

He answered, "I believe that Christ and his apostles were present. But if there is space left over in the picture I decorate it with figures of my own invention."

Said to him, "Did anyone commission you to paint Germans and clowns and the like in that picture?"

He answered, "No, my lords; my commission was to adorn that picture as I saw fit, for it is large and can include many figures, or so I thought."

It was said to him, "When you, the painter, add these decorations to your pictures, is it your habit to make them appropriate to the subject and to proportion them to the principal figures, or do you really do as the fancy takes you, without using any discretion or judgment?"

He answered, "I make the pictures after proper reflection, within the limits of my understanding."

He was asked, "Did he think it proper to depict at the Lord's last supper clowns, drunkards, Germans, dwarfs, and other lewd things?"

He answered, "No, my lords."

He was asked, "Why, then, did you paint them?"

He answered, "I did them on the understanding that they are not within the place where the supper is being held."

He was asked, "Do you not know that in Germany and other places infected with heresy they are accustomed, by means of outlandish paintings full of indecencies and similar devices, to abuse, mock and pour scorn on the things of the Holy Catholic Church, in order to teach false doctrine to foolish and ignorant people?"

He answered, "I agree, my lord, that it is bad; but I must say again that I am obliged to follow the example of my predecessors." [He was referring here to Michelangelo's Last Judgment in the Sistine Chapel of the Vatican.]

The inquisitors ordered Veronese to correct the painting, but he merely changed its name from The Last Supper *to* The Feast in the House of Levi. *It now hangs in the Academia Gallery in Venice.*

Source: From *Venice: A Documentary History, 1450–1630,* edited by David Chambers and Brian Pullan, with Jennifer Fletcher. Published by Blackwell Publishers (Oxford, 1992). Reprinted with permission.

CONCLUSION

Competing Understandings

During the Reformation the West was permanently divided into two discordant religious cultures of Protestant and Catholic. The religious unity of the West achieved during the Middle Ages had been fruit of many centuries of diligent effort by missionaries, monks, popes, and crusading knights. That unity was lost through the conflicts between, on the one hand, reformers, city magistrates, princes, and kings who wanted to control their own affairs and, on the other, popes who continued to cling to the medieval concept of the papal monarchy. In the West, Christians no longer saw themselves as dedicated to serving the same God as all other Christians. Instead, Catholics and Protestants emphasized their differences.

The differences between these two cultures had lasting implications for how people understood and accepted the authority of the Church and the state, how they conducted their family life, and how they formed their own identities as individuals and as members of a larger community. The next chapter will explore all of these themes.

As the result of intransigence on the part of both cultures, the division had tragic consequences. From the late sixteenth century to the late seventeenth century, European states tended to create diplomatic alliances along this ideological and religious divide, they allowed technical disputes about doctrine to prevent peaceful reconciliation, and they conducted wars as if they were a fulfillment of God's plan. Even after the era of religious warfare ended, Protestant and Catholic cultures remained ingrained in all aspects of life, influencing not just government policy but painting, music, literature, and education. This division completely reshaped the West into a place of intense religious and ideological conflict, and by the eighteenth century undermined the very idea that the West was necessarily a Christian civilization.

Suggestions for Further Reading

For a comprehensive list of suggested readings, please go to www.ablongman.com/levack/chapter13

Bireley, Robert. *The Refashioning of Catholicism, 1450–1700: A Reassessment of the Counter Reformation.* 1999. A fair reappraisal of the major events by one of the most prominent historians of Catholicism in this period.

Bossy, John. *Christianity in the West, 1400–1700.* 1985. A short study not of the institutions of the Church but of Christianity itself, this book explores the Christian people, their beliefs, and their way of life. The book demonstrates considerable continuities before and after the Reformation and is especially useful in understanding the attitudes of common lay believers as opposed to the major reformers and Church officials.

Cameron, Euan. *The European Reformation.* 1995. The most comprehensive general survey, this bulky book covers all the major topics in considerable detail. It is excellent in explaining theological issues.

Hsia, R. Po-chia. *The World of Catholic Renewal 1540–1770.* 1998. An excellent survey of the most recent research.

Koenigsberger, H. G., George L. Mosse, and G. Q. Bowler. *Europe in the Sixteenth Century,* 2nd ed. 1989. A good beginner's survey. Strong on political events.

McGrath, Alister E. *Reformation Thought: An Introduction,* 3rd. rev. ed. 1999. Indispensable introduction for anyone seeking to understand the ideas of the European Reformation. Drawing on the most up-to-date scholarship, McGrath offers a clear explanation of these ideas, set firmly in their historical contexts.

Muir, Edward. *Ritual in Early Modern Europe.* 1997. A broad survey of the debates about ritual during the Reformation and the implementation of ritual reforms.

Oberman, Heiko A. *Luther: Man Between God and the Devil,* trans. Eileen Walliser-Schwarzbart. 1992. First published to great acclaim in Germany, this book argues that Luther was more the medieval monk than history has usually regarded him. Oberman claims that Luther was haunted by the Devil and saw the world as a cosmic battleground between God and Satan. A brilliant, intellectual biography that is sometimes challenging but always clear and precise.

O'Malley, John. *Trent and All That: Renaming Catholicism in the Early Modern Era.* 2000. O'Malley works out a remarkable guide to the intellectual and historical developments behind the concepts of Catholic reform, the Counter Reformation, and, in his useful term, Early Modern Catholicism. The result is the single best overview of scholarship on Catholicism in early modern Europe, delivered in a pithy, lucid, and entertaining style.

Ozment, Steven. *The Age of Reform, 1250–1550: An Intellectual and Religious History of Late Medieval and Reformation Europe.* 1986. Firmly places the Protestant Reformation in the context of late medieval spirituality and theology, particularly strong on pre-Reformation developments.

Reardon, Bernard M. G. *Religious Thought in the Reformation,* 2nd ed. 1995. A good beginner's survey of the intellectual dimensions of the Reformation.

Scribner, R. W. *The German Reformation.* 1996. A short and very clear analysis of the appeal of the Reformation by the leading social historian of the period. Pays attention to what people actually did rather than just what reformers said they should do.

Notes

1. *Correspondence of Erasmus,* trans. R. A. B. Mynors and D. F. S. Thomson, annotated by Wallace K. Ferguson (1974–1994), no. 858, pp. 167–177.
2. *Desiderius Erasmus, The Essential Erasmus,* ed. John P. Dolan (1964), p. 148.
3. Quotation from Gordon Rupp, *Luther's Progress to the Diet of Worms* (1964), p. 29.
4. Ibid., p. 33
5. Quote from an anonymous caricature reproduced in A. G. Dickens, *Reformation and Society in Sixteenth-Century Europe* (1966), fig. 46, p. 61.
6. Translated and quoted in Thomas Head, "Marie Dentière: A Propagandist for the Reform," in Katharina M. Wilson, ed., *Women Writers of the Renaissance and Reformation* (1987), p. 260.
7. Quoted in Peter Blickle, "The Popular Reformation," in *Handbook of European History 1400–1600: Late Middle Ages, Renaissance and Reformation,* vol. II: *Visions, Programs and Outcomes,* eds. Thomas A. Brady, Jr., Heiko A. Oberman, and James D. Tracy (1995), p. 171.
8. Quoted in Heiko A. Oberman, *Luther: Man between God and the Devil,* trans. Eileen Walliser-Schwarzbart (1989), p. 240.
9. E. W. Ives, *Anne Boleyn* (1986), p. 398.
10. Quoted in Margery Stone Schauer and Frederick Schauer, "Law as the Engine of State: The Trial of Anne Boleyn," *William and Mary Law Review* 22 (1980), p. 68.
11. Quoted in Ives, p. 387.
12. Quoted in Schauer and Schauer, p. 70.
13. Quoted in Dickens, p. 134.
14. Quoted in Irving Lavin, *Bernini and the Unity of the Visual Arts* (1980), p. 107.

CHAPTER

14

The Age of Confessional Division, 1550–1618

Chapter Outline

- The Peoples of Early Modern Europe
- Disciplining the People
- The Confessional States
- States and Confessions in Eastern Europe

On July 10, 1584, a Catholic extremist François Guion, with a brace of pistols hidden under his cloak, surprised William the Silent, the Prince of Orange, as he was leaving the dining hall of his palace and shot him at point-blank range. William had been the leader of the Protestant nobility in the Netherlands, which was in revolt against the Catholic king of Spain. Guion masqueraded as a Protestant for seven years in order to ingratiate himself with William's party, and before the assassination he had consulted three Catholic priests who had confirmed the religious merit of his plan. Spain's representative in the Netherlands, the Duke of Parma, had offered a reward of 25,000 crowns to anyone who killed William, and at the moment of the assassination four other fanatics were in Delft trying to gain access to the duke.

The murder of William the Silent introduced an ominous new figure into Western civilization—the religiously motivated assassin. There had been many assassinations before the late sixteenth century, but the assassins had usually been motivated by the desire to gain political power or to avenge a personal or family injury, not by religious differences. The idea that killing a political leader of the opposing faith would serve God's plan injected into politics a measure of blind fanaticism that has persisted to our own times. The assassination of William introduced patterns of violence that have become all too familiar—deception by the assassin to gain access to his victim, the vulnerability of leaders who wish to mingle with the public, the lethal potential of easily concealed pistols (a new weapon at that time), the corruption of politics through vast sums of money, and the obsessive hostility of zealots against their perceived enemies. After the Protestant Reformation, the widespread acrimony among the varieties of Christian faith created a climate of religious extremism during the late sixteenth and early seventeenth centuries. These various forms or expressions of

St. Bartholomew's Day Massacre: This Protestant painter depicted the merciless slaughter of Protestant men, women, and children in the streets of Paris in 1572. The massacre was the most bloody and infamous in the French Wars of Religion and created a lasting memory of atrocity.

Christianity were called confessions° because their adherents believed in a particular confession of faith, or statement of religious doctrine.

Religious extremism was just one manifestation of an anxiety that pervaded European society at the time—a fear of hidden forces controlling human events. In an attempt to curb that anxiety, the European states allied themselves with the churches. The combined effort of state and church sought to discipline common people, persecute deviants of all sorts, and combat enemies through a religiously driven foreign policy. During this age of confessional division, European countries polarized along confessional lines, and governments persecuted followers of minority religions, whom they saw as threats to public security. During this period there was no place for the modern ethical principles of religious toleration, separation of church and state, and human rights. Anxious believers everywhere were consumed with pleasing an angry God, but when they tried to find God within themselves many Christians seemed only to find the Devil in others.

By attempting to discipline the people of Europe and make them better Christians, educated and elite society directly confronted a thriving popular culture. In many respects, the culture they encountered was nearly as alien as the native cultures in the newly discovered America. Certainly, the peoples of early modern Europe considered themselves Christian, but what they meant by Christianity was quite at odds with that of the reformers who had pushed through the Protestant and Catholic Reformations. In a confused, haphazard, and sometimes violent fashion, members of the elite attempted to blot out many elements of popular culture that they suspected might be remnants of pre-Christian beliefs and practices. One of the most curious consequences of the Reformations during the sixteenth and seventeenth centuries was a dramatic conflict between two cultures, that of the educated elite and that of the ordinary people. However, the disciplining of the people was primarily confined to western Europe. In eastern Europe religious diversity and popular culture thrived largely due to the relative weakness of the eastern European monarchs in comparison with those in western Europe.

The religious controversies of the age of confessional division redefined the West. During the Middle Ages, the West came to be identified with the practice of Latin Catholic Christianity. The Reformation of the early sixteenth century broke up the unity of medieval Christian Europe by dividing westerners into Catholic and Protestant camps. During the period from 1550 to 1618, governments reinforced religious divisions and attempted to unify their peoples around a common set of beliefs. Between the sixteenth century and the end of the eighteenth, these confessional religious identities changed in some places into more secular political ideologies, such as the belief in the superiority of a republic over a monarchy, but the assumption that all citizens of a state should believe in some common ideology remained. The period from about 1500 to 1800—the Early Modern period in European history—produced the lasting division of the West into national camps that were based on either religious confessions or ideological commitments.

The pervasive anxiety of the late sixteenth and early seventeenth centuries raises several questions that this chapter will explore: (1) How did the expanding population and price revolution exacerbate religious and political tensions? (2) How did religious and political authorities attempt to discipline the people? (3) How did religious differences provoke violence and start wars? (4) How did the countries of eastern Europe during the late sixteenth century become enmeshed in the religious controversies that began in western Europe during the early part of the century?

The Peoples of Early Modern Europe

During the tenth century if a Russian had wanted to see the sights of Paris—assuming he had even heard of Paris—he could have left Kiev and walked under the shade of trees all the way to France, so extensive were the forests and so sparse the human settlements of northern Europe. By the end of the thirteenth century, the nomadic Russian would have needed a hat to protect him on the shadeless journey. Instead of human settlements forming little islands in a sea of forests, the forests were by then islands in a sea of villages and farms, and from any church tower the sharp-eyed traveler could have seen other church towers, each marking a nearby village or town. At the end of the thirteenth century, the European continent had become completely settled by a dynamic, growing population, which had cleared the forests for farms.

As we saw in Chapter 10, during the fourteenth century all of that changed. A series of crises—periodic famines, the catastrophic Black Death, and a general economic collapse—left the villages and towns of Europe intact, but a third or more of the population was gone. In that period of desolation, many villages looked like abandoned movie sets, and the cities did not have enough people to fill in the empty spaces between the central market square and the city walls. Fields that had once been put to the plow to feed the hungry children of the thirteenth century were neglected and overrun with bristles and brambles. During the fifteenth century a general European depression and recurrent plagues kept the population stagnant.

In the sixteenth century the population began to rebound, but the sudden swell brought dramatic and destabilizing consequences that contributed to a pervasive anxiety. An important factor in the population growth was the transformation of European agriculture from subsistence to commercial farming, an uneven transformation that impoverished some villages while it enriched others. Moreover, the expanded population transformed the balance of power, as northern Europe recovered its population more successfully than southern Europe. As the population grew, young men and women flocked to the cities, creating enormous social strains and demands on local governments. Perhaps most disruptive was the price revolution, which brought inflation that ate away at the buying power of everyone from working families to kings and queens. The anxiety produced by these circumstances lasted into the early seventeenth century.

THE POPULATION RECOVERY

During a period that historical demographers call the "long sixteenth century" (ca. 1480–1640), the population of Europe began to grow consistently again for the first time since the late thirteenth century. In 1340, on the brink of the Black Death, Europe had about 74 million inhabitants, or 17 percent of the world's total. By 1400 the population of all of Europe had dropped to 52 million (less than one-fifth of the population of the United States today), or 14 percent of the world's total. Over the course of the long sixteenth century, Europe's population grew from 60.9 million to 77.9 million, just barely surpassing the pre-Black Death level.

The table to the right shows some representative population figures for the larger European countries during the sixteenth century. Two stunning facts emerge from these data. The first is the much greater rate of growth in northern Europe compared to southern Europe. England grew by 83 percent, Poland grew by 76 percent, and even the tiny, war-torn Netherlands gained 58 percent. During the same period Italy grew by only 25 percent and Spain by 19. These trends signal a massive, permanent shift of demographic and economic power from the Mediterranean countries of Italy and Spain to northern, especially northwestern, Europe. The second fact to note from these data is the overwhelming size of France, which was home to about a quarter of Europe's population. Once France recovered from its long wars of religion, its demographic superiority overwhelmed competing countries and made it the dominant power in Europe, permanently eclipsing its chief rival, Spain. Because Germany lacked political unity, it was unable to take advantage of its position as the second-largest land.

What explains the growth in the population and the economy? To a large extent, it was made possible by the transformation from subsistence to commercial agriculture in certain regions of Europe. Subsistence farmers, called peasants, had worked the land year in and year out, raising grains for the coarse black bread that fed their families, supplemented only by beer, grain porridge, and occasionally vegetables. Meat was rare and expensive. Peasants consumed about 80 percent of everything they raised, and what little was left over went almost entirely to the landlord as feudal dues and to the church as tithing—the obligation to give to God one-tenth of everything earned or produced. Peasant families lived on the edge of existence. In a bad year some starved to death, usually the vulnerable children and old people. But during the sixteenth century, in areas with access to big cities, subsistence agriculture gave way to commercial crops, especially wheat, which was hauled to be sold in town markets. Profits from this market agriculture stimulated farmers to raise even greater surpluses in the agricultural regions around the great cities—in southern England around London; in the Netherlands around Antwerp and Amsterdam; in France the Ile-de-France near Paris; in northern Italy near Milan and Venice; in Catalonia near Barcelona; and in scattered places in Germany. Commercial crops and the cash income they produced meant fewer starving children and a higher standard of living for those who were able to take advantage of the new opportunities. As commercial agriculture spread, the population grew.

European Population, 1500–1600 (in millions)

	1500	1550	1600
England	2.30	3.10	4.20
Germany	12.00	14.00	16.00
France	16.40	19.00	20.00
Netherlands	0.95	1.25	1.50
Belgium	1.25	1.65	1.30
Italy	10.50	11.40	13.10
Spain	6.80	7.50	8.10
Austria-Bohemia	3.50	3.60	4.30
Poland	2.50	3.00	3.40

Source: Handbook of European History 1400–1600: Late Middle Ages, Renaissance and Reformation, Vol. 1, *Structures and Assertions,* Jan de Vries, "Population," in Thomas A. Brady, Jr., Heiko A. Oberman, and James D. Tracy, eds., (1994), Table 1, p. 13.

THE PROSPEROUS VILLAGES

Success in commercializing agriculture could make an enormous difference in the lives of peasants. The village of Buia tells the story of many similarly prosperous hamlets. Situated in Friuli, a region in the northeast corner of Italy, it served as part of the agricultural hinterland of the great metropolis of Venice. For centuries the peasants of hilly and pleasant Buia had lived in thatched hovels surviving at the subsistence level. But during the fourteenth and fifteenth centuries serfdom disappeared in the region and the peasants' legal status changed. Now free to sell their labor to the highest bidder, peasant families contracted with a landlord to lease a plot of land for a certain number of years in

The Rise of Commercial Agriculture
During the sixteenth century commercial agriculture began to produce significant surpluses for the expanding population of the cities.

exchange for annual rent payments in kind. A typical yearly rent might include two bushels of wheat, two of oats, one of beans, one of millet, three barrels of wine, two chickens, one ham, three guinea hens, thirty eggs, two cartloads of firewood, and two days' work mowing hay. In contrast to the servitude of serfdom, which tied peasants to the land, agricultural leases created a measure of economic freedom. They allowed landlords to find labor at a time when laborers were scarce, and they enabled peasants to negotiate for a better reward for their labor.

Unlike some neighboring villages that were still under the heel of their lords, Buia had incorporated as a town, a status that provided it with more autonomy from its lords, the Savorgnan family. Moreover, Buia had diversified its economy, branching out into cattle raising and marketing its fierce pear brandy and smooth white wine. But Buia's crucial economic advantage derived from its access to capital. The Savorgnan lords liberally lent money to their tenants in Buia, which enabled them to survive hard times and to invest in commercial profit-making enterprises. Unlike other families, the Savorgnans were willing to invest in their tenants, because they had established political and economic ties with the nearby commercial metropolis of Venice whose bankers were more than happy to bankroll the Savorgnan family. From the commercial banks of Venice, money flowed through the hands of the Savorgnan to the peasants of the little village of Buia, who in turn produced crops that could be sold in the markets of Venice, a flow of money and goods that enriched everyone involved—the peasants, their Savorgnan landlords, and the Venetian bankers. With the increased income from commercial agriculture, Buia even began to look more affluent during the sixteenth century, boasting a substantial church, a tavern, and a simple one-room town hall where citizens could gather to debate their affairs.

The success of commercial agriculture during the sixteenth century depended on a free and mobile labor supply, access to capital for investment, and proximity to the markets of the big cities. What happened in Buia happened in many places throughout Europe, but overall the amount of land available could not provide enough work for the growing farm population. As a result, the growth of the rural population created a new class of landless, impoverished men and women, who were forced to take to the road to find their fortunes. These vagabonds, as they were called, foreshadowed the social problems that emerged from the uneven distribution of wealth generated by the new commerce.

THE REGULATED CITIES

By the 1480s cities began to grow, largely through migration from the more prosperous countryside, but the growth was uneven with the most dramatic growth occurring in the cities of the North, especially London, Antwerp, and Amsterdam (see Map 14.1). The surpluses of the countryside, both human and agricultural, flowed into the cities during the sixteenth century. Compared to even the prosperous rural villages, such as Buia, the cities must have seemed incomparably rich. Half-starved vagabonds from the countryside would have marveled at shops piled high with food (white bread, fancy pies, fruit, enormous casks of wine, roasting meats); they would have wistfully passed taverns full of drunken, laughing citizens; and they would have begged for alms in front of magnificent, marble-faced churches.

Every aspect of the cities exhibited dramatic contrasts between the rich and poor, who lived on the same streets and often in different parts of the same houses. Around 1580 Christian missionaries brought a Native American chief to the French city of Rouen. Through an interpreter he was asked what impressed him the most about European cities, so unlike the villages of North America. He replied that he was astonished that the rag-clad, emaciated men and women who crowded the streets did not grab the plump, well-dressed rich people by the throat.

The wretched human surplus from the farms continuously replenished and swelled the populations of the cities, which were frequently depleted by high urban death rates.

Map 14.1 Population Distribution in the Sixteenth Century
The population of Europe concentrated around the cities of northern Italy, the Danube and Rhine River valleys, Flanders and northern France, and southeastern England. During the late sixteenth century, northwestern Europe began to grow significantly more rapidly than southern Europe. (Source: Jan deVries, "Population," in *Handbook of European History 1400–1600: Late Middle Ages, Renaissance and Reformation, Vol. I: Structures and Assertions,* edited by Thomas A. Brady, Jr., Heiko A. Oberman, and James D. Tracy, (1994), Table 1, p. 13.)

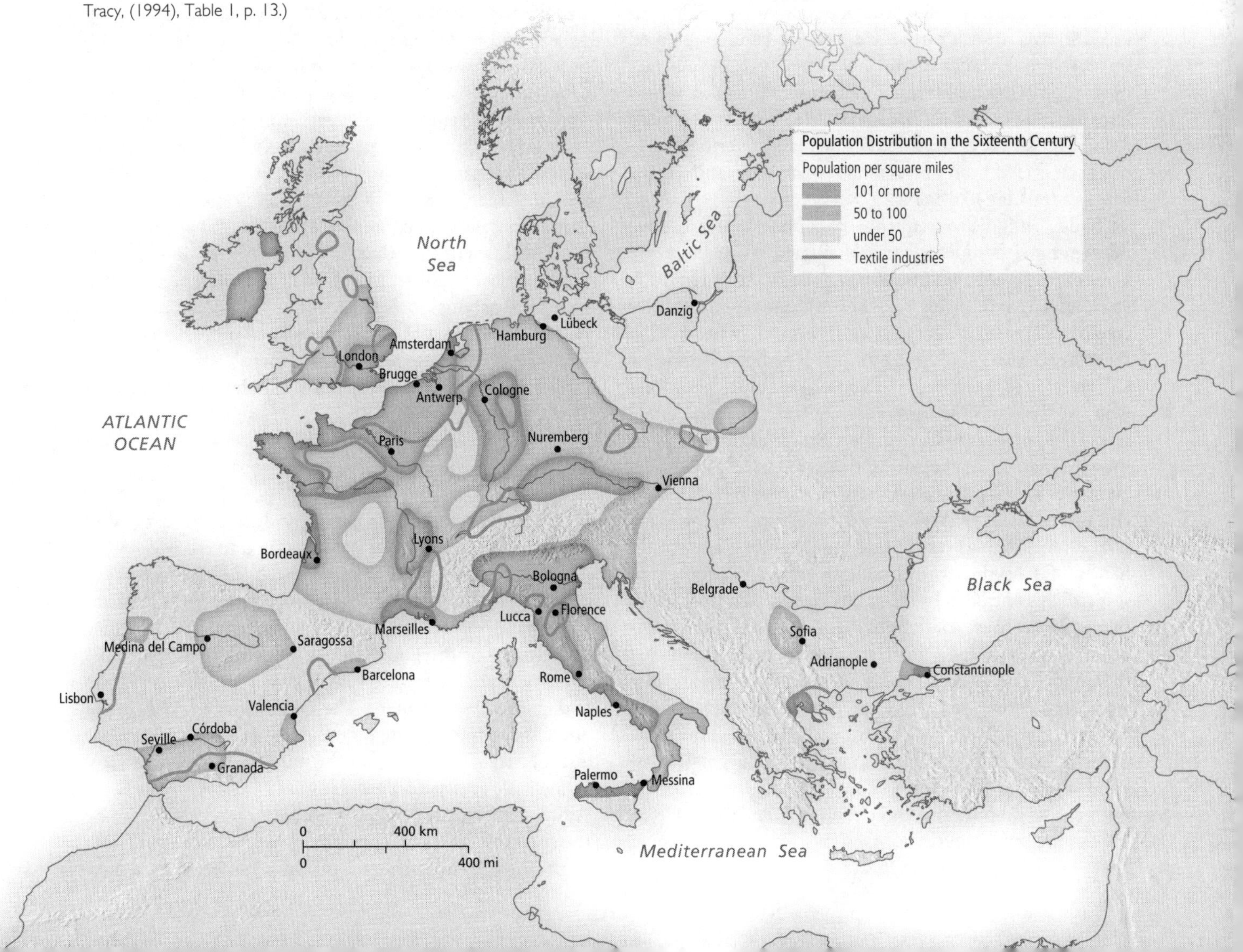

As wealthy as the cities were, they were unhealthy places: human waste overflowed from open latrines because there were no sewage systems; garbage, manure, dead animals, and roaming pigs and dogs made the streets putrid and dangerous; and water came from polluted rivers or sat stale in cisterns for months. Under such conditions, entire neighborhoods could be wiped out in epidemics. Both ends of the lifespan were vulnerable: one in three babies died in the first year of life; old people did not last long in cold, drafty houses. When the plague struck, which it continued to do about every twenty years until 1680, the rich escaped to their country retreats while the poor died in the streets or in houses locked up and under quarantine.

Despite the danger from disease in the cities, rural immigrants were less likely to starve than those who remained in small villages where they lacked land. Every city maintained storehouses of grain and regulated the price of bread and the size of a loaf so that the poor could be fed. The impulse to feed the poor was less the result of humanitarian motives than a recognition that nothing was more dangerous than a hungry mob. Given the contrasts in wealth among its inhabitants, cities guarded carefully against revolts and crime. Even for petty crime, punishment was swift, sure, and gruesome. The beggar who stole a loaf of bread from a baker's cart would have his hand amputated on a chopping block in the market square. A shabbily dressed girl who grabbed a lady's glittering trinket would have her nose cut off so that she could never attract a man. A burglar would be tortured, drawn, and quartered, and have his severed head impaled on an iron spike at the town gate as a warning to others.

To deal with the consequences of commerce and massive immigration, European cities attempted to regulate the lives of their inhabitants. Ringing bells measured each working day, and during the sixteenth century many cities erected a large mechanical clock in a prominent place so that busy citizens could keep to their schedules. The richer citizens elected from among themselves municipal officers who were responsible for protecting their financial interests. These officers inspected the weights and measures in the city market, regulated the distribution of produce to guarantee an abundant food supply, and repaired the streets and city walls. However talented or enterprising, new arrivals to the city had very limited opportunities. They could hardly start up their own business because all production was strictly controlled by the guilds. Recall from Chapter 10 that guilds were associations of merchants or artisans organized to protect their interests. Guilds rigidly regulated their membership; they required an apprenticeship of many years, prohibited technological innovations, guaranteed certain standards of workmanship, and did not allow branching out into new lines. A member of the goldsmiths' guild could not make mirrors; a baker could not sell fruit on the side; a house carpenter could not lay bricks. Given the limited opportunities for new arrivals, immigrant men and women begged on the streets or took charity from the public dole. The men picked up any heavy-labor jobs they could find. Both men and women became servants, a job that paid poorly but at least guaranteed regular meals.

Among the important social achievements of both Protestant and Catholic Reformations were efforts to address the problems of the destitute urban poor, who constituted at least a quarter of the population, even in the best of times. In Catholic countries such as Italy, Spain, southern Germany, and France, there was an enormous expansion of credit banks, which were financed by charitable contributions in order to provide small loans to the poor. Catholic cities established convents for poor young women who were at risk of falling into prostitution and for other women who had retired from the sex trade. Catholic and Protestant cities established orphanages, hospitals for the sick, hospices for the dying, and apartments lent out for a modest rent to poor widows. Both Catholic and Protestant cities attempted to distinguish between the "honest" poor—those who were disabled and truly deserving—and the "dishonest" poor who were thought to be malingerers. Protestant cities established poorhouses, which segregated the poor, subjected them to prisonlike discipline, and forced the able-bodied to work.

The more comfortable classes of the cities enjoyed large palaces and luxurious lifestyles. They hired extensive staffs of servants, feasted on meat and fine wines, and purchased exotic imports such as silk cloth, spices from the East, and, in the Mediterranean cities, slaves from eastern Europe, the Middle East, or Africa. The merchants whose fortunes came from cloth manufacturing, banking, and regional or international trade maintained their status by marrying among themselves, providing municipal offices to those whose fortunes had fallen, and educating their children in the newly fashionable humanist schools. The wealthy of the cities were the bastions of social stability. They possessed the financial resources and economic skills to protect themselves from the worst consequences of economic instability, especially the corrosive wave of price inflation that struck the West after about 1540.

THE PRICE REVOLUTION

Price inflation became so pervasive during the last half of the sixteenth century that it contributed to the widespread fear that events were being controlled by hidden forces. The effects of inflation are illustrated by the experience of the students at Winchester College in England. These young men were the privileged sons of English aristocrats and country gentlemen, who were destined for leisured wealth and public responsibility. The curriculum of Winchester emphasized the unchanging values of aristocratic privilege and Christian rectitude, but the dusty account books, kept in meticulous detail by generations of college stewards, reveal that change was very much a fact of college life during the sixteenth century. For example, in 1500 a piece of cloth large enough to make a student's uniform cost forty shillings. By 1580 the cost had doubled, and by 1630 it had tripled. During the sixteenth century the cost of a dozen sheets of parchment doubled, the cost of a dozen candles quadrupled, and the cost of a twelve-gallon barrel of wine (yes, the college served wine to its teenaged students) rose from eight to sixty-four shillings. English masons' experience of price inflation during this period was far more painful. Over the course of the century their wages doubled, but the price of bread increased four- or fivefold, and because the survival of their families depended on the cost of bread, price inflation seriously threatened their lives.

The finances of English college students and masons reveal the phenomenon that historians call the Price Revolution°. After a long period of falling or stable prices that stretched back to the fourteenth century, Europe experienced sustained price increases, beginning around 1540. The inflation lasted a century, forcing major economic and social changes that permanently altered the face of Western society. During this period overall prices across Europe multiplied five- or sixfold.

What caused the inflation? The basic principle is simple. The price paid for goods and services is fundamentally the result of the relationship between *supply* and *demand.* If the number of women who wish to wear silk gowns expands faster than the supply of silk, prices go up. This happens simply because those who most want silk will be willing to pay a higher price to get it. If the supply of available silk increases at a greater rate than the demand, then prices go down. The equation gets a little more complicated when taking into account two other factors that can influence price. One factor is the *amount of money in circulation.* If the amount of gold or silver available to make coins increases, there is more money in circulation. When more money is circulating, people have more money to buy more things, which creates the same effect as an increase in demand—prices go up. The other factor is called the *velocity of money in circulation,* which refers to the number of times money changes hands to buy things. When people buy commodities with greater frequency, it has the same effect as increasing the amount of money in circulation or of increasing demand—again, prices go up.

The precise combination of these factors in causing the great Price Revolution of the sixteenth century has long been a matter of considerable debate. Most historians would now agree that the primary cause of inflation was population growth, which increased demand. As Europe's population finally began to recover, it meant that more people needed and desired to buy more things. This explanation is most obvious for commodities that people need to survive, such as grain to make bread. These commodities have what economists call *inelastic demand,* that is, consumers do not have a great deal of discretion in purchasing them. Everybody has to eat. The commodities that people could survive without if the price is too high are said to have *elastic demand,* such as dancing shoes and lace collars. In England between 1540 and 1640 overall prices rose by 490 percent. More telling, however, is that the price of grain (inelastic demand) rose by a stunning 670 percent, whereas the price of luxury goods (elastic demand) rose much less, by 204 percent.

Monetary factors also contributed to inflation. The Portuguese brought in significant amounts of gold from Africa, and newly opened mines in central Europe increased the amount of silver by fivefold as early as the 1520s. The discovery in 1545 of the fabulous silver mine of Potosí (in present-day Bolivia) brought to Europe a flood of silver, which Spain used to finance its costly wars. As inflation began to eat away at royal incomes, financially strapped monarchs all across western Europe debased their money because they believed, mistakenly, that producing more coins containing less silver would buy more. In fact, the minting of more coins meant each coin was worth less and would buy less. Debasement was especially disastrous in England, where it was the major source of inflation during the 1540s and 1550s.

During the sixteenth century, no one understood these causes, however. People only experienced the effects of inflation, and then only gradually. The real wages of workers declined, causing widespread suffering and discontent. Incomes eroded for those dependent on fixed incomes—clergymen, pensioners, government clerks, and landlords who rented out land on long leases. Landlords who were willing to be ruthless and enterprising survived and even prospered. Those who were more paternalistic or conservative in managing their estates often lost their land to creditors.

The Price Revolution severely weakened governments. Most monarchs derived their incomes from their own private lands and from taxes on property. As inflation took hold, property taxes proved dangerously inadequate to cover royal expenses. Even frugal monarchs such as England's Elizabeth I were forced to take extraordinary measures, in her case to sell off royal lands. Spendthrift monarchs faced disaster. Spain was involved in the costly enterprise of nearly continuous war during the sixteenth century. To pay for the wars, Charles V resorted to a form of deficit financing in which he borrowed money by issuing *juros,* which provided lenders an annuity yielding between 3 and 7 percent on the amount of the principal. By the 1550s, however, the annuity payments of the *juros* consumed half of the royal revenues. Charles's son, Philip II, inherited such an alarming situation that in 1557, the year after he assumed the throne, he was forced to declare bankruptcy. Philip continued to fight expensive wars and borrow wildly, and thus failed to get his financial house in order. He declared bankruptcy again in 1575 and 1596. Philip squandered Spain's wealth, impoverishing his own subjects through burdensome taxes and contributing to inflation by borrowing at high rates of interest and debasing the coinage. As the greatest power of the sixteenth century, Spain sowed the seeds of its own decline by fighting on borrowed money.

Probably the most serious consequence of the Price Revolution was that the hidden force of inflation caused widespread human suffering. During the late sixteenth and early seventeenth centuries, people felt their lives threatened, but they did not know the source and so they imagined all kinds of secret powers at work, especially supernatural ones. Catholics suspected Protestants, Protestants suspected Catholics, both suspected Jews, and they all worried about witches. Authorities sought to relieve this widespread anxiety by looking in all the wrong places, by disciplining the populace, hunting for witches, and battling against enemies from the opposite side of the confessional divide.

Disciplining the People

The first generation of the Protestant and Catholic Reformations had been devoted to doctrinal disputes and to either rejecting or defending papal authority. Subsequent generations of reformers in the last half of the sixteenth and the early seventeenth centuries faced the formidable task of building the institutions that would firmly establish a Protestant or Catholic religious culture. Leaders of all religious confessions attempted to revitalize the Christian community by disciplining nonconformists and enforcing moral rigor. Members of the community came to identify responsible citizenship with conformity to a specific Christian confession.

Whether Lutheran, Calvinist, Catholic, or Anglican, godly reformers attacked popular culture. They reformed or abolished wild festivals, they imprisoned town drunks, they decreased the number of holidays, and they tried to regulate sexual behavior. Many activities that had once been accepted as normal came to be considered deviant or criminal. The process of disciplining the people required cooperation between church and secular authorities, but discipline was not entirely imposed from above. Some people wholeheartedly cooperated with moral correction and even encouraged reformers to go further. Others passively, actively, or resentfully resisted it.

Establishing Confessional Identities

Between 1560 and 1650 religious confessions reshaped European culture, and loyalty to a single confession governed the relationships between states. A confession consisted of the adherents to a particular statement of religious doctrine—the Confession of Augsburg for Lutherans, the Helvetic Confessions for Calvinists, the Thirty-Nine Articles for Anglicans, and the decrees of the Council of Trent for Catholics. Based on these confessions of faith, the clergy disciplined the laity, exiled nonconformists, and promoted distinct religious institutions, beliefs, and culture.

The process of establishing confessional identities did not happen overnight; it lasted for centuries and had far-reaching consequences. During the second half of the sixteenth century, Lutherans turned from the struggle to survive within the hostile Holy Roman Empire to establishing a confessional identity in the parts of the empire where Lutheranism was the chosen religion of the local prince. They had to recruit Lutheran clergy and provide each clergyman with a university education, which was made possible by scholarship endowments from the Lutheran princes of Germany. Once established, the Lutheran clergy became a branch of the civil bureaucracy, received a government stipend, and enforced the will of the prince. Calvinist states followed a similar process.

Catholics responded with their own aggressive plan of training new clergymen, propagandizing the laity, and reinforcing the bond between church and state. Just as with the Lutheran princes, Catholic princes in Germany associated conformity to Catholicism with loyalty to themselves, making religion a pillar of the state. Everywhere in western Europe (except for Ireland) the only openly practiced religion was the religion of the state.

The authorities primarily formed confessional identities among the laity by promoting distinctive ritual systems. These ritual systems embodied ways of acting and even of gesturing that literally transformed the way people moved their bodies so that a Catholic and a Protestant might be instantly recognized by certain telltale signs of posture, speech, and comportment.

The Catholic and Protestant ritual systems differed primarily in their attitude toward the sacred. Whereas Catholic ritual behavior depended on a repertoire of gestures that indicated reverence in the presence of the sacred, Protestant ritual depended on a demonstration of sociability that identified people as members of a certain congregation or church. For example, until the late sixteenth century Europeans greeted one another either by raising a hand, palm outward, which meant "welcome," or with a bow by which someone of lower status recognized the superiority of another. Some radical Protestants, however, insisted that all gestures of deference, such as bows and curtsies, were an affront to God and introduced a new form of greeting, the handshake. Shaking hands was completely egalitarian, and one could identify English Quakers or Scottish Calvinists, for example, simply by the fact that they shook hands with one another.

A particularly revealing ritual difference can be seen in the contrasting ways that Scottish Calvinists and Spanish Catholics reintegrated repentant sinners into the Church. In Calvinism disciplinary authority rested with the presbytery, a board of pastors and elders elected by the community. If a Scottish Calvinist blasphemed God, the presbytery could discipline him, shun him, or banish him from the community. If he wished to be reinstated and the presbytery agreed, he would be obliged to come before the entire congregation to confess sincerely his wrongs and beg forgiveness. The congregation would make a collective judgment about his acceptability for renewed membership. The pain inflicted on the Calvinist sinner was the social pain of having his transgression openly discussed and evaluated by his friends and neighbors.

If a Spanish Catholic blasphemed, he would be subjected to an extended ritual of penance, the auto-da-fé°, which meant a theater of faith. The auto-da-fé was designed to promote fear and to cause physical pain because, according to Catholic doctrine, bodily suffering in this world was necessary in order to free the soul from worse suffering in the next. An *auto* was a public performance in which dozens or sometimes hundreds of sinners and criminals were paraded through the streets in a theatrical demonstration of the authority of the Church and the power of penance. The *auto* culminated in a mass confirmation of faith in which the repentant sinners utterly subjected themselves to the authority of the clergy, while those who refused to repent or were relapsed heretics were strangled and their corpses burned.

Whereas the punishment of the Calvinist community was primarily a rite of social humiliation, the auto-da-fé involved physical torture as well as social degradation. The nub of the difference was that Calvinists had to demonstrate the sincerity of their social conformity; Catholics had to go through a performance that emphasized the authority of the clergy and that purified sin with physical pain.

Policing the Family

One matter on which Calvinists, Lutherans, and Catholics agreed was that the foundation of society was the authority fathers had over their families. This principle, known as patriarchy, was discussed in Chapter 11. The confessions that emerged from the Reformation further strengthened patriarchy because it so usefully served the authoritarian needs of church and state. According to an anonymous treatise published in 1586 in Calvinist Nassau, the three pillars of Christian society were the church, the state, and the household. This proposition made the father's authority a reflection of the authority of clergy and king—a position that all the confessions would have accepted. The enforcement of patriarchy required the policing of gender roles. And during the otherwise discordant sixteenth century, the one issue on which virtually all men and many women agreed was that women should be subservient to men.

Marriage and Sexuality: The Self-Restrained Couple

During the Early Modern period, the structure of the European family underwent a major transformation. The result was a new type of family that now seems normal to most people in the Western world. The new family type first appeared in northwestern Europe—in Britain, Scandinavia, the Netherlands, northern France, and western Germany. In these regions, couples tended to wait to marry until their mid- or late twenties, well beyond the age of sexual maturity. And when these couples married, they established their own household separate from either of their parents. Husbands were usually only two or three years older than their wives. By contrast, in southern Europe, men in their late twenties or thirties married teenaged women, and in eastern Europe, both spouses married in their teens and resided in one of the parental households for many years. The pattern established in northwestern European required that the couple be economically independent before they married, which meant both had to accumulate savings or the husband needed to inherit from his deceased father before he could marry.

This new marriage pattern required prolonged sexual restraint by young men and women until they were economically self-sufficient. In addition to individual self-control, sexual restraint required social control by church and secular authorities. These efforts seem to have been generally successful. For example, in sixteenth-century Geneva, where the elders were especially wary about sexual sins, the rates of illegitimate births were extremely low. The elders were particularly vigilant about disciplining women and keeping them subservient, often making and enforcing highly minute regulations. In 1584 Calvinist elders in another Swiss town excommunicated Charlotte Arbaleste and her entire household because she wore her hair in curls, which the elders thought were too alluring.

The new family also tended to be a smaller family. Despite the Christian precept that encouraged as many children as possible, married couples in northwestern European began to space their children through birth control and family planning. These self-restrained couples practiced withdrawal, the rhythm method, or abstinence. When mothers no longer relied on wet nurses and nursed their own infants, often for long periods, they also reduced their chances of becoming pregnant. Thus, limiting family size became the social norm in northwestern Europe, especially among the educated and urban middle classes. Protestant families tended to have fewer children than Catholic families, but Catholics in this region also practiced some form of birth control, even though Church law prohibited all forms except abstinence.

For prospective couples, parental approval remained more important than romantic love. In fact, a romantic attachment between a husband and wife was frowned upon as unseemly and even dangerous. More highly prized in a marriage partner were trust, dependability, and the willingness to work. Many married couples certainly exhibited signs of affection—addressing one another lovingly in letters, nursing a sick mate, mourning a dead one—but overly sentimental attachments were discouraged as contrary to the patriarchal authority that ideally characterized family life. Most husbands and wives seem to have treated one another with a certain coolness and emotional detachment.

JUSTICE IN HISTORY

The Spanish Auto-da-Fé: The Power of Penance

Performed in Spain and Portugal from the sixteenth to eighteenth centuries, the auto-da-fé merged the judicial processes of the state with the sacramental rituals of the Catholic Church. An *auto* took place at the end of a judicial investigation conducted by the inquisitors of the Church after the defendants had been found guilty of a sin or crime. The term auto-da-fé means "theater of faith," and the goal was to persuade or force a person who had been judged guilty to repent and confess. Organized through the cooperation of ecclesiastical and secular authorities, autos-da-fé brought together an assortment of sinners, criminals, and heretics for a vast public rite that dramatized the essential elements of the sacrament of penance: contrition, by which the sinner recognized and felt sorry for the sin; confession, which required the sinner to admit the sin to a priest; and satisfaction or punishment, by which the priest absolved the sinner and enacted some kind of penalty. The auto-da-fé transformed penance, especially confession and satisfaction, into a spectacular affirmation of the faith and a manifestation of divine justice.

The *auto* symbolically anticipated the Last Judgment, and it provoked deep anxiety among those who witnessed it about how God would judge them. By suffering bodily pain in this life the soul might be relieved from worse punishments in the next. The sinners, convicts, and heretics, now considered penitents, were forced to march in a procession that went through the streets of the city from the cathedral to the town hall or place of punishment. These processions would typically include some thirty or forty penitents, but in moments of crisis they could be far larger. In Toledo in 1486 there were three *autos*—one parading 750 penitents and two displaying some 900 each.

A 1655 *auto* in Córdoba illustrates the symbolic character of the rites. Soldiers bearing torches that would light the pyre for those to be burnt led the procession. Following them came three bigamists who wore on their heads conical miters or hats painted with representations of their sin, four witches whose miters depicted devils, and three criminals with harnesses around their necks to demonstrate their status as captives. The sinners carried unlit candles to represent their lack of faith. Criminals who had escaped arrest were represented in the procession by effigies made in their likeness, and those who had died before punishment were carried in their coffins. The marching sinners appeared before their neighbors and fellow citizens stripped of the normal indicators of status, dressed only in the emblems of their sins. Among them walked a few who wore the infamous *sanbenitos,* a kind of tunic or vest with a yellow strip down the back, and a conical hat painted with flames. These were the *relajados,* the unrepentant or relapsed sinners who were going to be "relaxed" (strangled and burned) at the culminating moment of the *auto.*

The procession ended in the town square at a platform from which penances were performed as on the stage of a theater. Forced to their knees, the penitents were asked to confess and to plead for readmission into the bosom of the church. For those who did confess, a sentence was announced that would rescue them from the pains of purgatory and the flames of the *auto.* The sentence required them to join a penitential procession for a certain number of Fridays, perform self-flagellation in public, or wear a badge of shame for a prescribed period of time. Those who failed to confess faced a more immediate sentence.

The most horrendous scenes of suffering awaited those who refused to confess or who had relapsed into sin or heresy, which meant their confession was not considered sincere. If holdouts confessed prior to the reading of the sentence, then the *auto* was a success, a triumph of the Christian faith over its enemies, and everything that could possibly elicit confessions was attempted, including haranguing, humiliating, and torturing the accused until their stubborn will broke. If the accused finally confessed after the sentence was read, then they would be strangled before burning, but if they held out to the very end, they would be burned alive. From the ecclesiastics' point of view, the refusal to confess was a disaster for the entire Church because the flames of the pyre opened a window into Hell. They would certainly prefer to see the church's authority acknowledged through confession than to see the power of Satan manifest in such a public fashion.

■ **Auto-da-fé in Lisbon**
A procession conducted the sinners, many with hats or aprons identifying their sins, to a stage and pyre where relapsed heretics were burned.

It is reported that crowds witnessed the violence of the autos-da-fé with silent attention in a mood of deep dread, not so much of the inquisitors, it seems, as for the inevitability of the final day of divine judgment that would arrive for them all. The core assumption of the auto-da-fé was that bodily pain could save a soul from damnation. As one contemporary witness put it, the inquisitors removed "through external ritual [the sinners'] internal crimes." It was assumed that the public ritual framework for the sacrament of penance would have a salutary effect on those who witnessed the *auto* by encouraging them to repent before they too faced divine judgment. ■

Questions of Justice

1. How did the auto-da-fé contribute to the formation of an individual and collective sense of being a Catholic?
2. How did the auto-da-fé reveal the difference between Spanish Catholic and Scottish Calvinist forms of discipline?
3. In the auto-da-fé, inflicting physical pain was more than punishment. How was pain understood to have been socially and religiously useful? Compare the role of pain here with that in St. Teresa of Avila's experience of pain, discussed in Chapter 13 (p. 000).

Taking It Further

Flynn, Maureen. "Mimesis of the Last Judgment: The Spanish *Auto de fe*," *Sixteenth Century Journal* 22 (1991): 281–297. The best analysis of the religious significance of the auto-da-fé.

Flynn, Maureen. "The Spectacle of Suffering in Spanish Streets," in Barbara A. Hanawalt and Kathryn L. Reyerson, eds., *City and Spectacle in Medieval Europe*. 1994. In this fascinating article Flynn analyzes the spiritual value of physical pain.

The moral status of marriage also changed during this period. Protestants no longer considered husbands and wives as morally inferior to celibate monks and nuns, and the wives of preachers in Protestant communities certainly had a respected social role never granted to the concubines of priests. But the favorable Protestant attitude toward marriage did not necessarily translate into a positive attitude toward women. In Germany the numerous books of advice, called the Father of the House literature, encouraged families to subordinate the individual interests of servants, children, and the mother to the dictates of the father, who was encouraged to be just but who must be obeyed. Even if a wife was brutally treated by her husband, she could neither find help from authorities nor expect a divorce.

Children: Naturally Evil?

Beginning in the fifteenth century, the middle classes began to adopt a new attitude toward children, placing greater emphasis on their welfare, education, and moral upbringing. The Reformation contributed to this process by emphasizing the family's responsibility for their children's moral guidance and religious education. One of the obligations of Protestant fathers was to read and teach the Bible in the home. This directive may have been more a theoretical ideal than a practical reality, but the rise in literacy among both boys and girls in Protestant countries attests to the increased importance of education.

Discipline also played a large role in the sixteenth-century family. Parents had always demonstrated love toward their children by indulging them with sweets and toys and protecting them from danger. But during the sixteenth century some authors of advice books and many preachers began to emphasize that parental love must be tempered by strict discipline. In effect, the clergy attempted to impose their own authoritarian impulses on the emotional lives of the family. The Protestant emphasis on the majesty of God and a belief in original sin translated into a negative view of human nature. Calvinist theologians who held such a view placed a special emphasis on family discipline. The *Disquisition on the Spiritual Condition of Infants* (1618) pointed out that from a theological point of view, babies were naturally evil. The godly responsibility of the father was to break the will of his evil offspring, taming them so that they could be turned away from sin toward virtue. The very title of a 1591 Calvinist treatise revealed the strength of the evil-child argument: *On Disciplining Children: How the Disobedient, Evil, and Corrupted Youth of These Anxious Last Days Can Be Bettered.* The treatise also advised that the mother's role should be limited to her biological function of giving birth. It directed fathers to be vigilant so that their wives did not corrupt the children, because women "love to accept strange, false beliefs, and go about with benedictions and witches' handiwork. When they are not firm in faith and the Devil comes to tempt them . . . they follow him and go about with supernatural fantasies."[1]

In order to break the will of their infants, mothers were encouraged to wean them early and turn them over for a strict upbringing by their fathers. The ideal father was to cultivate both love and fear in his children by remaining unemotional and firm. He was to be vigilant to prevent masturbation, to discourage frivolity, and to toughen little children by not allowing them to eat too much, sleep too long, or stay too comfortably warm. Although discouraged from being unnecessarily brutal, the godly father was never to spare the rod on either his children or his wife.

It is clear that disciplining children was an important theoretical guideline in sixteenth- and seventeenth-century Europe. It is less clear whether this was as true in practice as in theory. Historians disagree on the issue. It is likely that then, as now, there were many different ways of raising children, and each family exhibited its own emotional chemistry. And it is also likely that sixteenth-century parents did not consider firm discipline as unloving.

DISCIPLINING CHILDREN AND ENCOURAGING INFORMANTS

During the sixteenth and seventeenth centuries, schools began to rely on the monitor system for enforcing discipline among the pupils. The goal of the system was to control every moment of the students' lives, but it was impossible for school masters to achieve such regimentation by themselves, so they relied on student observers and informants. Youngsters were obliged to report any fellow student who spoke in the vernacular rather than Latin, lied, cursed, acted indecently, stayed in bed in the morning, talked in church, or missed prayers. The following account comes from a self-described "good pupil" at Cordier's College in Geneva.

We dined in the room, sitting quietly and making no murmur or noise; I gently reproved those whom I heard laughing foolishly or speaking in vain or frolicking; I told the observer about those who paid no attention to my warning so that he should take note of them . . . The master walked up and down the middle of the room, holding a book and frequently telling the observer to take note of those who played the fool . . . While we were finishing dinner, the last bell was rung, each of us picked up his books, and we went into the common room, the register of each class was read out according to custom, those who were present answered to their name, I answered too, and the absentees were recorded on the nomenclators' registers.

Source: From Philippe Ariès, *Centuries of Childhood: A Social History of Family Life,* translated by Robert Baldick, New York: Vintage Books, 1962.

The Ideal Family
During the late sixteenth century, idealized depictions of harmonious family life became very popular. This etching, which was sold in multiple copies at modest prices much as a wall poster would be today, depicts a prosperous peasant family.

SUPPRESSING POPULAR CULTURE

The family was not the only institution that sixteenth-century educated reformers sought to discipline. Their efforts also targeted many manifestations of traditional popular culture. The reformers or puritans, as they came to be called in England, wanted to purify society, to remake it into a "godly community" by imposing a rigid moral regimen, particularly on undisciplined youths and members of the lower classes. The suppression of popular culture had two aspects. One was a policing effort, aimed at ridding society of presumably un-Christian practices. The other was a missionary enterprise, an attempt to bring the Protestant and Catholic Reformations to the people through instruction and popular preaching.

Overall the godly reformers sought to encourage an ethic of asceticism, which valued thrift, modesty, chastity, and above all self-control. This ethic was neither Protestant nor Catholic but was promoted by clerics of all religious confessions. The traditional popular culture they so despised stressed other values such as spontaneity, emotional freedom, and generosity.

Once the reformers had cleaned up the churches by eliminating idolatry, unnecessary holidays, and superfluous rituals, they turned to the secular world, and they found much to criticize. The reformers saw impiety in comedians, dancing, loud music, rough sports, dice and card games, public drinking, dressing up in costumes, puppets, and above all actors. The Bishop of Verona condemned preachers who told stories that made the congregations laugh. To the reformers, these things were despicable because they seemed to be vestiges of pre-Christian practices and because they led people into sin.

The festival of Carnival° came under particularly virulent attack. The most popular annual festival, also known as Mardi Gras, Carnival took place for several days or even weeks before the beginning of Lent and included all kinds of fun and games—silly pantomimes, bear baiting, bullfights, masquerades, dances, lots of eating and drinking, and illicit sex. The *Discourse Against Carnival* (1607) complained about the temptations to sin and the money wasted in Carnival play. Catholics attempted to reform Carnival by eliminating the most offensive forms of behavior, especially those that led to violence or vice. Other popular festivals and entertainments suffered a similar fate of scornful criticism, regulation, or even abolition.

Pieter Brueghel the Elder's painting *The Battle Between Carnival and Lent* (1559) illustrates the role of festivals in the popular culture. In the painting, a fat man riding on a wine barrel engages in a mock joust with an emaciated, stooped figure of uncertain gender who rides a wheeled cart pulled by a monk and nun. The two figures represent two festival seasons. The fat man represents Carnival, a time of joyous, gluttonous, drunken feasting; the lean one represents Lent, a period of sexual abstinence and fasting that precedes Easter. The figures might also represent the passionate side of popular culture that was devoted to bodily pleasure (Carnival) and the clerical urge to suppress bodily desires and reform popular festivities (Lent).

What Catholics reformed, Protestants abolished. Martin Luther had been relatively tolerant of popular culture, but later reformers were not. The most famous German Carnival, the *Schembartlauf* of Nuremberg, was abolished; in England the great medieval pageants of York, Coventry, Chester, Norwich, and Worcester disappeared; in Calvinist Holland, the Christmas tradition of giving children gifts was strongly denounced.

The Carnival festival was highly resilient, however. Along with many other forms of popular culture, it persisted, even

The Battle Between Carnival and Lent

In this allegory, the festive season of Carnival is represented by a fat man riding a wine barrel. He is engaged in a mock joust with an emaciated figure representing Lent, the season for fasting. Behind Carnival, people engage in games, drinking, dancing, and flirtations. Behind Lent, a procession of the pious leads back into a church.

if less openly public. The moralist attack on popular culture meant that some activities retreated from outside to inside—into sports arenas, taverns, theaters, and opera houses. And some were professionalized by athletes, entertainers, actors, and singers. The attempts of dour clerics to abolish fun also provoked open resistance. In 1539 in Nuremberg the Lutheran pastor Andreas Osiander, who had preached against Carnival, found himself lampooned by a float in the shape of a ship of fools, in which he was depicted as the captain.

The attempts to suppress popular culture produced a confrontation between the educated elites of Europe and the workers, peasants, servants, and artisans who surrounded them and served them. Although not entirely successful, by the late sixteenth century the suppression had the effect of broadening the cultural gap between the educated few and the masses. Practices that previously had been broadly accepted forms of public entertainment, in which even members of the clergy participated, came to be seen as unworthy of educated people.

Hunting Witches

The most catastrophic manifestation of the widespread anxiety of the late sixteenth and seventeenth centuries was the great witch-hunt°. The judicial prosecution of alleged witches in either church or secular courts dramatically increased about the middle of the sixteenth century and lasted until the late seventeenth, when the number of witchcraft trials rapidly diminished and stopped entirely in western Europe.

Throughout this period, people accepted the reality of two kinds of magic°. The first kind was natural magic, such as the practice of alchemy or astrology, which involved the manipulation of occult forces believed to exist in nature.

The fundamental assumption of natural magic was that everything in nature is alive. The trained magician could coerce the occult forces in nature to do his bidding. During the Renaissance many humanists and scientific thinkers were drawn to natural magic because of its promise of power over nature. Natural magic, in fact, had some practical uses. Alchemists, for example, devoted themselves to discovering what they called the "philosopher's stone," the secret of transmuting base metals into gold. In practice this meant that they learned how to imitate the appearance of gold, a very useful skill for counterfeiting coins or reducing the content of precious metals in legal coins. Natural magic was practiced by educated men and involved the human manipulation of the occult, but it did not imply any kind of contact with devils. Most practitioners of natural magic desired to achieve good, and many considered it the highest form of curative medicine.

People of the sixteenth and seventeenth centuries also believed in a second kind of magic—demonic magic. The practitioner of this kind of magic—usually but not always a female witch—called upon evil spirits to gain access to power. Demonic magic was generally understood as a way to work harm by ritual means. Belief in the reality of harmful magic and of witches had been widespread for centuries, and there had been occasional witch trials throughout the Middle Ages. Systematic witch-hunts, however, began only when ecclesiastical and secular authorities showed a willingness to employ the law to discover and punish accused witches. The Reformation controversies of the late sixteenth century and the authorities' willingness to discipline deviants of all sorts certainly intensified the hunt for witches. Thousands of people were accused of and tried for practicing witchcraft. About half of these alleged witches were executed, most often by burning. Cases of alleged witchcraft rarely occurred in a steady flow, as one would find for other crimes. Typically, witchcraft trials took place during localized hunts when a flareup of paranoia and torture multiplied allegations against vulnerable members of the community. Most allegations were against women, in particular young unmarried women and older widows, but men and even young children could be accused of witchcraft as well.

People in many different places—from shepherds in the mountains of Switzerland to Calvinist ministers in the lowlands of Scotland—thought they perceived the work of witches in human and natural events. The alleged demonic magic of witchcraft appeared in two forms: *maleficia* (doing harm) and *diabolism* (worshipping the devil). The rituals of *maleficia* consisted of a simple sign or a complex incantation, but what made them *maleficia* was the belief that the person who performed them intended to cause harm to someone or something. There were many kinds of *maleficia,* including coercing an unwilling lover by sprinkling dried menstrual blood in his food, sickening a pig by

HOW WOMEN CAME TO BE ACCUSED OF WITCHCRAFT: A WITCH'S CONFESSION

Walpurga Hausmännin, an elderly widow and midwife from a small town near Augsburg in the Holy Roman Empire, was accused in 1587 of killing more than forty children. Her confession, extracted out of her through fear and torture, is tragic but typical, complete with lurid details of sexual intercourse with the Devil, the Devil's mark, a pact with the Devil, and riding on a broomstick to a witches' sabbath. This excerpt from her confession, which lists some of her alleged victims, illustrates how the collective fears of the community were channeled into imagined crimes against children.

[The Devil] also compelled her to do away with and to kill young infants at birth, even before they had been taken to Holy Baptism. This she did, whenever possible. These as follows:

1 and 2. About ten years ago, she had rubbed Anna Hämännin, who dwelt far from Dursteigel, with her salve on the occasion of her first childbirth and also otherwise damaged her so that mother and child remained together and died.

3. Dorothea, the stepdaughter of Christian Wachter, bore her first child ten years before; at its birth she made press on its little brain so that it died. The Devil had specially bidden her destroy the first-born.

5. When, four years ago, the organist's wife was awaiting her confinement, she touched her naked body with her salve whereby the child promptly died and came stillborn.

8. Three years ago when she was called to a mill to the miller's wife there she had let the child fall into the water and drown.

11. When six years ago, she partook of food with Magdalena Seilerin, called *Kammerschreiberin* (wife of the chamber scribe), she had put a salve in her drink, so that she was delivered prematurely. This child she, Walpurga, secretly buried under the doorway of the said wife of the scribe on the pretext that then she would have no other miscarriage. The same she also did with many others. When she was questioned under torture for the reasons of this burial, she admitted that it was done in order to cause disunion between two spouses. This her Devil-Paramour had taught her.

15. She had also rubbed a salve on a beautiful son of the late Chancellor, Jacob by name: this child had lovely fair hair and she had given him a hobby-horse so that he might ride on it till he lost his senses. He died likewise.

Source: From G. T. Matthews, ed., *News and Rumor in Renaissance Europe: The Fugger Newsletters,* 1959.

cursing it, burning a barn by marking it with a hex sign, bringing wasting diarrhea to a child by reciting a spell, and killing an enemy by stabbing a wax statue of him. Midwives and women who specialized in healing were especially vulnerable to accusations of witchcraft. The intention behind a particular action they might have performed was often obscure, making it difficult to distinguish between magic designed to bring beneficial results, such as the cure of a child, and *maleficia* designed to bring harmful ones. With the high infant mortality rates of the sixteenth and seventeenth centuries, performing magical rituals for a sick baby could be very risky. The logic of witchcraft beliefs implied that a bad ending must have been caused by bad intentions.

While some people may have attempted to practice *maleficia,* the second and far more serious kind of ritual practice associated with demonic magic, *diabolism,* almost certainly never took place. Diabolism was a fantasy that helped explain events that could not otherwise be explained. The theory behind diabolism asserted that the witch had sold her soul to the Devil, whom she worshipped as her god. These witches had made a pact with the Devil, worshiped the Devil in the ritual of the witches' sabbath, flew around at night, and sometimes changed themselves into animals. The two core beliefs of the pact with the Devil and the witches' sabbath created the intellectual and legal conditions for the great witch-hunt of the sixteenth and seventeenth centuries.

A pact with the devil was believed to give the witch the ability to accomplish *maleficia,* in exchange for which she was obliged to serve and worship Satan. The most influential witchcraft treatise, *The Hammer of Witches* (1486), had an extensive discussion of the ceremony of the pact. After the prospective witch had declared her intention to enter his service, Satan appeared to her, often in the alluring form of a handsome young man who offered her rewards, including a demonic lover, called an *incubus.* To obtain these inducements, the witch was obligated to renounce her allegiance to Christ, usually signified by stomping on the cross. The Devil rebaptized her in a disgusting substance, guaranteeing that her soul belonged to him. To signify that she was one of his own, the Devil marked her body in a hidden place, creating a sign, which could easily be confused with a birthmark or blemish. To an inquisitor or judge almost any mark on the skin might confirm guilt.

One of the fullest accounts of beliefs in the witches' sabbath comes from the tragic trial of the Pappenheimer family in Bavaria in 1600. The Pappenheimers, consisting of a mother, a father, and their sons, were vagrants arrested for killing babies and cutting off their hands for the purposes of witchcraft. In her confession under torture, Anna Pappenheimer gave a full account of her participation in a fantastic witches' sabbath that supposedly took place at night on a hill outside of the village of Tettenwang. She claimed that witches arrived from near and far flying in

The Witches' Sabbath

The myth of the witches' sabbath depicted witches paying homage to an enthroned Satan. The typical sabbath motifs included the ability to fly and cannibalism of Christian babies, as shown on the lower right. The figures walking on their hands reveal a world literally turned upside down.

Burning of Witches at Dernberg in 1555
One of the witches is being taken away by a flying demon to whom she had sold her soul.

on broomsticks and pitchforks. The assembled company largely consisted of women, young and old and most of them naked, but there were a few male witches (known as warlocks) and even some children. With a clap of thunder and a profusion of smoke, Satan himself suddenly appeared with his eyes glowing, dressed in black and smelling horribly. The assembled witches and warlocks bowed low before him, praying in a travesty of the Lord's Prayer, "Our Satan which art in Hell. . . ." There followed an infernal banquet of disgusting foods, including horse meat, ravens, crows, toads, frogs, and boiled and roasted infants. After the feast, an orchestra of demons played tuneless, screeching dance music that aroused a mad lust in the witches and their demon lovers, who began a wild spinning dance that finally broke down into a indiscriminate orgy. The family and some other drifters were grotesquely tortured and burned alive.

Between about 1550 and 1650, some 100,000 people in Europe were tried for witchcraft. About 50,000 of these were executed. Approximately half of the trials were in the German-speaking lands of the Holy Roman Empire. Prosecutions were also extensive in Switzerland, France, Scotland, Poland, Hungary, Transylvania, and Russia. Some 10,000 people were tried in Spain and Italy, but these were mostly for minor offenses of *maleficia,* and very few people were executed, probably none in Italy. As the product of collective beliefs and collective paranoia, witchcraft beliefs could be applied to all kinds of people, but allegations were most commonly lodged against poor, older women in small rural villages. In most of Europe, about 80 percent of the witches were female, but in Essex County, England, and Basel, Switzerland, more than 90 percent were female. In Russia and Estonia, however, men made up the majority of witches. These differences in the gender of alleged witches illustrate how the witchcraft myth was adapted to local conditions and assumptions about who was dangerous in society.

The Confessional States

The Religious Peace of Augsburg of 1555 provided the model for a solution to the religious divisions produced by the Reformation. According to the principle of *cuius regio, eius religio* (he who rules determines the religion of the land), each prince in the Holy Roman Empire determined the religion to be followed by his subjects, and those who disagreed were obliged to emigrate elsewhere. Certainly, forced exile was economically and personally traumatic for those who emigrated, but it preserved what was almost universally believed to be the fundamental principle of successful rulership—one king, one faith, one law. In other words, each state should have only one church. Except in the notoriously weak states of eastern Europe and a few small troubled ones in Germany, hardly anyone thought it desirable to allow more than one confession in the same state.

The problem with this political theory of religious unity, of course, was the reality of religious divisions created by the Reformation. In some places there were as many as three active confessions—Catholic, Lutheran, and Calvinist—in addition to the minor sects, such as the Anabaptists and the Jewish communities. The alternative to religious unity would have been religious toleration, but hardly anyone in a position of authority was willing to advocate that. Calvin had expelled advocates of religious toleration, and Luther had been aggressively hostile to those who disagreed with him on seemingly minor theological points. After 1542 with the establishment of the Universal Inquisition, the Catholic Church was committed to exposing and punishing anyone who professed a different faith with the exception of Jews in Italy who were under papal protection. Geneva and Rome became competing propaganda centers, each spewing out a

PLACES OF ENCOUNTER

Catholic and Protestant Churches

The distinction between Catholic and Protestant was clearly evident in the appearance of churches. Two fundamental assumptions governed what Catholics considered appropriate for a church. The first was the presence of relics on or beneath altars. A relic was the physical remains of a saint, usually the saint to whom the church was dedicated, or some object associated with the saint, and Catholics believed one of the purposes of a church was to house these sacred objects. As a result, Catholic churches tended to have many altars, each housing relics, because the more relics a church possessed the greater the presence of the sacred in it. The second assumption was that the more magnificent and beautiful the physical appearance of the church, the greater the honor offered to God. Relics were usually kept in reliquaries, boxes made of silver or gold and sometimes decorated with jewels. Altars were built of rare marbles, surrounded by rich brocades, covered by embroidered white lace altar cloths, and bedecked with enormous silver candelabra. Above the altars were paintings and sculptures, the more beautiful the better, because the mean, ugly, and cheap were considered an insult to God.

A Calvinist Church
Bare walls and clear glass windows characterized a Calvinist church. At the head of the congregation is a simple communion table, a lectern holding the Bible, and a raised pulpit for preaching.

A Catholic Church
A Catholic church is resplendent with marble, statues, and relics.

photo to come .509

In contrast, Protestant churches reflected a sense of cautious reserve and unease about material display. The vast majority of Protestant churches had once been Catholic. During the course of the sixteenth century they had to be converted to conform to Protestant sensibilities by stripping them of unnecessary vanities. Down came the statues and paintings, many of which were destroyed. The rich furnishings of silver and gold reliquaries were sold to provide alms for the poor. The walls of the churches were denuded

A Protestant Preacher Protestant preaching was always from the Bible. Both preacher and congregation followed the passage that was read from the scripture. Women, especially, found this helpful because it included them. Sermons were long—notice the hour-glass.

Separate Sides A blind man points to the separated sides of the Church, so bitterly divided in the sixteenth century. Attempts to unite the divided Church are known as "ecumenical movements," but none of the major divisions, despite far greater understanding, has yet been healed.

Catholic Preaching Catholic preaching in the years before the Reformation took place only on certain days. It was moralistic and wide-ranging, and could therefore move far from the text of the Bible. The preacher here is shown without a Bible before him. Preaching was not the high point of the service.

Plain and Simple Protestant ministers dress simply in a black gown and their pulpits are plain; there is no ornament to distract the congregation from the uplifting Word of God.

Teaching Children All Christians saw the importance of teaching children. In the Protestant tradition, schools, and in the eighteenth century, Sunday schools, were seen as an invitation to teach children the basic truth of Scripture.

Decoration in Devotion to God The decorated pulpit and the robes of the Catholic priest are aspects of the visual nature of Catholic devotion. The rest of the church would also have been decorated, and stained-glass windows may have shown stories from the Bible. Devotion was made tangible by the prayer beads used by the congregation, who are not necessarily listening to the sermon. "Telling the beads" is the practice of saying the sequence of prayers known as the rosary.

Two Kinds of Preaching
This German woodcut highlights the differences between Catholic and Protestant preaching. In Germany, the Bible, crudely set in wood type, was available by the end of the fifteenth century. It is arguable that this breakthrough in information technology was responsible for making the sixteenth-century Reformation possible.

of decorations. In Holland the walls were usually whitewashed, creating a visual impression of stark simplicity. In place of images, scriptural verses were sometimes painted on the bare walls. Altar screens were ripped out, and altars were turned around so that ministers would face the congregation. The focus of attention shifted from the altar to the pulpit from which the minister would preach the Word of God. The aim of the architecture in Protestant churches changed dramatically—from creating visual impressions that stimulated piety and honored God to facilitating the ability of the congregation to hear the preacher.

In both the Catholic and the Protestant worlds, the church was understood as the house of God. The difference, however, was in the kind of furnishings and the kind of behavior God found appropriate in His house. For the Catholic, the house was a place full of holy things and of reminders of the presence of the divine in the world, a place for touching and making physical demonstrations of pious emotions. For the Protestant, the house was an extension of the community, a place in which the holy might be found not within a material object but within oneself or perhaps within a neighbor.

For Discussion

Imagine a Catholic and a Protestant child living in the sixteenth century. How would their different experiences of being in a church and encountering God influence the understanding these children developed of their faith and confessional identity?

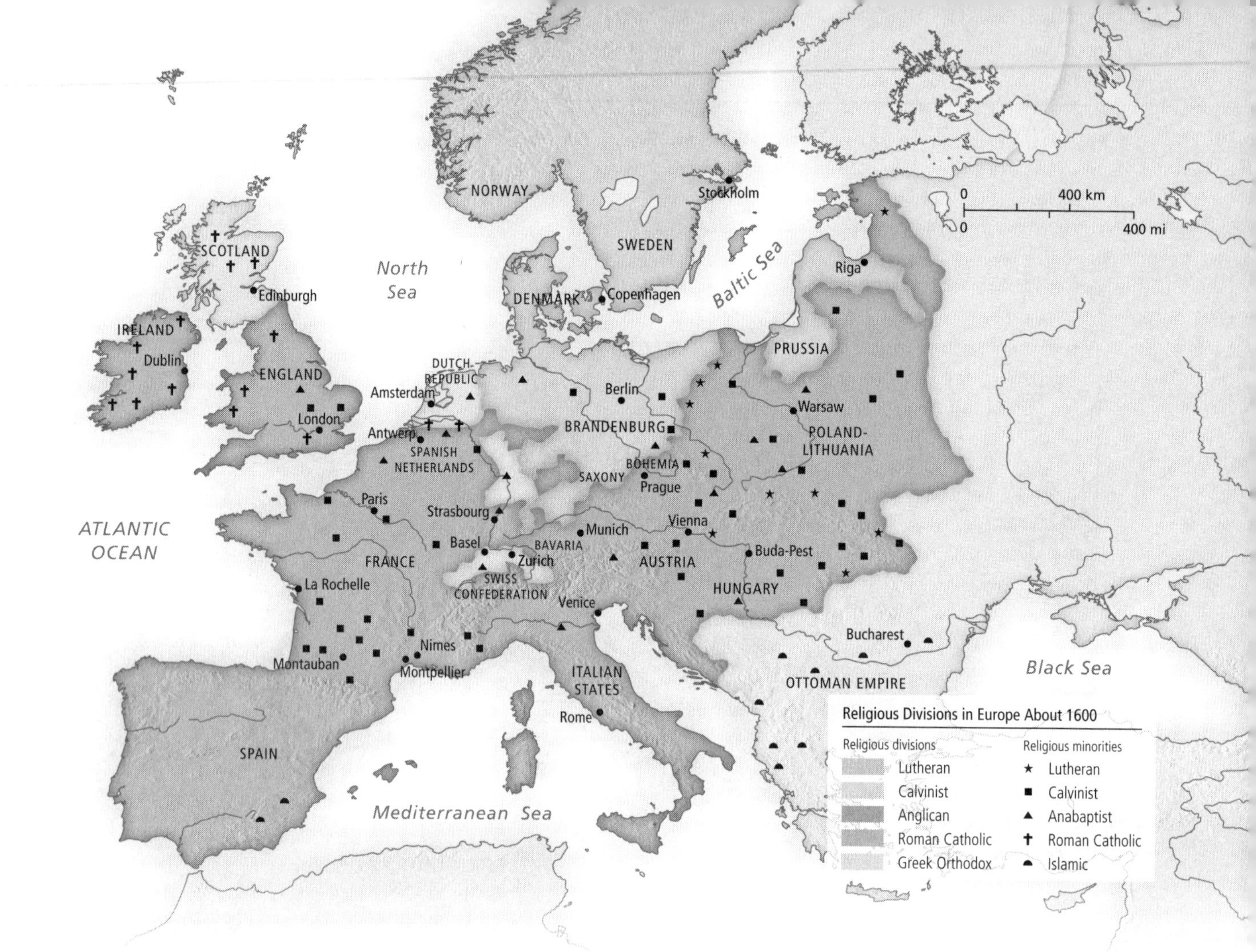

Map 14.2 Religious Divisions in Europe About 1600

After 1555 the religious borders of Europe became relatively fixed, with only minor changes in confessional affiliations to this day.

flood of polemical tracts and specially trained missionaries willing to risk their lives by going behind the enemy lines to console their co-religionists and evangelize for converts.

Wherever there were significant religious minorities within a state, the best that could be hoped for was a condition of anxious tension, omnipresent suspicion, and periodic hysteria (see Map 14.2). The worst possibility was civil war. Between 1560 and 1648 several religious civil wars broke out, including the French Wars of Religion, the Dutch revolt against Spain, the Thirty Years' War in Germany, and the English Civil War. (The latter two will be discussed in Chapter 15.)

During the late sixteenth century a new word appeared to describe a personality type that may not have been entirely new but was certainly much more common—the fanatic°. Originally referring to someone possessed by a demon, a fanatic came to mean a person who expressed immoderate enthusiasm in religious matters, a person who pursued a supposedly divine mission, often to violent ends. Fanatics from all sides of the religious divide initiated waves of political assassinations and engaged in grotesque massacres of their opponents. François Guion, the assassin of William the Silent, whose story began this chapter, was in many ways typical of fanatics in his steadfast pursuit of his victim and his willingness to masquerade for years under a false identity. During the sixteenth and seventeenth centuries, no religious community had a monopoly on fanatics. They presented themselves as serving the pope as well as the Protestant churches.

The sharp confessional divisions that produced fanatics and assassins also stimulated writers, poets, and dramatists to examine the human condition. Perhaps no period in the history of the West produced so many great works of literature as the late sixteenth and early seventeenth centuries.

The French Wars of Religion

When King Henry II (r. 1547–1559) of France died unexpectedly from a jousting accident, he left behind his widow, the formidable Catherine de' Medici (1519–1589), and a brood of young children—including his heir, Francis II

(r. 1559–1560), who was only 15. Henry II had been a peacemaker. He succeeded in keeping France from civil war by carefully pacifying the quarrelsome nobles of the realm, and at the Peace of Cateau-Cambrésis (1559) he finally brought an end to more than sixty years of war with Spain. In contrast, Catherine and her children, including three sons who successively ascended to the throne, utterly failed to keep the peace, and for some forty years France was torn apart by a series of desperate civil wars.

The Huguenots: The French Calvinist Community

By 1560 Calvinism had made significant inroads into predominantly Catholic France. Pastors sent from Geneva had been especially successful in the larger provincial towns, where their evangelical message appealed to enterprising merchants, professionals, and skilled artisans. Some 10 percent of the population had become Calvinists, or Huguenots° as French Protestants were called. The political strength of the Huguenots was greater than their numbers might indicate, because between one-third and one-half of the lower nobility professed Calvinism. Calvinism was popular among the French nobility for two reasons. One was patronage. The financial well-being of any noble depended on his patron, an aristocrat of higher rank who had access to the king and who could distribute jobs and lands to his clients. When a high aristocrat converted to Protestantism, he tended to bring his noble clientele into the new faith as well. As a result of a few aristocratic conversions in southwest France, Calvinism spread through "a veritable religious spider's web,"[2] as one contemporary put it.

Even more important than networks of male clientele was the influence of aristocratic women. The sister of King Francis I (r. 1515–1547), Marguerite of Angoulême (1492–1549), married the King of Navarre and created a haven in Navarre for Huguenot preachers and theologians. Her example drew other aristocratic ladies to the Huguenot cause, and many of the Huguenot leaders during the French Wars of Religion were the sons and grandsons of these early female converts. Marguerite's daughter, Jeanne d'Albret, sponsored Calvinist preachers for several years before she publicly announced her own conversion in 1560, and her son, Henry Bourbon, became the principal leader of the Huguenot cause during the French Wars of Religion° and the person responsible for eventually bringing the wars to an end.

The Origins of the Religious Wars

Like all civil wars, the French Wars of Religion exhibited a bewildering pattern of intrigue, betrayal, and treachery. Three distinct groups constituted the principal players. The first group was the royal family, consisting of Queen Catherine de' Medici and her four sons by Henry II—King Francis II (r. 1559–1560), King Charles IX (r. 1560–1574), King Henry III (r. 1574–1589), and Duke Francis of Alençon (1554–1584)—and her daughter, Marguerite Valois (1553–1615). The royal family remained Catholic but on occasion reconciled themselves with the Huguenot opposition, and Marguerite married into it. The second group was the Huguenot faction of nobles led by the Châtillon family and the Bourbon family who ruled Navarre. The third group was the hard-line Catholic faction led by the implacable Guise family. These three groups vied for supremacy during the successive reigns of Catherine de' Medici's three sons, none of whom proved to be effective monarchs.

During the reign of the sickly and immature Francis II, the Catholic Guise family dominated the government and raised the persecution of the Huguenots to a new level. In response to that persecution, a group of Protestant nobles plotted in 1560 against the Guises, and some Calvinist ministers provided scriptural justifications for vengeance against tyrants. The Guises got wind of a conspiracy to kill them and surprised the plotters as they arrived in small groups at the royal chateau of Amboise. Some were ambushed, some drowned in the Loire River, some hanged from the balconies of the chateau's courtyard. A tense two years later in 1562, the Duke of Guise was passing through the village of Vassy just as a large congregation of Protestants was holding services in a barn. The duke's men attacked the worshipers, killing some 740 of them and wounding hundreds of others.

Following the massacre at Vassy, civil war broke out in earnest. For nearly forty years a series of religious wars sapped the strength of France. Most of the battles were indecisive, which meant neither side sustained military superiority for long. Both sides relied for support on their regional bases: The Protestant strength was in the southwest, the Catholic in Paris and the north. Besides military engagements, the French Wars of Religion were characterized by political assassinations and massacres.

Massacre of St. Bartholomew's Day

After a decade of bloody yet inconclusive combat, the royal family tried to resolve the conflict by making peace with the Protestants, a shift of policy signified by the announcement of the engagement of Marguerite Valois, daughter of Henry II and Catherine de' Medici, to Henry Bourbon, the son of the Huguenot King of Navarre. At age 19, Marguerite—or Queen Margot, as she was known—was already renowned for her brilliant intelligence. But she was renowned also for her wanton morals, and to complicate the situation further, on the eve of the wedding she was having an affair with another Henry, the young new Duke of Guise who was the leader of the intransigent Catholic faction. The marriage between Marguerite and Henry of Navarre was to take place in Paris in August 1572, an event that brought all the Huguenot leaders to the heavily armed

Catholic capital for the first time in many years. The gathering of all their enemies in one place presented too great a temptation for the Guises who hatched a plot to assassinate the Huguenot leaders. Perhaps because she had become jealous of the Huguenots' growing influence on her son, King Charles IX, the mercurial Catherine suddenly switched sides and became implicated in the plot.

Catherine somehow convinced the weak-willed king to order the massacre of the Huguenot nobles gathered in Paris. On August 14, 1572, St. Bartholomew's Day, the people of Paris began a slaughter. Some 3,000 to 4,000 Huguenots were butchered in Paris and over 20,000 more were put to death throughout the rest of France. Henry of Navarre saved his life by pretending to convert to Catholicism, while most of his companions were murdered.

After the Massacre of St. Bartholomew's Day, both sides tried to interpret the events to their own advantage. Catholics celebrated. The pope marked the occasion by having a medal struck and frescoes painted in the Vatican. King Philip II of Spain wrote that the massacre "was indeed of such value and prudence and of such service, glory, and honor to God and universal benefit to all Christendom that to hear of it was for me the best and most cheerful news which at present could come to me."[3] For Catholics the massacre was a great service to God. Protestants had a very different reaction, and presented it as a great affront to God.

Catherine's attempted solution for the Huguenot problem failed to solve anything, however. Henry of Navarre escaped his virtual imprisonment in the royal household, set Marguerite up in an isolated castle, returned to Navarre and his faith, and reinvigorated Huguenot resistance. Two Huguenot political thinkers laid out a theory justifying political revolution, François Hotman in *Francogallia* (1573) and Théodore de Bèze in *Right of Magistrates* (1579). They argued that since the authority of all magistrates, including even low-ranking nobles, came directly from God, the Huguenot nobles had the right and obligation to resist a tyrannical Catholic king. During the same period, Catholic moderates known as the *politiques* rejected the excesses of the Guises and argued for an accommodation with the Huguenots.

The wars of religion continued until the assassination of King Henry III, brother of the late Charles IX. Both Charles and Henry had been childless, a situation that made Henry Bourbon of Navarre the rightful heir to the throne, even though he was a Huguenot. Henry Bourbon became King Henry IV (r. 1589–1610) and recognized that predominantly Catholic France would never accept a Huguenot king, and so in 1593 with his famous quip, "Paris is worth a mass," Henry reconverted to the ancient faith, and most opposition to him among Catholics collapsed. Once he returned to Catholicism he managed to have the pope annul his childless marriage to Marguerite so that he could marry Marie de' Medici and obtain her huge dowry. Affable, funny, generous, and exceedingly tolerant, "Henry the Great" became the most popular king in French history, reuniting the war-torn country by ruling with a very firm hand. With the Edict of Nantes° of 1598, he allowed the Huguenots to build a quasi-state within the state, giving them the right to have their own troops, church organization, and political autonomy within their walled towns, but they were banned from the royal court and the city of Paris.

Henry encouraged economic development under his minister the Duke of Sully, who retired the crushing state debt and built up a fiscal surplus by reforming finances and eliminating corruption. Henry declared that his ambition was for even the poorest peasant to be able to afford a chicken in his pot every Sunday, and even though he did not achieve this laudatory goal, his public works included

THE ST. BARTHOLOMEW'S DAY MASSACRE: THE POLITICS OF MEMORY

The Duke of Sully (1560–1641) became an ambassador and finance minister for French King Henry IV and was the principal architect of the Edict of Nantes, which provided a measure of religious toleration for Protestants in France after 1589. During the St. Bartholomew's Day Massacre he was 12 years old, but he never forgot what he witnessed. Sully was one of the few members of Henry of Navarre's personal entourage to survive the massacre.

Intending on that day to wait upon the king my master [Henry of Navarre, later King Henry IV of France], I went to bed early on the preceding evening; about three in the morning I was awakened by the cries of people, and; the alarm-bells, which were everywhere ringing. . . . I was determined to escape to the College de Bourgogne, and to effect this I put on my scholar's gown, and taking a book under my arm, I set out. In the streets I met three parties of the Life-guards; the first of these, after handling me very roughly, seized my book, and, most fortunately for me, seeing it was a Roman Catholic prayer-book, suffered me to proceed, and this served me as a passport with the two other parties. As I went along I saw the houses broken open and plundered, and men, women, and children butchered, while a constant cry was kept up of, "Kill! Kill! O you Huguenots! O you Huguenots!" This made me very impatient to gain the college, where, through God's assistance, I at length arrived, without suffering any other injury than a most dreadful fright.

Source: From "The Saint Bartholomew's Day Massacre" in Bayle St. John, ed., *Memoirs of the Duke of Sully, Vol. 1* (London: George Bell and Sons, 1877).

King Henry IV of France

This portrait of Henry "The Great" on horseback was painted in 1594 shortly after his conversion to Catholicism. The equestrian portrait recalled Henry's military victories.

the beautification of Paris and an impressive canal system to facilitate transportation.

Despite his enormous popularity, Henry too fell victim to fanaticism. After surviving eighteen attempts on his life, the king was fatally stabbed by a Catholic fanatic, who took advantage of the opportunity presented when the royal coach unexpectedly stopped behind a cart loading hay. Unlike the aftermath of the St. Bartholomew's Day massacre, Catholics all over France mourned Henry's death and considered the assassin mad. Henry's brilliant conciliatory nature and the horrors of the religious wars had tempered public opinion.

PHILIP II, THE KING OF PAPER

France's greatest rivals were the Habsburgs, who had regularly helped finance the Catholic cause during the French Wars of Religion. During the late sixteenth century, Habsburg Spain took advantage of French weakness to establish itself as the dominant power in Europe. When Emperor Charles V abdicated his thrones in 1556, the Habsburg possessions in Germany and the throne of the Holy Roman Empire went to his brother, Ferdinand I, and the balance of his vast domain to his son, Philip II (r. 1556–1598). Philip's inheritance included Milan, Naples, Sicily, the Netherlands, scattered outposts on the north coast of Africa, colonies in the Caribbean, Central America, Mexico, Peru, the Philippines, and most important of all, Spain. In 1580 he also inherited Portugal and its far-flung overseas empire, which included a line of trading posts from West Africa to the Spice Islands and the vast colony of unexplored Brazil.

CHRONOLOGY

The French Wars of Religion

1559	Peace of Cateau-Cambrésis between France and Spain
1560	Protestant Conspiracy of Amboise
1572	Massacre of St. Bartholomew's Day
1573	François Hotman publishes *Francogallia*
1579	Théodore de Bèze publishes *Right of Magistrates*
1593	King Henry IV of France converts to Catholicism
1598	Edict of Nantes granting Protestants religious toleration

Ruling over these enormous territories was a gargantuan task that Philip undertook with obsessive seriousness. From the rambling palace of El Escorial, which was also a mausoleum for his father and a monastery, Philip lived in semimonastic seclusion and ruled as the "King of Paper," an office-bound bureaucrat rather than the rule-from-the-saddle warrior his father had been and many of his contemporary monarchs remained. Philip kept himself to a rigid daily work discipline that included endless committee meetings and long hours devoted to poring over as many as 400 documents a day, which he annotated extensively in his crabbed hand. Because of his inability to delegate authority and his immersion in minutiae, Philip tended to lose his grasp of the larger picture, especially the shaky finances of Spain.

This grave, distrustful, rigid man saw himself as the great protector of the Catholic cause and committed Spain to perpetual hostility toward Muslims and Protestants. On the Muslim front he first bullied the Moriscos, the descendants of the Spanish Muslims. The Moriscos had received Christian baptism, but they were suspected of secretly practicing Islam, and in 1568 Philip issued an edict that banned all manifestations of Muslim culture and ordered the Moriscos to turn over their children to Christian priests to educate. The outraged Moriscos of Granada rebelled but were defeated with vicious cruelty. At first dispersed throughout Spain, the surviving Moriscos were eventually expelled from the country in 1609. Philip hardened his policy toward the Moriscos because he feared, not unreasonably, that they would become secret agents on Spanish soil for his great Mediterranean rivals, the Ottoman Turks. To counter the Turkish threat, Philip maintained expensive fortresses on the North African coast. In 1571 he joined the Venetians and the pope to check Turkish advances after the Ottomans captured Cyprus, Venice's richest colony. The Christian victory at Lepanto in the Gulf of Corinth, which destroyed more than one-third of the enemy's fleet, was heralded as one of the greatest events of the sixteenth century, proving that the Turks could be beaten. Lepanto renewed the crusading spirit in the Catholic world. Although the victory at Lepanto was a valuable propaganda tool, it had slight military significance because the Turks quickly rebuilt their fleet and forced Venice to cede Cyprus to them. The island remains divided between Christian and Turkish populations to this day.

Philip once said he would rather lose all his possessions and die a hundred times than be the king of heretics. His attitude toward Protestants showed that he meant what he said. Through his marriage to Queen Mary I of England (r. 1553–1558), Philip encouraged her persecutions of Protestants, but they got their revenge. After Mary's death her half-sister, Queen Elizabeth I, refused his marriage proposal and in 1577 signed a treaty to assist the Protestant Netherlands, which was in rebellion against Spain. To add insult to injury, the English privateer Sir Francis Drake (ca. 1540–1596) conducted a personal war against Catholic Spain by raiding the Spanish convoys bringing silver from the New World. In 1587 Drake's embarrassing successes culminated with a daring raid on the great Spanish port city of Cadiz where, "singeing the king of Spain's beard" he destroyed the anchored Spanish fleet and many thousands of tons of vital supplies. Philip retaliated by building a huge fleet of 132 ships armed with 3,165 cannons, which sailed from Portugal to rendezvous with the Spanish army stationed in the Netherlands and launch an invasion of England in 1588. As the Invincible Armada, as it was called, passed through the English Channel, it was met by a much smaller English fleet, assembled out of merchant ships refit for battle. Unable to maneuver as effectively as the English in the fluky winds of the channel and mauled by the rapid-firing English guns, the Spanish Armada° suffered heavy losses and was forced to retreat to the north, where it sustained further losses in storms off the coast of Scotland and Ireland. Barely more than half of the fleet finally straggled home. The Spanish quickly replaced the lost ships, but Philip's sense of invincibility was severely shaken.

The reign of Philip II illustrated better than any other the contradictions and tensions of the era. No monarch had at his grasp as many resources and territories as Philip, and yet defending them proved extremely costly. The creaky governmental machinery of Spain put a tremendous burden on a conscientious king such as Philip, but even his unflagging energy and dedication to his duties could not prevent military defeat and financial disaster. Economic historians remember Philip's reign for its series of state bankruptcies and for the loss of the Netherlands, the most precious jewel in the crown of Spain.

THE DUTCH REVOLT

The Netherlands boasted some of Europe's richest cities, situated amid a vast network of lakes, rivers, channels, estuaries, and tidal basins that periodically replenished

CHRONOLOGY

Spain and the Netherlands

1548	Annexation of the northern provinces of the Netherlands to the Spanish crown
1568	Edict against Morisco culture
1571	Christian victory over Ottoman Turks at Lepanto
1580	King Philip II inherits Portugal and the Portuguese Empire
1581	Seven northern provinces of the Netherlands declare independence from Spain
1584	Assassination of William the Silent
1588	Defeat of the Spanish Armada
1609	Expulsion of the Moriscos from Spain
1648	Treaty of Westphalia recognizes independence of the Netherlands

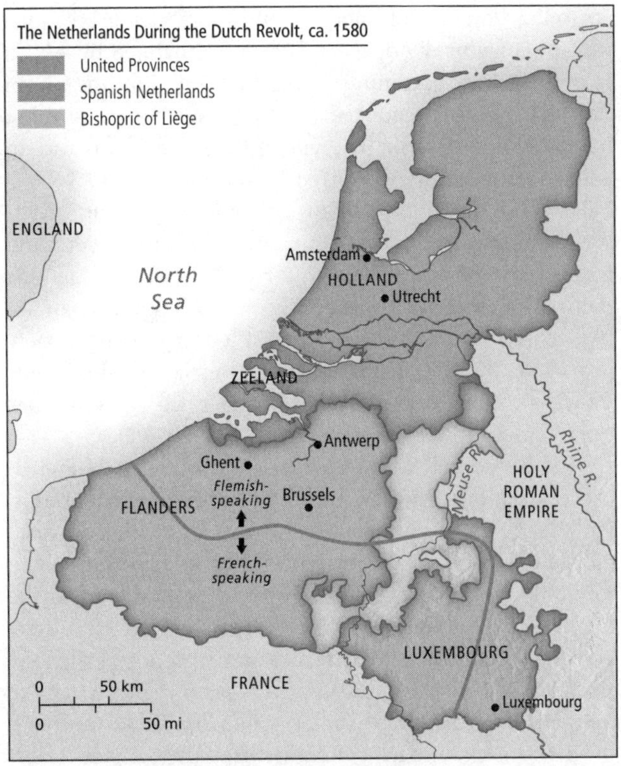

Map 14.3 The Netherlands During the Dutch Revolt, ca. 1580

During the late sixteenth century the northern United Provinces separated from the Spanish Netherlands. The independence of the United Provinces was not recognized by the other European powers until 1648.

the exceptionally productive soil through flooding. The Netherlands consisted of seventeen provinces, each with its own distinctive identity, traditions, and even language. The southern provinces were primarily French-speaking; those in the north spoke a bewildering variety of Flemish dialects. In 1548 Emperor Charles V annexed the northern provinces that had been part of the Holy Roman Empire to the southern provinces he had inherited from his father. His decision meant that when his son, Philip II, became king of Spain, all of the Netherlands was included with the Spanish crown. With his characteristic bureaucratic mentality, Philip treated Dutch affairs as a management problem rather than a political sore spot, an attitude that subordinated the Netherlands to Spanish interests. Foreign rule irritated the Dutch, who had long enjoyed ancient privileges including the right to raise their own taxes and muster their own troops.

Consolidating the Netherlands under the Spanish crown deprived the Dutch princes of the right to chose the official religion of their lands, a right they would have enjoyed had the provinces remained in the Holy Roman Empire where the Religious Peace of Augsburg granted princes religious freedom. Philip's harsh attitude toward Protestants upset the delicate balance among Catholic, Lutheran, Calvinist, and Anabaptist communities. Huguenot refugees from the French Wars of Religion heightened the anti-Catholic fanaticism of the local Calvinists, who in 1566 occupied many Catholic churches and destroyed paintings and statues.

In response to the rapidly deteriorating situation in the Netherlands, Philip issued edicts against the heretics and strengthened the Spanish Inquisition. The Inquisition in Spain was an arm of the monarchy charged with ensuring religious conformity among the extremely diverse cultures of the Iberian peninsula. The Spanish Inquisition had been preoccupied with investigating the Christian sincerity of former Jews, who after the expulsions of 1492 had converted to Christianity in order to stay in Spain. When introduced in the Netherlands, the Inquisition became an investigating agency devoted to finding, interrogating, and, if necessary, punishing Protestants. Philip also dispatched 20,000 Spanish troops under the command of the Duke of Alba (1508–1582), a veteran of the Turkish campaigns in North Africa and victories over the Lutheran princes of Germany. Alba directly attacked the Protestants. He personally presided over the military court, the Council of Troubles, which became so notoriously tyrannical that the people called it the Council of Blood. As an example to others, he systematically razed several small villages where there had been incidents of desecrating Catholic images, slaughtering every inhabitant. Alba himself boasted that during the campaign against the rebels, he had some 18,000 people executed, in addition to those who died in battle or were massacred by soldiers. The Prince of Orange, William the Silent (1533–1584), accompanied into exile some 60,000 refugees, who constituted about 2 percent of the population. While abroad William began to organize resistance to Alba.

Alba's cruelty backfired by steeling Protestant opposition to the Spanish. Alba also lost support among otherwise loyal Catholics when he attempted to introduce a 10 percent tax on trade. His policies a failure, Alba was recalled to Spain in 1573. Meanwhile the sea-beggars, as the Dutch Calvinist privateers were called, had begun to achieve some success against the Spanish. Within a few short years, William the Silent seized permanent control of the provinces of Holland and Zealand, which were then flooded by Calvinist refugees from the southern provinces. After Alba's departure, no one kept control of the unpaid Spanish soldiers, who in mutinous rage turned against cities loyal to Spain, including Brussels, Ghent, and most savagely Antwerp, the rich center of trade. Antwerp lost 7,000 citizens and one-third of its houses to the "Spanish fury," which permanently destroyed its prosperity. Alba's replacement, the shrewd statesman and general, the Duke of Parma (r. 1578–1592), ultimately subdued the southern provinces, which remained a Spanish colony. The seven northern provinces, however, united in 1579 and declared independence from Spain in 1581 (see Map 14.3). William the Silent became the *stadholder* (governor) of the new

United Provinces, and after his assassination his 17-year-old son, Maurice of Nassau, inherited the same title.

The Netherlands' struggle for independence transformed the population of the northern provinces from mixed religions to staunch Calvinism. The Dutch Revolt° became ensnared in the French Wars of Religion through Huguenot refugees, and the alliance with England, which provided much needed financial and moral support, reinforced the Protestant identity of the Dutch. The international Protestant alliance created by the Dutch Revolt and centered in the Netherlands withstood both Philip's fury and Parma's calm generalship. The failure of the Spanish Armada to land Parma's men in England guaranteed the survival of an independent Netherlands. The Dutch carried on a sporadic and inconclusive war against Spain until the end of the Thirty Years' War in 1648, when the international community recognized the independent Republic of the United Provinces.

LITERATURE IN THE AGE OF CONFESSIONAL DIVISION

Churches and monarchs everywhere demanded religious conformity in word and deed, a situation that would seem to stifle creativity, and yet the late sixteenth and early seventeenth centuries was one of the most remarkable periods in the history of creative literature. During this period the native or vernacular languages of western Europe became literary languages, replacing Latin as the dominant form of expression, even for the educated elite. Italian was the first vernacular to be prized for its literary qualities and considered a worthy alternative to Latin. The availability of cheap printed books and the Bible reading encouraged by the Protestant Reformation stimulated literature in other vernacular languages so that by the late sixteenth century great literary figures were writing in French, Portuguese, Spanish, and English.

French Literature During the Religious Turmoil

In France royal decrees in 1520 and 1539 substituted French for Latin in official legal and government documents. A century later with the founding of the Académie Française, it became government policy to promote, protect, and refine the French language. The greatest masters of French prose during this crucial period were François Rabelais (ca. 1483–1553) and Michel de Montaigne (1533–1592). Trained as a lawyer, Rabelais became a friar and priest but left the Church under a cloud of heresy to become a physician. Rabelais's satirical masterpiece, a series of novels recounting the fantastic and grotesque adventures of Gargantua and Pantagruel, combined an encyclopedic command of humanist thought with stunning verbal invention that has had a lasting influence on humorous writers to this day. One of Rabelais's most remarkable creations was the imaginary Abbey of Thélème, inhabited by a kind of antimonastic community of monks and nuns for whom "all their life was regulated not by laws, statutes, or rules, but according to their free will and pleasure." This was an abbey for hedonists who lived by the motto, "DO WHAT YOU WILL, because people who are free, well-born, well-bred, and easy in honest company have a natural spur and instinct which drives them to virtuous deeds and deflects them from vice."[4] Rabelais's optimistic vision of human nature represented a startling contrast to the growing anxiety provoked by the religious controversies of his time. Rabelais's controversial work was banned, and he was briefly forced into exile.

It is ironic that Montaigne became a master of French prose. His mother was a Catholic of Spanish-Jewish origins, and the young Michel spoke only Latin for the first six years of his life because his German tutor knew no French. After a modestly successful legal career, Montaigne retired to the family chateau to discover himself by writing essays, a literary form well suited to reflective introspection. In his essays, Montaigne struggled with his lasting grief over the premature death from dysentery of a close friend, reflected on his own experience of the intense physical pain of illness, and diagnosed the absurd causes of the French Wars of Religion. Montaigne's essays are a profound series of meditations on the meaning of life and death, presented in a calm voice of reason to an age of violent fanaticism. In one essay, for example, he exposed the presumption of human beings: "The most vulnerable and frail of all creatures is man, and at the same time the most arrogant." Montaigne thought it presumptuous that human beings picked themselves out as God's favorite creatures. How did they know they were superior to other animals? "When I play with my cat, who knows if I am not a pastime to her more than she is to me?"[5] His own skepticism about religion insulated him from the sometimes violent passions of his era.

Stirrings of the Golden Age in Iberia

The literary tradition in the Iberian peninsula differed from that of other regions in Europe in that Iberia is a polyglot region in which several languages are spoken—Basque, Galician, Portuguese, Castilian, and Catalan. The greatest lyric poet of the peninsula, Luís Vaz de Camões (1524–1580), lost an eye in battle and was sent to the Portuguese East Indies after he killed a royal official in a street brawl. When he returned years later, he completed his epic poem, *The Lusiads* (1572), which became the national poem of Portugal by celebrating Vasco da Gama's discovery of the sea route to India. This great work was modeled on the ancient epics, especially the *Aeneid,* the greatest Latin epic of ancient Rome, and even included the gods of Olympus as commentators on the human events of Camões's time. In the opening lines, Jupiter spoke of contemporary Portugal:

Eternal dwellers in the starry heavens, you will not have forgotten the great valor of that brave people the Portuguese. You cannot therefore be unaware that it is the fixed resolve of destiny that before their achievements those of Assyrians, Persians, Greeks and Romans shall fade into oblivion. Already with negligible forces—you were witnesses—they have expelled the Moslem, for all his strength and numbers . . .; while against the redoubtable Castilians they have invariably had heaven on their side. Always, in a word, they have known victory in battle and have reaped, with its trophies, fame and glory too.[6]

By connecting Portugal directly to the glories of the ancient empires, Camões managed to elevate the adventures of his fellow Portuguese in Asia to an important moment in the history of the world.

Because Spain was unified around the crown of Castile, the Castilian language became the language we now call Spanish. The period when Spain was the dominant power in Europe coincided with the Golden Age of Spanish literature. The greatest literary figure was Miguel de Cervantes Saavedra (1547–1616), an impoverished son of an unsuccessful doctor with little formal education. Like Camões, Cervantes survived many adventures, losing the use of his left hand at the naval battle of Lepanto and spending five years languishing in a Turkish prison after he was captured by Algerian pirates. In order to survive, the disabled veteran was forced to write plays for the Madrid theater and to work as a tax collector, but he was still imprisoned several times for debts. Desperate to make money, Cervantes published a serial novel in installments between 1605 and 1615. It became the greatest masterpiece in Spanish literature, *Don Quixote.*

The prototype of the modern novel form, *Don Quixote* was a satire of chivalric romances. Cervantes presented reality on two levels, the "poetic truth" of the master and dreamer Don Quixote and the "historic truth" of his squire and realist Sancho Panza. Don Quixote's imagination persistently ran away with him as he tilted at windmills, believing they were fierce dragons. It remained to Sancho Panza to point out the unheroic truth. Cervantes pursued the interaction between these two incongruous views of truth as a philosophical commentary on existence. For Cervantes there was no single, objective truth, only psychological truths revealed through the interaction of the characters, an idea that contrasted with the notion of dogmatic religious truth that dominated the time. Despite the extensive popularity of *Don Quixote,* Cervantes died a pauper, buried in an unmarked grave in Madrid.

The Elizabethan Renaissance

During the reign of Elizabeth I (r. 1558–1603), the Renaissance truly arrived in England. The daughter of Henry VIII and Anne Boleyn, Elizabeth faced terrible insecurity as a girl. Her father had her mother beheaded, she was declared illegitimate, and her sister Mary imprisoned her for treason in the Tower of London. After she ascended to the throne in 1558, however, she proved to be a brilliant leader. She prevented the kind of religious civil wars that broke out in France by establishing a moderate form of Protestantism as the official religion. She presided over the beginnings of England's rise as a major European power. Perhaps most remarkably, she became the patron and inspiration for England's greatest age of literature. Never mar-

Queen Elizabeth I of England

Elizabeth presided over the greatest age of English literature.

ried, Elizabeth used her eligibility for marriage as a lure in diplomacy, and even though she may have had real lovers, she addressed her subjects as if they were her only love. Her "golden speech" delivered before a divided House of Commons in 1601 exemplifies her ability to inspire exuberant loyalty:

> *Though God hath raised me high, yet this I account the glory of my crown, that I have reigned with your loves. . . . It is not my desire to live or reign longer than my life and reign shall be for your good. And though you have had, and may have, many mightier and wiser princes sitting in this seat, yet you never had, nor shall have any that will love you better.*[7]

Among Elizabeth's courtiers were major literary figures, including the adventurer-poet Sir Walter Raleigh (ca. 1552–1618), the soldier-poet Sir Philip Sidney (1554–1586), and Edmund Spenser (ca. 1552–1599), whose great poem *The Faerie Queen* was a personal tribute to Elizabeth.

The principal figure of the Elizabethan Renaissance, however, was not a courtier but a professional dramatist, William Shakespeare (1564–1616). In a series of theaters, including the famous Globe on the south side of the Thames in London, Shakespeare wrote, produced, and acted in comedies, tragedies, and history plays. Shakespeare's enormous output of plays, some of which made veiled allusions to the politics of Elizabeth's court, established him not only as the most popular dramatist of his time but the greatest literary figure in the English language. The power of his plays derives from the subtle understanding of human psychology found in his characters and the stunning force of his language. For Shakespeare, as for Montaigne, the source of true knowledge was self-knowledge. One character advises,

> *Neither a borrower nor a lender be,*
> *For loan oft loses both itself and friend*
> *And borrowing dulls the edge of husbandry.*
> *This above all: To thine own self be true,*
> *And it must follow, as the night the day,*
> *Thou canst not then be false to any man.*
> (Hamlet *I, iii, 75–80)*

Unlike most contemporary authors, Shakespeare wrote for a broad audience of paying theatergoers that included common workers as well as highly educated members of Elizabeth's court. This need to appeal to a large audience who gave instant feedback helped him hone his skills as a dramatist.

Some of these literary figures found their works banned, as did Rabelais. Some had political or personal troubles with their monarch, as did Montaigne, Camões, Raleigh, and Sidney. But the controversies of the day seemed to have stimulated rather than inhibited these writers. Political and religious turmoil led them to ask penetrating questions about the meaning of life and to rise above the petty squabbles that preoccupied so many of their contemporaries.

States and Confessions in Eastern Europe

In contrast to the confessional states of western Europe, eastern Europe during the early sixteenth century escaped the religious controversies that linked religious conformity to political loyalty. Bohemia and Poland, in particular, allowed levels of religious diversity unheard of in the West. During the last decades of the sixteenth and early seventeenth centuries, however, dynastic troubles compromised the relative openness of the eastern states, enmeshing them in conflicts among themselves that had an increasingly strong religious dimension. In Germany and central Europe, the weakness of the mad Emperor Rudolf permitted religious conflicts to fester, setting the stage for the disastrous Thirty Years' War (1618–1648) that pitted Catholic against Protestant.

Around the Baltic Sea, rivalries among Lutheran Sweden, Catholic Poland-Lithuania, and Orthodox Russia created a state of almost permanent war in a tense standoff among three very different political and religious states. The enormous confederation of Poland-Lithuania struggled to sustain the most decentralized, religiously diverse state anywhere in Europe. By the end of the century, it remained politically decentralized but had become an active theater of the Counter Reformation where dynastic policy firmly supported Catholicism. Russia began to strengthen itself from obscurity under the authoritarian rule of the tsars, who began to transform it into a major European power.

THE DREAM WORLD OF EMPEROR RUDOLF

In Goethe's *Faust,* set in sixteenth-century Germany, drinkers in a tavern sing:

> *The dear old Holy Roman Empire,*
> *How does it hang together?*[8]

Good question. How did this peculiarly decentralized state—neither Holy, nor Roman, nor an empire—hang together? In the late sixteenth century the empire consisted of the following components: 1 emperor; 7 electors, comprising 4 secular princes and 3 archbishops; 50 other bishops and archbishops; 21 dukes, margraves, and landgraves; 88 independent abbots and assorted prelates of the Church; 178 counts and other sovereign lords; about 80 free imperial cities; and hundreds of free imperial knights. The emperor presided over all, and the Imperial Diet served as a parliament, but the Holy Roman Empire was, in fact, a very loose confederation of semi-independent, mostly German states, many of which ignored imperial decrees that did not suit them. During the first half of the sixteenth century the empire faced a number of challenges—the turmoil within the empire presented by Martin

Luther, endless French enmity on the western borders, and the tenacious Ottoman threat on the eastern frontier. Only the universal vision and firm hand of Emperor Charles V kept the empire together. The universal vision and firm hand disappeared in the succeeding generations of emperors, to be replaced by petty dynastic squabbles and infirm minds.

The crippling weakness of the imperial system became most evident during the reign of Rudolf II (r. 1576–1612). The Habsburg line had a strain of insanity going back to Joanna "The Mad," the mother of Emperors Charles V (r. 1519–1558) and Ferdinand I (r. 1558–1564), who happened to be Rudolf's two grandfathers, giving him a double dose of Habsburg genes. Soon after his election to the imperial throne, Rudolf moved his court from bustling Vienna to the lovely quiet of Prague in Bohemia. Fearful of noisy crowds and impatient courtiers, standoffish toward foreign ambassadors who presented him with difficult decisions, paranoid about scheming relatives, and prone to wild emotional gyrations from deep depression to manic grandiosity, Rudolf was hardly suited for the imperial throne. In fact, many contemporaries, who had their own reasons to underrate him, described him as hopelessly insane. Rudolf certainly suffered from moments of profound melancholy and irrational fears that may have had genetic or organic causes, but he was probably unhinged by the conundrum of being the emperor, a position that trapped him between the glorious universal imperial ideal and the ignoble reality of unscrupulous relatives and petty rivalries.

Rudolf was not the only sixteenth-century prince in the Holy Roman Empire driven to distraction by the pressures of court life. At least twenty German princes and princesses were confined or deposed due to symptoms of serious mental disorder. Certainly inbreeding within a small pool of princely families contributed to the patterns of madness, but the most unhealthy emotional pressure was produced by the code of manners required of all courtiers, most particularly princes and princesses. This strictly-maintained code demanded the repression of all spontaneous feelings, a repression that resulted in a prevailing sense of shame. When religious rigidity and extreme political conflict were mixed into this volatile psychological concoction, it is not surprising that some personalities shattered. Since the entire political system depended on the prince's guidance, a mad prince could seriously disrupt an entire society.

Incapable of governing, Rudolf did not abandon the imperial ideal of universality, he just transmuted it into a strange dream world. In Prague he gathered around him a brilliant court of humanists, musicians, painters, physicians, astronomers, astrologers, alchemists, and magicians. These included an eclectic assortment of significant thinkers—the great astronomers Tycho Brahe and Johannes Kepler, the notorious occult philosopher Giordano Bruno, the theoretical mathematician and astrologer John Dee, and the remarkable inventor of surrealist painting Giuseppe Arcimboldo. As Chapter 16 will explain, many of these figures are considered the immediate forerunners of the Scientific Revolution. But Rudolf also fell prey to fast-talking charlatans, including the illusionist and opera-set designer Cornelius Drebber, who claimed to have invented a perpetual-motion machine. This weird court, however, was less the strange fruit of the emperor's hopeless dementia than the manifestation of a striving for universal empire. Rudolf sought to preserve the cultural and political unity of the empire, to eradicate religious divisions, and to achieve peace at home. Rudolf's court in Prague was perhaps the only place left during the late sixteenth century where Protestants, Catholics, Jews, and even radical heretics such as Bruno could gather together in a common intellectual enterprise, the goal of which was to discover the universal principles that governed nature, principles that would provide the foundations for a single unifying religion and a cure for all human maladies. It was a noble, if utterly improbable, dream.

While Rudolf and his favorite courtiers isolated themselves in their dream world, the religious conflicts within the empire reached a boiling point. Without a strong emperor, the Imperial Diets were paralyzed by confessional squabbles. In 1607 in the imperial free city of Donauworth in south Germany, a conflict between the Lutheran town council and the substantial Catholic minority gave the Catholic Duke of Bavaria the excuse to annex the city to his own territories. Despite the illegality of the duke's action, Rudolf passively acquiesced, causing fear among German Protestants that the principles of the Religious Peace of Augsburg of 1555 might be ignored. In the following decade, more than 200 religious revolts or riots took place. In 1609 the insane Duke John William of Jülich-Cleves died without a direct heir, and the most suitable claimants to the Catholic duchy were two Lutheran princes. Were one of them to succeed to the dukedom, the balance between Catholics and Protestants in Germany would have been seriously disrupted. Religious tensions boiled over. As Chapter 15 will describe, in less than a decade the empire began to dissolve in what became the Thirty Years' War.

The Renaissance of Poland-Lithuania

During the late sixteenth and early seventeenth centuries, Poland-Lithuania experienced a remarkable cultural and political renaissance. It was inspired by influences from Renaissance Italy linked to strong commercial and diplomatic ties to the Republic of Venice and intellectual connections with the University of Padua. As the major power in eastern Europe, Poland-Lithuania engaged in a tug-of-war with Sweden over control of the eastern Baltic and virtually constant warfare against the expansionist ambitions of Russia (see Map 14.4). The most remarkable achievement of Poland-Lithuania during this contentious time was its unparalleled and still controversial experiments in government. Poland-Lithuania had an elected king but called itself a republic. The king was a figurehead, and Poland-Lithuania was a republic in the sense that it was effectively governed by assemblies of nobles.

Very loosely joined since 1336, Poland and Lithuania legally merged in 1569, creating a confederation in which Poland supplied the king, but the Grand Duchy of Lithuania was considered an equal partner and allowed to retain its own laws, administration, and army. The novel feature of the confederation was how the nobles reserved power for themselves through their control of regional assemblies, which in turn dominated the central diet. These nobles elected the king and treated him, at best, as a hired manager. They resisted all attempts to exert royal power by asserting the legal right to form local armed confederations against the king and by exercising the principle of unanimity in the diet, which prevented the king or a strong faction from dominating affairs. In the last half of the seventeenth century Poland-Lithuania fell into chaos under this system, but for nearly three-quarters of a century it worked well enough—at least for the nobles.

The rule of the nobles in Poland-Lithuania came at a great cost to the Polish peasants, however, who were ruthlessly forced into serfdom and deprived of their legal rights. Peasants were prohibited from leaving the land without permission from their landlords, and they were denied the ability to appeal the legal judgments of their local lords. In this regard, Poland-Lithuania moved in the opposite direction from western European states, which at this time were extending the right of judicial appeal and allowing serfdom to fade away. Moreover, the Polish kings could not stop the gradual erosion of their authority so that Poland-Lithuania, the greatest power in the East, enfeebled itself through the

Map 14.4 Poland-Lithuania and Russia

These countries were the largest in Europe in the size of their territories but were relatively underpopulated compared to the western European states.

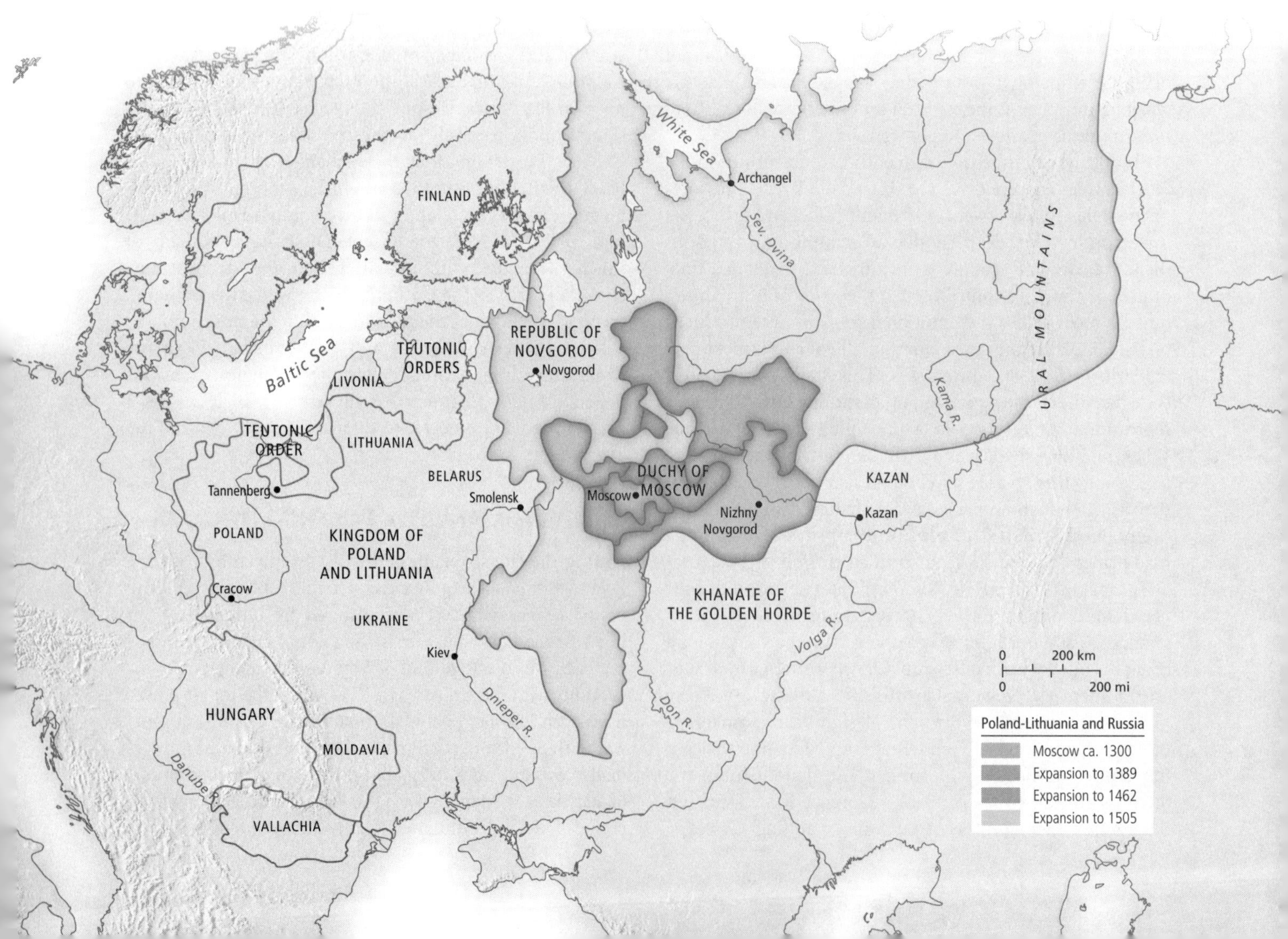

grasping hands of a notoriously self-interested and proud nobility.

Poland-Lithuania contained an incomparable religious mixture of Roman Catholics, Lutherans, Calvinists, Russian Orthodox, Anabaptists, Unitarians, and Jews, but these communities were strongly divided along geographic and class lines. Lutheranism was a phenomenon of the German-speaking towns, the peasants of Poland remained Catholic, those in Lithuania were Orthodox, and many of the nobles were attracted to Calvinism. During the late sixteenth century, however, Christians in Poland almost completely returned or converted to the Roman Catholic faith. The key to the transformation was the changing attitude of the Polish nobles, who had tolerated religious diversity because they believed that religious liberty was the cornerstone of political liberty. The return to Catholicism owed a great deal to Stanislas Hosius (1504–1579), who had studied in Italy before he returned to Poland to become successively a diplomat, bishop, and cardinal. Imbued with the zeal of the Italian Catholic Reformation, Hosius invited the Society of Jesus into Poland and worked closely with the papal *nuncios* (the diplomatic representatives of the pope), who organized a campaign to combat all forms of Protestantism. Between 1565 and 1586, forty-four young Polish nobles studied at the Jesuit college in Rome and when they returned took up the most influential church and government offices in Poland. Jesuit colleges sprouted up in many Polish towns, attracting the brightest sons of the nobility and urban bourgeoisie. A close alliance between the kings of Poland and the Jesuits enhanced the social prestige of Catholicism.

The cultural appeal of all things Italian helped lure the Polish nobility back to Catholicism. Through the spread of elite education, Catholicism returned to Poland largely through persuasion rather than coercion. But the transformation did not occur without violent repercussions. Lutheran, Calvinist, and Bohemian Brethren churches were burned. In Cracow armed confrontations between Protestant and Catholic militants led to casualties. However, Poland did not degenerate into civil war, as did France or the Netherlands over much the same issues. As the monarchy progressively weakened, the Catholic Church became the only solid institutional pillar of Polish national identity and Polish culture.

The Troubled Legacy of Ivan the Terrible

While Poland experimented with a decentralized confederation dominated by nobles that severely restricted the king's initiative, Russia evolved in the opposite direction. During the late fifteenth and sixteenth centuries, the grand dukes of Moscow who became the tsars of Russia eclipsed the authority of the great landed nobles and snuffed out the independence of the towns. The authoritarian tendencies of the tsars harmed the Russian peasants, however, just as royal weakness harmed the Polish peasants. After 1454 Moscow's creation of military fiefs (*pomestye*) to supply soldiers against the Tartars (Mongol tribes) allowed the nobles to push the peasants back into serfdom. Refusing to accept enserfment, the peasants fled the fields in massive numbers, depopulating central Russia as they found refuge among the Cossack colonies along the borders to the southeast.

Russia was already well-integrated into the European diplomatic community and engaged in trade with its Western neighbors. But for more than 300 years Russia had been under the "Tartar Yoke," a term describing the Mongolian tribes that overran the country, pillaging and depopulating it. Ivan III, "The Great" (1462–1505), succeeded in gradually throwing off the Tartar Yoke by refusing to continue to pay tribute to the Mongols. Ivan married Zoë, the niece of the last Greek emperor of Constantinople. The marriage gave him the basis for claiming that the Russian rulers were the heirs of Byzantium and the exclusive protectors of Orthodox Christianity, the state religion of Russia. Following the Byzantine tradition of imperial autocracy, Ivan practiced Byzantine court ceremonies, and his advisers developed the theory of the Three Romes. According to this theory, the authority of the ancient Roman Empire had passed first to the Byzantine Empire, which God had punished with the Turkish conquest, and then to Moscow as the third and last "Rome." Ivan celebrated this theory by assuming the title of tsar (or "Caesar"). With his wife's assistance, he hired Italian architects to rebuild the grand ducal palace, the Kremlin. Ivan captured the vast northern territories of the city-state of Novgorod, expanding the Russian state north to the White Sea and east to the Urals. Ivan's invasion of parts of Lithuania embroiled Russia in a protracted conflict with Poland that lasted more than a century. Like his fellow monarchs in western Europe, Ivan began to bring the aristocrats under control by incorporating them into the bureaucracy of the state.

CHRONOLOGY

States and Confessions in Eastern Europe

1480	Grand Duke and later Tsar Ivan III, "The Great," of Russia refuses to pay tribute to Tartars
1569	Merging of Poland and Lithuania
1606	Emperor Rudolf declared incapable of ruling by his family
1604–1613	Time of Troubles in Russia
1613	Michael Romanov elected Tsar of Russia

Ivan III's grandson, Ivan IV, "The Terrible" (1533–1584), succeeded his father at age 3 and became the object of innumerable plots, attempted coups, and power struggles among his mother, uncles, and the boyars (the upper-level nobles who dominated Russian society). The trauma of his childhood years and a painful disease of the spine made him inordinately suspicious and prone to acts of impulsive violence. When at age 17 Ivan was crowned, he reduced the power of the dukes and the boyars by forcing them to exchange their hereditary estates for lands that obligated them to serve the tsar in war. In weakening the boyars, Ivan gained considerable support among the common people and was even remembered in popular songs as the people's tsar. Nevertheless, Ivan distrusted everyone. He often arrested people on charges of treason, just for taking a trip abroad. In a cruel revenge on his enemies among the boyars, he began a reign of terror in which he personally committed horrendous atrocities. His massacre in 1570 of the inhabitants of Novgorod, whom he suspected of harboring Polish sympathies, contributed to his reputation as a bloody tyrant. By setting aside half of the realm as his personal domain, he created a strong financial base for the army, which led to military successes in the prolonged wars against Poland, Lithuania, and Sweden. During his reign, however, the Polish threat and boyar opposition to his rule revealed signs of the fragility of Russian unity.

During the "Time of Troubles°" (1604–1613), Russia fell into chaos. Boyar families struggled among themselves for supremacy, the Cossacks from the south led a popular revolt, and Poles and Swedes openly interfered in Russian affairs. Finally, the Time of Troubles ended when in 1613 the national assembly elected Tsar Michael Romanov, whose descendants ruled Russia until they were deposed in 1917. During the seventeenth century the Romanovs gradually restored order to Russia, eroded the independence of local governments, and strengthened the institution of serfdom. By the end of the seventeenth century Russia was strong enough to reenter European affairs as a major power.

CONCLUSION

The Divisions of the West

During the late sixteenth and early seventeenth centuries, hidden demographic and economic pressures eroded the confidence and security of many Europeans, creating a widespread sense of unease. Most people retreated like confused soldiers behind the barricades of a rigid confessional faith, which provided reassurance that was unavailable elsewhere. To compensate for the absence of predictability in daily life, societies everywhere imposed strict discipline—discipline of women, children, the poor, criminals, and alleged witches. The frenzy for social discipline displaced the fear of those things that could not be controlled onto the most easily controllable people, especially the weak, the subordinate, and those perceived to be different.

The union between religion and political authority in the confessional states bolstered official religious faith with the threat of legal or military coercion. Where different religious confessions persisted within one state—most notably France and the Netherlands—the result was riots, assassinations, and civil war. The West had become divided along religious lines in two ways. The first kind of division was within countries with religiously mixed populations, where distinctive religious communities competed for political power and influence. In these countries religion became the cornerstone to justify patriotism or rebellion, loyalty or disloyalty to the monarch. The second kind of division was international. The confessional states formed alliances, crafted foreign policies, and went to war, with religion determining friend and foe. The West split into religiously driven national camps. Over the subsequent centuries, religious differences mutated into ideological differences, but the sense that alliances among states should be linked together by a common set of beliefs has persisted to this day as a legacy from the sixteenth century.

During the period of the middle seventeenth to eighteenth centuries, confessional identity and the fear of religious turmoil led monarchs throughout Europe to build absolutist regimes, which attempted to enforce stability through a strengthened, centralized state. The principles of religious toleration and the separation of church and state were still far in the future. They were made possible only as a consequence of the hard lessons learned from the historical turmoil of the late sixteenth and seventeenth centuries.

Suggestions for Further Reading

For a comprehensive list of suggested readings, please go to www.ablongman.com/levack/chapter14

Anderson, M. S. *The Origins of the Modern European State System, 1494–1618.* 1998. The best short study for students new to the subject of the evolution of the confessional states in Europe. This book is very good at establishing common patterns among the various states.

Burke, Peter. *Popular Culture in Early Modern Europe.* 1994. This wide-ranging book includes considerable material from eastern Europe and Scandinavia, as well as the more extensively studied western European countries. Extraordinarily influential, it practically invented the subject of popular culture by showing how much could be learned from studying festivals and games.

Davies, Norman. *God's Playground: A History of Poland,* rev. ed., 2 vols. 1982. By far the most comprehensive study of Polish history, this is particularly strong for the sixteenth and seventeenth centuries. Davies offers a Polish-centered view of European history that is marvelously stimulating even if he sometimes overstates his case for the importance of Poland.

Dukes, Paul. *A History of Russia: Medieval, Modern, Contemporary, ca. 882–1996,* 3rd ed. 1998. A comprehensive survey that synthesizes the most recent research.

Dunn, Richard S. *The Age of Religious Wars, 1559–1715,* 2nd ed. 1980. An excellent survey for students new to the subject.

Evans, R. J. W. *Rudolf II and His World: A Study in Intellectual History, 1576–1612.* 1973. A sympathetic examination of the intellectual world Rudolf created. Evans recognizes Rudolf's mental problems but lessens their significance for understanding the period.

Holt, Mack P. *The French Wars of Religion, 1562–1629.* 1996. A lucid short synthesis of the events and complex issues raised by these wars.

Hsia, R. Po-chia. *Social Discipline in the Reformation: Central Europe 1550–1750.* 1989. An excellent, lucid, and short overview of the attempts to discipline the people in Germany.

Huppert, George. *After the Black Death: A Social History of Early Modern Europe.* 1986. Engaging, entertaining, and elegantly written, this is the best single study of European social life during the Early Modern period.

Levack, Brian P. *The Witch-Hunt in Early Modern Europe,* 2nd ed. 1995. The best and most up-to-date short examination of the complex problem of the witch-hunt. This is the place to begin for students new to the subject.

Ozment, Steven E. *Ancestors: The Loving Family in Old Europe.* 2001. This comprehensive study of family life demonstrates that families were actually far more loving than the theory of patriarchy would suggest.

Parker, Geoffrey. *The Dutch Revolt,* rev. ed. 1990. The classic study of the revolt by one of the most masterful historians of the period. This study is especially adept at pointing to the larger European context of the revolt.

Parker, Geoffrey. *The Grand Strategy of Philip II.* 1998. Rehabilitates Philip as a significant strategic thinker.

Wiesner, Merry E. *Women and Gender in Early Modern Europe.* 1993. The best short study of the subject. This is the best book for students new to the subject.

Notes

1. Quoted in R. Po-Chia Hsia, *Social Discipline in the Reformation: Central Europe, 1550–1750* (1989), 147–148.
2. Quoted in R. J. Knecht, *The French Wars of Religion, 1559–1598,* 2nd ed. (1996), 13.
3. Quoted in John Neale, "The Massacre of St. Bartholomew," reprinted in Orest Ranum, ed., *Searching for Modern Times,* vol. 1, 1500–1650 (1969), 176.
4. François Rabelais, *The Histories of Gargantua and Pantagruel,* trans. J. M. Cohen (1955), 159.
5. Michel de Montaigne, *Essays and Selected Writings,* trans. and ed. Donald M. Frame (1963), 219–221.
6. Luís Vaz de Camões, *The Lusiads,* trans. William C. Atkinson (1952), 42.
7. Quoted in "Elizabeth I," *Encyclopedia Britannica* 8 (1959), 364b.
8. Quoted in Norman Davies, *Europe: A History* (1996), 529.

CHAPTER

15

Absolutism and State Building in Europe, 1618–1715

Chapter Outline

- The Nature of Absolutism
- The Absolutist State in France and Spain
- Absolutism and State Building in Central and Eastern Europe
- Resistance to Absolutism in England and the Dutch Republic

In 1651 Thomas Hobbes, an English philosopher living in exile in France, was convinced that the West had descended into chaos. As he looked around him, Hobbes saw nothing but political instability, rebellion, and civil war. The turmoil had begun in the late sixteenth century, when the Reformation sparked the religious warfare described in the last chapter. In 1618 the situation deteriorated when another cycle of internal political strife and warfare erupted. The Thirty Years' War (1618–1648) began as a religious and political dispute in Germany but soon became an international conflict involving the armies of Spain, France, Sweden, and England as well as those of many German states. The war wreaked economic and social havoc in Germany, decimated its population, and forced governments throughout Europe to raise large armies and tax their subjects to pay for them. The entire European economy suffered as a result.

During the 1640s, partly as a result of that devastating conflict, the political order of Europe virtually collapsed. In England a series of bloody civil wars led to the destruction of the monarchy and the establishment of a republic. In France a civil war over constitutional issues drove the royal family from Paris. In Spain the king faced rebellions in no fewer than four of his territories, while in many European kingdoms peasants had risen in protest against the taxes their governments were collecting. Europe was in the midst of a profound and multifaceted crisis.

Hobbes, a man plagued by anxiety even since he was a child, proposed a solution to this crisis. In 1651 he published a book, *Leviathan,* about the origin and exercise of political power. He began by observing that people had a natural tendency to quarrel among themselves and seek power over each other. If left to their own devices in a hypothetical state of nature, in which government did not exist, they would find themselves in constant conflict. In these circumstances, which Hobbes referred to as a state of war, people would be unable to engage in

Louis XIV: Portrait of Louis XIV in military armor, with his plumed helmet and his crown on the table to the right. Drawn during the period of French warfare. In the background is a French ship.

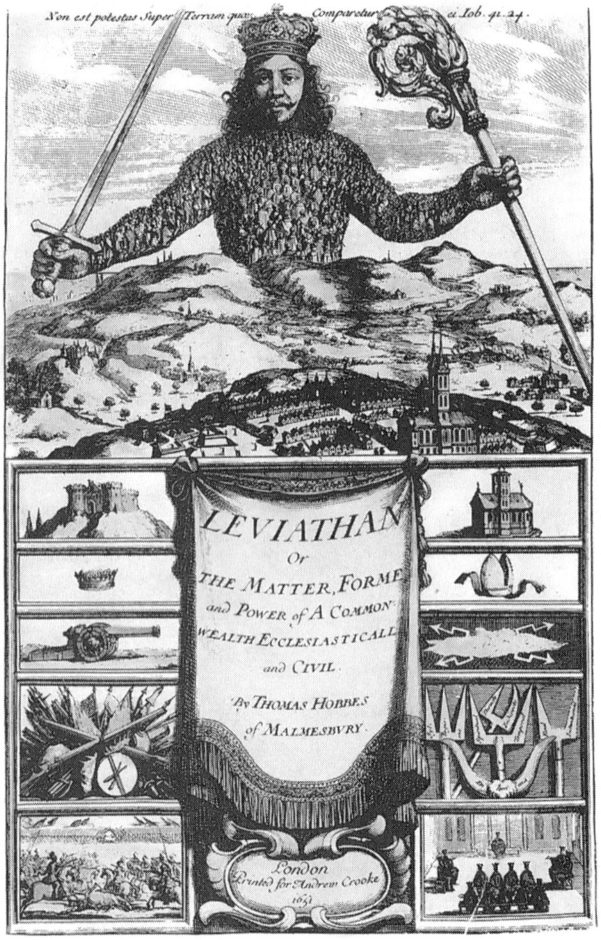

The Frontispiece of Thomas Hobbes's Treatise *Leviathan,* Published in London in 1651

The ruler is depicted as incorporating the bodies of all his subjects, since they collectively authorized him to govern.

trade or agriculture or pursue cultural interests. Life would soon become, in Hobbes's famous words, "solitary, poor, nasty, brutish, and short." The only way for people to find peace in this dangerous and unproductive world would be to agree with their neighbors to form a political society, or a state, by surrendering their independent power to a ruler who would make laws, administer justice, and maintain order. In this state the ruler would wield great power, and he would not share it with others. His subjects, having agreed to endow him with such extensive power, and having agreed to submit to his rule, could not resist or depose him.

Hobbes wrote *Leviathan* not simply as an abstract study of political philosophy but as a solution to the problems that plagued the West in the middle of the seventeenth century. He was suggesting that the best way to achieve peace and security was for people to submit themselves to the authority of a single ruler. The term used to designate the type of government is absolutism°. In the most general terms, absolutism means a political arrangement in which one ruler possesses complete and unrivaled power.

The political history of the West during the seventeenth and early eighteenth centuries can be written largely in terms of the efforts made by European monarchs to introduce absolutism. Those efforts were accompanied by policies intended to make the states they ruled wealthier and more powerful. Attempts to introduce absolutism and to strengthen the state took place in almost every country in Europe. In all these countries a succession of encounters took place between rulers who were trying to enlarge the power of the state and those who resisted their efforts. The outcome of these encounters varied from country to country, but for the most part the advocates of state building and absolutism prevailed. By the end of the seventeenth century the West comprised a number of large states, governed by rulers who had achieved unrivaled power and who commanded large, well-equipped armies. The West had entered the age of absolutism, which lasted until the outbreak of the French Revolution in 1789.

Not only did the West acquire a clear political identity during the seventeenth century, but its geographical boundaries also began to shift. Russia, which Europeans thought of as part of the East, began a program of imitating Western governments and became a major player in European diplomacy and warfare. At the same time Russia's southern neighbor, the Ottoman Empire, which had long straddled the boundary between East and West, was increasingly viewed by Europeans as part of a remote, Asian world.

This chapter will address the following questions: (1) What did absolutism mean, both as a political theory and as a practical program, and how was absolutism related to the growth of the power of the state? (2) How did the encounters that took place in France and Spain during the seventeenth century result in the establishment of absolutism, and how powerful did those two states become in the seventeenth century? (3) What was the nature of royal absolutism in central and eastern Europe, and how did the policies of the Ottoman Empire and Russia help to establish the boundaries of the West during this period? (4) Why did absolutism fail to take root in England and the Dutch Republic during the seventeenth century?

The Nature of Absolutism

Seventeenth-century absolutism had both a theoretical and a practical dimension. Theoretical absolutists included writers like Hobbes who described the nature of power in the state and explained the conditions for its acquisition and continuation. Practical absolutists were the rulers who took concrete political steps to subordinate all other political authorities within the state to themselves. Efforts to introduce royal absolutism in Europe began in the late sixteenth and early seventeenth centuries, but only in the late seventeenth century, after the Thirty Years' War and the political turmoil of the 1640s, did many European rulers consolidate their political positions and actually achieve absolute power.

The word *absolutism* usually conjures up images of despotic kings terrorizing every segment of the population, ruling by whim and caprice, and executing their subjects at will. Nothing could be further from the truth. Absolute monarchs succeeded in establishing themselves as the highest political authorities within their kingdoms, but they never attained unlimited power. Nor could they exercise power in a completely arbitrary manner. Theoretical absolutists never sanctioned this type of arbitrary rule, and the laws of European states never permitted it. Even if European monarchs had wished to act in this way, they usually could not because they did not have the political or judicial resources to impose their will on the people. The exercise of royal power in the seventeenth century, even when it was considered absolute, depended on the tacit consent of noblemen, office holders, and the members of local political assemblies. Kings usually could not afford to risk losing the support of these prominent men by acting illegally or arbitrarily, and when they did, they found themselves faced with rebellion.

THE THEORY OF ABSOLUTISM

When seventeenth-century political writers referred to the monarch as having absolute power, they usually meant that he possessed the highest legislative power in his kingdom. In particular, they meant that he did not share the power to make law with representative assemblies like the English Parliament. The French magistrate Jean Bodin (1530?–1596), who was one of the earliest proponents of absolutist theory, argued in *Six Books of a Commonweal* (1576) that absolute power consisted of several attributes, the most important of which was the power to make law. In similar fashion Hobbes referred to the absolute ruler as "sole legislator." Absolute monarchs, therefore, were rulers who could make law by themselves.

In order to bolster their authority, absolute monarchs frequently asserted that they received their power directly from God and therefore ruled by divine right. This idea was hardly new in the seventeenth century. The Bible proclaimed that all political authorities were "of God" and that people must therefore be obedient to them. In the fourteenth century European monarchs asserted that since God had given them the right to rule, the pope could not depose them. In the sixteenth century the idea of divine right was used to discourage rebellion, for to resist the king was to attack God's representative on Earth. In the seventeenth century many theorists of absolutism—although not Hobbes—used the idea of divine right to insist that kings were accountable only to God, rather than to their subjects.

Absolute rulers often claimed that they were above the law. This meant that when monarchs acted for reason of state, that is, for the benefit of the entire kingdom, they were not strictly bound by the law of their kingdoms. Being above the law also meant that they could not be held legally accountable for their actions, since they were the highest judges in the land. Being above the law did not mean kings or queens could act arbitrarily, illegally, or despotically, even though some of them did so from time to time. Absolute rulers, no less than those who shared power with representative assemblies, were always expected to observe the individual rights and liberties of their subjects as well as the moral law established by God. They were expected, for example, to try people in a court of law rather than execute them at will. The French preacher Jacques Bossuet (1627–1704), who wrote an absolutist treatise on the authority of kings in 1670, insisted that even though kings were not subject to the penalties of the law, they still were not freed from the obligation to observe that law. No less than their subjects, kings were subject to the "equity of the laws." This meant that they should not rule despotically or arbitrarily.

Theorists of absolutism made distinctions between European monarchs and rulers in other parts of the world, such as Turkish sultans, Russian tsars, and the kings of Asian and African lands. In those so-called Eastern countries, according to Bodin, "the prince has become the lord of the goods and the persons of his subjects," by which Bodin meant that the rulers of those lands could seize the possessions of their subjects or execute them without due process of law. Only in the West, wrote Bodin, did royal subjects live under a regime that abided by the rule of law. Bodin exaggerated the powers of both Turkish sultans and Russian tsars, who had much in common with the absolute rulers of western and central Europe. But by emphasizing the rule of law and the king's obligation to abide by it, Bodin identified one of the distinctive features of Western politics during the age of absolutism.

THE PRACTICE OF ABSOLUTISM

What steps did the European monarchs who claimed absolute power take to establish and maintain themselves as the supreme authorities within the state? The first strategy they employed was the elimination or the weakening of national representative assemblies, such as Parliament in England, *Diets* in German states, and the *Cortes* in Spain and Portugal. In France, which is considered to have been the most absolutist state in seventeenth-century Europe, the monarchy stopped summoning its national assembly, the Estates General, in 1614. This assembly did not meet again until the late eighteenth century. In similar fashion, the Portuguese Cortes did not meet after 1640. In

Brandenburg-Prussia the representative assembly for the entire electorate, the Diet, met for the last time in 1652.

In the main Spanish kingdom of Castile, the process was more gradual. Spanish kings gradually reduced the importance of the Cortes in the sixteenth century, but they did not stop calling them until 1664. In the kingdoms of England and Sweden, where absolutism never triumphed, kings who aspired to absolute rule succeeded in dispensing with representative institutions only for brief periods of time. Charles I of England (r. 1625–1649) refused to summon Parliament between 1629 and 1640, while Charles XII of Sweden (r. 1697–1718) did not convene the Swedish *Riksdag* during his entire reign. His successor, however, re-established parliamentary rule in 1722. Charles XII also indicated his preference for absolutism by crowning himself at his coronation, thus symbolizing his belief that he derived his power from no other human authority.

The second strategy of absolutist rulers was to secure the support of smaller regional, provincial, and municipal assemblies that controlled local government. These institutions represented much less of a direct challenge to royal authority, especially since they usually could not act in concert with other political bodies. Most of them therefore managed to survive during the age of absolutism. In fact, these local assemblies proved extremely useful to absolute monarchs, in that they could often be persuaded to grant taxes and recruit soldiers in exchange for the maintenance of their own institutional privileges and liberties. Thus French monarchs regularly convened the provincial assemblies of Languedoc, Brittany, and other provinces long after they had stopped calling the Estates General. The rulers of Prussia continued to meet with provincial *Landtagen* after they stopped calling the general Diet, while in Austria the Habsburg emperors summoned provincial diets throughout the seventeenth and early eighteenth centuries. The only time the king needed to control or suppress these smaller assemblies was when they threatened to become independent of the state. This is what happened when the Spanish principality of Catalonia staged a revolt against the crown in 1640. After the suppression of the revolt the king did not summon the Cortes of Catalonia again until 1701. Absolute monarchs tolerated provincial or local assemblies only to the extent that they served the purposes of the king.

The third strategy of absolute monarchs was to subordinate the nobility to the king and make them dependent on his favor. This was a demanding task, often requiring considerable political skill. After all, the king himself belonged to this wealthy and powerful social group. Traditionally noblemen participated in the government of the kingdom, serving as royal councilors and as members of the representative assemblies that the king summoned in order to make laws and levy taxes. Noblemen also provided the king with soldiers in time of war and led them into battle. The king was therefore dependent upon his noblemen, and to a certain extent he shared power with them. Their privileges and powerful political and social position, however, often led them to participate in rebellions and conspiracies against the king, with the goal of either replacing him or gaining control of his government.

Monarchs who aspired to a position of unrivaled power within their kingdoms could not tolerate challenges of this sort from the ranks of the nobility. They therefore took steps to keep the nobility in line, not only by suppressing rebellion and quashing conspiracies but also by appointing men from different social groups as their chief ministers. Another tactic was to demand that noblemen spend at least part of the year at court, where it was less likely that they could organize collective action against the king and where the king could keep an eye on them. At the same time, however, the king could not afford to alienate the same men, upon whom he still relied for running his government and maintaining order in the localities. Absolute monarchs, therefore, offered nobles special privileges, such as exemption from taxation, positions in the king's household, and freedom to exploit their peasants in exchange for their recognition of the king's superiority and their assistance in maintaining order in the localities. In this way nobles became junior partners in the management of the absolutist state.

The final strategy of absolute monarchs was to gain effective control of the administrative machinery of the state and to use it to enforce royal policy throughout their kingdoms. Absolute monarchs were by nature state builders. They established centralized bureaucracies that extended the reach of their governments down into the smallest towns and villages and out into most remote regions of their kingdoms. The business conducted by these centrally controlled bureaucracies included collection of taxes, recruitment of soldiers, and operation of the judicial system. Some absolute monarchs used the central machinery of the state to impose and maintain religious conformity. As the seventeenth century advanced, they also used the same machinery to regulate the price of grain, stimulate the growth of industry, and relieve the plight of the poor. In these ways the policies pursued by absolute monarchs had an impact on the lives of all royal subjects, not just noblemen and royal councilors.

WARFARE AND THE ABSOLUTIST STATE

Much of the growth of European states in the seventeenth century can be related in one way or another to the conduct of war. During the period from 1600 to 1721, European powers were almost constantly at war. The entire continent was at peace for only four of those years. To meet the demands of war, rulers kept men under arms at all times. By the middle of the seventeenth century, after the Thirty Years' War had come to an end, most European rulers had acquired such standing armies. These armies not only served their rulers in foreign wars but also helped them maintain order and enforce royal policy at home. Standing armies thus became one of the main props of royal absolutism.

During the seventeenth and early eighteenth centuries European armies became larger, in many cases tripling in size. In the 1590s Philip II of Spain had acquired mastery of Europe with an army of 40,000 men. By contrast, in the late seventeenth century Louis XIV of France needed an army of 400,000 men to become the dominant power on the continent. The increase in the size of these forces can be traced to the invention of gunpowder and its more frequent use in the fifteenth and sixteenth centuries. Gunpowder led to the widespread use of the musket, a heavy shoulder firearm carried by a foot soldier. The use of the musket placed a premium on the recruitment and equipment of large armies of infantry, who marched in square columns with men holding long pikes (long wooden shafts with pointed metal heads) to protect the musketeers from enemy attacks. As the size of these armies of foot soldiers grew, the role of mounted soldiers, who had dominated medieval warfare, was greatly reduced.

Changes in military technology and tactics also necessitated more intensive military training. In the Middle Ages mounted knights had acquired great individual skill, but they did not need to work in precise unison with other men under arms. Seventeenth-century foot soldiers, however, had to learn to march in formation, to coordinate their maneuvers, and to fire without harming their comrades in arms. Therefore they needed to be drilled. The introduction of volley fire, by which one successive line of soldiers stepped forward to fire while the others were reloading, placed an even greater premium on precise drilling. Drilling took place in peacetime as well as during war. The wearing of uniforms, which began when the state assumed the function of clothing its thousands of soldiers, gave further unity and cohesion to the trained fighting force.

The cost of recruiting, training, and equipping these mammoth armies was staggering. In the Middle Ages individual lords often had sufficient financial resources to assemble their own private armies. By the beginning of the seventeenth century the only institution capable of putting the new armies in the field was the state itself. The same was true for navies, which now consisted of heavily armed sailing ships, each of which carried as many as 400 sailors. To build these large armies and navies, as well as to pay the increasing cost of waging war itself (which rose 500 percent between 1530 and 1630), the state had to identify new methods of raising and collecting taxes. In times of war as much as 80 percent of the revenue taken in by the state went for military purposes.

The equipment and training of military forces and the collection and allocation of the revenue necessary to subsidize these efforts stimulated the expansion and refinement of the state bureaucracy. Governments found it necessary to employ thousands of new officials to supervise the collection of new taxes, and in order to make the system of tax collection system more efficient, governments often introduced entirely new administrative systems. Some states completely reorganized their bureaucracies to meet the demands of war. New departments of state were created to supervise the recruitment of soldiers, the manufacture of equipment and uniforms, the building of fleets, and the provisioning of troops in time of war. Rulers of European states recognized that the exercise of absolute power greatly facilitated the utilization of state power for these purposes.

The Absolutist State in France and Spain

The two European countries in which royal absolutism first became a political reality were France and Spain. The histories of these two monarchies in the seventeenth century followed very different courses. The kingdom of France, especially during the reign of Louis XIV (r. 1643–1715), became a model of state building and gradually emerged as the most powerful country in Europe. The Spanish monarchy, on the other hand, struggled to introduce absolutism at a time when the overall economic condition of the country was deteriorating and its military forces were suffering a series of defeats. Spain established the forms of absolutist rule, but the monarchy was not able to match the political or military achievements of France in the late seventeenth century.

THE FOUNDATIONS OF FRENCH ABSOLUTISM

Efforts to make the French monarchy absolute began in response to the disorder that occurred during the wars of religion in the late sixteenth century. Bodin wrote his treatises during those wars, and the threat of renewed civil war between Protestants and Catholics affected French politics throughout the seventeenth century. The first steps toward the achievement of absolutism were taken during the reign of Henry IV (r. 1589–1610), the Huguenot who converted to Catholicism in 1594 and who ended the wars of religion by granting freedom of worship and full civil rights to French Protestants by the Edict of Nantes (1598). This decree brought internal religious peace to the kingdom, while the progressive financial and economic policies of Henry's brilliant minister, the Duke of Sully, helped restore the financial strength of the crown and involve the government in a process of commercial recovery and expansion. Despite this success, Henry could not prevent the great nobles from conspiring against him, and his policy of religious toleration encountered resistance from Catholics committed to the suppression of Protestantism. In 1610 a fanatical

Catholic, François Ravaillac, stabbed the king to death in his carriage on a Parisian street.

On Henry's death the crown passed to his young son, Louis XIII (r. 1610–1643), while the queen mother, Marie de Medici, assumed the leadership of a government acting in the king's name during his youth. This period of regency, in which aristocratic factions vied for supremacy at court, exposed the main weakness of the monarchy, which was the rival power of the great noble families of the realm. The statesman who addressed this problem most directly was Louis's main councilor, Cardinal Armand Jean du Plessis de Richelieu (1585–1642). A member of an old and wealthy family, Richelieu rose to power through the patronage of the queen mother and then, after losing her support, maintained his preeminent position with the support of the king himself. He became the king's chief minister in 1628. Richelieu was arguably the greatest statebuilder of the seventeenth century. He directed all his energies toward centralizing the power of the French state in the person of the king.

Richelieu's most immediate concern was bringing the independent nobility to heel and subordinating their local power to that of the state. This he accomplished by suppressing several conspiracies and rebellions led by noblemen and by restricting the independent power of the provincial assemblies and the eight regional parlements°, which were the highest courts in the country. His great administrative achievement was the strengthening of the system of the intendants°. These paid crown officials, who were recruited from the professional classes and the lower ranks of the nobility, became the main agents of French local administration. Responsible only to the royal council, they collected taxes, supervised local administration, and recruited soldiers for the army. Since they could not come from the districts to which they were assigned, they had no vested interest in maintaining local customs or privileges.

Richelieu also modified the religious policy embodied in the Edict of Nantes. According to that document, Huguenots not only had freedom of worship but could also fortify the towns in which they lived. Richelieu resented the maintenance of these citadels of local power, which represented a challenge to the type of absolutist state he envisioned. He also suspected that rivals of the king from the nobility were using the Huguenot towns as a means of maintaining their independent power. A series of military confrontations between the government and the Protestants in the late 1610s and 1620s brought the country to the brink of civil war. Following the successful siege of the town of La Rochelle in 1627–1628, the government razed the fortifications of the Huguenot cities, melted down their cannons, and disarmed their Protestant citizens. A peace treaty signed in 1629 ratified the government's victory, but it did not deny the Huguenots their right to worship freely.

The most challenging task for Richelieu, as it was for all French ministers in the early modern period, was increasing the government's yield from taxation, a task that became more demanding during times of war. Levying taxes on the French population was always a delicate process, since the needs of the state conflicted with the privileges of various social groups, such as the nobles, who were exempt from taxation, and the estates of individual provinces such as Brittany that claimed the right to tax the people them-

Cardinal Richelieu
Triple portrait of Cardinal Richelieu, who laid the foundations of French absolutism.

selves. Using a variety of tactics, including negotiation and compromise, and relying heavily on the support of the provincial intendants, Richelieu managed to increase the yield from the *taille*, the direct tax on land, as much as threefold during the period 1635–1648. He supplemented the taille with taxes on office holding. Even then, the revenue was insufficient to meet the extraordinary demands of war.

Opposition to Richelieu's financial policies lay at the root of the main problem the government faced after the cardinal's death in 1642. The minister who succeeded him was his protégé Jules Mazarin (1602–1661), a diplomat of Italian birth who had entered French government service during Richelieu's administration. Mazarin dominated the government of Louis XIV (r. 1643–1715) during the period when the king, who inherited the throne at age 5, was still a boy and while his mother was serving as regent. Mazarin continued the policies of his predecessor, but he was unable to prevent civil war from breaking out in 1648. This challenge to the French state, known as the *Fronde* (a pejorative reference to a Parisian game in which children flung mud at passing carriages), had two phases. The first, the Fronde of the Parlement (1648–1649), began when the members of the Parlement of Paris, the most important of all the provincial parlements, refused to register an edict of the king that had required them to surrender four years' salary. This act of resistance led to demands that the king sign a document limiting royal authority. Barricades went up in the streets of Paris, and the royal family was forced to flee the city. A blockade of the city by royal troops led to an uneasy compromise in 1649. Revolts in three other parlements, each of which had its own dynamic and which were not coordinated with that of Paris, came to a similar resolution. The second and more violent phase was the Fronde of the Princes (1650–1653), during which the Prince de Condé and his noble allies waged war on the government and even formed an alliance with France's enemy, Spain. Only after Condé's military defeat did the entire rebellion collapse.

The Fronde stands as the great crisis of the seventeenth-century French state. It revealed the strength of the local, aristocratic, and legal forces with which the king and his ministers had to contend. These forces managed to disrupt the growth of the French state, drive the king from his capital, and challenge his authority throughout the kingdom. But in the long run they could not destroy the achievement of Richelieu and Mazarin. By the late 1650s the damage had been repaired and the state had resumed its growth.

CHRONOLOGY

France in the Age of Absolutism

1598	The Edict of Nantes grants toleration to French Calvinists, known as Huguenots
1610	Assassination of Henry IV of France, who was succeeded by Louis XIII (r. 1610–1643)
1628	Cardinal Richelieu becomes chief minister of Louis XIII of France
1643	Death of Louis XIII of France and accession of Louis XIV; Louis's mother, Anne of Austria, becomes queen regent with Cardinal Mazarin as his minister
1648–1653	The Fronde
1661	Death of Cardinal Mazarin; Louis XIV assumes personal rule
1685	Revocation of the Edict of Nantes
1715	Death of Louis XIV of France; succeeded by his grandson, Louis XV

ABSOLUTISM IN THE REIGN OF LOUIS XIV

The man who presided over the development of the French state for the next fifty years was the king himself, Louis XIV, who assumed direct control of his government after the death of Mazarin in 1661. In an age of absolute monarchs, Louis towered among his contemporaries. He is widely regarded as the most powerful king of the seventeenth century. This reputation comes as much from the image he conveyed as from the policies he pursued. Artists, architects, dramatists, and members of his immediate entourage helped the king project an image of incomparable majesty and authority. Paintings and sculptures of the king depicted him in sartorial splendor, holding the symbols of power and displaying expressions of regal superiority that bordered on arrogance. At Versailles, about ten miles from Paris, Louis constructed a lavishly furnished palace that became his main residence and the center of the glittering court that surrounded him. The palace was built in the baroque° style, which emphasized the size and grandeur of the structure while also conveying a sense of unity and balance among its diverse parts. The sweeping façades of baroque buildings gave them a dynamic quality that evoked an emotional response from the viewer. The baroque style, criticized by contemporaries for its exuberance and pomposity, appealed to absolute monarchs who wished to emphasize their unrivaled position within society and their determination to impose order and stability on their kingdoms.

Court life at Versailles revolved entirely around the king. Court dramas depicted Louis, who styled himself "the sun

Versailles Palace, Center of the Court of Louis XIV after 1682
The palace was constructed between 1669 and 1686. Its massiveness and grandeur and the order it imposed on the landscape made it a symbol of royal absolutism.

king," as Apollo, the god of light. The paintings in the grand Hall of Mirrors at Versailles, which recorded the king's military victories, served as reminders of his unrivaled accomplishments. Louis's formal routine in receiving visitors created appropriate distance between him and his courtiers while keeping his subjects in a state of subservient anticipation of royal favor. His frequent bursts of anger achieved the same effect. When an untitled lady took the seat of a noblewoman at a dinner in his presence, he described the act as one of "incredible insolence" that "had thrown him into such a rage that he had been unable to eat." After rebuking the offending lady for her "impertinence," he became so angry that he left the room.

The image of magnificence and power that Louis conveyed in art and ceremony mirrored and reinforced his more tangible political accomplishments. His greatest achievement was to solve the persistent problem of aristocratic independence and rebellion by securing the complete loyalty and dependence of the old nobility. This he achieved first by requiring the members of these ancient families to come to Versailles for a portion of every year, where they stayed in apartments within the royal palace itself. At Versailles Louis involved them in the elaborate cultural activities of court life and in ceremonial rituals that emphasized their subservience to the king. At the same time, he excluded the nobles from holding important offices in the government of the realm, a strategy designed to prevent them from building an independent power base within the bureaucracy. Instead he recruited men from the mercantile and professional classes to run his government. This policy of taming the nobility and depriving them of central administrative power could work only if they received something in return. Like all the absolute monarchs of western Europe, Louis used the patronage at his disposal to grant members of the nobility wealth and privileges in exchange for their loyalty to the crown. In this way the monarchy and the nobility served each other's interests.

In running the actual machinery of government Louis built upon and perfected the centralizing policies of Richelieu and Mazarin. After the death of Mazarin in 1661 the king, now 23 years old, became his own chief minister, presiding over a council of state that supervised the work of government. An elaborate set of councils at the highest levels of government set policy that was implemented by the department ministers. The provincial intendants became even more important than they had been under Richelieu and Mazarin, especially in providing food, arms, and equipment for royal troops. It was the intendants' job to secure the cooperation of the local judges, city councils, and parish priests as well as the compliance of the local population. If necessary they could call upon royal troops in order to enforce their will, but for the most part they preferred to rely on the more effective tactics of negotiation and compromise with local officials. The system, when it worked properly, allowed the king to make decisions that directly affected the lives and beliefs of his 20 million subjects.

A further manifestation of the newfound power of the French state in the late seventeenth century was the government's active involvement in the economic and financial life of the country. The minister who was most responsible for this series of undertakings was Jean Baptiste Colbert

(1619–1683), a protégé of Mazarin who in 1661 became controller general of the realm. Born into a family of merchants, and despised by the old nobility, Colbert epitomized the type of government official Louis recruited into his service. Entrusted with the supervision of the entire system of royal taxation, Colbert managed to increase royal revenues dramatically simply by reducing the cut taken by the agents whom the government hired to collect taxes.

Even more beneficial to the French state was the determination of Colbert to use the country's economic resources for its benefit. The theory underlying this set of policies was mercantilism°, which held that the wealth of the state depended on its ability to import fewer commodities than it exported. Its goal was to secure the largest possible share of the world's monetary supply. In keeping with those objectives, Colbert increased the size of France's merchant fleet, founded overseas trading companies, and levied high tariffs on France's commercial rivals. To make France economically self-sufficient he encouraged the growth of the French textile industry, improved the condition of the roads, built canals throughout the kingdom, and reduced some of the burdensome tolls that impeded internal trade.

The most intrusive exercise of this power of the state during Louis XIV's reign was the decision to enforce religious uniformity. The king always considered the existence of a large Huguenot minority within his kingdom an affront to his sense of order. Toleration was divisive and dangerous, especially to someone who styled himself as "Most Christian King." Even after Richelieu had leveled the walls of the fortified Huguenot towns, the problem of religious pluralism remained. In 1685 Louis addressed this problem by revoking the entire Edict of Nantes, thereby denying freedom of religious worship to about one million of his subjects. The enforcement of this policy was violent and disruptive, with the army being called upon to enforce public conversions to Catholicism. Protestant churches were closed and often destroyed, while large numbers of Huguenots were forced to emigrate to the Netherlands, England, and Protestant German lands. Few exercises of absolute power in the seventeenth century caused more disruption in the lives of ordinary people than this attempt to realize the king's ideal of "one king, one law, one faith."

LOUIS XIV AND THE CULTURE OF ABSOLUTISM

A further manifestation of the power of the French absolutist state was Louis's success in influencing and transforming French culture. Kings had often served as patrons of the arts by providing income for artists, writers, and musicians while endowing cultural and educational institutions. Louis took this type of royal patronage to a new level, making it possible for him to control the dissemination of ideas and the very production of culture itself. During Louis's reign royal patronage, emanating from the court, extended the king's influence over the entire cultural landscape. The architects of the palace at Versailles, the painters of historical scenes that hung in its hallways and galleries, the composers of the plays and operas that were performed in its theaters, the sculptors who created busts of the king to decorate its chambers, and the historians and pamphlet writers who celebrated the king's achievements in print all benefited from Louis's direct financial support.

Much of Louis's patronage went to cultural institutions, thereby enabling the king to influence a wider circle of artists and have a greater effect on the cultural life of the nation. He took over the Academy of Fine Arts in 1661, founded the Academy of Music in 1669, and chartered a theater company, the *Comédie Française,* in 1680. Two great French dramatists of the late seventeenth century, Jean Baptiste Molière (1622–1673), the creator of French high comedy, and Jean Racine (1639–1699), who wrote tragedies in the classical style, benefited from the king's patronage. Louis even subsidized the publication of a new journal, the *Journal des savants,* in which men of letters advanced their ideas. In 1666 Louis extended his patronage to the sciences with the founding of the Royal Academy of Sciences, which had the twofold objective of advancing scientific knowledge and glorifying the king. It also benefited the state by devising improvements in ship design and navigation.

Of all the cultural institutions that benefited from Louis XIV's patronage, the *Académie Française* had the most enduring impact on French culture. This academy, a society of literary scholars, had been founded in 1635 with the support of Cardinal Richelieu. Its purpose was to standardize the French language and serve as the guardian of its integrity. In 1694, twenty-two years after Louis became the academy's patron, the first official French dictionary appeared in print. This achievement of linguistic uniformity, in which words received authorized spellings and definitions, reflected the pervasiveness of Louis's cultural influence as well as the search for order that became the defining characteristic of his reign.

Louis introduced order and uniformity into every aspect of his own life and that of his country. He followed a precise routine in ordering his daily life, created ceremonies that ordered the life of his court, and insisted on the court's adoption of table manners that followed strict rules of politeness. He created a bureaucracy that was organized along rational, orderly principles, and he sought to ensure that all his subjects would practice the same religion. The establishment of a clearly defined chain of command in the army, which Louis's minister the Marquis de Louvois introduced, gave organizational cohesion and hierarchical order to the large military force the king and his ministers assembled. Nearly all areas of French public life were transformed by the king's desire to establish order and uniformity and his use of the power of the state to enforce it.

One indication of the extent of Louis's achievement was the conspicuous attempt of other monarchs to imitate

REVOCATION OF THE EDICT OF NANTES, OCTOBER 25, 1685

In 1685 King Louis XIV of France revoked the Edict of Nantes, the decree of King Henry IV that had granted freedom of worship to French Protestants in 1598. Before the revocation was published, the government sent dragoons (cavalry who arrived on horseback but fought on foot) to terrorize Protestant households and make them convert to Catholicism. The terms of the revocation were particularly harsh, and despite the prohibition against leaving the country, hundreds of thousands of Huguenots emigrated to England, the Dutch Republic, and North America.

. . . Therefore we decided that there was nothing better we could do to erase from memory the troubles, the confusion and the evils that the growth of this false religion had caused in our kingdom and that gave rise to the said Edict and to so many other edicts and declarations that preceded it, than to revoke entirely the said Edict of Nantes and the detailed articles attached to it and everything that has been done since on behalf of the said Supposedly Reformed Religion [Calvinism].

1. We therefore for these reasons and in full knowledge, power and authority, by means of the present perpetual and irrevocable edict, do suppress and revoke the Edict of the King, our grandfather, issued at Nantes in April 1598. . . . As a result we desire and it is our pleasure that all the temples of the Supposedly Reformed Religion situated in our kingdom, county, lands and seigneuries within our obedience be immediately demolished.
2. Our subjects of the Supposedly Reformed Religion are not to assemble for worship in any place or house for any reason.
3. Noble lords are not to hold worship services in their houses or fiefs of any sort on pain of confiscation of goods and property.
4. Ministers of the Supposedly Reformed Religion who have not converted are to leave the kingdom within fifteen days and are not to preach or perform any functions in the meantime, or they will be sent to the galleys.
5. Ministers who convert, and their widows after their death, are to receive the same exemptions from taxes and troop lodgings that they had as ministers . . .
6. Converted ministers can become lawyers or doctors of law without the usual three years of study and for half the fees usually charged by the universities.
7. Special schools for the children of the Supposedly Reformed Religion are prohibited.
8. Children of [Huguenot] parents are to be baptized by the chief priests of their parishes and raised as Catholics, and local judges are to oversee this.
9. If Protestants who left the kingdom before this edict was issued return within four months, they can regain their property and resume their lives. If, however, they do not return within four months, their goods will be confiscated.
10. All subjects belonging to the Supposedly Reformed Religion and their wives and children are forbidden to leave the country or to send out their property and effects. The penalty for men is the galleys and women confiscation of their persons and property.
11. The declarations already issued concerning those who relapse are to be executed in full.

And in addition, those who adhere to the Supposedly Reformed religion, while waiting until it pleases God to enlighten them like the others, may continue to live in the cities and communities of our realm, continue their commerce, and enjoy their property without being bothered or hindered because of the Supposedly Reformed Religion, on condition, however, of not practicing their religion or assembling for prayers or worship or for any other pretext, with the penalties stated above.

France, even in the eighteenth century. The absolute monarchs in Prussia, Austria, and Russia, as well as aspiring ones in England and Sweden, not only experimented selectively with French political methods but imported many of the features of French culture that Louis had supported. They built palaces in the same architectural style as that of Versailles, designed French gardens to surround them, imported the fashions and decorative styles of the French court, staged French ballets and operas in their capitals, and even spoke French, which had replaced Latin as the language of international diplomacy, when conducting official business. The power of the French monarchy had made French culture the dominant influence in the courts and capitals of Europe.

THE WARS OF LOUIS XIV, 1667–1714

The seventeenth-century French state was designed not only to maintain internal peace and order but also to wage war against other states. Colbert's financial and economic policies, coupled with the military reforms of the Marquis de Louvois, had laid the foundations for the creation of a formidable military machine. In 1667 Louis XIV began unleashing its full potential. Having assembled an army that was twenty times larger than the French force that had invaded Italy in 1494, Louis deployed this armed force against an array of European powers in no fewer than four separate wars between 1667 and 1714. His goal in all these wars, as it had been in all French international conflicts since 1635, was territorial acquisition (see Map 15.1). In this case Louis set his sights mainly on the German and Spanish territories in the Rhineland along the eastern borders of his kingdom. Contemporaries suggested, however, that he was thinking in grander terms than traditional French dynastic ambition. Propagandists for the king in the late 1660s claimed that Louis harbored visions of establishing a "universal monarchy" or an "absolute empire," reminiscent of the empires of ancient Rome, Charlemagne in the ninth century, and Charles V in the sixteenth century.

Louis never attained the empire of his dreams, but concerted action by almost all the other European powers was required to stop him. France's acquisition of new territories along its eastern boundaries between 1668 and 1684 confirmed the fears of other European states that the king had imperial ambitions. After Louis had launched an offensive against German towns along the Rhine River in 1688, signaling the beginning of yet another round of European warfare, Great Britain, the Dutch Republic, Spain, and Austria formed a coalition against him. Finally matched by the combined military forces of these allies, forced to wage war on many different fronts (including North America), and unable to provide adequate funding of the war on the basis of its system of taxation, France felt compelled to conclude peace in 1697. The Treaty of Ryswick marked the turning point in the expansion of the French state and laid the groundwork for the establishment of a balance of power° in the next century, an arrangement whereby various countries form alliances to prevent any one state from dominating the others.

The Treaty of Ryswick, however, did not mark the end of French territorial ambition. In 1701 Louis went to war once again, this time as part of an effort to place a French Bourbon candidate, his grandson Duke Philip of Anjou, on the Spanish throne. The impending death of the mentally weak, sexually impotent, and chronically ill King Charles II of Spain (1665–1700) without heirs had created a succession crisis. In 1698 the major European powers had agreed to a treaty in which Spanish lands would be divided between Louis himself and the Holy Roman Emperor, both of whom happened to be Charles's brothers-in-law. By his will, however, Charles left the Spanish crown and all its overseas possessions to Philip. This bequest offered France more than it would have received on the basis of the treaty. If the will had been upheld, the Pyrenees mountains would have disappeared as a political barrier between France and Spain, and France, as the stronger of the two kingdoms, would have controlled unprecedented expanses of European and American territory.

Dreaming once again of universal monarchy, Louis rejected the treaty in favor of King Charles's will. The British, Dutch, and Austrians responded by forming a Grand Alliance against France and Spain. After a long and costly conflict, known as the War of the Spanish Succession (1701–1713), the members of this coalition were able to dictate the terms of the Treaty of Utrecht (1713). Philip, who suffered from fits of manic depression and went days without dressing or leaving his room, remained on the Spanish throne as Philip V (r. 1700–1746), but only on the condition that the French and Spanish crowns would never be united. Spain ceded its territories in the Netherlands and in Italy to the Austrian Habsburg Monarchy and its strategic port of Gibraltar at the entrance to the Mediterranean to the British. The treaty not only confirmed the new balance of

Map 15.1 Territorial Acquisitions by France during the Reign of Louis XIV

The main acquisitions were lands in the Spanish Netherlands to the north and Franche Comté, Alsace, and Lorraine to the east. Louis thought of the Rhine River as France's natural eastern boundary, and territories acquired in 1659 and 1697 allowed it to reach that limit.

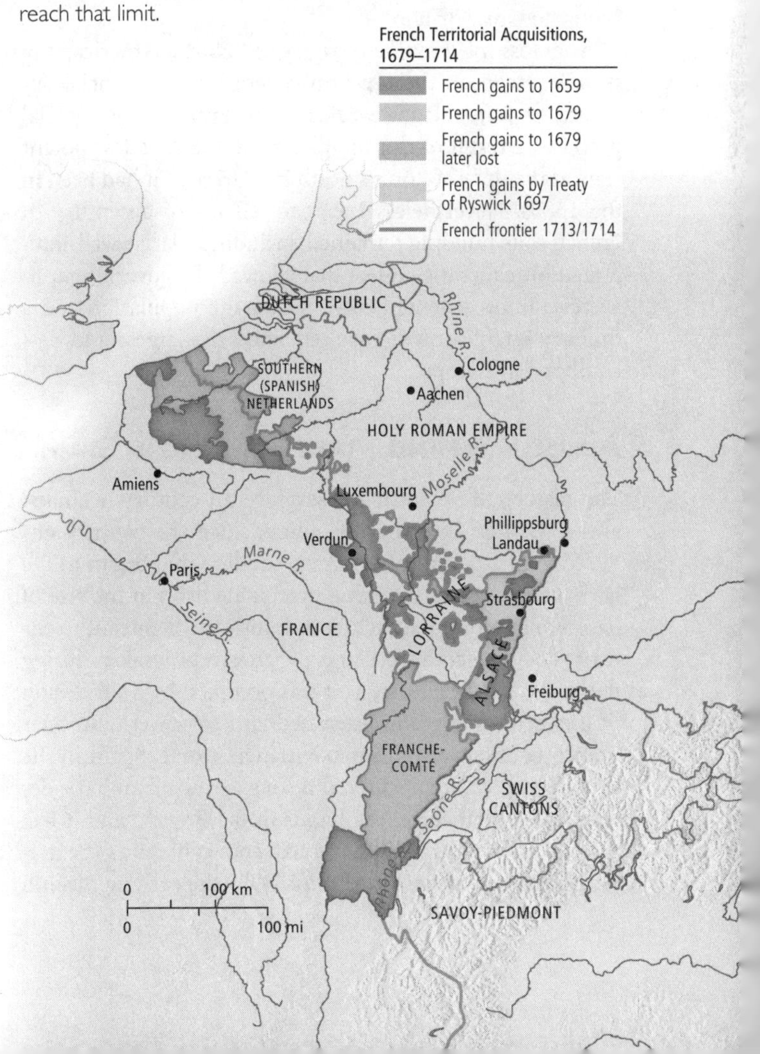

The French Bourbons and the Spanish Succession 1589–1700

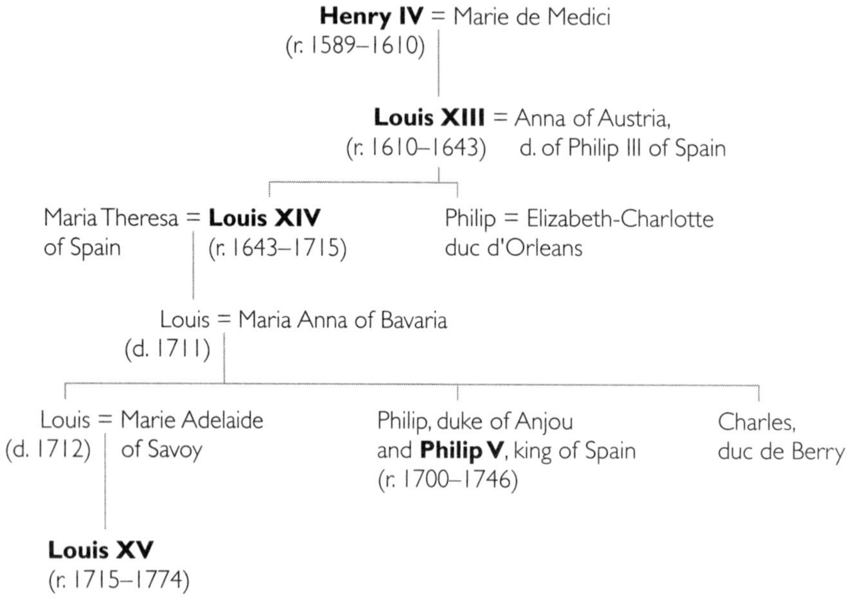

power in Europe but also resulted in the transfer of large parts of French Canada, including Newfoundland and Nova Scotia, to Great Britain.

The loss of French territory in North America, the strains placed on the taxation system by the financial demands of war, and the weakening of France's commercial power as a result of this conflict made France a less potent state at the time of Louis's death in 1715 than it had been in the 1680s. Nevertheless the main effects of a century of French state building remained, including a large, well-integrated bureaucratic edifice that allowed the government to exercise unprecedented control over the population and a military establishment that remained the largest and best equipped in Europe.

ABSOLUTISM AND STATE BUILDING IN SPAIN

The history of Spain in the seventeenth century is almost always written in terms of failure, since the country endured a long period of economic decline that began in the late sixteenth century with a precipitate drop in the size of its population and stretched well into the eighteenth century. The monarchy became progressively weaker during the seventeenth century, as it was occupied by a succession of ineffective kings who exercised far less power than their French counterparts. To make matters worse, Spain in the seventeenth century suffered a long series of military defeats, most of them at the hands of the French, and it lost the position it had held in the sixteenth century as the major European power (see Map 15.2). By the early eighteenth century Spain was a shadow of its former self, and its culture reflected uncertainty, pessimism, and nostalgia for former imperial greatness. None of this failure, however, should obscure the fact that Spain, like France, underwent a period of state building during the seventeenth century, and that its government, like that of France, gravitated toward absolutism.

The Spanish monarchy in 1600 ruled more territory than did France, and the various kingdoms and principalities that it comprised possessed far more independence than even the most remote and peripheral French provinces. The center of the monarchy was the kingdom of Castile, with its capital at Madrid. This kingdom, the largest and wealthiest territory within the Iberian peninsula, had been united with the kingdom of Aragon in 1479 when King Ferdinand II of Aragon (r. 1479–1516), the husband of Queen Isabella of Castile (r. 1474–1504), ascended the throne. These two kingdoms, however, continued to exist as separate states after the union, each having its own representative institutions and administrative systems. Each of them, moreover, contained smaller, semiautonomous kingdoms and provinces that retained their own distinctive political institutions. The kingdom of Valencia and the principality of Catalonia formed part of the Crown of Aragon, while in the sixteenth century the kingdoms of Navarre and Portugal had been annexed to the Crown of Castile. Outside the Iberian peninsula the Spanish monarchy ruled territories in the Netherlands, Italy, and the New World.

The only institution besides the monarchy itself that provided any kind of administrative unity to all these

■ **Map 15.2 The Decline of Spanish Power in Europe, 1640–1714**
Revolts in the United Provinces of the Netherlands and Portugal account for two of the most significant losses of Spanish territory. Military defeat at the hands of the French in 1659 and Austria in 1714 account for the loss of most of the other territories.

Spanish territories in the seventeenth century was the Spanish Inquisition, a centralized ecclesiastical court with a supreme council in Madrid and twenty-one regional tribunals in different parts of Spain, Italy, and America. Its function was to enforce religious uniformity and maintain the purity of the Catholic faith.

The great challenge for the Spanish monarchy in the seventeenth century was to integrate the various kingdoms and principalities of Spain into a more highly centralized state while at the same time making the machinery of that state more efficient and profitable. The statesman who made the most sustained efforts at realizing these goals was the energetic and authoritarian Count-Duke of Olivares (1587–1645), the contemporary and counterpart of Richelieu during the reign of the Spanish king Philip IV (1621–1665). The task Olivares faced was more daunting than anything the French cardinal had ever confronted. As a result of decades of warfare, the Spanish monarchy in the 1620s was penniless, the kingdom of Castile had gone bankrupt, and the entire country had already entered a period of protracted economic decline.

To deal with these deep structural problems Olivares proposed a reform of the entire financial system, the establishment of national banks, and the replacement of the main tax, the *millones,* which was levied on the consumption of basic commodities such as meat and wine, with proportional contributions from all the towns and villages in the kingdom. At the same time he tried to address the problem of ruling a disparate and far-flung empire, making all the kingdoms and principalities within the monarchy contribute to national defense on a proportionate basis. His ultimate goal was to unify the entire peninsula in a cohesive Spanish national state, similar to that of France. This policy involved suppression of the individual liberties of the various kingdoms and principalities and direct subordination of each area to the king himself. It was, in other words, a solution based on the principles of absolutism.

Olivares was unable to match the state-building achievement of Richelieu in France. His failure, which was complete by the time he fell from office in 1643, can be attributed to three factors. The first was the opposition he confronted within Castile itself, especially from the cities represented in the Cortes, over the question of taxation. The second, a problem facing Spain throughout the seventeenth century, was military failure, in this case the losses to France during the final phase of the Thirty Years' War. That failure aggravated the financial crisis and prevented the monarchy from capitalizing on the prestige that usually attends military victory. The third and most serious impediment was opposition to the policy of subordinating the outlying Spanish regions to the kingdom of Castile. The kingdoms and provinces on the periphery of the country were determined to maintain their individual laws and liberties, especially the powers of their own Cortes, in the face of the pressures to centralize power in Madrid. The problem became more serious as Olivares, in the wake of military defeat by the French and Dutch, put more pressure on these outlying kingdoms and provinces to contribute to the war effort.

Provincial resistance to a policy of Castilian centralization lay at the root of the Spanish crisis of the seventeenth century. This crisis did not throw Castile itself into a state of civil war. Unlike Paris during the Fronde, Madrid itself remained peaceful. Throughout the 1640s the crown managed to maintain order within its main kingdom, probably because it had learned the art of negotiating directly with the thousands of towns and villages that ran local government. Instead, the Spanish crisis took the form of separatist revolts in Portugal, Catalonia, Sicily, and Naples. With the exception of Portugal, which recovered its sovereignty in 1640, the monarchy met this test and managed to maintain control of its provincial and Italian territories. In the aftermath of the revolts, however, the monarchy failed to bring the areas within the sphere of effective central government control.

The relative weakness of the Spanish monarchy, especially in comparison with that of France, became most apparent in the late seventeenth century, the age of Louis XIV. In two important respects the Spanish government failed to match the achievement of the French. First, it could never escape the grip that the old noble families had on the central administration. The unwillingness of the nobility to recruit ministers and officials from the mercantile and professional groups within society (which were small to begin with in Spain) worked against the achievement of bureaucratic efficiency and made innovation virtually impossible. Second, unlike the French government during Colbert's ministry, the Spanish government failed to take steps to encourage economic growth. The hostility of the aristocratic ruling class to mercantile affairs, coupled with a traditional Spanish unwillingness to follow the example of foreigners (especially when they were Protestants) prevented the country from stemming its own economic decline and the government from solving the formidable financial problems facing it. To make matters worse, the Spanish government failed to make its system of tax collection more efficient.

The mood that prevailed within the upper levels of Castilian society in the seventeenth century reflected the failure of the government and the entire nation. The contrast between the glorious achievements of the monarchy during the reign of Philip II (r. 1555–1598) and the somber realities of the late seventeenth century led most members of the ruling class to retreat into that past, a nostalgia that only encouraged further economic and political stagnation. The work of Miguel de Cervantes (1547–1616), the greatest Spanish writer of the seventeenth century, reflected this change in the Spanish national mood. In 1605 and 1615 Cervantes published (in two parts) *Don Quixote,* the story

CHRONOLOGY

International Conflict in the Seventeenth Century

1609	Truce between the seven Dutch provinces and Spain
1618	Bohemian revolt against Habsburg rule; beginning of the Thirty Years' War
1619	Imperial forces defeat Bohemians at Battle of White Mountain
1648	Treaty of Westphalia, ending the Thirty Years' War; Treaty of Münster, ending the Dutch War of Independence
1667	Beginning of the wars of Louis XIV
1672	William III of Orange-Nassau becomes captain-general of Dutch; beginning of the war against France (1672–1678)
1688–1697	War of the League of Augsburg (Nine Years' War); England and Scotland join forces with Prussia, Austria, the Dutch Republic, and many German states against France
1697	Treaty of Ryswick
1700–1721	Great Northern War in which Russia eventually defeated Sweden; emergence of Russia as a major power
1701–1713	War of the Spanish Succession
1713	Treaty of Utrecht

■ **Diego de Velázquez, Portrait of the Prince Baltasar Carlos, Heir to the Spanish Throne**
The depiction of the six-year-old prince on a rearing horse was intended to suggest military and political power at a time when the monarchy was losing both. The prince died in 1646, before he could succeed to the throne.

of an idealistic wandering nobleman who pursued dreams of an elusive military glory. This work, which as we have seen in Chapter 14 explored the relationship between illusion and reality, served as a commentary on a nobility that had lost confidence in itself.

Spanish painting, which paradoxically entered its Golden Age at the time the country began to lose its economic, political, and military vitality, was less willing to accept the decline of Spain. There was very little in the paintings of the great Spanish artist Diego de Velázquez (1599–1660) that would suggest the malaise that was affecting Spain and its nobility at the time. Velázquez painted in the baroque style that was in favor at court throughout Europe, depicting his subjects in heroic poses and imbuing them with a sense of royal or aristocratic dignity. One of his historical paintings, *The Surrender of Breda* (1634), commemorated a rare Spanish military victory over the Dutch in 1625 and the magnanimity of the Spanish victors toward their captives. All this was intended to reinforce the prestige of the monarchy, the royal family, and the nation itself at a time when the imperial grandeur of the past had faded. Velázquez's painting reflected the ideals of absolutism but ignored the realities of Spanish political and military life.

■ **Diego de Velázquez, *The Surrender of Breda*, 1634**
The Spanish victory over the Dutch in 1625 gave Velázquez a rare opportunity to depict Spanish soldiers in a role they had frequently played in the sixteenth century.

Absolutism and State Building in Central and Eastern Europe

The forces that led to the establishment of absolutism and state building in France and Spain also made an impact on central and eastern Europe. In Germany the Thirty Years' War led to the establishment of two absolutist states, Prussia and the Austrian Habsburg Monarchy. Further to the East, the Ottoman and Russian Empires, both of them on the margins of the West, also developed absolutist political systems that shared many of the same characteristics as those in western and central Europe. Russia, previously thought of as belonging to an Eastern, Asian world, entered upon a program of Westernization and staked a claim to be considered a Western power. At the same time the Ottoman Empire, whose political development followed a Western pattern in many respects, was increasingly dismissed by Europeans as part of a distant, non-Western world.

GERMANY AND THE THIRTY YEARS' WAR, 1618–1648

Before 1648 the main political power within the geographical area known as Germany was the Holy Roman Empire. This large political formation was a loose confederation of kingdoms, principalities, duchies, ecclesiastical territories, and cities, each of which had its own laws and political institutions. The emperor, who was elected by a body of German princes, exercised immediate jurisdiction only in his own dynastic possessions and in the imperial cities. He also convened a legislative assembly known as the *Reichstag*, over which he exercised limited influence. But the emperor did not have a large administrative or judicial bureaucracy through which he could enforce imperial law in the localities. The empire was not in any sense a sovereign state, even though it had long been a major force in European diplomacy. It had acquired and maintained that international position by relying on the military and financial contributions of its imperial cities and the lands controlled directly by the Habsburg emperors.

A GERMAN WRITER DESCRIBES THE HORRORS OF THE THIRTY YEARS' WAR

In 1669 the German writer H. J. C. Grimmelshausen (1625–1676) published an imaginary account of the adventures of a German vagabond, to whom he gave the name Simplicissimus. The setting of the book was the Thirty Years' War in Germany, which Grimmelshausen had experienced firsthand. At age 10 Grimmelshausen, like the character Simplicissimus in the book, was captured by Hessian troops and later became a camp-follower. In this chapter Simplicissimus describes how the palace of his father was stormed, plundered, and ruined.

The first thing that these troops did was, that they stabbed their horses; thereafter each fell to his appointed task, which task was either more or less than ruin and destruction. For though some began to slaughter and to boil and to roast, so that it looked as if there should be a merry banquet forward, yet others there were who did but storm through the house above and below the stairs. . . . All that they had no mind to take with them they cut in pieces. Some thrust their swords through the hay and straw as if they had not enough sheep and swine to slaughter; and some shook the feathers out of the beds and in their stead stuffed in bacon and other dried meat and provisions as if such were better and softer to sleep upon. Others broke the stove and the windows as if they had a never-ending summer to promise. Housewares of copper and tin they beat flat, and packed such vessels, all bent and spoiled, in with the rest. Bedsteads, tables, chairs and benches they burned, though there lay many cords of dry wood in the yard. . . .

Our maid was so handled in the stable that she could not come out; which is a shame to tell of. Our man they laid bound upon the ground, thrust a gag into his mouth, and poured a pailful of filthy water into his body; and by this, which they called a Swedish draught, they forced him to lead a party of them to another place where they captured men and beasts, and brought them back to our farm, in which company were my dad, my mother, and our Ursula.

And now they began first to take the flints out of their pistols and in place of them to jam the peasants' thumbs in and so to torture the poor rogues as if they had been about the burning of witches. For one of them they had taken they thrust into the baking oven and there lit a fire under him, although he had as yet confessed no crime; as for another, they put a cord round his head and so twisted it tight with a piece of wood that the blood gushed from his mouth and nose and ears. In a word each had his own device to torture the peasants, and each peasant had several torture.

Source: Reprinted from *The Adventurous Simplicissimus: Being the Description of the Life of a Strange Vagabond Named Melchior Sternfels Von Fuchshaim* by H. J. C. Grimmelshausen. Published by the University of Nebraska Press.

■ **Map 15.3 Europe in 1648 after the Treaty of Westphalia**
The Holy Roman Empire no longer included the Dutch Republic, which was now independent of Spain. Some of the lands of the Austrian Habsburg Monarchy and Brandenburg-Prussia lay outside the boundaries of the Holy Roman Empire. Italy was divided into a number of small states in the north, while Naples, Sicily, and Sardinia were ruled by Spain.

The Thirty Years' War permanently altered the nature of this vast and intricate political structure. That war began as a conflict between Protestant German princes and the Catholic emperor over religious and constitutional issues. The incident that triggered it in 1618 was the so-called Defenestration of Prague, when members of the predominantly Protestant Bohemian legislature, known as the Diet, threw two royal officials out a castle window as a protest against the religious policies of their recently elected king, the future emperor Ferdinand II. The Diet proceeded to depose Ferdinand, a Catholic, and elect a Protestant prince, Frederick V of the Palatinate, to replace him. The war soon broadened into a European-wide struggle over the possession of German and Spanish territory, as the Danes, Swedes, and French successively entered the conflict against the emperor and his Spanish Habsburg relatives. For a brief period in the late 1620s England also entered the conflict against Spain. The war, which was fought mainly on German soil, had a devastating effect on the country. More than one million soldiers marched across German lands, sacking towns and exploiting the resources of local communities. Germany lost up to one-third of its population, while the destruction of property retarded the economic development of the country for more than fifty years.

The political effects of the war were no less traumatic. By virtue of the Treaty of Westphalia, which ended the war in 1648, the empire was permanently weakened, although it continued to function until 1806 (see Map 15.3). The individual German territories within the empire developed more institutional autonomy than they had before the war.

They became sovereign states themselves, with their own armies, foreign policies, and central bureaucracies. Two of these German states soon surpassed all the others in size and military strength and became major European powers. The first was Brandenburg-Prussia, a collection of various territories in northern Germany that was transformed into the kingdom of Prussia at the beginning of the eighteenth century. In the nineteenth century Prussia would unify Germany under its leadership. The second state was the Austrian Habsburg Monarchy, which in the eighteenth century was usually identified simply as Austria. The Habsburgs had long dominated the Holy Roman Empire and continued to secure election as emperors after the Treaty of Westphalia. In the late seventeenth century, however, the Habsburg Monarchy acquired its own institutional identity, distinct from that of the empire. It consisted of the lands that the Habsburgs controlled directly in the southeastern part of the empire and other territories, including the kingdom of Hungary, which lay outside the territorial boundary of the empire (see Map 15.1). Both Prussia and Austria developed their own forms of absolutism during the second half of the seventeenth century.

THE GROWTH OF THE PRUSSIAN STATE

In 1648, at the end of the Thirty Years' War, Prussia could barely have claimed the status of an independent state, much less that of an absolute monarchy. The core of the Prussian state was Brandenburg, which claimed the status of an electorate, since its ruler cast one of the ballots to elect the Holy Roman Emperor. The lands that belonged to the elector of Brandenburg lay scattered throughout northern Germany and stretched into eastern Europe. As

Map 15.4 The Growth of Brandenburg-Prussia in the Seventeenth and Eighteenth Centuries
By acquiring lands throughout northern Germany, Prussia became a major European power. The process began during the early seventeenth century, but it continued well into the eighteenth century. The Prussian army, which was the best trained fighting force in Europe in the eighteenth century, greatly facilitated Prussia's growth.

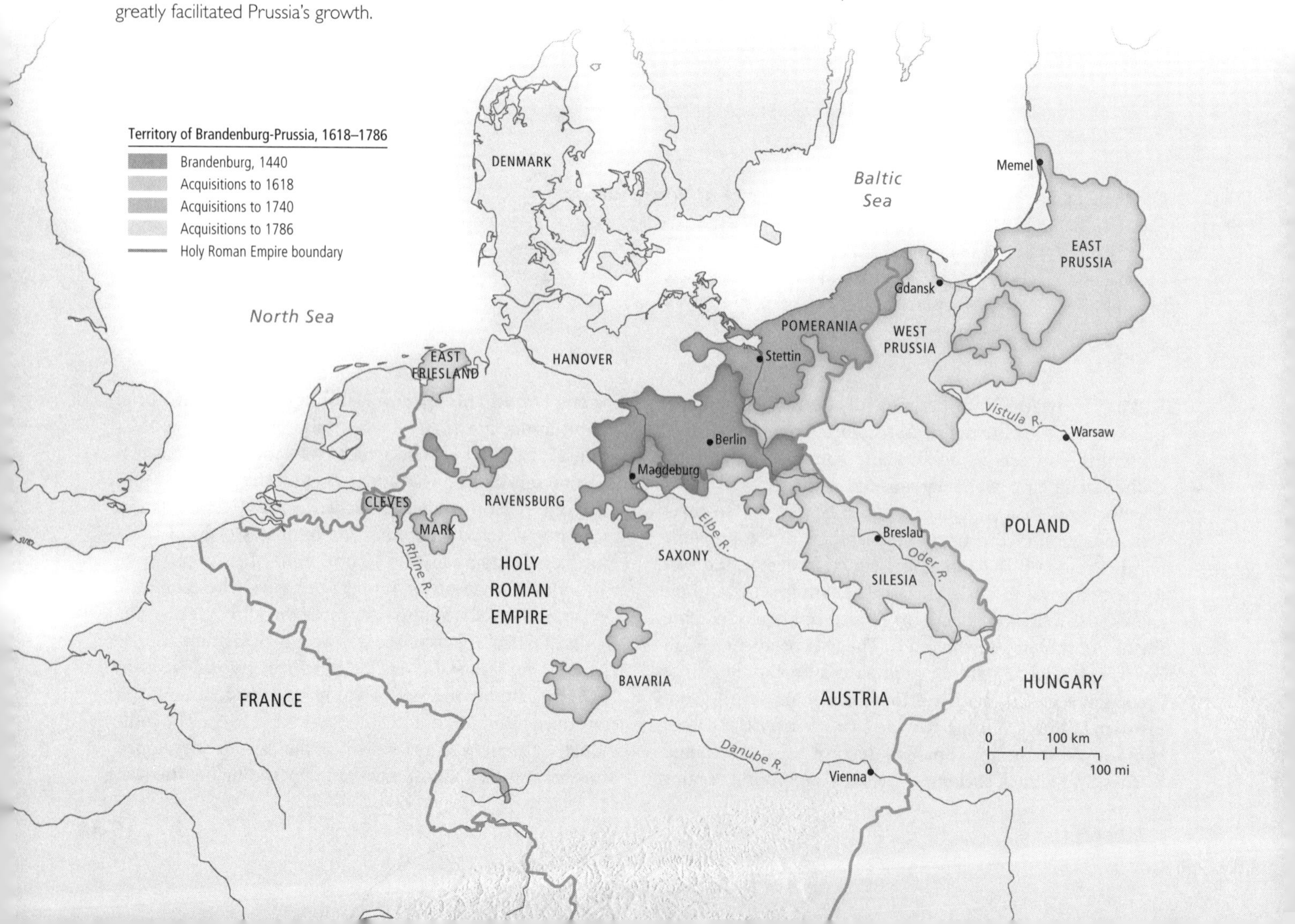

a result of the Thirty Years' War, the archbishoprics of Magdeburg and East Pomerania were annexed to Brandenburg. The Hohenzollern family, in whose line the electorate of Brandenburg passed, also owned or controlled various parcels of German territory in the Rhineland, near the borders of the Spanish Netherlands. In 1618 the Hohenzollerns had acquired the much larger but equally remote duchy of Prussia, a Baltic territory lying outside the boundaries of the Holy Roman Empire. As ruler of these disparate and noncontiguous lands, the elector of Brandenburg had virtually no state bureaucracy, collected few taxes, and commanded only a small army. Most of his territories, moreover, lay in ruins in 1648, having been devastated by Swedish and imperial troops at various times during the war.

The Great Elector Frederick William (r. 1640–1688) began the long process of turning this ramshackle structure into a powerful and cohesive German state (see Map 15.4). His son King Frederick I (r. 1688–1713) and grandson Frederick William I (r. 1713–1740) completed the transformation. The key to their success, as it was for all aspiring absolute monarchs in eastern Europe, was to secure the compliance of the traditional nobility, who in Prussia were known as Junkers°. The Great Elector Frederick William achieved this end by granting the Junkers a variety of privileges, including exemption from import duties and the excise tax. The most valuable concession was the legal confirmation of their rights over the serfs. During the previous 150 years Prussian peasants had lost their freedom, becoming permanently bound to the estates of their lords and completely subject to the Junkers' arbitrary brand of local justice. The Junkers had a deeply vested interest in perpetuating this oppressive system of serfdom, and the lawgiver Frederick was able to provide them with the legal guarantees they required.

With the loyalty of the Junkers secure, Frederick William went about the process of building a powerful Prussian state. A large administrative bureaucracy, centralized under a General Directory in Berlin, governed both financial and military affairs throughout the elector's lands. At first it was staffed by members of the nobility, but eventually educated commoners were recruited into the system. The taxes that the government collected, especially from the towns, went in large part to fund a standing army, which had come into being in the late 1650s.

The Prussian army grew rapidly, rising to 30,000 men in 1690 and 80,000 by 1740. It consisted of a combination of carefully recruited volunteers, foreign mercenaries, and, after 1713, conscripts from the general population. Its most famous regiment, known as the Blue Prussians or the Giants of Potsdam, consisted of 1,200 men, each of whom was at least six feet tall. Commanded by officers drawn from the nobility and reinforced by Europe's first system of military reserves, this army quickly became the best trained fighting force in Europe. Prussia became a model military state, symbolized by the transformation of the royal gardens into an army training ground during the reign of Frederick William I.

As this military state grew in size and complexity, its rulers acquired many of the attributes of absolute rule. Most significantly they became the sole legislators within the state. The main representative assembly in the electorate, the Diet of Brandenburg, met for the last time in 1652. Frederick William and his successors, however, continued to consult with smaller local assemblies, especially in the matter of taxation. The elevation of Frederick I's status to that of king of Prussia in 1701 marked a further consolidation of power in the person of the ruler. His son's style of rule, which included physical punishment of judges whose decisions displeased him, suggested that the Prussian monarchy not only had attained absolute power but could occasionally abuse it.

THE AUSTRIAN HABSBURG MONARCHY

The Austrian Habsburgs were much less successful than the Hohenzollerns in building a centralized, consolidated state along absolutist lines. The various territories that made up the Austrian Habsburg Monarchy in the late seventeenth century were larger and more diverse than those that belonged to the king of Prussia. In addition to the collection of duchies that form present-day Austria and that then served as the core of the monarchy, it embraced two subordinate kingdoms, which were themselves composed of various semiautonomous principalities and duchies. The first of these, lying to the north, was the kingdom of Bohemia, which had struggled against Habsburg control for nearly a century and included Moravia and Silesia. The second, lying to the southeast, was the kingdom of Hungary, including the large semiautonomous principality of Transylvania. The Habsburgs regained Hungary from the Ottoman Empire in stages between 1664 and 1718. In 1713 the monarchy also acquired the former Spanish Netherlands and the Italian territories of Milan and Naples.

The Austrian Habsburg monarchs of the seventeenth and early eighteenth centuries never succeeded in integrating these ethnically, religiously, and politically diverse lands into a unified, cohesive state similar to that of France. The problem was a lack of a unified bureaucracy. The only centralized administrative institutions in this amalgam of kingdoms were the Court Chamber, which superintended the collection of taxes throughout the monarchy, and the Austrian army, which included troops from all Habsburg lands. Like many European military forces it had become a standing army in 1648, and by 1716 it had a troop strength of 165,000 men. Even these centralized institutions had difficulty operating smoothly. The council of the army had trouble integrating units drawn from separate kingdoms, while the Court Chamber never developed a uniform system of tax collection. For all practical purposes the Habsburgs had to rule their various kingdoms separately.

In governing its Austrian and Bohemian lands, this decentralized Habsburg monarchy did nonetheless acquire some of the characteristics of absolutist rule. This development toward absolutism began long before the Treaty of Westphalia in 1648. After defeating the Bohemians at the Battle of White Mountain in 1620 during the Thirty Years' War, Emperor Ferdinand II (r. 1618–1637) had decided to strengthen his authority in the areas under his direct control. Bohemia, which had led the revolt against him, was the main target of this policy, but the emperor used this opportunity to increase his power throughout his territories. After punishing the rebels and exiling many of the Protestant nobility, he undertook a deliberate expansion of his legislative and judicial powers, and he secured direct control over all his administrative officials.

A policy of severe religious repression accompanied this increase in the emperor's authority. Like the French cardinal Richelieu, Ferdinand assumed that Protestantism served as a justification for rebellion, and he therefore decided that its practice could not be tolerated. Protestants in all the emperor's territories were forced to take a Catholic loyalty oath, and Protestant education was banned. Protestant towns were destroyed at exactly the same time that Richelieu was razing the fortifications of the Huguenot town of La Rochelle. These efforts at reconversion continued right through the seventeenth century. They amounted to a policy of religious or "confessional" absolutism.

While the Habsburgs succeeded in imposing some elements of absolutist rule on the Austrians and the Bohemians in the early seventeenth century, they encountered much more resistance when they attempted to follow the same course of action with respect to Hungary in the late seventeenth and eighteenth centuries. Hungarians had a long tradition of limited, constitutional rule in which the national Diet had exercised powers of legislation and taxation, just as Parliament did in England. Habsburg emperors made some limited inroads on these traditions but they were never able to break them. They also were unable to achieve the same degree of religious uniformity that they had imposed on their other territories. In Hungary the Habsburgs encountered the limits of royal absolutism.

THE OTTOMAN EMPIRE: BETWEEN EAST AND WEST

In the seventeenth and early eighteenth centuries the southeastern border of the Habsburg monarchy separated the kingdom of Hungary from the Ottoman Empire. This militarized frontier marked not only the political boundary between two empires but a deeper cultural boundary between East and West.

As we have seen in previous chapters, the West is not just a geographical but also a cultural realm, and the people who inhabit this realm, although distinct from one another, share many of the same religious, political, legal, and philosophical traditions. The Ottoman Turks, who posed a recurrent military threat to the Habsburg monarchy and who reached the gates of Vienna in 1683, were generally thought of as not belonging to this Western world. Because the Ottoman Turks were Muslims, Europeans considered them enemies of Christianity, infidels who were bent on the destruction of Christendom. In the sixteenth century Catholics and Protestants alike claimed that the military victories of the Turks over European forces were signs of divine punishment for the sins European Christians had committed. Ottoman emperors, known as sultans, were considered despots who ruled over their subjects as slaves. The sultans were also depicted in Western literature as cruel and brutal tyrants, the opposite of the ideal Christian prince of Europe. One French play of 1612 depicted the mother of the sultan Mehmet the Conqueror (r. 1451–1481) as drinking the blood of a victim.

These stereotypes of the Turks served the function of giving Europeans a sense of their own Western identity. Turks became a negative reference group with whom Europeans could favorably compare themselves. The realities of Ottoman politics and culture, however, were quite different from the ways in which they were represented in European literature. Turkish despotism, the name Europeans gave to the Ottoman system of government, existed only in theory. Ever since the fourteenth century Ottoman writers had claimed for the sultan extraordinary powers, including the right to seize the landed property of his subjects at will. In practice he never exercised unlimited power. His prerogatives were limited by the spirit of Muslim law, and he shared power with the grand vizier, who was his chief executive officer. In practice there was little difference between the rule of the sultans and that of European absolute monarchs.

Even the high degree of administrative centralization for which the Ottoman Empire was famous did not encompass all the regions under its control. Many of its provinces, especially those in the Balkans, enjoyed a considerable measure of autonomy, especially in the seventeenth century. The Balkans, which were geographically part of Europe, never experienced the full force of direct Turkish rule. In all the Ottoman provinces there was a complex pattern of negotiation between the central imperial administration and local officials. In this respect the Ottoman Empire was similar to the absolutist monarchies of western and central Europe. The Ottoman Empire bore the closest resemblance to the Spanish monarchy, which also ruled many far-flung territories in Europe. Like the Spanish monarchy, the Ottoman Empire declined in power during the seventeenth century and lost effective control of some of its outlying provinces.

Ottoman Turks and Europeans frequently went to war against each other, but there was a constant pattern of diplomatic, economic, and cultural interaction between them. The Turks had been involved in European warfare since the fifteenth century, and they had formed diplomatic alliances with the French against the Austrian Habsburgs on a number of occasions. Europeans and Ottomans often borrowed military technology from each other, and they also shared knowledge of administrative techniques. Trade between European countries and the Ottoman Empire remained brisk throughout this period. Europe supplied hardware and textiles to the Turks while they in turn shipped coffee, tobacco, and tulips to European ports. Communities of Turks and other Muslims lived in European cities, while numerous European merchants resided in territories under Ottoman control.

These encounters between Turks and Europeans suggest that the militarized boundary between the Habsburgs and the Ottoman Empire was much more porous than its fortifications would suggest. Military conflict and Western contempt for Muslim Turks disguised a much more complex process of political and cultural interaction between the two civilizations. Europeans tended to think of the Ottoman Empire as "oriental," but it is more accurate to view it as a region lying between the East and the West.

RUSSIA AND THE WEST

The other seventeenth-century power that marked the boundary between East and West was the vast Russian Empire, which stretched from its boundary with Poland in the west all the way to the Pacific Ocean in the east. Until the end of the seventeenth century, the kingdom of Moscovy and the lands attached to it seemed, at least to Europeans, part of the Asiatic world. Dominated by an Eastern Orthodox branch of Christianity, Russia drew very little upon the cultural traditions associated with western Europe. Unlike its neighboring Slavic kingdom of Poland, it had not absorbed large doses of German culture. It also appeared to Europeans to be another example of "Oriental despotism," a state in which the ruler, known as the tsar, could rule his subjects at will, "not bound up by any law or custom."

During the reign of Tsar Peter I, known as Peter the Great (r. 1682–1725), Russia underwent a process of Westernization, bringing it more into line with the culture of European countries and becoming a major European power. This policy began after Peter visited England, Holland, northern Germany, and Austria in 1697 and 1698. Upon his return he directed his officials and members of the upper levels of Russian society to adopt Western styles of dress and appearance, including the removal of men's beards. (Scissors were kept in the customs house for this purpose alone.) Beards symbolized the backward, Eastern, Orthodox culture from whose grip Peter hoped to extricate his country. Young Russian boys were sent abroad for their education. Women began to participate openly in the social and cultural life of the cities, in violation of Orthodox custom. Smoking was permitted despite the Church's insistence that Scripture condemned it. The calendar was reformed and books were printed in modern Russian type. Peter's importation of Western art and the imitation of Western architecture complemented this policy of enforced cultural change. Westernization, however, involved more than a change of manners and appearance. It also involved military and political reforms that changed the character of the Russian state.

During the first twenty-five years of his reign Peter had found himself unable to achieve sustained military success against his two great enemies, the Ottoman Turks to the south and the Swedes to the west. During the Great Northern War with Sweden (1700–1721) Peter introduced a number of military reforms that eventually turned the tide against his enemy. These reforms were based on the knowledge he had acquired of military technology, organization,

Peter the Great at the Battle of Poltava (1709), at Which Russia Defeated Swedish Forces

Standing 6 feet 7 inches tall, at a time when the average male height was 5 feet 8 inches, Peter was great in military and political achievements as well as in stature.

and tactics of Western European states, especially Prussia and, ironically, Sweden itself. Having introduced a program of conscription, Peter assembled a large standing army of more than 200,000 men, which he trained and disciplined in the Prussian manner. All of this was supported by the imposition of new taxes on a variety of commodities, including beards, and the encouragement of Russian industry in much the same way that Colbert had encouraged French industry. A central council, established in 1711, not only directed financial administration but also levied and supplied troops, not unlike the General Directory of the electorate of Brandenburg.

This new military state also acquired many of the centralizing and absolutist features of western European monarchies. Efforts to introduce absolutism in Russia had begun during the reigns of Alexis (r. 1645–1676) and Fedor (r. 1676–1682), who had achieved limited success in strengthening the central administration, controlling the nobility, and brutally suppressing peasant rebellions. Peter built upon his predecessors' achievement. He created an entirely new structure for managing the empire, appointing twelve governors to superintend Russia's forty-three separate provinces. He brought the Church under state control. By establishing a finely graded hierarchy of official ranks in the armed forces, the civil administration, and the court, Peter not only improved administrative efficiency but also made it possible for men of nonaristocratic birth to attain the same privileged status as the old landowning nobility. At the same time he won the support of all landowners by introducing primogeniture (inheritance of the entire estate by the eldest son), which prevented their estates from being subdivided, and supporting the enserfment of the peasants. In dealing with his subjects Peter claimed more power than any other absolute monarch in Europe. During the trial of his own son, Alexis, for treason in 1718, he told the clergy that "we have a sufficient and absolute power to judge our son for his crimes according to our own pleasure."

The most visible sign of Peter's policy of Westernization was the construction of the port city of St. Petersburg on the Gulf of Finland, which became the new capital of the Russian Empire. One of the main objectives of Russian foreign policy during Peter's reign had been to secure "a window to Europe" on the Baltic, which would open up trade with the West and allow Russia to become a Western naval power. By draining a swamp at the estuary of the Neva river, Peter laid the basis for the construction of an entirely new city, which was designed with the assistance of French and Italian architects in a style characteristic of European cities. In this enterprise Peter benefited from the nearly unlimited power he had over his subjects. He commanded every stonemason in Russia to relocate to the new construction site, and he used his powers over the serfs to assemble a labor force of more than 150,000 men. Construction began in 1703, and within twenty years St. Petersburg had a population of 100,000 people. With his new capital city now looking westward, and an army and central administration reformed on the basis of Prussian and French example, Peter could enter the world of European diplomacy and warfare as both a Western and an absolute monarch.

CHRONOLOGY

The Age of Absolutism in Central and Eastern Europe

1618	Ferdinand II becomes Holy Roman Emperor (r. 1618–1637)
1640	Beginning of the reign of Frederick William, the Great Elector of Brandenburg Prussia (r. 1640–1688)
1657	Leopold I becomes Holy Roman Emperor (r. 1657–1705)
1682	Accession of Tsar Peter the Great of Russia (r. 1682–1725)
1688	Accession of Frederick as elector of Prussia; becomes king of Prussia in 1701
1703	Foundation of St. Petersburg, Russia's new capital and "window on the West"
1705	Joseph I (r. 1705–1711) becomes Holy Roman Emperor
1711	Charles VI (1711–1740), brother of Joseph I, becomes Holy Roman Emperor

Resistance to Absolutism in England and the Dutch Republic

The kingdom of England and the northern provinces of the Netherlands stand out as the two great exceptions to the dominant pattern of political development in seventeenth-century Europe. Both of these countries successfully resisted the establishment of royal absolutism, and neither underwent the rigorous centralization of power and the dynamic growth of the state that usually accompanied the establishment of absolutist rule. In England the encounter between the proponents and opponents of absolute monarchy was more pronounced than in any other European country. It resulted in the temporary destruction of the monarchy in 1649 and the establishment of parliamentary supremacy after the Glorious Revolution of 1688. In the northern provinces of the Netherlands, known as the Dutch Republic, an even more emphatic rejection of absolutism occurred. During their long struggle to win their independence from Spain, the Dutch established a republican, decentralized form of government, but that did not prevent them from acquiring considerable military strength and dominating the world's economy during the seventeenth century.

THE ENGLISH MONARCHY

At various times in the seventeenth century English monarchs tried to introduce royal absolutism, but the political institutions and the political culture of the country stood as major obstacles to their designs. As early as the fifteenth century, the English writer and diplomat Sir John Fortescue (ca. 1395–1477) had celebrated England's parliamentary system of government by contrasting it with that of France, where he claimed the king could make laws by himself and impose his will on his subjects. Fortescue's treatise contributed to the pride Englishmen had in what they considered their distinctive set of political and legal traditions. The most important of these traditions was the making of law and the levying of taxes by the two Houses of Parliament, the House of Lords and the House of Commons, with the king holding the power to sign or veto the bills they passed.

In the early seventeenth century the perception began to arise, especially among certain members of the House of Commons, that this tradition of parliamentary government was under attack. The first Stuart king, James I (r. 1603–1625), who succeeded the last Tudor monarch, Elizabeth I, aroused some of these fears as early as 1604, when he called his first parliament. James thought of himself as an absolute monarch, and in a number of speeches and published works he emphasized the height of his independent royal power, which was known in England as the prerogative°. James also spoke often about his divine right to rule, and he claimed that the main function of Parliament was simply to give the king advice, rather than to make law. These statements had the effect of antagonizing members of Parliament, leading them to defend their privileges, including the right they claimed to discuss foreign policy and other affairs of state.

James believed that he was an absolute monarch, but he did not actually try to put his ideas into practice. For example, he did not try to make laws or levy taxes without the consent of Parliament or deny men their legal rights, such as freedom from arbitrary imprisonment. The real political fireworks did not begin until James's son, Charles I (r. 1625–1649), succeeded him. Charles believed in absolutism every bit as much as his father, but unlike James, Charles actually put his theories into practice. His efforts to force his subjects to lend money to the government during a war with Spain (1625–1629) and his imprisonment of men who refused to make these loans led Parliament to pass the Petition of Right in 1628. This document declared boldly that subjects possessed fundamental rights that kings could not violate under any circumstances, even when the country was at war.

Charles consented to the Petition of Right, but when Parliament met again in 1629, further conflict between the king and certain members of the House of Commons developed over taxation and the king's religious policies. Charles had been collecting duties on exports without parliamentary approval since 1625. He had also begun to favor conservative clergymen known as Arminians, leading the more zealous English Protestants, the Puritans, to fear that the English Church was leaning in the direction of Catholicism or "popery." Faced with this opposition over constitutional and religious issues, Charles decided to dismiss this parliament and to rule indefinitely without calling another one.

This period of nonparliamentary government, known as the *personal rule,* lasted until 1640. During these years Charles, unable to collect taxes by the authority of Parliament, used his prerogative to bring in new revenues, especially by asking all subjects to pay "ship-money" to support the outfitting of ships to defend the country against attack. During the personal rule the king's religious policy fell under the control of William Laud, who was named archbishop of Canterbury in 1633 and who became one of the king's main privy councilors. Laud's determination to restore many of the rituals associated with Roman Catholicism alienated large numbers of Puritans and led to a growing perception that members of the king's government were engaged in a conspiracy to destroy both England's ancient constitution and the Protestant religion.

This period of absolutism might have continued indefinitely if Charles had not once again been faced with the financial demands of war. In 1636 the king tried to introduce a new religious liturgy in his northern kingdom of Scotland. The liturgy included a number of rituals that the firmly Calvinist Scottish population considered popish. The new liturgy so angered a group of women in Edinburgh that they threw their chairs at the bishop when he introduced it. In response to this affront at their religion, the Scots signed a National Covenant (1638) pledging themselves to defend the integrity of their Church, abolished episcopacy (government of the church by bishops) in favor of a Presbyterian system of church government, and mobilized a large army. To secure the funds to fight the Scots, Charles was forced to summon his English Parliament, thereby ending the period of personal rule.

THE ENGLISH CIVIL WARS AND REVOLUTION

Tensions between the reconvened English Parliament and Charles led to the first revolution of modern times. The Short Parliament, called in April 1640, lasted only two months, but a Scottish military victory against the English in that year forced the king to call a second parliament. The Long Parliament, which met in November 1640, impeached many of the king's ministers and judges, and it dismantled the judicial apparatus of the eleven years of personal rule, including the courts that had been active in the prosecution of Puritans. Parliament declared the king's nonparliamentary taxes illegal, and it enacted a law limiting the time between the meetings of Parliament to three years.

This legislation did not satisfy the king's critics in Parliament. Their suspicion that the king was conspiring against them and their demand to approve all royal appointments created a poisoned political atmosphere in which neither side trusted the other. After the king and his armed guards forced their way into the House of Commons to arrest five members for treason, there was little hope of reconciliation. In August 1642 civil war began between the Parliamentarians, known as Roundheads because many of the artisans who supported them had close-cropped hair styles, and the Royalists or Cavaliers, who often wore their hair in long flowing locks. Parliament, which was supported by the Scots and which benefited from the creation in 1645 of a well-trained, efficient fighting force, the New Model Army, ultimately won this war in 1646 and took Charles prisoner. The king's subsequent negotiations with the Scots and the English Presbyterians, both of whom had originally fought against him, led to a second civil war in 1648. In this war, which lasted only a few months, the New Model Army once again defeated Royalist forces.

CHRONOLOGY

A Century of Revolution in England and Scotland

1603	James VI of Scotland (r. 1567–1625) becomes James I of England (r. 1603–1625)
1625	Death of James I and accession of Charles I (r. 1625–1649)
1628	Parliament passes the Petition of Right
1629–1640	Personal rule of Charles I
1638	Scots sign the National Covenant
1640	Opening of the Long Parliament
1642–1646	Civil War in England, ending with the capture of King Charles I
1648	Second Civil War; New Model Army defeats English Presbyterians and Scots
1649	Execution of Charles I of England and the beginning of the Republic
1653	End of the Long Parliament; beginning and dissolution of Barebones Parliament; Oliver Cromwell becomes Protector of England, Scotland, and Ireland
1660	Restoration of the monarchy in the person of Charles II; House of Lords and the Church of England also restored
1685	Death of Charles II and accession of his brother, James II (r. 1685–1688)
1688–1689	Glorious Revolution in England and Scotland
1707	England and Scotland politically joined to form the United Kingdom of Great Britain

This military victory led to a series of revolutionary changes in the English system of government. Believing with some justification that Charles could never be trusted, and eager to bring about an end to years of political uncertainty, members of the army purged Parliament of its Presbyterian members, leaving only a small group of Independents. These men, who favored a form of church government in which the congregations had a high degree of autonomy, had broken off negotiations with Charles I. The remaining members of Parliament were known as the Rump, because they were all that was left of the Long Parliament elected in 1640. This mall group of Independents in Parliament, following the wishes of the army, set up a court to try Charles in January 1649. The trial resulted in Charles's conviction and execution, and shortly thereafter the Rump destroyed the House of Lords and the monarchy itself. As Parliament had already destroyed the episcopal structure of the English Church in 1646, these actions completed a genuine revolution, a political transformation that destroyed the very system of government and replaced it with new institutions.

The revolution resulted in the establishment of a republic, in which the House of Commons possessed supreme legislative power in the name of the people of England. This change in the system of government, however, did not lead to the introduction of a more democratic form of government. A government of this sort, in which a very large percentage of the adult male population would be allowed to vote, was the goal of a political party, the Levellers, which originated in the New Model Army and attracted considerable support in London and the towns. In 1647 at Putney Bridge, near London, the Levellers participated in a debate with more conservative army officers concerning the future constitution of the country. The spokesmen for the Levellers called for annual parliaments, the separation of powers between the executive and legislative branches of government, and the introduction of universal suffrage for men. The army officers argued against this proposed constitution, arguing that the vote should be entrusted only to men who owned property. The officers made sure that the Leveller program would not be accepted. The Levellers eventually mutinied in the army, their leaders were imprisoned, and the party collapsed.

The fate of the Levellers and their program underlines the fact that the English revolution was brought about by men of property, especially by the gentry or lesser aristocracy who sat in the House of Commons and who served as officers in the New Model Army. Although these men defeated and executed the king and secured the right to participate regularly in the governance of the kingdom, they were also determined to keep political power in the hands of their own class.

The republican government established in 1649 did not last. Tension between the army and the Rump, fueled by the belief that the Rump was not creating a godly society, resulted in the army's dissolution of the Long Parliament in 1653 and the selection of a small parliament of zealous Puritans, nominated by the army. Known as the Barebones Parliament for one of its members, Praise-God Barebones, this assembly soon became hopelessly divided between radicals who wished to eliminate state support of the Church, the Court of Chancery, and the universities, and the moderates who opposed these measures. Unable to overcome its divisions, it too was dissolved after sitting for only five months.

At that point Oliver Cromwell (1599–1658), the commander-in-chief of the army and the most prominent member of the Council of State after 1649, had himself proclaimed Protector of England, Scotland, and Ireland. Cromwell had been a leader of the revolution, a zealous Puritan who had provided crucial support for the execution of the king and the establishment of the republic. At the same time, however, Cromwell feared that the Levellers and now the radical Puritans of Barebones Parliament would destroy the social order. The establishment of the Protectorate, in which Cromwell shared legislative power with Parliament, represented an effort to return to a more traditional system of government. Cromwell would not, however, go so far as to accept a petition of 1657 to make him king. After Cromwell's death in 1658 and the brief rule of his son Richard, the Protectorate collapsed. A period of political instability, in which there was renewed hostility between the army and the members of Parliament, led the army to restore the monarchy in 1660.

A LEVELLER ATTACKS THE LEADERS OF THE ENGLISH REVOLUTION

Within a month of King Charles I's execution in 1649, members of the Leveller party suspected that the officers of the army had abandoned their pledge to implement political reforms. They feared that the army was establishing an oligarchic regime that was just as repressive as that of Charles I. One of the Leveller leaders, John Lilburne, wrote this powerful and eloquent statement of the betrayal of the English revolution by its leaders.

Insomuch that we are even aghast and astonished to see that notwithstanding the production of the highest notions of freedom that ever this Nation or any people in the world have brought to light, notwithstanding the vast expense of blood and treasure that hath been made to purchase those freedoms, notwithstanding the many eminent victories God hath been pleased to honor our just cause withall, notwithstanding the extraordinary gripes and pangs this House hath suffered more than once at the hands of your own servants, and that at least for the obtaining these our native liberties. . . .

That yet after all these things have been done and suffered . . . behold, in the close of it all we hear and see what gives us fresh and pregnant cause to believe that the contrary is really intended, and that all those specious pretenses and high notions of Liberty with those extraordinary courses that have of late been taken . . . appear to us to have been done and directed by some secret powerful influences, the more securely and unsuspectingly to attain to an absolute dominion over the commonwealth.

Source: From *England's New Chains Discovered* by John Lilburne, 1649.

LATER STUART ABSOLUTISM AND THE GLORIOUS REVOLUTION

Charles II (r. 1660–1685) and his brother James II (r. 1685–1688) were both absolutists who admired the political achievement of their cousin, Louis XIV of France. At the same time, however, they realized that they could never return to the policies of their father, much less adopt those of Louis. Neither of them attempted to rule indefinitely without Parliament, as Charles I had. Their main objective was to destroy the independence of Parliament by packing it with their own supporters and use the prerogative to weaken the force of the parliamentary statutes to which they objected.

The main political crisis of Charles II's reign was the attempt by a group of members of Parliament, headed by the Earl of Shaftesbury (1621–1683) and known by their opponents as Whigs, to exclude the king's brother, James, from the throne on the grounds that he was a Catholic. Charles opposed this strategy because it violated the theory of hereditary divine right, according to which God sanctioned the right of the king's closest heir to succeed him. Those members of Parliament who supported Charles on

JUSTICE IN HISTORY

The Trial of Charles I

In January 1649, after the New Model Army had defeated the royalist forces in England's second civil war and purged Parliament of its Presbyterian members, the few remaining members of the House of Commons voted by a narrow margin to erect a High Court of Justice to try King Charles I. This trial, which resulted in Charles's execution, marked the only time in European history that a monarch was tried and executed while still holding the office of king.

The decision to try the king formed part of a deliberate political strategy. The men who arranged the proceeding knew that they were embarking upon a revolutionary course by declaring that the House of Commons, as the elected representative of the people, was the highest power in the realm. They also knew that the republican regime they were establishing did not command a large body of popular support. By trying the king publicly in a court of law and by ensuring that the trial was reported in daily newspapers (the first such trial in history), they hoped to prove the legitimacy of their cause and win support for the new regime.

The decision to bring the king to justice created two legal problems. The first was to identify a crime upon which the trial would be based. For many years members of Parliament had insisted that the king had violated the ancient laws of the kingdom. The charge read that he had "wickedly designed to erect an unlimited and tyrannical power" and he had waged war against his people in two civil wars. His prosecutors claimed that those activities amounted to the crime of treason. The problem was that treason in England was a crime committed by a subject against the king, not by the king against his subjects. In order to try the king for this crime, his accusers had to construct a new theory of treason, according to which the king had attacked his own political body, which they identified with the kingdom or the state.

The second problem was to make the court itself a legitimate tribunal. According to English constitutional law, the king possessed the highest legal authority in the land. He appointed his judges, and the courts represented his authority. Parliament could vote to erect a special court, but the bill authorizing it would become law only if the king agreed to it. In this case the House of Commons had set up the court by its own authority, and it had named 135 men, most of whom were army officers, to serve as its judges. The revolutionary nature of this tribunal was difficult to disguise, and Charles made its illegality the basis of his defense. When asked how he would plead, he challenged the legitimacy of the court.

> *"By what power am I called hither?" he asked. "I would know by what authority—I mean lawful authority. There are many unlawful authorities in the world—thieves and robbers by the highways. And when I know what lawful authority, I shall answer. Remember I am your king, our lawful king. . . . I have a trust committed to me by God by old and lawful descent; I will not betray it to answer to a new unlawful authority."*

By taking this position Charles put himself on the side of the law, and by refusing to enter a plea he also prevented his prosecutors from presenting the evidence against him.

The arguments that King Charles and John Bradshawe, the president of the court, presented regarding the legitimacy of the court reflected the main constitutional conflict in seventeenth-century England. On the one hand was the doctrine of divine-right absolutism, according to which the king received his authority from God. He was therefore responsible to God alone, not to the people. His subjects could neither try him in a court of law nor fight him on the battlefield. "A king," said Charles, "cannot be tried by any superior jurisdiction on earth." On the other hand was the doctrine of popular sovereignty, which held that political power came from the people. As Bradshawe said in response to Charles's objection, "Sir, as the law is your superior, so truly Sir, there is something that is superior to the law, and that is indeed the parent or author of law, and that is the people of England." This trial, therefore, involved not only a confrontation between Charles and his revolutionary judges but an encounter between two incompatible political ideologies.

In 1649 the advocates of popular sovereignty triumphed over those of divine right. Charles was convicted as a

Trial of Charles I at Westminster Hall, January 1649

The king is sitting in the prisoner's box in the foreground, facing the commissioners of the High Court of Justice. His refusal to plead meant that a full trial could not take place.

"tyrant, traitor, murderer, and public enemy of the good people of this nation." The verdict was never in doubt, although only 67 of the 135 men originally appointed as judges voted to convict the king, and a mere 59 signed the death warrant. The trial succeeded only to the extent that it facilitated the establishment of the new regime. With Charles gone, the Rump could move ahead with the abolition of the monarchy and the establishment of a republic. But in dramatic terms the trial was a complete failure. Charles, a small shy man with a nervous stammer, was expected to make a poor impression, but he spoke eloquently when he refused to plead, and he won support from spectators in the gallery. In the greatest show trial of the seventeenth century, the royal defendant stole the show.

When Charles's son, Charles II, was restored to the throne in 1660, royalists finally had their revenge against the judges of this court. Those who could be found alive were hanged, disemboweled, and quartered. For those who were already dead, there was to be another type of justice. In 1661 Royalists exhumed the badly decomposed corpses of Bradshawe, Henry Ireton, and Oliver Cromwell, the three men who bore the largest responsibility for the execution of the king. The three cadavers were hanged and their skulls were placed on pikes on top of Westminster Hall. This macabre ritual served as the Royalists' way of vilifying the memory of the judges of this illegal and revolutionary trial, and their unpardonable sin of executing an anointed king.

Questions of Justice

1. The men who brought King Charles to trial often spoke about bringing him to "justice." How is justice best understood in this context?
2. Why was it so important for the members of the High Court of Justice to make this trial conform to traditional common-law procedure? Did they succeed?
3. How does this trial reveal the limitations of divine-right absolutism in England?

Taking It Further

Peacey, Jason, ed. *The Regicides and the Execution of Charles I.* 2001. A collection of essays on various aspects of this episode and the men who signed the death warrant.

Wedgewood, C. V. *The Trial of Charles I.* 1964. Presents a full account and analysis of the trial by one of the great historical stylists of the twentieth century.

this issue, whom the Whigs called Tories, thwarted the designs of the Whigs in three successive parliaments between 1679 and 1681.

An even more serious political crisis occurred after James II succeeded to the throne in 1685. James began to exempt his fellow Catholics from the penal laws, which prevented them from worshipping freely, and from the Test Act of 1673, which had denied them the right to hold office under the crown. Catholics began to secure appointments in the army, the court, and local government. These efforts by the monarchy to grant toleration and political power to Catholics revived the traditional English fears of absolutism and popery. Not only the Whigs but also the predominantly Anglican Tories became alarmed at the king's policies. The birth of a Catholic son to James by his second wife, the Italian princess Mary of Modena, in June 1688 created the fear that the king's religious policy might be continued indefinitely. A group of seven Whigs and Tories, including the Bishop of London, drafted an invitation to William III of Orange, the captain general of the military forces of the Dutch Republic and James's nephew, to come to England to defend their Protestant religion and their constitution. William was married to James's eldest daughter, the Protestant Princess Mary, and as the king's nephew he also had a claim to the throne himself.

Invading with an international force of 12,000 men, William gathered substantial support from the English population, and when James's army defected, he was forced to flee to France without ever engaging William's forces in battle. The Convention, a special parliament convened by William in 1689, offered the crown to William and Mary while at the same time securing their assent to the Declaration of Rights, a document that later became the parliamentary statute known as the Bill of Rights. This bill, which is considered a cornerstone of the English constitution, corrected many of the abuses of royal power at the hands of James and Charles, especially the practice of exempting individuals from the penalties of the laws made by Parliament. By proclaiming William king and by excluding Catholics from the throne, the Bill of Rights also destroyed the theory of hereditary divine right.

It would be difficult to argue that this sequence of events, which is known as the Glorious Revolution, amounted to a revolution in the full sense of the word, since it did not change the basic institutions of English government. The revolution simply replaced one monarch with a king and queen who were more acceptable to the nation's political elite. But the events of 1688–1689 were decisive in defeating once and for all the absolutist designs of the Stuart kings and in guaranteeing that Parliament would

The House of Stuart
1603–1714

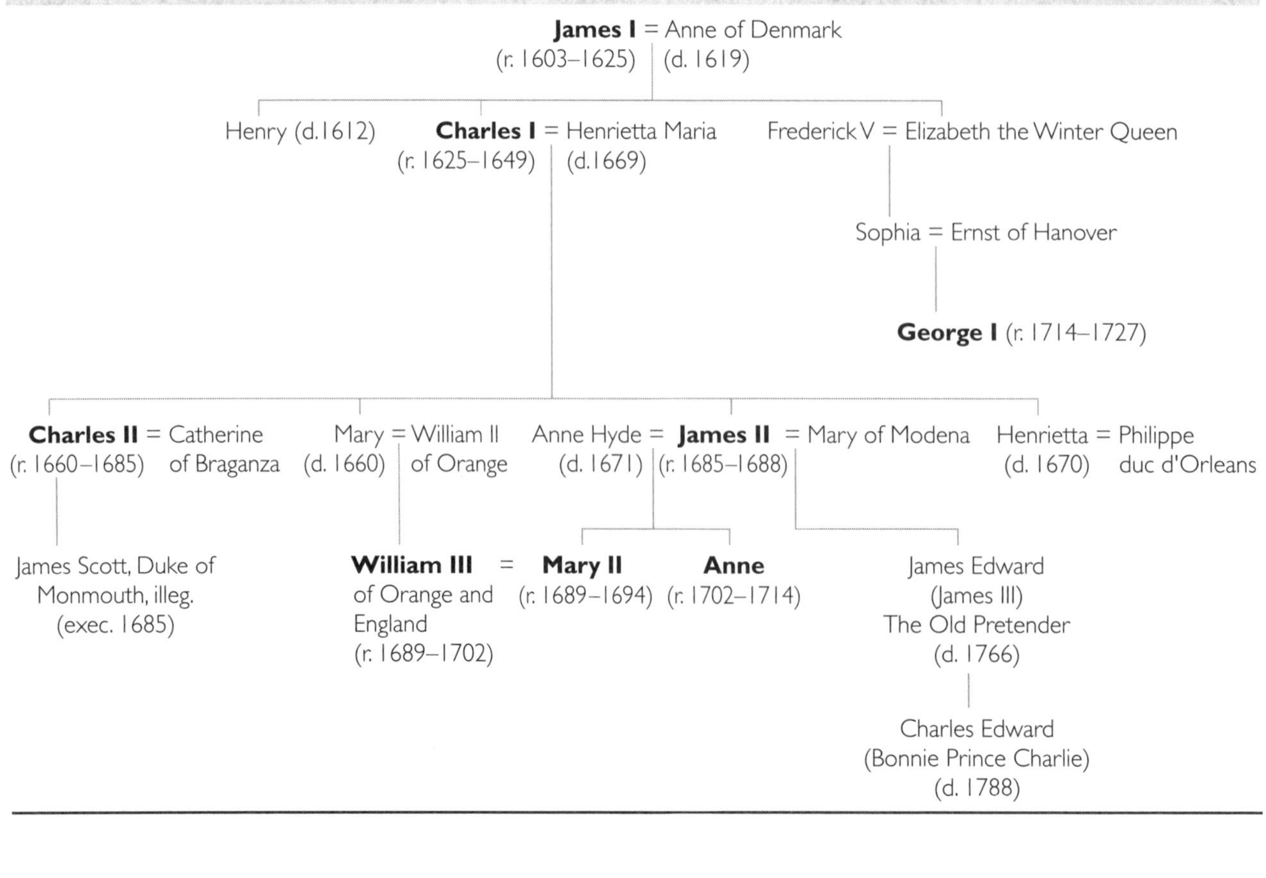

The Landing of William of Orange's Fleet in England, November 1688
The declared objective of this expedition was "for the restoration of the Constitution and the True Religion of England, Scotland and Ireland." After arriving in England, James II fled the country. William and his wife Mary became king and queen of England and Scotland in February 1689.

form a permanent and regular place in English government. That Parliament has in fact met every year since 1689, and its legislative power grew considerably when the crown vetoed a bill for the last time in 1707.

For the English aristocracy, the peers and gentry who sat in Parliament, the revolution guaranteed that they would occupy a paramount position within English politics and society for more than a hundred years. The revolution also had profound effects on British and European diplomacy, since it quickly brought England and Scotland into a war against Louis XIV of France, the great antagonist of William III. The main reason William had come to England and secured the crown in the first place was to secure British entry into the European alliance he was building against France.

Even if the Glorious Revolution has been misnamed, it prompted the publication of a genuinely revolutionary political manifesto, John Locke's *Two Treatises of Government* (1690). Locke was a radical Whig; he had written the *Treatises* in the early 1680s as a protest against the absolutist policies of Charles II, but only after the abdication and flight of James II could he safely publish his manuscript. Like Hobbes, Locke argued that men left the state of nature and agreed to form a political society in order to protect their property and prevent the chaos that characterized a state of war. But unlike Hobbes, Locke asserted that the government they formed was based on trust and that governments that acted against the interests of the people could be dissolved. In these circumstances the people, in whom sovereignty was always vested, could establish a new regime. Locke's treatises constituted an uncompromising attack on the system of royal absolutism, which he equated with slavery. His work gave the people permission to take up arms against an oppressive regime even before that regime had consolidated its power. Since its publication, the *Two Treatises of Government* have been pressed into the service of various revolutionary and radical causes, most notably in the Declaration of Independence by the United States of America in 1776.

The Glorious Revolution had a direct bearing on the growth of the English state. As long as Parliament had remained suspicious of the Stuart kings, it had been reluctant to facilitate the growth of the state, which until 1688 was under direct royal control. Once the king's power had been permanently restricted, however, and Parliament had begun to emerge as the highest power within the country, members of Parliament had less to fear from the executive branch of government. The inauguration of a long period of warfare against France in 1689 required the development of a large army and navy, the expansion of the bureaucracy, government borrowing on an unprecedented scale, and an increase in taxes. Members of Parliament, especially those in the Whig party, which had formed the main opposition to the monarchy before the revolution and had long opposed standing armies as a threat to English liberty, supported this expansion of the state as well as the war effort itself. By 1720 the kingdom of Great Britain, which had been created by the parliamentary union of England and Scotland in 1707, could rival the French state in military power, wealth, and diplomatic prestige. In fact, with its system of parliamentary government, Great Britain proved to be more successful than absolutist France in tapping the wealth of the people in the form of taxation to support its military establishment.

THE DUTCH REPUBLIC

In many respects the United Provinces of the Netherlands, known as the Dutch Republic, forms the most striking exception to the pattern of state building in seventeenth-century Europe. Formally established in 1588 during its revolt against Spanish rule, the Dutch Republic was the only major European power to maintain a republican form of government throughout the entire seventeenth century. As a state it also failed to conform to the pattern of centralization and consolidation that became evident in virtually all European monarchies. Having successfully resisted the centralizing policies of a large multinational Spanish monarchy, the Dutch Republic never acquired much of a centralized bureaucracy of its own. The provinces formed little more than a loose confederation of sovereign republican states. Each of the provinces sent deputies to the States General, where unanimity was required on all important issues, such as the levying of taxes, the declaration of war, and the ratification of treaties. Executive power was vested in a Council of State, which likewise consisted of deputies from the provinces. Even the individual provinces, the most important of which was Holland, were themselves decentralized, with the cities and rural areas sending delegates to a provincial assembly known as the States. Only the province of Holland invested one official, known as the grand pensionary, with extraordinary executive power.

This system of decentralized republican rule was much better suited for domestic affairs than the conduct of foreign policy. During most of the seventeenth century the Dutch were at war. After finally securing Spanish recognition of their independence by the Treaty of Münster in 1648, the Republic engaged in three commercial naval wars against England (1652–1654, 1665–1667, 1672–1674) and a much longer struggle against the territorial ambitions and economic policies of Louis XIV of France (1672–1678, 1689–1697, 1701–1713). The conduct of Dutch foreign policy and the coordination of the military forces of the seven provinces required some kind of central direction. During the 1650s John de Witt, the grand pensionary of Holland, assumed an informal presidency of the republic and directed the state's foreign policy in the first two wars against England. After 1672 William III, a prince of the hereditary house of Orange-Nassau, gave further unity and coordination to Dutch state policy. William, who served as the stadholder or governor of each of the seven provinces, became the captain-general of the republic's military forces when war with France began in 1672.

The House of Orange, which had a permanent vote in the States General, represented the royal, centralizing force within the Dutch Republic, and it led a party within the republic that favored a modification of republican rule. These princes never acquired the same type of constitutional authority that monarchs exercised in other European states. William III of Orange, who became William III of England and Scotland in 1689, exercised far more power in his new British kingdoms than he did in the Dutch Republic. Nevertheless the House of Orange played a crucial role in the rise of this tiny republic to the status of a world power. During the period of its influence the size of the Dutch military forces increased dramatically, from 50,000 men in 1670 to 73,000 in 1690 and 130,000 in 1710. During the same period of time the size of the Dutch navy doubled. In this one respect the republican, decentralized United Provinces participated in the same process of state building as the other great powers of Europe. The main reason the government was able to support this large standing army was the enormous wealth it had accumulated by virtue of the country's thriving international trade.

Political power in the Dutch Republic lay mainly with the wealthy merchants and bankers who served as regents in the councils of the towns. These same men represented the towns in the States of each province. The rural areas, which predominated only in the eastern provinces, were represented by the aristocracy. The country was therefore ruled by an oligarchy, but the men who belonged to it represented a predominantly urban, mercantile elite rather than a rural nobility. The members of this bourgeois elite did not tend to seek admission to landed society in the way that successful English merchants often did. Nor were they lured into becoming part of an ostentatious court in the manner of the French nobility. As men completely immersed in the world of commerce, they remained part of mercantile society and used their political power to guarantee that the Dutch state would serve the interests of trade.

The political prominence of Dutch merchants reflected the highly commercial character of the Dutch economy. Shortly after its truce with Spain in 1609, the Dutch cities, especially the rapidly expanding port city of Amsterdam in Holland, began to dominate European and world trade. The Dutch served as middlemen and shippers for all the other powers of Europe, transporting grain from the Baltic, textiles from England, timber from Scandinavia, wine from Germany, sugar from Brazil and Ceylon, silk from Persia and China, and porcelain from Japan to markets throughout the world. The Dutch even served as middlemen for their arch-enemy Spain, providing food and manufactured goods to

The Amsterdam Stock Exchange in 1668

Known as the Bourse, this multipurpose building served as a gathering point for merchants trading in different parts of the world. The main activity was the buying and selling of shares of stock in trading companies during trading sessions that lasted for two hours each day.

the Spanish colonies in the New World in exchange for silver from the mines of Peru and Mexico. As part of this process Dutch trading companies, such as the Dutch East India Company, began to establish permanent outposts in India, Indonesia, North America, the Caribbean, South America, and South Africa. Thus a relatively small country, with one-tenth the population of France and one-third that of Great Britain, became a colonial power.

To provide support for their dynamic mercantile economy, Dutch cities developed financial institutions favorable to trade. An Exchange Bank in Amsterdam, which had a monopoly on the exchange of foreign currencies, allowed merchants to make international transactions by adding sums to or deducting sums from their accounts whenever they imported or exported goods. The Dutch also developed rational and efficient methods of bookkeeping. A stock market, also situated in Amsterdam, facilitated the buying and selling of shares in commercial ventures. Even lawyers contributed to these commercial enterprises. In *The Freedom of the Sea* (1609), the great legal and political philosopher Hugo Grotius (1583–1645) defended the freedom of merchants to use the open seas for trade and fishing, thereby challenging the claims of European monarchs who wished to exclude foreigners from the waters surrounding their countries. Grotius, who also wrote *The Law of War and Peace* (1625), gained a reputation as the father of modern international law.

One of the most striking contrasts between the Dutch Republic and the kingdom of France in the seventeenth century lay in the area of religious policy. Whereas in France the revocation of the Edict of Nantes represented the culmination of a policy enforcing religious uniformity and the suppression of Protestant dissent, the predominantly Calvinist Dutch Republic gained a reputation for religious toleration. The Dutch Reformed Church did not always deserve this reputation, but secular authorities, especially in the cities, proved remarkably tolerant of different religious groups. Amsterdam, which attracted a diverse immigrant population during its period of rapid growth, contained a large community of Jews, including the philosopher Baruch Spinoza (1632–1677). The country became the center for religious exiles and political dissidents, accommodating French Huguenots who fled their country after the repeal of the Edict of Nantes in 1685 as well as English Whigs (including the Earl of Shaftesbury and John Locke) who were being pursued by the Tory government in the 1680s. In keeping with this Dutch tradition of toleration, Dutch courts became the first to stop the prosecution of witches, executing the last person for this crime in 1608.

This tolerant bourgeois republic also made a distinct contribution to European culture during the seventeenth century, known as its Golden Age. The Dutch cultural achievement was greatest in the area of the visual arts, where Rembrandt van Rijn (1606–1669), Franz Hals (ca. 1580–1666) and Jan Steen (1626–1679) formed only part of an astonishing concentration of artistic genius in the cities of Amsterdam, Haarlem, and Leiden. Dutch painting of this era reflected the religious, social, and

Rembrandt, *Syndics of the Clothmakers of Amsterdam* (1662)
Rembrandt's realistic portrait depicted wealthy Dutch bourgeoisie, who had great political as well as economic power in the Dutch Republic.

political climate in which painters worked. The Protestant Reformation had brought an end to the tradition of didactic and devotional religious painting that had flourished during the Middle Ages, leading many Dutch artists to adopt more secular themes for their work. At the same time the absence of a baroque court culture, such as that which still flourished in Spain and France as well as in the Spanish Netherlands, reduced the demand for royal and aristocratic portraiture as well as for paintings of heroic classical, mythological, and historical scenes. Instead the Dutch artists of the Golden Age produced intensely realistic portraits of merchants and financiers, such as Rembrandt's famous *Syndics of the Clothmakers of Amsterdam* (1662). Realism became one of the defining features of Dutch painting, evident in the numerous street scenes, still lifes, and landscapes that Dutch artists painted and sold to a largely bourgeois clientele. At the same time Dutch engravers perfected the art of political printmaking, much of it highly satirical, an achievement that was encouraged by the political tolerance of the country.

In the early eighteenth century the Dutch Republic lost its position of economic superiority to Great Britain and France, which developed even larger mercantile empires of their own and began to dominate world commerce. The long period of war against France, which ended in 1713, took its toll on Dutch manpower and wealth, and the relatively small size of the country and its decentralized institutions made it more difficult for it to recover its position in European diplomacy and warfare. As a state it could no longer fight above its weight, and it became vulnerable to attacks by the French in the nineteenth century and the Germans in the twentieth. But in the seventeenth century this highly urbanized and commercial country showed that a small, decentralized republic could hold its own with the absolutist states of France and Spain as well as with the parliamentary monarchy of England.

CONCLUSION

The Western State in the Age of Absolutism

Between 1600 and 1715 three fundamental political changes, all related to each other, helped redefine the West. The first was the dramatic and unprecedented growth of the state. During these years all Western states grew in size and strength. They became more cohesive as the outlying provinces of kingdoms were brought more firmly under central governmental control. The administrative machinery of the state became more complex and efficient. The armies of the state could be called upon at any time to take action against internal rebels and foreign enemies. The income of the state increased as royal officials collected higher taxes, and governments became involved in the promotion of trade and industry and in the regulation of the economy. By the beginning of the eighteenth century one of the most distinctive features of Western civilization was the prevalence of these large, powerful, bureaucratic states. There was nothing like them in the non-Western world.

The second change was the introduction of royal absolutism into these Western states. From one end of the European continent to the other, efforts were made to establish the monarch as a ruler with complete and unrivaled power. These efforts achieved varying degrees of success, and in two states, England and the Dutch Republic, they ended in failure. Nevertheless, during the seventeenth and eighteenth centuries the absolutist state became the main form of government in the West. For this reason historians refer to the period of Western history beginning in the seventeenth century as the age of absolutism.

The third change was the conduct of a new style of warfare by Western absolutist states. The West became the arena where large armies, funded, equipped, and trained by the state, engaged in long, costly, and bloody military campaigns. The conduct of war on this scale threatened to drain the state of its financial resources, destroy its economy, and decimate its civilian and military population. Western powers were not unaware of the dangers of this type of warfare. The development of international law and the attempt to achieve a balance of power among European powers represented efforts to place restrictions on the conduct of seventeenth-century warfare. These efforts, however, were not completely successful, and in the eighteenth and nineteenth centuries warfare in the West entered a new and even more dangerous phase, aided by the technological innovations that the scientific and industrial revolutions made possible. To the first of those great transformations, the revolution in science, we now turn.

Suggestions for Further Reading

For a comprehensive list of suggested readings, please go to www.ablongman.com/levack/chapter15

Aylmer, G. E. *Rebellion or Revolution.* 1986. A study of the nature of the political disturbances of the 1640s and 1650s.

Beik, William. *Louis XIV and Absolutism: A Brief Study with Documents.* 2000. An excellent collection of documents.

Collins, James B. *The State in Early Modern France.* 1995. The best general study of the French state.

Elliott, J. H. *Richelieu and Olivares.* 1984. A comparison of the two contemporary absolutist ministers and state builders in France and Spain.

Harris, Tim. *Politics under the Later Stuarts.* 1993. The best study of Restoration politics, including the Glorious Revolution.

Hughes, Lindsey. *Russia in the Age of Peter the Great.* 1998. A comprehensive study of politics, diplomacy, society, and culture during the reign of the "Tsar Reformer."

Israel, Jonathan. *The Dutch Republic: Its Rise, Greatness and Fall, 1477–1806.* 1996. A massive and authoritative study of the Dutch Republic during the period of its greatest global influence.

Parker, David. *The Making of French Absolutism.* 1983. A particularly good treatment of the early seventeenth century.

Parker, Geoffrey. *The Military Revolution.* 1988. Deals with the impact of the military revolution on the world as well as European history.

Rabb, Theodore K. *The Struggle for Stability in Early Modern Europe.* 1975. Employs visual as well as political sources to illustrate the way in which Europeans responded to the general crisis of the seventeenth century.

Schama, Simon. *The Embarrassment of Riches: An Interpretation of Dutch Culture in the Golden Age.* 1987. Contains a wealth of commentary on Dutch art and culture during its most influential period.

Wilson, Peter H. *Absolutism in Central Europe.* 2000. Analyzes both the theory and the practice of absolutism in Prussia and Austria.

CHAPTER

16

The Scientific Revolution

Chapter Outline

- The Discoveries and Achievements of the Scientific Revolution
- The Search for Scientific Knowledge
- The Causes of the Scientific Revolution
- The Intellectual Effects of the Scientific Revolution
- Humans and the Natural World

In 1609 Galileo Galilei, an Italian mathematician at the University of Padua, introduced a new scientific instrument, the telescope, which revealed a wealth of knowledge about the stars and planets that filled the night skies. Having heard that a Dutch artisan had put together two lenses in such a way that magnified distant objects, Galileo built his own such device and directed it toward the heavens. Anyone who has looked through a telescope or seen photographs taken from a satellite can appreciate Galileo's excitement at what he saw. Objects that appeared one way to the naked eye looked entirely different when magnified by his new "spyglass," as he called it. The Milky Way, the pale glow that was previously thought to be a reflection of diffused light, turned out to be composed of a multitude of previously unknown stars. The surface of the moon, long believed to be smooth, uniform, and perfectly spherical, now appeared to be full of mountains, craters, and other irregularities. The sun, which was also supposed to be perfect in shape and composed of matter that could not be altered, was marred by spots that appeared to move across its surface. When turned toward Jupiter, the telescope revealed four moons never seen before. Venus, viewed over the course of many months, appeared to change its shape, much in the way that the moon did in its various phases. This latter discovery provided evidence for the relatively new theory that the planets, including Earth, revolved around the sun rather than the sun and the planets around the Earth.

Galileo shared the discoveries he made not only with fellow scientists but with other Europeans. In 1610 he published *The Starry Messenger,* a treatise in which he described his discovery of the new moons of Jupiter. Twenty-two years later he included the evidence he had gained from his telescope in another book, *Dialogue Concerning the Two Chief World Systems,* to support the claim that the Earth orbited around the sun. He also staged a number of public demonstrations of his new astronomical instrument, the first of which took place on top of one

The Telescope: The telescope was the most important of the new scientific instruments that facilitated scientific discovery. This engraving depicts an astronomer using the telescope in 1647.

of the city gates of Rome in 1611. To convince those who doubted the reality of the images they saw, Galileo turned the telescope toward familiar landmarks in the city. Interest in the new scientific instrument ran so high that a number of amateur astronomers acquired telescopes of their own.

Galileo's observations and discoveries formed one facet of the development that historians call the Scientific Revolution. A series of remarkable achievements in astronomy, physics, chemistry, and biology formed the centerpieces of this revolution, but its effects reached far beyond the observatories and laboratories of seventeenth-century scientists. The Scientific Revolution brought about fundamental changes in Western thought, altering the way in which Europeans viewed the natural world, the supernatural realm, and themselves. It stimulated controversies in religion, philosophy, and politics and brought about changes in military technology, navigation, and economic enterprise. The revolution added a new dimension to Western culture and provided a basis for claims of Western superiority over people in other lands. For all these reasons the Scientific Revolution marked a decisive turning point in the history of Western civilization, and it set the West apart from contemporary civilizations in the Middle East, Africa, and Asia.

The scientific culture that emerged in the West by the end of the seventeenth century was the product of a series of cultural encounters. It resulted from a complex interaction among scholars proposing different accounts of how nature operated. In some cases the scientists who advanced the revolutionary ideas were themselves influenced by ideas drawn from different cultural traditions. Some of these ideas had originated in Greek philosophy, while others came from orthodox Christian sources. Still other ideas came from a tradition of late medieval science, which had in turn been heavily influenced by the scholarship of the Islamic Middle East. A skeptical refusal to rely on any inherited authority whatsoever had its own religious and philosophical sources.

In this chapter we will explore the scope and development of the Scientific Revolution and the changes it brought about in Western thought and culture. Five questions will structure our exploration of this subject: (1) What were the scientific achievements and discoveries of the late sixteenth and seventeenth centuries that historians refer to as the Scientific Revolution? (2) What methods did scientists use during this period to investigate nature, and how did they think nature operated? (3) Why did the Scientific Revolution take place in western Europe at this particular time? (4) How did the Scientific Revolution influence the development of philosophical and religious thought in the seventeenth and early eighteenth centuries? (5) How did the Scientific Revolution change the way in which seventeenth- and eighteenth-century Europeans thought of their relationship to the natural world?

The Discoveries and Achievements of the Scientific Revolution

Unlike political revolutions, such as the English Revolution of the 1640s discussed in the last chapter, the Scientific Revolution developed gradually and over a long period of time. It began in the middle and later decades of the sixteenth century and continued into the early years of the eighteenth century. Even though it took a relatively long time to unfold, it was revolutionary in the sense that it brought about a radical transformation of human thought, just as political revolutions have produced fundamental changes in systems of government. The most important changes in seventeenth-century science took place in the fields of astronomy, physics, chemistry, and biology.

ASTRONOMY: A NEW MODEL OF THE UNIVERSE

The most significant change in astronomy was the acceptance of the view that the sun, not the Earth, was the center of the universe. Until the middle of the sixteenth century, most natural philosophers—as scientists were known at the time—subscribed to the writings of the Greek astronomer Claudius Ptolemy (100–170 C.E.). Ptolemy's observations and calculations had given considerable support to the cosmology°, a theory regarding the structure and nature of the universe, proposed by the Greek philosopher Aristotle (384–322 B.C.E.). According to Ptolemy and Aristotle, the center of the universe was a stationary Earth, around which the moon, the sun, and the other planets revolved in circular orbits. Beyond the planets a large sphere carried the stars, which stood in a fixed relationship to each other, around the Earth from east to west once every twenty-four hours, thus accounting for the rising and setting of the stars. Each of the four known elements—earth, water, air, and fire—had a natural place within this universe, with the heavy elements, earth and water, being pulled down toward the center of the Earth and the light ones, air and fire, hovering above it. All heavenly bodies, including the sun and the planets, were composed of a fifth element, called ether, which unlike matter on Earth was thought to be eternal and could not be altered, corrupted, or destroyed.

This traditional view of the cosmos had much to recommend it, and some educated people continued to subscribe to it well into the eighteenth century. The authority of Aristotle, predominant in late medieval universities, was reinforced by the Bible, which in a few passages referred to the motion of the sun. The motion of the sun could be confirmed by simple human observation. We do, after all, see the sun "rise" and "set" every day, while the idea that the Earth rotates at a high speed and revolves around the sun contradicts the experience of our senses. Nevertheless, the Earth-centered model of the universe failed to provide an explanation for many patterns that astronomers observed in the sky, most notably the paths followed by planets. In the sixteenth century natural philosophers began to consider alternative models of the universe.

The first major challenge to the Ptolemaic system came from a Polish cleric, Nicolaus Copernicus (1473–1543), who in 1543 published *The Revolutions of the Heavenly Spheres,* in which he proposed that the center of the universe was not the Earth but the sun. The book was widely circulated, but it did not win much support for the sun-centered theory of the universe. The mathematical arguments Copernicus presented in the book were so abstruse that only the most erudite astronomers could understand them. Even those who could appreciate his detailed plotting of planetary motion were not prepared to adopt the central thesis of his book. In the late sixteenth century the great Danish astronomer Tycho Brahe (1546–1601) accepted the argument of Copernicus that the planets revolved around the sun but still insisted that the sun continued to revolve around the Earth.

Two Views of the Ptolemaic or Pre-Copernican Universe

(a) In this sixteenth-century engraving the Earth lies at the center of the universe and the elements of water, air, and fire are arranged in ascending order above the Earth. The orbit that is shaded in black is the firmament or stellar sphere. The presence of Christ and the saints at the top reflects the view that Heaven lay beyond the stellar sphere. (b) A medieval king representing Atlas holds a Ptolemaic cosmos. The Ptolemaic universe is often referred to as a two-sphere universe: The inner sphere of the Earth lies at the center and the outer sphere encompassing the entire universe rotates around the Earth.

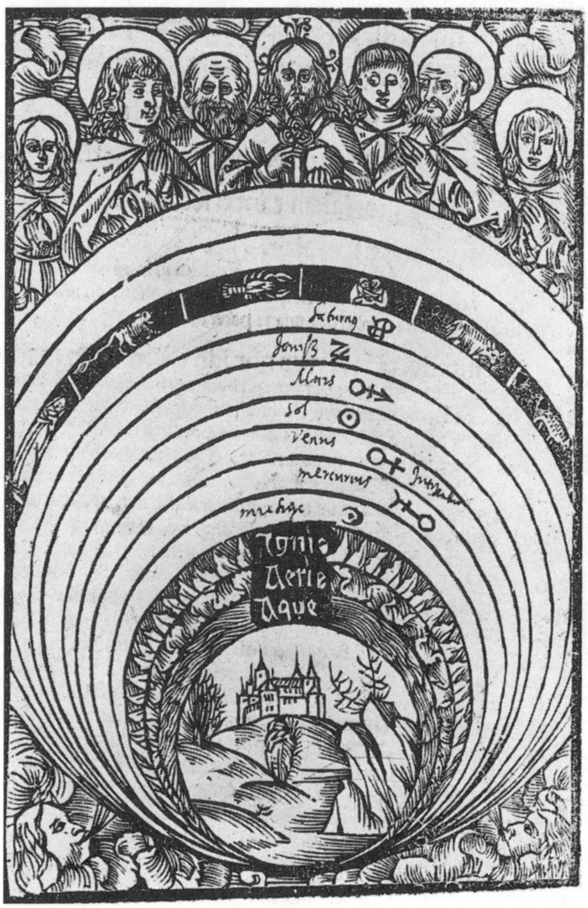

(a)

(b)

Significant support for the Copernican model of the universe among scientists began to materialize only in the seventeenth century. In 1609 a German astronomer, Johannes Kepler (1571–1630), using data that Brahe had collected, confirmed the central position of the sun in the universe. In his treatise *New Astronomy,* Kepler also demonstrated that the planets, including the Earth, followed elliptical rather than circular orbits and that the planets moved in accordance with a series of physical laws. Kepler's book, however, did not reach a large audience, and his achievement was not fully appreciated until many decades later.

Galileo Galilei (1564–1642) was far more successful than Kepler in gaining support for the sun-centered model of the universe. In some respects Galileo was more conservative than Kepler. For example, Galileo never took issue with the traditional idea that the planets followed circular orbits. But Galileo had the literary skill, lacking in Kepler, of being able to write for a broad audience. Using the evidence gained from his observations with the telescope, and presenting his views in the form of a dialogue between the advocates of the two competing worldviews, he demonstrated the plausibility and superiority of Copernicus's theory.

The publication of Galileo's *Dialogue Concerning the Two Chief World Systems—Ptolemaic and Copernican* in 1632 won many converts to the sun-centered theory of the universe, but it lost him the support of Pope Urban VIII, who had been one of his patrons. Urban believed that by naming the character in *Dialogue* who defended the Ptolemaic system Simplicio (that is, a simple person), he was mocking the pope himself. In the following year Galileo was tried before the Roman Inquisition, an ecclesi-

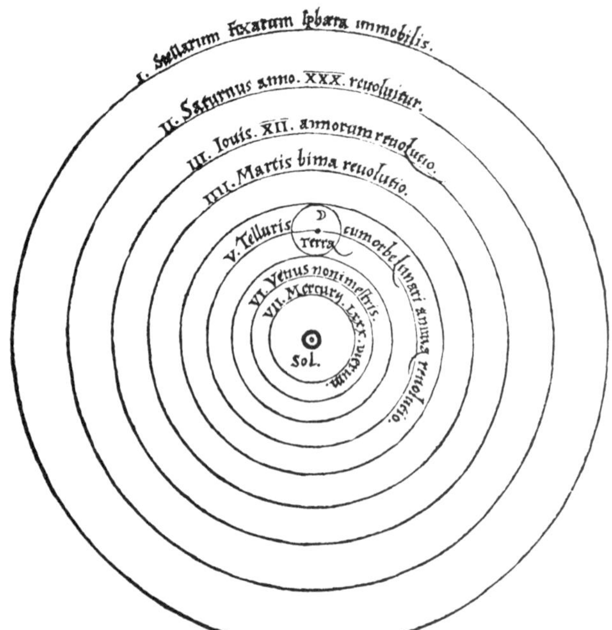

(a)

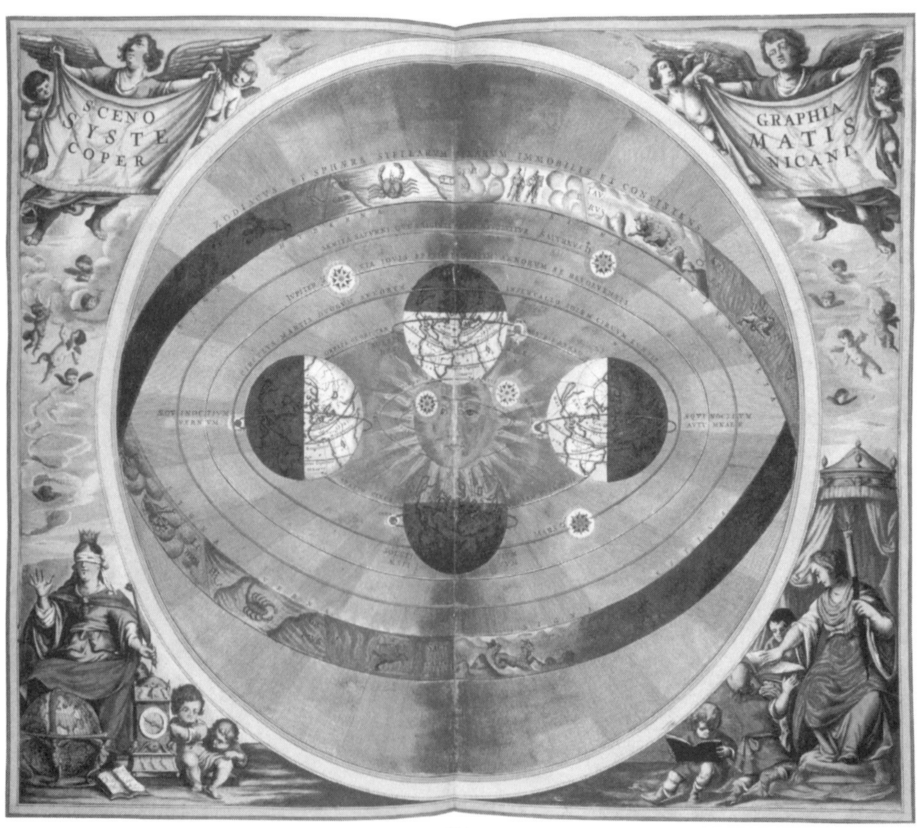

(b)

Two Sixteenth-Century Views of the Sun-Centered Universe
(a) The depiction by Copernicus. Note that all the orbits are circular, rather than elliptical, as Kepler was to show they were. The outermost sphere is that of the fixed stars. (b) A late-seventeenth-century depiction of the cosmos by Andreas Cellarius in which the planets follow elliptical orbits. It illustrates four different positions of the Earth as it orbits the sun.

COPERNICUS PROPOSES HIS SUN-CENTERED THEORY OF THE UNIVERSE

In the dedication of his book On the Revolution of the Heavenly Spheres *(1543) to Pope Paul III, Copernicus explains that in his search for an orderly model of the universe he drew inspiration from a few ancient philosophers who had imagined that the Earth moved. He then explained how he had bolstered his theory through long and frequent observations. Anticipating condemnation from those who based their astronomical theories on the Bible, he appeals to the pope for protection while showing contempt for the theories of his opponents.*

. . . I began to chafe that philosophers could by no means agree on any one certain theory of the mechanism of the Universe, wrought for us by a supremely good and orderly Creator . . . I therefore took pains to read again the works of all the philosophers on whom I could lay my hand to seek out whether any of them had ever supposed that the motions of the spheres were other than those demanded by the mathematical schools. I found first in Cicero that Hicetas had realized that the Earth moved. Afterwards I found in Plutarch that certain others had held the like opinion. . . .

Taking advantage of this I too began to think of the mobility of the Earth; and though the opinion seemed absurd, yet knowing now that others before me had been granted freedom to imagine such circles as they chose to explain the phenomena of the stars, I considered that I also might easily be allowed to try whether, by assuming some motion of the Earth, sounder explanations than theirs for the revolution of the celestial spheres might so be discovered.

Thus assuming motions, which in my work I ascribe to the Earth, by long and frequent observations I have at last discovered that, if the motions of the rest of the planets be brought into relation with the circulation of the Earth and be reckoned in proportion to the circles of each planet . . . the orders and magnitudes of all stars and spheres, nay the heavens themselves, become so bound together that nothing in any part thereof could be moved from its place without producing confusion of all the other parts and of the Universe as a whole. . . .

It may fall out, too, that idle babblers, ignorant of mathematics, may claim a right to pronounce a judgment on my work, by reason of a certain passage of Scripture basely twisted to serve their purpose. Should any such venture to criticize and carp at my project, I make no account of them; I consider their judgment rash, and utterly despise it.

Source: From Nicholas Copernicus, *De Revolutionibus Orbium Caelestium* (1543), translated by John F. Dobson and Selig Brodetsky in *Occasional Notes of the Royal Astronomical Society,* Vol. 2, No. 10, 1947. Reprinted by permission of Blackwell Publishing.

astical court whose purpose was to maintain theological orthodoxy. The charge against him was that he had challenged the authority of Scripture and was therefore guilty of heresy, the denial of the theological truths of the Roman Catholic Church. (See "Justice in History: The Trial of Galileo" later in this chapter.)

As a result of this trial Galileo was forced to abandon his support for the Copernican model of the universe, and *Dialogue* was placed on the Index of Prohibited Books, a list compiled by the papacy of all printed works containing heretical ideas. Despite this setback, support for Copernicanism grew during the seventeenth century, and by 1700 it commanded widespread support among scientists and the educated public. *Dialogue,* however, was not removed from the Index until 1822.

PHYSICS: THE LAWS OF MOTION AND GRAVITATION

Galileo made his most significant contributions to the Scientific Revolution in the field of physics, which deals with matter and energy and the relationship between them. In the seventeenth century the main branches of physics were mechanics (the study of motion and its causes) and optics (the study of light). Galileo's most significant achievement in physics was to formulate a set of laws governing the motion of material objects. His work, which laid the foundation of modern physics, effectively challenged the theories of Aristotle regarding motion.

According to Aristotle, whose views dominated science in the late Middle Ages, the motion of every object except the natural motion of falling toward the center of the Earth required another object to move it. If the mover stopped, the object fell to the ground or simply stopped moving. One of the problems with this theory was that it could not account for the continued motion of a projectile, such as a discus or a javelin, after it left the hand of the person who threw it. Galileo's answer to that question was a theory of inertia, which became the basis of a radical new theory of motion. According to Galileo, an object continues to move or to lie at rest until something external to it intervenes to change its motion. Thus motion is neither a quality inherent in an object nor a force that it acquires from another object; it is simply a state in which the object finds itself.

Galileo also discovered that the motion of an object occurs only in relation to things that do not move. A ship moves through the water, for example, but the goods carried by that ship do not move in relationship to the moving ship. This insight served the immediate purpose of explaining to the critics of Copernicus how the Earth can move even though we do not experience its motion. Galileo's most significant contribution to the study of mechanics was his formulation of a mathematical law of motion that explained how the speed and acceleration of a falling object are determined by the distance it travels during equal intervals of time.

The greatest achievements of the Scientific Revolution in physics belong to English scientist Sir Isaac Newton (1642–1727). Newton was one of those rare geniuses whose research changed the way future generations viewed the world. As a boy Newton found himself out of place while working on his mother's farm in a small hamlet in Lincolnshire and while attending school in the same county. Fascinated by mechanical devices, he spent much of his time building wooden models of windmills and other machines. When playing with his friends he always found ways to exercise his mind, calculating, for example, how he could use the wind to win jumping contests with his classmates. While he was still an adolescent, it had become obvious to all his acquaintances that the only place where he would be comfortable would be at a university. In 1661 he entered Trinity College, Cambridge, a step that introduced him to the broader world of ideas. In 1667 he became a fellow of the college and two years later, at age 27, he became the Lucasian Professor of Mathematics.

At Cambridge Newton pursued a wide range of intellectual interests, including the study of biblical prophecy. His great discoveries, however, were in the disciplines of mathematics and natural philosophy. During the 1680s Newton formulated a set of mathematical laws that governed the operation of the entire physical world. In 1687 he published his theories in *Mathematical Principles of Natural Philosophy.* The centerpiece of this monumental work was the universal law of gravitation°, which demonstrated that the same force holding an object to the Earth also holds the planets in their orbits. Newton established that any two bodies attract each other with a force that is directly proportional to the product of their masses and inversely proportional to the square of the distance between them. This law represented a synthesis of the work by Kepler on planetary motion, Galileo on inertia, the English physicist Robert Hooke (1635–1703) on gravity, and the Dutch scientist Christian Huygens (1629–1695) on centrifugal force. Newton's *Mathematical Principles* superseded the works of all these scientists by establishing the existence of a single gravitational force and by giving it precise mathematical expression. At the same time it revealed the unity and order of the entire physical world. It provided, in Newton's words, "a system of the world."

Newton extended his study of motion to the science of optics by demonstrating that light consists of small particles that also follow the laws of motion. Newton's theory prevailed until the early nineteenth century, when a series of experiments provided support for a new theory of light, according to which light should be thought of as waves, similar to those that cross a pond after a stone is dropped. Later in the nineteenth century the wave theory itself gave way to the view that light is a form of electromagnetic radiation. The most revolutionary change in our understanding of light, however, came with Newton in the seventeenth century.

CHRONOLOGY

Discoveries of the Scientific Revolution

1543 Andreas Vesalius publishes *On the Fabric of the Human Body,* the first realistic depiction of human anatomy; Copernicus publishes *The Revolutions of the Heavenly Spheres,* challenging the traditional Earth-centered cosmos

1609 Johannes Kepler publishes *New Astronomy,* identifying elliptical orbits of the planets

1628 William Harvey publishes *On the Motion of the Heart and Blood in Animals,* demonstrating the circulation of the blood

1632 Galileo publishes *Dialogue Concerning the Two Chief World Systems,* leading to his trial

1638 Galileo publishes *Discourses on the Two New Sciences of Motion and Mechanics,* proposing new laws of motion

1655 Evangelista Torricelli conducts experiments on atmospheric pressure

1659 Robert Boyle invents the air pump and conducts experiments on the elasticity and compressibility of air

1673 Christian Huygens publishes *On the Motion of Pendulums,* developing his theories of gravitation and centrifugal force

1687 Newton publishes his *Mathematical Principles of Natural Philosophy,* presenting a theory of universal gravitation

CHEMISTRY: DISCOVERING THE ELEMENTS OF NATURE

At the beginning of the seventeenth century, the branch of science today called chemistry had little intellectual respectability. It was not even an independent discipline, since it was considered a part of either medicine or alchemy°, the magical art of attempting to turn base metals into precious ones. The most famous chemist of the sixteenth century was the Swiss physician and natural magician Paracelsus (1493–1541), who rejected the theory advanced by the Greek physician Galen (129–200 C.E.) that diseases were caused by the imbalance of the four "humors" or fluids in the body—blood, phlegm, black bile, and yellow bile. The widespread medical practice of drawing blood from sick patients to cure them was based on Galen's theory. Paracelsus began instead to treat his patients with chemicals, such as mercury and sulfur, to cure certain diseases. Paracelsus and his followers also believed that chemistry would provide a new basis for the understanding of nature, and he interpreted the biblical account of the Creation as the chemical unfolding of nature. Paracelsus is often dismissed for his belief in alchemy, but his prescription of chemicals to treat specific diseases helped to give chemistry a respectable place within medical science.

During the seventeenth century chemistry became a legitimate field of scientific research, largely as the result of the work of the English natural philosopher Robert Boyle (1627–1691). Boyle destroyed the prevailing idea that all basic constituents of matter share the same structure. He contended that the arrangement of their components, which Boyle identified as corpuscles or atoms, determine their characteristics. Boyle also conducted experiments on the volume, pressure, and density of gas and the elasticity of air. His most famous experiments, undertaken with the help of an air pump, proved the existence of a vacuum. Largely as a result of Boyle's discoveries, chemists won acceptance as legitimate members of the company of scientists.

BIOLOGY: THE CIRCULATION OF THE BLOOD

The English physician William Harvey (1578–1657) made one of the great medical discoveries of the seventeenth century by demonstrating in 1628 that blood circulates throughout the human body. Harvey, who had studied medicine at the University of Padua and who became the royal physician to both James I and Charles I in England, challenged the traditional theory regarding the motion of the blood advanced by Galen and perpetuated by medieval philosophers. According to this traditional theory, blood originated in the liver, where it was converted from food and then flowed outward through the veins, providing nourishment to the organs and the other parts of the body. A certain amount of blood was also drawn from the liver into the heart, where it passed from one ventricle to the other and then traveled through the arteries to different parts of the body. During its journey this arterial blood was enriched by a special *pneuma* or "vital spirit" that originated in the atmosphere and was necessary to sustain life. When this enriched blood reached the brain, it became the body's "psychic spirits," which eventually traveled to the nerves and influenced human behavior.

During the late sixteenth century a succession of Italian scientists called specific aspects of Galen's theory into question. It was Harvey, however, who proposed an entirely new framework for understanding the motion of the blood. Through a series of experiments on human cadavers and live animals in which he weighed the blood that the heart pumped every hour, Harvey demonstrated that the blood circulates throughout the body, traveling outward from the heart through the arteries and returning to the heart through the veins. The heart, rather than sucking in blood, performed the essential function of pumping it by means of its contraction and constriction. The only gap in Harvey's theory was the question of how blood goes from the ends of the arteries to the ends of the veins. The answer to this question came in 1661, when scientists, using another new magnifying instrument known as a microscope, could see the capillaries connecting the veins and arteries. Harvey, however, had provided the basis for understanding how blood circulates through the body, and he had set a standard for the conduct of future biological research.

Biology
William Harvey discovered the circulation of the blood.

THE HUMAN BODY IN HISTORY

Dissecting the Human Corpse

As medical science developed in the sixteenth and seventeenth centuries, the dissection of human corpses became a standard practice in European universities and medical schools. Knowledge of the structure and composition of the human body, which was central to the advancement of physiology, could best be acquired by cutting a corpse to reveal the organs, muscles, and bones of human beings. The practice reflected the emphasis scientists placed on observation and experimentation in conducting scientific research. In the sixteenth century the great Flemish physiologist Andreas Vesalius (1514–1564), who published the first realistic drawings of human anatomy in 1543, cut limbs and extracted organs in his lectures on anatomy at the University of Padua. A century later, the English physician William Harvey dissected human cadavers in his path-breaking study of the circulation of the blood.

The physicians who performed dissections had difficulty securing an adequate supply of corpses. A preference developed for the bodies of recently hanged criminals, mainly because rulers claimed jurisdiction over the bodies of the condemned and could dispose of them at will. Criminals, moreover, were generally young or middle-aged and in fairly good health, thus making them desirable specimens for dissection. Demand for corpses became so great in the late seventeenth and eighteenth centuries that surgeons were willing to pay a price for them, thus turning the dead human body into a commodity. In eighteenth-century England the demand for bodies of the hanged often resulted in brawls between the agents whom the surgeons paid to snatch the bodies from the scaffold and the relatives and friends of the deceased, who wanted to claim the corpses in order to guarantee a decent burial.

During the sixteenth and seventeenth centuries, dissection underwent two transformations. The first was the expansion of the audience from a small group of medical students to a large cross-section of scholars who attended in order to learn more about the relationship between human beings and the natural world. The audiences also began to include artists, who learned from these exercises how to depict the human body more accurately. The second change was the transformation of dissection into a public spectacle, controlled by municipal authorities. During the seventeenth century, the city of Bologna staged dissections every year before crowds of as many as 200 people.

To these public dissections, which took place in many other European cities, people from the lower classes were often admitted together with scholars, students, and artists. The uneducated men and women who attended were attracted by the entertaining aspects of the event and the eagerness to witness the violence done to the corpse, just as they were at public executions. They were particularly eager to see the dissection of the genital organs, so much so that some authorities restricted access to that part of the dissection in the interest of public decency.

The holding of public anatomy lessons had much less to do with the popularization of science than with the satisfaction of the popular taste for blood and sex. Only in the late eighteenth century, during the age of the Enlightenment, did a new sensitivity to blood and human torment and an unprecedented repugnance of death bring about an end to public dissections, together with the public executions with which they were closely associated. ■

For Discussion

What interests were served by holding public dissections of human corpses in the seventeenth and eighteenth centuries?

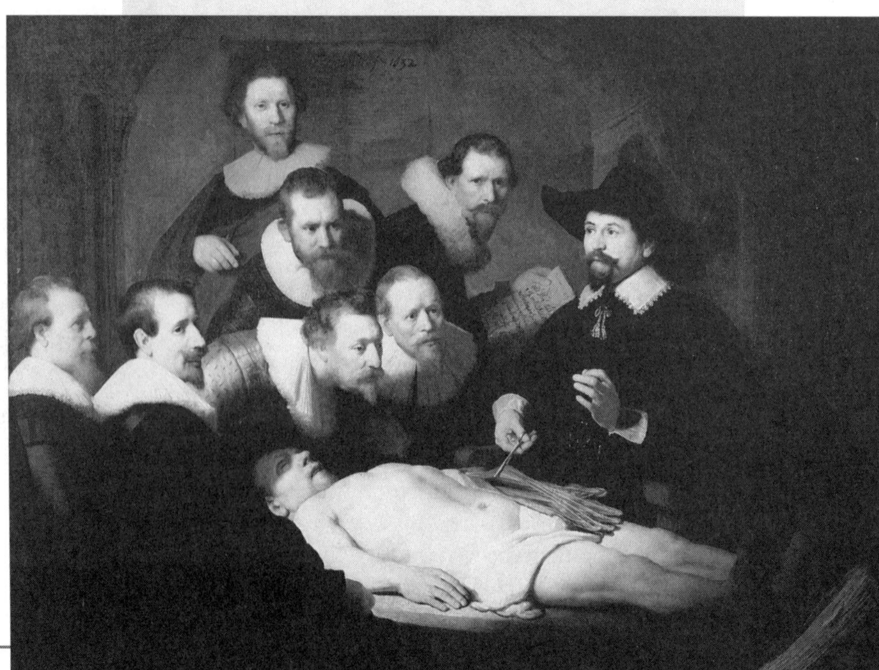

■ **Dissection**

Rembrandt van Rijn, *The Anatomy Lesson of Dr. Nicholaes Tulp* (1632). This dissection, unlike many others in Europe during the seventeenth century, was performed in private. The observers were not medical students or curious public observers but members of the Amsterdam Company of Surgeons.

The Search for Scientific Knowledge

The natural philosophers who made these various scientific discoveries worked in different academic disciplines, and each followed his own procedures for discovering scientific truth. In the sixteenth and seventeenth centuries there was no such thing as a single "scientific method." Many natural philosophers, however, shared similar views regarding the way in which nature operated and the means by which humans could acquire knowledge of it. In searching for scientific knowledge, these scientists engaged in extensive observation and experimentation, used a process of deductive reason to solve scientific problems, expressed their theories in mathematical terms, and argued that nature operated like a machine. Taken together, these common features of scientific research ultimately defined a distinctly Western approach to solving scientific problems.

Portrait of Robert Boyle with His Air-Pump in the Background (1664)

Boyle's pump became the center of a series of experiments carried on at the Royal Society in London.

OBSERVATION AND EXPERIMENTATION

The most prominent feature of scientific research in sixteenth- and seventeenth-century Europe was the extensive observation of nature, combined with the testing of hypotheses by means of rigorous experimentation. This was primarily a process of induction°, in which theories emerged only after the systematic accumulation and analysis of large amounts of data. It assumed a willingness to abandon all preconceived notions, whether they were those of Aristotle, Galen, or medieval philosophers, and to base scientific conclusions on experience and observation.

The English philosopher Francis Bacon (1561–1626) promoted this empirical, experimental approach in his book *New Organon* (1620), in which he complained that all previous scientific endeavors, especially those of ancient Greek philosophers, relied too little on experimentation. By contrast, Bacon's approach involved the thorough and systematic investigation of nature, a process which Bacon, who was a lawyer and judge, compared to the interrogation of a person suspected of committing a crime. Bacon claimed that scientific experimentation was "putting nature to the question" in order to obtain the truth, a phrase that referred to questioning a prisoner under torture to determine the facts of a case.

All the great scientists of the sixteenth and seventeenth centuries abandoned preconceived notions and based their theories on the facts of nature, but the most enthusiastic practitioners of carefully planned and controlled experimentation came from England. Two of its most tireless advocates were Boyle, who performed a succession of experiments with an air pump to prove the existence of a vacuum, and Robert Hooke, whose experiments with a pendulum provided one of the foundations for Newton's theory of universal gravitation. Harvey belongs to the same English experimental tradition, although his commitment to this methodology originated at the University of Padua. Galileo and some other Italian scientists matched the English in their insistence on experimentation, but Galileo's experiments were designed more to demonstrate the validity of his theories than to help him establish them in the first place.

DEDUCTIVE REASONING

The second feature of sixteenth- and seventeenth-century scientific research was the application of deductive reasoning to scientific problems. Unlike the inductive experimental approach, which found its most enthusiastic practitioners in England, the deductive approach had its most zealous advocates on the European continent. The men who took this approach were just as determined as Bacon and Boyle to replace the testimony of human authorities with what they discovered from nature itself. Their main method, however, was to establish basic scientific truths or propositions from which other ideas or laws could be deduced logically. The French philosopher and mathematician René Descartes (1596–1650) became the champion of this methodology. In his *Discourse on the Method* (1637) he recommended that in solving any intellectual problem a person should first establish fundamental principles or truths and then proceed deductively from those ideas to more specific conclusions.

The model for deductive reasoning was mathematics, in which one also moves logically from certain premises to conclusions by means of equations. Rational deduction° proved to be an essential feature of scientific methodology, although some scientists relied too heavily on it at the expense of a more experimental approach. The limitations of an exclusively deductive approach became apparent when Descartes and his followers deduced a theory of gravitation from the principle that objects could influence each other only if they actually touched. The theory, as well as the principle upon which it was based, lacked an empirical foundation, which is one based on observation and experience, and eventually had to be abandoned.

MATHEMATICS AND NATURE

The third feature of scientific research in the sixteenth and seventeenth centuries was the application of mathematics to the study of the physical world. The mathematical treatment of nature was undertaken by scientists working in both the experimental and the deductive traditions. Descartes shared with Galileo, Kepler, and Huygens the conviction that nature had a geometrical structure and that it could therefore be understood in mathematical terms. The physical dimensions of matter, which Descartes claimed were its only properties, could of course be expressed mathematically. Galileo claimed that mathematics was the language in which philosophy was written in "the book of the universe."

This mathematical way of looking at the physical world had a long history. The Greek philosophers Pythagoras (582–507 B.C.E.) and Plato (ca. 428–348 B.C.E.) had both emphasized the geometric structure of the cosmos and therefore considered numbers to hold the key to its secrets. In the fifteenth century Renaissance philosophers revived this ancient Greek emphasis on mathematics. Copernicus, who was influenced by Platonic thought, criticized the Islamic and western European medieval philosophers who had accepted an Earth-centered universe for their mathematical miscalculations. Copernicus advocated a rigorous application of mathematics to astronomical writing. One of the reasons his book *The Revolutions of the Heavenly Spheres* was so demanding was that he described planetary motion in technical, mathematical terms.

In the seventeenth century Isaac Newton's work provides the best illustration of the application of mathematics to scientific problems. Newton used observation and experimentation to confirm his theory of universal gravitation, but the work in which he presented his theory, *The Principles of Mathematics,* was written in the language of mathematics. Just as Newton had synthesized previous work in physics to arrive at the law of universal gravitation, he also combined the experimental and deductive approaches to acquire scientific truth. His approach to solving scientific problems, which became a model for future scientific research, involved generalization on the basis of particular examples derived from experiments and the use of deductive, mathematical reasoning to discover the laws of nature.

THE MECHANICAL PHILOSOPHY

Much of the scientific experimentation and deduction undertaken in the seventeenth century proceeded on the assumption that the natural world operated as if it were a machine made by a human being. This philosophy of nature, which is often referred to as the mechanical philosophy°, cannot be attributed to a single person; but its most comprehensive statement can be found in the work of Descartes. The scholastic philosophers of the fourteenth and fifteenth centuries insisted that nature was fundamentally different from a machine or any other object built by man. According to the scholastics, natural bodies had an innate tendency to change, whereas artificial objects, that is, those constructed by humans, did not. Descartes, Kepler, Galileo, and Bacon all denied that assumption, arguing that nature operated in a mechanical way, just like a clock or some other piece of machinery. The only difference was that we cannot readily observe the structures of natural mechanisms, in the way that we can see the structure of a pump or a wagon.

According to mechanists—scientists who subscribed to the mechanical philosophy—nature consisted of many machines, some of them extremely small. The human body was itself a machine, and the center of that human machine, the heart, was in Harvey's words "a piece of machinery in which, though one wheel gives motion to another, yet all the wheels seem to move simultaneously." Since the human body was made by God, it was superior to any human-made machine, but it was still nothing more than a machine.

According to Descartes, the only part of a human being that was not a machine was the mind, which was completely different from the body and the rest of the material world. Unlike the body, the mind was an immaterial substance that could neither be extended in space nor divided. Nor could it be measured mathematically, in the way one could record the dimensions of the human body. Because Descartes made this sharp distinction between the mind and the human body, we speak of his philosophy as being dualistic°.

The mechanical philosophy presented just as bold a challenge to those philosophers known as Neoplatonists° as

■ **René Descartes**

Although Descartes was a scientist who made contributions to the study of biology and optics, he is best known for the method he proposed to attain certain knowledge and his articulation of the mechanical philosophy.

it did to the scholastics. Neoplatonists were inspired by the work of Plotinus (205–270 C.E.), the last great philosopher of antiquity who had synthesized the work of Plato with that of other Greek philosophers. Plotinus also drew on many traditions of ancient Persian religion. Neoplatonic thought experienced a revival in the fifteenth and sixteenth centuries at the time of the Renaissance (see Chapter 11). Neoplatonists believed that the natural world was animistic—that is, it possessed a soul (known to them as a world soul) and was charged with various occult forces and spirits. The English natural philosopher William Gilbert (1544–1603), who wrote extensively on the phenomenon of magnetism, adopted a Neoplatonic worldview when he declared that the Earth and other planets were actually alive. Kepler clearly recognized the incompatibility of this outlook with that of the mechanical philosophy when he insisted that "the machine of the universe was not similar to a divine animated being."

Descartes and other mechanists argued that matter was completely inert or dead. It had neither a soul nor any innate purpose. Its only property was extension, or the physical dimensions of length, width, and depth. Without a spirit or any other internal force directing its action, matter simply responded to the power of the other bodies with which it came in contact. According to Descartes, all physical phenomena could be explained by reference to the dimensions and the movement of particles of matter. He once claimed, "Give me extension and motion and I will construct the universe." Even the human body contained no "vital spirits." It consisted only of flesh and the blood pumped by the mechanism of the heart. The only difference between the human body and other machines was that the mind (or soul) could move it, although how it did so was a matter of great controversy, as we shall see in a later section.

The view of nature as a machine implied that it operated in a regular, predictable way in accordance with unchanging laws of nature. Scientists could use reason to discover what those laws were and thus learn how nature performed under any circumstances. The scientific investigations of Galileo and Kepler were based on those assumptions, and Descartes made them explicit. The immutability of the laws of nature implied that the entire universe was uniform in structure, an assumption that underlay Newton's formulation of the laws of motion and of universal gravitation. Newton's theory of gravity denied Descartes's view of matter as inert, but he nonetheless accepted his view that the universe operated like a machine.

The Causes of the Scientific Revolution

Why did the Scientific Revolution take place at this particular time, and why did it originate in western European countries? What prompted natural philosophers in Italy, France, England, and the Dutch Republic to develop new ways of looking at the world? There are no simple answers to these questions. We can, however, identify a number of developments that inspired this remarkable set of scientific discoveries. Some of these developments were internal to science, in the sense that they arose out of earlier investigations conducted by natural philosophers in the late Middle Ages, the Renaissance, and the sixteenth century. Others were external to the development of science, arising out of the religious, political, social, and economic life of Europe during the early modern period.

DEVELOPMENTS WITHIN SCIENCE

The three internal causes of the Scientific Revolution were the research into the motion conducted by scholastic natural philosophers in the fourteenth century, the scientific investigations conducted by humanists at the time of the Renaissance, and the collapse of the dominant conceptual frameworks that had governed scientific inquiry and research for centuries.

Late Medieval Science

Modern science can trace some of its origins to the fourteenth century, when the first significant modifications of Aristotle's scientific theories began to emerge. These challenges came not only from theologians, who objected that Aristotle was a pagan philosopher, but from natural philosophers, who refined some of the basic ideas of Aristotle's physics.

The most significant of these refinements was the theory of impetus. Aristotle, as we have seen, had argued that an object would stop as soon as it lost contact with the object that moved it. The scholastic philosophers who modified this principle claimed that objects in motion acquire a force that stays with them after they lose contact with the mover. The theory of impetus did not bring about a full-scale demolition of Aristotle's mechanics, but it did begin to call Aristotle's authority into question. The theory of impetus was known in Galileo's day, and it influenced some of his early thought on motion.

Scholastic philosophers of the fourteenth century also began to recommend direct, empirical observation in place of the traditional scholastic tendency to accept preconceived theories regarding the operation of nature. This approach to answering scientific questions did not result in the type of rigorous experimentation that Bacon demanded three centuries later, but it did encourage scientists to base their theories on the facts that emerged from an empirical study of nature.

The contribution of late medieval science to the Scientific Revolution should not be exaggerated. Scholastic natural philosophers continued to accept the cosmology of Ptolemy. They still perpetuated the anatomical theories of Galen. The restraints that theology exercised over scientific thought in the Middle Ages also prevented the emergence of new scientific ideas.

Renaissance Science

Natural philosophers during the Renaissance made more tangible contributions to the rise of modern science than the scholastics of the late Middle Ages. Renaissance natural philosophers made those contributions despite the fact that the Renaissance, the revival of classical antiquity in the fifteenth and sixteenth centuries, was not conducive to the type of scientific research that Galileo, Descartes, Boyle, and Newton conducted. Renaissance humanism was mainly a literary and artistic movement, and humanists were not particularly interested in scientific knowledge. Humanism also cultivated a tradition of deferring to the superior wisdom of classical authors, whereas the new science defined itself largely in opposition to the theories of the ancients, especially Aristotle, Ptolemy, and Galen. The main philosophical movement of the Renaissance, moreover, was Neoplatonism, which as we have seen, promoted an animistic view of nature that mechanists like Descartes and Kepler rejected.

The natural philosophers of the Renaissance did nonetheless make a number of important contributions to the birth of modern science. Many of the discoveries of the late sixteenth and seventeenth centuries drew their inspiration from Greek scientific works that had been recovered in their original form during the Renaissance. Copernicus found the original idea of his sun-centered universe in the writings of Aristarchus of Samos, a Greek astronomer of the third century B.C.E. whose work had been unknown during the Middle Ages. The theory that matter was divisible into small measurable particles known as atoms was inspired at least in part by the recovery of the texts of the ancient philosophers, most notably Democritus, who flourished around 480 B.C.E. Sixteenth-century editions of the works of Archimedes (287–212 B.C.E.), which had been virtually unknown in the Middle Ages, stimulated interest in the science of mechanics. The recovery and translation of previously unknown texts also made scientists aware that Greek scientists did not always agree with each other and thus provided a stimulus to independent observation and experimentation as a means of resolving their differences.

The Renaissance philosophy of Neoplatonism, despised by mechanists, also played an important role in the Scientific Revolution. In addition to the belief that the natural world had a soul, Neoplatonists adopted a geometric view of the universe and therefore encouraged the application of mathematics to the study of the natural world. Kepler developed his third law of planetary motion by applying to the cosmos the Neoplatonic idea of a harmony between numbers. The Neoplatonic tendency to think in terms of large, general categories also encouraged scientists like Kepler, Galileo, and Newton to discover universal laws of nature. Even alchemy, which many Neoplatonists practiced during the Renaissance, involved natural philosophers in experiments that gave them a limited sense of control over the operations of nature. The followers of Paracelsus, whose alchemy was tinged with Neoplatonic mysticism, were firm advocates of the observation of nature and experimentation.

Even the men identified with the later phase of the Scientific Revolution were influenced to some extent by the cultural traditions that we associate with the Renaissance. Kepler became involved in the study of magic at the court of the Holy Roman Emperor Rudolf II. From his reading in Neoplatonic sources, Kepler acquired his belief that the universe was constructed according to geometric principles. Bacon gained some of his enthusiasm for experimentation from his interest in natural magic, which was the use of magical words and drawings to manipulate forces in the physical world without calling on supernatural beings for assistance. Newton was fascinated by the subject of magic and studied alchemy intensively. The original inspiration of

Newton's theory of gravitation probably came from his professor at Cambridge, the Neoplatonist Henry More, who insisted on the presence of spiritual and immaterial forces in the physical world.

These contributions of the Renaissance to the new science were so important that some historians have identified the sixteenth century, when learned magic was in vogue and when the mechanical philosophy had not yet taken hold, as the first stage of the Scientific Revolution, to be followed by the mechanical phase when the discoveries of Galileo, Boyle, and Newton took center stage. Modern science resulted not so much from the victory of the mechanical philosophy over its Neoplatonic predecessor but from this encounter between these two worldviews.

The Collapse of Paradigms

The third internal cause of the Scientific Revolution was the collapse of the intellectual frameworks that had governed the conduct of scientific research since antiquity. The key to understanding this development is the recognition that scientists in all historical periods do not strive to introduce new theories but prefer to work within an established conceptual framework, or what the scholar Thomas Kuhn has referred to as a paradigm°. Scientists strive to solve puzzles that are presented by the paradigm. Every so often, however, the paradigm that has governed scientific research for an extended period of time collapses because it can no longer account for many different observable phenomena. A scientific revolution occurs when the old paradigm collapses and a new paradigm takes its place.

The revolutionary developments we have studied in astronomy and biology can be explained at least in part by the collapse of old paradigms. In astronomy the paradigm that had governed scientific inquiry in antiquity and the Middle Ages was the Ptolemaic system, in which the sun and the planets revolved around the Earth. Whenever ancient or medieval astronomers confronted a new problem as a result of their observations, they tried to accommodate the results to the Ptolemaic model. In the process they had to refine the basic concept that Ptolemy had presented. By the sixteenth century the paradigm had been modified or adjusted so many times that it no longer made sense. As scientists gradually added numerous "epicyles" of planetary motion outside the prescribed spheres, and as they identified numerous "eccentric" or noncircular orbits around the Earth, Ptolemy's paradigm of a harmoniously functioning universe gradually became a confused collection of planets and stars following different motions. Faced with this situation, Copernicus began to look for a simpler and more plausible model of the universe. The sun-centered theory that he proposed became the new paradigm within which Kepler, Galileo, and Newton all worked.

In the field of biology a parallel development occurred when the old paradigm constructed by Galen, in which the blood originated in the liver and was drawn into the heart and from there traveled through the arteries to the brain and nerves, also collapsed. By the seventeenth century the paradigm of Galen could no longer satisfactorily explain the findings of medical scholars, such as the recognition that blood could not easily pass from one ventricle of the heart to the other. It was left to Harvey to introduce an entirely new paradigm, in which the blood circulated through the body. As in astronomy, the collapse of the old paradigm led to the Scientific Revolution, and Harvey's new paradigm served as a framework for subsequent biological research.

DEVELOPMENTS OUTSIDE SCIENCE

A number of nonscientific developments also encouraged the development and acceptance of new scientific ideas. These developments outside science include the spread of Protestantism, the patronage of scientific research, the invention of the printing press, military and economic change, and voyages of exploration.

Protestantism

The growth of Protestantism in the sixteenth and seventeenth centuries encouraged the rise of modern science. Catholics as well as Protestants engaged in scientific research, and some of the most prominent European natural philosophers, including Galileo and Descartes, were devout Catholics. Protestantism, however, encouraged the emergence of modern science in three indirect ways.

First, Protestant countries proved to be more receptive than Catholic ones to new scientific ideas. Protestant churches, for example, did not prohibit the publication of books that promoted novel scientific ideas on the grounds that they were heretical, as the Papal Index did. The greater willingness of Protestant governments, especially those of England and the Dutch Republic, to tolerate the expression of unorthodox ideas helps to explain why the main geographical arena of scientific investigation shifted from the Catholic Mediterranean to the Protestant North Atlantic in the second half of the seventeenth century.

The second connection between Protestantism and the development of science was the emphasis Protestant writers placed on the idea that God revealed his intentions not only in the Bible but also in nature itself. Protestants claimed that individuals had a duty to discover what God had revealed to them in this way, just as it was their duty to read the Scripture to gain knowledge of God's will. Kepler's claim that the astronomer was "as a priest of God to the book of nature," a reference to the Protestant idea of the priesthood of all believers, serves as an explicit statement of this Protestant outlook.

The third contribution of Protestantism to the new science was the strong Protestant belief in the millennium, the second coming of Christ predicted in the Book of Revelation in the New Testament. Many Protestants believed that the event was about to occur and after Christ's arrival he would rule the world with the saints for a thousand years. In preparation for this climactic event, many English scientists, including Boyle and Newton, called for the use of scientific knowledge to achieve the general improvement of society. They also took seriously the biblical prediction that as the millennium approached, knowledge and understanding would increase.

Patronage

Although the intellectual problems that scientists grappled with may have inspired them to pursue their research and conduct experiments, they could not have succeeded without some kind of financial and institutional support. Only with the acquisition of an organizational structure could science acquire a permanent status, develop as a discipline, and give its members a professional identity. The universities, which today are known for their support of scientific research, did not serve as the main source of that support in the seventeenth century. One reason was that most universities, which were predominantly clerical institutions, had a vested interest in the defense of scholastic theology and Aristotelian science. They were therefore unlikely to provide the type of free academic atmosphere in which new scientific ideas might flourish. Moreover, within the university the only subject that allowed for the exploration of nature was that of philosophy. As long as science was considered a branch of philosophy, it could not establish its autonomy as a discipline and gain recognition as a legitimate pursuit in its own right.

Given limited support from the universities, scientists became dependent upon the patronage of wealthy and politically influential individuals. For the most part this patronage came from the kings, princes, and great noblemen who ruled European territorial states. During the seventeenth century, scientists found this type of patronage in two different types of institutions. The first were the courts of Italian and German princes. Galileo, for example, was the beneficiary of the patronage of Vincenzio Pinelli of Padua, the Venetian patrician Giovanfrancesco Sagredo, the Grand Duke of Tuscany Cosimo II de' Medici, the Roman aristocrat Prince Federico Cesi, and even Pope Urban VIII. These patrons, who were eager to display their interest in and support of learning, were actually responsible for securing Galileo's university appointments.

The terms of these appointments could be very generous. Galileo's appointment as Chief Mathematician at the University of Pisa, which Cosimo II secured for him in 1610, did not even require him to reside or teach there. Galileo's patrons gave him the opportunity to engage in his scientific work, and they circulated his publications at foreign courts. They did not, however, provide him with a permanent institutional base in which he could work.

Patronage from one politically powerful ruler rarely outlived the death of the patron, and the client could also lose the support of his patron, as Galileo did when he fell out of favor with Pope Urban VIII in 1632. Scientists who secured their livelihood at court also had to conduct themselves and their research in such a way as to maintain the favor of their patrons. Galileo referred to the new moons of Jupiter that he observed through his telescope as the Medicean stars in order to add luster to the image of the Medici family. His publications were inspired as much by his obligation to glorify Cosimo as by his belief in the validity of the sun-centered theory.

The second type of scientific institutions that provided patronage to scientists were academies in which groups of scientists could share ideas and work collectively. One of the earliest of these institutions was the Academy of the Lynxes in Rome, founded in 1603 by Prince Cesi. In keeping with the aristocratic values of its founder, it was modeled on an order of knights. Galileo became a member of this academy in 1611, and it published many of his works. In 1657 Cosimo II founded a similar institution, the Academy of Experiment, in Florence. These academies offered a more regular source of patronage than scientists could acquire from individual positions at court, but they still served the function of glorifying their founders, and they depended on patrons for their continued existence. The royal academies established in the 1660s, however, especially the Royal Academy of Sciences in France and the Royal Society in England, reduced that dependence on their patrons. These academies became in effect public institutions; even though they were established by the crown, they operated with a minimum of royal intervention. The royal academies also acquired a permanent location that made possible a continuous program of work.

The mission of the Royal Society in England was the promotion of scientific knowledge through a program of experimentation. It also served the political purpose of placing the results of scientific research at the service of the state, as we shall see shortly. This had been Francis Bacon's objective in his *New Organon,* and many of the members of the society, including Robert Boyle and Robert Hooke, were

CHRONOLOGY

The Formation of Scientific Societies

1603	Prince Cesi founds the Academy of the Lynxes in Rome
1657	Cosimo II de' Medici founds the Academy of Experiment in Florence
1662	Founding of the Royal Society of London under the auspices of Charles II
1666	Founding of the Academy of Sciences in Paris

■ **The Frontispiece of Thomas Sprat's *The History of the Royal Society of London* (1667)** Fame places a laurel on a bust of Charles II, the patron of the society, while the president of the society, Lord Brouncker, sits to the left, pointing to the king. The late Sir Francis Bacon, whose emphasis on experimentation defined the purpose of the society, sits to the right and points to the navigational devices and firearms that he had predicted would lead to European control of the globe. They are sitting in a room filled with books and scientific instruments, including a telescope. In the background the Thames River, the gateway to the British Empire, suggests a further link between science and empire.

committed to the implementation of Bacon's plans. The research that members of the Royal Society did on both ship construction and military technology gave some indication of this commitment. These attempts to use scientific technology to strengthen the power of the state show that two of the most important developments of the seventeenth century, the growth of the modern state and the emergence of modern science, were related.

The Printing Press

The scientific academies and societies of the seventeenth century gave natural philosophers an opportunity to discuss their findings among themselves, but these scientists also needed to communicate the results of their research to scientists in more distant localities. The introduction and spread of printing throughout Europe made it much easier for scientists to share their discoveries with others who were working on similar problems. During the Middle Ages, when books were handwritten, the dissemination of scientific knowledge was limited by the number of copies that could be made of a manuscript. Moreover, errors could easily creep into the text as it was being copied. The advent and spread of printing helped to correct this problem: Scientific achievements could be preserved in a much more accurate form and presented to a broader audience. The availability of printed copies also made it much easier for other scientists to correct or supplement the data that the authors supplied. In this way the entire body of scientific knowledge became cumulative, as it is today. Printing also made possible the reproduction of illustrations, diagrams, tables, and other schematic drawings that helped to convey the author's findings.

It remains uncertain how large a role printed materials played in the development of science. Scientists certainly read the work of others, but they also devoted large amounts of time to their own experiments, and those experiments in the long run were more important than books in the development of scientific knowledge. Printing may have accomplished more by making members of the nonscientific community aware of the latest advances in physics and astronomy than by leading scientists themselves to make new discoveries. In this way printing helped to make science an integral part of the culture of educated Europeans. The printing press also facilitated the growth of opposition to the new science, since it made possible the publication of treatises attacking the theories of Copernicus, Galileo, and Descartes.

Military and Economic Change

The Scientific Revolution occurred at roughly the same time that both the conduct of warfare and the European economy were undergoing dramatic changes. As territorial states increased the size of their armies and their military arsenals, they naturally demanded more accurate weapons with longer range. Some of the work undertaken by physicists during the seventeenth century, especially concerning the trajectory and velocity of missiles, gravitation, and air resistance, had the specific intention of improving military weaponry. Members of the Royal Society in England conducted extensive scientific research on these topics, and in so doing followed Francis Bacon's recommendation that scientists place their research at the service of the state.

The practical needs of capitalist enterprise also had a bearing on the direction of scientific research. The seventeenth century was a formative period in the emergence of a new capitalist economy, one in which private individuals engaged in trade, agriculture, and industry in order to realize ever-increasing profits. Some of the questions discussed at the meetings of the Royal Society suggest that its members undertook research with the specific objective of making such capitalist ventures more productive and profitable. The research did not always produce immediate results, but ultimately it increased economic profitability and contributed to the growth of the English economy in the eighteenth century. Knowledge of the displacement of water by ships led to improvements in methods of ship construction, which benefited merchants engaged in overseas trade. The determination of longitude by means of an accurate measurement of time at sea, a problem with which many seventeenth-century scientists grappled and which was finally solved in the eighteenth century with the invention of the chronometer, improved navigation. The study of mechanics led to new techniques to ventilate mines and raise coal or ore from them, thus making mining more profitable.

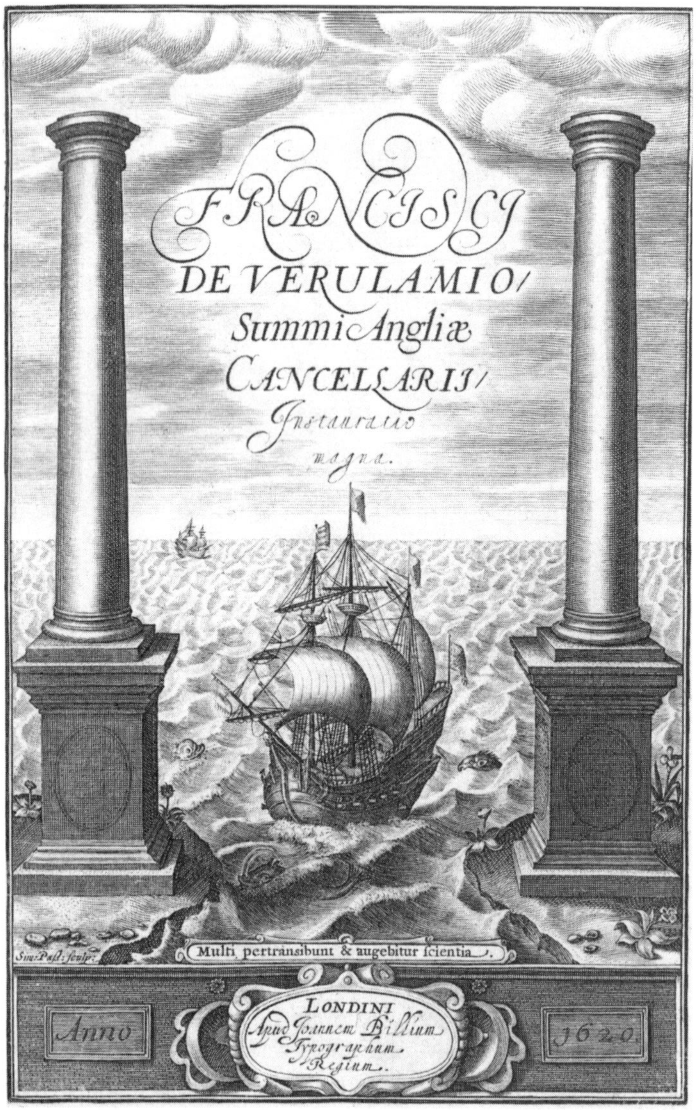

■ **The Frontispiece to Francis Bacon's *The Great Instauration* (1620)**

The ship is shown sailing beyond the Straits of Gibraltar and the two pillars of Hercules, which had symbolized the limits of human knowledge. The biblical prophecy below the engraving reads: "Many shall pass to and fro and science will be increased." Bacon intended to show that the opening of the world to navigation and commerce complemented the further discovery of scientific knowledge. Both involved the discovery of new worlds.

Voyages of Exploration

Closely related to the economic causes of the Scientific Revolution were the oceanic voyages of exploration that European mariners began to make in the late fifteenth century. As these voyages began long before the seventeenth century, they did not exercise an immediate or direct influence on the development of science. Most of the voyages, moreover, were undertaken by Portuguese and Spaniards, who did not play a major role in the Scientific Revolution. Nevertheless, these voyages revealed to mariners a number of natural phenomena that conflicted with the inherited traditions of Greek and late medieval science. They disproved, for example, much of what Ptolemy had written about the moistness of land in the Southern Hemisphere and what Aristotle had written about the difficulty of living in tropical areas. These inconsistencies led European natural philosophers to call into question the inherited authority of the Greeks on a variety of scientific matters and to base their views on the empirical observation of nature. In writing about the experimental method, Bacon frequently cited the body of evidence that had come from these voyages.

The Intellectual Effects of the Scientific Revolution

The Scientific Revolution had a profound impact on the intellectual life of educated Europeans. The discoveries of Copernicus, Kepler, Galileo, and Newton, as well as the assumptions upon which their work was based, influenced the subjects that people in the West studied, the way in which they approached intellectual problems, and their views regarding the supernatural realm.

EDUCATION

The philosophy of Aristotle, especially in its Christianized, scholastic form, had proved remarkably durable at European universities during the sixteenth century. It had successfully withstood the challenge of Neoplatonism, but the new science and the mechanical philosophy represented a more potent challenge to its supremacy. Over the course of the seventeenth and early eighteenth centuries, especially between the years 1680 and 1720, science and the new philosophy that was associated with it acquired academic respectability and became an important component of university education. Outside academia, knowledge of science increased as the result of its promotion by learned societies, attendance at public lectures, the discussion of science in coffeehouses, and the publication of scientific textbooks. As this knowledge was diffused among the educated classes, science secured a permanent foothold in Western culture.

The spread of science did not go unchallenged. It encountered academic rivals committed not only to traditional Aristotelianism but also to Renaissance humanism, which had gradually penetrated the curriculum of the universities during the sixteenth and seventeenth centuries. Beginning in the late seventeenth century a conflict arose between "the ancients," who revered the wisdom of classical authors, and "the moderns," who emphasized the superiority of the new scientific culture. The most concrete expression of this conflict was the Battle of the Books, an intellectual debate that raged in England and on the Continent in the late seventeenth and early eighteenth centuries over the question of which group of thinkers had contributed more to human knowledge. The battle accentuated the differences between two distinct components of western European culture. The Battle of the Books ended with no clear winner, and the conflict between the ancients and the moderns has never been completely resolved. The humanities and the sciences, while included within the same curriculum at many universities, are still often regarded as representing two separate cultural traditions.

SKEPTICISM AND INDEPENDENT REASONING

One of the most significant intellectual effects of the Scientific Revolution was the encouragement it gave to the habit of skepticism, the tendency to doubt what we have been taught and are expected to believe. This skepticism formed part of the method that seventeenth-century scientists adopted in their efforts to solve philosophical problems. As we have seen, Descartes, Bacon, Galileo, and Kepler all refused to acknowledge the authority of classical or medieval texts, preferring instead to rely upon the knowledge they acquired from the observation of nature and the use of their own rational faculties.

In *Discourse on the Method,* Descartes showed the extremes to which this skepticism could be taken by doubting the reality of his own sense perceptions and even his own existence. He eventually found a way out of this dilemma when he realized that the very act of doubting proved his existence as a thinking being. As he wrote in words that have become famous, "I think, therefore I am." Upon this foundation Descartes went on to prove the existence of God and the material world, thereby conquering the skepticism with which he began his inquiry. In the process, however, Descartes had promoted an approach to solving intellectual problems that asked people to question the authority of others and to think clearly and systematically for themselves. The effects of this method began to become apparent in the late seventeenth century, when Descartes's methodology was invoked in challenging a variety of orthodox opinions regarding the supernatural world.

Some of the most radical of those opinions came from the mind of Baruch Spinoza (1632–1677), who grew up in Amsterdam in a community of Spanish and Portuguese Jews who had fled the Inquisition. Although educated in the Orthodox Jewish manner, Spinoza also studied Latin and read widely the work of Descartes and other Christian writers of the period. From Descartes, Spinoza had learned "that nothing ought to be admitted as true but what has been proved by good and solid reason." This skepticism and independence of thought led to his excommunication from the Jewish community at age 24, at which time he changed his first name from its Jewish form, Baruch, to Benedict. A skilled lens grinder by trade, Spinoza spent much of his life developing his philosophical ideas.

Spinoza challenged Descartes's separation of the mind and the body and the radical distinction between the spiritual and the material. For Spinoza there was only one substance in the universe, which he equated with nature or God. This pantheism, in which all matter became spirit and was comprehended within God, challenged not only the ideas of Descartes but also a fundamental tenet of Christianity—the distinction between God as pure spirit and the material world that he had created. In his most famous book, *A Treatise on Religion and Political Philosophy* (1670), Spinoza developed these ideas and also called for complete freedom from intellectual restraints.

The type of freethinking that Spinoza advocated aroused considerable suspicion. His followers, most of whom lived in the Dutch Republic, were constantly exposed to the danger of prosecution for atheism and blasphemy. Spinoza's skeptical approach to solving philosophical and scientific problems revealed the radical intellectual potential of the new science. The freedom of thought that Spinoza advocated, as well as the belief that nature followed immutable laws and could be understood in mathematical terms, served as important links between the Scientific Revolution and the Enlightenment of the eighteenth century. Those connections will be studied more fully in Chapter 17.

CHRONOLOGY

The Impact of the Scientific Revolution

1620	Sir Francis Bacon publishes *The New Organon,* arguing for the necessity of rigorous experimentation
1633	Galileo tried by the Roman Inquisition
1637	René Descartes publishes *Discourse on the Method,* recommending the solution of intellectual problems through a process of deduction
1670	Baruch Spinoza publishes *Treatise on Religion and Political Philosophy,* challenging the distinction between spirit and matter
1686	Bernard de Fontenelle publishes *Treatises on the Plurality of Worlds,* a fictional work exploring the possibility of extraterrestrial life
1682	Edict of Louis XIV ending most witchcraft trials in France
1684	Last execution for witchcraft in England
1691–1693	Balthasar Bekker publishes *The Enchanted World* in four volumes, denying the intervention of the devil in the operation of the natural world
1709	Thomas Newcomen invents the first steam engine

SCIENCE AND RELIGION

The most profound intellectual effects of the Scientific Revolution occurred in the area of religious thought. The claims of the new science presented two challenges to traditional Christian belief. The first involved the apparent contradiction between the sun-centered theory of the universe and biblical references to the sun's mobility. Since the Bible was considered the inspired word of God, the Church took everything it said, including any passages regarding the operation of the physical world, as literally true. The Bible's reference to the sun moving across the sky served as the basis of the official papal condemnation of sun-centered theories in 1616 and the prosecution of Galileo in 1633.

The second challenge to traditional Christian belief was the implication that if the universe functioned as a machine, on the basis of immutable natural laws, then God apparently played a very small role in its operation. This position, which was adopted by the late-seventeenth- and eighteenth-century thinkers known as Deists°, was considered a denial of the Christian belief that God superintended the operation of the world and was continually active in its governance. None of the great scientists of the seventeenth century actually adopted this position, but the acceptance of the mechanical philosophy made them vulnerable to the charge that they denied Christian doctrine. Because of his support for the mechanical philosophy, Descartes was suspected of atheism.

Although the new science and seventeenth-century Christianity appeared to be on a collision course, a number of scientists and theologians insisted that there was no conflict between them. One argument they made was that religion and science were separate disciplines that had very different concerns. Religion dealt with man's relationship with God, while science explained how nature operated. As Galileo wrote in a letter to the Grand Duchess Christina of Tuscany in 1615, "The Holy Ghost teaches us how to go to Heaven, not how the heavens go." Scripture was not intended to explain natural phenomena, but to convey religious truths that could not be grasped by human reason. In making these points Galileo was pleading for the separation of religion and science by freeing scientific inquiry from the control of the Church. To some extent, that separation has taken place over the course of the last three centuries. Theology and science have gradually become separate academic disciplines, each with its own objectives and methodology. Even the papacy eventually accepted the position of Galileo on this question in 1992. Nevertheless, conflicts between the claims of science and those who believe in the literal truth of the Bible have not disappeared, especially regarding the theory of evolution.

Another argument for the compatibility of science and religion was the claim that the mechanical philosophy, rather than relegating God to a role of a retired engineer, actually manifested his unlimited power. In a mechanistic universe God was still the creator of the entire physical world and the formulator of the laws of nature that guaranteed its regular operation. He was still all-powerful and present everywhere. According to Boyle and Newton, moreover, God played a supremely active role in governing the universe. Not only had he created the universe, but, in a theory developed by Boyle, he also continued to keep all matter constantly in motion. This theory served the purpose of redefining God's power without diminishing it in any way. Newton arrived at a similar position in his search for an immaterial agent who would cause gravity to operate. He proposed that God himself, who he believed "endures always and is present everywhere," made bodies move according to gravitational laws. Throughout the early eighteenth century this feature of Newtonian natural philosophy served as a powerful argument for the existence and immanence of God.

As the new science became more widely accepted, and as the regularity and immutability of the laws of nature became more apparent, religion itself began to undergo a transformation. Instead of denying the validity of the new science, many theologians, especially Protestants, accommodated scientific knowledge to their religious beliefs. Some Protestants welcomed the discoveries of science as an opportunity to purify the Christian religion by combating the superstition, magic, and ignorance that they claimed the Catholic Church had been promoting. Clerics who accepted the new science, including those who became members of the Royal Society, argued that since God worked through the processes of nature, human beings could acquire theological knowledge of him by engaging in scientific inquiry. For them religion and science were not so much separate but complementary forms of knowledge, each capable of illuminating the other.

The most widespread effect of the new science on religion was a new emphasis on the compatibility of reason and religion. In the Middle Ages scholastic theologians such as Thomas Aquinas had tried to reconcile the two, arguing that there was a body of knowledge about God, called natural theology, that could be obtained without the assistance of revelation. Now, however, with the benefit of the new science, theologians and philosophers began to expand the role that reason played in religion. In the religious writings of the English philosopher John Locke, the role of reason became dominant. In *The Reasonableness of Christianity* (1695), Locke argued that reason should be the final arbiter of the existence of the supernatural and it should also determine the true meaning of the Bible. This new emphasis on the role of reason in religion coincided with a rejection of the religious zeal that had characterized the era of the Reformation and the wars of religion. Political and ecclesiastical authorities looked down on religious enthusiasm not only as politically dangerous, since it had inspired revolution and rebellion throughout Europe, but as a form of behavior that had no rational basis.

The new emphasis on the reasonableness of religion and the decline of religious enthusiasm are often viewed as evidence of a broader trend toward the secularization of European life, a process in which religion gave way to more worldly concerns. In one sense this secular trend was undeniable. By the dawn of the eighteenth century, theology had lost its dominant position at the universities, the sciences had become autonomous academic disciplines, and religion had lost much of its intellectual authority. Religion also began to exercise less influence on the conduct of politics and diplomacy and on the regulation of economic activity.

Religion had not, however, lost its relevance. Throughout the eighteenth century it remained a vital force in the lives of most European people. Religious books continued to be published in great numbers. Many of those who accepted the new science continued to believe in a providential God and the divinity of Christ. Moreover, a small but influential group of educated people, following the lead of the French mathematician, physicist, and religious philosopher Blaise Pascal (1623–1662), insisted that although reason and science have their place, they represent only one sphere of truth. In his widely circulated book *Reflections*, which lay unfinished at his death but was published in 1670, Pascal argued that religious faith occupied a higher sphere of knowledge that reason and science could not penetrate. Pascal, the inventor of a calculating machine and the promoter of a system of public coach service in Paris, had been an advocate of the new science. He endorsed the Copernican model of the universe and opposed the condemnation of Galileo. But on the question of the relationship between science and religion, Pascal presented arguments that could be used against Spinoza, Locke, and all those who considered reason the ultimate arbiter of truth.

MAGIC, DEMONS, AND WITCHCRAFT

The new science not only changed many patterns of religious thought but also led to a denial of the reality and effectiveness of magic. Magic is the use of a supernatural, occult, or mysterious power to achieve extraordinary effects in the physical world or to influence the course of human events. The effects can be beneficial or harmful. Magicians claimed to be able to use their special powers to cure a person or inflict disease, acquire political power, stimulate love or hatred in another individual, predict the future, or produce any number of natural "marvels," including changes in the weather. In the sixteenth and seventeenth centuries men and women believed in and practiced two forms of magic. Natural magic°, such as the practice of alchemy, involved the manipulation of occult forces that were believed to exist in nature. As we have seen, many

JUSTICE IN HISTORY

The Trial of Galileo

The events leading to the trial of Galileo for heresy in 1633 began in 1616, when a committee of eleven theologians reported to the Roman Inquisition that the sun-centered theory of Copernicus was heretical. Those who accepted this theory were declared to be heretics not only because they called the authority of the Bible into question but because they denied the exclusive authority of the Catholic Church to determine how the Bible should be interpreted. The day after this report was submitted, Pope Paul V instructed Cardinal Robert Bellarmine, a theologian who was on good terms with Galileo, to warn him to abandon his Copernican views. Galileo had written extensively in support of the sun-centered thesis, especially in his *Letters on Sunspots* (1613) and his *Letter to the Grand Duchess Christina* (1615), although he had never admitted that the theory was proved conclusively. Now he was being told that he should not hold, teach, or defend in any way the opinion of the sun's stability or the Earth's mobility. If he were to ignore that warning, he would be prosecuted as a heretic.

During the next sixteen years Galileo published two books. The first, *The Assayer* (1623), was an attack upon the views of an Italian philosopher regarding comets. The book actually won Galileo considerable support, especially from the new pope, Urban VIII, who was eager to be associated with the most fashionable intellectual trends. Urban took Galileo under his wing and made him the intellectual star of his court. Urban even went so far as to declare that support for Copernicanism was not heretical but only rash.

The patronage of the pope may have emboldened Galileo to exercise less caution in writing his second book of this period, *Dialogue Concerning the Two Chief World Systems* (1632). This treatise was ostensibly an impartial presentation of the rival Ptolemaic and Copernican cosmologies, but in its own quiet way it served the purpose of promoting Copernicanism. Galileo sought proper authorization from ecclesiastical authorities to put the book in print, but he eventually allowed it to be published in Florence before it received official approval from Rome.

The publication of *Dialogue* precipitated Galileo's fall from the pope's favor. Urban, who at this time was coming under criticism for leniency with heretics, ordered the book taken out of circulation in the summer of 1632 and appointed a commission to investigate Galileo's activities. After receiving the report from the committee a few months later, he turned the matter over to the Roman Inquisition, which charged Galileo with heresy.

The Roman Inquisition had been established in 1542 to preserve the Catholic faith. Its main concern was the prosecution of heresy. Like the Spanish Inquisition, this Roman ecclesiastical court has acquired a reputation for being harsh and arbitrary, for administering torture, for proceeding in secrecy, and for denying the accused the right to know what the charges were in advance of the trial. There is some validity to these criticisms, although the Roman Inquisition did not torture Galileo or deny him the opportunity to present a defense. The most unfair aspect of the proceeding, and of inquisitorial justice in general, was the determination of the outcome of the trial by the same judges who had brought the charges against the accused and conducted the interrogation. This meant that in a politically motivated trial such as Galileo's, the verdict was a foregone conclusion. To accept Galileo's defense would have been a sign of weakness and a repudiation of the pope.

Although the underlying substantive issue in the trial was whether Galileo was guilty of heresy for denying the sun's motion and the Earth's immobility, the more technical question was whether by publishing *Dialogue* he had violated the prohibition of 1616. In his defense Galileo claimed that the only reason he had written *Dialogue* was to present "the physical and astronomical reasons that can be advanced for one side or the other." He denied holding Copernicus's opinion to be true.

In the end the court determined that by publishing *Dialogue,* Galileo had violated the injunction of 1616. He had disseminated "the false opinion of the Earth's motion and the sun's stability" and he had "defended the said opinion already condemned." Even Galileo's efforts "to give the impression of leaving it undecided and labeled as probable" was still a very serious error,

The Trial of Galileo, 1633
Galileo is shown here presenting one of his four defenses to the Inquisition.

since there is no way that "an opinion declared and defined contrary to divine Scripture may be probable." The court also declared that Galileo had obtained permission to publish the book in Florence without divulging to the authorities there that he was under the injunction of 1616.

Throughout the trial every effort was made to distance the pope from his former protégé. There was real fear among the members of the papal court that since the pope had been Galileo's patron and had given him considerable latitude in developing his ideas, he himself would be implicated in Galileo's heresy. Every step was taken to guarantee that information regarding the pope's support for Galileo did not surface. The court made sure, for example, that no one from the Medici court, which had provided support for Galileo, would testify on Galileo's behalf. The trial tells us as much about the efforts of Urban VIII to save face as about the Catholic Church's hostility to the new science.

Galileo was required to formally renounce of his views and to avoid any further defense of Copernicanism. After making this humiliating submission to the court, he was sent to Siena, and later that year was allowed to return to his villa in Arcetri near Florence, where he remained under house arrest until his death in 1642. ■

Questions of Justice

1. Galileo was silenced because of what he had put into print. Why had he published these works, and why did the Church consider his publications a serious threat?
2. Why did Galileo accept the verdict of the court?
3. Is a court of law an appropriate place to resolve disputes between science and religion? Why or why not?

Taking It Further

Finocchiaro, Maurice, ed. *The Galileo Affair: A Documentary History.* 1989. A collection of original documents regarding the controversy between Galileo and the Roman Catholic Church.

Sharratt, Michael. *Galileo: Decisive Innovator.* 1994. A study of Galileo's place in the history of science that provides full coverage of his trial and papal reconsiderations of it in the late twentieth century.

SKEPTICISM REGARDING THE DEVIL

Balthasar Bekker, a Dutch Calvinist minister, wrote a four-volume attack on the belief in witchcraft entitled The Enchanted World *in 1691–1693. The book denies the possibility that the Devil could exercise power over the natural world or that he could appear as a human being. Bekker reflects the skepticism and rationalism of Descartes as well as the belief of natural theologians that God works through the processes of nature.*

There is no argument so absurd as that of attributing an unusual effect to an occult or unknown cause, but above all, to these sorts of intellects [demons], as people want to do, in order to draw as a consequence that they have the power and the capacity to do such things. Why not rather investigate deeply into the knowledge of Nature in order to unite things corporeal to things corporeal? For if I encounter something which has not yet been proven, but which nevertheless is of the same nature as something else, what reason do I have to look for another cause than that which I already have found at work in the other? . . . I have not investigated the secrets of nature in such a way that I could know what she is yet capable of doing again, and I have not thumbed through books in such a way that there could not be in them certain things formerly known to be natural things, but that pass today for witchcraft. . . .

Man is forced, as soon as he meets something that arrests his judgment, to throw it back upon the Devil. He can do this in all safety, and without being fearful of passing for idiotic, stupid, wicked or impious. But if he should happen to put into doubt, and even more if he should deny that the Devil can be the author of the thing, he is called an atheist. . . . As if there had to be no God if it were not true that the Devil acted upon men in all sorts of encounters? If you answer yes, why could He not do by means of his angels the things which cannot be done naturally, or rather, by the force of nature, of which man still does not know the thousandth part?

Source: From Balthasar Bekker, *The Enchanted World* (1691) in Alan C. Kors and Edward Peters, *Witchcraft in Europe, 1100–1700: A Documentary History.*

Neoplatonists believed in the possibility of this type of magic, and many of them actually practiced it. Demonic magic°, on the other hand, involved the invocation of evil spirits so that one might gain access to their supernatural power. The men who were most committed to the mechanical philosophy denied the effectiveness of both types of magic. By claiming that matter was inert, they challenged the central notion of natural magic, which is the belief that material objects are animated by occult forces, such as a sympathy for another object. If matter was not alive, it contained no forces for a magician to manipulate.

The denial of the reality of demonic magic was based on a rejection of the powers of demons. Seventeenth-century scientists did not necessarily deny the existence of angelic or demonic spirits, but the mechanical philosophy posed a serious challenge to the belief that those spirits could influence the operation of the physical world. The belief in demons experienced a slow death. Many scientists struggled to preserve a place for them in the physical world, arguing that demons, like God, could work through the processes of nature. Ultimately, however, the logic of the mechanical philosophy expelled them from the world-view of the educated classes. By the beginning of the eighteenth century, scientists and even some theologians had labeled the belief in demons as superstition, which originally had meant false or erroneous religion but which was now redefined to mean ignorance of mechanical causes. As Thomas Sprat, an English clergyman, declared in his history of the Royal Society, "Experiments have proven demons don't exist."

The denial of the power of magic, together with the rejection of the belief in the power of demonic spirits, also explains why many educated Europeans began to deny the reality of witchcraft in the later half of the seventeenth century. Witches were individuals, mostly women, who stood accused of using magic to bring harm upon their neighbors, their animals, or their crops. They were also accused of having made a pact with the Devil, the means by which they received their magical powers. In many cases it was claimed that witches worshipped the Devil collectively at nocturnal orgies known as sabbaths. At these assemblies, so it was claimed, witches danced naked, had sexual intercourse with demons and other witches, and sacrificed unbaptized children to the Devil. To someone who subscribed to the mechanical philosophy, this entire set of beliefs about witches was highly questionable. Demons could not intervene in the operation of the physical world, much less make pacts with human beings and copulate with them at the sabbath.

The most emphatic, comprehensive, and unequivocal attack on the entire body of witch beliefs during the seventeenth century came from the pen of a Dutch minister and follower of Descartes, Balthasar Bekker, whose four-volume study, *The Enchanted World* (1691–1693), denied that the Devil could exercise any jurisdiction over the natural world. The mechanical philosophy was not the only basis for Bekker's skepticism. A biblical scholar, Bekker produced many passages from Scripture indicating that God exercised complete sovereignty over the Devil and had in fact chained him to Hell. In this way the Devil had been rendered incapable of causing physical destruction in the world, either with or without the assistance of witches.

Skeptics such as Bekker played only a minor role in bringing about the decline and end of witchcraft prosecutions. As we discussed in Chapter 14, thousands of Europeans, most of them women, were tried and executed for witchcraft during the sixteenth and seventeenth centuries. These unfortunate people were accused not only of harming their neighbors but of belonging to a vast diabolical conspiracy to destroy Christian civilization. Beginning in the 1620s the number and frequency of these witchcraft trials began to decline. The reason for this decline was not so much the triumph of the mechanical philosophy, which spread within ruling elites only gradually, but the growing recognition by judges and magistrates that large numbers of innocent people had been forced under torture to confess to crimes they had not committed. In order to avoid any further miscarriages of justice, courts abandoned the use of torture and demanded that convictions for witchcraft satisfy very strict standards of legal proof. In such circumstances the number of convictions and executions was reduced to a mere trickle. The trials did not come to a complete end, however, until political authorities recognized that witchcraft was an impossible crime. Only then did they take steps to ensure that no one could ever be tried for it again. Between 1682 and 1776 the laws that had authorized the prosecution and execution of witches in France, Prussia, Great Britain, Sweden, Austria, Poland, and Russia were all repealed.

The skeptical views that many educated people acquired regarding witchcraft and magic were usually not shared by people who remained illiterate. For them magic and witchcraft remained very real, and they continued to suspect and accuse their neighbors of engaging in diabolical practices until the early nineteenth century. In a number of instances they took the law into their own hands, stoning accused witches, drowning them, or burning them alive. All of this served to highlight a widening gap between the views of the educated and those of the common people. There had always been differences between learned and popular culture, but there also had been many aspects of culture that educated and uneducated people shared. Both groups, for example, took part in the same religious services and rituals, and both groups also shared some of the same beliefs about magic and witchcraft. In the late seventeenth century, however, this common cultural ground began to disappear, and members of the educated classes began to develop unprecedented contempt for the ignorance and superstition of the common people. The education of the upper classes in the new science and in Descartes's philosophy only aggravated what was already a noticeable trend.

The development of two separate realms of culture became one of the main themes of eighteenth-century history, and it contributed directly to the formation of class divisions. On the one side were the educated upper classes who prided themselves on their rational and enlightened views; on the other were the illiterate peasants who continued to believe in magic, witchcraft, and what the educated referred to as "vulgar superstition."

Humans and the Natural World

The spread of scientific knowledge not only redefined the views of educated people regarding the supernatural realm, but it also led them to reconsider their relationship to nature. This process involved three separate but related inquiries. The first was to determine the place of human beings in a sun-centered universe; the second to investigate how science and technology had given human beings greater control over nature; and the third to reconsider the relationship between men and women in light of new scientific knowledge regarding the human mind and body.

The Place of Human Beings in the Universe

The astronomical discoveries of Copernicus and Galileo offered a new outlook regarding the position of human beings in the universe. The Earth-centered Ptolemaic cosmos that dominated scientific thought during the Middle Ages was also human-centered. Not only was the planet that human beings inhabited situated at the center of the universe, but on Earth humans occupied a privileged position. This is not to say that the human condition was always viewed in positive terms. Trapped on a stationary Earth, which itself was corruptible, individuals were always vulnerable to the temptations of the demonic spirits that medieval clerics told them were constantly hovering in the atmosphere. But human beings nonetheless remained the absolute physical and moral center of this universe. They were, after all, created in the image of God, according to Christian belief. Renaissance Neoplatonism reinforced this medieval view. By describing human beings as having the characteristics of both angels and beasts, with the capacity to ascend toward God or descend to the level of animals, Neoplatonists accentuated the centrality and importance of humankind in the world.

The acceptance of a sun-centered model of the universe began to bring about a fundamental change in these views of humankind. Once it became apparent that the Earth was not the center of the universe, human beings began to lose their privileged position in nature. The Copernican universe was neither Earth-centered nor human-centered. Scientists such as Descartes continued to claim that human beings were the greatest of nature's creatures, but their habitation of a tiny planet circling the sun inevitably reduced the sense of their own importance. Moreover, as astronomers began to recognize the incomprehensible size of the cosmos, the possibility emerged that there were other habitable worlds in the universe, calling into further question the unique status of humankind.

In the late sixteenth century and seventeenth centuries a number of literary works explored the possibility of other inhabited worlds and forms of life. In *The Infinite Universe and World* (1584), the Neoplatonist monk Giordano Bruno (1548–1600), who was eventually burned as a heretic, postulated the existence of other rational beings and suggested that they might be more intelligent than humans. Kepler's *Somnium,* or *Lunar Astronomy* (1634), a book that combined science and fiction, described various species of moon dwellers, some of whom were rational and superior to humans. This was followed by a number of works of fiction on travel to the moon, including Francis Godwin's *The Man in the Moon* (1638) and Cyrano de Bergerac's *The Other World* (1657). The most ambitious and fascinating of all these books was a fictional work by the French dramatist and poet Bernard de Fontenelle, *Treatises on the Plurality of Worlds* (1686). This work, which became immensely popular throughout Europe, was more responsible than any purely scientific discovery of the seventeenth century for leading the general reading public to call into question the centrality of humankind in Creation.

THE CONTROL OF NATURE

The Scientific Revolution bolstered the confidence human beings had in their ability to control nature. By disclosing the laws governing the operation of the universe, the new science gave humans the tools they needed to make nature serve their own purposes more effectively than it had in the past. This confidence in human mastery over nature found its most articulate expression in the writings of Francis Bacon. Instead of accepting the traditional view that humans were either passively reconciled with nature or victimized by it, Bacon believed that knowledge of the laws of nature could restore the dominion over nature that humans had lost in the biblical Garden of Eden. Bacon believed that nature existed for human beings to control and exploit for their own benefit. His famous maxim, "knowledge is power," conveyed his confidence that science would give human beings this type of control over nature.

In the same spirit Descartes announced that as human beings we had the capacity "to turn ourselves into the masters and possessors of nature." For him nature included animals or beasts, which, unlike human beings, did not have souls and were therefore merely corporal machines. (For this reason, he was not at all reluctant to dissect live animals.) Later in the seventeenth century the members of the Royal Society proclaimed their intention to make scientific knowledge "an instrument whereby mankind may obtain a dominion over things." This optimism regarding human control of nature found support in the belief that God permitted such mastery, first by creating a regular and uniform universe and then by giving people the rational faculties by which they could understand nature's laws.

Many scientists of the seventeenth century emphasized the practical applications of their research, just as scientists often do today. Descartes, who used his knowledge of optics to improve the grinding of lenses, contemplated ways in which scientific knowledge might improve the drainage of marshes, increase the velocity of bullets, and use bells to make clouds burst. He even dreamed of making the blind see and enabling men to fly. As we mentioned earlier, members of the Royal Society discussed how their experiments would help miners, farmers, and merchants. They even discussed the possibility of making labor-saving machines. These efforts to apply scientific knowledge to practical problems encouraged the belief, which has persisted to the present day, that science could improve human life.

The hopes of seventeenth-century scientists for the improvement of human life by means of technology remained in large part unfulfilled until the eighteenth century. Only then did the technological promise of the Scientific Revolution begin to be realized, most notably with the innovations that preceded or accompanied the Industrial Revolution. The first steam engine, for example, which utilized the scientific study of atmospheric pressure conducted by a student of Galileo in the 1650s, was not invented until 1709. The great improvements in the construction of canals and the use of water power to drive machinery, which were based upon the study of Newtonian mechanics, likewise did not take place until the eighteenth century. In similar fashion, research on the internal structure of grains and the breeding of sheep did not significantly increase food production until the eighteenth century, at the time of the agricultural revolution.

By the middle of the eighteenth century, the belief that science would lead to an improvement of human life became an integral part of Western culture. Much less apparent at that time, however, was a recognition of the destructive potential of applied science. Governments supported scientific research on ballistics to gain military advantage, but it was not until the twentieth century, especially with the construction of engines of mass destruction, that people began to recognize technology's potential to cause permanent harm to the human race. In the seventeenth and eighteenth centuries, those who possessed scientific knowledge thought mainly in terms of the benefits that science and technology could confer. Their faith in human progress became one of the main themes of the Enlightenment, which will be discussed in Chapter 17.

WOMEN, MEN, AND NATURE

The new scientific and philosophical ideas of the seventeenth century challenged ancient and medieval notions regarding women's physical and mental inferiority to men. At the same time the new science left other traditional ideas about the roles of men and women unchallenged.

Until the seventeenth century, a woman's sexual organs were thought to be imperfect versions of a man's, an idea that made woman an inferior version of man and in some respects a freak of nature. During the sixteenth and seventeenth centuries, a body of scientific literature advanced the new idea that women had sexual organs that were perfect in their own right and served distinct functions in reproduction. Another traditional biological idea that came under attack during this period was Aristotle's view that men made a more important contribution to reproduction than did women. The man's semen was long believed to contain the form of the body as well as the soul, while the only contribution the woman was believed to have made to the process was the formless matter upon which the semen acted. By the beginning of the eighteenth century, a scholarly consensus had emerged that recognized equal contributions from both sexes to the process of reproduction.

Some seventeenth-century natural philosophers also called into question ancient and medieval ideas regarding women's mental inferiority to men. In this regard Descartes supplied a theory that presupposed intellectual equality between the sexes. In making a radical separation between the mind and the human body, Descartes found no difference between the minds of men and women. As one of his followers wrote in 1673, "The mind has no sex." A few upper-class women provided solid evidence to support this revolutionary claim of female intellectual equality. Princess Elisabeth of Bohemia, for example, carried on a long correspondence with Descartes during the 1640s and challenged many of his ideas on the relationship between the body and the soul. The privately educated English noblewoman

ELISABETH OF BOHEMIA CHALLENGES DESCARTES

Elisabeth of Bohemia, the daughter of King Frederick of Bohemia and granddaughter of King James I of England, engaged in a long correspondence with Descartes regarding his philosophy. Privately educated in Greek, Latin and mathematics, Elisabeth was one of a small group of noblewomen who participated in the scientific and philosophical debates of the day. The letter concerns the relationship between the soul (or mind), which Descartes claimed was immaterial, and the body, which is entirely composed of matter. One of the problems for Descartes was to explain how the mind can move that body to perform certain functions. In the letter Elisabeth plays a deferential, self-effacing role but in the process exposes one of the weaknesses of Descartes's dualistic philosophy.

The Hague, 20 June 1643

Monsieur Descartes,

. . . The life I am forced to lead does not leave me the disposition of enough time to acquire a habit of meditation according to your rules. So many interests of my family that I must not neglect, so many interviews and civilities that I cannot avoid, batter my weak spirit with such anger and boredom that it is rendered for a long time afterward useless for anything else. All of which will excuse my stupidity, I hope, not to have been able to understand the idea by which we must judge how the soul (not extended and immaterial) can move the body by an idea we have in another regard of heaviness, nor why a power—which we have falsely attributed to things under the name of a quality—of carrying a body toward the center of the Earth when the demonstration of a contrary truth (which you promised in your Physics) confirms us in thinking it impossible. The idea of a separate independent quality of heaviness—given that we are not able to pretend to the perfection and objective reality of God—could be made up out of ignorance of that which truly propels bodies towards the center of the Earth. Because no material cause represents itself to the senses, one attributes heaviness to matter's contrary, the immaterial, which nevertheless I would never be able to conceive but as a negation of matter and which could have no communication with matter.

I confess that it is easier for me to concede the matter and the extension of the soul than to concede that a being that is immaterial has the capacity to move a body and to be moved by it. For if the former is done by giving information, it is necessary that the spirits which make the movement be intelligent, which you do not accord to anything corporal. And although, in your meditations, you show the possibility of the soul being moved by the body, it is nevertheless very difficult to comprehend how a soul, as you have described it, after having had the faculty and habit of good reasoning, would lose all that by some sort of vapors, or that being able to subsist without the body and having nothing in common with it, would allow itself to be so ruled by the body.

Source: From *The Princess and the Philosopher: Letters of Elisabeth of the Palatinate to René Descartes* by Andrea Nye.

■ **Astronomy**
Elisabetha and Johannes Hevelius working together with a sextant in a German astronomical observatory. More than 14 percent of all German astronomers were female. Most of them cooperated with their husbands in their work.

Margaret Cavendish (1623–1673) wrote scientific and philosophical treatises and conversed with the leading philosophers of the day. In early eighteenth-century France, small groups of women and men gathered in the salons or private sitting rooms of the nobility to discuss philosophical and scientific ideas. In Germany it was not uncommon for women to help their husbands run astronomical observatories.

Although seventeenth-century science laid the theoretical foundations for a theory of sexual equality, it did not challenge other traditional ideas that compared women unfavorably to men. Most educated people continued to ground female behavior in the humors, claiming that because women were cold and wet, as opposed to hot and dry, they were naturally more deceptive, unstable, and melancholic than men. They also continued to identify women with nature itself, which had always been depicted as female. Bacon's use of masculine metaphors to describe science and his references to "man's mastery over nature" therefore seemed to reinforce traditional ideas of male dominance over women. His language also reinforced traditional notions of men's superior rationality. In 1664 the secretary of the Royal Society, which excluded women from membership, proclaimed that the mission of that institution was to develop a "masculine philosophy." At the same time the tradition of depicting science as a female goddess, such as Minerva, began to disappear.

The new science provided the theoretical foundations for the male control of women at a time when many men expressed concern over the "disorderly" and "irrational" conduct of women. In a world populated with witches, rebels, and other women who refused to adhere to conventional standards of proper feminine behavior, the adoption of a masculine philosophy was associated with the reassertion of patriarchy.

CONCLUSION

Science and Western Culture

The Scientific Revolution was a uniquely Western phenomenon. It had no parallel in the Eastern world. During the Middle Ages the Islamic civilizations of the Middle East produced a rich body of scientific knowledge that had influenced the development of science in western Europe, but by the time of the Scientific Revolution Islamic science had entered a period of decline. Other civilizations, most notably in China and India, also possessed impressive scientific traditions, but they too failed to undergo a transformation similar to that which occurred in western Europe in the seventeenth century.

In all these non-Western civilizations, religious traditions had prevented philosophers from undertaking an objective study of the natural world. Either nature was viewed as an entirely secular (that is, not religious) entity and hence not worthy of study on its own terms, or it was viewed as something so heavily infused with spiritual value that it could not be subjected to rational analysis. Only in Europe did religious and cultural traditions allow the scientist to view nature as both a product of supernatural forces and something that was separate from the supernatural realm. Nature could therefore be studied objectively without losing its religious significance. Only when nature was viewed in this dual way, as both the creation of God and as something independent of the deity, could it be subjected to mathematical analysis and brought under human domination.

The Scientific Revolution gave the West a new source of identity. The West could be distinguished not only by its Christianity, its capitalist economic system, its large bureaucratic states, and its massive standing armies, but also by the scientific content of its education, its approach to the natural world, and its science-based technology. By the beginning of the eighteenth century, modern science became an essential component of Western culture. It also laid the foundations of the Enlightenment, another distinctively Western phenomenon, which will be discussed in the next chapter.

The rise of Western science and technology had profound implications for the encounters that took place between Western and non-Western peoples in Africa, Asia, and the Americas. By the eighteenth century, European science provided explicit support for European empires, which will be discussed in Chapters 19 and 23. Science gave Western states the military and navigational technology that allowed them to establish their control over non-Europeans. Knowledge of botany and agriculture allowed Western powers to develop the resources of the areas they colonized and to use these resources for the improvement of their own societies. Most important, the possession of scientific knowledge and technology encouraged people in the West to think of themselves as superior to the people they subjugated or controlled. Scientific theories regarding biological and physiological differences between the people who inhabited the West and natives of other countries also contributed to those attitudes. Western imperialism had its roots in the Scientific Revolution of the seventeenth century.

Suggestions for Further Reading

For a comprehensive list of suggested readings, please go to www.ablongman.com/levack/chapter16

Biagioli, Mario. *Galileo, Courtier: The Practice of Science in the Culture of Absolutism.* 1993. Argues that Galileo's desire for patronage determined the type of research he engaged in and the scientific questions he asked.

Cohen, H. Floris. *The Scientific Revolution: A Historiographical Inquiry.* 1995. A thorough account of all the different interpretations of the causes and significance of the Scientific Revolution.

Dear, Peter. *Discipline and Experience: The Mathematical Way in the Scientific Revolution.* 1995. Explains the importance of mathematics in the development of seventeenth-century science.

Debus, Allen G. *Man and Nature in the Renaissance.* 1978. Deals with the early history of the Scientific Revolution and develops many of its connections with the Renaissance.

Drake, Stillman, ed. *Discoveries and Opinions of Galileo.* 1957. Includes four of Galileo's most important writings, together with a detailed commentary.

Easlea, Brian. *Magic, Witch-Hunting and the New Philosophy.* 1980. Relates the end of witch hunting to the spread of mechanical philosophy.

Kuhn, Thomas S. *The Copernican Revolution.* 1957. The most comprehensive and authoritative study of the shift from an Earth-centered to a sun-centered model of the universe.

Popkin, Richard. *The History of Skepticism from Erasmus to Spinoza.* 1979. Discusses skepticism as a cause as well as an effect of the Scientific Revolution.

Schiebinger, Londa. *The Mind Has No Sex? Women in the Origins of Modern Science.* 1989. Explores the role of women in all aspects of scientific endeavor.

Shapin, Steven. *The Scientific Revolution.* 1996. A study of the origins of the modern scientific worldview that emphasizes the social influences on the production of knowledge and the social purposes for which scientific knowledge was intended.

Shapin, Steven, and Simon Schaffer. *Leviathan and the Air Pump.* 1989. Study of the difference between Robert Boyle and Thomas Hobbes regarding the value of experimentation.

Thomas, Keith. *Man and the Natural World. A History of the Modern Sensibility.* 1983. A study of the shifting attitudes of human beings toward nature during the period from 1500 to 1800.

Webster, Charles. *The Great Instauration: Science, Medicine and Reform, 1626–1660.* 1975. Explores the relationship between Puritanism and the Scientific Revolution in England.

Westfall, Richard S. *Never at Rest: A Biography of Isaac Newton.* 1980. A superb biography of the most influential scientist in the history of the West.

Credits

Unless otherwise acknowledged, all photographs are the property of Pearson Education, Inc. Page abbreviations are as follows: (T) Top, (B) Bottom, (L) Left, (R) Right, (C) Center.

Justice in History title panel image: Don Mason/Corbis

The Human Body in History title panel image: Cameraphoto/Art Resource, NY

What Is the West?
I-2 Canali Photobank; **I-4** European Space Agency/Photo Researchers, Inc.; **I-6** Courtesy of Adler Planetarium & Astronomy Museum, Chicago, Illinois (W-264); **I-7** American Museum of Natural History Library (AMNH#314372)

Chapter 1
1-2 Victor R. Boswell, Jr./National Geographic Image Collection; **1-4** Augustin Ochsenreiter/South Tyrol Museum of Archaeology; **1-12 (L)** Courtesy of the Trustees of the British Museum, London (BM116730); **(R)** Courtesy of the Trustees of the British Museum, London (WA15285); **1-15 (T)** Robert Harding Picture Library; **(B)** George Gerster/Photo Researchers, Inc.; **1-17** Nimatallah/Art Resource; **1-19** Erich Lessing/Art Resource, NY; **1-20** Scala/Art Resource, NY; **1-22** Staatlisches Museum Ägyptischer Kunst; **1-23** Dagli Orti/The Art Archive; **1-24 (T)** Borromeo/Art Resource, NY; **(B)** Robert Harding Picture Library; **1-28** Neolithic farm, ca. 5000 B.C.E.; **1-29** Roger Ressmeyer/Corbis

Chapter 2
2-2 National Archaeological Museum, Athens/Dagli Orti/The Art Archive; **2-6** Réunion des Musées Nationaux/Art Resource, NY; **2-7** The Art Archive; **2-9** British Museum, London/Bridgeman Art Library; **2-11** Osiride Head of Hatshepsut, originally from a statue. Provenance: Thebes, Deir el Bahri. Limestone, painted. H. 64 cm. H. with crown 124.5 cm. The Metropolitan Museum of Art, Rogers Fund, 1931, (31.3.157) Photograph © 1983 The Metropolitan Museum of Art, New York; **2-13** AKG London; **2-16 (L)** Gérard Degeorge/Corbis; **(R)** AKG London; **2-20** Private Collection, Paris/Dagli Orti/The Art Archive; **2-22** Nimatallah/Art Resource, NY; **2-24** Scala/Art Resource, NY; **2-26** Hirmer Fotoarchiv, Munich; **2-34 (T)** Erich Lessing/Art Resource, NY; **(B)** Oriental Institute, University of Chicago

Chapter 3
3-2 Erich Lessing/Art Resource, NY; **3-8** Drawing from *In the Shadow of the Temple* by Meir Ben-Dov, translation by Ina Friedman. Copyright © 1982 by Keter Publishing House Jerusalem Ltd.; English translation © 1985 by Keter Publishing House Jerusalem, Ltd. Reprinted by permission of HarperCollins Publishers; **3-10** State Hermitage Museum, Moscow, Russia; **3-16 (TL)** American Numismatic Society; **(TR)** American Numismatic Society; **(CL)** American Numismatic Society; **(CR)** American Numismatic Society; **3-20** Lipke/Trireme Trust USA; **3-24 (L)** Foto Marburg/Art Resource, NY; **(BR)** Index s.a.s.; **3-25** Staatliche Äntikensammlungen und Glyphtothek, Munich; **3-26** Robert Harding Picture Library; **3-27** Museum of Fine Arts, Boston; **3-30** Scala/Art Resource, NY; **3-30** Scala/Art Resource, NY; **3-33** Scala/Art Resource, NY

Chapter 4
4-2 Scala/Art Resource, NY; **4-6** Dagli Orti/The Art Archive; **4-9** Réunion des Musées Nationaux/Art Resource, NY; **4-11** Nimatallah/Art Resource, NY; **4-14** Réunion des Musées Nationaux/Art Resource, NY; **4-15** Erich Lessing/Art Resource, NY; **4-20 (T)** Erich Lessing/Art Resource, NY; **(B)** Staatliche Museen, Berlin/Bildarchiv Preussischer Kulturbesitz; **4-22** Robert Harding Picture Library; **4-29** Statue of Cybele, Roman, II Century A.D., Bronze, Length 139.1 cm. The Metropolitan Museum of Art, Gift of Henry G. Marquand, 1897. (97.22.24) Photograph by Schecter Lee, Photograph © 1985 The Metropolitan Museum of Art; **4-35** Alinari/Art Resource, NY

Chapter 5
5-2 Erich Lessing/Art Resource, NY; **5-8** SEF/Art Resource, NY; **5-9** Erich Lessing/Art Resource, NY; **5-10** Oplontis Fresco Mimmo Jodice/Corbis; **5-12** Index s.a.s; **5-13** Leo C. Curran; **5-14** © Dorling Kindersley; **5-15 (TL)** © Dorling Kindersley; **(TR)** Staatliche Antikensammlung und Glyptothek, Munich; **(B)** © Dorling Kindersley; **5-16** Robert Harding Picture Library; **5-25** AKG London; **5-31** Scala/Art Resource, NY; **5-32** Dura Europa Fresco Art Resource, NY; **5-35** Courtesy of the Trustees of the British Museum, London (BMC Vespasian 16)

Chapter 6
6-2 Österreichische Nationalbibliotek, Vienna; **6-4** Scala/Art Resource, NY; **6-5** SEF/Art Resource, NY; **6-6** Erich Lessing/Art Resource, NY; **6-9** Alinari/Art Resource, NY; **6-12** Victoria & Albert Museum, London/Art Resource, NY; **6-16** Réunion des Musées Nationaux/Art Resource, NY; **6-18** Corbis; **6-25** Alinari/Art Resource, NY; **6-30** Erich Lessing/Art Resource, NY; **6-33** Réunion des Musées Nationaux/Art Resource, NY; **6-36** Courtesy of the Trustees of the British Museum, London

Chapter 7
7-2 Art Resource, NY; **7-6 (T)** Balatoni Museum, Keszthely, Hungary; **(B)** Balatoni Museum, Keszthely, Hungary; **7-7** *David and Goliath*, Byzantine, Made in Constantinople, 629–630; Early Byzantine, Silver, D. 1 ½ in. (3.8 cm); Diam. 19 ½ in (49.4 cm); The Metropolitan Museum of Art, Gift of J. Pierpont Morgan, 1917 (17.190.396) Photograph © 2000 The Metropolitan Museum of Art; **7-9** The Art Archive; **7-10 (L)** Monastery of St. Catherine, Mt. Sinai, Egypt/Bridgeman Art Library; **(R)** Scala/Art Resource, NY; **7-15** AP/Wide World Photos; **7-17** Bibliothèque Nationale de France, Paris (RC A 69284); **7-18** Robert Harding Picture Library; **7-22 (TL)** The Nasser D. Khalili Collection of Islamic Art; **(TR)** The Nasser D. Khalili Collection of Islamic Art; **(BL)** Bibliothèque Nationale de France (2001 A 83707); **(BR)** Bibliothèque Nationale de France (2001 A 83705); **7-25** The Art Archive; **7-33 (T)** Courtesy of the Trustees of the British Museum, London (EPS200642); **(B)** Courtesy of the Trustees of the British Museum, London (EPS200646); **7-34** By permission of the British Library (Cotton.Nerod.iv. fol. 211)

Chapter 8
8-2 Art Resource, NY; **8-7** Bibliothèque Nationale de France, Paris (Latin 9428 f. 71v/RC A 39420); **8-10** Erich Lessing/Art

Resource, NY; **8-13** AKG London; **8-14** AKG London; **8-16** Bodleian Library, Oxford University (Ms Bodl. 624 fol. 81r); **18-17** Réunion des Musées Nationaux/Art Resource, NY; **8-18** Cambridge University Collection of Aerial Photography (ATV76); **8-20** Chitter Åhlin/The Museum of National Antiquities, Sweden; **8-21** Scala/Art Resource, NY; **8-23** State Historical Museum, Moscow; **8-30** Scala/Art Resource, NY

Chapter 9

9-2 Giraudon/Art Resource, NY; **9-6** Dagli Orti/The Art Archive; **9-7** Werner Forman Archive/Art Resource, NY; **9-11** Arthur Thévenart/Corbis; **9-13** Scala/Art Resource, NY; **9-14** Musée Condé, Chantilly/Bridgeman Art Library; **9-15** Cameraphoto/Art Resource, NY; **9-17** Bridgeman Art Library; **9-19** Bibliothèque Nationale de France, Paris; **9-23** Art Resource, NY; **9-29** Bildarchiv Preussischer Kulturbesitz; **9-32** Courtesy Achim Bednorz; **9-33** **(T)** Marc Garanger/Corbis; **(B)** Courtesy Achim Bednorz

Chapter 10

10-2 Snark/Art Resource, NY; **10-6** Réunion des Musées Nationaux/Art Resource, NY; **10-7** Scala/Art Resource, NY; **10-15** Bibliothèque Nationale de France, Paris (M. 2643, folio 226 v.); **10-17** Santa Maria Novella, Florence/Index a.s.a; **10-19** Honourable Society of Inner Temple London/Eileen Tweedy/The Art Archive; **10-20** Bibliothèque Nationale de France, Paris (MS. Fr. 2644 fol. 135); **10-22** Bibliothèque Nationale de France/Harper Collins Publishers/The Art Archive; **10-23** By permission of the British Library (Addt. mss.42130 fol 147v); **10-25** Bibliothèque Nationale de Rouen (MS U 49 fol. 1); **10-26** Stadtarchiv Soest (Bestand A Nr. 2771); **10-27** Tomb Effigy of Jean d'Alluy, mid-13th century, Limestone, 83 $\frac{1}{2} \times 34\ \frac{1}{4}$ in. (212.1 × 87 cm) The Metropolitan Museum of Art, The Cloisters Collection, 1925. (25.120.201) Photography © 1979 The Metropolitan Museum of Art; **10-28** **(T)** Réunion des Musées Nationaux/Art Resource, NY; **(B)** Bibliothèque Nationale de France, Paris (MS. Lat. 1156B, fol 163); **10-29** Réunion des Musées Nationaux/Art Resource, NY; **10-30** Réunion des Musées Nationaux/Art Resource, NY

Chapter 11

11-2 Scala/Art Resource, NY; **11-8** Scala/Art Resource, NY; **11-9** Ravenna/Index s.a.s; **11-13** Kunsthistorisches Museum, Vienna/Art Resource, NY; **11-14** Erich Lessing/Art Resource, NY; **11-20** **(L)** Orsi Battaglini/Index s.a.s.; **(R)** Orsi Battaglini/Index s.a.s.; **11-21** Art Resource, NY; **11-22** **(T)** Alinari/Art Resource, NY; **(B)** Bridgeman Art Library; **11-23** **(L)** Scala/Art Resource, NY; **(R)** Scala/Art Resource, NY; **11-24** Scala/Art Resource, NY; **11-25** Petrus Christus (Flemish [Bruges], active by 1444–died 1475–76), *A Goldsmith in His Shop*, Possibly Saint Elegius, 1449, Oil on wood; Overall: 39 $\frac{3}{8} \times 34\ \frac{3}{4}$ in. (100.1 × 85.8 cm); Painted surface: 38 $\frac{5}{8} \times 33$ 1-/? in. (98 × 85.2 cm). The Metropolitan Museum of Art, Robert Lehman Collection, 1975 (1975.1.110) Photograph © 1993 The Metropolitan Museum of Art

Chapter 12

12-2 Courtesy of the Trustees of the British Museum; **12-5** Bibliothèque Nationale de France, Paris (RCC1619); **12-7** The Art Archive; **12-8** Bridgeman Art Library; **12-11** Scala/Art Resource, NY; **12-12** Scala/Art Resource, NY; **12-15** Snark/Art Resource, NY; **12-16** **(T)** American Museum of Natural History Library (AMNH#314372); **(B)** American Museum of Natural History (AMNH# 315459); **12-18** New York Public Library, Rare Books Division. Astor, Lenox and Tilden Foundations; **12-21** Georgius Hoefnagle plate from Georg Braun (1542–1622), 5 vols. *Civitatis Orbis Terrarum* (Colonia Agrippinae, 1572–1618), Maps Division, Sterling Memorial Library, Yale University; **12-27** The Library of Congress; **12-28** Biblioteca Medicea Laurenziana (Med. Palat. 220, c. 460v)

Chapter 13

13-2 Scala/Art Resource, NY; **13-5** Das Standebuch, 1568; **13-6** Erich Lessing/Art Resource, NY; **13-7** Foto Marburg/Art Resource, NY; **13-12** M. Schneiders/Artephot; **13-19** By courtesy of the National Portrait Gallery, London (NPG668); **13-26** Scala/Art Resource, NY; **13-28** The Granger Collection, New York; **13-30** Scala/Art Resource, NY; **13-31** Alinari/Art Resource, NY

Chapter 14

14-2 The Art Archive; **14-6** Art Resource, NY; **14-13** AKG London; **14-15** Adriaen van Oastade (Dutch, 1610–1685). *The Family*, 1647. Etching on paper, 7 $\frac{1}{2} \times 6\ \frac{5}{8}$ in. Georgia Museum of Art, University of Georgia; gift of Alfred H. Holbrook, GMOA 1967.1820.; **14-16** Erich Lessing/Art Resource, NY; **14-18** New York Public Library, Astor, Lenox and Tilden Foundations; **14-19** Mansell Collection/Time Life Pictures/Getty Images; **14-20** Index s.a.s.; **14-21** Germanisches National Museum, Nürnberg; **14-25** Réunion des Musées Nationaux/Art Resource, NY; **14-29** Bedford Estate/Marquess of Tavistock

Chapter 15

15-2 Réunion des Muées Nationaux/Art Resource, NY; **15-4** Hobbes, *Leviathan*; **15-8** Philippe de Champaigne, 1602–1674. Triple Portrait of Cardinal Richelieu, oil on canvas, 58.4 × 72.4 cm. © The National Gallery, London (NG798); **15-10** Réunion des Musées Nationaux/Art Resource, NY; **15-17** **(T)** Museo del Prado/Art Resource, NY; **(B)** Scala/Art Resource, NY; **15-23** Scala/Art Resource, NY; **15-29** This item is reproduced by permission of the Huntington Library, San Marina, California; **15-31** AKG London; **15-33** Museum Boijmans van Beuningen, Rotterdam; **15-34** Rijksmuseum Foundation, Amsterdam

Chapter 16

16-2 Archivo Iconografico, S.A./Corbis; **16-5** **(L)** © 1982 Instructional Resources Corporation; **(R)** From *The Cosmographical Glass*, 1559; **16-6** **(L)** The Library of Congress (LC USZ62-95165); **(R)** By permission of the British Library (Neg No. 2204); **16-9** By courtesy of the National Portrait Gallery, London (NPG5115); **16-10** Photograph © Mauritshuis, The Hague; **16-11** Ashmolean Museum, Oxford University (BI313); **16-13** Erich Lessing/Art Resource, NY; **16-17** From Thomas Sprat's *The History of the Royal Society of London*; **16-18** From Francis Bacon's *The Great Instauration*; **16-23** Erich Lessing/Art Resource, NY; **16-28** Corbis